Psychiatric-Mental Health Nursing

Adaptation and Growth

 **J. B. Lippincott Company**   *Philadelphia*

London   Mexico City   New York   St. Louis   São Paulo   Sydney

Barbara Schoen Johnson
R.N., M.S.
Coordinator/Instructor
Nursing
El Centro College
Brookhaven College Satellite
Dallas, Texas

Psychiatric- Mental Health Nursing

Adaptation and Growth

Sponsoring Editor: William Burgower/David T. Miller
Manuscript Editor: Leslie E. Hoeltzel
Indexer: Carol M. Kosik
Design Director: Tracy Baldwin
Designer: Anne O'Donnell
Production Supervisor: Kathleen P. Dunn
Production Coordinator: Susan Hess
Compositor: Circle Graphics
Printer/Binder: The Murray Printing Company

Cover Photography by Michael E. Frankel, Dynamic Images

6 5 4 3 2 1

Library of Congress Cataloging in Publication Data

Main entry under title:

Psychiatric-mental health nursing.

    Includes bibliographies and index.
    1. Psychiatric nursing.   I. Johnson, Barbara Schoen.
[DNLM: 1. Mental Disorders—nursing.   2. Mental Health—
nurses' instruction.   3. Psychiatric Nursing.
WY 160 P97204]
RC440.P737   1986   610.73'68   85-16047

ISBN 0-397-54393-X

The authors and publisher have exerted every effort to ensure that
drug selection and dosage set forth in this text are in accord with
current recommendations and practice at the time of publication.
However, in view of ongoing research, changes in government regulations, and the constant flow of information relating to drug therapy
and drug reactions, the reader is urged to check the package insert
for each drug for any change in indications and dosage and for added
warnings and precautions. This is particularly important when the
recommended agent is a new or infrequently employed drug.

to Barry

Contributors

Cheryl Lindamood Anderson, R.N., M.N., PH.D
Assistant Professor of Nursing
Baylor University School of Nursing
Dallas, Texas

Deborah Jackson Antai-Otong, R.N., M.S., C.S.
Instructor, Nursing
El Centro College
Dallas, Texas

Virginia Trotter Betts, R.N., M.S.N., J.D.
Academic Chair, Behavioral Sciences as Applied to
    Nursing
Associate Professor, Psychiatric-Mental Health Nursing
Vanderbilt University School of Nursing
Nashville, Tennessee

Patriciann Furnari Brady, R.N., M.A., M.S.
Assistant Professor, Department of Nursing
University of South Dakota
Vermillion, South Dakota

Patricia Flatley Brennan, R.N., M.S.N.
Assistant Professor of Nursing
Marquette University College of Nursing
Milwaukee, Wisconsin

Sharon Byers, R.N., M.S.N., C.S.
Clinical Nurse Specialist, Older Adult Services Program
Hennepin County Mental Health Center
Minneapolis, Minnesota

Barbara G. Tunley Crenshaw, R.N., M.S.
Professor, Division of Science and Health
Front Range Community College
Westminster, Colorado

Joy Randolph Davidson, R.N., M.S.N.
Instructor, Nursing
El Centro College
Dallas, Texas

Cheryl Steudtner Detwiler, R.N., M.S.N.
Instructor/Coordinator, Nursing
El Centro College
Brookhaven College Satellite
Dallas, Texas

M. Suzanne Doscher, R.N., M.S.
Associate Professor
Medical University of South Carolina College of Nursing
Charleston, South Carolina

Peggy J. Drapo, PH.D., R.N.
Associate Professor
Texas Woman's University College of Nursing
Denton, Texas

Sally Francis, M.S., M.A.
Director, Child Life–Child Development Department
Children's Medical Center of Dallas
Assistant Professor of Clinical Pediatrics
University of Texas Health Science Center
Southwestern Medical School
Dallas, Texas

Judith A. Greene, PH.D., R.N.
Associate Professor
Coordinator, Psychosocial Long-term Nursing and
    Community Mental Health Nursing
University of Tennessee, Knoxville
Knoxville, Tennessee

Christina R. Hogarth, R.N., M.S., C.S.
Director, Mental Health Unit
Dettmer Hospital, Inc.
Troy, Ohio

Marilyn Jaffe–Ruiz, ED.D., R.N., C.S.
Chairperson/Associate Professor
Lienhard School of Nursing
Pace University
New York, New York

Susan Kah, B.S.N., M.N., ED.D.
Professor and Chairperson, Special Programs in Nursing
Miami-Dade Community College
Miami, Florida

James McColgan, Jr., R.N., M.S., PH.D. CAND.
Assistant Professor of Nursing
Boston College
Chestnut Hill, Massachusetts

Mary Snyder McElvain, R.N., M.S., C.S.
Formerly Instructor, Nursing
University of Nevada, Las Vegas
Las Vegas, Nevada

Patricia N. Mahon, R.N., PH.D.
Professor
Texas Woman's University College of Nursing
Denton, Texas

Cynthia Ann Pastorino, R.N., M.S.N.
Clinical Nurse Specialist, Orthopaedics
Methodist Medical Center
Dallas, Texas

Sandra L. Patterson, R.N., M.S.
Instructor/Coordinator, Nursing
El Centro College
Dallas, Texas

Juliann Casey Reakes, R.N., ED.D.
Professor of Nursing
Abilene Intercollegiate School of Nursing
Abilene, Texas

S. Robin Shanks, R.N., M.S.N., J.D.
Treatment Coordinator
Forensic Services Division
Middle Tennessee Mental Health Institute
Nashville, Tennessee

Margie N. Slaughter, R.N., M.S.
Assistant Dean, Health Sciences
Trinity Valley Community College
Kaufman, Texas

Mary Anne Sweeney, R.N., PH.D.
Associate Professor
San Diego State University School of Nursing
San Diego, California

Barbara A. Thurston, R.N., M.S.
Assistant Professor, Department of Nursing
Saint Anselm College
Manchester, New Hampshire

Anne Warner Toothaker, R.N., B.S.N.
Formerly Staff Nurse
The Veterans Administration Medical Center
Boise, Idaho

Sylvia M. Anderson Whiting, R.N., M.S., C.S.
People Helpers, Mental Health Nurse Specialists
Summerville, South Carolina
Adjunct Associate Professor
Medical University of South Carolina
Charleston, South Carolina
Consultant and Associate Professor of Nursing
South Carolina State College Department of Nursing
Orangeburg, South Carolina

Rhea P. Williams, R.N., M.N.
Associate Professor of Nursing
Azusa Pacific University
Azusa, California

Foreword

I wish to commend the editor and authors of *Psychiatric-Mental Health Nursing: Adaptation and Growth* for the creation of a comprehensive, readable, and relevant textbook. The student will find within these pages every content and process ingredient essential to nursing psychiatric patients. The notion of a practice framework and the therapeutic use of self provides the "springboard" for the theoretical perspective of human development. Armed with that background, the student is presented with the art and science of nursing the mentally ill in subsequent chapters. Material dealing with intervention and disturbed behavior is presented in a manner that establishes a sophisticated foundation for interdisciplinary communication. Through the skillful blending of dynamic and descriptive psychiatry, the common language of mental health is recognized and accorded status. Amidst this orientation, the nursing process and the distinctive role of the nurse remain constant and visible. Neither are the authors so conceptual that they lose sight of the developmental and situational crises that create special challenges for contemporary practice. The issues of family violence, rape, the aged and adolescents and more are presented in sufficient depth and breadth for entry into practice.

Both students and educators will find the chapter previews and summaries helpful and chapter-specific learning objectives invaluable. I congratulate Barbara Johnson and her contributing authors for writing an educationally and professionally sound textbook that prepares the student for entry into practice in psychiatric-mental health nursing.

Lucille A. Joel, R.N., Ed.D., F.A.A.N.
Professior and Director for Clinical Affairs
Rutgers—The State University
    College of Nursing
Newark, New Jersey

Foreword

I first became acquainted with *Psychiatric-Mental Health Nursing: Adaptation and Growth* when I was asked to review chapters. This was, of course, a blind review. I had no idea who the editor/authors were, and they did not know who I was. (I assumed that I was just one of several reviewers.) As the chapters arrived in packs of ten or so, I began to look forward to the task; over several years I came to feel a part of this project, as some chapters came around for the second time. Thus I saw the book grow, expand, and flesh out into a comprehensive and touching work. In this age, when we are beginning to understand the multidimensional aspects of phenomena in our field, it is a pleasure to find a textbook that addresses so many levels.

For *Psychiatric-Mental Health Nursing: Adaptation and Growth* reaches the reader in many ways. It is factual, well organized, theoretically based, and yet deeply humanistic. The client is presented not as a clinical case with a deadful set of symptoms, but rather as a person who might be our mother, brother, friend, or lover. We are drawn into the existential world of the clients and their families and are helped to understand their feelings and actions. In turn, we learn about ourselves.

Psychiatric-Mental Health Nursing: Adaptation and Growth is also characterized by its lack of jargon and by its creative departures from other textbooks in the field. One example is the career profiles of psychiatric nurses. This is an interesting idea that I have never seen in a psychiatric nursing textbook, and which should prove both enjoyable and inspirational to students.

I commend Barbara Schoen Johnson and all the contributors for putting forth a work that I believe will make an outstanding contribution to our field. I am honored to have had a small part in its creation.

Suzanne Lego, R.N., Ph.D., C.S.
Demarest, New Jersey

Preface

When I undertook to write this textbook of psychiatric-mental health nursing, I had several goals in mind. First, I wanted to compile accurate, comprehensive, and up-to-date material that would stimulate the reader to seek out more information and experience in this area of nursing. Second, I wanted to produce good-quality writing that would not only communicate in a clear, concise, and interesting manner, but also touch the reader's emotions as well as his thinking processes. Third, I wanted to expose the reader to some exciting applications of psychiatric-mental health nursing concepts not ordinarily found within the realm of the traditional textbook.

As *Psychiatric-Mental Health Nursing: Adaptation and Growth* becomes a reality, I feel confident that I have achieved what I set out to do. The outcome of striving toward those three goals is contained within these pages.

To produce a textbook with current, comprehensive, and factual content, I turned to the 29 nurse practitioners, educators, and researchers who became the book's contributing authors. Each nurse-writer had specific tasks to accomplish—to research the topic of the chapter thoroughly, gather both the classic and the newest material, and put the chapter together in a comprehensive and logical manner.

The results, I believe, are significant. Patricia Brennan's chapter on suicide also addresses the needs of the survivor-victims; her chapter on trends in psychiatric-mental health care examines the issue of the impaired nurse and the approaches being considered to move beyond punishment to rehabilitation. Christina Hogarth's chapter on families and family therapy includes the topic of children of divorce. Virginia Betts' and Robin Shanks' discussion of least restrictive treatment environment provides clear guidelines to this legal implication of psychiatric nursing. Judith Greene's chapter on milieu therapy explains why and how the milieu benefits psychiatric clients. These, of course, are just a few examples of the thought-provoking content that the contributing authors have brought to this new book.

My second goal focused on the affective domain. Nursing, after all, is more than an aggregate of cognitive and psychomotor learnings. Psychiatric-mental health nursing requires the integration into one's professional repertoire of certain affective behaviors such as self-awareness, objectivity, and acceptance of the other. The use of the self as a therapeutic instrument calls on a person's ability to employ honesty, openness, trustworthiness, and caring within a professional nursing role.

The writing in *Psychiatric-Mental Health Nursing* has been designed to impact the reader's emotions as well as his understanding and knowledge. Discussing individual therapy, Joy Davidson writes, "People hope for more happiness and less pain. They fear change in themselves and in the people they love." In her chapter on mood disorders, Susan Kah describes depression as a "lonely, loveless, and hopeless state." These and similar examples seek to speak to the reader directly, meaningfully, and without the interference of confusing jargon.

There are also personal accounts, the recounting of unique experiences generously shared by the authors. In the chapter on family violence, a member of Parents Anonymous describes the abuse of her own children and her present work, as a sponsor of other abusing parents, to prevent child abuse. In the chapter on death and dying, Fela Alfaro relates her personal experiences with death, from her earliest awareness that her mother died giving birth to her to her more recent encounters, as an adult, with the deaths of family members and friends. Explaining the need of the rape victim to be believed, Sally Francis uses the words of a victim to make the point: "A part of me was relieved when the police came—that I looked so bad, that there was blood, that the door had been broken open, the house was torn up, and there were fingerprints. There couldn't be any doubt that something awful had happened to me."

The third goal, that of including in this work a variety of topics not ordinarily found in psychiatric-mental health nursing textbooks, warrants the reader's attention. Besides the usual topics included in a psychiatric nursing book, *Psychiatric-Mental Health Nursing* has a section on the emotional aspects of medical care—trauma, surgery, and critical care, the physically ill or handicapped child, women's health issues of pregnancy, childbearing, mastectomy, and hysterectomy, and death and dying. There is also a section on crisis situations, with chapters on crisis theory and intervention, rape, suicide, and abuse. Other content that is not ordinarily found in psychiatric-mental health nursing textbooks includes the topics of mental retardation, organic mental disorder, sociocultural aspects of nursing care, mental health of the aging, trends in psychiatric-mental health care, nursing research, and career profiles of psychiatric-mental health nurses.

Selye's stress/adaptation theory forms the conceptual framework for this book. According to this theory, stress is an ever-present human state, and any biophysical or psychosocial factor causes stress to a human being. These stressors, or factors requiring a response or change in the individual, are perceived in various ways by different individuals. A person's perception of the stressor influences his manner of coping with it. Adaptation, says Selye, is the end-state of adjusting to the changes in a person's internal or external environment.

This book is also about growth—using one's problems or crises to grow to higher levels of mental health and toward self-awareness and empathy.

Nursing process is a strong emphasis that is integrated throughout *Psychiatric-Mental Health Nursing*.

Rather than focusing on the client's mental disorder, its etiology, symptoms, and medical treatment, with nursing interventions tucked in, almost as an afterthought, at the end of each discussion, this book is a book about *nursing*, first and foremost. *Psychiatric-Mental Health Nursing* demonstrates the application of the nursing process in a wide variety of client situations.

Several noteworthy features of the book include

a clear, concise manner of presentation;
an emphasis on nursing process integrated throughout the text;
nursing assessment and nursing diagnosis guidelines;
attention to the guiding principles of psychiatric-mental health nursing and the specific nursing actions derived from those principles;
a theoretical framework built on stress and adaptation;
a humanistic approach that catches up the whole person;
adherence to the current DSM-III criteria of mental disorders;
attention to the affective realm—the development of empathic responses, insight, respect for human dignity, and growth through experiential exercises;
the exemplification of behavioral dysfunctions and their theoretical bases through clinical case studies, nurse-client dialogues and interactions, and a view of the nursing process at work through nursing care plans;
a focus on self-awareness in the nurse, that is, the nurse as a very human being, a person in touch with his or her own feelings;
an emphasis on cross-cultural aspects of psychiatric-mental health nursing;
reinforcement of the nurse's significance and role in the collaborative efforts of the entire mental health team; and
an eclectic approach to the therapeutic possibilities for any client.

It has been a joyful experience to put together *Psychiatric-Mental Health Nursing: Adaptation and Growth.* I believe that it will help open up for the reader the exciting world of psychiatric-mental health nursing. That was, and is, my most important goal.

Barbara Schoen Johnson, R.N., M.S.

Acknowledgments

I recognize that I owe thanks to many people who offered me encouragement during this rigorous writing adventure. To include all of their names here, regretfully, would produce an extensive and unwieldy list. I will name, therefore, only a few of the many I acknowledge:

Barbara Burke, whose friendship and honesty I can count on;

the valuable friends and colleagues—Juanita Zapata Flint, Sondra George Flemming, Felicitas "Fela" Alfaro, Sandy Patterson, Marjorie Schuchat, Pattie Murphey Lucas, Margie Slaughter, Kathy Pritchett, Cheryl Detwiler, Elizabeth Winslow, Dana Stahl, Mandie Turner, Sharon Sonkin, Gayle Varnell, Sue McLelland, Fran Duplan, Nancy Scott, and Betty Nelson—who seemingly never tired of hearing about and encouraging my efforts;

the nurses who helped me lay down the foundation of the work I love—Helen Czarnecki, Dolores Cleveland, Catherine Thayer, and Marianne Mosley;

my Dean and Associate Dean, Kay Kiefer Eggleston and Carol Lipin Speyerer, who offered me support during a sometimes trying experience;

Jalane A. Pearcy, who typed (and retyped) every word of this manuscript and kept her good humor during it all;

the primary developmental reviewers for the text, Sandra B. Fielo, Ed.D., R.N., Associate Dean, College of Nursing, State University of New York, Downstate Medical Center, Brooklyn, New York, and Suzanne Lego, Ph.D., R.N., Private Practice, New York, New York, whose ideas and suggestions provided valuable input and often started me thinking again;

my two superb sponsoring editors, Bill Burgower, who helped me formulate the plans for this book, and Dave Miller, who helped me bring them to reality;

my parents, Roy and Marie Schoen, who have always believed in me;

my sisters and brother, Roberta Schoen Ravagnani, Mary Ellen Schoen Makkos, and Jeffrey Schoen, who have put up with me over the years;

my children, Eric and Jessica, who give meaning to my life and bring me joy and hope for the future; and,

my husband, Barry, whose love and gentleness provide the "wind beneath my wings."

Contents

Part I
Introduction

Chapter 1
Entering Psychiatric-Mental Health Nursing

I do not know what causes insanity or what can cure it, and I don't really believe that anyone else knows either. I do not even think that it is a constant condition, much less an "illness," or that the crazy people live over there on that side of the line, and the rest of us over here. I think that madness is part of all of us, all the time, that it comes and goes, waxes and wanes. . . . I myself don't think that madness can be fully understood, only experienced—in oneself or in one's friends or in the people one sees crumbling at the office or on the streets.

Otto Friedrich,
Going Crazy: An Inquiry into
Madness in Our Time,
1976

Barbara Schoen Johnson

Chapter Preview

This chapter introduces the reader to the field of psychiatric-mental health nursing. Often mystifying or frightening to the novice, psychiatric-mental health nursing draws upon the knowledge bases of mental health and nursing to create an integrated and unique discipline. The principles of psychiatric-mental health nursing permeate all areas of nursing practice, such as helping new parents recognize and respond to the needs of their infant, calming the fears of a hospitalized child, talking with an adult facing surgery, or intervening in a disturbed family system.

This chapter examines mental health and mental disorder, the present and past roles of psychiatric-mental health nursing, and the application of the nursing process to client problems. It explores nurses' and clients' views of each other, their feelings, reactions, expectations, and attitudes and values regarding mental health. The individual's responses to stress and his use of coping mechanisms are also discussed.

The importance of nurses' taking care of themselves and attending to their own needs is emphasized throughout the chapter. Measures such as ventilation to understanding friends or colleagues, attention to one's physical health through diet and exercise, and involvement in absorbing hobbies or activities are explored as concrete ways to reduce stress and burnout and to promote optimal effectiveness in psychiatric-mental health nursing.

Learning Objectives

On completion of this chapter, the reader should be able to accomplish the following.

1. Discuss the parameters of mental health and mental illness
2. Identify the challenges facing mental health care
3. Differentiate between stress and distress
4. Explain the three stages of the General Adaptation Syndrome
5. Give examples of coping mechanisms
    Denial
    Regression
    Displacement
    Projection
    Reaction formation
    Repression
    Suppression
    Identification
    Rationalization
    Fantasy
    Intellectualization
6. Describe the roles of psychiatric-mental health nurses
7. Compare the views and perceptions of psychiatric nurses and clients
8. Discuss nurses' reactions to clients exhibiting disturbed behavior
9. Identify measures to prevent job stress and burnout
10. Describe the steps of the nursing process

Mental Health and Mental Illness

The states of health and illness are defined according to the values of a society. Generally, when a person's behavior is adaptive to his environment, we say that he is healthy, and when his behavior is maladaptive, we say that he is ill. Culture greatly influences these determinations about health and illness. Behavior that is acceptable in one cultural group may or may not be tolerated in another group.

Mental Health

The World Health Organization defines health as "a state of complete physical, mental and social well-being, not merely the absence of disease or infirmity." The significance of this definition is that it emphasizes the positive—a state of well-being—and does not focus on the lack of illness, disease, or disorder.

In this aforementioned state of emotional well-being, or *mental health,* the person functions comfortably within his society and is satisfied with himself and his achievements.[10] Mental health implies mastery in the areas of life involving love, work, and play. Some definitions of mental health also include the criterion of happiness as an important component.

Five "freedoms" that mentally healthy people demonstrate, according to Satir and associates, are as follows.

1. The freedom to see and hear what is here instead of what should be, was, or will be
2. The freedom to say what one feels and thinks, instead of what one should
3. The freedom to feel what one feels, instead of what one ought
4. The freedom to ask for what one wants, instead of always waiting for permission
5. The freedom to take risks in one's own behalf, instead of choosing to be only "secure" and not rocking the boat.[24]

Androgyny in Mentally Healthy Persons
Androgyny is the interaction and balance of "feminine" and "masculine" characteristics in an individual. Sex-role stereotypes, such as "Men should be strong and not express their feelings" or "It's OK for women to cry and ask for help," are often inflexible and limit a person's adaptive and interpersonal effectiveness.

Androgyny, on the other hand, allows an individual to adapt his or her behavior according to different situations or needs. The result is a greater degree of mental health and personal fulfillment. One study, however, suggests that there may be a double standard of mental health for men and women among mental health professionals. Androgynous behavior, in this study, was seen as more acceptable in female than male clients.[15]

Mental Illness or Disorder

Historical Views of Mental Illness

Historically, mental illness was viewed as demonic possession, the influence of ancestral spirits, the result of violating a taboo or neglecting a cultural ritual, and spiritual condemnation.[10] The mentally ill have been ridiculed, neglected, banned, persecuted, and deprived of their freedoms.

The common belief that mental disturbance was related to supernatural phenomena meant that healing, if it were to take place at all, must involve supernatural intercession. Other beliefs have held that the "passions" that interfered with proper reasoning were responsible for mental illness. Melancholia, now called depression, at one time was thought to result from an imbalance of body systems, which caused an excess of bile in the body.[10]

In the 19th century, mental illness was viewed as incurable and little, if any, humane treatment existed. Until 1820, the mentally ill were exhibited, for a fee, as diversion and entertainment for the public. Until 1886, the mentally ill were restrained in iron manacles.[7]

Beginning in the 1950s, pharmacotherapy changed the picture of mental health care. The discovery of neuroleptic and, later, antidepressant drugs brought about a more hopeful attitude regarding the prognoses of the mentally ill, particularly those with psychotic disorders.[13] The psychoactive drugs gave the psychotic client some relief from his symptoms and allowed him greater benefits from other therapies.

Defining Mental Disorder

Precise definitions of mental illness or disorder are elusive and impractical. Some would define mental illness as "psychiatric disease."[10] A noted nurse–author describes mental distress as "the mind expressing its discomfort through thoughts, feelings, and behaviors."[3] General criteria for *mental disorder* include the following.

1. Dissatisfaction with one's characteristics, abilities, and accomplishments
2. Ineffective or unsatisfying interpersonal relationships
3. Dissatisfaction with one's place in the world
4. Ineffective coping or adaptation to the events in one's life as well as a lack of personal growth

Attitudes Toward Mental Illness

When our attitudes toward understanding and accepting mental illness are examined over centuries, we find that they have not progressed dramatically.[9] Our approaches to the mentally ill are determined not only by medical and psychiatric theory, but also by the political and social climates of the time. For example, on February 5, 1963, President John F. Kennedy delivered his well-known "bold new approach" address to the United States Congress. The result of this address and subsequent legislation was the creation and growth of the community mental health movement in the United States. Unfortunately, after the 1970s, interest in community mental health waned, and currently there are vastly unserved and underserved populations in our country (see Chaps. 5 and 41).

The judicial system in the United States is influential in psychiatric-mental health treatment issues. In recent years court decisions have affirmed individuals' right to treatment, right to refuse treatment, and right to treatment in the least restrictive setting.[9] These rulings influence our attitudes about mentally disturbed persons and their rights and responsibilities (see Chap. 39).

An individual's values and personal beliefs affect his attitudes about mental illness, people with mental disorders, and treatment of mental illness. If, for example, a person holds independence and being a "self-made man" as strong values, he may disdain the apparent dependence or weakness of a disturbed individual. If a person values his liberty and personal freedom highly, he may fail to appreciate the need for physical or chemical restraint of an aggressive client. If he values stoicism, he may find it difficult to understand the usefulness of the expression of feelings in regaining or maintaining one's mental health.

There still exists a stigma surrounding individuals who need or use psychiatric-mental health services. The need continues for public education to modify or alter misconceptions about mental illness and persons with mental disorders.

Mental Health Care Today

Many problems face mental health care today. Psychiatric-mental health treatment is costly, and until recently, most medical insurance plans did not cover treatment for mental disorders. If a client is hospitalized in a state institution for the mentally ill, he is removed from his support system and often receives little more than custodial care.[30] The lack of governmental support for community mental health centers hastened the centers' narrowing of services and populations served. There exists in the United States unequal access to health care. Consumer advocate groups have not demanded improved mental health care, although their voice is now becoming stronger (see Chap. 5).[30]

The 1971 White House Conference on Aging acknowledged the need for comprehensive health care (including mental health care) for the aged.[29] It called for the diagnosis, treatment or safe transfer to a more adequate site for care, and rehabilitation of aged persons with emotional disorders, as well as their return home to family and community. The Conference also recommended alternatives to institutional care: training of mental health care providers to work with the aged, an allotment of an increased amount of research monies to the treatment of the aged, and the development of innovative therapeutic services to currently institutionalized older persons.[29]

Stress: Mechanisms and Responses

Hans Selye, a renowned biological scientist, defines *stress* as the "nonspecific response of the body to any demand made upon it."[26] Although *stressors*, or stress-producing factors, are different, such as the physical stressors of heat and cold and the psychological stressors of failure, success, and a new challenge, they elicit essentially the same biologic stress response. It is even immaterial, he claims, whether the situation or challenge we face is a pleasant one (success) or an unpleasant one (failure). Stress is not a synonym for distress; it is not anxiety or tension, nor is it something to be avoided at all costs. The absence of all stress is death.

General Adaptation Syndrome

To cope with any type of increased demand made upon it, the body responds in a stereotyped manner, with identical biochemical changes.[26] These responses are termed the *General Adaptation Syndrome* (GAS). The General Adaptation Syndrome demonstrates the body's manifestations of stress as they develop over a period of time.

The General Adaptation Syndrome evolves in three stages.

1. *Alarm reaction* is the stage in which the body begins to respond and adjust to the stressor; the body's resistance is being diminished and death may occur if the stressor is sufficiently strong.
2. *Stage of resistance* is the stage in which the body continues to resist the stressor and no longer evidences signs of the initial reaction; the person's level of resistance is greater than normal.
3. *Stage of exhaustion* is the stage in which the body's ability to resist the stressor, or adaptation energy, becomes exhausted following lengthy exposure to the same stressor; the signs of the initial reaction return but are irreversible and the person dies.[26]

For a more in-depth look at the body's physiological response to stressors, see Figure 1-1.

Distress

Damaging or unpleasant stress is *distress*. The body's biologic responses to stressors cause psychophysiological disorders. According to Selye, damaging stressors (*e.g.*, anxiety, frustration, insecurity, and aimlessness) may result in a variety of physical and emotional disorders, such as migraine headaches, peptic ulcers, myocardial infarctions ("heart attacks"), hypertension, suicide, mental illness, and "hopeless unhappiness."[26]

What is the ultimate aim of people? Is it, as Selye suggests, to express ourselves as fully as possible, according to our own talents and desires, and to achieve a sense of security? If so, then we must learn how to accomplish this. Selye's solution is to find our own optimal stress level and then to use our adaptive energy at a rate and in a direction adjusted to our own qualifications and preferences.[26]

Selye's own philosophy gives us a guideline for using our adaptive energy.

> "Fight for your highest attainable aim
> But never put up resistance in vain."[26]

Coping Mechanisms

Coping mechanisms are also referred to as ego-defense mechanisms, mental mechanisms, and defense mechanisms. Coping mechanisms function to protect the ego from overwhelming anxiety; for the most part, they operate on an unconscious level.

Denial

Denial is a commonly used coping mechanism wherein a person denies the existence of some external reality. The person using denial is unaware that he is using it. When a patient is informed of his medical diagnosis, for example, he usually denies its existence for some period of time.

> "Oh no, this is a mistake."
> "It's not true."
> "There's nothing wrong with me."
> "I can't have diabetes (multiple sclerosis, cancer, heart attack), I'm too young and healthy."

For a brief or lengthy periods of time, denial generally operates as a protective and often a healthy mechanism, protecting the individual from the shock of reality until he is better able to deal with it. In time, denial usually diminishes and the person gradually begins to face, accept, and deal with the harsh realities.

There are varying degrees of denial. A person who has been told that he has had a heart attack, which caused a great deal of damage to the heart muscle, may deny that he has had a heart attack at all. Another person facing the same diagnosis may acknowledge that he has suffered a heart attack and recognize the need for treatment and for modification of his lifestyle, but may not believe that the extent of heart damage is as serious as his doctors have described.

Denial may also have treatment implications. If a child exhibits overtly disturbed behavior but his parents deny that a problem exists, the parents will not seek treatment for their child and may, in fact, become indignant

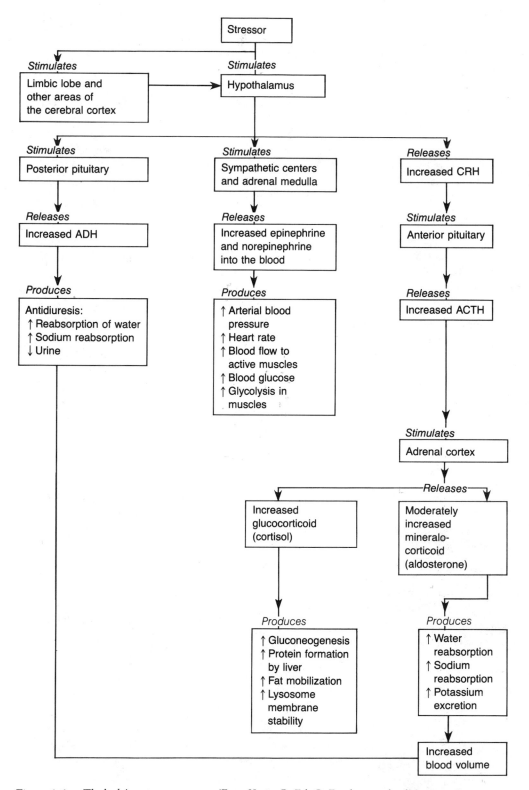

Figure 1-1.   *The body's response to stress.* (From Kozier B, Erb G: Fundamentals of Nursing: Concepts and Procedures, 2nd ed, p 186. Menlo Park, California, Addison-Wesley, 1983)

when a teacher or school nurse recommends psychologic assessment of the child.

A person may deny selectively; that is, deny certain facts but accept, or seem to accept, others.

> A husband and wife in their early thirties were told by the pediatric neurologist that their son, 10 months of age, had static congenital encephalopathy, commonly called cerebral palsy, evidenced in right-sided hemiparesis. While dealing with their shock, anger, and the other facets of grief, they began to plan and implement various therapies needed by their son—passive exercising of his right arm and leg and an active swimming program.
>
> Eight months after the diagnosis of the child's condition, the couple sat in their living room watching the Summer Olympic Games on television. The woman turned to her husband and asked, "Do you think someday our son will be an olympic athlete?" "What?!" replied the man, looking at his wife in disbelief.

Denial takes many forms and serves many functions. In this situation, it protected the woman from the full force of her grief over the loss of the ideal or "perfect" child.

Regression

Through the use of *regression,* a person avoids anxiety by returning to an earlier, more comfortable time in his life, a time when his needs were met more completely.

A 3-year-old child might regress in response to the birth of a sibling and begin again to soil her pants, suck her thumb, talk "baby talk," and ask for a bottle. An adult undergoing any physical or emotional stress might regress by becoming irritable, demanding, and whining; or the adult might take to his bed for a "sick day," thereby giving up his responsibilities for the day and allowing others to meet his needs.

Play is one important form of regression. It is our way of voluntarily relinquishing our adult concerns and duties and engaging in a child-like state of spontaneity and enjoyment. For children, of course, play serves many functions, including fantasy, learning, and opportunity for mastery of physical and emotional challenges.

Like the other coping mechanisms, regression may be a useful and healthy response to stressors, but may become maladaptive if used excessively or exclusively.

Displacement

Displacement is the transfer of an emotion from its original object to a substitute object. For example, if a person is angry with his superior at work or school, he may feel too threatened to confront that individual with his anger; instead, he may go home and vent his anger on a family member. The person has displaced his feeling (anger) from its original object (his superior) to a substitute object (a family member).

It is likely that the individual who displaces his feelings has no awareness that he is using displacement. Later, however, he may look back on the events and realize that, because he was angry with someone to whom he could not comfortably express his feeling, he "took it out" on a member of his family.

Projection

Projection is the displacement of feelings, usually feelings perceived as "negative," onto another individual. If, for example, a person feels guilty (or angry, dependent, aggressive, or hostile) and this feeling is unacceptable to him, he may project it onto another rather than owning it.

> "I'm not angry, but she's mad at me."
> "I don't have any bad feelings toward him, but he sure hates me."

Individuals with paranoid behavior frequently overuse the mechanism of projection. If the person is fearful of his environment, he may project those feelings onto the external world and develop the delusion that forces in the environment, such as the FBI, CIA, or Soviet spies are "out to get him." He may believe that others are constantly watching him and plotting his demise.

Sometimes, projection of feelings functions as an adaptive mechanism, protecting us from feelings that we find unacceptable in ourselves until we can learn to own up to them and acknowledge that having both "positive" and "negative" feelings is part of our humanity.

Reaction Formation

When a person uses *reaction formation,* he acts in a way that is the opposite of how he feels. For example, if a person feels aggressive or hostile toward another, he might, because these feelings are unacceptable to him, behave very kindly and politely toward the object of his feelings. The individual who uses reaction formation is not consciously aware of the great disparity between his feelings or ideas and his actions.

> A student seemed to be angry at one particular instructor. She was displeased with her grades on the instructor's exams and with the many criticisms and corrections she received from the instructor. When she interacted with the instructor, however, she wore a frozen, continuous smile on her face, was excessively polite, and talked in a high-pitch, "little girl" tone of voice. Frequently, she gave the instructor gifts.

If a person cannot acknowledge his own feelings of dependency, he may behave in ways that emphasize his independence. He may assert that he "needs no one," and verbally and nonverbally drive others away.

Repression

Through *repression,* an individual forces certain feelings or thoughts into his unconscious. The repressed material, such as painful memories or feelings, remains in the person's unconscious, although it may surface from time to time in his dreams or "slips of the tongue." Repression is a mechanism that occurs at the unconscious level.

The usefulness of repression, again, is to protect the individual from overwhelming anxiety. He involuntarily "forgets" certain events or feelings that evoke a great deal of anxiety.

Suppression

Suppression takes place when a person consciously excludes certain thoughts or feelings from his mind. The excluded thoughts or feelings are those that cause him anxiety. This coping mechanism operates at the conscious level. When a person decides to "put something out of his mind" or "not worry about it until tomorrow," he is using suppression.

> A student was assigned a major research paper to write. Every time he thought about the length and depth of the paper and the amount of hard work it would require, he felt extremely anxious.
>
> To overcome his anxiety and initiate work on the paper, he decided he would not think about it as a total, completed project, but would break it down into smaller, more manageable units. He listed each component of the assignment—choosing and delineating the topic, outlining the scope of the topic, researching each subtopic, and so on—and then proceeded to tackle each component systematically.
>
> When his anxiety surfaced from time to time, he forced himself to push aside fears about the total undertaking and concentrate on the smaller unit of work before him.

Identification

Identification is the unconscious adoption of the personality characteristics, attitudes, values, and behavior of another person. Children frequently identify with their parents, a favorite aunt, uncle, or teacher, and even well-known public figures in sports or entertainment. Adults also use identification as a means of continued growth by adopting some of the attributes of their role models. When this process becomes conscious, however, it is called *imitation.*

The person using identification is unaware of doing so, although others may recognize that he is identifying with another. Overuse of identification may result in a person developing low self-esteem and little individuality because he has relied heavily on the advice and support of others.

Rationalization

Rationalization is the substitution of acceptable reasons for the real or actual reasons motivating behavior. Through rationalization, a person justifies his behavior or conceals his disappointments.[31] For example, if a person interviews for a job but is not hired, he may rationalize that the interviewer for the company did not spend enough time with him to get a fair impression of his strengths. He may also rationalize that he did not really want the job or that the job would have required more time than he was willing to devote to it. In each of these rationalizations, the person covers his real feelings of failure and disappointment with ones that will protect him from the anxiety associated with failure and disappointment.

Fantasy

Fantasy is nonrational mental activity that allows an individual to escape from his daily pressures and responsibilities.[31] Through fantasy, a person temporarily breaks through the boundaries of reality and enters a place where he can daydream about whatever is most pleasurable to him. For example, if a person is overwhelmed by the pressures of a task he has undertaken, he may imagine the completion of the task and the feelings of satisfaction and pride he will experience at its completion. These feelings may spur him on to work harder toward his goal.

The thinking of children, particularly young children, is characterized by fantasy. Often, adults become stifled by the realities of the world and abandon their use of fantasy. The ability to fantasize, however, provides an effective escape valve for people of all ages and promotes childlike creativity. The excessive use of fantasy, on the other hand, reduces an individual's contact with reality and may render him incapable of dealing with the demands of his life.

Intellectualization

Through *intellectualization,* a person uses his intellectual powers of thinking, reasoning, and analyzing to blunt or avoid emotional issues. Talking about or dealing directly with feelings are too threatening or painful for him.

Sometimes, an individual with significant emotional problems (*e.g.,* a severe lack of interpersonal skills) will intellectualize his problems. He may discuss Sullivan's interpersonal theory and the effect of childhood interpersonal experiences on adult functioning and he may weigh the value of one therapeutic intervention over another, but he will avoid the more difficult discussion of his feelings. Feelings are often the heart of the issue in psychiatric-mental health nursing, but they require a degree of courage and confidence to face.

The usefulness of these various coping mechanisms lies in their protection of the person from intolerable anxiety. We all use these mechanisms at one time or another, particularly in situations that elicit threatening or painful feelings; however, their value depends on their judicious use. The continuous, exclusive use of these mechanisms would inhibit or prevent the person from learning other, more effective ways to cope with, adapt to, and grow in relation to his environment.

Psychiatric-Mental Health Nursing

One of the most significant figures in the history of psychiatric nursing in the United States was Dorothea Lynde Dix (1802–1887). During her time, the standard treatment of the mentally ill ranged from negligence to brutality. She found patients confined in cages and cellars, chained, and beaten.[7] She pioneered the crusade for reforms in the treatment of the mentally ill and gained the support of influential citizens by describing to them the abhorrent conditions in which mental patients lived.

Psychiatric-mental health nursing has evolved, from those times to the present, into a unique discipline. It now combines the knowledge, experience, and skills of nursing and mental health. In actuality, the name psychiatric-mental nursing implies two different areas of nursing that often interact and overlap. Psychiatric nursing focuses on the care and rehabilitation of those with identifiable emotional disorders. Mental health nursing focuses on well populations; it intervenes in crisis situations and with high-risk individuals or groups to prevent the development of mental illness or disorder.

Roles of Psychiatric-Mental Health Nurses

Some of the roles of the psychiatric-mental health nurse include skilled communicator, role model of adaptive behavior, director of the therapeutic milieu, advocate for the client and family, member of the mental health care team, primary nurse for specific clients, and therapist with individuals, groups, and families. This last role, nurse–therapist, requires advanced education, supervision, and experience. Many of these roles are approached in depth in other chapters of this book (see Chaps. 3, 4, 14, 15, and 31). The reader is encouraged to explore these and other chapters for a greater understanding of the roles of nursing.

Views of Novice Nurses

The impressions, perceptions, and fears of nurses new to psychiatric-mental health nursing are important to examine. If unexamined or ignored, they may hamper the nurse's effectiveness in intervention. A noted psychiatric-mental health nurse and author, Ann W. Burgess, has described the feelings common to nursing students facing their first psychiatric nursing experiences. They are listed below.

Feeling useless
Appearing like a novice
Anxiety
Fear of being rejected by the client
Fear of hurting the client
Fear of being hurt by the client
Depression
Anger
Embarrassment
Concerns about their own mental health[3]

The following display will also help mental health nurses prepare for their experiences.

Clients' Views of Mental Health Care

The clients' views and feelings are likewise important to consider. Often, clients are frightened or relieved in response to being hospitalized in a psychiatric unit. They may fear that treatment will dehumanize them or that mental health care providers will overmedicate, discount, or neglect them.[3] Clients may also be suspicious of the new environment (if they are hospitalized for psychiatric treatment) and the strange, but seemingly well-intentioned, mental health professionals.

Clients seeking psychiatric treatment often expect that the care providers will be able to solve their problems for them. They may expect to play a passive role while the psychiatrist, nurse, psychologist, or social worker actively "cures" them. It is necessary for mental health care professionals to clarify these client perceptions and provide clients with straightforward information about the processes of mental health care and the expected behavior of the client as a member of the health care team. The insert, The Mental Health Nurse As Person, explores the phenomenon of clients ascribing omnipotence to mental health care professionals and ways to deal with this occurrence.

(Text continues on p 14)

Preparing for Psychiatric-Mental Health Nursing Experiences

Johnnie Bonner, R.N., M.S.N.
Clinical Manager, Adult Unit
Brookhaven Psychiatric Pavilion
Farmers Branch, Texas

Philosophies and theories about the nature of human behavior and what constitutes competent, ethical treatment of individuals with emotional disorders vary greatly. In addition to philosophic and theoretical differences, treatment settings, researchers, educators, and the literature usually focus on limited aspects rather than the entire continuum of possible services and knowledge. You may be exposed to a variety of settings or you may realize that your textbook or instructor describes different kinds of treatment from what you observe. If you think of the inconsistencies as differences and refrain from making judgments about "right or wrong" or "good or bad," you may be more open to learning from what you see and hear.

Sometimes, the structure or the day-to-day tasks and functions are not as easy to identify on a psychiatric unit as they are in other services. This apparent lack of specific treatments and tasks may leave you wondering whether you can make any meaningful or helpful contribution to clients and the agency providing the learning experience for you. Most psychiatric-mental health professionals and agencies believe that contributing to your learning experience is an investment that is expected to pay off indirectly; it will also pay off in the long term by adding some of you to the ranks of clinicians or by providing you with a constructive awareness of psychiatric nursing, regardless of the field within nursing that you choose for a career. Psychiatric-mental health staff do not expect you to do anything but learn; however, they also know from experience that you will make significant contributions. Your energy and enthusiasm are refreshing. Your relatively unbiased exploration of what staff are doing and why will raise important questions and issues that need to be reviewed in the ongoing process of evaluating care.

You may wonder, particularly during your initial psychiatric nursing experience, "What will I discuss with the client?" The client may choose to keep the process of your interactions superficial, partially due to the dynamics of his problems and partially due to the reality that the time limits of a student's rotation will not allow the development of an in-depth therapeutic alliance. Focus initial questions or interview openings on what led to the client's or others' decision to seek treatment. This will help you become acquainted with the client and give him an opportunity to reflect again on the nature of his difficulties or treatment issues. Discussing the decision to seek treatment can be genuinely helpful, even when it is repeated many times, because it is an opportunity to examine the same set of circumstances from a different perspective. The simplicity of these natural and expected kinds of questions does not negate their therapeutic value.

There are also other areas that you may invite clients to explore with you. These include their expectations of the treatment facility and services and their responses to them. Thoughtful reflection on progress in the course of treatment can help build the client's self-esteem and hope for change.

The issue of confidentiality assumes an important and perhaps somewhat different perspective within the psychiatric–mental health team. The potential situation exists in which you are asked by the client not to share some information that he has revealed. I can think of *no* situation in which agreeing to this kind of request would be therapeutic. This may be a difficult dilemma, often preceded by the client's flattering comments about your attributes as a good listener or an understanding and trustworthy person. You may even be lured by the hope that the client will reveal something that will have great impact on his treatment. The client will need to be reminded, kindly but firmly, that it is important for all members of the therapeutic team to share any information that might contribute to his treatment. In addition, you might ask the client to explore why he is unable to trust the other members of the treatment team. As a student, you might try to understand the dynamics of how accepting and keeping the client's "secrets" separates you from the rest of the team.

Another crucial issue in psychiatric-mental health nursing is that of maintaining a "separateness" in the therapeutic role. You may hear this called "detachment," "objectivity," or "distance," but despite how thoughtfully this topic is discussed with you, you may bristle and think that others are suggesting that you develop an attitude of coldness. On the contrary, your values of compassion and empathy are not being challenged; indeed, it is virtually impossible to be therapeutic without those qualities. What experienced psychiatric-mental health clinicians recommend is that in order for you to use your knowledge and skills therapeutically, compassion and empathy must be expressed in a manner that leaves your personal life separate from the client's. Clients do not need us personally, as friends or companions, as much as they need us to teach them how to have (or why they don't have) friendship and companionship outside of treatment. Identifying your own feelings and attitudes and discussing them with an experienced clinician may help you develop as a professional who is both caring and effective in relationships with clients.

As you work with clients, keep in mind that, although you may provide an opportunity and an environment in which change may occur, you cannot make a client change. You cannot transfer your observations, knowledge, and assessment of what you believe is best for him into his awareness. Try to imagine, at times, what it would cost the client to make the changes you feel would benefit him.

Change is the client's choice. He may need our skills, knowledge, and a safe place to work; and although he may sometimes borrow our hope, he makes the choices, he does the internal work, and he needs to feel the pride and take the credit. He lives with the choices.

The Mental Health Nurse As Person

Janet W. Dalsheimer, R.N., M.S.
Mental Health Nurse Consultant
Dallas, Texas

Entering mental health nursing may be a career choice that appears exciting and sometimes a little overwhelming. We may wish to understand all of the intricacies of human behavior to work more effectively with our clients, but a sometimes overlooked fact is that people are complex. Even with many years of study and experience in the field of mental health, we cannot hope to comprehend every facet of being a person. We can, however, strive toward greater understanding of the people to whom we give care if we initially embody some concepts about people in general. Next, undertaking the complex task of understanding ourselves and our needs can further reduce the risk of relating to clients in less-than-effective ways.

It is helpful to remember that, as people, we share more similarities than differences. We all have concerns about our lives, our health, our relationships, and our well-being. As human beings, we experience happiness, anger, loneliness, joy—literally, a full spectrum of emotions. Within this framework of our thoughts and feelings, we then function with varying degrees of mental health.

Because mental health cannot be demonstrated at the cellular level, in order to examine this phenomenon, we must rely on theoretical constructs and symptoms reflective in behavior. How do we know when we have mental health? Is it an "all or nothing" condition? Mental health has been defined as the most appropriate adjustment a person can make at a particular time based on internal and external resources. This definition implies that mental health is like physical equilibrium—it is necessary to constantly adjust it in order to retain it. Continuous effort is needed to cope with new situations.[4]

When we are mentally healthy, we experience some of the following "inner signals."

Self-esteem; self-respect that prevails even in the face of discouragement, failure, or frustration

An open, flexible approach to life; being able to experience a failure without berating ourselves or others

A spontaneous, outgoing temperament; possessing the ability to enjoy others and the capability of giving and accepting love; being able to express strong feelings appropriately

Minimal nervous tension; being free from crippling worry and strain; facing life in a relaxed, confident manner

Appropriate depression, anxiety, and anger under stress; drawing upon a philosophy that facilitates the handling of frustration and pressure reasonably well.[1]

Needless to say, the complete and constant attainment of the above criteria is practically impossible. No one can be expected to cope with, or adapt perfectly to, every one of life's crises. Nevertheless, can we, as mental health professionals, help others if our own mental health is not perfectly intact? If we accept the fact that people are not perfect, and that we are likewise human, then part of our self-understanding is to accept thankfully that we can, indeed, fit into an imperfect world. Like everyone else, we are in the process of striving toward higher levels of mental health.

Despite our understanding of life's imperfections, a myth persists that mental health professionals are all-knowing or possess magical powers. This is a problem of "imbued omnipotence," a term referring to a complex of unrealistic beliefs held about mental health professionals by others outside of the profession.[5] Some of these "beliefs" may be that mental health professionals have the ability to read minds or predict the future. Mental health care providers may be regarded as people who should cope with and act appropriately in every situation or, even more unrealistically, as people who have no problems at all.

It is important to understand this external view of the mental health nurse in order to avoid the subtle trap of an omnipotent image. Inexperienced nurses who believe that they must produce a "magic" answer that will solve a client's problems, or who even believe that there is one such "magic" solution, will find this expectation terribly self-defeating. It is a self-expectation that will crush professional spirit and create insurmountable distance between nurses and their clients.

What, then, is the dividing line between nonhospitalized persons and those who are hospitalized with an emotional disorder? It is simply the ability to cope at a given point in time—the ability to draw upon available resources and weather life's daily stresses.

When mental health is viewed within this framework, it is easier to recognize that, as creatures who are vulnerable, none of us are immune to the possibility of needing professional help at some point in our lives. We, as mental health nurses, are in no way dramatically different from our clients. If we see our clients as "different" or as persons to be pitied, we are behaving defensively to protect ourselves. This stance may be antitherapeutic or unhelpful, for we are at risk of thinking and acting in ways that lack compassion and sensitivity to our client's needs.

If, on the other hand, we adopt the philosophy that mental health, like physical health, is a matter of degree and is a fluctuating condition, we leave ourselves open to experiencing empathy, or *feeling with* our clients. Perhaps some of us may have developed an interest in mental health nursing after a personal experience with therapy, or we may find a need for therapy at some point in our careers. The self-understanding attained through therapy not only provides personal benefits, but it also facilitates further understanding of the process through which our clients travel. Remembering the feelings of pain and those of satisfaction that may be evoked in therapy can provide us with personal experiences from which to draw and can help us approach others with greater empathy.

In addition to understanding ourselves as people in the role of mental-health nurse, we should also remember that the role itself has limitations. We often need the ideas of our colleagues, and we may need other disciplines. Collegial support can come from a clinical nurse specialist as well as from staff nurses. We should also feel free to consult the chaplain, social worker, occupational therapist, psychiatrist, and psychologist. Each specialty has much to contribute to the client's care, yet each has its own limitations. By working together as a team, we provide better care for the client.[2]

Finally, self-understanding means knowing how to take care of ourselves mentally and physically. Again, we must know our limitations and be kind to ourselves. We cannot perform emotionally draining work and ignore the importance of replenishing ourselves. A great deal of material has been written in recent years on the topics of stress and burnout. To remain effective as mental-health professionals and to avoid becoming "burned out," it is important to incorporate strategies for coping with stress into our daily lives. The following suggestions will help prevent stress from turning into distress.

Take care of your body. This is a two-fold process that involves paying attention to diet and exercising regularly. To avoid feeling overwhelmed while trying to change old patterns, set small goals and reward yourself for accomplishments. For example, if you have decided to cut down on refined sugar, you might decide to substitute fruit for candy during the next week. You might also think about several pleasurable activities that could be substituted for eating when a craving for sugar surfaces. In the area of exercise, it is important to pick an enjoyable activity, a form of exercise you will stick with. Setting a goal of walking around the block or campus every day may be just the starting point that is needed to embark on an exercise program. A balanced diet and adequate exercise are essential for an overall feeling of well-being.

Learn to play. We need to escape from the pressures of life and have fun on a regular basis. Resurrecting old board games from childhood, such as Monopoly, can be fun. It is important to pick an activity that is absorbing and enjoyable. Remember to use vacation time to get away, both physically and mentally, from work or school.

Make some friends with people outside of nursing and mental health. It is mentally refreshing to learn and talk about subjects other than work-related topics.

Learn to plan. Whenever possible, take on projects one at a time and work on them until they are completed. Making lists, rather than committing tasks to memory, aids organization tremendously.

Learn a substance-free method of relaxing. While they may be more socially acceptable than other habits, excessive eating, drinking, and smoking are health-damaging means to relaxation. More positive ways to relax include yoga, meditation, and progressive relaxation techniques.

Attempt to solve problems when at your best mentally and physically. Determining what time of day you feel most alert and functional may be helpful in getting difficult tasks completed.

Do something simple that can be accomplished easily, something over which you have a high degree of control. Tasks such as washing clothes or sweeping the walk are nearly always available to undertake.

Break your routine by seeking new experiences. Give of yourself in a non-nursing area. Select a cause that is of genuine interest and volunteer your time.

Talk out your troubles. We need to remind ourselves that expressing concerns to an understanding friend or counselor is important. We set an example for our clients by not bottling up problems.[3,6]

By understanding and nurturing ourselves, we will become healthier and will strengthen our sense of well-being. Our clients, in turn, will benefit from this self-understanding by which we learn to identify commonalities among people. A mixture of theoretical knowledge about people and self-understanding allows us to bring to our practice the highest level of mental health nursing care.

References

1. Didato SV: Am I "Normal"? Parade, p 22, September 11, 1983
2. Lipkin GB, Cohen RG: Effective Approaches to Patients' Behavior. New York, Springer–Verlag, 1973
3. Robinson AM: Stress Can Make You—or Break You. RN 38: 73–77, 1975
4. Robinson, L: Psychiatric Nursing as a Human Experience, 2nd ed. Philadelphia, WB Saunders, 1977
5. Travelbee, J: Intervention in Psychiatric Nursing: Process in the One-to-One Relationship. Philadelphia, FA Davis, 1969
6. Woolfolk, RL, Richardson FC: Stress, Sanity, and Survival. New York, Monarch, 1978

Nurses' Reactions to Disturbed Behavior

Like everyone else, nurses are affected by the behavior of the people around them. When nurses work with clients with psychiatric problems, they may encounter various forms of disturbed behavior—bizarre, aggressive, hostile, suspicious, dependent, and violent. Their reactions to these behaviors are likely to reflect the range of their experiences and values.

The nurse reacting to disturbed behavior may be offended, repulsed, threatened, annoyed, angered, surprised, or shocked. She may be confused and frightened by these feelings. She may view her feelings as "unprofessional" and be ashamed of them. If the goal of nursing is to provide the highest quality nursing care for patients, then nurses must first examine their own values, feelings, and reactions. Self-exploration and working through difficult issues, such as how to interpret and deal with manipulation or hostility, are critical developments in the nurse's professional growth.

There is no one "right way" to intervene therapeutically in disturbed behavior. Mental health care providers explore their thoughts and feelings, follow certain broad guidelines, and experiment with what works for them. Nurses and other care providers cannot impart wisdom to anyone, but they can give of themselves—their caring and hopes—to the other.[14]

Stress and Burnout Among Nurses

The pressures of psychiatric-mental health nursing are significant. Intervening daily with individuals whose behavior is disordered or maladaptive requires a great deal of personal and professional resources. The toll on the nurse can be heavy.

The nurse should be alert to certain warning signs of increasing job stress. These include job dissatisfaction, loss of enthusiasm and energy, fatigue, sleep disturbances, and escape activities (such as alcohol and drug use).[6]

More severe, chronic, or crisis symptoms of stress include exhaustion, chronic fatigue, physical illness that may become critical (such as a bleeding ulcer), loss of control of emotions, obsession with problems, withdrawal, moodiness, and increased use of escape activities.[6]

Positive coping with job stress and burnout requires a concerted effort by the nurse or other mental health care provider. Support systems, at work and away from work, are necessary to allow the nurse to ventilate feelings and help keep events in perspective. It is also useful if the nurse does not expect 100% satisfaction from her job, because this expectation is destined to failure. Taking frequent, brief vacations, or minivacations, has been found to be more refreshing and relaxing than infrequent, longer vacations. Positive imagery, such as imagining job success and satisfaction, is an effective use of fantasy and provides a mental minivacation.[6] Specific measures for preventing job burnout are described in the insert, The Mental Health Nurse As Person.

Use of Nursing Models

There is some truth or usefulness to all models of nursing, given the diverse problems and needs of diverse clients in diverse settings.[5] Important issues to explore in various models include the following.

Who defines the client problems?
Is the client blamed for his problems?
Is the client expected to take responsibility for arriving at solutions to his problems?
Who evaluates the success or failure of the solutions?[5]

Providing people with increased responsibility for solving their own problems develops competence and independence. The medical model of helping, wherein the helpers decide the solutions to client problems, promotes the client's dependence on health care providers.

Roy's model of nursing aims to promote adaptation of the client to a changing environment. The nurse assesses the adaptiveness or maladaptiveness of client behaviors and plans interventions to modify maladaptive behaviors.[5]

The goal of nursing intervention may be regained stability for the client; that is, adaptation of the client to his environment. On the other hand, the goal may be more dynamic and change-oriented, related to an improved level of wellness or mental health.

The Nursing Process

The nursing process is a problem-solving approach to effect change in client problems. The steps of the nursing process—assessment, analysis and nursing diagnosis, planning, intervention, and evaluation—allow a systematic method by which nurses deliver care to clients. The American Nurses' Association's Standards of Psychiatric and Mental Health Nursing delineate the scope of nursing practice (see also the insert entitled Standards of Psychiatric and Mental Health Nursing at the end of this chapter).

Assessment

Assessment, the first step of the nursing process, is the systematic collection of comprehensive data about clients and their problems and needs. Psychological, social, and cultural influences on an individual's functioning are explored.

Analysis and Nursing Diagnosis

The second step of the nursing process, analysis or nursing diagnosis, includes the organization of data into categories, the determination of actual and potential client problems, analysis of the causes of the problems, if possible, and the formulation of conclusions.

Planning

Planning, the third step of the nursing process, involves the determination, in cooperation with the client and his family, of goals and interventions to achieve the goals.

Intervention

Intervention, the fourth step of the nursing process, is the implementation of nursing activities designed to reach client goals.

Evaluation

Evaluation, the fifth and final step of the nursing process, is the determination of outcomes of nursing interventions. Evaluation of present services may demonstrate the need for additional services. Burgess and Holmstrom's work entitled Rape: Crisis and Recovery, for example, demonstrates the need for services to rape victims to prevent more serious disturbances later.[4]

Section III of this text, The Process of Psychiatric–Mental Health Nursing, studies in depth each step of the nursing process.

Summary

This chapter introduced the reader to the basic principles of the psychiatric field of nursing. Some of the major emphases of the chapter include the following.

1. Mental health and mental illness are imprecisely defined states.
2. Satisfaction with one's characteristics, abilities, and accomplishments, effective and satisfying interpersonal relationships, effective coping or adaptation to one's life events, and personal growth characterize mental health.
3. The stigma attached to mental illness or disorder may hamper an individual's willingness to seek treatment and his rehabilitation.
4. Problems hindering the progress of mental health care today are cost of treatment, separation of clients from their support systems, lack of governmental support of community mental health centers, and unequal access to care.
5. Stress is the nonspecific response of the body to any demand made on it.
6. Stressors, or stress-producing factors, whether physical or psychological, pleasant or unpleasant, elicit the same biologic stress response.
7. The General Adaptation Syndrome evolves in three stages—alarm reaction, stage of resistance, and stage of exhaustion.
8. Coping mechanisms, such as denial, rationalization, regression, fantasy, and so forth, protect the individual from anxiety.
9. Roles of psychiatric-mental health nurses include advocate, communicator, role model, member of the health team, and nurse–therapist.
10. Self-awareness, self-exploration, and working through feelings and reactions to disturbed behavior are necessary for nurses to intervene in therapeutic ways.
11. Job stress and burnout can be minimized through an early detection of symptoms of stress, regular attention to physical health and exercise, and involvement in non-nursing activities.
12. The nursing process—assessment, analysis and nursing diagnosis, planning, intervention, and evaluation—is a problem-solving approach by which nurses deliver care to clients.

Standards of Psychiatric and Mental Health Nursing

American Nurses' Association
Division on Psychiatric and Mental Health
Nursing Practice, 1982

Professional Practice Standards

Standard I. Theory
   The nurse applies appropriate theory that is scientifically sound as a basis for decisions regarding nursing practice.

Standard II. Data Collection
   The nurse continuously collects data that are comprehensive, accurate, and systematic.

Standard III. Diagnosis
   The nurse utilizes nursing diagnoses and/or standard classification of mental disorders to express conclusions supported by recorded assessment data and current scientific premises.

Standard IV. Planning
   The nurse develops a nursing care plan with specific goals and interventions delineating nursing actions unique to each client's needs.

Standard V. Intervention
   The nurse intervenes as guided by the nursing care plan to implement nursing actions that promote, maintain, or restore physical and mental health, prevent illness, and effect rehabilitation.

Standard V-A. Intervention: Psychotherapeutic Interventions
   The nurse uses psychotherapeutic interventions to assist clients in regaining or improving their previous coping abilities and to prevent further disability.

Standard V-B. Intervention: Health Teaching
   The nurse assists clients, families, and groups to achieve satisfying and productive patterns of living through health teaching.

Standard V-C. Intervention: Activities of Daily Living
   The nurse uses the activities of daily living in a goal-directed way to foster adequate self-care and physical and mental well-being of clients.

Standard V-D. Intervention: Somatic Therapies
   The nurse uses knowledge of somatic therapies and applies related clinical skills in working with clients.

Standard V-E. Intervention: Therapeutic Environment
   The nurse provides, structures, and maintains a therapeutic environment in collaboration with the client and other health-care providers.

Standard V-F. Intervention: Psychotherapy
   The nurse utilizes advanced clinical expertise in individual, group, and family psychotherapy, child psychotherapy, and other treatment modalities to function as a psychotherapist, and recognizes professional accountability for nursing practice.

Standard VI. Evaluation
   The nurse evaluates client responses to nursing actions in order to revise the data base, nursing diagnoses, and nursing care plan.

Standard VII. Peer Review
   The nurse participates in peer review and other means of evaluation to assure quality of nursing care provided for clients.

Standard VIII. Continuing Education
   The nurse assumes responsibility for continuing education and professional development and contributes to the professional growth of others.

Standard IX. Interdisciplinary Collaboration
   The nurse collaborates with other health care providers in assessing, planning, implementing, and evaluating programs and other mental health activities.

Standard X. Utilization of Community Health Systems
   The nurse participates with other members of the community in assessing, planning, implementing, and evaluating mental health services and community systems that include the promotion of the broad continuum of primary, secondary, and tertiary prevention of mental illness.

Standard XI. Research
   The nurse contributes to nursing and the mental health field through innovations in theory and practice and participation in research.

This material has been published by the American Nurses' Association and is being reprinted with the ANA's permission.

References

1. Antonovsky A: Health, Stress, and Coping. San Francisco, Jossey-Bass, 1979
2. Bruch H: Learning Psychotherapy: Rationale and Ground Rules. Cambridge, Harvard University Press, 1974
3. Burgess AW: Psychiatric Nursing in the Hospital and the Community, 3rd ed. Englewood Cliffs, New Jersey, Prentice-Hall, 1981
4. Burgess AW, Holmstrom LL: Rape: Crisis and Recovery. Bowie, Maryland, Robert J Brady, 1979
5. Cronenwett LR: Helping and Nursing Models. Nurs Res 32 (November/December): 342–346, 1983
6. Dillon A: Reducing Your Stress: Six Experts Tell You How. Nursing Life 3 (May/June): 17–24, 1983
7. Dolan JA, Fitzpatrick ML, Hermann EK: Nursing in Society: A Historical Perspective, 15th ed. Philadelphia, WB Saunders, 1983
8. Dongier M, Wittkower ED (eds): Divergent Views in Psychiatry. Hagerstown, Harper & Row, 1981
9. Flagg JM: Public Policy and Mental Health: Past, Present, and Future. Nursing and Health Care 4 (May): 246–251, 1983
10. Freedman AM, Kaplan HI, Sadock BJ: Modern Synopsis of Comprehensive Textbook of Psychiatry. Baltimore, Williams & Wilkins, 1972
11. Friedrich O: Going Crazy: An Inquiry into Madness in Our Time. New York, Simon and Schuster, 1976
12. Haber J, Leach AM, Schudy SM, Sideleau BF: Comprehensive Psychiatric Nursing, 2nd ed. New York, McGraw-Hill, 1982
13. Kalinowsky LB, Hippius H, Klein HE: Biological Treatments in Psychiatry. New York, Grune & Stratton, 1982
14. Kaslow FW et al: Supervision, Consultation, and Staff Training in the Helping Professions. San Francisco, Jossey-Bass, 1977
15. Kravetz D, Jones LE: Androgyny as a Standard of Mental Health. Am J Orthopsychiatry 51 (July): 502–509, 1981
16. Laing RD: The Facts of Life: An Essay in Feelings, Facts, and Fantasy. New York, Pantheon Books, 1976
17. Langner TS, Michael ST: Life Stress and Mental Health: The Midtown Manhattan Study, vol II. London, The Free Press of Glencoe, 1963
18. Lewis JM, Usdin G (eds): Treatment Planning in Psychiatry. Washington, DC, American Psychiatric Association, 1982
19. Looney JG, Blotcky MJ: Special Perspectives on Treatment Planning for Children. In Lewis JM, Usdin G (eds): Treatment Planning in Psychiatry, pp 289–336. Washington, DC, American Psychiatric Association, 1982
20. Luckey JW, Berman JJ: Effects of New Commitment Laws on the Mental Health System. Am J Orthopsychiatry 51: 479–483, 1981
21. Mallick M: Nursing Diagnosis and the Novice Student. Nurs Health Care 4: 455–459, 1983
22. Peplau HE: Interpersonal Relations in Nursing. New York, G. P. Putnam's & Sons, 1952
23. Rosenhan DL: On Being Sane in Insane Places. In Brink PJ (ed): Transcultural Nursing: A Book of Readings, pp 175–197. Englewood Cliffs, NJ, Prentice-Hall, 1976
24. Satir V, Bernhard YM, Macdonald N: Using the Family Unit for Change. In Beiser M, Krell R, Lin T, Miller M (eds): Today's Priorities in Mental Health: Knowing and Doing, pp 35–39. Miami, Symposia Specialists, 1978
25. Schwab JJ, Schwab ME: Sociocultural Roots of Mental Illness: An Epidemiologic Survey. New York, Plenum Medical Book Company, 1978
26. Selye H: Stress Without Distress. New York: The New American Library, 1974
27. Shore MF: Marking Time in the Land of Plenty: Reflections on Mental Health in the United States. Am J Orthopsychiatry 51 (July): 391–402, 1981
28. Shires B: Nurses Need Nurturing, Too. Nursing Life 3 (January/February): 40–43, 1983
29. Toward a National Policy on Aging. Proceedings of the 1971 White House Conference on Aging, Vol II. Washington, DC, 1971
30. Westlake RJ (ed): Shaping the Future of Mental Health Care. Cambridge, Ballinger, 1976
31. Wilson HS, Kneisl CR: Psychiatric Nursing. Menlo Park, California, Addison-Wesley Publishing Co, 1979

Chapter 2
Conceptual Frameworks for Care

The intimate union of theory and practice aids both.

Alfred North Whitehead

Judith A. Greene

Chapter Preview

A *theory* is a conceptual system that describes and explains selected phenomena. In this way, theory serves as a tool to guide and shape human understanding and behavior. To the extent that theories apply to real events, they are considered useful. When theories apply to real nursing events, they serve to guide the understanding and behavior of nurses.

Nurses use theories of human behavior to understand clients and to intervene therapeutically. Theories used by psychiatric-mental health nurses fall into four basic theoretical viewpoints:

1. Psychoanalytic theory
2. Behavioristic theory
3. Biologic theory
4. Systems theory

Although these four theoretical perspectives represent different views of humankind, they are nevertheless equally useful to nurses.

Learning Objectives

On completion of this chapter, the reader should be able to accomplish the following.

1. Explain the purposes of theoretical or conceptual frameworks
2. Discuss the basic assumptions underlying the psychoanalytic, behavioristic, biologic, and systems theories
3. Apply these four theoretical perspectives to the nursing care of clients
4. Compare psychoanalytic, behavioristic, biologic, and systems theories and their applications to nursing

The Psychoanalytic Theoretical Perspective

The psychoanalytic theoretical perspective is derived from the work of Sigmund Freud and his followers. The basic assumptions underlying this theoretical perspective include the following.

1. All human behavior is caused and can therefore be explained. Slips of the tongue, accidents, dreams, artistic creations, and all other forms of human behavior have meaning and can therefore be explained. This psychoanalytic theory states that all human behavior, however obscure, does not occur randomly or by chance; rather, all human behavior is determined by antecedent life events.

2. All human behavior from birth to old age is driven by an energy force called the *libido*. The goal of the libido is tension reduction through the attainment of pleasure. The libido is closely associated with the physiological or instinctual drives (hunger, thirst, elimination, sex). Release of these drives results in the reduction of tension, which is experienced as pleasure; hence, the *pleasure principle* becomes operative when pleasure-seeking behaviors are employed.[9]

3. Human behavior that channels impulsive pleasure-seeking behaviors into creative pursuits (sublimation) is considered the highest form of human expression. Maturity, therefore, is associated with the ability to invent and use substitutive or disguised forms of gratification.[9] This ability to delay pleasure in favor of more socially acceptable behavior is referred to as the *reality principle*.

4. The personality of the human being can be understood by means of three major hypothetical structures—id, ego, and superego. The *id* represents the most primitive structure of the human personality in that it houses the instincts. The id cannot delay the attainment of pleasure. When human behavior originates from the id, it is impulsive, pleasure-oriented, disconnected from reality, and, consequently, often inappropriate. Thought processes deriving from the id are characterized by their illogical, confused form and their preverbal, or preoperational, content.[9] Such thought patterns are referred to as *primary process*. Examples of primary-process thought patterns are often reflected in the verbalizations of psychotic schizophrenic individuals (see Chap. 22).

The *superego* is the personality structure that contains the values, legal and moral regulations, and social expectations that thwart the free expression of pleasure-seeking behaviors. The superego, in this way, functions to oppose the id. Society and the family determine the content of the superego and the kinds of limitations it imposes on the individual.[9] Severe limitations enforced by the superego can lead to maladaptive patterns. For example, many depressed individuals feel excessive guilt because they cannot possibly live up to the strict, harsh standards imposed on them by their superego.

The *ego* represents that part of the human personality that has the greatest contact with reality. Unlike the id, the ego is capable of postponing pleasure until an appropriate time, place, or object is available. Unlike the superego, the ego is not driven to blind conformity to rules and regulations. Rather, the ego, acting as a mediator between the id and superego, gives rise to more mature and adaptive behavior.[9] To illustrate, mentally healthy individuals are neither driven toward impulsive, pleasure-seeking behavior nor toward rigid, moralistic behavior. Instead, these individuals live adaptively in the present, free of the ceaseless pursuit of pleasure or pain (see Chap. 1).

With the id and superego constantly at odds with one another, the ego is faced with the task of maintaining control over instinctive impulses while simultaneously taking into consideration moral values and injunctions. Understandably, the human being, from time to time, experiences anxiety when confronted with situations that challenge the tenuous balance between the id and superego. At these times, the ego employs defense mechanisms to ward off anxiety.[7] Repression, denial, regression, rationalization, reaction formation, undoing, projection, displacement, sublimation, isolation, and fixation are among the commonly used defense mechanisms.

5. The human personality functions on three levels of awareness—the conscious, the preconscious, and the unconscious. *Consciousness* refers to the perceptions, thoughts, and feelings existing in a person's immediate awareness. *Preconscious* content, on the other hand, is not immediately accessible to awareness. The person must make an effort to retrieve this content before it reaches awareness. Unlike both conscious and preconscious content, *unconscious* material, for the most part, remains inaccessible to the individual.

6. The unconscious affects all three structures of the personality—the id, the superego, and the ego. Although the id's content resides totally in the unconscious, the superego and ego exist in all three levels of consciousness.[9] Freudian slips, word choices, jokes, and many nondeliberate nonverbal behaviors are examples of the id, ego, and superego operating at all three levels of consciousness. Through these three levels of consciousness, the ego maintains contact with reality as well as with the id and superego.

7. Human personality development unfolds through five innate stages referred to as the *psychosexual stages*. The sequence of these stages corresponds to the changing manner in which the individual seeks pleasure. The stages are called psychosexual stages because the theory further assumes that all pleasure is essentially sexual in nature. These stages include the oral, anal, phallic, latency, and genital stages. Although these stages extend throughout the lifespan, the theory also maintains that the first 6 years of life determine the individual's long-term personality characteristics[9]; that is, early-life events, especially with regard to parent-child ex-periences, determine the individual's behavior throughout life;

8. Despite this theory's deterministic view of human behavior, it is further assumed that human personality and behavior possess sufficient flexibility to permit slow progress toward change.[6]

Therapeutic Approaches

In keeping with these basic assumptions, the psychoanalytic view of human behavior relies on the therapeutic approach of psycholanalysis. This therapeutic approach is exercised by psychiatrists, psychologists, and psychiatric mental-health nurses who have undergone extensive education and training in its use. *Psychoanalysis* employs strategies such as hypnosis, dream interpretation, and free association, in which the client verbalizes every idea that come to mind regardless of how trivial or shameful it may sound. The psychoanalyst attempts to maintain a relatively passive demeanor in order to create a neutral environment devoid of approval or disapproval and to encourage the client to be his natural self from moment to moment. When the psychoanalyst interacts with the client, it is usually to make an interpretation of the client's verbal or nonverbal behavior. No touching occurs between the client and psychoanalyst. Usually, the psychoanalyst remains out of the client's visual field.[6]

The primary goal of psychoanalysis is to create a permissive-yet-safe situation in which the client can recall past traumatic events and work through residual conflicts and emotions that have thwarted or fixated his growth and integration as a person. In short, the goal of this approach is to help the client release his full potential as a healthy, well-integrated human being.

Application to Nursing

Psychoanalytic theory has influenced psychiatric-mental health nursing in many ways. This theoretical perspective, perhaps more than any other, has helped mental health professionals understand psychopathology and stress-related behaviors. More importantly, this theory illustrates the importance of not taking human behavior at face value. That is, psychoanalytic theory helps the psychiatric-mental health nurse and other health care providers discern and explore the meaning behind human behavior.

The Behavioristic Theoretical Perspective

The behavioristic theoretical perspective is derived from the works of Ivan Pavlov, John Watson, and B. F. Skinner. Several basic assumptions underlie this theoretical perspective:

1. All human behavior is a response to a stimulus or stimuli coming from the environment.
2. Human beings are passive organisms that can be conditioned or shaped to do anything given that correct responses to specific stimuli are rewarded or reinforced.
3. Human beings can control or determine the behavior of others, whether or not they wish to be controlled.
4. The human personality is a mere pattern of stimulus–response chains or habits.
5. Both adaptive and maladaptive behaviors are learned and perpetuated through reinforcements.
6. Maladaptive behavior can therefore be unlearned and replaced by adaptive behavior, provided that the human being receives exposure to specific stimuli and reinforcements for the desired adaptive behavior.[5]

Therapeutic Approaches

Several therapeutic approaches stem from the behavioristic theoretical perspective. *Token reinforcement* is one such approach. With this approach, the use of direct reinforcers is delayed through the administration of tokens. When desired adaptive behavioral responses are emitted, tokens are awarded to the client. After a specific number of adaptive behavioral responses occur, the tokens can then be redeemed for actual reinforcers, such as an extra cup of coffee or a higher level of privileges.[9]

Shaping is another behavioral reinforcement technique used to condition close approximations of some desired adaptive behavior. In applying this technique, reinforcement of successively closer approximations occurs until the terminal adaptive behavioral outcome is reached.[9] Shaping requires careful observation and a great deal of patience to identify and reinforce desired behavior approximations.

Other behavior-change techniques derived from the behavoristic approach include relaxation therapy, aversive conditioning, implosion, flooding, and assertiveness training. The behavior therapist usually determines what behavior of the client's should be changed and what behavioral approach to use in order to effect that change.

Application to Nursing

Nurses with advanced psychiatric-mental health education often employ behavioristic techniques when working with long-term mentally ill clients in one-to-one, as well as group, situations. Nurses use behavioral strategies in the management of psychiatric clients within a therapeutic milieu; clients are often rewarded or reinforced with privileges such as attendance at a certain activity or a weekend pass. Behavioristic strategies are also useful tools to nurses working with physically disabled clients in rehabilitation settings.

The Biologic Theoretical Perspective

The biologic theoretical perspective originated in the early era of psychiatric medicine. This theoretical perspective assumes the following.

1. Departures from normal adaptive behavior are due to illnesses, structural or genetic defects, or biochemical imbalances affecting the central nervous system.
2. Restoration to adaptive mental health usually requires somatic therapy, such as psychotropic medications, psychosurgery, hormonal therapy, or electric shock therapy.
3. Mental or psychological illnesses are like all other illnesses.

Application to Nursing

The biologic theoretical perspective places little if any emphasis on psychosocial explanations or treatments of abnormal or maladaptive behavior. This theory, however, does provide explanations or rationale for the effectiveness of somatic therapies.

The Systems Theory Perspective

The systems theory perspective is derived chiefly from the work of Ludwig von Bertalanffy. Basic assumptions of this theory include the following.

1. The human being is a living, open system consisting of interrelated subsystems.[4, 12]
2. These interrelated subsystems are components or parts of the total human organism.[4, 12]
3. These subsystems, in relation to each other, tie the human system together and form a whole.[12]
4. Individual subsystems, or "subwholes," possess attributes in common with each other and the human system as a whole. Consequently, every part of the human system is so related to its fellow parts that a change in one part or subsystem will cause a change in the remaining parts or subsystems.[12]
5. The human system therefore behaves not as a composite of independent elements, but coherently and as an inseparable whole.[4, 12]
6. The human system is surrounded by a boundary that serves to separate the human system from its surrounding environment. Information may cross this boundary in order to enter or leave the human system.[12]
7. The five sensory channels plus the verbal and nonverbal behavioral modes of the human system serve as a boundary separating the human system from the surrounding environment. Information may

cross this boundary, thereby providing sensory *input* to the human system. The human system then transforms this sensory input into useful, meaningful forms. This transformation process, referred to as *thruput,* involves feeding this sensory input through thoughts, feelings, memories, values, attitudes, intelligence, physiological structures, and so forth. In turn, the human system produces information (or *output*) that is fed back to the human organism itself or to the environment and other human beings via verbal and nonverbal behaviors. Output, also referred to as *feedback,* is not always appropriate to input; furthermore, output is not always predictable on the basis of input. The reason for this lack of predictability is that the transformation of input (the thruput process) is unique for each human system.

8. The human system tends to favor a steady state in which there is an orderly exchange of information or input within the human system and between the human system and the environment.[4]

9. Disruption of stability results in stress on the total human system, and this stress affects the amount of energy available to activate or maintain the human organism. A depletion of energy lessens the amount, type, and intensity of informational inputs accepted by the human organism, which in turn affects the correctness and efficiency of information processing (or thruput). Finally, a weakened input and thruput affects the correctness of the human organism's output; that is, verbal and nonverbal behavior.

Application to Nursing

According to the systems theory, the goal of nursing care is to assist clients to maintain or regain a steady state. This theory also provides the nurse with a holistic, theoretical perspective from which to understand the human being. The systems theory resolves the mind–body dispute by viewing the human organism from a perspective of matter–energy–information.

Recognizing that human beings are not simple, passive organisms, the systems theory assists the nurse to observe and understand how clients affect and are affected by the environment, other people, and themselves. In providing such a holistic viewpoint, the systems theory allows the nurse to identify client strengths that can be used to overcome or compensate for weaknesses and limitations. Moreover, the systems theory views the human being as a complex organism and, thereby, acknowledges that human behavior has multiple causes and meanings. By making such an acknowledgement, this theory performs its most valuable function—capturing the uniqueness and complexity of human life.

Summary

This chapter has examined various theoretical bases for understanding human behavior and for intervening in maladaptive behavior. Some of the major points of the chapter include the following.

1. Psychoanalytic, behavioristic, and biologic theoretical perspectives (Table 2-1) emphasize that hu-

Table 2-1. **Conceptual Models of Treatment**

MODEL	SUBJECT	INTERVENTIONS
Biologic	Physical illness or defect causing mental illness	Chemotherapy Psychosurgery Insulin coma therapy Electroconvulsive therapy
Behavioristic	Stimuli causing human behavior	Token economy Behavior modification Shaping Operant conditioning
Psychoanalytic	Developmental events causing mental illness	Psychoanalysis Free association Dream interpretation Hypnosis
Systems	Whole system and subsystems	Interpersonal Environmental Physical treatment Social change Family treatment

man behavior is largely determined by external forces or other factors outside the individual's control; that is, the human being is viewed as a passive organism.

2. The system theory (Table 2-1) acknowledges the effects of external forces on human behavior, but maintains that the individual can either influence these outside forces or can compensate for them; that is, the individual is viewed as an active and interactive human system.

3. The psychoanalytic, behavioristic, and biologic theoretical perspectives hold that human behavior is monocausal, that it is determined by one cause.

4. According to the psychoanalytic theory, behavior is determined by early life events with parental figures.

5. The behavioristic theory holds that exposure to given stimuli and reinforcements determine how the human being learns to behave.

6. The biologic theory states that human behavior is determined by the genetic and biologic make-up of the individual.

7. The systems theory asserts that human behavior has multiple causes.

8. All four theoretical perspectives are useful to nurses in assessing, planning, implementing, and evaluating nursing care.

References

1. Boulding, KE: General Systems Theory: The Skeleton of Science. In Walter B (ed): Modern Systems Research for the Behavioral Scientist, pp 3–10. Chicago, Aldine Publishing, 1968

2. Freud, Sigmund: Civilization and Its Discontents. New York, WW Norton & Co, 1961

3. Hilgard ER, Bower GH: Theories of Learning, 4th ed. Englewood Cliffs, NJ, Prentice-Hall, 1975

4. Miller JG: General Living Systems Theory. In Freedman AM, Kaplan HI, Suddock BJ (eds): Comprehensive Textbook of Psychiatry, 3rd ed, Vol 1, pp 98–114. Baltimore, Williams & Wilkins, 1980

5. Nye RD: Three Views of Man. Monterey, California, Brooks/Cole, 1975

6. Offenkrantz W, Tabin A: Psychoanalytic Psychotherapy. In Arieti S (ed): American Handbook of Psychiatry, 2nd ed, Vol 5, pp 183–205. New York, Basic Books, 1975

7. Roberts SL: Behavioral Concepts and Nursing Throughout the Life Span. Englewood Cliffs, NJ, Prentice-Hall, 1978

8. Snelbecker GE: Learning Theory, Instructional Theory, and Psychoeducational Design. New York, McGraw-Hill, 1974

9. Starr BD, Goldstein HS: Human Development and Behavior. New York, Springer, 1975

10. Sutherland JW: A General Systems Philosophy for the Social and Behavioral Sciences. New York, George Braziller, 1973

11. von Bertalanffy L: General System Theory. New York, George Braziller, 1968

12. von Bertalanffy L: General System Theory and Psychiatry. In Silvano A (ed): American Handbook of Psychiatry, 2nd ed, Vol 1, pp 1095–1117. New York, Basic Books, 1975

Chapter 3
Communication

So healthy, sound, clear, and whole.

Alfred Lord Tennyson

Juliann Casey Reakes

Chapter Preview

Adaptation to the environment is one of the goals of productive living. The interpersonal process is an indispensable component of psychiatric-mental health nursing that facilitates the adaptation process. This chapter focuses on the experiences that assist the client to understand and learn new, adaptive ways of dealing with the environment and developing patterns of productive living.

Both the client and nurse make interpretations and evaluate each other's behavior in an interactive process.[6] This chapter emphasizes how nurses learn to become skillful communicators who extrapolate from both the nursing and communication processes to build a relationship with a client that is therapeutic for the client and professionally functional for the nurse.

Learning Objectives

Upon completion of the chapter, the reader should be able to accomplish the following.

1. Define communication and the communication process
2. Describe the nursing communication model
3. Discuss the interrelationships of the components of the communication process
4. Assess the communication needs and problems of clients
5. Explain the nurse's use of listening and observation skills in the therapeutic communication
6. Identify therapeutic uses of self-disclosure
7. Apply the techniques of therapeutic communication, including the following

> Clarification
> Reflection
> Confrontation
> Verification
> Self-disclosure
> Informing
> Silence
> Summarizing
> Directing
> Questioning

8. Identify barriers to therapeutic communication
9. List goals for intervening in psychotic communication

Communication Process

Each person has a unique relationship with the environment that is manifested in behavior. The transport system for behavior is the process known as communication. *Behavior* can be thought of as a transmission or series of transmissions that take place when the individual interacts with the environment. Communication is the conveyor of these transmissions and is always present and occurring.[26] Even if an individual tried, he could never *not* communicate; his lack of verbalization, eye contact, and so forth would communicate something to others.

Communication is a personal, interactive system—a series of every-changing, ongoing transactions in the environment. Transmissions are simultaneously received (or decoded), are sent (or encoded), and are influenced by the sum total of the experiences and perceptions of the receivers and senders.

Purpose of Communication

Interaction with others gives the individual a sense of identity and being. A person's concept of self and the relationship of this self to another individual, to a group of people, and to the world occur because of communication.

Communication System

Communication, whether verbal or nonverbal, includes three essential aspects:

1. The transmission of information
2. The meaning of the transmission
3. The behavioral effects of the transmission

The transmission of information is the sending and receiving of *messages* or units of information. Through the feedback process, every person in the transaction is affected by the behavior of everyone else involved.

Communication Models

Communication models, or graphic representations of various approaches to communication, provide overviews or perspectives about communication. The following adapted model serves as a pattern that outlines the essential components of communication.[26]

A model of communication compatible with the nursing process is an adaptation of the Wenburg and Wilmot process model of communication.[26] This model is particularly useful for nursing application because it emphasizes the behavioral aspects of the communication process and the internal and external environmental variables that influence the process. Use of this model assists the nurse to explore the communication process and identify those elements pertinent to the communication and nursing processes.

Components of the Communication Process

Communication is an ongoing, every-changing, infinite transmission system influenced by all the participants in the transmission. Components of the communication process

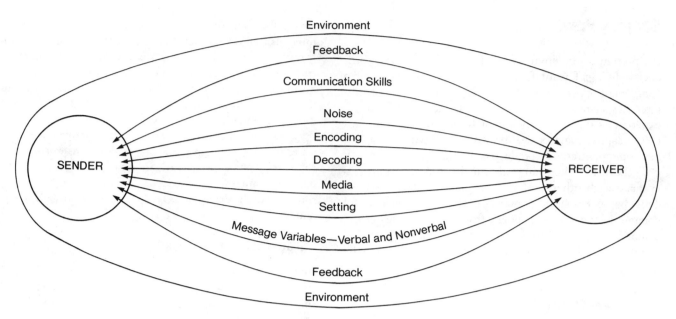

Figure 3-1. *Nursing communication model.*

include the sender, the receiver, the message, message variables—verbal and nonverbal communication, noise, communication skills, setting, media, feedback, and environment (see Fig. 3-1).

Sender

The sender is the encoder, the person who initiates the transmission. This event, the transmission of the message, is both verbal and nonverbal.

Receiver

The receiver of the message is the decoder. Encoding and decoding occur simultaneously and are activities of both sender and receiver. The past and present experiences of sender and receiver influence the transaction.

Message

The message is the unit of information received. A message is made up of many variables that can be verbal or nonverbal.

Message Variables

Message variables are selective verbal and nonverbal stimuli from the internal or external environment that give shape, direction, and focus to the message. The written and spoken language are examples of verbal communication; gestures, smiles, and dress are examples of nonverbal communication.

Verbal Communication. Language is the expression of ideas according to society's shared format for sentence structure and grammatical rules.[15] Language is an acquired form of symbolization, a verbal behavior specific to humans.[28]

Although speech is ongoing social behavior, it frequently fails to explain behavior accurately. Speech itself is a complex activity involving the oral, respiratory, auditory, and nervous-system components of the body. Structural defects, malfunctioning due to disease, auditory and verbal impairments, sensory deprivation or overload, and learning disabilities may affect its use and decrease its transmission accuracy.

The schizophrenic person is characterized by his inability to abstract and use word symbolization to translate meaning that is reality-oriented. The stutterer experiences an interruption in the normal rhythm of speech sounds and he, too, is impaired in his ability to express his relationship with the environment. The mentally retarded child may be unable to learn language and is deprived of an expected social behavior. The autistic child exemplifies the individual who cannot symbolize with words.

In addition to attending to words and sounds, the nurse recognizes that nonverbal behaviors, such as voice pitch, voice quality (that is, harsh, weak, or strained), and voice amplification (that is, soft or loud) influence the message and are essential components of communication assessment. The choice of words, grammar, and understanding of language also influence the nature of the nurse–client relationship and, therefore, are included in the assessment.

Nonverbal Communication. Approximately 35% of the meaning of a communication transaction is due to verbal variables; the remaining 65% represents the impact of nonverbal communication. Nonverbal communication may do the following.

1. Contradict verbal behavior
2. Emphasize an emotional tone or mood

3. Complement verbal behavior
4. Control the environment
5. Be the communication of choice[10]

Many nonverbal behaviors are associated with messaages. The familiar behaviors of crying, screaming, laughing, moaning, giggling, and sighing are examples of nonverbal communication. Other forms of nonverbal communication include facial expressions, body posture and gait, tone of voice, and gestures.

Noise

Noise refers to interferences within the communication system that hinder the accuracy of the transmission.

Communication Skills

Communication skills include the abilities of the sender and receiver in using message variables to observe, listen, clarify, and validate the meaning of the transmission.

Setting

The setting refers to the place or location where communication takes place.

Media

Media are the sensory channels that carry the message. Sensory channels include auditory, visual, touch, taste, and smell. A client's verbal message to the nurse for medication to relieve his anxiety will be carried via the nurse's auditory channel. The nurse, through the visual channel, sees tears in the client's eyes. The client leans forward and grasps the nurse's hand, emphasizing his need through touch. More than one sensory channel is involved in communication.

Feedback

Feedback is inherent in the communication system. Negative feedback functions to regulate the system to maintain the steady state, and positive feedback is responsible for change and disruption within the system. When applied to the communication system, feedback functions as a regulatory mechanism in the communication process. The receiver may see a sad or depressed expression on the sender's face but decide not to share this perception with the sender, thereby failing to clarify the communication. If the receiver had told the sender of his perceptions and the sender had explained that his sad expression had nothing to do with the present communication, a positive change might occur and the facial expression might change to reflect the ongoing transaction.

Feedback involves the continuous interpretation of responses of the sender and receiver as messages are simultaneously encoded and decoded. Private variables experienced by the sender and receiver are continually being communicated to each other and therefore influence the transaction.

Environment

The internal and external influences affecting the communication process make up the environment. Contextual cues affect the quality and sometimes the content of communication. Factors in the external environment are seen by everyone, but may be perceived differently by each individual. Room temperature, noise levels, smells, and lighting are examples of external environmental factors. Influences in the internal environment are known only to the individual and are not experienced in the same way by other people. Feeling tired, experiencing stomach discomfort, and feeling cold are examples of internal environmental factors.

Levels of Communication

A basic premise of the communication process is that it is intrapersonal in nature; all reactions to communication take place within one's self regardless of the number of people involved in the transaction. Communication occurs intrapersonally, interpersonally, in small groups, and in public or large groups. A characteristic of group communication is that the members are interdependent (*e.g.*, in social, therapy, or task groups). Public communication refers to the public speaking setting in which one person sends a verbal message to a number of receivers. In psychiatric-mental health nursing, the main focus of interaction occurs at the interpersonal and group levels.

Interpersonal Needs

Individuals have interpersonal needs that include knowing that the self is personable, worthy, and able to interact with and use the environment satisfactorily. An individual whose interpersonal needs are not met adequately may be withdrawn, cold, and superficial in relationships. An overly friendly, possessive, and confiding individual may also be giving cues of a less-than-satisfying self-image. A loner, a shy and passive sort, as well as a talkative "attention getter" may present behaviors that display feelings of unworthiness.

Submissiveness, lack of confidence, inability to make decisions, as well as domination and aggressiveness may indicate an inability to use and control the environment.[26] The communication process is a potent approach to assisting others in making adaptive changes to the environment.

Interpersonal Communication

Interpersonal communication is affected by the sensitivity of the participants to their own feelings and to the feelings of the other participants. Verbal and nonverbal communication may be spontaneous or calculated to affect the receiver. In therapeutic communication, for example, the nurse communicates to the client by arrangement of the environment, use of space, touch, voice inflection, dress, and so forth. Interpersonal communication is the most direct and pertinent form of communication, because it is through this transaction that needs are met.

Communication and the Nursing Process

Client problems may involve a variety of maladaptive patterns of communication. The nurse identifies these problems as objectively as possible and uses a systematic approach, utilizing listening skills and the nursing process to formulate tentative nursing disgnoses or to identify client problems. During the assessment interview, the interaction between the nurse and client is not designed exclusively for data collection purposes. The nurse's creation of an environment that is conducive to communication conveys to the client that she is attuned to his feelings and needs. Within a therapeutic atmosphere, change can occur and the client can be helped to identify and understand his behavior in a neutral, caring atmosphere.

Assessment of Communication

Congruence Between Verbal and Nonverbal Communication

A goal of the nurse in a therapeutic relationship is to assess the *congruence,* or agreement between the client's verbal and nonverbal communication. The client may not be aware that disharmony between his verbal and nonverbal communication exists.

If the client tells the nurse that he feels fine but has a sad facial expression and tear-filled eyes, his nonverbal communication does not agree with his words and the nurse is alerted to incongruent behavior. Assessment of nonverbal communication is an integral part of the communication assessment process. Facial expressions, motor activity, gestures, feeling tone, and congruence between verbal and nonverbal message variables are important categories for assessment (refer to the insert, Communication Assessment Tool).

Use of Space and Territory

The use of space and territory is a form of nonverbal communication. The distance a person places between himself and another person or between himself and a group of people is a significant factor in interpersonal activities.

The concept of distance as a communication variable has been categorized as meeting public, social, and personal needs. The interpersonal aspects of public space involve the most distancing of people, while intimate personal space involves close contact. Personal (nonintimate) and social space are often reflected in informal gatherings, and interpersonal contact falls between the public and intimate distancing.

The goals and duration of the nurse–client relationship determine the space and distancing involved in the interaction. When designing a therapeutic milieu, the nurse assesses space and territorial needs of all clients.[12, 24, 27]

The nurse may observe certain behaviors that indicate a client's personal space and territory are being invaded. *Personal space* refers to the space preferred for interaction, whereas *social space* has a connotation of companionship.

Territory implies assigned space, such as a client's room, public room, or a specific seating arrangement. Territory is a designated place that implies ownership or personal possession. Intrusion or violation of someone's space or territory can distract and distort communication.[2]

Therapeutic Communication

Listening

Listening, or focusing on all of the behaviors expressed by a client, is the foundation of therapeutic communication. Listening requires energy in a form of concentration that does the following.

1. Minimizes distractions
2. Conveys objectivity
3. Is not evaluative in terms of agreeing or disagreeing with the communicator
4. Focuses on the client's behavior
5. Uses feedback objectively.[13]

Listening is an active process that focuses objective, empathic attention on the client. Maintaining eye contact, facilitating close proximity (if not threatening to the client), projecting a relaxed physical orientation and closeness, and speaking in a normal, audible voice are all characteristics of this process.[5, 6, 8]

The nurse attends to physical cues, such as room temperature and physical comfort. She tries to eliminate noise from the listening environment and tries to discontinue other media channels, such as the telephone, television or radio, in order to meet therapeutic listening goals and prevent interruption of the interaction.

Listening to another person requires the decoding of both the content and the feelings expressed in the message. Verbalizations, opinions, thoughts, and impressions make up the *content* part of messages. The *feeling* portion of a message is the emotional one, which may be described verbally (although this verbal description may or may not be accurate) or nonverbally.[24] A client who speaks in a relaxed voice may nevertheless reveal his anxiety by his nonverbal behaviors of chain smoking, clenching his hands, tense body posture or movement, and so forth. To individualize approaches to clients, the nurse notes congruence or incongruence between verbal and nonverbal communication and then validates her observations with the client. The anxiety or preoccupation of either nurse or client may be reflected

Communication Assessment Tool

Name_____ Age_____ Sex_____ Diagnosis_____

I. Sender or receiver impairments
  A. Structural deficit
  B. Sense deficits: hearing, sight, smell, touch, taste
  C. Loss of functions
  D. Disease
  E. Drugs
  F. Other
II. Message variables
  A. Nonverbal communication
    1. Facial expression
    2. Gestures
    3. Body movements
    4. Affect
    5. Tone of voice
    6. Posture
    7. Eye contact
    8. Voice volume, quality, pitch
    9. Other
  B. Verbal communication
    1. Content of message
    2. Communication patterns
      a. Blocking
      b. Slow
      c. Rapid
      d. Quiet
      e. Halting
      f. Aphasic
      g. Continuity
      h. Excessive
      i. Detailed
      j. Stammering
      k. Circumstantial
      l. Tangential
      m. Long silences
      n. Other
III. Noise
IV. Communication skills
  A. Openness, spontaneity
  B. Use of clarification
  C. Request for feedback
  D. Tolerance of silence
  E. Acceptance of confrontation
  F. Other
V. Setting
  A. Inpatient unit
  B. Community settings
  C. Other
VI. Media
VII. Feedback
  A. Precise
  B. Pertinent
  C. Goal-directed
  D. Informative
  E. Solicited
  F. Positive
  G. Negative
  H. Clarified
  I. Opportune
VIII. Environment
  A. External influences
    1. Temperature
    2. Physical arrangement
    3. Lighting
    4. Noise level
    5. Other
  B. Internal influences
    1. Beliefs
    2. Experiences
    3. Thoughts
    4. Attitudes
    5. Other
IX. Cultural influences
  A. Health practices
  B. Religious implications
  C. Language barriers
  D. Food preferences
  E. Other

in nonverbal communication that interferes with the therapeutic listening environment.

Observation

The nurse carefully observes for the client's communication of internal influences that may prevent the attentiveness needed for the therapeutic communication process. The nurse, too, is influenced by internal variables and may be sleepy, hungry, thinking about a meeting with a supervisor, and so on. These kinds of influences can interfere with the nurse–client relationship and should be evaluated and modified, if necessary, to maintain an objective and empathetic environment conducive to the communication process.

Self-Disclosure

One of the major goals of therapeutic communication is to use a planned, systematic approach to foster the client's self-disclosure so that he can make adaptive changes.[21, 23] In our culture, we learn at an early age to control or conceal our authenticity—we disguise, hide, or deny our feelings.[13]

Diagnosing Communication Needs

The nurse analyzes assessment data and formulates nursing diagnoses that may include the following.

The client's maladaptive behaviors, as manifested in
>   Low self-esteem
>   Poor self-concept
>   Feelings of unworthiness
>   Inability to express anger

The client's use of the communication process
>   Inability to speak
>   Limited understanding of language
>   Nonassertive communication
>   Distorted decoding
>   Inability to send an accurate message
>   Incongruence in verbal and nonverbal communication

The client's expression of feelings about his communication abilities
>   Anxiety when talking to authority figures
>   Withdrawal when involved in group communication
>   Continuous talking when interacting with certain individuals

Feelings are expressed in behavior, however, and the client can learn to recognize these inner experiences and express them as adaptively as possible.

> A 35-year-old woman was able to identify her promiscuous sexual behavior as a way of dealing with her self-deprecatory feelings resulting from an incestuous relationship with her step-father during early adolescence. Her suicide attempt, at the age of 14 years, symbolically ended the relationship, but her sexual behavior during adulthood continued to express her rage and low self-esteem.

Feelings form the bases for intervention that aims to deal with those feelings realistically.[14]

Cultural Influences. A person's culture influences how he expresses his feelings, and each culture has certain sanctioned verbal and nonverbal channels of expression. Whereas an American conceals his feelings, a member of an Eastern culture openly and loudly expresses his grief, anger, or joy. Communication is an integral part of the culture of a group, and the nurse must therefore understand how a specific culture uses it. Cultural variables, such as the perception of time, bodily contact, and territorial rights, also influence communication. The communication practice of different cultures affects their expression of ideas and feelings, decision-making, and communication strategies.[12]

The nurse is less concerned with the causes of behavior than with the effect of the client's behavior on the immediate environment. The "now," "how," and "what" of behavior are major areas of nursing assessment and intervention. The nurse's specific communication skills allow her to use the communication process as a vehicle for implementing the nursing process.[13]

Communication Techniques

Communication techniques include clarification, reflection, confrontation, informing, verification, self-disclosure, silence, summarizing, directing, and questioning.

The feeling and content components of communication are usually presented simultaneously in a transaction. The client's abilities to label feelings and to identify whether his behavior is adaptive or maladaptive represent therapeutic progress to the psychiatric-mental health nurse. When a feeling has been labeled, the nurse then uses a translating or paraphrasing technique to help the client focus on this feeling, correct his misperceptions, and alter the resultant maladaptive or distorted behavior. In this way, the client learns new interpersonal skills; he learns to explore his feelings and express them in an adaptive manner.[13]

The content portion of the message is also important because it enables the client to repeat or describe an experience from his point of reference. The nurse identifies similarities in themes or concerns of the client and develops an appreciation of the uniqueness of the client's situation. The following are examples of therapeutic communication techniques.

Clarifying Feelings. When clarifying the client's feelings,

1. repeat the feeling tone of the message in your own words, or restate an emotional word or a phrase used by the clients;
2. use an open, questioning tone of voice; that is, a nondirective and noninterrogating one;
3. wait until the client responds.

Marian, a 31-year-old married woman is admitted to the unit because of depression and recent alcohol abuse.

Client (Marion): I don't know what happened—I left the children at the neighbor's and went to a bar just to see who was there. I woke up the next morning in a motel with a strange man (begins to cry, puts her clenched fists to her eyes).

Nurse: You're frightened and ashamed because you don't know what happened and you woke up in a strange place?

Client: It was so scary. I'm afraid it will happen again. I wouldn't leave even when my husband came for me. I feel so humiliated.

Admission to a Mental Health Unit: Communication and Perceptions

Tom, an 18-year-old, is admitted to a mental health unit because of a chronic problem with "stomach ailments," insomnia, and anorexia. Tom was reluctant to enter the unit, but his physician had told him he would learn new ways of handling his stressful environment, which involved many family problems related to his divorced parents and drug-dependent brother and sister.

Tom was admitted at 3:30 pm, experienced a 30-minute structured intake interview by the nurse, was oriented to the unit by another client assigned to this task, and went to his room. Thirty minutes into the dinner hour, the nurse realized that Tom hadn't been informed of the unit's dinner time. She escorted him to the dining room and asked a client Tom's age to help him.

Because Tom was admitted to the unit on a "pass day" for many of the residents (therefore, group activities were not being held), Tom went back to his room to read. Meanwhile, the nurse and other staff were busy admitting another new client and assisting clients with passes. Tom was given sleep medication at 9:30 pm and was asleep at 10:30 pm.

The next day, Tom checked out against medical advice because, he said, "The unit wasn't what I expected." Tom's perception of this new environment was of a polite but uncaring, strange new environment that was not very different from the one he was trying to escape. The communication and behavior of the nurse and others in the environment reinforced Tom's perception of the unit and his low self-esteem.

The nurse tried to help Marian label her feelings to create a clearer, more meaningful picture of her behavior. The nurse attended to the client's nonverbal cues and the feeling tone of her communication. Marian verified the message the nurse perceived.

Reflecting Feelings. When reflecting the client's feelings,

1. state your comprehension of the feeling message, using emotional and feeling descriptive words;
2. use a nonquestioning tone of voice;
3. wait until the client responds.

Client (Marian): I don't know who I am anymore (wipes eyes, lights a cigarette, talks in a whisper). I'm drawn to go to any barroom even though I tell myself it won't happen again.

Nurse: You feel frightened and ashamed that you're not in control of yourself.

Client: I can't seem to conrol my actions when these feelings come over me.

The nurse identified the feelings of shame and depression that Marian verified as being a part of her behavior and one of the reasons for her voluntary admission to the mental-health unit.

The nurse may use the clarifying technique to help the client label any other feelings she is experiencing, before reflecting on those feelings. The reflecting technique helps build a trusting nurse–client relationship because the client can express painful or uncomfortable feelings that are empathetically received by the nurse.

Clarifying Content. When clarifying the content of the client's communication,

1. repeat your comprehension of the thought or idea in your own words;
2. repeat a specific word or idea used by the client;
3. use an open, questioning tone of voice;
4. wait until the client responds.

Client (Marian): The man who brought me back to the motel was a gentleman.
Nurse: The man in the bar?
Client: Yes, the one I went with to the motel. I didn't even know him.

The nurse clarified the content part of Marian's message. This clarification acknowledged the client's recollection of her experience. The client needs to know and believe that the nurse has an accurate picture of her perceptions of the experience. Reflecting the content part of the message is another way of telling the client that the nurse is actively listening to obtain an accurate picture of his behavior.

Reflecting Content. When reflecting the content of the client's communication,

1. state your comprehension of the content message using descriptive or cognitive words;
2. use a nonquestioning tone of voice;
3. wait until the client responds.

Client (Marian): My brother is a diabetic and my sister has hypoglycemia problems. I read in a magazine that people who drink a lot may have trouble burning up sugar in their blood.
Nurse: You think because of the history of diabetes and your sister's glucose tolerance, you may have a glucose problem, too.
Client: Yes, I'm wondering if the doctor would check my blood.

The nurse informed Marian that a blood sugar test had been completed and the results were within normal limits.

Confronting Feelings.

When confronting the client's feelings,

1. describe the emotional message or feelings you are perceiving;
2. describe the client's ongoing behavior that is influencing your perceptions;
3. identify the contradictions using a questioning tone of voice;
4. wait for the client's response.

Marian has been less depressed since intensive therapy began 2 weeks ago. She is taking an antidepressant medication and is participating actively in the unit program.

The team has noticed incongruence in Marian's expression of feelings toward her husband. Marian discusses her feelings of love and need for closeness with her husband, but refuses his phone calls and does not open his letters. The team has decided to confront Marian with her behavior.

Client (Marian): I love my husband so much, and I know he understands why I go to bars when I'm upset.

Nurse: You feel your husband knows you love him so much that he accepts your behavior when you become anxious. Is refusing his calls and not opening his letters contrary to these strong feelings of love you say you feel for him?

Client: Sometimes I feel so confused. I hate him at times and then, at other times, feel overwhelming love for him.

Confronting Content.

When confronting the content of the client's communication,

1. describe the message you are perceiving, using cognitive terms;
2. describe the mixed-content messages you are perceiving using the specific cognitive terms of the client;
3. identify the contraindications using a non-questioning tone of voice;
4. wait for the client's response.

Client (Marian): My husband isn't interested in visiting me. I know 50 miles is a long way to come, but he won't make the effort.

Nurse: You think your husband doesn't care about you because he hasn't visited you, but you told me you sent him a letter asking him not to come. I'm confused, Marian.

Client: Well, don't you think he should know I really didn't mean for him not to come?

Nurse: I'm sure he's trying to do what you want and not visit you if that's your request. He has called every day.

Verifying Perceptions.

When verifying or "checking out" your perceptions of the client's behavior,

1. describe your perceptions of the client's behavior, using terms similar to his own descriptions of content or feelings.
2. use an open, questioning tone of voice to enable the client to verify your perceptions.
3. wait for the client's response.

Client (Marian): I don't think I have a drinking problem. I think all my trouble stems from my parent's divorce when I lost my friends and home.

Nurse: You're having difficulty accepting the fact that you are an alcoholic, and it's easier to blame your parents for your problems.

Client: I feel so uncomfortable when I look at the other people at our meetings who are so open about being alcoholics—I guess I can't or don't want to accept the fact that I'm like them.

Self-Disclosure.

The nurse reinforces the genuine regard for, and respect of, the client by means of the therapeutic use of self. Self-disclosure may be used after the client describes a feeling or an emotional message. When self-disclosing,

1. clarify the client's message or feeling tone;
2. describe similar experiences or feelings of your own;
3. wait for the client's response.

Client (Marian): I'm very frightened to go to the employment agency and apply for a job.

Nurse: I think I know what you mean. I've always felt "scared" when I had to apply for a new job.

The nurse avoids asserting "I know how you feel" because this response may be interpreted by the client to mean that his experience is a common one or that the nurse is far superior to him. On the other hand, the nurse's self-disclosure helps the client realize that his feelings, thought, or behaviors are shared and appreciated by others. It reinforces the nurse's empathy and willingness to share an experience with the client.

Bear in mind that this technique and all techniques of therapeutic communication are designed to meet a specific goal, after which the nurse immediately refocuses on the client. The nurse uses the technique of self-disclosure judiciously and sparingly so that the interaction does not become one dominated by the nurse's disclosures.

Giving Information.

Communicating facts to the client is a frequent component of intervention. It is a cognitive, goal-directed function and meets an identified objective for the client. When giving information to the client,

1. state the purpose of an activity, procedure, or situation;
2. describe an activity, procedure, or situation;
3. identify the components of an activity, procedure, or situation.

Client (Marian): I signed some kind of a contract yesterday about drugs and passes, but I can't remember all the facts.

Nurse: Each client signs a contract with our unit within 24 hours of admission. This contract identifies the rules and regulations about drugs and 20-minute, free-time passes. The contract you signed stated the following.
1. I do not have any drugs with me nor will I take any drugs that are not a part of my treatment.
2. I will sign out when I leave the unit, identifying where I'm going in the hospital, and will return in 20 minutes.

The nurse removed Marian's contract from the chart to show her the contract and her signature.

Silence.

When using silence,

1. describe the behavior that needs the client's response;
2. use an open, questioning, or declarative tone of voice;
3. wait for the client's response.

Marian had signed a behavioral contract to attend Alcoholics Anonymous meetings, which were being held at another area in the hospital.

Nurse: You didn't attend the AA meeting last night.

Client (Marian): I—just . . . (Marian puts her head in her hands; silence followed for about 2 to 3 minutes. Marian had recently talked about her feeling that she was not an alcohol abuser. She then begins to cry.) It's so hard for me to see myself as an alcoholic. (Silence for about 1 minute) I feel so ashamed and even unclean when I go to those meetings.

Nurse: You feel humiliated and dirty.

Client: I know it's not the people there. It's accepting myself as I am and not the make-believe I've been living.

Although it is often uncomfortable for nurse and client alike, using silence therapeutically is a very effective measure to encourage the client's communication. Silence provides time for the client to contemplate a thought, feeling, or decision. If a client is not comfortable with or trusting of the situation, he may use silence as a way to resist the interaction.

Summarizing.

When summarizing the interaction with the client,

1. review the interaction in specific terms;
2. wait for and listen to the client's response;
3. clarify any misunderstandings.

Nurse: Marian, during the last month you've said that you accept the fact that you abuse alcohol, you have complied with the behavioral contract, and you have attended two AA meetings a week for the past 4 weeks.

Client: I've gotten something out of them, too. I'll continue until my stay here ends, right?

Nurse: As I recall that is correct, but let's look at the behavioral contract.

Summarizing is an effective way to assist the client to examine themes in the interaction and to examine progress in general. It is also an appropriate technique for terminating a nurse–client counseling session, but may be useful at any time in the interaction to emphasize progress or focus on specific areas that are of concern to the client.

Directing.

When directing the client's interaction,

1. use nonverbal or succinct, open-ended questioning, or declarative statements;
2. wait for client's response.

Nurse: You were saying—.

Client (Marian): I know that when my husband called last night, I wanted to be kind and considerate about the out-of-town trip he needs to take, but—.

Nurse: Please go on, Marian.

Directing encourages the client to explore and express his thoughts and feelings. It also communicates the nurse's interest and attentiveness. Expressions such as "you were saying," "you mentioned this previously," "please continue," "Mmm-hmmm", or a nod of the head function as cues for the client to continue. Allowing the client time to respond is an essential part of this therapeutic technique.

Questioning. Frequently, the nurse uses direct questions or indirect questioning-like responses during therapeutic communication. A client, however, may become defensive or may intellectualize when asked the "why" of his behavior. Open-ended questions are helpful ways to elicit the "how," "what," "where," and "when" of the client's behavior. Questions such as "Will you elaborate?" "Will you give me an example?" and "Am I correct?" are examples of these responses. The nurse avoids asking questions that require an answer of "yes" or "no" and those that are probing and interrogative during therapeutic communication.[3, 5, 6, 13]

Interviewing

Interviewing is a specific type of guided and limited intercommunication with an identified purpose. An interview is usually conducted to collect a data base for analysis and decision-making purposes. The nurse often employs structured assessment tools and questionnaires to gather and categorize data.[11, 17]

Some guidelines for interviewing include the following.

1. Conduct sessions seated in a private, comfortable area with adequate lighting and hearing distance.
2. At the beginning of each session, plan and discuss with the client the length and purpose of the session.
3. Observe, listen, and use facilitative communication techniques.
4. Convey a professional demeanor through dress and manner.
5. Summarize the interaction at the end of the session and make arrangements with the client for the next session.
6. Positively reinforce the client for his attention, effort, and so on.

(For more information about interviewing techniques, refer to Chap. 9)

Barriers to Therapeutic Communication

Barriers to therapeutic communication inhibit or interfere with nurse–client communication (note italicized subjects below). Lack of planning or inadequate preparation by the nurse during the communication process may result in failure to meet the client's identified goals. The goal of precise data collection directs communication assessment; *inadequate data collection* is a significant barrier to facilitative communication.

Nurse–client interaction is built on the development of a trusting relationship. *Lack of regard* for the other person in an interaction inhibits, or functions as a barrier to, therapeutic communication.

Other verbal and nonverbal communication of the nurse may cause disruption or cessation of the nurse–client interaction. *Changing the subject* indicates to the client that the nurse is uncomfortable with the present communication and has therefore introduced a new, and usually superficial, topic of conversation. The client may perceive the nurse's *probing questions* as morbid curiosity, threatening elements, and an intrusion into his privacy.

Advising the client, or telling him what he should do, what he should think, or how he should feel, is a dangerous trap into which any helping professional may inadvertently slip. To advise the client impinges on his individuality and his right to determine his own behavior.

Belittling the client, such as discounting his feelings, tells him that he and his feelings are not important or worthy of others' attention. *Defending* the hospital or agency, staff, therapy, or other aspect of treatment usually fails to respond to whatever the client is saying or asking, and it reduces the liklihood of continued communication with the client.

Closed-ended questions limit the client's responses to one- or two-word answers, such as questions that require answers of "yes" or "no." These questions inhibit the client's freedom to elaborate on his thoughts and feelings.

False reassurance is a common barrier to therapeutic communication. Telling the client that "everything will be all right," unless, of course, the nurse is absolutely sure that everything will end satisfactorily, is an attempt to give a pat solution to what may be complex questions or problems. This reassurance, arising out of habit rather than the facts of the situation, tends to eliminate the client's further elaboration of his thoughts and feelings and tends to terminate communication with the nurse.

Intervening in Psychotic Communication

The nurse does not reinforce the client's psychotic communication. Initial interaction with an individual demonstrating psychotic behavior involves showing interest in, and concern for, the client. A realistic approach to the client may be spending time with him in an activity, such as walking.

The tasks of recognizing his feeling messages, decoding his content, and clarifying his feelings without causing him to be overstimulated by the interaction are difficult ones for the psychiatric-mental health nurse. Frequent use of silence may increase the client's anxiety and his hallucinatory behavior. Saying "I can't follow your thinking" to the client who evidences psychotic communication is a way to introduce him to the reality of interpersonal communication.

Listening for and clarifying themes or needs with the psychotic client is difficult and often perplexing for the nurse. The client who needs time to develop a trusting relationship with another may continue to use psychotic communication and behavior to test the relationship. The nurse continuously evaluates the relationship and the effectiveness of communication with the client.

Summary

This chapter has explored the purposes, systems, and models of communication. Other emphases of the chapter include the following.

1. The components of the communication process are the sender, receiver, message, message variables, noise, communication skills, setting, media, feedback, and environment.
2. The communication and nursing processes interweave to provide the nurse with a foundation to assist clients' progressions toward optimal adaptation.
3. Empathy enables the nurse to view the client in a caring and objective manner and to interact with him in a planned, systematic way.
4. The techniques of therapeutic communication—clarification, reflection, confrontation, verification, self-disclosure, informing, silence, summarizing, directing, and questioning—are the nurse's tools to elicit helpful or facilitative interaction with the client.
5. Barriers to therapeutic communication, such as defending, lack of regard for the other person, and advising, interfere with, or inhibit, communication between the nurse and client.
6. Therapeutic communication is one of the most powerful tools of the psychiatric-mental health nurse.

The following is an example of an interaction between a psychiatric-mental health nurse and a client who is using psychotic communication. The nurse has been meeting and spending time with the client since his admission a week ago and has been using various activities within the milieu during their sessions to develop a relationship.

Client: The voices are talking to me again and told me not to go with you on this walk today, but to stay in my room and talk to them.

Nurse: Are you confused about whether I want to be with you?

Client: The voices (puts hands to head) are mad at me, and they're saying awful things and using bad words because I'm with you.

Nurse: I look forward to our walks and getting to know you better.

Client: The voices tell me you're just saying that because you want to trick me.

Nurse: I care about you and want to be able to help you. I will be with you every day at this time for the next week.

The nurse was aware of the client's history of abuse by his parents and of spending his adolescence in foster homes. He was diagnosed as schizophrenic and has had repeated admissions to the psychiatric hospital. He has been in a rehabilitation-work program successfully for the past year but became psychotic again when he learned his mother died. Eventually, the nurse and client talked about his feelings of rejection and helplessness. The client was able to return to his rehabilitation-work program and outpatient care.

Process Recording

Applying Therapeutic Communication Techniques

A 24-year-old man is admitted voluntarily to a mental health unit. The following recording is part of an admission interview.

Client's Verbal and Nonverbal Communication	Nurse's Verbal and Nonverbal Communication	Therapeutic Technique	Evaluation
	Will you tell me your reasons for admitting yourself to the unit (relaxed, open posture, maintaining eye contact)?	Clarifying content	The nurse asks the client to identify his reasons for seeking mental health treatment. The nurse is likely to have already completed introductions

(Continues on p 36)

Client's Verbal and Nonverbal Communication	*Nurse's Verbal and Nonverbal Communication*	*Therapeutic Technique*	*Evaluation*
Well, my wife left me 2 weeks ago, and I (starts to cry, speaking between sobs) feel like my world has come to an end.			and the sharing of initial information about the purpose, length, and process of the admission interview. Instead of relying on the views or opinions of others, the nurse seeks information and perceptions directly from the client.
I can't sleep or eat—I want her back and I know I've got to get my head together (holds head in hands, elbows resting on knees).	(She allows silence for 2 to 3 minutes.)	Silence	Although it is often tempting to say something to stop the client fom crying, it is therapeutic to allow him free expression of his feelings and his thoughts.
I've been feeling this way since she left. I love her so much, but I've never been able to tell her until the day she was packing to leave.	You're feeling sad and hurt right now (softer voice).	Clarifying feelings	The nurse tries to help the client identify his feelings, an important initial step before he can begin to cope with, or work through, them.
Betty and I have been together for 3 years—we lived together for 1½ years. Those were good times, and then we got married (looks away, fidgets with ring on finger).	Not able to tell her you love her—	Reflecting feelings	The nurse focuses on the issue of the client's feelings, which are usually more difficult to express, or to deal with.
Yeah, see ever since we met, Betty thought I was a macho man, and I tried to be that kind of guy, and I'm not.	You were saying that you couldn't tell her you loved her (looks directly at client, nods).	Reflecting content	The nurse again tries to focus the interaction on what appears to be a significant issue for him— his inability or failure to express his love for his wife. This is also a useful technique when the client's communication is rambling or difficult to follow.
I thought she wanted the strong, silent type, but I seemed to drive her away (shakes his head from side	If you were macho, you couldn't tell her you loved her—is that what you're saying?	Clarifying content	

Client's Verbal and Nonverbal Communication	Nurse's Verbal and Nonverbal Communication	Therapeutic Technique	Evaluation
to side, sad facial expression).			
Betty is just 19—we met when she was 16. She never went out much, and lately she's been going out with my sister—to the clubs to dance, and I felt it was OK because I go out with the boys.	Go on (nods).	Directing	The nurse encourages the client to continue, verbally and nonverbally. She informs him that she is interested in what he is saying and how he is feeling.
She seemed always ready to go out but didn't pay attention to the house or meals—so I shook her and slapped her. I'm no good (starts to cry)—she was scared of me.	Go on.	Directing	
Yeah, scared and felt all I thought about was work—and I did. I wanted Betty to have things—she's had it hard.	Scared of you?	Reflecting content	Reflection of a word, a phrase, or a sentence encourages the client to elaborate on his statements.
I played a role with her so long that I hated myself—and I took it out on her.	You felt you could show Betty your love by giving her things.	Clarifying feelings	The nurse explores how the client feels about his wife and his pattern of relating to her; she also gives him the opportunity to evaluate the accuracy of her clarification.
(He puts head in hands and begins to cry.) I'm no good—I love Betty, and I finally told her I wasn't a big tough guy, but just an ordinary person—	You say you love her, but you slapped and shook her.	Confronting content	The nurse verbalizes the incongruence between the client's verbalizations (his love for his wife) and his actions (physically abusing her).
Oh, I am—even though I told her the truth, she still packed up.	You're feeling down, and upset about your past behavior with Betty?	Reflecting feelings	Again the nurse reflects the client's feelings to help him identify and own them.
	(She remains silent for 1–2 minutes; looks at client.)	Silence	The nurse's use of silence offers client and nurse a time to reflect on what's been said and collect their thoughts for the next interchange.

(*Continues on p 38*)

Client's Verbal and Nonverbal Communication	Nurse's Verbal and Nonverbal Communication	Therapeutic Technique	Evaluation
	You said the 1½ years you two lived together were the good times.	Clarifying content	The nurse next returns to an earlier point in the discussion, encouraging the client to elaborate, if he wishes.
Yeah, we weren't around any family, and I didn't drink like I do now.			
	You abuse alcohol?	Verifying	In response to the client's communication about his drinking the nurse verifies this information which he has shared.
Yes, that's another problem I have.			

Discussion

A process recording is an analysis of an interpersonal interaction. It examines closely the verbal and nonverbal communication of the nurse-helper and the client seeking help. Specific therapeutic techniques are identified at each point of intervention during the interaction. Evaluation of the helpfulness of the interaction—both verbal and nonverbal communication—is an integral part of the recording.

References

1. Applebaum R, Anatol KW, Jenson O, Porter RE, Mandel JE: Fundamental Concepts of Human Communication. San Francisco, Canfield Press, 1973

2. Ardrey R: The Territorial Imperative. New York, Atheneum, 1966

3. Authier J, Authier K, Lutey B: Clinical Management of the Tearfully Depressed Patient: Communication Skills for the Nurse Practitioner. J Psychiatr Nurs Ment Health Serv 17 (February): 34–41, 1978

4. Berne E: Games People Play. New York, Grove Press, 1964

5. Brammer LM: The Helping Relationship. Englewood Cliffs, NJ, Prentice-Hall, 1973

6. Carkhuff RR: The Art of Helping, IV, 4th ed. Amherst, Mass, Human Resources Development Press, 1980

7. Crouch L: Disturbance in Language and Thought. J Psychiatr Nurs Ment Health Serv 10 (May–June): 5–8, 1972

8. Dominick AB (ed): How to Make People Listen to You. Springfield, IL, Charles C Thomas, 1971

9. Doona ME: Travelbee's Intervention in Psychiatric Nursing, 2nd ed. Philadelphia, FA Davis, 1979

10. Edwards BJ, Briehart JK: Communications in Nursing Practice. St Louis, CV Mosby, 1981

11. Enelow AJ, Swisher SN: Interviewing and Patient Care. New York, Oxford Press, 1972

12. Hall, ET, Whyte WF: Intercultural Communication: A Guide to Men of Action. In Brink PJ (ed): Transcultural Nursing, pp 44–62. Englewood Cliffs, NJ, Prentice-Hall, 1976

13. Headington BJ: Communication in the Counseling Relationship. Cranston, RI, Carroll Press, 1979

14. Longo DC, Williams RA: Clinical Practice in Psychosocial Nursing: Assessment and Intervention. New York, Appleton-Century-Croft, 1978

15. Miller GA: The Magical Number Seven, Plus or Minus Two: Some Limits on Our Capacity for Processing Information. In Silverstein A et al (eds): Human Communication: Theoretical Explorations, pp 81–97. New York, John Wiley & Sons, 1974

16. Ong WJ: The History and the Future of Verbal Media. In Silverstein A et al (eds): Human Communication: Theoretical Explorations, pp 165–183. New York, John Wiley & Sons, 1974

17. Peplau H: Basic Principles of Patient Counseling, 2nd ed. Philadelphia, Smith, Kline & French Laboratories, 1964

18. Phillips LW: Language in Disguise: Nonverbal Communication with Patients, Perspect Psychiatr Care 4 (July–August): 18–21, 1966

19. Pryser PW: The Psychological Examination: A Guide for Clinicians. New York: International Universities Press, 1979

20. Rickelman B: Bio-Psycho-Social Linguistics. Nursing Research 20 (September–October): 398–403, 1971

21. Ruesch J: Therapeutic Communication. New York, WW Norton, 1961

22. Sielski LM: Understanding Body Language. Personnel and Guidance Journal 57 (January): 238–242, 1979

23. Smitherman C: Nursing Actions for Health Promotion. Philadelphia, FA Davis, 1980

24. Vance B: Human Relationships in Nursing. Provo, Utah, Brigham Young University, 1979

25. Watzlawick P: Pragmatics of Human Communication. New York, WW Norton, 1967

26. Wenburg JR, Wilmot WM: The Personal Communication Process. New York, John Wiley & Sons, 1973

27. Wilson JS: Deciphering Psychotic Communication. Perspect Psychiatr Care 18 (November–December): 254–256, 1979

28. Wolfgang A (ed): The Teacher and Nonverbal Behavior in the Multicultural Classroom. Nonverbal Behavior, Application and Cultural Implication, Part 3, pp 159–174. New York, Academic Press, 1979

Chapter 4
Therapeutic Relationships

How strange is the lot of us mortals! Each of us is here for a brief sojourn; for what purpose he knows not, though he sometimes thinks he senses it. But without deeper reflection one knows from daily life that one exists for other people—first of all for those upon whose smiles and well-being our own happiness is wholly dependent, and then for the many, unknown to us, to whose destinies we are bound by the ties of sympathy. A hundred times every day I remind myself that my inner and outer life are based on the labors of other men, living and dead, and that I must exert myself in order to give in the same measure as I have received and am still receiving.

Albert Einstein,
Ideas and Opinions

Patriciann Furnari Brady

Chapter Preview

During hospitalization and many other health care experiences, the nurse is the primary person accessible to the client to meet his physical and psychological needs. To maximize effectiveness in communication and intervention, nurses strive to develop therapeutic relationships with their clients.

This chapter focuses on the therapeutic relationship—what it is and what it is not, its purposes and phases. The attitude of the nurse helper and the measures that facilitate growth are examined as critical issues affecting the development of the therapeutic relationship.

Learning Objectives

After studying this chapter, the reader should be able to accomplish the following.

1. Define therapeutic relationships
2. Differentiate between social, intimate, and therapeutic relationships
3. Describe the characteristics of a therapeutic relationship
4. Identify the anxieties of the nurse and client in a therapeutic relationship
5. Discuss the expectations of the nurse and client in a therapeutic relationship
6. Discuss the impact of the attitude of the nurse helper on a therapeutic relationship
7. Describe ways in which the nurse facilitates the growth of clients

Dynamics of the Relationship

Definition and Purposes of Relationships

A *relationship* is a state of being related or a state of affinity between two individuals. Clients and nurses have an affinity for each other or are related to each other within the health care system.

Nursing is a dialogue—a human-to-human event.[21] Clients enter the health care system with an awareness of their expected role behavior and with certain expectations of the nurse. Most of these behaviors focus on the "ill client" and the "nurse caregiver" roles. Explicit in the nurse caregiver role is the provision of physical care; implicit in the role is the meeting of client's psychological needs and the facilitation of growth. The development of a therapeutic relationship enables the nurse to meet client needs and intervene in client problems.

Hildegard Peplau describes nursing as an educative instrument—a maturing force—that aims to promote forward movements of personality in the direction of creative, constructive, productive personal, and community living.[28] Nurses provide for clients the opportunity for an honest relationship. The care dimensions in such a relationship promote human growth through empathic understanding in an atmosphere conducive to the client's self-exploration.[1]

Types of Relationships

In relationships with clients, the temptation to see the person as a friend may arise. The nurse who says, "I feel so close to the client, I feel he is my friend" is altering the implied focus of the interaction between professional and one seeking help. Three possible types of relationships—social, intimate, and therapeutic—are observed between individuals.

Social Relationship

The *social relationship* is one we experience most commonly in our everyday lives. Both individuals are equally involved in this relationship and are concerned with meeting their own needs through the relationship. There is neither a predetermined goal or focus in the social relationship, nor is the continuation of the relationship determined at its outset.

Intimate Relationship

An *intimate relationship* is a relationship between two individuals committed to one another, caring and respecting each other. Intimacy is usually exclusive to those involved and implies that they love each other.

According to Erikson, the ability to develop an intimate relationship with an adult of the opposite sex is highly dependent on completing developmental tasks.[8] The intimate relationship forms the basis for procreation of future generations.

Therapeutic Relationship

A *therapeutic relationship* is one in which the nurse and client work together toward the goal of assisting the client meet his needs and facilitate growth. The interaction is purposefully established, maintained, and carried out with an anticipated outcome of assisting the client obtain new coping and adaptation skills. The most basic assumptions underlying the therapeutic relationships are as follows.

1. The client's difficulties are expressed in the relationship.
2. The previous, learned difficulties of former relationships are amenable to change in this relationship.[11]

The nurse–client relationship is a helpful, purposeful interaction between an authority in health care (the nurse) and a person or group with health care needs.[26] The one-to-one psychiatric nurse–client relationship is an interpersonal relationship between a psychiatric-mental health nurse and a client for the purpose of brief counseling, crisis intervention, or psychotherapy.[21]

Phases of a Therapeutic Relationship

Initial or Introductory Phase

The *initial phase* or introductory contact between a client and nurse can occur in a variety of settings. The initial admission procedure or provision of technical care for the client offers opportunities for an initial interaction. Often, nursing students ask "What do I say first?" The nurse should acknowledge the client by name and should then introduce herself. Establishing the frequency and length of contact and establishing a reason for the contact assists the client to clarify the purpose and particulars of the relationship.[13] Structuring the interaction avoids the client's misunderstanding or misinterpreting the relationship, and it helps the nurse and client establish goals for the relationship.

During this phase of a therapeutic relationship, the nurse must demonstrate acceptance of the client's behavior, must establish rapport, and must provide an opportunity for the client to begin to develop trust. Frequently, clients test the nurse's commitment by missing appointments or by exhibiting acting-out behavior. In this phase of the relationship, the client's problems are identified, nursing diagnoses and goals are determined, priorities are set, and plans are formulated to achieve the goals.[5]

During this initial interaction, the nurse and client may also establish a contract to formalize the terms of their relationship. The contract may include designating a time and place to meet, finding alternatives for initially contracted goals, keeping appointments, exploring problems, maintaining confidentiality, and re-evaluating the expectations at any point in the relationship (see the insert Treatment Contract).[5]

The nurse and client must recognize and differentiate what types of problems are amenable to intervention. When setting goals with clients, the nurse also recognizes that, because patterns of behavior are not developed in a short period of time, brief or short-term interventions may not be appropriate for "deep-rooted" problems and behavior.

The nurse informs the client when his desired goals are beyond her realm of expertise or the duration of the interaction. Failure of the nurse to share this information with the client in an open and honest manner will interfere with the establishment of trust and the ultimate outcome of the relationship.

The nurse and client affect each other; the nurse should recognize the effect she has on the client and his

Treatment Contract

Formalizing Expectations and Consequences

John W., 24 years old, was admitted to a psychiatric hospital with a diagnosis of antisocial personality 2 weeks prior to his initial contact with Ms. G., who was assigned as his primary nurse. John was having difficulty following the routines of the ward, was missing group therapy, was frequently demanding the nurses' and doctors' attention, and was borrowing cigarettes and money from other clients.

In their initial contact, John and Ms. G. decided to meet weekly to assist him to follow his treatment plan and discuss problems he was having during his hospitalization. After identifying together his areas of concern and what privileges he hoped to attain, they established the following contract.

"I, John W., agree to follow this contract outlining the expected behavior and will then receive the privileges listed below.[11]

1. Attend meals as scheduled.
2. Shower and change clothes daily.
3. Attend group sessions on time, as established in my treatment plan.
4. Participate as an active member in group therapy.
5. Meet Ms. G. at 10:00 am, Wednesdays, on the Unit.

6. Not ask other patients for cigarettes or money.
7. Ask nurses for assistance with problem areas and leave the nurses' station when requested.
8. Make an appointment to see the physician, when needed, and not try to talk to him without an appointment unless permission is given by ward nurses.
9. Report to the ward staff prior to leaving the ward.

John W. agreed to abide by the contract immediately, and when he demonstrated the expected behavior for three days, the following schedule of privileges was established.

John W. will be permitted the following.

1. One hour off ward every shift for 1 week
2. Two hours off ward every shift for 1 week
3. Four hours off ward every shift for 1 week
4. May be off ward at all times except during therapy time and must report to nursing staff prior to meals

John W. and Ms. G. discussed the consequences of his failure to follow one of the expected behaviors and decided that, in that instance, he would lose his current privilege level and would be moved back to the previous privilege level.

effect on her. The nurse strives to care for the client in such a manner that a sense of trust and confidence develops.[26] Therapy begins when the nurse and client progress beyond exchanging information and the client begins to share subjective content underlying his behavior.[5]

During the initial phase of a relationship, the nurse also gathers data about the following.

1. How the client views himself and his problems
2. Problematic areas of interpersonal relationships
3. Problematic areas the client denies[29]

Before moving to the next phase of the relationship, the nurse and client evaluate the initial phase and assess whether the following tasks have been accomplished.

1. Security is being established through continued development of trust.
2. The client is being assisted to verbalize thoughts and feelings.
3. Areas of inadequate stress adaptation are being identified.
4. Strengths and weaknesses are being assessed.
5. Goals for the relationship are established.

Middle or Working Phase

The *working phase* of the relationship occurs when the client and nurse are actively involved in meeting the goals established during the initial phase of the relationship. The client may fluctuate between dependence and independence in an attempt to acknowledge the painful and unpleasant aspects of his life and begin to try out healthy, adaptive behavior.[26] The nurse encourages the client to express his feelings and attempt new adaptation approaches without danger of punitive treatment; she also reinforces his effective problem-solving.

In this phase of the relationship, the client is also likely to feel more secure and will openly discuss topics that he was unable to discuss previously.[5] The client is more likely to successfully learn new behaviors because his anxiety level decreases when trust is reinforced through the nurse's acceptance. The nurse and client continue to discuss his problems and conflicts and the nurse encourages him to try new ways of resolving his conflicts.[24]

The *therapeutic tasks* of the working phase of the nurse–client relationship include the following.

1. Increase awareness and perception of the reality of specific personal experiences.
2. Develop realistic self-concept and promote self-confidence.
3. Recognize areas of discomfort and verbalize these feelings.
4. Attempt to make comparisons between the ineffective behavior within the relationship and the ineffective behavior outside the relationship and draw conclusions regarding these comparisons.

5. Encourage a plan of action, implement the plan, and evaluate the results of the plan to alter the client's behavior.
6. Assess readiness for, and provide opportunities for, independent functioning.[19]

Termination Phase

The *termination phase* of the therapeutic relationship is bound by the time restriction established during the initial phase. As time of termination draws near, the nurse reminds the client (or the group of clients) of the agreed-upon duration of the relationship and assists him to socialize with others.[24]

The termination of the relationship represents possible traumatic difficulties for the client. The nurse recognizes his imminent loss and helps him adapt to this stressor.[13, 27, 37] If the client feels rejected, insecure, and unloved at the time of termination, he may regress. The nurse recognizes that termination provokes stress, she supports the client's coping behaviors, and she is sensitive to his individual needs. Other members of the mental health team also help the client deal with termination issues.

Tapering off contact with the client is a helpful way to encourage his independence. The nurse summarizes the client's progress toward attaining his goals and freely expresses her own feelings regarding the termination.

Termination means dissolving a relationship. The primary tasks for the nurse during termination include the following.

1. Space contacts with each client further apart and begin to decrease the amount of time of each contact.
2. Establish a more relaxed, less intense interaction.
3. Focus on the future.
4. Discourage cues that lead to new areas of exploration.
5. Provide necessary referral to others in the health care team.[19]

Dimensions of a Therapeutic Relationship

Conceptual Framework

For clients with emotional problems, nursing provides a unique opportunity to deal with problems of living. "Emotional illness is a pattern of living—of thinking, feeling, and behaving—that a person adopts in an attempt to lessen his anxiety and solve his problems of relating to others."[14] Although this pattern of adaptation may temporarily relieve stress for the individual, it merely postpones the resolution of problems. As an active member of the treatment team, the nurse provides opportunities for the development of a relationship with the client that can be close enough to deal with his special fears, symptoms, and interpersonal problems.

In a therapeutic relationship, the nurse and client purposefully strive to establish goals. The kinds of interactions in which nurses participate vary from assisting a client to eat to undertaking individual, group, or family therapy with him. The nurse recognizes that, although not all contacts with clients are therapy sessions, each contact with a client has the potential for being therapeutic, for promoting interpersonal growth, for changing behavior, or for benefiting the client in some way.[5] Nurses identify the adaptive skills a client uses to relieve his stress, assess effectiveness of such skills, and help him develop new adaptive skills.

Characteristics of the Therapeutic Relationship

The core of nursing is the relationship between the nurse and the client. This therapeutic relationship is a goal-directed relationship that helps the client develop more appropriate coping skills and offers him the potential for growth.

Carl Rogers has described the benefits of a helping relationship in these words.

> If I can provide a certain type of a relationship, the other person will discover within himself the capacity to use that relationship for growth and change and personal development will occur.[32]

The nurse's behaviors and attitudes affect the client's view of himself. Her effectiveness depends on the qualities of genuineness, honesty, and authenticity. The nurse cares about the humanism and dignity of the client. Mentally disturbed clients often misinterpret reality, they lack interpersonal skills, and they interpret a nurse's aloofness as rejection. Therefore, the nurse maintains constant self-awareness of both verbal and nonverbal behavior. Consistency in approach fosters the development of trust, particularly when the client tests the relationship.

The client's behavior is his best adaptation to stress. Unconditional acceptance of him as a person reinforces his worth and dignity. If the client must perform ritualistic behavior, for example, care is planned to allow him time to complete his rituals.

One of the client's rights is to be involved in his own care. Together, the nurse and client determine the goals of the relationship, although the primary responsibility for maintaining the relationship falls within the nurse's realm. The nurse acknowledges the potential for growth and movement toward mental health. Her hopefulness and faith support the client's newly learned coping skills.

Anxieties of Nurse and Client

In a therapeutic relationship, both nurse and client are involved in a stress-producing situation. The openness and honesty inherent in the relationship make them vulnerable to its impact.

Dealing with the client's dependency needs requires a great deal of skill and self-awareness. Dependency needs may elicit within the nurse a feeling of having the sole solution to the client's problems. If the nurse does not recognize the potential or actual growth of the client, perhaps because it does not match her expectations, a relationship may develop that meets the nurse's needs instead of the client's needs. It is always a temptation to try to make the other person into a reflection of ourselves or our ideals rather than to help him develop his individual potential.[15] The nurse constantly re-evaluates her feelings, thoughts, and behavior within a relationship.

When the client does not meet the ideals of the nurse, for example, when he does not appear to be gaining insight into his behavior, the nurse may view the relationship as lacking progress. In turn, the client feels internal stress trying to please the nurse and may test her commitment to the relationship. At this point, the nurse may realize that she cannot meet all the client's needs and may seek assistance from others within the health care team.

The nurse and client may also need to discuss honestly the course of the relationship. Perhaps the goals of the relationship should be re-evaluated. The nurse must be able to tolerate, accept, and redirect the anxiety that accompanies the recognition of possible failure. The tension required to produce action must be differentiated from the hostility resulting from frustration.[15]

The client and nurse may elicit in each other feelings that are hard to admit. Testing the nurse and the relationship may indicate that the client is unable to express his feelings. Likewise, a difficult situation exists when the nurse experiences feelings of anger and frustration. An inability to verbalize these feelings by either member of the relationship places a strain on the relationship and affects trust and honesty. The nurse strives to become aware of her own feelings and to help the client identify and deal with his feelings.

Expectations of the Client and Helper

Clients seeking medical or psychiatric treatment expect to experience the relief of anxiety. This can result from the health care team's response to the client's physical or emotional stress.

The nurse initiates a relationship with a client in which he is free to verbalize needs; as the relationship progresses, he also verbalizes fears and anxieties. The nurse urges him to evaluate his adaptive pattern and the consequences of his defensive behavior. The therapeutic relationship provides the client with the opportunity to test new adaptive skills. As the client receives positive feedback within the relationship and experiences growth and increased self-esteem, he is able to relinquish ineffective behavioral patterns. As the relationship leads to termination, the nurse encourages the client to use healthier skills in interactions outside the relationship. The ultimate goal is one of independence for the client.

Family and friends of the client have expectations of treatment as well. The nurse acknowledges the family unit as a significant part of the treatment process. At times, however, the family and friends of the client may encourage, elicit, or reinforce his inappropriate or maladaptive behavior. The client must determine what type of relationship, if any, he wants to continue with his family. Frequently, nurses believe that union with one's family is the ultimate goal of healthy adaptation, but this is not always true.

Issues in a Therapeutic Relationship

Attitudes of the Nurse Helper

Our attitudes, developed at a young age, determine our behavior. Each attitude is a signal of a need present in the individual. To facilitate growth in an individual, nurses first identify attitudes present within themselves. Mentally disturbed clients are often viewed by our society as hopeless and helpless individuals. The presence of these attitudes, either consciously or unconsciously, prevents the nurse from intervening in ways that encourage the client's independence. Feelings of hopelessness are particularly evident when working with clients who have long-term emotional disorders. Nurses and other care providers may question, "What is the use of working with these individuals when they are not likely to return home ever again?" Failure to recognize and modify their own attitudes results in failure to provide quality nursing care to clients.[17]

The nurse offers hope that the client will lead a productive life within his environment. Regardless of the client's present level of adaptation, growth is possible. Assisting a client to move from one level of functioning to another is progress, although it may seem minimal to the observer. For example, a withdrawn client who establishes even brief periods of eye contact with the nurse demonstrates a beginning trust level.

Each client, regardless of his status or place within our environment, has worth and dignity. Respect for the individual is an essential component of nursing. When respect of others is lacking, the client experiences worthlessness, anxiety, and disturbed behavior.

The difference between tolerance of behavior and acceptance of behavior is often a misunderstood concept. Tolerance is a passive activity; no action is required of the nurse. Acceptance is an active process that requires recognition of the client's behavior as meeting a need and representing his best adaptation at the time. Respecting the human dignity of the individual, hoping for potential growth, and accepting the client's behavior are beginning steps in facilitating growth for the client.

How Can I Create a Helping Relationship?

Self-understanding is the nurse's responsibility in a nurse–client relationship. The following questions may help the nurse examine the relationship.

1. Can I *be* in some way that will be perceived by others as trustworthy, dependable, or consistent?
2. Can I be expressive enough as a person so that what I am will be communicated unambiguously?
3. Can I let myself experience positive attitudes toward this other person— attitudes of warmth, caring, liking, interest, respect?
4. Can I be strong enough as a person to be separate from the other?
5. Am I secure enough within myself to permit him his separateness?
6. Can I let myself enter fully into his world of his feelings and personal meaning and see these as he does?
7. Can I receive him as he is?
8. Can I act with sufficient sensitivity in the relationship so that my behavior will not be perceived as a threat?
9. Can I free him from the threat of external evaluation?
10. Can I meet this other individual as a person who is bound by his past and my past?

(From Rogers CR: On Becoming a Person. Boston, Houghton Mifflin, 1961)

Facilitating Growth

An important objective of therapeutic intervention is to provide the client with opportunities to recognize the needs his behavior meets and to develop more effective attitudes and behaviors. The approach of the nurse in the therapeutic relationship should be one of consistency. The nurse's behavior and approach give the client feedback about the appropriateness of his behavior.

The nurse's consistency also provides the client with security. In this environment, he is free to deal with problems and develop adaptation skills. When the client experiences inconsistency in the nurse's behavior, he often focuses his attention on pleasing the nurse, rather than on his own personal growth.

To encourage the client to try out new adaptive behaviors, the nurse provides emotional support by assisting him to pay attention to his feelings, to link his feelings to his troublesome behaviors, and then to explore alternate behaviors. The nurse creates a relationship in which the client shares decision-making and validates his perception of the outcome of his decisions. This offers the client an opportunity to try his new behavior without penalty (wherein he can receive feedback from others and can evaluate the outcome of his behavior) as he develops a new set of adaptation skills that are less destructive than those he previously used. During the client's growth process, the nurse supports and reinforces the healthy aspects of his personality, assesses the client's movement toward independence, and encourages him to assume more responsibility for himself.

Interpersonal Skills

Carl Rogers states, " . . . the degree to which I can create a relationship which facilitates growth of others as a separate person is a measure of the growth I have achieved myself." Self-awareness is an essential component of effective therapeutic relationships. The nurse also takes responsibility for examining her own behavior and for making the necessary changes in behavior when that is indicated. To function as a healthy adult role model, the nurse must demonstrate sufficient emotional maturity to be able to postpone the satisfaction of her own needs and allow the client's needs to take precedence.[15]

The nurse's most basic and important therapeutic tool is herself, her own personality. Many physical, cultural, psychological, social, and environmental factors interact to create a unique personality; the nurse's awareness of these factors increases her insight into her own and others' feelings and behavior. Objectivity and empathy grow out of the nurse's self-awareness, emotional maturity, responsibility, and insight and these tools prevent misinterpretation of the client's needs through interference of the nurse's own needs.

Transference and Countertransference

The client who is functioning at a regressed level may misinterpret or unconsciously displace onto the nurse his earlier feelings about important persons, such as his parents.[35] This misinterpretation or unconscious displacement of feelings is termed *transference*. Transference distortion, based on unconscious conflict, is the inevitable consequence of human encounter.[35]

The nurse recognizes and accepts that the client is responding to her on the basis of a previous relationship. Lack of recognition of the transference would lead the nurse to respond to the client's behavior in ways that may negate its effectiveness.

Countertransference is the helping person's distorted or inappropriate responses to clients due to the helper's unconscious conflict.[35] A nurse, for example, may displace feelings for her younger brother onto a young male client for whom she is caring. Nurses should attend to the feelings they experience when interacting with clients, particularly when they differ from usual feelings. If the nurse identifies or suspects that transference or countertransference is occurring, she may solicit the aid of clinical supervisors or other mental health team members to help her develop objectivity in the relationship.

Summary

This chapter has presented the dynamics and dimensions of a therapeutic relationship, as well as the issues that may arise in such a relationship. It has also included the following.

1. A therapeutic relationship is one in which the nurse and client participate and work toward the goals of meeting the client's needs and facilitating his growth.
2. There are three possible types of relationships— social, intimate, and therapeutic.
3. Therapeutic relationships progress through initial or introductory, middle or working, and termination phases.
4. The core of nursing is the relationship between the nurse and the client.
5. The nurse recognizes that the client's behavior is his best possible adaptation to stress at the time.
6. The therapeutic relationship provides the client with an opportunity to examine unsuccessfully adaptive (or maladaptive) behaviors, and to explore and try out new adaptive skills.
7. The nurse's self-awareness, responsibility, emotional maturity, objectivity, and empathy are powerful tools of intervention.

References

1. Aiken L, Aiken JL: A Systematic Approach to the Evaluation of Interpersonal Relationships. Am J Nurs 73 (May): 863–866, 1973
2. Bailey DS, Dryer S: Therapeutic Approach to the Care of the Mentally Ill. Philadelphia, FA Davis, 1971
3. Campaniello JA: The Process of Termination. J Psychiatr Nurs Ment Health Serv (February): 29–32, 1980
4. Carser DL: Primary Nursing in Milieu. J Psychiatr Nurs Ment Health Serv 19 (February): 35–41, 1981
5. Carter FM: Psychosocial Nursing, 3rd ed. New York, Macmillan, 1981
6. Clemence M, Sr: Existentialism: A Philosophy of Commitment. Am J Nurs 66 (March): 500–505, 1966
7. Egan G: The Skilled Helper. California, Brooks/Cole, 1982
8. Erikson EH: Childhood and Society, 2nd ed. New York, WW Norton, 1964
9. Fagin CM: Psychotherapeutic Nursing. Am J Nurs 67 (February): 298–304, 1967
10. Fitzpatrick JJ, Whall AL, Johnston RL, Floyd JA: Nurs-

ing Models and Their Psychiatric Mental Health Application. Bowie, MD, John J Brady, 1982

11. Grace HR, Camilleri D: Mental Health Nursing, 2nd ed. Dubuque, IA, Wm C Brown, 1977
12. Haber J et al: Comprehensive Psychiatric Nursing. New York, McGraw-Hill, 1978
13. Hale JS, Richardson J: Terminating the Nurse–Patient Relationship. Am J Nurs 63 (September): 1116–1119, 1963
14. Hays JS, Larson KH: Interacting with Patients. New York, Macmillan, 1964
15. Irving S: Basic Psychiatric Nursing, 2nd ed. Philadelphia, WB Saunders, 1978
16. Jensen HN, Tilloston G: Dependency in the Nurse–Patient Relationship. Am J Nurs 61 (February): 81–84, 1961
17. Johnson MM: Self-Disclosure: A Variable in the Nurse–Client Relationship. J Psychiatr Nurs 18 (January): 17–20, 1980
18. King I: A Conceptual Frame of Reference for Nursing. Nurs Res 17 (January–February): 27–31, 1968
19. Kriegh HZ, Perko JE: Psychiatric and Mental Health Nursing: A Commitment to Care and Concern. Reston, VA, Reston Publishing, 1979
20. Lamonica EL: The Nursing Process: A Humanistic Approach. California, Addison-Wesley, 1979
21. Lego SM: The One-to-One Patient Relationship. Perspect Psychiatr Care 18 (March/April): 67–88, 1980
22. Leininger M: Caring, A Central Focus of Nursing and Health Care Services. Nursing and Health Care 1 (Oct): 135–143, 1980
23. Long L, Prophit P, Sr: Understanding/Responding: a Communication Manual for Nurses. California, Wadsworth Health Science Division, 1981
24. Manfreda M, Krampetz SD: Psychiatric Nursing, 10th ed. Philadelphia, FA Davis, 1977
25. McCann J: Terminating of the Psychotherapeutic Relationship. J Psychiatr Nurs 17 (October): 37–39, 1979
26. Murray RB, Zentner JP: Nursing Concepts for Health Promotion, 2nd ed. Englewood, NJ, Prentice-Hall, 1979
27. Nehren J, Gillian NR: Separation Anxiety. Am J Nurs 65 (January): 190–112, 1965
28. Peplau H: Interpersonal Relations in Nursing. New York, GP Putnam's Sons, 1952
29. Rector C: Content in the Initial Therapeutic Patient Interview. Perspect Psychiatr Care 3 (March): 33–35, 1965
30. Robinson L: Psychiatric Nursing as a Human Experience, 2nd ed. Philadelphia, WB Saunders, 1977
31. Rogers CR: Client-Centered Therapy. Boston, Houghton Mifflin, 1951
32. Rogers CR: The Characteristics of a Helping Relationship. Personnel and Guidance Journal 37 (September): 6–16, 1958
33. Rogers CR: On Becoming A Person. Boston, Houghton Mifflin, 1961
34. Schoffstall C: Concerns of Student Nurses Prior to Psychiatric Nursing Experience: An Assessment and Intervention Technique. J Psychiatr Nurs Ment Health Serv 19 (November): 11–14, 1981
35. Schwartz LH, Schwartz JL: The Psychodynamics of Patient Care. Englewood, NJ, Prentice-Hall, 1972
36. Sene B: Termination in the Student–Patient Relationship. Perspect Psychiatr Care 8: 39–45, 1969
37. Taylor MC: Mereness' Essentials of Psychiatric Nursing, 11th ed. St Louis, CV Mosby, 1982
38. World Health Organization: Expert Committee on Psychiatric Nursing, First Report. World Health Organization technical report series, No 105, July, 1956. In Hays JS, Larson KH (eds): Interacting with Patients. New York, Macmillan, 1964
39. Yura H, Walsh M: Human Needs and the Nursing Process. New York, Appleton-Century-Croft, 1978

Chapter 5
Community Mental Health

A good part of the struggles of mankind center around the single task of finding an expedient accommodation—one, that is, that will bring happiness—between this claim of the individual and the cultural claims of the group; and one of the problems that touches the fate of humanity is whether such an accommodation can be reached by means of some particular form of civilization or whether the conflict is irreconcilable.

Sigmund Freud,
Civilization and Its Discontents

Marilyn Jaffe-Ruiz

Chapter Preview

"Community mental health" is an idea, a philosophy, an enactment that came to fruition in 1963 with the late President John F. Kennedy's "Bold New Approach."[22] Before that time, interest in the care of mentally ill people in the community waxed and waned, depending upon the political/social/economic climate of the times. Through the 1960s and early 1970s, the community mental health thrust enjoyed momentum and prosperity, but has again waned in the late 1970s and early 1980s. Although the enthusiasm and political support for community mental health has diminished, many important principles of care can be applied to an evolving form of psychiatric-mental health treatment in which nurses can, and do, play an important role.

The purpose of this chapter will be to present a brief history of community mental health—its current determinants and parameters—and to provide a look at the existing trends as well as a forecast for the future. The role of the nurse in community-focused mental health care delivery is essential for providing comprehensive mental health services.

Learning Objectives

Upon completion of this chapter, the reader should be able to accomplish the following.

1. Define community mental health
2. Describe the philosophy upon which community mental health is based
3. Identify five essential services of the community mental health care delivery system
4. Differentiate among primary, secondary, and tertiary prevention in community mental health nursing
5. Analyze various factors that influence trends in community mental health
6. Describe the role of the nurse in community mental health

Defining Community Mental Health

Community mental health is best defined both philosophically and operationally. The phrase *community mental health* describes a change in focus of psychiatric-mental health care from the individual to the individual in interaction with his environment. It also describes a place where comprehensive care is delivered; that is, outside of hospitals, in the least restrictive setting and hopefully, at home or as close as possible to where the client lives. Community mental health is "all activities undertaken in the community in the name of mental health."[7]

Additionally, community mental health focuses on an assessment of the community—its populations, stressors, and strengths. Mental health problems are seen not only as residing within an individual whom it would be advantageous to treat in a noninstitutional setting, but as residing within specified groups as well. To accomplish treatment for these groups, the Community Mental Health Centers Act of 1963 identified five components of service, which have become almost synonymous with community mental health. These five components of community mental health care are as follows.

1. Inpatient services
2. Outpatient services
3. Partial hospitalization
4. Emergency services
5. Consultation and education

Primary, Secondary, and Tertiary Prevention

The treatment focus incorporates public health precepts of prevention of occurrence (or primary prevention), early case finding and prompt intervention (or secondary prevention), rehabilitation (or tertiary prevention), and mechanisms for continuity of care.

On a community level, prevention is geared to individuals and to larger specialized populations. For example, early childhood–parent education programs, infant stimulation programs, and early socialization play groups attempt to effect *primary prevention* of mental disorders. Although these programs would be valuable for most families, they are considered especially preventive in those families where there are more apparent risk factors (*e.g.*, in families with pregnant teenagers).

Secondary prevention is provided by crisis intervention services, including hot lines, walk-in services, brief psychotherapy, and hospitalization when necessary. Consumer education groups and self-help groups also play a role in providing support to individuals and families during periods of increased stress or exacerbation of symptoms of mental disorders. Psychoactive medications are also therapeutic measures of secondary prevention.

Rehabilitation, or *tertiary prevention*, and continuity of care need to be available to all socioeconomic groups in the way of family supports, home services, residential placements, and halfway houses. Liaison workers, reliable friends, family members, or sponsors need to be helped to negotiate complex systems of care and to advocate for the client. Short-term and long-term hospitalization may be necessary for certain clients and should be available as a part of the mental health service delivery system.

Changes in the focus of mental health care during recent years also brought about a belief that the patient (frequently now called the client) should be an active participant in his care and should be a co-partner in his treatment planning. The mental health worker does not have to be a doctor or a trained professional, but could be an indigenous worker who would be knowledgeable and responsive to the community members and who could also, therefore, gain employment.[7] The ambiguity in the definition of mental health worker is similar to the ambiguity in the definition of client. There is a need to differentiate the individual who responds to stress with recognizable mental illness, the one who responds with a milder stress state, and the one who is chronically ill.

Philosophical Bases of Community Mental Health

Today, there is an important new philosophical premise of community mental health: There is now a shift from the belief that all mental illness is intrapsychic and amenable to psychoanalytic treatment to a belief that whole populations may need psychiatric treatment. The interaction of man and his environment, rather than his early psychological struggles, is viewed as the cause of emotional disorders. Societal stressors are seen as contributing to, if not the cause of, a person's ills.

Another premise of community mental health is the belief that mental health services should be available to all who need them regardless of personal characteristics, such as age, ability to pay, or place of residence. Individual freedom, long-term relationships in small groups, and community organization are valued activities and qualities that have been incorporated into the community mental health movement.[36] There has been a change from the biologic or medical model to a biopsychosocial model, encompassing services from all of the health and social science disciplines.

Service delivery to clients has been modified to include the examination of long-term custodial care and the exploration of new avenues for treatment in free-standing community mental health centers or in treatment units of general hospitals. Nurses and other mental health professionals have become increasingly involved in the assessment and treatment of social ills. Mental health workers have undertaken involvement in tenant advocacy, legal issues, and school problems, as well as traditional psychological issues.

Community mental health has tried to be all things to all people, perhaps to its detriment. Now, however, is the time for mental health professionals to determine how they can best provide comprehensive services to those in need.

History and Influences on Community Mental Health

The community mental health movement has been hailed as a revolution in psychiatry, with the shift of care from individuals in institutions to populations in the community. This change in the focus of care, or movement, may be viewed as having the same magnitude of impact as that of Phillippe Pinel removing the chains from mental patients and Sigmund Freud's introduction of psychodynamic concepts.[29, 34]

Advances in psychopharmacology have played a large, but often unstated, role in community-based mental health treatment. With the advent of major tranquilizers in the early 1950s, individuals could be treated in less restrictive environments and were psychologically amenable to other treatment modalities, such as the verbal therapies of individual, group, and family therapy.

Although the Community Mental Health Centers Act of 1963 was the first piece of federal legislation aimed at large-scale funding for the building and staffing of treatment centers for the mentally ill, important events preceded this major one.[6] It is interesting to note that, before 1963, responsibility for care and treatment of the mentally ill fell to state and local governments; currently, there is a trend to return this responsibility to state and local governments. (The insert Historical Review of Community Mental Health presents a brief review of these events.)

The historical overview tells a story of increasing federal responsibility for funding of mental health services through the 1970s. Mandated by the 1963 Community Mental Health Centers Act, the focus of mental health care

Historical Review of Community Mental Health

1930s	Two Federal Narcotics Hospitals were established.
1946	Congress passed the National Mental Health Centers Act. National Institute of Mental Health was created.
1955	Mental Health Study Act—Congress establishes Joint Commission on Mental Illness and Mental Health.
1960	Report of The Joint Commission on Mental Illness and Mental Health, *Action for Mental Health,* published.
1963	Report from the President on Mental Illness and Mental Retardation to Congress—stimulated Community Mental Health Centers Act. Congress passed Community Mental Health Centers Act to provide federal funding for building and staffing of Community Mental Health Centers.
1973	Joint Commission on Mental Health of Children established.
1975	Congress extends Community Mental Health Centers Act.[27]
1978	Report to the President from the President's Commission on Mental Health.[28]

(From Beigel A, Levinson A: The Community Mental Health Center: Strategies and Programs. New York, Basic Books, 1972)

shifted from the individual in institutions to communities organized into catchment areas of populations between 75,000 and 200,000.[6] Community mental health centers were built and staffed to provide comprehensive and continuous care with an emphasis on prevention. Minorities, children, and the elderly were identified as particular groups whose needs were incorporated into the legislation of the 1970s. Direct service gave way to indirect services that provided consultation and education to schools, religious organizations, courts, nonpsychiatric health professionals, and others in the community.

Community Mental Health and the Nursing Process

The community mental health nurse has the opportunity to work with the individual and the social system in which he lives. Stressors that impinge upon people in the human–environment interaction are often social in nature. At the same time, the human–environment interaction provides the health professional with an opportunity to supply interactions to improve a persons' coping ability.

Historically, nurses have played a key role in providing mental health services in the community by combining public health and psychiatric nursing knowledge. One study identified 22 roles nurses play in community mental health; the most frequently identified roles included therapist, cotherapist, collaborator on the interdisciplinary team, consultation, liaison, case finder, and crisis intervention worker.[19]

Assessment and Analysis

The community mental health nurse assesses the individual and his community resources, living arrangements (including housing and significant others), job status, economic status, cultural background, and religious affiliation. Stress in any one or more of these areas may interact with a vulnerable individual to produce psychiatric-mental health problems.

The nurse's assessment of the client in the community takes in many factors (see italicized below). Generally, *economic conditions* contribute to the rate of mental hospital admissions. There is a relationship between a depressed economy and increased social stress resulting in an increased number of psychiatric hospitalizations.[9] For that reason, the nurse asks the following questions: What is the current economic, social, and political climate? How is it likely to affect the client system? What additional services might need to be provided during times of financial need?

Sociocultural status often affects economic conditions of a particular client. Many minority groups in this country are disproportionately represented among the underemployed and unemployed members of our society. Additionally, many people use health care providers who are indigenous to their cultural group. In some communities, "medicine men," herbalists, and spiritualists may be frontline primary care providers. The nurse needs to be sensitive to how the health care system is viewed by the client and vice versa. Often, because of economic, cultural, or language barriers, obtaining health care has been a frustrating or discouraging experience for the client.

Transportation to a health-care agency is often problematic. How accessible is the agency to the client? Are outreach services provided? Are alternative means of transportation available? Is reimbursement provided? Transportation is of particular concern for the elderly.[17]

It is commonly agreed that, when a client has a strong *support system,* he will be better able to solve his problems effectively. Who are the important persons to the client? What are their relative states of health or illness? How involved are they able to be or willing to be? What role or roles does the client serve for them?

Many people who are mentally disturbed, especially if they are chronically ill, live in isolation. What service groups are available? Religious groups? Self-help groups?

Some clients are representatives of *populations with special needs* and communities have organized services around such people. Examples of special populations are the elderly, the young, substance abusers, and the developmentally disabled. Does this client or his family fit into any of those or other categories of individuals with special needs? If so, what resources are available for referral in his community?

The type of *living facilities* available certainly reflects how a person cares for himself. In what type of dwelling does the client live? Is it safe? Is there adequate plumbing, heating, refrigeration, and so forth? Can this person live without supervision? Are there halfway houses, group homes, or adult homes available, if necessary? How receptive is the community to the mentally ill individual?[20, 27]

The community mental health nurse assesses both the client's needs and the services available to him. For example, if the nurse thinks a client could manage at home if he could attend a day treatment program but there is not any day treatment program available, acute care hospitalization may be necessary.

The nurse analyzes the data gathered about the client and his life situation and determines the level of his needs. This analysis leads the nurse to identify client problems or nursing diagnoses, which, in turn, prompt plans and nursing interventions.

Planning

The nurse and other members of the treatment team estimate carefully the client's needs and the community resources before beginning the planning process. Planning takes into consideration what goals the mental health care providers, the client, his family, and significant others want to achieve. Realistic, attainable, short-term goals are imperative to reduce frustration and facilitate successful treatment outcomes.

Intervention

Community mental health intervention is planned along the public health model of primary, secondary, and tertiary prevention. The nurse may be a primary care provider by working with clients—individuals, families, or groups—to identify their needs and facilitate treatment through collaboration and referral.

Primary Prevention

Primary prevention aims at preventing illness or disorder before it occurs. In order to accomplish this goal the nurse must anticipate the needs of special populations and provide counseling and other needed services; for example, to those undergoing a developmental or situational crisis. Brief, short-term, supportive services to families undergoing bereavement or experiencing other losses fall under the rubric of primary prevention. Nurses provide these services in public health as well as mental health settings by identifying and strengthening the person's coping abilities; for instance, the nurse might foster an individual's use of intellectualization in order to mobilize his energies to find resources during a family crisis. Another nursing intervention is the development of appropriate community mental health services, such as the implementation of senior citizens' hot-lunch and drop-in programs to reduce the isolation of the elderly and meet their nutritional needs.

Goals of primary prevention are tailored to the individual, to the entire community, or both. For example, a husband who lost a wife at a recognized disaster (*e.g.*, the collapse of a midwestern hotel) may engage in bereavement therapy. At the same time, the surrounding community may use crisis intervention groups to deal with the impact of the disaster on their lives.

Another example is that of a middle-aged male who is depressed after losing a job due to a particular industry's slowdown. The man may require individual therapy to intervene in the depression, while his family may need help adjusting to the modification of roles resulting from this loss. On a community scale, food subsidies, housing programs, and stimulation of employment may be needed to promote mental health (refer to the Case Study).

Secondary Prevention

Secondary prevention reduces prevalence through early case-finding and prompt intervention. Rapid, available, and accessible treatment and referrals to appropriate services are essential. Short-term hospitalization, intensive outpatient treatment, medication, and partial hospitalization are some of the approaches through which secondary prevention is accomplished. Nurses frequently provide this care in emergency rooms to the suicidal client, in inpatient units, and in psychiatric and other health care clinics. The nurse intervenes by fostering a therapeutic relationship, by re-

structuring the environment, by bringing in services, by providing respite or halfway-house care, and by using psychopharmacological agents to strengthen the client's coping mechanisms.

Tertiary Prevention

Tertiary prevention aims to reduce long-term disability through a program of rehabilitation, after care, and resocialization. Its aim is also to prevent the exacerbation of acute symptoms or a worsening of symptoms. The nurse assesses individuals' stress levels and coping behaviors and encourages them to develop new patterns of adaptive behavior and to adopt new coping skills. One goal of a client, for example, may be to learn to talk out his problems rather than attacking someone.

Deinstitutionalization of large numbers of psychiatric clients during the late 1960s and 1970s made the tertiary prevention level of care the focus of much attention by communities, politicians, and health care workers. Many communities with insufficient resources were not equipped to absorb large numbers of psychiatric clients into their neighborhoods. Additionally, the stigma attached to psychiatric illness and the possible occurrence of deviant social behavior resulting from mental disturbance make this type of disorder not acceptable to the vast majority of people. Much work remains to be done in the areas of public attitude, education, and support of communities to cope effectively with the care of people with psychiatric illness who are in the community.

The overall goal of community mental health nursing is to provide the optimum level of mental health for a community and its members. It is not sufficient to treat the individual's ills without treating the larger societal issues. It is counterproductive for a person who has been deinstitutionalized to come to a mental health clinic and receive medication, supportive psychotherapy, supplemental security income, and food stamps if he has inadequate housing and no meaningful work.

Nurses in community mental health assist clients, through the nursing process, by identifying needs, problems, strengths, and resources, by making referrals, by offering therapeutic support, and by encouraging the use of an effective problem-solving process. In addition, the nurse needs to work actively as an advocate toward promoting legislation for innovative approaches to preventing and caring for the mentally disturbed in our communities.

Evaluation

Legislative pressures are moving the mental health system from process to outcome evaluations. Funding, policy-setting, and clinical issues are dependent on the clarity of outcome studies. To say a client is or is not better, or that a community has mental health services adequate for its

(Text continues on p 55)

Case Study: Intervening in a Family's Crisis

Mr. Alan is a 45-year-old engineer in the aircraft industry. He lives with his 42-year-old wife and two daughters, Mary, age 14, and Jane, age 18.

The aircraft plant in their community has recently been shut down because of a slowdown of growth in that industry. Mr. Alan has lost his $35,000-a-year position, as have most of his neighbors.

Mrs. Alan is a homemaker. She has not worked outside the home since her older daughter was born. Prior to that time, she worked as an executive secretary. Periodically during their marriage, Mrs. Alan suffered from periods of depression, specifically after the loss of her parents and when the family moved from an urban to a more suburban environment. Each episode of depression was treated by brief psychotherapy and antidepressant medication.

This year, Jane has begun college in a neighboring state and Mary is a freshman in high school. Mary has had increasing difficulty academically. She has been truant from school and her grades have fallen from her usual As to barely passing marks. In the classroom, she seems lethargic and demonstrates a poor attention span. Because of these problems, the home-room teacher referred Mary to the school nurse.

The school nurse took a complete health history and performed a physical assessment of Mary. In the course of the interview, Mary told the nurse that she is upset and worried about her parents. She said that they have been fighting constantly since her father lost his job 1 month ago and she's worried that her mother will get "sick" again. Mary also told the nurse that she has been frightened and unable to sleep.

During their conversation, the nurse observed that Mary's speech was slurred and her reaction time slowed. The nurse asked Mary if she was using any drugs. Mary stated that since she has been unable to sleep, she has been smoking marijuana and sometimes takes "downs" a friend gave her.

The nurse realized that in order to help Mary, she would have to meet with the whole family. She told Mary that she was going to call her parents in to meet with them and Mary's teacher together.

The next day, the meeting took place. Mr. and Mrs. Alan were very concerned about the teacher's report of Mary's behavior. They, too, were upset about their home situation and were therefore not paying as much attention to Mary, although they noticed and were worried about the changes in her behavior. Mrs. Alan admitted to feeling depressed and worried that she might not be able to function in a job outside her home. Mr. Alan expressed that he felt numbed by his job loss. Their financial problems are further compounded by the expenses of Jane's tuition and room and board. Also, because Mr. Alan's job is terminated, so are his health insurance benefits.

The school nurse helped the family recognize their need for help and suggested that she refer them to the community mental health center. The family seemed relieved by the suggestion and cautiously accepted the referral.

The Alan family (including Jane) visited the community mental health center 2 days later. The community mental health center nurse gathered the initial intake and assessment information. She identified the family to be in crisis precipitated by Mr. Alan's recent job loss. This loss of job has meant a loss of family income, alteration in roles with resultant marital discord, and drug abuse by the younger daughter. The older daughter, Jane, felt guilty about being away, worried, and angry about the possibility of being made to return home from college.

After the assessment and during the planning of strategies for intervention, the nurse realized that, even though the Alan family is unique, these same issues were confronting many other families in the area. The family as a whole, as well as each individual member, needed assistance.

The nurse analyzed her data and shared with the Alan family her assessment, validating their concerns and desires. She elicited their thoughts and ideas about the interventions, which she then presented to the Mental Health Center's treatment team.

Her suggestions are incorporated into the following nursing care plan.

Community Mental-Health Nursing Care Plan

Alan Family Care Plan

	Goals	Intervention	Evaluation
Mr. Alan	To grieve his loss of position; to establish new employment	Participate in support group with others who have lost their jobs; vocational counseling with job placement	Mr. Alan successfully finds new employment.
Mrs. Alan	To prevent further depression	Individual, brief psychotherapy; possible medication; opportunity for job placement; support group for women re-entering job market	Mrs. Alan mourns the loss of status and is able to be flexible in assuming a new role without incapacitating depression.
Mary	To find alternate ways, besides drugs, of coping with her feelings and family events	Drug-abuse therapy program; group for adolescents	Mary is able to stop abusing drugs and is able to form positive identifications in an adolescent group.
Jane	To find alternate payment options at school; to learn to cope effectively with family crisis	Explore school work/study program or part-time job to help defray college living expenses; apply for scholarship aid; telephone availability to clinic staff with referral to college health service	Jane is able to stay at college and participate in decision-making regarding family's and her own future.
Whole family	To resolve family role and functions	Financial assistance; health-insurance provisions; food subsidy program; family therapy	Family members are able to be more flexible in roles while satisfying their individual and family needs.
Community	To assist specialized groups to maintain optimal health	Education about effects of job loss and its consequences; drug consultation and education to the schools; community action involving legislators, business people, clergy, and health professional to prevent further community problems	Legislative programs are established to prevent social, economic, and psychological breakdown in the community.

Questions for Discussion

1. Which of the five essential components of community mental health did the nurses use to intervene with the Alan family?
2. What other alternatives, based on the principles of community mental health, might the school nurse have suggested if a community mental health center was not available in the community?
3. Which of the interventions planned for the Alan family are examples of primary prevention? Which are examples of secondary prevention?
4. What are the various biopsychological stressors that contributed to the Alan family's problems?
5. How is the role of the community mental health nurse similar to, and different from, other nursing roles?
6. How do you compare the principles and philosophy of community mental health with other treatment appraoches?

population is difficult in the absence of clear-cut criteria.[32] Identified areas for study include the following.

1. Program quality that conforms to standards
2. Values of specific treatment
3. Safety and efficacy, rather than usual and customary practice
4. Administrative structure
5. Program designs
6. Target populations of clients
7. Outcome indices, such as reduction of symptoms and vocational and social rehabilitation[32]

Unfortunately, even if ideal conditions are set up for research, little research in the social sciences shows direct cause-and-effect findings. Instead, results are likely to be descriptive and inconclusive. The ambiguities of the social systems model, though frustrating, offer the mental health practitioner an opportunity for diverse and creative practice. A shift from a single-causality to a multicausality mode of explanation of emotional disorder, which includes biologic, psychological, sociologic, and spiritual stressors, is essential for providing holistic care.

Trends Affecting Community Mental Health Care Delivery

The hopes, enthusiasm, and plentiful federal funding that characterized 1963 have diminished in the 1980s. Inflation, the state of the economy, unemployment, high crime rates in the major cities, suburbs, and rural areas, and a conservative political climate all serve to diminish the prospects of community mental health making a significant impact in reducing the ills of the individual in this country. Nevertheless, these times may spawn some new ideals for effective community-based mental health services in which nurses may play an important therapeutic role. Much research is needed to demonstrate beneficial outcomes with cost-effective service. Preventive treatment, identification of potential at-risk populations, and diverse treatment modalities using a variety of practitioners need to be examined.

Some gains of the community mental health movement include a reduction of population and an unlocking of doors of state mental hospitals, both literally and figuratively, to operationalize the notion of treatment in the least restrictive setting; a decreased emphasis on expensive analytic therapies as a major form of psychiatric treatment; and a de-emphasis on psychiatrists as the only legitimate care providers in order to enable other professionals (*e.g.*, registered nurses, social workers, psychologists, and paraprofessionals) to play a more active role in care. Mental health care providers have broadened the scope of services available to a wider range of the population.

Community mental health must provide for comprehensive and continuous care, available and accessible to all members of the population. It must involve the orderly uninterrupted movement of clients among the diverse elements of the service delivery system. Strong linkages and communication networks need to be established without a duplication of efforts or negation of important components.[3]

There remains a need to develop, in a systematic way, primary prevention ranging from prenatal care to care for the elderly. Secondary prevention, acute care, and early case-finding should be available through community hospitals. Those persons with emotional disorders require services to alleviate stressors and to strengthen coping skills; these services (or tertiary care) include financial, housing, food, recreational, and social services in a home-like setting with backup services as needed.

Greater emphasis and appreciation should be given to self-help groups, transitional facilities, and respite facilities. Families of the mentally ill are better equipped to provide supportive care on a continual basis if they, too, have support services as well as a chance for separation from the disturbed family member.

It is clear that the need for mental health services will not diminish; if anything, it will increase in the future. Fifteen percent of the American population suffers from some emotional disorder, and of these 32 million people nearly 7 million do not receive any care.[31] At the same time, unfortunately, funding for mental health services is disappearing. With the shift of funding from the federal level to the state level, mental health services, including research and aid to the handicapped, are being reduced. The "Bold New Approach" of the 1960s must be evaluated and redesigned in the 1980s to preserve the humanistic intent of community mental health.

Summary

This chapter has traced the development of the community mental health movement in the United States and the current challenges facing our communities. Other points of the chapter include the following.

1. Community mental health services are designed to provide comprehensive, continuous care to populations of people who need them.
2. The aims of community mental health are the prevention of illness or disorder (primary prevention), limitation of disability (secondary prevention), and rehabilitation (tertiary care).
3. Mental health workers, professional and paraprofessional, are used in addition to psychiatrists to provide mental health care to individuals, families, and communities.
4. The shift in funding from the federal to state level has reduced mental health services and endangered the viability of community mental health.

5. The community mental health nurse applies the nursing process—assessment and analysis, planning, intervention, and evaluation—to provide comprehensive services to clients.

References

1. Albee G: Psychiatry's Human Resources: Twenty Years Later. Hosp Community Psychiatry 30:11 (November): 783–786, 1979
2. Albee G: The Fourth Mental Health Revolution. J Prevention 1: 67–70, 1980
3. Bachrach L: Community of Care for Chronic Mental Patients: A Conceptual Analysis. Am J Psychiatr 138:11 (November): 1449–1451, 1981
4. Barton W, Sanborn C: An Assessment of the Community Mental Health Movement. Lexington, DC Heath, 1975
5. Bellak L: A Concise Handbook of Community Psychiatry and Community Health. New York, Grune & Stratton, 1974
6. Biegel A, Levinson A: The Community Mental Health Center: Strategies and Programs. New York, Basic Books, 1972
7. Bloom B: Community Mental Health: A General Introduction. Monterey, Brooks/Cole, 1977
8. Bloom B: The Logic and Urgency of Primary Prevention. Hosp Community Psychiatry 32:12 (December): 839–843, 1981
9. Brenner MH: Mental Illness and The Economy. Hosp Community Psychiatry 26:7 (July): 451, 1975
10. Butler R: Psychiatry and the Elderly: An Overview. Am J Psychiatr 132:9 (September): 893–900, 1975
11. Caton C: The New Chronic Patient and the System of Community Care. Hosp Community Psychiatry 32:7 (July): 475–478, 1981
12. Chu F, Trotter S: The Madness Establishment. New York, Grossman, 1974
13. Cohen G: Mental Health Services and the Elderly: Needs and Options. Am J Psychiatr 133:1 (January): 65–68, 1976
14. Estroff S: Making It Crazy. Berkeley, University of California Press, 1981
15. Fagin C: Psychiatric Nursing at the Crossroads: Quo Vadis. Perspect Psychiatr Care XIX(3, 4): 79–106, 1981
16. Freud S: Civilization and Its Discontents. New York, WW Norton, 1961
17. Hagebak J, Hagebak B: Serving the Mental Health Needs of the Elderly: The Case for Removing Barriers. Community Ment Health J 16(4): 263–275, 1980
18. Hollingshead August de Belmont, Redlich F: Social Class and Mental Illness. New York, John Wiley & Sons, 1958
19. Howard L, Baker F: Ideology and Role Function of the Nurse in Community Mental Health. Nurs Res 20:5 (September/October): 450–454, 1971
20. Johnson P, Beditz J: Community Support Systems: Scaling Community Acceptance. Community Ment Health J 17:2 (Summer): 153–160, 1981
21. Joint Commission on Mental Illness and Mental Health: Action for Mental Health. New York, Basic Books, 1961
22. Kennedy JF: Message from the President of the United States Relative to Mental Illness and Mental Retardation. House of Representatives, Document No. 58, 88th Congress, 1st Session. Reprinted in Bloom B: Community Mental Health: A General Introduction. Monterey, Brooks/Cole, 1977
23. Lamb HR, Zusman J: A New Look at Primary Prevention. Hosp Community Psychiatry 32:12 (December): 843–848, 1981
24. Lancaster J: Prospects for Mental Health in the 80's. Responding to Stress: Community Mental Health in the 80's, pp 1–9. New York, National League for Nursing, 1981
25. Laster R: Community Mental Health. J Psychiatr Nurs Ment Health Serv 15:3 (March): 19–22, 1977
26. Leiberman EJ (ed): Mental Health: the Public Health Challenge. Washington DC, American Public Health Association, 1975
27. Ozarin L: Community Alternatives to Institutional Care. Am J Psychiatr 133:1 (January): 69–72, 1976
28. President's Commission on Mental Health: Report to the President from the President's Commission on Mental Health, Vols 1 and 2. Washington DC, Government Printing Office, 1978
29. Ramshorn MT: Mental Health Services. In Haber J et al (eds): Comprehensive Psychiatric Nursing, pp 10–17. New York, McGraw-Hill, 1978
30. Report of the Task Force on Community Mental Health Programs. Am J Psychiatr 139:5 (May): 705–708, 1982
31. Reiger DA, Goldberg ID, Taube CA: The De Facto U.S. Mental Health Services System. Arch Gen Psychiatry 35 (June): 685–693, 1978
32. Schulberg H: Outcome Evaluations for the Mental Health Field. Comm Ment Health J 17:2 (Summer): 132–142, 1981
33. Weissman CM, Klerman GL: Epidemiology of Mental Disorders: Emerging Trends in the U.S. Arch Gen Psychiatry 35 (June): 705–712, 1978
34. Wilson H, Kneisl C: Psychiatric Nursing. Menlo Park, Addison-Wesley, 1979
35. Yolles S: The Future of Community Psychiatry. In Barton W, Sanbonn C (eds): An Assessment of the Community Mental Health Movement. [Edited by Walter Barton and Charlotte Sanbonn.] Lexington, DC Heath, 1975
36. Zusman J: The Philosophic Basis for a Community and Social Psychiatry. In Barton W, Sanbonn C (eds): An Assessment of the Community Mental Health Movement. Lexington, DC Heath, 1975

Part II
Human Development

Chapter 6
Development of the Person

To venture causes anxiety, but not to venture is to lose oneself.

Søren Aabye Kierkegaard

Sylvia M. Anderson Whiting

Chapter Preview

Development is the result of a combination of factors and forces that impel the individual toward a characteristic style. The nature–nurture controversy has created diverse and sometimes conflicting schools of thought. It is generally agreed, however, that development proceeds along certain specific lines called developmental phases or stages.

Although most adults can identify significant life events that they believe have impacted the present, the debate continues about how these influences come about, about their effects upon the emerging personality, and about the resolution of problems. The student of psychiatric-mental health nursing needs to understand the factors influencing human development and needs to formulate a conceptual framework of mental health problems and treatment approaches.

Newborn infants subjected to identical stimuli display a wide variety of responses. These differing reaction patterns of newborns are termed constitutional baselines or complexes. Therefore, one infant may remain placid whereas another may react intensely to stimuli. Feeding and crying behaviors also differ widely from infant to infant. These infant behaviors require adaptive responses from the mothering or parenting figure. The resulting maternal–child or parental–child interactions are responsible for multiple adaptive or maladaptive responses affecting maturation and development. The unfolding of development has been thought to occur over a period of 2 decades to form the functioning personality.[1] Current theory asserts, however, that development is a continuous process occurring throughout the lifespan and is not limited to a few years in early life.

The reader may sometimes hear references to normal or abnormal development. These terms, it must be remembered, are relative and dependent upon many factors, such as averages or statistical norms, social norms, individual response patterns, and the presence or absence of psychopathology.[1]

This chapter will introduce the reader to theories about human development from intrapsychic, interpersonal, social learning, cognitive, and behavioristic viewpoints.

Learning Objectives

On completion of this chapter, the reader should be able to accomplish the following.

1. Discuss the phases of psychosexual development according to Freud's intrapsychic theory
2. Describe the development of self-concept according to Sullivan's interpersonal theory
3. Explain the developmental tasks of the eight stages of development described in Erikson's social learning theory
4. Describe the thinking of children during each of the four periods of cognitive development according to Piaget's theory
5. Discuss the effects of reinforcement on learning according to behavioristic theory
6. Apply developmental criteria to the assessment of clients evidencing physical and emotional health problems

Theories of Development

Intrapsychic Theory

Sigmund Freud, credited with being the father of psychiatry, was a Viennese physician whose work continued until his death in 1939. Freud utilized hypnosis in the treatment of psychiatric patients and, in this way, became interested in the processes of the unconscious. The art and science of psychoanalysis developed from his description of the unconscious, which is thought to contain the repressed memories of all experiences from the first 6 years of life. An extension of this concept states that, although memories may be repressed, they continue to influence or drive all behavior. Chapter 2 also provides information about the development of psychoanalytic and other theories and their application to the treatment of mental disorders.

Libidinal or instinctual drives influence behavior and are related to a person's attempt to gain pleasure or satisfaction through the mouth, anus, or genitalia. The three periods during which the infant and young child focus on these orifices are known correspondingly as the oral, anal, and phallic (or oedipal) phases of development.

The psychoanalytic theorist relates psychological (often referred to as psychosexual) problems to the child's experiences during these three phases of development. Individuals with severe disturbances of the mind are believed to have experienced maladaptive maternal–child relationships during the early infantile period, the oral phase. Those with less severe mental disturbances are thought to have encountered difficulties during the later periods of early childhood; that is, during the anal phase (approximately from 18 months to 3 years) or during the phallic phase (approximately from 3 to 6 years).

Oral Phase

Encountering difficulties in any of these three phases results from anxiety of the mother or mothering person. The development of the infant's ego strength depends on the mother's security in herself and in her mothering role. During the oral phase, the infant experiences whatever the mother feels; that is, he introjects the person of closest attachment and takes on the anxiety or serenity of that person.[11] When the anxiety of the mothering person is all-pervasive, the infant is particularly vulnerable and begins life with a deficit in adaptive abilities.

Anal Phase

The mothering person may encounter no particular difficulty during the period of infancy but may cope ineffectively with the young child as a mobile toddler. The anal phase challenges the mother's coping ability because she must allow him to move away—in effect, to seek freedom or a greater sense of self. Toilet training of the toddler and other issues of the anal phase often arouse psychological problems, particularly related to the rules of custom and culture.

While the toddler strives for mastery over certain aspects of his life, he may not be ready to comply with the social expectations of his parents or other significant adults. The child's strivings in two directions, compliance and noncompliance, is termed *ambivalence*. He may comply through proper elimination, thereby introjecting the values of his parents, or he may not comply through retention or inappropriate discharge of feces, which then brings retribution and further anxiety. This "holding on" and "letting go" leads to various behaviors that psychoanalytic clinicians refer to as *anal characteristics*.

Phallic Phase

As the child moves into the phallic (or oedipal) phase of development, the foundation has usually been well established for what occurs during this stage. When anxiety has been present throughout the parent–child relationship, it is likely that it will continue to manifest itself in the ongoing relationship.

In addition, a problem of a different nature may evidence during the phallic phase, when the child begins to develop an awareness of gender. The child recognizes his or her own gender and manifests an interest in the sexuality of others. He or she may also engage in sexual exploratory play, which may cause parents considerable anxiety.

The term *oedipal* refers to the Greek myth about Oedipus Rex who was separated from his mother in childhood, was reunited with her in adulthood, and, not knowing that she was his mother, fell in love with her. Freud postulated that, during the years from 3 to 6, the child is unconsciously driven toward the parent of the opposite sex and, in effect, desires to possess that parent for himself or herself. For the male child, the issue is less complex than it is for a female child because the mother is the primary love object; for the female, however, it means competing with mother, the young girl's primary love object. The child often resolves the oedipal complex by becoming like, or identifying with, the same-sex parent.

Latent and Genital Phases

Freud called the next two stages of development the latent and genital phases. His use of the term *latent* refers to his belief that sexuality in the child from 6 to 10 or 12 years does not disappear but becomes hidden. At this age, the child engages in the larger world and is absorbed by its challenges to such an extent that his libidinal drive seems to assume less importance and attention.

Then, during the adolescent period, the oedipal strivings reawaken and stir a need for the adolescent child to rework and settle his or her libidinal drive toward the parent of the opposite sex. One way in which this is accomplished is by the adolescent rechanneling his or her energies toward peers of the opposite sex.

An individual's responses during the infantile or early childhood periods, which are carried into adulthood, may cause maladaptation and serious adjustment problems. When a person senses himself to be in constant jeopardy, he is unable to turn his energy away from the self and toward more productive activity. In this way, a person may become self-absorbed and defensive in the protection of the self or ego. Defensive maneuvers arising from these early phases of development include repression, introjection, projection, denial, isolation, ambivalence, regression, and sublimation.

Interpersonal Theory

The work of Harry Stack Sullivan, one of psychiatry's most influential thinkers, began in the 1920s and continued to evolve until his death in 1949.

Departing from Freudian concepts, Sullivan used the term *integrating tendencies* to describe behavior by which one moves toward others.[13] These behaviors include smiling, eye contact, verbal communication, offering an object, and so on. This interpersonal relating of one individual to another takes place, according to Sullivan, to convert us "into human beings instead of merely members of the species by assimilating and becoming part of a vast amount of culture."[13]

Security and Self-Concept

The integrating tendencies are related to the pursuit or maintenance of security or the avoidance of insecurity, so that the individual does not experience anxiety. The self comes into being through the young child's experiences. When the child experiences satisfactory fulfillment of his needs, he senses a "good mother" who relaxes the tension of his recurrent needs; this "good mother" becomes introjected as the "good me." When the child receives inadequate mothering and his needs are not satisfactorily met, he senses the "bad or evil mother" associated with the experience of anxiety, which he then introjects as the "bad me."[14] If the maternal–child relationship is, in effect, nonexistent, the child faces a more serious situation from which there develops no sense of self or "not me." According to Sullivan's interpersonal theory, self-concept and anxiety are closely related to an individual's early-life experiences and continue their influence throughout the lifespan.

Social Learning Theory

Psychologist Erik Erikson has contributed a theory of development that has gained prominence during the past 2 decades. Erikson's theory is formulated according to three principles of organization—the somatic process, the ego process, and the societal process.

In the infantile period, the individual is influenced by somatic processes through exposure to pain, such as colic, earaches, and hunger pains, and by ego processes through exposure to anxiety, such as anxiety that is introjected from the mothering figure. Through societal processes, such as the experience of a family crisis, the infant may be exposed to panic, which impacts on him through the method and quality of care administered by his caretaker.

Erikson describes the psychoanalyst as a kind of historian and the history of childhood as the basis for understanding human anxiety. According to this theory, anxiety is the outcome of the ongoing interaction of somatic, ego, and societal processes.

Developmental Tasks
The eight stages of developmental tasks or ego qualities devised by Erikson are as follows.

1. Trust versus mistrust—infancy
2. Autonomy versus shame and doubt—toddlerhood
3. Initiative versus guilt—preschool years
4. Industry versus inferiority—school age
5. Identity versus role confusion—adolescence
6. Intimacy versus isolation—young adulthood
7. Generativity versus stagnation—middle adulthood
8. Integrity versus despair—older adulthood

(See Erikson's Stages of Development.)

Through satisfactory completion of the developmental task of each stage, the individual becomes ready to move on to each succeeding stage feeling strong and able to meet the requirements for that stage. If the individual experiences failure in any stage, he is likely to have greater difficulty achieving success in future stages of development. Each stage is also significant in its own right and results in satisfaction and need fulfillment to the individual who meets the challenges of that stage.

A further distinction of Erikson's social learning theory is his concept linking the developmental stages of individuals to certain social institutions or values (see the extract below). Success in living is described by Erikson in this way: "Healthy children will not fear life if their elders have integrity enough not to fear death."[4]

Cognitive Theory

Jean Piaget's theory of cognitive development states that motor activity involving concrete objecs results in the de-

(Text continues on p 36)

Erikson's Stages of Development with Adaptive or Maladaptive Characteristics Within each Stage

Infant

Trust	Versus	*Mistrust*	*Societal Institution*
Ease in feeding		Withdrawal into	Religious affiliation
Depth of sleep		schizoid and depressive states	
Relaxation of bowels			
The first social achievement allows mother out of sight without undue anxiety or rage.			

Toddler

Autonomy	Versus	*Shame and Doubt*	*Societal Institution*
Self-control without loss of self-esteem		Low self-esteem	Law and order
Good will and pride		Secretiveness	
Rightful dignity		Feelings of persecution	
Lawful independence			
Sense of justice			

Preschooler

Initiative	Versus	*Guilt*	*Societal Institution*
Loving		Hysterical denial	Economic ethos
Relaxed		Paralysis, inhibition, or impotence	
Bright in judgment		Overcompensatory showing off	
Energetic			
Task-oriented			

Initiative	Versus	*Guilt*	*Societal Institution*
		Psychosomatic disease	
		Self-righteousness	
		Moralistic surveilance	

School-aged

Industry	Versus	*Inferiority*	*Societal Institution*
Productivity		Sense of inadequacy	Technologic ethos
Task completion		Mediocrity	
Steady attention		Self-restriction	
Perseverance		Constricted horizons	
Manipulation of tools		Conformity	

Adolescent

Identity	Versus	*Role Confusion*	*Societal Institution*
Idealistic		Delinquency	Ideology and aristocracy
Integration of identifications with libidinal vissicitudes		Psychotic episodes	
Integration of aptitudes with opportunity		Doubt and sexual identity	
Confidence		Overidentification with heroes, cliques, and crowds	

Young Adult

Intimacy	Versus	*Isolation*	*Societal Institution*
Commitment		Self-absorption	Ethical sense
Sacrifice		Distancing behaviors	
Compromise		Character problems	
True genitality			
Work productivity			
Satisfactory sex relations			

Middle-aged Adult

Generativity	Versus	*Stagnation*	*Societal Institution*
Establishing and guiding the next generation		Regression to an obsessive need for pseudo intimacy	Ethos of generative succession
Productivity		Personal impoverishment	
Creativity		Early invalidism	
		Self-love	
		Lack of faith	

Older Adult

Integrity	Versus	*Despair*	*Societal Institution*
Assurance of order and meaning		Fear of death	Charity
Experience conveying world order and spiritual sense		Sense time as too short	
New and different love of one's parents		Disgust	
Defends the dignity of own lifestyle against threat			
Emotional integration			
Fellowship with others			
Acceptance of leadership			

(From Erikson EH: Childhood and Society. New York, WW Norton, 1968)

velopment of mental functioning. For example, as an infant discovers his hand that is holding a rattle, he begins to recognize a sound that occurs every time he moves his hand with the rattle in it. Therefore, reflex activity drops out as repetition produces a result that the infant observes; his activity begins to take on purpose. Eventually, the infant identifies the shaking rattle as a producer of sound. Later, he will realize that he is able to create the sound.

Piaget's four periods of cognitive development are as follows.

1. Sensorimotor (0–2 years), during which time development proceeds from reflex activity to representation and sensorimotor learning
2. Preoperational (2–7 years), during which time development proceeds from sensorimotor representation to prelogical thought
3. Concrete operational (7–11 years), during which time development proceeds from prelogical thought to logical, concrete thought
4. Formal operational (11–15 years), during which time development proceeds from logical, concrete thought to logical solutions to all kinds or categories of problems

Tenets of Piaget's Theory

The basic tenets of Piaget's theory of cognitive development are as follows.

1. Every child passes through each stage and substage of cognitive development in the same sequence, although not according to a given timetable.
2. Every child develops strategies for interacting with the environment and knowing its properties.
3. There is a gradual progression from one period of cognitive development to another, with the acquisition of each new operation building on already existing ones.
4. The process of development is one in which increasing differentiation and complexity is matched by increasing integration and coordination of schemata.[2]

Early Learning

Maximal learning, said Piaget, takes place through the process of contemplative recognition, which precedes intentionality. During the period from 4 to 8 months of age, the infant evidences interest in the results of his own behaviors on the environment, and he invents procedures to make interesting sights last. These reactions of the infant are forerunners of contemplative recognition.

Contemplative recognition is the function of recognizing and remembering that what has disappeared will reappear. In other words, the infant sees mother appear, disappear, and reappear frequently enough to anticipate a recurrence of the experience. This ability to recognize when

an object has reappeared extends to many other objects. From approximately 6 to 11 months of age, the infant demonstrates this cognitive process when he repeatedly throws an object and waits expectantly for someone to pick it up. The game of peek-a-boo also reinforces this process.

Representational intelligence refers to the manipulation of mental representations of things and actions, the anticipation of events and consequences of actions, and the ability to evoke an image of an absent object rather than simply recognizing it when it appears. The development of representational intelligence leads to the preoperational stage, wherein objects are classified and categorized. Rudimentary cognitive function precedes language development.[2]

Piaget emphasized the maturation of the nervous system in his theory of cognitive development. The abilities developed within each stage evolve according to the individual's unique timetable of maturation.

Behavioristic Theory

According to behavioristic theory, development is influenced by the stimulus–response interaction; behavior is shaped through the consistency of responding. Researchers have conducted studies to determine the effects of reinforcement of newborns' sucking behaviors, older infants' smiling behaviors, and other developmental skills, such as toilet training, sharing, helping, and cooperating.[7]

Reinforcement of Learning

The neonate is able to learn much more than is usually recognized by parents and professionals. Neonate learning occurs through reinforcement that coincides with need satisfaction.[16] Perceptual discrimination and active learning are possible for the newborn. Therefore, when a mothering person consistently appears along with a need-fulfilling stimulus (*e.g.*, the breast or bottle) the neonate relates the two and prefers that person over all others.

Differentiation between two faces and voices has been demonstrated during the first 2 weeks of the neonate's life. Furthermore, this recognition seems to be related to the infant's development of social communication skills by means of bodily movements and, within a short period of time, by means of the smile. These forms of social communication occur through mutual interaction of mother and neonate, which is reciprocally rewarding and reinforcing.

Current Developmental Theory

The newest model of development, a biopsychosocial model, discounts the idea that the optimal period for certain developmental behaviors is always in early childhood. It asserts, rather, that the human organism possesses a complexity that defies easy or simple classifications or comparisons.

Two attributes of the human brain, flexibility and plasticity, are developmentally significant and allow for a variety of adaptive sequences.[15] Therefore, although early life influences are considered very important, they are no longer thought to produce irreversible effects on the personality.

Consonance Versus Dissonance

An interactionist model of development focuses on the concept of "goodness of fit" and the related ideas of consonance and dissonance. This model demonstrates that development in a progressive direction occurs when consonance (or goodness of fit) exists and that dissonance (or poorness of fit) involves discrepancies between the individual and the environment. Such discrepancies result in distorted development and maladaptive functioning.[15] The goodness-of-fit concept implies that environmental demands and expectations are in accord with the individual's capacity to respond. This results in consonance or a sense of comfort, which makes progressive, optimal development possible.

Consider the following application of this concept: Mary is a shy, introverted individual who has just completed college with a bachelor's degree in biology. She restricts relationships to one or two people. She has two job opportunities from which to choose, one as a research assistant in a laboratory and the other as a public relations coordinator. Both pay equitable and similar salaries. Using the goodness-of-fit concept, it is likely that Mary would be more comfortable and more adaptive as a research assistant than as a public relations coordinator and that her development would continue more smoothly.[16,17]

Developmental Issues in Nursing

Nurses are frequently called upon to assess developmental processes and progression in the course of implementing the nursing process. They frequently refer to any of these theories, or a combination of them, to determine probable causes of behavior and interventions that will facilitate effective behavior change. Psychiatric-mental health nurses are necessarily interested in developmental issues, because physical and emotional health are, in large part, determined by adaptive or maladaptive responses along the developmental continuum.

One useful framework considers the presence of dependency, independency, or interdependency in progressive stages on a continuum (see Table 6-1). This framework establishes that in healthy, adaptive states, there is progressive movement away from dependency, totally evident at birth, to the ultimate adult position of interdependency.

The great struggle for independence takes place during the adolescent period and is responsible for creating marked equilibrium. Ego crystallization, the crucial issue during adolescence, occurs through the process of achieving independence. When this process is incompletely experienced, often observed in adolescent rebellion, it is usually worked out during later periods of life at a time when other processes should be occurring, thereby hindering the development of those phases.

Dependency is closely related to anxiety and an emotionally restricted self. Interdependency, on the other hand, is found in persons who are relatively free of anxiety and able to view themselves as capable individuals interacting with other capable individuals.

The overall goals of human development include social competence and mastery. Many believe that the first year of life is the most important; some would even propose that the first day of life may well be the most significant one.

It is clear that the study and understanding of development is complex and multifaceted even before the added influence of cultural differences. The development of a child in America and another in Samoa will demonstrate obvious differences in the manner in which tasks are mastered, the time when they occur, and the utilization of skills. Nevertheless, there will be consistent sequential development in numerous areas of functioning across cultures; the children within a given culture will evidence linear progression toward mastery of certain tasks expected within the cultural group.

To understand development, the nurse must consider genetic transmission, cultural transmission, temperament, motivation, physical endowment, stimulus provision, and interaction with others. The fact that these forces contribute to development lends credence to the notion that developmental outcomes are not the responsibility of one person. In the past, mothers were viewed as totally responsible for the healthiness of a child's development. Fathers, siblings, extended family, and even the child himself were seen as mere bystanders in the scenario. Furthermore, it was held that the child's development was essentially completed in 6 years and that, from the age of 6 on, only modification of the personality took place. Little attention

Table 6-1. **Progression from Dependence to Interdependence**

INFANCY (0–1)	CHILDHOOD (1–12)	ADOLESCENCE			ADULTHOOD
		Early	*Middle*	*Late*	
Dependency	Decreasing dependency	Conflict in dependency	Struggle toward independence	Independence	Interdependency

focused on adult development, particularly on the mid-age and late-age periods.

Current developmental theories give rise to the hope that there is continuity in the process of development, and that self-actualization may occur even in the late-age period. Many examples of persons who achieved their greatest potential only after reaching elderly status are available. Some adults appear to progress, regress, and progress according to life circumstances or crises. Late-age development was a less prominent issue in the years when life expectancy did not exceed the mid-age period for most, but survival past the age of 100 years is not uncommon anymore. The 1970 United States census revealed that there were more than 10,600 Americans past the age of 100 years.[15]

Generally, development in the elderly is not as much a matter of achieving a higher level of functioning as it is a transformation, qualitative in nature, that is concerned with maintaining adaptive behavior governed by weakened physiological structure and increased egocentricity.[14] Adaptation requires considerable compensation for the individual whose sensory apparatus, from the 4th decade on, begins to limit function. As the 7th decade begins, the person's sensory and perceptual processes become slower, requiring a longer period of time to arrive at accuracy in problem-solving. Research findings suggest that the major change in intellectual functioning from mid-life to early old age is related to reaction time. An understanding of this concept is important if nurses are to avoid infantilizing the aged individual who may respond to the label if he is regarded as incapable.[9] Often, people conclude that because the elderly person does not function as well physically as the young person, he is also less capable intellectually. Nurses are in a position to reinforce the elderly individual as a person who has wisdom, responsibility, and prestige.[9]

Summary

This chapter has presented an overview of five different developmental theories—intrapsychic, interpersonal, social learning, cognitive, and behavioristic. The integration of these theories has evolved into a body of knowledge permitting further study of developmental issues. Some of the major points of the chapter are as follows.

1. Human development is a complex and multifaceted process involving a variety of forces that effect unique personalities.
2. Development is currently considered to be a continuous process, unfolding throughout the lifespan, rather than being limited to a few years in early life.
3. No longer is the responsibility for development placed on the mothering person alone, but on the complex and interacting influences on the individual.
4. The developmental period of old age is a focus of current attention. Evidence supports the idea that a qualitative level of development continues in the increasing numbers of elderly persons in our population.
5. Healthy, adaptive adult functioning occurs at a level of interdependency.

References

1. Call JD: Normal Development. In Noshpitz JD (ed): Basic Handbook of Child Psychiatry, Vol I, pp 1–10. New York, Basic Books, 1979
2. Drucker J: Development from One to Two Years: Ego Development. In Noshpitz JD (ed): Basic Handbook of Child Psychiatry, Vol I, pp 157–164. New York, Basic Books, 1979
3. Emde R, Robinson J: The First Two Months: Recent Research in Developmental Psychobiology and the Changing View of the Newborn. In Noshpitz JD (ed): Basic Handbook of Child Psychiatry, Vol I, pp 72–105. New York, Basic Books, 1979
4. Erikson EH: Childhood and Society, 2nd ed. New York, WW Norton, 1963
5. Mausch I: Old Age in the U.S.: A Time to Wait. Geriatric Nursing 1 (May/June): 42–43, 1980
6. May R: The Meaning of Anxiety. New York, The Ronald Press, 1950
7. O'Leary KD, Wilson GT: Behavior Therapy: Application and Outcome. Englewood Cliffs, New Jersey, Prentice-Hall, 1975
8. Pierce P: Intelligence and Learning in the Aged. Journal of Gerontological Nursing 6 (May): 268–270, 1980
9. Plawecki H, Plawecki J: Act Your Age. Geriatric Nursing 1 (September/October): 179–181, 1980
10. Robson KS: Development of the Human Infant from Two to Six Months. In Noshpitz JD (ed): Basic Handbook of Child Psychiatry, pp 106–112. New York, Basic Books, 1979
11. Roiphe H: A Theoretical Overview of Preoedipal Development During the First Four Years of Life. In Noshpitz JD (ed): Basic Handbook of Child Psychiatry, pp 118–127. New York, Basic Books, 1979
12. Rosen H: Pathway To Piaget. Cherry Hill, New Jersey, Postgraduate International Inc, 1977
13. Sullivan HS: Clinical Studies in Psychiatry. New York, WW Norton, 1956
14. Sullivan HS: The Fusion of Psychiatry and Social Science. New York, WW Norton, 1964
15. Schaie KW: Psychological Changes From Midlife to Early Old Age: Implications for the Maintenance of Mental Health. Am J Orthopsychiatry 51 (April): 199–218, 1981
16. Thomas A: Current Trends in Developmental Theory. Am J Orthopsychiatry 51 (October): 580–609, 1981
17. Thomas A, Chess S: The Dynamics of Psychological Development. New York, Bruner/Mazel, 1980

Chapter 7
Sociocultural Aspects of Care

If we are to achieve a richer culture, rich in contrasting values, we must recognize the whole gamut of human potentialities, and so we are a less arbitrary social fabric, one in which each diverse human gift will find a fitting place.

Margaret Mead

Margie N. Slaughter

Chapter Preview

A variety of ethnic groups presently call America home. In addition, members of ethnic minorities continue to arrive daily from other countries. Psychiatric-mental health problems increase in relation to unemployment, economic decline, and interpersonal alienation. An individual's culture encompasses many factors that influence his perceptions of health and illness and whether he seeks assistance from mental health care professionals.

This chapter is written to help the health care provider understand and appreciate how a person's culture affects his perceptions of, and reactions to, health and illness, emotional problems, and disorder. The overview of culture focuses on the specific aspects of ethnicity, lifestyle, religion, and family influences. The nursing process—assessment, analysis, planning, implementation, and evaluation—is applied to psychiatric-mental health clients of different cultures.

Learning Objectives

The reader, upon completion of the chapter, should be able to accomplish the following.

1. Define culture
2. Discuss the influence of culture on the health beliefs and practices of individuals
3. Recognize the existence of racial and cultural diversity in American society
4. Recognize and discuss own feelings and behaviors that influence one's ability to interact with individuals of another culture
5. Apply the nursing process to clients of different cultures

    Assess clients of different cultures

    Describe the problems or potential problems of clients of different cultures

    Formulate nursing diagnoses for clients of different cultures

    Identify nursing goals and actions designed to alleviate the problems of clients and families of different cultures

    Formulate nursing care plans for clients and families of different cultures

    Evaluate the effectiveness of nursing interventions

Culture

Culture is man's basic roadmap for living.[23] Specific cultural beliefs include an individual's values and patterns of living, and these beliefs have always been a part of human existence. How a person reacts to illness, his health mainte- nance, daily activities, food preferences, interpersonal relationships, patterns of action, beliefs, and feelings are all culturally linked.

Culture is learned behavior—dynamic and ever-changing. Culture is transmitted from one generation to another through socialization practices that are reinforced by cultural and social interactions. As an individual matures, he may accept or reject certain portions of his culture, thereby inducing cultural changes.

Subculture and Ethnicity

A *subculture* is a group of people who may be distinguishable by ethnic background, religion, social status, or other similar characteristics; at the same time, they may share certain features with larger social segments.[20] Nevertheless, although some of these features are shared, certain differences exist due to ethnic background. An *ethnic group* is a group of people with a common origin who hold basically similar values, beliefs, and means of communication.[31]

Why Study Culture?

The concept of culture provides a comprehensive framework for care providers to understand and appreciate the cultural differences and similarities essential to providing quality patient care. Being knowledgeable about cultural similarities enables care providers to appreciate common human behaviors and bonds. Failing to appreciate cultural differences leads to ineffective communication and relationships between clients and care providers and limits the providers' ability to work effectively with members of other cultures.

Culture is a patterned way of life with special meaning to the individual members of the culture. To develop a therapeutic plan of care, the health care provider needs to be aware of the client's way of thinking, feeling, and responding. Knowledge of the client's background helps health professionals understand cultural factors related to health care, their role in working with clients and families of different cultures, and approaches they might take in order to facilitate changes in health practices.

Multiethnicity of the United States

For many years, people in the United States have lived with the myth of the "melting pot," or cultural homogeneity. According to this myth, various European people immigrating to the United States were absorbed into America's mainstream.[9] This process of assimilation required that the particular European ethnic groups relinquish those behavioral practices that failed to fit into their new culture. Although some European ethnic groups, such as the Italians, Irish, Jews, and Polish, were persecuted for certain beliefs, practices, and behaviors, they were nevertheless absorbed into the main culture. This was not true, however, of all ethnic groups.

Ethnic groups of color, those with yellow, brown, black, or red skin, have never been totally assimilated into the main culture. Their color, as well as other distinctive racial characteristics such as facial features, body build, and hair texture, made it impossible for them not to be noticeable. Ethnic groups of color have been, and still are, oppressed and discriminated against.

A new ethnicity movement began in the early 1970s that focused on the multiethnicity of the United States and attempted to dispel the melting-pot myth. This movement encouraged ethnic awareness, ethnic traditions, and the practice of specific ethnic customs. The movement further stressed that it was not necessary to relinquish all cultural differences to become totally assimilated into American society.[37]

American Cultural Values

Cultural values are powerful forces that govern an individual's behavior.[20] Many times, people are not fully aware of these American values and their effect on the individual's manner of thought and behavior.

The white middle-class American represents the norm of behavior for the people of the United States. Growth and development theories pertaining to family structure and function, personality development, and physiologic and anatomic characteristics are based on this norm of white America.[20]

American culture stresses the values of automation, time, success, cleanliness, and optimal health.[26] Health care providers are also members of a subculture and influenced by the overall American culture; the values of the dominant culture are reflected in the administration of health care.

Automation

Modern technology has hurled American society toward increasing automation. Some of the positive results of technology are improvements in the quality of life by early detection of certain diseases of adults, children, and the unborn. On the other hand, today's technology has provided us with the ability to annihilate life.

Through automation, jobs that were formerly held by human beings may be performed faster and more efficiently by machines. Automation has altered the job market and has caused many people to seek career changes. The need for career changes and the rise in unemployment when jobs are unavailable, increase stress in individuals, families, and communities.

Modern technology has also had its impact on nursing. Nurses and other health care providers use computers in the processes of gathering and categorizing client data and administering health care services. They operate sophisticated, efficient machines in the treatment of selected diseases. Some subtle dangers exist when health professionals utilize and rely on particularly advanced machinery.

One growing concern is the tendency of people to relate more readily to machines than to other humans. Health care providers may become so involved in technical skills that the client and his stresses, anxieties, and fears are overlooked.

Time

Time is valuable and not to be wasted in America. Time dominates work, sleep, and play. Time influences economic, political, and social values. Time also stimulates emotional reactions in people who are influenced by its power. For example, an individual may feel guilt if he believes he is wasting time, fear or stress if he fails to be on time for an appointment, and anger or frustration if he has to wait for another person who is not on time.

Many other cultures of the world do not view time as such a priority consideration as we do in the American culture. Some countries have no clocks; many depend on the sun and moon to influence their actions and activities. The failure or the need to adhere to a time schedule does not seem to create a problem for these cultural groups.[35]

Success

Successful people are perceived as those who keep busy, work hard, and strive to reach the top. Americans continue to push themselves to greater achievements, to compete, to increase their salaries, and to become more successful socially, economically, and politically. Having the power to control others is equated with success. In conjunction with this continual push for upward mobility, Americans are resorting to more over-the-counter medications, illegal drugs, prescribed drugs, and alcohol to alleviate their daily stresses and problems.

Nursing is likewise influenced by the cultural value of success. Nurses are perceived by others as achievers and are measured by their ability to perform. Nurses themselves often measure their success by their ability to complete tasks. Nursing education in the past stressed actions and tasks; nursing students were rewarded for their task performance, and often not for being active listeners or for being independent, critical thinkers. In more recent years, however, the nursing profession has emphasized the need for nurses to be thinkers, planners, and assessors of health care.[27]

Cleanliness

Bathing, using of deodorants, and wearing clean clothes are stressed through media advertisements, through health education in school, and through education by parents and others. Americans spend billions of dollars on body soaps, washing powders, house cleaners, and other products that promote optimum cleanliness and physical aesthetics. During toilet training, children quickly learn that it's not okay to get soiled; children are often reprimanded for dirtying their clothes.

America's cultural attitude toward cleanliness often conflicts with the attitudes of other cultures. Some cultures feel that exposure to dirt enhances health. Other cultures do not believe that deodorants should be used and do not find the body odor offensive. Some cultures do not think that it is necessary to wash as frequently as Americans do and believe that frequent washing wastes valuable water. Many of these attitudes and values of other cultures are difficult for health care providers to understand and accept because they conflict with their own beliefs about cleanliness.

Nurses strive to maintain a clean, orderly, and relatively germ-free environment for the patient. They spend an enormous amount of time keeping the patient and his environment tidy and clean. The nurse's personal cleanliness is effected by her wearing clean uniforms and maintaining an odor-free body.

American culture stresses that a patient should feel better when he is clean. Assessment of an individual's emotional status includes an evaluation of his physical appearance. For example, are his clothes clean? Is he unkempt; that is, is his hair dirty, does he have body odor, or does he have an unwashed body? Lack of cleanliness often indicates to mental health professionals that the individual is experiencing some type of emotional upset or disorder. Lack of attention to one's personal appearance is frequently interpreted according to American cultural values, as a sign of depression or decompensation.

Optimal Health

The maintenance of health is held as a human right, as well as a civil right, by health officials and by national, state, and local governments. According to middle-class norms, the culturally disadvantaged and deprived experience poor health practices. Senior citizens on fixed income and low-income families who fail to consider health a primary goal are identified as part of these culturally disadvantaged.

Members of many cultures do not view health maintenance as a primary need as long as they are free of pain and have no symptoms that indicate a need to seek health care. The members of some cultures, when interacting with health care providers, may subtly or overtly receive a message that their health practices are unacceptable. Many of these patients will listen politely and then choose either to ignore the information or simply not return to the health care facility. Health care providers may inadvertently attempt to impose their own health practices on members of other cultures without realizing that each individual has health norms and practices that are governed by his own culture.[33]

Process of Enculturation

Enculturation is the process by which an individual learns the expected behavior of the culture. These behaviors incorporate that culture's specific values, beliefs, sanctions, and constraints.[26] The primary goal of enculturation is to provide the individual with the skills needed to function within a given community. This community may consist of people of the same ethnic group, or of a different ethnic group.

Agents of Enculturation

It is the responsibility of the agents of enculturation to convey values and a sense of belonging, warmth, and cohesion within a culture. The family, neighborhood, religion, and educational system are agents of enculturation.

Family

The family is the earliest and most effective agent of enculturation. Each unique family interaction conveys to its members communication patterns, role behavior, values, beliefs, and views of the world. Within the family, the individual learns fear, love, hatred, and hope. He develops his aspirations, even those of an intense and deeply personal nature, within the family, and is both positively and negatively affected by others' perceptions of who and what he is.

A family, particularly a minority family, transmits not only what is valued by the group, but also clues regarding how members of the group are likely to be perceived and received by others outside the group.[4] For minority groups and those suffering the effects of discrimination, ethnic identity and its transmission serve to protect their members from the larger world.[8] The larger world belittles or demeans the members of minority groups, often out of ignorance and frequently intentionally. Ethnicity protects against the insinuation that, if the members abandon their ethnic group identity or related behaviors, discrimination against them will cease. This insinuation has proved to be false; blacks or hispanics who have chosen to abandon subtle, but characteristic, speech patterns still experience job discrimination in certain areas of America.[6]

Neighborhood

The *neighborhood* is another agent of enculturation. Neighborhoods consist of shops, church, school, taverns, and many members of a social network. An ethnic group residing together over a long period of time develops a strong sense of belonging and community. This social network helps members develop and structure relationships outside the home and maintain endangered values, customs, and beliefs when individual members of the ethnic group begin to move into mainstream America.

Neighborhood networking varies according to geographic locations and different ethnic groups. For example, in large urban areas, only pockets of stable neighborhoods may be found. Many inner-city neighborhoods are being destroyed by vandals, are sold to land developers, or are slowly deteriorating due to neglect. When neighborhoods change rapidly, the stability of the social network is threatened or lost. In some cases, when mothers and fathers both work outside of the home, members of the neighborhood may offer the primary means of socialization and protection for children. From these neighbors, children may learn how to protect themselves from strangers and criminal elements in the community.

Religion

Religion plays an important role in the life of many ethnic groups. Some people look to religion for answers to their questions about why certain events, such as illness or injury, occur in their lives. Religion also affects the way in which people interpret the signs and symptoms of illness. Religious beliefs often influence the course of the illness and the person's willingness to seek medical care. For example, members of religions that promulgate a belief that God ultimately controls all that happens on the earth and teach that man should accept with humility and resignation the fate to which he has been assigned, may tend to avoid the use of medical services.[19]

Church attendance provides spiritual involvement for some and a basis of social life for other members of the church community. Religious groups also act as enforcers of ethnic values, customs, and behaviors. Through their church participation and involvement, some church members gain status that is self-affirming and confers on them the respect and honor of the community.[26]

Educational System

Within the schools, children begin to relate with others outside of their immediate environment. Often, the school environment provides the child with his first opportunity to encounter someone from a different ethnic group. The teacher becomes a critical figure to the child. The child's ability to adjust to school progresses effectively when the child is able to relate with a teacher of the same ethnic group or with a teacher who is culturally sensitive and supportive.

Busing has probably contributed to the problem of maintaining ethnic identity. In the pursuit of better educational opportunities for all children, many children coming from schools and teachers who promote adjustment to the process of formal education are bused to other schools and teachers who are not sensitive to cultural differences. A teacher may be unsuccessful in interacting with children of different ethnic groups due to the lack of educational preparation in working with children of different cultures, the fear of not being an effective teacher of the child, the mistake of "trying too hard" to help the child succeed in school, the fear of identification with the child, and the bigotry and prejudices that the teacher may be unable to deny. The child quickly learns that the teacher is the authority figure. If a child receives negative responses from the teacher or other person in the authority role, he may react to them strongly; that is, negative responses may have profound effects on him and his behavior.

Process of Acculturation

Acculturation is the process in which groups with different cultures and backgrounds meet and live together. Efforts to understand and accurately describe acculturation were triggered by the mass migrations of Europeans to the United States, by the importation of slaves, and by the contacts between the original settlers and the American Indians.[12]

Cultural change takes place gradually and in any degree. Acculturation makes one group's culture the point of reference and focuses upon the events and processes by which that group responds to continuous contact with another group.[31] The group may accept, reformulate, or reject elements of the other culture.

During the process of acculturation, the ethnic group may adopt only the major themes or behaviors of the dominant society, such as its language, or the ethnic group may establish even deeper relationships with the dominant society, such as through intermarriage. Many ethnic groups value their traditions and differences and actively attempt to prevent total assimilation into the dominant culture, while at the same time they seek social and economic equality.[37] On the other hand, not all members of an ethnic group necessarily believe or practice all aspects of that culture. One reality to bear in mind is that, because of intermarriage within different cultures, there are few people who can be considered culturally pure.[39]

Aspects of Cultural Learning of Specific Ethnic Groups

Each ethnic group has a unique history with respect to oppression and discrimination, the value attached to academic pursuits, the roles of men and women, the value of the family, and the translation of religious teachings into dicta for daily living.

The traditions transmitted by the family, the special inflection of language, and even the foods a person eats let him know that he is with his own. For the lower-class white, as well as for ethnic groups of color, the reality of cultural distinctions has also perpetuated continuing and persistent discrimination in jobs, in housing, in schooling, in the reception received in the work place, and often in institutions providing health care.[15]

The term *ethnic people of color* has been designated to persons belonging to the four large minority groups in the United States. These four minority cultures have been defined by the Federal Government and include the Spanish-speaking, American Indian or native American, Asian American, and Black American. It should be noted that subcultures exist within each of the ethnic groups discussed. Specific nursing actions and implications related to each ethnic group are also discussed.

Spanish-Speaking Americans

Three major subcultures—the Mexican-American, Hispanic, and Puerto Rican—comprise the Spanish-speaking people in America. Mexican-Americans represent the majority of the Spanish-speaking people. Although each of these subcultures is distinctive in origin and characteristics, they share some commonalities in relation to health practices, the use of healers, attitudes toward health care providers, and so forth.

Health Practices

In the Spanish-speaking culture, a sick person remains within his group or family. The danger of illness or harm is perceived as coming from outside the patient, such as from the impersonal physical world or from the unknown.

Generally, an older family member within the home, usually the grandmother, treats mild illnesses by means of various herbs and home remedies. Illness, harm, and the hazards of the unknown are prevented by men and women wearing certain objects, such as copper pennies, cloves of garlic, or a "deer's eye," or by performing certain rites. A piece of red cloth may be worn over the heart to prevent angina. The health care provider should not remove these objects unless their removal is absolutely necessary, because they provide comfort and security to the Spanish-speaking patient. Men and women believe that by observing the ritual calendar, by being a good Catholic, and by being a respected member of the community, a person is able to maintain balance in his life.

Attitudes Toward Health Care Providers

Many Spanish-speaking patients are uncomfortable when treated by a physician. They often perceive the doctor's professional approach as being indifferent to personal needs.[30] Spanish-speaking women may feel embarrassment and bashfulness in the presence of male physicians or medical students and may prefer to have a female conduct the interview or examination. A male would prefer, likewise, not to be cared for by a female health provider. In the hospital, the fear of surgery, the impersonality of the doctors and nurses, the infringement on one's modesty, and the possibility of death contribute to the anxiety of being hospitalized.

Healers

It is important for the health care provider to be aware that a Spanish-speaking patient may consult both a faith healer and a physician. Many times, the patient may be referred to a physician by a healer who determined that the patient was too critically ill for him to treat.

Two kinds of healers are involved in folk medicine. The curandero (male) or curandera (female) is seen when a person is ill. The curandero or curandera uses rituals, massages, and herbs to combat the illness, and he or she involves the patient and his family in the treatment. These healers are believed to be chosen by God to heal natural folk illnesses.[30] (See the essay on Curanderismo.)

The second healer is known as the epiritualisto (male) or epiritualista (female). The spiritualist is usually consulted when there is a need to remove hexes, communicate with the dead, or a desire to predict the individual's future.[37]

Social and Kinship Ties

The family is a cherished institution, probably second only to God and the church. Typically, the father is the patriarch whose authority is recognized and exercised. He is responsible for providing guidance and leadership to the family and for making all major decisions.

The mother is subordinate to her husband or to the head of the household. The mother's interests primarily include bearing children and caring for her family, home, and close kin.

Respect is accorded to members of the family on the basis of age and sex. The old are accorded more respect than the young, and men more respect than women.

Religion

Religion is an important influence because the Spanish-speaking peoples believe that religion unifies and integrates their life in the family and the community. The predominant religion is Roman Catholicism.

A strong belief of Spanish-speaking people is that God gives health and allows illness for a reason. They also believe that faith in God is necessary for recovery from illness.

The priest continues to be recognized as a spiritual leader, even though some of the religious activities of the Catholic church are changing. The priest also serves as a counselor in temporal, religious, and community matters.

Language

Many Spanish-speaking patients and families experience their language as a barrier to health care in institutions that expect an individual to be proficient in English. The language difference further isolates Spanish-speaking clients from organizations and services that could help improve their living conditions.

Mental Illness

Research has demonstrated that there is less incidence of mental illness among Spanish-speaking people in part because there are fewer role conflicts; that is, the rules of behavior of the culture are clearly defined.[30] The family also serves as a buffering mechanism that allows members to share, and thereby reduce, anxiety and stressful situations. Their view of the world enables them to blame external forces for failures, and this further reduces guilt. Spanish-speaking people are also likely to be averse to hospitals and are reluctant to seek treatment for mental illness.

Curanderismo

Juanita Zapata Flint, R.N., M.S.
Coordinator/Instructor, Nursing
El Centro College
Brookhaven College Satellite
Dallas, Texas

Curanderismo is the practice of folk healing that evolved from European medical practices of the 15th and 16th centuries and that continues today within the Mexican American community. The Aztecs, Mayas, and other Indian groups left these folk beliefs and curing practices to the Spanish Catholics in Mexico. Curanderismo has persisted as a tradition in the Mexican American culture because of its members' rural background, illiteracy, poverty, and distrust of the modern medical care system.[2]

Curanderos, or folk healers, are usually women who believe they are endowed with curing powers from God. The healer comes to hold this belief by experiencing a dream or a vision or by being involved in the care of a sick person who recovers. Curanderos are sincere in their belief that they were chosen by God and, therefore, do not usually charge fees for their healing services. They believe that if they expected or demanded payment, their divine gift of healing would be taken away. Recently, however, it has become common for curanderos to develop a fee system, although their charges are minimal.[3]

The diseases treated by the curandero are thought to be due to the will of God or to witchcraft. *Susto*, or fright, is a condition that follows an emotional upset and is characterized by depression, restlessness, loss of strength, and anorexia. If the patient suffers from susto, the curandero will be asked to intervene, because curanderos are the only ones believed to have the power to perform the necessary healing rituals.[4]

Mal ojo, or evil eye, is thought to be caused by envy, covetous expressions, or attention paid by one person to another. For example, telling a mother that her child is attractive, but failing to touch the child after making that statement will cast the spell of mal ojo and the child will become ill with fever. The person complimenting the child should also touch him, thereby breaking the spell of mal ojo.

The belief in mal ojo is widespread. Mexican Americans may take preventive measures, such as wearing amulets, gold earrings, snakes' fangs, garlic, or oil crosses on the head; to deflect the mal ojo.[1,5]

These diseases, mal ojo and susto, are only two of the many folk diseases that the nurse might encounter when caring for the Mexican American patient. The nurse should not assume that, because a patient is educated or acculturated, he does not hold these beliefs in curanderismo. A patient's perceptions of health and illness are influenced strongly by his cultural beliefs; health care services must acknowledge and understand those cultural beliefs to provide optimal care to Mexican American patients.

References

1. Ingham JM: On Mexican Folk Medicine. American Anthropologist, 1970
2. Kiev A: Curanderismo: Mexican-American Folk Psychiatry. New York, The Free Press, 1968
3. Madsen W: The Mexican-American of South Texas. New York, Holt, Rhinehart, and Winston, 1964
4. Rodriguez J: Mexican Americans: Factors Influencing Health Practices. The Journal of School Health 53 (February): 136–140, 1983
5. Swafford-Gonzalez MJ, Gutierrez MG: Ethno-Medical Beliefs and Practices of Mexican Americans. Nurse Practitioner 8 (November–December): 29–34, 1983

Implications for Nursing Actions

1. Recognize and attend to the role of the nuclear and extended family in Spanish-speaking cultures. Illness of the Spanish-speaking patient tends to be a social, family, and, oftentimes, a community matter rather than an isolated illness state of one person.
2. Provide explanations that take into account the extent to which the client and his family are acculturated.

   Define and clarify any technical or professional terms.
   Use audiovisual aids whenever possible.

   Obtain an interpreter or bilingual health care provider if needed.
3. Avoid cultural labeling, which might contribute to degrading attitudes toward the patient and family.
4. Accord respect by using proper forms to address Spanish-speaking patients, instead of using first names.
5. Listen attentively to the comments and responses of client and family and validate with them their perception of the communication.
6. Recognize that ritual acts and health practices are important to the Spanish-speaking patient and his family.

Native Americans

There are more than 200 American Indian, or native American, tribes in the United States; the greatest portion of these reside in Oklahoma, Alaska, Arizona, California, and New Mexico.[2] More than one half of these tribes reside on reservations. In recent years, increasing numbers of native Americans are migrating from reservations to the larger cities in search of educational and employment opportunities. Although each of these tribes has its own language, customs, beliefs, and practices, there are some commonalities that guide the nurse in working with the native American.

Family Structure and Roles

The native American family includes both the nuclear family and the extended families and the community. Each family member has rights and specific duties. The native American family is also child-oriented and all family members participate in the childrearing process.

Food, shelter, and survival are supported on a community basis.[36] Adoption rituals are performed within tribal ceremonies to prevent a family's loss of ties due to death and to ensure that the individual will always have a family. When an individual member of the culture becomes hospitalized, family members and friends may travel a great distance to visit him.

Native American families of many tribes are experiencing serious disorganization. This has been attributed to the changes in the native American's way of life on the reservation and to his difficulties in adapting to the expectations of the dominant society.[36]

Food

Food has both religious and social value to native Americans. Food is incorporated into religious ceremonies. It is also an integral part of any social gathering. Good, plentiful food increases a family's reputation in their tribe.

Time

The native American's life is not dictated by a clock. Rather, actions are initiated and develop, not according to a time schedule. Time is viewed as a continuum without a beginning or an end.[2]

Religion

The members of native American tribes hold a holistic view of life and believe that God is the giver of life. Illness is perceived in association with religion. An individual who becomes ill is likely to seek intervention from a medicine man and subscribe to religious rituals to remove the illness.

Values

Some of the values upheld by native Americans on the reservations are in transition for those who are moving to the city. An important value of the native American is the importance of sharing, rather than possessing, material objects.

Healers and Health Practices

Many native Americans view the world through the realm of the supernatural and seek assistance from the medicine man or Shaman. Although most native Americans recognize the value of modern medicine, they may continue to use native healers in addition to medical intervention.[36] The native healers' use of herbs, plants, and other healing techniques have been proven effective.[39]

Healing ceremonies usually take place in the home and involve the participation of family members and other members of the tribe. It is not unusual for a hospitalized native American to desire to use a native healer. The family of the hospitalized member may want to leave certain objects in the patient's room, objects which they believe caused the illness and can also effect the cure.

Mental Illness

The impoverishment of native American life has contributed to the high incidence of such health problems as tuberculosis, communicable diseases, malnutrition, and high maternal and infant mortality rates.[39] There are, among native Americans, high rates of suicide, alcoholism, and homocide.[36] There is also a high rate of automobile accidents, which many researchers suspect are, in actuality, undocumented suicides.[2]

The native American community experiences social and personal disorganization as a result of the dominant society's insistence that the Indian community relinquish their own culture and religion. This leads to a loss of an integrated value system, leaving the individual with feelings of hopelessness, despair, and anger as he attempts to cope with everyday problems.

Though geographically different, the Alaskan native American experiences similar difficulties trying to live in two different cultures. There are no native reservations in Alaska. The Alaskan native American's villages are located within the interior of Alaska. The only means of transportation to some of these villages is by air. Many Alaskan natives experience anger and frustration about the changes in their villages and way of life, and they experience depression and helplessness about their dependence on the dominant society.

Implications for Nursing Actions

1. Remember that the family and community play important roles in the care of the individual native American.
2. Do not prevent the hospitalized patient and family from seeking treatment from a native healer. Using a healer may reduce some of the client's feelings of alienation in the health care system and may therefore contribute to his psychological well-being.

3. Be aware that native Americans may perceive hospitals as places that isolate them from their major cultural and social group.

4. Recognize that time does not have the same value for native Americans as it does for the dominant society and that an individual who keeps an appointment at a health clinic or hospital may not necessarily be on time.

5. Listen attentively to the native American's words; he often speaks softly and expects the listener to pay careful attention.

6. Observe and assess nonverbal behavior of native American clients; they are likely to watch the health care provider but say little or nothing.

7. Avoid note-taking and the extensive use of questions during the history-taking process. The native American resents excessive questioning and believes that writing while he is talking shows disrespect.

8. Break eye contact with the client intermittently when interacting with him; maintaining continuous eye contact is perceived by the native American as an invasion of privacy.

Asian Americans

The numerous cultures from eastern Asian countries include the Chinese, Japanese, Philippine, Korean, and Vietnamese peoples. Although each culture has distinct differences, there are some similarities that help the health care provider administer quality health care.

The Family

The family plays a significant role in all of the Asian cultures. Asian American families are controlled by the father who has total authority over the members. The traditional wife may or may not speak English and is responsible for maintaining the home life.

The family assumes greater importance than the individual; family loyalty binds the individual to his home. For most Asian Americans, emotional security and economic well-being depend on the family. The individual will compromise other personal obligations in the interest of family ties and the family unit.

Socialization

Family members of the Asian American cultures convey their caring for each other with less verbalization than the dominant society. Parents expect that their child will submit to their guidance without disagreement, hesitation, or questioning. "Back-talk" from a child is shocking and distressing to adults and marked independence of the child is discouraged. Although the main responsibility for a child's socialization rests with the parents, extended kin actively participate in helping the child become a respected and wanted person in society.

In the traditional Asian home, the child learns from his parents to respect, admire, and fear the family ancestors whose strength and virtue are extolled.[35] The child is encouraged to follow the example of his ancestors for moral, ethical, and social behavior.

Food

Asian cultures believe that it is necessary to eat a balanced diet of foods containing the properties of yin and yang. The forces of yin and yang are believed to control nature and the body. Yin is the negative force—dark, cold, and empty; yang is the positive force—light, warm, and full.[39]

Members of Asian cultures believe that too much of the wrong foods could lead to illness and that certain illnesses can be cured by proper foods. When an imbalance of food exists, an increase in the opposite force is needed to bring the body back into harmony. Vegetables are mixed together to balance yin and yang forces. Diets consisting entirely of high-protein foods, raw fruits and vegetables, or extremely cold or hot foods are viewed unfavorably by Asian Americans. The classification of yin and yang foods is traditional and passed down through generations.

Health Practices

Asian medicine is based on the concept that the universe and man are susceptible to the laws of five elements—fire, earth, metal, water, and wood. Every organ of the body is believed to possess the properties of taste, emotion, sound, odor, season, power, climate, and other elements. Health is perceived as the balance of yin and yang; imbalance leads to dysfunction and disease.

Folk medicine practitioners, or herbalists, practice widely and actively in Asian American homes. Other Asian Americans may use spiritual healing, the transfer of psychic healing energies from the person administering care to the one who is ill.

Implications for Nursing Actions

1. Remember that Asian Americans may experience language difficulties

    Request a bilingual staff member or interpreter.
    Use creativity to develop alternate means of communication when an interpreter is unavailable.

2. Recognize that members of Asian cultures may be upset by the drawing of blood, because blood is viewed as the source of the body's life.

3. Be aware that Asian Americans may be reluctant or unable to express feelings of anger, frustration, or pain.

4. Realize that the patient may refuse surgery unless under critical circumstances, because he believes it is best to die with an intact body.

5. When familiarizing Asian American patients with

the hospital, be sensitive to their perception of the hospital as an alien place and to their feeling of isolation from the rest of the family.

6. Intervene by fostering communication between patient and physician. Members of the Asian culture may perceive the physician as the authority and be reluctant to complain or inform him of their problems. Talking to a physician about their concerns may be perceived as disrespect.

7. Plan meals for Asian American patients according to a balance of foods containing yin and yang properties and appealing arrangement and taste.

Black Americans

Black Americans originated in Africa from a culture that reflected skill in agriculture, government, scholarship, and the fine arts.[14] The largest importation of slaves to the United States occurred in the 1700s. Once brought to this country, blacks were unable to preserve their customs, religion, or family traditions because the institution of slavery actively discouraged enculturation.

All blacks can probably trace their heritage to some part of Africa. The slave trade dispersed them throughout America. Isolated and faced with an alien environment, each group of blacks was forced to develop its own language, folklore, music, and religion.

Within the United States, there are considerable differences between blacks in the upper class, blacks in the middle class, and blacks who are poor. Nevertheless, their similarities, including a commonality of suffering, are stronger than the differences.

When a group of people are in a subjugated position in a culture, they will, in order to survive, band together and form a subculture. Therefore, to survive in a dominant society that has historically and repeatedly ignored them, blacks have developed, as a means of identification, different ways of living, eating, dressing, and, in some cases, different ways of speaking.[6] Continued discrimination has been a chief factor in the confinement of blacks to ghettos and in their inability to become a part of the dominant society.

The Family

The concept of the family as an important unit has been traced to ancient Africa. The union between two people benefited both families economically, politically, religiously, and socially.[3] During the era of slavery, men and women were perceived as commodities to be bought and sold by their owners as they deemed necessary and marriages between two slaves were therefore often not recognized. Members of the extended family, which may include uncles, aunts, boyfriends, girlfriends, and other members of the community, participate in and influence childrearing.

Language

Language is one of the most important means of comprehending reality. For the black culture, language has presented a reality of insults, confusion, and depression.[6] Black language has been denigrated by whites, contributing to self-deprecation and insecurity among some blacks.

Historically, black language evolved for a definite purpose. Slaves borrowed or adapted language forms from their white masters to deceive or make fun of their masters, to communicate secretly with each other, and to plan revolts and methods of escape.[22]

The black slaves soon learned that whatever they said to each other or to their masters must be couched in words with double meanings, in half truths, and in other forms that would not endanger their own safety. As a result, black slaves became adept at verbal survival mechanisms.

The reasons for the development of black language have changed with the times. The language spoken by black Americans varies according to socioeconomic status as well as geographic areas. Even educated blacks who speak perfect standard English can speak the black language when the situation demands it. This does not hold true, however, for a person who has not been exposed to the black culture.

Religion

Religion has been a source of strength for black Americans in times of trouble or stress. A strong religious orientation has provided a strong foundation for the development, survival, and stability of the black family. The predominant religion of the black American is Baptist.

It is not unusual to see some members of a religious congregation of blacks come together to pray for a hospitalized patient. The meeting may include prayer, singing, and religious readings. This support is comforting to black Americans during stressful times.

The black minister is a significant member of the black community and often serves as a counselor for members of his community. The church provides emotional and often financial support to members of the community in need.

Food

Food habits of black Americans are influenced by both heritage and by socioeconomic factors. Hogs, chicken, corn, and beans were food products of the early United States, particularly the southern region. Parts of hogs that were not considered good enough for the plantation master to consume, such as the head, brains, intestines (chitterlings), stomach (maw), and feet were fed to the slaves. These parts of the hog, as well as greens, yams, and other foods, are considered "soul food." Many blacks still prefer to eat these parts of the hog due to their low price. Although this type of food is preferred by many black Americans, it would be incorrect to assume that all black Americans enjoy and eat the same kinds of food.

Health Practices

Many black Americans will not seek health care assistance until the health problem is a serious one. Some of the factors that influence this behavior include fear of health care providers and hospitals, fear of death, refusal or inability to consider health maintenance a priority, and the belief that he can use home remedies to cure the problem. Other blacks may rely on healers to restore their health.

Mental Illness

The greatest proportion of clients in mental institutions are black.[10] There are many factors contributing to this phenomenon. Fewer blacks can afford a private physician and, therefore, do not seek treatment until their psychiatric–mental health problem reaches a state requiring hospitalization.[34] Some black Americans fail to develop the kinds of qualities, such as extensive verbal skills and adequate insight, needed by people in order to respond appropriately to psychotherapeutic assessments.[27] Because they fail to develop these skills, blacks receive custodial forms of care more frequently than the dominant culture.[34]

Implications for Nursing Actions

1. Use nonverbal behavior carefully designed to convey an accurate message. Black Americans are skilled at assessing others' nonverbal behavior and may be particularly observant when interacting with health care providers.
2. Speak to the patient with courtesy and respect. Do not address him by first name unless he has asked you to do so.
3. Ask food preferences rather than assuming that black Americans prefer the same kinds of food.
4. Plan interventions to reduce the hostility and suspiciousness that patients may demonstrate within the health care setting. People who have been lonely or rejected by others over long periods of time or during their formative years, such as black Americans, are frequently not brave enough to risk the possible pain of new human relationships.
5. Attend to client and family communication, which may be extremely difficult and frustrating for the health care provider. Many black Americans will

assume an exaggerated air of indifference or ignorance in the health care environment and this behavior may result in cultural mislabeling.

Culture and the Nursing Process

Assessment and Analysis of Cultural Factors

Although most nurses recognize the need for cultural sensitivity, many experience frustration when developing this awareness and sensitivity. Some of the factors related to this frustration are lack of knowledge regarding different cultures and fear of offending a person of a different ethnic group. One cannot be expected to know everything about every ethnic group. People of the same ethnic group do not know everything about their own ethnicity. Neither should one pretend to know about a different cultural group when interacting with members of that group. A more honest approach is to admit lack of knowledge and carry out an assessment that encourages rapport between client and health professional and that gathers information needed to formulate nursing care plans. The assessment and analysis of cultural factors include the client's language skills, behavior related to health care, taboos and prohibitions, and coping behaviors.

Languages

Language differences between staff and patients, and even between staff members themselves, are significant barriers to communication in the health care environment. Language differences may create or further complicate health care problems. Even individuals who speak the same language but are members of different cultural groups may have difficulties understanding each other. For example, a health care provider from the North may experience difficulty in understanding a patient from the South whose speech patterns may be slower and who may pronounce certain letters and words less clearly.[16]

Another language difficulty may occur when different age groups or generations within the same culture do not understand each other. For example, young black Americans may use a slang word or idiom that an older black health care provider does not understand.[14]

(*Text continues on p 79*)

Case Study: Cultural Implications of Therapeutic Planning

Presenting Information

Mrs. P., a 36-year-old black woman and mother of three children (ages 6, 9, and 11½), was seen in a psychiatric treatment setting for the first time. She was described as being out of touch with reality and mumbling about the "judgment day" when she would be punished. She was diagnosed as paranoid schizophrenic, acute onset. Her family refused to admit her to a psychiatric institution. She was placed on high doses of Thorazine and her family was instructed to bring her for daily therapy. Her husband was also instructed to attend therapy.

Discussion

1. What goals had been developed for Mrs. P. and her family?
2. Who developed these goals?

Continuing Problems

Mrs. P. was very depressed when she returned to the mental health clinic. She remained uncooperative with the assigned therapist. Her affect was described as flat and she did not establish eye contact with the therapist. The therapist observed that Mrs. P. became agitated when the discussion turned to Mr. P. or their children, particularly their 11½-year-old son. She also noted that Mr. P. failed to accompany Mrs. P. to her therapy sessions.

The therapist, who was white, expressed her frustration and inability to establish rapport with Mrs. P. to other health team members. She expressed doubts that Mrs. P. could remain functional in her home and community. Furthermore, Mrs. P. was not taking the medication prescribed for her.

Discussion

1. Why did Mrs. P. and her husband not cooperate with the therapist?
2. Describe the therapist's feelings.
3. What is the significance of Mrs. P.'s agitation?

New Information

The therapist decided to discuss Mrs. P. at the next staff meeting and seek others' suggestions. The staff physician believed that Mrs. P. should be admitted to an inpatient treatment unit where her medication regimen would be followed. He predicted that she would become increasingly nonfunctional without the medication. Some of the therapists questioned the sincerity and committment of the husband who failed to attend the therapy sessions with Mrs. P. A black therapist expressed interest in Mrs. P. and her situation and volunteered to work with her. A few therapists questioned the effectiveness of any therapeutic approaches to Mrs. P. because she was obviously seriously mentally ill. Nevertheless, Mrs. P.'s case was reassigned to the black therapist.

At subsequent meetings, the newly assigned therapist was able to supply additional information regarding Mrs. P. and her life. Mrs. P. informed the therapist that she stopped taking her medication because it made her feel sleepy and unable to care for her son who was severely retarded as a complication of meningitis at the age of 5 years.

Mrs. P. believed that it was her fault that her child was retarded because she had taken him to the state where the meningitis outbreak occurred. She stated that God was punishing her for being so careless with her child's life and she must therefore suffer the burden. She was totally responsible for caring for her son during the day and part of the night, 7 days a week, and the care included diaper changing and gastrostomy feedings. Her son also needed suctioning via his tracheostomy and his need for suctioning had increased within the last few months.

The doctor had told Mrs. P. that her son would not live to be older than 12 years of age. The child would become 12 years old 2 months from the day Mrs. P. suffered her apparent psychotic break.

Mrs. P. further related that her husband worked two jobs and that they "just didn't talk about" their son's illness. After she began to talk about her son and his special needs, she no longer seemed delusional. The therapist described the behavioral changes as marked. Although she still spoke in monosyllables, Mrs. P. displayed a wider range of affect and sometimes established eye contact. Mrs. P. defined "judgment day" as her son's 12th birthday and her "punishment" as his death.

What Was Done

The therapist and Mrs. P. worked out an acceptable agreement regarding the issue of her medication. Mrs. P. agreed to continue attending and participating in therapy; she also agreed that if she or the therapist observed that her emotional well-being was endangered, they would again consider the resumption of medication.

The therapist focused on helping Mrs. P. accomplish the following.

1. Identify positive qualities in herself.
2. Set realistic goals regarding what she could and could not do for her son.
3. Seek outside sources of help with her son's care. (Mrs. P.'s devotion to her son was her "penance" for her "sin.")
4. Develop effective communication with her husband (Mrs. P. saw herself as self-sufficient and needing no one; to tell him of her feelings, she felt, may make her "weak and beholding to him.")
5. Deal with her grief and work on anticipatory grief

It is possible that mental health care providers may overlook the cultural implications of a client's problems. Health care workers must be aware of their own behavior, feelings, and values when interacting with members of different ethnic groups. The client's behavior may represent coping with what is perceived as a hostile environment. The nurse responds, without labeling, to the client's behavior within its context.

Nurses and other health professionals may overestimate how much language a member of another cultural group understands. They may also fail to appreciate the degree of fear and anxiety a patient feels when he is unable to understand what is being said to him. One bilingual nurse described the feelings of Asian patients who recently immigrated to the United States.

> Nothing is more frightening and frustrating than to be in a foreign country and to visit the doctor and not understand what is being said. That is frequently one of the reasons why some patients are hesitant to go to the doctor. First, they have to find someone to go with them to translate. It is a frightening feeling to go to a hospital of any type where no one understands or speaks the same language.[20]

Some patients may feel so ashamed that they are unable to speak the language expected of them that they pretend to understand when they do not. Some are afraid to admit that they do not understand the language for fear of being labeled "dumb" or "ignorant."

Health care providers often unconsciously treat patients, families, and other staff members who are unable to speak their language in an insensitive manner. When health care providers try to communicate with an individual who speaks a different language, they may experience anger and exasperation.

Assessing Barriers to an Effective Nurse–Client Interaction.

Barriers to effective interaction between the health care provider and the client are influenced by many factors. These factors include cultural beliefs and practices, education, sex, socioeconomic status, and values. To effectively communicate with another person, these barriers must be overcome.

Problems of communication often arise during the process of history-taking and, consequently, diminish the effectiveness of the nurse's clinical expertise. Problems with communication may prevent the patient from even reaching the examining room. A nurse practitioner in an American Indian health service hospital related the following incident.

> The nurses would call out each patient's name as he was to see the physician. Many of the patients were not only old and hard of hearing, but also were not accustomed to the anglicized version of their names. Quite often, the patient failed to respond unless a younger member of the family who understood English was present and responded to the name.
>
> Often the patient's name was just skipped over when the patient did not respond immediately. Consequently, a patient might sit in the waiting room the entire day unless the waiting room personnel either noticed this patient's continual presence or the patient got up and left.[32]

What to Assess

1. How do members of the family communicate with each other?
2. Which languages are used in the home? Outside of the home?
3. How much English do the patient and family understand?
4. Do the patient and family speak English well enough to communicate their needs?

Taboos and Prohibitions

The areas of conversation that are sensitive or even taboo vary according to geographic locations, customs, values of the culture, and values of the individual. In one culture, a person may be forbidden to mention certain animals; in another, certain secret words may be prohibited. In a third culture, certain political issues or particular types of illness are forbidden topics for discussion.

Prohibitions against discussion of bodily functions and display of parts of the body are more pronounced in some cultures than in others. In some cultures, an individual is not permitted to discuss issues related to the family outside of the family system.

What to Assess

1. What are the norms of confidentiality?
2. Are there certain health topics about which patients may be sensitive or unwilling to talk?
3. Are there behaviors expected in the health care setting that may be embarrassing or unacceptable to the patient?
4. How might the nurse best approach sensitive-but-necessary topics?

Coping Behaviors

Individual coping behaviors are culturally influenced. The emotions of anger, love, frustration, and embarrassment are universal, but the indications of their presence and the manner of their expression vary in each culture.

Health care professionals must be aware of cultural differences regarding the display of emotions and expression of feelings. Understanding how a particular culture expresses feelings and displays emotions helps health care providers behave in ways that are consistent with those values. In the following situation, the mental health caregivers did not provide care consistent with the client's values.

> Mrs. Lu, an Asian American, visited a local mental health center with the complaint of inability to communicate with her husband. The mental health center staff, however, were uninformed regarding the cultural values and expected behavior of the Chinese people. Mrs. Lu's therapist encouraged her to express her anger directly

and also to express her affection for her husband openly through such behaviors as holding his hand.

When Mrs. Lu tried out these new behaviors, her husband became distraught and feared that his wife was losing her mind because her behavior was unfamiliar and unacceptable. The Chinese community neither understands nor accepts the open expression of anger or of warm feelings by holding hands.[26]

What to Assess

1. How does the client show approval or disapproval? Agreement or disagreement?
2. How are anger, embarrassment, love, and other emotions expressed?
3. What are the cultural norms concerning raised voices, arguments, expressions of humor, and so forth?

Analysis of the assessment data allows the nurse to classify and categorize client information and formulate nursing diagnoses that then direct nursing care planning.

Planning

After implementing the first two steps of the nursing process (assessment and analysis or nursing diagnosis), the nurse begins planning nursing care that will meet the identified health care needs of the client and family. This planning process must incorporate the goals of the individual and his family. The health care provider attends to such factors as who stays with the patient in the hospital or health care agency and who is the spokesperson. In some cultures, the male speaks for the female; in other cultures, the elder or another respected member of the family may speak for the patient. This situation may be particularly uncomfortable for the health care provider if her culture dictates that each individual has the right to speak for himself.

The nurse or other health professional may request the help of clergy or another influential person outside of the family to assist the client and family adapt to the available health care services. Acceptance of the patient and family without imposing more hospital rules or regulations than necessary will foster effective nurse–client relationships.

The health care provider should communicate honestly with others when she lacks knowledge of the behaviors, rules, values, and lifestyles of other cultures. Seeking information from the patient and family about their culture is an effective tool. To pretend to be knowledgeable about different cultures only alienates people and induces fear and distrust of the health care system.

Developing a quality plan of care takes time. When health care providers lack the time needed to make adequate plans, they experience stress, which the culturally different patient and family perceive as frustration directed at them personally.

Intervention

After assessing the patient and family, formulating nursing diagnoses, and identifying goals, the care provider identifies nursing interventions to meet identified health needs and to resolve patient problems. Cultural awareness and sensitivity should guide the nurse's implementation of each stage of the nursing process. Intervening with clients and families of different cultural groups also requires that the nurse examine her own biases, fears, and prejudices. Specific nursing actions have been outlined in the discussion of the four large minority groups in the United States.

Evaluation

The effectiveness of the plan of care is evaluated by observing, interacting with, and reassessing the patient and family and their problems and needs. The nurse collects further data from other health professionals who are involved with the patient and family. The patient's and family's participation in their own care and their volunteering of information beyond what is requested by the caregiver may indicate that nursing intervention has been effective. The evaluation process is continuous, but ever-changing, as the health care provider reassesses and redefines the needs of the patient and family.

Attitudes, Values, and Prejudices of the Health Care Provider

The health care provider is a product of an ethnic group that has its own set of values and attitudes and that has influenced the development of prejudices. Nursing education may serve as a vehicle to enlighten an individual about different ethnic groups and about the importance of being culturally sensitive and aware.

The assessment of cultural sensitivity starts with the self. What makes you who you are? What do you value most? About which group or groups of people do you feel prejudice? All of us have prejudiced feelings about something or someone. These feelings may be mild (*e.g.*, we'd rather not be with a certain person) to strong (*i.e.*, we feel great hostility toward, and fear of, a certain person). Prejudices, biases, and fears are less likely to interfere with a care provider's ability to administer quality patient care when she is aware of these feelings, admits their presence, and fills in her knowledge gaps with information about the feared cultural groups.

Members of minority groups may have never had the opportunity to experience what is taken for granted by the dominant culture. Nevertheless, they want neither the pity of members of the dominant society nor their apologies for being who they are or who they desire to become. Cultural conflict develops when one culture attempts to impose its values on another.

People of different ethnic groups, particularly minority groups, are not patterned after people of the dominant western civilization. They are people who have distinctive histories, who have a set of distinctive life experiences, who deserve a distinctive place in American society, and who are capable of making a distinctive contribution to the wider society.[37]

If the health care provider has negative or unresolved feelings related to her own cultural background, she may be unable to take a genuine interest in assisting the client of any culture. It is difficult to work with a client who activates your own unresolved feelings.

Another difficulty may be encountered when a health professional is expected to be an expert about her own culture and is also expected to relate well with every client of the same culture. The interaction of two people of the same culture will not guarantee the development of a therapeutic relationship, just as two individuals of different cultures will not prevent its development. Many factors, including goals of care, nature of the health problem, interpersonal skills, and degree of enculturation influence the development of an effective nurse–client relationship when the two are members of different cultures.

Summary

This chapter has focused on the concept of culture, cultural similarities and differences, the health care needs of clients of different cultures, and the nursing intervention designed to meet those needs. Some of the major ideas of the chapter include the following.

1. Culture is learned behavior that is transmitted from one generation to another.
2. Culture governs an individual's patterns of action, beliefs, and feelings.
3. Awareness of cultural similarities allows health care providers to appreciate common human behaviors and bonds; failure to appreciate cultural variations results in ineffective communication and ineffective relationships between the client and the health care providers.
4. Health care providers are members of a subculture influenced by the values of their (in our case, American) culture and these values are reflected in the administration of health care.
5. Enculturation is the process whereby an individual learns the expected behavior of a culture; acculturation is the process whereby two cultural groups come into contact with each other.
6. Each ethnic group has a unique history.
7. The four large minority groups in the United States are Spanish-speaking Americans, native Americans, Asian Americans, and black Americans.
8. No form of behavior can be judged normal or abnormal outside of its cultural context.
9. The nurse recognizes that the quality of communication between health care provider and client directly affects the quality of health care.
10. The health care provider needs to be aware that, in some cultures, the family assumes greater importance than the individual.
11. Failure to identify the decision maker in the client's family may result in sabotage of the plan of care.
12. Nursing intervention is planned with sensitivity to the client and family's unique health needs and cultural influences.
13. Knowledge of cultural similarities and differences is essential in the delivery of quality health care.

References

1. Atkinson D, Morten G, Sue DW: Counseling American Minorities: A Cross-Cultural Perspective. Dubuque, IA, Wm C Brown, 1979
2. Beuf AH: Red Children In White America. Philadelphia, University of Pennsylvania Press, 1977
3. Billingsley A: Black Families in White America. Englewood Cliffs NJ, Prentice-Hall, 1968
4. Blumberg P: The Impact of Social Class. New York, Thomas Cromwell, 1972
5. Branch MF, Paxton PP: Providing Safe Nursing Care for Ethnic People of Color. New York, Appleton-Century-Crofts, 1976
6. Brown C: The Language of Soul. In Kochman T (ed): Rapping and Styling Out. Chicago, Chicago University Press, 1972
7. Brownlee AT: Community, Culture, and Care: A Cross-Cultural Guide For Health Workers. St Louis, CV Mosby, 1978
8. Bullough E, Bullough M: Ethnic Identity and Health Care. New York, Appleton-Century-Crofts, 1972
9. Carter FM: Psychosocial Nursing: Theory and Practice in Hospital and Community Mental Health. New York, Macmillan Publishing, 1976
10. Cheek D: Assertive Black, Puzzled White. California. Impact Publishers, 1977
11. Chohen E, Eames E: Cultural Anthropology. Toronto, Little Brown, 1982
12. Clark AL: Culture, Childbearing: Health Professionals. Philadelphia, FA Davis, 1978
13. Cleckly H: The Mask of Sanity. St Louis, CV Mosby, 1976
14. Delaney AJ: Black Task Force Report. New York, Family Service Association of America, 1979
15. Devore W, Schlesinger EG: Ethnic-Sensitive Social Work Practice. St Louis, CV Mosby, 1981
16. Dillard JJ: Black English. New York, Random House, 1970
17. Eaton J, Weil R: Culture and Mental Disorders. New York, The Free Press, 1955

18. Erikson EH: Identity, Youth and Crisis. New York, WW Norton, 1960

19. Fish S, Shelley J: Spiritual Care: The Nurse's Role. Downer's Grove, IL, Inter Varsity Press, 1978

20. Folta JR, Deck E: A Sociological Framework For Patient Care. New York, Wiley Medical Publications, 1979

21. Glazer N, Moynihan P: Beyond The Melting Pot. Cambridge, Harvard University Press, 1963

22. Haskins J: The Psychology of Black Languages. New York, Barnes and Nobles, 1973

23. Henderson G, Primeaux M: Transcultural Health Care. Menlo Park, CA, Addison-Wesley, 1981

24. Howze B: Black Suicides: Final Acts of Alienation. Human Behavior (February): 10–15, 1979

25. Jones RL: Black Psychology. New York, Harper & Row, 1972

26. Keesing FM: Acculturation: A Dictionary of The Social Sciences. New York, Macmillan, 1974

27. Leininger M: Cultural Diversities of Health and Nursing Care. Nurs Clin North Am 12 (March): 5–18, 1977

28. McDonald M: Not By The Color of Their Skin: The Impact of Racial Differences on the Child's Development. International Press, 1970

29. Moore BM: Cultural Differences and Counseling Perspective. Texas Personnel and Guidance Association Journal, pp 39–44, 1974

30. Murillo N: The Mexican American Family. In Martinez RA (ed): Hispanic Culture and Health Care: Fact, Fiction, Folklore. St Louis, CV Mosby, 1978

31. Pasquali EA, Alesi EG, Arnold HM, DeBasio N: Mental Health Nursing: A Bio-Psycho-Cultural Approach. St Louis, CV Mosby, 1981

32. Primeaux MH: American Indian Health Care Practices. Nurs Clin North Am 12 (March): 55–65, 1977

33. Saunders L: Cultural Differences and Medical Care: The Case of the Spanish Speaking People. New York, Russell Sage Foundation, 1959

34. Seham M: Blacks and American Medical Care. Minnesota, University of Minnesota Press, 1973

35. Spector RE: Cultural Diversity in Health and Illness. New York, Appleton-Century-Crofts, 1979

36. Westmeyer J: The Drunken Indian: Myth and Realities. In Unger S (ed): The Destruction of the American Indian Family. New York, Association of American Indian Affairs, 1974

37. White EH: Giving Health Care to Minority Patients. Nurs Clin North Am 12 (March): 27–39, 1977

38. Williams RL: The B.I.T.C.H. Test (Black Intelligence Test of Cultural Homogeneity). Black Studies Program, St. Louis, Washington University, 1974

39. Wolff L, Weitzel M, Zornow R, Zshohar H: Fundamentals of Nursing. Philadelphia, JB Lippincott, 1983

Chapter 8
Sexuality and Sexual Concerns

I am a sexual being. So is she. Together, we produce an experience that is exquisite for both of us. She invites me to know her sexually, and I invite her to know me sexually. We share our erotic possibilities in delight and ecstasy. If she wants me and I don't want her, I cannot lie. My body speaks only truth. And I cannot take her unless she gives herself. Her body cannot lie.

Sidney M. Jourard,
The Transparent Self,
1971

Sharon Byers

Chapter Preview

Sexuality is an integral part of the personality, a significant aspect of the functioning of the identity during varied states of wellness. Sexual activity is a form of communication, a method of self-affirmation, a pleasurable form of play, and a reflection of the individual's value system.

This chapter explores the development of sexuality throughout the life span. A humanistic perspective emphasizes the importance of identifying the client's sexual norms and needs and facilitating adaptation accordingly. The chapter describes the four stages of the human sexual response cycle (*i.e.*, excitement, plateau, orgasm, and resolution), traditional lifestyles and nontraditional methods of sexual expression, and sexual dysfunctions and their treatment approaches. The nurse's role and intervention with clients manifesting sexual problems or concerns are also discussed.

Learning Objectives

On completion of the chapter, the reader should be able to accomplish the following.

1. Define sexuality, sensuality, sex role, and gender identity
2. Differentiate between sex derivative, adjunctive, and arbitrary differences
3. Discuss the genetic, hormonal, and psychological influences on sexual development
4. Describe the four stages of human sexual response—excitement, plateau, orgasm, and resolution
5. Compare traditional and alternative sexual lifestyles
6. Discuss the client's sexual needs during specific physical or emotional disorders
7. Describe the common sexual problems of men and women clients who seek sex therapy
8. Apply the nursing process to the care of a client manifesting a sexual problem

The Meaning of Sexuality

Sexuality is the expression and experience of the self as a sexual being. It is, therefore, a state of both the body and mind and a crucial part of the personality. Sexuality is not limited to overt sexual activity, such as sexual intercourse, but includes solitary activities like studying, walking, and relaxing. Sexuality is a part of every relationship, whether it is primarily a sexual relationship or not; it is the rapport that is established between the self and the other.[15]

An important aspect of sexuality is *sensuality*, which is the expression and experience of self as a sensual being. Sensuality means the ability to experience enjoyment through the senses, such as touching a pleasing fabric, listening to good music, or touching the skin of a loved one. Sensuality is a necessary component of fulfilled sexuality. Sensual attraction, however, does not necessarily lead to a wish for sexual activity; it refers merely to pleasure in the company of the other.

One key to unlocking one's enjoyment of sexuality and sensuality is through body awareness and acceptance. *Sex roles* are culturally determined patterns associated with male and female social behavior and may be accepted or rejected by the individual. *Gender identity*, or how one chooses to view oneself as a male or female in interaction with others, is an individual and unique expression.

Body appearance holds some limitations for self-direction. The *transsexual*, for example, is a person who is able to clearly reject his or her physical sexual appearance and prefers to undergo surgery, psychotherapy, and hormone treatments to make a complete "sex change." More common are the problems of men's and women's inabilities to accept their bodies to the fullest extent to enable sexual fulfillment. To ease the acceptance of their bodies, men and women may perceive a need to change their bodies through dieting or exercise. Nevertheless, body acceptance ultimately depends on one's ability to relax with one's body and to allow physical sensations to be accepted and experienced as they are, without defensively screening out unwanted sensations or perceptually twisting sensations.

Many people view sexual activity through a structure made up of religious values and stereotypical myths. Reality is shaped by choice, our assigned sets of meanings, and even by anxiety, fear, and lack of knowledge.[5] Religious beliefs and other sets of personal values usually result in our classification of sexual activity into one of three categories.

1. Procreational sex refers to sexual activity for the purpose of conceiving children.
2. Relational sex refers to sexual activity for the purpose of strengthening or fulfilling committments of a relationship.
3. Recreational sex refers to sexual activity for the purpose of play and personal enjoyment.[13]

Sexual Differences

Sex Derivative Differences

The body holds the only inevitabilities of sexuality. These inevitable differences are that men normally impregnate women and women are normally able to lactate, gestate, and menstruate. Nothing else, including aggressivity, strength, or sex role has been found to be strictly related to either male or female.[7] The other differences are relatively arbitrary, some appearing as predispositions created by atomic differences, such as the position one must take to urinate and baldness. These are called *sex derivative* differences and they are not absolutes. These differences vary from individual to individual according to familial tendencies, physical make-up, and personality preferences.

Sex Adjunctive Differences

Sex adjunctive differences are those seen fairly consistently from culture to culture but are even less related to real physical differences than to the sex derivative differences. Examples of sex adjunctive differences are the choice of male or female to earn money for the household and the traditional role of the woman in childrearing. These differences are based on some physical differences, such as muscle mass and the ability to lactate, but were more important determinants of male and female preferred roles in the past. These roles tend to persist due to historic precedence, but are now being questioned and challenged frequently by modern "house husbands" and career women.[7] These sex adjunctive differences are of great political importance today in the liberation of men and women; stereotypical roles have become chains to people who prefer to use choice rather than history to determine their daily activities.

These sex adjunctive differences may have been linked to hormonal or genetic programming during the days of our early primate ancestors. For example, one male hormone, androgen, does increase physical activity in the individual; however, whether this activity is expressed as physical aggression or dominance is not related to hormonal factors but rather to individual choice and learning[10]—that is, androgen may influence one to be more aggressive, but ultimately the personality structure and choices of modern men and women determine behavior.

Sex Arbitrary Differences

Sex arbitrary differences are purely determined by culture and therefore vary from culture to culture. Such differences include face painting and genital mutilation. In the Anglo-Saxon cultures, it is acceptable for the female to wear colors on her face, called make-up. In other cultures men wear face paints. In Judeo-Christian cultures, it is common for men to be circumcised as infants. In other cultures, the young female undergoes similar procedures, such as removing or cutting away a part of the clitoris or the hood of the clitoris. In most of these situations of genital mutilation of infants, the procedure is believed to be painless, despite the infants' cries to the contrary, and is undergone without anesthetic. The procedure is also usually explained as required by hygienic, as well as religious, needs.[7]

It is sometimes difficult to understand how basically arbitrary distinctions can be viewed as unquestionable and inevitable differences between the sexes. The explanation for this view lies in the fact that our world is shaped by a basic he-schema and she-schema.[8] Our expectations, habits, traditions, mores, customs, norms, and the wielding of power throughout history form the basis for these schema.

The interpretations of difference between the sexes are evident from the first days of life, when baby boys and baby girls are handled and talked to in measurably different ways.[7] The infant's behavior is also interpreted differently according to sex-related expectations and perceptions. Choices of gifts, colors, and activities are determined according to the child's sex and perceptions of how a child of that sex should behave.

There are also age-related distinctions regarding sexual differences. For example, in our culture, children are not generally considered to be sexual. Therefore, we observe the panic of a mother finding her toddler son fondling his penis, or the horror of parents discovering their 13-year-old daughter's birth control pills. The infant's first erection and lubrication occurs soon after birth, indicating the pervasive nature of sexuality. Elderly people are also thought of as asexual by many in the American culture. Two hundred years ago, few individuals lived long enough to become elderly; we have no precedence on which to form our view of sexuality in the elderly. Our cultural perspective on the sexual needs of the elderly has not progressed as rapidly as the average life span has grown.

Nurses' Knowledge of Sexual Differences

The task of the nurse regarding sexuality is threefold.

1. To be knowledgeable about sexuality and the "norms" of society
2. To use this knowledge to understand others' behaviors and attitudes that differ in cultural and individual perspectives from our own
3. To use this understanding to facilitate the client's adaptation and optimal health

Adaptation does not mean conforming to others' expectations or norms, but rather, responding to the world without losing the unique qualities of oneself. Through adaptation, a person maintains his choices and values while accepting those of differing choices and values.[15] The nurse's awareness of her own and others' feelings and attitudes about sexual behavior and differing choices enables her to respond to an encounter based on a sincere understanding of the needs of the client, rather than in response to emotional taboos or her own stereotypical beliefs.

Sexual Development

Sexual development occurs in the embryo and continues throughout the life span. A variety of influences (genetic, hormonal, and psychological) have an impact on this development.

Genetic Influences

Chromosomes initiate sexual development. Chromosomes, found in every cell of the body, are the carriers of genetic programming information. Within the ovum and sperm are the chromosomal offerings of the two parents, which determine the genetic makeup of the child. The male's sperm cell determines the sex of the embryo at conception by adding either an X chromosome or a Y chromosome to the X chromosome contained within the ovum. Two X chromosomes result in a female fetus; an X and a Y chromosome result in a male fetus.[12]

Sometimes, these groupings of chromosomes occur differently, resulting in such variations as XXY, or *Klinefelter's syndrome*. This extra X chromosome produces a male who appears normal until adolescence, when decreased production of the male hormone (testosterone) results in small testes, infertility, and a low libido (or sexual interest). Behavioral differences associated with Klinefelter's syndrome include generalized passivity, lack of ambition, and a predisposition to sudden outbursts of aggression. These behavioral and libido differences are reversed with treatments of testosterone, even when undertaken as late as in adulthood.[3] Apparently, hormonal therapy affects the libido to enable a broader range of behavioral choices.

Turner's syndrome occurs when the second sex chromosome is missing, producing the pattern XO. This syndrome results in short females without functioning gonads. Until puberty, no problems are noted; however, at the normal age of puberty, the breasts do not develop and there are no menses. The psychological problem associated with this chromosomal variation involves the impact of stigma caused by the differences between this person and the female norm. The absence of hormones during fetal development results in possible deficits in motor coordination, range of affect, and directional sense. The patient with Turner's syndrome seems more complacent and seems to have less initiative than other girls or women of similar age.[8] Although it is uncertain why these traits are found in women with Turner's syndrome, an answer offered by research seems to be that genetic patterning creates a predisposition that is fostered by cultural influences. Hormone therapy results in normal breast development and menses in the female with Turner's syndrome, but the short stature does not change, resulting in a woman no taller than 4½ to 5 feet tall.

The XYY chromosomal pattern produces a male with few physical differences from an XY male, except for a slightly taller stature and some abnormalities of the seminiferous tubules.[9] As children, these boys appear less socially mature, more impulsive, and less successful in interpersonal relationships than their peers. As adults, these men are often found in penal institutions, perhaps due to some intellectual deficit making them more prone to break the law. These men tend to commit crimes, but not necessarily crimes of an aggressive nature.[3]

Nursing implications of the diagnosis of one of these chromosomal abnormalities include counseling with parents and child regarding the impact of the diagnosis on the developing self-image of the child. The nurse educates parents and child about the typical behavioral and appearance differences associated with the syndrome. The nurse explains that, although hormone therapy is a useful means of reducing the difference between the child and the normal male or female, it is not a "cure" for the syndrome. In all cases, hormone therapy can only change superficial differences. Counseling is recommended for intervention in, or prevention of, a crisis in response to the diagnosis as the client and family experience the loss of a "normal" identity.[1]

Hormonal Influences

During the first 6 weeks of development, male and female fetuses are anatomically alike. At 6 weeks, primitive gonads are beginning to develop but are not yet differentiated as male or female. Following this time period, hormones have the greatest effect on the sexual differentiation of the fetus. At 8 weeks, if testosterone is present in sufficient levels, testes develop from the indistinct gonads. If no testosterone or a less-than-normal amount of testosterone for a male of this age is secreted by the 12th gestational week, ovaries are formed. Even if the genotype is XY, the absence of testosterone at this partricular time of fetal development causes female differentiation to occur. This would result in an anatomic female who is capable of procreation but who bears a XY genotype.

These sexual differentiations occur in the external genitalia, the internal sex structures, and the delicate nervous pathways and other portions of the brain to create the pattern for further development. The ambiguous gonadal structures develop into uterus, fallopian tube, and vagina in the absence of testosterone. With testosterone and androgen secretion at sufficiently high levels, the same structures become the vas deferens, seminal vesicles, and ejaculatory ducts.

Externally, androgen stimulation results in the urogenital folds joining to form a penis. Without androgen, this fold becomes the labia minora. The hypothalamic-pituitary-gonadal system in the brain responds to the presence of androgen by becoming noncyclic. Without androgen, female hormones result in female structures and a cyclic system, with fluctuating hormonal levels producing menses and fertility (see Fig. 8-1).[9]

A variety of hormonal imbalances may affect the development of the fetus, so that a genetic female develops male genitalia or, more likely, ambiguous genitalia with a hypertrophied clitoris. A genetic male could develop internal or atrophied testes, ambiguous genitalia (such as a penis and a small vaginal opening), or an atrophied penis. Such variations differ from those seen in chromosomal abnormalities in that the original structures determined by the genotype are sex-appropriate, but an improper balance of male and female hormones results in an ambiguous stage of sexual development of the fetus.

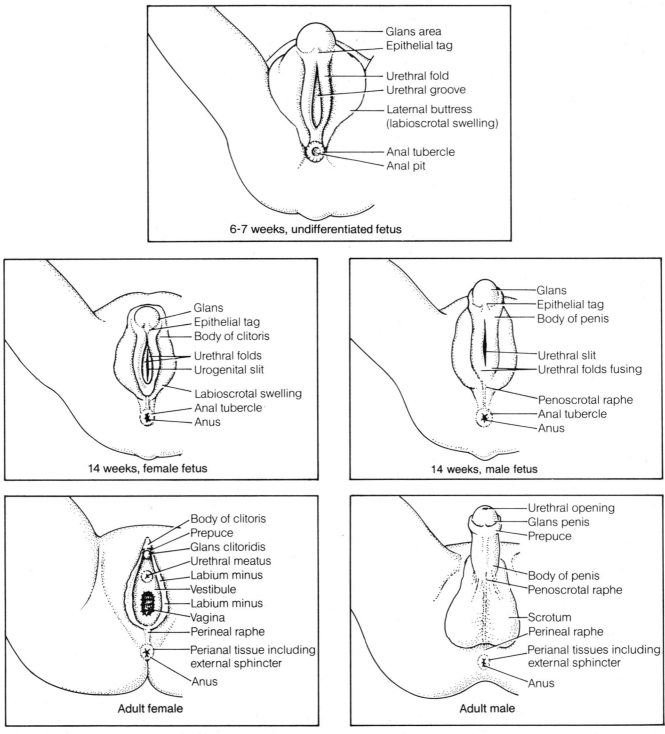

Figure 8-1. *Sexual differentiation.*

Diagnosis and treatment with hormone therapy assists the child with ambiguous genitalia to have a near-normal life. Many times, the fetal development is so different from the genetic structure that the best decision is to raise the child as a child of the sex of the genitalia rather than the genotype. The learned element of sexuality is apparently the most important influence after birth, be-cause these children rarely have problems developing gender identity if they were treated consistently as the sex assigned early in life.[10] Surgery, hormone therapy, and counseling with the parents are critical elements in a healthy pattern of development. During such procedures, the child is less confused and traumatized if the situation is described as a "hormone imbalance" rather than referring to "male" or "female" characteristics. Parents will adapt more readily to the birth of a child with ambiguous genitalia if the delivery room staff do not refer to the child as either sex, until careful study results in the assignment of sex of greatest likelihood of development.[3]

Development of Gender Identity

Infants are treated differently according to their sex. Undoubtedly, differences of parental behavior result in differences of behavior of the child. According to Freudian or psychodynamic theory, the first 3 years of life are crucial in the development of gender identity because, during this time, the child identifies with the parent of the same sex and develops a complementary relationship with the parent of the opposite sex. Biochemically, these first 3 years are possibly crucial in the development of neural pathways that further result in certain predispositions of behavior according to sex. According to learning theory, the responses of others teach the child to develop a gender identity of male or female early in life. Another theory, the "cognitive switch theory," states that genetic as well as environmental influences result in the development of a stable gender identity of male or female at a set age of 3 to 4 years.[13]

Many theorists, although accepting the importance of early experience, development, and learning, reject the idea of a fixed identity at such a young, and seemingly arbitrary, age. These theorists believe that a variety of influences develop predispositions (that may or may not be realized) in response to lifelong experience, development, and learning. These theorists believe that maleness and femaleness are not fixed points but exist on a continuum that is open to interpretation and expression according to cultural pressures and preferences. The choices of the individual ultimately become decisive in developing the gender identity in response to the experiences of life.[12] The normally developed male and female human share most of the same "male" and "female" hormones, but in differing proportions according to the genetic and hormonal development of the individual. Although they are normally differentiated, the male and female are much more like one another than they are like less differentiated individuals having genotypes other than XX or XY, or than they are like individuals who developed without the influence of both types of sex hormones.

The first step of gender-identity development occurs as the child becomes aware of the differences of the sexes and perceives that he or she is male or female, as compared to others. This basic recognition of one's sex (whether anatomically clear or assigned due to anatomic ambiguity) is called *sexual identity*.[10] Sexual identity allows the child to clearly interpret the behaviors of others as behavior appropriate for a male or female, and as different or the same as the sex of the child.

During early childhood, the child forms bonds between himself and male and female significant people. How these bonds are formed affects how the child will prefer to develop his or her sexual identity. Parents and other important adults serve as role models and teachers about how men and women act and relate with each other.

Gender identity refers to how the child feels about his or her sexual identity; that is, how the child decides to interpret his or her sexual identity for himself or herself. The development of *gender role* refers to how the child's gender identity will be expressed socially, in behavior with others of the same and opposite sex.

Children tend to prejudge themselves and others regarding sexual orientation and identity based on information and attitudes mimicked from parental behavior, because they have little real experience on which to base their own behaviors. Often, this results in very rigid distinctions of gender roles. On the other hand, if children are told about sexuality, about differences and similarities between the sexes, and about sexual behavior between the sexes before puberty, they develop a more matter-of-fact approach to sex.[7] Later on, they are able to make important decisions about their own behavior based on information, rather than on emotions, stereotypes, or expectations of others.[7]

During early childhood, fantasies also play an important role in the child's developing gender identity. These fantasies include images of ultimate self-satisfaction and feelings of self-fulfillment. Children's fantasies do not tend to be as structured or realistic as those of adults. These fantasy associations are formed according to feelings of pleasure, and are instrumental in the development of the child's system of symbols pertaining to self. These symbols are uncensored by the expectations of society and loved ones, and are therefore truly creative events of the child. This system of symbols and fantasies takes on an erotic quality when the child reaches puberty.[7]

These fantasies guide the *choice of sexual object*; that is, the individual's choice of an object for sexual expression. For most people, symbols and fantasies are abstractions during childhood, but in adolescence they develop into an image of the ideal man or woman. For others, the system of abstractions persists, and the adult's sexual interest is invested in objects, events, or particular types of people; this is termed *paraphilias*. The fantasies of the child before puberty probably correlate with later choices of sexual expression when he becomes sexually active.[14]

The preadolescent years are an important period in the development of gender identity because, during these years, the child experiences his first bond of an adult nature. The preadolescent usually forms this intense bond or friendship with a peer of the same sex, although he may have a strong case of "hero worship" of an older person. This sensitive preadolescent period enables the child to begin to shed childhood values and interests and replace them with those of the adult world. The intense preadolescent relationship is not unlike a love relationship. It is usually not one-sided like the "crushes" of earlier childhood but may be just as fantasy-oriented and romantically obsessive, whether the romantic element is covert or overt. These intense relationships sometimes become sexual, resulting in an early homosexual or heterosexual experience. This does not, however, indicate the life-long sexual object choice of the preadolescent. Nevertheless, the resolution and success of this bond creates early perceptions about roles in a sexual relationship.

During the adolescent phase of development, the adolescent expresses his perceptions of roles through sexual interest in another. Although sexual object choice is usually determined during adolescence, this choice can, and frequently does, change in adult years. The way in which early romantic relationships develop and satisfy the adolescent's needs and desires greatly affects his future behavior in relationships.

Life experience and opportunities and increasing self-awareness influence gender identity, gender role, and sexual object choice throughout the adult years. The early and middle adult years focus on sexually solidifying a long-term relationship and procreating. In middle age and later maturity, the focus turns again to the self and to personal fulfillment. In older age, sexual activity becomes symbolic of the continuation of social abilities and the reaffirmation of the self.

Sexual Expression

Sexual object choice determines sexual expression. This choice is formed by an internal fantasy image of the "ideal other." Dating behaviors are attempts to find this perfect other and develop a relationship rich in personal satisfaction. The success or failure of early adolescent relationships depends greatly on how well the fantasy actually fits the person. As people mature, their fantasies change. The "ideal-person" image is usually altered by learning more about the needs, desires, and behaviors of others. A more mature person may be successful in falling in love because the fantasy may be more realized.[7] If the individual's fantasy is of an object, as in the paraphilias, he may still develop feelings of concern, affection, and erotic interest in another person in response to experience.

The state of "being in love" means total involvement with, and devotion to, another person. In this state, sexual activity is undertaken according to perceived mutual needs and desires, which are expressed nonverbally during acts of love making. The ability to send and receive these nonverbal cues accurately is necessary in sexual relationships. Also, people usually engage in sexual activity in a state of *abandonment,* in which each partner abandons his or her body to the pleasure of the other, and becomes totally immersed in delighting the body of the other.[7]

"Being in love" is obviously not the sole motivation for sexual activity. Sometimes, people are unable to integrate their images of an ideal relationship partner and an ideal sexual partner. They then find themselves in a relationship with one person, with whom they are "in love," but deeply sexually attracted to another person. Some people do not like the man or woman with whom they enjoy the most intense sexual pleasure. Some men and women, perhaps due to conflicting feelings about sexual activity, believe that they can only experience sexual abandonment with someone they do not personally like or respect. It is probably true that relationships endure when they contain the potential for both sexual and personal pleasure for both parties.

Human Sexual Response

The human sexual response cycle consists of four phases—excitement, plateau, orgasm, and resolution.

Excitement

The first phase, the excitement phase, is brought on by psychological stimulation, such as fantasy or romantic communication; or by physiological stimulation, such as touching, kissing, fondling, licking, or biting erotic parts of the body. The areas on the body that are particularly sensitive to erotic stimulation are called *erogenous zones.* These zones differ among individuals, but generally include the neck, mouth, breasts, inner thighs, and genital areas. The anus and navel are also erogenous areas for some people.

The petting and fondling activities engaged in during the excitement phase of the sexual response cycle are called *foreplay.* For many people, foreplay is the most important part of sexual activity. The caring, nurturing, and attentive behaviors between the sexual partners communicate concern and appreciation for the needs, desires, and sexual nature of the other. Young men and women of various ages sometimes reach orgasm (or climax) in response to intense foreplay alone. Nevertheless, this phase of sexual activity is the one most frequently omitted, especially if the couple perceive sex as relational or procreational, rather than recreational.

The excitement phase in the female is characterized by lubrication, expansion of the clitoris, and nipple erection. There is a generalized tensing of muscles throughout the body, and increased heart rate, respirations, blood pressure, and motor restlessness. A fine rash or "sex flush" also appears over the abdomen and chest of many women.

In males, the first phase consists of erection of the penis, elevation of the testes, nipple erection, and sometimes a sex flush. Heart rate, respiratory rate, blood pressure, and motor restlessness increase in men as in women.

Plateau

The second phase of sexual response is the *plateau* phase, which lasts from 30 seconds to several minutes in men and women. In the female, vaginal vasocongestion results in a reduction of the opening of the vagina, and the development of a swollen and tensing area called the *orgasmic platform* in the lower third of the vagina and the labia minora. The clitoris retracts from the normal position. Breasts enlarge through areolar engorgement. The sex flush, generalized muscle tension, rising heart rate, blood pressure, and respiratory rate continue.

In men, the plateau phase consists of an increase in size of the coronal area of the glans penis. The testes continue to increase in size and elevate. The sex flush and motor restlessness increase. Heart rate, blood pressure, and respiratory rate rise.

Orgasm

The next phase of sexual response is called *orgasm*. In females, orgasm consists of three to fifteen strong, rhythmic contractions of the orgasmic platform of the vagina. These may be followed by spastic contractions. During this phase the vagina remains enlarged, and the uterus contracts irregularly. There is generalized muscle spasm and loss of voluntary muscle control throughout the body. Hyperventilation, blood pressure, heart rate, and sex flush reach a peak. The rectal sphincter may contract and the urinary meatus may dilate.

In males, the orgasm phase is characterized by ejaculatory contractions along the entire length of the penis, three or four expulsive contractions, then several contractions of less intensity. Response patterns of muscles, rectal sphincter, heart rate, blood pressure, and respiratory rate are the same as those seen in women during this phase.

Resolution

The *resolution* phase is the final phase of human sexual response. In the female, this stage is marked by the return of the orgasmic platform to its normal size and position. The clitoris returns to normal size and position in 5 to 30 minutes. Breasts return to their normal size. Sex flush and muscle tension disappear as heart rate, blood pressure, and respiratory rate return to normal. In many women, lubrication recurs during the resolution phase, indicating an ability to reach orgasm again if stimulated.

In the male, the resolution phase is a similar return of the genitalia to their normal sizes and positions, but it also includes a *refractory period*, during which time ejaculation cannot occur. This refractory period varies in length widely among individuals and changes throughout the life span. During the resolution phase, the penis reduces in size about 50% almost immediately after orgasm. The remaining enlargement of the penis disappears more slowly, sometimes over 2 hours. Similarly, vasocongestion of the scrotum and testes reduces by 50% rapidly, then continues to resolve over a longer period of time. Sex flush, nipple erection, muscle tension, heart rate, blood pressure, and respiratory rate all normalize fairly quickly during this phase.

Methods of Experiencing Orgasm

Orgasm may be reached through a variety of techniques. *Masturbation* refers to the self-stimulation of erogenous areas to the point of orgasm. In men, masturbation is usually performed by gripping the shaft of the penis and moving the hand up and down. Vibrators are also commonly used in masturbation, by rubbing the moving area of the machine over and around the penis. Women masturbate by either directly or indirectly stimulating the clitoris, by rubbing over or around the clitoris, or by inserting an object into the vagina to simulate the action of the penis in intercourse.

Cunnilingus is oral–genital stimulation performed on a woman. *Fellatio* is oral–genital stimulation performed on a man. Many men and women prefer this method of reaching orgasm over other methods. Lips, tongue, and teeth are used to stimulate the clitoris and vagina in cunnilingus and the penis in fellatio. Sucking, licking, nibbling, and blowing activities are used in this method of sexual stimulation.

Anal intercourse is common among male homosexuals and also occurs in heterosexuals. A lubricant is necessary because the anus does not have the natural lubrication of the vagina. Anal intercourse is very stimulating to the penis because the anal opening is tight. The penis inserted into the anus stimulates the clitoris or penis of the receiving partner indirectly and is psychologically erotic for many people. For others, anal intercourse does not produce erotic sensations and may result in pain. Some women and men are excited by their partner stimulating the anus with a finger during intercourse. The finger or penis inserted into the anus should be washed before insertion into the vagina to avoid infecting the vagina with the normal bacteria of the rectum.

Sexual intercourse, or *coitus*, is penetration of the vagina by the penis. Coitus is performed in a variety of positions. Face-to-face–woman-above and face-to-face–side-lying positions allow more control by the woman and usually result in less depth of vaginal penetration than many other positions for intercourse. The face-to-face–man above position facilitates deeper penetration, especially if the woman has her legs over the shoulders of the man. This position does not facilitate as much ejaculatory control by the man. The rear-entry position allows deeper penetration and manual clitoral stimulation. Seated and standing positions offer varying degrees of control for either partner, depending on the position of each partner, and they tend to decrease the depth of penetration.[4]

Other activities for reaching orgasm include penetrating the vagina or anus with the hand, vibrator, or other object, simulating actions of the penis. The hand and fingers create widely different sensations than does the penis or other penis-shaped objects, and offer variations for heterosexual couples and a principle method of sexual activity for homosexual and lesbian couples. In addition, the penis, scrotum, clitoris, and vagina may be stimulated by the hand or other body part of the partner to result in orgasm.

Traditional Lifestyles of Sexual Expression

In the current, dominant society of this country, some sexual activity occurs in most men and in many women before marriage. Although this is counter to the teachings of most American religions, this practice does allow the adolescent to survive sexual attractions and erotic relationships before making a lifetime choice of marriage.[7] In addition, masturbation is common among adolescents and may help the adolescent and young adult develop his or her sexual responsiveness and range of sexual preference.[2] Dating extends through the high-school years, and the time of marriage generally depends on career choices. Many men and women choose to establish themselves in a profession or other career before marriage; however, subcultural as well as individual values, goals, and norms help determine the time of marriage.[7] Heterosexual relationships are now commonly formed as partnerships, in the true sense of the word, with marriage contracts defining the shared responsibilities and the obligations of both partners.

Alternative Sexual Lifestyles

Homosexuality, Lesbianism, and Bisexuality

For about 10% of the population, the sexual object choice is a member of the same sex. For another 20% to 40%, the sexual object choice could be either male or female. Preferring a member of the same sex as a sexual partner is referred to as *homosexuality* among men and *lesbianism* among women. *Bisexuality* refers to an equal, or almost equal, preference for either sex. In addition, many bisexuals do not feel fulfilled with a solitary (or monogamous) relationship with a member of either sex, but prefer to be involved in equally intense and meaningful relationships with a man and a woman. Other people may refer to themselves as bisexual if they have had an intense sexual relationship with a person of the same sex, even if they generally prefer and are engaged in a heterosexual relationship.

The development of the homosexual, bisexual, and lesbian is probably not very different from that of the heterosexual. The homosexual who identifies himself as such is open to nonconformity and is able to tolerate risk. The imagery and early bonds of homosexuals may have been related to developing an appreciation of people of the same sex or, in the case of the bisexual, an equal appreciation of both sexes. There may be biochemical differences present in people who choose alternative sexual lifestyles, but these probably represent potentialities rather than inevitabilities, and are probably also present in many people who choose heterosexual lifestyles.[14]

These choices of alternative sexual lifestyles are made not only due to preferences for sexual activities, but also due to a perceived ability to share emotional intimacy with either a man or a woman, and with that particular man or woman chosen for a sexual relationship. Some people choose to follow an alternative sexual lifestyle for political reasons, even if they believe they could succeed in a less controversial sexual lifestyle. The radical feminist who is also a lesbian is an example of this. She may choose lesbianism because of her political differences with men and her dislike of the traditional female role in heterosexual relationships. Some people believe that everyone is bisexual to one extent or another and that situations create the lifestyle choice.[14]

Homosexuals, lesbians, and bisexuals are sometimes referred to collectively as "gays." There is, in some areas of the country, a united force of gay people working through political means for greater sexual freedom and less stigma in society. Aside from this one aggregate created primarily for political purposes, there exists very little similarity among homosexual men, lesbians, and bisexuals. Each represents a distinct subculture with differing values, norms, and mores. There is really no such thing as a typical "gay person," just as a typical heterosexual person exists only statistically. The mannerisms and preferences of dress that are seen as associated with gay people are many times subcultural artifacts, like any fashion trend, and are sometimes exaggerated in response to stigma from the heterosexual world.

The sexual behavior of gay people varies as much as the sexual behavior of heterosexuals. There is no more prevalence of sexual dysfunction, bizarre sexual practices, child molestation, or sadomasochistic sexual activity among homosexuals, lesbians, and bisexuals than that found among heterosexual groups.[14] Neither is promiscuity more common among homosexuals than heterosexuals. Gay people do tend to enter a greater number of sexual relationships, perhaps because there are no societal supports of long-term relationships among gay people. Nevertheless, their relationships tend to last for 2 to 3 years, and they tend to be monogamous.[11] For many homosexual people, the "gay bar" provides an opportunity, and one of the few places where it is acceptable, to meet with and talk to other homosexuals; the heterosexual, or "straight" world, on the other hand, has a variety of places within which heterosexuals can display affection for each other and be considered socially acceptable.

Transsexuality

The *transsexual,* in most cases, presents an entirely different lifestyle choice than the homosexual. Many transsexuals do not desire a homosexual relationship and are, perhaps, in successful heterosexual relationships.[14] The transsexual believes he or she is psychologically of the sex opposite his or her anatomic gender. Surgery, hormone treatment, and psychotherapy are sought as a "sex change" process by the transsexual. The impetus for this change process is rarely a sexual relationship but is a need to ensure the integrity of his or her identity.[14]

Paraphilias

Other variations in sexual preferences and lifestyles are termed *paraphilias* (*i.e.,* sexual or erotic attraction to objects, events, or superficial aspects of certain types of people). Although these variations are manifested by people who also have very normal sexual habits and vocational interests, the paraphilic activities may occur more often during times of stress or difficulty in heterosexual relationships. The common factor of these variations is erotic pleasure received from the inanimate and unreciprocated sexual activity. One example of the paraphilias is *transvestitism*, or a sexual desire to dress in the clothing, or adopt the mannerisms, of the opposite sex. *Voyeurism* refers to a desire to watch others in sexually vulnerable or erotic positions, such as those who are engaged in sexual activity with another or those who are undressing alone. *Exhibitionism* is an erotic desire to expose one's genital or erogenous areas to others. Voyeurism and exhibitionism sometimes involve anger toward the victim (the unsuspecting person who is observed or is the recipient of the exhibitionism) or anger toward something the victim represents. An exhibitionist, for example, may be angry with all women and may believe he hates them; he then expresses his anger through the victim's response of shock. In most cases, however, the impetus for the behavior involves no attempt at psychological violence.

The paraphilias include a sexual preference for children (pedophilia), a preference for sexual activity with animals (bestiality or zoophilia), and a sexual attraction to the smell and sight of death (necrophilia). *Sadism* is a paraphilia in which the man's or woman's preferred sexual object choice is not a type of person but is the act of inflicting pain on someone else. A *masochist* is a person whose sexual object choice is the experience of pain. In sadistic and masochistic relationships, erotic fulfillment is not achieved without either psychic or physical pain.

The paraphilias are not easily "treated," just as the sexual object choice of a heterosexual is not easily changed. Desensitization has been effective in dissociating the erotic experiences from the image of the paraphilia when the person is fully motivated to change.[1]

Variations in Sexual Expression Due to Physical or Mental Conditions

The Client's Sexual Needs

Illness, disability, hospitalization, and surgery are frequent factors in the disruption of the self-concept, including the sexual identity and gender identity. The client may demonstrate these disruptions as withdrawal from the family, anger toward the hospital or clinic staff, and deterioration of normal practices of hygiene and dress. Sometimes, hospitalized clients respond to crises by making obscene or sexually suggestive remarks or gestures toward nursing personnel. Although this behavior cannot be reinforced by the nurse, the response should not be one of anger. The nurse first clarifies the nature of the nurse–client relationship, and then clearly states that the nurse is interested in maintaining this therapeutic, nonsocial relationship. If the client is persistent, the nurse repeats the limits of the relationship and that she will not tolerate violation of these limits. Often, the client accepts the more clearly defined relationship and, perhaps, indicates a need for a closer relationship with staff on a therapeutic level. Illness and hospitalization weaken most normal coping mechanisms of clients and remove them from significant relationships, thereby creating a need for intimacy on some level with staff members. This need is met by an understanding nursing staff responding with emotional warmth and support within a professional relationship.

Many nurses are bothered by the client who masturbates. Perhaps one reason for this lack of tolerance and empathy is a mistaken belief that seriously ill people do not have sexual needs and desires. The nurse should provide for, and respect the privacy of, the client by knocking on the door before entering, by keeping the curtain drawn around the client's bed unless requested otherwise, and so forth. If the nurse finds a client masturbating, she should apologize for the invasion and provide the necessary privacy. It is important to convey respect and appreciation for the needs and individual values of the client. Similarly, a client may need sexual activity with his or her sexual partner while hospitalized. The nurse should be sensitive to cues of these needs and should respond by providing needed privacy. When the sexual relationship of the client is not a marital one, or is not heterosexual, the nurse may be less understanding of his needs. This is an example of the nurse's own value system being forced on the client and represents a nontherapeutic act of stigmatization.

Changes in Sexual Abilities

Certain physical and mental conditions affect one's ability to perform sexually and create a threatening crisis for the client's self-esteem. The nurse needs to be aware of such conditions and needs to encourage the client to verbalize feelings and frustrations. Many times, if the usual mode of sexual expression is not possible, an alternative method could be successful in meeting the client's sexual and relationship needs. For example, the quadriplegic client can participate in sexual intercourse if she or he is comfortable taking on a new role, perhaps a more passive one. A man who has lost the ability to achieve and maintain an erection may undergo a relatively simple procedure to have a penile implant placed surgically that enables erection, although not ejaculation. Many times, the client will feel satisfied with the ability to please his or her partner sexually, even if orgasm, as formerly experienced, is impossible.

Many surgical treatments of disease result in impotency in the male. These include perineal prostatectomies and, sometimes, ileostomies and colostomies. The client is encouraged to try alternative methods of pleasing his sexual partner other than intercourse. A penile implant may also be suggested. Some women experience a loss of libido following bilateral oopherectomies, and difficulty reaching orgasm following abdominal surgeries to create a colostomy or ileostomy. In these situations, it is imperative that both partners are fully aware of the physiological causes of such difficulties and establish clear communication regarding both partners' sexual needs and desires. Diabetes mellitus may result in orgasmic dysfunctions in some men and women, and sometimes impotence in men. Again, one solution may be the clear communication between the client and sexual partner. Some women experience *dyspareunia*, or pain with sexual intercourse, following hysterectomies and radiation treatments for uterine or cervical cancer. Coital positions that provide the woman with more control in directing the penis and that prevent deep penetration may restore sexual satisfaction in the relationship.[3]

The aged person experiences changes in sexual abilities that are sometimes perceived by the elderly as an inability to engage in any sexual activity. The elderly person should be counseled regarding the normalcy of changes, such as a longer refractory period in the male, less firmness of the male erection, a longer time period required to achieve erection and reach orgasm, and occasional incidents of inability to achieve erection. Many men adapt to such changes by trying alternative sexual activities, such as having the partner stimulate the penis manually before attempting coitus, and oral sex if erection cannot be achieved fully enough to engage in coitus. Women tend to experience a loss of lubrication and some dyspareunia with the normal physical changes of aging. Sexual activities other than coitus and new coital positions allow the elderly woman to enjoy a full sex life.[3]

The Effects of Drugs

Some drugs affect libido and sexual abilities. When possible, the drug should be discontinued and a drug without this side effect should be administered. If this is not possible, the nurse explains to the client the cause of the problem and encourages him to alter his or her sexual activity as necessary. One such alteration might be the adoption of new coital positions or longer periods of foreplay before attempting coitus. Again, it is necessary that the client's sexual partner know the reason for the client's changing sexual abilities. Alcohol affects sexual interest and abilities in many men and women, but these changes are reversed when the alcohol use is curbed or stopped. On the other hand, chronic alcohol or drug use may affect the relationship to an extent that it interferes with normal sexual activity. Couples therapy or counseling may be needed to help restore open communication between the partners.

Sexual Behavior During Psychoses

The schizophrenic client may evidence bizarre sexual habits during psychotic episodes. These are usually part of the client's delusional system and probably do not represent his covert sexual desires. The client with manic behavior often exhibits increased sexual interest along with the loss of his usual inhibitions, this results in a period of sexual promiscuity and flirtatious behavior. The depressed client may experience a loss of sexual interest and ability during the acutely depressive period. It is important that family members, friends, and sexual partners of these clients be informed of the causes of erratic behavior and understand that the behavior may never recur during healthier periods for the client. The client should be protected by limit-setting of the staff; punishment or chastisement will not change his inappropriate behavior.

Nursing Interventions

The attitudes held by health care providers can make the occurrences of sexual problems more difficult or less difficult for the client and family to cope with and overcome. During the early recovery period, the nurse or other staff member who works with the client who underwent injury or surgery resulting in a change in body image must convey an attitude of acceptance of the ostomy, the amputation stump, or the paralyzed limbs. Nurses must be sensitive to the client's cues that a concern exists, and support his attempts to discuss the problem or fear. The nurse must be aware of the sexual needs of the hospitalized client, the elderly client, and the clients' sexual partners. It is also important for the nurse to facilitate the family's understanding of the client's condition. This may be done by suggesting a family meeting be held, during which the nurse supports the client in talking with the family or sexual partner. The nurse may wish to suggest a private meeting between the client and the sexual partner or the family. The nurse helps the client prepare for such a meeting by talking about the problems that need to be discussed and, perhaps, by role-playing a situation of talking with the family member about a sensitive topic. The nurse may also decide to talk with the family member or members about changes and needs of the client, with the client's permission, to make future discussions easier for him. Clear communication is an essential element in the relationship between client and family or sexual partner.

Sex Therapy

Sex therapy is a particular approach to sex counseling that is practiced by master's-level clinicians with additional training in this therapy specialty. Sex therapy involves gathering careful assessments and histories of a couple's sexual difficulties, then clarifying each member's perceptions of the other and of sexual activities in general. The therapist facilitates communication between the two partners and their acceptance of each others' feelings and attitudes.[5] The approach of sex therapy is that sex is to be enjoyed and must not be viewed as an obligation of a relationship. The therapist may suggest certain exercises for the couple, most of which focus the couple on the sensual pleasures of touching and foreplay and de-emphasize the demand aspects of sexual activity. One such exercise is called the *Sensate Focus* exercise, a sense awareness activity during which the partners are not to attempt any activity to achieve orgasm but are to spend time relaxing and enjoying the physical closeness of the other. The couple may also be taught new coital positions or different sexual activities that may better suit the needs of both partners. Other types of exercises assist the client to maintain more control during the sexual activity and to help him or her overcome fear or anxiety about sexual behavior. The *Squeeze technique* is an exercise suggested to help a man prolong ejaculation during coitus to promote a mutually more pleasurable experience for the couple. This technique involves the woman stimulating the penis until near orgasm, then firmly squeezing the head of the penis with her thumb and two fingers, until the urge to ejaculate has subsided. This may be done during coitus also, if the woman is on top of her partner and can remove the penis from the vagina when her partner informs her of nearing orgasmic inevitability.[2]

Common Sexual Problems

Impotence, the inability to achieve or maintain erection sufficiently to perform coitus, is a problem commonly seen in sex therapy. It is termed *primary impotence* when the man has never been able to achieve erection, and *secondary impotence* when the man has developed an inability to achieve or maintain erection but has successfully achieved erections in the past. *Premature ejaculation* is the condition in which the man is unable to control ejaculation as long as he wishes to please himself or his partner. Both impotence and premature ejaculation may be caused by physical problems or by psychological conflict, such as stress or difficulties in the relationship. The cause of the sexual problem is ascertained before attempting treatment. The sensate focus exercise is often suggested as a treatment for impotence, and the squeeze technique is employed as a treatment for premature ejaculation.[2]

Women seeking sex therapy often present with the problems of vaginismus or orgasmic dysfunction. *Vaginismus* is a spastic contraction or tightening of the vagina during or before penetration for coitus. *Primary orgasmic dysfunction* is an inability to achieve orgasm with no history of having had orgasm. *Secondary orgasmic dysfunction* refers to the development of difficulty attaining orgasm in certain situations. Physical causes for these problems, such as infection or nerve damage, are first ruled out. The therapist then ascertains that the woman wishes to be able to enjoy sexual activity with her partner. The woman and therapist discuss any conflicts about sexual activity or the relationship. Vaginismus is frequently treated by the insertion of graduated plastic catheters into the vagina for several minutes at a time, or even overnight. After the woman is able to tolerate one size, a larger catheter is inserted until she can tolerate penetration by a penis. When intercourse is attempted, the woman should assume a position that enables her to control the thrusts of the penis. Orgasmic dysfunctions are treated by suggesting the sensate focus exercise and periods of sexual activity during which the woman is not expected to "perform" or achieve orgasm. Coital positions are suggested that allow clitoral and breast stimulation by the partner or by the woman herself.[2]

Sexual Problems and the Nursing Process

Assessment and Analysis

Assessment, the first step of the nursing process, includes reviewing the client's record for a clearer understanding of all aspects of the sexual problem. A sex history is obtained in which the client's earliest sexual experiences are described, along with the method the client first learned about sex. The nurse compiles data that clarify the client's feelings and attitudes about sex. The assessment process also focuses on the sexual relationship. What are the sex roles and gender roles taken by each partner? How well do the partner's attitudes agree with those of the client? How do each perceive the needs of self and the other? How are sexual needs and preferences expressed in the relationship? Is there equal consideration of the needs of the other? The nurse may also wish to investigate the past relationships of the client and his or her partner. How have these prior relationships affected the client's current situation? Finally, how clearly defined is the client's gender identity, and how is this perceived by the partner? This information facilitates a clarification of the problems and assists the nurse in identifying educational deficits and other needs.

It is important for the nurse to include cultural data in the assessment process. The religious and ethnic influences on the client's perceptions of sexuality assist the nurse in understanding the client's responses and determining realistic treatment approaches. If the client has rejected his or her culture of origin and adopted another lifestyle or subculture, the culture of origin may still have a covert influence on his behavior and responses. If the client has chosen a lifestyle that is nontraditional, the nurse may be helpful in suggesting ways the client can respond to stigma, either in preventing exposure in society, or in establishing a support group and alternative system of approval. (See the dialogue and diagnosis guidelines below.)

Planning

Treatment approaches are planned following the data-gathering and analysis processes. These approaches may be suggested by the nurse or other health care professional, based on an understanding of the cultural and religious preferences that influence one's sexuality and sexual activity. The nurse ascertains the client's acceptance of the suggested interventions and explains the processes involved. In most situations, it is necessary that both sexual partners accept and understand the therapy program. It is

(Text continues on p 97)

Therapeutic Dialogue

Talking with the Client About Sexual Concerns

Nurse: What is the part about your relationship you dislike most?

Client: Our sex life.

Nurse: Your sex life doesn't suit you. In what ways is it unsatisfactory for you?

Client: I don't know. It's good for him, I guess. I guess that's how it always is?

Nurse: That's how what always is?

Client: It's always what suits him. I just think something ought to go my way too.

Nurse: How does sex not go your way?

Client: Well, it's when he wants it and how he wants it and you know—I never have time.

Nurse: Does your husband rush sexual activity a little too fast for you?

Client: Too much, too fast.

Nurse: It sounds like you feel your husband doesn't take enough time to get you ready for intercourse. And that maybe he doesn't ask what you like. Is that right?

Client: Yeah. And he always wants to do it.

Nurse: If he were trying things that you liked more, and taking it a little slower, would you like to have sex more often than you do now?

Client: Well, yeah, maybe. But he won't change anything.

Nurse: How much do you talk about sex, and what each of you likes and dislikes?

Client: Never.

Nurse: Have you ever told him how you feel about your sexual pattern together?

Client: He knows. I've never told him, but he has to know.

Nurse: I don't really think he can know unless you tell him. Have you ever told him what you like and don't like in sexual activity?

Client: Well, no, but I thought he was supposed to know that.

Nurse: Actually, it sounds like both of you could benefit by learning to talk about this openly.

Discussion

The client in this dialogue has been married to her sexual partner for 18 months. The couple has not as yet established satisfactory communication patterns. Difficulty expressing and discussing needs and wants is frequently manifested as a sexual problem.

Nursing Analysis and Diagnosis of Sexual Problems

The following are nursing diagnoses of sexual problems and assessment data supporting each diagnosis.

Assessment and Analysis of Data

Thirty-year-old woman, three pregnancies, three abortions

Anxiety experienced during entry of penis during intercourse and during fantasy of intercourse

No anxiety during foreplay or masturbation or cunnilingus

Discomfort during entry of finger into vagina and pain during intercourse

Complaints began 3 months earlier, 2 months after last abortion

Reported similar but milder problems following each abortion, but of brief duration (4–6 weeks)

No signs of vaginal infection or tissue damage of any kind

Nursing Diagnosis

Pain with intercourse (vaginismus) related to fear of pregnancy

(Continues on p 96)

Assessment and Analysis of Data	Nursing Diagnosis
Stated fear of pregnancy but no recognition of this as cause of problem	
Observed adequate communication between partners and an apparently supportive and "healthy" relationship	
Twenty-eight-year-old woman, states she is a lesbian, complaining of boredom in sexual relationship of 2 years	Lack of sexual enjoyment related to stress in relationship (unresolved anger)
Client denies any problem with her lesbianism; is open about this at work and with peers	
Client denies any other problems in the relationship; states she has never had this problem in previous long-term relationships	
Client describes her partner as an "unusually good lover," despite complaints of "boredom" and disinterest	
Client's partner appears to be a controlling person, insists on managing many aspects of the client's life	
Client has admitted difficulty expressing anger in the relationship	
Thirty-four-year-old male, married and divorced twice; states that he cannot enjoy sex and other aspects of intimacy in these relationships	Lack of sexual enjoyment related to possible transsexualism
Reports successful sexual performance but denies comfort or pleasure in the role	
Three homosexual relationships of short duration; reportedly unsatisfactorily	
Reports sexual fantasies usually include self as female	
Has long felt he is more "like a woman in a man's body"	
Twenty-four-year-old male, single, complains of frequently being unable to reach orgasm or ejaculation, except when masturbating	Difficulty with ejaculation (retarded ejaculation) related to discomfort in relationships with women
Reports satisfactory erections during all sexual encounters	
Reports normal ejaculation when alone and occasionally when with a "casual sexual partner—somebody I just met"	
Reports this problem persists even when highly sexually aroused and sufficiently stimulated by partner	

Assessment and Analysis of Data   *Nursing Diagnosis*

Reports no long-term sexual relationships or close friendships with women; states he feels "too shy with women"

Fantasies include successful sexual encounters with women—denies any homosexual fantasies or experiences

Discussion

The nurse compiles and examines assessment data to place historical and descriptive information in the appropriate context. By considering as many aspects of the problem as can be explored, the nurse strives to understand it from the perspective that is most helpful to the client. This approach to analysis of sexual concerns is particularly important, because the problem may be related to a multiplicity of factors, including self-image, physiologic conditions, genetic tendencies, communication abilities, sensitivity to nonverbal cues, and erotic-fantasy images.

Analysis of assessment data results in a nursing diagnosis that describes briefly the problem and identifies the immediate etiology or etiologic factors. Formulation of a nursing diagnosis enables the nurse to understand the client's sexual problem in greater depth and to develop a precise, helpful care plan or initiate a timely referral to another mental health professional.

the couple, not one or the other partner, who is the client in sex therapy. The client (*i.e.*, the couple) works with the nurse through the planning process.

Intervention

The nurse's role in the intervention process is frequently one of clarification of communication. The nurse encourages expression of feelings by both partners, eliciting feedback, separating thoughts and feelings, and helping the clients learn other means of clear, open communication. The nurse or other health care provider often suggests activities for the couple to try to encourage the development of new sexual patterns. Many times, the nurse acts as a teacher, clarifying vague information for the client and giving him new information about sex positions or habits. The nurse might help the client explore why he or she has some preference or fear, based on historical or cultural information.

Evaluation

Nursing interventions are evaluated by follow-up sessions with the client. The nurse explores with the client whether he accepted or tried the suggested interventions. Evaluation also includes determining whether the suggested activities or positions were realistic for the client's situation. In some cases, the client may not wish to change or may not be ready to try something new. The nurse assesses the client's progress and suggests new activities, if appropriate. The nurse

may decide to refer the client to someone else (perhaps, someone with a perspective more consistent with the client's) or to a clinician more experienced or with greater training in sex therapy.

Summary

This chapter has discussed the development of sexuality as an integral part of the personality. Some of the major points of the chapter include the following.

1. The sexual nature of the personality affects the emotional, spiritual, and psychological natures of the self; indeed, they are not separate "natures" but parts of the personality, the self.
2. Sexual development is·influenced by genetic and hormonal factors and by the development of gender identity.
3. The human sexual response cycle consists of four phases—excitement, plateau, orgasm, and resolution.
4. Traditional and alternative sexual lifestyles, such as homosexuality, transsexuality, and paraphilias, are contrasted.
5. Clients who undergo injury or surgery resulting in a changed body image often suffer a blow to their sexual identity.
6. Nursing interventions with clients whose physical

or mental disorders interfere with their sexual abilities include client and family teaching, support, and counseling.

7. Sex therapy may be the treatment of choice for certain common sexual problems—impotence, premature ejaculation, vaginismus, and orgasmic dysfunction.

8. The steps of the nursing process are applied to clients with sexual problems.

References

1. Bancroft J: Deviant Sexual Behavior. Oxford, Clarendon Press, 1974

2. Kaplan HS: The New Sex Therapy. New York, Brunner/Mazel Publications, 1974

3. Kolodny RC, Masters WH, Johnson VE, Biggs MA: Textbook of Human Sexuality for Nurses. Boston, Little, Brown, 1979

4. Masters W, Johnson V: Human Sexual Response. Boston, Little, Brown, 1966

5. Masters W, Johnson V: The Pleasure Bond. Boston, Little, Brown, 1970

6. Mims F, Swenson M: Sexuality: A Nursing Perspective. New York, McGraw-Hill, 1980

7. Money J: Love and Love Sickness. Baltimore, Johns Hopkins Press, 1979

8. Money J, Ehrhardt A: Man and Woman, Boy and Girl. Baltimore, Johns Hopkins Press, 1972

9. Money J, Musaph H (eds): Handbook of Sexology. New York, Excerpta Medica, 1977

10. Money J, Tucker P: Sexual Signatures: On Being a Man or a Woman. Boston, Little, Brown, 1975

11. Saghir M, Robins E: Male and Female Homosexuality. Baltimore, Williams & Wilkins, 1973

12. Stoller RJ: Sex and Gender. New York, Jason Aronson, 1974

13. Wilson H, Kniesl C: Psychiatric Nursing. Menlo Park, California, Addison-Wesley, 1979

14. Wolff C: Bisexuality: A Study. New York, Quartet Books, 1977

15. Woods NF: Human Sexuality in Health and Illness. St Louis, CV Mosby, 1979

Part III
The Process
of Psychiatric-Mental Health
Nursing

Chapter 9
Psychosociocultural Assessment

Even as a melody is not composed of tones, nor a verse of words, nor a statue of lines—one must pull and tear to turn a unity into a multiplicity—so it is with the human being I say You. I can abstract from him the color of his hair or the color of his speech in the color of his graciousness; I have to do this again and again; but immediately he is no longer You.

Martin Buber:
I and Thou, 1958

Sharon Byers

Chapter Preview

Psychosociocultural assessment is the first step of the nursing process employed in psychiatric-mental health care. It is a holistic assessment process that is designed to provide efficiency, reliability, and adaptation to the needs of the client and nurse. The conceptual framework for this approach is based on the nursing process, Selye's stress–adaptation model, and Maslow's formulation of the hierarchy of needs. This chapter emphasizes the nurse's relationship skills as the most critical assessment tool. To facilitate the novice interviewer's development of competence and confidence, client expectations of assessment interviewers are behaviorally defined and described. The hypothesis approach to structuring the interview presents a multidimensional and comprehensive system of assessment.

Learning Objectives

On completion of this chapter, the reader should be able to accomplish the following.

1. Define psychosociocultural assessment
2. Distinguish the types and purposes of assessment used in clinical situations
3. Describe various tools of psychosociocultural assessment
4. Discuss the importance of the relationship aspect of the interview in the assessment process
5. Describe the role and expectations of the nurse interviewer
6. Identify stages and other structural aspects of the interview
7. Apply the hypothesis approach to structure a psychosociocultural assessment
8. Compare methods of recording assessment data

Assessment: First Step of the Nursing Process

The effectiveness of the nursing process depends on the accurate completion of each step of the process. Assessment begins this process and is therefore the foundation. *Nursing assessment* is defined as the gathering, classifying, categorizing, and analyzing of client information and forms the basis of nursing care planning. A nursing assessment is a holistic assessment; that is, all areas of the client's life are examined as possible sources of important assessment data. The recovery of a surgical patient, for example, is enhanced by basing his nursing care on a solid understanding of his cultural background, sexual beliefs and fears, spiritual needs, social activities, and psychological status.

The nurse exercises professional judgment to determine the depth of the assessment of each area of client functioning and to choose the methods of gathering needed data, especially data that include sensitive or emotionally laden topics. The nurse also uses assessment information gathered by other psychiatric-mental health professionals, when possible, to protect the client from frequent and repetitious interviews.

Conceptual Frameworks

The use of theoretical models to form a conceptual framework of the nursing assessment process allows a more precise definition of that process. Accordingly, Maslow's hierarchy of needs and Selye's stress–adaptation syndrome form a framework for assessment that focuses on the needs of the individual, the adaptation resources of the individual, and the methods by which the nurse may facilitate the individual's meeting those needs and may facilitate his adaptation process.[20] Although this chapter will emphasize the assessment of the psychological, sociologic, and cultural aspects of the client's life, it is understood that the processes of adaptation on both physiological and psychological levels are intertwined and inseparable; they are, therefore, equally important for examination.

Assessment in Various Health Care Settings

The setting of a nursing assessment does not necessarily determine the focus of the assessment. In the medical areas of a hospital, as in a psychiatric treatment center, it is essential to attend to the psychosocial needs of the individual. In the nursing care planning of a patient experiencing postoperative psychosis or sensory deprivation delirium, for example, careful assessment of psychosociocultural aspects of the patient's condition will facilitate intervention in responses that can be life-threatening.

It cannot be assumed that psychosocial needs and problems of clients are readily apparent to the nurse in any health care setting. Studies show that clients and their family members are reluctant to report "nonmedical" problems or fears, because they do not believe these are within the realm of concern for the nurse or physician.[21] A purposeful, comprehensive psychosociocultural assessment should be conducted in all health care settings and should include the collecting and analyzing of information not always identified as problematic for the client at that time.[23]

Analysis of Assessment Information

Following data gathering and an ongoing exploration of client problems, an analysis of the data should be completed. During the *analysis*, the second step of the nursing process, assessment information is examined and categorized according to the goals of "making sense" of the data and clarifying a picture of the client as a whole person.

The nurse records the information obtained during the assessment process according to the policies of the health care facility and professional nursing judgment. Formulation of a *nursing diagnosis* or diagnoses is based on the nurse's assessment and analysis of client data, which, in turn, form the basis for planning nursing care (see Chap. 10).

Types of Assessment

Problem Identification

The type of assessment employed is usually determined by the nature of the client's problem and needs. Various purposes, goals, objectives, and methods distinguish assessments. In a crisis or emergency situation, the purpose of the assessment is to identify the problem, formulate a brief, clear statement of the problem, form a working hypothesis regarding the nature, intensity, and cause of the problem, and begin some type of therapeutic intervention. The goal of a crisis assessment is to furnish some measure of relief to the client and family in acute distress. This necessitates delaying a comprehensive data gathering. A suicidal and intensely disturbed client who presents himself in the psychiatric emergency room of a hospital is an example of a person in need of crisis assessment and intervention.

Problem Clarification

If a problem has been identified but is of a less urgent nature, the purpose of the assessment is clarification of the problem. The nurse systematically assesses the client concerning his perspective of the identified problem and his psychosocial and cultural history. A client who presents himself at a community mental health center to receive treatment for stress-related dysfunctions of eating and sleeping is an example of a person in need of problem clarification. In attempting to clarify the problem, the assessor's questions focus on the following.

1. The nature and intensity of the disruption caused by the problem
2. The time and context, or circumstances, wherein the problem was first noticed
3. Situations in which the problem is most and least disturbing
4. Specific fears concerning the problem and the changes it has caused in the client's life

In addition to clarifying the problem, the assessment usually includes a search for potential problems, strengths, resources, and normal habits of living in healthy and disrupted times. This kind of information about a client might assist in planning nursing interventions that would prevent a health disruption or that would facilitate client adaptation to a major change in role, image, or social space.

Special Considerations: Age, Cultural Background, and Physical Health Status. Priorities in the assessment process vary according to client factors that represent special needs, such as age, cultural background, and physical

health condition. Briefer assessment tools are used when assessing the elderly client, with greater emphasis placed on observation of the client rather than on information obtained during the interview. Assessment of children requires increased attention to observation of the child's interaction, communication, and play.

The client's sociocultural group also determines priorities in assessment. *Client norms,* or expected behavior and experience in particular life situations, guide the nurse's assessment, analysis, and diagnosis of client problems and needs. The assessment process discussed in this chapter primarily focuses on the adult client in the middle years, although the nurse may apply this basic approach to any client by taking into consideration the client's special needs. (The reader is also encouraged to refer to chapters that deal with special populations—children, adolescents, aged.)

Holistic Assessment

Hypothesis Approach to Assessment. Based on an understanding of the holistic nature of people, the nurse assesses all aspects of the client's life and experience. According to the hypothesis approach to assessment, the nurse considers key and probable questions about the client's life in each of the areas of biologic, psychological, social, cultural, cognitive, and behavioral experience.[4, 16] Consideration of these hypotheses guides the nurse's questioning during the interview process. This guidance assures that the assessment is comprehensive, complete, and directed by the needs of the client. The following discussion includes hypotheses that address many possible etiologies of, and explanations for, the client's behavior.

Psychological Hypotheses. Psychological hypotheses are explored through various psychological assessment tools, such as psychological tests, the mental status exam, history taking, and the interview. The assessor evaluates the results of these examinations and considers certain psychologic theories during the client interview.

The client's problem, according to psychological hypotheses, is related to, or caused by, the following factors.

1. The client's personality style and pattern of response to others
2. The dynamics of unresolved conflicts (such as early relationships, self-image, interaction with significant people)
3. A maturational or situational crisis
4. Psychodynamic issues (such as impaired or weak ego functioning)
5. Self-image, body image, or sexual identity

Social Hypotheses. The nurse–assessor gathers social information about the client; including socioeconomic status, social habits, social skills, and social values. Data should also be collected to explain how the client views society, socialization, and significant others with whom he interacts. The assessor must also understand how the client is, in turn, viewed by society, social groups significant to him, and those individuals who comprise his significant relationships.

The client's problem, according to social hypotheses, is related to, or caused by, the following factors.

1. A change in the client's social space (such as role, support system, and social boundaries)
2. Social isolation
3. The impact of the client's behavior, attitudes, or lifestyle on society or significant social groups
4. His communication of a social statement (such as a form of rebellion or refusal to cooperate with society)

Biologic Hypotheses. Biologic hypotheses refer to assumptions that the client's behavior is partially due to some biologic factor (*e.g.*, a disease process, neurochemistry, endocrine activity, physical dependence on some substance, or a biologic reaction to an internal or external environmental event). Methods of gathering data about biologic problems of the client include laboratory tests, x-rays, general physical examinations, and neurologic assessments.

The client's problem, according to biologic hypotheses, is related to, or caused by, the following factors.

1. An affective disorder caused by a biologic imbalance or dysfunction
2. A schizophrenic disorder caused by a biologic problem
3. An organic disease
4. Stress
5. Physical dependence on alcohol or other drugs
6. A response to a psychotropic agent or other chemical taken as part of a therapy regime
7. An allergic response to some environmental substance

Behavioral Hypotheses. Behavioral hypotheses focus on the assumption that the client's maladaptive behavior is socially learned and can therefore be "unlearned" and replaced with more adaptive behavior. Target behaviors, that is, the particular maladaptive response patterns, are identified and manipulated by the therapist. To increase the client's repertoire of responses, the therapist teaches him adaptive behaviors.

The client's problem, according to behavioral hypotheses, is related to, or caused by, the following factors.

1. Learned, undesirable behavior patterns or emotional patterns
2. Inattention to, or misperception of, cues in the environment
3. Deficits in learning or skills

Cognitive Hypotheses. Cognitive hypotheses are based on the assumption that the client's thoughts or thinking processes result in the identified problem. Underlying this assumption is the belief that an individual's perceptions and images of self and others, messages to self, and perceptions of the world are learned and may be identified as incorrect or maladaptive; they also may be replaced by more positive thoughts.

The client's problem, according to cognitive hypotheses, is related to, or caused by, the following factors.

1. The client's negative perception of self
2. The client's negative statements to self that increase his anxiety, fear, hopelessness, and maladaptive behavior
3. The client's maladaptive view of others, the world, and others' expectations of him
4. The client's faulty expectations of others
5. The client's inconsistent thoughts, values, and attitudes

Cultural Hypotheses. The nurse–assessor accurately evaluates client behavior as adaptive, maladaptive, or disturbed in relation to cultural norms, expectations, and beliefs of the client's reference group. The cultural reference group refers to the group of people with whom the client most closely shares beliefs, behaviors, and attitudes. This group determines norms and values with and for the client, and is, in effect, the "in group" by whom the client wishes to be accepted.

Cultural beliefs and values affect how an individual interprets the behavior of a health care provider. Cultural conflicts and pressures explain client behavior that may otherwise be misunderstood by the mental health professional. The cultural beliefs and values of the health care provider, in turn, influence his or her understanding and acceptance of the client. (Further discussion of the cultural aspects of psychiatric-mental health care may be found in Chapter 7.)

The client's problem, according to cultural hypotheses, is related to, or caused by, the following factors.

1. The culture into which the client was born, or in which he grew and developed
2. The adoption of a cultural pattern different from, or in addition to, the culture of origin
3. An identifiable conflict between the client's culture of origin and his adopted culture (such as a culture of origin that has faded for an elderly client and has been replaced by a new and strange culture)
4. Norms, values, and expectations of the client's reference group
5. The cultural reference group's view of the world and the group's place in, and treatment by, the world at large
6. Cultural taboos and myths
7. Acceptance, encouragement, discouragement, and prohibition of variations of group members' behaviors
8. Rituals practiced in response to events of transition

within, separation from, and incorporation into the cultural group

9. The cultural group's definition of health and illness
10. The cultural practice of caring, nurturing, and healing

Tools of Assessment

The nurse gathers assessment information using a variety of structural approaches and perspectives of inquiry, which are called *assessment tools*. A comprehensive psychosociocultural assessment necessitates the use of several tools; a variety of perspectives are provided by an interdisciplinary mental health team. Within the team that is functioning, the nurse administers some of these assessment tools, interprets the results, formulates a list of client problems and nursing diagnoses, and plans and evaluates nursing interventions. The psychologist administers psychological tests, analyzes the test results, and formulates a diagnostic impression from his disciplinary perspective. Other disciplines also use certain assessment tools to gather essential client data.

Gathering Historic Information

The client's historic data are collected in a holistic assessment. The depth of the history is determined by the problem area and the purpose of the assessment. The history's function is to form a background against which current client functioning may be measured and to gain an understanding of the client's past, present, and potential.

Objectives of the history-taking include the following.

1. To describe adaptive and maladaptive patterns of behavior
2. To formulate priorities of care
3. To identify client problems and analyze client data in the proper context
4. To consider the client's probable responses to potential therapeutic interventions
5. To analyze the client's perception of the world, health, and illness[26]

The history format chosen by a discipline is generally consistent with its philosophy and approach. A nursing history, for example, focuses on the problems and needs of the client and gathers information to assist in nursing care planning in health and illness adaptation. Medical histories are often oriented toward the client's symptoms and the diagnosis of an illness state. A psychiatric history, for example, centers on the client's psychodynamics, or internal conflicts, conflict resolution, and previous psychiatric difficulties.

A nursing history form is a vehicle for organizing and recording client information prior to, during, and following the interview. The sample questions and general categories of examination should be adapted to the client's personality, needs, wishes, and level of communication.[26] (See inserts, Guide to Client Assessment and Summary of Nursing History: Mr. S.G.)

(Text continues on p 107)

Guide to Client Assessment

Demographic Data:

Name
Age
Sex
Marital status
Religion
Height
Weight
Date of admission
Admitting diagnosis

Client's Perceptions and Expectations

How does the client define "the problem" and its cause?
What are the client's expectations of treatment?
What is the length of time client expects to be involved in treatment?
What are the client's discharge plans

History

Social and Cultural Data
Occupation

Educational background
Race/national origin
Who lives with the client?
Availability of family or significant others
Client's view of society/world
Recent loss or change in social space, role, habits
Leisure-time activities
Use of tobacco, alcohol, and other drugs

Sexual
Is client satisfied with his sexual activity and identity?
What is the effect of current problems on sexual functioning?

Medical
Allergies
Previous major illnesses, surgeries, and hospitalizations
Medications taken regularly
Review of systems
  Sensory
  Musculoskeletal

(Continues on p 106)

Circulatory
Integumentary
Respiratory
Gastrointestinal
Urinary
Reproductive
Neurologic
   Mental status
   Thought content and form

Basic Needs

Dietary preferences, habits, allergies, and restrictions
Rest/sleep/comfort
Personal hygiene
Eliminatory habits and needs
Psychosocial

General Observation

Appearance
   Posture

Gait
Dress
Jewelry, makeup
Facial expression
Behavior
   Motor activity
   Eye contact
   Purposeful or goal-directed actions
Communication
   Verbal (rate, pace, flow of speech)
   Nonverbal (gestures, body language)
   Clarity of communication
   Communication of feelings
   Communication with family and significant others

Summary

Client functioning and problems
Identified needs and resources
Suggested interventions

Summary of Nursing History: Mr. S. G.

Mr. S. G. is a 26-year-old married male admitted to the psychiatric-mental health unit with a diagnosis of *schizophrenia, paranoid type.* His weight is 160 pounds, height is 5 feet 11 inches. The client is a practicing Catholic from Center City, admitted for the first time to this facility. He has no history of previous admissions to any psychiatric facility, but he has been seen in outpatient therapy for 6 years by his admitting psychiatrist, Dr. R. B.

S. G. stated his reason for admission is to "hide until the heat is off," referring to his apparently delusional belief that he is being searched by the mafia. This fear has recently caused S. G. to quit his job, following 2 weeks of absenteeism. S. G. does not expect the hospital to help with his fear, but he does feel he will be protected here.

S. G. is an attorney who graduated from law school in Minnesota and has been practicing law for 1 year at the Office of legal Services. He is white, of middle-class background, and comes from the midwestern United States. He lives with his wife and 6-month-old son in an apartment complex near his office. He generally enjoys tennis and jogging.

He states that he does not smoke tobacco but does drink alcohol moderately—about one to two drinks or beers, about once or twice weekly. He denies the use of other drugs.

S. G.'s wife is frightened by her husband's behavior but appears supportive and concerned. S. G.'s parents have also expressed support and concern and are now staying in town, although they live in Texas. S. G. has had many changes in his life in the past 2 years—graduation from law school, accepting his first full-time job, marriage, and a child.

S. G. does not have any physical complaints. He has had no major illnesses, nor does he have any allergies. His sexual interest has decreased recently in relation to the increase in his fear and anxiety, but he has expressed no anxiety regarding his sexual identity.

S. G. is alert and attentive to the interviewer. He is disoriented to the situation at times, believing he is being interviewed for acceptance into a refugee camp. Memory, retention, judgment, and intellectual ability are all appropriate upon questioning. His affect is intense, labile, and indicative of anxiety and fear. His behavior appears normal for the situation. He relates to the interviewer in a somewhat friendly manner.

S. G. described his self-image by saying, "I am a failure. I've lost it all to the mafia." His body image appears normal. The client believes people are watching him and that he is usually being followed. No abnormalities of speech are assessed. His flow of thought appears to be racing at times, and the client agrees with this description. The client's thought content is obsessed with fear of the mafia.

Review of systems are, otherwise, unremarkable. Eating and drinking habits are normal for the client. He expresses no special diet preference and has had no trouble with his appetite since the delusional system developed, but has had difficulty sleeping, with early morning waking. Hygiene habits appear normal for the client's situation—clean, neat, casually dressed. Eye contact is good. The client states that he has no problems communicating his feelings to others, and that marital communication is "excellent"; however, eye contact between the client and his wife during the admission interview appeared, at times, to indicate tension and avoidance of conflict.

The client is an intelligent, 26-year-old man who appears his stated age and is functioning normally except for overwhelming fear and obsession related to a delusion of persecution. He responds to this delusion with anxiety, sometimes panic, and withdrawal from normal activities. His marital relationship appears to be a supportive factor, as does the presence of his parents and other family and friends in the area.

His strengths include intelligence, family support, understanding coworkers (his boss called to express support), and a history indicative of strong previous coping skills and interpersonal relations. His needs include control of anxiety, reinforcement of reality, acceptance of therapeutic relationships with staff, and exploration of stressors that resulted in this apparent psychotic break. Stressors evident at this time include several changes in the life space of the past 2 years—graduation, marriage, new job, new baby, new location. Further assessment of the marital relationship is warranted.

Diagnostic Impression

Disturbance in mood related to delusional
    thought content
Poor anxiety control related to delusional
    thought content
Disturbance in motivation related to delusional
    thought content
Disturbance in thinking related to inadequate
    coping with environmental stressors

Psychological Testing

Psychological testing is a structured and systematic process of observing and describing specific behaviors through the use of a numeric or category system.[7] The usefulness of such tests depends on their proper administration and the accurate interpretation of the test results. The significance of psychological test results depends, in turn, on the degree of agreement of several assessment tools (*e.g.*, a battery of psychological tests administered in conjunction with a diagnostic interview and history taking). There are three general categories of psychological tests—projective tests, personality inventories, and intelligence tests (see Table 9-1).

Projective Tests. The projective test is designed to reveal the structure of the client's mind by focusing on his verbalized projections onto ambiguous figures. Although these projections have been shown reliably to identify patterns of thinking, they only represent potential states and not the client's current or highest level of functioning. Projective tests are not standardized, objective, or predictive of behavior in actual situations.[17]

Personality Inventories. Personality inventories are standardized, objective tests usually in the form of a questionnaire, that measure attitudes, inhibitions, and action tendencies. The liabilities of personality inventories lie in the limited response choices offered by these tests and the

artificial nature of the situation in which the questions are asked. Nevertheless, these tests have been shown to be reliable indicators of thought patterns and potential behavior.

Intelligence Tests. Intelligence tests measure intellectual functioning on verbal and nonverbal levels. These tests are standardized according to age but do not usually take into account sociocultural influences on the individual's vocabulary and reasoning. The purpose of administering intelligence tests to a psychiatric-mental health client is to determine the role of intellectual functioning in the development and existence of his problem.[24] (The reader will find examples and uses of a variety of psychological tests in Table 9-1.)

Mental Status Exam

The mental status exam is an assessment tool that was developed primarily from the medical model perspective. This examination aims to identify psychopathologic symptoms and also assesses the current mental status of the client (*i.e.*, his intellectual and emotional functioning). The tool is useful for identifying acute psychotic features of the client quickly and for distinguishing functional conditions from organic conditions.

As with all assessment tools, the significance of the results of the mental status exam can only be understood in

Table 9-1. **Psychological Tests**

PSYCHOLOGICAL TEST	CATEGORY	AREA ASSESSED	DESCRIPTION	PURPOSE
Rorschach	Projective	Pattern of thinking; level of development of thinking, reasoning and association	The client interprets ambiguous figures (inkblots).	To rule out psychosis; to determine potentialities of personality
Thematic Apperception test (TAT)	Projective	Pattern of thinking; responses to hypothetic situations	The client interprets ambiguous figures (drawings).	To rule out psychosis; to predict social response patterns
Draw-a-Person test	Projective	Pattern of thinking; self-image and image of others	The client draws self or another person, or an anonymous human figure.	To rule out organic impairment; to determine image of self or others; to rule out psychosis
Bender–Gestalt	Projective	Cognitive abilities; pattern of perception; coordination of intellectual, perceptual, and psychomotor functions	The client is asked to copy nine designs from memory or with design in sight.	To rule out organic brain syndrome; to differentiate some psychotic states
Sentence Completion/Word Association	Projective	Prominent themes and patterns of thinking; areas of thought that are threatening to client	The client is asked to respond spontaneously to a stated or written word or phrase with an associated word or phrase.	To identify areas of fear, preoccupation, and image of self and others; to rule out psychosis; to rule out personality disorder
Minnesota Multiphasic Personality Inventory (MMPI)	Personality inventory; objective	Personality patterns; characteristic responses to stress	Paper-and-pencil standardized test	To rule out dangerous personality patterns, such as suicidal or homicidal thinking, or bizarre psychotic states; to identify general response patterns
Tennessee Self-Concept Scale	Personality inventory; objective	Personality patterns; image and concept of self in relation to others and the environment	Paper-and-pencil standardized tests	To rule out dangerous personality patterns or potentials of behavior; to predict behavior in social situations; to define feelings about self
Wechsler Adult Intelligence Survey	Intelligence test	Intelligence; cognitive abilities	The client completes 11 tasks that give overall information about intelligence.	To assess current intellectual functioning, as compared to potential; to rule out organic impairment; to rule out intellectual impairment due to functional psychosis
Sanford–Binet Intelligence Test	Intelligence test	Intelligence; cognitive abilities	This paper-and-pencil test is only accurate for clients under age 16.	To assess current intellectual functioning, as compared to potential; to assess ability to learn in a structured setting

relation to the client's history, sociocultural status, and physical condition. A hearing impairment, religious belief or custom, or subcultural jargon may cause the nurse–assessor to misinterpret the client's response as evidence of psychopathology, when the response actually represents normal behavior for him.

Level of education, degree of social interaction, and environmental stimulation at home are other factors that influence client responses. The assessor evaluates test results and the client's current level of functioning in relation to these factors and compares the client's responses to the average responses of a person of similar age, religion, ethnic group, and past experiences. (See the insert Mental Status Exam for the categories and approaches to explore each area of client functioning.)

Self-Assessment

Ever since the civil rights movement of the 1960s, people have been increasingly aware of their personal rights, including the right to understand one's body and mind and determine one's own health care. The nursing profession has fostered this self-help movement by emphasizing client education and support, rather than labeling and directing the client.[22]

This self-help trend is also evident in the assessment process. Today's professional nurse may encourage the cli-

Mental Status Exam

The following general categories should be explored during the mental status exam. Suggestions for pursuing each area are included.

Appearance. General appearance, grooming, motor behavior, mannerisms, posture, gait (Assess through general observations and recorded as a general impression.)

Behavior. Speech patterns, tone of voice, use of slang, flow of speech, eye contact, body language, general behavioral responses to others and environment (Assess through general observation; compare findings to the client's usual behavior.)

Orientation. Awareness of reality of person, place, time, situation, relationship with others (Assess through direct questioning.)

Memory. Immediate recall, recent memory, remote memory (Assess through direct questioning.)

Sensorium. Ability to attend and concentrate; perception of stimuli—internal and external (Assess through direct questioning.)

Perceptual Processes. Processing of information received through sensorium; includes awareness of self and one's thoughts, reality, and fantasy (Assess by asking questions about delusions, illusions, and hallucinations.)

Mood and Affect. Mood refers to the prevailing emotion displayed. Affect refers to the range of emotion displayed, (happy, sad, unchanging). Emotion refers to subjective physiological changes in response to thoughts and perceptions. (Assess through observation and judge the appropriateness of the behavior in relation to the client's usual behavior.)

Intellectual Functioning. General fund of knowledge; cognitive abilities, such as the ability to calculate simple arithmetic problems; ability to abstract, or think symbolically and according to categories of association (Assess through direct questioning, such as requesting the client to solve simple math problems or interpret a simple proverb or analogy.)

Thought Content. Recurrences of topics of thinking, themes of conversation (Assess by observing what the client discusses spontaneously in conversation.)

Thought Processes. Stream of conscious or mental activity, as indicated in speech (Observe for rate, flow, associations made, and ability to pursue a topic logically.)

Insight. Awareness of one's own responsibilities and abilities, especially regarding the current area of concern; ability to analyze problem with objectivity. (Ask the client to explain the current problem.)

Judgment. This refers to decision-making abilities, especially regarding delaying gratification for an ultimate gain. Describe the style as impulsive, rational, methodological, or "trial-and-error." (Assess by asking the client what he would do in dilemmas requiring important decisions involving personal welfare, such as if he inherited a large sum of money or smelled smoke in a theatre.)

(Taken from Crary WG, Johnson CW: The Mental Status Exam. In Johnson CW, Snibbe JR, Evans LE (eds): Basic Psychopathology: A Programmed Text, pp 50–89. New York, Spectrum, 1975. Also taken from Margolin C: Assessment of Psychiatric Patients. J Emergency Nursing 6 (July–August): 30–33, 1980)

ent to assess himself through the use of such tools as life-stress scales and assertiveness scales. Many self-assessment scales center on the client's wellness and strengths and help him identify and interpret his own personality, perceptions, anxieties, coping patterns, and needs.

Another tool of self-assessment is called the algorithm, which offers a structured decision-making method for self-assessment, self-diagnosis, and evaluation of need for further assessment and treatment.[3] The algorithm is sometimes referred to as a "decision-making tree." Individuals may use the decision-making tree to help them reach sensitive, personal decisions as objectively as possible, while considering the possible results of each option (see Fig. 9-1). Algorithms provide a model for understanding such an abstract concept as a diagrammatic definition.[30]

The liabilities of these self-assessment approaches concern the apparent simplification and generalization of very complex and individually specific situations. In addition, the value of all self-help assessment techniques depends on the client's insight, self-awareness, and motivation. These approaches assume that, with appropriate education and support, the individual has the potential for accurate self-assessment, self-diagnosis, and self-improvement.

The Interview

The most important assessment tool is the interview process. The hypothesis method of structuring the interview insures that no essential information is overlooked; it also gives the client an opportunity to "tell his story" in response to open-ended questons.

The findings of social research have defined the qual-

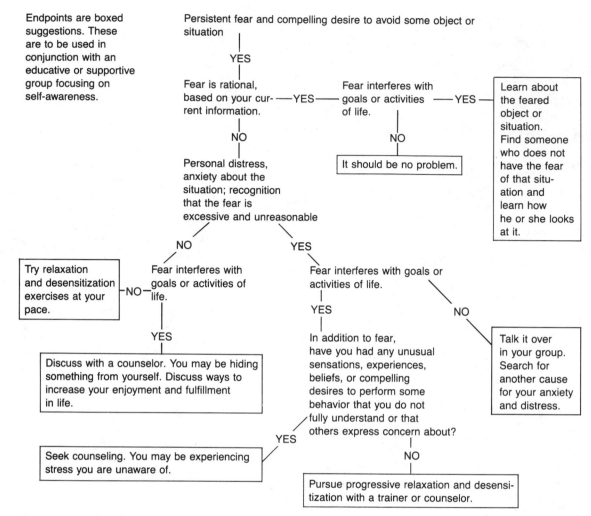

Figure 9-1. *Algorithm for fear and phobia.*

ities, appearance, and attitudes of an effective interviewer.[25] The interviewer's sensitivity and skill can be developed through training. The critical element in the psychiatric-mental health interview is the human element—spontaneity, warmth, and caring. The goal of an interviewer is to develop these qualities to such an extent that they become a part of her, so that they flow with the qualities she has always owned.

Conducting the Interview. The interview is a purposeful, goal-directed interaction between two people.[31] A powerful implication in this definition is that both participants share actively in the process, and each is influenced by the other. The relationship-building interaction of nurse and client determines the success or failure of the interview as an assessment tool.

Professional therapeutic relationships differ from social interaction. The professional interview has a select purpose, unlike the casual nature of social interaction. The professional interview also has unity, progression, and the-

matic continuity.[31] The roles of interviewer and client in the interview do not reflect the equality seen in most social situations; the client may, in fact, view the interviewer as the "expert" and feel in awe of her. Spontaneity, always present in human interaction, may be less evident during the interview. Social taboos, which usually demand that a person avoid the discussion of unpleasant facts and feelings, do not apply during a professional interview.

In a professional relationship, therapeutic rapport must progress from a superficial to an intimate level in a brief period of time to enable the client to feel comfortable in self-revelation. The image of the nurse as a professional facilitates the client's acceptance of such an unusual situation. To foster the development of this relationship, the nurse maintains a nonjudgmental attitude and responds to self-disclosure with honesty, support, and acceptance.[5] The client discloses at his own rate and in whatever manner is comfortable for him. The professional nurse usually limits self-disclosures to demographic data and here-and-now perceptions.[26]

The Role of the Nurse–Interviewer. Either in an overt or subtle manner during the interview, the content, or factual aspect, of the interaction is related to the process, or relational aspect, of the interaction. The nurse–interviewer must continuously observe both major levels of interaction—process and content—that take place. The nurse's subjective emotional responses often serve as a barometer to assess these two levels of interaction.[12] The nurse's experience of comfort during the interview probably reflects the client's feeling of security; her experience of anxiety or fear probably indicate that he is uneasy or lacking control of angry impulses. Maturity and self-awareness help the nurse distinguish between personal conflict and an honest sharing of the client's experience.

The nurse assumes a participant–observer role during the interview. On one hand, the nurse empathizes and imagines the client's experience and the expectations placed on him by self and society. On the other hand, the nurse observes the progression of the relationship, the client's patterns of interaction, the information he discloses, and her own subjective responses to him. Therefore the nurse participates actively in the interaction of the interview while still observing it. It is necessary to attend to the client's cues that indicate his preferences for timing (when to discuss what topic), pacing (how fast or slow to proceed with the data gathering), and his expectations and needs.

Skills of the Nurse–Interviewer. A client usually prefers an active, friendly interviewer who verbalizes minimally and uses effective communication techniques.[36] The functions of communication techniques during the interview are to assist the client make transitions in his thinking, label amorphous experiences, and gain a clearer understanding of the situation.[15] The key elements in facilitative communication include the following.

Careful listening
Attending
Demonstration of sincere interest in the importance of
    the client's words

The nurse–interviewer expresses the quality of attentiveness through eye contact, body language, verbal feedback, and the appropriate use of silence.

Other techniques of facilitative communication are concreteness (*i.e.*, the interviewer's specificity of communication) and persistence in requesting the client to describe feelings and events in specific, rather than vague or abstract, terms.

Immediacy, a critical skill, refers to the interviewer's ability to recognize feelings and thoughts of immediate importance to the client and to deal with those issues first. Immediacy also facilitates data gathering, because the client distracted by strong emotion cannot concentrate on the interview.

Experiential and didactic confrontations are also techniques that facilitate authentic relationships. A didactic confrontation occurs when the interviewer objectively offers the client relevant information to correct misinformation. Experiential confrontation involves the nurse's consistently pointing out discrepancies and generalizations in the client's conversation as they occur; this provides first-hand and immediate feedback.[15] (The reader is encouraged to refer to Chapter 3.)

Client Expectations of the Interviewer. Client expectations influence the interview process. At least initially, clients respond more positively to interviewers who meet their expectations and preferences.[33] The preferred image of the nurse–interviewer is that of an expert who is confident in personal and professional roles.[9] The client prefers the professional who conveys warmth and authentic concern and, simultaneously, maintains emotional objectivity.[31] This quality of *emotional objectivity* is the ability to express feelings and responses about the client in a professional and nonjudgmental manner.[2]

The nurse is expected to be competent at starting an interview and keeping the flow of conversation moving.[30] Clients tend to feel uncomfortable during lengthy pauses in conversation, unless the silence is obviously allowing the client to reflect on a question or response.

The client expects the nurse–interviewer to be knowledgeable about human behavior and to interpret *his* behavior, in particular, within the proper context. The client also expects the interviewer to realize that the client is an "expert on himself."[2] The nurse should recognize her powerful position, the client's relative dependency, and the importance of ethics and self-responsibility in accepting the client's trust.[25]

The effects of an interview may be therapeutic or deleterious. A personal and professional code of ethics guides the nurse's actions in the following ways.

1. The nurse does not engage in social, physical, or business contacts with the client.
2. The nurse respects the client's right to confidentiality.
3. The nurse determines when it is necessary to refer a client to another professional.
4. The nurse accepts the role of client advocate and teaches and supports the client regarding his rights.

Finally, the mental health professional is aware that clients seldom fit the ideal image (*i.e.*, the energetic, verbal, motivated partner in the interview process). To work effectively with an uncooperative client, the mental health care provider must find his areas of motivation and nurture them.

Stages of the Interview

Introductory Stage. The introductory stage of the interview consists of the client and interviewer introducing themselves, stating their goals and expectations, and discussing the purposes of the interview. This stage is crucial because it allows the client to dispel or maintain his expectations and establish the rules and roles of the interview relationship. For example, the interviewer informs the client how long the interview will last. During this initial stage, the interviewer "scans" the client, gathers superficial information about the problem, and makes general observations of the client.

Working Stage.   The second stage of the interview is the middle or working phase. This stage begins when the client permits a serious pursuit of the problem, to which the interviewer responds with therapeutic skills of problem identification or clarification. During this phase, the nurse–interviewer focuses in depth on the emergence and development of the problem, the extent of disruption caused by the problem, and the client's approaches to the problem thus far. The nurse also assesses the strengths and resources of the client and begins to consider possible intervention strategies.

During the working phase, the nurse and client influence each other; a process of change occurs in both. This is the enactment of the participant–observer role.[29] The middle stage of the interview concludes with an exploration of all potential problems not previously examined.

Termination Stage.   The termination stage of the interview begins with a reminder to the client that the interview will soon be ending. This reminder should be given 5 to 10 minutes before the interview is scheduled to end or 5 to 10 minutes before the interviewer has decided to terminate it based on the client's responses. The interviewer then reviews and summarizes what has been accomplished and asks the client to add, clarify, or correct information reviewed. The need for follow-up sessions or referrals to other professionals is suggested at that time.

Finally, in recognition of the difficulty the client endures in revealing so much of himself and his past experiences, the nurse–interviewer informs the client that she appreciates his cooperation and intrinsic worth. This should consist of a positive and entirely truthful statement that gives the client something to go away with and helps him to feel better because of the interviewer.

Professional Handling of Client Data.   The information gathered in a nursing assessment should be treated as vital and strictly confidential material, even if it does not seem to be of a "private" nature.

Recording Interview Data.   Recording of data gathered during the interview can be completed in a variety of ways, depending on the needs and wishes of the client and nurse. One method is for the interviewer to keep a verbatim written recording. This method, although allowing accuracy, disrupts the flow of the interview process. Sometimes, students of mental health professions use this method as a learning experience to examine communication patterns.

Another method of recording is to use a third-person nonparticipant to record the verbatim interview conversation and to note, as much as possible, the nonverbal communication. The presence of the third person, however, may significantly alter the dynamics of the interview, particularly trust, and may be perceived as a violation of psychological privacy.

Probably the most widely used approach is the recording of brief notes throughout the interview or the making of "mental notes," followed by the writing of a summary of verbal and nonverbal client data later. Although this method offers greater comfort for the client, it may not provide optimal accuracy.

Audio- and video-tape recordings are the most reliable methods of recording during the interview. Videotaping allows a review of the session and gives the most complete information about the client's communication within the environmental context. Audiotaping, however, is usually seen as a less formidable recording method than videotaping. Before planning to tape record an interview, the nurse must ascertain that institutional policies permit taping and that the client has given his approval by signing a permission form. The permission form should clearly state the purpose of the taping, who will have access to the tape, and when and how the tape will be destroyed or erased. Problems related to taping an interview include client discomfort, irritation, and suspicion.

Regardless of the method of recording chosen, a concluding summary should complete the report. The summary should consist of the following.

1. A demographic description of the client, such as age, sex, and so forth.
2. Major patterns of behavior
3. A comparison of the client's behavior to accepted norms
4. Suggestions for further assessment, referral, or intervention strategies
5. Subjective impressions of the client, identified as such
6. Client strengths and resources, as well as problem areas of functioning
7. A reasonable approach to the client's situation

Recording of assessment information, including a thorough client history, description of the problem, and the client's abilities and potential sources of motivation, allows for an accurate analysis of the data. Gathering client-assessment data enables the nurse to formulate accurate diagnoses, which form the bases for nursing care plans.

Summary

This chapter has discussed the first step of the nursing process and has examined its characteristics, components, and structure. The major emphases of the chapter have included the following points.

1. Nursing assessment is the gathering of client data, which is then classified and categorized in the analysis step of the nursing process.
2. Nursing assessment explores the needs, problems, and adaptive resources of the individual, and the means by which the nurse may help the client move to a higher level of health.
3. Identification and clarification of the client's problems are major purposes of nursing assessment.
4. Through the hypothesis approach to assessment, the nurse–interviewer explores client functioning in the psychological, social, biologic, behavioral, cognitive, and cultural areas of his life.
5. A variety of assessment tools should be used to conduct a comprehensive assessment of the psychiatric–mental health client.
6. The communication and relationship skills of the nurse comprise the most essential element of the assessment interview.

References

1. Argyle M, Dean J: Eye Contact, Distance, and Affiliation. Sociometry 28: 289–304, 1965
2. Bernstein L, Bernstein RS, Dana RH: Interviewing: A Guide for Health Professionals, 2nd ed. New York, Appleton-Century-Crofts, 1974
3. Blattner B: Holistic Nursing. Englewood Cliffs, NJ, Prentice-Hall, 1981
4. Burgess AW, Lazare A: Community Mental Health. Englewood Cliffs, NJ, Prentice-Hall, 1976
5. Coad-Denton A: Therapeutic Superficiality and Intimacy. In Clinical Practice in Psychosocial Nursing: Assessment and Intervention, pp 23–48. New York, Appleton-Century-Crofts, 1978
6. Crary WG, Johnson CW: The Mental Status Exam. In Basic Psychopathology: A Programmed Text, pp 50–89. New York, Spectrum, 1975
7. Cronback LJ: Essentials of Psychological Testing, 3rd ed. New York, Harper & Row, 1970
8. Diagnostic and Statistical Manual of Mental Disorders, 3rd ed. Washington, DC, The American Psychiatric Association, 1980
9. Dixon DN, Heppner PP: Effects of Client Perceived Needs and Counselor Role on Clients' Behaviors. J Counseling Psychology 25: 514–519, 1978
10. Dubbert P, Eisenmann E: The Mental Health Assessment Interview. In Backer B, Dubbert PB, Eisenmann E (eds): Psychiatric Mental Health Nursing: Contemporary Readings, pp 5–33. New York, Van Nostrand Reinhold, 1978
11. Feinsterheim H: The Initial Interview. In Lazarus A (ed): Clinical Behavior Therapy, pp 22–40. New York, Brunner/Mazel, 1972
12. Francis G, Munjas B: Manual of Socialpsychologic Assessment. New York, Appleton-Century-Crofts, 1976
13. Gilmore SK: The Counselor-in-Training. New York, Appleton-Century-Crofts, 1973
14. Hall ET: The Anthropology of Manners. Scientific American 192: 84–90, 1955
15. Hubble M, Gelso C: Effect of Counselor Attire in an Initial Interview. J Counseling Psychology 28: 581–584, 1978
16. Lazare A: The Psychiatric Examination in the Walk-In Clinic: Hypothesis Generation and Testing. Arch Gen Psychiatr 33 (January): 96–102, 1976
17. Maloney MP, Ward M: Psychological Assessment: A Conceptual Approach. New York, Oxford University Press, 1976
18. Margolin C: Assessment of Psychiatric Patients. J Emergency Nursing 6 (July–August): 30–33, 1980
19. Mehrabiam A: Inference of Attitudes from the Posture, Orientation, and Distance of a Communicator. In Argyle M (ed): Social Encounters, pp 103–118. Oxford, England, Aldine Publishing, 1973
20. Miller JF, Hellenbrand D: An Eclectic Approach to Practice. Am J Nurs 81 (July): 1339–1343, 1981
21. Nishiura E, Whitten C, Jenkins D: Screening for Psychosocial Problems in Health Settings. Health and Social Work 5 (August): 22–28, 1980
22. Orem D: Nursing: Concepts of Practice. New York, McGraw-Hill, 1971
23. Reynolds J, Logsdon J: Assessing Your Patients' Mental Status. Nursing 79 9 (August): 26–33, 1979
24. Sands W: Psychiatric History and Mental Status. In Freedman A, Kaplan H (eds): Diagnosing Mental Illness, pp 20–40. New York, Atheneum, 1972
25. Shapiro MB: Assessment Interviewing in Clinical Psychology. Brit J Soc Clin Psychology 18 (June): 211–218, 1979
26. Simonson NR: The Impact of Therapist Disclosure on Patient Disclosure. J Counseling Psychology 23 (January): 3–6, 1976
27. Sommer RK: The Distance for Comfortable Conversation: A Further Study. Sociometry 25: 111–116, 1962
28. Stevens B: First Line Patient Care Management. Wakefield, Massachusetts, Contemporary Publishing, 1976
29. Sullivan HS: The Psychiatric Interview. Swick H, Gawel P, Gawel ML (eds) New York, WW Norton, 1954
30. Vickery DM, Fries JF: Take Care of Yourself: A Consumer's Guide to Medical Care. Reading, Massachusetts, Addison-Wesley, 1977
31. Weins A: The Assessment Interview. In Weiner I (ed): Clinical Methods in Psychology, pp 3–61. New York, John Wiley and Sons, 1976
32. Wilson H, Kniesl C: Psychiatric Nursing. Menlo Park, California, Addison-Wesley, 1979
33. Ziemelis: Effects of Client Preference and Expectancy Upon the Initial Interview. Counseling Psychology 21: 23–30, 1974

Chapter 10
Analysis/Nursing Diagnosis

It has been said and written scores of times, that every woman makes a good nurse. I believe, on the contrary, that the very elements of nursing are all but unknown.

> Florence Nightingale,
> Notes on Nursing: What It Is and What It Is Not

Sharon Byers

Chapter Preview

Analysis is a cognitive process, utilizing skills of critical thinking. The second step of the nursing process focuses on analysis of the data so that a nursing diagnosis may be established. The nurse demonstrates comprehension of the significance of the information gained from the client, applies theoretical knowledge in comparing the client's status with established norms, describes client information in terms of various categories and classes, synthesizes new categories and descriptive labels to assign to categories, and evaluates actions, needs, and possible gaps in care.

The formal step of analysis, or nursing diagnosis, follows the initial step of assessment and verifies that behaviors have been observed in their proper contexts and placed in appropriate clusters or categories. The nurse next formulates or chooses a suitable label or diagnosis, either according to broad guidelines or through the use of a taxonomy. Nursing's use of various diagnostic systems and the accepted diagnostic system of psychiatry (Diagnostic and Statistical Manual, Third Edition [DSM-III]) are discussed in this chapter.

Learning Objectives

On completion of this chapter, the reader should be able to accomplish the following.

1. Identify and describe the steps of the cognitive process of analysis

   Examination
   Synthesis
   Categorization
   Evaluation

2. Discuss the importance of formal analysis in the diagnostic process
3. Formulate a client problem list based on analysis of client data and review of strengths, resources, and motivations
4. Discuss the advantages and disadvantages of applying diagnoses to clients
5. Explain the use of the five axes of the DSM-III classification of psychiatric diagnoses
6. Define nursing diagnosis
7. Compare various formats of writing nursing diagnoses

   Problem statement
   Problem–etiology–sign/symptom
   Alternatives

8. Formulate a nursing diagnosis based on client assessment data

Analysis of Client Information

The analysis phase, also called the nursing diagnosis phase, is probably the step of the nursing process least discussed in the nursing literature; however, recent journal articles and books have begun to focus on defining and categorizing nursing diagnostic labels.

Is one reason for the dearth of literature on clinical analysis in nursing due to nurses' inclination to prefer to use intuition rather than more scientific or rigid methods of clinical thinking?[17] Computerization and other complex changes in the health care system are prompting greater accountability in the health care professions. Health care disciplines are reviewing their boundaries and attempting to clarify the processes that uniquely define them. The student is often expected to emerge on the health care scene at an advanced level of functioning, requiring that cognitive processes that come naturally with experience must be defined operationally to enable the novice to demonstrate proficiency.

Cognitive Processes Comprising Analysis

Analysis of assessment data includes several cognitive processes—examination, synthesis, categorization, and evaluation.[14] Examination involves taking apart pieces of information, studying the data to determine relationships with other pieces of information, and placing the information within its proper context. During synthesis, pieces of information are reassembled according to their relationships. Categorization requires the clustering of pieces of information according to common themes and their similarities and differences. Evaluation is the appraisal of the analytical processes and outcomes for applicability to client problems and needs.

Examination

In the process of examination, the nurse reviews client information for its significance, its reliability, and its validity. What, the nurse asks, is the data's relevance to the client's stated problem and the nurse's initial clinical impression? Significance of client information is also examined according to the following.

1. Priority of importance to the client's current situation
2. Immediacy of need for resolution
3. Pertinence to the stated complaints of the client
4. Limitations of the clinician and the clinical setting
   The client's pattern of behavior is examined during this step of analysis. The nurse also explores various feeling states associated with the behaviors, possible motivations for the behavior pattern, and thought patterns that result in the behavior or af-

fective state. In addition, the nurse weighs the cultural and social implications of the client's behavior.

Synthesis

Synthesis means that information is assembled to form a new understanding or a new concept. When the behavior pattern is analyzed, new relationships among behaviors may become clear. Several behavior patterns, seemingly unrelated, may now appear to have a common motivation or reinforcement, to be related to a common pattern of thinking, or to result from a common feeling state. These new understandings involve dissecting complex observations and putting them together in new relationships that guide the clinician in understanding the client's problem and its etiology. The experienced nurse has seen these patterns develop and unfold before and may, therefore, identify relationships readily. Conversely, the inexperienced nurse may need to examine, individually, each observation of the client according to possible motivation, feeling state, pattern of thinking, and sociocultural implications.[12]

Categorization

During the phase of categorization, new relationships are grouped according to common themes for ease of labeling.[15] A descriptive phrase is assigned according to these new groupings. The categories used may be derived from the particular assessment tool or from the format of the assessment interview. For example, several behaviors may indicate a clouding of the sensorium, and when seen as related behaviors, they may be described with one phrase or sentence rather than listing discrete behaviors.

A clinician's training and experience help create potential categories in which to place several experiences or observations. The scope or perspective of the discipline may limit possibilities unless the clinician has a broad vocabulary of descriptive terminology to apply when viewing appropriate categories.[14] Nursing, as a profession based on many different bodies of knowledge, uses descriptive terminology blended from a variety of disciplines. For example, terms referring to role conflicts are derived from sociology, terms referring to perceptual problems are derived from psychology, and terms referring to physiological imbalances are derived from biology. Categorization is a less formal step than diagnosis or formulation of a problem statement.

Evaluation

At this point, the entire process of analysis is reviewed for accuracy, thoroughness, and applicability to the client's situation. For example, a person's problems may be examined, synthesized, and neatly categorized; however, leaving out a detail of age, marital status, previous experience, or cultural background may result in an inappropriate diagnosis or problem statement.

During the evaluation phase, the nurse also adds the valuable perspective of intuition about a client to the analysis process. The nurse who is not besought with her own personal and esteem needs is free to observe and respond to the client's feeling-level responses. The self-aware nurse reliably detects the client's feelings of warmth, fear, suspicion, or anger. This intuitive information is examined in conjunction with the analysis of other assessment data, and, if validated, is instrumental in problem identification. If the perception is not validated, the nurse explores possible gaps in both client assessment data and her own self-awareness.

Formulating the Problem List

Formulating the problem list includes reviewing, analyzing, synthesizing, and categorizing data according to the client's problems, strengths, motivations, and resources. It is necessary, before beginning this discussion, to reflect on the nurse's role within the framework of a nursing philosophy and its impact on the nurse's approach to problem identification. Without this perspective, the listing of problems may become a useless theoretic exercise.

Although the clinician attempts to identify all problems, only those identified as problems by the client, with the exception of life-threatening problems, are relevant. Nurses espouse a philosophy of holism and self-determination of the client. This philosophy is translated as sensitivity to the experiences and needs of the whole person and respect for the individual values of the person and his right to make independent decisions. When nurses become overly "problem-oriented," they may evaluate the client's data from the value perspective of the nurse assessor, of nursing as a profession, or of society at large. It is widely accepted that, with the exception of superficial behaviors, lasting behavior change is motivated internally, not from external pressure. It is therefore critical to examine the context of each aspect of client information to prevent mislabeling an adaptive process or an intrinsic aspect of the personality as "a problem."

Reviewing Client Strengths

Strengths are those factors that help a client adapt and assist him toward a favorable prognosis, such as youth, physical health, freedom from previous psychiatric problems, and intelligence. Ability to form relationships, flexibility, and a wide range of problem-solving experiences are also strengths of the client. The nurse usually asks the client to list his strengths and reviews the assessment data to determine other strengths that he has not identified.

Strengths may be more difficult to identify in a long-term or regressed client. When working with this client, the nurse may need to rely heavily on historical information, such as the client's abilities and potentialities prior to the onset of the health disruption. The client's strengths are used in therapeutic planning to help him regain self-esteem, set goals for higher levels of functioning, and mobilize hope for change.

Reviewing Client Resources

The client's resources are external factors that are helpful to him in the adaptation process. These resources include his support networks, such as family and friends, financial stability, or proximity to community agencies. Resources may be real or potential strengths of the client (*i.e.*, not all friends and family members can be relied on during times of crisis or need). Sometimes, a resource, unused by the client, may not be realized as a strength. For example, if a client perceives a specific community agency as an unacceptable resource, that agency remains a potential resource and the nurse attempts to give the client necessary information that may alter his value judgment of the agency.

Reviewing Client Motivations

Psychiatric-mental health clients are not typically highly motivated for change. Many factors, including high levels of anxiety and difficulties in thinking productively, tend to cast a hopeless aura over the client. Motivation is generally present in one who expects to succeed. Most people who seek out mental health assistance have experienced, probably recently, failure of their coping abilities and lowering of self-esteem. This presents one of the most important challenges for the nurse—identifying potential sources of motivation for the client and encouraging him to adopt these as motivations for change. Because change produces anxiety, it is avoided by many, especially by those who are already experiencing a great deal of stress. Therefore, the client might be more highly motivated to maintain the status quo than to change, unless he recognizes and accepts potential sources of motivation.

Potential motivations might include present or previous interests of the client, aspects of independence he desires, decreasing of his medication, opportunity to engage in some enjoyable activity, or attention from the therapist or other mental health care provider. The latter source of motivation must be used cautiously, however, because the desired result is not for the client to "be good for the nurse," but to make lasting behavior changes.

These potential sources of motivation are both long- and short-term reinforcements. Long-term reinforcements are more appropriate for clients who can tolerate delayed gratification of their needs and are, therefore, self-motivated to some degree. These clients may need some stimulation and support from mental health professionals. Conversely, other clients require immediate gratification and short-term, specific reinforcement. Negative reinforcement or withdrawal from the client are not effective approaches to the client lacking self-motivation because they increase anxiety and reinforce a negative self-image, which are not conducive to learning or adaptive, lasting behavior change.

Evaluating Client Problems Within Their Contexts

During this evaluation step, the nurse reviews those concepts previously phrased as potential or real problems of the client and attempts to word them in concise, descriptive terminology. The nurse avoids jargon and relies on precise, clear descriptions of the problems. These may be listed with subproblems and should represent the client's behaviors that impede adaptation or interfere with independent functioning.

The problem list should be complete and should include those factors that are "constants" with the client, whether they are recognized by the client as a problem or are clearly distinguished as a behavior, attitude, or pattern of response resulting in dysfunction or disturbance in his adaptation. It should be remembered that these "problems" may not be resolved; on the contrary, the client may learn to hide the behavior or cope more adaptively with the resulting disturbance.

The Diagnostic Statement

A *diagnosis* is defined as a label that represents a disease, problem, or situation and is based on examination and analysis. The implication is that a diagnosis expresses the cause of some human misery and more easily leads the professional to a cure.

The labeling process, in any condition, involves the use of power. It may be construed that one person (*i.e.*, the professional) is reducing the complexities of another person to a single label. Labeling often results in self-fulfilling prophecies, stigma, chronicity, and isolation. Many people believe that the act of labeling is a form of social control that results in the removal of people from the mainstream of society and interference with their basic rights, because they exhibited behavior that is "socially unacceptable." Most people carry their labels with them for life; many are considered to be "former mental patients" whenever their behavior appears aberrant.

Regardless of philosophical implications, the usefulness of a diagnostic label is irrefutable. A diagnosis, like any label, allows a person to attach a cognitive image to an abstraction. Professionals from a variety of disciplines communicate more clearly due to the common language of diagnosis. The determination of a diagnosis may help the professional formulate intervention approaches, although this is not necessarily true.

In the field of mental health, the link between diagnosis and treatment is tenuous. People, after all, require individual attention in response to unique individual needs and characteristics, despite whatever diagnostic category they fall in. Also, certain psychiatric diagnoses are considered "untreatable," and the client is treated, or not treated, accordingly. It is important that any professional, especially one delving into human feelings and needs, view the client as a person with a problem, not as a diagnosis.

Although the term diagnosis is generally associated with the medical profession, the need for a diagnostic process in every helping profession has been well documented.[1] Diagnoses are peculiar to a disciplinary perspective and are generally tied to treatment approach preferences.

The Diagnostic and Statistical Manual, Third Edition

The psychiatric-mental health nurse frequently uses the American Psychiatric Association's Diagnostic and Statistical Manual, Third Edition (commonly called the DSM-III). This manual consists of a number coding system for psychiatric diagnoses (see the Case Study of Ella C. at the end of the chapter). Included also in the DSM-III is a clearly written text of diagnostic categories, which lists acceptable psychiatric diagnoses, suggestions for structuring a diagnosis and differentiating similar diagnoses, and specific behavioral criteria that must be met before a diagnostic label is assigned to a client. These criteria, along with a "multiaxial evaluation" system that offers a holistic view of the client, make this edition of the diagnostic manual a great improvement over what seemed to be a vague and value-laden system.[3] This edition also avoids the over-use of jargon and phrases descriptions in an atheoretical manner, which encourages professionals other than psychiatrists to use the system.[19] The student is encouraged to thoroughly review this manual.

Multiaxial Diagnosis

This major improvement in the manual consists of a five-axis system of diagnosis to insure that important information about the client as a whole person is included in both the labeling process and the interpretation of the label. Each axis lists a separate diagnosis of a different aspect of the client's situation, and together, the axes form one major holistic diagnosis in five parts.[19]

Axis I consists of the primary diagnosis of an acute disruption. This is any mental disorder other than a personality disorder or developmental disorder. *Axis II* describes the longer-standing personality disorder or developmental disorder that may be considered the client's "baseline."[19] Some clinicians list here, in descriptive terms, the personality type of the client to give a clear picture of a client whose personality does not meet criteria as a personality disorder. *Axis III* states the diagnosis of any physical condition, whether or not this condition seems to greatly affect the psychiatric status of the client. *Axis IV* indicates the severity of the psychosocial stressor within the past year. Many times, this is a precipitating event and indicates how fragile the client is. A clearly stated table is included with examples, and the stressor is rated on a range of "none" to "catastrophic." *Axis V* describes the highest level of adap-

tive functioning in the past year, allowing a view of the "premorbid personality," as well as an idea of how quickly and dramatically functioning has disintegrated. A table with descriptors and examples is included here also. The client's functioning within the last year is rated from "superior" to "grossly impaired."[19]

Diagnostic Criteria of the Manual

The diagnostic criteria offer the greatest advantage of the DSM-III. These criteria are statements that have been clinically demonstrated to be critical elements of the common behavioral syndromes. The criteria are essential characteristics that must be found in the client's pattern of behavior or experience before the client is to be assigned a particular diagnosis.

The diagnostic criteria are inclusive and allow room for individual differences within a pattern of behavior by including phrases such as "at least one of the following" or "for at least a 6-month period." They also focus on the determination of a significant change in the level of functioning. To assist in making the differential diagnosis, the criteria include statements that eliminate the client from another diagnostic classification, such as "absence of psychotic features" or "not due to another mental disorder."[3]

Nursing Diagnosis

Many theorists believe that nursing is still undecided about the primary area of concern of nursing practice. This slow evolution of the art and science of nursing has hindered efforts to develop a well-structured system of nursing diagnoses.[7] Such a system, or taxonomy, is not considered by all to be a positive addition to nursing practice because it discourages the use of intuition and that a labeling system cannot possibly include the variety of client responses that nurses address.[16] Others believe that a taxonomy is necessary as the first level of theory building, progressing toward a unified theory of nursing practice.[10] Such unity seems remote in the varied fields of nursing now, but it would strengthen nursing as a profession.

Another objection to a nursing taxonomy, especially in psychiatric-mental health nursing, concerns the fact that the DSM-III is already a highly descriptive and holistic tool. It has been suggested that psychiatric nurses spend their efforts further developing this tool instead of working on a separate taxonomy.[19] One objection to this approach is that the DSM-III is atheoretical, and is therefore not specific enough to fit the perspective of nursing. Some say nursing diagnoses could more clearly guide the practice of nursing and foster its development as an autonomous profession.

Taxonomies developed for nursing have been refuted or criticized by some nurses because of their noninclusive theoretical perspective, their absence of nursing theory, or their unwieldly nature.[11] Another objection is that most current systems do not accurately address the value system of nursing. Nevertheless, these criticisms and conflicts are considered by many to be a normal growth process in the development of nursing.[10]

The system being developed by the Task Force of the National Group for the Classification of Nursing Diagnosis is an ambitious effort drawing upon the work of many major nursing theorists and the expertise of nurses from all areas of the profession. Conferences are held by this group every 2 years to update and further develop their work.[9] Despite the incompleteness of this body of work, the reader is encouraged to become familiar with this system, as well as other systems of diagnosis developing within nursing. Hopefully, convergence of thought, brought on by clinical testing of such systems, will result in a unified system of diagnosis that better defines the profession, theory, and practice of nursing.[15]

A *nursing diagnosis* is a statement of a client's response pattern to a health disruption. This response pattern is one that is less than adaptive and can be interrupted through nursing intervention.[8] A nursing diagnosis is not a nursing problem, but a client problem that is stated in such a way as to guide the formulation of a behavioral objective or goal and the development of therapeutic nursing actions. The nursing diagnosis is the end-product of the analysis of the nursing assessment of a client.[6]

Nursing Diagnosis As a Problem Statement

Formulating the nursing diagnosis as the real or potential problems of the client may still be its most commonly used form in the clinical setting. It is discerned by comparing client behavior with norms appropriate for the client's situation or the client's normative baseline.[13] This form of nursing diagnosis generally reflects those aspects of the client that impede his progress toward the attainment of his own goals, or those aspects that are judged by others to represent a dysfunction or disability, often resulting in hospitalization for treatment.

The phrasing of the nursing diagnostic statement should be clear, concise, and descriptive and should avoid jargon and abstractions that are incomprehensible to non-nursing staff. The use of medical terminology is avoided because this is a statement reflecting a client problem in which the nurse can intervene through independent nursing measures. For example, schizophrenia may be considered a psychiatric diagnosis treated through psychiatric interventions, such as psychotropic medications. The regressed hygiene measures, limited social skills, and agitation in response to hallucinations, however, are client responses to the schizophrenic condition and can be treated with nursing interventions. Generally, the acting-out or withdrawn behaviors that the client exhibits in response to hallucinations and delusions are seen as problems amenable nursing treatment rather than the hallucinations or delusions themselves. (See the insert, Errors in Writing Nursing Diagnoses.)

Problem–Etiology–Sign/Symptom Format

The approach Problem–Etiology–Sign/Symptom (or P-E-S) format is being developed by the National Group for the Classification of Nursing Diagnosis.[5] The taxonomy devel-

Errors in Writing Nursing Diagnoses

Error	Example
Use of medical diagnoses, pathologies, treatments, or diagnostic procedures	Hallucinations related to schizophrenia
Wording nursing diagnostic statements in terms of nursing problems or client needs, goals, inferences, or symptoms	Need for constant attention related to insecure ego
Phrasing the etiologic statement so that it essentially repeats the problem, rather than stating the etiology	Sexual dysfunction related to inability to maintain an erection
Use of judgmental statements or statements implying legal responsibility in the nursing diagnosis	Fluid volume excess related to inadequate monitoring of IV fluids by nursing staff

(From Carpenito LJ: Nursing Diagnosis: Application to Clinical Practice. Philadelphia, JB Lippincott, 1983. Also from Marriner A: The Nursing Process: A Scientific Approach to Nursing Care, 3rd ed. St Louis, CV Mosby, 1983)

oped by this group is based on an assumption that the profession of nursing is aligned with the theory of "Unitary Man."[6] This theory basically addresses the holism of the individual in his relationship with the environment.[5] (The reader is referred to Classification of Nursing Diagnoses: Proceedings of the Third and Fourth National Conferences for an excellent discussion of the overall development of this approach.[9])

This taxonomy includes 50 nursing diagnoses (see the list below). The format of these diagnoses is a two-part statement—problem statement (first part), related to (joining phrase) etiologic statement (second part), followed by further descriptive signs and symptoms. The problem statement fits the stated criteria. The phrase "related to" is used instead of "due to" to avoid the implication of singular etiology; holistic principles hold that every aspect of the individual and his functioning is caused by many internal and external factors. Etiologic factors are underlying sources of the identified problem and are also amenable to nursing

intervention.[5] An example of this type of nursing diagnosis is *Sexual Dysfunction related to loss of body part.*

Sometimes, etiologic statements are deleted to guide nursing interventions more clearly and to avoid referring the nurse to dependent or interdependent nursing functions related to ordered medical interventions, such as medication administration. Instead, an aspect of the problem that is amenable to nursing intervention is listed. For example, instead of *Alteration in Cardiac Output: Decreased, related to congestive heart failure,* the nursing diagnosis would be stated as *Alteration in Cardiac Output: Decreased: Exercise intolerance.*[2]

Some client problems are so thoroughly developed in the most recent classification of diagnoses that they include etiologic statements, common signs and symptoms, expected outcomes of the nursing measures, and nursing interventions. Also included in the classification are problem statements that need no etiologic statement, such as *Rape Trauma Syndrome.* Some problem statements have many,

List of Nursing Diagnoses from the Fifth National Conference, 1984

Accepted Diagnoses

Activity intolerance
Airway clearance—ineffective
Anxiety
Bowel elimination—alteration in: constipation
Bowel elimination—alteration in: diarrhea
Bowel elimination—alteration in: incontinence
Breathing pattern—ineffective
Cardiac output—alteration in: decreased
Comfort—alteration in: pain
Communication—impaired verbal
Coping—ineffective individual
Coping—ineffective family: compromised
Coping—ineffective family: disabling
Coping—family: potential for growth
Diversional activity—deficit in
Family processes, alteration in
Fear (specify)
Fluid volume deficit—actual
Fluid volume deficit—potential
Fluid volume excess
Gas exchange—impaired
Grieving—anticipatory
Grieving—dysfunctional
Health maintenance, alteration in
Home maintenance management—impaired
Injury—potential for; poisoning, potential for; suffocation, potential for; trauma, potential for
Knowledge deficit (specify)
Mobility—impaired physical
Noncompliance (specify)
Nutrition—alteration in: less than body requirements

Nutrition—alteration in: more than body requirements
Nutrition—alteration in: potential for more than body requirements
Oral mucous membrane, alteration in
Parenting—alteration in: actual
Parenting—alteration in: potential
Powerlessness
Rape—trauma syndrome: rape trauma, compound reaction, silent reaction
Self-care deficit (specify level): feeding, bathing/hygiene, dressing/grooming, toileting
Self-concepts—disturbance in: body image, self-esteem, role performance, personal identity
Sensory perceptual alteration: visual, auditory, kinesthetic, gustatory, tactile, and olfactory perceptions
Sexual dysfunction
Skin integrity—impairment of: actual
Skin integrity—impairment of: potential
Sleep pattern disturbance
Social isolation
Spiritual distress (distress of the human spirit)
Thought processes—alteration in
Tissues perfusion—alteration in: cerebral, cardiopulmonary, renal, gastrointestinal, peripheral
Urinary elimination—alteration in pattern of
Violence—potential for

(From Kim MJ, McFarland GK, McLane A: Classification of Nursing Diagnoses: Proceedings of the Fifth National Conference, pp 472–524. St Louis, MO, CV Mosby, 1984)

varied etiologies and the nurse then develops the etiologic statement in response to the client's unique situation.[2]

Problems are worded to specify *actual,* or present, problems, as well as potential and possible problems. *Potential problems* are those frequently observed in clients with certain conditions or predisposing factors and alert the nurse to "observe for" and "prevent" them.[13] *Possible problems* are those indicated in the client but unconfirmed by existing data.[2]

Sometimes, the problem statement is related to more than one distinct, identified etiology. In this case, all of the etiologies are listed, such as *Ineffective Individual Coping related to depression in response to identifiable stressors: Institutionalization, unsatisfactory support system, and inadequate psychologic resources.* Examples of problems seen in association with diagnoses are listed in the insert, Suggested Nursing Diagnoses and Client Problem List.

The primary aim of the nursing diagnosis is clear direction to nursing intervention. Clarity and individualization of nursing interventions are possible if the second part of the nursing diagnosis, the etiologic statement, is written in specific terms. Outcome criteria and behavioral objec-tives can be made more specific if the first part of the diagnosis, the problem statement, is also written in precise terms.[11] An accurate nursing diagnosis assists in determining the priority of care needs.[15]

Writing nursing diagnoses is a complex task for both experienced and novice nurses. A manual listing the taxonomy and explaining each diagnostic category should be consulted until the nurse becomes familiar with the diagnoses and their application in care planning. For additional and updated information on this taxonomy the reader is directed to: The Clearinghouse for Nursing Diagnoses, St. Louis University School of Nursing, 3525 Caroline Street, St Louis, Missouri, 63104. This group publishes a newsletter on a regular basis. Through this newsletter, nurses are encouraged to share their experiences applying these diagnoses to clients in clinical settings and to share their work toward developing other diagnostic categories.

Alternatives in Writing Nursing Diagnoses

Some institutions have devised their own categories of nursing diagnoses that are used consistently within their set-

Suggested Nursing Diagnoses and Client Problem List

The underlined phrase is the first part of a diagnostic statement and the phrases below are examples of problems seen in association with that diagnosis. The second part of the diagnostic statement begins with "related to" and represents, in some way, an etiology of the syndrome described in the first part of the diagnostic statement. The complete diagnosis represents a syndrome that is disruptive to the health or adaptation of the client.

Disturbance in Self-Concept

Potential for self-injury
Withdrawn behavior
Poor hygiene habits
Ruminations

Ineffective Coping

Acting out
Ruminations
Withdrawn behavior

Impaired thought processes

Acting out
Social isolation
Restless behavior

Fear
Poor social skills

Lack of Social Skills

Acting out
Aggressive behavior
Limited self-care abilities

Limited Communication Abilities

Acting out
Disorganized speech
Social isolation

Potential for Injury

Inability to communicate impending seizure

Note that problems appear under several different diagnostic statements. A phrase listed as a problem in one situation is listed as a diagnostic syndrome statement in another situation. Making these distinctions carefully and accurately are important when planning nursing interventions. Such decisions must be based on thorough knowledge of the client's problem, of the client as a diagnostic entity, and of the client as a person with a set of behavioral responses.

ting.[4] Other institutions offer not a taxonomy, but guidelines for constructing and using nursing diagnoses. The advantage of such approaches are the ability to individualize the nursing diagnosis according to the needs of the client and the descriptive clarity that can be achieved with the use of regionally familiar terms. Some nurses voice specific objections to the taxonomy developed by the national group; it is impossible, they say, to be descriptive when using such a taxonomy in every setting and field of nursing.[19] For example, many psychiatric nurses believe that psychiatric–mental health problems are underdeveloped in the taxonomy. To some nurses, the advantages of using a nationally standardized, unified system are paramount; to others, the unwieldy nature of the taxonomy diminishes its usefulness.

Current variations in the use of nursing diagnoses show that some nurses are deleting the use of qualifying phrases, such as "alterations in," "dysfunction in," and "impairment of," and are in favor of what they consider to be clearer, more descriptive terms, such as "limited," "inadequate," and "ineffective."[4] In some institutions, nurses prefer to use broader diagnostic statements, such as "impaired thought processes related to chronic delusional system," with specific substatements listed below the diagnosis, such as "suspicious of staff" and "distorted self-image." Other nurses prefer to incorporate medical terminology in nursing diagnoses in order to establish uniformity and in order to avoid developing another system of jargon, nursing terminology.[18]

The nursing diagnosis, whether formulated according to a developed taxonomy, a problem statement, or another approach, should be specific enough to give the nurse who is unfamiliar with the client a clear picture of his current status within the context of his problem and situation. If necessary, specific behavioral manifestations are listed to guide the nurse in developing specific behavioral objectives. The nursing diagnosis leads clearly to specific, individualized nursing interventions.

Summary

This chapter has discussed the second step of the nursing process as two distinct phases by which the nurse analyzes client assessment data, looks for patterns and incongruencies, categorizes the information into meaningful groups and subgroups of data, evaluates the entire process, and then formulates a diagnosis. Some of the major points of the chapter have included the following.

1. The analysis process is one carried out almost unconsciously by the experienced nurse, but it can be examined and adopted by the novice nurse.
2. Analysis involves the distinct cognitive processes of examination, synthesis, categorization, and evaluation.
3. The formulation of the problem statement involves choosing descriptive phrasing for problem behaviors, which are those identified by the client as problematic or are those seen by mental health care providers as disruptive or maladaptive.
4. Problem statements are compiled after reviewing client strengths, motivations, and resources within their appropriate context.
5. The DSM-III is an atheoretical classification system fostering a holistic approach to the client; it also includes specific behavioral criteria promoting greater accuracy in diagnosis.
6. The process of analysis culminates in the formulation of a diagnosis.
7. A nursing diagnosis is a statement of a client's response pattern to a health disruption.
8. Nurses are struggling to develop consistent approaches in writing nursing diagnoses, including a taxonomy developed by a national group, the use of a problem statement as a nursing diagnosis, and institutional variations on the approach adopted by the national group.

Case Study: Ms. Deborah K.

Analysis of Assessment Data

Examination

Ms. Deborah K., R.N., is a 30-year-old unmarried woman and a chiropractic student in her second year of school. She presented at the community mental health center complaining of anxiety attacks, withdrawal from significant relationships, headaches, sleep disturbances, and "feeling like I'm falling apart." These symptoms, of 5-weeks duration, lack a clearly identified precipitating factor. She stated that her primary affect is anger that is un-focused and pervasive. She reported the ending of a romantic relationship 3 months prior to the appearance of her symptoms, which, she stated, was in response to a mutual decision and acceptable to her. She also reported anxiety over finances and grades, compounded by her difficulty finding a job, which would fit with her demanding schedule.

Deborah is the middle child of a large Polish Catholic, upper-middle-class family. Most of her siblings are successfully employed, financially secure, and in stable marital relationships. There is no history of psychiatric disturbances of the client or other family members. The client has had successful intimate relationships.

By means of analysis, the nurse recognized the need for ongoing assessment throughout the development of a therapeutic relationship. Certain topics may be explored more openly and thoroughly after the nurse and client have established rapport and the client's symptoms have been somewhat controlled. The reduction of anxiety would allow introspection and learning.

Synthesis

There seems to exist a relationship among Deborah's anxiety attacks, physical complaints, and feelings of impending loss of control. Anger may or may not be related to frustrations experienced in school, financial worries, and the loss of a significant relationship, which may be perceived as a failure by the client. Anxiety may be related to her need for achievement and the high expectations set by herself and her family. No relationships among data seem to indicate severe psychopathology at this point.

This client has successfully dealt with responsibilities, intimate relationships, and normal living demands, and has been viewed as a high achiever. Single marital status is described as her choice due to her many personal goals and not having found a partner who would fit in that personal goal pattern.

Categorization

An appropriate descriptor of this client's experience, including her complaints of sleep disturbance, anxiety attacks, headaches, and "feeling like I'm coming apart," is *Anxiety Reaction*. This anxiety may also be placed in another category of *perception of loss of control*, as seen in the many obstacles to goal attainment in the client's life and the implications of her expectations of achievement and success. The subjective feeling of "coming apart" may be an indicator of this perceived loss of control.

The client's angry affect and withdrawal in relationships may be seen as "stress reactions" in response to a variety of frustrations.

It can be assumed by the previous personal and family history that the client's self-concept includes an achievement orientation in all areas of her life, which would be threatened during this period of mental and physical distress. This *threat to self-image* would result in anxiety, and might also lead the caregiver to place this problem in the category of *unrealistic or overly rigid expectations for self*. Considering the stress of graduate-level education, the expense and financial burden incurred in professional tuitions, and the overall impact these factors have on lifestyle and relationships, an expectation to succeed at all endeavors during this time could be termed *unrealistic*.

Evaluation

In this situation, the nurse working with Deborah K. would identify the need for further questioning and would identify the need for further exploration in the areas of goals and expectations of self, perceived need for control, previous experiences with disappointment, family relationships and expectations, and the recent romantic relationship. The impeding factor in this process seems to be the client's lack of insight, which is incongruent with her history and accomplishments. Further exploration of the client's prior experiences with failures, crises, or losses is indicated.

Problem List for Ms. Deborah K.

Strengths

1. Youth and physical health
2. No history of psychiatric disturbances of self or family members
3. Previous successful employment
4. Previous successful intimate relationships
5. Intelligence
6. Ambition and motivation
7. Short-term duration of symptoms
8. Adaptability to lifestyle changes
9. Generally high self-esteem and self-confidence
10. Previous positive experiences with health care system
11. Pleasant appearance and manner

Resources

1. Large, supportive, involved family
2. At least three, concerned, close friends
3. School counselors and resource people
4. Ability to earn money (if work can be scheduled around school commitments or in the event that she has to withdraw from school)
5. Community mental health center near her home

Motivations

1. Goal of becoming a chiropractor
2. Interest and belief in feedback from others
3. Goal of self-actualization

Problems

1. Overwhelming anxiety and lack of experience with, and knowledge of, coping skills
2. Withdrawal from friends
3. Possible unrealistic expectation of self and need to compete with family members
4. Lack of significant other to provide support
5. Real concerns and problems in meeting goals, possibly due to external causes
6. Possible grief or guilt over recent failure of romantic relationship
7. Apparent lack of insight regarding relationships between symptoms or origin of feelings

Case Study: Ms. Ella C.

Analysis/Nursing Diagnosis

An Assessment Report

Ella C., a 30-year-old woman appearing slightly older than her stated age, was admitted for the first time to City General Hospital Mental Health Unit. The client was accompanied by her sister, Mrs. Sadie R., who appeared concerned, but reluctant to obligate herself. Ms. C. has had no previous psychiatric admissions or treatment. Mrs. R. described her sister as "a loner" who has, in the past 6 months, appeared increasingly withdrawn, neglectful of her appearance, preoccupied, and disinterested in her environment. Ms. C.'s stated reason for admission was "I just can't go on." Mrs. R. stated that her sister lives alone in a rooming house, was employed by a shoe factory for 11 years until 4 months ago when she was "laid off," along with several hundred other workers. Ms. C. is currently on unemployment compensation, and has no insurance or cash savings.

Methods of Assessment

A mental status exam, a personal history, and an open-ended interview were used in the assessment process. Ms. C.'s sister was present during most of the history-taking. Ms. C. was interviewed according to hypotheses of psychological, social, biologic, cultural, and behavioral theories of the etiology of her problems.

Results of Assessment: Mental Status Exam

Ms. C. is a thin, poorly nourished, poorly groomed woman who states she has not eaten in 4 days. Her explanation for this behavior was "I don't care." Ms. C.'s gait, posture, and mannerisms are that of a much older woman, and convey an attitude of defeat. Ms. C. is oriented in all five spheres, is alert when spoken to, exhibits normal attention and concentration, denies any unusual experiences, sensations, morbid thoughts, suicidal thoughts, and complains only of extreme fatigue. Her memory appears intact on all three levels. Her mood is of despair, with physiologic complaints indicative of grief. Her affect is sad, with limited affective response to the environment. Intellectual functioning appears normal for the client's educational and occupational status. She was able to subtract by 3's from 100, although slow in her responses. Abstraction abilities are normal; she is able to compare apples and oranges, cats and trees; she can explain the proverb "A rolling stone gathers no moss." Ms. C. speaks in a soft voice, and psychomotor retardation is notable. Recurring themes of conversation are fatigue and sadness. Her judgment appears appropriate. She responded normally for her sociocultural group to the question, "What would you do if you inherited

$10,000?" Her insight appears poor, with the client blaming herself for the loss of her job, although this was clearly due to economic problems within the company.

Social History

Ms. C.'s parents were described by the client's sister as "uninvolved." The mother and father were of middle-income status, and both were killed in a car accident when the client was 8 years old. The client and her sister, then 16-years-old, were taken in by the maternal grandmother, who was described as "moody, always angry" by the client. The grandmother was reportedly of middle income, unemployed, and supported by her deceased husband's retirement.

The client's sister stated that Ms. C. had few friends while growing up but appeared happy. The client was reportedly punished frequently by the grandmother (especially for loud or "excessive" talking) by being sent to the basement or a similar place of isolation for over an hour. The client's sister feels this method of discipline increased Ms. C.'s shyness and social isolation.

The client's grandmother died suddenly of a "heart attack" when the client was 17 years old. Ms. C. and Mrs. R. lived in the grandmother's house for 2 years, until the client's sister's marriage, at which time the client moved out into a rooming house and began working for a shoe factory, where she was employed for 11 years.

Summary of Interview Findings

Although the client related in a distant fashion throughout the mental status exam and history, eye contact and mannerisms indicated increasing trust and comfort in the interview, as well as responsiveness to the interviewer. Ms. C.'s withdrawn behavior appears somewhat related to social learning from parents and grandmother and was reinforced by multiple losses. Ms. C. believes she was mistreated by her grandmother, and appears to hold some anger toward the deceased grandmother, although she denies any anger. The client appears to believe she has been defeated by life and is perhaps communicating her need to be dependent, nurtured, and given attention now as she has not been treated in her past. The vegetative signs of depression warrant consideration for psychotropic medication. Ms. C. denies suicidal thoughts, but she is obviously apathetic about her welfare. Although no disorder in thinking was noted, a schizophrenic condition cannot be ruled out at this time, in view of a lifelong pattern of isolation and withdrawn behavior. Ms. C. has an obvious deficit of social skills, is retarded in emotional development, and appears aware that she is different from most 30-year-old women, which is perhaps another source of stress. Ms. C.'s response to the interviewer indicates a potentially successful response to one-to-one counseling of an educative and supportive nature, at this time.

Summary and Suggestions

Ms. C. is a 30-year-old woman admitted to the Mental Health Unit for depression with no history of psychiatric admissions or treatment. She has a lifelong pattern of withdrawal and isolation. She has no friends and, although accompanied to the hospital by her sister, does not appear to have a substantial support system. The client is recently unemployed due to economic cut-backs. She is, perhaps, feeling victimized by multiple losses since childhood—of her parents, grandmother, home, relationship with sister, and now, job. There is evidence of poor adaptation to these crises. Ms. C. has appeared to be unsuccessful in completion of developmental tasks since the death of her parents, 22 years ago. Ms. C.'s immediate needs concern her anorexia and apathy about her own welfare. She will be referred for psychological examination to rule out a psychotic condition, and will be assessed for possible medication intervention. Ms. C. was assigned a primary nurse and will meet with the undersigned clinical nurse specialist in daily one-to-one sessions. A support network assessment will be considered, if approved by the client, involving interviews with the client's landlady, and seemingly involved neighbors, and the client's sister's family. No group interactions are suggested at this time.

Diagnoses

Nursing Diagnoses

These are to be modified as appropriate following further observation.

1. Alterations in self-concept, related to multiple losses and unresolved grief
2. Limited social skills, related to social isolation
3. Potential for organic injury, related to anorexia and apathy regarding self-welfare

Diagnostic and Statistical Manual, Third Edition Diagnoses

Axis I—269.33 Major depression, recurrent, with melancholia (Provisional: R/O schizophrenic condition)

Axis II—301.82 Avoidant personality disorder

Axis III—Poorly nourished, dehydrated state due to anorexia

Axis IV—Psychosocial stressors: Loss of job and economic security. Severity: 5, severe

Axis V—Highest level of adaptive functioning past year: 5, poor

References

1. Briar S: Toward Autonomous Social Diagnosis. Bulletin of the Menninger Clinic 40: 593–601, 1976
2. Carpenito LJ: Nursing Diagnosis: Application to Clinical Practice. Philadelphia, JB Lippincott, 1983
3. *Diagnostic and Statistical Manual of Mental Disorders*, 3rd ed. Washington, DC, The American Psychiatric Association, 1980
4. Dossey B, Guzzetta C: Nursing Diagnoses. Nursing, 81 11 (June): 34–38, 1981
5. Dossey B, Guzzetta C: Nursing Diagnosis: Framework, Process, and Problems. Heart Lung 12 (May): 281–291, 1983
6. Gordon M, Sweeney MA: Methodological Problems and Issues in Identifying and Standardizing Nursing Diagnosis. Adv Nurs Science 2 (October): 1–15, 1979
7. Henderson B: Nursing Diagnoses: Theory and Practice. Adv Nurs Science 1 (October): 75–83, 1978
8. Jauron GD, Mundinger MO: Developing a Nursing Diagnosis. Nursing Outlook 23 (February): 94–98, 1975
9. Kim MJ, Moritz DA (eds): Classification of Nursing Diagnosis: Proceedings of the Third and Fourth National Conferences. New York, McGraw-Hill, 1982
10. Kritek PB: Commentary: The Development of Nursing Diagnosis and Theory. Adv Nurs Science 2 (October): 73–79, 1979
11. Lunney M: Nursing Diagnosis: Refining the System. Am J Nurs 82 (March): 456–459, 1982
12. Mallick J: Nursing Diagnosis and the Novice Student. Nursing and Health Care 4 (October): 455–459, 1983
13. Marriner A: The Nursing Process: A Scientific Approach to Nursing Care, 3rd ed. St Louis, CV Mosby, 1983
14. Matthews C, Gaul A: Nursing Diagnosis from the Perspective of Concept Attainment and Critical Thinking. Adv Nurs Science 2 (October): 17–26, 1979
15. Perry A: Nursing Diagnosis Research. J Neurosurg Nurs 14 (April): 108–111, 1982
16. Shamansky S, Yanni C: In Opposition to Nursing Diagnosis: A Minority Opinion. Image: The Journal of Nursing Scholarship 15 (Spring): 47–50, 1983
17. Shoemaker J: How Nursing Diagnosis Helps Focus Your Care. RN 42 (August): 56–61, 1979
18. Williams AB: Rethinking Nursing Diagnosis. Nursing Forum 19: 357–363, 1980
19. Williams J, Wilson H: A Psychiatric Nursing Perspective on DSM-III. J Psychosoc Nurs Ment Health Serv 20 (April): 14–20, 1982

Chapter 11
Planning

Hold fast the time! Guard it, watch over it, every hour, every minute! Unregarded, it slips away, like a lizard, smooth, slippery, faithless, a pixywife. Hold every moment sacred. Give each clarity and meaning, each the weight of thine awareness, each its true and due fulfillment.

Thomas Mann,
The Beloved Returns,
1940

Anne Warner Toothaker

Chapter Preview

Through planning, the third step of the nursing process, the nurse determines from client data and diagnosis what needs to be accomplished, in what order it needs to be done, how it will be done, who will do what, and who is responsible for seeing that the plan of care is completed. The client entering the mental health arena is trying to find order in a chaotic existence; his world is awry and a change is necessary.

The nurse, through assessment and analysis, examines the client's physical and mental health, his social and economic stressors, and his functioning in his family, work setting, and community. Planning is the ordering of that information and the use of it, in collaboration with the client and the other members of the treatment team, in order to deal effectively with the client's mental health needs and problems.

Learning Objectives

On completion of the chapter, the reader should be able to accomplish the following.

1. Define the planning process
2. Differentiate between long-term and short-term goals
3. Discuss one's own ability to accept the values and goals of the client and his family
4. Formulate a nursing care plan including

   Client problems or nursing diagnoses
   Client outcomes
   Deadlines
   Nursing orders or approaches

5. Explain the use of standardized nursing care plans and the balanced service system in psychiatric-mental health care

Planning and the Nursing Process

This chapter is about planning—how to devise a plan, how to write a plan, how to rewrite a plan. Despite its commonality and universality, planning is a learned procedure. We learn to plan each day. Time-management and self-improvement courses devote much attention to the topic of planning. But what is it? *Planning* is the structuring of needs and problems in an orderly manner to achieve an end or a goal. A plan provides a map of how to reach a certain point and also provides reference markers to allow us to observe and evaluate progress along the way.

Organization

Planning is common to everyone; however, that very universality obscures its difficulty. If everyone can plan, why are some people more organized than others? The organiza-tion of a plan determines its workability. Through ordering or structuring, one chooses not to be chaotic, because chaos serves to defer decision-making, responsibility-taking, and choice.

Nursing care planning is intrinsic to the profession. A nursing plan provides structure to care-giving and measures what a nurse thinks and does. Just as the student plans for school work, the student nurse learns to plan care for and with the client. Planning is also a growth-producing experience because one's choices in weighing and selecting alternatives, in prioritizing, and in assigning values are, inherently, judgments. The plans of the nurse must reflect the choices of the client. Growth occurs as the nurse reflects, "Whose choices are these? Whose plan is this? Whose values does this plan reflect?"

Purposes of Planning

After a need is recognized or determined, and a goal (or goals) has been established, planning begins. The purposes of planning are to

1. establish the process or direction of change;
2. measure progress during the change.

Process of Planning

Planning is a learned activity. It necessitates the establishment of limits to determine how much detail is necessary and when detail becomes awkward, cumbersome, and constricting.

The writing of a plan enhances its workability and usefulness, because the concreteness of words on paper clarifies one's thinking. A written plan solidifies choices, keeps the planner on track, and serves as a reminder of where the planner has been and is heading.

Goal Setting

A long-term goal is determined when a need for change is established. Short-term goals provide direction and concreteness to change. (See the insert, Long-Term and Short-Term Goals.) They are determined by prioritizing, or choosing the order in which changes will occur. Completion of short-term goals is an indication that one is on the way to the accomplishment of long-term goals. The time frames that determine long-term and short-term goals depend on the end one wishes to achieve. A freshman student with a career goal measures short-term goals in terms of semesters or courses. A person facing spring house cleaning measures short-term goals in hours and days. Short-term and long-term goals are not inflexible time determinates.

Another important use of time is determining when a step in a plan will be completed or reviewed. A college student may set a long-term goal of graduation, but his short-term goal is passing a particular semester with a grade average of "B"; his daily study sessions are check points.

Long-Term and Short-Term Goals

Changes require goal setting. Long-term goals are oriented toward the future, whereas short-term goals are the markers of achievement that one attains along the way toward a goal. Goals are observable and measurable by others.

Long-Term Goals	Short-Term Goals
To achieve independence through employment	1. To graduate from high school or passing of equivalency exam 2. To graduate from an appropriate vocational or collegiate program 3. To apply for and attain a job
To increase ability to cope with stress, as demonstrated by decreased angry outbursts	1. To seek counseling and/or self-help group and attend meetings regularly 2. To identify one coping strategy and "try on" that coping method for 1 month
To improve organization and promptness	1. To organize and list responsibilities of home, work, school, children 2. To prepare general schedules based on prioritizing or responsibilities 3. To prepare individual daily schedules with daily tasks, appointments
To increase self-esteem by altering body image	1. To achieve ideal body weight 2. To improve body tone through daily exercise 3. To assess and redo wardrobe

Learning to plan is learning time management. Dealing with smaller time increments provides the manageability to achieve short-term goals and, eventually, long-term goals.

Method

Finally, the planner determines what will be necessary to accomplish the goals (*i.e.*, what method or approach will be needed). The method is a list of instructions one writes to oneself in order to complete the step. A junior student planning study time would not necessarily include on his list "bring pens, scratch pads, and calculator"; however, a freshman student might need those specifics in order to not waste study time. The method may be as individual as the planner. It is important to strive for detail and not take too much for granted.

Nursing Care Planning and Change

The nursing care plan is a remarkable document—a reflection of the professionalism of the nurse. It allows everyone to learn what nursing is and does and helps define nursing's relationship to other disciplines. The nursing care plan in the treatment of the mental health client is a fluid document. Treatment may be crisis-oriented, continuous, or both. Therefore, the plan reflects the current problems and goals identified by the client. This is a crucial aspect of psychiatric-mental health nursing. The plan is created *with* the client, not *for* the client. The essence of mental health treatment is change and change is unlikely unless the client and his family believe it is necessary.

Change is demanded and expected when the client seeks professional assistance. The circumstances surrounding the client become increasingly uncomfortable and intolerable. The client or family usually demand a very general change. "Change her," or "I can't control him anymore," parents may say about a troubled child. "I can't take it anymore," a woman may declare. The changes involved in psychiatric-mental health treatment are not unilateral. The changes in behavior made by the client affect his relationships and threaten his social structure.

Nurses teach, counsel, nurture, and facilitate change. Their ability to understand and appreciate other disciplines places nurses in facilitator roles between clients and various

Negotiating Goals: A Case Example

A 15-year-old boy, John, is brought to a mental health clinic for counseling because of his continued drug addiction and delinquent behavior. John is well-known to the courts and juvenile detention authorities and is brought to the clinic by his probation officer. John's parents have previously requested that the state assume his custody due to his uncontrolled behavior. The state has been reluctant to fulfill their request because of lack of funding. The probation officer has been meeting weekly with John, but there have been no changes in his drug addiction and truancy.

At the completion of the assessment, the treatment team identified the following objectives of each of the people involved with John.

1. John's goal: to be "left alone"
2. State's goal: to minimize the amount of money that will be spent for John
3. John's parents: to control John's behavior, "make him a good boy"
4. John's probation officer: to remove John from his case load
5. John's therapist: to eliminate John's drug addiction

The therapist is working with John individually, not with any family members. The overall treatment goal is written to reflect John's desire for independence, and is stated as a positive, concise, measurable goal.

Treatment Plan Goal: Increasing independence through responsible behavior as demonstrated by graduation from high school or obtaining a G.E.D.

Increasing independence allows John a means so that he can be "left alone." High-school graduation or the equivalent provides the means for measurement of his change. Allowing John to choose treatment outcomes permits him an active role in his treatment. Studying for his classes and exams will provide structure for John. His graduation from high school will promote future employment and meet the state's goal of spending less money. John will be meeting regularly with his counselor, which should reduce the amount of time he spends with his probation officer. The nurse in this situation acts as a liaison and communicates the treatment goal and rationale to all members of the mental health team.

---

therapeutic modalities. Nursing incorporates into the treatment plan all members of the mental health team. This liaison role assists the client and those close to him during the changing process.

When the client enters a mental health facility, the goals that are established must be understandable and acceptable to all those associated with the client. These objectives are established by the client, the family, and the treatment team; they also take into account the mores and support systems in the community. When many people are involved in the goal-setting process, negotiations leading to acceptable long-term objectives are imperative. (See the insert, Negotiating Goals: A Case Example.)

Hidden Agenda

Sometimes, a goal is not stated directly or even alluded to, but is a "hidden agenda," a secret. For example, before exposing a family secret or directly confronting a hidden rationale for therapy, the nurse carefully evaluates what purpose will be served by exposing the "secret." In this delicate situation, the benefit of discussing or exploring the hidden agenda must clearly outweigh the pain the client and family will endure. Because mutual trust and respect are critical for successful therapy and change, the nurse builds rapport and trust before approaching these problems.

Accepting Others' Values

The goals that are established in treatment planning must be acceptable to the client and his family. This requires that the nurse be familiar with, and accepting of, differing cultures and values. Learning about different cultures and examining one's own values are growing experiences and responsibilities of psychiatric-mental health nurses.

Formulating the Nursing Care Plan

Nurses use nursing care plans throughout their professional lives, from student to practitioner. The purposes of the care plan vary. During the educational process, the care plan assists the student identify health care problems and effective ways to deal with them. The nurse practitioner uses the care plan to communicate data about the client and therapeutic approaches to other members of the treatment team.[15]

Format of the Plan

A nursing care plan includes diagnosis (medical or nursing), client problems, expected outcomes (short-term and long-term goals), deadlines, and nursing orders.

The purpose of the care plan is to communicate information and rationale clearly, effectively, and quickly. For this reason, care plans are written in columns. Reading horizontally, the nurse can readily identify problems, goals, approaches, and deadlines, thereby expediting daily care.

Defining the Client Problem or Nursing Diagnosis

It is important that the nurse phrase the client problem or nursing diagnosis so that it conveys the same meaning to many people. The use of the simple declarative sentence insures that the team will begin at the same point. Defining the cause of the problem focuses the team in one direction. Establishing a causal tone also allows all members the freedom to address their areas of expertise and bias.

The problem statement or nursing diagnosis contains a "due to" clause. These words define the nurse's analytic ability. The observable problem is generally an indication of a more serious difficulty that must also be addressed. This statement reflects the effectiveness of the assessment and analysis processes and direct nursing approaches.

Defining Expected Outcomes

When defining outcomes, the nurse is actualy stating short-term treatment goals. The outcome statement requires a measurable action by the client that is observable by other persons. Outcomes are client-related and the nurse reflects, once again, "Is this best for the client? Whose choice is this?"

Defining Deadlines

Time clarifies, solidifies, and anchors a plan. Without deadlines for completion or evaluation, a plan is an idea. Deadlines are not absolute, but serve as a reminder for the nurse. Deadlines may be instructions of when to evaluate or record progress. Frequently, deadlines structure the type of care the nurse provides for a client.

Delineating Nursing Orders or Approaches

Nursing orders or approaches define what nurses do—their judgments, actions, and choices. Included in the nursing orders may be statements of activities performed by other members of the mental health team.

The mental health nurse is in a unique position to be familiar with many aspects of the client's treatment plan—medical, psychologic, and social. The challenge to the nurse is to include in the care plan orders, which are client-centered, approaches that may be directed by other disciplines, yet that still reflect nursing care.

Examples of Client Problems

Client Problem	Discussion
1a. Poor hygiene	If a person is unwashed and dirty, nursing care is directed by the cause. A brain-damaged client may never be independent in his self-care. A person preoccupied with differentiating reality from fantasy will require guidance with hygiene. A depressed client may lack the energy to wash himself or change his clothes.
1b. Poor hygiene due to low self-esteem	The treatment is now directed by the client's lack of self-interest and self-respect. A change in this behavior indicates a change in self-perception.
2a. Hallucinating	The nursing approaches to a client who is hallucinating is decidedly different if the cause of the hallucination is chemical, physiological, or psychological.
2b. Hallucinating due to lack of sleep.	The nursing care is now directed toward creating an environment in which the client can rest.

Example of Client Outcomes

Client Problem

1a. Poor hygiene due to low self-esteem

Client Outcome

His hygiene improves.

Discussion

Which aspect of hygiene—washing hair, wearing clean clothes? Who measures improvement? Whose idea is it to wash? The vagueness of this outcome statement does not give direction to treatment activities.

Client Problem

1b. Poor hygiene due to low self-esteem

Client Outcome

The client initiates and follows through with washing hair and wearing clean clothes.

Discussion

Clean hair and clothing are readily observable and measurable. If the client initiates bathing and changing of clothes, it is meaningful behavior. Conversely, if the client performs these actions to comply with a staff member's request, his behavior may express no more than his reluctance to argue. A person with low self-esteem may interpret the staff's suggestion as further proof of his inherent worthlessness.

Client Problem

1a. Hallucinating due to lack of sleep

Client Outcome

The client sleeps.

Discussion

How does one determine whether another is sleeping unless the person is deliberately awakened? If the client states that he has slept well, how does the nurse diagnose hallucinatory behavior?

Client Problem

1b. Hallucinating due to lack of sleep

Client Outcome

The client verbalizes that he is no longer hallucinating.

Discussion

The outcome is now measurable; the client reports a change.

Example of Deadlines

Client Problem	**Client Outcome**	**Deadline**
1a. Poor hygiene due to low self-esteem	The client initiates and follows through with washing hair and changing clothes.	Observe client daily at 2 p.m.

Discussion

Reviewing the care plan early in the day, the nurse knows that observation and documentation are required regarding the progress of the client in performing his self-care.

Examples of Nursing Orders or Approaches

Client Problem	Client Outcome	Deadline	Nursing Orders
1a. Poor hygiene due to low self-esteem	The client initiates and follows through with washing hair and changing clothes.	Observe daily at 2 p.m.	Beginning treatment: 1. a. In the morning, schedule shower time. b. Assist the client as needed. 2. Observe clothing and condition of hair in morning; note any changes throughout the day

Discussion

These nursing approaches are readily applied in psychiatric-mental health care settings.

Client Problem	Client Outcome	Deadline	Nursing Orders
2a. Inability to form meaningful relationship due to lack of self-worth	The client identifies one person as a friend.	Client discharge from in-patient facility	1. Involve the client in group therapy daily (led by group therapist) and note the client's reaction after the group. 2. Provide activities through occupational therapy. Note where the client sits and whether he interacts with anyone. 3. Seek the client out during "non-prime-time" hours and engage him in superficial, social conversation.

Discussion

The nursing orders provide an overview of the treatment program. Although two of the activities are directed by other team members, the nurse is able to observe and measure outcomes during and after these therapies.

Standardized Nursing Care Plans

The use of standardized nursing care plans allows the nurse to achieve the goal of communicating objectives of care and efficient planning. The acknowledgement of behavioral similarities permits more time for nurses to recognize and deal with the client's uniqueness. (See examples of standardized nursing care plans at the end of the chapter.)

Purposes of Standardized Care Plans

Standardized nursing care plans serve several functions in assisting the nurse to maintain high level care. Standardizing of care plans acknowledges the similarities of symptoms and evaluates current nursing practice within a particular treatment setting. These care plans also serve as educational and orientation tools for new employees of an agency. Standard care plans serve to insure comparable levels of nursing care within a treatment setting. The standardization of plans allows the nurse time to focus on the individual problems, needs, and goals of the client. Finally, the standard care plan is utilized to communicate information about client problems and therapeutic approaches when clients move from one treatment setting to another.

Forms of Standardized Care Plans

Standard nursing care plans are drafted according to medical or nursing diagnoses and generalized treatment goals. Client problems, for example, may be differentiated as actual, potential, possible, and unusual problems. *Actual problems* are those behaviors or symptoms usually seen in that category or diagnosis. Examples of usual problems are listed below.

Depression: low self-esteem and poor hygiene
Manic behavior: loud, rapid speech; grandiosity

Potential problems are those behaviors or symptoms that might occur when a client has that particular diagnosis; the nurse should observe for their occurrence and take preventive measures. Examples of potential problems are listed below.

Depression: potential suicidal ideation due to low self-esteem; potential malnourishment due to anorexia
Manic behavior: potential violent outbursts due to emotional lability

Possible problems are those behaviors or symptoms that may or may not occur. Possible problems are the "rare quirks" of a diagnosis that are sometimes forgotten in the day-to-day concerns of nursing. Possible problems are reminders that a particular problem, although rare, is related to the client's diagnostic classification. Examples of possible problems are listed below.

Depression: Possible auditory and visual hallucinations due to sleep disturbances
Manic behavior: Possible suicidal attempt due to grandiosity; possible legal difficulty due to excessive buying

Finally, the standardized nursing-care plan provides blank spaces labeled *unusual problems,* which are the identified problems unique to the client. A blank column is also provided for dates and initials, which notify the mental health team when problems are identified and nursing approaches are initiated.

Balanced Service System

Mental health care is a team approach, and the team members are often public and private sector agents of health care delivery—social workers, psychologists, physicians, nurses, clinics, hospitals, schools. Treatment may take place in an inpatient or outpatient setting.

The client seeking help dealing with mental health problems is often overwhelmed by the number and diversity of agencies available to him and involved with him. Although the goals of treatment are continuity and consis-

tency, these goals are not always met. A client may enter an inpatient facility, be discharged, and continue therapy in an unrelated outpatient clinic. As treatment progresses, the client may be referred to other agencies to assist in rehabilitation, such as agencies involved with vocational training, housing, and foster-child services. Each agency employs professionals with their own philosophies and biases. Each professional feels responsible for knowing all aspects of the client's situation and status. Consequently, there are overlaps of information and, often, a time-wasting repetition of history-taking. The client is constantly beginning again.

The *balanced service system* permits the professionals to know what aspects of the client's problems are being handled and by whom. It dignifies the client by allowing him to progress.[14] The balanced service system also allows the members of the team to focus on their areas of expertise, thereby reducing the duplication of services. Time is used more efficiently because one therapist knows with whom to speak at another agency.

Clients are frequently overwhelmed when entering new agencies or meeting new therapists. Utilizing a balanced service system, clients and therapists can arrange introduction prior to therapy times and the responsibilities of everyone involved in the client's care become clear. The treatment plan is truly the client's. (See the Case Study at the end of the chapter.)

Summary

This chapter has explored the third step of the nursing process. Planning is a structuring of needs and problems in an orderly manner so that a goal may be achieved. Some of the important points of the chapter include the following.

1. When a client seeks therapy, he is mandating change that will affect all his relationships.
2. The writing of a plan clarifies the planner's thinking and details the choices available to him.
3. Establishing time frames within the plan provides guidelines for review and evaluation of the plan.
4. Nursing care plans provide structure for care and define nursing.
5. Nursing care plans contain the diagnosis, problems, long-term and short-term goals, outcomes deadlines, and nursing orders or approaches.
6. Standardized nursing care plans acknowledge the similarities of behavior, and therefore allow the nurse in the workplace to focus on the client's uniqueness.
7. Consistency and effectiveness of care is promoted by a system of care planning that identifies the responsibilities of each team member.

Sample Nursing Care Plan #1

SAINT ALPHONSUS REGIONAL MEDICAL CENTER
Boise, Idaho 83706

STANDARD NURSING CARE PLAN #
ALTERATIONS IN COPING

Initiated by: _____

_____
Patient name or Addressograph

COMPLETE AS APPROPRIATE

DATE	NURSING DIAGNOSIS	EXPECTED OUTCOME	TARGET DATE	NURSING ORDERS AND CHECKING INTERVALS
	1) Ineffective individual coping, 2° _____ _____ _____	1a) Verbalizes positive statements about self _____ _____		1a) Teach patient positive reinforcement: _____ _____
		b) Demonstrates insight into needs and problems _____ _____ _____		b) Assist patient with identification and seeking realistic solutions: _____ _____
		c) Increased appropriate behavior _____ _____ _____ _____		c) Encourage patient to accept responsibility for own behavior: _____ _____ _____

Consider also:
   Noncompliance
   Family coping
   Parenting, alterations
   Alterations in nutrition

5/83

Sample Nursing Care Plan #2

SAINT ALPHONSUS REGIONAL MEDICAL CENTER
Boise, Idaho 83706

STANDARD NURSING CARE PLAN #
PATIENT WITH DISTURBANCE IN AFFECT

Initiated by: _____

Patient name or Addressograph

COMPLETE AS APPROPRIATE

DATE	NURSING DIAGNOSIS	EXPECTED OUTCOME	TARGET DATE	NURSING ORDERS AND CHECKING INTERVALS
	1) Self-concept, disturbance in: _____ _____ _____ _____ 2° _____	1) Participates in therapies: a) _____ b) _____ c) _____ d) _____ b) Socialization: Specify _____ _____ _____		1) Assist patient in developing realistic goals and plans involved: _____ _____ b) Involvement in unit activities: _____ _____ c) Type of participation/ frequency: _____ d) Provide patient education _____ _____
	2) Violence, potential for: _____ _____ 2° _____	2) Will not hurt self or others.		2) Provide safe environment: _____ _____ _____
	3) Injury, potential for: _____ 2° _____	3) Will not injure self.		3a) Develop realistic controls: _____ b) Safety precautions: ___ _____ _____
	4) Grieving, dysfunctional, 2° _____ _____	4) Expresses normal grieving.		4a) Help patient understand grieving process. b) Identify present stage of grieving. _____ _____ c) Intervene appropriately: _____

Consider also:
Sleep pattern disturbance
Self-care deficit
Bowel elimination, alterations
Spiritual distress
Sexual dysfunction
Diversional activity, deficit
Alterations in nutrition

5/83

Standard Nursing Care Plan

Depression (Exogenous, Neurotic)

Overall criteria for discharge:
1) Sleep pattern approximates normal
2) Affect brighter
3) Verbalizing no suicidal concerns

Please circle appropriate problem number and orders.

Date	Problems	Expected Outcome	Checking Intervals	Nursing Orders
	I. Usual problems Core symptoms of depression due to the interaction of: Blunted flat affect Repetitive, ruminative thoughts Hopeless, helpless feelings Psychomotor retardation			
	1) Anorexia due to Lack of activity Flat affect Preoccupation with disturbing thoughts	1a) The client maintains weight. b) Eats 75% of all meals.	Tues. & Fri.	1a) Accompany patient to meals b) Do not make eating a major issue. c) Weigh Tues., and Fri. d) Record appetite.
	2) Sleep disturbance: Difficulty falling asleep and/or Early morning awakening (EMA)	2) Client sleeps in his predepression pattern	Nightly	2a) Assess patient's normal sleep pattern—insomnia remedy if has developed one b) Encourage light, nonstimulating activity before bedtime. c) Do not let patient take daytime naps unless medically contraindicated.
	3) Social isolation and withdrawal due to negative attitude	3a) Participates in basic unit social activities b) Controls negative outlook so that he does not talk about how hopeless everything is around other patients.	Daily	3a) Discourage patient from using room *excessively* to avoid social contact. b) Encourage participation in social activities. c) Make time to discuss with patient problems he has in social situations. d) Try to lead conversation away from totally negative preoccupation; try physical, food, occupational therapy, or game activity

Date	Problems	Expected Outcome	Checking Intervals	Nursing Orders
				e) Do not try to argue patient out of negative attitude.
	4) Somatic complaints due to preoccupation with self and anxiety (headache, backache, nausea)	4) After medical testing has ruled out physical cause, the patient is able to state that symptoms may be a result of stress.	Daily	4a) Give medication as ordered in a nonpunitive manner. Do not comment or criticize. b) Offer some time to talk with the patient about physical complaints.
	5) Inability to make decisions due to lack of concentration and ambivalence	5a) Rejects decisions made for him b) Demonstrates ability to make appropriate decisions from simple to complex	Daily	5a) Assign primary staff member to plan with the client a simple daily schedule, with short duration activities at which he can succeed. b) Do not ask the patient to decide activities if he is unable—rather, make decision and tell him, "it is time for . . . ." or "you can have your bath at 9 or 10 . . . do you have a preference?" c) Discourage major decision-making. d) Make fewer decisions for patient as he begins to reject them.
	II. Potential Problems 1) Constipation and/or urinary retention due to Inadequate fluid intake Lack of activity	1a) Bowel movement at normal pattern for patient b) Voids q shift c) Drinks at least 8 glasses fluid/24 h (if no fluid volume problems)	Daily	1a) Assess the patient's normal bowel, bladder routine, and record. b) Encourage fluids at meals—q2h. c) Encourage physical rather than sedentary activity.
	2) Suicide due to feelings of helplessness, hopelessness, or as a manipulation or in response to hallucinations	2a) No suicide gestures or actions b) Verbalizes rather than acts out desires for suicide.	Every 15–30 minutes	2a) Be aware of possibility of suicide as patient gets "better," is more spontaneous, energetic. b) Make sure patient swallows all prescribed medicines (to prevent hoarding)

(Continues on p 138)

Date	Problems	Expected Outcome	Checking Intervals	Nursing Orders
				c) If patient is giving suicide "clues," ask him if he is indeed thinking about suicide, if he has made any plans, what the plans are.
				d) Do not be afraid to approach subject of suicide with patient (usually it is a relief for him to be able to talk about it).
				e) Room search with patient in attendance may be necessary, looking especially for hoarded, over-the-counter, or other medicines; sharps; long belts, cords.
				f) Notify patient's physician.
				g) Check patient every 15–30 minutes or be in constant attendance if necessary.
				h) May ask patient to sign in at nursing station as often as checks are ordered.
	III. Possible Problems 1) Delusions, hallucinations (in endogenous, psychotic depression) is a coping mechanism with anxiety.	1) See SNCP Schizophrenia section: impairment in reality testing.		

	IV. Unusual Problems
	  1) Feelings of isolation due to family's inability to communicate effectively
		1) Client reports to nurse a conversation between herself, husband, and children.	Discharge	1a) Allow the family to visit at times convenient to them.
				  b) Nurse visit with family and observe interaction and do social group leading.

Case Study: Planning Care for the H. Family

Carol H. is a 34-year-old mother of two children; Amy, 10, and Justin, 7. She has been married 13 years to Henry H., a 35-year-old salesman. While Henry has been moderately successful at his job, Carol has remained at home to raise the children.

Presently, Carol is hospitalized following a suicide attempt. The nursing assessment reveals a woman who has been increasingly "homebound" for 3 years, since Justin started school. She has many recriminations that her suicide attempt failed and declares, "That proves I can't do anything right." She has no hobbies or interests outside of the home and says, "My house keeps me busy."

Henry expresses bewilderment that his wife is unhappy and has attempted suicide. Henry is a firmly voiced, positive man. He informs the nurse that he and his wife do little together "because I'm selling." The house is generally clean and "that counts, or at least, that's what I thought." Henry believes there must be a marital problem, but doesn't know what it is.

Amy is having trouble in school paying attention. Justin is "perfect"; his school work is immaculate and he is overly polite and cooperative at school and at home.

A team conference is held to formalize care planning for Carol. Carol's therapist has determined that the conference would be too overwhelming for Carol to attend. She is unable to make decisions and this is further eroding her self-esteem. Henry would like to know the options he has to "get his family back the way it was before 'this' happened." An initial plan is formulated that states that when Carol verbalizes that she is no longer suicidal, has an alternative to suicide when she feels hopeless and help-less, and has met twice with her after-care counselor, she will be evaluated for discharge. To facilitate Carol's recovery, she will be given antidepressant medication. Recognizing the impact of a suicide attempt upon children, plans are made to notify Amy's and Justin's teachers. A hospital plan and a systems plan are initiated to monitor progress and to coordinate treatment efforts.

As Carol's hospitalization progresses, Henry becomes less positive and asks for more direction in caring for the children. He continues to ask for help to "fix the family . . . make it the way it was." A conference of the treatment team, including Carol and Henry, is held. Options for after-hospitalization treatment are discussed and the decision is made to begin marital counseling and family therapy. The systems plan is amended to reflect these additions. Appointments with the therapists are made so that marital counseling can begin prior to Carol's discharge. The nurse–facilitator coordinates these efforts.

Carol will continue her antidepressants and marital counseling after discharge from the psychiatric facility. When Carol is discharged, the school teachers and counselors continue to be actively involved in monitoring the children's behavioral reactions to the changes at home. Goals are established to increase Amy's attention span and for Justin to become less "perfect." These goals are communicated to the school nurse who then incorporates them in the Systems Plan.

Use of the Balanced Service System Plan helps to coordinate the H. family's treatment. Each agency uses both their own detailed plan and a systems plan to insure that they do not duplicate efforts.

Balanced Service System: the H. Family

Goal: To increase H. family's self-awareness and awareness of each other as measured by depression of mother

Date	Problem	Outcome	Modality	Deadline	Approach
4/14	1. Carol (mother) suicidal due to ↓ self-esteem and ↑ deep depression	Verbalize alternatives to suicide ↓ depression as demonstrated by ↑ in activity level and return to "presuicide attempt" dress: clean clothes, make-up, hair washed, set	Hospitalization: St. Georges Antidepressant, as prescribed by Dr. Jones	Weekly Discharge from hospital	a. Standardized Nursing Care Plan: Depression St. Georges (M. Allen to coordinate) b. Routine medication education to be done by R. Rose c. Establish rapport with client and collaborate with husband and record. d. Monitor activity level on unit's record.
4/14	2. Potential school behavior problems by children due to anxiety caused by mother's suicide attempt	Children verbalize fear re suicide attempt.	School	weekly Monthly	a. Inform school teacher and counselors and record response. This is to be done by M. Allen. b. Identify and record on Systems Plan name of teachers and counselor.
4/26	3. Lack of individual understanding between Carol and Henry due to ↓ communication and time spent together	Verbalize new information about each other	Mental health clinic	Weekly	a. Marital counseling by R. Smith weekly to begin prior to discharge from hospital
4/23	4. Lack of familial interaction due to ineffective communication	Family interactions ↑ as measured by spontaneous conversation	Family therapy at mental health clinic	Every 2 weeks	a. Family therapy: R. Smith (therapist)

References

1. Altschul AT: Psychiatry Under Review—1: The Care of Mentally Disordered: Three Approaches. Nursing Times 76 (March 13): 452–454, 1980

2. Altschul AT: Psychiatry Under Review—3: The Role of Professionals. Nursing Times 76 (March 27): 555–556, 1980

3. Baker BW, Kastelic FA: Patient Care: Four Steps to Increasing Positive Interactions Between Hospital Staff and Patients. Hospital Forum 23 (April–May): 12–15, 1980

4. Cady JW, Freshman DJ, Nroby RB: Taking the Pain Out of Care Planning. Medicus Systems Corp, 1975

5. Fowler G: A Needs Assessment Method for Planning Alternatives to Hospitalization. Hosp Comm Psychiatr 31 (January): 41–45, 1980

6. Giovannetti P: Understanding Patient Classification Systems. J Nurs Admin 9 (February): 4–9, 1979

7. Gladstone TU, McKegney FP: Relationship Between Patient Behavior and Nursing Staff Attitudes. Supervisor Nurse 2 (June): 32–35, 1980

8. Glazer WM, Aaronson HS, Prusoff BA, Williams DH: Assessment of Social Adjustment in Chronic Ambulatory Schizophrenic. J Nerv Ment Dis 168 (August): 493–497, 1980

9. Hessler I: Psychiatry Under Review—2: Roles, Status and Relationships in Psychiatric Nursing. Nursing Times 76 (March 20): 508–510, 1980

10. Huey K: Conference Report: Patient Reentry into Community. Hosp Community Psychiatr 31 (January): 52–55, 1980

11. Johnson MN: Self-Disclosure: A Variable in the Nurse–Client Relationship. J Psychiatr Nurs Ment Health Serv 18 (January): 17–20, 1980

12. Joseph B, Ryan CF, Boudveault TM: Evaluating the Impact of a Continuity-of-Care Program on Discharged Inpatients. Hosp Community Psychiatr 32 (August): 574–575, 1981

13. Kelly JA, Patterson J, Laughlin C, Urey J, Snowden EE: Objective Evaluation and Prediction of Client Improvement in Mental-Health Aftercare. Soc Work in Health Care 5 (Winter): 187–202, 1979

14. Krispin AL: Nursing—A Role in Multidisciplinary Treatment Planning. J Psychiatr Nurs Ment Health Serv 18 (April): 14–17, 1980

15. Mayers MG: A Systematic Approach to Nursing Care Plan. New York, Appleton-Century-Crofts, 1972

16. Newberry P, Weissman MM, Myers JK: Working Wives and Housewives: Do They Differ in Mental Status and Social Adjustments? Am J Orthopsychiatry 49 (April): 282–291, 1979

17. Schain W: Patients' Rights in Decision Making: The Case for Personalism versus Paternalism in Health Care. Cancer (Supplement) 46 (August 15): 1035–1041, 1981

18. Skodel AE, Plutchik R, Kardsu TB: Expectations of Hospital Treatment: Conflicting Views of Patient and Staff. J Nerv Ment Dis 168 (February): 70–74, 1980

19. Standard Nursing Care Plan: Depression. Saint Alphonsus Regional Medical Center, Boise, Idaho, 1981

20. Syson-Nibbs L: Progress Through a Planned Approach. Nursing Mirror 150 (February 14): 41–44, 1980

21. Tsuang MT, Dempsey M: Long-Term Outcome of Major Psychoses, Parts One and Two. Arch Gen Psychiatr 36 (November): 1295–1304, 1979

Chapter 12
Intervention

If the wrong man uses the right means, the right means work in the wrong way.

Ancient Chinese Saying

Patricia N. Mahon

Chapter Preview

This chapter presents an eclectic, developmentally based approach to the process of psychiatric-mental health nursing. Each developmental stage and its needs and associated tasks are discussed in relation to adult psychiatric problems and the approach to their treatment. Nursing interventions, specifically helping relationships, are explored; the value of such relationships is also discussed.

Learning Objectives

On completion of the chapter, the reader should be able to accomplish the following.

1. Identify the role of the psychiatric-mental health nurse
2. Discuss the assumptions underlying an eclectic approach to psychiatric-mental health nursing
3. Summarize the developmental tasks and issues of each stage of development
4. Explain the developmentally based nursing approaches for various psychiatric-mental health disorders
5. Describe the usefulness of an eclectic approach to mental health care

Role of the Psychiatric-Mental Health Nurse

The psychiatric-mental health nurse is an active, respected member of the mental health team in a variety of treatment settings. Definitions of the role of the psychiatric nurse have become increasingly blurred over the years. As their therapeutic skills and education grow, nurses are assuming the role of primary therapist in addition to their more traditional roles.

The focus of therapeutic nursing intervention is not the personality disorder, psychosis, depression, or any other diagnostic category; it is the individual with specific needs and developmental tasks. The individual's disorder does not arise as a phoenix from an obscure niche of the unconscious; it is formed in the totality of a person's life experiences and interactions.

Many theories and techniques of psychotherapeutic treatment have been utilized as if each one were the only theory or technique in existence. These individual schools of thought speak only to a small part of the whole person and his needs and purport a narrow etiologic view. Nurses assess the needs of the individual client and employ the appropriate approach for meeting the identified needs. This process and a holistic orientation imply the need for more than a single theoretical and therapeutic approach to client care. In addition to learning appropriate approaches for holistic individualized care, we must keep in mind the individual nurse's personality. Self-awareness and understanding form the basis of our psychiatric-mental health nursing practice (see the essay A Historical Perspective).

Assumptions Underlying An Eclectic Approach

Any approach to psychotherapeutic treatment presupposes a certain underlying philosophy and set of beliefs. The following are beliefs or assumptions about human individuals, interactions, growth, maturity, and behavior that underlie an eclectic approach to psychiatric-mental health nursing.

Individuals develop and make choices about their life experiences.

An individual constantly interacts with his environment and assumes a major role in determining the types of experiences he eventually integrates. Each person's environment presents a plethora of situations from which he can select experiences. Selecting experiences that are meaningful can create situations that engender growth experiences. The greater the individual's developmental maturity, the more this selection process is under his control.

Individual personality growth is aided by significant human interactions.

Interpersonal relationships constitute the center of our life experiences. The types of relationships we choose change or differ according to our level on the developmental ladder. Therefore, the quality, depth, and appropriateness of interpersonal interactions become the determinants of our growth.

For example, to a newly born individual, a relationship engendering security inherently provides a growth potential for the infant. On the other hand, a relationship offering self-acceptance or "belongingness" offers nothing for growth at this stage of development.

Immaturity is the main impetus for seeking emotional treatment.

Psychopathology may be defined as the difference or gap between the existing emotional developmental level of an individual and the expected emotional developmental level that corresponds to his chronological age. If one accepts this premise, emotional disturbance may be equated with developmental immaturity. It is important, then, that the nursing process be based on an accurate assessment and analysis of the individual's level of emotional maturity and the corresponding needs. The planning of care calls for a relationship that is consistent with the assessed level of functioning in order to provide the interpersonal experience necessary for optimum developmental and emotional growth.

A Historical Perspective

Psychiatric Nursing in 1920

From the publication of the first psychiatric nursing textbook, Nursing Mental Diseases (Bailey H, R.N., Macmillan, New York), in 1920, psychiatric nursing has maintained and refined its active role in the treatment of clients. The role of the psychiatric nurse, at the time of its formal academic beginning, included the skills of observation (the most important nursing activity, according to Bailey), recognition of symptoms, limit setting, and the use of "sympathies of the heart." Nursing intervention during that era was based on the observation of symptoms and the inherent needs of the client that were communicated through those symptoms. "While signs are the province of the doctor," said George H. Kirby, M.D., in 1920, "symptoms are in a peculiar way that of the nurse." Growth and development were approached from a purely neurophysiological stance rather than from the standpoint of developmental tasks.

In this historic book, Bailey also described the qualifications that she believed were necessary for a nurse working with clients with mental disorders. To function in this area of nursing, she said, is "a task which calls for the full use of all the powers of the mind, sympathies of the heart, and skill of hand." Bailey's expectations of the effective psychiatric nurse are contemporarily expressed in familiar terms—self-knowledge, self-understanding, emotional maturity, and strength of personality. She emphasized the importance of not only the special knowledge and skill acquired by the nurse's training, but also the benefits of culture, social accomplishments, and "reading, study, and travel in the broader school of life."

A list of the expectations of the psychiatric nurse in 1920 declared that the individual must

1. be intelligent (because no form of nursing makes such a constant appeal to the intellect);
2. possess observational skills;
3. possess accurate reasoning;
4. possess the ability to make quick judgments;
5. have the mastery of her own emotions;
6. have more than ordinary capability;
7. be versatile;
8. be resourceful;
9. be mature;
10. be educated.

Developmental Issues, Needs, and Tasks

To use an eclectic approach to psychiatric-mental health nursing, the nurse must have an understanding of the developmental levels and their inherent relationship needs. The developmental stages are presented in the familiar hierarchical order and each stage is discussed in relationship to the needs, issues, and tasks.

Infancy

The first 2 years of life, or infancy, is designated as the *oral period*, in which the personality structure of the individual is centered around the issue of impulsivity. Until the infant begins to develop speech, his behavior and interpersonal relationships are autistically motivated. The ego is still in a primitive stage with its minimal strengths and abilities focused on the management of impulses and impulse gratification. Impulse identification and communication of a need (for example, crying for a bottle, fussing when wet) are the important developmental tasks during this early period. Successful mastery of this developmental period includes the expression and gratification of impulses.

The infant experiences security through interaction with parental figures who create a protective and secure atmosphere, which is necessary for growth to take place. Crucial aspects of this stage of development are the effectiveness of the mother figure and the establishment of trust.[9]

Toddlerhood

Late infancy, or toddlerhood, which may extend from 2 years of age to 3 or 4 years of age, is referred to as the *anal period*. The core needs during this period are for support in the appropriate expression of feelings and the control of impulses. During this period, the child is involved in the development of social, emotional, and physiological control, such as bowel and bladder control. A major task is learning that there is not only an appropriate time and place to defecate, but that other types of feelings can also be modulated and expressed at appropriate times and in an appropriate manner.

The child's ego functions begin to take root during the battle for control of impulsivity. The pleasure principle is slowly being displaced by the reality principle and the child begins to relate and deal with the world in a new way.[12] The child responds to the world in terms of societal demands and expectations. During this stage, the superego is born.

The parents' role of providing security seems to be less important than providing support in impulse control. The child experiences feelings such as shame, guilt, and depression during this stage and needs parental support to begin to face superego demands.

Preschool Years

From the ages of 3 or 4 to 6 years, the child is in the *oedipal stage* of development. During this stage, the child's dominant developmental needs are to deal with sexual and aggressive impulses and to come to terms with parental and societal demands. The development of the ego is of primary importance during the preschool years. The child engages in a struggle between sexual impulses and their appropriate expression.

This stage is one in which one parent is seen as an unobtainable love object due to the threat of the more powerful and potent parent of the same sex. An unconscious decision, the only feasible way out of the threatening dilemma, is to become as much like the parent of the same sex as possible; that is, to identify.[15] The child identifies with the parent of the same sex in order to cope with the impossible, internal interaction between the id, ego, and superego, and the external family situation. Growth and healthy identification require a healthy dependency on the same-sexed parent, the parent with whom the child identifies.

A successful resolution of this developmental stage increases ego strength and assists the child in changing his or her role within the family unit. The evolution of certain life skills and the realization that gratification of impulses involves a time-delay factor are significant hallmarks of learning during this stage of development.

Early School-Age

The years from 6 to 9, identified as *early latency*, constitute a stage in which learning, the acquisition of knowledge, and the development of the social role outside the protection of the home and family take place. During the earlier stages of development, the child established some peer relationships, although the primary relationships were focused on the "all important" family. During the early school-age years, however, the child begins to make his way into the world and develop relationships with significant adult and authority figures such as neighbors. The child's control over the environment increases greatly as he acquires knowledge and new learning.

At this developmental stage, the self-concept is still in a primitive, rudimentary form. The self is the *perceived self*; that is, the individual as he observes himself operating in the larger world and in varied situations. The child now possesses the beginning ability to "step outside" of, and observe, himself in various situations. With growth come the ability and power to modify or change behavior. The prime developmental task during this stage is to relate specific "self" concepts to specific interactional situations with

others and the environment. The ability to differentiate the self and the ego is a necessary skill in the process of interaction. The "self-sets" that begin to form are the forerunners of an integrated, adult sense of self.

The early-latency-age child needs guided experiences from reliable adults in authority. Guidance from the father or mother figure as a social representative within the family setting is necessary; guidance is also necessary from a teacher, coach, neighbor, or other important adult outside the nuclear family.

Late School-Age

Latency, the period that precedes adolescence, stretches from the ages of 9 to 12 years. The harmonization of various aspects of the differentiated self-concept occurs during this time, although several areas of the self, including sexual, vocational, and scholastic development, are neither owned nor integrated. The integration of these facets of the self are slowed because they inherently carry with them the threat of independence and separation from the family. The continuing need for dependency is transferred from family to peer relationships. In the process of forming peer relationships, experiences with independence are accumulated through new self-concept structures that carry very little or no threat at all (sports teams, boy and girl scouts, clubs), while those that pose the greatest threat (sex, vocation) are denied and avoided.

Adolescence

The stage of adolescence brings with it the physiological changes of puberty, the full blown emergence of the self-concept, and the integration of the biopsychosocial aspects of the individual. The young adolescent who is just beginning to integrate a sense of self may swing violently from viewing self as completely inadequate to the opposite end of the continuum, that of pridefulness and being puffed up over a sense of adequacy. The underlying theme of adolescence is a sense of striving, a need for a feeling of adequacy, and the search for an opportunity to test out the "self."

Equipped with the psychological skills for adult maturity, the adolescent must distance himself from the child–parent–family relationships and move toward adult relationships in the larger world. The intellectual choices made for adulthood must be actualized and the associated responsibilities must be accepted in this stage.

The major developmental tasks during adolescence are making a commitment, working through the commitment, and solidifying the personality structure so that the self is viewed as a participant in the larger world. This is a painful, but necessary, process in the movement up the developmental ladder to adulthood.

The adolescent's need to prove himself as a person in his own right, as an adequate and independent human being, gives rise to conflicts with parents and authority over power issues. This conflict is usually the rule rather than the exception.

Adulthood

The successful completion of adolescence, which is a difficult task for many, can lead to what has been referred to in modern times as the *existential crisis*. The individual, at this point in development, is no longer in need of the family constellation for self-identity. The person is faced with life, in the form of aloneness, the absurdity of existence, and all the responsibilities inherent in his attained freedom. The standards and structures by which the adolescent had previously structured his life are no longer seen as meaningful. A reorganization of the meaning of life, along with the blatant knowledge that he is no longer a child in an adult world, confronts the individual. The "adult" must be an active, productive participant in the activities and responsibilities of the larger, nonprotective world. The emotional development of the human being is not at all completed at this stage. During adulthood, various issues, problems, and stresses arise and confronting them is another, separate phase of development.

Developmental Framework for Nursing Intervention

Knowledge and understanding of the stages of development and the issues, tasks, and needs of each period form the framework within which the planning of nursing intervention takes place. For example, the drives of infancy center around impulsivity and immediate need gratification. These issues are eloquently discussed by Harry Stack Sullivan, whose theoretical discussion centers on impulse gratification, maternal empathy, and autism. These psychological factors provide an understanding of behavior dominated by the primary process, as in schizophrenia.

If the individual's emotional needs are not met and the tasks of a developmental stage are not completed, "lags" in maturity may be identified. Such deficits at various developmental levels result in emotional fixations that halt the natural movement through the remainder of the developmental stages and, hence, result in immaturity. As a result, psychopathology, or emotional disorder, arises from the fixation at a specific stage of development. Certain disorders can, in fact, be linked to fixations at these specific stages. The following are examples.

Schizophrenia—Infancy

Schizophrenic individuals function at the level of extreme dependence and are preoccupied with the fulfillment of their basic security needs. The impetus behind schizophrenic behavior is the gaining of greater security experiences from the world around. One finds that schizophrenic clients become intensely involved with their therapists and those who are identified as significant to them in an attempt to gain security. Security is also found within the hospital setting in which the basic needs of the individual are met by another.

The schizophrenic's life revolves around the meeting of basic security and dependency needs. When these basic, infantile needs are not fulfilled, the individual engages in delusional and hallucinatory behavior. The symbolism of the delusional and hallucinatory material usually reflects impulses and needs that center on dependency and security.

Manic Depression—Toddlerhood

Problems revolving around the issue of impulse control can be traced to the anal phase of development. Primitive attempts at impulse control by a child in the anal period of development can also be similarly observed in the individual with a diagnosis of manic-depressive disorder.

An individual with this affective disorder is torn between the expression and the avoidance of aggression, impulse, and feelings. The major objective of the professional mental health caregiver, in working with this client, is to create a learning environment in which the client can learn how to express his impulses and feelings appropriately.

Neurotic Disorder—Preschool Years

Ego development emerges out of the process of dealing with the aggressive and sexual impulses that arise during the oedipal period of development. The preschool child becomes an enigmatic challenge for his parents because, if he is limited too severely, he may develop a punitive superego that restricts and punishes him and limits his effectiveness as an adult with adult ego functioning. This may be observed in the individual exhibiting neurotic or maladaptive behavior.

The neurotic personality is laden with unacceptable impulses that must be severely restricted and controlled or the individual becomes overwhelmed by anxiety. The individual attempts to maintain internal homeostasis of impulse control and restriction by continuing an overdependency on parental figures or on some significant individual who is placed in a parental role.

Neurotic disordering that begins early in the oedipal stage may result in obsessive–compulsive behavior. The obsessive–compulsive conflict of the adult is closely associated with anality, in which depression and repressed aggression exist. The hysterical neurotic personality is fixated at a later oedipal stage and focuses more on concerns with sexuality. The obsessive–compulsive individual utilizes the defense of denial in a primitive manner to attempt to rid the self of threatening, unacceptable impulses. The hysterical individual, more mature on the developmental scale, utilizes more sophisticated defenses, is easier to interact and develop a relationship with, and is easier to treat.

Personality Disorder—Early School-Age

The demands of a formal education and of society are issues that must be dealt with in the early latency or school-age period. In the process of functioning and judging that functioning, in the world larger than the family, the child's ego and superego merge into what has been termed the *developing self*. Individuals with personality disorders, which represent a fixation at the early latency stage, are continually struggling with their unsuccessful transition from the ego mechanisms that controlled impulses during the oedipal period to the expression of the self in a world viewed as confusing.

A successful transition into the larger world requires the individual to compile and index the self-images that have been tested in the larger world of peers and adult authority. The person discovers acceptable channels for the expression of impulses and incorporates them into his repertoire of behavior. The pathology of a personality disorder is expressed by the rejection of cultural systems and values (as in antisocial individuals) or by the identification with a subculture that possesses its own values different from those of the large society (as in members of street gangs). Both of these pathologic expressions are found in clients who desire the gratification of impulses as their end; therefore, both types of clients attempt to manipulate the world to attain this end.

Behavior Disorder—Late School-Age

The individual with a behavioral disorder is viewed as being fixated late in the latency period of development. During this period, the individual's self-concept is being integrated into the personality. Fixations at this level of development are characterized by very adequate functioning in all areas of life, with the exception of one area. Not unlike a preadolescent child, an individual with a behavioral disorder utilizes certain symptoms to maintain dependency and avoid the impending conflict of dependency–independency; that is, he tries to avoid growing up! Individuals with behavioral disorders use avoidance behaviors to relate with others. "Gamesmanship" is easily observed as their mode of operation in relationships and in the avoidance of the decisions and choices needed to move toward maturity.

The individual with a behavioral disorder does not typically seek help until he reaches a point of being overwhelmed by his symptoms. He seeks out peer relationships that protect and reinforce his avoidance of maturity. Generally, such individuals get along well with others, function at a satisfactory level, maintain friendships, work and do superficially well in their life . . . with the exception of never achieving what is needed to "move on" in life, such as finishing school, achieving job promotions, and so on. If asked how things are going for them, their usual response would be, "Everything is fine . . . just great." When verbally confronted with their behavior in regards to achievement,

they will usually respond by stating, "Sure, everything is great, but that," and then proceed to avoid the problem. Such individuals possess an unlimited catalog of rationalizations to explain why they haven't succeeded at any particular time or in any particular endeavor. They possess extensive knowledge about a variety of topics—cars, stereos, hobbies, the stock market, and others—but never utilize that knowledge for their own movement to a more mature, responsible level of development.

The behavior of the individual diagnosed with a behavioral disorder is used to prevent progress toward maturity and the responsibilities inherent in adult roles. The individual may be well-versed in the responsibilities that he is avoiding and is conscious of his avoidance behaviors. He copes with the independence–dependence conflict by maintaining the dependence of a more immature level of development. Those individuals who appear to be frightened by success and those who become dependent on chemical substances (drugs and alcohol) are identified in this developmental fixation.

Adolescent Reaction—Adolescence

The problem for the adolescent is two-fold—that of conflict between independence and dependence, and the growing sense of awareness of the self's operation within the larger world of adulthood. In the attempt to attain and maintain a sense of social adequacy, the individual faces the feared possibility of finding the self adequate and acceptable. Many of the symptoms observed in the adolescent reaction are the social and behavioral reflections of an attempt to gain a sense of social adequacy and acceptance. Adolescents are frequently plagued with feelings of inadequacy when their accomplishments do not meet their unrealistic expectations of themselves.

During adolescence, the individual is expected to make choices of goals in life and move actively toward attaining these goals. The growing of sexual and social adequacy along with the commitment to grapple with the problems of life are the areas that need to be supported during this stage of development. Fixation at the adolescent level of development produces an individual who is neither able to move forward with a decision nor able to carry through with it energetically once a decision has been made.

At the adolescent stage of development, a fairly high level of personality development has been achieved and the superego and ego have been integrated into the personality. The identified needs of an individual fixated at the adolescent phase of development are acceptance and support during the decision-making process, and the peer group is naturally sought out to meet these needs.

Existential Crisis—Adulthood

With the successful attainment of maturity and the confrontation of the self with the idea of freedom of choice, the individual must then deal with the meaning of life and aloneness. Inherent in this phenomenon is the concept of a *transcendental self,* a self that exists beyond one's individual self-image, or a self in relation to the larger universe.

The developmental crisis during this period includes profound anxiety, depression, and exploration of the meaning of death and its finality. The crisis is intense and the associated painful emotions are exquisitely experienced. The needs of an individual travailing such a crisis include mature relationships that provide an environment in which to interact, react, and act on choices made. At this developmental stage, a meaning in life can only be ascribed by the individual himself or herself.

Nursing Interventions

Helping Relationships

At the foundation of a helping relationship is a basic belief that individuals grow as a result of positive interpersonal interactions. Therapeutic relationships are sought because of earlier developmental needs that have not been satisfactorily met. A helping relationship that identifies developmental needs and provides the appropriate behavioral learning leads to developmental and emotional growth.

The therapeutic aspect of nursing care is the relationship shared by the professional and client. This relationship is an intense involvement in which resistance and defenses are lifted and in which direct, honest communication occurs. The relationship is based on trust and involves individualized nursing approaches according to the identified developmental needs of the client.

Eclectic Therapeutic Approach

Theorists have conceptualized therapeutic approaches from specialization with diagnostic categories of clients; such as Sullivan's work with schizophrenic individuals, Freud's work with neurotic clients, and Rogers' work with individuals with adolescent reactions. Each of these therapists conceptualized a framework that was applicable to their specific group of clients and developed appropriate interventions that met identified needs.

Nursing calls for an eclectic understanding and approach to treatment based on the specific needs of the client, rather than on any one specific framework. A developmental approach provides the nurse with a framework for assessment, analysis, planning, and the implementing of care based on the individual client's developmental needs. The initial interviews call for the nurse's assessment of the individual and his family and the generation of a series of questions or hypotheses about his developmental level and needs. Based on this assessment, the nurse then applies the theoretical approaches and interventions that appropriately meet the identified needs.

For example, the schizophrenic individual relates to others and the world in terms of security and need fulfillment. These communications are seen in his concrete thinking, dream-like fantasy (hallucinations), and demands upon the nurse to assume a maternal role. Basically, the schizophrenic message is that others, including the nurse, are not providing motherly care. In the relationship, it is necessary to search out the meaning of the client's symbolic expressions, as a loving mother must, in order to "understand" the needs of her child. The most imperative aspects in working with a schizophrenic patient are to accept the commitment that is necessary in the relationship, to take the risks involved, and to meet the client's oral-dependent needs in a therapeutic and growth-producing manner.

The behavioral cycles in the affective disorders, such as manic-depression, are attempts at impulse control utilizing an archaic ego structure. Delusional systems and primary thought processes can be observed in this pathological fixation. During the normal anal period, the mother meets needs for superego control and shares in ego functioning with the child. This is done while providing the support needed as the child attempts to develop self-control and higher ego functioning. Similarly, the nurse's role with the manic-depressive individual focuses on supporting the existing ego strength while providing external limits and protection.

The phenomenon of transference within helping relationships aids in the resolution of turbulent, neurotic interactions based in oedipal fixations. Interpretation, another psychotherapeutic technique, is an advanced skill that is important for the resolution of intrapsychic and developmental conflicts and movement toward greater maturity.

In a helping relationship with an individual with a personality disorder, the nurse is viewed as a societal representative of authority and must possess a clarity of her own values to help the client develop healthy behaviors for dealing with the world. Theoretically, ego psychology, neoanalytic approaches, and group therapy are appropriate treatment approaches for the individual fixated in early latency.

The helping interpersonal relationship needed to treat a person with a behavior disorder calls for a less intensive, peer-type relationship in which exploration may occur. Because of a more highly developed personality structure, the individual is agile in avoiding situations that pose a threat. Appropriate nursing interventions focus on exploring the effectiveness of specific behaviors used to maintain pathology and on examining the "games" used in gaining "payoffs." Such approaches open the door to the formation of peer relationships needed for the movement toward growth.

The relationship needs of an individual with an adolescent reaction are minimal and are most appropriately met with a nondirective approach encompassing a permissive atmosphere and the reflection of feelings, genuineness, and unconditional positive regard. The client-centered approach of Carl Rogers is the appropriate interpersonal approach for an individual fixated at the adolescent stage of development.[29]

A therapeutic helping interaction with an individual experiencing an existential crisis involves two individuals (client and professional) who are able to share their common struggles and find meaning in their existence. Therapists such as May, Frankl, and other existential theorists and philosophers present extensive conceptualizations regarding the existential crisis.[10,23,24] The nurse, in this type of helping relationship, must be armed with a vast, organized body of understanding, knowledge, and maturity from which to interact, evaluate, and treat the individual experiencing an existential crisis.

Summary

This chapter has explored the role of the psychiatric-mental health nurse and the developmental issues, needs, and tasks of each stage of development on which nursing interventions are based. Some of the emphases of the chapter include the following.

1. In the treatment of psychiatric-mental health clients, it must be remembered that individuals do not move from their fixation, or pathology, to maturity in one leap, but move from one level of fixation to the next, higher level toward maturity.
2. Underlying helping relationships is the basic belief that individuals grow as a result of positive interpersonal interactions.
3. The helping person has a responsibility to be knowledgeable in varied theoretical and conceptual approaches, in order to be consistent with the growth of the client.
4. The developmental eclectic approach should ultimately provide a framework to help individuals resolve developmental fixations and reach the level of a mature, fully functioning person.

References

1. Alexander F, Eisentein G, Grotjahn M: Psychoanalytic Pioneers. New York, Basic Books, 1966
2. American Psychiatric Association: Diagnostic and Statistical Manual of Mental Disorders, 3rd ed. Washington, DC, American Psychiatric Association, 1980
3. Berne E: Games People Play. New York, Grove Press, 1964
4. Berne E: Transactional Analysis in Psychotherapy. New York, Grove Press, 1961
5. Brenner C: Psychoanalysis. New York, Doubleday, 1957
6. Brill A: Psychoanalysis. New York, Washington Square Press, 1960
7. Bruch H: Learning Psychotherapy. Cambridge, Harvard University Press, 1974
8. Ellis A: The Rational Emotive Approach. New York, Julian Press, 1973
9. Erikson E: Childhood and Society. New York, WW Norton, 1963
10. Frankl V: Man's Search for Meaning: An Introduction to Logotherapy. New York, Washington Square Press, 1971
11. Freud A: Normality and Pathology in Childhood—Assessments of Development. New York, Internal University Press, 1965
12. Freud S: Beyond the Pleasure Principle. New York, Bantam Books, 1959
13. Freud S: Character and Culture: General Psychological Theory. New York, Collier Books, 1963
14. Freud S: Dora: An Analysis of a Case of Hysteria. New York, Collier Books, 1963
15. Freud S: Early Psychoanalytic Writings. New York, Collier Books, 1963
16. Freud S: New Introductory Lectures on Psychoanalysis. New York, Norton Press, 1965
17. Fromm-Reichman F: Principles of Intensive Therapy. Chicago, University of Chicago Press, 1950
18. Goffman I: Asylums. New York, Anchor Books, 1959
19. Hartman H: Essays on Ego Psychology. New York, Internal University Press, 1964
20. Horney K: Collected Works of Karen Horney, David Rapport (ed). New York, Basic Books, 1967
21. Luchins AS: Group Psychotherapy. New York, Random House, 1967
22. Luft J: Group Process. California, National Press Books, 1970
23. May R: Courage To Be. New York, Norton Co, 1975
24. May R: Power and Innocence. New York, Harper & Row, 1972
25. Patterson CH: Relationship Counseling and Psychotherapy. New York, Harper & Row, 1974
26. Perls F: Gestalt Therapy. New York, Dell Publishing, 1951
27. Perls F: Gestalt Therapy Verbatim. New York, Bantam Books, 1970
28. Perls F: In and Out of the Garbage Pail. New York, Bantam Books, 1971
29. Rogers C: On Encounter Groups. New York, Harper & Row, 1970
30. Rosenbaum M, Berger M: Group Psychotherapy and Group Function. New York, Basic Books, 1963
31. Sullivan HS: Interpersonal Theory of Psychiatry, Helen Perry (ed). New York, Norton Books, 1953

Chapter 13
Evaluation

Institutions are weighted with the past; the individual is on the side of vitality and the future.

John W. Gardner,
In Common Cause

Susan Kah

Chapter Preview

Evaluation is the process of determining the value of something in the attainment of preset goals.[13] Evaluation of nursing practice is an essential component of professional accountability. Nurses are answerable to clients and their families. They are also answerable to themselves, to others who participate in the client's care, to the agencies in which they practice, to the community, and to the profession of nursing; which, in turn, is accountable to society.[15]

One focus of this chapter is the exploration of the process of evaluation as an essential component of the nursing process. The chapter also addresses the broader issue of self-regulation to assure quality in professional performance. The evaluation of client progress and nursing care in a psychiatric-mental health setting is discussed. Also included in the chapter are descriptions of various approaches to evaluation and the components of quality assurance programs in nursing.

Learning Objectives

The reader, on completion of the chapter, should be able to accomplish the following.

1. Define the process of evaluation
2. Explain the relationship of the evaluation phase with the other phases of the nursing process
3. Discuss the difficulties that the nurse may encounter when evaluating the care of clients with psychiatric-mental health problems
4. Compare three different, but interrelated, approaches to evaluation—structure, process, and outcome
5. Describe how the phases of the nursing process—assessing, diagnosing, planning, implementing, and evaluating—provide data or input for quality assurance programs in nursing.

Evaluation: A Component of the Nursing Process

Evaluation is the fifth component of the nursing process and should follow the implementation of actions designated by the nursing care plan.[18] The nursing process is cyclic; evaluation serves as the catalyst for modifying the other components of the care plan. (The dynamic nature of the nursing process and the significance of evaluation are illustrated in Figure 13-1.)

Evaluation has two targets.

1. The changes experienced by the client as a result of the actions of the nurse
2. The quality or effectiveness of the nursing care itself

The nurse compares the changes experienced by the client with the client-centered objectives specified in the care plan. These objectives are the criteria for evaluation. For example, the nurse may assess a withdrawn client as being disoriented and specify "client awareness of time and place" as an objective of nursing care. Subsequent nursing actions may include visual clues placed in the client's environment, such as a clock and calendar, and verbal reinforcement of time and place. The nurse accompanies and follows these actions with observations of the client's behavior.

Does he keep appointments?
Is he present at activities he is expected to attend?
Are his eating and sleeping patterns fairly regular?

If the client's behavior does not change, then the nurse must review and modify the assessment, planning, and implementation phases of care.

Review and modification of the care plan provide nurses with important information about their practice. Was the original assessment of the client complete? Was the nursing diagnosis correct? Was the identified problem a problem for the client or for the nurse? Were the objectives realistic for the client? Did new problems cause a change in the client that was not recognized? Did the client participate in the planning of care? Were the nursing actions appropriate for the identified problem? Is documentation of care available? Is the client's response described completely enough to provide a basis for evaluation? Finding the answers to these and other similar questions engages nurses in the problem-solving that is essential to accountable practice.

Evaluation of the Client with a Mental Health Problem

It is often difficult, for a variety of reasons, to appraise changes experienced by the client and to determine which resulted from nursing intervention. Nurses in psychiatric-mental health care settings assess clients who have difficulty with thinking, feeling, and behaving rather than with more objectively measurable changes in physical status, such as vital sign changes. Thinking and feeling are subjective processes; behavior has multiple causations and is frequently open to many interpretations. Detecting changes in another person's self-image and perceptions of reality requires not only knowledge of human behavior but sensitivity and skillful communication as well.

Another difficulty in evaluating changes in the client's condition stems from the nature of mental illness. Clients with mental health problems usually do not recover quickly, and they may never be completely free of problematic behaviors. If nurses are not perceptive of minor changes in the client's condition, they may overlook progress. A client's decision to eat with others or to join a therapy group may be a milestone in his recovery. Some-

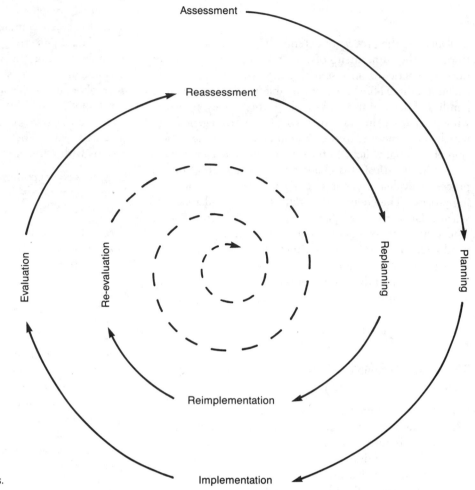

Figure 13-1. *The nursing process.*

times, clients take three steps toward health and two backward before they continue on again. This regression is not uncommon. After examining possible reasons for this regression, the nurse must be sufficiently patient to recognize the client's progress that is occurring.

The nurse must also take care to maintain realistic expectations when formulating objectives of care for, and with, the client. Client care resources must be considered. The level of staffing of a psychiatric unit is frequently a limitation. The nurse must also maintain an awareness that some clients will not be able to reach a high level of achievement or functioning. When beginning nurses recognize this possibility, they are more likely to see clients as they really are.

Evaluation of Psychiatric-Mental Health Nursing Practice

Evaluating nursing practice itself can be as difficult or elusive as evaluating changes in the client's condition. One reason for this difficulty is the multidisciplinary and closely collaborative nature of client care. Nurses usually function as part of a health care team, each member contributing to the client's recovery. The client may receive medication, psychotherapy, and occupational therapy, live in a therapeutic environment, and interact with significant others as well as with nurses. Nurses participate in and influence many of these therapies and also make their own unique contribution to client care; however, it is frequently impossible for nurses to determine that a particular change in client behavior resulted from a specific nursing action or series of actions. Nursing research may lead in this direction, but nurses caring for clients with mental health problems must be able to derive satisfaction from a collaborative role and must not underestimate their own significance.

Another factor that makes care evaluation difficult is the predominance of psychosocial nursing approaches or actions employed in the care of a client with mental health problems. The nature of an interaction with a client is very difficult to quantify, describe, or reproduce. The psychiatric-mental health nurse practices an art as well as a science. In order to modify an action or approach, nurses must be able to define what they are already doing. This is a goal worthy of pursuit.

Evaluation: A Broader View

Although novice nurse practitioners are not expected to assume administrative or nursing management responsibilities, they practice within a system that they must be familiar with. Nursing managers, as well as others responsible for the effectiveness of health care delivery systems, are experiencing increasing pressures to demonstrate commitment to improved client care. As a result, evaluation has become "an open-ended and continuous variable aiding growth and change in outcomes," rather than remaining a closure for a process.[9] Because nurses are becoming increasingly accountable for their practice, as in primary care, a broader view of evaluation is necessary.

Approaches to Evaluation

A view of nursing evaluation that addresses and goes beyond changes in the client's condition encompasses three approaches: structure, process, and outcome.[7] These three approaches are reflected as evaluation criteria in the Standards of Psychiatric and Mental Health Nursing Practice enunciated by the Division on Psychiatric and Mental Health Nursing Practice of the American Nurses' Association.

Structure

An evaluation of structure includes a consideration of the purpose of the health care facility, organizational characteristics, fiscal resources and management, qualifications of health care personnel, physical facilities and equipment, and the facility's status regarding accreditation or approval by appropriate bodies. The public usually assumes that these structural attributes are related to the quality of client care; however, this assumption does not obviate the need to evaluate the care clients actually receive.

Nurses have traditionally been more involved in process-and-outcome evaluation than in structure evaluation. Nevertheless, structural attributes, such as written policies and procedures, job descriptions, and the availability of supervision, consultation, and continuing education, have a very strong influence on the nature of nursing care provided in a facility.

Process

Evaluation of the process of care entails an appraisal of all major and significant minor steps in the care of the client. In this type of appraisal, the standards of practice of the profession serve as the basis for judgments of quality.[15] The American Nurses' Association has established general Standards of Nursing Practice to fulfill the nursing profession's obligation to provide and improve practice in any setting.[1] The Standards, utilizing a systematic approach to nursing practice, provide a means for determining the quality of nursing care received by the client.

The Division on Psychiatric and Mental Health Nursing Practice of the American Nurses' Association has also identified Standards of Psychiatric and Mental Health Nursing Practice. They too reflect the steps of the nursing process and are accompanied by rationale and lists of structure, process, and outcome criteria that are useful in measuring the achievement of each standard. The rationale and criteria are included at the end of the chapter in an extract entitled Nursing Care Plan; the Standards of Psychiatric and Mental Health Nursing Practice are presented here.

Whether nurses use these standards or develop their own guidelines for practice, a process approach to evaluation reflects the assumption that the process of care (*e.g.*, discussing client-related data and reviewing clinical practice with peers) is directly related to general or specific outcomes of care for clients.

Outcome

Evaluation of the outcomes of care centers on the end results of care.[15] Outcomes are, in fact, the ultimate validators of care.[7] Evaluation of outcomes focuses on the status of the client following assessment, diagnosis, and a specific period of nursing and other health care intervention. As discussed earlier in this chapter, it is often difficult to specify those nursing activities that are directly related to client care outcomes, such as the client's acquisition of knowledge and self-care activity. Nurses are challenged, nevertheless, to analyze and document nursing actions that make a difference in the client's situation or condition.

Quality Assurance in Nursing

Quality assurance is the delivery of health care to all individuals at the optimum level of excellence and the persistent endeavor to obtain continued improvement.[13] Quality assurance focuses on what should be done to achieve desired objectives. The American public has become increasingly concerned that health care be appropriate and acceptable, as well as available and accessible. Federal legislation, which is intended to prevent the unnecessary utilization of costly resources, has reflected this concern for quality. The Social Security Amendments of 1972 mandated professional review of health care delivered to recipients of Medicare, Medicaid, and Maternal and Child Health Programs through Professional Standards Review Organizations.

Professional Standards Review Organizations (PSROs) were created to serve as external control mechanisms for quality assurance. The PSROs involve local practicing physicians in ongoing review and evaluation of health care services, and reflect the belief that effective peer review at the local level is the best method for assuring the appropriate use of health care resources and facilities. Although a review of nursing care is not a specific legal mandate, the implications are present. Professional Standards Review Organizations are expected to provide evidence over time that

Standards of Psychiatric and Mental Health Nursing Practice

Standard I. Theory

The nurse applies appropriate theory that is scientifically sound as a basis for decisions regarding nursing practice.

Standard II. Data Collection

The nurse continuously collects data that are comprehensive, accurate, and systematic.

Standard III. Diagnosis

The nurse utilizes nursing diagnoses and standard classifications of mental disorders to express conclusions supported by recorded assessment data and current scientific premises.

Standard IV. Planning

The nurse develops a nursing care plan with specific goals and interventions delineating nursing actions unique to each client's needs.

Standard V. Intervention

The nurse intervenes as guided by the nursing care plan to implement nursing actions that promote, maintain, or restore physical and mental health, prevent illness, and effect rehabilitation.

Standard V-A. Psychotherapeutic Interventions

The nurse (generalist) uses psychotherapeutic interventions to assist clients to regain or improve their previous coping abilities and to prevent further disability.

Standard V-B. Health Teaching

The nurse assists clients, families, and groups to achieve satisfying and productive patterns of living through health teaching.

Standard V-C. Self-Care Activities

The nurse uses the activities of daily living in a goal-directed way to foster adequate self-care and physical and mental well-being of clients.

Standard V-D. Somatic Therapies

The nurse uses knowledge of somatic therapies and applies related clinical skills in working with clients.

Standard V-E. Therapeutic Environment

The nurse provides, structures, and maintains a therapeutic environment in collaboration with the client and other health care providers.

Standard V-F. Psychotherapy

The nurse (specialist) utilizes advanced clinical expertise in individual, group, and family psychotherapy, child psychotherapy, and other treatment modalities to function as a psychotherapist and recognizes professional accountability for nursing practice.

Standard VI. Evaluation

The nurse evaluates client responses to nursing actions in order to revise the data base, nursing diagnoses, and nursing care plan.

Standard VII. Peer Review

The nurse participates in peer review and other means of evaluation to assure quality of nursing care provided for clients.

Standard VIII. Continuing Education

The nurse assumes responsibility for continuing education and professional development and contributes to the professional growth of others.

Standard IX. Interdisciplinary Collaboration

The nurse collaborates with interdisciplinary teams in assessing, planning, implementing, and evaluating programs and other mental health activities.

Standard X. Utilization of Community Health Systems

The nurse (specialist) participates with other members of the community in assessing, planning, implementing, and evaluating mental health services and community systems that include the promotion of the broad continuum of primary, secondary, and tertiary prevention of mental illness.[2]

This material has been published by the American Nurses' Association and is being reprinted with the ANA's permission.

---

nonphysician health care practitioners have become involved in the development of standards for their areas of practice, peer review mechanisms, and continuing education that reflect evaluation of care. Nurses and nursing care must be an integral part of any quality assurance program.

Quality assurance in nursing is an effort requiring the time and commitment of nurses. The exact process will be unique to the health care facility and the individuals who practice there. Generally, several steps must be taken.

1. Identifying desirable outcomes for defined populations of clients

2. Relating the nursing process to these outcomes
3. Using established guidelines to assess the care actually given

Nurses have already developed tools and methods designed to assure the quality of nursing care.

Components of a Quality Assurance Program

The tools and methods used by nurses to assure the quality of nursing care generally provide for either concurrent evaluation or periodic retrospective evaluation. *Concurrent evaluation* takes place while the client is receiving care; *periodic evaluation* occurs retrospectively, or after the fact, such as monthly or quarterly.

Concurrent evaluation, which focuses on both processes and outcomes of care, continually compares the planned for, or expected, result with what is actually being accomplished.[13] Bases for concurrent evaluation include, but are not limited to, nursing histories, nursing care plans, problem-oriented records or other nursing notes, nursing rounds, and client feedback. One retrospective evaluation tool is the nursing audit. The *nursing audit* is a method for evaluating quality of care through appraisal of the nursing process as it is reflected in the client care records for discharged clients. Both concurrent and retrospective evaluation methods or tools may be combined in a systematic manner to become a quality assurance program. Each method will be briefly discussed in relation to its quality control function. Froebe and Bain conceptualize a quality assurance program (QAP) "package" in Figure 13-2.

Nursing History

The inclusion of the nursing history in a quality assurance program is necessitated by the fact that it provides the base for other components in the program. This logical data gathering technique culminates in an original nursing assessment of client problems from which the problem-oriented record or care plan develops. Clients, families, other health care team members, and earlier records are major resources for the nursing history. The nursing history should be concise and comprehensive; data should clearly support the identified problems.

Problem-Oriented Records

Kerr asserts that "the primary reason for the existence of the hospital chart is to record problems and solutions, i.e., that care of the client."[12] *Problem-oriented records* (POR), a concept that is implemented by all persons contributing to the client's care, have four components.

1. A defined data base
2. The problem list
3. The initial plan
4. The progress notes[13]

The nursing history provides information for the data base, from which client problems are identified. Additional problems are added to the list as they are identified. Problems may be socioeconomic and physical, as well as psychosocial. The problem-oriented method of charting assures that the client is viewed holistically by all members of the health care team. All data, health care interventions, and client responses can be found in one place on the client's record (*i.e.*, the progress notes) that are documented by the nurse, physician, and other health care professionals. These notes, written in the SOAP format (Subjective data, Objective data, Assessment, and Plan) reflect the client's response to care as well as the reasoning process for the plan of care. This systematic form facilitates both concurrent evaluation of client care and the retrospective evaluation of auditing the client's record. (See the insert Problem-Oriented Record.)

Nursing Rounds

"*Rounds*, by definition, are planned, purposeful excursions by administrators into a work area to experience and to see first hand the climate and interactions of staff within the client care delivery areas."[9] Direct encounters with clients and their care, as well as with the staff, provide nursing managers with feedback about the quality of care and the overall achievement of nursing goals.

Nursing rounds can also be made by nurses to formulate the client's plan of care. The nurse visits and interacts with each client to validate the plan, ask questions, answer questions, clarify misunderstandings, and evaluate progress. "There is nothing as reassuring as a nurse who takes the time with the rest of the nursing team to visit each client to update the nursing care plans..."[5] This reassurance is especially meaningful to clients with mental health problems.

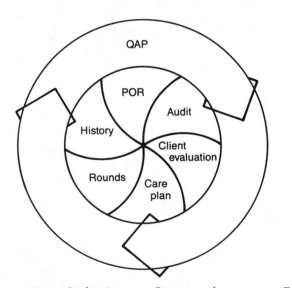

Figure 13-2. *Quality Assurance Program package concept. (From Froebe D J, Bain R J: Quality Assurance Programs and Controls in Nursing. St Louis, CV Mosby, 1976)*

Problem Oriented Record

Problem List

Date	Problem #	Problems	Date Resolved
5/06/84	1	Self-destructive behavior, related to rejection by husband and guilt associated with abandonment of children	
	2	Low self-esteem related to childhood rejection and unrealistic expectations of self	
	3	Inability to express anger, related to fear of rejection	

Progress Notes

5/10/84   6:00 a.m.   #1 Self destructive

S—She says she is unable to sleep because she hates herself so much.

O—Pacing in the hall; hair disheveled; in night clothes; talking to self at intervals

A—She is experiencing high level of anxiety, which may indicate an increase in suicide risk.

P—Stay with the client and encourage verbalization of feelings. Continue assessment of suicidal risk.

Signature, R.N.

Nursing Care Plans

A well written plan provides a central source of information about the patient and a description of his nursing needs. . . . A nursing care plan does not insure optimal patient care, but it will never be attained without a plan.[11]

Care plans are an effective measure of accountability in nursing. Unfortunately, the use of care plans has not always been embraced by nurses. A well-written care plan takes time, takes intellectual effort, and reflects continual

practice. Nurses, for many reasons, do not always have these to give. Unless the situation is remedied by nurses, they may find it increasingly difficult to overcome the task-oriented image that has plagued the profession of nursing for so long. Nurses caring for clients with mental health problems must substantiate how they use a therapeutic milieu, the surrogate parent role, their knowlege of somatic therapies and related clinical skills, health teaching, and psychotherapeutic intervention in order to solve these problems.

Client Feedback

An accepted fact is that any successful business, to maintain its success, must know whether it is satisfying its consumer. Any business receiving its direction from sources other than its customers may be led to false conclusions and ultimate disaster.[9]

Nursing rounds have already been mentioned as one way of eliciting client feedback. Other methods can be used as well. A well-structured questionnaire given to clients and their families can formalize opinions so they are not lost to those who could do most with the information. Meetings with groups of clients can be held to explore client perceptions regarding all aspects of care and to problem-solve issues as they arise. Discharge interviews and suggestion boxes on psychiatric-mental health units can also be used to elicit feedback.

Nurses who ask for client feedback are risk-takers. They may get more than they bargained for; they may also be pleasantly surprised. Most important, they may learn how to improve client care. Feedback is not used to assign blame but to appraise care and identify areas for improvement. Defensiveness in response to client feedback is a confusing message, one that is especially inimical to a psychiatric care setting.

Nursing Audit

The nursing audit is a means of looking into the charts of discharged clients to appraise the type of care they received. For this reason, it may be difficult to determine whether deficiencies in nursing care lie in the documentation of the care or in the actual care. The nursing audit centers on professional standards or processes that have been developed internally or adopted and, perhaps, adapted from an external source. The American Nurses' Association, the National League for Nursing, and the Joint Commission for Accreditation of Hospitals have all developed guides for periodic nursing audits.

The focus of the nursing audit is on the client and his nursing care. Nurses or peer reviewers make the final appraisal of the "extent to which nursing care has measured up to the characteristics that are specified."[8] The nurses' records and care plans are examined to determine the completeness and accuracy of all phases of the nursing process.

To exemplify the client care focus, the six points included in the audit plan of the Joint Commission of Accreditation of Hospitals are summarized.

1. Establishment of criteria for patient care
2. Comparison of criteria and actual practices
3. Analysis of actual practice findings
4. Corrective action
5. Follow-up studies to determine whether the corrective action was effective
6. Report of the results of the audit activity to those to whom one is accountable with accompanying notations describing the actions of the governing body in response to all the foregoing.[10]

The nursing audit, in addition to delineating professional responsibility, has other uses. It can serve as an educational tool and team builder within and across professional disciplines. The criteria developed by those practicing in the facility determine definite goals for client progress. A final use of the nursing audit is the way in which audit criteria become the focus for uniformity of planning and recording.[3]

Summary

Evaluation has been presented as an essential but sometimes elusive component of the nursing care provided for clients with mental health problems. Some of the information presented in this chapter includes the following.

1. The manifestations and long-term nature of mental illness, as well as the artful and collaborative qualities of psychiatric care, work against "cause and effect" appraisals.
2. The broader and timely issue of self-regulation aims to assure quality in professional performance.
3. Approaches to evaluation—structure, process, and outcome—are related to quality assurance programs, the goal of which is improvement in health care.
4. Nursing histories, problem-oriented records, nursing rounds, nursing care plans, client feedback, and nursing audits are all tools or methods that can be used by nurses to maintain quality of care.

Nursing Care Plan

Evaluating Nursing Interventions

Nursing Diagnosis	Goal	Intervention	Evaluation
Moderate anxiety possibility related to agitation and hospitalization The client was admitted with agitated depression, was unable to sit during the interview, and was fidgeting with clothes and necklace.	The client will verbalize her feelings concerning hospitalization.	Observe for behavioral symptoms of anxiety that may be expressed as muteness, hyperactivity swearing, striking out, complaining, or crying. Observe for physiological symptoms of anxiety, such as tachycardia, increased blood pressure, increased respirations, decreased peristalsis, vasoconstriction, sweating, dry mouth, or dilated pupils. Use therapeutic communication techniques. Explain the unit routine to the client and enlist participation in all aspects of care. Encourage visits from significant others. Include family in the provision of care, when possible, and as they express a desire to participate.	Goal is not met; client has less interaction with health care team since initial assessment, speaks only when spoken to, frequently stares out the window, and cries during the evening. Continue interventions. Additional nursing actions: Observe for an increase in depression (apathy, decreased ability to concentrate, insomnia, fatigue, anorexia). Spend at least 15 to 30 minutes with the client in am and pm. Specifically use techniques of silence, directing, reflection, and clarification during interactions Show acceptance by encouraging free verbalization of anger and other feelings
Possible nutritional deficit due to anorexia The client is on a regular diet; weighs 115 lbs., is 5′5″.	The client will attain adequate nutritional intake by eating at least half of each offered meal.	Offer small frequent feedings with supplemental high-protein nourishments. Encourage oral hygiene before and after meals. Maintain an attractive environment during meals.	The goal is currently met; client is maintaining weight. Continue interventions and stay with client during meals.

References

1. American Nurses' Association: Standards of Nursing Practice. Kansas City, MO, American Nurses Association, 1973

2. American Nurses' Association: Standards of Psychiatric and Mental Health Nursing Practice. Kansas City, MO, Division on Psychiatric and Mental Health Nursing, 1982

3. Betts V: Using Psychiatric Audit as One Aspect of a Quality Assurance Program. In Kneisel C, Wilson H (ed): Current Perspectives in Psychiatric Nursing, Vol II, pp 202–208. St Louis, CV Mosby, 1978

4. Blackwell BL, Bolman WM: The Principles and Problems of Evaluation. Community Ment Health J 13 (February): 175–186, 1977

5. Bower FL: The Process of Planning Nursing Care: A Theoretical Model. St Louis, CV Mosby, 1972

6. Debski-Himberger A: A Quality Assurance Program for Psychiatric Nursing. Supervisor Nurse 11 (November): 25–26, 1980

7. Donabedian A: A Guide to Medical Care Administration, Vol II. New York, American Public Health Association, 1969

8. Donabedian A: Some Issues in Evaluating the Quality of Nursing Care. Am J Public Health 59 (October): 1833–36, 1969

9. Froebe DJ, Bain RJ: Quality Assurance Programs and Controls in Nursing. St Louis, CV Mosby, 1976

10. Joint Commission on Accreditation of Hospitals: Accreditation Manual for Hospitals. Chicago, The Commission, 1970

11. Kelly N: Nursing Care Plans. Nursing Outlook 14 (May): 61–64, 1966

12. Kerr AH: Nursing Notes, That's Where the Goodies Are. Nursing, 75 5 (February): 34–41, 1975

13. Kron T: The Management of Patient Care, 5th ed. Philadelphia, WB Saunders, 1981

14. Miller TW, Lee LI: Quality Assurance: Focus on Environmental Perceptions of Psychiatric Patients and Nursing Staff. J Psychiatr Nurs 18 (December): 9–14, 1980

15. Phaneuf MC: The Nursing Audit: Profile for Excellence. New York, Appleton-Century-Crofts, 1972

16. Phaneuf MC: The Nursing Audit: Self Regulation in Nursing Practice. New York, Appleton-Century-Crofts, 1976

17. Ryan LJ, Gearhart MK, Simmons S: From Personal Responsibility to Professional Accountability in Psychiatric Nursing. J Psychiatr Nurs 15 (June): 19–24, 1977

18. Yura H, Walsh M: The Nursing Process: Assessing, Planning, Implementing, Evaluating, 3rd ed. New York, Appleton-Century-Crofts, 1978

Part IV
Intervention Modes

Chapter 14
Milieu Therapy

Once from a big, big building,
When I was small, small
The queer folk in the windows
Would smile at me and call.

And in the hard wee gardens
Such pleasant men would hoe:
"Sir, may we touch the little girl's hair!"
It was so red, you know.

They cut me coloured asters
With shears so sharp and neat,
They brought me grapes and plums and pears
And pretty cakes to eat.

And out of all the windows,
No matter where we went,
The merriest eyes would follow me
And make me compliment.

There were a thousand windows.
All latticed up and down.
And up to all the windows,
When we went back to town,

The queer folk put their faces,
As gentle as could be;
"Come again, little girl!" they called, and I
Called back, "You come see me!"

Edna St. Vincent Millay,
A Visit to the Asylum

Judith A. Greene

Chapter Preview

This chapter defines concepts related to the creation and maintenance of a therapeutic milieu in the hospital setting. Components, characteristics, and goals of a therapeutic milieu are described and functions of the mental health team are delineated. Furthermore, the role of the nurse and the use of the nursing process in milieu therapy are discussed. Guidelines for managing and coordinating a therapeutic milieu, or milieu therapy, are introduced and then applied in illustrative case examples.

Learning Objectives

The reader, on completion of this chapter, should be able to accomplish the following.

1. Discuss concepts related to the creation and maintenance of a therapeutic milieu
2. Identify the components, characteristics, and goals of a therapeutic milieu
3. Describe the functions and humanistic attributes of a mental health team
4. Discuss the nurse's role and functions within the therapeutic milieu
5. Apply general guidelines for facilitating a therapeutic milieu

Therapeutic Milieu Defined and Described

The term *milieu* is a French word meaning middle place. In the English language, milieu means environment or setting. The term milieu, as used in psychiatric-mental health nursing, refers to the people and all other social and physical factors within the environment with which the client interacts.

More specifically, a *therapeutic milieu* is a 24-hour environment designed to provide asylum, in the truest sense of the word, to individuals whose capacities for coping with reality have deteriorated. As such, the therapeutic milieu affords clients refuge while also supplying them with opportunities to acquire adaptive coping skills. Offering secure, comfortable physical facilities for sleeping, dining, bathing, and engaging in recreational, occupational, social, psychiatric, and medical therapies enables the therapeutic milieu to

1. shelter clients physically from what they may perceive as painful, terrifying stressors;
2. protect clients physically from discharges of their own and others' maladaptive behaviors;
3. support the physiological existence of clients; and,
4. provide pleasant, attractive sensory stimulation to clients.

To assist clients in acquiring adaptive coping skills, the therapeutic milieu must also consist of caring, concerned, intelligent persons who can work together effectively as a mental health team. A mental health team is composed of nurses, occupational and recreational therapists, psychiatric nurse clinical specialists, social workers, dance and art therapists, psychologists, psychiatrists, pastoral counselors, paraprofessionals, and other mental health caregivers.

Characteristics of a Therapeutic Milieu

The overall goal of the mental health team within a hospital setting is to create and maintain a therapeutic milieu program. The following elements characterize a therapeutic milieu.

Individualized Treatment Programs

A therapeutic milieu is tailored to the client's individual needs as much as possible without infringing on the needs and rights of other clients and mental health team members. Nevertheless, a definite structure, overall guidelines, and social controls are set forth to provide order and predictability within the environment.

Self-Governance

To avoid the cultivation of dependence and regression, a therapeutic milieu must provide some formal mechanism whereby clients participate in decision-making regarding milieu issues. Structured community meetings, client–team meetings, or client–team committee meetings held at regularly scheduled intervals are examples of approaches used to elicit client involvement in milieu decisions. Furthermore, involving clients in such approaches enables them to exert a therapeutic influence upon the environment and each other.

Progressive Levels of Self-Responsibility

In a therapeutic milieu, clients are expected to assume a responsible role in the maintenance of the environment. The degree of responsibility expected of clients is commensurate with their individual capabilities at any given point during their treatment. Matching expected responsibilities with client capabilities promotes feelings of self-responsibility in clients. A variety of approaches may be used to assist clients in becoming self-responsible. Some approaches include client–client or client–team member collaboration in performing tasks essential to milieu maintenance (*e.g.*, serving meals, cleaning, gardening, and providing appropriate entertainment).

A Variety of Meaningful Activities

To minimize social withdrawal and regression, a therapeutic milieu must provide each client with an individualized activity schedule. Such activities may include structured exercise classes, jogging, training in interpersonal skills (*e.g.*, assertiveness), grooming classes, arts, crafts, relaxation training and stress management classes, dance classes, dances and other social functions, and work and occupational therapies.

Links with the Client's Family

In addition to providing refuge to clients, a therapeutic milieu also provides opportunities for clients to re-enter the mainstream of family life at their own pace. Links with the family may be accomplished in several ways. Family visits can be incorporated into the overall therapeutic milieu program by including family members in selected milieu activities. Involving family members in this manner may necessitate "on-the-spot" family counseling from time to time to help clients and their families work through conflicts and problems inevitably arising during visits. Brief, "on-the-spot" family counseling is directed toward helping clients and their families acquire more adaptive modes of relating to each other. Including family members in selected milieu activities such as dining, social dances, arts and crafts classes, and medication classes enables mental health team members to observe family dynamics and to role model adaptive interpersonal behaviors to both clients and their families. Providing such links with the family hopefully serves to decrease the likelihood of clients becoming institutionalized to the hospital setting.

Links with the Community

Activities occurring outside the structured milieu such as going on shopping trips, picnics, hikes, and camping trips, visiting museums and zoos, and attending concerts, plays, and movies serve to link clients to community life. Participating in such activities with mental health team members helps clients to develop the social skills and confidence needed to re-enter the community. Additionally, such activities provide clients with opportunities to acquire or rekindle enjoyable leisure-time or cultural interests. Again, establishing such links with the community helps prevent client institutionalization to the hospital.

Effective Working Relationships Among Mental Health Team Members

Interpersonal conflict periodically occurs in any group of individuals. A mental health team, like all other groups, experiences such conflicts. Consequently, mental health team members must have the ability to resolve interpersonal conflicts effectively and promptly. If mental health team members cannot do so, then the effectiveness of the therapeutic milieu may decline to the point where clients are placed in serious jeopardy. When mental health team members can engage in effective conflict resolution, they are more apt to trust each other, to communicate accurately and completely with each other, and to act and interact as a mental health team and not as "lone therapists." Furthermore, mental health team members who resolve interpersonal conflicts will serve as effective role models to clients.

Humanistic Mental Health Team Members

For a therapeutic milieu program to be effective, mental health team members need to possess high degrees of the following attributes.

Optimistic attitudes toward people in general

The ability to inspire hopefulness in clients and co-team members

Creativity in working toward more effective ways of involving clients and co-team members in the environment

Lack of fear and prejudice when confronted with persons exhibiting unconventional or aberrant behaviors

Willingness to maintain frequent personal contacts with clients on a daily basis[10]

The ability to set limits on their own behavior and the behavior of others in a nonpunitive manner

A willingness to share control and responsibility with clients as well as co-team members

The belief that controls and limits should be provided by people to the greatest extent possible, rather than by locked doors, physical restraints, or chemotherapeutic agents.

Facilitating a Therapeutic Milieu: Milieu Therapy

Components of a Therapeutic Milieu

Comfortable, secure physical facilities, the mental health team, and the therapeutic milieu program constitute the essential components of a therapeutic milieu. These essential components enable the milieu to exert a therapeutic influence upon clients. In other words, the total milieu, not just one component or mental health team member, serves as the primary therapeutic agent. The total milieu acting as the primary therapeutic agent is referred to as *milieu therapy*.

Milieu therapy is a group therapy approach that uses a total living experience—recreational, occupational, social, psychiatric, and medical therapies, plus mental health team–client relationships—to accomplish therapeutic objectives.[6, 13] These therapeutic objectives include assisting clients to

1. correct or redefine their perceptions of stressors;
2. correct maladaptive coping behavioral patterns;
3. develop adaptive coping behavioral patterns[5]; and,
4. acquire interpersonal and stress management skills in order to conduct themselves more effectively in the environment and strengthen or correct their coping abilities.

Facilitating a therapeutic milieu that assists clients to achieve these objectives requires management of the environment and coordination of the mental health team's collaborative efforts.

It is important for the therapeutic milieu, which is a

microcosm of society, to match the client's cultural background. The absence of such a match can create greater cognitive dissonance or conflict within the client. Therefore, prior to recommending milieu therapy, mental health team members must ascertain that the therapeutic milieu is, to some extent, compatible with the client's cultural background.

Nursing in the Therapeutic Milieu

Applying the Nursing Process

Traditionally, nurses have assumed responsibility for managing and coordinating milieu activities.[12] Viewing clients from a holistic, rather than a fragmented, frame of reference enables nurses to fulfill these responsibilities. In other words, unlike many other mental health team members, nurses possess both the knowledge and skills to help clients meet their physiological, psychological, and social needs. Furthermore, because nurses maintain continuous 24-hour contact with clients, they have a greater opportunity to assume management and coordination responsibilities than do other mental health team members (see the insert on this page).

To manage and coordinate a therapeutic milieu effectively, nurses use the nursing process to assess clients within the milieu, plan and implement milieu strategies, and evaluate client as well as milieu outcomes. More specifically, nurses assess the physiological and social states of each client within the milieu. Making these assessments on a continual basis enables nurses to play a major role in the individualization of clients' treatment plans and activity schedules. Assessing the influence of the milieu on each client and the influence of each client on the milieu is another important aspect of the nursing role in the therapeutic milieu. Such assessments are invaluable in assisting the mental health team to understand the group dynamics of the milieu and to select and implement appropriate milieu strategies and activities. Other ways in which nurses contribute to the management and coordination of the therapeutic milieu include the following.

1. Providing physical care
2. Medication administration
3. Providing psychosocial care
4. Mental health teaching

Providing Physical Care

Providing physical care to clients in the therapeutic milieu falls within nursing's realm of responsibilities. Therefore, nurses assess the extent to which clients are able to engage in daily living activities—eating, eliminating, bathing, dressing, and so forth. For example, some clients may require considerable assistance with daily living activities; other clients, however, may be entirely self-sufficient in these tasks. In any event, nurses are responsible for assessing client capabilities in this area and implementing directly or indirectly an individualized treatment plan designed to reinforce or promote client independence in performing daily living activities. Assessing the physical status of clients in order to detect signs of physical illness or adverse physical reactions to rigorous activity schedules also constitutes an important nursing care function. The inserts on pages 167–168 help to illustrate ways in which nurses provide physical care within a therapeutic milieu.

Medication Administration

In the therapeutic milieu, as in other hospital settings, nurses manage the administration of medications. Some of the methods used to administer medications, however, differ significantly from those used in other hospital settings. For example, in the therapeutic milieu, clients are often expected to approach the nurse for their medication at specific times and places. In some progressive settings, capable clients are given responsibility for administering their own medications. Whatever method is used, the goal is to assist clients to assume responsibility for taking their own medications. Nurses assist clients to reach this goal by providing a humane approach to medication administration and by observing and recording desired and undesired medication effects.

Nursing in the Therapeutic Milieu

Managing and Coordinating the Therapeutic Milieu

Direct Client Care

Effectively manages the day-to-day care of individual clients

Assists as necessary in contributing to the formulation and implementation of individualized treatment plans for clients—
assessment; diagnosis; treatment; evaluation; discharge planning; re-entry into the community

Indirect Client Care

Maintains ongoing communication with other mental health team members

Enforces rules, policies, and regulations of the therapeutic milieu with sound clinical judgment

Maintains cooperative, supportive working relationships with other mental health team members

Schedules, assigns, and manages work effectively

Nursing in the Therapeutic Milieu

Providing Physical Care: Nutrition

Client Problem	*Goal*	*Nursing Intervention*
Nutritional disturbance, due to paranoid ideation; client believes food is poisoned	Establish adequate dietary intake	Serve meals "family style."
		Point out that all plates are filled from the same containers.
		Taste client's food to demonstrate that it is safe to eat.
		Invite client to picnic held on unit patio
		Invite client to have refreshments served during unit party
		Unobtrusively observe client's intake and output and assess actual or potential nutritional problems

Nursing in the Therapeutic Milieu

Providing Physical Care: Sleep Disturbances

Client Problem	*Goal*	*Intervention*
Insomnia, due to hypersensitivity to external stimuli	Establish adequate sleep pattern	Provide a restful, quiet environment by reducing external stressors.
		Move the client to a quiet area if necessary.
		Provide relaxation therapy shortly before bedtime.
		Allow the client to stay up, if indicated, and provide him with quiet activities.

Providing Psychosocial Care

Providing psychosocial care to clients consumes the greatest proportion of nursing time and effort in a therapeutic milieu.[3] To provide such care, nurses engage in a variety of helping behaviors. One area of helping behavior involves reducing stressors within the milieu that may be perceived as psychonoxious by some clients. To illustrate, stimuli such as loud voices, televisions or radios, unsightly visual stimuli, and crowded spaces may be psychonoxious to schizophrenic clients demonstrating hypersensitivity to external stimuli.[2] To reduce the frequency and intensity of hallucinations and illusions experienced by such clients, the minimization of such stressors may be helpful.[7]

Encouraging clients to express their problems and conflicts, to attempt to understand them, and to experiment with new ways of handling problems and conflicts constitutes another form of helping offered by nurses in the therapeutic milieu. To provide such help, nurses may use informal group interventions such as community meetings and structured or unstructured counseling sessions to assist clients with problems operative in their current life situations (see the insert on p. 168).

Conducting brief, "on-the-spot" counseling with clients and families to help them deal with problems arising during visits is another important aspect of the nursing role. Periodically, nurses may also need to engage in limit-setting in order to assist clients in dealing with behaviors destructive to the self, others, or the environment (see the insert Protection of Client and Staff). Other helping behaviors important to the nursing role include helping clients use

Nursing in the Therapeutic Milieu

Providing Physical Care: Hygiene/Self-Care

Client Problem
Poor Hygiene and Self-Care, due to withdrawal and low self-esteem

Goal
Become independent in hygiene and self-care

Nursing Intervention
Teach the client hygiene and self-care skills by means of formal or informal classes.

Gently confront the client regarding hygiene and self-care behaviors.

Offer kind, consistent encouragement to the client in attempts to become independent in self-care.

Act as a role model by following sound hygiene and grooming habits.

Guide the client verbally and nonverbally, with gradual withdrawal of assistance, until client becomes independent in self-care.

Use peer group pressure, as appropriate.

Positively reinforce signs suggestive of progress in hygiene and self-care.

Nursing in the Therapeutic Milieu

Providing Psychosocial Care: Setting Limits on Manipulative Behaviors

Client Problem
Manipulative Behavior: A group of clients conspired to receive extra privileges by requesting them from various mental health team members; they then attempted to pit staff members against each other by repeating different versions of staff responses.

Goal
Learn to interact more directly with individual and groups

Intervention
Initiate a mental health team meeting to discuss the problem and arrive at a group decision regarding milieu strategy.

Initiate a community group meeting to share mental health team's assessment of the problem.

Inform the group that each client will be assigned to one specific team member, and that seeking extra privileges from other team members will not be allowed.

Confront client everytime he or she attempts to revert to former behavior pattern.

Initiate subsequent mental health team and community meetings if inconsistencies arise.

time productively for leisure and work, involving withdrawn clients in the milieu, and serving as a role model by demonstrating interpersonal effectiveness in dealing with clients and other mental health team members.

Attitude Therapy. Another aspect of psychosocial nursing care in the therapeutic milieu involves the use of *attitude therapy*. This therapy is based upon five fundamental attitudes.

1. *Active friendliness,* with which the client is helped to move out of his or her social withdrawal
2. *Passive friendliness,* when the nurse is available for interaction but makes no friendly overture and merely waits for the client to make the first move
3. *Kind firmness,* by which the nurse directs the client into rewarding activities in a kind, but firm, manner

4. *Matter-of-factness,* or responding to the client in a calm, casual manner
5. *No-demand,* used especially when the client is in a state of panic or disintegration and in which nothing is requested of him or her[4]

In applying attitude therapy, each client's predominant behavioral style is identified. Then, nurses and other mental health team members jointly decide which of the preceding attitudes should be prescribed for each client. For example, passive friendliness might be prescribed for a highly suspicious client, whereas active friendliness might be used to draw out a client immobilized by feelings of worthlessness.[13] Although collaborative efforts of the mental health team are essential to implement attitude therapy successfully, the nursing role is the mainstay of this therapeutic approach. (See the insert on p. 170.)

Nursing in the Therapeutic Milieu

Protection of Client and Staff from Discharges of Maladaptive Behavior

Client Problem	*Goal*	*Intervention*
Agitated, destructive, combative behavior	Promote client understanding, control, and acceptance of responsibility for his or her behavior	Intervene promptly when controls and limits are needed.
		Approach in a nonthreatening manner; allow physical space.
		Use kind firmness; do not behave fearfully.
		Refrain from provoking or arguing with client.
		Attempt to determine antecedents of disturbance.
		Remove to a nonstimulating, safe area.
		Provide appropriate diversional/physical activity.
		Use seclusion or other physical restraints only if other approaches fail; be prepared with an adequate number of personnel to assist in enforcing limits consistently.
		Verbally and nonverbally assure client that his or her behavior has not alienated staff.
		Reinforce and support adaptive behaviors.
		Help the client verbalize thoughts, feelings and problems.
		Explore with the client alternative ways of coping with stress.

Nursing in the Therapeutic Milieu

Attitude Therapy

Client Behavior

The client refused to do finger painting prescribed by the art therapist

Attitude Prescription

The nurse used kind firmness by directing the client in activity; eventually the client complied without directives.

Client Behavior

The client ran to his room when he was enrolled in the medication class.

Attitude Prescription

The nurse slowly followed client to his room and then matter-of-factly told him to join the class; the client responded immediately.

Client Behavior

A tearful, dependent, depressed client continually criticized her self-care abilities

Attitude Prescription

The nurse used a matter-of-fact approach in expressing the expectation that the client would perform self-care; avoided sympathizing with client. Gradually, the client became self-sufficient in self-care.

Client Behavior

A suspicious client refused to attend community meetings.

Attitude Prescription

The nurse used passive friendliness by telling the client the time and place community meetings occurred. Also, she told the client that she could come when she decided to do so. Later, the client began attending community meetings on her own initiative.

Mental Health Teaching

Mental health teaching represents another important function of the nursing role in the therapeutic milieu. Mental health teaching that centers around psychotropic medications, or methods of coping with psychiatric illnesses, is often provided by nurses to clients and their families in order to increase their understanding of, and compliance with, treatment plans. Nurses and other mental health team members also teach classes focusing on interpersonal effectiveness (*e.g.*, assertiveness training, communication and problem-solving skills, parental effectiveness, and so forth) to clients and their families. Such classes help clients relate to others more effectively in the milieu and helps them prepare for their return to families, friends, and community. Similarly, involving families in such classes assists them to cope with, and adapt to, the client's changed behavior, and therefore prepares the family for the client's re-entry into the home and community.

A newer area of mental health teaching offered by nurses as well as other mental health team members deals with stress management. In the therapeutic milieu, this form of mental health teaching focuses on helping clients learn to cope with stress through jogging, aerobic exercise, dance, and relaxation techniques. For example, jogging is thought to reduce stress and to foster a sense of well-being or mild euphoria by permitting or encouraging clients to indulge themselves in pleasurable, self-esteem-enhancing fantasies.[1] For reasons that are currently unknown, engaging in aerobic exercise or dance also tends to promote similar reactions. In addition to reducing stress, it is probably safe to assume that the aforementioned activities also contribute to self-esteem through weight loss, increased muscle tone, poise, and balance. In some instances, such classes may also promote increased social interaction among clients.

Relaxation training is another useful method for helping clients to learn to cope with stress. Progressive relaxation, a method originally presented by Jacobson, is appropriate for some clients hospitalized in a therapeutic milieu.[8] For example, clients with psychiatric disorders characterized by nonadaptive anxiety (*i.e.*, chemical dependencies, anxiety reactions, depressive states, and so forth) may respond favorably to this form of mental health teaching.[9, 12]

Teaching progressive relaxation involves teaching clients to tense and then relax major muscle groups of the body in a prescribed, systematic order, usually working downward from the forehead to the feet. Ordinarily, this training occurs in group situations within the therapeutic milieu. Usually, a few members of the mental health team need to participate in the program with clients in order to encourage client involvement.

The nurse or other mental health team member leading the class may wish to use an audio-training-cassette to teach progressive relaxation. The purchase of such audio-training-cassettes for the therapeutic milieu affords an additional advantage; selected clients may use the cassettes to practice relaxation on their own as needed.

Other Nursing Considerations in the Therapeutic Milieu

Depending on the organizational structure of the milieu, nurses may be responsible for developing individualized

Nursing Behaviors for a Therapeutic Milieu

> Encourage clients to help and support each other individually and as a group.
>
> Assist clients to understand each others' feelings and problems.
>
> Conduct community meetings in which clients have the opportunity to discuss their concerns with each other and the mental health team, and if appropriate, give them the opportunity to determine group actions and rules.
>
> Support community/group rules and actions by assisting clients to work through or overcome specific difficulties (*i.e.*, noncompliance with community or group decisions or rules; issues such as stealing, pranks, excessive noise).
>
> Participate freely in milieu activities (*i.e.*, exercise, art, craft classes, social functions).

nursing care plans, rather than contributing assessment data to an overall interdisciplinary treatment plan. In either case, however, nurses must function within the context of the total mental health team in order to manage and coordinate milieu activities in an effective, harmonious manner. Failure to do so can result in clients pitting mental health team members against one another, thereby sabotaging the therapeutic milieu's effectiveness.

Usually, nurses are also responsible for making assignments for nursing and paraprofessional personnel. In making these assignments, nurses must remain cognizant of the overall purposes of the therapeutic milieu program, clients' individual needs, and the needs and capabilities of personnel. Inasmuch as it is possible, nurses need to avoid assigning personnel to clients having exaggerated forms of problems similar to their own. By doing so, nurses can help minimize the extent of perceptual distortions originating within personnel toward clients. For example, a psychiatric-mental health nurse whose spouse has a substance abuse problem may tend to perceive and react to clients with similar problems as she would react to the spouse. In this situation, the nurse would fail to respond to the client's uniqueness. This type of perceptual distortion may also be referred to as countertransference.

Moreover, although it would be ideal for personnel to be able to work effectively with all clients, such an expectation is extravagant, if not totally unrealistic. Nurses and other personnel constituting the mental health team are human and are therefore subject to many of the same life stressors and strains affecting clients. Nevertheless, the list of nursing behaviors on this page can be used as a guideline when setting up and maintaining an effective therapeutic milieu.

Summary

This chapter has described what constitutes a therapeutic milieu, how the total milieu acts as the primary therapeutic agent, and what functions nurses perform in creating and maintaining a therapeutic milieu. The following information has been discussed.

1. From a stress-adaptation framework, clients may require milieu therapy in a hospital setting as a result of a decreased ability to cope with, and adapt to, life stressors.
2. The therapeutic milieu provides a temporary, safe haven from these life stressors while also offering clients opportunities to acquire adaptive coping behaviors; that is, the therapeutic milieu affords asylum while simultaneously extending an invitation to clients to return to the mainstream of living and being in the world.
3. Essential characteristics of a therapeutic milieu include individualized treatment programs, self-governance, progressive levels of responsibility, meaningful activities, links with the client's family and community, effective relationships among members of the mental health team, and humanistic attributes of the mental health team members.
4. Milieu therapy is a group therapy approach that uses the client's total living experience as the primary therapeutic agent.
5. Nurses have traditionally assumed the responsibility for managing and coordinating therapeutic milieu activities and they also serve as a link between clients and the socially constructed reality of everyday life.
6. One important nursing function in the therapeutic milieu is mental health teaching of clients (*e.g.*, information about psychotropic medications, psychiatric disorders, interpersonal and communication skills, stress management, and relaxation training).
7. Nurses in the therapeutic milieu must communicate the following message by their every action and word—"Come, come join us in the world, You are welcome here."

References

1. Altshul VA: The Ego-Integrative (and Disintegrative) Effects of Long-Distance Running. Curr Concepts Psychiatr 1 (July–August): 6, 1978
2. Arieti S: Interpretation of Schizophrenia, 2nd ed. New York, Basic Books, 1974
3. Carleton EJ, Johnson JC: A Therapeutic Milieu for Borderline Patients. In Mereness D (ed): Psychiatric Nursing, Vol 1, 2nd ed, pp 288–293. Dubuque, Iowa, Wm C Brown, 1971

4. Hayden LK, Hannah HD, Cozart NR: Attitudes in Action. Am J Nurs 69 (December): 2693–2695, 1966

5. Holmes MJ: Psychiatric Mental Health Nursing. In Arieti S (ed): American Handbook of Psychiatry, Vol 5, 2nd ed, pp 652–665. New York, Basic Books, 1975

6. Holmes MJ, Werner JA: Psychiatric Nursing in a Therapeutic Community. New York, Macmillan, 1966

7. Jacobs AM, Brotz CA, Gamel NN: Critical Behaviors in Psychiatric-Mental Health Nursing, Vol II: Behavior of Nurses. Palo Alto, CA, American Institutes for Research, 1973

8. Jacobson E: Progressive Relaxation. Chicago, University of Chicago Press, 1938

9. Lazarus AA: The Practice of Multi-Modal Therapy. New York, McGraw-Hill, 1981

10. Linn L: Occupational Therapy and other Therapeutic Activities. In Kaplan HI, Freedman AM, Saddock BJ (eds): Comprehensive Textbook of Psychiatry/III, Vol 3, pp 2382–2390. Baltimore, Williams & Wilkins, 1980

11. Nemiak JC: Anxiety State (Anxiety Neurosis). In Kaplan HJ, Freedman AM, Saddock BJ (eds): Comprehensive Textbook of Psychiatry/III, Vol 2, pp 1483–1493. Baltimore, Williams & Wilkins, 1980

12. O'Toole AW: Psychiatric Nursing. In Kaplan HJ, Freedman AM, Saddock BJ (eds): Comprehensive Textbook of Psychiatry/III, Vol 3, pp 3001–3004. Baltimore, Williams & Wilkins, 1980

13. Robbins LL: The Hospital as a Therapeutic Community. In Kaplan HJ, Freedman AM, Saddock BJ (eds): Comprehensive Textbook of Psychiatry/III, Vol 3, pp 2362–2368. Baltimore, Williams & Wilkins, 1980

Chapter 15
Individual Psychotherapy

With them it is as though an artist were to gather the hands, feet, head and other members for his images from diverse models, each part excellently drawn, but not related to a single body, and since they in no way match each other, the result would be a monster rather than man.

Copernicus,
De revolutionibus orbium caelestium

In each of us, there was, like unused muscle and organs of the Spirit, courage and energy and responsibility never employed in our time in the world. The blessed one was he who confronted with a crisis in life was driven to call upon those resources, to use them to survive, even triumph over life itself. One so challenged and so triumphant had won the only prize that counted . . . the prize of the Maker of the spirit . . . the rebirth of a withering soul, and, as such, a Homeric victory over life's disaster.

Author Unknown

Joy Randolph Davidson

Chapter Preview

Psychotherapy is a method of facilitating change in a person's feelings, attitudes, and behaviors. For most of us, this is both intriguing and disturbing. The idea that major changes can be brought about by talking with another person seems almost like magic; it brings out hopes and fears in everyone.

People hope for more happiness and less pain. They fear changes in themselves and in the people they love. How will change, no matter how desirable it may be, affect important relationships? What does it mean in terms of time, effort and responsibility for the individual? What will the person have to do in therapy, and how can the habits and feelings of a lifetime be altered?

This chapter discusses how people can change in therapy by becoming able to use their own hopes, dreams, and strengths. Emphasis is placed on the origins of therapy, the evolution of therapeutic techniques, and the qualities that are necessary for effective therapy. Certain commonly used terms are defined and discussed in relation to the specific meanings and concepts they convey about the nature of human behavior.

Although psychotherapy is based, in large part, on Freudian theory, it is now viewed as a mixed discipline, the result of many contributions from many areas. Therapy is an open-ended process that continues throughout a person's life. New ways of perceiving, relating, and being are learned as life situations change and as the individual reaches new developmental stages.

Learning Objectives

On completing this chapter, the reader should be able to accomplish the following.

1. Discuss the purposes of individual psychotherapy
2. Describe levels and stages of psychotherapy
3. Contrast social and therapeutic relationships
4. Identify the qualities of an effective therapist
5. Compare client and therapist expectations of therapy
6. Discuss concepts of psychotherapy

What Is Psychotherapy?

Psychotherapy is the use of a group of techniques to modify feelings, attitudes, and behavior in people. The therapist uses both verbal and nonverbal means of communication to build a relationship with the client. The basic concept of therapy involves understanding—both self-understanding and being understood by another, to achieve relatedness and to relieve emotional pain.

Psychotherapy may be a treatment choice for a variety of reasons—to treat an emotional disorder, to deal with problems in people who would not be described as emotionally ill, to gain insight and self-knowledge, and to train people in the helping professions. Still other indications for therapy are the reduction of stress and the treatment of medical problems, especially those illnesses with psychosomatic features.

How does psychotherapy work? An onlooker might look at a therapy situation and see that two people meet and talk to each other very regularly over a period of time. One of the two people might seem to be very emotional—angry, happy, crying at times, and sometimes in despair. Nevertheless, these brief meetings, only an hour long, would appear to have profound effects on both the person and his family.

In therapy, two people come together in an encounter that is specifically designed for the purposes of relieving emotional pain, treating mental illness, and facilitating growth. The dialogue between them is focused on issues of great importance to the client. To enter therapy, most people must have a strongly perceived need to understand themselves, to make some kind of change in themselves, or to get relief from pain. Often, more than one of these factors motivates the client to enter therapy. In a therapy situation, one person is designated as the helping person and the other is called the client (*i.e.*, the person who is seeking help).

Specificity of purpose of the interaction, identification of the roles of therapist and client, and the use of primarily verbal means of communication mark the differences between psychotherapy and other human relationships. Nonverbal techniques used in therapy include the use of silence, body language, and facial expression, and respect for personal space.

Levels of Psychotherapy

The abilities, needs, and motivation of the client and the resources available to him help determine the level of psychotherapy in which he participates. These levels of therapy are generally classified as supportive, re-educative, and reconstructive.

Supportive Therapy
Supportive therapy allows the client to express feelings, explore alternatives, and make decisions in a safe, caring relationship. It may be needed briefly or over a period of years. In supportive therapy, there is no plan to introduce new methods of coping; instead, the therapist reinforces the client's existing coping mechanisms.

Re-educative Therapy
Re-educative therapy involves learning new ways of perceiving and behaving. The client explores alternatives in a

planned, systematic way, which requires a longer period of time. Often, the client enters into a contract that specifies desired changes in behavior. Changing a behavior may change the way in which the client perceives himself. Talking about alternative ways of coping opens up new options that the client may then try. Examples of re-educative therapy include short-term psychotherapy, reality therapy, cognitive restructuring, and behavior modification.

Reconstructive Therapy

Reconstructive therapy typically involves deep psychotherapy or psychoanalysis, it may take 2 to 5 or more years of time, and it delves into all aspects of the client's life. Emotional and cognitive restructuring of the self takes place. Positive outcomes of reconstructive therapy include greater understanding of self and others, more emotional freedom, development of potential abilities, and heightened capacity for love and work. The focus of this chapter is long-term, reconstructive therapy.

Stages of Psychotherapy

Introductory Stage

The introductory stage is the stage in which the client and therapist meet and begin to work together. This stage usually involves taking a history of the client's life, including any medical problems. It is important to realize that many physical illnesses resemble emotional problems and that the opposite is also true. Referrals or consultations may be indicated at this time to understand the problem.

The exploration of the client's background and problems should include any precipitating factors or events that caused him to seek help. The client should discuss his perceptions of his problems and needs and his expectations of therapy.

The therapist, during this introductory stage, forms some preliminary ideas about the client and his needs. Together, client and therapist discuss issues such as the length of time therapy will require, meeting dates, fees, and so forth. These issues are more fully described in the chapter section further on dealing with client and therapist expectations.

During the introductory phase, the client and therapist also begin to form some ideas about each other regarding personality compatibility, whether there is mutual respect or liking, and whether they can work together. The ability to work together and to be invested emotionally in the task of therapy is known as the *treatment alliance.*

The introductory phase may last from a few weeks to 2 or more years in a situation with an extremely withdrawn, defended, or psychotic person. The goal of this first stage of therapy is to establish a degree of trust that will allow the client to give up his defenses as he enters into the second, or working, stage of treatment.

Working Stage

As the client becomes able to trust and to disclose more about himself in the *working stage* of therapy, the client and therapist begin to explore the thoughts, feelings, and behaviors that have caused him pain or problems. This exploration may take months or years to accomplish. Often, the client reworks material previously explored as his level of trust deepens. Deeper trust allows the client to experience greater recall and insight and to express his previously repressed feelings. As the client comes to understand and function more effectively, the last stage, working through, is reached.

Working Through Stage

In the final stage of therapy, the *working through stage,* the client understands much more about himself and his relationships and begins to try out new ways of perceiving, thinking, feeling, and behaving. As he interacts with others and uses his newly acquired coping skills, changes occur, both in the client and the people around him. In other words, his inner emotional changes are reflected in his external behaviors and in his interactions with others. The client may need a great deal of support and encouragement and may rework emotional material during this stage. *Termination* of therapy may be viewed as a kind of separation. The client becomes more autonomous and ready to live his own life.

Client and Therapist

During individual psychotherapy, the client explores issues of such an intimate and personal nature that they can only be discussed with a person who is felt to be trustworthy. Trust is a necessary condition for growth and change. Let's examine how trust comes about.

Many of us have experienced change in our own lives—it probably happened because someone was therapeutic at a time of need. Looking back, we remember a grandparent, a parent, a friend, or maybe a teacher or minister who had a profound effect on our lives. Somehow, the presence, the understanding, or the example of that person helped us to understand, to feel better, or to make a needed change. Some quality in that person met our own need to find meaning or direction in life.

Our own change and growth may have resulted from a love that made no demands and set no conditions. Or, we may have responded to another's acceptance or ability to see worth in another human being. Perhaps it was the integrity of mind and spirit that made it safe to confide in him or her. We say of such people, "he always loved me and believed in me" . . . "she understands me, she was always there when I needed her" . . . "he is solid as a rock" . . .

These qualities that are so powerful in our personal lives are the qualities that are effective in therapy. In therapy, there is a person, the client, who is in conflict or in a process of growth and change. The client is experiencing enough pain or discomfort to cause him to perceive a need for help. Another person, the therapist, has the essential qualities to provide that help.

Why is it necessary to go to a therapist to get help? Why can't we achieve the same results by talking to the people who are important in our lives? All of us have families, friends, doctors, teachers and ministers available to us in time of need. Even the poorest and most lonely have some available resources.

Many people can, and do, use these resources. One of the goals of therapy is to learn to relate more effectively to others to meet more of our own, and their, needs. Another goal is to grow so that we have more strengths and are able to give more of ourselves to others.

For many people, however, the realities of living and relating to others have been difficult and painful. Perhaps, the person has grown up in a family that was conflicted, chaotic, or dysfunctional to a greater extent than most families. Perhaps, family members were locked into constricting roles; there were hidden agendas, unclear communication patterns, or incidents of physical and emotional abuse. Ways of relating and expressing feelings may have been distorted, causing painful, unproductive encounters with the people most important to the client as a child. Perhaps they were not able to understand the child or give him what he needed.

Early ways of relating and early experiences are carried from the past into the present. Often, faulty or unproductive ways of relating are modified by other experiences and other relationships. Relearning and emotional repair take place. These processes are normally seen as children enter school and form friendships; adolescence is also a time of major reworking and relearning. This reworking and relearning is what therapy is designed to do. The client experiences emotional relearning in a safe relationship.

In therapy, the client relates to the therapist and behaves in the same way as he does with the significant other people in his life. Patterns of client behavior become evident as the process of therapy continues. In traditional psychotherapy, a great deal of emphasis is placed on the client's childhood memories of relationships and events. In present-oriented therapies, the emphasis is on the client's behavior in current relationships. In both kinds of therapy, however, distortions or problem areas in interpersonal relations are identified and become the foci of therapy.

Therapist Versus Family or Friends: Whom to Choose?

When faced with a problem, the client may consult any helping person—a family member, friend, minister, or therapist; he may choose a therapist because of his *objectivity.* The therapist is not related to, or involved with, the client outside the therapy situation. This is one of the therapist's

important ethical responsibilities. The therapist should not engage in a social relationship, and particularly not in a sexual relationship with a client. If this should occur, the relationship can no longer be considered therapeutic. Obviously, people may consult friends or those who are already known to them for therapy. In this situation, it is important that the therapist discuss the need for objectivity with the client and, if there is a conflict, refer him to another therapist. Often, however, a friend or acquaintance is able to be both objective and therapeutic.

The therapist provides a *different perspective* for the client and offers him alternative ways of perceiving, thinking, feeling, and behaving. Often, a client is locked into one mode of being, like "being in a rut" and unable to get out. The therapist is not limited by the client's special set of circumstances.

The therapist also brings *specialized knowledge* to the relationship with the client. The specialized knowledge is in the area of human behavior and includes understanding problems and problem-solving techniques. In addition, the therapist brings a background in medicine, nursing, psychology, social work, the ministry, or counseling.

Because of these qualifications—objectivity, perspective, and specialized knowledge—the therapist operates outside the framework of the client's life and within the context of stated goals designed jointly by client and therapist for the client's benefit.

Qualities of the Therapist

Carl Rogers identified the qualities that promote a therapeutic relationship.[16] Rogers believes that therapist attitudes provide "necessary and sufficient conditions" for therapeutic change. These attitudes are congruence, unconditional positive regard, and accurate empathic understanding.

Congruence or genuineness, means that the feelings, thoughts, and behaviors of a person are consistent. To be congruent, the therapist needs to understand himself, to be aware of his feelings, and to be free of deceit or misleading behaviors. This does not imply that the therapist expresses or acts on every thought or feeling; awareness, rather, allows for a choice of behaviors.

Clients are often incongruent; that is, they are not aware of their feelings or thoughts. They may express feelings and ideas that do not match what is really felt or thought. Congruence in the therapist allows the client to become aware of his true feelings and thoughts and to feel free to express them.

Unconditional positive regard involves being able to feel concern and caring for the client without making any value judgments. This means being able to accept both positive and negative statements made by the client and being able to have faith in his potential as a human being. This attitude allows the client to accept and value himself, and to move toward realizing his potential.

Students and Therapy

Students sometimes work with psychiatric-mental health clients on a one-to-one basis in inpatient and outpatient settings. The students usually function as members of a treatment team and participate in carrying out a plan of care.

Members of the treatment team have input in planning and implementing client goals, and regularly provide feedback on client and team interaction. Within this setting, the nursing instructor acts as a resource person and supervisor to the student. Together, the treatment team and instructor provide direction and support for the student.

The central, or most important, element of therapy is the ongoing process that involves the client, the student, and the staff. By the term *process*, we mean the experience of self-discovery, understanding, and relating. This process extends to everyone involved and, in a truly therapeutic setting, leads to growth and self-actualization.

Students have a great deal to contribute to clients; they bring interest, concern, and caring to the clinical setting. Clients respond to this and often feel less threatened by students than they do by the professional staff.

Problems may arise because of the students' vulnerability and tendency to become over-involved with a client. Both of these tendencies are also related to the students' therapeutic qualities. Without empathy and concern, little therapy could occur.

As the clinical experience progresses, students often begin to realize that they and their family and friends are really not very different from the client. There is a common humanity and most human problems are similar. It is difficult for the student in the sense that he or she begins to question long-held values and beliefs and to wonder just how healthy he is. The student's personal problems often become more visible.

Over-identification with the client seems to be related to this awareness that we are not very different from each other. As increased self-awareness, recognition of similarities, and empathy occur, the student may develop very intense emotional ties with the client. Furthermore, the emphasis on congruence and positive regard will affect the student as it does the client. A staff member who has these qualities brings out feeling, and the student experiences a therapeutic environment in action.

The student needs to realize that his feelings and concerns are not "wrong" or "bad," but need to be shared with the nursing instructor and staff. This openness will keep the student–client relationship in a therapeutic framework and will help to relieve the student's anxiety.

A large part of the anxiety many students feel stems from the fear of harming the client. They often express this fear as "What if I say the wrong thing?" or "Do you think I said the right thing?" The student's fear or anxiety, therefore, relates to both the self and the client.

A student may want or need to work further on personal problems and may be referred for counseling. A need for counseling does not have to be considered a weakness. Insight, empathy, and therapeutic concern are typical of people in helping professions. Working out one's own problems allows for personal and professional growth.

Accurate empathic understanding involves feeling and experiencing with the client "almost as if" the therapist were having those feelings and experiences. This empathy allows the client to become more aware of his feelings and to feel validated. Someone, he realizes, has heard what he is trying to express and understands him.

The therapist, because of what he or she is, facilitates growth and development in the client. It is not a matter of giving to, or doing for, someone; rather, it is a way of reaching the client's energies and potentials and freeing them for use.

Client Expectations

The energies and potentials of the client are powerful. The wishes, hopes, and dreams of our lives have great emotional energy invested in them, and this provides a key to understanding what motivates people to go into therapy. To understand themselves or to change behavior in even small ways, people must have a strongly perceived need to change, the hope that change is possible, and at least some belief that someone can help.

Usually, the client realizes that something in his life is causing so much emotional pain that something needs to be done. The need must be strong enough to cause the client to risk self-disclosure and to continue in therapy even when it is painful and embarassing.

Sometimes, the client seems to expect the therapist to solve all his problems. This may not be a conscious thought; however, it is a very human one and probably a wish that all of us have had at one time or another. We wish that someone would love us, take care of us, and make things right.

The therapist usually makes it clear from the beginning that therapy is a joint effort in which the client will come to understand what the problems are and what he

Nursing Process and Individual Therapy

The nursing process is a form of problem-solving. The steps of collecting and analyzing data, identifying problems, formulating goals, planning actions, and evaluating progress are also those of the process of therapy.

It is important to remember that the major focus of therapy is how the process is carried out. In a team approach, physicians, nurses, psychologists, social workers, occupational therapists, mental health technicians, and nursing students work in collaboration to meet the client's needs. Students work with the staff and with clinical nursing supervision in interaction with clients; these interactons may be on a one-to-one basis with inpatients or outpatients.

Client goals need to be jointly determined by the client, therapist, and staff. Goals and actions should be simple, measurable, and stated in behavioral terms.

An example of this process applied to a withdrawn adolescent client follows:

Problem: Fourteen-year-old Mary has difficulty in forming relationships with peers. She neither talks with them nor joins in their activities.

Goal: Mary will relate more effectively to her peers.

Action: 1. Mary will talk with at least two peers daily for a minimum of 10 minutes each.
2. Mary will use "I" messages to express feelings and thoughts.

Evaluation: Mary has been able to carry out the actions planned this week. The "I" messages are difficult for her, but the result of using this method has been the expression of more feeling. Her speech is less flat. Peers have been more responsive to her.

needs to do. To "help" or "do for" the client would take away from the growth and autonomy that therapy is designed to accomplish.

The client can expect confidentiality, specialized knowledge, and skill from the therapist. In addition, he needs to know how often therapy will take place, the probable length of treatment, and how much it will cost. He should know how to contact the therapist in case of an emergency or a change in plans. Usually, there is some formulation of the situation and an explanation of how therapy will be conducted.

Therapist Expectations

The major expectation of the therapist is that the client will be as open and honest in discussing his situation as he is consciously able to be. This is sometimes referred to as the *therapeutic contract.*

Other therapist expectations include keeping appointments on time and being paid for services. The therapist should arrange ways in which the client can contact him in case of need. He should also schedule holidays and vacations in such a way as to let the client know well in advance and provide for another therapist to take care of any problems that arise.

Usually, the therapist will use a collaborative approach in planning therapy, identifying problem areas, and setting goals. This may take several sessions or may evolve as therapy continues and a better understanding of the situation comes about. Therapy is almost always a process of verbal interaction between the client and the therapist. Sometimes, it is difficult to put feelings into words, but this is a very valuable kind of learning, because it allows other people to understand one another and helps to clarify feelings for the client.

Physical acting out of loving or hostile feelings between client and therapist is inappropriate and this should be clarified with the client if any confusion or misunderstanding is present.

The therapist may also expect rewards such as receiving pleasure from facilitating growth and change, or from understanding more about human behavior. The therapeutic relationship is always maintained within the orientation of a professional person working with a client to meet the client's needs. Personal and social needs of the therapist are properly met through family, friends, and the community.

The therapist has a further obligation—that of protecting the client who is suicidal or likely to harm another person. In this situation, it may be necessary to hospitalize the client. Taking steps to protect the client is often reassuring to him, even though he is angry and protests. Hospitalization, for example, supplies external control at a time when the client feels out of control. Being out of control or feeling out of control is very frightening for both the client and the people around him.

Sometimes, people use threats of suicide to get attention or to manipulate others. The nurse must realize that, even when the client threatens suicide for these reasons, the possibility of suicide is real. This kind of behavior also provides fertile ground for exploring the client's need to manipulate others and the feelings that would lead to such behavior.

How client problems are defined and what kind of therapy is engaged in depends to a great extent on the therapist's orientations. The therapist forms a theoretical framework of values and beliefs, or concepts, derived from his education and life experiences. The next section of the chapter will discuss how some of the concepts used in individual therapy came about.

Origins and Development of Psychotherapy

There is a tremendous amount of information available dealing with human behavior. Some of it is old, some is new. Contributions to the study of human behavior have come from medicine, psychiatry, psychology, and biology. A particularly interesting area has been that of ethnology. Studies of animal behavior have inspired much of the current research on human behavior. Such seemingly diverse areas as Harlow's work with monkeys and studies of imprinting in animals have helped us to understand ourselves.[9] Studies of social behavior have also broadened our conceptions of how people develop and relate to each other. Many of the original ideas of Freud and his colleagues about individuals and therapy are still in use; others have been modified as new information and new perspectives became available.

As we review some of the thinking and major concepts that have shaped the development of therapy as we know it today, it is important to keep in mind that all theories and concepts are formed within the context of a historical period. They arise in a given culture out of the general level of knowledge of that time. That is one reason why theories change over time as the culture changes. Another reason for ongoing change in theories is that research techniques are constantly being improved and each period of active research provides us with more accurate information. Theories, or hypotheses, are ideas that try to explain how or why something occurs. By understanding behavior, we can predict it and can, perhaps, make changes.

Theories or concepts are formed by individuals. The therapist shapes his beliefs and values out of his own experiences within the larger cultural framework. For example, a person who had difficulty forming a warm, close relationship with parents during infancy might grow up to form a theory that interpersonal difficulties during infancy may cause or contribute to mental illness. Research on infant attachment, in fact, tends to support this belief.[1, 3, 4, 5] Self-understanding helps the therapist to understand others.

In therapy, both the client and therapist are involved in trying to understand and form ideas as to what causes problems, and are trying to find solutions to those problems. To do this, they must explore the client's beliefs and values.

Freud's Theories

Freud, who is known as the father of psychiatry, certainly was affected by his culture and the state of knowledge at that time. His genius was his ability to transcend culture and, from his observations of his patients, develop ideas that are still influential in therapy.

He studied in Vienna, which was the world center for medical education at that time. He could be described as a middle class, Jewish, professional male who had access to the new knowledge of that day. There was a tremendous amount of work being done in all the sciences in the Victorian era and in the first part of the 20th century. Application of the scientific method, the use of the microscope and telescope, and the new theory of evolution had opened up whole new areas for investigation.

Freud was a neurologist. He was interested in applying the scientific method to his work. At that time, people in the sciences were engaged in describing, classifying, and labeling their discoveries. Mental illness and the workings of the mind could be studied, described, labeled and classified. The medical model originated in this way and proclaimed that mental illness is a disease manifested by symptoms. This was a radical idea at the time and represented a significant change from older ideas that mental illness was caused by sin or constitutional inferiority.

Freud became convinced that the mind was a major factor in mental illness when he observed that patients suffering from amnesia or from hysterical paralysis became symptom-free under hypnosis. The patient was able to remember, or was able to use the previously paralyzed body part, thereby demonstrating that the illness was not an organic impairment, but a functional one. This distinction is still utilized in health care. Organic illness can be demonstrated by alterations in the anatomy or physiology of the body; in functional illness, an organic cause cannot be demonstrated. (Note: with improved diagnostic studies such as Positron Emission Tomography, Nuclear Magnetic Imaging, and the Dexamethasone Suppression Test, these classifications may change.)

As Freud talked with patients and they told him about their lives and experiences, some interesting things happened. The patients often remembered previously forgotten experiences. Talking allowed them to express some of the painful thoughts and feelings attached to those experiences and, sometimes, their physical or emotional distress would be relieved; that is, they became free of symptoms. Freud began to try to understand and account for what he experienced. In time, he called this work *analysis* or *psychoanalysis,* a study of the workings of the mind. From his experiences with patients and his self-analysis, Freud formed major concepts about mental functioning.

Concepts of Psychotherapy

Insight

A person is said to gain *insight* when he becomes consciously aware of the odd, painful, angry, or socially unacceptable thoughts or feelings that he had repressed. *Intellectual insight* is an understanding of the origins and consequences of a symptom or behavior. *Emotional insight* involves both understanding and re-experiencing the very painful, frightening, or angry feelings that are associated with that symptom or behavior. This re-experiencing, also called *catharsis,* frees a person's fixed emotions and allows for emotional growth.

Repression

The concept of repression is central to Freudian theory. Through the mechanism of *repression,* feelings, thoughts, and experiences that are too painful or threatening to the person to be allowed to remain in conscious awareness, or to become conscious, are pushed back into the unconscious part of the mind. *Unconscious* means, literally, not available to consciousness. Repression is an unconscious phenomenon; that is, the person does not try to forget. Instead, events or ongoing situations that threaten the ego integrity, (*i.e.,* the person's self-image or safety) are too painful to realize. Sometimes, there is partial repression. For example, knowledge of a situation may be in a person's awareness, but the feelings about the situation are repressed.

Repressed knowledge and feelings exert powerful influences on people that come out in all kinds of ways. Freudian slips or "slips of the tongue" occur. Sometimes, a word or phrase that seems funny or inappropriate in the context of a sentence makes very good sense in expressing the person's real feelings.

Dreams also provide a way of getting at repressed thoughts and feelings. People in therapy often have vivid, and sometimes recurring, dreams. In fact, recurring dreams may be present for a long time and may represent the client's attempt to solve a problem. It is fairly common to have vivid dreams or to remember more dreams when we are anxious or excited. Therapy represents both a form of stress that causes anxiety, and an emotionally secure situation. The security offered by the therapist allows for weakening of repressions and access to emotionally important material. The client's emotional content may be disguised in dreams.

Originally, therapists attempted to analyze both manifest and latent dream content; that is, they believed that a specific kind of dream had a specific meaning. Now, therapists believe that the most productive use of dream material comes from the client's discussion of his thoughts and feelings and what the dreams mean to him.

Free Association

Free association is the free expression of thoughts and feelings just as they come to mind. This method encourages the lowering of the client's defenses. It is the primary method of treatment in psychoanalysis and in much of psychotherapy.

Resistance

Resistance means that the client resists recalling information or recalling feelings. It often occurs as *blocking,* wherein a client will suddenly "blank out" and be unable to finish a thought or idea. He may suddenly change the subject without any cue or obvious reason to do so. In blocking, there is not only repression of painful knowledge and feelings, but also resistance to recall and understanding.

Techniques such as having the client lie on a couch and face away from the therapist are used in psychoanalysis to avoid influencing the client as to what he should say. These are ways of trying to decrease resistance. Therapeutic attitudes of being accepting and nonjudgmental are also ways of decreasing resistance and allowing the client to express his thoughts and feelings.

Maslow helps us to understand resistance through his assertion that people have both a need to know and a fear of knowing.[12] Knowing and understanding may imply action and change. In therapy, the therapist supports the client's need to know. This support is needed because the knowledge that has been repressed is literally unthinkable, the feelings are too painful to feel. Therapy, then, represents both threat and opportunity.

What is so terrible that it cannot be thought or felt or said? Each of us has secrets, things we would not want other people to know because they would disapprove, reject us, stop loving us, or be very angry. In unconscious material, the fear that derives or mediates the repression is so strong that it is experienced as a threat to the person's existence—a fear of total rejection, abandonment, loss of existence, or intolerable feelings of being worthless or bad.

Infants and small children are literally dependent on significant adults, usually parents, for survival in both a physical and an emotional sense. Lack of love, disapproval, or an inability to accept the child and love him as he is is a threat to that child's survival.

Sometimes, a family will place adult burdens of emotional responsibility on a child and expect that child to meet the dependency needs of the parents. Each family also has standards of behavior for children that include which feelings may be expressed and how they may be expressed. If a child learns that it is not safe to express pain and anger or that it is not safe to express love, tenderness, and vulnerability, then repression is the price the child pays for surviving in that family. The effects of that repression may include shame and guilt.

Reworking

Through *reworking*, children learn other ways of behaving as they grow and develop. Other family members, peers, and people outside the immediate family model different ways of feeling and behaving. Adolescents, especially, rework earlier developmental stages and modify earlier feelings, beliefs, and attitudes.

To a great extent, this *emotional relearning* is what happens in psychotherapy. Early therapists believed that the personality was fairly rigid and could only be modified slightly. Now we believe that there is far more plasticity and potential for change, even in middle age or old age.

Transference

Transference is a major tool or technique—a powerful force—in psychotherapy. In therapy, the client transfers feelings and attitudes held toward significant others onto the therapist. The client then reacts toward the therapist in the same ways he reacts, or reacted, toward the important people in his life. There may be different sets of feelings and attitudes for each person in the client's life. At times, for example, he may behave as if the therapist is mother, father, brother, or sister. The sex of the therapist doesn't seem to make much difference. In *transference*, the client is deeply involved with the feelings and experiences of his own life and projects these experiences onto the therapist. The transference may be *positive*, in which all good qualities are transferred onto the therapist, or it may be *negative*, in which the therapist becomes all bad. A positive transference may become negative as the client gets in touch with his feelings of pain and anger and hurt. A negative transference may become positive as the client begins to establish trust with the therapist and work through his hurt and anger.

The term *significant others* seems very pale and weak; these are, after all, the people who have profound importance in our lives. We love, hate, fear, want, and depend on them. We are often almost as concerned with their feelings and needs as our own.

In transference, the client realizes, as therapy continues, that the therapist is not like the significant others in his life. The projection or transference allows both client and therapist to understand the feelings, attitudes, and behaviors that the client has learned. An important part of emotional relearning is the client's realization that other people do not possess the stereotyped or punitive reactions that have been present in his relationships in the past. The client also realizes how he or she contributes to, or feeds into, present relationships to maintain the faulty, incongruent, or inappropriate perceptions and behaviors. The experience of being valued and understood allows the client to have new perceptions and form new perspectives.

Countertransference

In *countertransference*, the therapist sometimes experiences a transference of his or her feelings for significant others onto the client. Usually, something about the client; appearance, tone of voice, mannerisms, or behavior; will trigger countertransference. An unusual like or dislike of the client is a clue to the therapist that countertransference is operating. This clue can be very useful if it alerts the therapist to analyze the reaction. If not detected, countertransference can cause problems. Therapists will often consult with a colleague or request supervision to deal effectively with this kind of situation. Consultation or supervision allows for working through both client's and therapist's feelings in a therapeutic way with benefits for both.

Ambivalence

Ambivalence is the experience of two strong, opposing feelings or wishes toward the same object, or person, at the same time. It could equally well be described as the conflict experienced when strong approach/avoidance tendencies are present. Dollard, Miller, and others were able to create ambivalence in laboratory rats by giving them an electric shock while they were eating. A strong drive or need (hunger) caused approach to food; the painful shock caused strong avoidance tendencies.[7]

In human beings, the opposite feelings or needs are almost always love/hate, love/fear, or some combination. Anger usually results when strong drives or needs are frustrated; that is, not allowed appropriate expression. Another outcome of this frustration may be what is called *learned helplessness*, which is believed to be a major component of depression.[17]

Ambivalence, then, causes a great deal of conflict that may be expressed as feelings of distress, anxiety, tension, or an inability to make decisions or to move at all. In extreme states, this would be called panic, if it manifested as anxiety, or immobility, if the client were frozen in conflict.

Ambivalence is present in all of us. We have differing feelings toward people that vary with the amount of closeness in the relationship and with different situations. A small child expresses feelings very directly and can say, "I hate you" when frustrated, and a few minutes later say, "I love you" with equal intensity. Both feelings are real and, as the child grows up, he comes to realize that being angry at a person does not mean not loving the person also.

In a "good enough" family, children are taught to own their feelings and to label them correctly. The family functions to meet the child's needs for love and security and socializes the child by teaching him to get his needs met in socially acceptable ways.

Problems arise when parents are unable to fulfill these

necessary functions for their children. Parents who cannot allow a child to separate and become autonomous contribute to ambivalence over dependence/independence and love/hate issues. If being dependent means being loved and being independent means being emotionally abandoned, a tremendous amount of conflict and anger will be generated within the child.

Parents who have difficulty allowing feelings of anger, aggression, or sexuality may react to the child's expression of these feelings in such a punitive way that these feelings are repressed. In our culture, it is particularly true that girls repress angry, aggressive, and sexual feelings. Boys are more likely to repress feelings of love, tenderness, and dependency. By repressing strong feelings, we not only inhibit emotional development in regard to the feeling repressed, but we also inhibit the appropriate expression of its opposite feeling.

Ambiguity

Ambiguity describes the experience of uncertainty. One measure of emotional competence is how well a person is able to tolerate living with a degree of uncertainty. An element common to many people in therapy is difficulty in tolerating ambiguity, which indicates a strong need for certainty and stability. Most of us would like to live in what has been referred to as a reasonably predictable environment.

We need to feel that we have some control over our lives. Children who live in a chaotic or deprived environment and children who never experience stability in their lives will be at risk in the world. Often, when they become adults, they will cling to very rigid ideas to feel secure.

Tolerating ambiguity means that we are able to perceive the world and the people around us in a way that allows for shades of meaning and also allows for many feelings about a given person or situation. Sometimes, we think it would be easier or safer to live in a world where things could be categorized as good or bad, either this or that. Perhaps, though, there would be fewer possibilities and our experiences would not be as rich in meaning. Part of becoming adult is the ability to accept in each of us, the subtle shifting of complex thoughts and feelings toward other people in our lives.

Object Constancy

The feeling of security or stability in our lives is known as *object constancy* or *object permanence*. It is a general feeling that people are reliable and that the world is a pretty good place. There are several influences during an individual's growth and development that help to establish this feeling.

One very useful concept is that of the "good enough mother" and the expansion of that to the idea of the "good enough" family. No family is perfect and no mother could possibly be all-loving and all-giving. Most of us, in fact, would be pretty uncomfortable with perfection, having not quite achieved that state for ourselves. Nevertheless, families, mothers in particular, do some very important things.

Object constancy comes about partly as the result of a secure maternal–infant attachment.[1,3,4,5] A secure maternal–infant attachment has survival value for the infant and for the human species. It is manifested by the infant's maintenance of proximity to the mother in times of stress and by his exploration from a safe base (mother) in times of security.

Maternal qualities that foster attachment are sensitivity to the infant's needs, warmth, and nurturance. The infant both initiates and limits interaction with the mother or primary caregiver. This is done by eye contact or vocal cues (*i.e.*, crying or vocalizing). Mother cues in to the baby's signals, mirrors, and selectively emphasizes the behavior. The first faint twitch of the baby's lips is identified as a smile and positively reinforced by mirroring the behavior.

Accurate empathic mirroring reinforces desired social behaviors. The sensitive mother is aware that her baby is tired when he ends eye contact. This is a signal to end the interaction. Soon after birth, the parents identify the baby's cries as indicating hunger, pain, or a cry for attention. This concern and care for the infant's needs and individuality insures that the infant's needs will be met and that he can depend on his mother or father to do this. Babies seem to be genetically programmed to prefer the human face and their eyes focus best at a distance of about 9 inches in early infancy. Babies quickly learn to recognize and prefer mother. After about 7 months, the baby begins to discriminate and prefer mother, father, and known others to strangers, and to be anxious with strangers. Distinctions made between self and others and between known people and strange people are precursors of a clear sense of self or identity.

As the baby becomes more mobile, we can observe the gradual processes of separation and individualization. Babies love games. In peek-a-boo, the very young baby loves the experience of hiding and then being seen. A young baby will hide his or her eyes. The belief seems to be that if the baby can't see, then he can't be seen! If a person or an object can't be seen, does it exist? The fun of peek-a-boo and hide and seek is finding that people do still exist even though we can't see them for a little while. As the baby becomes a toddler, we can watch him play happily for a while, go to another room, come back to his parent, and then return to play. The parent, the infant discovers, still exists even if he or she is in another room.

The ability to say "No" and to control bowel and bladder functions also reinforces the experience of being autonomous. This experience further emphasizes the distinction between what is I and mine and what is you and yours.

As these processes of identification, separation, and autonomy occur, there is a corresponding internalization of the feelings, attitudes, and behaviors of the parents or significant others. This internalization is known as *introjection*. The infant incorporates aspects of significant others as part of the self. At the same time, he internalizes constructs, or conceptions, of the significant others or object. This internal representation of others supplies object constancy. Later in life, even when death occurs, we continue to carry a realistic conception of those we love; they remain constant for us as they were experienced. The feeling of being loved and being able to depend on others to meet accurately our needs for both security and autonomy allows for a sense of self-identity and a sense of the identity, or object permanence, of others.

In therapy, clients may need to achieve object constancy and may need to separate from a fused sense of identity with a parent or other person. This may require a considerable amount of work and sometimes involves multiple types of therapy, utilizing an inpatient milieu structure.

All of these aspects of therapy sound simple, as though therapy follows an outline or sequence of mental or emotional events. That is the plan, but not at all the usual situation. Each success of the client's is reinforcing and leads to more work, but the repressed material is both painful and powerful. Resistance is seen in other forms.

Acting In

Acting in is the kind of resistance that circumvents therapy through blocking, forgetting, changing the subject, or trying to elicit the therapist's approval or disapproval while trying to recall or express feelings. Consciously, the client is earnestly trying to express everything as it comes to mind.

Acting Out

In *acting out,* the client substitutes some kind of action for feeling or thinking. As memories, feelings, and thoughts begin to reach awareness, a kind of reflex substitution of action occurs. The painful awareness is not allowed to reach consciousness.

The defenses seen in acting out are learned ones and the client may show a pattern of defensive acting out. Common defenses are the use of alcohol or drugs, getting involved in fights, running away, or the compulsive or promiscuous use of sexual activity. Even ordinary activities like work or exercise can be used or overused as defenses, instead of thinking or feeling.

Sometimes in therapy, a client will get married, divorced, form new friendships, and so on as a "short cut" to getting support or getting dependency needs met. This is another way of avoiding the more difficult task of becoming aware of one's feelings and understanding one's self. The therapist may ask the client to sign an agreement or contract to postpone major lifestyle changes during therapy until a better self-understanding exists.

Interpretation

Interpretation appears very exciting in movies in which the analyst arrives at a brilliant interpretation of the patient's problem. The patient would say, "Aha! That explains everything!"

Actually, the important aspect of *interpretation* is the client's understanding of his feelings and behavior. The client's insight is the therapeutic element. A therapist may make beautiful formulations of the client's problems and their origins and causes, but this is not helpful unless the client arrives at self-understanding.

Sometimes, the therapist will offer a tentative explanation or ask whether it is possible that a particular feeling or experience is connected to another. Questions such as this are best asked infrequently and with respect for the client's anxiety and need for his defenses. Even a cautious and accurate comment may arouse a good deal of anger or denial. Interpretation of this kind is useful when the client is ready to deal with this aspect of himself and when his awareness is just below the surface.

Working Through

Working through comes in the last phase of therapy. At this point, the client has reached a fairly good understanding of the feelings and patterns of behavior that have caused him distress. The client has more emotional energy available and is able to perceive more of the world around him and to form new perspectives.

Working through means that the client's insights have to be discussed and reworked over a period of time. The long repressed pain, guilt, anger, shame, grief, or sadness must be expressed—not just once, but many times—in order to be owned and integrated into the self. This takes a lot of work and there are often periods of regression, discouragement, or acting out. At the end, however, the pain is gone.

Part of the process of working through is the knowledge that therapy will eventually end. A relationship that has been of great importance will gradually become less important and then end, usually by agreement of the therapist and client.

Translating

Translating insight and understanding into new behaviors is the final aspect of working through. Discussion is not enough; success in trying new behaviors is highly reinforcing. As the client feels less angry, vulnerable, or frightened, he feels more freedom to try new ways of behaving. The client becomes more autonomous, more aware of options. Feelings are often more vivid and more consciously experienced. The client is better able to live with tensions, ambivalence, and ambiguity.

The process of emotional re-education is now internalized so that, as time goes on, the client's emotions become more congruent, and a greater choice of behaviors are available to him. Psychotherapy then becomes a process of being—a process of learning, trying out, and adapting that continues through the client's life.

Summary

This chapter has discussed how people change their feelings, attitudes, and behaviors through therapy. Some of the important points discussed in the chapter are as follows.

1. An individual may choose to engage in the process of psychotherapy to treat an emotional disorder, to deal with his problems, or to gain insight and self-understanding.
2. Various levels of psychotherapy—supportive, re-educative, and reconstructive—describe the depth of therapy and the degree of change undertaken by the client.
3. During each of the three stages of individual psy-chotherapy, the client and therapist have certain tasks to accomplish, such as exploring the client's history and current problems and needs during the introductory stage.
4. Because of his objectivity, perspective, and special-ized knowledge, a therapist can generally be more effective than a person's family or friends in help-ing him deal with problems and growth needs.
5. The client and therapist need to clearly com-municate their expectations of each other and of therapy.
6. The important concepts of psychotherapy, such as insight, repression, resistance, and reworking, are explored and applied to the client involved in indi-vidual psychotherapy.

Case Study

Using Individual Psychotherapy to Foster Lifestyle and Behavior Changes

Ms. Jane V. is an attractive young woman in her early twenties. She is slender, of average height, well-developed, and well-nourished. Her posture is erect. She seems a little overactive, perhaps due to anxiety.

"I came to see you because my family doctor recommended you," she said during her first inter-view with a therapist. She added that since her en-gagement ended recently, she has been unable to sleep and has had suicidal thoughts.

When the therapist asked her to talk more about her feelings, she stated, "I feel like my world has ended. I've been abandoned again. I just want to die. This always happens—everytime I love someone, I lose. At first everything is so wonderful, but it doesn't work out. They just can't meet my needs."

The therapist then asked Jane how she handles disappointments. "Well," she responded, "I have wondered if I drink a little too much. Sometimes I smoke a joint—just to relax, you know—or maybe a Valium will help. That scares me, though. I cut my-self once—see my wrists. Maybe the Valium makes it worse."

The therapist also learned that Jane has done well in school and is now a junior in college, but has no clear idea of what she wants to do for a career.

Jane is the third child of a highly achievement-oriented family. An older brother has just finished law school, her sister is a graduate student in busi-ness, and a younger brother is interested in computer science. Her father is an attorney and her mother is a homemaker.

Jane described her father as distant, but de-manding, and her mother as very protective and with few interests outside the family. She related that she had asthma when she was a child, and that her mother has "always babied" her. (Later, in ther-apy, Jane expressed her difficulty in identifying with her weak but manipulative mother, and her own poor self-image as a woman.)

At times, Jane tried to hold summer jobs, which she always left because of personality differ-ences with her employers. While talking about these experiences, she became quite angry and expressed that people had been unfair to her. She became tear-ful at this point in the interview and said, "You know I always try so hard, but everything goes wrong. No matter what I do, it falls apart. I feel so helpless! Sometimes I think things will never be better."

Subsequent therapy sessions tended to confirm the therapist's impressions that Jane has a Borderline Personality Disorder. Specific problems of Jane's include

1. an overly close, dependent relationship with her mother;
2. a distant and hostile relationship with her father;
3. lack of a clear sense of self, especially in rela-tion to gender identity and self-esteem;
4. indecisiveness about a career choice;
5. habitual use of alcohol or drugs to cope with emotional pain;
6. a pattern of unstable relationships; and,
7. depression, evidenced by self-mutilation and feelings of helplessness and hopelessness.

Initial goals set up by Jane and the therapist are

1. to form a treatment alliance; and,
2. to involve the family in the therapeutic process.

The treatment alliance requires that Jane attend therapy sessions and express her feelings openly and honestly.

Family involvement is expected as Jane and her family meet every 2 weeks with a family therapist to work on the family's definition of itself and its problem areas. The therapist explains that Jane might need 2 or more years of therapeutic work and suggests that two therapy sessions per week would be useful at this time to deal with her severe depression.

The purposes of the treatment alliance are to reduce Jane's extreme dependency on her mother and encourage exploration of her problems from the safe base the therapist provides. The difficulty in these tasks occurs because of the symbiotic state that exists between Jane and her mother. Jane's mother rewards her dependency (*i.e.*, she responds to Jane's dependency with love and approval). Jane's efforts at becoming independent have, in the past, been punished by the withdrawal of her mother's love and approval—in essence, abandonment.

Jane has learned to get her needs met primarily by manipulating her mother and other people. She also has a feeling of "entitlement," which means that she feels special and deserves special privileges.

Jane also has a number of strengths that have allowed her to experience some successes. Her compulsiveness has helped her to do well in school and to finish tasks. She has talent in painting and has sold a little of her work. She is intelligent and tries to understand and make sense of her life.

Family therapy will relieve some of the pressure from Jane as the identified patient. The pattern of an over-functioning, but emotionally distant, father and an over-emotional, but under-functioning, mother can be addressed. Therapy will redefine Jane's privileged and emotionally damaging position in the family. Her brothers and sister can also learn to relate better to each other and to redefine themselves.

As therapy progresses, Jane will become aware of her role in the dependent, too-close, and too-distant relationships with her parents. Jane and the therapist first address the hostile relationship with her emotionally distant father and the distress and anger she feels about it. Later, they examine both Jane's anger at her all-powerful mother and her own dependent and manipulative behaviors.

Giving up dependency means taking on responsibility for one's own feelings and behavior. This is a difficult task and small gains need to be repeated. The therapist might encourage Jane to decide on an area of study and finish college. Another goal might be to form friendships with peers to provide a supportive network and meet some of the needs previously met by her mother.

Success is highly reinforcing. As Jane succeeds in mastering the smaller goals, she will become able to attempt greater tasks. Self-understanding and mastery will help to improve her self-esteem and provide feelings of self-worth.

Gender identity is achieved partly by modeling or identifying with women whom one would like to emulate. Feelings of mastery and achievement also help to change the idea of being helpless and dependent to feeling good about being a woman.

Relationships also solidify as a result of therapy. The experience of the therapist as a dependable person helps to relieve fears of abandonment. Through this therapeutic relationship, achievement and independence are rewarded.

Feelings of depression and fears of abandonment should decrease as Jane improves. Friends and social activities can replace alcohol and other drugs as more effective ways to get her needs met. When Jane begins to place greater value on herself, her relationships with family and friends will strengthen.

Major tools of individual psychotherapy are the setting of firm, consistent limits and the use of confrontation. In addition, clients like Jane may need hospitalization with the use of an entire milieu to provide support and emotional relearning. Other clients may be able to take advantage of outpatient care. Jane was able to make changes in herself and within her family.

Questions for Discussion

1. Can you identify client problem areas other than those listed?
2. What are the purposes and tasks of the therapeutic alliance?
3. Goals are identified for Jane during the introductory stage of therapy; what goals would you formulate for the working and working through stages of Jane's therapy?
4. Explain Jane's perceptions of her problems and needs. Are these consistent with expected behavior of a client with Borderline Personality Disorder?

References

1. Ainsworth MD, Blehar MD, Waters E, Wall S: Patterns of Attachment: Assessed in the Strange Situation and at Home. Hillsdale, NJ, Lawrence Erlbaum, 1978

2. Arieti S: On Schizophrenia, Phobias, Depression, Psychotherapy and the Farther Shores of Psychiatry. New York, Brunner/Mazel, 1978

3. Bowlby J: Attachment, Vol I. New York, Basic Books, 1969

4. Bowlby J: Separation, Anxiety and Anger, Vol II. New York, Basic Books, 1973

5. Bowlby J: Loss, Sadness and Depression, Vol III. New York, Basic Books, 1980

6. Carkhuff RR, Truax CB: Training, Counselling and Psychotherapy: An Evaluation of an Integrated and Experiential Approach. J Consult Psychol 29:333–336, 1965

7. Dollard J, Doob LW, Miller N, Mowrer OH, Sears RR: Frustration and Aggression. New Haven, CT, Yale University Press, 1939

8. Fromm-Reichman F: Principles of Intensive Psychotherapy. Chicago, The University of Chicago Press, 1950

9. Harlow HF, Zimmerman RR: Affectional Response in the Infant Monkey. SCIENCE 130:421–432, 1959

10. Korchin SJ: Modern Clinical Psychology: Principles of Intervention in the Clinic and Community. New York, Basic Books, 1976

11. Kvarnes RC, Parloff GH (eds). A Harry Stack Sullivan Case Seminar. New York, WW Norton, 1976

12. Maslow AH: The Need to Know and the Fear of Knowing. J Gen Psychol 68:111–124, 1963

13. Masterson JF: The Narcissistic and Borderline Disorders: An Integrated Developmental Approach. New York, Brunner/Mazel, 1981

14. Meninger K: The Vital Balance, pp 79–152. New York, The Viking Press, 1967

15. Rioch MJ, Coulter WR, Weinberger DM: Dialogues for Therapists. San Francisco, Josey Bass, 1976

16. Rogers C: On Becoming A Person. Boston, Houghton Mifflin, 1961

17. Seligman MP: Helplessness: On Depression, Development, and Death. San Francisco, WH Freeman, 1975

18. Sullivan HS: Interpersonal Theory of Psychiatry. New York, WW Norton, 1953

Chapter 16
Groups and Group Therapy

No man is an island, entire of itself;
every man is a piece of the continent,
a part of the main; . . .
any man's death diminishes me,
because I am involved in mankind;
and therefore never send to know for whom
the bell tolls;
it tolls for thee.

John Donne,
Devotions XVII

Barbara G. Tunley Crenshaw

Chapter Preview

We live and work in groups. Each of us is born into a family, we attend school with groups of our peers, we enter into friendship and work-related groups, and we establish our own groups of family or significant others. In psychiatric-mental health and other areas of health care, nurses interact with groups of students, faculty, professional colleagues, and clients and their families. An understanding of group dynamics and their application is essential to effective functioning.

The family may be defined as the individual's primary group. The characteristics of this primary group influence how the individual is socialized into future groups, and how he adopts various roles within groups.

This chapter discusses group process, dynamics, theory, group norms, roles, decision-making, and outcome. It examines various types of groups and the advantages and disadvantages of group therapy. An overview of theoretical frameworks for group therapy, such as Rogerian, Gestalt, Transactional Analysis, and T (training)-groups are also presented. The chapter focuses on nursing intervention through the media of group process and therapy.

Learning Objectives

On completion of the chapter, the reader should be able to accomplish the following.

1. Identify the characteristics of a group
2. Explain group norms and how they are developed and enforced
3. Compare styles of group leadership and their effects on group members' functioning
4. Describe the process of structuring a group
5. Define three major categories of group roles
6. Discuss the purposes, advantages, and disadvantages of group therapy
7. Discuss the curative factors of group therapy
8. Compare the various types of therapy and self-help or growth groups
9. Describe the stages of group development
10. Apply therapeutic interventions to groups of clients
11. Identify process communication in group behavior

Group Process

What Is a Group?

A *group* is three or more persons with related goals. These goals of group members are influenced by many forces—intrapersonal, interpersonal, need, the physical environment, and the unique interaction of the group.

The physical environment is one factor that affects group development. For example, the physical environment

or climate in some countries is so severe that the survival of the individual depends on his relationship to other individuals. The individuals form bonds of relationship that develop into groups. These groups develop structure, characteristics, and roles. The further creation of systems and subsystems leads to the development of more complex societies that display certain characteristics called culture.

Characteristics of Groups

Characteristics of groups include the following.

1. The size of the group
2. The homogeneity or heterogeneity of group members
3. The stability of the group
4. The degree of cohesiveness, or "bonding power," between members
5. The climate of the group (*i.e.*, warm, friendly, cold, aloof, and so forth)
6. The group's conformity to group norms
7. The degree of agreement of the leader's and the group's norms
8. The group's ability to deal with members' infractions
9. The goal-directedness and task orientation of the group's work

Types of Groups

Groups may be primary or secondary, formal or informal. Members of *primary groups* have face-to-face contact. They have boundaries, norms, and explicit and implicit interdependent roles. An example of a primary group is a family.

Secondary groups are usually larger and more impersonal than primary groups. Members of secondary groups do not have the relationship bonds or emotional ties of members of a primary group. An example of a secondary group is a political party or a business.

A *formal* group has structure and authority. Authority in a formal group usually emanates from above and interaction in the group is usually limited. A faculty meeting is an example of a formal group. *Informal* groups provide much of a person's education and contribute greatly to their cultural values. The members of an informal group are not dependent on each other, such as in friendship groups and hobby groups.[5]

Group Norms

A *group norm* is the development, over a period of time, of a pattern of interaction within a group to which certain behavioral expectations are attached. Group norms affect the scope and functioning of a group. Norms also help to structure role expectations. Norms provide sanctions, taboos, and reference power to the group.

To explain group norms, let us examine a nursing

team meeting, designed to discuss both client care planning and communication among the nursing staff. A role expectation norm is that the team leader will chair the meeting. A norm of the membership is that the members will be on time and will, possibly, sit in certain places. There may be a formalized norm called an agenda of the meeting, which states that communication among nursing staff members will occur before the discussion to plan client care. Other group norms may be universal with regard to the task role of one member, such as the role of the secretary who records the minutes of the meeting. Group members who present their client's history and assessment accurately, clearly, and with organization receive sanction. A group taboo is to fall asleep and snore while another member is talking. When a group member falls asleep and snores during meetings, especially if this occurs numerous times, he is viewed as a deviant. A deviant may eventually be isolated by the group. Members neither speak to him nor listen when he speaks. They may physically isolate him by not sitting next to him. Therefore, punishment, formal or informal, is metered out to the deviant along with criticism.[77]

Norms exert a controlling element over groups by setting the boundaries of group activities. To promote the growth and stimulation of group members, it is important that groups learn to change their norms when they are no longer functional for the group. A group remains more creative if each member becomes a "change agent" for norms no longer needed (see Nursing Care Plan, "Intervention in Group Process" on p. 200).

Group Leadership

To become an effective group leader, the nurse must understand the concepts of leadership and the forces, scope, and limitations inherent in each concept. The three concepts of influence, power, and authority have an impact on leadership.[79] *Power* is the perceived ability to control appropriate reward, therefore lending *influence* to the leader.[7] The nurse leader gains *authority* through influence, power, and her knowledge or expertise. The leader also understands that there are effective ways of using authority and she decides to what extent she will expand or limit her authority.

The effective leader also decides to what extent her authority will be autocratic; that is, centralized, or democratic (*i.e.,* decentralized). The leader reaches this decision, in part, according to the type of group. For example, the leader may relinquish authority readily in a training group. The purpose of the T-group (or training group) is to improve the group members' ability to communicate or relate to others in the group. The members, however, generally possess a certain degree of knowledge and experience in relating to others and are therefore capable of imparting their skills to other group members.

In psychoanalytic groups, where members are likely to exhibit high degrees of personality disorganization and faulty communication and interpersonal skills, the leader may exercise centralized authority. In other types of therapy groups, such as Gestalt groups, which deal with the "here and now" and whose members are generally healthy, the distribution of power within the group may depend on the age and emotional maturity of the group members.

Styles of Group Leadership

Leadership styles are influenced by several factors, including the following.

1. The philosophy of treatment
2. The personality of the leader
3. The traits and characteristics of the group
4. The purpose of the group
5. The degree of mental, emotional, or cognitive impairment of the group members

The nurse group leader alters her style of group leadership according to the demands of the therapeutic situation. The three basic styles of group leadership are as follows.

1. Autocratic style
2. Democratic style
3. Laissez-faire style

An *autocratic* leader is one who exercises significant authority and control over group members, who rarely, if ever, seeks or uses input from the group, and who does not encourage participation or interaction of the group.

In some circumstances, such as in emergencies, the autocratic style of leadership may be the most effective; it conserves time and energy and dictates roles and responsibilities to members. On the other hand, constant use of an autocratic leadership style may cause hostility, scapegoating behavior, dependence on the leader, and limitation of growth potential for group members.

The *democratic* style of leadership encourages group interaction and participation in group problem-solving and decision-making. A democratic group leader values the input and feedback of each group member, seeks spontaneous, honest interaction among members of the group, and creates an atmosphere in which members are rewarded for their contributions. The group's opinions are solicited and the group's work is tailored to their common goals. A group with a democratic leadership style may require more time and effort than an autocratic group to accomplish its goals; however, the group's efforts are more productive and cohesive and instill in members a sense of participation in decision-making.

In a *laissez-faire* style of leadership, group members are free to operate as they choose. This style of group leadership may be effective if the members are highly knowledgeable, task-oriented, and motivated. On the other hand, the laissez-faire approach is time-consuming and often inefficient in the accomplishment of group tasks.

Responsibilities of Group Leaders and Members

Sandra Patterson, R.N., M.S.
Coordinator/Instructor-Nursing
El Centro College
Dallas, Texas

Group leaders' responsibilities to members include

1. insuring the psychological safety of group members;
2. establishing and maintaining group norms;
3. role-modeling relationship skills;
4. commenting on group process.

To receive gratification from group membership, members must

1. introspect;
2. self-disclose;
3. nurture others;
4. express their feelings;
5. contribute to the maintenance of the group.

Decision-Making

Decision-making is a necessary component of leadership, power, influence, authority, and delegation of authority. In formal groups, specific guidelines determine which decisions will be made by the leader and which decisions will be delegated to group members; that is, decentralized decision-making.

The ability to make effective decisions depends on the following.

1. The group's knowledge of the subject
2. The group's ability to choose appropriate methods to solve specific problems
3. The group's ability to test and evaluate problem-solving decision-making, after a decision has been put to the test
4. The group's maturity and its ability to reverse or modify a decision that has proved to be unwise, unfair, or otherwise unacceptable.

Decisions may be made by consensus, majority vote, or minority decision. In a *consensus*, all members of the group agree on a decision. Although consensus may prove to be time-consuming and costly, especially in a large group, it gives more satisfaction to the total group. The democratic leader uses consensus whenever possible.

Majority vote is a form of decision-making in which the issue is decided by the larger number of group members. This method is often used by democratic leadership when it is not possible to reach a consensus.

A *minority decision* may be formulated by a self-delegated subgroup or a group appointed as a subcommittee to explore the situation in greater depth and reach a decision.

Structuring the Group

The group leader is instrumental in establishing and maintaining cohesiveness in the group. She selects and orients new group members in both beginning and continuing groups. An effective leader insures that the structuring process for the group defines group norms, clarifies expectations, sets standards for group performance, and works to maintain cohesiveness as new members are introduced into the group. The leader discusses some of these issues with new members before introducing them to the group. An example of such a discussion follows.

Leader: Jane, welcome. I am Ms. C., the group leader. I always meet with new members to share with them the goals and expectations of the group. (pause)

Leader: The group will have eight members, including you. We will meet from 1 to 2 pm each day in the Blue Room. Members will enter and leave the group as their behavior and needs change. (pause)

Jane: What are we expected to do?

Leader: Group members are expected to share their problems and their feelings about those problems with other members of the group.

Jane: Is that all?

Leader: No, it is also my expectation that group members will discover techniques of problem-solving through exploring these problems and feelings and that, eventually, when members learn to relate more effectively to each other, they will transfer these newly acquired skills to other relationships.

Jane: That sounds difficult and frightening.

Leader: Changing and growing have a certain amount of pain.

The leader therefore structures the group by determining its size, homogeneity of group members, and leadership style. The group's purpose and goals define its scope, limitation, and hoped-for accomplishments.[19]

Roles in Groups

The functioning of group leaders and members are interdependent. Member roles can enhance the effectiveness of a group leader and vice versa.

Roles observed in groups are categorized as follows.

1. Group task roles
2. Group building and maintenance roles
3. Individual roles

Group task roles identify group problems and select methods to solve those problems.[51] Problem-solving helps the group to reach its goal or mission. Some examples of group task roles are as follows.

1. The initiator–contributor, who suggests or proposes to the group new ideas or different ways of regarding the group problem or goal
2. The information seeker, who asks for clarification
3. The opinion seeker, who does not ask primarily for facts of the case, but for a clarification of values pertinent to what the group is undertaking
4. The information giver, who offers facts or generalizations that are "authoritative" or who shares his own experience in relation to the group problems
5. The opinion giver, who states his ideas and values about group suggestions
6. The elaborator, who develops the meaning of suggestions offered to the group
7. The coordinator, who shows or clarifies how ideas can work
8. The orienter, who keeps the group on target by defining where the group is in relationship to its goal
9. The evaluator–critic, who sets standards by evaluating the accomplishment of the group in relation to its task, using previously set standards of group functioning
10. The energizer, who arouses the group to greater productivity by prodding members
11. The procedural-technician, who speeds up group movement by doing things such as handing out material and so forth
12. The recorder, who is the "group memory," who writes down productive discussions and group decisions[51]

Group building and maintenance roles are oriented toward the functioning of the group as a whole. They are designed to alter or maintain the group's way of working to strengthen, regulate, and perpetuate the group as a group. Some examples of group building and maintenance roles are as follows.

1. The encourager, who gives acceptance to the contributions of others
2. The harmonizer, who reconciles differences between group members
3. The compromiser, who admits his error to maintain group harmony and meets the person with an opposing idea halfway
4. The gate-keeper, who facilitates the contributions of others, thereby keeping communication open through his encouraging remarks about these contributions
5. The standard setter, who sets group goals to be achieved and evaluates the functioning of the group
6. The group-observer, who notes what is occurring in the group and feeds it back to the group with his evaluation or interpretation of the group's procedure
7. The follower, who goes along with the ideas of other members, assuming more of an audience role[52]

Individual roles are roles that meet only the needs of the group member, not of the group. They do not enhance; rather, they hamper group functioning. They support individual needs and goals, not group needs and goals. Some examples of individual roles are as follows.

1. The aggressor, who deflates the status of individual and group accomplishment
2. The blocker, who resists progress by arguing or disagreeing beyond reason
3. The recognition-seeker, who calls attention to himself through boasting and pointing out his achievements
4. The self-confessor, who expresses feelings and ideology not related to the group, but uses the group as an audience
5. The play-person, who "horses around," demonstrating his lack of involvement
6. The dominator, who asserts his authority and superiority in manipulating the group or certain members of the group
7. The help-seeker, who tries to elicit sympathy from the group or individual members
8. The special interest pleader, who tries to have his own biases and prejudices accepted through the use of others

All of these roles are observed in group behavior. Individually oriented behavior, which often grows out of personal anxiety, detracts from and temporarily stymies the group and its progress, whereas task, maintenance, and building roles promote group growth and productivity.[52]

Group Therapy

Purposes

One of the purposes of group psychotherapy is to intervene in psychopathology. Group therapy offers multiple stimuli for distortions in interpersonal relationships to be revealed, examined, and resolved.[1]

The purpose of a group is related to its goals and expected outcomes. For example, a training group's purpose is to help members improve their present style of relating of others. An individual needing to develop or heighten these skills would join a T-group instead of a psychotherapy group.

Advantages and Disadvantages

Group therapy, as a form of treatment for psychiatric-mental health clients, has advantages and disadvantages. The advantages of group therapy include the following.

1. A greater number of clients can be treated in group therapy, making the method cost-effective.
2. Members profit by hearing other members discuss their problems. This discussion decreases the member's feelings of isolation, alientation, and uniqueness, and encourages him to share his feelings and problems.
3. Group therapy provides an opportunity for clients to explore their specific styles of communication in a safe atmosphere where they can receive feedback, and can undergo change.
4. Members learn multiple ways of solving a problem from other group members and group exploration may help them discover new ways of solving a problem.
5. Members learn about the functional roles of individuals in a group. Sometimes, a member shares the responsibility of the co-therapist. Members become culture carriers.
6. The group provides for its members' understanding, confrontation, and identification with more than one individual. The member gains a reference group.[55]

There are also disadvantages of group therapy. An individual's privacy may be destroyed; for example, when a conversation shared within the group is repeated outside of the group. This behavior obstructs confidentiality and hampers complete and honest participation in a group.

Clients may experience difficulty exposing themselves to a group or believe that they lack the skills to communicate effectively in a group. Some clients may use these factors as resistance; others may be reluctant to expose themselves to the group because they do not want to "change."

Group therapy will not be a helpful form of therapy if the therapist conducts the group as if he is giving individual therapy. Such a therapist may see dynamics and group processes as incidental or antagonistic to the therapeutic process. The effective group leader must be skilled in techniques and interventions that foster group interaction and shape group behavior and growth.[38,74]

Curative Factors of Group Therapy

Yalom[78] described ten curative factors of group therapy.

1. Imparting of information
2. Instillation of hope
3. Universality
4. Altruism
5. The corrective recapitulation of the primary family group
6. Development of socializing techniques
7. Imitative behavior
8. Interpersonal learning
9. Group cohesiveness
10. Catharsis

Imparting of information is the use of information in a planned, structured manner, such as didactic instruction given in a lecture format. These lectures may be accompanied by audio-visual and other teaching aids. The topic of the lecture or didactic presentation is clear.

Instillation of hope helps the client maintain faith in the therapeutic modality. The client is optimistic; he believes that he will get better.

Universality prevents the client from feeling unique and different. Within the group, he begins to feel less isolated and more like other people. This feeling is strengthened by the client's learning that others in the group have problems, thoughts, and feelings similar to his own.

Altruism is the process of clients' aiding or helping each other. The act of giving to others becomes therapeutic for the giver, which increases the self-esteem of the giver.

The corrective recapitulation of the primary family group means that the client is influenced in therapy group by his history. Initially in group therapy, the client usually perceives the behavior of other members as being like his siblings, and the behavior of the leader (or therapist) as being like his parents. When neither the members nor the leader respond to him as his siblings or parents have in the past, the client begins to gain insight into his own behavior.

Development of socializing techniques occurs in group therapy. Social skills are related to interpersonal success in our society. Feedback and role-playing of social events are two techniques employed in group therapy that develop social skills. It is expected that clients will terminate their group therapy experience with greater social skills than they previously had. Clients with regressed behavior may learn elementary social skills such as not belching during group, whereas clients in higher functioning groups may learn to attend to feedback about styles of communication such as rushing one's words, repeating oneself, and interrupting other members when they are speaking.

Imitative behavior is a powerful therapeutic tool through which a group member identifies with the healthier aspects of the other members and the leader. Imitating the behavior of an assertive group member or leader, for example, demonstrates growth.

Interpersonal learning results from therapy groups because the groups are, in effect, microcosms of society. Learning from a therapy group can be transferred to other groups. The client learns to profit from the therapeutic use of anxiety. When anxiety is minimized, the client relates more openly, he learns to trust, to expose himself, to give of himself, to expect from others, to test reality, and therefore to experience growth.

Group cohesiveness relates to bonding or solidarity, the feeling of "we" instead of "I."[48] Cohesiveness is demonstrated through group attendance and the ability of the group to communicate positive and negative expressions to each other without the group disintegrating. In cohesive groups, members try hard to impress one another, are accepting of each other, and enter and leave the group with minimal disruption of the process.

Catharsis is the expression of feelings, especially those that involve deep emotions. Expression of feelings is particularly important in the curative process.[70]

Nurses and Group Process and Therapy

Historically, nurses have used groups and group process in hospitals and other health care settings. As nursing progressed from functional assignments to the team approach, many studies were undertaken to gather information on the most effective ways to use the team's task and maintenance roles. The search for this information led nurses to collaborate with colleagues in examining group theory, group dynamics, and group functioning in various health care delivery systems. Psychiatric-mental health nurses have specifically explored the use of groups as a teaching method, a therapeutic tool with clients, and a form of peer group supervision.

Nurse educators have employed group seminars as part of the teaching-learning process to enable nursing students to participate in groups, to learn group roles, and to learn the function and dynamics of the student-participant role. Instructors delegated a certain amount of authority to the nursing students, yet also served as democratic leaders, structuring the course to a certain degree and defining expectations of the class. This methodology of experiential learning sparked an exciting involvement in learning group theory, enabling students to transfer their knowledge of, and experience in, group dynamics to other arenas of therapy, such as milieu, client groups, and supervision groups. Often, these seminars served as prerequisites for advanced courses in group therapy in graduate nursing programs.

Psychiatric-mental health nurses learned group therapist and co-therapist roles and responsibilities. Dr. Hildegard Peplau, an early authority on psychiatric nursing specialist programs, augmented nurses' involvement in group therapy through "experiential learning." Nurses developed increasing skill in the techniques of group therapy; psychiatric nursing clinical specialists became highly skilled in group intervention.

The Mental Health Revolution, sponsored by President John F. Kennedy, demanded greater numbers of health professionals to administer formal and informal group therapy in community mental health centers. Responding to this need, psychiatric-mental health nurses, and, particularly, psychiatric clinical nurse specialists, became more active in group leader roles in therapeutic communities, outpatient settings, and private therapy, and also became more active as liaison psychiatric nursing consultants in general hospital settings.

Psychiatric-mental health nurses participate as leaders or co-leaders in many formal and informal group therapies including revitalization, resocialization, reeducation, supportive therapy, insight, psychoanalytic therapy, transactional analysis, family therapy, couples therapy, adolescent therapy, T-groups, and prevention groups in the community.[13]

Types of Therapy Groups

Growth Groups and Psychotherapeutic Groups

In the past three decades, numerous forms of growth groups, such as self-help groups and group counseling, have developed. Guidelines to determine the maximal therapeutic benefit of a growth or therapy group for an individual participant include the following.

1. The extent of personality disorganization of the participant
2. The effect of personality disorganization on interpersonal functioning, as a family member, provider, productive citizen, and so on
3. The degree of functional ability and role success or failure of the participant
4. The participant's ability to harness his impulses in stressful group situations; for example, does the member become verbally or physically disruptive or destructive in anxious situations?
5. The member's purpose or goals in joining a group, both articulated goals and those of hidden agenda status
6. The participant's ability to share and support each other around problem-solving tasks
7. The participant's ability to use the material produced in group to problem-solve his own situation

There are different functions of the leader in psychotherapeutic and self-help groups. The leader in the psychotherapy group assumes more responsibility for the group than does a leader of a self-help group. In the psychotherapy group, the group members or clients may have limiting neurotic or maladaptive-to-severe emotional disturbances. The member may be referred to the group from individual therapy, where he was seen in an initial crisis state but is now able to tolerate the group setting. Clients in a therapy group do not become the therapist and the therapist never assumes the client's role in the group. The leader may also provide more support for members of a therapy group who may have less tolerance for stress.

In a growth or self-help group, such as a T-group, both leader and members have attained a certain degree of emotional stability and one does not observe a great discrepancy between their functioning by the end of the growth group experience. The group initially uses the leader to provide guidance and clarification; however, toward the end of the group experience, he becomes a part of the group and several of his functions may be performed by the group members. In a growth group, the members may receive less support from the leader while dealing with their anxiety, but there is conflict resolution by the end of the group.

Psychoanalytic Group Psychotherapy

In a psychoanalytic group, the therapist holds a prominent position. Each individual client in the group has a relationship with the therapist. Group communication is focused on the three levels of unconscious, semiconscious, and conscious material. The group focuses on interpretation of dreams, free association, and other latent content produced in the group. The therapist turns these experiences into conscious, healthy learning experiences for the client. This process is accomplished by transference to the therapist and multi-transferences to group members.

Transactional Analysis

The three ego states of the individual—the parent, the child, and the adult—are examined in transactional analysis groups. A goal of T. A. groups is that individuals in the group will communicate from the proper ego state for the situation and responses of others, thereby lessening conflict and promoting mature relationships.

Rational-Emotive Therapy

Based on the theory of Albert Ellis that human beings, although subject to powerful biologic and social forces, still have the capacity for being rational, rational-emotive group therapy aims to maximize a person's rational thinking. People, says Ellis, tend to overgeneralize situations when they are anxious. If they do not employ thinking and reasoning at this point, they become irrational. The therapist designs activities to rid the members of the group of their irrational ideas.

Rogerian Group Therapy

In a Rogerian group, the therapist's goal is to help the members express their feelings toward one another during group sessions. The therapist's role is one of encouraging this expression of feelings, clarifying these feelings with clients, and accepting clients and their feelings nonjudgmentally. Through this process, the client learns to accept his own feelings, a first step toward self-acceptance. The client gains positive self-regard through his relationship with the therapist.[13] Inherent in Rogerian theory is the belief that change and growth can take place at any age.

Gestalt Therapy

Fritz S. Perls pioneered the techniques of Gestalt therapy. Gestalt theory emphasizes the "here and now"; that is, it emphasizes self-expression, self-exploration, and self-awareness in the present. Clients and therapist focus on everyday problems and try to solve them. The individual becomes aware of his "total self" and "the world" that surround him; awareness of the problem renders him capable of change. The leader's role in Gestalt therapy groups is to help members express their feelings and grow from their experiences.

Interpersonal Group Therapy

Interpersonal theory development is attributed to Harry Stack Sullivan, who also worked extensively with Peplau to introduce interpersonal theory into nursing. Anxiety is the focus of interpersonal therapy—how the individual develops anxiety and how he resolves it. Anxiety has the potential to hamper, distort, or enhance relationships between individuals. Interpersonal group therapists explore the members' anxiety and stress and their effects on the individual.

It is believed that anxiety arises from interpersonal relationships and is reduced or relieved through interpersonal support. One of the main goals of interpersonal group therapy is to promote the individual's comfort with others in the group, which then transfers to other relationships.

Psychodrama Groups

Psychodrama in the United States has its origin, implementation, and direction in the work of Jacob L. Moreno. He promoted this method of group therapy with individuals, small groups, and large groups. He even tried to help the citizens of America resolve their guilt over John F. Kennedy's assassination through sociodrama.

Psychodrama can be used as a form of group psychotherapy that explores the truth through dramatic methods. During *psychodrama*, the subject (or client) produces a topic to be explored. The director (or therapist) directs the subject through role-playing of scenes related to the topic and incorporates the use of auxiliary egos (or therapeutic aides) in the action. The audience experiences the feelings and identifies with the action on the stage. A catharsis occurs for the subject and also for the audience.

Bion Method

Also termed the Travistock conference, the *Bion method* emphasizes experiential learning that is translatable into action in work and community life. The group provides a setting in which experience can be studied and partially understood as it occurs. The group examines transactions, boundaries, the function of leadership, and attitudes toward authority.[10]

Marathon Groups

The term *marathon group* refers to the amount of concentrated time the participants spend together as a group. Marathon groups are similar to each other, not by virtue of the leaders' theoretical orientations or techniques, but because each is a single uninterrupted session. These sessions may last from 12 hours to 2, 3, or more days, allowing short periods away from the group for sleeping and eating. These groups have a clearly stated goal of personal change or growth of the participants.

Encounter Groups

The purpose of an encounter group is personal change, often as a result of deeply felt experiences. The differences between marathon and encounter groups are minimal, and the theoretical orientations of group leaders are diverse.

Example of themes of encounter groups are

"The Challenge of Change, Danger, and Fulfillment";
"Closeness, can it hurt?";
"Marriage, how to survive it."

T-Groups

The *T-group* is the oldest and best known therapeutic method coming out of the sensitivity training group movement. The first T-group conference was held in Bethel, Maine in 1946. The goal of each T-group conference is to verify experimentally the T-group method. This involves the study of group norms, roles, communication distortions, and the effects of authority on behavior patterns, personality, and coping mechanisms. Group members receive feedback by exposing themselves to others in the group and they also experiment with new and more productive behavior.

Other sensitivity groups may have similar objectives, such as interpersonal skill groups, discussion groups, self-analytic groups, and process groups. All of these groups focus on the growth process of the individual through the help of the leader and the group.

Stages of Group Development

Initial Stage

The initial stage of group development is likely to involve more superficial, rather than open, trusting communication. The members are becoming acquainted with each other and are searching for similarity between themselves and other group members. Members may also be unclear about the purposes or goals of the group. A certain amount of structuring of group norms, roles, and responsibilities takes place (see the insert, Stages of Group Development).

Working Stage

During the working stage of group development, the real "work" of the group is accomplished. Because members are already familiar with each other, with the group leader, and with the group's rules, they are free to approach their problems and to attempt to solve their problems. Conflict and cooperation surface during the group's work.

Characteristics of a Mature Group. The mature group demonstrates the following characteristics.

1. The group develops workable norms, a group culture.
2. Conflict exists but resolution follows; when it occurs, conflict arises due to issues of importance, not emotional issues.
3. Members evaluate their own work and assume responsibility for their work.
4. Members are accepting of each others' differences without placing value judgments on them.
5. Role assignment is sanctioned by members of the group.
6. Topics are discussed and decisions are made by means of rational behavior such as sharing information and open discussion.
7. The group provides a feeling of "we" for the leader and members.
8. The group has cohesion.
9. The group is willing to validate itself, it has a "group image."[12]

Termination Stage

During termination, the group evaluates the experience and explores members' feelings about it and the impending separation. The termination of the group may be an opportunity for group members who have difficulty with "goodbyes" to learn to deal more realistically and comfortably with this normal part of human experience, separation. (The inserts on p. 196 further illustrate the stages of group development.)

Group Communication and Nursing Intervention

Therapeutic Interventions with Groups

The use of therapeutic communication techniques with groups requires that nurses possess considerable preparation and skill in group work. Some of these therapeutic group interventions include the following.

Approval—condoning or encouraging an attitude, feeling or action

Acceptance—an attitude or a relationship that recognizes the worth of a person without implying either approval of particular behaviors or personal affection

Clarification—restatement by another, in what is hoped to be clearer terms, of the substance of what the client has said

Exploration—a shift from considering one aspect of a situation to considering another

Identification—delineating specific factors for the purposes of understanding or clarifying

Stages of Group Development

Stages	Characteristics of Stages
Initial stage	Getting acquainted with group leader and members
	Dependency on the leader
	Searching for meaning and purpose of the group
	Restricted content and communicational style
	Search for similarity among members
	Giving advice
Working stage	Solving some of the problems of working together
	Conflict between members or between members and leader
	Working on issues of dominance, control, and power within group
	Cooperating to accomplish the group's work
Termination stage	Evaluating and summarizing the group experience
	Exploring positive and negative feelings about the group experience

(Adapted from Clark CC: The Nurse As Group Leader. New York, Springer–Verlag, 1977; also from Yalom ID: The Theory and Practice of Group Psychotherapy. New York, Basic Books, 1970)

Stages of Group Development: A Basketball Team

Group growth, functioning, and development can be compared to a basketball team. The team has appointed members designated to play certain roles, a leader (coach), and a co-leader (captain or point guard).

The team enters its *initial stage* of group development when the team members become acquainted. The leader (coach) *structures* the group by informing members of the frequency and time of practice and the expectations of the team, such as, "team members will work together to develop a winning team." Another group *norm* is that members (players) respect each other and their contributions.

Players are instructed to be on time for practices and for games; a player who persists in arriving late becomes a *deviant*. Together, players and coach decide that chronically late members will not be permitted to play the next game (sanctions).

The group learns to depend on the leader for guidance and instruction in certain skills. The leader uses the didactic method and group participation exercises to effect the skills of basketball during the *working stage*.

The coach and team study and practice different plays. They change plays, however, if they do not achieve the *goal* of winning basketball games. The coach functions as a "change agent" because his *interventions* impact the direction of the team and promote growth.

The captain or point guard may be the team's *co-leader* who brings in the plays from the coach to the team during the game or calls the plays in the role of "playmaker."

The team guards work at *maintenance and building roles*, while the team forwards work at the *task roles* of scoring points. *Individual roles* are observed when players make fouls and tempers flare.

The team demonstrates both competition and cooperation. The coach strives to build cohesion and a feeling of "we." Members symbolically show this identification through team uniforms, team colors, and team mascot.

Toward the end of the basketball season, the team enters its *termination stage*. Players and coach evaluate and summarize their group and individual performance for the season. Players also evaluate the coach's leadership skills. They express feelings of happiness and sadness. As an open-ended group, senior players face leaving the team at the end of the school year and younger players are added to the squad. Farewells and good wishes are spoken; an awards ceremony or party may mark the goodbyes.

Interpretation—finding or explaining the meaning or significance of the information

Information-giving—stating facts about a problem

Encouraging expression of feelings or ideas—indicating in some way that it is permissible or desirable to talk about feelings or ideas

Reassurance—offering the client confidence of a favorable outcome through suggestion, through persuasive arguments, or through comparing similar cases

Support—giving comfort, approval, or acceptance to a person

Intervention—an action that directs or influences the client's behavior

Understanding—indicating verbally or nonverbally that one knows or comprehends what is being communicated by the client and what he is feeling

Reflection—repeating back to the client what he has said, mirroring his statement

Listening—concentration on the client's communication without interruption

Teaching—helping the client learn specifics in relation to events and behavior

Silence—the use of no verbal or spoken words

Structuring—shaping the content of the group meeting

Limit-setting—deciding how far group members and the group may go before the therapist ceases or restricts, to a point, the behavior, activity, or verbal expression of members

Latent and Manifest Communication

Groups use both latent and manifest communication. *Latent content* is that content which is not discussed, that which occurs on a feeling level and is seldom verbalized, such as hidden agenda; *manifest content* involves spoken words (see Fig. 16–1). Groups are most effective when their latent content and manifest content are similar. The further apart these levels of communication are, the more problems in communication are experienced by the group.

A group may not solve its problems readily, due to the interference of latent content. Hidden agendas hinder group communication. For example, if a group member feels that he would be punished if he verbalized his opinion in the group, especially if he disagrees with the leader, his latent communication would influence his overt behavior and interfere with group growth.

Content and Process Communication

Content and process are other ways of observing group communication. When we observe the group's discussion, we are focusing on the *content*. When we observe how the group is handling its communication, then we are focusing on *process*. Who talks to whom, what is said, and what is left unspoken are examples of process.[34] An example of content and process communication follows.

Content	Process
1. Discussing how a mother does not take care of her children may mean...	the leader or therapist is not meeting the dependency needs of the group.
2. Talking about the fighting of sisters and brothers at home may mean...	there is a lot of conflict and fighting in the therapy group.

An effective group leader brings the group's attention to the issues of process and their meaning.

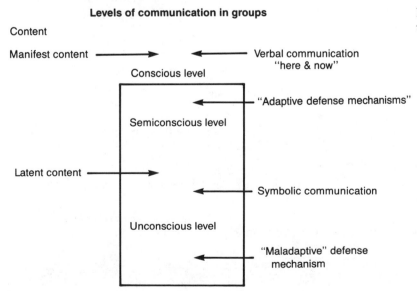

Figure 16-1. *Communication diagram: "the group mind."*

Transference and Countertransference

Transference occurs when a client attributes characteristics and behavior of a family member or significant other to the therapist, thereby causing himself to respond to the therapist in a certain manner.[77] The clarification of this distortion with the client helps to create a therapeutic process of learning. Countertransference occurs when the therapist responds in a negative manner to the client's transference, further complicating communication.

Themes

The group leader observes for themes in the group's communication that recur or relate one group session to another and then explores the meanings of these themes. Through therapeutic communication, the leader may help the group uncover and problem-solve the issue. Group functioning is also evaluated by observing changes in members' behavior, such as their ability to apply these new techniques to problem-solving future tasks. The insert below illustrates the way in which communication themes are used.

Higher functioning groups or those with less overt psychopathologic symptomatology will work through problems with minimal hidden agenda and symbolic language. The therapist can encourage the group to deal with "here and now" material and can manage anxiety more readily than in a group that communicates on a symbolic level.

Group Case

Theme: The group theme is "authority," or more pointedly, transference. Our therapist is punitive to the group, like our mothers, if we disagree.

Countertransference:
Therapist I, Mrs. A, became angry and stated: "You are rebellious and don't want to listen to reason. I am particularly angry at Marty because she started this...

Resistance:
Three-fourths of the group did not attend the next meeting.

Interpretation:
Therapist II, Mr. B, (at a later session): Marty, when you stated we were like your mother, it sounded as if you were angry.

Acceptance:
Marty: Yes, and afraid.

Exploration:
Therapist I, Mrs. A: Marty, I wonder if you felt your weekend pass being cancelled was related to you disagreeing with me in group?

Acknowledgement:
Marty: Yes.

Consensual validation:
Group: "You know, Mrs. A, we all thought that."

Insight:
Group: "Later we realized that there was no connection between the cancellation of Marty's pass and the group meeting."

Problem solving:
Group: "We decided next time we would check out the situation before coming to a conclusion."

The co-therapist, in this example, listened for latent and manifest content to identify the group theme and used techniques of communication to help the group solve the problem.

Summary

This chapter has discussed group process and theory and their application to therapeutic needs. Some of the major foci of the chapter have included the following.

1. A group is three or more persons with related goals.
2. Groups vary according to their size, homogeneity of membership, climate, norms, and goal-directedness.
3. Group norms are the patterns of interaction that develop over time within a group.
4. A group leader designs the group's structure, style of leadership, and decision-making policies.
5. Roles in groups are task, building and maintenance, and individual roles.
6. The advantages of group therapy include its effectiveness and efficiency in time and cost.
7. Nurses participate as leaders and co-leaders in multiple formal and informal groups.
8. Most therapeutic group experiences can be categorized as psychotherapy or growth groups.
9. The three stages of group development are the initial, working, and termination stages.
10. Nurses and other group leaders employ a variety of therapeutic interventions with groups and identify and explore latent versus manifest communication, and process versus content communication.

Therapeutic Intervention in Groups

Reflection:

Mr. B: "All this talking is really a pain in the neck."

Nurse: "This talking is a pain in the neck."

Interpretation:

Mr. B: "All this talking is really a pain in the neck."

Nurse: "Mr. B, you seem annoyed at all the talking."

Encouraging Expression of Feelings:

Mr. W: "It takes me about 10 or 15 minutes to get oriented again in the morning and then I'm all right."

Nurse: "Are there others who feel this way?"

Ms. S: "I always get up to eat and have some coffee. Then I feel more like facing others."

Offering Support:

Marty: "Well, I don't know. My busted arm has played heck with me. Getting anything for it has been a federal case. And I am not one who shows pain easily."

Nurse: "This must be pretty infuriating."

Marty: "Well, it really bugs me."

Structuring:

Frank: "I'm going home soon."

Mrs. C: "Really?"

Nurse: "Maybe you would like to talk about going home?"

Teaching:

Abel: (spoken to nurse) "You were irritated at me, weren't you, but we were able to talk about it and work it out."

Nurse: "Yes, we did, Abel. I was irritated because I felt you were not listening. And we did talk about it."

Understanding:

Marty: "Nurse, I feel frightened about discharge."

Nurse: "I can understand your feeling frightened. Leaving the hospital is not always easy."

(*Continues on p 200*)

Exploration:

  Frank: "My son decided to leave the business."

  Nurse: "Tell me how that came about."

Clarification:

  Abel: "I feel hopeless, no way out."

  Nurse: "You feel you have no way out?"

Interpretation:

  Abel: "I feel hopeless, no way out."

  Nurse: "You sound suicidal."

Giving Information:

  Marty: "All the staff write notes in the charts after the group meeting and put their own interpretation on what we say, don't they?"

  Nurse: "I can only speak for myself. I write notes in the chart, but I try hard not to misinterpret what members state in the group."

Approval:

  Frank: "I decided to move to a new apartment."

  Nurse: "You made a wise decision."

Reassurance:

  Frank: "I was afraid to move at first."

  Nurse: "Frank, we are always here to listen to your fears and try and help you work them out."

Limit-setting:

  Marty: "I feel we need to cancel our therapy session next week since the next day is a holiday and we need a long weekend to travel."

  Nurse: "Holiday weekends are difficult; however, we will not cancel our group session."

Acceptance:

  Marty: "Nurse, I was angry at you for not cancelling the session."

  Nurse: "It's all right for you to get angry at me, Marty."

Nursing Care Plan

Interventions in Group Process and Group Therapy

Client Problem	*Goal*	*Intervention*
Fear of authority, resulting in timid, hostile, aggressive, or withdrawn behavior	To diminish the client's problem in dealing with authority	Use nonverbal and verbal communication techniques; listen to the client and encourage him to share and explore his feelings.
		Reassure the client that the nurse-therapist will not respond punitively when he expresses his feelings.
		Respond in an understanding manner when the client presents his feelings (even when they are hostile).

Client Problem	Goal	Intervention
		Role-play various patterns of authority to determine which ones cause the client to become defensive or uncomfortable.
		Provide the client with "desensitization" problem-solving situations related to his specific problem (*e.g.*, record conversations with persons of authority and analyze them for problematic areas, themes, patterns, and other situations resulting in the client's discomfort or maladaptive behavior).
		Help the client develop problem-solving strategies around the identified problem situations.
Initial anxiety in a group, displayed by silence, fidgeting, nervous movement, and selective hearing	To lessen the client's anxiety so he can function more effectively in a group	Give "strokes" for positive interaction.
		Help the client establish a role in the group related to his skills.
		Share with the client that discomfort in the initial stage of group development is not uncommon.
		Meet the client's dependency needs.
Hidden agenda	To help the client express communication and action in an open manner	Identify the source of individual and group anxiety causing the hidden agenda.
		Explore the hidden agenda with the group and its meaning and effect on the group's functioning.
Subgrouping	To eliminate unproductive subgroups	Establish clarifying goals and purpose of the group (thereby lessening the group's anxiety and aiding in elimination of subgroups).
		Direct subgroup interest toward the goals of the group, thereby lessening subgroup preoccupation with outside themes.
		Shorten the group's "fight and flight" stage through the use of independent members as catalysts to speed up the group process.
Difficulty in giving and receiving information in a group	To increase the client's comfort in giving and receiving information	Help the client explore his feelings about receiving objective data about himself.
	To teach the client techniques in giving and receiving feedback	Help the client to connect the feedback he is giving and receiving with a specific incident to lessen ambiguity and distortion.

(Continues on p 202)

Client Problem	Goal	Intervention
		Help the client explore the advantage of giving feedback at the proper time.
		Help the client learn how to validate his feedback with others for accuracy and tact.
Feeling threatened to the point of defensiveness and verbal outbursts	To decrease the client's anxiety	Reduce the anxiety of the group by reassuring the client.
		Assess the group's level of anxiety to determine its effect on the client
		Assess your own level of anxiety to determine its effect on the client's feeling of threat.
		Explore the topic being discussed in the group to see what meaning this topic holds for the client (*i.e.*, is the topic a "high impact" one?).
Discomfort with established group norms	To increase the client's comfort with group norms	Help the client evaluate the purpose of the norm (*i.e.*, why it is developed and how it represents group standards).
		Help the client understand the result of breaking the group norm, such as increased anxiety of the group.
		Help the client learn methods of changing norms, such as present the change to the group, state rationale for change, allow discussion by the group, and so forth. Remind the client that there is a definite risk in violating a current norm in order to challenge its desirability.
Deviant behavior	To modify deviant behavior	Identify deviant behavior and discuss it with the client.
		Identify sources of discomfort in the environment that affect the client.
		Explore with the client whether or not he identifies his behavior as deviant.
		Help members of the group identify deviant behavior.
		Help the client explore how his behavior affects his relationship in the group.
		Use group pressure to help the deviate change or conform to group norms.
		Help the group identify which behavior is destructive and which might foster group growth.
Indecision	To improve the client's decision-making ability	Help the client develop assertive communication skills.

Client Problem	Goal	Intervention
		Help the client explore methods of decision-making in a group.
		Help the client implement conflict resolution strategies in the group to arrive at the most productive decision for the group.
		Help the client explore all aspects or data related to the decision, thereby reaching a broader view of the issue before coming to closure.
Overdependency	Appropriate independence of clients in accomplishing the group's task	Provide a leadership void to make the client more independent.
		Explore with the client his feelings about dependency and how it affects the group's growth.
		Share specific techniques with the client, such as a list of the group's tasks and requesting that he volunteer for the job for which he is most suited.
Role confusion or lack of clarity of membership activity	Increased understanding of his role in the group Understanding of group norms relating to specific roles within the group	Ask the client to express his ideas about his perception of roles in the group.
		Help the client express how he perceives his role in the group in relationship to other client–members' roles.
		Clarify distortions of interpretation about role and role-taking
Lack of interpersonal closeness or trust Feeling frightened when he shares himself with others	Increased ability to trust Lessened fear of himself and others	Display consistent behavior as the group leader.
		Listen to the client's fears.
		Explore with the client the reality of his fears.
		Show respect, dignity, and caring when the client discusses closeness.
		Reassure the client that closeness is possible.
		Time interventions involving closeness carefully.
Resistance to therapy (*e.g.*, grunting, moaning, staring into space, overresponding to situations, changing the subject)	Increased acceptance of, and participation in, therapy	Explore with client his resistant behavior.
		Confront the client with his actions and behavior, utilizing an understanding approach.
Competition that stimates group progress	Increased skill and comfort with competition, compromise, and cooperation	Help the client learn how to gain recognition for his effort in socially acceptable ways.

(*Continues on p 204*)

Client Problem	Goal	Intervention
		Explore the concepts and goals of competition, compromise, and cooperation with client.
Termination of the group, resulting in increased anxiety and self-defeating behavior	Acceptance of group termination Growth from termination experience	Help the client identify his accomplishments while he has been a member of the group.
		Help the client work through feelings of loss during termination (*i.e.,* feelings of anger, depression, euphoria, rejection).
		Help the client express both positive and negative feelings about the group and evaluate the group experience realistically.
		Plan a termination activity that allows expression of group members' feelings.

References

1. Armstrong SW, Rouslin S: Group Psychotherapy in Nursing Practice. New York, Macmillan, 1963

2. Bach G: Intensive Group Psychotherapy. New York, Ronald Press, 1954

3. Battery R, Schill S, Durking HE, Friedmann A, Krasner T, La Hullier D: The Challenge for Group Psychotherapy: Present and Future. New York, International Universities Press, 1974

4. Benne KD, Sheats P: Functional Roles of Group Members. Group Development (Selected Series Number I), pp 51–59. Washington, DC, National Training Laboratories, National Education Association, 1961

5. Benne K (originally presented by), Bennett TR (revised by), Thornton R (further abbreviated by), Gertz B (final revision): Examples of Decision Making. Unpublished handout of National Training Laboratories Workshop, Washington DC, 1972

6. Bennis W, Shepard H: A Theory of Group Development. Human Relations 9 (November): 415–437, 1956

7. Bennis W: Leadership Theory and Administrative Behavior, Administrative Science 4 (December): 259–302, 1959

8. Berne E: Transactional Analysis in Psychotherapy. New York, Grove Press, 1961

9. Berne E: Principles of Group Treatment. New York, Oxford University Press, 1966

10. Bion WR: Experiences in Groups and Other Papers. New York, Basic Books, 1961

11. Bonner H: Group Dynamics: Principles and Application. New York, Ronald Press, 1959

12. Bradford L, Gibb J, Benne K: T-Group Theory and Laboratory Method, 2nd ed. New York, John Wiley & Sons, 1964

13. Burgess AW: Psychiatric Nursing in the Hospital and the Community, 3rd ed. Englewood Cliffs, NJ, Prentice-Hall, 1981

14. Cathcart RS: Small Group Communication: A Reader, 2nd ed. Dubuque, IO, Wm C Brown, 1974

15. Cartwright D, Zander A: Group Dynamics, 3rd ed. New York, Harper & Row, 1968

16. Clark CC: Teaching Nurses Group Concepts: Some Issues and Suggestons. Nurse Educator 1 (January–February): 17–20, 1978

17. Clark CC: The Nurse As Group Leader. Springer Series on the Teaching of Nursing, Vol 3. New York, Springer-Verlag, 1977

18. Corsino RJ: Methods of Group Psychotherapy. New York, McGraw-Hill, 1957

19. Crosbie P: Interaction in Small Groups, p 2. New York, Macmillan, 1975

20. Douglass LM: The Effective Nurse Leader and Manager, 2nd ed. St Louis, CV Mosby, 1984

21. Durald MM, Hanks D: The Evaluation of Co-Leading a Gestalt Group. J Psychiatr Nurs Ment Health Serv 18 (December): 19–23, 1980

22. Eaton MT, Peterson MH, Davis JA: Psychiatry, Medical Outline Series, 3rd ed. New York, Medical Examination Publishing, 1976

23. Fields SJ: The Person Circle: A First Book On Group Psychotherapy and The Small Group Field. Hickville, NY, Exposition Press, 1976

24. Fisher BA: Small Group Decision Making: Communication And The Group Process. New York, McGraw-Hill, 1974

25. Foulks SH, Anthony ET: Group Psychotherapy: The Psychoanalytic Approach. Baltimore, MD, Penguin Books, 1965

26. Gazda GM: Basic Approaches To Group Psychotherapy

and Group Counseling. Springfield, IL, Charles C Thomas, 1971

27. Gazda GM: Innovations to Group Psychotherapy. Springfield, IL, Charles C Thomas, 1968

28. Gibbs JR, Smith EE, Roberts AH: Effects of Positive and Negative Feedback Upon Defense Behavior In Small Problem-Solving Groups. Paper read at the American Psychological Association Meeting, 1955

29. Gibbs TR, Platts GN: Role Flexibility in Group Interaction. American Psychologist 5:491, 1950

30. Goldberg AA: Group Communication: Discussion Processes Application. Englewood Cliffs, NJ, Prentice-Hall, 1975

31. Goldberg C: Encounter: Group Sensitivity Training Experience. New York, Science House, 1970

32. Ginott HG: Group Psychotherapy With Children. New York, McGraw-Hill, 1961

33. Glassman SM: Some Considerations in Building an Effective Group. Journal of the Fort Logan Mental Health Center 3 (Fall): 47–60, 1965

34. Glassman SM, Schiff S: Basic Concepts in Group Psychotherapy. Unpublished paper presented at Fort Logan Mental Health Center, Denver, CO, 1972

35. Glassman SM, Wright TL: A Conceptual Framework For Group Therapy. Unpublished paper for classroom presentation, 1974

36. Glassman SM, Schiff S: Large and Small Group Therapy In a State Mental Center. International Journal of Group Psychotherapy 19 (April), 1969

37. Haber J, Leach A, Schudy S, Sidelean BF: Comprehensive Psychiatric Nursing, 2nd ed. New York, McGraw-Hill, 1978

38. Heckel RV, Salzberg HC: Group Psychotherapy: A Behavioral Approach. Columbia, SC, University of South Carolina Press, 1976

39. Hill J: Power in Therapy. Unpublished paper presented to the Fourth Annual Alumni Meeting of Graduate Psychiatric Nursing Specialists, University of Colorado Health Science Center, 1980

40. Hoppock R: The Real Problem. American Psychologist 9:81–82, 1954

41. Horwitz M, Cartwright OP: A Projectile Method for the Diagnosis of Group Properties. Human Relations 6:397–410, 1953

42. Hurley EA: An Investigation of Therapeutic Intervention as Practiced By Four Psychiatric Nurses In Group Work With Selected Psychiatric Patients. Masters Thesis. University of Colorado, 1960

43. Jackson EN: Group Counseling: Dynamic Possibilities of Small Group. Philadelphia, Pilgram Press, 1969

44. Johnson DW, Johnson FP: Joining Together Theory and Group Skills. Englewood Cliffs, NJ, Prentice-Hall, 1975

45. Johnson JA: Group Therapy, a Practical Approach. New York, McGraw-Hill, 1963

46. Jones M: The Therapeutic Community: A New Treatment Method In Psychiatry. New York, Basic Books, 1953

47. Kadis AL, Kasner JD, Weiner MF: Practicum of Group Psychotherapy, 2nd ed. New York, Harper & Row, 1963

48. Kaplan JW: Group Psychotherapy Theory and Practice, 2nd ed. New York, Grune & Stratton, 1959

49. Kaplan-Koehne N, Levy K: An Approach for Facilitating the Passage Through Termination. J Psychiatr Nurs Ment Health Serv 16 (June): 11–14, 1978

50. Kassaz D: The Development of a Psychiatric Team in the Light of a Group Development Theory. Journal of the Fort Logan Mental Health Center 2:101–115, 1965

51. Kozier B, Erb G: Fundamentals of Nursing Concepts and Procedures, 2nd ed. Menlo Park, CA, Addison-Wesley Publishing Co, 1983

52. Lippit GL, Seashore E: Leadership in Nursing Theories: The Professional Nurse Looks At Group Effectiveness. Washington, DC, Leadership Resources, 1966

53. Loomis ME: Group Process For Nurses. St Louis, CV Mosby, 1979

54. Luft J: Group Processes: An Introduction to Group Dynamics, 2nd ed. Palo Alto, CA, National Press, 1970

55. Marram GD: The Group Approach in Nursing Practice. St Louis, CV Mosby, 1973

56. Moreno JL: Common Grounds for All Group Psychotherapists: What is a Good Psychotherapist? Group Psychotherapy 15:263–264, 1962

57. Moreno JL, Friedemann A: The International Handbook of Group Psychotherapy. New York, Philosophical Library, 1966

58. Moreno JL: Who Shall Survive The Foundation of Sociometry, Group Psychotherapy and Sociodrama? 2nd ed. New York, Beacon House, 1978

59. Morris KT: A Handbook of Non-Verbal Group Exercises. Springfield, IL, Charles C Thomas, 1975

60. Morris KT: A Handbook of Verbal Group Exercises. Springfield, IL, Charles C Thomas, 1974

61. Mueller A, Metzbaugh C: Nursing Home For Student Learning. Nurse Educator 3 (January–February): 14–16, 1978

62. Murray RB, Huelskoetter MW: Psychiatric/Mental Health Nursing. Englewood Cliffs, NJ, Prentice-Hall, 1983

63. Napier RW, Gersherfield MK: Groups: Theory and Experience. Boston, Houghton Mifflin, 1973

64. Nixon HL: The Small Group. Englewood Cliffs, NJ, Prentice-Hall, 1979

65. Pasquali EA, Alesi E, Arnold H, De Basio N: Mental Health Nursing: A Bio Psychocultural Approach. St Louis, CV Mosby, 1981

66. Patterson CH: Theories of Counseling and Psychotherapy. New York, Harper & Row, 1966

67. Robinson L: Psychiatric Nursing as a Human Experience. Philadelphia, WB Saunders, 1977

68. Roich MJ: Dialogues For Therapies: Dynamics of Learning and Supervision. San Francisco, Jossey-Bass, 1976

69. Singerman B, Higgins C, Warring B: An Evening Diversional Activity Program for Psychiatric Patients. J Psychiatr Nurs Ment Health Serv 18 (December): 28–31, 1980

70. Stuart G, Sundeen SL: Principles and Practice of Psychiatric Nursing. St Louis, CV Mosby, 1979

71. Thelen HA: Dynamics of Groups at Work, 4th ed. Chicago, The University of Chicago Press, 1958

72. Trousley MM: The Use of Family Therapy In Terminal

Illness and Death. J Psychosoc Nurs Ment Health Serv 20 (January): 17–22, 1982

73. Veninga R, Fredland D: Teaching the Group Approach. Nursing Outlook 22 (June): 373–376, 1974

74. Whitaker D, Lieberman MA: Psychotherapy Through The Group Process. New York, Atherton Press, 1964

75. White O, Block D, Smith K: Nursing In Community Mental Health Services: An Interdisciplinary Team In A Therapeutic Community Setting, Chap II. National Institute of Mental Health Pilot Project Grant, University of Colorado, 1967

76. Wikler L, Savins A: Behavior Modification Parent Groups: A Training Manual for Professionals. Thorofare, NJ, Charles B Slack, 1976

77. Wilson H, Kneisel C: Psychiatric Nursing, 2nd ed. Menlo Park, CA, Addison-Wesley, 1983

78. Yalom ID: The Theory and Practice of Group Psychotherapy. New York, Basic Books, 1970

79. Yura H, Ozimek D: Nursing Leadership: Theory and Process, 2nd ed. New York, Appleton-Century-Crofts, 1981

80. Zander A: Motives and Goals in Groups. New York, Academic Press, 1971

81. Zander A: Leadership and Organizational Functioning: Organizational Regression. International Journal of Group Psychotherapy 3:25–28, 1978

82. Zander A: Types of Leadership Styles, National Training Laboratories, Series I (revised handout). Washington DC, National Educational Association, 1961

Chapter 17
Families and Family Therapy

... And what of Marriage, Master?
You shall be together when the white wings of death scatter
your days.
Ay, you shall be together even in the silent memory of God.
But let there be spaces in your togetherness,
And let the winds of the heavens dance between you.
Love one another, but make not a bond of love:
Let it rather be a moving sea between the shores of your souls.
... Sing and dance together and be joyous, but let each one of
you be alone.
Even as the strings of a lute are alone though they quiver with
the same music.
Speak to us of children...
... They are the sons and daughters of Life's longing for itself.
They come through you but not from you.
And though they are with you yet they belong not to you.
You may give them your love but not your thoughts.
You may house their bodies but not their souls,
For their souls dwell in the house of tomorrow, which you
cannot visit, not even in your dreams.
You may strive to be like them, but seek not to make them like
you:
For life goes not backward nor tarries with yesterday.
You are the bows from which your children as living arrows are
sent forth.

Kahlil Gibran,
The Prophet,
1923

Christina R. Hogarth

Chapter Preview

Fairy tales, television, and the wedding industry would have us believe that marriage is finding the prince or princess and living happily ever after. In recent years, however, "happily ever after" has given way to unprecedented rises in divorce, child and spouse abuse, substance abuse, adolescent suicide, crime, teenage pregnancy, and heavy reliance on social welfare and mental health services. During these troubled times, many families have lost hope and control over their own destinies, but others have organized to avoid becoming one of these alarming statistics. For many years, sociologists, anthropologists, psychiatrists, psychologists, social workers, and, to some extent, nurses have studied the family, have explored the structure and form of the family, and, more recently, have examined the dynamics and interactions of the family as a system. Initially, systems theorists studied families that had a schizophrenic member, but have now focused on the less disturbed and, importantly, successful families.

Stress and change are present in the lives of all families. How the family adapts to these stresses and changes depends on the ability of the adults to love and care for each other, while providing a caring atmosphere for children to learn and grow to capable adulthood. Parents are indeed, as Kahil Gibran says, "the bow from which (their) children as living arrows are sent forth." The static fairy tale is truly a myth.

This chapter presents the major theories of family functioning with particular emphasis on the family systems approach, common stressors and changes that affect families, an assessment methodology based on Beavers' and Satir's work with families, family therapy approaches, and other nursing interventions used when working with families who fall on a continuum from optimum to troubled.

Learning Objectives

On completion of the chapter, the reader will be able to accomplish the following.

1. Define family
2. Describe four theoretical approaches to the study of family

   Developmental theory
   Structure and function analysis
   Communication theory
   Systems theory

3. Identify the characteristics of living systems
4. Discuss eight variables of the family that are instrumental in producing competent individuals
5. Discuss the historical, developmental, role-related, and environmental stressors affecting families

6. Apply the nursing process to healthy and dysfunctional families

   Identify assessment criteria for optimal, adequate, midrange, and troubled families
   Formulate nursing diagnoses for dysfunctional families
   List goals for nursing interventions with families
   Describe interventions of nurses who work with midrange to troubled families and of nurse–family therapists
   Identify evaluation criteria of family functioning

7. Describe characteristics and skills essential to psychiatric-mental health nurses who work with troubled or dysfunctional families

Family Theories

Defining Family

Most definitions of family describe the traditional nuclear family. There are, however, many types of family structures that need to be included in a comprehensive definition. A *family* is a "culturally produced social system," made up of two or more people in a primary group. The persons in this primary group may be related by blood, marriage, adoption, or mutual consent, they may interact through certain familial roles, and they may create and maintain a common subculture.[37]

Family functions include at least two of the following.

1. Maintenance of a common household
2. Rearing of children
3. Companionship and mutual support among members
4. Sexual relationship between one or more pairs of adults
5. Financial cooperation
6. Enculturation of members[37]

These components of a definiton of a family take into account varying compositions of family members, such as the traditional nuclear family, homosexual couples, elderly persons not related by blood living together as a family group, and variant family forms such as single parent families and extended family groupings. Although the form or structure of the family is changing considerably, the family persists as the most important force in providing economic necessities, socialization, and companionship for people of all ages.

Although families are small in size, they are typically complex and difficult to analyze. Anthropologists, sociologists, and mental health professionals and researchers have studied the family from various theoretical perspectives including developmental stages, structure–function analysis, communication theory, and systems theory.

Developmental Stages of the Family

Development refers to an orderly evolution of events moving from simple to more complex. Human development has been studied extensively in all spheres of human experience including biologic, psychological (*i.e.,* cognitive and emotional), social, and spiritual realms. The family is both a group of people in varying stages of development and a family group in a stage of development.

Duvall has described the basic tasks and development stages of families. The eight basic tasks of families are as follows.

1. Physical maintenance
2. Allocation of resources—meeting family needs and costs; apportioning goods, facilities, space, authority
3. Division of labor
4. Socialization of family members
5. Reproduction; recruitment and release of family members
6. Maintenance of order
7. Placement of members into the larger society
8. Maintenance of motivation and morale—encouragement and affection, meeting personal and family crises, refining a philosophy of life and sense of family loyalty through rituals.[13]

The eight stages of family development are as follows.

1. Beginning families (married couple)
2. Early childbearing families (oldest child infant to 30 months)
3. Families with preschool children (oldest child 2½–5 years)
4. Families with school children (oldest child 6–13)
5. Families with teenagers (oldest child 13–20)
6. Launching center families (children leaving home)
7. Families of middle years (empty nest through retirement)
8. Family in retirement and old age (retirement to death of both spouses).[14]

The insert on page 210 describes stage-critical family developmental tasks based on critical issues facing the couple or oldest child.

Stevenson has identified four stages of family development based on the length of the couple's relationship.

Stage I—emerging family
Stage II—crystallizing family
Stage III—integrating family
Stage IV—actualizing family[37]

The *emerging family* encompasses the first 7 to 10 years of the relationship. The couple is initiating their work and career paths, and children often enter the family during this stage. Both developments—career and children—are stressful events, as are the beginning stages of the relationship.

By the end of this period of the emerging family, patterns of family life are established.

The *crystallizing family* stage extends from 10 to 25 years of cohabitation. This period of family life is usually calm until children reach adolescence. There is also considerable contact between children and parents before the children are launched from the family. The adults continue to grow and begin to participate in community life.

The *integrating family* stage lasts from about the 25th year of the relationship until the 40th. Usually, the children are young adults by this time and the couple or adults who lead the family renew and enhance their relationship. Although work roles continue to be important, humanistic tendencies appear and leisure is significant to the couple during this stage. The grown children may need to make adjustments to aging parents.

The *actualizing family* period encompasses the years past 40 years of living together. The couple continues to grow, hopefully, or, if one partner dies, the remaining partner grieves and continues to grow. Family members deal with aging, chronic illness, dying parents, and death.

Family Structure and Function

Structure refers to the organization of the family. Structure includes type of family (*i.e.,* nuclear or extended) and the value system of the family, which in turn dictates roles, communication patterns, and power distribution within the family.[14] The value system includes basic beliefs about man, nature, the supernatural, time, and family relationships. Value systems tend to cluster by socioeconomic status or ethnic group.

Families of lower-class status, for example, tend to have a present-time orientation and view themselves as subjugated to the environment and supernatural (fate). Family relationships tend to be disrupted by desertion of spouses and early emancipation of children due to severe economic difficulties. Families cope, however, by taking in other extended family members' children and often by the grandmother's provision of direct assistance to family members. Power is usually authoritarian or not exerted.

Middle-class families espouse the Protestant work ethic prevalent in this country. This ethic dictates the importance of work and planning for the future, and the belief that man is somewhat evil but changeable by hard work. Financial stability and success are viewed as rewards for hard work. Family relationships center around the nuclear family with socialization among work-related or neighborhood friendships. Power is more egalitarian in middle-class than in lower-class families, but it becomes more male-dominated as the economic level of the family rises. Middle-class families see themselves as able to control, and work for mastery over, the environment. These statements are broad generalizations of social class values and do not account for cultural differences. Many ethnic groups, for example, place great importance on extended family relationships,

Stage-Critical Family Developmental Tasks Through the Family Cycle

Stage of the Family Life Cycle	Positions in the Family	Stage-Critical Family Developmental Tasks
Married couple	Wife Husband	Establishing a mutually satisfying marriage Adjusting to pregnancy and the promise of parenthood Fitting into the kin network
Childbearing	Wife–mother Husband–father Infant daughter or son or both	Having, adjusting to, and encouraging the development of infants Establishing a satisfying home for both parents and infant(s)
Preschool-age	Wife–mother Husband–father Daughter–sister Son–brother	Adapting to the critical needs and interests of preschool children in stimulating, growth-promoting ways Coping with energy depletion and lack of privacy as parents
School-age	Wife–mother Husband–father Daughter–sister Son–brother	Fitting into the community of school-age families in constructive ways· Encouraging children's educational achievement
Teenage	Wife–mother Husband–father Daughter–sister Son–brother	Balancing freedom with responsibility as teenagers mature and emancipate themselves Establishing postparental interests and careers as growing parents
Launching center	Wife–mother–grandmother Husband–father–grandfather Daughter–sister–aunt Son–brother–uncle	Releasing young adults into work, military service, college, marriage, and so on with appropriate rituals and assistance Maintaining a supportive home base
Middle-aged parents	Wife–mother–grandmother Husband–father–grandfather	Rebuilding the marriage relationship Maintaining kin ties with older and younger generations
Aging family members	Widow/widower Wife–mother–grandmother Husband–father–grandfather	Coping with bereavement and living alone Closing the family home or adapting it to aging Adjusting to retirement

(From Duvall E: Family Development, 4th ed, p 151. Philadelphia, JB Lippincott, 1971)

rather than on the individualism valued by middle-class Americans.

Functions of the family include procreation and socialization of children, maintenance of a household, affection, health and illness care, adapting to change within and from outside the family, and providing necessities for family members.

Family Communication Theory

The family communication theory developed from research at the Mental Research Institute in Palo Alto, California. Jackson, Watzlawick, Haley, Beaven, and Satir have become well-known theorists for their contributions to the understanding of family dynamics in schizophrenia and double-bind communication, and for their pioneering and still relevant efforts in family therapy. These researchers and practitioners state that the child learns and develops by responding to verbal and nonverbal communication. The child's interpretation of himself and the environment depend on messages received from parents. The messages are powerful because the child depends on his parents for survival. Communication, says Satir, is the way members "work out to make meaning with one another." In nurturing families, communication is congruent, "direct, clear, specific and honest." Self-worth is high in nurturing families; the family members have positive feelings about themselves. Rules are norms for how people in the family should think and act. In nurturing families, the rules are "flexible, human, appropriate, and subject to change." Links to society are the ways family members relate to the community. The linking in nurturing families is "open and hopeful." Satir views families as peoplemaking factories with the parents as engineers or architects of the family.[33] Communication, self-worth, rules, and links to society are assessed by observing interactions among family members. Communication is the focus of intervention in the family.

Family Systems Theory

The family systems theory developed during the 1950s on both the East and West coasts of the United States. The West coast group of Jackson, Haley, and associates in Palo Alto explored the notions of communications theory (*i.e.*, cybernetics and feedback loops) and homeostasis applied to the family with a schizophrenic member.[3, 34, 43] In Washington, DC, Bowen based his family systems concepts on a biological systems model.[6] In Philadelphia, Minuchin utilized the systems model in his research with families exhibiting psychosomatic disorders.[26] Most recently, Lewis and Beavers have explored not only disturbed families, but healthy families from a systems viewpoint.[4, 24]

A system is a whole that consists of more than the sum of its parts. Although a system can be divided into subsystems, the subsystems are not representative pieces of the whole. Human beings are complex organisms who respond, grow, and change in the context of relationships with others and in response to the environment. To study family research, theory, and therapy, one must understand the basic characteristics of living systems.

Characteristics of Living Systems

Boundaries are limits, or imaginary lines drawn to define the limits, beyond which one may intrude. Boundaries pertain to the system as a whole, as well as to subsystems within it. Concrete examples of boundaries are the use, or nonuse, of bedroom doors. Boundaries exist between individuals, between subsystems, and between the family system and the environment. The families' values, style, and self-worth determine the permeability of the boundary to outside influences, such as the media, friends, school, church, and so forth. Boundaries may be clearly defined but open to change and input, or so poorly defined that confusion and chaos exist, or so rigid that little input can permeate.

Negentropy is a tendency toward openness to the environment, both inside and outside the family. Living, open systems tend to increase in complexity over time; this increase in complexity is called *differentiation*. An example of differentiation is human growth and development. The child grows from a dependent infant to a child with concrete thinking and a short attention span who feels safe at home to a young adult with abstract thinking and a lengthy attention span who is capable of living on his own in a complex environment. *Entropy* is the tendency of a system to be closed to the environment. If a person remains closed to feedback from others, he tends to develop distorted and peculiar perceptions, thoughts, and feelings.

Time is an important entity in families because systems change with the passage of time, as people age and children are born and leave home. *Stresses* and strains impinge on and occur within family systems. Stress is normal and inevitable as change occurs. Adolescence is an example of a common developmental stressor. *Conflict* often results from stress and change, and is also a normal and common phenomenon. A family's ability to manage change and conflict is termed *adaptation*. Adaptation may range from failure to adapt to mere survival to growing and changing into a more highly differentiated system.

It is useful to view families on a continuum from most negentropic to most entropic, or from more growth-oriented to less growth-oriented. Families that are most negentropic, or more open and growth-oriented, are those that produce the most personally and interpersonally capable people. Families that are more entropic, or less open and growth-oriented, produce less capable people who often come to the attention of health care workers, mental health care providers, educators, and law enforcement personnel.

Producing Competent People

Beavers describes eight variables that are critical for producing competent people.[4] Optimal families have an open system orientation. This orientation assumes that an individual needs a group from which he derives satisfaction and personal definition, and that life is complex with experience flowing not from a single cause, but from multiple factors.

These optimal families have permeable boundaries. The family views the world outside of itself positively, utilizes input from society and the environment to enrich their lives, and discards input that they do not value. The boundaries between subsystems within the family, such as the subsystems of parents and children, permit privacy and aloneness, but allow for the inclusion of others.

The optimum family experiences contextual clarity, which means that verbal and nonverbal communication are congruent and clear, and that generational lines are clear with a strong parental coalition. Oedipal issues in these families are resolved appropriately.

Power in optimal families is shared and flows from the parental couple. The parental pair have an egalitarian partnership that consists of complementary role behaviors. Roles are not shared, but complement one another; for instance, one partner relates as the more aggressive one and the other relates as the more supportive. These complementary roles exist without sexual stereotyping, but follow the prevalent social patterns of the time. Sex does not define overt power in optimal families. Neither do people in these families lose their power by becoming close and intimate. Children do not assume parental responsibilities; parents use authoritarian approaches, if needed.

Optimal families encourage autonomy. They consciously believe that children are being prepared to leave the family and live interdependently, and progressively encourage independent thinking and behaviors. Each member's views are respected and each member claims responsibility for, and communicates clearly, his or her thoughts, feelings, and actions. People from optimal families possess a high degree of initiative and performance.

The affective tone in optimum families is caring, warm, empathic, and hopeful. Members ask about and attend to feelings; they are involved with one another. Conflict, which is inevitable, is dealt with and resolved. The family members believe that they are able to survive difficult or unpleasant situations and occurrences. Their management or resolution of conflict strengthens their relationships and increases their confidence in the relationships.[1] Negotiation and task performance are accomplished with input from all members and attention to the developmental capabilities of children. No one is excluded. Parents lead the negotiations, typically in family meetings.

The optimum family has transcendent values; that is, the family has a belief system that tolerates and transcends the pain of loss and change. This belief system may be in part based on conventional religious beliefs, but is usually an intrinsic belief that love is a worthwhile risk even though the loved one may be lost. The family has an altruistic bent toward society. Children, of course, cannot conceptualize these notions until they are nearing adulthood. Nevertheless, mature parents set the tone for the family with their own abilities to transcend the inevitability of loss, death, and change.

Change

It is evident that the concept of change is central in the family systems theory. Western, particularly American, views about marriage and family are influenced by fairy tales and the media wherein the hero and heroine find each other and live "happily ever after." The couple soon find, however, that living happily ever after is, indeed, a fairy tale. They discover, instead, that their lives and the environment are constantly changing. If children enter the family, change and conflict are inherent. Every system, though, works to maintain homeostasis; that is, some kind of stability that provides a balance between what is valued and desired and the changes that impinge on, and disrupt, that homeostasis or steady state. Change causes stress within the system.

Stressors and Their Impacts on Families

Historical Development

During this century and particularly during the past 30 years, enormous technological and social change has occurred in the United States. Following the sacrifices and pain of World War II, families settled into a conservative

pattern of the nuclear family wherein the wife–mother gave up her job in the factory to the returning veteran and stayed home to raise the children while the husband–father went to work. In greater numbers, families moved away from the city to suburban areas, a sign of increasing affluence and materialism. The adults of the 1950s were children of the depression who feared economic deprivation and wished to spare their children the pain of poverty.

During the 1960s, tremendous, indeed revolutionary, changes took place. The civil rights movement and college-age children's rebellion against the materialistic society and the United States' increasing involvement in Vietnam disrupted the long-accepted values of patriotism and the work ethic. Humanitarian social values became prevalent; minority groups in the United States insisted on their rights to participate in the affluent life of the middle-class American. Their insistence took place through political influence, through passive tactics (*e.g.*, civil disobedience), or through violence. The rights of the individual became paramount in education, health care, hiring practices, housing, and business opportunities.

The 1970s brought the women's movement and emphasis on self-awareness and fulfillment. Divorce rates skyrocketed and the family, in its normal configuration of homemaker–mother, breadwinner–father, and children, was threatened. Individual freedom was important. Inflation was rampant.

By the end of the 1970s, the dual-earner family was the majority family form and half of the mothers in the work force had preschool children.[5,46] Violent crime, sexual promiscuity, adolescent pregnancy, substance abuse, mental health problems, and suicide were epidemic, particularly among adolescents. The era of self-fulfillment appeared to have exacted a high toll among the youth of the country. The emergence of ultra-conservative groups, such as the "moral majority," and increased membership in fundamentalist churches signaled a swing of the pendulum toward more traditional values.[45] Universities raised standards and were unwilling to provide tutorial services to substandard students. High schools began to reinstitute stiff discipline. The public demanded heavier penalties for crime.[41]

The families of the 1980s have the challenge and opportunity of choosing those values and lifestyles that best meet the needs of the adult and child members. The forging of competent selves remains the mission of family life, with the parents providing competent leadership within the family. Assisting families with this monumental task is the focus of nursing intervention in numerous health care settings.

Developmental Stressors

In addition to developing as a unit in the context of historical events, the family undergoes changes related to the growth and development of its members. The birth of the first child, whether unplanned and unwanted or planned and anticipated with joy, is a significant stressor. The physiological and emotional changes of pregnancy test the couple's ability to be supportive of one another. Lifestyle changes related to nausea or fatigue may also be difficult for the couple. The birth of the child is now usually a shared experience for the couple and often a peak experience in their lives. The demanding infant, however, soon commands a central position in the family by requiring a great deal of energy, time, and emotional investment. The couple must learn to meet the baby's needs without neglecting their own, a task that persists through the childhood and adolescence of their children.

The adolescent period is a highly stressful time for families. The teenager's ambivalence about dependence versus independence and his resultant limit-testing are frightening and frustrating experiences for parents. Finding a balance between giving the child freedom to grow and learn, while protecting him from harmful experiences until his judgment is sound, is a difficult job, requiring time, energy, careful thought, and sensitivity. Open communication centered on the teenager's thoughts and feelings regarding issues important to him, such as money, rules, school achievement, sex, love, career choice, and friends, is critical. Parents of the adolescent need to know his friends and his whereabouts and they need to set appropriate, fair limits with consequences for the breaking of rules. On the other hand, every aspect of the adolescent's life should not be subjected to scrutiny, probing, and checking up. Trust should be established through childhood and early adolescence, and opportunities for role-taking, examining moral ethical issues, and developing good judgment should be provided *with* the child.[17]

The middle years present two major crises, the midlife crisis and dealing with aging parents. The crisis of midlife begins when the middle-ager confronts the fact of his own mortality, often triggered by the appearance of wrinkles or competition from younger people at work. The middle-aged person confronts his or her own limitations and hopes for success, and comes to terms with accomplishments in life thus far, including work, family relationships, sexuality, and hopes for children. This is a painful time for the adult and often coincides with the presence of teenagers in the family. Diminished health and death of parents leaves the middle-ager responsible for two generations, a considerable burden.[35, 37]

The older adult must cope with the loss of work, friends, spouse, and often economic resources. He also looks back on his life and concludes that it has been a meaningful experience with which he is satisfied, or that it has not been meaningful, which leads to despair.

Role Development and Change

Role development and change cause considerable challenges or difficulties for families. Since the late 1970s, the predominant family structure is the *dual-earner family*, in which there are often preschool children. The physical and emotional care of children, maintenance of the household, participation in children's activities, providing transportation to children's activities, as well as maintaining and developing self and the relationship with a spouse dictate a full, interesting life or a frustrating and exhausting one. Women in these families experience more role strain and stress and spend more hours on household chores than men. Household help is expensive to hire.[5] Child care facilities are often inadequate in quantity or quality and are rarely available at the workplace.

The skyrocketing divorce rate profoundly affects the families involved. Self-esteem of the spouses suffers a severe blow, and the children become angry and confused, are often forced to choose the parent with whom they will live, and feel they are to blame for the breakup of their parents' marriage. Most families cannot recover from divorce without counseling, usually instigated by the mother–wife's pain or by the acting-out behavior of the children. Serious economic setbacks occur when one household becomes two households with the same income. Women usually earn less money than their male counterparts and are more likely to receive custody of the children than men. Child support payments may or may not be paid regularly. Children of divorce undergo moves to new schools, loss of friends and activities, and loss of the parent who does not have custody. The grief process is prolonged because of the proximity of the spouse–parent; that is, the parent without custody.[10]

Loss of a family member through death or desertion is not uncommon. The family may grieve the loss of the parent, spouse, or child and move on. Economic conditions in these families vary according to socioeconomic class, whether the lost member was a breadwinner or the sole breadwinner, and whether the death was due to catastrophic illness.

The single-parent family is at risk because of its limited financial resources and the parent's limited time and energy. Because one parent is absent from the home, that parent's role modeling is not available for the children.[20]

An increase in remarriages has resulted in the blended family. Putting two families together, particularly if there are children in the families, takes time and patience. The adoptive family of an older child must have considerable patience and love for the child who has often been in a succession of foster homes.[9]

Another increasing phenomenon is the adolescent parent. A dramatic rise in teenage pregnancy, with large numbers of teenage mothers keeping their babies, has resulted in increasing numbers of teenaged parents. The adolescent girl may opt for marriage or may opt to live at home and finish school. Nevertheless, adolescent parents have not reached adulthood themselves, but have the responsibility for a baby for which they are emotionally and financially ill-equipped. In addition, the adolescent mother and her infant are often at physiological risk.

Surviving Divorce: the Children

In addition to the already strenuous developmental tasks of childhood and adolescence, children of divorce must master six more psychological tasks, according to Judith Wallerstein, who has conducted a longitudinal study of children of divorce. This study has produced some sobering data.

The process of recovery from divorce is a lengthy one lasting through late adolescence or early adulthood. Even when the psychological tasks of coping with divorce are mastered, the child of divorce experiences "some residue of sadness, of anger and of anxiety about the potential unreliability of relationships . . ." The tasks of coping with divorce include the following.

Task I, *acknowledging the reality of the marital rupture,* is usually completed within a year, although usually accompanied initially by considerable regression. Younger children have more difficulty with this task because of their inability to conceptualize time, space, and the nature of relationships.

Task II, *disengaging from parental conflict and distress and resuming customary pursuits,* is also usually completed by the child within a year or two of the divorce. In the year following the divorce or separation, the child often has difficulty in learning and has other school problems. Some children become involved in sexual activity or stealing. All children must distance themselves from their upset parents and overcome their own depression and anxiety. After the initial upset, most children resume their usual activities.

Task III, the *resolution of loss,* takes many years. In addition to grieving the multiple losses that the divorce precipitates, the child strives to recover from an overwhelming sense of rejection. This sense of rejection is diminished by frequent, reliable visiting arrangements and by the development of the relationship with the noncustodial parent.

Task IV, *resolving anger and blame,* also takes many years to accomplish. Usually in late adolescence, the child begins to understand the parents and the reasons for the divorce. Typically, the child forgives the parents and, perhaps, himself or herself.

Task V, *accepting the permanence of divorce,* is a gradual process during which the child wishes intensely for and fantasizes the restoration of the family. It is not uncommon for mature adults to continue to wish for and fantasize the reconciliation of their parents.

Task VI, *achieving realistic hope regarding relationships,* is a normal task of adolescence, but for the child of divorce, it is complicated by fears of rejection and failure based on his earlier experience.

Clearly, the child of divorce faces a dilemma—to learn to trust in his own lovability, in his capacity to love, in his self-worth, and in the reliability of relationships.

(From Wallerstein JS: Children of Divorce: The Psychological Tasks of the Child. Am J Orthopsychiatr 53 [April]: 230–242, 1983)

Environmental Influences on the Family

Although descriptions of the family primarily refer to middle class families or those with middle class values, a variety of cultures are represented in the United States. The family cannot be adequately assessed or effectively treated without an understanding of the ethnic group from whence it came. Different cultures have different orientations to time and relationships that the health care provider must comprehend and appreciate in order to assist the family in maximizing their potential.[8, 27, 29, 39, 40] For further exploration of this topic, the reader is encouraged to examine Chapter 9, which deals with cultural variations.

Poverty is an overwhelming obstacle for many families. The struggle for existence in terms of obtaining food, clothing, and shelter, all substandard and far from the American dream, occupies the family's time and energy and depletes its dignity. Frustration is high, desertion and violence are common. Reliance on public assistance is demeaning and undermines individual initiative.

Television and other media have been significant influences on families during the past 20 years. The ubiquitous presence of the TV set has contributed to unprecedented materialism, increase in violent crime among young people, irresponsible sexual behavior, sapping of creative thinking, undesirable dietary practices, and lack of communication between family members.[17, 25] Family members eat many dinners in the 25-inch, full-color presence of murder and mayhem. One may wonder whether Americans can face each other without the television intervening.

The changing values of society have an impact on schools and churches. Schools at all levels have been concerned with students' rights and with providing curricula for the development of the whole self, which inadvertently resulted in a decline in college entrance exam scores and serious discipline problems, particularly in high schools. As funding shrinks and conservative values return, high schools are raising academic standards and adopting stricter discipline policies. Church membership has decreased overall since 1970, but an increase of one per cent (1%) was noted in 1980 with increases among Catholics, Mormons, and Southern Baptists.[41]

The rise in violent crime and in the incidence of family violence is staggering. The cluster of factors contributing to the occurrence of family violence include low income, unemployed husband, husband and wife under age 30 and married less than 10 years, higher-than-average levels of conflict in the family, excessively high number of stressors, non-white racial group, lack of church membership, parental disagreement over children, presence of verbal aggression, residence in neighborhood less than 2 years, and abusiveness of the couple's parents.[38]

The presence of chronic illness or handicap in a family member taxes physical and emotional energy, time, and economic resources of both the ill or handicapped person and of the other members of the family.

Although these stressors are significant and prevalent, a critical variable in whether the family survives and produces capable people is the self-esteem of the parents. The family can tolerate and cope with a great deal of stress if parents feel satisfied with themselves and their relationship. Low self-esteem is a stressor to the family.

Application of the Nursing Process to the Family

Assessment and Analysis

The assessment framework presented in this chapter incorporates a number of variables found to effect the development of competent people and a category related to health.[21] (See also the insert Guide to Family Assessment below.)

People are continually subjected to stress and change; it is how one manages stresses that determines one's relative wellness. Individuals' ability to adapt and grow stems directly from their experiences in family life. Families' levels of adaptation fall on a continuum from optimal to midrange to severely disturbed functioning.[4] Families may also be described as nurturing or troubled.[33] (See Family Mental Health Continuum on page 216.)

Optimal Families

The optimal family has been described earlier in this chapter in the section dealing with systems theory and the development of competence in people. The *optimal family* also has little physical illness and usually practices high-level health care including excellent nutrition and abstinence or near abstinence from alcohol, drugs, tobacco, caffeine and

Guide to Family Assessment

1. Open-system orientation
   Multiple causation of events
   Need for each other and other people
2. Boundaries
   Touching
   Interaction between family members
   Allocation of space in household
   Links to society
3. Contextual clarity
   Oedipal issues resolved
   Clear generational lines
   Strong parental coalition
   Communication
     Clear, direct, honest, specific
     Congruent
4. Power
   Flows from parental coalition
   Delegated to children appropriate to age
   Clear role definition
   Not sex-defined
   Rules
5. Encouragement of autonomy
   Differentness accepted

6. Affective issues
   Warmth–caring
   Empathy
   Feelings attended to
   Amount of conflict
   Resolution of conflict
   Self-esteem of members high
7. Negotiation and task performance
   Input from all members
   Led by parents
   Little amount of conflict
8. Transcendent values
   Expect loss
   Recover from, prepare for loss
   Hopeful
   Altruistic
9. Health measures
   Healthy diet
   Freedom from drugs and chemicals
   Regular exercise and recreation
   Concern for the environment
   Abstinence from dangerous activities

Family Mental Health Continuum

Family:	Troubled	Midrange	Adequate	Optimal
Children evidencing:	Process schizophrenia Severe behavior disorder Borderline personality disorder	Neuroses Behavior disorders	No obvious pathology	Unusual individual competence

(Adapted from Beavers RW: Psychotherapy and Growth: A Family Systems Perspective. New York, Brunner/Mazel, 1977)

saccharine; he also participates in regular exercise and recreation, avoids dangerous activities, and demonstrates concern for the environment. The optimal family is, indeed, the ideal family. Most families function in the adequate and midrange area and a smaller proportion of families function in the troubled range.

Adequate Families

Adequate families produce people who do not have mental health problems. The adequate family maintains an open systems orientation; the family is flexible and open, does not believe causation of events is linear, and expresses need for each other and other people. The intrasystem boundaries are clearly defined but open. Members of the family respect each others' privacy, but there is considerable face-to-face interaction and touching.

The family's links to society are numerous and viewed positively. The societal links are likely to include work, schools, church, friends, extended family, family physician, and community service organizations. The family is not likely to have connections with social welfare agencies. Contextual clarity is present in these families. Oedipal issues are resolved appropriately according to the ages of the children. The parents provide strong leadership and maintain their relationship as a couple. Communication is clear, direct, honest, specific, and congruent.

Power in adequate families flows from the parents who use authoritarian measures when necessary. Parents delegate responsibility to children as it is deemed appropriate for their age and stage of development. Roles are clear; that is, family members know and agree on their functions and performance of activities. Family members understand and generally respect family rules. Power and authority are not ascribed by sex, although the mother in the family generally has less power than her husband for two reasons— she earns less money and she is more likely to set aside her goals, including her employment responsibilities, to meet the needs of children.[5] It is rare to find a truly egalitarian couple with children with equally divided family and work responsibilities. Achievement of an egalitarian relationship

necessitates an enormous output of energy, and probably occurs with paid help or extended family providing some of the nurturing of children and household chores.[30,31] For children's needs to be met in an adequate or optimal manner, at least one of the marital partners must sacrifice some aspect of self-realization and, at present, that person is most likely to be the mother.

Adequate families encourage autonomy by encouraging children and adults to try new activities and express their ideas, even when they are divergent with the families' values. Family members are valued for their differences as well as their similarities with others. Idiosyncrasies are tolerated with good humor.

The affective tone in adequate families is warm and caring. Members are empathetic, often at early ages. Members consider and ask about others' feelings. Although there is more conflict in the adequate family than in the optimum family, it is resolved without loss of self-esteem. Self-esteem is high in these families; however, the mother may experience more stress, loneliness, or depression than other family members.

Negotiation and task performance are accomplished with considerable ease, but not as easily as in optimal families. Decisions are often reached at family meetings; parents lead the discussions and have the final say in decisions. Some conflict over household work exists and the mother is likely to assume a disproportionate share of the work, which may be self-imposed or may be due to the many activities in which the other family members engage. Nevertheless, the adequate family can usually work out ways to prevent the overload of one person. Family members are competent and excel in some areas. The family is less likely to be an entire group of superachievers than the optimal family. There exists no significant deviance in performance in school or work or in relationships with others.

Transcendent values include a hopeful, positive outlook, the expectation and preparation for loss of children, retirement, and so forth, and an altruistic bent toward neighbors. These families also practice adequate health measures and do not suffer significant health problems.

Midrange Families

Midrange families produce people who evidence mental health problems. The "identified patient" in the family is likely to be neurotic or behaviorally disordered, depending on the family style. Family members may also have physical illnesses. Although family members are reasonably effective, they are restricted. An open-system orientation is absent in these families; family members need others but under certain conditions. The family tends to believe that there are causes for events, but they are not sure what they are. They continuously strive to find answers and to do well.

Boundaries remain fairly clear in these families, although, when under pressure, the family will solidify its boundaries and turn inward (*i.e.*, keep the trouble inside) or lose its boundaries and spill into the environment. Interaction between family members (intrasystem interaction) is restricted.

Links to society are present, but they disrupt when the family is under unusual pressure. Families who tend to externalize trouble (*i.e.*, push it into the environment) have contact with law enforcement agencies.

Midrange families also have difficulty with contextual clarity. Oedipal issues are not resolved because expressions of sexuality are stereotyped and stifled. The parental coalition is present but weak, and other coalitions develop that undermine the effectiveness of the parents. Communication in these families is generally clear, but expressed with fear, guilt, or anger.

Power is the central difficulty in midrange families. The family confuses love and power. Love is a feeling that moves one to care about the life and growth of another.[15] Midrange families often believe that caring is controlling the life of another and, by means of overt or covert coercion, applying a system of "oughts" and "shoulds." The "shoulds" are often sex-stereotyped. The parents believe in doing the "right" thing and are constantly struggling for control of the children through discipline, money, and so forth. Children become powerful by manipulating the parents, not by learning to assume power and responsibility. Family roles are defined by sex or by other beliefs about the family member, such as "she's so good and never causes any trouble," or "Johnny's the athletic one." The family behaves as if there is someone judging the family's actions, thoughts, and feelings as to their goodness or badness.

Encouragement of autonomy is not found in midrange families; on the contrary, children are expected to adhere to the family's norms. The constant power struggles and repression of feelings and ideas within the family sap family member's creativity. Children tend to stay in the parental home well into adulthood, or leave home very early—a kind of pseudoautonomy.

The affective issues that characterize midrange families are depression, anxiety, and anger. The enormous resultant conflict may be overtly expressed in angry exchanges or repressed through submission to the "oughts" and "shoulds." As a result, members display little empathy, conflict over rules and norms, considerable frustration, and caring that is controlling rather than growth-producing. The self-esteem of the family members is low, and the identified patient has very low self-esteem.

Negotiation and task performance is accomplished by coercion because the parental team cannot agree on who does what. Nevertheless, the work of the family is accomplished. These families do not hold family meetings.

Transcendent values of hope and altruism are lacking in midrange families. The family eventually accepts change and loss, but with a great deal of pain, anger, and frustration. They look toward the future as if to say, "What difficulty will present itself?" Martyrdom is not an unusual stance for members of these families.

Health problems in midrange families include excessive use of alcohol, prescription tranquilizers, and other drugs for relief of the pain of daily living. The stressful existence of midrange families produces some psychophysiologic illnesses, such as headaches, ulcers, obesity, and so forth. Because the family is concerned with doing the "right" thing, they meet their basic health needs. The family attempts recreation and exercise, but the conflict that surfaces during the planning of events reduces their pleasure. In some families, the presence of a great deal of anger leads to dangerous activities, such as hitting, driving at excessive speeds, and running away. The midrange family is too preoccupied with daily events to explore health promotion and wellness activities.

Troubled Families

Families who function on the more entropic end of the family health continuum tend to produce people who exhibit antisocial disorders, borderline personality disorders, or psychotic disorders. *Troubled families* display qualities that are the opposite of the optimal family's characteristics. The family tends to be very rigid or disordered, rather than open and flexible.

The boundary issues in troubled families are problematic. The family system boundary is rigid with minimal links to society. The links are tentative and mistrustful and input from the larger society is limited. Troubled families may also have diffuse boundaries, which means that family business tends to spill over into the environment. Interpersonal boundaries in these families are also diffused, resulting in family members' global response to input. Distancing between people is prevalent.

Contextual clarity is blurred in troubled families. Due to a weak parental coalition, cross-generational clinging occurs and oedipal issues remain unresolved. The parents deal with their pain of disappointment in each other by reaching across generational boundaries for comfort or control of the situation. Often this cross-generational clinging takes the form of a triangle; that is, mother and son form a coalition against father. Often, there is covert or overt incestuous behavior. The child who is "triangled" is usually the symptom-bearer in the family. This child (or young adult) responds to these pressures with mental disorder, physical illness, or delinquent behavior.

Communication in troubled families is not clear, congruent, specific, direct, or honest. Because people in troubled families have low self-esteem, they fear rejection from others and are embarrassed about it. To "cover up" their fear of rejection, members of troubled families tend to use the four following patterns of communication described by Satir:

1. Placating or doing anything to prevent others from getting angry
2. Blaming or attempting to look strong and reject first
3. Computing or treating the other as if they were insignificant by using big words
4. Distracting or eliminating the possibility of rejection by changing the subject or talking in a "crazy" way[33]

Another characteristic of communication in troubled families is the lack of congruence between the content of what is said and the feeling beneath it (*i.e.*, incongruence between verbal and nonverbal communication); for example, smiling when talking in an angry tone of voice. *Double-bind communication* occurs when an incongruent message is sent that includes a direction to do something with a nonverbal message to do the opposite, and, furthermore, the receiver of the message is not permitted to comment on it. For example, a father says to his child, "Come here and let me hug you. You know Daddy loves you" (in angry tone of voice). The child answers, "You sound mad." The father responds, "I don't know what you're talking about." The child is then faced with the dilemma of choosing to which communication he will respond. A child faced with continuous double-bind communication is unable to determine the true meaning of verbalizations and to identify and name normal feelings. As the child's ability to test reality becomes impaired, he may invent his own language and peculiar explanations for events; that is, the child becomes schizophrenic. In some troubled families, anger is communicated through hitting and other forms of assault.

Another communication difficulty found in troubled families is disqualifying. *Disqualifying* takes place when an individual fails to attend to another's message by silence, ignoring, or changing the subject. Evasiveness in communication is also common in these families.

Power is diffuse in the troubled family and does not flow from the parents. Autonomy is discouraged, rather than encouraged. In fact, the troubled family does not tolerate differentness. Paradoxically, the family tends to view one of its members as "different" and the cause of its trouble; this process is called *scapegoating*.

The affective tone in troubled families with diffuse boundaries tends to be exaggerated. The members react inappropriately to threats or one member's difficulties. In families with rigid boundaries, the affective tone is restricted, depressed, and despairing, there is a lack of empathy, and great distance exists between the members. Undue attention, which is confusing, smothering, or rejecting, is paid to one member. Self-esteem in troubled families is low, and hate, inability to respond empathetically to others, loneliness, and hopelessness predominate. Negotiation is not accomplished and performance of tasks varies widely. Conflict may be a constant, overt, and unresolved presence in families with diffuse boundaries; this conflict is denied, not commented on, and unresolved in families with rigid boundaries. Transcendent values are absent. The inability of troubled families to tolerate loss or differences leads to a cynical, hopeless outlook, rather than an altruistic, hopeful one. The stresses of unhappy family life often produce serious physical illness, usually in one member.

Planning

The optimal and adequate families are not likely to present themselves for assistance at traditional mental health care settings. These families are found at church activities, P.T.A. meetings, community functions, adult education centers, and other such events. They read newspapers, magazines, and books and select television programs. Therefore, the nurse plans to reach optimal and adequate families in nontraditional health care settings. These families do, however, participate in preventive and health maintenance programs where nurses come into contact with them. Family members may be enriched in four areas: enhancement of existing strengths, anticipatory guidance, parenting education, and holistic health measures.

Enhancement of existing strengths may be as simple as a word of praise or as complex as a series of structured, goal-directed activities. Providing encouragement and praise for the successful performance of parental functions develops trust and increased self-esteem. Anticipatory guidance refers to teaching parents and families what to expect next, particularly in terms of developmental events and crises. Childbirth education is an example of anticipatory guidance. Classes on adolescence and aging parents are also very useful. Parenting programs may be formal or informal.[11, 12, 18] There is currently a need for parenting programs adapted to the teenage years. Holistic health principles, including nutrition with natural foods, exercise, and stress management techniques, are still unknown to, or are not practiced by, many people.[46] Stress management focuses on relaxation techniques, meditation, and leisure activities.

Midrange families utilize mental health facilities and interact with nurses in community health settings. The midrange family with school-age children is likely to come in contact with the school nurse. These families benefit from enhancement of their strengths and parenting programs. The nurse may help the family with problem-solving, conflict management, and education of the family about normal growth and development, especially as it relates to their present difficulties. The nurse may also refer the family for family therapy if problem-solving and education approaches fail to relieve the family problems.

Troubled families require family therapy for resolution of their difficulties. Family therapy is available through therapists in private practice, community mental health centers, and psychiatric inpatient units. Networking is often essential for troubled families, particularly if economic problems exist, if protection for one or more members is needed, or if there is involvement with the legal system. The therapist, nurse, social worker, or other health care professional responsible for service to the family seeks sources of support for the family and assists them in arranging for these services. Some examples of these services are churches, social welfare agencies, emergency pantry service, Red Cross, voluntary agencies, hospice, and community health services. Another source of assistance to families is multiple family group therapy.[19]

Intervention

Characteristics and Skills of the Nurse

To work effectively with families, the nurse must possess self-awareness, empathy, therapeutic communication skills, and knowledge of family theory. The nurse expands her understanding of family life through formal education, self-directed learning, observation, and supervised practice.

Self-awareness is critical for understanding the behaviors of others. One must be able to identify and "own" one's own thoughts, feelings, and biases before understanding others' feelings and behaviors. The psychiatric-mental health nurse pursues personal growth as part of ongoing education. The nurse must also become aware of her own family dynamics, roles, and values so that she will not confuse, compare, or impose her own family style upon others.

Another critical characteristic of the psychiatric-mental health nurse working with families is empathy. The nurse interacts and intervenes with many different families who possess varying problems and strengths. The ability to experience the family's trouble "from their shoes," and then step back to analyze and intervene, is essential for helping relationships of all kinds, including those with the family. Empathy is essential to building trust.

Therapeutic communication skills are essential for health-care providers working with families. The nurse serves as a role model of clear, open, direct, honest, and congruent communication and as a clarifier of the family's unclear communication. The nurse who works with families possesses certain beliefs about families. These include the beliefs that families are functioning as well as they are able, that no one is to blame, that parents want very much to do a good job, and that people behave in nonproductive ways because they are in pain. The nurse, empathizing with the family's pain, works from the position of their strengths and assists them, primarily through communication skills, to learn that the problem is a family problem and that there are more satisfying ways to live as a family, and as people.

There are additional skills that nurses utilize in caring for families. Skillful use of the nursing process, particularly taking adequate time to define the problem accurately, leads to a more productive plan with successful outcomes. So-called "noncompliance" is usually a result of failure of the nurse or other health care provider to discover underlying issues that result in nonresolution of the problem. Knowledge of various teaching strategies, an understanding of learning principles, and the ability to make adequate referrals for other services are important.[44] The nurse actively assists the family through the steps to assure entry into the desired system.

Collaboration is working with others, as an equal, toward a common goal. The nurse serves as a peer on the mental health team and strives to provide the best service to clients by utilizing the contributions of other disciplines in the interest of the family.[2] Nurses also serve as consultants on family health in the community by serving on advisory boards, committees, and school boards, and by communicating with legislators and candidates about the needs of families.

The development of personal coping skills is essential to the well-being of the nurse who works with families. The intensive nature of family health nursing, especially psychiatric-mental health nursing, requires that the nurse obtain sufficient rest, exercise, relaxation, and nurturance and support from colleagues, friends, and significant others in her personal life. Adequate supervision from an experienced clinician promotes objectivity, continued professional growth, and support of the nurse.

Family Therapy

Family therapy is undertaken by clinicians of various disciplines, including nurse–therapists, who have undergone formal training in family therapy during graduate or postgraduate education. Sometimes, nurses without graduate education practice family therapy under close supervision, although graduate preparation is preferred and usually required for family therapy.

Family therapy is a specific intervention mode based on the premise that the member with the presenting symptoms signals the presence of pain in the whole family. This pain arises from the disappointment of the marital partners with each other. Their unhappiness, anger, and hurt are expressed overtly or covertly in a number of ways, such as triangling, scapegoating, psychophysiological illness, mental illness, and substance abuse. Whatever the presenting diagnosis, the therapist works in similar ways to assist the family to identify and express their thoughts and feelings, define family roles and rules, try new, more productive styles of relating, and restore strength to the parental coalition.

Taking the Family's History. Initiation of family therapy necessitates exploring the family's history, starting with the beginning of the relationship of the parents. This strategy starts the process of focusing on the couple as leaders of the family and takes the pressure off the "identified patient." During the history-taking, each person in the family is identified and recognized in chronological order, thereby acknowledging each member's uniqueness and defining his role(s) (see the insert below).

Another historical approach to family therapy is the

Family Assessment Guidelines

1. Open system orientation
   What do you believe are the reasons for the difficulty?
   What do you think the solution is?
2. Boundaries
   (Notice who touches whom, who talks to whom, presence of eye contact.)
   (Notice whether the touching is parental, kind, loving, seductive, rough, or violent.)
   Where does everyone sleep?
   Do you all have time alone?
   How do you get along with Johnny's teacher? scout leader? other significant people in Johnny's life?
   How do you like Johnny's friends? Are you in touch with Johnny's friends' parents?
3. Contextual clarity
   Who's in charge in this family?
   Who gets along best with whom?
   Who does what around the house?
   (Notice whether parents agree on what is happening.)
   (Notice whether there is unusual closeness between child and opposite sex parent.)
   (Is communication clear, honest, specific—do members make "I statements" or blaming "you statements"?)
   (Can the interviewer get an answer to a question? Can family members get an answer?)
   (Can the interviewer follow the family conversation?)
   (Are verbal and nonverbal communications congruent?)
   How much is your TV turned on?
4. Power
   (Do the parents set the tone for the interview, set limits on children's behaviors? Are the limits reasonable, not just talk or punitive?)
   (Does one person control the group by talking or distracting?)
   (Does everyone talk or at least seem involved?)
   Tell me your rules. What happens if they are broken?
   What are everyone's jobs at home?
5. Encouragement of autonomy

If you, Sue, like to stay home and read and you, Bob, like to go to parties, how do you deal with these different desires?
   (Are members stereotyped as "the angel," "the wild one," "just like his Uncle Joe," and so on?)
   What kinds of things are you, Johnny, interested in?
   How are you different from your sister?
6. Affective issues
   (Can the interviewer feel warmth and caring, or does the interviewer feel uncomfortable, fearful?)
   (What do you think Johnny is feeling? What are you feeling as you listen to Johnny?)
   (Notice whether family members seem ashamed or embarrassed.)
   (Are conflicts resolved?)
   What do you do when you get angry?
7. Negotiating and task performance
   Do you argue about household chores?
   (Can the family solve a problem with parents having final say in the issue?)
   Do you have meetings?
8. Transcendent values
   (Do family members believe that problems can be solved?)
   What do you think and feel about Johnny going to camp? getting married? and so on?
   What do you (parents) do for fun?
   (Do family members accept that life is complicated, difficult, joyous, routine?)
   What kinds of community activities are you involved in?
   (Do family members laugh at themselves, have a sense of humor?)
9. Health measures
   When, where do you eat meals? Do you eat one meal each day together? What kinds of things do you eat?
   How often do you have a drink? Does anyone take medications?
   Tell me how you have fun.
   Do you participate in sports or other exercise? What do you do to relax yourself?

use of the genogram. The genogram is a three-generation map of the family structure and relationships.[19] As the therapist draws the map, she questions the family about significant events and identifies family roles. The therapist and family gain an enormous amount of knowledge about the family through the genogram. The genogram is a nonthreatening technique that may be used for diagnosing the family's problems and for helping the family members understand that their present structure, roles values, and entire system evolved from the past. The use of the genogram is an excellent approach for nurse–therapists and other psychiatric-mental health professionals who work with dysfunctional families (see Fig. 17-1 and the case study on p. 222).

Communication Techniques in Family Therapy.

Family therapy may be initiated by asking the family to talk together about the trouble and "monitoring the family conversation."[1,22] The therapist intervenes in the family's conversation by clarifying, by interpreting double level, double-bind, and nonverbal communication, and by assisting members to own their own thoughts, feelings, and actions and to communicate them clearly and congruently to others. The therapist deals with anger by talking about it openly and nonjudgmentally, by interpreting anger as hurt, by handling emotionally loaded issues by moving from the least to most emotionally loaded material, and by tying feelings to the facts.[34] The therapist uses humor and empathy, points out positive aspects of the individuals, never blames anyone, and assumes good will even when it is expressed poorly.[34]

Experiential Activities.

Other therapeutic techniques available to the nurse–family therapist and the family are homework assignments, paradoxical injunction, and sculpting. Homework assignments might require family members to engage in one recreational activity together during the next week, to eat one third of their meals together, or to verbally reinforce each family member once each day. Paradoxical injunctions are instructions to perform the opposite of what is intended, also called the therapeutic bind.[23] Sculpting is a technique wherein the family enacts an experience without words, then "freezes." The sculpture expresses the feeling tone without word games and is a powerful device for assisting families to understand their relationships. The therapist instructs a particular member to arrange the sculpture as he or she would like it to be, thereby initiating change with action.[28]

Evaluation

Successful outcomes of work with families can be measured by comparing family functioning to the assessment criteria described in this chapter. The family that functions opti-

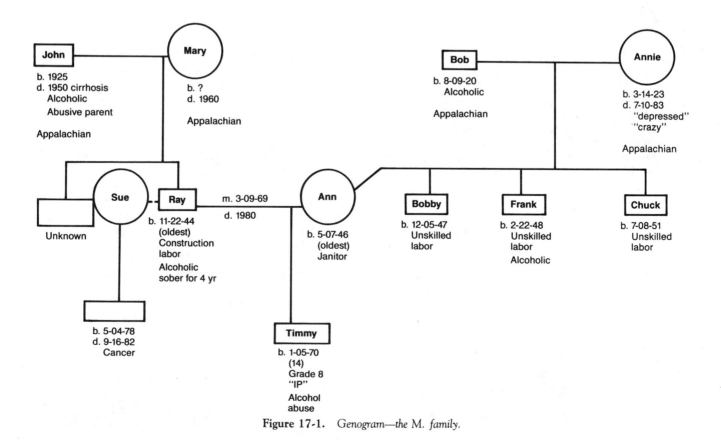

Figure 17-1. *Genogram—the M. family.*

mally has an open systems orientation, clear boundaries, positive links to society, contextual clarity with clear and congruent communication, a strong parental coalition, appropriate power distribution, autonomous people, a warm, caring, affective tone with high self-esteem of members, efficient negotiation and task performance, and transcendent values of hope and altruism. As Satir summarizes, "Family therapy is terminated when everyone in the family can use the first person singular followed by an active verb and ending with a direct object."[34] At that point, family members are free to express feelings and thoughts without fear of loss of self-esteem.

Summary

This chapter provides an overview of theories of family development, roles, structure, and functioning. Some of the critical points discussed in this chapter include the following.

1. A family is a culturally produced social system made up of two or more people in a primary group.
2. Stages of family development may depend on the adult members or the oldest child as an index of family development.
3. According to the family systems theory, the whole (the family) is more than the sum of its parts (the members of the family).
4. Living systems possess clear, but open, boundaries, negentropy, differentiation, and adaptation.
5. Successful families produce competent people through mature leadership of parents.
6. Historical, developmental, role-related, and environmental stressors influence today's family.
7. Assessment of families includes examination of the family's open system orientation, boundaries, contextual clarity, power, encouragement of autonomy, affective tone, negotiation and task performance, transcendent values, and health.
8. Goals planned for optimal to troubled families are enhancement of existing strengths, anticipatory guidance, parenting education, and holistic health measures.
9. Nurses working with families need to possess self-understanding, empathy, therapeutic communication skills, and knowledge of family theory.
10. The family therapist helps the family identify and express their thoughts and feelings, define family roles and rules, try more productive styles of relating, and restore strength to the parental coalition.

Family Case Study: the M. Family

Assessment

Fourteen-year-old Timmy called the adolescent inpatient facility saying he wanted to "get off drugs and alcohol" and that he could not get along with his parents. An appointment was made with him and his family. Timmy and his mother, Ann, came for several appointments. When outpatient family therapy failed to assist the family, and the potential for violence increased, inpatient admission was arranged.

Timmy is the only child of Ann and Ray M. They were divorced years ago and are now "getting back together." The couple have known each other from childhood. Ann is a small, obese, woman who wore the soiled jacket from her janitor's uniform on every occasion that the therapist saw her. Ann talks continuously in a low voice and tells her "story" at every opportunity, whether or not it is relevant. Ann is a high-school graduate. She is one female of four siblings of an alcoholic father and a "mental case" mother. Two brothers are alcoholics. She describes her childhood as working very hard at keeping house, studying, and later working as a nurse's aide at an early age. She was, and remains, ashamed of her family or origin and is angry and ashamed that her son, whom she had hoped would be President of the United States, has been drinking for 2 years, cursing, skipping school, and generally not meeting her expectations.

Ray is angry that his son is in the hospital and believes that, with some reasonable rules, Timmy can behave and quit drinking. Ray quit drinking 4 years ago. Ray's father was an alcoholic and physically abused him and his siblings until about age 6; then his father died. His mother was ineffectual, and Ray left home in early adolescence. He was befriended by, and lived with, Ann's family. He learned to drink with her father and brothers.

Several years ago, Ray became involved in an affair during which a child was born. The child became ill with cancer and died. He has ended the relationship with the child's mother and is attempting to reestablish his marriage. He has maintained regular contact with his son throughout the separation and divorce.

Ray has a sixth-grade education. Both parents work two jobs and neither parent is in the home after 4 pm on weekdays or before 4 pm on weekends.

The jobs are needed to provide necessities, but both parents work extra, in part, to buy Timmy a moped, computerized video games, and other expensive items. They do this so he will not have the childhoods they had. Ray also works so that he won't drink and because he cannot tolerate his wife's unpredictable behavior: her "telling her story" and blaming him for his affair. Ray tried to leave or end the assessment interview when he became upset. Ann works because it raises her self-esteem, and she knows no other way to accomplish this. Timmy was cared for by his maternal grandmother, who died 6 months ago after a year's illness. He was then supervised by his alcoholic grandfather.

Timmy is a very pleasant youth who is working hard on his goals in the program and is determined to stop drinking and maintain sobriety. He finds the treatment program's privilege level system logical and helpful. He is outgoing and friendly but angers quickly. He has average intelligence. He complains about his mother's overprotectiveness and says he has to leave the house during his parents' arguments.

This family has deficits in all nine areas of assessment and is described as a midrange family with some characteristics of a troubled family.

Open Systems Orientation

Ann believes the family's problems are unilaterally her son's failure. Initially, Ray stated that the problems are Ann's fault, but quickly decided that placing Timmy with his alcoholic grandfather for care, buying him too many things, and failing to set rules with logical consequences are errors. Timmy believes that being with his alcoholic grandfather and his parents' fighting are the problems. All family members imply or express a need for others in their lives.

Boundaries

No touching was noted during the assessment interview. Interaction occurs between parent and child with very little between parents. Ann has very few relationships outside the family.

Contextual Clarity

The parental coalition is absent. Ann uses her son, rather than her husband, for companionship and support. Ray behaves in a parental role but is unavailable to both his wife and Timmy because of his long work hours and his inability to negotiate with his wife. The parents use blaming patterns of communication and communicate with each other through their child. Only Ray is able to make "I statements."

Power

Ray and Timmy are essentially powerless. Although Ann is very passive superficially, she manipulates her family by not communicating in any other way than "telling the story," thereby inducing guilt and frustration. Her manipulations are a result of her very low self-esteem, shame, and loneliness. Role definitions are based on each individual's perception. Ann's role with her husband is that of a punitive parent; with her son, she assumes a peer role and expects her son to behave like an adult. Ray has a parental role but no husband role. Timmy wishes he were treated like an adolescent son, which his father does but his mother does not. Apparently, his grandmother fulfilled the role of parent for Timmy, but this was offset by the grandfather's treating Timmy as a peer.

Ann and Ray have different sets of expectations that are not clearly defined. Ann expects Timmy to stay at home at all times and bring his friends to their home; however, she does not approve of his friends. When Ray directs Timmy to perform a household chore without consulting Ann, she then tells Timmy not to do it. Timmy, in turn, becomes angry and confused, leaves the house, and drinks.

Encouragement of Autonomy

Although family members identify differences in each other, they are unable to accept them and they hold distorted, unrealistic, and unexpressed expectations of each other.

Affective Issues

Although this family has intense, painful conflicts, the very intensity indicates their concern about losing each other. Both parents care deeply for their son, who reciprocates the feeling. The parents were seriously hurt by their experiences in their families of origin and in their experiences with each other. The family earnestly desires to be together as a family but has been unable to negotiate the changes needed. Self-esteem is low in all three members of the family with Timmy having the highest levels.

Negotiation and Task Performance

This family is unable to negotiate.

Transcendent Values

This family is in a great deal of pain and not hopeful because Timmy's drinking has upset their hopes for him to have a better life than the parents had.

Health Measures

Although the family has a regular dinner daily, other meals are irregular and unplanned. Timmy abuses alcohol and marijuana. Ann is obese. Ray has regular recreation with his friends, but Ann and Timmy do not. There is no family recreation at all. Ann and Timmy's recreation together is watching soap operas. (*Continues on p 224*)

Although there are deficits in all nine assessment areas, several major themes emerge as appropriate areas for nursing intervention. These are expressed as nursing diagnoses. Because the parental coalition is the critical factor in family functioning, the therapy is directed toward the couple.

Nursing Diagnoses

1. Ineffective parenting related to parental conflict
2. Family conflict related to ineffective communication patterns:

Ann "telling the story"
Ray not talking, then leaving
Timmy talking angrily, then leaving; being "in the middle" of the parents

3. Excessive work hours related to low self-esteem and fear of intimacy
4. Alcohol abuse (Timmy)

Goals and Interventions

(See Family Nursing Care Plan)

How to Prepare a Three-Generation Genogram

General Instructions

Divide the paper sideways into three levels.
Begin in the middle, with husband on left.
Males are in squares; females are in circles.
Place birthdates below symbol, prefaced by a "b."
Place deathdates below symbol, prefaced by a "d."
Place marriage date, preceded by "m" on the paired solid line. Separation = "s." Divorce = "d."
Adoption date is "a."
For first generation (the grandparents), indicate the sibling structure by "oldest of ____," or "youngest of ____," and so on.
Indicate occupation and ethnicity of the first generation along with symbols.
Indicate the occupation of the middle generation.
Indicate the school year or occupation of the third generation (children of major couple).

Notations

(Illustrated on genogram and marked as 1/, 2/, and so forth
1/ Solid paired line indicates marriage.
2/ Broken paired line indicates nonmarriage relationship.
3/ Solid vertical line indicates children of the couple.
4/ Date of doing genogram and clinician's name

Adapted from Smoyak S: Family Systems: Use of Genograms as an Assessment Tool. In Clements IW, Buchanan DM (eds): Family Therapy: A Nursing Perspective. John Wiley & Sons, 1982

Family Nursing Care Plan

The M. Family

Nursing Diagnosis	Goal	Intervention	Evaluation
2/1 Ineffective parenting related to parental conflict	1. Ray and Ann will determine a list of expectations for Timmy with consequences for unmet expectations by 2/7.	1–3. Family therapy sessions with T. Robbins, R.N., M.S., Tuesdays and Thursdays from 12 to 1 pm, discussion of goals achieved through homework assignments	1. Goal was met by 2/7.
	2. Ray and Ann will decide what age-appropriate recreation activities they will permit their son to participate in by 2/14.		2. Goal was met by 2/14.
	3. Ray and Ann will adjust their work hours so that each parent is more available during nonschool hours by 2/14.		3. Ray changed hours to be home by 10 p.m. and more weekend hours. Ann plans to stop her weekend job.
	4. Timmy will experience success and/or consequences in levels system by 2/14.	4. Milieu supervised by C. Smith, R.N., primary nurse, daily, and in privilege levels meeting Tuesday and Friday, 3:45 pm.	4. Timmy kept all rules and met daily goals by 2/14.
2/1 Family conflict related to ineffective communication patterns	1. Ann will say what she wants specifically from her husband and from her son by 2/21	1–3. Family therapy sessions with T. Robbins, Tuesdays and Thursdays, 12 to 1 pm. for 3 weeks.	1. Ann said specifically what she wanted from her son by 2/16 but not her husband.
	2. Ray will stay in the sessions and say what he thinks and feels by 2/21.	a. Therapist will direct family members to use "I statements" and eye contact.	2. Ray refused to come to sessions after 2/14.
	3. Timmy will stay in the sessions and say what he feels and wants without cursing by 2/21.	b. Therapist will direct family to stay in "here and now."	3. Timmy was able to stay in sessions, state feelings, and not curse, with coaching, by 2/21.
		c. Therapist will emphasize (praise) family members' goodwill, attempts to change, and successes.	

(Continues on p 226)

Nursing Diagnosis	*Goal*	*Intervention*	*Evaluation*
		d. Therapist will name feelings, etc., as concretely as possible.	
	4. Parents will stop communicating through Timmy by 2/14.	4. Therapist will redirect communication.	4. Parents attempted to communicate through the therapist and school teacher. They talked to each other on the phone.
		a. Primary nurse will direct parent communication to family therapist.	
		b. Primary nurse encourages verbalization of feelings and insight into his "being in the middle."	
2/1 Excessive number of work hours due to low self-esteem and fears of intimacy	1. Ann will reduce her work hours and find one social activity outside the home by 2/21.	1–3. Therapist will facilitate couple's talking together about positive aspects of their long relationship. Therapist will explore with couple and family possible fun activities.	1. The family did not meet these goals.
	2. Ann and Ray will spend 1 hour per day in household without arguing.		
	3. Ray will reduce work hours so that there is time for family activity and time with Ann alone by 2/21.		
2/21 Alcohol abuse	1. Timmy will maintain sobriety through 2/21.	1. Participate in chemical dependency program.	1. Timmy did maintain sobriety including weekend day passes.
		a. Group 10:30–11:30 am Monday through Friday, A. Budd, M.S., therapist.	
		b. Education and Big Book discussion 1–2 pm, Monday through Friday with B. Brown, C.A.C.	
		c. AA meeting, Friday, 6 pm at Good Samaritan Youth Services.	

Nursing Diagnosis	Goal	Intervention	Evaluation
	2. Family will verbalize understanding of family dynamics that contribute to Timmy's drinking by 2/21.	2. a. Family sessions will include a discussion of this problem. Therapist will point out dynamics as they occur. b. Adolescent group therapy 2–3 pm, Monday through Friday, T. Poffer, M.S.	2. Parents verbalized understanding of some contributing factors.
	3. Parents will verbalize commitment to attend Alanon (Ann) and AA meeting with Timmy (Ray) once weekly by 2/21.	3. Discharge planning in family session.	3. Ray verbalized commitment but did not follow through.

References

1. Andrews E: The Emotionally Disturbed Family. New York, Jason Aaronson, 1977

2. Aradine C, Pridham KF: Model for Collaboration. Nursing Outlook 21 (October): 655–657, 1973

3. Bateson G, Jackson D, Haley J, Weakland J: Toward a Theory of Schizophrenia. In Jackson DD (ed): Communication, Family, and Marriage. Palo Alto, CA, Science & Behavior Books, 1968

4. Beavers WR: Psychotherapy and Growth: A Family Systems Perspective. New York, Brunner/Mazel, 1977

5. Bohen HH, Viveros-Long A: Balancing Jobs and Family Life. Philadelphia, Temple University Press, 1981

6. Bowen M: Family Therapy in Clinical Practice. New York, Jason Aaronson, 1978

7. Brallier L: The Nurse as Holistic Health Practitioner. Nurs Clin North Am 13 (December): 643–655, 1978

8. Braxton E: Structuring the Black Family for Survival and Growth. Perspectives in Psychiatric Care 14 (October/November/December): 165–173, 1976

9. Brockhaus J, Brockhaus R: Adopting an Older Child: The Emotional Process. Am J Nurs 82 (February): 288–291, 1982

10. Collison C, Futrell J: Family Therapy for the Single-Parent Family System. J Psychosoc Nurs Ment Health Serv 20 (July): 16–20, 1982

11. Dreikurs R, Soltz V: Children, the Challenge. New York, Duell, Sloan & Pearce, 1964

12. Dinkmeyer D, McKay G: Systematic Training for Effective Parenting. Circle Pines, Minnesota, American Guidance Service, 1975

13. Duvall E: Family Development, 4th ed. Philadelphia, JB Lippincott, 1971

14. Friedman MM: Family Nursing: Theory and Assessment. New York, Appleton-Century-Crofts, 1981

15. Fromm E: The Art of Loving. New York, Harper & Row, 1956

16. Gibran K: The Prophet. New York, Alfred A. Knopf, 1968 (Original copyright, 1923)

17. Glenn SH, Warner JW: The Developmental Approach to Preventing Problem Dependencies. Family Development Institute, Bethesda, Maryland.

18. Gordon T: Parent Effectiveness Training. New York, PH Wyden, 1970

19. Guerin PJ, Pendagast EG: Evaluation of Family System and Genogram. In Guerin PJ (ed): Family Therapy. New York, Gardner Press, 1976

20. Horowitz J, Perdue B: Single-Parent Families. Nurs Clin North Am 12 (September): 503–511, 1977

21. Kelly A: Evaluating and Improving Family Health. The Holistic Health Handbook. Berkeley, California, And/Or Press, 1978

22. Kempler W: Principles of Gestalt Family Therapy. Salt Lake City, UT, Deseret Press, 1974

23. Lantz JE: Family and Marital Therapy. New York, Appleton-Century-Crofts, 1978

24. Lewis JM, Beavers WR, Gossett JT, Phillips VA: No Single Thread: Psychological Health in Family Systems. New York, Brunner/Mazel, 1976

25. Mc_____ D: TV: Its Problems for Children. Pediatr Nurs (M____ il): 17–19, 1979

26. Minuc___ ___ Families and Family Therapy. Cambridge, Harvard ___ ersity Press, 1974

27. Murray R ___ ner J: Nursing Concepts for Health Pro-

motion, 2nd ed. Englewood Cliffs, NJ, Prentice-Hall, 1979

28. Papp P: Family Choreography. In Guerin PJ (ed): Family Therapy. New York, Gardner Press, 1976

29. Prattes O: Beliefs of the Mexican-American Family. In Hymovich D, Barnard M (eds): Family Health Care. New York, McGraw-Hill, 1973

30. Rapoport R, Rapoport R: Dual-Career Families. Baltimore, Penguin Books, 1971

31. Rapoport R, Rapoport R: Dual-Career Families Re-examined. New York, Harper Colophon Books, 1976

32. Richardson DB, Thornton J, Gest T, Wellborn S: End of the Permissive Society? U.S. News and World Report, pp 45–48, June 28, 1982

33. Satir V: Peoplemaking. Palo Alto, CA, Science and Behavior Books, 1972

34. Satir V: Conjoint Family Therapy. Palo Alto, CA, Science and Behavior Books, 1967

35. Sheehy G: Passages: Predictable Crises of Adult Life. New York, Bantam Books, 1976

36. Smoyak S: Family Systems: Use of Genograms as an Assessment Tool. In Clements IW, Buchanan DM (eds): Family Therapy: A Nursing Perspective. New York, John Wiley & Sons, 1982

37. Stevenson J: Issues and Crises during Middlescence. New York, Appleton-Century-Crofts, 1977

38. Straus M, Gelles R, Steinmetz SK: Behind Closed Doors: Violence in the American Family. Garden City, NY, Anchor Books, 1980

39. Sue S: Asian Americans: Psychological Perspectives. Ben Lomond, CA, Science and Behavior Books, 1973

40. Tripp-Reimer T, Friedl M: Appalachians: A Neglected Minority. Nurs Clin North Am 12 (March): 41–54, 1977

41. *U.S. News and World Report.* S. V. "Tomorrow," pp 11–12. June 28, 1982

42. Visher EB, Visher JS: Step Families: A Guide to Working with Step Parents and Stepchildren. New York, Brunner/Mazel, 1979

43. Watzlawick P, Beaven J, Jackson D: Pragmatics of Human Communication. New York, Norton, 1967

44. Wolff I: Referral: A Process and a Skill. Nursing Outlook. 10 (April): 253–256, 1962

45. Yankelovich D: Stepchildren of the Moral Majority. Psychology Today (November): 5–10, 1981

46. Yankelovich, Skelly and White Inc: Family Health in an Era of Stress: The General Mills American Family Report, 1978–1979. Minneapolis, Minnesota, General Mills, 1979

Chapter 18
Behavioral Approaches

We are controlled by the world in which we live, and part of that world has been and will be constructed by men. The question is this: are we to be controlled by accident, by tyrants, or by ourselves in effective cultural design?

> B. F. Skinner,
> Freedom and the Control of Men,
> 1955

Juliann Casey Reakes

Chapter Preview

This chapter discusses principles of behavior therapy, strategies of learning theory, and the application of these principles and strategies in assisting clients to replace maladaptive behavior with adaptive behavior.

Learning refers to that process that brings about a change in behavior. For example, if a client stops abusing alcohol after serving 90 days in jail and seeks counseling after his release, learning may be inferred from his behavior.

Behavior therapy has proven to be a practical, efficient, parsimonious way of assisting clients and families to change their behavior by the application of learning theories. Behavior therapy is the essence of behaviorism. Behaviorism is a philosophical approach to life, as well as a psychological discipline built on a precise scientific orientation to the problems of man and other living organisms. Behaviorism represents reality and therefore views behavior that is outside of the expected social norm as maladaptive, not as a symptom of disease, a form of deviance, or a deficit. The cause of maladaptive behavior is not a relevant issue, because the focus of behavior therapy is to assist a person to adapt objectively to the real world by learning ways to change his responses to the internal and external environments.

The components of both the nursing process and the process of behavior analysis and application are similar. Assessment, analysis, planning, intervention, and evaluation by means of specific outcome criteria are inherent in both methodologies. The goals of nursing and behavior therapy are also parallel—to help people deal more effectively with reality.

Learning Objectives

On completion of the chapter, the reader should be able to accomplish the following.

1. Define terms specific to behavior therapy
2. Apply principles of behavior therapy to nursing practice and client problems
3. Discuss the goals of behavioral therapeutic approaches
4. Differentiate between classical conditioning, operant conditioning, cognitive therapy, and other forms of behavior modification
5. Discuss the use of various forms of behavioral intervention
6. Apply the steps of the nursing process to the process involved in behavior therapy

Principles of Behavior Therapy

The term *behavior* implies an open and wide range of overt and covert responses that include emotions and verbaliza-

tions.[28, 44] The contemporary use of behavior therapy refers to a group of diversified approaches for dealing with maladaptive behavior. Maladaptive behavior may either be learned or may be a result of a failure to learn adaptive behavior (see the insert below for a further description). The basic premise of behavior therapy is that most behaviors are learned. This, however, does not rule out the biologic implications of maladaptive behavioral responses; that is, biochemical, genetic, or cellular disturbances.[9]

In behaviorist terms, maladaptive behavior is a way of

Describing Adaptive and Maladaptive Behavior

Thorough data collection, thoughtful analysis, and specific behavioral descriptions result in accurate problem identification.

These are some descriptions of maladaptive behavior identified for a client.

1. Continually tells anyone who listens that she talks on the phone everyday to the President of the United States
2. Sits in a chair in activity room with head bowed and hands tightly clasped in lap
3. Drinks only liquids on meal tray
4. Throws food on the floor at every meal
5. States continual preoccupation with thoughts of her son's death
6. Paces the length of the floor in her room
7. Complains of feeling a "tight, narrow band" around her head
8. Stares at the floor or ceiling when talking with other clients or staff members

Descriptions of a client's adaptive behavior include the following.

1. Completes assigned ceramic activities
2. Initiates conversation with group members
3. Volunteers to obtain equipment for outdoor games
4. Explains decision in an assertive manner to husband
5. Requests help in seeking solutions to a problem
6. Contracts with the staff to complete daily goals
7. Speaks with reality orientation and realism
8. Expresses angry feelings about marriage failure

Note that these descriptions of behavior do not imply judgment, that is, "good" or "bad" or "positive" or "negative" behavior. They are simply objective verbal or written pictures of behavior observed.

dealing with stress. Obvious or overt responses are measured; hidden or covert responses are subjective, but can be described in behavioral terms and changed. Mediating processes or cognitions (*i.e.*, thoughts, feelings, and attitudes) are subjective variables and, similar to objective variables or events that are situation-specific (*i.e.*, birth, marriage, and job), they can be described in behavioral terms and influenced to effect behavioral change.[6]

The process of behavior therapy is a precise approach to bringing about behavioral change. Concepts, thoughts, or subjective representations (*e.g.*, anxiety, guilt, depression, anger, joy, and hope) are described in specific behavioral terms to present a detailed, finely tuned approach to client needs.[16]

The work of John B. Watson, an early 20th-century psychologist, formed the foundation for behavior therapy and for applying objective methodology to solving maladaptive behavioral problems. Learning, or behavioral change, occurs because of experiences that, over a period of time, result in conditioned response learning or classical conditioning, as described by Ivan P. Pavlov.

Classical Conditioning

In Pavlovian learning, an *unconditioned stimulus*, food, elicits an *unconditioned response*, salivation, in a hungry dog. When a bell, a *conditioned stimulus*, is paired with the food, an unconditioned stimulus, over a period of time the conditioned stimulus results in salivation in the dog, a *conditioned response*. The unconditioned stimulus, food, is a reinforcer for the conditioned stimulus and the conditioned response. This type of learning is affected by events that occur before the behavior. The preceding events elicit a certain response. The unconditioned stimulus may be rewarding or pleasant (*e.g.*, a smile from the nurse) or unpleasant, noxious, painful or aversive (*e.g.*, as a drug that induces nausea). Aversive therapy has been used to treat alcoholism by pairing the drinking of alcohol with a nausea-producing drug.

There are many examples of classical conditioning in health care. Fear of injections may be conditioned by the nurse's white uniform or by the sight of the needle or syringe. The nurse's uniform, as unconditioned stimulus, elicits discomfort or fear, the unconditioned response. The needle becomes a conditioned stimulus, and fear, a conditioned response. For example, fear of arguing or fighting may result from an association with a traumatic event that involved arguing or fighting. When a child receives a toy after each visit to the doctor and is told by the doctor, nurse, and his mother how well he behaved, eventually praise alone is sufficient to elicit his positive behavior.

More than one stimulus not originally associated with a response may reinforce this learning by serving as a link in binding a response to a series of stimuli. By the process of chaining, more than one unconditioned stimulus may become a conditioned stimulus and higher-order conditioning, or learning, can result. For example, a child receives a

toy at the doctor's office when he responds favorably to the doctor's examination and treatment. The office nurse verbally praises the child and hands him a toy while giving him a hug or a pat on the back. At the same time, the child's mother tells him his reward is a stop at McDonald's for a special treat because he was such "a good boy." The toy is a primary reinforcer for the child's behavior in the doctor's office; the praise, pleasant physical contact (touch), and the treat at McDonald's are successive reinforcers. Many emotional responses, such as an unfounded fear of objects, may become a conditioned response due to a higher order conditioning, despite the fact that there may have been no direct association with the feared object. Words, which can be symbols of experiences or events, may become conditioned stimuli that trigger respondent behavior or that signal dangerous or feared situations.[6]

The classic example of respondent conditioning is the work of psychologist, John B. Watson, and nurse, Rosalee Rayner, of John Hopkins Hospital. Albert, an 11-month-old child was conditioned by noise association with a white rat and other white furrylike objects. This illustrates the behavioristic view that phobias are conditioned fears learned when a stimulus is paired with a feared object or event.[53]

Several years later, in 1924, Mary Cover Jones, a psychologist, used clinical conditioning theory to counter conditioned fear to furrylike objects experienced by a young boy. Pairing food eaten by the child in various distances from a rabbit, representing the class of feared objects, the child was able eventually to eat with the rabbit sitting on his table and his lap.[22]

In 1952, H. J. Eysenck conducted a survey of neurotic patients following psychotherapy and concluded that about two thirds of the patients would have recovered eventually from their illness with or without psychiatric treatment. A few years later, Eysenck suggested a new approach for dealing with maladaptive behavior—behavior therapy. Behavior therapy is not concerned with dialogue as a treatment, as is traditional psychotherapy. On the contrary, behavioral therapy deals with changing the individual's maladaptive behavior by a planned, objective approach, such as respondent conditioning and counter-conditioning techniques.[14]

A contemporary of H. J. Eysenck, Joseph Wolpe, built on the theory of classical conditioning to demonstrate clinically that learned anxiety may be inhibited by another behavioral response. When behavioral responses, such as muscle relaxation, assertive responses, and sexual arousal responses, occur in the presence of cues that originally triggered anxiety, anxiety is lessened. These responses eventually become associated with the cues and weaken the anxiety response. Wolpe called this counter conditioning process *reciprocal inhibitiion*.[54] For example, the person who experiences unsatisfactory job interviews and becomes anxious may become conditioned to employment situations because of encounters with similar cues and stimuli. The anxiety that is evoked may result in avoiding job situations. Learning to deal assertively with this situation in the presence of these cues can reduce his anxiety. Assertive responses, sexual responses, and muscle relaxation are associated with the parasympathetic nervous system; increased activity of this system decreases anxiety responses associated with the sympathetic nervous system, such as dilated pupils, increased blood pressure, heart rate, and increased blood supply to voluntary muscles.[54] Systematic desensitization based on reciprocal inhibition theory has been effective with a broad group of client problems including phobias, obsessive-compulsive disorders, sexual disorders, psychosomatic disorders, and alcoholism.[9]

In 1962, Lazarus and Abramovitz applied the principles of systematic desensitization to treat children's fears. A child's phobic behavior toward a dog was eliminated in a short 5-week session. A pleasant wished-for scene imagined by the child and the gradual introduction of the phobic object dissipated the anxiety originally associated with the dog.[29]

Operant Conditioning

Until B. F. Skinner and a colleague introduced a specific type of behavior therapy, operant conditioning, in 1954, classical conditioning was the force of behaviorism. Operant or instrumental behavior (such as eating or writing) refers to activity strengthened or weakened by its consequences (such as weight loss or weight gain). Operant behavior is under the control of the individual who can use behavior to change or modify the environment.

Operant conditioning is also called operant reinforcement theory. A *reinforcer* is anything that increases the probability of a response. In respondent conditioning, the unconditioned stimulus, paired with the conditioned stimulus, is the reinforcement that brings about specific behavior. In operant conditioning, reinforcement strengthens the emitting of a wide range of behaviors. The client learns to duplicate the response. The criteria for reinforcement are that the reinforcer meet a need and be goal-directed. Food, for example, may not always emit an adaptive behavior if hunger is not a priority need for the individual.[49] A positive reinforcer, or reward, strengthens a behavior; the removal of a negative reinforcer strengthens or facilitates adaptive behavior when the client is able to evade or avoid the harmful reinforcer.

Both positive and negative reinforcers are specifically defined with regards to prior impact on the behavior to be changed. Punishment is not a negative reinforcer because it is designed to eliminate a behavior, whereas true negative reinforcement produces adaptive behavior.[49] Punishment often suppresses the maladaptive behavior, but does not eliminate it from the client's behavioral pattern.[13] If the individual is not offered a specific alternative, he may respond with a behavior that is more maladaptive than the original behavior. Regressive behavior or generalization to other situations may also occur if an alternative behavior is not available.[44] For example, a child may be punished for eating "junk food" at home and may, therefore, learn to eat his "junk food" at fast-food stands. Children often become enuretic when punished, whereas adults may resort to overeating, drinking alcoholic beverages, or retaliating with aggressive behavior toward spouse or children.

Operant conditioning has been successfully used with many clinical and behavioral problems that have not responded to other treatments. By means of negative and positive reinforcement, speech was successfully restored in a schizophrenic client who had not spoken for 30 years. Candy, cigarettes, magazines, books, and praise were successfully used as positive reinforcers to increase verbal communication in mute chronic schizophrenic clients.[4]

Free Operant Conditioning

In addition to operant conditioning, Skinner demonstrated a type of instrumental conditioning called free operant conditioning. Skinner also used this method, termed *free operant study*, to study behaviors. A response easily emitted is selected to be measured while other emitted behavior is also studied.

To study the effect of a drug on hallucinatory behavior, a hospitalized psychotic male was the subject of a free operant study. Two behaviors were first measured, hallucinatory behavior and the specific activity of pulling a plunger that was intermittently reinforced. A psychotropic drug was given to the client for the experimental phase and the same activities by the client were recorded. It was found that, when the plunger activity was decreased, the hallucinatory behavior increased. The experimenter concluded that the drug actually increased the hallucinatory behavior rather than decreasing it.[31] In a similar free operant study, a researcher found that a chronic schizophrenic client responded more positively following therapeutic interactions with a nursing student than from psychotropic drug therapy.[30]

Operant Control of Verbal Behavior

According to Skinner, verbal behavior is also under operant control. Verbal behavior is influenced by its relationship to the behavior of other people. Like other operant conditioning, verbal behavior is influenced by its outcome. It influences personal interaction and is maintained by social behavior. Verbal behavior translates other behavior into word symbols but, like any translation, there is subjectivity in the interpretation. Words, when reinforced and under similar contingencies, become maintained as behavior patterns.[49] For example, the psychotic verbal behavior of one long-term schizophrenic client was eliminated by positively reinforcing rational verbal behavior with cigarettes and by withholding cigarettes when the client demonstrated irrational verbal behavior.[2]

Generalization

Adaptive behavior specific to one situation may occur in similar situations because of a phenomenon called *generalization*. Rational verbal behavior learned in a client–health team interaction may generalize in client–family and client–friend relationships.

Discrimination

Discrimination refers to a specific response occurring in a given situation. The client who is positively reinforced for completing an activity task and who is ignored when the task is not completed, then who consistently completes his assigned work, is making a differential or a discriminating response.

Extinction

Extinction is the withholding of reinforcers and reducing the probability of the response occurring. If the staff ignore the client's attention-seeking behavior and positively reinforce group-participating behavior, the former behavior may be extinguished by the increase in the latter response.[50]

Prompting and Fading

Prompting and fading refer to creating conditions that facilitate or accentuate the reinforcer. *Prompting* is a cuing process; *fading* is the gradual reduction of this process. Enunciating a word carefully for an aphasic client who is learning to identify objects again following a stroke may be eliminated or faded as soon as the client begins to name the object without cuing by the nurse.

The following example illustrates the application of fading and prompting. A program was initiated to emphasize the need for client compliance with a prescribed daily activity program. The client was instructed to notify a staff member hourly when an activity was completed. The staff member prompted the client to check the schedule and reinforced the client's actions with praise when the task was completed. After a 3-day compliance with this plan, the hourly check was expanded to 2 hours for another 3-day period, 4 hours for the next 3 days, and as compliance increased, the schedule was checked once a day.

Shaping

Shaping behavior refers to the patterning of a group of actions by the continued reinforcement of responses essential to the desired target behavior.[9] A neat, clean physical appearance is targeted as the priority behavior to be achieved by the client. When the client is consistently rewarded with verbal praise and attention from the health team when his hair is combed, teeth are brushed, nails are trimmed and clean, the overall target behavior—a neat, clean physical appearance—is often achieved.

Reinforcers

The choice of reinforcers, as well as the timing, is important for adaptive change. When the response or operant occurs and is recognized by the individual as bringing about a desired action or modification in the environment, the client has discovered a potent tool for change.[25] *Social reinforcers* may include praise, attention, touch, or interest. *Material reinforcers* may include food, prizes, redeemable tokens, or money. *Activity reinforcers* may include watching television, attending plays or movies, attending dances, playing cards, or shopping.

Reinforcement Schedules

Reinforcement may be associated continuously with a specific target behavior or may occur at fixed or varying intervals.[44] Designing reinforcers and schedules of reinforcement for a specific client requires careful planning of the nurse. All of the staff involved in the client's 24-hour care must be consistent and must follow the schedule according to the protocol set for the client.

Reinforcement schedules may be

1. continuous—every expected response is reinforced;
2. intermittent—every expected response is not reinforced—only those responses selected are reinforced;

    fixed ratios—every certain response is reinforced, such as the third, eighth, or tenth response;

    variable ratio—the responses being reinforced are changed at certain times; at first, the third response may be reinforced and, the next day, the sixth response may be reinforced;

3. at intervals—variable or fixed ratios that are concerned with the time between reinforcement.[44]

Nursing Process and Behavior Therapy

Assessment and Analysis

Collection of Data

The first step in both the nursing process and the application of behavioral principles is assessment. Assessment includes the collection of objective and subjective data. Objective data are data that can be measured, observed, or validated. Subjective data are data that reflect the client's feelings, perceptions, and "self talk" about his problems.

Information about the client's problem may be obtained from the following.

Nursing history
Systems review
Physical examination findings
Psychosocial, cultural, or mental status findings including developmental data, demographic data, and the length of time, frequency, and extent of the presenting problem
Description of the behavior and situation before and after the problem

Consequences of the problem behavior
Client resources; that is, likes, dislikes, support systems, and interests
Client expectations and motivations

The nurse may identify other problem areas that the client does not recognize, but that influence the presenting problem. For example, the nurse may perceive that the client has poor verbal communication skills, which may be directly related to his presenting problem of feeling anxious in situations with strangers. Cultural influences may have a direct effect on the presenting problem and cultural data should be included in an assessment.

Listening to the client is as necessary as the accurate recording and validating of data. Observation of the client during the interview, examinations, and testing situations contributes valuable information in identifying the following.

1. The problem behavior
2. The situations in which the behavior occurs
3. The consequences of the behavior

Therapeutic Dialogue

Identifying the Client's Perception of the Problem

The following dialogue between the nurse and client illustrates the importance of the client's identification of the problem.

Nurse: Tell me in your own words your feelings about what's happened.

Client: I've been laid off again. This is the second time in 6 months. My parents are elderly and barely making it financially. My brother and sister send them $50 a month and I can't even send $5. My son blames me for using his college money to keep the family going. He went into the service to get away from me. My brother refuses to talk to me. My wife and daughter ignore me—nobody listens to me.

Nurse: You're feeling very alone and sad, but angry that no one listens to you.

Client: They all hate me and blame me for their problems.

Nurse: You're feeling...

Client: It's like I told you. It's my mistakes. Yes, I feel sad and responsible. Why can't I stop crying—a grown man?

Nurse: You've felt this way before?

Client: Even in grade school when my friends were not happy, I always felt it was me. When things didn't go right at work, I would feel the same way. I was demoted 6 months ago and would have been let go but I took a lower paying job. I wanted to try something different—I like carpentry but I was afraid...

Nurse: You've been afraid a lot?

Client: Well, when my wife had to go back to work and I couldn't continue helping my parents (begins to tear again and voice trembles)...

Nurse: You feel responsible for your wife, your parents, and your children?

Client: Yes, I feel I have lost control over life. I feel hopeless and responsible but I know I can't take care of everybody. I guess it's my "head trouble."

Discussion

The client is beginning to identify his irrational belief that he should be responsible for his wife, children, parents, and other family members. The nurse's therapy plan will be to assist the client in using the problem-solving process to identify the problem specifically, realistically, and logically, and identify adaptive ways to cope with the problem. Problem-solving is an essential intervention for clients who lack these skills or for those who are reluctant to use the process when faced with problems.

4. The parameters of the problem
5. The client's perception of the problem.[14]

Problem Identification

The behavior or target problem should be clearly identified. Problems might include inadequate social skills, overwhelming anxiety when talking with strangers (as seen by perspiring, headache, dizziness, faltering speech), or the inability to use family resources, when necessary, without feeling guilty.

Planned observations by the members of the psychiatric-mental health team may disclose the modifying of a favorable response other than the target behavior. An unplanned event may become a reinforcer. For example, smiling associated with verbal praise, the primary reinforcer, may strengthen the target behavior when used alone. Withdrawing a reinforcer to bring about a desired behavior is an excellent intervention in many client management situations. Sending a disruptive client to a "time-out" area may increase a targeted behavior.

Chance Reinforcement

Chance reinforcement may also result in strengthening maladaptive behavior. When the nurse gives immediate attention to the client who refuses to eat by spoon feeding him, even though extra cigarettes might be given to the client for eating without help, the nurse may be unknowingly reinforcing the noneating behavior.

Secondary Reinforcement

Secondary reinforcers or conditioned responses are as influential in changing behavior as primary reinforcers.[19] Participation with others by playing bingo, the primary reinforcer, may become a secondary reinforcer for increasing verbal communication and illustrates the application of the Premack Principle. The *Premack Principle* states that a high-probability behavior can reinforce a low-probability response. For example, a client who likes to watch television may be allowed to watch his favorite program if he attends his occupational therapy activity. Another example of this principle occurs when anorexic clients are rewarded for weight gain by being permitted to participate in desired activities.[33]

Behavior includes aspects of both operant and respondent conditioning and behavior can be modified and adapted by the use of a variety of techniques. The response to be modified requires data about the behavior's frequency rate of occurrence and the specific situation in which the behavior occurs. The choice of effective reinforcers, the selection of a reinforcement schedule, and a precise plan to initiate behavioral techniques are essential.

Planning

Planning of behavioral interventions occurs as a cooperative effort of the psychiatric-mental health team. Objectivity of team members is a necessary component of planning behavioral methods; subjectivity affects the evaluation of clients' behavioral progress and treatment planning.[8]

Goal-Setting

Based on the assessment and analysis of client behavior, treatment goals are identified. These goals may include the following.

1. To provide a safe physical environment
2. To increase a defined behavioral performance
3. To promote self-care and independence
4. To implement competent, individualized care
5. To select learning methods

A treatment plan format for each client may incorporate the following elements.

Client's name
Purpose of the behavior modification program
Goals of the program
Place where the behavior occurs
Target behavior (see the sample protocol below)
Reinforcement schedule
Staff objectives (how to record behavior, reinforcement
    protocol, and so forth)
Time the behavior is to be observed or is to occur
Data-collection methods[47]

Adaptive (Target) Behavior Protocol

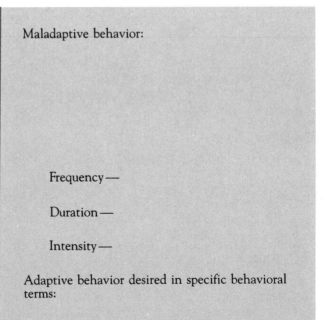

Maladaptive behavior:

Frequency—

Duration—

Intensity—

Adaptive behavior desired in specific behavioral terms:

Intervention

Following the observation and recording of baseline data, the nurse employs the fourth step of the nursing process, intervention. Intervention includes compliance with reinforcement schedules, manipulations of the environment, and other treatment activities.

Self-Management Programs

Nurses have directed self-management programs with clients motivated for behavior change in the areas of weight control and smoking control. Self-management programs follow the same format as other modification programs; observing and recording one's own behavior are additional reinforcers.[11]

Contracting

The nurse has many interventions to use in behavior therapy programs in addition to reinforcement applications. *Behavioral contracting,* an agreement with a client for a specific behavior is often used in self-control programs. Contracting may be an oral or a written agreement. If it is written, the contract is usually dated, behavior or other criteria are identified, and it is signed by the nurse and the client (see the sample contract).

Other Behavioral Activities

Positive or negative reinforcement of behavior, *prompting* (cues), *fading* (removing cues), extinction (ignoring a behavior), *time out,* and *revoking privileges* are activities that may be included in the nursing plan (see the sample time-out record on p. 237). Teaching the client to *discriminate* (make a certain response) or *generalize* (apply a response to other situations) may also be goals of a treatment plan. The use of *over correction* (another behavior is added to one that the client is repeating in an acceptable way) or *simple correction* (a repeat of the acceptable behavior) are examples of interventions that may be useful in treatment planning.

Cognitive Therapy

Cognitive therapy applies principles of behavior and uses specific methodologies to change thought patterns ("self-talk") that are illogical, irrelevant, distorted, and inhibiting.[44] The major tool in cognitive therapy is the use of speech to change events that the client views negatively, irrationally, and illogically.

Rational Emotive Therapy. One form of cognitive therapy is rational emotive therapy (RET). Rational emotive therapy is built on the premise that an individual's values and beliefs control his behavior. Many beliefs and assumptions are illogical and irrational. People often evaluate their behavior by using these faulty illogical thoughts. Some of these false assumptions include the following.

1. A person should be loved and approved by all.
2. A person should be competent and talented and prove himself.

Contract

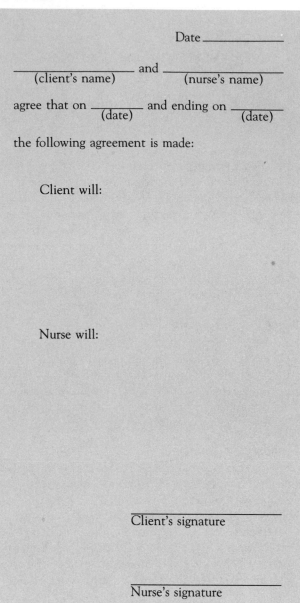

Date _____

_____ and _____
(client's name)   (nurse's name)

agree that on _____ and ending on _____
                  (date)   (date)

the following agreement is made:

Client will:

Nurse will:

_____
Client's signature

_____
Nurse's signature

3. A person has little control over his life and pressures make one feel angry, hostile, and depressed.
4. Dangerous and threatening situations should be feared.
5. Past experiences are the most important influence on present behavior.
6. Order and understanding of the world are necessary for well-being.
7. Dependency on stronger individuals or a supernatural power is necessary for living.
8. Understanding of the world is necessary for a happy life.
9. Performing well and being liked are necessary to feel adequate as a person.

Time Out Record

Behavior Before Intervention	Time Out		Behavior During Intervention	Behavior After Intervention
	Begins	*Ends*		

10. Being depressed, angry, or anxious is giving in to situations or feelings that should be faced.
11. Beliefs of society and authority figures should not be questioned, and if they are, punishment will follow.

The following example illustrates the RET model (see also Fig. 18-1).

> A 42-year-old engineer is admitted to the hospital because he is experiencing severe anxiety, diarrhea, a "pounding" feeling in his chest, difficulty breathing, insomnia, a sensation of suffocation, and difficulty swallowing. His behavioral pattern occurred after his 17-year-old daughter told him and his wife that she was pregnant and wanted an abortion (A).
>
> The client told the nurse that he is "no good" and a "harsh disciplinarian," that his wife and children do not love him, that he is to blame for his daughter's problems, and that he is worthless (B).
>
> This father is experiencing anxiety, guilt, depression, and anger (C). The nurse focuses with the client on his self talk, or assumptions, and the validity of these beliefs (D). The client is helped to discriminate between infor-

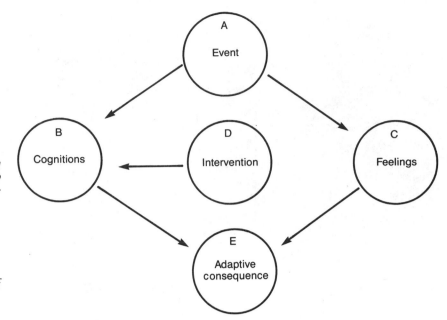

Figure 18-1. *The rational emotive therapy model. Rational emotive therapy uses this model to illustrate a therapeutic approach to faulty assumptions or beliefs.*
  A—the external event
  B—the cognitions associated with A
  C—the feelings emotions associated with A
  D—the interventions that modify B
  E—the adaptive consequences
(From Ayllon T, Houghton E: Modification of Symptomatic Verbal Behavior of Mental Patients. Behav Res Ther 2:87–97, 1964–1965)

mation that is rational and logical and information that is distorted and negative. The nurse and the client focus on his feelings that he is "no good" and worthless because he is to blame for his daughter's pregnancy.

The client realized his thinking was illogical, and that it would not be catastrophic if his family did not love him. The client was able to think logically and realize that he is not responsible for his daughter's behavior. He also realized that he quickly assumed responsibility for all family problems, which excluded his family from responsibility (E).

Cognitive methodologies involve the client and nurse in approaches whereby specific objectives and structured interventions apply learning principles to increase the client's problem-solving, social skills, and assertive communication. Self-assessment, self-monitoring, behavior reversal, role playing, modeling, visual imagery, and thought stopping, as well as interventions with operant and respondent conditioning, are included in this diversified approach to meeting clients' needs.[20]

Cognitive therapy has been successful in treating individuals with depressive behaviors. Based on the assumption that people are depressed because of inadequate social skills, lack of positive social reinforcement, and negative environmental events, emphasis is placed on increasing the client's social skills through assertive training, assessing events that may reinforce his negative feelings, setting goals, and rehearsing new social skills. The depressed person interprets cues and data illogically, thereby deprecating affirmative information and enlarging negative data.[24]

Thought Stopping. *Thought stopping,* developed by Wolpe, has been successful in treating individuals with depressive behaviors.[18, 37, 51] Behaviors that are irrational, of a

brooding type, and anxiety-provoking are inhibited by a specific therapy approach. By shouting the word, "stop" after he expresses his illogical behavior, the client realizes he can control his own thoughts.[54] Another approach to thought stopping is to request the client to substitute a positive thought for a negative, distorted thought.[52]

Thought stopping has been reported to be useful in treating obsessive–compulsive disorders. The word "stop" initiated by the therapist is often followed by an oversized stimulus, such as a loud noise or by the client's loudly echoing the word "stop." The troublesome thought is interrupted or blocked by counter-conditioning principles.[48]

Modeling

Learning through another's performance, even if the behavior is not practiced or rewarded, is a principle of social learning theory. *Modeling,* or imitation, is a method of behavior change. Individuals learn vicariously by observing others' behavior or by verbal descriptions of a desired behavior, which serve as cues for initiating new responses. Both aggressive and nonaggressive behavior may be demonstrated by modeling techniques. For example, in one study, children who watched aggressive actions by real-life models on film and by cartoon characters displayed more aggressive behavior than children exposed to nonaggressive behavior or children in a control group.[7] Modeling strategies have also been effective in reducing children's fears. Brief, filmed experiences showing a child overcoming fear in certain situations, such as visiting a dentist's or physician's office or interacting with a feared animal, were shown to children who then rehearsed their own responses to the feared situation.[7]

Many studies have used modeling to promote adaptive behaviors in adolescents. To illustrate, peer modeling has helped teach young offenders to postpone rewards, and has helped mentally retarded boys use questions in a learning situation.[35]

Imagery

Imagery is an adaptable therapeutic approach used to facilitate positive self-talk. Mental pictures under the control of, and initiated by, the client may correct faulty cognitions.[28] The client pictures past significant memories and present events that, combined with relaxation therapy and role playing, increase his awareness of situational events and other variables resulting in maladaptive behavior.

Imagery techniques have been used with a couple with severe marital problems. The marital partners complained of being depressed, anxious, unable to sleep, and sexually dysfunctional. Both were unable to express anger. The partners were asked to picture the parent of the opposite sex, imagine their spouse standing next to the parent, and note characteristic similarities. They therefore identified characteristics in each other they remembered in their parents with whom they had poor interpersonal relationships. When their perceptions of each other were changed, their relationship improved.[34] Imagery is also an important aspect of systematic desensitization and has been successfully used with clients experiencing phobias.[38]

Behavior Rehearsal

Behavior rehearsal, or role playing, is a therapy approach used in conjunction with modeling. Clients rehearse new responses to problem situations after learning new adaptive responses portrayed through modeling. The nurse's specific attention to detail reinforces characteristics of assertive behavior, such as eye contact, clear and audible vocal tone, posture, and gait.[28]

Behavior rehearsal is advantageous in group settings for teaching social skills and for meeting specific therapy goals. The sharing of simulated situations as well as modeling approaches provides opportunities for participation by the group members.[16]

Assertiveness Training

Role playing is the technique most often used to teach assertiveness training. Assertiveness training deconditions anxiety arising from interpersonal relationships, because assertive behavior is an interfering emotional process free of anxiety.[54] Assertive behavior is expressive, spontaneous, goal-directed, and self-enhancing.[1]

Assertiveness training has been successful with a variety of client populations.[10, 39, 42, 46] One nurse therapist used behavior rehearsal, modeling, imagery techniques, and reports of self-monitoring behavior in assertiveness training with women over 60 years of age. The following are examples of material discussed in the third session of the assertiveness training group. The objectives were to model, rehearse, and discuss these situations.

1. Telling a relative you do not want to vacation with her
2. Telling your daughter or son something positive about him or her
3. Telling a grocery clerk that you were overcharged for an item you bought the previous day
4. Talking to a group of women about volunteering for the local hospital

Modeling, role-playing exercises, and sharing experiences with practicing assertive responses were incorporated into each group session.[42]

Problem-Solving

Behavioral goals include increasing adaptive behavior and learning problem prevention and problem-solving.[26] Problem-solving involves various phases.

1. A general approach to the problem situation
2. A specific definition of the problem and its parameters
3. Generation of possible solutions and implications
4. Selection of a solution
5. Testing and evaluation of the solution

A lack of problem-solving skills is often associated with maladaptive behaviors and interpersonal problems.[16, 20] In conjunction with other cognitive therapy methods, the client is taught to identify the situational and personal aspects of the problem that may be inhibitory to the problem-solving process.[25]

Problem-solving has been effective in helping parents adapt successfully to childrens' needs and problems. In one study, parents identified a need for assertive communication with their children by self-monitoring their interactions with their children. Children, both pre-school and school-aged, were taught and practiced problem-solving skills.[20]

Progressive Muscle Relaxation

Muscle relaxation is a potent treatment strategy for dealing with a variety of client problems such as psychophysiological distress, chronic sleeplessness, and so forth. Anxiety lessens when muscles relax.[44] More than 40 years ago, Edmund Jacobson recognized that muscle relaxation was a therapeutic tool for stress-related problems. After studying the physiological and psychological effects of muscle relaxation, he comfortably positioned clients and taught them to tense and relax the main muscle groups of their bodies. He then shared the monitoring information with the clients who were eventually able to use only passive activity to relax.[21]

Wolpe demonstrated that progressive muscle relaxation, combined with mental pictures (images) of a feared situation or increased association with the feared object in graduated increments, could desensitize phobic clients. Muscle relaxation is physiologically incompatible with the anxiety-evoking response.[54] Natural childbirth practices are based on muscle relaxation to decrease anxiety and facilitate delivery.[27]

The following guidelines are suggested when using relaxation therapy.

Keep the environment as quiet as possible and request that the client sit comfortably in a chair or lie down to facilitate muscle relaxation. Tell the client that he is learning a technique that may help him reduce tension and anxiety. Encourage him to close his eyes and let his thoughts focus on pleasant, quiet scenes, as he tenses and relaxes various muscle groups.

The nurse may demonstrate the technique and may emphasize that muscles should not be strained, but should be tensed to about 75% of their potential. In some client situations, a doctor's order and a careful physical assessment may be necessary to reduce the risk of any complications of this procedure. Use a ratio of a 5-to-10-second cycle of tension followed by a 20-second cycle of no tension.

Instruct the client in a quiet, calm way to "tense his hands by making a fist and then relax" . . . You may suggest that the client feels he is "letting go" and becoming very relaxed and comfortable. The biceps, triceps, shoulder, neck, mouth, tongue, eyes, back, midsection, thighs, stomach, calves, feet, and toes are tensed and relaxed in the same manner.

Breathing in a deep relaxing way and "letting it all out" is usually the final relaxation technique. It is important that the client not overexert the breathing exercise and cause hyperventilation.[16, 44]

Evaluation

Objectives of behavioral change, which are stated in specific performance terms or in terms of detailed and precise outcome criteria, are measurable. Although careful monitoring is necessary to validate the desired behavioral outcome, evaluation is more simplified than in client situations with highly subjective descriptions of behavior.

During assessment, behavior is measured over time until a clear response is identified. An intervention is then applied and the behavior measured again for a specific period of time. If there is a change in behavior, the intervention is removed to validate that the intervention was responsible for the behavioral change. (It is not always possible to use this type of evaluation when working with people because of infringement or interference with therapeutic goals.) This technique is called the *reversal technique*. Is a daily recording of weight associated with the client's small, but continual, weight loss, or does a weight change occur when the recording is eliminated?

Multiple base line recording is another technique for both assessing and evaluating interventions. Through this technique, a number of behaviors are measured over time and an intervention is applied to one of these behaviors until a change in the behavior is noted. Little or no change may occur in the other behaviors. The intervention is then applied to one of the other behaviors to determine if there is a change (see the sample base line recording below and Figs. 18-2 and 18-3). Tidy dress, combed hair, and weight loss may be three base line behaviors recorded; recording weight may continue to be an intervention, although tidiness of dress or combed hair is now noted instead of weight change.[5]

The importance of evaluation cannot be overemphasized, because the effect of interventions may be unique to one targeted behavior or may influence other behaviors. Revising treatment plans and recognizing the need for modifications help to individualize care for psychiatric-mental health clients.

Base Line Recording

Hallucinatory Behavior

Time	M	T	W	TH	FRI	SAT	SUN
8 am–10 am	—	—	—	—	—	—	—
10 am–12 noon	—	—	—	—	—	—	—
12 noon–2 pm	11	11	1	—	—	—	11
2 pm–4 pm	11	11	1	1	—	1111	111
4 pm–6 pm	1111	111	11	1	—	111	111
6 pm–8 pm	11	11	11	1	1	11	111
8 pm–10 pm	11	1	1	1	1	1	1
Total Records	12	10	7	4	2	10	12

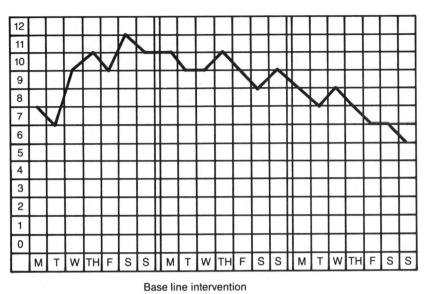

Base line intervention

Figure 18-2. *Frequency of hallucinatory behavior before and during intervention.*

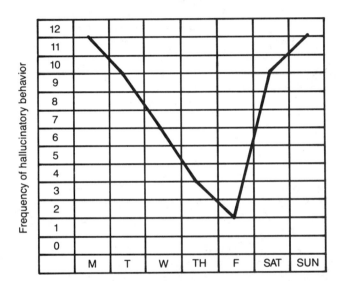

Figure 18-3. *Graph of hallucinatory behavior.*

Summary

Twenty years ago, the psychiatric nurse was described as a behavioral engineer who has a unique position to assist clients to learn adaptive behaviors.[3] The goals of nursing intervention and behavior therapy are both concerned with predicting behavior and providing accurate interventions for client problems. Some of the major points of the chapter have included the following.

1. Following a complete data collection, which includes health history, physical and mental status examinations, laboratory tests, and client and family interviews, objective observation of the maladaptive behavior for a period of time is essential for accurate behavioral assessment.

2. The health team documents the observation period and the frequency of the behavior.

3. Specificity, a key factor in behavioral analysis, results from objective systematic approaches to client problems.

4. Descriptions of both adaptive and maladaptive behavior and behavioral outcomes must be detailed in performance expectation to allow precise measurement and evaluation.

5. Behavioral interventions, including behavioral contracting, cognitive therapy, modeling, imagery, assertiveness training, and progressive muscle relaxation, are powerful approaches to client problems and needs.

Case Study

Behavior Therapy with a Suspicious Client

Marian Spivak, a 38-year-old housewife and part-time graphic artist for a building firm, is admitted to the psychiatric unit with the diagnosis of paranoia. Marian has two children—a boy, 15 years old, and a girl, 17 years old. Marian was working full-time until a year ago when she felt her co-workers were talking about her. Her husband stated that, at that time, she was very hostile, both at home and at the office, "flying off the handle," when there was no provocation or logical reason. Marian decided to work part-time because she couldn't tolerate the "mean looks" and "laughing" that were going on around her.

Dave, her husband, an accountant who works for the same company, realized Marian was not herself. "Things came to a head," said Dave, "when Marian locked herself in her room and would not eat anything that she did not prepare"; she said that Dave and the children as well as her parents were against her.

Marian was unable to function at work, refused to do anything at home, and neglected her appearance because she had to be "on guard." She had not slept for 3 days before admission to the treatment facility and had barricaded herself in her room refusing to answer the phone or allow anyone in. Marian was an avid reader of mystery and historical novels, and she spent all day and night reading books she had stockpiled.

After a complete assessment, the nurse identified the following maladaptive behaviors:

Sits rigidly in large chair with hands clenched and held tightly to body; head and neck rigid; eyes shifting rapidly from side to side; legs bent and knees drawn close to body	Tension in body
Hair uncombed and snarled; cotton shirt wrinkled and collar ripped; slacks unpressed; tennis shoes unlaced and dirty.	Unkempt appearance
Refuses to eat any food unless she prepared it herself from unopened packages or cans.	Controls her eating
Verbalizes that the staff is laughing at her and she cannot leave her room because they intend to harm her.	Suspicious of others
Verbalizes that the newscaster on the television told her to stay in her room and not to eat anything she has not prepared.	Illogical thinking

Marian was placed on fluphenazine (Prolixin) while the identified behaviors continued to be observed and measured by the staff over a 7-day period of time. A staffing conference was arranged to discuss a treatment plan for Marian.

During the conference, the following information was shared among team members. Marian began sleeping through the night on her 4th day of admission. The behaviors observed initially were recorded at the same frequency by the staff over the 3-day period. Marian was observed calling the staff into her room and she drank milk and juice at mealtime and at bedtime, although she still refused solid food. She requested books to read and asked if her husband could bring her books from home.

The staff discussed Marian's treatment plan and explained what was expected of her. Marian was told that she could control her behavior by helping with her treatment plan. The staff believed that Marian needed to receive positive behaviors from the staff and residents, they believed that she needed to examine the effect of her behavior on other people, and they hoped that she would realize that other people could have pleasant and rewarding effects for her.

Because Marian was an avid reader of historical and mystery novels and had requested books to read, the treatment team selected books as the primary reinforcer and reading as the secondary reinforcer. Marian was placed on a token program, and when she participated in activities or completed a goal that indicated adaptive behavior, she earned tokens that could be redeemed for reading material and time to read. Refusing to eat, suspicious behavior, illogical thinking, body tension, and unkempt appearance were identified as priority target behaviors to be changed.

Reinforcers—tokens earned to be redeemed for historical and mystery novels and reading time on a daily basis:

Three tokens—30 minutes reading	11 am
Six tokens—30 minutes reading	11 am; 2 pm
Eight tokens—30 minutes reading	11 am; 2 pm; 7 pm
Ten tokens—45 minutes reading	11 am; 2 pm; 7 pm; 9 pm
Twelve tokens—60 minutes reading	11 am; 2 pm; 7 pm; 9 pm
Fifteen tokens and over—anytime when planned activities are not involved	

Refusing to eat—Marian was allowed to serve her food, under supervision, from the main food carts (food was served family style at small tables seating six residents). Marian was to receive the following tokens immediately after eating.

    One token for eating one half of the main course
    One token for drinking 6 oz of liquid
    Three tokens if she ate all of the food and drank liquid (excluding dessert); no tokens awarded for dessert

The illogical thinking and suspicious self-talk were to be ignored by the staff. The staff was instructed to leave Marian immediately when she began to talk in a suspicious or illogical manner, such as if medication needed to be administered. When Marian's verbal behavior was logical, her tone of voice normal, and her behavior not indicative of unfounded suspiciousness, the staff was instructed to interact with her and praise her behavior. After a week, Marian began to eat most of the food on her tray. She redeemed her tokens for books and reading time. Her suspicious and illogical thinking decreased, although at stressful times (*e.g.*, following a visit with family, dialogue with her therapist, and psychological testing), suspicious behavior would increase for 2 or 3 hours.

The following week, Marian's unkempt appearance was targeted for change. Marian had requested phone privileges and the staff decided tokens could be redeemed for phone privileges when her appearance improved.

Unkempt appearance: Marian was to receive one token for combing her hair, one token for wearing make-up, and one token for wearing suitable attire and shoes.

    One token—could be used for a
      3-minute call
    Two tokens—could be used for a
      5-minute call

    Three tokens—could be used for a
      10-minute call

The staff was also instructed to praise Marian for her improved appearance. At the end of the 4th week, Marian was eating satisfactorily, suspicious behavior and illogical thinking had not been observed, and Marian was interacting with the staff and seeking out other residents.

Marian still displayed body tension, and she was assigned to a relaxation therapy group led by a resident of the treatment unit who initially had been taught relaxation therapy and who was supervised by a staff member. This group met daily for 30 minutes and members were encouraged to practice the relaxation exercises on their own during the day.

Marian was assigned to assist the personnel in food service. There, she helped serve the food to other residents of the unit and helped to plan table decorations and special parties that were held weekly under the supervision of the unit's activity director.

Marian continued to improve and was discharged to outpatient treatment after a 60-day period. Family therapy was begun and Marian attended the day hospital activities from 9:00 am to 3:00 pm 5 days a week. Marian eventually returned to work, after an additional 3 months of outpatient treatment. Family therapy continues.

References

1. Alberti RE, Emmons ML: Your Perfect Right, 2nd ed. San Luis Obispo, CA, Impact, 1974

2. Ayllon T, Houghton E: Modification of Symptomatic Verbal Behavior of Mental Patients. Behav Res Ther 2: 87–97, 1964–1965

3. Ayllon T, Michael J: The Psychiatric Nurse as a Behavioral Engineer. J Exp Anal Behav 2 (October): 323–334, 1959

4. Baer DM, Wolf MM, Risley TR: Some Current Dimensions of Applied Behavior Analysis. J Appl Behav Anal 1: 91–97, 1968

5. Baker R: The Use of Operant Conditioning to Reinstate the Speaking Mute Schizophrenics: A Progress Report. In Burns LE, Worsley JL: Behavior Therapy in the 1970s. Bristol, John Wright & Sons Ltd, 1970

6. Bandura A: Principles of Behavior Modification. New York, Holt, Rinehart and Winston, 1969

7. Bandura A, Walters RH: Social Learning and Personality Development. New York, Holt, Rinehart and Winston, 1963

8. Buckholdt DR, Gubruin JF: The Underlife of Behavior Modification. Am J Orthopsychiatr 50 (April): 279–290, 1980

9. Burns LE: Introduction. In Burns LE, Worsley JL (eds): Behavior Therapy in the 1970s, pp 1–3. Bristol, John Wright & Sons, 1970

10. Butler P: Assertive Training: Teaching Women Not to Discriminate Against Themselves. Psychotherapy: Theory, Research and Practice 13 (Spring): 56–60, 1976

11. Carignan ST: Self-Motivation and Self-Control in Operant Conditioning. Perspect Psychiatr Care 13: 36–41, 1974

12. Ellis A, Grieger R: Handbook of Rational-Emotive Therapy. New York, Springer-Verlag, 1977

13. Estes WK: An Experimental Study of Punishment. Psychological Monographs 57, 1944

14. Eysenck HJ: The Effects of Psychotherapy: An Evaluation. Journal of Consulting Psychology 16: 319–324, 1952

15. Fallon IH, Lloyd GG, Harpen RE: The Treatment of Social Phobia. J Nerv Ment Dis 169: 180–184, 1981

16. Goldfried MR, Davison G: Clinical Behavior Therapy. New York, Holt, Rinehart and Winston, 1976

17. Graziano AM, DeGiovanni S, Garcia K: Behavioral Treatment of Children's Fears: A Review. Psychological Bulletins 86: 804–830, 1970

18. Hackmann A, McLean C: A Comparison of Flooding and Thought Stopping in the Treatment of Obsessional Neurosis. Behav Res Ther 13: 263–269, 1975

19. Hall CS, Gardner L: Theories of Personality, 2nd ed. New York, John Wiley & Sons, 1970

20. Hauser MJ: Cognition Commands Change. J Psychiatr Nurs Ment Health Serv 19 (February): 19–26, 1981

21. Jacobson E: Progressive Relaxation. Chicago, University of Chicago Press, 1938

22. Jones MC: A Laboratory Study of Fear: The Case of Peter. Pedagogical Seminary and Journal of Genetic Psychology 31: 308–315, 1924

23. Kazdin AE: Effects of Covert Modeling and Coding of Modeled Stimuli on Assertive Behavior. Behav Res Ther 17: 53–61, 1979

24. Kovacs M: The Efficacy of Cognitive and Behavior Therapies for Depression. Am J Psychiatr 137 (December): 1495–1501, 1980

25. Krech D, Crutchfield RS, Livson N (with the collaboration of Wilson WA): Elements of Psychology, 3rd ed. New York, Alfred A. Knopf, 1974

26. Krumbaltz JD: Behavioral Goals of Counseling. J Counseling Psychology 13 (Summer): 153–159, 1966

27. Lamaze F: Painless Childbirth: Psychoprophylactic Method. London, Burk Publishing Company, 1958

28. Lazarus AA: Multi-Modal Behavior Therapy. Springer Series in Behavior Modification. (Cyril M. Franks, series ed) New York, Springer-Verlag, 1976

29. Lazarus AA, Abramovitz A: The Use of "Emotive Imagery" in the Treatment of Children's Phobias. J Ment Science 108 (March): 191–195, 1962

30. Lindsey OR: Characteristics of the Behavior of Chronic Psychotics as Revealed by Free-Operant Conditioning Methods. Dis Nerv Syst (Manager Supp) 21: 66–78, 1960

31. Lindsey OR: Operant Conditioning Techniques in the Measurement of Psychopharmacologic Response. The First Hahnemann Symposium on Psychosomatic Medicine, pp 373–383. Philadelphia, Lea & Febiger, 1962

32. Marks IM: Review of Behavioral Psychotherapy, I: Obsessive-Compulsive Disorders. Am J Psychiatr 138 (May): 584–592, 1981

33. McMorrow MJ, Cullinan D, Epstein MH: The Use of the Premack Principle to Motivate Patient Activity Attendance. Perspect Psychiatr Care 16 (January–February): 14–18, 1978

34. Morrison JK: The Use of Imagery Techniques in Family Therapy. Am J Family Therapy 9: 52–56, 1981

35. Moss GR, Rick GR: Overview: Application of Operant Technology to Behavioral Disorders of Adolescents. Am J Psychiatr 138 (September): 1161–1169, 1981

36. Mowrer OH: The Present State of Behaviorism. Educational Journal 97 (Spring): 4–23, 29, 1977

37. Nigl AJ: Use of Thought Stopping and Self-Reinforcement in Treatment of Depression. Psychol Rep Part 1, 38 (June): 843–846, 1976

38. Öst Lars-Göran: Fading vs. Systematic Desensitization in the Treatment of Snake and Spider Phobia. Behav Res Ther 16: 379–389, 1978

39. Percell LP, Berwick PT, Bergel A: The Effect of Assertive Training on Self-Concept and Anxiety. Arch Gen Psychiatr 31 (October): 502–504, 1974

40. Pratt SJ, Fischer J: Behavior Modification: Changing Hyperactive Behavior in a Children's Group. Perspect Psychiatr Care 13: 37–42, 1975

41. Reakes J: Behavior Reversal Revisited; A Multi-Faceted Love for the Instructor. J Nurs Ed 18 (February): 48–51, 1979

42. Reakes J: The Effects of Two Approaches to Assertive Training on Self-Esteem, Assertiveness, Laws of Control and Life Satisfaction with Women Sixty Years of Age or Over. Unpublished doctoral dissertation, August, 1979

43. Riehl JP, Roy Sr C: Conceptual Models for Nursing Practice, 2nd ed. New York, Appleton-Century-Crofts, 1980

44. Rimm DC, Masters JC: Behavior Therapy: Techniques and Empirical Findings. New York, Academic Press, 1974

45. Roberts MJ, Canfield M: Behavior Modification with a Mentally Retarded Child. Am J Nurs 80 (April): 679, 1980

46. Russel A, Winkler R: Assertive Training and Homosexual Service Groups. J Counsel Clin Psychol 45 (February): 1–13, 1977

47. Sabulsky DJ: Behaviorism and Its Application to the Profoundly Retarded. Psychiatr Nurs (September–October): 10–13, 1979

48. Salzman L, Hales FH: Obsessive Compulsive Disorders: A Review of the Literature. Am J Psychiatr 138 (March): 286–296, 1981

49. Skinner BF: About Behaviorism. New York, Vintage Books, 1976

50. Skinner BF: Freedom and the Control of Men. American Scholar 25: 56, 1955

51. Stern R: Treatment of a Case of Obsessional Neurosis Using Thought Stopping Technique. Br J Psychiatr 117 (October): 441–442, 1970

52. Teasdale JD, Rezin V: Effect of Thought Stopping on Thoughts, Mood and Corrugator EMG in Depressed Patients. Behav Res Ther 16: 97–102, 1978

53. Watson JB, Rayner R: Conditioned Emotional Reactions. J Exp Psychol 3: 1–14, 1920

54. Wolpe J: The Practice of Behavior Therapy, 2nd ed. New York, Pergamon Press, 1973

Chapter 19
Psychopharmacology

There are drugs to numb experience and drugs to intensify it; drugs to put a person to sleep and drugs to awaken him; drugs to intoxicate and drugs to detoxify; drugs to energize and drugs to tranquilize; drugs to expand experience and drugs to eliminate consciousness.

Deborah Jackson Antai-Otong

Sidney M. Jourard,
The Transparent Self,
1971

Chapter Preview

The focus of this chapter is the study of psychopharmacology and its impact on psychiatric-mental health nursing. The advent of psychotropic medication has generated dramatic results in the treatment of the mentally ill. The role of the psychiatric-mental health nurse is critical in the client's understanding of the importance and usefulness of these medications. Responsibilities of the nurse include recognizing the desired actions and adverse reactions of the drugs and normal therapeutic dosages, documentation of medication administration, and keeping abreast of current literature on the psychotropic drugs. Another nursing responsibility involves teaching the client and family members about the client's medication.

This chapter discusses the psychoactive drugs according to their major classifications, desired effects, adverse effects, side effects, normal dosage ranges, and nursing implications. Drug interactions and contraindications are also discussed to facilitate safe administration of the psychoactive drugs.

Learning Objectives

On completion of the chapter, the reader should be able to accomplish the following.

1. Discuss the historical development of psychopharmacology
2. Identify the nursing responsibilities in administering psychoactive drugs
3. Formulate a teaching plan for a client who is taking psychotropic medication
4. Identify nursing actions to promote clients' compliance with medication regimes
5. Discuss nursing responsibilities in administering research drugs
6. Identify the actions, therapeutic dosages, uses, side effects, toxic effects, routes of administration, contraindications, and nursing implications of the

   antipsychotic agents,
   antidepressant agents,
   antianxiety agents,
   antimanic agents,

7. Plan nursing actions to prevent or alleviate the side effects of psychoactive drugs

Historical Review of Psychopharmacology

Man's search for relief from the miseries, anxieties, and worries of everyday life has probably existed since the beginning of time. In each age, man has sought to find a means of decreasing his anxiety and elevating his moods.[22] He has experimented with some brews or natural derivatives to alter his mood, whether for medicinal, religious, or recreational purposes. He has chewed coco leaves, consumed coffee, smoked cannibus, injected opiates, and indulged in alcohol.[19]

Psychopharmacology has emerged during recent decades as a scientific discipline within the field of psychiatric-mental health care. The first accessible synthetic compounds, which appeared at the end of the 19th century, were the bromides, chloral hydrate, and morphine. World War II marked the beginning of the modern era of clinical pharmacology.[10] Barbiturates were discovered in the 20th century; the amphetamines became available initially in the 1950s.[19]

In Australia during the 1950s, Cade accidently observed the calming effects of lithium on animals. His findings of the efficacy of lithium in the treatment of manic agitation were reported almost 10 years after his initial observations.[10] Also in the 1950s, lysergic acid diethylamide (LSD)-25 was synthesized, tested, and its effects were studied.[16]

In France during the 1950s, Laborit discovered the tranquilizing effects of chlorpromazine (Thorazine) while the drug was being initially tested as an anesthetic.[26] It was then tested on schizophrenic clients in 1952.[20] Chlorpromazine was first used in the United States in 1954 and quickly became the drug of choice in the treatment of schizophrenia. By 1970, 85% of all institutionalized psychiatric clients were receiving either this drug or other phenothiazine drugs. Because of their usefulness in managing the schizophrenic individual, the phenothiazines became known as "antipsychotic" drugs.[13]

Monoamine oxidase inhibitors were also accidently discovered in the mid-1950s. The compound iproniazid closely resembled isoniazid, a drug used to treat tuberculosis. Early investigators observed that tuberculosis patients became less depressed and demonstrated elevations in mood during their lengthy stays in the tuberculosis sanitoria. Some patients even exhibited manic behavior in response to this antituberculosis medication. These observations and the acknowledgement that this compound produced inhibition of the enzyme monoamine oxidase (MAO) led to early speculation that a correlation existed between brain chemistry and mood.[22]

The tricyclic antidepressants were initially discovered during the 1960s in an attempt to find new and more effective antipsychotic drugs. The first tricyclic antidepressant identified was imipramine (Tofranil). The discovery of the antidepressants have brought to light the biochemical mechanisms of the brain in both normal and chemically altered emotional reactions. At the present time, the tricyclic drugs are by far the most commonly used class of antidepressants.[22]

Over a span of several decades, the psychotropic drugs

demonstrated effectiveness in controlling a broad range of mental and emotional disorders. They have revolutionized the treatment of psychiatric illness.[27] The safety of administering these medications and of monitoring their actions and side effects has similarly increased during this time. With the rapid proliferation of knowledge, the field of psychopharmacology has evolved into a group of scientific disciplines seeking to test the efficacy of various drugs and to understand their mode of action on various neuroendocrine systems.[6]

Nursing Responsibilities in Medication Administration

Ensuring Client Safety

The nurse who administers a drug is responsible for knowing the drug's action and potentialities. In addition, the nurse must know the following.

1. The prescribed dose and the maximum amount of the drug that may be safely given to the client
2. The method of administration
3. The expected action of the drug
4. The side effects
5. The adverse effects (short-term and long-term)
6. The nursing implications of the drug

In addition, the nurse is responsible for the safekeeping and storage of the drug and for the proper identification of the client, particularly the psychiatric client.[1]

The client's response to medication requires continuous monitoring of expected, adverse, and toxic effects. Nurses observe, assess, and evaluate the client's response to psychopharmacologic treatment.[8]

Documentation of these therapeutic and adverse effects of the client's medication enhances communication among mental health team members and also enhances continuity of client care (see the sample charting on this page). The courts have recognized nursing's responsibility for this documentation and have held nurses accountable when appropriate communication and follow-up are not undertaken.[8]

Teaching the Client About Medication

Client teaching has always been a responsibility of the nurse; this responsibility is particularly a priority with the psychiatric-mental health client.[2] Teaching facilitates and promotes understanding of the medication that is prescribed for the client and encourages medication compliance. Compliance with his medication regime is especially important when the client is discharged from a treatment facility.

The nurse generates the client's teaching plan after assessing his individual needs, problems, diagnoses, support systems, and level of understanding (see Medication Teach-

Charting Medication Reactions

A client who was discharged 5 days ago is now in the lobby of the outpatient Crisis Unit and requests to see the physician because "something is wrong" with him. The receptionist calls the nurse to come and see the client. He was discharged on Navane, 20 mg daily.

S—"My neck is stiff, I can't move it! What's wrong with me? I can't talk right. Help me!"

O—Client is standing in the lobby of the Crisis Unit with his head in a fixed position to the right side, his tongue protruding from his mouth, with some increased salivation. Speech slurred.

A—Patient is experiencing a dystonic reaction from psychotropic medication, Navane.

P—1. Give (ordered) prn dose of Cogentin, 2 mg IM now.
2. Evaluate client's response to Cogentin.
3. Reassure client that he will feel better in several minutes.
4. Contact physician and arrange follow-up with client today.
5. Reinforce teaching about taking oral Cogentin if symptoms recur.

Signed by N. Luke, R.N.

ing Plan on p. 248). To compile a thorough history and assessment, the nurse interacts with the client and his family or friends. The data gathered from the client and his significant others facilitate the development of an individualized treatment plan and provide information about his past responses to medications and past compliance or noncompliance with prescribed medication regimes.

The following is an example of nursing plans to address the client's and family's teaching needs concerning the client's prescribed medication.

1. Establish family contact, preferably on the client's admission to the psychiatric treatment setting

   a. Provide information.
   b. Provide support and empathy.

2. Involve family members.

   a. Focus on family needs.

3. Structure the setting.

   a. Negotiate time.
   b. Arrange the environment.

Medication Teaching Plan

A 21-year-old man has been discharged from an inpatient psychiatric facility on thiothixene (Navane), 20 mg at bedtime. A prn medication, benztropine (Cogentin) 2 mg, has also been ordered if extrapyramidal symptoms develop. He has been given a month's supply of medications and a follow-up appointment for the outpatient Day Center activities program. His medication teaching plan follows.

These are directions that will assist you in taking your medications:
Take Navane, 20 mg, 2 tablets (10 mg each), at bedtime by mouth.

1. Your medication should not make you sleepy or drowsy during the day, but if your doctor increases your medication, you may be sleepy for 2 to 4 days, so give your body time to adjust to the medicine by being careful when driving or using heavy machinery during this time.
2. Your medication should not cause you to have stiffness in your back, neck, tongue, or eye muscles. If these symptoms occur, you need to take your side effect medicine, which is Cogentin, 2 mg, by mouth.
3. It is expected that your mouth may become dry; drink plenty of water. Constipation might be a problem, but do not rely on laxatives; increase the roughage in your diet or ask your physician to prescribe a stool softener.
4. Anxiety (nervousness) is a normal human emotion, but if it should get out of hand or excessive, you need to report this to your doctor as soon as possible.
5. For Navane to be effective, you must take it every night as prescribed. For example, do not wait to take it when you feel the need; if you miss a dose, make it up as soon as you remember.
6. Navane is not addictive. It is not habit-forming. You will not get "hooked" on it.
7. If you develop any of the following symptoms, you need to report them immediately to your doctor.

   Muscular twitching
   Weakness
   Dizziness
   Difficulty swallowing
   Disturbances or changes in your walking

4. Instruct the client regarding the following.

   a. Mental disorder
   b. Medications
      Drug name
      Dose prescribed
      Time of administration
      Desired action
      Self-care
      Side effects to report to doctor or clinic

   c. Importance of follow-up, including follow-up laboratory work for clients on lithium or medications that produce blood dyscrasias or other dangerous effects

Promoting Compliance with Medication Regimen

A major problem in psychiatric-mental health care involves the client's failure to adhere to a prescribed medical regimen. Most people who are physically or mentally ill and hospitalized express a sense of loss of control over their lives. They may become dependent on the medical and nursing care providers and may feel left out of the decision-making processes regarding their daily care.

Noncompliance is influenced by the client and his family and friends (see the therapeutic dialogue on p. 249). For example, when a psychiatric client is hospitalized with symptoms of mental illness such as psychosis, the family

Therapeutic Dialogue

Assessment of Noncompliance with Medication Regimen

Nurse: (seated at desk, facing client and his wife) What has brought you to the clinic today, Mr. A.?

Client: (avoiding eye contact, looking at wife) My wife told me I needed to come in.

Nurse: Your wife told you to come in? Do you know why your wife wanted you to come in?

Client: I don't know. Ask her! (pointing to his wife)

Client's Wife: He has been doing things that do not make sense. He's done this before and he needs medicine.

Nurse: (turning to client again) Will you tell me what your wife is talking about?

Client: I don't know, ask her! (voice becoming louder, fidgeting in his chair)

Client's Wife: He has been getting up at night and going outside in his underwear. All he needs is his medicine.

Nurse: More medicine? When is the last time you took your medication, Mr. A.?

Client's Wife: He ran out of medicine 3 months ago and at the time he was feeling good.

Discussion

One of the major problems in treating the psychiatric client is medication compliance. It is valuable to have a family member present during these discussions to substantiate what the client is or is not saying about his medications and his behavior when he takes his medicine and when he does not take his medicine. The nurse assesses his behavior and ascertains how he has responded to medication in the past and how he is responding to it presently. It is also necessary to assess the family members' knowledge and understanding of the client's need for medications, particularly long-term medications for the treatment of schizophrenia and bipolar disorders.

may have requested that the client be "fixed." The client may exhibit impaired judgment, insight, and understanding of the disorder.[3] When these symptoms abate, the family may believe that the client is "cured." This information is conveyed by the family to the client, who has little reason to doubt that this is true because, indeed, he "feels better" and even "cured." When the discharge order is written, usually when the individual is no longer a threat to the family, both client and family members believe that the disappearance of symptoms equates "cure" and medications are therefore no longer important.

Another misconception about psychotropic medication involves the client's and family's fear that he will become "addicted" to the drug. It is the nurse's responsibility to initiate a teaching plan for the client and family to provide them with accurate information about the psychoactive medications and the importance of following the prescribed medication regimen.[20]

The majority of psychiatric clients who do not take their medication as prescribed are those with a diagnosis of *schizophrenia*. Several variables are responsible for this noncompliance, including the following.

1. The need for maintenance medication over a lengthy period of time
2. The experience of uncomfortable side effects from the medications
3. The nature of the schizophrenic disorder in which the client who stops taking his medication may "feel better" or, at least, no worse[7]

The health professional may inaccurately assume that the schizophrenic client is taking his medication when, in fact, he is not. On the other hand, if the client's disturbed behavior does not change after the medication is prescribed, mental health care providers may incorrectly assume that he is not taking his medication.[14]

One study that involved the use of two groups of outpatients diagnosed with schizophrenia examined the effects of compliance with medication regimens. One group of clients was treated with parenteral fluphenazine decanoate and the other group was given the oral form of the same medication with questionable compliance. The results of the study revealed equal rates of relapse between the two groups. This picture suggests that there are other factors to be examined when one concludes that a client is compliant or noncompliant with his prescribed medication.[30]

Self-medication helps to promote a sense of being in control of oneself. The capabilities of individual clients and the availability of their support systems influence who will be able to administer their own medications. Taking control over one's life and one's medication facilitates the development of confidence and self-respect and minimizes the pervasive pathologic dependence that often surfaces in the psychiatric-mental health client. Care providers need to encourage this control and sense of confidence.

Another factor influencing compliance is the fact that people want to feel as good as they possibly can. Many clients will stop taking their antipsychotic medication when they begin to feel worse. Part of this discontinuation of medication is related to the client's poor judgment inherent in the psychotic process, but there are other factors.[14] Akathisia and other side effects may be more distressing to the client than the medical and nursing staff realize. Sometimes, psychiatric-mental health caregivers tend not to listen to what the client is saying about the medication's side effects, especially if the client is not exhibiting common physical aberrations.[20] It is essential that each of the client's complaints be attended to, assessed, and documented to alleviate these side effects.[28]

The final area to examine in relation to compliance with medication regimens is, "What meaning does the client attach to taking medications?" The symbolism of taking medication is another reminder to psychiatric clients that they are mentally ill or disturbed.[13] This issue may be neglected by many mental health professionals who interact with clients; however, if this issue and other issues of concern to the client and family are examined and explored, nurses can provide factual, useful information about psychotropic medications and can alleviate the client's fears about taking medication over a prolonged period of time.

Working with Research Drugs

During the last 3 decades, the introduction of new psychotropic drugs has transformed the treatment of psychiatric-mental health clients. Present research is examining the effects of psychoactive drugs on the nervous system. Research findings have demonstrated that some drugs have specific effects on psychological processes and these findings have generated a need for further research into the nature of mental illness. Examples of such effects are the chemical changes that take place in depressive and manic states characteristic of bipolar disorders.[3]

Drug treatment is based on scientific research more so than other somatic therapies.[1] Nursing professionals contribute to the success of the research findings through the provision of continuous, 24-hour-per-day monitoring. Medication regimens are prescribed primarily by means of the documented observations of the nursing staff.[8]

Initially, the effects of a new drug is researched with the use of laboratory animals. When the drug is considered safe for the use of humans, drug trials are instituted to determine the effects of the drug on human subjects. The subjects selected have a common set of target symptoms that are expected to benefit from the drug. These clients must have explicit reports available to them regarding their disorders, severity of the symptoms, and degree of incapacity. Nursing responsibilities include careful documentation of all therapeutic effects observed and the client's reactions to them. Usually, the study involves a control group and it is the responsibility of the nurse to administer the drug to one group and withhold it from the other group, utilizing other forms of treatment as ordered.[1]

In addition to monitoring the psychological responses of clients who are involved in psychopharmacologic research, the nurse is also responsible for monitoring and documenting the physiological responses. Physiological monitoring includes assessment of the vital signs, particularly the blood pressure, prior to and after administration of the drug. Changes in the heart rate and rhythm, palpitations, and any signs indicative of blood dyscrasias should be reported and documented carefully.[1]

Nurses involved in research of psychotropic drugs must be aware of negative feelings that may be generated by the research itself. The nurse needs to acknowledge honestly the client's participation in research that is not willingly undertaken. Ambivalence may interfere with the client's progress as well as with the benefits of the study.[1]

Finally, it is imperative that nurses who are involved in research are familiar with proper research guidelines peculiar to the health care institution.[25] These guidelines include the signed informed consent of each participant in the research study (see the insert Consent to Act as a Subject for Research and Investigation on p. 251).

Psychotropic Medication

Table 19-1 lists names, classifications, and dosages of the psychotropic medications.

Consent to Act as a Subject for Research and Investigation

I hereby agree to participate voluntarily in a study of the following experimental procedure or treatment:

_____
(Name of procedure or treatment)

conducted by:

_____
(Name of person (s) or institution conducting investigation)

After careful explanation, I agree to,

1. Voluntarily participate in this study and I may withdraw at any time without interference with my treatment at _____
(Health care institution)

2. My individual results will not be identified or reported; my name will not be associated with the findings.

3. The information from these tests may help the investigators learn the best method of treatment for this participant and other patients with similar difficulties in the future.

4. According to the investigators, every effort will be made to prevent physical injury or reaction that could result from the administration of this procedure or treatment.

5. The investigators are prepared to advise in the event that medical treatment is needed due to adverse reactions. I agree to report these adverse effects.

I have received a verbal description of this study, including a fair explanation of the procedures and their purpose, any associated discomfort or risks, and a description of the possible benefits. An offer has been made to me to answer all questions about the study after its completion. I further understand that no medical service or compensation is provided to subjects by this institution as a result of injury from participation in this research.

_____   _____
(Signature of patient or person authorized to   (Date)
consent for patient)

_____   _____
(Signature of witness)   (Date)

Antipsychotic Agents

Approximately 20% of the prescriptions currently written in the United States are targeted toward altering mental processes. That translates to hundreds of thousands of individuals who presently take these medications.

Antipsychotic (or neuroleptic) agents comprise a group of widely used drugs in the field of psychiatry (see the insert on p. 252). They are used primarily to treat severe psychiatric disorders (*i.e.,* psychoses).[5]

The antipsychotic drugs change or alter the moods and thoughts of individuals who recognize and respond to reality with difficulty, such as clients with hallucinations, delusions, disordered thinking, and emotional withdrawal. The drugs are not selective for schizophrenia, but have other forms of clinical usefulness, including their antiemetic properties, their antihistaminic effects, their ability to potentiate analgesics, and their ability to treat hiccoughs.

Clients taking antipsychotic agents must be closely

Table 19-1.   **Psychotropic Medications**

CLASSIFICATION	CHEMICAL GROUP	GENERIC NAME	TRADE NAME	DAILY DOSAGE
Antipsychotic/ Neuroleptics	Phenothiazines	Chlorpromazine	Thorazine	200–1000 mg
		Trifluoperazine	Stelazine	6–20 mg
		Thioridazine	Mellaril	150–600 mg
	Butyrophenones	Haloperidol	Haldol	0.5–15 mg (PO) 2–5 mg (IM/IV)
	Thioxanthenes	Chlorprothixene	Taractan	100–500 mg
Antidepressant Agents	Tricyclics	Imipramine	Tofranil	100–200 mg
		Amitriptyline	Elavil	75–200 mg
		Doxepin	Sinequan	75–150 mg
	Triazolopyridine	Trazodone	Desyrel	150–400 mg
	Tetracyclic	Maprotiline	Ludiomil	150–200 mg
	Monoamine oxidase inhibitors	Phenelzine sulfate	Nardil	15–90 mg
		Tranylcypromine sulfate	Parnate	10–40 mg
Antianxiety Agents	Benzodiazepines	Alpraxolam	Zanax	0.75–1.5 mg
		Diazepam	Valium	4–40 mg
		Chlordiazepoxide	Librium	15–40 mg
	Propanediols	Meprobamate	Equanil/ Miltown	1200–1600 mg
Antimanic Agents	Lithium carbonate	Lithium carbonate	Lithium, Eskalith	600–1800 mg

Antipsychotic/Neuroleptic Agents

Classification: Antipsychotics, Neuroleptics

Formerly called "major tranquilizers"
Improve the mood and behavior of psychotic clients without excessive sedation and without causing addiction

Actions

Block and potentiate the uptake of norepinephrine and receptor effect
Sites of action: both nervous system (limbic, reticular activating system, extrapyramidal) and peripheral
Anticholinergic effects
Antihistamine, antipruritic
Sedation, antipsychotic effects without clouding of consciousness

Side Effects

Central nervous system: extrapyramidal with motor restlessness (akathisia), parkinsonism, seizures, dystonias
Autonomic nervous system: dry mouth, mydriasis, nasal congestion, constipation, urinary retention

Cardiovascular: reversible arrythmias, orthostatic hypotension, tachycardia
Gastrointestinal: anorexia, constipation, diarrhea, hypersalivation, nausea and vomiting, obstructive jaundice
Hematopoietic: agranulocytosis (especially with chlorpromazine), leukopenia, leukocytosis
Endocrine: amenorrhea, changes in libido, lactation, gynecomastia, impotence
Allergic: dermatitis, photosensitization

Drug Interactions/Contraindications

Central nervous system depressants (alcohol, narcotics, barbiturates) are potentiated
Anticonvulsives—seizure threshold is lowered
Antiemetics—effects are potentiated
Tricyclics—anticholinergic effects are potentiated
Levodopa—inhibits antiparkinsonism effects
General anesthesia—effects are potentiated
Lithium—can cause encephalopathic syndrome (*i.e.,* weakness, fatigue, irreversible brain damage)
Anticoagulants—effects inhibited
Monoamine oxidase inhibitors—effects inhibited

monitored for adverse side effects including extrapyramidal reactions and tardive dyskinesia. There is a wide margin of safety between the doses of antipsychotic agents necessary to produce therapeutic effects and those that can cause fatal overdose. Although they are capable of producing toxic effects, neuroleptic agents have a low incidence of lethality.[29]

Nurses are responsible for observing the client for adverse as well as therapeutic effects and for reporting and documenting these effects. Client and family teaching is essential to promote medication compliance and to minimize the incidence of exacerbation. Support is necessary for the client experiencing adverse effects, particularly if there is any impairment in sexual functioning.

Extrapyramidal Side Effects

The central nervous system's potential responses to antipsychotic drugs are great. Because of the high incidence of extrapyramidal side effects of antipsychotic agents, it is imperative to discuss this subject with the client and his family. These side effects, predicted to develop in 5% to 15% of all clients who are taking antipsychotic drugs, are usually frightening, embarrassing, and uncomfortable to the client.[4, 15]

Extrapyramidal side effects of antipsychotic agents are difficult to prevent, but can be alleviated if they are diagnosed early and accurately. The alleviation of these symptoms decreases the client's distress and, therefore, contributes to his willingness to adhere to a medication regimen. A study involving 85 long-term schizophrenic clients demonstrated that there was a significant association between clients' taking their medications and the occurrence of extrapyramidal side effects, particularly akathisia, regardless of the severity of the symptoms.[27]

The antipsychotic agents that are associated with the highest incidence of precipitating extrapyramidal symptoms are the low-dose phenothiazine drugs (such as fluphenazine [Prolixin]) and haloperidol. The four groups of major toxic effects associated with the development of extrapyramidal symptoms are as follows.

1. Pseudoparkinsonism
2. Akathisia
3. Dystonia/dyskinesia
4. Tardive dyskinesia[4]

Pseudoparkinsonism symptoms, those symptoms that mimic Parkinson's disease, are characterized by akinesia, rigidity, and tremors. These symptoms, accounting for about 40% of all extrapyramidal side effects, may be caused by the blockage of dopamine receptors in the basal ganglia and substantia nigra.

Akathisia is characterized by a syndrome involving motor restlessness. These symptoms account for about 50% of all extrapyramidal side effects.[4]

Dystonia and *dyskinesia* are characterized by involuntary, jerking, uncoordinated body movements. *Tardive dyskinesia* normally occurs as a late symptom and is associated with the long-term use of high-dose phenothiazine drugs. Symptoms characteristic of tardive dyskinesia are mainly buccolingual movements, such as "fly catcher" tongue movements, pursing of the lips, and jaw movements. There can also be involvement of the limbs and trunks that sometimes mimics Huntington's chorea. Unfortunately, there is no treatment for tardive dyskinesia.[4]

Clients who are taking antipsychotic (or neuroleptic) drugs should be examined for the development of neurologic symptoms at least every 3 months. "Drug holidays," brief periods of time during which the client is taken off his medication, are recommended at least two times per year in order to decrease the risk of tardive dyskinesia. This respite from medication allows symptoms that have been masked to surface.[11] (The nursing care plan on p. 254 further illustrates precautions and interventions needed for clients on phenothiazines.)

Prevention of tardive dyskinesia is a crucial aspect of administering psychotropic drugs. Psychiatric nurses participate in this preventive effort by providing information to the client and family members; this information assists them in detecting the early signs and symptoms of these side effects and helps them recognize the importance of reporting them immediately. Client and family teaching also diminishes the distress and embarrassment associated with the symptoms. Nursing care providers must also be aware of the times of maximal risk for the development of the extrapyramidal side effects of antipsychotic agents (see Table 19-2).

Antiparkinsonism Medication

Antiparkinsonism drugs are used to treat the side effects and toxic effects precipitated by antipsychotic medications, with the exception of tardive dyskinesia. The controversy continues regarding the prophylactic use of these drugs when antipsychotic medication is initiated. Several factors feed this concern over the use of antiparkinsonism drugs.

1. There is a low incidence of extrapyramidal symptoms in clients who take antipsychotic medication.
2. Antiparkinsonism drugs produce additional anticholinergic side effects.
3. Antiparkinsonism drugs add additional cost of treatment for the client and family.

There is some evidence that antiparkinsonism drugs become unnecessary after 1 to 3 months of treatment and should be discontinued.[4] The antiparkinsonism drugs should not be administered until there are overt signs and symptoms of extrapyramidal side effects that respond favorably to this type of intervention (see Tables 19-3 and 19-4).[5]

Antidepressant Agents

Affective disorders, or mood disturbances, include depression and mania. *Depression* is characterized by dysphoric

Nursing Care Plan

The Client Taking Phenothiazines

Client Problem	Intervention	Rationale
Drowsiness	1. Administer medication at bedtime. 2. Report to the physician if drowsiness persists longer than several weeks. 3. Advise the client not to operate hazardous machinery or drive a vehicle while taking phenothiazine.	1. To maximize sedation 2. This is usually a temporary condition; continued sedation may indicate a need to decrease or change medication. 3. To prevent injury to self or others
Orthostatic hypotension	1. Encourage the client to progress slowly from a supine or sitting to a standing position (over one minute) 2. Record the blood pressure with client in lying, sitting, and standing positions. Call the physician if blood pressure drops 20 to 30 mm Hg. 3. Teach the client to keep head up while ambulating. 4. Apply elastic hose as ordered. 5. Reassure the client that this is a temporary occurrence and should disappear in several weeks.	1. To enable automatic nervous system to equalize blood throughout body and decrease venous pooling in lower extremities 2. To monitor changes in blood pressure 3. To minimize dizziness 4. To promote venous return 5. To alleviate anxiety
Weight gain	1. Monitor weight daily. 2. Teach the client how to plan well-balanced meals and avoid salt.	1. To determine weight fluctuations 2. To provide nutritious, low-calorie, and low-salt foods that are acceptable to client
Melanosis	1. Teach the client to apply sunscreen when exposed to sunlight and to wear protective clothing and sunglasses.	1. To protect the skin from sunlight and prevent pigmentation

Table 19-2.   Time of Maximal Risk of Extrapyramidal Side Effects of Antipsychotic Agents

SIDE EFFECTS	SYMPTOMS	TIME OF MAXIMAL RISK
Dystonia/dyskinesia	Involuntary jerking, uncoordinated body movements	1–5 days
Pseudoparkinsonism	Akinisia, rigidity, tremors	5–30 days
Akathisia	Syndrome of motor restlessness, inability to sit still	5–60 days
Tardive dyskinesia	Pursing and sucking movements of lips, "fly catcher" tongue movements (symptoms become more severe on withdrawal of medication)	Months to years

Table 19-3. **Antiparkinsonism Medications**

CLASSIFICATION	GENERIC NAME	TRADE NAME	DOSE (MG/DAY)	ROUTE
Anticholinergic	Benztropine	Cogentin ✓	0.5–6.0	PO, IM, IV
	Biperiden HCl	Akineton	2.0–8.0	PO
	and Biperiden lactate		6.0–10.0	
	Trihexyphenidyl HCl	Artane ✓	6.0–10.0	PO
Antihistamine	Diphenhydramine	Benadryl ✓	75–150	PO, IM, IV
Other	Amantadine	Symmetrel ✓	100–200	PO

Table 19-4. **Side Effects of Antiparkinsonism Drugs**

SYSTEM AFFECTED	SYMPTOMS	TREATMENT RECOMMENDATIONS
Central nervous	Drowsiness	Administer at bedtime; decrease dose of drug
Autonomic	Dry mouth, blurred vision, urinary retention	Sugar-free candy or gum; avoid activities requiring visual acuity
Cardiovascular	Orthostatic hypotension	Antiembolism hose; assist client to sit or stand slowly
Gastrointestinal	Jaundice	Stop medication; bedrest
Endocrine	Weight gain	Weight reduction diet; physical exercise
Allergic	Transient skin rashes, photosensitivity	Antihistaminic drugs; avoid sunlight

mood, changes in appetite, changes in sleep patterns, and slowing of mental processes. Proper treatment of depression necessitates accurate diagnosis.[3] Physical problems underlying the depression are explored and treated before the antidepressant drug treatment is initiated.

Depression may be treated with tricyclic antidepressant agents and monoamine oxidase inhibitors (MAO inhibitors). Tricyclic antidepressants and related compounds are the most widely used agents for the treatment of depression (see the insert on p. 256); their efficacy in the alleviation of depression has been established by numerous research studies.[24]

Antidepressant medications are particularly effective in the treatment of endogenous depression, which is marked by vegetative symptoms, such as regression and decreased productivity. The therapeutic value of these agents depends on the client receiving adequate doses of the drug for a sufficient period of time. The onset of drug action for most antidepressant agents occurs in approximately 2 to 3 weeks and the optimal response takes place in 1 month. Some sedation is often desirable during early treatment with antidepressants and is noted during the administration of both amitriptyline and doxepin.[5, 24]

The nurse is responsible for client teaching and emotional support during treatment with antidepressant agents (see the nursing care plan on p. 257). The client needs to be informed of the length of time necessary for optimal response of his medication. Some clients may become discouraged and, possibly, even more depressed if they are not told about this delayed therapeutic response.[21]

Tricyclic Antidepressants

Tricyclic antidepressant agents are potentially lethal if they are taken in amounts that are 10 to 30 times the daily recommended dose. A nursing implication is therefore to monitor the ingestion of the tricyclic antidepressants to prevent the client from hoarding the medications for a future suicide attempt. Individuals who overdose on these medications do not respond to treatment by dialysis or forced diuresis. Rather, the treatment for tricyclic antidepressant overdosage includes supportive measures and the administration of physostigmine to manage atropine overdose effects.[4]

There exists a high relapse rate with antidepressant medication treatment during the first year after recovery from acute, severe, depressive illness. The client is therefore usually treated with antidepressants for a period of at least several months.[18] The nurse provides further support to the client by sharing information with him that reinforces his positive response to the medication.

Antidepressant Agents

Classification: Antidepressants

Used in the treatment of clients with regressed and agitated depressive states

Actions

Possibly inhibits the membrane pump mechanism responsible for the uptake of norepinephrine and serotonin in adrenergic and serotonergic neurons

Reverses psychomotor retardation in depressed individuals

Improves insomnia by increasing state-4 slow wave and decreasing rapid eye movement (REM) sleep

Potent anticholinergic

Monoamine oxidase inhibitors—increase concentration of epinephrine, norepinephrine, and storage sites thoughout the central nervous system that increases the concentration of monoamines in brainstem

Side Effects

Central nervous system: drowsiness, sedation, muscle tremors, paresthesias, delusions, hallucinations

Autonomic nervous system: dry mouth, urinary retention, constipation, mydriasis

Cardiovascular: postural hypotension, sinus tachycardia, cardiac arrythmias, pedal edema, electrocardiogram (ECG) changes (ST-segment depression, T wave flat, prolonged QRS)

Gastrointestinal: nausea and vomiting, anorexia, obstructive jaundice

Hematopoietic: agranulocytosis

Endocrine: gynecomastia, galactorrhea, hyperglycemia, and hypoglycemia

Allergic: allergic rash

Withdrawal symptoms: abrupt cessation leads to nausea, headache, malaise (not indicative of addiction)

Drug Interactions

Antihypertensives—action/effects may be blocked

Thyroid medications—effects are potentiated

Central nervous system depressants—effects are potentiated

Monoamine oxidase inhibitors—causes hypertensive crisis, severe convulsions, and death

Antipsychotics—potentiate anticholinergic effects

Atropine—potentiates anticholinergic effects

Contraindications

Caution in clients with cardiovascular disorders (causes arrythmias)

Increases or exacerbates psychosis in schizophrenics

Increases or exacerbates mania in manic-depressives

Increases hazards in clients receiving electroconvulsive therapy (ECT)

Caution in clients with impaired liver disorders

Caution in clients who are suicidal or who have a history of suicidal attempts (dialysis is of little value in overdoses because of decreased plasma levels)

Monoamine Oxidase Inhibitors

Drug Interactions

Tricyclics and tyramine-containing foods—causes serious hypertensive crises

Antihistamines—increases the accumulation of norepinephrine in nerve endings

Central nervous system depressants—decrease metabolic breakdown by liver

Levodopa—potentiates action

Antihypertensives/diuretics—decreases the action

Amphetamines—potentiates the action

Dibenzypines—causes hypertensive crisis and severe convulsions

Contraindications

Foods that are high in tyramine—aged cheeses, beer, pickled herring, sherry, sour cream, chocolate, raisins, and many others

Clients with cerebrovascular defects or cardiovascular disorders

Presence of pheochromocytoma

Persons with liver impairment

Clients older than 60

Monoamine Oxidase Inhibitors

The MAO inhibitors are generally considered not as effective as other forms of treatment for acute depression. The severe side effects of these drugs and their complex interactions with other drugs and foods limit their usefulness. Although MAO inhibitors are not used as often as other antidepressant drugs, they may also provide selective benefits for conditions other than depression, such as those disorders characterized by phobias and anxiety.[5]

The nursing implications of administration of MAO inhibitors include observing the client for untoward side effects, particularly hypertensive crises resulting from interaction with specific drugs and foods. It is essential for the nurse to educate the client and family about certain foods

Nursing Care Plan

The Client Taking Antidepressants

Client Problem	Intervention	Rationale
Dry mouth	1. Teach the client to drink frequent sips of water or lemonade and chew sugarless gum and candy. 2. Reassure the client that dryness of his mouth is a temporary reaction.	1. To moisten mucous membranes 2. To decrease anxiety and increase his compliance with medication regime
Constipation	1. Teach the client to include in his diet foods that are high in bulk and fiber, (*i.e.*, brans, fresh fruits, and vegetables) 2. Encourage drinking adequate amounts of fluids. 3. Encourage ambulation. 4. Administer stool softeners as ordered.	1. To increase bulk in stools and promote peristalsis 2. To soften stools and prevent constipation 3. To promote peristalsis 4. To lower surface tension, permitting water to penetrate and soften stool
Sedation	1. Encourage the client to take medication at bedtime. 2. Teach him the importance of avoiding alcohol and other sedatives and depressants. 3. Advise the client to avoid driving and using hazardous equipment.	1. To promote sleep and rest 2. The antidepressants potentiate sedative effects of CNS depressants. 3. To prevent accidents and injury
Urinary retention	1. Monitor intake and output. 2. Check the abdomen for distention. 3. Catheterize prn. 4. Assess for the history of prostatic hypertrophy. 5. If urinary retention persists, report to the physician.	1. To assess if the client is adequately emptying bladder 2. To assess bladder distention 3. To empty bladder and decrease the risk of bladder infection 4. This condition will further increase the risk of urinary retention 5. This may be a temporary effect of the medication; therefore, persistent retention should be investigated further
Hypertensive crisis (due to monoamine oxidase inhibitors)	1. Monitor the client's blood pressure in lying, sitting, and standing positions. 2. Assess neurological signs, including complaints of headache and blurred vision. 3. Teach the client to avoid foods that contain tyramine, such as aged cheese, wine, beer, chicken livers, and so forth. 4. Warn the client to avoid over-the-counter cold and sinus medications and amphetamines.	1. To provide baseline blood pressure and to assess cardiovascular changes in response to position changes 2. Headache may be an initial sign of hypertensive crisis. 3. These foods will precipitate hypertensive crisis. 4. These drugs have adrenergic properties and increase the potential of developing hypertensive crisis.

(Continues on p 258)

Client Problem	Intervention	Rationale
Risk of suicide	1. Monitor the client's swallowing of medications.	1. To prevent the client from hoarding lethal dose of medications
	2. Inform the client and his family of the time required for the drug's therapeutic effects to occur.	2. To encourage and reassure the client that depressions are usually time-limited
	3. Assess the suicide potential; that is, previous attempts, family history, possession of a weapon, lethality of the plan, and so on.	3. These drugs are potentially lethal and may be included in the client's suicide plan.
	4. Instruct the client not to take antidepressants with central nervous system depressants.	4. To minimize central nervous system depression resulting from potentiation
	5. Assist the client to explore alternatives in dealing with feelings of hopelessness and despair.	5. To provide options and increase availability of support systems

and drugs that the client must avoid while taking these medications. These foods and drugs that contain tyramine and produce a synergistic effect with the MAO inhibitors include aged cheese, wine, beer, yogurt, chocolates, pickled herring, and bananas.

Antianxiety Agents

Anxiety is both a normal aspect of universal human behavior and a cardinal symptom of many psychiatric disorders. Anxiety is also associated with fear and serves psychobiological adaptive purposes.

Antianxiety agents, among the most widely prescribed drugs, are usually the drugs of choice to treat overt anxiety and somatic complaints. They are also useful in the treatment of convulsions and muscle spasms. (See the insert on this page.)

The benzodiazepines comprise the most useful group of antianxiety agents. The conditions that respond most favorably to the benzodiazepines are those involving acute anxiety reactions of medical and psychiatric clients. It is imperative that medical causes contributing to the client's anxiety are ruled out before this medication is begun.

The nursing implications of administering antianxiety agents are recognizing the potential for both physical and psychological dependence and abuse of these agents. Abuse of these drugs may be attributed, in part, to the development of tolerance to them after approximately 3 to 4 weeks. During this time, the client may increase the dosage that was originally ordered in order to regain the initial euphoric effect.[4] The client needs to be informed that these drugs are not a "cure" for his anxiety and that the

Antianxiety Agents

Classification: Antianxiety Agents

Formerly called "minor tranquilizers"
Reduce anxiety, tension, and agitation
Sedative effects

Actions

Possibly act on limbic system, thalmus, and hypothalmus
Produce calming effect

Side Effects

Central nervous system: drowsiness, ataxia, confusion, depression, blurred vision
Cardiovascular: hypotension, palpitations, syncope, transient ECG changes
Gastrointestinal: nausea, vomiting, diarrhea
Hematopoietic: neutropenia, aplastic anemia, agranulocytosis
Endocrine: changes in libido
Allergic: skin rash
Physical/psychological dependence: withdrawal can cause convulsions, tremors, and abdominal and muscle cramps

Drug Interactions

Central nervous system depressants—actions are potentiated

Contraindications

Clients with renal or liver impairments

Nursing Care Plan

The Client Taking Antianxiety Agents

Client Problem	Intervention	Rationale
Sedation	1. Teach the client to administer medication at bedtime. 2. Caution the client about the use of hazardous equipment and driving a vehicle.	1. To maximize the sedative effects and promote sleep 2. To prevent or minimize the possibility of accidents and injury
Physical and mental dependency	1. Assist the client to view his problems realistically. 2. Assist the client to examine other alternatives in dealing with anxiety, such as physcial exercise, gardening, and relaxation techniques. 3. Teach the client the signs of dependency, such as the need to increase dose to obtain same effect, nervousness, and abdominal cramping 4. Instruct the client not to suddenly stop medications without consulting the physician.	1. To resolve conflicts and underlying anxieties 2. To promote tension release, goal-setting, and relaxation 3. To minimize physical and psychological dependency on medications and to encourage the client to assume responsibility and control over the use of drugs. 4. Abrupt withdrawal can precipitate seizures and, possibly, death

identification of the source of his anxiety may help reduce its effects. The nurse also assists the client in exploring methods of dealing with his feelings (see the nursing care plan above).

Antimanic Agents

The primary indications for the use of lithium carbonate are treatment for acute mania and long-term prophylactic treatment of bipolar disorder, formerly termed manic-depressive illness (see the insert on p. 260). Lithium is particularly efficacious in the prevention of recurrent manic episodes.

Lithium is ideally used to treat clients with normal sodium intake and normal cardiac and renal functioning. Prior to initiating lithium administration, the individual must undergo an adequate medical evaluation consisting of electrolyte studies, thyroid function tests, complete blood count, blood urea nitrogen, urinalysis, and electrocardiogram.

Lithium, a salt, is not metabolized by the body. It is easily absorbed via the oral route and exists in body fluids. During the process of renal excretion of lithium, it competes with sodium for reabsorption in the proximal tubules of the kidneys.[4]

Most clients demonstrating severely manic behavior are initially treated with large doses of antipsychotic drugs.

When the client evidences less disturbed behavior, in approximately 5 to 10 days, lithium is gradually introduced.

There is a low therapeutic index for lithium salts. Lithium is a potentially toxic drug that can produce degenerative changes primarily in the kidneys.[12] Despite its toxic effects, lithium may be safely administered through careful monitoring of the client's serum level of lithium. The therapeutic serum lithium range for the treatment of acute mania is 0.9 to 1.4 mEq/liter; long-term maintenance level of lithium is 0.6 to 1.2 mEq/liter. Serum lithium levels should be measured about 10 to 14 hours after the last dose of the drug. Once a maintenance level of serum lithium has been reached, blood levels should be measured about every 3 months. It normally takes 2 to 3 weeks of lithium administration to produce a therapeutic level of the drug.[4]

An important nursing responsibility is client and family education, aimed at preventing toxicity and manicdepressive recurrences. The necessity of taking the medication as prescribed should be stressed. Clients and family members should be instructed to notify their physician if the client experiences increased sweating, takes diuretics, or decreases his salt intake. These conditions lower the body's sodium levels and increase the risk of overdose. The client needs to be able to recognize the possible side effects of lithium, such as diarrhea, tremors, and nausea, and needs to report them to his physician immediately. The client and

Antimanic Agent: Lithium

Classification: Antimanic Agent

Used to treat mania and recurrent manic episodes

Actions

Alters sodium transport in nerve and muscle cells and effects a shift toward intraneuronal metabolism of catecholamines; however, specific biochemical mechanism of action on mania is unknown

Side Effects

Central nervous system: tremors, muscle hyperirritability, tinnitis, confusion, slurred speech, clonic movements

Autonomic nervous system: blurred vision

Cardiovascular: cardiac arrythmias, hypotension, bradycardia

Gastrointestinal: anorexia, nausea, vomiting, diarrhea, excessive salivation

Endocrine: euthyroid goiter, hypothyroidism (myxedema)

Urinary: albuminuria, oliguria, polyuria, decreased creatinine clearance

Allergic: drying and thinning of hair, alopecia, itching

Note: Plasma lithium levels require close monitoring. Therapeutic level is 0.9–1.4 mEq/liter. The therapeutic level and toxic levels are very close in reading. Lithium levels more than 1.5 mEq/liter produce signs of toxicity.

Drug Interactions

Diuretics—increase risks of lithium toxicity

Antipsychotics—can cause encephalopathic syndrome (*i.e.*, weakness, fatigue, irreversible brain damage)

Neuromuscular blocking agent—prolong their effects

Nonsteroidal/anti-inflammatory agents—increase the plasma levels of lithium

Contraindications

Clients with renal impairment

Cardiovascular disease

Clients taking diuretics

The presence of severe debilitation or dehydration, sodium depletion

Pregnant women (causes fetal anomalies)

Clients with hypothyroidism require close monitoring

family must also be informed of the need for regular monitoring of serum lithium levels.

Nurses provide psychological support to clients and their families in dealing with their feelings about this bipolar disorder. Parents or grandparents, for example, may experience guilt associated with feeling responsible for the client's emotional disorder. Stressing the importance of preventing recurrences by taking the medication as prescribed may encourage hopefulness for the client and family.

Summary

This chapter has focused on several areas that are significant for the safe and therapeutic use of psychotropic medication. The historical perspective presented information about the revolution of psychotropic drugs and their influence on the field of psychiatric-mental health care. Some of the other major points of the chapter have included the following.

1. The introduction of psychotropic agents has revolutionized the treatment of institutionalized psychiatric clients and has facilitated their return to community life.

2. One of the more important theories of the action of psychotropics is based on the biochemical activities of the neurotransmitters, specifically norepinephrine and dopamine.

3. The psychotropic medications are classified into the antipsychotic or neuroleptic, antidepressant, antianxiety, and antimanic agents.

4. Nurses play a significant role in the development of new information from research studies of psychotropic drugs.

5. Noncompliance with medication regimens is a major problem in the field of psychiatric-mental health care.

6. One of the variables that may reduce this noncompliance with regimens and may prevent recurrences of emotional disorder is client and family teaching, an integral part of the psychiatric treatment plan.

7. The revolution that heralded the advent of psychopharmacology several decades ago has developed into continuous research processes that lead to the important drug discoveries of today and tomorrow.

Nursing Care Plan

The Client Taking Lithium

Client Problem	Intervention	Rationale
Toxicity	1. Monitor the client for early toxic signs, such as diarrhea, nausea, and vomiting. 2. Teach signs and symptoms of toxicity to the client and his family members. 3. Obtain baseline levels of renal and cardiovascular functioning prior to beginning medications (*i.e.*, BUN, ECG, and so on). 4. Monitor laboratory results associated with renal functioning. 5. Monitor lithium serum levels and teach the client and his family the importance of follow-up. 6. Teach the client how to maintain adequate sodium intake and the necessity of calling the physician if there is an increase in sodium loss via diaphoresis, vomiting, or diarrhea	1., 2. There is a small index between the therapeutic level and toxicity; noting these early symptoms assists in preventing toxic effects. 3., 4. Lithium is excreted by the kidneys; ineffective functioning of the kidneys may result in cumulative toxicity. 5. To provide objective data about serum levels of lithium 6. Sodium competes with lithium in the kidneys for reabsorption; a decrease in sodium due to these conditions contributes to an increased risk of lithium toxicity.
Recurrence of manic behavior	1. Teach the client and his family the signs and symptoms of recurring mania, such as talkativeness, increased motor activity, racing thoughts, inability to rest, decreased attention span, and so forth.	1. To alert the client and his family that psychiatric attention is required
Recurrence of depression	1. Teach the client and his family the symptoms of recurring depression, such as crying, feelings of hopelessness, lack of attention to personal hygiene, lack of energy, and so on.	1. To alert the client and his family that psychiatric attention is required

References

1. Altshul AT: Psychiatric Nursing, 4th ed. pp 256–261. Baltimore, Williams & Wilkins, 1973
2. American Nurses' Association: Standards of Psychiatric and Mental Health Nursing Practice. Kansas City, American Nurses' Association, 1982
3. American Psychiatric Association: Diagnostic and Statistical Manual of Mental Disorders, 3rd ed. Washington, DC, American Psychiatric Association, 1980
4. Appleton WS: Fourth Psychoactive Drug Usage Guide. J Clin Psychiatr 43 (January): 12–27, 1982
5. Baldessarini RJ: Drugs and the Treatment of Psychiatric Disorders. In Gilman AG, Goodman LS, Gilman A (eds): The Pharmacological Basis of Therapeutics, 6th ed, pp 391–442. New York, Macmillan, 1980
6. Bernstein JG: Handbook of Drug Therapy in Psychiatry. Boston, John Wright & Sons, 1983
7. Blackwell B: Drug Therapy: Patient Compliance. N Engl J Med 289 (August): 249–252, 1973

8. Brands AJ, Brands AB: Responsibility. Family and Community Health 6 (April): 63–71, 1983

9. Burgess AW: Psychiatric Nursing in the Hospital and the Community, 3rd ed. Englewood Cliffs, NJ, Prentice-Hall, 1981

10. Cade JJ: Lithium Salts in the Treatment of Psychotic Excitement. Med J Aust 2 (September): 349–352, 1949

11. Crane GE: Prevention and Management of Tardive Dyskinesia. Am J Psychiatr 129 (October): 466–467, 1972

12. Davis JM: Overview: Maintenance Therapy in Psychiatry, Affective Disorders. Am J Psychiatr 133 (January): 1–13, 1976

13. Davison G, Neale JM: Abnormal Psychology: An Experimental Clinical Approach. New York, John Wiley & Sons, 1978

14. Diamond RJ: Enhancing Medication Use in Schizophrenic Patients. J Clin Psychiatr 44 (June): 7–14, 1983

15. Harris E: Extrapyramidal Side Effects to Antipsychotic Medications. Am J Nurs 18 (July): 1324–1328, 1981

16. Hofmann A: The Discovery of LSD and Subsequent Investigations on Naturally Occurring Hallucinogens. In Ayd FJ, Blackwell B (eds): Discoveries in Biological Psychiatry, pp 91–106. Philadelphia, JB Lippincott, 1970

17. Hollister LE: Current Antidepressant Drugs: Their Clinical Use. Drugs 22 (August): 129–152, 1981

18. Hollister LE: Tricyclic Antidepressants. N Engl J Med 299 (November): 1106–1109, 1168–1172, 1978

19. Jaffe JH: Drug Addiction and Drug Abuse. In Gilman AG, Goodman LS, Gilman A (eds): The Pharmacological Basis of Therapeutics, 6th ed, pp 535–584. New York, Macmillan, 1980

20. Kane JM: Problems of Compliance in the Outpatient Treatment of Schizophrenia. J Clin Psychiatr 44 (June): 3–6, 1983

21. Klein DF, Davis JM: Diagnosis and Drug Treatment of Psychiatric Disorders. Baltimore, Williams & Wilkins, 1969

22. Klein DF, Gittelman R, Quitkin F, Rifkin A: Drug Treatment of Psychiatric Disorders of Adults and Children, 2nd ed. Baltimore, Williams & Wilkins, 1980

23. Kline NS: Antidepressant Medications: A More Effective Use by General Practitioners, Family Physicians, Internists, and Others. J Am Med Assoc 227 (March): 1158–1160, 1974

24. Kuhn R: The Treatment of Depressive States With G22355 (Imipramine Hydrochloride). Am J Psychiatr 115 (November): 459–464, 1958

25. Laben JK, Mclean CP: Legal Issues and Guidelines For Nurses Who Care for the Mentally Ill. New York, Slack Inc, 1984

26. Laborit H: Note: Complimentaire concernant L'Utilisation des Antihistaminiques des Synthése en Anesthésie. Acta Chirurgica Belgica 49 (March): 390–391, 1950

27. Newton M, Godbey KL, Newton DW et al: How You Can Improve the Effectiveness of Psychotropic Drug Therapy. Nursing '78 8 (July): 46–55, 1978

28. Rifkin A, Quitkin F, Kane JM et al: Are Prophylactic Antiparkinson's Drugs Necessary? A Controlled Study of Procyclide Withdrawal. Arch Gen Psychiatr 35 (April): 483–489, 1978

29. Rodman MJ, Smith DW: Pharmacology and Drug Therapy in Nursing, 3rd ed. Philadelphia, JB Lippincott, 1985

30. Schooler NR, Levine J, Severe J et al: Prevention of Relapse in Schizophrenia: An Evaluation of Fluphenazine Decanoate. Arch Gen Psychiatr 37 (January): 16–24, 1980

31. Van Patten T: Why Do Schizophrenic Patients Refuse to Take Their Drugs? Arch Gen Psychiatr 31 (July): 67–72, 1974

Part V
Application
of the Nursing Process
to Disturbed Behaviors

Chapter 20
Anxiety and Maladaptation: The Personality Disorders

Grief has limits, whereas apprehension has none. For we grieve only for what we know has happened, but we fear all that may possibly happen.

Pliny the Younger,
Letters

Judith A. Greene

Chapter Preview

The current period of history is rapidly becoming known as the age of narcissism.[4,5] *Narcissism*, a love for the self, stands as a counter example to a love for humanity. Given that many of today's most popular life philosophies advocate individual self-growth, individual rights, and self-improvement to the exclusion of concern for others, narcissism is an appropriate metaphor for the recent state of the human condition.[4,5]

With this change in how individuals view themselves in relation to others, the incidence and prevalence of psychiatric syndromes have also changed. More specifically, unlike the age of anxiety, when people succumbed to a variety of neuroses (now referred to as anxiety states), the age of narcissism is resulting in the increased incidence and prevalence of personality disorders.[4] Although typologies and diagnostic criteria for personality disorders have undergone many changes so that it is now virtually impossible to ascertain valid statistics regarding their exact incidence and prevalence, experts agree that personality disorders constitute a significant psychiatric-mental health problem.[4,17]

Learning Objectives

Upon completion of the chapter, the reader should be able to accomplish the following.

1. Define personality and personality disorder
2. Identify common characteristics of personality disorders
3. Describe the position of the personality disorders on the mental health–illness continuum
4. Discuss the concept of anxiety and its physiologic, perceptual, cognitive, and behavioral effects
5. Identify the ways in which anxiety manifests itself in selected personality disorders
6. Discuss selected personality disorders in terms of their perceptual, cognitive, affective, and behavioral disturbances, their adaptation levels, and their mental health care seeking behaviors.
7. Apply the nursing process—assessment, analysis, planning, intervention, and evaluation—to clients with personality disorders.

Personality and Personality Disorder Defined

The concept of *personality* may be defined as " . . . a consistent and stable pattern of behavior shown by a person in meeting a variety of challenges and opportunities, consistent over long periods of his life and recognized as special to each person."[16] The individual's personality is an indispensable aspect of self-identity in that it is ego-syntonic with the individual's self-definition. Personality patterns or styles

may be adaptive or maladaptive. When the personality of an individual is maladaptive, the designation *personality disorder* is appropriately applied.

Common Characteristics of Personality Disorders

Although several distinct types of personality disorders exist, the following characteristics are commonly found in all of the disorders.

1. A deeply ingrained, inflexible, maladaptive response to anxiety
2. Maladaptation that is most apparent within an interpersonal or social context
3. The capacity to induce others to feel irritation and annoyance
4. A self-centered, inflexible approach to work and interpersonal relationships.[17]

Adjectives or descriptive phrases applicable to many persons with personality disorders include narcissitic, unempathic, inordinate sense of entitlement, dependent, lack of self-insight while giving evidence of pseudo self-knowledge, unable to self-evaluate, cynical, pessimistic, depressed, lack of objectivity, egocentric, selfish, lonely, immature, manipulative, aggressive, hostile, and suspicious.[1,4,17] While these terms concretize, to some extent, the four characteristics associated with all personality disorders (listed above), they also indicate the severity of these disorders.

Personality Disorders in Relation to the Health–Illness Continuum

The health–illness continuum may be used to classify personality disorders in terms of severity, with adaptive mental health at one extreme and psychoses at the other extreme (see Fig. 20-1). Neuroses or anxiety states follow adaptive mental health on the continuum. The personality disorders then fall between the anxiety states and psychoses. This schematic classification therefore illustrates that the personality disorders constitute one of the most severe groups of psychiatric syndromes.

Etiology of Personality Disorders

Because typologies and diagnostic criteria for personality disorders have changed frequently, exact sources of etiology remain unverified through clinical research. It is commonly believed, however, that genetic, constitutional, maturational, and environmental factors may play a role in their emergence.[17] The social fabric of today's world, with its emphasis on self-indulgences of all kinds, is also thought to play a major role in the development of some personality disorders.[4,5]

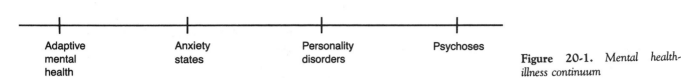

Figure 20-1. *Mental health-illness continuum*

Anxiety and Maladaption

Although personality disorders represent a major discrete group of psychiatric syndromes, they, like all other psychiatric syndromes, are associated with anxiety. Before discussing the ways in which anxiety manifests itself in each of these disorders, it is essential to review the nature of anxiety. Peplau's theory of anxiety provides a point of departure for this review.[8,9]

Defining Anxiety

According to Hildegard Peplau, *anxiety* is defined as the initial response to psychic threat.[8,9] In other words, anxiety occurs as the initial response to psychic stressors. Because anxiety is a form of energy, it is not accessible to direct observation; however, the presence of anxiety may be ascertained through the individual's self report. For example, anxious individuals may describe the subjective experience of anxiety as vague discomfort, uncertainty, self-doubt, diffuse apprehension, dread, restlessness, or feeling jumpy, jittery, helpless, powerless, or irrational.[8] On a more objective basis, the effects of anxiety may be inferred from the individual's verbal and nonverbal behaviors and physiological responses. These behaviors and responses indicating the presence of anxiety occur along a continuum ranging from mild, moderate, and severe degrees of anxiety to panic (see Figure 20-2).[8,9]

Physiological Effects of Anxiety

Anxiety causes certain physiological responses within the individual. Initially, epinephrine and norepinephrine are released from the adrenal medulla and cortisone is secreted by the adrenal cortex. The secretion of these hormones produces an increased heart rate, elevated blood pressure, and an increase in the rate and depth of respiration. Other physiological effects accompanying anxiety include systemic and localized changes in body temperature, urinary frequency and urgency, dryness of the oral mucosa, anorexia, excessive perspiration of the palmar surfaces of the hands and feet, increased muscular tension, changes in the woman's menstrual cycle, sexual dysfunction of both men and women, decrease in the blood's clotting time, and release of glycogen by the liver. The extent to which these physiological effects occur depends largely on the degree and duration of anxiety. Generally, mild and moderate anxiety enhance these effects whereas severe anxiety and panic tax the individual's capacity to exhibit these physiological responses.

Perceptual Effects of Anxiety

Anxiety also affects the ways in which an individual perceives and processes sensory input. In *mild anxiety*, the human organism is capable of grasping increased sensory input. The five sensory channels—sight, hearing, taste, smell, touch—are more open to sensations. Mild anxiety therefore heightens the individual's sensory awareness. *Moderate anxiety*, on the other hand, dulls perception; that is, the individual's sensory channels are less open to sensory input. If, however, the individual is directed to do so, he can attend to greater sensory input.[8]

With the occurrence of *severe anxiety*, perception becomes increasingly distorted and sensory input reduced. The processing of sensory stimuli occurs in a scattered, disorganized manner. In *panic level* anxiety, perception becomes grossly distorted.[8] At this point, the individual is incapable of differentiating real from unreal stimuli.

Effects of Anxiety on Cognition

Cognition, the ability to concentrate, learn, and problem-solve, is influenced by anxiety. Mild and moderate anxiety levels are most conducive to concentration, learning, and problem-solving. The normally intelligent individual who is mildly to moderately anxious discerns relationships between and among concepts with relative ease. His concentration and problem-solving occur without undue difficulty.

In contrast, severe anxiety seriously hinders cognitive function. The severely anxious individual has difficulty concentrating and often fails to discern even obvious relationships between and among concepts. The panic-stricken individual suffers even greater cognitive impairment. Concentration, learning, and problem-solving are virtually impossible during panic episodes.[8]

Figure 20-2. *Anxiety continuum.*

Effects of Anxiety on Verbal and Nonverbal Behavior

Mild Anxiety. The speech content and form of the mildly anxious individual reflect heightened sensory awareness and cognitive function. Thoughts are logically verbalized; speech rate and volume are appropriate to content and communication context. Nonverbally, the mildly anxious person appears alert, confident, and relatively secure.

Moderate Anxiety. Verbal behavior of the moderately anxious individual is often characterized by frequent changes of topic, repetitive questioning, joking, and wordiness. Blocking, or loss of train of thought, may also occur. Speech rate often accelerates and speech volume often increases.

Nonverbally, the moderately anxious individual may change body positions frequently, use excessive hand gestures, and assume aggressive body postures toward others. Furthermore, because moderately anxious individuals do not perceive and process sensory input as efficiently as mildly anxious individuals, they tend to hesitate and procrastinate in meeting routine social and vocational expectations. Such behaviors often present an overall picture of restlessness and discontent that may provoke others' feelings of irritation toward the moderately anxious individual.

Severe Anxiety. The severely anxious individual displays verbal behavior indicative of highly distorted perceptual and cognitive function. Severely anxious individuals often verbalize their emotional pain by making such assertions as, "I can't stand this," "I can't think," or by vociferously demanding help and relief.

Nonverbal behavior usually reveals both fine and gross motor tremors, facial grimaces, as well as other forms of purposeless activity, such as pacing and hand wringing.[8] Severely anxious individuals present an overall picture of extreme emotional discomfort and behavioral disorganization.

Panic. Panic level anxiety results in even greater emotional pain and behavioral disorganization of the individual. Both verbal and nonverbal behaviors suggest a psychotic-like state in which panic-stricken individuals are virtually helpless to defend themselves and to negotiate simple life demands. These individuals may scream incoherently and run about wildly or may cling tenaciously to something or someone accurately or inaccurately perceived as a source of safety and security. Protective and calmative measures must be initiated promptly because prolonged panic states are incompatible with life.[8,9]

Behavioral Patterns Employed to Cope with Anxiety

Individuals attempt to cope with anxiety by employing the following major behavioral patterns.

1. *Withdrawal*—the behavioral or psychological retreat from anxiety-provoking experiences
2. *Acting out*—the discharge of anxiety through aggressive behavior
3. *Psychosomatization*—the visceral or physiological expression of anxiety
4. *Avoidance*—the management of anxiety-ladened experiences through evasive behaviors
5. *Problem-solving*—using anxiety in the service of learning adaptive behavior[8,9]

With the exception of the last item, the preceding behavioral patterns are maladaptive. These patterns are considered maladaptive because they function to replace feelings of anxiety with feelings of pleasure and comfort at the expense of accurate reality perception and growth toward maturity. Therefore, the primary goal for treating individuals with personality disorders is to assist them in using anxiety as a means to increase their commitment to reality and growth toward maturity.

Application of the Nursing Process to Personality Disorders

Compulsive Personality Disorder

Assessment and Analysis

Perception. Perceptual, cognitive, affective, and behavioral disturbances accompany compulsive personality disorder. Perceptual disturbances associated with this disorder include inattention to new facts or different viewpoints, sharp focus on selected details, and the inability to focus on casual or peripheral details.

Cognition. This narrow perceptual focus leads to a variety of cognitive disturbances. Intellectual rigidity or the inability to voluntarily shift attention and concentration to another topic is prominent in the compulsive personality.[15] The cognitive content associated with this tenacious cognitive form usually centers around rules, standards, or codes of a moralistic or legalistic nature.[7] Consequently, the compulsive personality is often described as dogmatic.

Affect. The compulsive personality's narrow, yet tenaciously sharp, perceptual focus also reflects an underlying affective disturbance. Anxiety and ambivalence lie at the heart of this disturbance. Specifically, the individual with a compulsive personality experiences anxiety concerning the ability to control a variety of desirable, but forbidden, emotions and impulses. Moralistic or legalistic injunctions serve to defend the compulsive personality against those feelings and impulses.[7] Therefore, the individual with a compulsive personality avoids experiencing anxiety by tenaciously clinging to a set of fixed beliefs or injunctions.

Emotional constriction evidenced by lack of mirth, affection, lust, or frivolity occurs as an outgrowth of this concentrated focus on rules and regulations and represents another feature of the compulsive individual's affective disturbance. Furthermore, whimsical, frivolous behavior demonstrated by others often precipitates feelings of resentment and contempt in the person with a compulsive personality.[15]

Behavioral Disturbance. *Behavioral disturbances* exhibited by individuals with compulsive personalities include inflexible stubbornness, blind conformity and obedience, excessive prudence, neatness, and cleanliness, and undue preoccupation with work, efficiency, and productivity.[7] In interpersonal relationships, compulsive personalities show little ability to "give and take." Instead, these individuals insist upon doing things the right way; that is, their way.[17] Issues of control and dominance therefore take precedence over issues of human care and concern. For this reason, it is not surprising that the person with a compulsive personality is often perceived as cold, self-centered, and demanding. Because individuals with compulsive personalities often display verbal and nonverbal disapproval of persons whose behavior departs from their standards, these perceptions have some grounding in reality.[15]

Additionally, persons with compulsive personalities engage in a variety of behaviors designed to convince others to behave in accordance with their own rules and regulations. This need to control others stems from the compulsive individual's unconscious battle to control the self.[15] In other words, the person with a compulsive personality seeks to control the self through the control of others.

Level of Adaptation. Despite the limitations to the compulsive personality's perceptual, cognitive, affective, and behavioral functions, this disorder is adaptive and even rewarded in some occupational settings. Therefore, individuals affected by this disorder are rarely viewed as "mentally ill."[7] At worst, they are considered obstinate and boring, and at best, the "ideal, efficient worker."

Moreover, individuals with compulsive personalities are not drawn to seek therapy, which would necessitate change. Because change is threatening, therapy is usually sought only if and when these individuals experience unanticipated stress that over-taxes their coping mechanisms.[7]

When persons with compulsive personalities do appear for treatment, they commonly present with psychophysiologic discomforts, anxiety attacks, sexual problems, exhaustion, or depression.[7, 15, 17] Treatment, therefore, centers around amelioration of these presenting symptoms rather than the compulsive personality disorder itself.

Passive-Aggressive Personality

Assessment and Analysis

The term *passive-aggressive personality* refers to a specific way of perceiving, thinking, feeling, and behaving.

Perception. Individuals with passive-aggressive personalities tend to perceive the world, other persons, life in general, and themselves through a negative "lens." For example, these persons search for faults, flaws, injustices, and mistakes in almost any situation or environment in which they find themselves.[7] This pessimistic perceptual filter not only influences the kinds of sensory input received by persons with passive-aggressive personalities, but also influences their cognition, affect, and behavior.

Cognition. *Cognition* in the passive-aggressive personality reflects a negative mindset filled with negative thoughts about the future and criticisms of self and others. Indecisiveness about how, when, and under what circumstances to act also stands as a major characteristic of the passive-aggressive personality's cognitive set. Deficient regulatory control of impulsive, fleeting thoughts largely accounts for the passive-aggressive personality's indecisiveness.[7]

Affect. Underlying the passive-aggressive personality's indecisiveness is an ambivalent affect. In other words, these persons are characteristically torn between enthusiasm and pessimism, hope and hopelessness, compliance and noncompliance, love and hate, respect and envy, independence and dependence, and action and inaction. Understandably, such ambivalence leads to irritable moodiness, discontent, dissatisfaction, and contrariness. Low self-confidence and resentment toward authority figures on whom the passive-aggressive individual depends and whom he views as superior to himself are also associated with this ambivalent affect. Consequently, jealousy, hostility, and aggressive strivings occur to a significant degree in this disorder.

Behavior Patterns. The verbal behavior of passive-aggressive personalities reflects their characteristic manner of perceiving, thinking, and feeling. The passive-aggressive individual verbally displays negativism through incessant complaining, grumbling, and fault finding. The content of his verbalization usually centers around themes of feeling unappreciated, unloved, overworked, overburdened, and being unfairly treated, misused, and abused.[7]

Nonverbal behavioral patterns stemming from the passive-aggressive individual's indecisiveness and ambivalence include procrastination, delay tactics, dawdling, inefficiency, obstructionism, and errors of omission.[17] These behaviors serve to vent hostile, envious feelings, and aggressive strivings while simultaneously permitting the passive-aggressive personality to appear ingratiating, friendly, and even submissive. Furthermore, these covertly aggressive tactics manipulate, maneuver, or induce others to behave in a manner that will increase the passive-aggressive person's feelings of safety and security. These passive attack techniques thereby enable individuals with this personality type to avoid experiencing anxiety.

If these passive attack techniques fail and anxiety and frustration continue to mount, then the individual with a passive-aggressive personality may resort to occasional angry, emotional outbursts. The content of these angry outbursts usually centers around issues of exploitation, unfair treatment, and unappreciation. The underlying intent of the outbursts is to elicit sympathy and, therefore, to manipulate others to decrease their demands and expectations.[7] In this way, the passive-aggressive person can also escape experiencing anxiety.

Level of Adaptation.
Individuals with passive-aggressive personalities are usually articulate in reporting their subjective distress. Rarely, however, do they exhibit insight regarding the origins of their distress.[7] Therefore, the inner conflicts and ambivalences underlying their distress remain unrecognized.

Although these individuals complain about their discomfort and express a desire to rid themselves of it, they nevertheless avoid seeking adaptive solutions through learning and problem-solving. Consequently, it is not surprising that passive-aggressive personalities often develop anxiety and depressive episodes as well as suicidal crises. In such cases, treatment is aimed at crisis resolution and reinforcement of a more consistent and adaptive approach to life. To fulfill these treatment goals, behavior modification, family and group therapies, and crisis intervention techniques are often employed. In more severe cases, extensive, long-term psychoanalytic therapy may be indicated.[7]

Antisocial Personality Disorder

Assessment and Analysis
The term *antisocial personality* refers to an aggressive behavioral pattern. This aggressive personality type is described as "... the acting out kind of person, the adventurer, the explorer, the athlete, the soldier, and the pioneer..." as well as the delinquent and criminal.[13] While individuals with antisocial personalities use action as a primary form of expression, they also possess characteristic ways of perceiving, thinking, and feeling.

Perception.
Antisocial personalities perceive other people and the world as hostile, harmful, and out to undermine their independence. Consequently, these individuals expect to experience malice, humiliation, and betrayal at every turn.[7] Viewing the world and other people from such a "hostile lens" results in the antisocial person experiencing continual threat.

Individuals with antisocial personalities view others as sources of threat to their independence because they perceive themselves as "super-independent" individuals capable of negotiating life demands alone. More specifically, these persons see themselves as assertive, self-sufficient, tough-minded, competitive, powerful, and superior. Valuing these characteristics highly, individuals with these personality types reject attributes associated with warmth, caring, or tenderheartedness in both themselves and others.

Cognition.
This hostile perceptual style influences what persons with antisocial personalities think and believe about themselves and others in rather drastic ways. To illustrate, the slogans "might makes right" and "beat the other guy to the punch" could very well serve as life mottos for antisocial personalities. To state more simply, antisocial persons believe that human beings are basically evil; therefore, they believe they are entitled to take a highly antagonistic stance toward other people and society in general. Holding these beliefs, individuals with antisocial personalities use their cognitive capacities, for the most part, to design schemes, tactics, or strategies to outwit and punish their perceived adversaries. The terms *rigid, dogmatic,* and *cunning* describe the cognitive style of these personality types.[7]

Affect.
Affectively, antisocial individuals are hostile, punitive, and vengeful. Because these persons project their own malevolent attributes onto others, they mistrust people. Individuals with antisocial personalities are especially mistrustful of people who display warm, caring, or tender behaviors, because they fear that such persons are insincere, deceitful, and out to undermine their independence.[7]

Antisocial personalities also experience feelings of anxiety; they feel anxious when they cannot become independent of individuals or situations perceived as threatening.[7] To reduce their anxiety level and to increase their feelings of powerfulness and independence, those with antisocial personalities act out in a variety of ways.

Behavior Patterns.
Behavioral manifestations characteristic of an antisocial personality disorder reflect the perceptual, cognitive, and affective patterns described above. Nonverbally, antisocial persons appear cold, callous, and insensitive to the feelings and values of others. Although they may periodically display gracious, cheerful, and socially clever behaviors, they express neither warmth nor compassion toward others.[7]

Because individuals with antisocial personality disorders become easily bored, restless, and frustrated when faced with the tedium of day-to-day routines and responsibilities, they often impulsively seek thrills and dangers to buffer these feelings.[10] Examples of such acting-out behaviors include aggressive sexual behavior, vandalism, fighting, dangerous sports, outbursts of explosive anger, chemical abuse, and violent abuse and exploitation of other persons.[17]

Verbal behaviors reflecting the antisocial personality style include derogating, humiliating, brusque, and belligerent verbalizations directed to or about persons perceived as threatening, vicious argumentation and insults, and other forms of violent, verbal abuse. Such verbal behaviors betray the tendency of antisocial personalities to become furious and vindictive when faced with threats to their independence. In other words, the first inclination of these persons is to attack the perceived threat by resorting to demeaning and controlling behaviors.[7, 10 14]

Despite the fact that most antisocial individuals manifest abrasive, crude, and callous behaviors, some can sensitively discern the subtleties of human interaction.[7] More specifically, these persons are not only keenly aware of the moods and feelings of other persons, they can also use these perceived weaknesses to manipulate, exploit, and control others. In short, individuals with antisocial personalities use both verbal and nonverbal behaviors to accure power and independence and to cope with anxiety.

Level of Adaptation. At one time, the term *antisocial personality* suggested criminal and delinquent behaviors.[10] More recently, however, clinicians have come to believe that only a very small proportion of antisocial personalities actually come into conflict with the law.

Currently, it is thought that many individuals with antisocial personalities receive societal reinforcements and rewards for their tough, realistic, competitive approaches to life. In fact, most persons with these personality types find socially valued positions in business, politics, or the military. Still others find their places in society as harsh, punitive parents or spouses, "fire and brimstone" evangelists, vengeful bosses, or as irritable, punitive teachers.[7]

In any case, aggressive, action-oriented, antisocial personalities seldom seek mental health services. If and when such services are sought, antisocial individuals are unlikely to make significant progress in the direction of adaptive mental health.

Paranoid Personality

Assessment and Analysis

The term *paranoid personality* applies to individuals who display pervasive and long-standing suspiciousness. This suspicious pattern affects the perceptual, cognitive, affective, and behavioral functions of paranoid persons in some specific ways. Alterations in these functions reflect the great efforts individuals with paranoid personalities must make to counter the anxiety they experience in everyday life.

Perception. The perception of individuals with paranoid personalities is extremely acute, intense, and narrowly focused in search of "clues" or the "real" meaning behind the behavior of other persons or life events in general. To a great extent, paranoid persons perceive the world as being composed of clues to hidden or special meanings; hence, they disregard or even disdain manifest reality. Moreover, paranoid personalities perceive unexpected or unpredictable events and behaviors as highly threatening.[15]

Paranoid individuals generally perceive other persons as dishonest, full of trickery, and out to undo them. Their extreme distrust of others stems largely from their distorted perception of self. These individuals usually view themselves as self-sufficient, objective, rational, emotionally balanced, and very important.[7]

Cognition. The great degree of perceptual distortion present in persons with paranoid personality disorder significantly influences their cognitive function. Cognitive disturbances may range from transient ideas of reference, in which they believe that others are giving them special attention or gossiping about them, to delusional systems, in which they grossly misinterpret trivial events or achievements to fit their grandiose self-perceptions. These delusional systems may also be of a persecutory nature in which paranoid individuals believe that others are being unduly critical or are being purposefully deceptive or malicious toward them.[7]

Paranoid persons are hypercritical of others and prone to collect real or imagined injustices. Often, they seek retribution for such injustices through the legal system. Although these persons criticize others freely, they regard criticisms directed at themselves as signs of betrayal, jealousy, envy, or persecution.[7] Their cognitive function therefore deals primarily with making the imagined real and the real invalid.

Affect. The paranoid individual's affective domain reflects a lack of basic trust. Extreme suspiciousness, vigilance, mistrust, guardedness, and hostility characterize this lack of basic trust. Other affective attributes of paranoid personalities include abrasive irritability, defensiveness, envy, jealousy, serious-mindedness, and emotional coldness. Typically, paranoid persons assume a callous, unsympathetic approach to others in an effort to purge themselves of any tendencies to experience humor or affectionate and tender feelings. Moreover, when others express affection or tenderness toward a paranoid individual, that expression of warm feelings is likely to arouse in him fears of entrapment, deceit, and domination.[7] When confronted with humorous situations, persons with paranoid personalities often react with anger, hostility, and extreme suspiciousness.

Paranoid individuals experience profound emotional constriction in that they are virtually unable to reach out or connect with other persons in an emotional sense. Consequently, they experience little, if any, interpersonal or sensual pleasure. Furthermore, they must resort to fault-finding and projection of their own shortcomings onto others to preserve their own sense of self-esteem.[15] Through projection and psychological and social withdrawal, individuals with paranoid personalities maintain control of their fears and anxieties. Their behavioral patterns reflect these maladaptive approaches to anxiety control.

Behavioral Manifestations. Nonverbally, paranoid personalities present as hypervigilant, mobilized, prepared individuals who are ready for attack. Rarely do they appear relaxed or unguarded. For the most part, they remain coldly reserved on the periphery of events, and seldom do they mix smoothly with people in social situations. On the contrary, these individuals remain withdrawn, distant, and secretive in social situations. Because they lack the capacity for spontaneity and abandonment, their nonverbal behaviors appear very deliberate, tense, and, at times, even rehearsed.[7, 15]

Paranoid persons often engage in a variety of verbal interchanges designed to test the honesty of their associates. Because of the nature and lengthiness of these interchanges, their associates may become quite exasperated and angry with them. In addition to testing the trustworthiness of others, persons with paranoid personalities may also display argumentative, contentious, intimidating, and cajoling verbal behaviors.[7] The content of their verbalizations usually reflects themes of blame, deceit, control, persecution, and self-aggrandisement.

Level of Adaptation.
Most individuals with paranoid personalities experience lifelong effects of the disorder. In some, this disorder may precede the development of schizophrenia. In still others, a paranoid personality disorder may remit with maturity and the reduction of life stressors.[17]

Few individuals with paranoid personalities, however, voluntarily seek mental health services. When these persons appear for treatment, it is usually at the insistence of family members or associates.[7]

Individual, rather than group, psychotherapy is indicated for persons with paranoid personalities.[17] At the outset of therapy, trust formation must take place before other therapeutic techniques are employed.[7] Genuineness, respect, courtesy, and a formal, instead of an overly warm approach facilitate the process of trust development.[17] After trust is established between client and therapist, cognitive restructuring or psychoanalytic techniques may prove beneficial.[7] Behavioristic techniques, however, are usually contraindicated because of their intrusive nature.[17] Such behavioristic therapeutic interventions serve to palliate, rather than reverse, the paranoid personality disorder.[7]

Schizoid Personality Disorder

Assessment and Analysis
Socially detached, shy, and introverted persons may be described as having schizoid personality disorders. This classification refers to individuals who exhibit perceptual, cognitive, affective, and behavioral patterns that fall within the healthier end of the schizophrenic spectrum.[17] This personality disorder differs from schizotypal personality disorder in that the latter's symptomatology more closely resembles schizophrenia. Schizoid personalities, in contrast to both schizotypals and schizophrenics, do not demonstrate

odd or eccentric perceptual, cognitive, and behavioral patterns.[17]

Perception.
Despite the fact that individuals with schizoid personalities exhibit healthier behavior patterns than schizotypals and schizophrenics, the perception of these individuals does reflect a distorted pattern. This pattern is characterized by a reduced ability to attend, select, differentiate, and discriminate adequately between and among interpersonal and social sensory inputs. Consequently, the person with a schizoid personality tends to blur or mix up such inputs and this results in disorganized perceptual function. This perceptual dysfunction appears largely confined to interpersonal and social contexts.[7] Because illusions and hallucinations do not occur as part of this dysfunction, persons with schizoid personalities remain able to recognize reality despite their faulty interpersonal or social perception.

Cognition.
The cognitive pattern of schizoid personality types is consistent with their perceptual style. With regard to interpersonal and social situations, schizoid individuals demonstrate vague, impoverished thought processes; that is, they possess little social intelligence.[7]

Individuals with schizoid personalities are more apt to apply their cognitive abilities to mechanical problems, artistic pursuits, or metaphysical questions and are likely to excel in these areas.[12, 13, 17] Inanimate objects and ideas, instead of real people, become prominent topics within the schizoid's thoughts.[17]

Affect.
Indifference characterizes the affect of the schizoid personality. This indifference manifests itself in a variety of ways. First of all, these individuals appear totally indifferent to the thoughts and feelings of other people. They appear emotionally constricted, aloof, and inappropriately serious. Some clinicians believe that fear underlies the schizoid's aloofness.[17] Even in the face of considerable provocation, however, they rarely express feelings of anxiety, anger, or depression.[7] Although they seldom become emotionally involved with people, individuals with schizoid personality disorders invest emotionally in imaginary friends and a variety of cognitive activities.[17]

Behavior Patterns.
The nonverbal and verbal behaviors evident in schizoid personalities reflect a socially detached life pattern. Some prominent nonverbal behaviors include blank and affectless facial expression, an inability to tolerate eye contact, lethargic, awkward body movements, social withdrawal and aloofness, and unfashionable dress.[17] Often, schizoid individuals appear so drab and inconspicuous that they escape the attention of other people altogether.

Verbally, persons with schizoid personalities are unproductive. While their speech is goal-directed, their verbal emissions are short and to the point. They avoid spontaneous conversation and usually remain silent.[17] Their slow, monotonous speech form reveals the use of an occasional odd metaphor or word selection.[7] Both verbal and nonverbal behaviors of these personalities can best be described as underresponsive.

Level of Adaptation. Persons with schizoid personality types live out their lives in a socially detached way; they neither desire nor enjoy social interaction. They prefer to be alone and keep other people and life experience itself at arm's length.

Very few schizoid individuals ever seek mental health services. Their social isolation and indifference reduce their motivation for doing so. When they do come for assistance, their treatment is similar to that of paranoid personalities; however, unlike paranoid personalities, they may eventually tolerate, and even profit from, group psychotherapy.[7, 17]

Borderline Personality Disorder *p.5'*

Assessment and Analysis

The person with borderline personality disorder exhibits a cross section of almost all the perceptual, cognitive, affective, and behavioral disturbances present in the other personality disorders. In many ways, borderline personality disorder corresponds to the infantile personality described by Ruesch.[11, 12] These individuals typically cannot tolerate anxiety and, as a result, employ all the major maladaptive coping behaviors—avoidance, denial, withdrawal, acting out, and psychosomatization—to defend themselves against anxious feelings.

Perception. An outstanding feature of the borderline personality's perceptual pattern is the tendency to view people in "either-or" categories. For example, people are seen as either "all good" or "all bad"; that is, the borderline personality may view other persons as either kind, rewarding, and supportive or hateful, distant, and punitive.[6, 7, 17] This tendency to pigeon-hole individuals into "all good" or "all bad" categories is termed *splitting.*[17]

The self-perception of individuals with borderline personalities is also distorted. Often, they lack a clear, internal picture or image of who they are as individuals. Consequently, borderline individuals often suffer identity disturbances with regard to their self-image and their sexual, social, and occupational roles.[17]

Cognition. The perceptual distortion evident in the borderline personality disorder affects the individual's cognitive function significantly. Because these clients tend to perceive other individuals in such narrow, rigid ways, their cognitive function is impaired. Holding diametrically opposed and rapidly shifting beliefs about the "goodness" or "badness" of other people contributes to the borderline

personality's almost constant state of cognitive confusion.[7] Lacking a clear self-perception results in a confused self-concept.

Individuals with borderline personalities also manifest cognitive dysfunction in that they fail to learn from their life experiences.[7] For this reason, they continue to repeat their mistakes over and over again. Their ability to problem-solve; that is, to cope adaptively with anxiety, is seriously impaired.

Affect. Affective instability, marked by shifts from normal mood to anger or depression with return to normal mood often within only a few hours, stands as a cardinal sign of borderline personality disorder.[7] Another striking characteristic of this personality disorder is intensity of affect.[6] Anger, loneliness, depression, emptiness, impatience, self-pity, low self-esteem, and deficient self-confidence are some of the emotions experienced intensely and erratically by the person with a borderline personality.[1, 2] They experience fears of loss and abandonment, intense dependency longings, as well as feelings of entitlement to special care or privileges. Furthermore, when authority figures do not provide immediate relief for their uncomfortable feeling states, these individuals may become rageful, hostile, and jealous.[6]

Subjectively, persons with borderline personalities report feeling scattered, unintegrated, and incapable of following self-chosen pursuits.[7] Instead, they depend on others, not themselves, to give their lives direction and meaning. In this sense, the borderline personality bears an exaggerated resemblance to Reisman's "other-directed person," and as such, stands as a pitiful caricature of today's average person in the street.[11]

Behavioral Disturbances. The behavior of those with borderline personalities dramatically reflects the perceptual, cognitive, and affective disturbances associated with this disorder. Nonverbally, these individuals display their highly changeable and intense affect through impulsive behaviors. Some of these behaviors include extravagant spending, sexual promiscuity, hyperingestion of food and mood-altering chemicals, and, sometimes, antisocial behaviors such as lying and stealing.[7] Furthermore, during stressful periods, they frequently exhibit self-multilative acts, recurrent accidents, and other forms of impulsive self-destructive behavior.[1, 2] To a great extent, whimsical acting-out characterizes the nonverbal behavior of borderline personalities.

The individual with borderline personality disorder may display verbal behaviors that are self-critical, demanding, whining, threatening, manipulative, argumentative, complaining, ingratiating, and blaming.[7] Periodically, these individuals even become verbally abusive to others.[2]

The verbal and nonverbal behaviors of borderline personalities function to anger those individuals with whom they associate. Often, others feel imposed upon or manipulated by the person with a borderline personality disorder and, as a result, they may wish to punish him. The verbal and nonverbal expressions of intense emotions emitted by those with borderline personalities also tend to arouse feelings of fear in others. Sometimes, their families, friends, and associates may actually fear for their own safety. Seldom, however, do borderline individuals become physically assaultive.[2] Nevertheless, persons with borderline personalities are unequaled in their ability to arouse intense and contradictory emotions in their associates.

Level of Adaptation. The life histories of persons with borderline personalities reveal a series of beginnings and endings. Numerous, intense, short-term interpersonal relationships, checkered school and work records, and drastic lifestyle changes reflect the borderline personality's overall unstable pattern. Getting into and out of difficulty becomes a way of life for these persons; consequently, they seldom realize their full potential. Some may even succumb periodically to brief psychotic episodes. Their major strength, however, lies in their ability to recruit enough interpersonal or social support to make another beginning.[7]

Many individuals with borderline personality disorders seek mental health care services. Usually, they present with symptoms of depression, psychosis, or suicidal crisis. Short-term institutionalization may be needed in these instances. Treatment is aimed at reducing the presenting symptoms. Because the borderline personality disorder is a deeply ingrained pattern, it is resistant to treatment. Only the most intensive and prolonged psychotherapy can effect substantial long-term personality and behavioral changes.[2,5,7]

Planning and Implementing Nursing Care for Individuals with Personality Disorders

Nurses may encounter individuals affected with personality disorders in many settings within the health care system (see Nursing Diagnoses on p. 274). Usually, these individuals receive labels such as crock, grump, complainer, or manipulator. Despite the fact that these persons usually are not hospitalized for their personality disorders *per se*, the nurse needs to take their personality behavioral patterns into account when planning and implementing nursing care.

Self-Awareness

To work with personality-disordered individuals, nurses need to develop a high degree of self-awareness. Nurses and other health care providers often experience a number of emotional reactions to these individuals: anger toward the client, defensiveness, wanting to control and dominate the client, excessive preoccupation with the client, and becoming flustered and unable to concentrate during interactions with the client.[17] The nurse needs to tolerate and accept these feelings as natural reactions to personality-disordered clients, and, at the same time, she needs to

Nursing Diagnoses: Personality Disorders

The following nursing diagnoses may be used to describe the behavior of clients with personality disorders.

1. Acting-out to gain control
2. Acting-out to reduce tension/anxiety
3. Manipulation to gain control
4. Violent (verbal/nonverbal) behavior to release tension and/or to reestablish control
5. Blaming to relieve self of guilt/shame or to project own defects to others
6. Decreased impulse control due to weak ego boundaries
7. Low frustration tolerance
8. Ineffective social relations due to
   Excessive need for control or independence
   Excessive dependency needs
   Poor social skills
   Fear of intimacy
   Hostile or angry abusive behavior
9. Splitting
10. Suspiciousness
11. Hyperingestion
12. Depression
13. Clinging "demandingness"
14. Rage
15. Avoidance
16. Shyness

refrain from acting on these feelings. Discussing emotional reactions to these clients with a trusted nurse colleague can increase the nurse's self-awareness and emotional control.

Trust Development

Because many personality-disordered clients tend to mistrust other people, the nurse needs to exercise special care to establish trust. A straightforward, matter-of-fact approach, as opposed to an overly warm approach, is indicated in working with these clients. Punctuality, honesty, respect, and genuineness also add significantly to trust formation.

In verbal interactions with personality-disordered individuals, the nurse should avoid interpreting the client's behavior. The reason for this is that mistrustful clients tend to view interpretations as intrusive and controlling. Instead, the nurse needs to employ open-ended questions designed to help these clients focus on their behavior and its consequences. Nurses must also maintain congruence between their verbal and nonverbal behaviors; incongruent behavior of the nurse often results in these clients becoming more suspicious of her.[17] Some clients may attempt to use such discrepancies to manipulate the nurse and other health care providers.

Confrontation

Confrontation may be necessary to work effectively with personality-disordered clients who attempt to use manipulation.[17] Pointing out a client's problematic behavior to him or her is termed *confrontation*. The purpose of confrontation is to assist the client to become more self-aware.

The keys to effective confrontation include the following.

1. Pointing out the behavior as soon after its occurrence as possible
2. Being specific in describing the behavior
3. Using a nonaccusatory, nonjudgmental, matter-of-fact manner
4. Maintaining the focus on the client's actual behavior rather than the client's explanation of it

Furthermore, confrontation needs to occur in a setting in which the client feels safe and supported. The nurse must exercise sound and sensitive judgment in planning and implementing confrontations with the client. A trusting relationship between the nurse and the client is a prerequisite to the use of confrontation.

Limit-Setting

Manipulative, dependent, and acting-out behaviors displayed by personality-disordered clients may necessitate the nurse's use of limit-setting.[2] It is important to remember that limit-setting is not punitive in nature. Furthermore, limit-setting includes more than merely telling a client to stop a particular behavior. Specifically, limit-setting involves the following.

1. Identifying the behavior that the client needs to control
2. Matter-of-factly requesting the client to control the behavior
3. Offering an appropriate, alternative behavior for the client to pursue
4. Anticipating that the client will test the nurse to determine if she will back down
5. Remaining steadfast and consistent in the use of limit-setting.

Limit-setting must be sensitively and judiciously applied to ensure its effectiveness. Vacillation and backing down after setting limits with a client seriously jeopardizes the development and maintenance of a trusting nurse–client relationship.

Setting limits with clients can pose significant problems for nurses who lack maturity, self-confidence, and the ability to control their own anger and acting-out tendencies. Similarly, nurses who meet their own psychological needs by seeking the approval and affection of clients will be unable to set limits effectively. Effective limit-setting therefore requires both clinical skill and personal maturity.

Summary

This chapter presents the concepts of personality, personality disorder, and anxiety. These concepts provide the necessary background for discussing the perceptual, cognitive, affective, and behavioral disturbances evident in the compulsive, passive-aggressive, antisocial, borderline, schizoid, and paranoid personality disorders. Some of the major points of the chapter include the following.

1. Maladaptive personality patterns or styles may be described as a personality disorder.
2. The behavior of individuals with personality disorders is often narcissistic, dependent, depressed, egocentric, immature, hostile, and manipulative.
3. Anxiety, says Peplau, is the initial response to a psychic threat.
4. Mild anxiety brings with it heightened sensory awareness and alertness.
5. Moderate anxiety may be characterized by frequent changes of topic, wordiness, repetitive questioning, blocking, procrastination, and general restlessness.
6. Severe anxiety state is marked by perceptual distortion and cognitive impairment and may be demonstrated through the individual's tremors, facial grimaces, pacing, and hand wringing.
7. During panic states, concentration, learning, and problem-solving are virtually impossible.
8. A compulsive personality disorder is marked by narrow perceptual focus, intellectual rigidity, anxiety and ambivalence, lack of mirth, inflexible stubbornness, and attempts to control others.
9. The person with a passive-aggressive personality perceives others and the world in general pessimistically, is indecisive and ambivalent, feels unappreciated and misused, and procrastinates or works inefficiently.
10. An antisocial personality disorder is characterized by hostility, antagonism, punitiveness, mistrust, callousness, and insensitivity.
11. Paranoid personalities display pervasive suspiciousness, cognitive disturbances ranging from ideas of reference to delusional systems, hypercritical attacks on others, hostility, projection, guardedness, jealousy, and emotional coldness.
12. Schizoid personality disorder is marked by social withdrawal and extremely shy behavior, impoverished thought processes, indifference, and underresponsiveness.
13. The individual with a borderline personality disorder uses many maladaptive patterns to avoid anxiety—splitting, avoidance, withdrawal, acting-out, and psychosomatization.
14. Nursing care of personality disordered clients requires that nurses develop a high degree of self-awareness, form trusting relationships with clients, and use confrontation and limit-setting techniques effectively.

Therapeutic Dialogue

Confronting a Client with a Personality Disorder

Mr. Samuels has been hospitalized for treatment of an irritable colon. He initially presented with symptoms of abdominal cramps, diarrhea, and dehydration. Additionally, Mr. Samuels displays some behaviors associated with borderline personality disorder, such as erratic and intense moodiness, dependence, hyperingestion of foods and beverages that aggravate his irritable colon, and splitting. Despite Mr. Samuels' tendency to split staff into two groups, "the good guys and bad guys," he has come to trust his primary nurse, Ms. Brown.

Ms. Brown has noticed that Mr. Samuels departs from his therapeutic diet frequently and that his presenting symptoms continue to persist. Mr. Samuels avoids eating his therapeutic diet by being unavailable for meals. Specifically, he is usually sleeping, feeling too ill to eat, or preoccupied with phone calls or visitors when meals are served. In place of the therapeutic diet, Mr. Samuels requests either his mother or girlfriend to bring him unsuitable meals and snacks. Because Ms. Brown has observed these behaviors, she decides to confront Mr. Samuels about his behavior.

Nurse: Have you noticed how frequently you've skipped your prescribed diet?

Client: I guess I've been too sleepy and sick to eat. (whining voice tone)

Nurse: Why do you think you are either asleep or sick at mealtimes? (focusing on the meaning of the client's behavior)

Client: (Mr. Samuels changes the subject and begins talking about his desire to find a new job.)

Nurse: We were discussing your not eating your prescribed diet when you started talking about something else. (re-focuses client on the topic of his eating behavior)

Client: Really. I guess I didn't realize what I was doing. I'm just so tired. Anyway, what difference does it make if I don't eat what they bring me? The hospital gets paid for the food, anyway. (begins to sound somewhat defensive)

Nurse: I don't know if it makes a difference or not. I do know, however, that your irritable colon symptoms have increased. (pointing out a change in his physical condition)

Client: Yeah, I've had some diarrhea, some stomach cramps. So what? (stated in a nonemotional blasé manner)

Nurse: (Remains silent. Further talking would merely be repetitious of what she's already said. Ms. Brown must be able to deal with her own feelings of anxiety during silence and to resist the client's maneuvering her into assuming the major responsibility for the interaction.)

Client: I guess my symptoms are worse but I don't understand why. (unaware of how his eating behavior affects his physical condition)

Nurse: What have you been eating in place of your prescribed diet? (uses open-ended question to gently focus client on his behavior)

Client: Well, either my mom or girlfriend brings me something to eat and drink. But, but I only eat a little. (sounds defensive)

Nurse: What do they usually bring you?

Client: Oh, stuff, you know. Regular food.

Nurse: This seems difficult for you to talk about. (points out client's behavior)

Client: Difficult? No, I don't think so. (facial expression looks somewhat puzzled)

Nurse: (Remains silent to permit Mr. Samuels time to collect his thoughts.)

Client: I always eat just what I'm supposed to. (a somewhat defensive tone of voice)

Nurse: I'm sure you intend to, yet at times it's hard to stick to a diet. (gently interjects possibility of his deviating from diet without being accusatory)

Client: Maybe, uh, uh, you know, sometimes it is.

Nurse: I wonder if there are times that maybe you eat foods you aren't supposed to? (a gentle confrontation)

Client: Once in a while. Mostly, when my mom or girlfriend brings me food.

Nurse: How do you feel physically after eating these foods?

Client: Sometimes O.K. but I guess most of the time I get sick, more diarrhea. Then, I just want to sleep.

The goal of this confrontation is to increase Mr. Samuel's self-awareness regarding how his eating behaviors affect his physical health. Toward the end of the conversation, he begins to recognize that his behavior may lead to an exacerbation of symptoms.

References

1. Chessick RD: The Borderline Patient. In Arieti S (ed): American Handbook of Psychiatry, Vol 3, 2nd ed, pp 808–819. New York, Basic Books, 1975

2. Dubovsky SL: Psychotherapeutics in Primary Care. New York, Grune and Stratton, 1981

3. Ehrmann M: Desiderata. Los Angeles, Brooke House, 1972

4. Lasch C: The Culture of Narcissism. New York, WW Norton, 1978

5. Marin P: The New Narcissism. Harper's (October issue), pp 45–56, 1975

6. Masterson JF: Psychotherapy of the Borderline Adult. New York, Brunner/Mazel, 1976

7. Millon T: Disorders of Personality. New York, John Wiley & Sons, 1981

8. Peplau HE: A Working Definition of Anxiety. In Burd SF, Marshall MA (eds): Some Clinical Approaches to Psychiatric Nursing. New York, Macmillan, 1963

9. Peplau HE: Interpersonal Relations in Nursing. New York, GP Putnam's Sons, 1952

10. Rappeport JR: Antisocial Behavior. In Arieti S (ed): American Handbook of Psychiatry, Vol 3, 2nd ed, pp 253–269. New York, Basic Books, 1975

11. Riesman D: The Lonely Crowd. New Haven, Yale University Press, 1961

12. Ruesch J: Disturbed Communication. New York, WW Norton, 1957

13. Ruesch J: Therapeutic Communication. New York, WW Norton, 1973

14. Salzman L: Other Character-Personality Syndromes: Schizoid, Inadequate, Passive-Aggressive, Paranoid, Dependent. In Arieti S (ed): American Handbook of Psychiatry, Vol 3, 2nd ed, pp 224–234. New York, Basic Books, 1975

15. Shapiro D: Neurotic Styles. New York, Basic Books, 1975

16. Stanton AH: Personality Disorders. In Nicholi AM Jr (ed): Harvard Guide to Modern Psychiatry, pp 283–295. Cambridge, Belknap Press of Harvard University Press, 1978

17. Vaillant GE, Perry J: Personality Disorders. In Kaplan HI, Freedman AM, Saddock BJ (eds): Comprehensive Textbook of Psychiatry/III, Vol 2, 3rd ed, pp 1562–1590. Baltimore, Williams & Wilkins, 1980

Chapter 21
Disorders of Mood: Depressed and Manic Behavior

To die: to sleep:
No more; and by a sleep to say we end
The heartache and the thousand natural shocks
That flesh is heir to, 'tis a consummation
Devoutly to be wish'd. To die, to sleep.

Hamlet

Susan Kah

Chapter Preview

Disturbances of mood or affect illustrate, perhaps more than any other response to stress, that human feelings and behaviors exist on a continuum with no clear demarcation between "normal" and "abnormal" or between health and illness. This chapter focuses on the feelings, thoughts, and ineffective behaviors that characterize individuals who are depressed or struggling against depression. The overview of depressed and manic behavior discusses the incidence, possible causes, and types or diagnostic categories currently employed to facilitate the care and treatment of clients. A major emphasis of this chapter is the application of the steps of the nursing process—assessment, analysis, planning, implementation, and evaluation—to individuals suffering from disturbances in mood.

Learning Objectives

The reader, upon completion of the chapter, should be able to accomplish the following.

1. Compare the biologic and psychosocial theories regarding the etiology of mood disorders
2. Contrast the incidence and symptomatic behaviors of mania and depression
3. List the types of mood disorders according to current diagnostic categorization
4. Discuss primary prevention of disorders of mood
5. Apply the nursing process to the care of manic and depressed clients

   Assess the verbal and nonverbal behavior of clients with disorders of mood

   Describe the problems and potential problems commonly experienced by clients with disorders of mood

   Identify nursing goals and actions designed to alleviate the problems of manic and depressed clients and their families

   Formulate a comprehensive nursing care plan for a client with a mood disorder

   Evaluate the effectiveness of the nursing intervention
6. Recognize and discuss her own feelings and behaviors that may influence the therapeutic use of self

Incidence and Significance of the Problem

Unhappiness that is pathologically intense is called *depression*.[22] Depression has been described as the number one mental health problem in the United States; an estimated 10% to 20% of the population experiences significant episodes of depression.[2,6] Data from the National Institute of Mental Health indicate that one in five Americans has at least moderate symptomatology of depression.[13] The critical nature of the problem is underscored by the fact that an estimated 12% to 14% of depressed individuals die from suicide.[26]

Manic behavior, like depression, is also a disturbance in mood. *Mania*, believed to be a defense against depression, is characterized by varying degrees of elation, hyperactivity, agitation, and accelerated thinking and speaking.

Depression occurs at all ages and does not seem to be related to the pressures produced by any particular civilization or historic age. Infants are described as exhibiting *anaclitic depression* when deprived of a warm, close experience with another individual. This early form of depression in response to neglect is characterized by a lack of social responsiveness and an apathetic mood. School-age children may mask depression with aggressiveness, problematic behavior in school, and psychosomatic complaints.[1] Adolescents frequently abuse drugs and exhibit violent and sexually promiscuous behavior in their struggle against depression. It is also during adolescence that the behavioral manifestations of the depression begin to take on the characteristics of adult depressions.

Depressed adults are overwhelmed by feelings of helplessness, hopelessness, and sadness. These individuals have extremely low self-esteem and experience a decrease in physical and psychic energy, which results in an apathetic withdrawal from the environment. In older adults, depression may take the form of a *pseudodementia*, a false picture of senility caused by depressive symptoms.

History of Depression

The history of depression includes such ancient victims as Nebuchadezzar, Saul, and Herod. Hippocrates believed depression was caused by excessive black bile or melan cholé, from which the word *melancholy* derived. Today this term is sometimes used to denote severe depression. The pains of depression have also been felt by such notables as Dostoevski, Poe, Hawthorne, Darwin, Lincoln, Churchill, and, more recently, vice-presidential candidate Thomas Eagleton and astronaut Edwin "Buzz" Aldrin. It seems that from the dawn of history, depression has been a prevalent disorder, even though an individual's specific reaction to the disturbance may have been shaped by the society in which he lived.

Etiologic Theories

As with many other mental health problems, the cause or causes of depression and mania are not definitely known. Many authorities do agree, however, that in the case of depression, either biologic or psychological factors may result in the same pathological or disturbed behavior. Consequently, theories that focus primarily on biologic or psychological causes should not be interpreted as mutually exclusive theories.

Biologic Influences

Amine Hypothesis

As a biochemical disorder, depression has been associated with a functional deficit of one or more of the brain neurotransmitter amines—serotonin, norepinephrine, and dopamine—at specific nerve cell synapses. This deficit interferes with the transmission of electrochemical impulses from one nerve cell to another. In effect, the cells are "switched off." Conversely, mania is associated with a functional excess of one or more of these amines. This amine hypothesis of the affective disorders provides a basis for understanding the pharmacologic treatment of depression. This mode of treatment of depression through medication will be described more fully later in this chapter.

Evolutionary Development

It has been hypothesized that depressive mechanisms may exist in the biochemical system because they have survival value in the evolution of the human race.[14] The dampening of emotional response may serve as a protective device when submission, passivity, and withdrawal are the most effective reactions to a particular stressful situation. Depression can, therefore, be perceived as a malfunction of an attempt to conserve energy when it would prove fruitless to do anything else.

Familial Influence

Depression seems to occur more frequently in certain families; consequently, it is believed that the predisposition for depression may be inherited. This tendency alone, however, does not necessarily result in clinical symptoms. The depressive process may be triggered by some insult to the integrity of the individual, which overwhelms the person's defenses. Scientists continue to search for the specific genetic link to depression and hope that such knowledge will help identify those who are most susceptible to the disorder. Early identification of susceptible persons should then be followed by primary preventive efforts.

Physical Influences

Depression may occur as a secondary effect of some medications, particularly hormones, sedatives, and antibacterials, and may also occur in conjunction with certain viral infections, such as mononucleosis and hepatitis. Depression that accompanies such physical states presents a much simpler mental health problem than other types of depression.

Psychosocial Influences

A frequently encountered interpersonal theory regarding the cause and dynamics of depression focuses on the importance of a real or perceived loss that the distressed individual has experienced. This sense of loss follows such events as death, divorce, physical separation, or a change in status, role, or state of health. In response to such a loss, the individual becomes profoundly depressed if resolution, the expected outcomes of the adaptive grieving process, is not attained. The depressed individual responds to the loss with feelings of abandonment, frustration, and conscious or unconscious anger, much of which is turned inwardly against the self.

Psychoanalytic View

This view of depression is closely related to the Freudian or psychoanalytic belief that depression has its foundation in oral needs for love and gratification that have been frustrated, usually by a mothering figure. The resulting ambivalent feelings of love and hate produce strong feelings of guilt and a pattern of adult behavior characterized by dependency and a low frustration tolerance. The person may employ various techniques, such as submissive, manipulative, coercive, piteous, demanding, or placating behavior, to maintain this relationship that is desperately needed but that the person has essentially ambivalent feelings about.[7]

Cognitive View

A cognitive model of depression refutes the belief that depression is anger turned inwardly and, instead, conceptualizes depression as a negative way of thinking about one's self, one's future, and one's environment.[4] The individual experiences sadness, loss of spontaneous motivation, loss of interest, indecisiveness, and suicidal wishes because of his idiosyncratic or peculiar views. This theory holds that the individual's cognitive disturbances precede his affective changes. The mobilization of hostility may be helpful, not because it decreases the amount of self-hate, but because it gives the individual a greater sense of control over his environment.

Behavioral View

The behavioral view of depression is illustrated by the assertion that learned helplessness plays a central role in the development of depression. Behaviors that define "learned helplessness," such as passivity, negative expectations, and feelings of helplessness, hopelessness, and powerlessness, are also major symptoms of depression. Those persons who are susceptible to depression have encountered a lifetime of experiences that have taught them that they are ineffective and lack the ability to influence their sources of suffering and gratification.

A review of these and other etiologic theories of mental disorders leads to the conclusion that one cannot deal with the causation and symptomatology of any emotional disorder in terms of a single, discrete influence; depression is no exception. Although perceived as a primarily psychological disturbance in mood or affect, there are significant cognitive and biologic components.

Those treating and caring for the depressed client must ask several questions.

What made the client vulnerable?
What triggered the disturbance?
Why did the client's defenses fail?
What kinds of interventions will help the client to grow?

Types of Affective Disorders

The affective disorders may be categorized in a variety of ways. It may be that the various states commonly called depression are really several different disorders. It is important to remember, however, that such theoretical concerns do not necessarily interfere with offering effective help to depressed clients, especially if that help is based on specific knowledge of the individual and his environment.

If one perceives depression as existing on a continuum from health to illness, and as sometimes serving a useful function, the reaction of *grief* and the process of *mourning* would be placed at the healthy end of the continuum. Most individuals respond to losses in their lives in a fairly predictable way. Denial, usually short-lived, progresses to a developing awareness of the loss, followed by anger mixed with sadness, and then finally a resolution characterized by acceptance of the loss, and, perhaps, idealization of the lost object or individual. Grief, in response to a psychic wound, such as the death of a loved one, can be compared to the pain that accompanies a physical wound. The mourning process, which may take as long as a year, can be compared to the usually more rapid healing of a physical wound. This ability to resolve losses varies greatly among individuals and is dependent upon previous interpersonal experiences, one's ego strength, and the support and resources that are available. Some depressions can be linked to unresolved grief.

Nonpsychotic Affective Disorders

If one moves along the continuum from health toward illness, it becomes apparent that there are some individuals who live out most of their lives in chronic states of depression, which sometimes alternate with periods of *hypomania,* an abnormality of mood ranging between normal euphoria and mania. These individuals, however, do maintain contact with reality and do not experience a personality disintegration that makes hospitalization necessary.

Cyclothymic Disorder

Those clients experiencing numerous periods of nonpsychotic depression and hypomania are described as having a *cyclothymic disorder*. Hypomania or mania is considered to be a defense or reaction formation against the painful experience of depression. Manic behavior has also been associated with an increase or surplus of neurotransmitter amines in the brain. The opposing manifestations of depression and hypomania are seen in the following pairs of symptoms: feelings of inadequacy (during depressed periods) and inflated self-esteem (during hypomanic periods); social withdrawal and uninhibited people-seeking; sleeping too much and not sleeping enough; diminished productivity at work and increased productivity.[2]

Dysthymic Disorder

Clients with *dysthymic disorders* experience periods of chronic depression or a loss of interest or pleasure in all, or almost all, usual activities and pastimes. Periods free from these depressive states may be as brief as a few days or a few weeks. The person with a dysthymic disorder does not evidence hypomanic behavior.

The chronic nature of this disorder is cause for concern because it may be accompanied by a lifelong struggle against depression, which may assume various maladaptive forms. In the attempt to escape feelings of inadequacy, emptiness, loss of energy and vigor, a pessimistic attitude toward the future, and recurrent thoughts of death or suicide, the client may intensify certain activities to generate excitement. Gambling, criminal behavior, promiscuity, and illegitimate pregnancy are examples of such "acting out" behaviors. Intensification of work, spending money, homosexual behavior, mysticism, and intensification of religious interest can also be used in the struggle against depression.

The depressed client may also turn to substance abuse (*i.e.*, the abuse of alcohol and other drugs) to dull or escape his psychic pain. The problems created by the tendency toward depression extend beyond the clinical state that is called depression.[7]

Major Affective Disorders

At the illness end of the mental health continuum, one finds the most severe disorders, which may include psychotic features. A *psychosis* implies an extreme response to stress, such as impaired reality testing and the development of delusions, hallucinations, and affective, as well as psychomotor and physical, disturbances. The client frequently becomes unable to function either at work or as a family member, and may become a danger to himself as well as to others. This client usually requires hospitalization and responds to the structure and milieu he finds in the psychiatric facility. Psychotic episodes are also usually treated vigorously with psychotherapeutic agents. The major affective disorders can become psychotic in nature.

The major affective disorders are divided into two major categories—bipolar disorders and major depression.[2] The essential feature is disturbance involving either a manic episode or a major depressive episode. Although psychotic features may not always be present in the major affective disorders, there is extreme social and occupational impairment.

Bipolar Disorders

A *bipolar disorder* consists of one or more manic episodes, with or without subsequent or alternating major depressive episodes. These manic episodes typically begin suddenly, with a rapid escalation over a few days.

The first manic episode usually occurs before age 30, but is very rare in children and adolescents.[2,8] Most individuals who have manic episodes will eventually have a major depressive episode; however, only about 20% of the adults who experience depression have manic episodes.[8]

The bipolar disorder seems to be equally common in men and women and is frequently described as having a strong genetic or familial component. The not uncommon occurrence of bipolar disorder in the same family suggests that a biogenetic factor may be at least a contributory cause.[18]

Major Depression

Major depression is a disorder of mood wherein an individual experiences one or recurrent major depressive episodes without signs of manic or hypomanic behavior. The onset is variable in length, with symptoms usually developing over a period of days to weeks. It is estimated that at least half of those who experience a major depressive episode will have another one.[2] Major depression seems to occur more frequently in women.

Mental health professionals who work with depressed clients may encounter descriptors of mood disorders that have been used to enhance understanding of the client's situation and condition. Major depression is also referred to as a *unipolar depression*. If the major depression occurs after childbirth, it is called a *post-partum depression*. When it occurs around the 6th decade of life, it may be described as an *involutional melancholia*. If the depressed client is agitated, one says that he has an *agitated depression*; when he is almost inert, one speaks of a *retarded depression*. Depression that seems to occur without any relationship to external events is sometimes referred to as an *endogenous depression*. This is in contrast to a *reactive* or *exogenous depression*, the cause of which is evident in the client's history.

The many terms that are currently in use or have been used in the past to label depression are the result of the efforts of mental health caregivers to provide accurate descriptions of the depressive process. By formulating specific descriptions of the disorder, caregivers are better able to plan the most therapeutic nursing approaches for the depressed client.

Application of the Nursing Process to Disorders of Mood

The application of the nursing process to disorders of mood must focus on primary prevention; that is, the maintenance of mental health, as well as secondary and tertiary preven-

tion, through the provision of care and treatment to those already identified as mentally ill. Primary prevention of the affective disorders is closely related to the etiologic theories previously presented in this chapter. Through secondary and tertiary prevention, the nurse provides needed support and resources to the client. Hopefully, mental health treatment will prevent the possible complications and long-term effects of the major disorders and will promote a higher level of functioning of the client.

Primary Prevention

Primary prevention of mental illness is specifically described as biologic, social, or psychological intervention that promotes emotional well-being or reduces the incidence and prevalence of mental illness in populations.[19] The incidence of depression as a syndrome has been described as increasing, although the presence of severe depressive illness has decreased.[3]

The rapid changes in society with the concomitant stresses and losses of the traditional support systems, such as family, church, and neighborhood, may be contributing to this increasing incidence of depression. One model of the causation of depression in the 20th century indicates that those most prone to depression seem

1. to be women, the poor, young adults, the elderly, and the previously married;
2. to have experienced a previous loss and be subjected to economic, isolating, parental, or marital stressors;
3. to lack both employment outside the home and an intimate relationship;
4. to have three or more children living at home;
5. to earn feelings of love, respect, recognition, and worth in life through another person or group.[13]

Primary prevention of the affective disorders, whether for the vulnerable members of society described or for others, cannot currently be achieved through biologic intervention. There are no physical means, such as a blood test, that can be used to predict depression for specific individuals. In the present absence of biologic intervention, psychological and social preventative efforts assume major importance.

Planning Primary Prevention

Two major goals in the primary prevention of the affective disorders are as follows.

1. The development of a positive self-concept, as demonstrated by self-confidence, self-respect, and even self-actualization
2. Healthy adaptation to loss

The nurse, by virtue of her professional role, finds herself in a variety of situations, such as child health care settings, in which these goals can be pursued.

The self-concept has its foundation in infancy and childhood, and reflects parental perceptions and messages. The parent teaches the child overtly and covertly about his lovability, his worth as an individual, and his ability to master the environment. It is important to assess whether the child learns to initiate ideas and follow through with activity because these activities are recognized and reinforced. Instead of doing this, the child may perceive that he and his efforts are inadequate, useless, and not wanted. Rejection can be devastating to the development of a positive self-concept. Children who experience rejection sometimes conclude that they can only elicit love and approval from significant others if they assume guilt and punish themselves. Children who fail to learn to love themselves may become adults who measure their own worth solely according to the perceptions of others. These "dominant other" individuals become prime candidates for depression.

Promoting Adaptation to Loss

The nurse functions in many practice settings where children and adult clients and families are experiencing growth, development, change, and loss. Hospitalization itself results in loss of status, loss of self-determination, loss of usual family relationships, and perhaps loss of wage-earning ability. In addition, clients may be adapting to a changing body image, a changing lifestyle, and even the loss of life.

Some of these losses can be anticipated, and clients can be helped to adapt through anticipatory guidance and other supportive nursing actions that allow for verbalization, sharing of feelings, and problem solving. Some situations involving loss, such as death of a child or rape, can become crises for the individuals involved. The nurse's ability to recognize the existence of crisis and to intervene or arrange for others to do so may facilitate adaptive behaviors and may prevent depression. The reader is referred to Chapter 31 for more information on helping individuals deal with overwhelming stressors in their lives.

Nurses who participate in health education programs, such as prenatal and postnatal education, sexuality and family planning, genetic counseling, age-specific parenting groups, and support groups for those in transition, widows, divorcees, retirees, and so forth, are providing knowledge and exploring feelings so clients can maintain control over, and derive satisfaction from, their own lives. Nurses who practice in community health agencies, in doctors' offices, in well baby clinics, and in pediatric care settings have many opportunities to promote healthy parent–child relationships. The nurse's knowledge of growth and development can be used to help parents understand their children's behavior and, just as importantly, feel more positively about themselves.

In summarizing, the nurse, regardless of the nature of her practice, provides health education and reinforces the self-esteem of clients as integral aspects of her care. The nurse participates in the primary prevention of depression, which is certainly not limited to psychiatric treatment settings, where only a small percentage of potential and existing depression is recognized and treated.

Secondary and Tertiary Prevention

Secondary prevention seeks to reduce the prevalence of mental disorder by providing intervention that decreases the number of stressors and shortens the duration of disequilibrium. Tertiary prevention refers to measures used to reduce the level of social defects that result from mental disorder. This type of prevention often includes rehabilitation and readaptation to the environment.[19]

The nurse participates in the secondary and tertiary prevention of the affective disorders through the application of the nursing process—assessment, analysis, planning, implementation, and evaluation—in client care settings. Although individuals with affective disorders can be found virtually anywhere, the following discussion focuses on the client in a psychiatric care setting. The nurse is reminded, however, that the application of nursing knowledge and skill is never bound by a location or setting.

Assessment and Analysis

Nursing assessment and analysis of depressive and manic behaviors can be systematically accomplished through a thorough consideration of the client's affect, thought processes, intellectual processes, and physiological and psychomotor activity. The nurse both identifies problems that the client has in these areas of functioning and begins to chart the course for the goal-setting nursing intervention that will follow the assessment process. The following discussion includes observations that the nurse commonly makes when encountering clients with manic or depressive disorders. Bear in mind that no two clients present exactly the same history and behavior and the nurse should avoid the tendency to perceive clients with a mind set created by "textbook" descriptions.

Affective Changes

Affect in Depression. One area of assessment that provides essential data in the determination of a nursing diagnosis is the client's affect. Because depression and mania manifest themselves primarily as disturbances in mood or affect, the emotional tone of the client may be the most obvious deviation from healthy behavior. The depressed client appears sad, dejected, apathetic, and uncomfortable in his painful suffering, but does not usually exhibit bizarre behavior. He feels hopeless and, at the same time, helpless to do anything about his situation. He may verbalize feelings of guilt as well as feelings of anger or hostility. The client is unable to feel pleasure or experience joy.

These verbalized and, perhaps, unverbalized feelings are consistent with the physical appearance of the depressed client. There is frequently a disregard for grooming, cleanliness, and personal appearance. The client's stooped posture and dejected facial expression are also nonverbal messages of depression. During observation and communication with the depressed client, the nurse may begin to perceive that depression can actually be a defense against sadness and grief. Depression seems to raise the client's threshold for pain, thereby protecting the client from more pain than what is already being experienced by him.

Depression in Children. Because children are frequently unable to express feelings verbally, childhood depression is difficult to detect and may be reported less frequently than it actually occurs. Children tend to act out their emotional problems. Anger, aggressiveness, hyperactivity, delinquency, and school problems may be just as indicative of depression as sad, tearful faces, withdrawal from activities, and verbal expression of poor self-esteem.[1]

Affect in Mania. The manic client's mood is in direct contrast to that of the client experiencing depression. The manic client is self-satisfied, confident, and aggressive, and feels "on top of the world" and in control of his destiny. His flight into the external world, however, is also a defense against sadness and grief. The client's anger, sarcasm, and irritability become evident when the nurse attempts to set limits on his behavior or when he is frustrated by other individuals or objects in the environment.

When assessing the client's affective changes, the degree of the change is one of the most important judgments the nurse makes. Is the client mildly depressed, severely depressed, exhibiting retarded depression, or in depressive stupor? The mildly depressed client requires a less intensive approach than the severely depressed client, who sees no reason to continue living. The nurse must also observe for changes in the client's affective state, which would indicate that he is responding to other modes of therapy.

Thought Processes

Thought Processes in Depression. The thoughts of the depressed or manic client are congruent with his feelings; there is no dichotomy between thought and affect. The depressed client ruminates about his unhappy situation, discussing it repeatedly and asking the same questions to which no one can give a satisfactory answer. Thinking may be difficult and slow; the content becomes limited to a few topics. Replies to the nurse's questions may be delayed and condensed, and the client does not reveal his private thoughts.[25]

In depression, there is frequently a heightening of awareness of inner sensations and a reduction in the awareness of external events.[22] This inability to mobilize attention to events in the outside world may lead to delusional thinking. These delusions or false beliefs, however, are consistent with the client's affective state. Delusional content is frequently characterized by self-deprecation, ideas of guilt, and remorse. There may also be a suspicious and persecutory trend to the client's ideas; that is, he may believe that he is being persecuted by others. Delusions may

also be hypochondriacal in nature. The client sometimes believes he has a consuming illness that is destroying him from within, perhaps cancer.

The depressed individual thinks he is a failure and is totally pessimistic about his future. He believes that his life will not improve and he will not be convinced otherwise. The depressed client is filled with self-reproach, thinks in absolute terms, and becomes averse, rather than simply indifferent, to opportunities for change.

Suicidal Ideation. Because depression is characterized by many negative thoughts and accompanying feelings of self-hate and hostility, one of the most critical areas for the nurse to assess is the degree of the client's suicidal ideation. What thoughts does the client have about taking his own life? How great is the risk that he might try to do so? An accurate assumption for the nurse to make is that all depressed clients are potentially suicidal. The question is not "is he?" but "to what degree is he?"

Although a data base for the assessment of suicide risk has not been scientifically established, statistics have been recorded that point toward some helpful generalizations. It has been estimated that more than 80% of the 22,000 to 25,000 suicides reported annually can be traced to a previous depressive episode.[6,10] In addition to the severity of depression being directly related to the degree of suicidal risk, there are other behaviors or symptoms that the nurse must include in the assessment of the depressed client. The presence of anxiety, hopelessness, withdrawal, disorientation, and hostility all indicate a higher risk of suicide than in depressions that are not characterized by these feelings and behaviors. Those clients who do not have social and personal resources, such as housing, transportation, money, employment, and available significant others are also at higher risk for suicide than those who do have these resources. A history of alcohol and drug abuse is a likely cause for added concern in the assessment of suicidal potential. Substance abuse behaviors are predominantly self-destructive coping strategies. Clients who have a history of multiple, high lethality suicide attempts, such as by shooting, are also greater suicide risks than those who have no such history. The client who frequently verbalizes the desire to die and describes a very specific plan is also someone who requires immediate intervention.

Depression, like suicide, is an attempt by the client to communicate a state of deprivation. If the depression does not elicit the desired responses from others, suicide may become the next course of action. Suicide can be viewed as a last desperate cry for help or love when no other avenues of communication exist for the client.

Thought Processes in Mania. Nursing assessment and diagnosis of the hypomanic or manic client's thought processes reveals different kinds of material. In all degrees of mania, there is little introspection.[18] In fact, the manic individual evades thinking and is occupied with phonetics rather than meaning in his thinking and speech. His stream of thought is characterized by a rapid association of ideas, termed *flight of ideas*, with rhyming and play upon words. Although these thoughts seem illogical, the client's remarks are very similar to free associations prompted by unconscious thoughts and feelings. The following is an example of flight of ideas.

"How do I feel? I feel with my hands. How do you feel? No, seriously, everything is wonderful; couldn't be better. Going 'from bad to worse' Benchley said. Really, honey, this is a marvelous place you've got here. Mar-vel-ous. Mar-vel-ous. Vel. I really must shampoo my hair.

In his euphoric state, the manic client is full of ambitious schemes and exaggerations that belie reality. Delusions often occur and are usually expansive, fleeting, and wish-fulfilling. The manic client may erroneously believe that he has great wealth and power. He is too busy to submit his ideas and impressions to critical examination. His desperate need to convince others of his grandiosity should alert the nurse to the very strong feelings of inadequacy that he is trying to overcome.

Intellectual Processes. Intellectual processes included in the nursing assessment of the client with a disorder of mood are perception, consciousness, and orientation. Disorders of these processes, in conjunction with the changes in affect and thinking already described, often leave the client with decreased powers of judgment and decision-making. In such instances, the nurse must determine to what extent it may be necessary to assume decision-making for the client and when this action is therapeutically warranted. Although autonomous behavior is a long-term goal for every client, there are times during acutely severe depression and mania when the nurse must make decisions for the client because he is unable to do so for himself.

Perception. The depressed client's perception may be distorted because of his intensive affective state. He perceives the world as strange and unnatural. A client with deep feelings of guilt may interpret the sound of wind in the trees as reproaching voices. This misinterpretation of a real sensory experience is called an *illusion*. The severely depressed client may less frequently experience *hallucinations*, perceptions that occur when there is no impulse created by the stimulation of a receptor. Auditory hallucinations are the most frequent form of perceptual disturbance and, if they do occur, they usually represent the projection of affective distress. An example of this projection occurs when the depressed client hears voices blaming him or telling him that he is worthless.

Hallucinations may occur in manic excitement but are not common.[18] As is the case with depression, perceptual disorders of manic clients usually take the form of illusions.

Consciousness. Among disturbances of consciousness are those imposed by disordered attention. Attention is the conscious, selective reaction by which an individual examines the external world for useful data.[18] Feeling and attitudes influence attention, and both depressed and manic clients may exhibit problems in the area of attention. The depressed client's attention may be so tenaciously directed toward his limited mental content that nothing will divert his energy elsewhere.

The severely depressed client may be so fearful of some impending disaster that he may actually become confused. Retarded depression, in which there is an inhibition of stream of thought and psychomotor activity, may result in *stupor*. In depressive stupor, there is almost complete immobility, a clouded sensorium, and intense preoccupation.

The manic client, on the other hand, is easily distracted by people, noises, and activity in the environment. Because of this inattention or distractibility, the manic client may fail to discriminate among objects and people. The most severe form of mania, called delerious mania, is characterized by purposeless and continuous activity.

Orientation. Disorientation as to who one is, to where one is, and to time may occur in any mental disorder in which there is extensive impairment of the client's memory, the extent or accuracy of his perception, or his attention.[18] Because the intensely depressed or manic client may experience such impairments in orientation, the nurse assesses the client's understanding of his environment and how he locates himself in it.

A consideration of the client's intellectual processes also includes the assessment of the client's insight. *Insight,* which depends upon perceptual accuracy and consciousness, refers to the client's ability to observe and understand himself, or to the extent of self-knowledge.[18] The depressed client, acutely aware of his suffering, knows he is ill and usually demonstrates some desire to end his suffering. Unfortunately, his ambivalence and mistrust of others may interfere with an effective use of the resources available. The manic client, on the other hand, denies his many conflicts as well as the awareness that he is coping with them in a very unhealthy way.

Physiological and Psychomotor Activity. Depression and mania are physical states as well as psychological ones. An assessment of the client with an affective disorder would be incomplete without a thorough consideration of his physiological status and psychomotor activity.

Physical Effects of Depression. The depressed client has been described as an individual in whom a deficit in psychic energy is accompanied by a decrease in physical energy. All erotic, constructive, and reproductive activities come to a standstill.[22] Physiologically, depression manifests itself in a variety of ways. The client has difficulty sleeping, is anorectic, and loses weight. His muscle tone is decreased. Constipation may result from poor eating patterns and inactivity. Women may experience menstrual irregularities and amenorrhea. Sexual desire is decreased; the male client may be impotent. The client feels continually fatigued and may complain of physical symptoms for which no organic basis can be found. A delusional client may refuse to eat or drink because he believes he is undeserving of sustenance.

Unless agitated by feelings of anxiety, most depressed clients are lethargic and withdrawn, and resist social contacts. The depressed client lacks interest in personal hygiene and normal grooming routines. His hair and clothes may be unkempt and his body may be in need of bathing.

Physical Effects of Mania. The manic client presents some of the same problems for care but for different reasons. Nutritional deficits may exist because the client will not take the time to eat or cannot attend to this activity for sufficient amounts of time. Dehydration may occur for the same reasons. Because the manic client's continuous activity may not result in a feeling of fatigue, exhaustion may result.

The manic client may dress in bizarre ways and may use make-up inappropriately. He does not attend to personal hygiene. Acute episodes of mania may be accompanied by singing, shouting, writing, or destruction of clothing and property. The client may intrude in the activities of others or may collect objects. Although this overactivity is purposeful, the client does not attain his objective or goal because he does not complete tasks or projects.

The overactivity of the manic client makes it difficult for the nurse to detect signs and symptoms of physical illness that may accompany his physical debilitation. Careful nursing observation may detect signs of an infection, such as pneumonia, to which the client may be too busy to attend.

Nursing assessment of the client with an affective disorder must be a continuous process. The client's mood may change quickly and the potential for suicide is great. Physical illness may complicate the client's care. The disturbances in affect, thought, intellect, and psychomotor activity described should serve as general guidelines. The changes from the normal to depressed state are summarized in Table 21-1. When the client begins to receive treatment, especially through medication or electroconvulsive therapy, his behavior may change. The nurse must remember that somatic treatment of depression, although helpful for the client, makes nursing assessment more difficult to accomplish.

Planning

The nurse can plan care for the client with an affective disorder with a legitimate feeling of optimism. Both mania and depression are time-limited conditions; in most instances, the nurse will see the client return to a healthier, functioning state. This does not mean, however, that nursing and medical care are not needed. Both can shorten the intensity and length of these affective states and can, perhaps, save the client's life.

There is no single way to approach depressed or manic clients. It is essential that the nurse perceive the client as an individual. The nurse's perceptions should be shared and compared with those of other members of the health care team. Client-centered goals should be a combined effort of those associated with, or responsible for, the care of the client, including the client and his family when possible.

Goal Setting for the Depressed Client. Frequently, assessment of the depressed client will result in goals that are related to the following needs.

1. Physical safety and health
2. Expression of painful negative feelings
3. Love, acceptance, a feeling of belonging rather than one of isolation
4. Feelings of being useful and needed
5. Opportunities to achieve worthwhile accomplishments
6. Opportunities for autonomy and self-actualization

These client needs are quite naturally a direct consequence of the essence of depression—a lonely, loveless, and hopeless state. They are realistic goals for the nurse to pursue as they all depend upon relationships with other human beings. They are also goals that transcend the experience of hospitalization.

Goal Setting for the Manic Client. Assessment of the manic client will result in a somewhat different list of needs during the manic state.

1. Physical safety and health
2. Opportunities to channel physical and psychic energy
3. Accurate perception of reality

The manic client has the same underlying needs for love and autonomy that the depressed client exhibits in a more obvious manner. During the manic episode, however, the client's strong denial necessitates that the nurse postpone most interpersonal actions that may help the client meet these needs.

Discharge Planning. Most clients with affective disorders have functioned in society as adult family members and will be able to do so again in the future. Planning, therefore, must extend beyond the time and place of hospitalization. The client's family must be incorporated into the plan of care to prevent the client from feeling abandoned and alone.

Other resources, such as church, work, and social groups, must be maintained if at all possible.

What employment opportunities will be available to the client?

What opportunities for socialization will present themselves to the client?

Who can the client turn to when he feels stressed?

Table 21-1.   **Changes from Normal to Depressed State**

ITEMS	CHANGES	
	Normal State	*Depressed State*
Stimulus		**Response**
Loved object	Affection	Loss of feeling, revulsion
Favorite activities	Pleasure	Boredom
New opportunities	Enthusiasm	Indifference
Humor	Amusement	Mirthlessness
Novel stimuli	Curiosity	Lack of interest
Abuse	Anger	Self-criticism, sadness
Goal or Drive		**Direction**
Gratification	Pleasure	Avoidance
Welfare	Self-care	Self-neglect
Self-preservation	Survival	Suicide
Achievement	Success	Withdrawal
Thinking		**Appraisal**
About self	Realistic	Self-devaluating
About future	Hopeful	Hopeless
About environment	Realistic	Overwhelming
Biologic and Physiological Activities		**Symptom**
Appetite	Spontaneous hunger	Loss of appetite
Sexuality	Spontaneous desire	Loss of desire
Sleep	Restful	Disturbed
Energy	Spontaneous	Fatigued

(From Friedman J, Katz MM (eds): The Psychology of Depression: Contemporary Theory and Research. New York, John Wiley & Sons, 1974)

These and similar questions must be answered as the nurse and other members of the mental health team plan with the client and his family for his return to home and community.

Intervention

Nursing Intervention for the Depressed Client. After assessing the client's needs and identifying goals for the client with an affective disorder, the nurse identifies nursing actions that are designed to achieve these goals. It is important that the nurse remember that behavior changes slowly and the client may have periods of regression. Realistic expectations about behavior change must accompany the nurse's actions. Even minor changes in the client's behavior should be considered significant; nursing approaches should not be discarded prematurely.

Physical Safety and Health

Decreasing Suicidal Risk. The depressed client's needs for physical safety and health require that the nurse maintain a constant vigil for the possibility of suicide and other self-destructive behaviors. Once the nurse has determined that the client is suicidal, several actions are warranted. The client should be observed frequently or continuously on a one-to-one basis. Most obviously, the nurse must make sure that the environment is as free from poten-

tial danger as possible. Items such as belts, razor blades, scissors, and other sharp objects should be removed from the client's immediate environment. The nurse should also be very aware of the medications that the client is taking and the possibility of his hoarding dosages for future lethal ingestion. Pill overdosage is the most common form of successful suicide and suicidal gesture.[10] If the client leaves the unit or hospital for any reason, he and his belongings should be carefully searched upon return. Psychiatric facilities should have a detailed written description of "suicidal precautions," which are implemented when clients are identified as suicidal. The nurse should become very familiar with these and assume responsibility for their initiation, enforcement, and modification.

There is a close relationship between suicide and crisis theory. The nurse may view the suicidal state as a therapeutic opportunity. The client may be ready to learn new coping skills that he can continue to use after the crisis has subsided. If the nurse has not already established a relationship with the client, it is imperative that the nurse or some other member of the health care team do so at this time. If suicide is a cry for love, help, and attention, the client must feel that these needs are perceived by someone in the environment and that he is cared for. The risk of suicide may be so great that the nurse may determine that the client should not be left alone, even in the bathroom. Letting the client know that his stressful situation is acknowledged and communicating that he will receive support and help in controlling his impulses are important interventions. Gratifying dependency needs during this acutely stressful period may reduce the client's level of anxiety, which, in turn, decreases the risk of suicide.

The nurse, in addition to meeting dependency needs, should also use the therapeutic relationship with the depressed client in order to help him gain an understanding of the crisis, to help him become aware of and accept his feelings, which may be very hostile, and to explore coping mechanisms other than self-destruction.

The nurse bases her reactions to the suicidal client on certain beliefs. The client who talks about suicide does commit suicide, and threats and attempts must be taken seriously. The nurse must not deny the client's feelings by shying away from discussing suicidal thoughts. Such discussions will not cause the client to commit suicide or make him more suicidal; they will probably reduce some of his anxiety. Suicidal clients are ambivalent about dying, and the nurse should maximize those arguments the client accepts or offers for living. The client who commits suicide is not necessarily psychotic or even mentally ill. In fact, in many instances, the risk of suicide is greatest when the client is emerging from the depths of depression and appears to be improving. The client then has the physical and mental energy to conceive a plan and carry it out. The client may actually feel and communicate relief once he has found a final solution (*i.e.*, suicide) to his problems. For more indepth information about suicide, the reader is referred to Chapter 34.

Ensuring Physical Health. The client's physical health and safety are frequently concerns when the nurse cares for the depressed client. The severely depressed client does not attend to bodily needs and may not have the energy to care for himself. The nurse should consider the following actions as long as the client cannot do these for himself.

1. Bathing the client
2. Assisting with the client's grooming, such as care of hair and nails
3. Selecting appropriate clothing
4. Ensuring the intake of nutritious food, which may mean sitting with the client as he eats
5. Clearing the environment of potential hazards, such as misplaced furniture, slippery rugs, and poorly lighted areas
6. Maintaining a record of sleeping patterns, bowel function, and menstrual function
7. Identifying the need for further nursing and medical actions

Promoting Physical Activity. The depressed client should be encouraged to engage in physical activity for several reasons: 1) to expel energy, 2) to produce feelings of physical well-being and control, and 3) to produce feelings of accomplishment (see insert, The Brain–Body Phenomenon). Because joy accompanies activity, it is suggested that the client participate in active behaviors that were previously reinforcing to him, such as jogging, tennis, or housekeeping chores, even if he doesn't want to do them.[16] The client progresses from solitary activity to noncompetitive activity with others to competitive activity with others.

Monitoring Side Effects of Medication. Because the depressed client is usually receiving antidepressant medication, the nurse should also be familiar with the side effects of these medications. These frequently include constipation, dry mouth, and sedation. Other side effects are loss of

The Brain–Body Phenomenon

Walking, Running, and Dancing Your Way to Mental Health

Although it is unclear why, physical fitness enhances mental health. Walking, jogging, bicycling, swimming, and aerobic dance are popular forms of exercise that may be powerful antidotes to depression and anxiety.

Exercise produces a sense of enhanced mental energy and concentration. Joggers express feelings of heightened mental acuity and hours of clear-headedness after running.

Exercise relieves tension. Strenuous activity is all-absorbing, not allowing the participant to worry about anything else. Tension may not return until hours after exercise. Stress on one body system may help relax another.

Exercise is adult play, accompanied by joy and lightheartedness.

Exercise produces a sense of self-worth. Participants set progressive goals that are achievable and not in competition with others. It's hard to feel sorry for yourself and exercise at the same time.

Exercise produces a sense of control. It gives the participant freedom not experienced in other aspects of life. The cyclist or jogger does not depend on anyone else for exercise.

Exercise can symbolize active participation in life and serve as a socially acceptable way of asserting oneself.

Mental energy, lightheartedness, self-worth, autonomy, and assertiveness are the antitheses of depression. Movement, through physical exercise, may be a prescription of choice for disturbances in mood.

visual accommodation, headache, dizziness, nausea and vomiting, increased perspiration, and weight gain. These side effects can be minimized or avoided by gradually increasing the dosage to the optimal therapeutic level.[9] The nurse should discuss possible side effects with the client and should encourage him to report them to members of the health team.

Expression of Feelings

Exploration of Anger and Sadness. The depressed client fears open communication and intimacy; nevertheless, feelings that rage inside him need some form of expression. In every phase of its development, depression includes a component of anger, whether that anger is visible or invisible, conscious or unconscious.[22] Regardless of whether the client appears angry or not, he needs someone with whom he can share his sadness and verbalize his guilt. The nurse must not be intimidated or discouraged by these interactions with the depressed client. Sometimes, nurses mistakenly assume that it is a nursing responsibility to "make things better" for the client. Even if the client professes extreme helplessness, the nurse must not approach him as though he were a helpless being.

The nurse may find it useful to explore with the client what is helping to maintain his depression. Once the client identifies his own depression-reinforcing behaviors used to elicit sympathy from others, such as crying, the client may decide to stop engaging in these behaviors. He may even decide to stop talking about his depression.

Therapeutic Communication. The nurse engages in active listening and demonstrates acceptance of whatever feelings and thoughts the client communicates (see the sample dialogue, Encouraging the Expression of Feelings). If the nurse withdraws or more overtly rejects the client or his feelings, she reinforces his belief that it is not safe to express oneself and that others don't care about him. It is very important that the nurse does not try to talk the client out of his sadness by being inappropriately cheerful and optimistic or by offering false reassurance.

Therapeutic Dialogue

Encouraging the Expression of Feelings

Nurse: Sarah, you mentioned you were in the hospital because you attempted suicide; tell me more about that. (sitting on a bed next to the client, maintaining eye contact, leaning toward the client)

Client: I took an overdose of Elavil. I ended up in Intensive Care for 4 days. I just couldn't take it anymore. I had to get out of the house. (looking at the nurse, speaking calmly and deliberately)

Nurse: Then you didn't intend to kill yourself? (asked in a questioning manner, trying to make eye contact with the client)

Client: No, it was the only way I could get away from my parents. (The client, Sarah, is a 32-year-old woman with muscular dystrophy who is confined to a wheelchair.) They don't support me; they didn't even come to see me when I was in Intensive Care. (maintaining intermittent eye contact with the nurse, wiping tears off cheeks)

Nurse: You wanted them to care? (speaking softly)

Client: Yes. You know it's hard watching your body deteriorate a little bit at a time. Every day I lose something. I remember when I could dance like everybody else. (affect very sad, still maintaining intermittent eye contact) I'm depressed, but I've got a good reason to be depressed. There's no cure for me; I'm just getting worse.

Nurse: It's a heavy burden for you. (maintaining eye contact with the client)

Client: Yes. (nodding head) So I've got to use my mind. That's the only thing I have left.

Discussion

Sarah voluntarily mentioned her suicidal behavior to the nurse who did not hesitate to explore this further. Suicide is accompanied by an intense feeling state; there is a need to verbalize and share.

The nurse attempts to clarify Sarah's feelings and the meaning of her suicidal behavior. Sarah expresses ambivalent feelings toward her parents; she wants to leave them, but she wants them to care. The nurse has not yet begun to explore the origin of these feelings, nor the alternative ways to express them.

The nurse conveys a sincere interest in the meaning of, and the feelings associated with, the client's behavior. The nurse neither moralizes about the act of suicide, nor challenges the client with the possibility that she really had no intent to take her own life.

As Sarah has explained, her depression can be associated with a very real, ongoing loss. She seems to be communicating that she needs more help to cope with the feelings of anger and frustration inherent in her situation. The nurse identifies this need, which will become an important focus in Sarah's plan of care.

Cultural Influences. The expression of feelings is greatly influenced by one's cultural heritage. Southern Europeans and Latins tend to be very expressive; Northern Europeans and orientals do not. Some believe that to express one's feelings is a sign of weakness to be avoided at all costs. This belief is demonstrated in the subculture of sex. In many societies, it is acceptable for girls and women to express their feelings, but not for boys and men. As the nurse implements care, these cultural differences must be considered.

Positive Reinforcement. Another helpful approach in the treatment of depression is the concept of positive reinforcement. The nurse may advocate the use of an "anti-depression" kit, which contains pleasuring items, memorabilia of happy times, or reminders of future activity.[17] The client creates this kit for himself and resorts to it when he feels depressed.

Effects on the Caregiver. Depression is contagious, and depressed people tend to drive others away from them. Depressed clients are repetitively negativistic and sometimes clinging and manipulative. Nurses often feel frustrated and angry at themselves in return. Planning and sharing the client's care with other members of the health team provide the nurse with an opportunity to express and explore her own feelings and a means of group support. The client's family, who may have been likewise frustrated, may be encouraged by learning that depression is self-limiting and that they can look toward a time when the client will recover and return to a more normal level of functioning. The family members' involvement in the client's plan of treatment may help to determine the degree of adaptation and growth that the entire family is able to achieve as a result of the depressive episode.

Feelings of Acceptance and Belonging. The nurse can initiate a therapeutic relationship with the depressed client to facilitate his feelings of acceptance and belonging. The nurse may schedule regular times to meet with the client, thereby ensuring privacy and communicating that he is important as an individual. These individual appointments with the client should be arranged only as the nurse can realistically implement and follow through. The nurse's trustworthiness and consistency are paramount issues in providing care for the depressed, or any, client.

The nurse must also maintain a sensitivity to the environment and constantly question how other clients and staff influence the depressed client. Is he being included in activities? Is he relating to others and on what level? The psychiatric-mental health nurse generally has more opportunity to make such observations and manipulate the environment to the client's benefit than anyone else on the health team.

Feelings of Being Useful and Needed and Feelings of Accomplishment. Hospitalization and illness, whether for mental or physical reasons, usually imply that the client will experience a certain degree of helplessness and dependency.

Consequently, it is often a difficult task to engender in the client feelings of being useful and needed. Nevertheless, the nurse should use whatever opportunities arise to promote the development and reinforcement of these feelings in the client. As soon as he is ready, the client should participate in client groups that share in decision-making for the unit or facility in which he is receiving care. The client should also be encouraged to assume some responsibility for planning and carrying out social activities and share in other unit tasks.

A severely depressed client may not be able to function as an effective member of a group; expecting him to do so may reinforce a negative view of himself. The nurse must assess the client carefully before communicating her expectations. Perhaps the severely depressed client would benefit from an initial one-to-one relationship that is gradually expanded to include a larger sphere of people.

The nurse can foster the client's sense of accomplishment by encouraging him to identify what achievements would make him feel better about himself and to focus on one of them. These achievements could be very simple, such as getting out of bed at a certain time, dressing oneself, not spilling coffee. It is beneficial to encourage the client to focus on what he has done, rather than on what needs to be accomplished, and never to miss an opportunity to congratulate himself.[15]

The nurse should not overwhelm the client but should encourage him to spend time only with those people with whom he feels comfortable. Successful achievement within the hospital may help the client feel that he can also be effective outside the hospital. Discharge planning must include a consideration of what in this client's future life will permit him to feel needed and useful.

Are there family members to whom he is important?
Is there an occupation in need of his talent?
To whom or what does he make a difference?

Opportunities for Autonomy and Self-Actualization. Autonomy and self-actualization are frequently identified as characteristics of the mentally healthy individual.[20] Autonomy is a component of self-actualization and implies a relative independence of the physical and social environment. The autonomous individual is not dependent for his main satisfactions on the real world, including the people in it, their opinions and affections. The need for self-actualization is exhibited by the individual who must do what he, individually, is fitted for. He must be true to his own nature. Both autonomy and self-actualization are long-term goals toward which many individuals strive during most of their lifetime.

Learned helplessness and dependency, the opposites of autonomy and self-actualization, are frequent companions of depression. The severely depressed client may not be able to take care of his own bodily needs, decide how to dress in the morning, or choose what to have for breakfast.

He is, therefore, even less able to make decisions about relationships, financial needs, or occupational matters. In some situations, the nurse must make such decisions for the client until his anxiety level decreases and he shows other indications of increased decision-making ability. The nurse does what must be done to mobilize the client and this frequently requires a very directive approach. The client is not asked if he would like to have breakfast; he is told that it is time for him to have breakfast. If given a choice, most depressed clients would decline such invitations to eat. In this instance, the nurse may appear to be taking away the client's autonomy; however, this is not so. The client cannot be deprived of his autonomy when, in fact, he has surrendered it to his depression.

As the client progresses, the nurse encourages the client to listen to himself and assume more of his own decision-making. The nurse's own problem solving skills provide both support and a corrective educational process for him. What does he perceive as his problems? What are possible solutions to these problems? What are the possible outcomes of such solutions? What puts the client in control of himself and his situation? If the client can recognize his potential for self-direction and development, he is taking a step toward health and away from a mode of thinking that plays a central role in depression—helplessness.

Nursing Intervention for the Manic Client. Nursing care of the manic client is focused primarily on maintaining the physical health of the client until his manic state subsides, usually as the result of medication. A client who is in a manic state seeks to release tension through physical activity and may not be aware of his other physical or psychological needs. The client's flight of ideas prevents significant interpersonal contact.

Physical Safety and Health. The increased mobility of the manic client ranges from mild motor excitement to incessant activity. The client's talking, singing, dancing, and teasing is frequently accompanied by weight loss, a decrease in food consumption, insomnia, and constipation. The nurse intervenes by keeping environmental stimuli to a minimum. For example, the nurse may keep the client away from areas where others are engaging in noisy physical activity. The client is extremely distractible and reacts to almost any stimulus in the environment.

Unrealistic demands by the client are also a potential problem and are best approached with partial fulfillment of the demand whenever possible. The nurse tries to avoid direct confrontations by letting the client know what he can do rather than what he can't do. A client's request to go outside at night, for example, could be answered with the information that he will have the opportunity to go out in the morning, if this is in fact so. In this manner, the client is able to focus on the positive aspects, rather than the limitations placed on his behavior.

At times, it may be necessary to use the client's distractibility to ease him out of a troublesome situation. The client's euphoric mood can change quickly to one of irritation, or even rage, when he sees that others don't respond to his enthusiasm or react in accordance with his expectations.

Promoting Physical Health. By not aggravating the client's excitability, the nurse may find it easier to attend to his physical needs. The client cannot be expected to sit down for complete meals, but he can be given foods and liquid to carry around with him. These foods should be high-calorie and high-protein substances to meet his increased energy expenditure. The nurse should also monitor the client's sleeping and elimination patterns because these basic needs may be neglected. Nursing or medical intervention may be necessary to promote proper rest and elimination. The client should also be observed carefully for signs of illness because he may be in a debilitated state and may ignore or be unaware of developing symptoms of physical disease.

Lithium Therapy. Nursing actions to promote physical health must also include close observation of the client who is taking lithium to counteract manic behaviors. Lithium is a potentially dangerous drug that is 80% effective in the short-term management of the manic phase of a bipolar disorder.[11] The amount of drug that is therapeutic is only slightly less than the amount that produces toxicity. This difficulty in regulating the precise dosage of the drug is compounded by the fact that no two clients respond entirely the same to lithium or absorb or excrete it at exactly the same rate.[11]

Lithium therapy requires the monitoring of clients' blood levels at frequent intervals. The initial stabilization phase may be followed by a maintenance phase during which the dose is reduced. Because some clients may be maintained on lithium for an indefinite period of time, the nurse should ascertain what the client understands about his need for lithium and should help him accept the probability of continuing therapy for an extended length of time.

The nurse should also consider introducing the client to another individual who is taking lithium so they may share information and problems. The client's family also needs to be alerted to the effects and side effects of lithium, as well as to the importance of monitoring the reappearance of manic behavior. The reappearance of manic behaviors may first evidence as a sleep disturbance or an increase in alcohol consumption by the client.

Because the client must be able to eliminate lithium from his system, kidney function tests are desirable before therapy is initiated. An electrocardiogram (ECG) and electrolyte and thyroid studies should also be performed to determine if the client is a suitable and safe candidate for lithium therapy.

Clients and their families must know that lithium should not be taken with diuretics and should be advised of the signs of lithium toxicity. Fortunately, when toxicity

Case Study

Caring for the Client Who Is Struggling Against Depression

The S. Family consists of Mr. and Mrs. S. and their two sons, 15-year-old Robert and 12-year-old Andy. Robert, tall and blond, was brought to an inpatient psychiatric treatment facility by his mother who verbalized great concern about Robert's abuse of drugs and alcohol. The admitting physician diagnosed Robert as being "depressed" and "anxious."

During the admission process, the mental health care team gathered additional data from both Mrs. S. and Robert. Approximately 3 days before this admission, Robert had been treated in a hospital emergency room for a drug overdose. At that time Robert did not know what drugs he had taken and he was very angry and fearful.

Mrs. S. described Robert as being a "bright" and "good" child, although he never seemed interested in cuddling or kissing. She perceived him as being self-sufficient and hyperactive. Mrs. S. explained that Robert's behavior changed about 1 year ago. At that time, he started missing school, he failed a grade, and his abuse of drugs escalated to the point that Mrs. S. feared for Robert's life.

Family interaction, according to Mrs. S.' description, appears chaotic and turbulent. Mrs. S. indicated that she believes in physical discipline of her children but receives very little support with them from her husband. She described Mr. S. as uninterested in the family and pointed out that she even manages the financial affairs of the family.

Upon admission, Robert stated, "I don't have a problem," but was willing to put in the necessary time so he "could get out of here." Robert described his mother as being physically abusive to both him and his brother since Robert was 5 or 6 years old. Robert related that when he was 6, he put a plastic bag over his head and said he wanted to die.

The nurse gathered Robert's history a short time after he was admitted for treatment. When the nurse and Robert talked alone, he answered questions very briefly and offered no spontaneous comments or conversation. Robert's eye contact with the nurse was minimal; his affect was moderately depressed.

The nursing history resulted in the following additional data. Robert is enrolled in a work-study program and plans to continue with school when he returns home. Robert stated that no one at school really cared whether he attended or not. He also said he would like to enlist in the Air Force after completing high school or earn an equivalency diploma and learn to fly. If he doesn't learn to fly, he said, he'd like to work around planes in some capacity, perhaps as a mechanic. Robert's vocational experience is limited; he worked as a delivery boy for 2

weeks, but quit because he wasn't earning enough money.

Robert's interests are presently limited to drugs and rock music. He stated that he has no close friends, even though he abuses drugs in the company of others (it's "no fun", he said, to do it alone). He perceives his relationship with his parents as "not too good" because they don't approve of his behavior. Robert said he doesn't have much to do with his younger brother, Andy. When asked to describe himself, Robert replied, "I'm a regular kid doing what I want to do."

This is Robert's first hospitalization for any illness. He considers himself physically healthy. When the nurse inquired about his use of drugs and alcohol, he stated matter-of-factly that he consumes about two quarts of whiskey per week and smokes marijuana daily. During the last 2 years, he has also used mescaline, LSD, oxycodone (Percodan), and methaqualone (Quaalude). Although not clearly relating it to his use of drugs, Robert also mentioned that he is currently on probation for trespassing.

During his first week of hospitalization, Robert gradually became acquainted with the staff and some of the other clients. He was perceived as being intelligent, sometimes sociable, and usually cooperative, although somewhat guarded. He frequently paced the floor. At times, he played pool or ping pong with one or two young male clients or watched television. Robert went to bed late and got up late, sleeping 10 to 12 hours a night.

Robert's treatment included occupational therapy, recreational therapy, psychotherapy, and family therapy. The latter was considered to be especially crucial to Robert's treatment. The staff also projected that Robert would need to become involved in a drug rehabilitation program following hospitalization.

The initial family therapy session was attended by Mrs. S., Andy, and Robert. Mrs. S. described herself as being at her "wits end" and expressed a great deal of hostility toward her husband, whom she perceived as undermining everything she tried to do. During this first session, Robert was not communicative—he denied having problems and wanted to know "what all the fuss was about."

The entire family, including Mr. S., attended subsequent family therapy sessions, and Robert was gradually able to express how his feelings were related to his parents' dysfunctional relationship. His desire to modify his behavior, however, remained questionable.

The nursing care plan for Robert focused on establishing a relationship with him to facilitate expression of feelings about his family and hospitalization. Because his inability to function at home and school precipitated his admission, Robert's day was carefully structured with activities in which he was expected to participate.

After almost 3 weeks of inpatient treatment, Robert was discharged to a drug rehabilitation program. Robert's physician judged that Robert's prognosis was guarded, however, because he lacked motivation and insight.

Questions for Discussion

1. Which of Robert's behaviors are "typical" for the adolescent? Which ones are not?
2. To what possible "losses" can you relate Robert's struggle against depression?

3. How has the relationship between Robert's parents affected him?
4. Can Robert's drug abuse be related to his mother's past physical abuse of him? How are they similar or different?
5. For Robert, could drug abuse be a form of suicide? Explain why or why not.
6. What other nursing care approaches would you formulate for this client?
7. Robert's physician indicated that Robert's prognosis was guarded because he lacks motivation and insight and his behavior is ego syntonic. Do you agree with this? Why or why not?

occurs, it usually occurs in progressive fashion and is detected before harm comes to the client.[11]

If mania is severe, the client may initially be given a major tranquilizer because lithium's therapeutic effects require at least 1 week of administration to manifest themselves. During this lag phase in the treatment, the nurse should keep in mind that high doses of drugs such as chlorpromazine (Thorazine) and haloperidol (Haldol) will mask the nausea and vomiting of lithium toxicity. Close and continuous nursing observation is essential to safeguard the client during psychopharmacological therapy.

Opportunities for Channeling Physical and Psychic Energy. A creative nursing approach to the manic client is critical in the planning of his treatment. The nurse attempts to reduce the client's accelerated manner of thinking and speaking by presenting accurate feedback to him. For example, when the client moves rapidly from one topic to the next, the nurse informs him that she does not understand him and asks for clarification. When interacting with this client, the nurse may find it necessary to refocus or redirect the conversation so that only one topic is being discussed at a time. Although these nursing approaches may meet with limited success, the nurse has an obligation to provide accurate information to the client about how he is being perceived by others. It is usually best to avoid long discussions with the manic client. If he has access to paper and pen or pencil, the manic client will often write voluminously. Writing may, in fact, provide a therapeutic benefit to the individual who can use this medium to express his feelings. The nurse may involve the client in gross motor activities, such as sweeping, mopping, or other tasks, and some noncompetitive physical exercises to channel his hyperactivity. The client's attention span is short; therefore, his participation in games and sports, which require sustained interest and adherence to rules, is usually unsuccessful. Monitoring and directing of the client's activity are essential components of the nursing care designed to prevent his exhaustion.

Reinforcement of Reality. The manic client is expansive in his thinking and may be delusional. He may believe he exerts great power and control and possesses great wealth. He may identify with the influential people in the environment; for example, he may be found making rounds with doctors or nurses. The client may communicate to other clients that he can secure hospital passes for them. The nurse mirrors reality for the client by responding to him as the client he is. The nurse does not challenge the client's beliefs, but neither does she encourage his delusional thinking.

Consistency in Approach. Because of the manic client's propensity to manipulate those in his environment, it is essential that those responsible for his care communicate with one another and respond to the client in a consistent manner. The client can be argumentative and demanding; the nurse should not respond in kind. The nurse and other mental health caregivers set limits on the client's behavior consistently and with confidence, knowing that they have planned and chosen the most appropriate interventions according to the client's need.

Other Therapies. The nurse should be aware of, and may be involved in, various other forms of therapy indicated for the client with a disturbance in mood. These therapies include various forms of group therapy, chemotherapy, and electroconvulsive therapy.

Group Therapy. Depending on his level of wellness and his ability to interact with others, the depressed client may benefit from involvement in remotivation therapy. This structured form of group therapy focuses on reality orientation, building self-esteem, relationships with other clients in the group, and family therapy. A group comprised entirely of depressed clients is usually avoided, because the nature and extent of the interaction within the group would be limited. The manic client is usually disruptive to others in a structured group situation and may not benefit from this therapeutic approach.

Chemotherapy. Chemotherapy plays a significant part in the treatment of both depression and mania. Antidepressant and antimanic drugs are employed to alleviate the client's symptoms but do not resolve the psychosocial issues that may hve precipitated the client's disorder. Because these drugs help make the client more amenable to other types of intervention, those responsible for the client's care must take advantage of this effect. Chemotherapy should never be the sole form of treatment for the client.

The nurse who administers antidepressant and antimanic drugs to clients must be familiar with the intended therapeutic effects, the signs of toxicity, the side effects, the contraindications, and the usual dose and route of administration. The nurse must observe the client carefully to verify that he is taking his medication. Both manic and depressed clients may have perceptions that convince them that drugs are not necessary or that drugs are even harmful to them.

Antidepressant medications are expected to increase the client's level of activity, increase his appetite, and improve his sleep patterns. They are also expected to elevate mood and decrease self-accusatory or delusional thoughts. Lithium, the drug usually prescribed to treat mania, effectively decreases the client's excessive elation, hyperactivity, and accelerated thinking and speaking. A complete review of the medications indicated for disorders of mood is included in Chapter 19.

Convulsive Therapies

Insulin Therapy. Before the advent of chemotherapy in the treatment of psychiatric disorders, various types of shock therapy were administered to the client in the hope that behavior change would result. The use of shock therapies dates from 1933, when large doses of insulin were injected into the schizophrenic client to produce a deep hypoglycemic state as a form of treatment of schizophrenia.

Electroconvulsive Therapy. Electroconvulsive therapy (ECT), first used in 1938, is the application of a small dose of electricity through electrodes placed on the client's temples. Both insulin and electroconvulsive therapy are in use today. There is still no satisfactory explanation for the therapeutic action that results from either type of shock therapy.

The primary indication for electroconvulsive therapy is depression. Acutely manic clients who are threatened by exhaustion may also benefit from this type of treatment. Because chemotherapy has proved to be effective in the treatment of mood disturbances, electroconvulsive therapy may be less often indicated or may be considered only when the client does not respond satisfactorily to medication.

Electroconvulsive therapy, a relatively safe procedure, sounds more ominous than it actually is. Nevertheless, the nurse should keep in mind, that strong feelings of fear and anxiety may be elicited when one mentions this type of treatment to clients and families. The client may envision electrocution or death or may anticipate permanent intellectual changes. Both the physician and nurse must carefully explain what the treatment is like and prepare the client for the aftereffects. The nurse can be supportive of the client to the extent that she has knowledge about, and has resolved her own feelings about, the use of ECT. The client's fear of ECT should never be used against the client in the form of a threat or coercion.

The client is prepared for ECT in a manner similar to preparation for surgery. The nurse assures that he has no food or drink the morning of the treatment, voids just prior to the procedure, removes dentures, and wears a hospital gown or loose clothing. The client must give his informed consent and the appropriate form must be signed. A complete physical examination of the client is required, including a spinal x-ray. Vital signs are monitored before and after the treatment.

The ECT treatment is usually administered in a room that is designated for this purpose and that adjoins a recovery area. The client is placed on a stretcher or firm bed. A rubber mouthpiece is inserted in the client's mouth to maintain an airway. In some instances, the client is given intravenously a short-acting anesthetic, such as methohexital (Brevital), and a muscle relaxant, frequently succinylcholine (Anectine), just before the electric shock is administered. Electrodes are applied to the client's temples, the shock is administered, and the client experiences a typical grand mal seizure with tonic and clonic phases. The nurse and others in attendance should not attempt to restrain the client's body but should guide the extremities so that they do not become injured during the seizure activity.

When the seizure ends, oxygen may be given as a safety measure because apnea may occur physiologically in any general convulsive seizure. Consequently, airways and equipment for oxygenating the client should be readily available in the treatment area.

Once the client is transferred to the recovery area, he will regain consciousness quickly. While he is awakening, he should be positioned on his side to prevent aspiration of oral secretions. The nurse monitors the client's vital signs during the recovery period. It is usual for the client to be confused. The client must be observed carefully to insure his safety and must be reoriented to his surroundings. The client should be permitted to rest after the treatment and should then be helped to get his breakfast.

The client may or may not be hospitalized for ECT treatments. Such treatments are usually given three times a week; the number of treatments the client receives depends upon the results obtained. The physician may originally plan six treatments, but may continue to 25 or 30 treatments according to the client's response. The nurse's observations of the client during this time are important in the decision-making regarding the number of future treatments.

A frequent aftereffect of ECT is memory impairment that may range from a mild tendency to forget details to severe confusion. This memory impairment may persist for weeks or months following the last ECT treatment. The nurse prepares the patient for this confusion and assures him that it is expected and that full return of his memory will eventually occur.

There are many theories about why ECT is effective in depression. Some authorities believe that the confusion and impairment of memory the treatment produces permit a denial that reduces the intensity of the client's conflict and his awareness of anger and disappointment.[22] Other theories hold that the client perceives ECT as well-deserved punishment and therefore feels less guilty. Electroconvulsive therapy has also been described as a "flight into health" that the client chooses over the threat of ECT. Others maintain that physical changes occur (*e.g.*, cerebral anoxia) that cause improvement in some unknown way.

Evaluation

The nurse evaluates care of the client with a mood disorder by observing the client's behaviors and comparing them with previously formulated client-centered objectives. The nurse also collects data relating to the client's behavior by talking with the client's family and other health team members who are involved in his care. The nursing process is cyclical in nature, and evaluation results in a reassessment of client problems, the formulation of new or modified objectives, and the specification of additional or modified nursing actions that are intended to bring the client even closer to his optimal state of health.

As the depressed client interacts with the nurse and others during this evaluation phase, the nurse can consider the following questions: Has the client's self-concept become more positive? Does the client give any indication of suicidal ideation? Has the client's outlook become more optimistic? Has the client's dependency decreased? Is decision-making easier for the client? Does the client interact more frequently with others? Does the client sleep more and complain less of fatigue and other physical maladies? Is the client's appetite improved? Is he gaining weight? Is the client attending to personal hygiene and grooming? Positive responses to questions such as these usually indicate that the client has begun to assume control over his own life and is motivated to participate in some of the activities of daily living.

When evaluating care of the manic client, the nurse may ask the following questions: Are the client's psychomotor activity and speech becoming slower and more regulated? Is the client less distractible? Does the client have a more realistic perception of his influence and abilities? Is the client more introspective? Are the client's dress and use of make-up more appropriate? Is the client sleeping more and able to monitor his own physical needs?

The client's return to a healthier state is dependent upon the efforts of all members of the health care team, including family members, friends, and the client himself. When the client returns home, these resources must still be accessible as he encounters many stressors that will test his newly acquired confidence. The client may have new living arrangements to which he must adapt, a new job in which he must succeed, and altered or new relationships to establish and maintain. The client must continue to have someone with whom to share his feelings and validate his perceptions and problem-solving skills.

Summary

This chapter has focused on the characteristics of two very different but related behavioral patterns, depression and mania, and the nursing care that may be indicated for each. Both depression and mania have been presented as extreme feeling states with cognitive and physical components that differ primarily in degree, rather than in kind, from those experienced by healthier individuals. The following facts and ideas have been presented.

1. Mood disorders, described early in recorded history, are a major mental health problem in the United States.

2. The cause or causes of mood disorders have not been established with any certainty; etiologic theories include both biologic and psychosocial influences.

3. Mood disorders can be chronic as well as acutely psychotic and can be masked by various maladaptive behaviors, such as alcoholism and promiscuity.

4. Manic behavior is psychodynamically perceived as a defense against depression.

5. The nurse has a responsibility to participate in the primary prevention of mood disorders as well as in the secondary and tertiary prevention.

6. The nurse is a collaborator with other members of the health care team, including the client and his family, and assumes an influential role in determining the client's care and treatment, which have both psychosocial and biologic components.

7. Nursing assessment and intervention for the depressed client focus on the client's physical health and safety, his feelings about himself and others and the expression of these feelings, and distorted perceptions and false beliefs about the environment and himself.

8. Suicide, frequently an outcome of depression, can be prevented.

9. Nursing assessment and intervention for the manic client focus on the client's physical health, the channeling of the client's energy, environmental manipulation, and reinforcement of reality.

10. Somatic therapy, including chemotherapy and electroconvulsive therapy, is a vital component of the treatment plan for a client with a disturbance in mood.

11. Nurses and other mental health professionals need opportunities to express, explore, and resolve their feelings of anger and frustration that may develop as a result of their work with depressed and manic clients.

Nursing Care Plan

The Depressed Client

Client Problem	Goal	Intervention
Suicidal ideation	Prevention of suicide	Establish a nurse–client relationship to meet client's dependency needs, reduce his anxiety, monitor risk of suicide, and help client identify alternatives to self-destructive behavior.
		Carefully monitor ingestion of medication.
		Control the client's access to objects in the environment that can be used for self-destructive purposes, such as pointed objects, belts, light bulbs, and mirrors.
		Maintain constant observation by nurse and other members of the health care team.
		Engage the client in diversional activities; avoid constant focus on suicidal preoccupations.
		Follow "suicide precautions" established by treatment facility, if warranted by client's behavior or ordered by client's therapist.
		Encourage the client to take responsibility for his own behavior whenever this behavior is a therapeutic possibility.
Inability to care for self	Provision of adequate nutrition	Expect the client to eat regular meals; do not give him a choice about whether or not to eat.
		Remain with the client during meals to determine his eating patterns; maintain intake and output records if necessary.
		Allow as much time as client may need for eating; client may need to be fed.
		Encourage the client to eat with whom he feels comfortable.
	Promotion of personal cleanliness and attractive appearance	Bathe client daily, if necessary, and supervise related activities, such as mouth and skin care.
		Shampoo and comb hair if client cannot do it for himself.
		Assist the client with other aspects of grooming, such as the use of deodorant, make-up, and nail care.
		Select appropriate clothes for the client and assist with upkeep as necessary.

Client Problem	Goal	Intervention
		Recognize the client's efforts to maintain his own appearance; do not become impatient if his self-care is slow.
		Reinforce what the client can do for himself rather than focus on what must be done for him.
	Promotion of rest and exercise	Expect the client to participate in physical exercise on a daily basis; try to incorporate activities the client previously enjoyed.
		Gradually encourage the inclusion of others in physical activities, as they become more enjoyable for the client.
		Prevent accidents; maintain a safe environment for the client.
		Establish regular hours for sleeping and wakefulness.
		Consider prohibiting day time sleeping if the client has difficulty sleeping at night.
Inability to express feelings	Expression of negative feelings, especially those of isolation and anger	Initiate interaction with the client on a regular basis.
		Be direct and honest with one's own feelings.
		Allow for verbalization of feelings, "You look very annoyed this morning."
		Encourage physical expression of feelings, such as striking pillows or a punching bag and hammering appropriate objects.
		Avoid impulses to cheer up the client or to try to talk him out of his depression.
		Explore with the client what is helping to maintain his feeling of depression (What are the secondary gains?).
		Avoid focusing on physical complaints (for which there are no organic bases); redirect the client to other topics and areas of concern.
		Share the responsibility for this intervention with other members of the health care team.
Negative view of self, low self-esteem, feelings of worthlessness	Encouragement of positive view of self and feelings of usefulness	Schedule regular times with the client that ensure privacy and communicate his importance as an individual. *(Continues on p 298)*

Client Problem	Goal	Intervention
		Do not overwhelm the client with attention or with too many ideas at one time.
		Point out to client that self-deprecating comments block communication.
		Do not allow the client to ruminate about failures in the past; redirect the client to present problems or involve the client in another type of activity.
		Identify with the client achievements that would make the client feel better about himself and ask the client to focus on *one* of these.
		Help the client recognize opportunities to congratulate himself, however modest his accomplishment may seem.
		Include the client in group activities that provide for some degree of success.
		Assign responsibilities that are important yet not too difficult for the client to assume.
Interpersonal dependency	Development and reinforcement of autonomy	Make decisions for the client during those periods when the client is unable to assume this responsibility.
		Support the client's attempts at decision making.
		Encourage and role model the use of the problem-solving process in decision-making.
		Insist that the client delineate the problem, propose alternate solutions, and consider the outcomes.
		Allow sufficient time for the client to think and act.
		Clearly communicate what is expected of the client (attendance at meals, etc).
		Be specific about the amount of time that can be spent with the client and adhere to this limit.
		Spend time with the client in group situations.
		Point out to the client his insensitivity to others' needs and help him identify other ways of behaving.
		Help the client formulate a written schedule of activity, first on a day-to-day basis, then for longer periods of time, to foster feelings of control.

Nursing Care Plan

The Manic Client

Client Problem	*Goal*	*Intervention*
Hyperactivity, accelerated thinking, and speaking	Sufficient rest, decrease in rate of verbal and motor activity	Keep environmental stimuli to a minimum.
		Provide the client with sufficient room in which to move about.
		Engage the client in physical activities or tasks that channel his energy, such as writing, drawing, or sweeping.
		Interrupt impulsive acting out behavior whenever possible and encourage the client to work towards self-control; respond to dangerous or destructive behavior with swift and coordinated intervention.
		Try to minimize the client's activity at night.
		Offer warm baths or soft music to promote sleep.
		Tell the client when his conversation is not understandable; help him focus on one idea at a time.
Inability to care for self	Adequate nutrition	Provide finger foods for the client to carry around with him; do not expect him to sit down for three meals a day.
		Choose foods for the client that will provide needed additional calories and will also meet basic nutritional needs.
		Provide abundant fluids.
		Maintain an intake and output record, if warranted.
	Personal cleanliness, appropriate dress	Remind the client to bathe, brush teeth, use toilet.
		Help the client select clothing that is appropriate to the climate and situation and that is easy to take on and off.
Delusional thinking grandiosity	Accurate perception of self and abilities	Do not reinforce the client's delusions through discussion or validation.
		Do not challenge the client's beliefs.

(Continues on p 300)

Client Problem	Goal	Intervention
		Reinforce reality by responding to him as the person he is; do not laugh at him.
		Be prepared to protect the client from himself; he may give away possessions.
Demanding behavior	Adherence to limits	Set no more limits than are necessary for the client, then enforce the limits.
		Provide simple explanations when denying requests; avoid argumentation whenever possible.
		Use persuasion rather than force.
		Partially fulfill a demand, if this is feasible, to spare the client complete frustration.
		Consider postponing a decision about a client's request if more data are needed.
Manipulative behavior	Perception of others as individuals	Maintain close communication with other members of the health care team so all are responding to the client in the same way.
		Control own feeling of anger toward the client to prevent loss of the situation.
		Point out to the client his manipulative behavior and interrupt the pattern.

References

1. Albright A, Murphy CM, Rhyne MC: Depression in Children: Reasons and Risks. Pediatric Nursing 6 (July/August): 9–13, 1980

2. American Psychiatric Association, Diagnostic and Statistical Manual of Mental Disorders, 3rd ed. Washington DC, American Psychiatric Association, 1980

3. Arieti S: The Power of the Dominant Other. Psychology Today 12 (November): 54–58, 92–93, 1979

4. Beck A: The Development of Depression: A Cognitive Model. In Friedman RJ, Katz MM (eds): The Psychology of Depression: Contemporary Theory and Research, pp 3–27. New York, John Wiley & Sons, 1974

5. Beck CT: The Occurrence of Depression in Women and the Effect of the Women's Movement. J Psychiatr Nurs Ment Health Serv 17 (November): 14–16, 1979

6. Brown BS: Forward to Friedman RJ, Katz MM (eds): The Psychology of Depression: Contemporary Theory and Research. New York, John Wiley & Sons, 1974

7. Chadoff P: The Depressive Personality: A Critical Review. In Friedman RJ, Katz MM (eds): The Psychology of Depression: Contemporary Theory and Research, pp 55–69. New York, John Wiley & Sons, 1974

8. Chapman AH: Management of Emotional Problems of Children and Adolescents, 2nd ed. Philadelphia, JB Lippincott, 1974

9. DeGennaro M, Hymen R, Crannell AM, Mansky PA: Antidepressant Drug Therapy. Am J Nurs 81 (July): 1304–1310, 1981

10. Fuller E (ed): Caring for the Suicidal Patient. Patient Care 14 (November 30): 101–134, 1980

11. Harris E: Lithium. Am J Nurs 81 (July): 1311–1315, 1981

12. Hatton C, Rink A, Valente SM: Suicide: Assessment and Intervention. New York, Appleton-Century-Crofts, 1977

13. Jacobson A: Melancholy in the 20th Century: Causes and Prevention. J Psychiatr Nurs Ment Health Serv 18 (July): 11–21, 1980

14. Kline N: From Sad To Glad. New York, Ballantine Books, 1974

15. Knowles RD: Coping With Lethargy. Am J Nurs 81 (August): 1465, 1981

16. Knowles RD: Handling Depression Through Activity. Am J Nurs 81 (June): 1187, 1981

17. Knowles RD: Handling Depression Through Positive Reinforcement. Am J Nurs 81 (July): 1353, 1981

18. Kolb L: Modern Clinical Psychiatry, 9th ed. Philadelphia, WB Saunders, 1977

19. Lancaster J: Community Mental Health Nursing: An Ecological Perspective. St Louis, CV Mosby, 1980

20. Maslow A: Motivation and Personality, 2nd ed. New York, Harper & Row, 1970

21. Nelms BC, Brady MA: Assessment and Intervention: The Depressed School Age Child. Pediatric Nursing 6 (July/August): 15–19, 1980

22. Ostow M: The Psychology of Melancholy. New York, Harper & Row, 1970

23. Rosenbaum M: Depression: What to Do, What to Say. Nursing 80 10 (August): 65–66, 1980

24. Seligman MP: Depression and Learned Helplessness. In Friedman RJ, Katz MM (eds): The Psychology of Depression: Contemporary Theory and Research, pp 83–125. New York, John Wiley & Sons, 1974

25. Swanson A: Communicating With Depressed Persons. In Backer B, Dubbert P, Eisenman E (eds): Psychiatric/ Mental Health Nursing: Contemporary Readings, pp 165–173. New York, Van Nostrand Reinhold, 1978

26. Wold CI, Tabachnik N: Depression as an Indicator of Lethality in Suicidal Patients. In Friedman RJ, Katz MM (eds): The Psychology of Depression: Contemporary Theory and Research, pp 187–202. New York, John Wiley & Sons, 1974

Chapter 22
Retreat from Reality:
The Schizophrenic Disorders

While I was at Grace Hospital, it was my sense of hearing which was the most disturbed. But soon after I was placed in my room at home, all of my senses became perverted. I still heard the "false voices"—which were doubly false, for Truth no longer existed. The tricks played upon me by my senses of taste, touch, smell, and sight were the source of great mental anguish.

> Clifford Beers,
> A Mind That Found Itself: An Autobiography
> 1923

Barbara Schoen Johnson

Chapter Preview

This chapter focuses on the disturbances in reality orientation, thought processes, and social involvement that are known as *schizophrenia*. These serious emotional disorders cause an untold burden on human lives. The overview of schizophrenic disorders will discuss its incidence, current theories of etiology, and types or diagnostic categories of the disorder. The following sections of the chapter will apply the steps of the nursing process—assessment, analysis/nursing diagnosis, planning, intervention, and evaluation—to individuals with schizophrenia and their families and communities.

Learning Objectives

On completion of the chapter, the reader should be able to accomplish the following.

1. Discuss biologic and psychosocial theories of the etiology of schizophrenia
2. Identify the types of schizophrenia
3. Describe the behaviors of schizophrenic disorders, particularly the thought, affective, and social/behavioral disturbances
4. Formulate nursing diagnoses and goals for the schizophrenic client and his family
5. Intervene therapeutically in the schizophrenic client's thought, affective, and behavioral disturbances
6. Discuss the effects of chemotherapeutic agents in the care of schizophrenic clients
7. Evaluate the effectiveness of nursing actions designed for clients with schizophrenic disorders
8. Identify means of intervention with populations at risk for the development of schizophrenic disorders
9. Discuss own feelings and attitudes when caring for schizophrenic clients

Schizophrenic Disorders

Schizophrenia is a common and unsolved mental health problem in the world today. It is estimated that 1% of the United States population is, or has been, affected by the disorder. Its onset usually occurs early in life—adolescence or young adulthood—and often becomes a progressive and disabling condition. Far-reaching economic, family, and community effects add further stress to the lives of these severely disturbed individuals and their loved ones.

Although multiple etiologic theories have been proposed and studied, the definitive cause, or causes, of schizophrenia remain unknown. Current methods of prevention and treatment are often inadequate and fall into the category of "too little, too late."

Some types of schizophrenia appear to exist in all populations, regardless of culture.[23, 24] There are, however, different incidence rates of schizophrenia when compared cross-culturally.

Most likely, schizophrenia is not a single disease, but a *heterogeneous disorder*; that is, a group of several distinct disorders, or a collection of disorders, with some common features.[11, 33] These common features include a disturbance in thinking and an extreme preoccupation with the self and with inner fantasies.

The person who has a schizophrenic disorder may live in his own world—a world inhabited by "voices" that condemn or accuse him of vile acts, and "visions" of frightening animals, monsters, or scenes. The person may be totally withdrawn from the external environment and may invest all of his energy in an internal fantasy life. He may regress to a level wherein he does not attend to personal hygiene, activities of daily living, interpersonal contacts, or even the presence of physical illness or pain.

Etiologic Theories

There exist today many theories of the etiology of schizophrenia (see the insert, Historical Perspectives). The search for a cause is spurred on by the hope that discovery of the cause, or causes, of schizophrenia will result in the determination of a cure.

Currently, there are two main groups of theories regarding the etiology of schizophrenia—the biologic theories and the psychosocial theories. The view that schizophrenia is a collection of disorders, rather than a single disorder, implies a variety, or combination, of etiologies.[33]

Biologic Theories

According to the biologic theories, the etiology of schizophrenia is related to organic or physiological factors. These biologic theories are discussed according to genetic and biochemical influences.

Genetic Influences. There is evidence of a genetic factor in the causation of schizophrenia.[10] A higher incidence rate of schizophrenia occurs in the relatives of schizophrenics than in the general population. It has also been demonstrated that the closer the family relationship, the higher the incidence of schizophrenia in the relatives. For example, if a man is known to have schizophrenia, the chance that his son will also develop schizophrenia is much greater than the chance that his nephew will become schizophrenic. In addition, the incidence rate of schizophrenia will be greater for both the man's son and his nephew than it would be for the general population.

Genetic influences in the development of schizophrenia have been demonstrated through the study of twins. Twin studies have shown that if one of monozygotic ("identical") twins becomes schizophrenic, the incidence

Historical Perspectives: Views of Schizophrenia

Some important figures in medical history have conceptualized, developed, and refined what today is known as "schizophrenia."

Emil Kraepelin

At the end of the 19th century, Emil Kraepelin (1855–1926) differentiated from the rest of mental disorders a condition he called Dementia Praecox. This diagnosis implied a fatalistic prognosis, because dementia, Kraepelin believed, occurred precociously or early in life and led a gradual, but continual, downhill course leading to intellectual deterioration. Kraepelin attributed the etiology of this disorder to an endogenous factor such as organic pathology or an error of metabolism, not to societal influences.

The identified symptoms of Dementia Praecox included hallucinations, delusions, disorders of thought and consequently speech, poor insight and judgment, flat affect, and reduced attention to the outside world.

Eugen Bleuler

The Swiss psychiatrist Eugen Bleuler (1857–1930) renamed the syndrome "schizophrenia" to indicate the "splitting" of various mental functions. Bleuler classified the disorder's symptoms into two major categories.

1. Fundamental symptoms (also known as the "four As"), symptoms that indicated the underlying process specific to schizophrenia, including

   associative disturbance, or thought disturbance;

   affective disorder; that is, a flat or blunted affect or one which was inappropriate or incongruous to the thought or situation;

   autism; that is, detachment from external reality and withdrawal into fantasies;

   ambivalence, or the simultaneous existence of opposing feelings, thoughts, and desires.

2. Accessory symptoms, or symptoms that were frequently present but not specific to schizophrenia nor diagnostic of it, including hallucinations, delusions, and catatonic posturing.

Sigmund Freud

Sigmund Freud (1855–1939) emphasized the importance of psychological factors in the etiology of schizophrenia. He described the process of the development of hallucinatory psychoses, which, he felt, originated from frightening and unbearable ideas. He coined the term *projection* and described it in relation to paranoid disturbances.

Adolf Meyer

Attention to the psychological factors in the development of schizophrenia was also advocated by Adolf Meyer (1866–1950), a Swiss-born and Swiss-educated psychiatrist who became a prominent medical authority in America. Meyer proposed that the longitudinal study of schizophrenic patients would offer insights into various etiological influences.

Carl Jung

Carl G. Jung (1875–1961) discussed the idea of certain individual's "predisposition" to emotional disturbance. He saw the schizophrenic patient as an "introvert" who directs a great deal of energy into himself. Jung also considered the possibility of a psychosomatic factor in operation in schizophrenia; he proposed that an emotional disorder could cause a metabolic disturbance and, eventually, physical brain damage in psychotic patients. One of Jung's important concepts was the "collective unconscious," which stores the archetypes, or mythological images, of all people. Jung thought that the symptoms of schizophrenia were "reproductions of the archetypes deposited in our collective unconscious."

Harry Stack Sullivan

An American psychoanalyst, Harry Stack Sullivan (1892–1949), examined the impaired interpersonal relations, not the intrapsychic forces, that predominate in schizophrenia. He believed that children who were later to become schizophrenic adults had undergone disturbed interpersonal relations with their parents and significant others. Sullivan's major life work was the psychotherapy of schizophrenia in which he interacted, not as an observer, but as a participant with the patient.

(From Arieti S: Interpretation of Schizophrenia, 2nd ed. New York, Basic Books, 1974; Cancro R: Individual psychotherapy in the Treatment of Chronic Schizophrenic Patients. Am J Psychother 37 (October): 493–501, 1983; and Goldstein WN: DSM-III and the Diagnosis of Schizophrenia. Am J Psychother 37 (April): 168–181, 1983)

rate for the other twin is significantly higher than for dyzygotic ("fraternal") twins.

Lastly, it has been shown that the rate of schizophrenia in the children of schizophrenic mothers when the child was adopted away in the first few weeks of life equals the rate that would have been expected had they been reared by their biologic mothers. The incidence rate of schizophrenia for children of nonschizophrenic mothers when the child was adopted away early in life equals that incidence seen in the general population.

Biochemical Influences. Much recent research has focused on the biochemical influences on the development of schizophrenia. There may be biochemical differences in the nervous system of the person with schizophrenia that cause him to process sensory information in an abnormal manner. An alteration in this important mental function of information processing could result in disturbances of attention, inadequate social interaction, isolation, and hypersensitivity.[10] The attentional disorder in schizophrenia is a well-documented event and is observed especially in clients whose condition has been chronic.

Schizophrenic disorders may be associated with a disturbance in the adrenergic systems of the brain.[19, 28] An overactivity of dopamine or an insufficiency of norepinephrine at certain central synapses of the brain, or an imbalance between the two substances could be a part of the biologic factors present in schizophrenia. Lending support to the dopamine theory of schizophrenia is the positive behavioral effect that results from the biochemical action of the antipsychotic medications, and the fact that an amphetamine-induced psychosis mimics acute paranoid schizophrenia.

It has been proposed that there may be an immunological imbalance or, perhaps, a defect in the regulation of the immune system in some clients with schizophrenia. Nevertheless, the role of the immune system in the etiology and development of the schizophrenic syndrome is still undetermined.

Brain impairment does exist in a substantial number of schizophrenic clients.[29] Certain structural brain abnormalities in clients with chronic schizophrenia have been visualized by computed tomography (CT) scanning techniques.[31] Currently, available data suggest a complex picture of brain dysfunction in schizophrenic individuals that includes cerebral atrophy, enlargement of the ventricles of the brain, disturbances in cerebral metabolism and electrical activity, neurologic soft signs, and a variety of neuropsychological deficits.[29] These findings further support the belief that schizophrenia is not one disorder, but a group or collection of disorders.

Psychosocial Theories

The psychosocial theories of the etiology of schizophrenia focus on the intrapsychic and interpersonal dimensions of the client's development and life experiences.

Intrapsychic Influences. An individual becomes schizophrenic, says one theorist, not because of what others did to him, but "because of what he does with what was done to him."[4] An intrapersonal approach to the etiology of schizophrenia is based on the theory that there exists a predisposition of the personality to break down under high levels of stress. Certain characteristics of the individual (*e.g.*, hypersensitivity, increased anxiety, and social detachment) may, under extensive stress, escalate into suspicion, intolerable fears, withdrawal, and isolation from others.

The child who later becomes schizophrenic may be extremely sensitized to certain negative characteristics of a parent (*e.g.*, emotional detachment or hostility) and may incorporate these feelings into his own distorted self-image.[3] His view of himself is that of a worthless, guilty, helpless individual.

Another vulnerability model proposes that schizophrenia is an episodic, and not a continuous, disorder.[34] "Triggering" life events, such as the death of a loved one, may exacerbate a crisis and emotional collapse for the person who is predisposed to schizophrenia. Some of the potential factors in the development of vulnerability include low socioeconomic status, crowding, community disorganization, lack of acculturation, social isolation, and minority status. The individual's social network, which is often diminished in schizophrenia, is an important determinant in whether he is accepted and supported or isolated and vulnerable to a schizophrenic episode.

Interpersonal Influences. An interpersonal view of schizophrenia is based on the premise that a person learns values, attitudes, and communication patterns through his family and culture. Disordered communication and interaction may, therefore, be a learned phenomenon that may also be unlearned through therapeutic intervention.

Communication within the family of a schizophrenic client is often indirect, unclear, incongruent, and growth-impeding.[26] For example, members of a family that produces a schizophrenic member often feel that they are not free to comment on whatever they observe in the family. This stifling of communication is typical of a closed family system.

Another aspect of disturbed communication is the lack of adequate feedback mechanisms. Normally, when two people communicate, one person sends a message to the other and the second person sends back a response that informs the first person of the effect of his message. Feedback and the correction of information are essential components of effective interpersonal interaction but are absent or defective in the family communication patterns of the schizophrenic.[25]

The communications of all family members are frequently discounted in the family that has a schizophrenic member. The members of the schizophrenic's family may also be forbidden to enter into any close relationships with others from outside the family.[16] The "rules" of the family of a schizophrenic often seem strange and rigid compared to other families in the community; typically, the family appears aloof and isolated.

The schizophrenic process is thought to begin early in the child's life and to destroy the emotions and personality structure of the individual as it grows. Inherent in the schizophrenic process is the fact that the parents notoriously implicate their children in their personal life.[32] Because the parents are disappointed in their mutual relationship, they may turn to their child (who later becomes schizophrenic) and expect from him all the love, acceptance, and affection they did not receive from each other.

Double-bind communication is considered to be at the core of schizophrenic maladaptation. The basic nature of the double-bind phenomenon is that the child receives two opposing messages from the parent and both of the messages must be obeyed. For example, the parent holds out his arms and says, "Come here and give me a hug, son," and then when the child runs to him, the parent pushes the child away and says, "Why would I want to touch a bad boy like you?" The child is punished if he expresses love for the parent and punished if he does not, and he can find no way out of the situation.[6]

Some families with a schizophrenic member are found to be severely *fused*, wherein the members have never adequately separated or developed into individuals with their own viewpoints, thoughts, and feelings. Rather than having separate identities, members of this family possess an *undifferentiated family ego mass*.[8] It seems that the member with the least amount of differentiation from the others is the person who often becomes psychotic in the family.

Types of Schizophrenia

The types of diagnostic classifications of schizophrenia, according to the criteria of the Diagnostic and Statistical Manual of Mental Disorders, third edition (DSM III), are as follows.

1. *Schizophrenia disorganized* (formerly called hebephrenic). The client is frequently incoherent and displays a flat, silly, or inappropriate affect. No delusional system is evident.
2. *Schizophrenia catatonic*. Usually, the client exhibits one or more of the symptoms of catatonic rigidity, stupor, mutism, negativism, posturing, or excitement.
3. *Schizophrenia paranoid*. The client is preoccupied with delusions of persecution, delusions of grandeur, ideas of reference, or hallucinations that involve persecutory or grandiose material.
4. *Schizophrenia undifferentiated*. The client evidences psychotic symptoms but either does not meet the

criteria of one of the subtypes or meets the criteria of more than one subtype.
5. *Schizophrenia residual*. The client, at one time in the past, exhibited the psychotic symptoms of schizophrenia, but is not psychotic at present. The client may still show signs of some emotional disturbance, such as withdrawal from others or flat affect.[1]

When a client is diagnosed as having a schizophrenic disorder, it is also noted whether the course of the disturbance is *chronic* (with or without an acute exacerbation of symptoms), *subchronic*, (with or without an acute exacerbation of symptoms), or *in remission*.

Another approach to the classification of schizophrenia is based on prognosis.[22] *Reactive schizophrenia*, which carries the expectation of a positive treatment outcome, refers to a disorder with a rapid onset and a relatively satisfactory level of functioning before the breakdown. *Nuclear* or *process schizophrenia*, on the other hand, has a gradual onset, and is seen in persons with a socially inadequate premorbid personality. The expected treatment outcome in nuclear schizophrenia is less positive than in reactive schizophrenia.

Application of the Nursing Process to the Client with a Schizophrenic Disorder

In this section of the chapter, the steps of the nursing process—assessment, analysis/nursing diagnosis, planning, intervention, and evaluation—are applied to the client who exhibits behaviors exemplifying retreat from reality.

Assessment and Analysis

Nursing assessment and diagnosis of the client with a schizophrenic disorder are complex processes. Chapter 9 offers general guidelines for providing the nurse with a base of information about the client. This foundation of client data, identified problems, and nursing diagnoses serve as sources of information from which treatment goals and interventions are derived. Specific nursing approaches, such as openness, honesty, cultural appreciation, and acceptance of the unique properties of the individual are essential to any comprehensive assessment.

The nursing assessment and analysis of the client who exhibits behaviors of the schizophrenic disorders are presented by addressing the major areas of

1. disturbances of thinking;
2. disturbances of feeling;
3. social/behavioral disturbances.

Disturbances of Thinking

One of the classical signs of schizophrenia, said Eugen Bleuler, is an *associative disorder* (see the previous insert,

Historical Perspectives: Views of Schizophrenia). This disturbance in thinking has generally been considered the primary characteristic of schizophrenia. The client gives evidence of his "loose associations" or disconnectedness of thought through his verbal patterns. Because a person's speech is the only means through which an individual can understand another person's thought, the nurse must be attuned to the client's communication.

Listening to the client's speech, the nurse may soon realize that his thoughts are not leading logically to the next ones. Instead, the thinking is chaotic, disorganized, and confusing. The listener feels ill at ease, unable to comprehend what is being said, and unable to take part in the conversation. At times when the client becomes more anxious, his thinking (and, likewise, his speech) becomes increasingly illogical. The uncomfortable feeling experienced by the nurse who is trying to establish communication with this client is very difficult to describe; it is, however, a readily identifiable and diagnostically important feeling once it has been experienced.

Evidence of *magical thinking* is seen in the client who believes that his thoughts or wishes can control other people or events. This form of primary process thinking can be observed as part of the normal development of the preschool child, as suggested by the familiar sight of a child skipping down the sidewalk and chanting, "Step on a crack, break your mother's back." Its presence in an adult, however, who believes that he can manipulate the actions of others through "mind control" is neither acceptable nor appropriate behavior in our society.

A schizophrenic client may have minimal or seemingly no awareness of his environment. He may wander as though he were in foreign surroundings or appear to be in a dream world. An important safety-related factor is the client's lack of regard for his own well-being. He may step in the path of oncoming traffic or perform other potentially dangerous acts, while giving the impression that he does not grasp the obvious danger.

The client may also experience feelings of *depersonalization*, wherein he feels that his body belongs to another person or that he is somehow removed from his body. He may believe that his spirit is hovering above his body and watching its movements and behavior with detachment.

The client may attempt to communicate with others through the use of *symbolism*. Again, his symbolic words and actions can be viewed as a part of his disordered thinking. Language may be private and idiosyncratic. The client may create new words, called *neologisms*, which have meaning and purpose to him alone. *Cryptic language* refers to the client speaking in an abbreviated fashion; that is, he may speak aloud only every fourth, or sixth, or tenth word of his thoughts.

Illusions may be another sign of the client's thought disorder. An *illusion* is a misinterpretation of a real sensory experience. An example of an illusion is the experience of seeing a shadow in the room when awakening in the middle of the night and immediately concluding that a robber has broken into the house. Schizophrenic clients are often disturbed and frightened by illusions.

A *delusion* is a fixed, false belief of the client's that cannot be corrected by reasoning with him. The client with paranoid schizophrenia generally has *delusions of persecution* (*i.e.*, that others are planning to harm him in some fashion, that there is a conspiracy to follow him at all times and "bug" his telephone, that creatures from other planets are controlling his mind, and so forth) or *delusions of grandeur* (*i.e.*, that he is Jesus Christ, the Virgin Mary, Napoleon, or some other important, famous, or historically significant personage [see the dialogue, Gathering Information About the Client's Perceptions]).

To identify the presence of a delusion, the nurse must first understand the beliefs characteristic of a culture, because a delusion is a belief that is not in keeping with the beliefs accepted by a person's culture. For example, in the United States, we would term it delusional for a person to believe that semen could wander up into a man's head and cause his brain to deteriorate, and yet that belief is culturally acceptable in parts of India.[23]

A *hallucination* is a false sensory perception, (*i.e.*, without external stimulus) or a sensory perception that does not exist in reality, such as seeing "visions" or hearing "voices" (see the insert, Hallucinations and Delusions: How Do They Develop?).

A client may "hear" the voice of God, the devil, or a close relative. The voice is frequently one that berates or condemns him for his past and present evils. *Auditory hallucinations* are the most common form of hallucinations; *visual hallucinations* occur second most frequently. What the client sees in his visual hallucinations are likely to be threatening, frightening monsters or scenes. Although hallucinations involving the other senses (gustatory, tactile, olfactory) do occur, they are less common.

In American society today, there are probably only a few small religious groups that sanction hallucinations. Nevertheless, hallucinations that are not part of a psychiatric disorder may be acceptable phenomena in other societies.[23] A question that must be asked is whether the hallucination is appropriate or even expected within the cultural framework. For example, a person's role in society (*e.g.*, a medicine man or an artist) may necessitate or utilize some of the symptoms that appear to be schizophrenic in nature.

Disturbances of Feeling

The term *affect* refers to one's mood or feeling tone. Frequently, in schizophrenic disorders, there is a marked absence of affect or there is flat, blunted, or inappropriate affect. The client's apparent lack of emotional expression may cause the nurse to feel as if she is trying to communicate with a machine or inanimate object. The individual's affect may also seem inappropriate in relation to the conversation

Therapeutic Dialogue

Gathering Information About the Client's Perceptions

Nurse: (seated at table near client, looking directly at her) You were telling me, Mrs. D., about how you came to this hospital.

Client: I know why I came here. (throws her head back, stiffens her neck, and grips the arms of her chair) I have a calling.

Nurse: A calling? What kind of a calling?

Client: To help my friends. (expansive, sweeping gesture of her hand toward the others in the room)

Nurse: Who do you think called you, Mrs. D.? (questioning tone of voice, maintaining eye contact)

Client: (winks one eye and hunches forward as though sharing a secret) The Master Doctor, the Big Physician.

Nurse: Do you mean God? (straightforward, inquiring facial expression and voice)

Client: Of course, I mean God. (impatient tone of voice, frowning, stands up and shouts) Who else would I mean?

Discussion

Often, the nurse wishes to gather information regarding the client's perception of the reason for, and events surrounding, her admission to the psychiatric unit. At times, the client's perception is at odds with the reality-based facts of the situation.

Mrs. D. believes that she has been chosen as a special person and received this "calling" to come into the hospital to help other people.

The nurse, in interacting with Mrs. D., is asking her for clarification about this "calling," which she believes has come from God.

The nurse neither agrees nor disagrees with Mrs. D. about the truth of her beliefs. Such agreement or attempts to disprove her beliefs usually serves to reinforce or strengthen the delusional material of the client. Instead, the nurse proceeds to gather information in a nonthreatening, supportive manner and to communicate acceptance of Mrs. D. as a valuable human being. A subsequent nursing goal will focus on the clarification of reality with the client.

---

or the context of the situation (*e.g.*, the client who laughs and smiles in response to hearing some piece of sad news).

The client's apathy may increase the nurse's sense of frustration. This seeming absence of caring about himself or his situation may depress and anger the nurse who believes that the client must first want to improve before he will begin to make therapeutic gains. Once again, the nurse must examine the client's affective state in relation to his cultural context.

Social/Behavioral Disturbances

The client with a schizophrenic disorder retreats from the reality of interpersonal contact. He appears aloof, uninterested in others, and content with his own inner fantasies.

His communication is either lacking or directed toward private, idiosyncratic goals. Rather than using language and nonverbal communication to establish rapport with other persons and to derive pleasure from those relationships, the schizophrenic client uses his communicative efforts as a means of self-stimulation or reinforcement of his preoccupying fantasies.

A pronounced fear of others and of himself prevents the schizophrenic client from making contact or responding to the social overtures of others. It is probable that he fears harm from other people or fears that he may not be able to control his own impulses and may therefore bring harm to others.

Impulsive, bizarre, or otherwise uninhibited behavior, such as masturbation in public, gesturing, or posturing, may also be signs of the behavioral disturbances of schizophrenia.

The client may show signs of extreme dependency or

Hallucinations and Delusions: How Do They Develop?

A well-known theorist and writer about schizophrenia, Silvano Arieti, has proposed that hallucinatory voices occur only in particular situations; that is, when the client expects to hear them. The client, for example, perceives hostility around him, expects to hear the neighbors talking about him, puts himself into a "listening" attitude, and then experiences the hallucination (he hears them talking about him).

Another example of this phenomenon occurs in ideas of reference. The client thinks that people are laughing at him, hears laughing and giggling, and looks at people and sees them smiling. They may not be smiling, but he may have misinterpreted their facial expressions. Or, if they are smiling, it may be for reasons that have nothing to do with the client.

The goal, says Arieti, in treating this client is to help him recognize that he sees or hears people laughing at him when he expects to. Next comes the recognition that he feels people *should* laugh at him because he is a "laughable" individual. He hears laughing, in fact, because he thinks people should laugh at him; that is, "what he thinks of himself has become the cause of his symptom."

The return to reality is slow because the client's reality is sad and worsened by his vulnerability. Therapists must be careful to promote the client's return by improving his reality. Eventually, the client moves toward mastery of his own situation, no longer the victim of external forces.

helplessness. This behavior is often repulsive to individuals who value independence and assertiveness and may elicit anger and frustration in even the most conscientious and self-aware mental health professionals.

The client with schizophrenia may have concerns about his sexual identity. Although little research has been conducted on this topic, a change in sexual behavior has been noted during periods of psychotic decompensation.[30] The schizophrenic client's inadequate social skills, withdrawal, and isolation contribute to his lack of sexual partners. In psychiatric hospitals, where sexual activities are generally discouraged or prohibited, chronic schizophrenic clients encounter medical, social, and cultural obstacles to their sexual expression.[30]

Assessment of the client's ability to perform his own self-care and activities of daily living, to function in his work setting, and to respond appropriately to his own physical needs are critical issues for the psychiatric-mental health nurse. At times, a client may be so removed from contact with reality that he is unaware of his body's need for food, water, and rest.

The client's role in his family and community and the availability and responsiveness of his support system are important variables in the assessment process. His eventual level of adaptation may be strongly influenced by the presence of supportive, caring significant others. The absence of a support system, on the other hand, may reinforce a lifetime of failure and rejection and may offer the client little hope for a satisfying future.

The nurse needs to assess the client's *relationships with the significant figures* in his life. From these observations and objective descriptions of family and community interactional patterns, the nurse will later formulate treatment goals and interventions for and with the client and the people who are important to him.

Other Unique Characteristics

In addition to these general factors that the nursing assessment of a client with a schizophrenic disorder must address, multiple variations in behaviors will also be observed by the astute and perceptive nurse. No symptom picture that is characteristic of a psychiatric disturbance is ever the same in two individual clients. Because every person is different and has unique distinguishing characteristics, he will never appear "just like all the others"—whether he is emotionally disturbed or healthy and adapting. Individualization and objectivity are key words in any nursing assessment and analysis.

Planning

Preparation of the client's treatment plans is best approached as a collaborative effort of the mental health team, which includes the client and his family. Flexibility and creativity are essential ingredients in the continuous process of planning, evaluation, and replanning of therapeutic efforts. No single treatment modality will effect the desired behavioral changes for all clients.

Although preoccupation with fantasies, poor reality contact, and symbolic forms of communication are characteristic of schizophrenia, each client exhibits specific disturbances that require individualized nursing approaches. Some psychiatric inpatient facilities may prepare standardized nursing care plans or treatment plans that offer general principles of care; these standard plans then require individualization in nursing diagnoses and interventions for the client.

Goal-Setting

The major goals for the schizophrenic client include

1. promotion of trust;

2. establishment of a nonthreatening environment for the client;
3. encouragement of satisfactory social interaction;
4. increase of the client's self-esteem;
5. validation of the client's perceptions;
6. clarification and reinforcement of reality;
7. promotion of physical safety;
8. encouragement of independent behavior;
9. attention to the client's physical needs;
10. reduction of anxiety and psychotic symptoms through chemotherapeutic agents;
11. coordination of therapy with the client's family or significant others.

Discharge Plans

Discharge planning begins at the time of the client's admission to the psychiatric inpatient unit. Many schizophrenic clients suffer not only the long-term effects of their disorder, but also "the Rip Van Winkle syndrome"; that is, they awaken from a long sleep to find a world with changed technologies, cultural values, and economics.[22] It is a frightening world for discharged clients who may cling tenaciously to the hospital environment.

An adequate discharge program needs to foster social skills, work/job skills, self-confidence in dealing with problems, and involvement in the outside community.[22] For example, before discharge from a psychiatric facility, the long-term client must learn, practice, and be tested in the basic, practical aspects of daily living, such as how to ride a bus, shop for groceries, apply for a job, cook a meal, and take his own medication.

Community involvement before discharge means that the client should be familiar with his future landlord and employer. These people, after all, are the individuals who will play a significant role in his adjustment to life outside the hospital versus his readmission to a psychiatric facility. Employers and landlords must know the discharged client as a person and must realize that he needs direct and constructive feedback. He is not a fragile or helpless person and should not be treated as such. A 24-hour, 7-days-per-week, crisis telephone line to the client's former psychiatric-mental health care providers also help smooth his discharge to his family and community.

Intervention

Certain personal characteristics are considered necessary when working therapeutically with a schizophrenic client. The mental health professional needs to be straightforward, simple, and accepting, and must hold unconditional regard for the dignity of another human being—even when that person is severely withdrawn and regressed.[3] This mandate includes, for example, demonstrating respect for the client's desire for silence, so that the nonverbal communication becomes a shared experience.

Influencing the Client's Disturbances of Thinking

Deciphering Meaning. When confronted with the client's symbolic words, actions, or other examples of his disordered thinking, the nurse remembers that, although his behavior may seem, at times, almost impossible to understand, it does have meaning to the client. The nurse tries to listen for the themes and search for the hidden meanings in his communication. The client's verbal and nonverbal behaviors cannot be dismissed as senseless or as gibberish.

The client's rhyming communication may also give clues to the nurse about his thoughts and feelings.

Mary Mary dictionary
blowing smoking
not even caring

In these words, the client, Mary, conveys to the nurse several possible routes to explore. Is she feeling apathetic ("not even caring")? Angry ("blowing" or "smoking")? Is there a meaning to "Mary dictionary"? The nurse listens to these unusual forms of communication and attempts to decode the communication and determine, through validation, what meanings they hold for the client.

Reinforcing Reality. Much of the nurse's focus in working with the schizophrenic client will be centered on helping him to clarify reality and validate his perceptions. This is accomplished both by describing a real event or circumstance to the client and by involving the client in conversations or activities that focus on the here-and-now.

When dealing with the client with feelings of depersonalization, the nurse will need to state what she sees as a real fact (*e.g.*, that one part of his body is not dead, or that he has not become an inanimate object, and so forth) but will also need to avoid getting involved in an argument with the client. No one can argue away feelings of depersonalization or hallucinations or any other disturbances in reality-testing. Nevertheless, psychiatric-mental health professionals are responsible for stating the facts, as they see them, to the client in a manner that is simple, concise, and non-threatening.

While she is stating these facts, the nurse also attempts to bring the client back into contact with reality by involving him in some reality-oriented activity. Perhaps the nurse could talk with the client about a picture in a magazine and attempt to interest him in this concrete topic. Perhaps involving the client in a physical activity, such as taking a walk and conversing about the objects he sees while walking, will be therapeutic for him. These are both reality-oriented activities that the nurse may employ in day-to-day contact with persons who have withdrawn from reality.

When the client is overcome with the idea that he is living in an unreal environment, he should not be left alone for long periods of time. Staying with the client is an essential step in reinforcing reality because the nurse signifies a major link with the real world for the client. Allowing the client to remain isolated only encourages him to become more involved or preoccupied with his fantasies. Again, the nurse's engagement of the client in reality-oriented activities and conversations is a helpful intervention.

Promoting Clarification. The client who has a confused sense of identity will require much clarification from the nurse. In conversations, the nurse must help the client realize what he said or did versus what others said or did. When ambiguous and confusing topics arise, the nurse must stop the conversation and request clarification from the client. Because the client will often hide behind a "you know what I mean . . . ", the nurse must not assume that she does know what the client means unless she has first asked for clarification. Finding out directly from the client is the only sure way to understand the message he is conveying.

The schizophrenic client's loose associations are extremely difficult to understand. Pretending to understand his line of thought only widens the gap between client and nurse. The most helpful approach to what may seem incoherent ramblings is to ask clarifying questions. Perhaps the nurse may also determine a recurrent idea or theme in the speech and further pursue its meaning for the client. The nurse and other psychiatric-mental health caregivers act as healthy role models for the client by communicating with him in a clear and concise manner.

Intervening in Hallucinations. The client who is hallucinating is one who is preoccupied and frightened; leaving him alone only deepens his preoccupation and fear. The nurse's very presence is a reassuring force that helps calm his fears. It is crucial for the nurse to remember that the hallucination is real to the client. When working with the hallucinating client, the nurse communicates to him concern that he is upset or bothered by the things he hears or sees.

At the same time, the nurse makes it clear to the client that she does not see or hear the hallucinations that he is describing. It is critical to know that the nurse never agrees with him about hearing the "voices" or any hallucinatory experience. Because it is the mental health professional's function to serve as the healthy role model for the client, the nurse cannot reinforce his retreat from reality through hallucinations or delusions. Neither is it beneficial to argue about whether or not the hallucination or delusion is real. Rather than engage in activities that strengthen the client's withdrawal, the nurse encourages the client to regain his contact with reality by gently directing him into conversation or activities focused on the here-and-now (see the dialogue, Dealing with Hallucinations).

It has been suggested that the "voices" appear in specific situations, when the client expects to hear them. This expectation causes him to develop a "listening attitude," especially in times of stress.[3] The nurse may help the client actively fight the hallucination first by discovering the relation between his feelings (anxiety) and the "listening attitude," and second by disrupting the process of falling into the next stage of experiencing the "voices."

Interrupting the Client's Disturbances of Feeling

Role Modeling. The nurse models appropriateness of affect by displaying a somber facial expression when discussing a serious topic or a joyful expression when engaging in a happy or pleasant topic of conversation. Using body language to convey a mood appropriate to the thought is one aspect of the nurse's repertoire of communication skills.

Developing Tolerance. Bizarre or inappropriate behavior or affect of the client must not be reinforced by nurses' smiles, nods, anger, or laughter. Although they need to demonstrate tolerance of the client's behavior, nurses and other mental health caregivers may, at times, feel disgust or amusement. It is often difficult to admit negative feelings to oneself, especially while trying hard to become therapeutic. Nevertheless, the therapeutic self is primarily a person of honesty, and any insights about one's feelings must be acknowledged openly before they can be faced. It is particularly important to deal honestly with feelings because the schizophrenic client has often learned from his family and culture to discount his own feelings. During interactions with psychiatric-mental health staff, the client may communicate that he perceives certain feelings as "dangerous." Feelings must be examined in a supportive, open environment.

Diminishing the Client's Social/Behavioral Disturbances

Developing Trust. The development of a trusting relationship is basic to nursing care approaches to the schizophrenic client. It is essential that nurses and other psychiatric-mental health professionals show interest in, and acceptance of, the total person who is the client. Although this goal is partly accomplished by means of the nurse's words, it is also heavily influenced by nonverbal behavior. The nurse's nonjudgmental attitude and genuineness cannot be manufactured. A genuine desire to offer assistance will be perceived accurately by the client and he will begin to view the nurse as a person who is helpful and sincere.

Through the nurse's body language, facial expression, eye contact, tone of voice, and verbalizations, the client receives messages about the nurse's trustworthiness. The client, in turn, responds to these messages. It is likely that because the schizophrenic client's past interpersonal experiences have been unsuccessful or unsatisfying, he is unwilling to take risks in his encounters with another person.

Therefore, the client's response to a nurse, even if the nurse is warm, open, and genuine, may be reticent. Estab-

Therapeutic Dialogue

Dealing with Hallucinations

Nurse: What has been troubling you, Jeff? (sitting with the client, trying to establish eye contact)

Client: I hear voices. (looking down at the floor, shoulders hunched forward) They are punishing me and want me to repent.

Nurse: Do you want to share with me your thoughts on what you believe you heard? (leaning toward client, arms and hands open and resting on lap)

Client: (sitting very quietly, brow furrowed, staring at his hands) There were two men—one was 62 and one was 42. The 42-year-old was good. His face was in stone on the floor. When you went by, he went into your mind. It was like a strong wind. (pauses, looks at the nurse's face) You really don't want to hear this.

Nurse: (softly, maintaining eye contact) You don't think I want to hear about these "voices," Jeff?

Client: Two weeks after I was discharged from this hospital, I was walking down this road—the voices started, then the wind telling me to kill myself for my repentence. (stands up, begins to pace back and forth in front of the couch, his eyes cast downward)

Nurse: (still seated, looking up at the client as he paces) Do the wind and noises bother you a lot, Jeff?

Client: Yes, and it's always at six o'clock. (walks away from the nurse)

Discussion

Communicating, verbally and nonverbally, with the client who experiences hallucinations requires skilled use of therapeutic techniques.

Jeff is open in expressing the torment he is experiencing from the punishing "voices." Many clients lack the trust, reality contact, or verbal skills needed to share these hallucinatory events with psychiatric-mental health care providers.

The nurse verbalizes concern for Jeff and offers him the opportunity either to share or withhold information about "what he believes he hears." In discussing hallucinatory material, the nurse demonstrates acceptance of the client's hallucination as a "real" event to him. At the same time, the nurse neither agrees with the client nor tries to dissuade him or convince him that the "voices" are not really occurring. For the client, we must assume, the "voices" are present, and they are likely to be a source of anxiety, fear, and agitation for him.

A strong theme of guilt/repentance/punishment is evident in Jeff's conversation. The nurse has not yet begun to explore the sources of these feelings of worthlessness nor the possible ways to intervene with Jeff to reduce his unpleasant, and perhaps unbearable, feelings.

This interaction represents one aspect of the process of establishing trust and building rapport with the client.

lishing rapport with the client, although it is essential, will not be easy to accomplish. Gradually, as a result of continued, consistent, and pleasant interpersonal experiences, his level of trust in another person will increase. The nurse slowly breaks through his wall of isolation and assumes more and more significance for him. At this point the nurse can begin to introduce other people into his experiences. Hopefully, the client will transfer some of his trust in the nurse to another, second person, and then to a third person, and so on, until he has learned meaningful ways to interact with a larger sphere of people. If the initial interpersonal contact with the nurse is pleasant and rewarding to the client, he will be more inclined to risk opening himself to others.

On the other hand, if the nurse does not regard the client positively, fears him, or finds him repulsive or hopeless, this attitude will also be sensed by him. Sometimes, the client's perceptions are so painfully acute that he will overtly respond to whatever he senses in the other person;

he will respond to the "vibes" he receives from the other person. The nurse in this situation may be saying all the correct words but will not establish a therapeutic rapport if sincerity is lacking. In fact, if one had to choose the more important factor in dealing with the psychiatric client, the actual words used by the intervener or the nonverbal behavior, nonverbal communication would probably be judged more influential in conveying empathy toward the client. The goal, of course, is to combine both verbal and nonverbal communication skills in order to deal effectively and therapeutically with clients.

Approaching the Client. Because the client tends to withdraw from others, the nurse needs to make the initial approach to the client. Waiting for him to make the first contact is fruitless because he often lacks the self-confidence necessary to initiate contact with another person. Remembering that the client is likely frightened of others, the nurse approaches him in a nonthreatening way. The nurse is encouraged to sit near him (but not crowding him or impinging on his personal space, because he may fear harm from close contact with others), and to speak in a soothing voice. Both of these approaches demonstrate to the client that the nurse is interested in him but willing to advance slowly and respond to his cues.

The close interpersonal relationship that develops in the therapeutic environment is, for the client, a new kind of close relationship. Other people, the client learns, can care for him, not just take care of him.[2]

Encouraging Independence.

Encouraging the client's self-help skills and rewarding or reinforcing his participation in activities of daily living will help promote independent behavior. The client may need the opportunity to make simple decisions and experience small successes over a period of time. As the client is able to tolerate and accept more responsibility, he is given these opportunities in a progressive fashion.

Dealing with Hostility.

The problem of dealing with the client's hostility may be of significance, because the nature of the close therapeutic relationship may engender angry outbursts from the client. It is probably the intensity of the closeness and the fear of rejection that prompt the client to reject the mental health professional. Hostility, on the other hand, may be disguised and evidenced as extreme passivity, testing behaviors, or projection.[2]

It is critical that the nurse avoid overwhelming the client with too much talk or too much closeness. Although touch is an important therapeutic technique, it must be used judiciously. Touch can be very frightening to the client if the nurse employs it indiscriminately. For example, the paranoid schizophrenic client who thinks that he can be destroyed by someone's touch will become very agitated if he is touched by psychiatric caregivers. (For a detailed explanation of interventions with the client with paranoid ideas and actions, the reader is referred to Chapter 23.)

Approaching the Client's Family

Denial of the client's feelings has often been learned from, and reinforced by, the client's family. Any therapeutic work with the client who is withdrawn from reality must also be implemented with the client's family. Supportive measures must be employed to enlarge the client's and the family's social sphere, to raise their level of interpersonal functioning, and to increase their ability to become aware of feelings and learn to handle them effectively (see the case study at the end of the chapter). A significant degree of the success of any treatment plan depends on the mental health team's ability to effect change in the client together with his family and significant others, not as separate entities.

Couples therapy groups for married schizophrenic clients or parents groups for young, unmarried schizophrenic clients offer problem-solving skills and provide outside contacts for the family members. Often, the discharged client will not return to his home, but to a group home or some alternative living arrangement. Plans for this move to a new living situation need to be examined and worked out in detail long before the client is ready to leave the psychiatric facility.

An optimal approach to the client's family is to view the family not as a source of pathology, but as a means of restoration to health.[4] Psychiatric-mental health professionals work with family members to help them add understanding to their personal concern, to explore the client's areas of particular vulnerability, and to learn to clarify the client's communications. The goal is to reintegrate the client into his family whenever possible.

Important Therapies

Individual Psychotherapy.

The client with a schizophrenic disorder experiences difficulty relating to others and these difficulties with others are reflected in behaviors such as anxiety in interpersonal contacts, mistrust, fear, and misinterpretation of others' behavior. The therapist tries to counteract the client's anxiety, offer warmth and reassurance, and remove the fear "almost automatically aroused by interpersonal contact."[4] The client and therapist must first learn to know, trust, and not be afraid of each other.[4]

The principles of psychotherapy of the schizophrenic client are as follows.

1. Stimulate very little or create no anxiety and diminish the anxiety already present in the client.
2. Prevent the client from returning to his premorbid (prepsychotic) state, which would promote continued vulnerability for psychosis.
3. Achieve and maintain a state of "delicate balance" prior to the client's independence from treatment, because of his continued poor tolerance for frustration, discomfort, and anxiety.
4. Employ a therapeutic approach by which the client moves toward gradual and progressive self-acceptance.[4]

Therapists who have proved to be very successful individual psychotherapists with schizophrenic clients demonstrate certain process and personal attributes. These personal and process variables include the following.

Sense of self-confidence and self-worth
Honesty
Commitment to the client and his welfare
Flexibility and the ability to follow the client's lead
Persistence and hope
Ability to postpone the gratification of feeling professionally competent
Tolerance for uncertainty

Tolerance for madness without becoming frightened or
    rejecting
Tolerance for error[11]

The important commonalities in different effective psycho-
therapies may, in fact, be therapists' attitudes and attributes
rather than their theoretical beliefs.

Group Therapy.   Various forms of group therapy may
be employed as a psychosocial form of treatment for psychotic clients in mental health facilities. Communication with
the psychotic person, in group and other kinds of therapies,
may be concrete, brief, and direct, or may be psychoana-
lytically oriented, depending on the therapist's theoretical
framework.

Behavior Therapy.   In a behavioristic approach, the
schizophrenic client is seen as an individual with specific
and measurable problems.[21] These problems, it is believed,
are treated by certain behavioral interventions, such as positive and negative reinforcement.

Milieu Therapy.   Milieu therapy is a team effort
whose therapeutic effect for schizophrenic clients is related
to its abilities to communicate and work together as a
team.[5] The psychiatric-mental health staff must feel free to
talk about clients, families, events, and their own feelings
to prevent a dangerous buildup of anger and frustration. The
overall milieu attitude reflects the therapeutic effectiveness
of the environment that has been designed for clients. Client or ward government activities may offer opportunities
for clients to participate in decision-making relevant to
their living situation.

Keeping in mind that the client's judgment may be
impaired will alert the nurse to important safety needs. Due
to his poor reality contact, the client may place himself in
potentially dangerous situations both indoors and out-of-
doors. Nursing responsibility dictates that the environment
must be safety-oriented and that care providers must attend
to the client in a conscientious manner.

If left alone, the client may neglect his basic physical
needs. The nurse, therefore, assumes the responsibility for
physical health when the client is unable to meet his own
needs. The nurse must observe him carefully and frequently
for signs of possible illness, physical deprivation, medication reaction, and so on.

Pharmacotherapy.   The nurse is often called upon
to administer psychotropic drugs to the schizophrenic client. Antipsychotic medication will act to decrease extra-
neous stimuli, thereby strengthening the client's contact
with reality. The nurse responsible for administering this
medication to the client must be aware of the drug's action,
use, usual dosage, route of administration, side effects,
contraindications, and nursing implications.

In the past 20 years, psychopharmacology has moved
from the status of an adjunct to psychological therapies to
the dominant form of treatment for psychiatric disorders. It
has been found that the psychotropic drugs are useful in
preventing relapse and hospital readmissions for a substantial number of, but not all, psychiatric clients.[10, 27] These
drugs reduce a wide range of symptoms very effectively,
especially over the short term, but they do not maintain
effectiveness over some of the symptoms of chronic schizophrenia, such as flattened affect.[27] They do not significantly
affect the quality of the client's social or personal adjustment to life outside of the hospital.[10]

Administration of an antipsychotic medication
should be a part of a comprehensive treatment program for
the client with a psychotic disturbance, not the sole method
of treatment. The psychoactive drugs control some of the
symptoms of the schizophrenic psychoses, such as withdrawal, aggression, extreme anxiety, hallucinations, and
delusions. The client who receives antipsychotic medication is, therefore, more amenable to the various forms of
social, recreational, and rehabilitative therapies. The
choice of any psychotropic medication depends on its effectiveness and its safety for the individual client. Most schizophrenic clients are helped by antipsychotic medications;
some are unaffected and some become worse.[18]

The side effects of antipsychotic medications are distressing and harmful. The watchful nurse consistently observes the client for any of the following side effects of the
antipsychotic medications: extrapyramidal effects (including tardive dyskinesia), autonomic effects, metabolic and
endocrine effects, hypersensitivity reactions, and sedative
effects.[13, 18] (For a thorough review of the actions, side effects, and nursing implications of the antipsychotic medications, the reader is referred to Chapter 19.)

To decrease the incidence of tardive dyskinesia, psychoactive medication is currently being administered in
reduced amounts. This reduction in medication is accomplished either through low-dosage treatment or through intermittent or targeted medication treatment.[27] Intermittent
medication administration is the episodic, rather than the
continuous, use of medication for symptom reduction in
some schizophrenic clients who do not need medication
continuously. This method of medication administration
requires the identification of prodromal symptoms, (*e.g.,*
feeling "tense and nervous" or experiencing difficulty sleeping or decreased enjoyment) and the early resumption of
medication before the client becomes so disturbed that he
requires hospitalization.

Intervening with High-Risk Populations

The children of schizophrenic women comprise a population at risk for emotional problems.[15] Often, the children's
behavioral deviations are evident by the ages of 1 to 5 years.
Families with a psychotic mother or father cope with their
life stresses less adequately than families with nonpsychotic
parents.

The children of these families are at a greater risk of educational, social, and economic deprivation. The chronic stresses facing these children include the unpredictable behavior of the psychotic parent, a chaotic household, the repeated hospitalizations of the parent, and resulting socioeconomic stress.

Suggestions for intervention with high-risk groups are

1. continuing help to the children of psychotic parents;
2. teaching the mother and father parenting skills to care for their children;
3. contraceptive information and services.[15]

Evaluation

The "success" of any treatment program is measured not only by how many clients are discharged from the program, but also by the availability of community support services and aftercare resources, and by the local community's tolerance of behavioral deviance.[22]

The schizophrenic client who is prepared for discharge needs to know that he will not be abandoned, that he will be helped to succeed in the community, and that the psychiatric-mental health staff are confident in his ability to succeed.

Evaluating the effectiveness of nursing interventions requires a reassessment process to determine what therapeutic results or gains have occurred. Has a specific nursing action had an impact on a specific disturbed behavior of the client? What is the nature of the change in affect, thinking, or social relationships? The evaluation process is a continuous one. By constantly examining changes in the client's behavior, the nurse has the opportunity to decide to strengthen or alter certain aspects of the treatment plan.

Humanistic influences that reflect on the care of the mentally disturbed today include the voiced rights of mental patients, a multidimensional understanding of peoples' behavior, respect for the basic worth and dignity of each individual, and community education that promotes acceptance and tolerance of the mentally ill.[22]

Similarly, more humanistic forms of treatment, such as open-door policies and client government, are being employed as the therapeutic modality of choice. Evaluation of these modalities and their benefit to schizophrenic clients may encourage us to examine and critique the philosophy and practices of our own psychiatric-mental health setting.

The Nurse's Feelings and Attitudes

The nurse's own feelings are an area that deserves, but rarely receives, considerable attention. Working with the schizophrenic client, the nurse is confronted with a wide range of unusual, and sometimes threatening, client behaviors. The nurse must, in the face of "madness," remain sane and secure—essential ingredients in therapeutic effectiveness.

On the other hand, it is not recommended that the nurse stay aloof or emotionally distant.

Working with a client who is in poor contact with reality is often a frustrating and frightening experience for the nurse. The delusional or hallucinatory material produced by the client is at a very primitive level and may be likened to the nightmares that each of us has experienced at one time or another. Some of our own most basic fears may be put into words or acted out by the client with a schizophrenic disorder.

It is encouraged that nurses and other mental health professionals become involved with their clients as an essential part of the therapeutic process. The client who is withdrawn from reality, however, may elicit great anxiety or similar disturbing feelings in the nurse. Seeing a person who is severely regressed, withdrawn, and apathetic is likely to be a tragic experience for any of us. Employing a repertoire of therapeutic skills with such a client may seem an overwhelming task because of the emotionally draining side effects. Although nurses need to maintain and convey hope for the client's improvement, they may find themselves distraught over the difficulties inherent in that responsibility. Feelings of guilt over "not getting through" or "not doing enough" may arise in the nurse and may further complicate the therapeutic assignment.

Understanding the facts of the client's situation and the treatment possibilities will help the nurse to set realistic goals for the client. Professional supervision sessions and involvement in a support group among colleagues in the work setting will also assist the nurse to keep a balanced view of the client's needs and gains. Nurses must cultivate close, rewarding relationships with family and friends as part of the process of personal growth and self-renewal, and to insure their own therapeutic effectiveness.

Human involvement and caring are prerequisites to therapeutic intervention. The nurse's caring manner demonstrates to the client that he is accepted and respected as a fellow human being. In time, it will be evident to the client that he is not viewed as hopeless, but as a person of dignity and worthy of respect.

The client who is schizophrenic is likely to be very sensitive to others' feelings and to see through facades; he may arouse strong feelings of anxiety, anger, and depression in mental health professionals. The intensity of the relationship with a schizophrenic client often brings to the surface these interpersonal and emotional issues. The nurse needs to address these issues to prevent their hindering therapeutic effectiveness.

Summary

This chapter has presented two major areas of information—an overview of the schizophrenic disorders and the application of the nursing process to the client with a schizophrenic disorder. Some of the major foci of the chapter include the following.

1. Because it is estimated to affect 1% of the population and its onset occurs during adolescence and young adulthood, schizophrenia is considered a common and tragic emotional disturbance, or group of disturbances.

2. The biologic theories are built on data that support genetic, biochemical, immunological, or structural influences on the client and his behavior.

3. The psychosocial theories of the etiology of schizophrenia focus on the intrapersonal and interpersonal factors that lead to its development.

4. The five types of schizophrenia—disorganized, catatonic, paranoid, undifferentiated, and residual—have been explained in terms of their operational criteria.

5. Assessment and analysis of the client is approached by examining the three major areas of disturbances of thinking, disturbances of feeling, and disturbances of behavior.

6. The foundation of an accurate assessment is a nonjudgmental attitude and careful, objective observation and description of client behaviors.

7. The psychiatric-mental health nurse is involved in treatment planning as a collaborative effort with other members of the mental health team, which includes the client and his family or significant others.

8. Specific goals are set for, and with, the client and his family to intervene in the present behavior and to begin preparation for discharge to the community.

9. The nurse is encouraged to be consistent and genuine in her approach to the schizophrenic client.

10. The nurse's own feelings while working with the schizophrenic client must be addressed openly as they are an important part of the therapeutic process.

11. Individual, group, and family therapy, the behavioristic approach, milieu therapy, and chemotherapy are discussed as useful modalities.

12. Interventions are proposed and advocated with high-risk populations, such as the children of psychotic parents.

13. Evaluation of nursing intervention is the continuous process of examination and assessment of the therapeutic effectiveness of each specific intervention.

Nursing Care Plan

The Client Who Retreats from Reality

Client Problem	Goal	Intervention
Disturbances of thinking: use of symbolism	To clarify meanings	Validation of perceptions
		Detection of themes or hidden meanings
Hallucinations and delusions	To decrease fear and anxiety	Remaining with client
	To clarify reality	Calm, directive approach
		Disruption of events or circumstances leading to retreat from reality
		Orientation to nurse's name, position, and purpose in the interaction
		Acceptance of hallucinatory or delusional experience without agreement or disagreement with client
		Encouragement of reality-oriented conversation and activities
		Role-modeling of clear communication
		Consensual validation of experiences
Disturbances of feeling: incongruent, blunted, or disordered affect	To reinforce spontaneity and congruence of mood	Role-modeling appropriateness of affect
		Tolerance of bizarre behavior or affect
		Reinforcement of appropriate, socially acceptable interaction
Social/behavioral disturbances: withdrawal and isolation	To establish rapport	Nonverbal communication of acceptance and trustworthiness
		Initiation of interaction
		Consistent nonthreatening approach
		Availability of support
	To encourage social interaction	Rewarding interpersonal experiences
		Development of trust on one-to-one basis
		Gradual increase in the social sphere
Noncommunicativeness	To facilitate communication	Respect for silence
		Nonverbal communication through presence, consistency, and positive regard
		Acceptance of any communicative attempts
Dependency	To promote independent behavior	Provision of decision-making opportunities
		Rewarding of independent behavior, such as self-care activities
		Gradual increase in responsibility

Case Study

Approaching the Family System After a Member's Repeated Psychiatric Hospitalizations

The R. Family, consisting of 53-year-old grandmother, Helen, a 28-year-old mother, Linda, and a 3-year-old son, Tommy, was referred to the community health nurse following Linda's third psychiatric hospitalization for a schizophrenic episode. When asked by the nurse if she knew why the follow-up visits had been recommended, Linda replied that she thought the nurse could help her with Tommy "who was still not potty-trained." This problem perceived by Linda and her mother Helen to be the focus of concern, served as the vehicle through which the community health nurse was permitted to approach the family.

Initial contact with the R. family struck the nurse as a picture of the three family members against the world—protected in their high-rise fortress, 11 stories above street level, behind a door secured by multiple bolts and locks, and surrounded by the aged inhabitants of their apartment building. Lacking a car, a telephone, and daily newspapers, the family was fairly well-isolated (except for television contact or an occasional bus trip to a store) from the rest of society. Rarely would outside contacts touch the family's firmly entrenched homeostatic mechanisms. They had no relations in the southwestern United States, but Linda had a few friends and someone to date every 2 or 3 weeks. Tommy's father was not presently, nor had he ever been, involved with either his son or Linda, a fact which left her with much bitterness and distrust. Although it appeared at first that she assumed responsibility for her child, it soon became apparent that Helen fulfilled the mothering role for Tommy. Linda's relationship with her son resembled that of an older sibling, rather than a mother, to Tommy. Neither Helen nor Linda worked outside of the home; they derived their income from Social Security and Linda's disability checks.

Working with the discharged schizophrenic client means also working with the family members to promote a healthier level of functioning of the entire family system. One of the nurse's early concerns centered on Tommy and his environment. How was he to be removed from his present isolating experience and exposed to other children and adults? Research into the family backgrounds of schizophrenic clients has shown that the children at risk often require special assistance in broadening their social experiences outside their families.[9] Day care was suggested for Tommy, but until he was toilet-trained, this was not possible. It seemed that neither Helen nor Linda actively attempted to toilet train Tommy because he was needed at home; without Tommy through whom to interact, the two women might have had considerably more difficulty interacting with each other.

Communication within the R. family was not the clear, direct, and congruent pattern of a healthy, adapting family. Often, Linda and Helen carried on parallel monologues and made no attempt to respond to each other's statements. Without the reaffirmation of each other's thoughts and feelings, they were both operating as isolated individuals who had no corrective mechanisms for keeping information up to date and reality-oriented. The nurse realized that neither Helen nor Linda were hearing the impact of their own or each other's messages. Focus of the intervention soon shifted from Tommy's lack of toilet-training to the family's interactional patterns and payoffs.

Certain aspects of "undifferentiated family ego mass" and fusion in members' thoughts and feelings could be seen in the R. family's interaction.[8] Often, Linda would begin a sentence dealing with her emotions about a particular issue and Helen would complete the sentence. Or, Helen might speak to the nurse while Linda listened and continuously nodded her head in agreement. Rarely, especially during the initial visits, were differences of opinion expressed by the two women.

As the story of this family unfolded after several visits, it became clear to the nurse that Helen's marriage had been a source of unhappiness and frustration to her. Her husband had been a weekend drinker who, when drinking, would "lose his temper," destroy furniture, and verbally abuse her and their daughter, Linda. Helen grew increasingly alienated from him and in turn, focused a great amount of attention on Linda. The mother–child relationship became the all-important aspect of her life.

Goals of the nurse's therapeutic intervention included helping Linda and Helen develop a clearer perception of events and a greater awareness of their own and others' thoughts and feelings. Such growth in perception and awareness would permit these insecure, anxious persons to deal more effectively and less fearfully with life's problems.[9]

By helping the family members to tolerate periods of increased anxiety, the nurse hoped to demonstrate that they were not fragile, helpless people who would be harmed by their feelings. Rather, it was essential for the family to learn that anxiety is inevitable during all problem-solving situations, it is necessary for any individual's growth, and it would eventually subside. By demonstrating in face-to-face contacts that anxiety can be tolerated, the nurse hoped to show the R. family that they could live with, and learn from, anxiety. To help build the weakened self-esteem in the R. family, the nurse offered a consistently accepting and nonjudgmental relationship with them.

The nursing approach to the R. family centered on support of the family leader, Linda, in making her own decisions about her future. In the past, Linda had been fearful about any ventures outside of her family. At times, she expressed ambivalence about her confining world at home and wondered aloud to the nurse if she were "smart enough to make it" on her own. Gradually, she began to make more independent choices regarding her own actions. The nurse reinforced any behavior that indicated an opening of this closed family system.

As Linda became more comfortable with her occasional social contacts (a trip shopping or iceskating), her desire for them seemed to increase. Slowly, the nurse introduced the idea of vocational training to Linda. Again, gradually, Linda decided to investigate and, with the nurse's support and presence during the initial visit to the Vocational Rehabilitation Center, followed through with this suggestion.

A job for Linda was not without its reverberations throughout the whole family system. The job could mean loneliness and rejection to Helen, the introduction of new people and new ways of living into the family, increased self-esteem and independence for Linda, and the opening up of a wider, more reality-based world for Tommy.

Certain family "secrets" about Linda's father's drinking and abuse, Linda's repeated psychiatric hospitalizatons, and Helen's feelings of guilt and responsibility for Linda's disturbance were uncovered and addressed within the family setting. Hopefully, dealing with the secret, unspoken issues openly would improve the family's abilities to interact genuinely with each other in the future. Controversial topics between Helen and Linda, such as whether they should move to another location, were not ignored but were explored with the nurse. This was done to demonstrate to them that differences of opinion do not kill either the people or the relationship involved—rather, differences offer stimulation and the opportunity for growth.

Increasing the family's interchanges with the larger community occurred most significantly through Linda's decision to enter vocational testing and later training, through the State Rehabilitation Commission, and through the family's decision to move to a neighborhood that offered a more open environment to the family. The new neighborhood consisted of a younger population of residents, a peer group for Tommy, and easier access to a variety of activities for all family members. The R. family made use of, and benefited from, some planned interventions to influence their interactional patterns—both within and beyond the family.

Questions for Discussion

1. What are the potential problems facing the psychiatric client after discharge from inpatient care? How might these unique needs be met by the mental health team, the client, and his family?
2. Describe the patterns of behavior and communication that are observed in families with a schizophrenic member.
3. Discuss the therapeutic techniques that promote trust and open communication in a closed family system.
4. Create a "family nursing care plan" for the R. family.

References

1. American Psychiatric Association, Diagnostic and Statistical Manual of Mental Disorders, 3rd ed. Washington, DC, American Psychiatric Association, 1980
2. Arieti S: Interpretation of Schizophrenia, 2nd ed. New York, Basic Books, 1974
3. Arieti S: Psychotherapy of Schizophrenia. In West LJ, Flinn DE (eds), Treatment of Schizophrenia: Progress and Prospects, pp 115–130. New York, Grune & Stratton, 1976
4. Arieti S: Psychotherapy of Schizophrenia: New or Revised Procedures. Am J Psychother 34 (October): 464–476, 1980
5. Artiss Lt Col KL, MC: Milieu Therapy in Schizophrenia. New York, Grune & Stratton, 1962
6. Bateson G et al: Toward a Theory of Schizophrenia. In Jackson DD (ed): Communication, Family, and Marriage, pp 31–54. Palo Alto, Science and Behavior Books, 1968
7. Beers CW: A Mind That Found Itself: An Autobiography. New York, Doubleday & Co, 1923
8. Bowen M: Family Psychotherapy. In Howells JL (ed): Theory and Practice of Family Psychiatry, pp 843–862. New York, Brunner/Mazel, 1971
9. Bruch H: Learning Psychotherapy: Rationale and Ground Rules. Cambridge, Harvard University Press, 1974
10. Cancro R: The Healer and Madness. Strecker Monograph Series, No 15. The Fifteenth Institute of Pennsylvania Hospital Award Lecture, 1978
11. Cancro R: Individual Psychotherapy in the Treatment of Chronic Schizophrenic Patients. Am J Psychother 37 (October): 493–501, 1983

12. Deutsh M, Katz I, Jensen AR (eds): Social Class, Race, and Psychological Development. New York, Holt, Rinehart, 1968

13. Ezrin-Waters C, Seeman MV, Seeman P: Tardive Dyskinesia in Schizophrenic Outpatients: Prevalence and Significant Variables. J Clin Psychiatr 42 (January): 16–22, 1981

14. Goldstein WN: DSM-III and the Diagnosis of Schizophrenia. Am J Psychother 37 (April): 168–181, 1983

15. Grunebaum H: Preventive Intervention with Psychotic Mothers: A Controlled Study. In Primary Prevention of Schizophrenia in High-Risk Groups, pp 32–37. Copenhagen, Regional Office for Europe, World Health Organization, 1977

16. Haley J: The Family of the Schizophrenic: A Model System. In Jackson DD (ed): Communication, Family, and Marriage, pp 171–199. Palo Alto, Science and Behavior Books, 1968

17. Jackson DD: The Question of Family Homeostasis. In Jackson DD (ed): Communication, Family, and Marriage, pp 1–11. Palo Alto, Science and Behavior Books, 1968

18. Jarvik ME, Flinn DE, West LJ: Psychopharmacological Treatment of Schizophrenia. In West LJ, Flinn DE (eds): Treatment of Schizophrenia: Progress and Prospects, pp 79–98. New York, Grune & Stratton, 1976

19. Kety SS: Progress in the Psychobiology of Schizophrenia: Implications for Treatment. In West LJ, Flinn DE (eds): Treatment of Schizophrenia: Progress and Prospects, pp 35–43. New York, Grune & Stratton, 1976

20. Laing RD, Esterson A: Sanity, Madness and the Family, 2nd ed. New York, Basic Books, 1971

21. Liberman RP: Behavior Therapy for Schizophrenia. In West LJ, Flinn DE (eds): Treatment of Schizophrenia: Progress and Prospects, pp 175–206. New York, Grune & Stratton, 1976

22. Ludwig AM: Treating the Treatment Failures: The Challenge of Chronic Schizophrenia. New York, Grune & Stratton, 1971

23. Murphy JM, Leighton AH: Approaches to Cross-Cultural Psychiatry. Ithaca, Cornell University Press, 1965

24. Rin H: Schizophrenia: Its Crosscultural Aspect. In Fukuda T, Mitsuda H (eds): World Issues in the Problems of Schizophrenic Psychoses, pp 90–101. Tokyo, Igaku-Shoin, 1979

25. Ruesch J: Synopsis of the Theory of Human Communication. In Howells JG (ed): Theory and Practice of Family Psychiatry, pp 227–266. New York, Brunner/Mazel, 1971

26. Satir V: Peoplemaking. Palo Alto, Science and Behavior Books, 1972

27. Schooler NR, Levine J: Strategies for Enhancing Drug Therapy of Schizophrenia. Am J Psychother 37 (October): 521–532, 1983

28. Seeman P et al: Elevation of Brain Neuroleptic/Dopamine Receptors in Schizophrenia. In Baxter CF, Melnechuk T (eds): Perspectives in Schizophrenia Research, pp 195–202. New York, Raven Press, 1980

29. Seidman LJ: Schizophrenia and Brain Dysfunction: An Integration of Recent Neurodiagnostic Findings. Psychol Bull 94 (September): 195–238, 1983

30. Verhulst J, Schneidman B: Schizophrenia and Sexual Functioning. Hosp Comm Psychiatr 32 (April): 259–62, 1981

31. Weinberger DR, Wyatt RJ: Structural Brain Abnormalities in Chronic Schizophrenia: Computed Tomography Findings. In Baxter CF, Melnechuk (eds): Perspectives in Schizophrenia Research, pp 29–38. New York, Raven Press, 1980

32. Wolman BB: Children Without Childhood: A Study of Childhood Schizophrenia. New York, Grune & Stratton, 1970

33. Zigler E, Glick M: Paranoid Schizophrenia: An Unorthodox View. Am J Orthopsychiatr 5 (January): 43–70, 1984

34. Zubin J: Chronic Schizophrenia from the Standpoint of Vulnerability. In Baxter CF, Melnechuk T (eds): Perspectives in Schizophrenia Research, pp 269–294. New York, Raven Press, 1980

Chapter 23
Suspicious, Hostile, and Aggressive Behavior: The Paranoid and Acting-Out Disorders

Growing up often means facing the anguished isolation of no longer belonging as we wander in exile through a strange world that makes no sense. Each of us must make his or her separate way through an indifferent, unfamiliar landscape in which good is not necessarily rewarded, nor evil punished. Adding to the confusion, at times we find ourselves or others graced with unearned love and happiness or burdened with "undeserved" calamity and pain.

Sheldon Kopp,
An End to Innocence:
Facing Life Without Illusions,
1978

Mary Snyder McElvain

Chapter Preview

Clients exhibiting paranoid and acting-out disorders experience a number of different behaviors and motivations. Nurses observe suspicious, hostile, and aggressive behavior in a variety of situations—in the behavioral pattern of a client with a diagnosed emotional disorder and in the repertoire of responses available to any individual, in any given interaction, without that person being labelled according to a particular clinical category.

This chapter introduces the reader to the concepts of suspicion, hostility, and aggression and explores various theoretical frameworks underlying these concepts. The chapter also reviews the incidence, etiology, and dynamics of the paranoid and acting-out disorders, and focuses on the application of the nursing process to suspicious, hostile, and aggressive behavior. It is through the creative use of personality, a knowledge base, and specific techniques that the nurse, within the format of the nursing process, cares for unique and individual clients.

Learning Objectives

After completing the chapter, the reader will be able to accomplish the following.

1. Differentiate between suspicious, hostile, aggressive, and acting-out behaviors
2. Discuss the incidence of paranoid and acting-out disorders
3. Discuss the psychological, biologic, and sociocultural theories of the etiology of suspicious, hostile, and aggressive behaviors
4. Discuss the dynamics underlying hostility and suspiciousness, impulsivity and acting-out, and anger and aggression
5. Apply the nursing process to clients who demonstrate suspicious, hostile, and aggressive behavior
6. Verbalize awareness of one's own feelings and attitudes when interacting with a person exhibiting hostile, suspicious, or aggressive behavior.

Defining Suspicious, Hostile, and Aggressive Behavior

Suspicious behavior involves hypersensitivity, alertness, and some distortion of reality.[62] The suspicious person uses selective attention to gather information that will fit his schema, confirm his beliefs, and allow rigid conclusions to be drawn.

Hostility is defined as a feeling of antagonism accompanied by a wish to hurt or humiliate others.[32, 56] Because hostility is a sustained feeling, it produces responses that range from overly polite behavior to murderous rage or

suicide.[33] Anger may be differentiated from hostility in that anger does not necessarily involve a wish to harm. *Anger is a physical and emotional state in which an individual experiences a sense of power to compensate for an underlying feeling of anxiety.*[56] In this way, anger may be viewed as a second-level emotion involving the wish to overpower.

Aggression is any behavior that expresses anger or its related emotions.[56] It is also a natural drive that has been classified by Freud and Lorenz as instinctive, classified by others as an elicited drive (described in the frustration–aggression hypothesis), or described as learned social behavior.[32] Aggressive drives are greatly influenced by cultural conditioning and may therefore be turned toward constructive or destructive goals. Many people learn to sublimate, repress, or displace expressions of anger. The struggle for control of these expressions uses much psychic energy and is considered a crucial factor in determining the level of one's mental health.[25, 56]

It is paradoxical that persons who find it intolerable to acknowledge their own hostility tend to perceive the world as hostile, unfriendly, and dangerous.[33] When a person fails to recognize feelings of anger in himself, he may use his anger in a destructive way, and may therefore feel helpless. From this helpless and distorted perspective, the individual is constantly distrustful of others' intentions and continually disappointed because others do not meet his needs. There becomes evident, then, a link between paranoid thinking and hostile, aggressive behavior.

Acting-out behavior consists of impulsive actions or inappropriate verbalizations to express unconscious conflicts. It may be an episodic or a lifelong pattern of behavior and does not automatically include aggressive or antisocial behavior.[7] Even when a person acknowledges his acting-out behavior, he is usually unaware of what motivates the behavior or even what it may communicate to others.[25] For example, some persons who chronically act-out with physical violence do not perceive themselves as having a problem with anger.[35]

Incidence of Paranoid and Acting-Out Disorders

The suspicious and acting-out disorders encompass multiple behaviors and diagnostic categories, thereby making it difficult to arrive at accurate statistical data to explain the incidence. We could, for example, include behaviors as diverse as child abuse, vandalism, and self-mutilation in these disorders.

There exist no valid statistics on the incidence of paranoid disorders due to poor definition, imprecise instruments, and haphazard investigation. Although in one study, paranoid psychoses were found in 12% of psychiatric clients, this fact does not take into account the number of people with some clinical symptoms of paranoia in the general population.[32] The prevalence of antisocial personality disorders ranges from 0.05% to 15%, according to the literature; in prison populations, the prevalence may be 75%.[32]

Persons with socially deviant behavior do not usually seek mental health services voluntarily. The incidence of socially deviant behavior traditionally has been two to three times higher among males than among females.[32] With the changing role of women, however, this trend may already be altered.

Etiologic Theories

Like so many of the behaviors studied in psychiatric-mental health nursing, suspicious, hostile, and aggressive behaviors are multi-determined. In this chapter, the antecedents of these behaviors will be discussed by means of psychological, biologic, and sociocultural theories.

Psychological Theories

Intrapsychic Approaches

Freud believed that aggression stems from redirecting the death instinct away from the self toward others.[32] Antisocial behavior, he said, involves a defective ego that is combined with a weak or immature superego, resulting in the person being unable to control or regulate his behavior but feeling little or no guilt because of the inability.[45] Freud also portrayed paranoid processes as unconscious homosexual tendencies, which an individual defends against through the use of denial and projection.[32]

Other intrapsychic theorists view hostile and aggressive behavior as a result of anxiety and inner conflict, or as energy that is directed into specific character orientations in relating to the world.[30] Specifically, Fromm describes an "exploitative orientation," wherein the source of good and bad lies outside the self. With this orientation, a person values other people and things only for their usefulness.[21]

Another psychological factor in the development of paranoid or antisocial behavior may include "malevolent transformation," in which an individual turns rejection and hatred from the self toward others. On the other hand, the person may use "desensitization," wherein his defense mechanisms operate to deaden feelings toward others.

Other research has supported the *stimulation-seeking hypothesis*; that is, that psychopathic individuals engage in more stimulus-seeking than do neurotic persons.[4, 12] Such findings imply that when intervening with psychopathic individuals, diverse stimuli may be needed to cue and to reinforce behavior, and a particular stimulus may work for only a brief period of time.

A *cognitive model* explains how appraisals, expectancies, and private speech mediate between aversive stimuli and aggressive reactions. Results of one study show that as aggressive behavior becomes more marked, subjects were biased to infer hostility in interpersonal relationships. The threshold for aggressive acts seem to be related to an expectation of hostility from others.[43]

Interpersonal Approaches

Antisocial behavior is often thought to stem from childhood. If, for example, parents alternately infantalize their children and then expect perfection, the child cannot internalize conflicts due to superego defects.[36] Another theory proposes that there is an interactional pattern to antisocial behavior because the behavior is unconsciously encouraged by a parent who obtains vicarious satisfaction from his or her own antisocial impulses.[58] Bowlby feels that lack of attachment to a mother figure during the first 3 years, whether by absence, changes, or deprivation, leads to acting-out behavior later in life.[5]

Considering the importance of the second stage of growth and development, Autonomy versus Shame, in learning controls, it is understandable that parental neglect or inconsistency during this period might have undesirable consequences. This is not to say that a direct cause-and-effect relationship exists between early parental deprivation and later development of an impulsive lifestyle. There is, however, some evidence that relates lack of close emotional ties early in life to affectionless lifestyles.[63]

The third stage of growth and development, Initiative versus Guilt, has also been cited as a crucial time in the formation of social or antisocial traits. If the child lacks a warm, trustworthy role model during this period, he may fail to introject societal values adequately.

Biologic Theories

Biochemical Theories

Biochemical theories of suspicious, hostile, and aggressive behavior focus on the fact that changes in blood chemistry may sensitize or desensitize neural systems for aggression. Underlying those theories is the premise that particular stimuli activate certain neural systems in the brain resulting in a tendency for the organism to behave destructively toward those stimuli complexes. Another stimulus change thereby turns off aggression.

Blood chemistry variables always interact with social, environmental, and learning factors; however, other things being equal, increased androgen levels are associated with increased hostile behavior of some kind. If the progesterone–estrogen ratio is altered, it is possible to decrease feelings of irritability accompanying the premenstrual tension syndrome. Exact endocrine–brain chemistry interactions and their causal relationship to aggressive behavior remain to be discovered.[41] Allergic aggressive reactions have been reported, but their physiology is unclear.

Physiological Theories

Physiological theories have examined the functional integrity of relevant neural systems. The neural system for aggression is found in much of the limbic system. For example, limbic tumors result in personality changes with irritability as a predominant symptom. It is postulated that tumors irritate neurologic mechanisms for aggression or destroy inhibitory mechanisms to aggression. Certain types of brain trauma, rabies, and encephalitis, all of which damage particular portions of the limbic system, are associated with a loss of impulse control. Temporal lobe epilepsy may also activate the neural system for aggression. Specific brain lesions can, likewise, reduce or eliminate excessive hostile behavior.

Genetic Theories

Certain chromosomal abnormalities such as Klinefelter's syndrome and XYY syndrome may result in a lack of impulse control. This occurrence of these disorders points to the existence of a genetic theory. Nevertheless, more evidence is needed to support genetic theories of hostile and aggressive behavior.

Alcoholism and aggressive behavior are certainly linked phenomena, as police and emergency room staffs could verify. Researchers have found that a variation in level of intoxication results in different levels of aggression.[47] Violent behavior associated with alcohol intoxication is related to 64% of all murders, 41% of all assaults, 34% of all rapes, 29% of other sex crimes, and 60% of all cases of child abuse.[50]

Sociocultural Theories

When a person perceives society's norms as ambiguous, weak, or conflicting, he may develop socially deviant behavior.[45] This "social strain theory" proposes that misunderstanding of, or rebellion against, values leads to criminal acts. Certainly, the crises of everyday life among the poor are a social strain. Because different social classes hold different norms for behavior, behavior that is tolerated or promoted in one class becomes deviant when judged by members of another social class.

Another sociocultural theory, the "urbanization theory," states that socialization and its concommitant controls are more effective in folk or rural societies, although urban societies are now more prevalent.[49] Disorganization occurs in some urban families, particularly in slums and ghettos, where bad behavior is punished, but good behavior is rarely rewarded. Children in these families learn to respond to parental moods and discipline, which are external controls, but do not develop internal controls.[40]

One study of boys from a lower-class urban environment examined the three major elements that have an impact on their level of aggression. The first element was the emotional relationship between the boy and his parents.

When parents frequently used physically punitive discipline, threats, or parental rejection, such as unfavorable comments on the boy's worth, their sons were likely to behave in a highly aggressive manner. The second factor was direct control over the boys' behavior. High demands, over-controlled or under-controlled supervision, and inconsistent discipline tended to increase the level of the boys' aggressive behavior. A third element was the family milieu. There was higher aggression in families where one parent undermined or attacked the other; that is, where parental conflict and antagonism were pervasive.[38]

Exposure to aggressive models, especially television violence, has also been studied as a social determinant of aggressive behavior. Researchers have shown that subjects who viewed aggressive human and cartoon models on film showed almost twice as much aggression, when they were later frustrated, than did a control group. One can conclude that filmed aggression facilitates the expression of aggression and shapes the form of subjects' aggressive behavior.[3]

Why is television violence important? After all, it does not control instigators to aggression nor does it provide reinforcement for aggression in real life. It does, however, teach us how to aggress. It also portrays for us the functional value of coercive behavior in achieving material rewards, social recognition, increased self-esteem, or successful retaliation against enemies.[2]

Other research found a strong positive relationship between the violence ratings of favorite programs and aggressive behavior of boys, although there was no corresponding relationship for girls.[16] The single best predictor of how aggressive a young man would be at age 19 was the violence of television programs he preferred at age 8. This seems to be a critical developmental period when the child is very susceptible to violence on television. Girls may have a differential ability to use television as a fantasy experience rather than a realistic one, so that the modeling effect is decreased.[15]

Environmental determinants of aggressive behavior include noise, crowding, and heat. These extrapersonal stressors and situational determinants (*e.g.,* heightened arousal and drugs) have shown inconclusive results as determinants of human aggression.[32] Recently, however, an interesting 18-year study has drawn a profile of 66 aggressive individuals from adolescence into adulthood. A few of the characteristics of children with the most extensive continuing antisocial activity include the following.

1. They are mostly boys.
2. They have the longest preadmission history of childhood problems.
3. Their antisocial and behavioral disturbances are the chief complaints, rather than psychiatric symptoms.
4. Their families have more antisocial backgrounds and there are more single-parent homes.
5. There are more minority children from deprived and disadvantaged areas.[19]

Dynamics of the Paranoid and Acting-Out Disorders

Our curiosity as psychiatric nurses leads us to ask many "why" and "how" questions about human behavior and the situations, predicaments, and crises in which people find themselves. In studying patterns of behavior, the student needs to consider behavior dynamics; that is, what forces within the individual explain particular symptoms or psychiatric syndromes. This chapter considers the dynamics of hostility and suspiciousness, impulsivity and acting-out, and anger and aggression.

Dynamics of Hostility and Suspiciousness

In paranoid disorders, delusions are dominant behavioral symptoms. These delusions may be well-systematized and developed logically, or they may be bizarre and changeable. In either case, suspiciousness, which results in delusions, is a defense against the disintegration of the person's ego.

Paranoid styles of behavior usually involve projection of attitudes about the self, especially feelings of rejection, inadequacy, and inferiority. As the client becomes increasingly anxious in response to intrapersonal, interpersonal, or extrapersonal stressors, his uncomfortable inner feelings are projected and are therefore perceived as a growing danger or threat from without. The client finds a focus for his projected feelings resulting in delusions about the FBI, mafia, extraterrestrial beings, and so on. The client's projection may result in overaggressiveness. On the other hand, the client may use other ego defense mechanisms, such as reaction formation against aggression, dependency needs, and feelings of affection, or denial of certain painful realities.[32]

Lack of trust, the hallmark of suspicious behavior, is probably the result of early parenting in what the child perceives as a hostile environment within an authoritarian or critical family atmosphere. The child becomes hypersensitive to imagined slights.[32] At the same time, the environment may place on the child high expectations for performance. An insecure child may use fantasy to increase his self-esteem or may develop over-determined goals. Social failure later in life may result from rigid or unrealistic goals.

As paranoid ideation progresses, a "pseudocommunity" may develop, wherein the paranoid person ascribes malevolent motivations to real and imagined people.[32] This pseudocommunity can be thought of as the significant others of the paranoid person. The person uses considerable energy in watching for and defending against these negatively significant others.

A very rare occurrence is a shared paranoid disorder, which is called "folie a deux." In "folie a deux," two persons, most commonly sisters, develop a shared delusional system. One of the individuals is likely to have an already established paranoid psychosis and the second person develops a close relationship with her.[32]

Focusing on disrupted communication rather than intrapersonal stressors constitutes an interactionist approach to suspicious behavior. This approach explains that, by exclusion and mutually perceived mistrust, delusions develop over time. In fact, by examining the social environment of the identified client, one may find that the client's significant others use many pretexts, or misstatements, to influence him or gain his cooperation.[63] This pattern of altered communication continually feeds into and fuels his mistrust of others.

Dynamics of Impulsivity and Acting-Out

As with suspicious behavior, impulsive and acting-out behavior has the common dynamic element of mistrust. The impulsive client demonstrates a low frustration tolerance and an inability to postpone gratification. His behavior seems to say, "If I can't have it now, I don't trust either you or me to be able to get it for me later." The client's excessive dependency, combined with a low frustration tolerance, may lead the nurse to feel conflicted and to want to withdraw from him.

Impulsive and acting-out behavior styles are generally characterized as disorders of the superego. Due to faulty identification and learning, the client does not see himself from the perspective of inner ethical principles (conscience), nor from outer standards of authority (morality). He tends to blame all of his difficulties on others; that is, he projects, which usually comes across as a "victim posture" or the attitude that "the world has the problem and must change—not me."

Although the person exhibiting impulsive or acting-out behavior does not have a thought disorder in the sense of the psychotic person's break with reality, his thinking is deficient in being able to predict effects of actions or to problem-solve in terms of long-range consequences. He appears egocentric and without a sense of direction, so the whim becomes all important in his thinking.[63] He views the world as inconsistent, rather than as hostile.

The impulsive or acting-out person denies responsibility for the results of his behavior. He lacks the controls that refine the thinking process; he has not, however, lost control of his aggressive feelings.[26] Although he engages in a great deal of manipulation of the social environment, he feels no guilt about his exploitations.[45]

Impulsive behavior may be described as active or passive. In actively impulsive behavior, the person acts on a whim with contempt for others' feelings or rights. This type of behavior is often found among criminal or delinquent populations. The second, passive type of impulsive behavior is a "giving in" to temptation. This person has lost interest in resisting whatever stimulus is presented and usually possesses a weak or inadequate personality.

A child may develop mistrust and faulty superego functioning when parents delay meeting his needs or act indifferently or rejecting toward him. The child who later exhibits impulsive behavior may have had no role models or may have had models who were deceitful, superficial, or narcissistic.[26]

A newer method of studying and formulating impulsive, acting-out behavior is based on the rational-emotive therapy of Albert Ellis. Impulsive behavior, says Ellis, results from philosophic distortions or irrational beliefs. For the impulsive person, "wants" become "needs" and once a person "needs" something, he is no longer responsible for the behavior it takes to meet that need. This is an example of "the end justifies the means" philosophy. Rational-emotive therapy, however, is descriptive and does not answer why a person confuses his wants and his needs in the first place. Nevertheless, it does offer a framework for intervention with persons with egocentric belief systems and will be discussed further in the chapter.

Dynamics of Anger and Aggression

Anger is a universal human emotion. Some people deny their anger at the expense of considerable psychic energy. Anger is expressed through a wide range of behaviors that are learned and shaped through the socialization process. By identification with role models, by subtle nonverbal cues, and by the consequences of aggressive actions during childhood, individuals grow to learn both healthy and harmful ways to deal with angry feelings.

Anger is also a cover-up. It "veils the original threat which gave rise to anxiety."[29] Anger is a means of neutralizing or avoiding anxiety that arises in response to an interpersonal threat. The insert below shows a model of the development and release of anger.

A Model of Anger

Perceived threat (Frustration, unmet expectations, loss of self-respect)

↓

Anxiety is felt

↓

Anxiety is transformed to anger (Anger gives one a sense of power, and, resultingly, increased self-esteem, which is a stimulus for action.)

↓

Feel relief (If the expression of anger has been forbidden, ignored, or ineffective in the past, the individual will likely experience guilt or lowered self-esteem)

Anger and aggression may be channeled externally or internally.[10, 56] The direct outward expression of anger and aggression may take place through verbal or physical means; it may overpower others or take into consideration the rights of others. There are degrees of direct outward expression of aggression. For example, a person may calmly state, "I am feeling angry enough to hit you," or may shout, "Get out of here or I'll kill you." A person may break a cigarette, hit a wall, turn over a chair, break a window, or break someone's nose. These behaviors occur on a continuum from less severe to more severe and, as a consequence, may result in different kinds of responses to the aggressor.

The indirect, outward expression of anger and aggression may occur through ego defense mechanisms or passive-aggressive behavior. A person may use several defense mechanisms to deal with angry feelings. Through rationalization, a person tries to justify angry behavior by giving motives other than the real ones, for example, "When I get tired, I get grouchy." A person may use reaction formation to disown angry feelings; while actually seething inside, an individual may show undue concern or an oversolicitous attitude toward others. By using fantasy, a person may belittle the object of anger so that it becomes less threatening. Sarcasm or ironical remarks are examples of the magical attack that fantasy entails. Through somatization, a person focuses on bodily aches and pains rather than the anger that festers inside his body. Displacement is used to direct anger toward a safer target. For example, family members are often the recipients of displaced angry feelings from the work setting or vice versa.

A person exhibiting passive-aggressive behavior uses passivity or submissiveness to express hostility or destructive feelings. This is a resistive form of behavior often seen as procrastination, dawdling, stubbornness, intentional inefficiency, or forgetfulness. Parent–child interactions that lead to passive-aggressive behaviors probably involve some inhibition of the child's assertiveness, with only partial and grudging satisfaction of his dependency needs. The child, therefore, develops a behavior pattern wherein he learns to attract attention and, at the same time, cause discomfort to authority figures. His dependency needs insure that he seldom, if ever, expresses anger directly.

Psychoanalytic theory proposes that the inward expression of angry feelings is seen as depression or self-destructive acts. Another view, however, states that hostility is a defense against depression, rather than a cause of it.[33]

A therapist who works within a psychoanalytic framework supports the client in expressing his repressed angry feelings in order to relieve the depression. When angry feelings are viewed as a defensive mechanism, however, the therapist may only be strengthening the client's defenses through attention to angry feelings rather than focusing on depressive ones.

Application of the Nursing Process to Suspicious, Hostile, and Aggressive Behavior

Assessment and Analysis

The astute nurse assesses clients for cues indicating suspicious, hostile, and aggressive behavior (see the insert, Diagnosing the Suspicious Client). The nurse then uses the nursing process to defuse volatile situations or to channel the expression of these emotions as constructively as possible.

Therapeutic assessment begins with asking questions. It never assumes that the nurse knows the meaning behind a given behavior or that a certain client will respond in a particular fashion in a particular situation. To describe and explain behaviors, it is useful and helpful to ask, "Which are the problematic behaviors, for whom, and why?"

Nursing Diagnosis

Diagnosing the Suspicious Client

The nurse selects, from among a list of standardized nursing diagnoses, those which are relevant to a particular client. The data gathered about an individual client form the basis for the determination of the final nursing diagnosis or diagnoses. The nurse considers the following probable and possible nursing diagnoses when working with a client who is suspicious.

Probable Nursing Diagnosis	*Type of Data Supporting the Nursing Diagnosis*
1. Anxiety	1. Client perceives threat to self-concept and lacks trust in new environment and strangers.
2. Impaired verbal communication	2. Client withdraws and refuses to speak or becomes argumentative over the precise meanings of words. Either pattern of communication disrupts usual flow of conversation.
3. Coping, ineffective individual	3. Client demonstrates distortion or confusion of roles, difficulty making decisions, destructive behavior, and inappropriate use of defense mechanisms.
4. Powerlessness	4. Issues of control are manifest in client's interactions. Client has heightened awareness of need to control.
5. Self-concept, disturbance in	5. Client's negative view of self is often displayed as attack on, or withdrawal from, others. Client may inappropriately attempt to direct own treatment.
6. Social isolation	6. Client withdraws from others due to mistrust.
7. Thought processes, alterations in	7. Client has difficulty evaluating reality problem-solving, and poor judgment, and may have hallucinations or delusions.
Possible Nursing Diagnosis	*Supporting Data*
8. Activity intolerance	8. Client does not tolerate an incease in activity, lacks

Possible Nursing Diagnosis	*Supporting Data*
	incentive to participate, and lacks trust in the person asking him to participate.
9. Ineffective family coping	9. Client's history shows evidence of ineffective or abusive relationship with parents, spouse, children.
10. Diversional activity deficit	10. Hospitalized client feels trapped in inpatient unit with nothing he wishes to do.
11. Health maintenance, alterations in	11. Client does not perceive threat to health (*e.g.*, "There's nothing wrong with me"), resulting in refusal of medications or other therapies.
12. Home maintenance management, impaired because of mental status	12. Client exhibits delusional thinking. He doesn't assume usual responsibilities around the home, or he takes control inappropriately.
13. Potential for injury related to perceptual deficit	13. Hallucinations may direct or command the client to harm self or others. Poor judgment may lead client to put self in dangerous situations.
14. Knowledge deficit	14. Client denies his situation or inaccurately perceives his health status. Client's anger may interfere with adherence to prescribed health behavior.
15. Mobility, impaired physical	15. Client who is physically restrained has impaired mobility.
16. Noncompliance	16. Client does not comply with therapeutic regimen due to prior negative experiences with psychiatric personnel, lack of trust in general, nontherapeutic environment, or unsatisfactory relationship with caregiver, expensive therapy, health beliefs that are different from professional advice, poor self-esteem, or negative side effects from psychotropic medication.
17. Nutrition, alterations in: less than body requirements	17. Client believes that food is poisoned, or that staff has slipped unwanted medication into food or drink, and stops eating due to mistrust. If nutritonal status changes, client may suffer from alterations in bowel elimination or fluid volume deficit.
18. Parenting, alterations in	18. Stress of entire family unit is

Possible Nursing Diagnosis	*Supporting Data*
	increased when one member has psychiatric problems.
19. Self-care deficit	19. Client is unwilling to eat, bathe, or groom self satisfactorily.
20. Sensory-perceptual alterations	20. Psychotropic medications may slow reactions to environment. Client undergoes physical isolation if he is in restraints or otherwise secluded from others.
21. Sexual dysfunction	21. Client experiences decreased libido or impotence as side effects of some of the psychotropic medications. Lack of trust limits selection of sexual partner or hinders sexual performance. Hospitalization results in separation from partner.
22. Sleep pattern disturbance	22. Hospital environmental or anxiety decreases ability to sleep. Tranquilizing medication increases sleep or drowsiness.
23. Violence, potential for	23. Perceived threat to self-esteem, misperceived messages from others, dysfunctional verbal communication patterns to relieve stress, and hostility lead to violent behaviors. Client has history of lack of control or acting-out behavior.

Environmental Factors

Environmental influences are important factors in assessing suspicious, hostile, and aggressive behavior. New and unfamiliar surroundings may increase the client's mistrust or frighten him to such an extent that he feels the need to protect himself. The amount of stimulation in the environment (*i.e.*, the noise, lighting, temperature, clutter, or crowding) may also cue suspiciousness and hostility. In locked psychiatric units, the locked door may symbolize entrapment or punishment against which a client feels powerless and, eventually, angry. Uniforms, whether worn by professionals from the emergency room, security guards, or police, may trigger feelings of rebellion against authority in a client with poor impulse control or poor reality testing. Nurses are able to regulate environmental stressors when these stressors impact negatively on clients.

Indicators of Dangerous Behavior

The unpredictability of suspicious, hostile, and aggressive behavior bothers many beginning practitioners in psychiatric-mental health nursing. Watching for behavioral cues and listening carefully for the feeling tone or latent communication of a client enables the nurse to prevent hostile feelings from escalating into dangerous actions. Some indicators of suspicious or dangerous behavior include the following.

1. Thinking and perception
   Hallucinations or delusions that threaten the client with harm or command the client to harm; for example, a new father hears voices telling him to take his baby to another town to save him from murderers
2. Motor activity
   Increased psychomotor agitation, which is often a signal that the client cannot tolerate physical closeness; for example, a client begins to pace the hall rapidly
3. Mood or affect
   Increased intensity of affect or verbalizations or a noticeable change in the manner in which

a client expresses wants and needs; for example, a client's voice quivers and she pleads with psychiatric staff to let her out of the hospital before she loses control

4. Physical state

Organic states in which the client may be unable to communicate a warning, such as beginnings of seizures, delirium, brain lesions, or withdrawal states

5. Context

History of violent outbursts against self or others, which may include repeated criminal behavior or multiple suicide attempts; for example, a client is known to engage in physical fights with other clients and staff on previous admissions

Use of alcohol, other addictive drugs, or hallucinogenic drugs that remove controls on behavior; for example, a client is admitted with known phencyclidine (PCP) ingestion.[1, 26, 45, 53]

These predictors indicate that the impulse control of an adult or adolescent is disturbed in some way. There is a "childhood triad" of behaviors that is used to ascertain the seriousness of impulse control disturbance in children. These three behaviors are firesetting, bedwetting, and cruelty to animals. The consistency of this particular combination of behaviors has been found to correlate with some degree of socially aberrant behavior in children.[54]

Assessing Potential for Violence. One aspect of every mental status assessment is assessing the individual's potential for violence. During initial interviews with the client, or whenever the nurse suspects the possibility of suicidal or homicidal behavior, the nurse should ask, "Do you feel like hurting yourself or anyone else?" The nurse will not introduce ideas of violence into the client's head. Instead, by asking the question directly, the nurse promotes a healthy role model of verbalization in place of acting-out behavior. If the client is a poor historian or is unable to respond, the nurse may need to interview people who accompany the client to the clinic or hospital regarding the client's impulse control. The nurse asks those accompanying the client how he has managed aggressive feelings in the past.[32] At this time, the nurse may also offer information about how the hospital will help the client control his behavior.

Degrees of Suspicion, Hostility, and Aggression

Just as there are four stages of anxiety, there are several degrees of suspicious, hostile, and aggressive behavior. Some of the terms used to describe these various degrees are vigilant, sensitive, hypersensitive, paranoid, underlying

hostility, thinly-veiled hostility, overt hostility, belligerent, aggressive, and assaultive. The aim of nursing, of course, is not to eradicate the client's feelings, but to teach the constructive expression of these feelings and to provide a safe environment for staff and clients.

Assessing Client's Control and Knowledge

Suspicious, hostile, and aggressive feelings and behaviors may be assessed on a continuum from less severe to more severe, or they may be assessed in relation to two ego functions, control and knowledge. By considering the correlation of control of behavior and knowledge of feelings, the nurse gains direction in planning nursing interventions. In Table 23-1, possible nursing interventions are suggested for different levels of client ego functioning and different degrees of control and knowledge.

The nurse uses assessment skills to decide if a given client is in control and knows what he is feeling and doing. Judging whether someone is in control of his behavior is easier than deciding whether someone understands his feelings. Many times, nurses confuse these two ego functions, control and knowledge, and insist that a client "should control" his behavior whenever he exhibits self-awareness; however, any of us may have habits of behavior that have harmful effects, yet we are not "in control" or able to stop the habits at will.

Transactional Analysis Framework for Assessment

Transactional analysis has been suggested as a helpful way to assess nurse–client interactions.[27, 56] Using the framework of adult, parent, and child ego states, the nurse determines that the suspicious, hostile, and aggressive client is most often responding on the basis of his "child" state. Ideally, in these situations, the nurse responds from an "adult" state, which is logical, factual, and assertive, but not aggressive. The goal of the nurse is twofold—to respond from an adult state and to guide the client to respond from his adult state also.

Table 23-1. **Control and Knowledge of Suspicious, Hostile, and Aggressive Feelings and Behavior: Possible Nursing Interventions**

	CONTROL OF BEHAVIOR	NO CONTROL OF BEHAVIOR
Knowledge of feeling	No intervention needed	Behavior modification Psychotherapy Medication (chemical restraint)
No knowledge of feeling	Confrontation Role-playing Insight therapy Education	Chemical restraint Physical restraint Isolation from others

Planning

Goal Setting

How the nurse assesses the multiple factors involved in the client's expression of suspicious, hostile, and aggressive feelings will determine how she plans appropriate interventions. Overall goals for paranoid or acting-out clients are consistent with the stages of growth and development that have been negatively resolved. These goals include the following.

1. To increase trust in interpersonal relationships and trust in self
2. To maintain control over the expression of feelings and resultant behavior
3. To increase social awareness
4. To promote the development of values and conscience

In addition to setting these goals, the nurse plans secondary prevention activities designed to intervene with the client's dependency needs, level of anxiety, self-esteem, low frustration tolerance, and physical needs. Planning also takes into account the greater potential for manipulation in relationships with these clients.

Discharge Planning

Discharge planning for paranoid and acting-out clients may involve coordination with social agencies other than mental health facilities (*e.g.*, public health agencies, probation departments, and welfare services). New support systems must be developed if a client has exhausted or "worn out" his former supports. Families may be frightened of a returning client if incidents of hostile and aggressive behavior were traumatic and family members have not worked through their feelings.

Paranoid and acting-out clients are likely to have many resistive defenses. They do not feel that their behavior or attitude requires any modification, and they demand instead that others change their behavior. Some clients have been through their communities' legal, mental health, and various assistance programs to the extent that workers and officials offering these services are "worn out" by the client. The inclination of some mental health professionals may be to discharge them "to the streets" without referral or follow-up treatment. Other clients may be discharged on the condition that they "get out of town" and cause no further trouble in a particular community. A change of scenery for the client does not, however, alleviate stressors, nor is it a way to decrease impulsive, antisocial behavior. An exception to this is the situation in which a person may be removed from a particular community for the purpose of changing friends who trigger certain undesirable behaviors.

Intervention

Nurses are challenged when intervening with clients who demonstrate paranoid and acting-out behavior because they frequently also exhibit hostility and resistance. These clients are usually not asking for help from mental health professionals; in fact, they may say directly, "go away." The nurse who understands the client's sense of inadequacy and inferiority will decode his verbal and nonverbal communications as "go away closer" and, therefore, will not be put off by the client's often involuntary status, resistance, and noncompliance.

Primary Prevention

Suspicious, hostile, and aggressive behavior is other-directed, social behavior; therefore, the nurse must take into account the context in which it occurs. Primary prevention must be addressed if mental health professionals do not wish to perpetrate conditions that foster this behavior. Our communities are often breeding grounds for continued rage and violence.[8, 26] The insanity of hunger, poverty, unemployment, and overcrowding cannot be accepted as "givens" in society. Strengthening family systems, identifying and treating maternal depression, and preventing and treating child abuse and neglect are specific areas for primary prevention efforts by mental health professionals.[45]

Intervening Before the Outbreak of Aggression

Do studies dealing with decreasing aggression among children have any bearing on reducing the frequency of aggressive behavior in adults? One study, for example, showed that aggressive behavior in children could be reduced through decreasing aggressive models.[17] Similarly, on psychiatric units, could not criticism, bickering, and dissension among staff members be reduced and greater nurturing of clients be provided as a corrective emotional experience? Modeling includes gentle but firm attitudes of staff members and the selection of nonviolent television programming on units.

An "ounce of prevention" is worth more than a pound of cure when it applies to the prevention of violence in a psychiatric-mental health facility. Loss of control accompanied by violence always damages self-esteem and interpersonal relationships. Skill in detecting the client's wish for control and the ability to set limits without being punitive are professional hallmarks toward which nurses strive. It greatly reassures clients to know that they will not be allowed to be destructive.

A first step in intervening before the outbreak of aggression is to remember that hostility is a second-level emotion. The nurse constantly assesses the client's feeling tone and then deals with signs of his anxiety or fear that could escalate into angry feelings and behaviors. Genuineness and empathy are attitudes to be cultivated when working with hostile clients. These attitudes serve to elicit responses that are incompatible with anger or violent acts and may deter such behavior. The nurse also keeps her verbal tone light and matter-of-fact, rather than intense and authoritarian to avoid challenging or provoking the client who has poor impulse control.

Humor that does not demean the client may be used in some situations to elicit feelings of amusement. Humor is not useful, however, with paranoid clients because it is too likely to be misinterpreted.

The use of humor is demonstrated in the following incidents.

Client: "Who do you think you are, telling me I seem angry this morning?"
Nurse: "You're saying that, if I were an umpire in a baseball game, that would have been a bad call?"

or

Client: "If that lady doesn't shut up, I'll punch her lights out."
Nurse: "That would be great on a movie set in some violent scene, but here in the hospital, control is the name of the game."

People want to be listened to and understood. When a client is angry, the nurse can reduce his feelings of being threatened and minimize defensiveness by restating the feeling and content of what he has communicated.[31] For example, the client says, "I've been in this ___ ___ hospital for 4 days and no one will go to my apartment and get my clothes. I'm being held against my will and I'm going to sue everyone involved on this ward." The nurse might respond, "I hear how frustrated you are to be here and not to believe anyone is doing anything for you."

The initial interview is an important time to try to defuse anger and convey the attitude that psychiatric-mental health professionals are willing and able to work with the client. The client may stare angrily at the nurse without speaking. To meet that gaze directly communicates that the nurse is trustworthy. Instead of trying to convince the client of the nurse's friendliness, the nurse portrays professional understanding by commenting on the client's anger and mistrust. Feelings that are brought out into the open can be discussed. If the client tries to control the interview with myriad complaints, the nurse refocuses his attention by asking him how the nurse can be of help.[32]

Dealing with Manipulation.

When a client is struggling with the issue of control, the probability increases that he will use manipulation. *Manipulation* is the process of influencing another to meet or comply with one's own needs and wishes, regardless of the needs and wishes of the other.[25] When manipulation exists, the goals of the nurse and client conflict. If the nurse is manipulated into believing an untrue story about the client or is manipulated into meeting his dependency needs, such as dressing him when he is able to dress himself, the nurse may be ridiculed by peers or counseled to "be more firm" with clients. In this situation, the nurse often feels powerless and "used." As a consequence of having been manipulated, many nurses refuse to meet any dependency needs of clients and overreact to clients' need to control interactions. If nurses respond to clients with defensiveness and anger, this cycle continues and sets up barriers to effective communication.

The key to avoiding manipulation is to be as clear as possible about each other's goals; that is, to verbalize conflicts rather than operating out of "hidden agendas." The nurse's own annoyance at meeting a client's request or demand is an early clue that manipulation may be occurring. The nurse then asks what is happening in the nurse–client relationship and how she feels about it. Restating what each person wants from the other may correct misperceptions of roles and expectations.

Preventing Loss of Control.

Whenever the nurse feels as though she must be very careful not to upset the client, the nurse may be detecting subtle cues of the client's impending loss of control. In this event, the astute nurse will intervene in one of several ways.

1. Environmental manipulation by decreasing frightening stimuli or by giving the client more space
2. A calm, self-assured, and helpful attitude toward the client by identifying self and giving succinct explanations of what is happening or what is expected of him. (Allowing the client to "save face" by suggesting alternatives, such as "let's walk off some of that energy," is more helpful than issuing commands, such as "stop what you're doing or you'll go into the seclusion room.")
3. Offering medication, usually the major tranquilizers, which decrease anxiety, agitation, and delusions[26, 63]

Indications for Medication.

Often, major tranquilizers are offered to clients to help control their agitation or rage. It should be noted that paradoxical rage has been observed in a few individuals receiving benzodiazepines.[5] Chlordiazepoxide may tend to increase aggressiveness and is therefore useful with clients who are inhibited and could benefit from expressing aggression. On the other hand, oxazepam seems to have no effect on aggression and may be a better medication for clients with poor impulse control.[5, 22] Initial studies also indicate that lithium may have a reasonably specific antihostility action, but further investigation is needed to confirm that finding.[55, 59]

Validating and Expressing Feelings.

If the nurse has previously established a therapeutic relationship with the client, she may intervene to prevent the outbreak of aggression by talking with him, usually on a one-to-one basis, to validate assumptions about his feelings. The nurse encourages the client to describe and clarify the present experience to increase his awareness of feelings and what triggers them. The nurse then helps the client choose to express his feelings in a socially acceptable manner. The nurse may direct the client to sublimate the energy generated by his feelings

Case Study

Inpatient Treatment for an Impulsive and Aggressive Young Adult

Johnny M. was admitted to the psychiatric inpatient unit at the local general hospital for the fifth time in 2 years. Johnny is 23 years old, from a minority ethnic background. He quit school at age 15, supposedly to start working, but he drank and caroused so extensively that he was unable to hold even menial jobs. He spent several short periods of time in the county jail before he was 21 years old. It was during his time in jail that he was first referred for psychiatric observation because he had many physical fights with other inmates; however, when placed in a cell by himself, he would be self-destructive. Presently, when police pick him up for fighting or destroying property, they bring him to the psychiatric unit, rather than booking him into jail. He is often drunk or high on street drugs when he comes to the attention of authorities.

Johnny has an older brother with whom he lives from time to time. When they have a disagreement, one of them throws the other one out. Johnny supports himself on disability checks he gets for a back injury sustained at age 19, when he worked at a construction job for 3 months. He still portrays a "macho" image and has some skill at finding women with whom to live and who are willing to support him for awhile. He was married for 6 months at age 17, still talks about the girl because "she messed up my head," and, in fact, stabbed himself when she divorced him.

When the nurse admitting Johnny asked him to comment on his frequent admissions to the psychiatric unit over the past 2 years, he said, "Hey, my friends have split and nobody wants to help me out. Everybody's interested in locking me up and throwing away the key. Only the nurses know there's nothing wrong with me. I think the cops get their kicks out of hassling me." The nurse also noted Johnny's lack of insight, his loneliness, and his use of projection. She decided to ask the treatment team to discuss Johnny's plan of care to try to break the discouraging cycle of admissions.

When the team met the next day, they decided that treatment must include attention to Johnny's psychological needs, his diminishing relationships with family and friends, and his social environment, including the drug culture and lack of job training.

Johnny is an example of the "fuzzy distinction between criminal justice and the mental health systems."[37] Because he bounces from legal system to mental health system to social or disability payment systems, his care has been fragmented, repetitive, and ineffective. Some professionals in each system have been only too glad to pass him to another system because working with him is frustrating.

At this point, the treatment team acknowledged accountability for Johnny's care. They invited Johnny to the team meeting and obtained his permission to contact family members and agency workers. They explained to Johnny that "help" involves working together to move forward, not "passing the buck" and moving in circles. Johnny's loneliness is an emotion from which he cannot escape as he has done in the past. He has finally experienced enough pain to agree to start a new treatment plan. The treatment team has no illusions that Johnny's progress will be rapid or easy to effect. His impulsiveness and hostile-aggressive feelings are habitual and, in response to stress, he is likely to regress to those styles of behaving and feeling.

Questions for Discussion

1. What is the connection between the legal system and the mental health system? What does "accountability" in those systems mean?
2. How are issues of authority, responsibility, trust, and control manifest with the young adult client who displays impulsive and aggressive behavior?
3. Discuss the therapeutic techniques that are useful and those that are noneffective in an initial interview with a client who is toxic on alcohol or street drugs.
4. Describe the new, young, chronic population of psychiatric clients.
5. Formulate a nursing care plan for Johnny M. based on needs and problems identified by the treatment team.

---

in a number of activities, or the nurse may role play with the client the direct expression of feelings in hypothetical situations.[33,45] In these instances, the nurse uses the positive aspects of her relationship with the client to neutralize his aggressive drives.[19] (See the dialogue, De-escalating Angry Feelings.)

Removing Sensory Reinforcement. There are research data to suggest that sensory reinforcement maintains some instances of aggression.[28] The treatment implications of this finding indicate that undesirable behavior may be suppressed by removing sensory consequences (*e.g.*, by not yelling or acting startled if someone bangs a fist on the

Therapeutic Dialogue

De-escalating Angry Feelings

The client is sitting alone in the day room of an inpatient unit where several other clients are talking quietly or involved in activities.

Nurse: (approaches client) You've been sitting here for some time by yourself, Mike. I'd like to sit with you now. (sits down)

Client: Ah, get out of here. Just go.

Nurse: You're very firm in that command, Mike. I'm concerned about your feelings being bottled up.

Client: (sarcastic tone of voice) Oh sure, everyone is so concerned about me. (voice becomes louder) Then why did they drag me in here so I'll lose my job?

Nurse: That's a lot to sort out. (continuing in matter-of-fact tone) You don't want to be here, you're upset with someone, and you're afraid you'll lose your job.

Client: If you can solve all that, sister (snicker), you're a better man than I am.

Nurse: Which part of it do you want to tackle first?

Client: I just want you to get out of here and leave me alone before I blow my stack.

Nurse: You haven't blown your stack yet, which shows good control of your behavior. One way to stay in control here is to talk things out a little at a time. For now, how would you like some coffee or juice?

Discussion

When a client "looks" angry, it may be difficult for the nurse to approach him because of the nurse's fear of rejection. In many cases, however, the nurse must assume responsibility for initiating the interaction or the client will remain withdrawn. In this situation, the nurse tells Mike she will sit with him rather than asking his permission to sit; he still has a choice of whether or not he wants to talk. The nurse's metacommunication says, "You are worth my time."

Mike's initial attitude suggests that he may be testing others' concern for him because of prior negative experiences. When the nurse encounters a defensive, angry client, data must be collected regarding his skill in relating to others in the past. The nurse looks for patterns of behavior which indicate that the client is developing a beginning level of trust. During this interaction, Mike continues to "push away"; therefore, the nurse proceeds slowly.

Initially, the nurse informs Mike that she hears his wish to be left alone. The nurse then continues to verbalize her interest in him. Mike's response shows a defensive, victim posture ("they dragged me in here"), which tells the nurse his anxiety level is rising. Again, the nurse uses the communication technique of paraphrasing to list the various ideas Mike has expressed both overtly and covertly. The nurse tries to help Mike focus his thoughts and feelings rather than making global statements.

In the midst of this interaction, the nurse detects Mike's feelings of low self-esteem and of being overwhelmed. Instead of assuming the client's sense of powerlessness, the nurse conveys the ideas that he can approach his problems bit by bit. By asking Mike what *he* wants, the nurse conveys to him that, with the nurse's help, he is responsible for setting goals in his treatment.

Mike's response to the nurse's attempt at goal-setting is to push the nurse away again. His response indicates a low level of frustration tolerance to demands being placed on him. The nurse recognizes his rising anxiety level for the second time and his need to distance people. The nurse compliments Mike on his control, although it may be tenuous, and makes the covert issue of control overt. It is also necessary for the nurse to educate the client about the unit's expectations for maintaining control. The stated expectations offer the client the alternative of ventilating at his own pace rather than acting-out.

Finally, the nurse gives the client another alternative to his angry posture in her suggestion to use a socially approved means of relaxing. The nurse may use the client's reaction to her offer of coffee or juice for further assessment of whether an alliance is forming.

This interaction shows that nursing interventions do not have to be "heavy" to be therapeutic. In this brief encounter, the nurse was constantly aware of the client's varying anxiety level and his need for increased self-esteem. Nursing interventions, therefore, were directed to those two areas of need while attempting to build rapport and help the client focus on goals.

---

table). On the other hand, aggressive acts may be replaced with more socially acceptable behavior that still has sensory consequences (*e.g.*, hitting a pillow or a punching bag, rather than a human).

Decreasing the Client's Suspicious Behavior

The suspicious client is one who uses avoidance, resistance, testing, and manipulation to protect a fragile self. The client will respond more readily to one or two mental health

Therapeutic Dialogue

Interacting with a Paranoid Client

Nurse: (approaching client on an inpatient unit) Mr. W., would you like to attend group therapy this afternoon?

Client: Is it recorded?

Nurse: No, Mr. W, there are no tape recorders in the room.

Client: But everything we say right now is being heard through those vents (points to air conditioning vents near ceiling).

Nurse: Mr. W, those are air conditioning vents to keep the temperature comfortable. You are safe here in the hospital.

Client: They would love to know what I'm saying.

Nurse: Who is "they"?

Client: You'll probably run tell them.

Nurse: Mr. W., I'm Jack, the nurse working with you here in the hospital. You sound anxious. Did my asking about group therapy lead to anxious feelings?

Discussion

The client with whom the nurse is interacting is severely paranoid as evidenced by his delusional thinking. Many people approach novel situations with caution, but for clients who mistrust, making a choice involving some interpersonal risk is especially frightening.

The nurse approaches the client with a clear, direct question regarding an activity. Throughout the interaction he clarifies misperceptions in a straightforward but nonargumentative manner. The nurse reaffirms his own identity and assures the client of his safety as necessary. Emphasis is placed on reality orientation to person and place because the client's delusional thinking may confuse this experience with future fantasies or past memories.

Finally, the nurse externalizes the feeling (in this case, anxiety) that may have precipitated the suspicious sequence. If the client can begin to connect his feeling state with his thought processes, he may begin to understand and to control some of the faulty conclusions he draws.

The nurse does not pursue the global pronoun, "they," at this time because the client's guardedness serves a defensive function and the nurse is working to establish trust. It would be appropriate to do so in another context. Too many questions, especially with no comments or statements interspersed with the questions, are likely to be attacked by the paranoid client.

By focusing on process, or what is happening in the relationship, rather than on content, the nurse avoids the trap of trying to talk a client out of delusional thinking and, instead, gives feedback and allows the relationship to develop at the client's pace.

care providers working with him consistently, rather than a number of different staff members. Gradually, he will form relationships with a few significant others. The nurse makes undemanding, brief contacts with the client at first, knowing that he needs to distance to preserve his sense of self (see the dialogue, Interacting with a Paranoid Client). The client may perceive the approaches of others as attacks.

Maintaining honesty, adhering to a schedule, and following through on commitments made to the suspicious client are important ways for the nurse to increase her credibility. A matter-of-fact, rather than a warm, approach allows the client to set the pace for closeness.[45]

Counteracting Misperceptions. The nurse does not touch a client who exhibits suspicious behavior. Again, touch may be perceived as an attack, even a sexual advance or threat, by a delusional client. Likewise, the nurse is careful to do nothing that may be construed as secretive in front of the suspicious client. The nurse is honest in answering questions about medication that may be mixed with fruit juice, or any other questions about various treatment approaches. Simple, straightforward explanations are best in that they provide the client with less material for distortion. The nurse neither whispers in front of the client nor discusses other clients within the hearing range of the suspicious client.

Decreasing the Client's Hostile Behavior

The nurse assists the hostile client to move from reliance on external controls to his own internal controls. Nevertheless, the nurse does not hesitate to apply external controls when necessary for safety. If the client's hostility escalates to the level of assaultiveness, the psychiatric nursing staff should initiate the quick, decisive teamwork. The guiding principle in applying external controls is to assemble and use sufficient staff members to deal with the situation safely. Often, a "show of force" alone will subdue a client who is out of control (see Nursing Care Plan, The Client Who Is Hostile and Suspicious).

Applying External Controls. On units where there is an increased possibility of physical assaultiveness, such as emergency rooms, intensive care units, and psychiatric in-patient units, all staff should be aware of a general plan of action and should also be familiar with their responsibility should an incident occur. During an incident of assaultive behavior, one staff member acts as the leader and issues directions to other staff with key words, such as "now," to approach the client and take hold of his limbs. The team surrounds the client rather than backing him into a corner, because the client may decide that his only way out of a corner is to attack. Team members remain calm while the leader communicates to the client in direct terms, "We are not going to allow you to hurt yourself or anyone else."

Anxiety is communicated interpersonally—it is contagious. During an incident of aggressive behavior, everyone's adrenalin seems to flow. It is the nurse's responsibility to manage anxiety levels and especially to keep herself in a mild to moderate range of anxiety. At all times, staff members strive to maintain the client's self-esteem. The nurse's attitude of being authoritative rather than authoritarian, and setting limits rather than punishing are the media through which the client's self-esteem is maintained.

When the client returns to a moderate level of anxiety, the nurse clarifies with him what occurred, what feelings were involved, and what might be learned from the situation. The nurse uses this problem-solving approach with all clients who are capable of learning from their behavior. The nurse conveys the message "Your behavior was/is unacceptable, but you are acceptable."[45]

Use of Restraints and Seclusion.

There are several treatment alternatives to intervene in assaultive behavior. Chemical restraints (major tranquilizers), physical restraints, and seclusion rooms may be used separately, or in combination, according to protocols in given treatment settings. Because these three forms of restraint are restrictive therapies, there must be clear guidelines and a physician's order for their use. The purposes of restraint are containment of injurious actions, isolation to reduce difficult interpersonal relationships, and decreased sensory input to relieve sensory overload.[62] There must also exist objective criteria for terminating the use of seclusion rooms or restraints, rather than relying on arbitrary feeling states of the nursing staff. Criteria for release from restraint or seclusion may be grouped in the following categories.

1. Psychomotor agitation, assessed by means of decreased restlessness, lowered blood pressure, and pulse rate
2. Stabilization of mood, assessed by means of absence of physical threats, lowered anxiety level, consistency of verbal and nonverbal behavior, and feelings of trust in staff
3. Cognitive processes, assessed by means of insight and ability to look at precipitating incident in objective manner, increased ability to concentrate, and improved reality testing[62]

The seclusion process is more likely to meet client needs, rather than staff needs, when standards for the use of seclusion rooms and restraints are developed and employed. One study found that, during evening and night shifts, staff use seclusion rooms more frequently than do staff on day shifts. Also, shifts that are staffed primarily with female employees use seclusion more often than shifts during which numbers of male staff predominate. Seclusion is, in effect, an "intensive care environment" in which the client requires additional monitoring and staff involvement.[11, 52]

Nursing intervention with a client who is hostile but not assaultive may require "waiting him out." Dr. Karen Horney conceptualized all behavior as being motivated by the desire to move toward, move away from, or move against someone else. When we assess the angry client as moving against us in a self-defensive maneuver, we can show a willingness to listen and demonstrate respect and caring for the individual.[42] When we assure the client that he is safe with us, his defensive, hostile behavior often subsides.

Exploring and Controlling Angry Behavior.

The nurse may observe various types of hostile behavior exhibited by psychiatric-mental health clients. A *grandiose* client may state, "When I get out of here, I'll buy a decent hospital for anyone who wants to be admitted," implying that the present treatment is inadequate. The client with *hyperreligiosity* may become angered when others challenge his claims to be a deity or disagree with his interpretation of theology. Likewise, the client who is a *champion of causes* arouses hostility when followers are not forthcoming. Lastly, the client (seen especially in involuntary settings) with a *propensity for litigation* can be verbally threatening to psychiatric staff members who, in turn, often react in defensive, sarcastic, or placating manners. A guiding principle of intervention with each of these hostile clients is to avoid power struggles and, instead, focus on establishing a therapeutic alliance where trust and learning occur.

Although the nurse may assess a client as angry or hostile, the client may not be aware of those emotions or may deny them. In trying to validate her perceptions, the nurse uses terms such as "you seem upset (or irritated, or frustrated)," rather than "you seem angry (or mad)," because the latter terms are emotionally loaded words that provoke an even more intense reaction.[56] Helping clients explore their anger is often a lengthy process and involves a great deal of reteaching, redirecting, and resetting of priorities.

Research on cognitive techniques to control anger has determined that it is important to remain task-oriented when faced with a provocation.[44] Less anger is aroused if one defines a situation as a problem that calls for a solution, rather than as a threat that calls for an attack. Early recognition of arousal is also an important principle of anger control. The further a person has progressed into the provocation sequence, the less likely he is to initiate effective self-control.[44]

Behavior therapists may help an individual become more aware of angry feelings by requesting the client to count the number of times each day when he experiences the feeling of irritation or anger, no matter how slight the feeling. To understand better what triggers the feelings, the therapist then asks the client to describe the situations surrounding these incidents. Imagery and role playing are other techniques by which an individual may become more aware of his feelings and may practice his responses in given situations.[35]

Frequently, the nurse is the recipient of the client's hostility. If the nurse's actions have led to the client's angry response, it is helpful to let him ventilate those emotions directly. Often, however, the nurse is a victim of displaced anger and the nurse can point out to the client that she is not the correct target by saying, "I seem to be getting intense feelings from you that may belong somewhere else." At times, the client reacts with hostility to the nurse because the nurse symbolizes the rules and regulations of the therapeutic regimen. The nurse should then recognize the importance of the issue of control and provide the client with opportunities to exercise choice; for example, on daily menus, in requesting passes from inpatient units, or in voluntary participation in selected activities.

Decreasing Antisocial Behavior

Interventions with impulsive, acting-out behavior often call for the application of external controls prior to initiating the problem-solving aspect of the therapeutic process. The nurse's aim is not to resolve the client's unconscious conflicts, but to support his basic needs regarding dependency and fear of intimacy. Due to developmental deficits in the character of the person with impulsive behavior, therapy with this individual is likely to be a long-term process incorporating education about mature ways of handling stressors.

Because the impulsive person is often oblivious to anxiety as a warning that something is amiss in interpersonal relationships, the nurse must give feedback to the impulsive client about the consequences of his behavior, any self-destructive results, and the social reality in which the behavior took place.[9] Offering alternatives, rather than telling him to stop a certain behavior, helps the impulsive client retain a sense of freedom and choice, which are essential in assisting him take control of, and responsibility for, his actions.

Modeling Communication. Communication skills of clients with impulsive behavior are notoriously poor. Why else would these individuals act-out, rather than talk out, conflicts? Indeed, the nurse intervenes by modeling the expression of feelings, especially those feelings regarding the effect a client's behavior has on the nurse and others.[63]

Needs Versus Wants. One interesting approach to clients with impulsive behavior is to demonstrate to them that their impulsive actions are often the result of thoughts that confuse "need" and "want" statements. "I need something and therefore I should have it" is often substituted for "I want something and will be frustrated not to have it." When wants become needs, the person may feel that he is no longer responsible for behavior necessary to fulfill those needs. On the other hand, wants are preferences one can choose to act upon or not. Such patterns are pointed out in rational-emotive therapy, a form of cognitive therapy.[61] Challenging need–want confusion may help a client redefine a situation, thereby eliciting new or different emotions. It is one way to help a client learn to tolerate anxiety.

Group therapy is often a more desirable treatment modality than one-to-one therapy with clients who use antisocial behaviors because their manipulative style, which is often very draining on one therapist, can be diluted or exposed in group settings. Peer pressure for socially acceptable behavior is an effective method of treatment.[7]

Whenever acting-out behavior occurs, the nurse should examine her own behavior in relation to the client's. Inadvertently, the nurse may encourage or reinforce acting-out behavior by being very angry or very pleased with the client's behavior. The nurse questions how provocative she is being with the client.[7] New rules and limits may be needed.

Evaluation

Evaluation of nursing interventions with clients demonstrating suspicious, hostile, and aggressive behavior takes into account several factors.

1. Was the behavior controlled although feelings may have been intense?
2. Was everyone's safety maintained?
3. Did symptoms of paranoia and acting-out decrease?
4. Did the client and nurse learn any problem-solving techniques for handling these behaviors in the future?
5. Was the client's self-esteem maintained?

The nurse's effectiveness in evaluating what occurs in nurse–client relationships involving anger, suspicion, and impulsivity often depends on the nurse's self-awareness or recognition of these emotions in herself. While evaluating nursing interventions, the nurse is also reassessing client behavior and beginning the nursing process again.

Nurses working in outpatient settings may evaluate their interventions in supervisory conferences. Informal chats with colleagues or formal staff conferences on inpatient units should be used to discuss the effectiveness of various forms of intervention. By answering questions like the five listed above, nurses can analyze techniques and feelings and propose alternative behaviors necessary to improve the outcomes in future situations. For example, during a mental health team conference, the staff members may discuss that, while restraining a client in leather restraints, his safety was assured and dangerous behavior was stopped, but that his suspicious symptoms increased. Therefore, the staff might decide that fear was an important motivator to the client's acting-out behavior. Closer observation of the client and assurances to him of his safety therefore need to be accomplished to prevent his further acting-out.

Nurse's Feelings and Attitudes

The qualities most useful in working with paranoid and aggressive clients are nondefensiveness, realism, acceptance, consistency, and kind firmness.[45] Nevertheless, when a client is noncompliant and defiant, the nurse is likely to react with uncomfortable, if not negative, feelings. It is frustrating not to have clients welcome our good intentions to help. If nurses remember, however, that the client is in the treatment setting because of such defensive behavior, they are less likely to insist that he relinquish his defensiveness as a condition of treatment.[26]

The nurse should neither ignore defensive symptoms nor run from them. The client who says in an angry tone, "Go on and talk to some other poor fellow who really needs help," challenges the nurse to pass him by. Instead of leaving him, the nurse may suggest, "Let's get to know each other without focusing on problems." In this way, the nurse offers an interaction wherein the client can feel comfortable.

Some nurses have great difficulty saying "no" to clients. Their own need to be liked by others overrides their ability to be firm. If the nurse vacillates and conciliates aggressive clients, the client gains control. If the nurse reacts kindly and with submissive reassurance, the client may become passively dependent.[6] For example, the client who tests the nurse with requests or demands for special privileges often reacts to fulfillment of each one by asking another favor. The nurse readily feels manipulated in these situations. The nurse may avoid feelings of powerlessness by meeting the client's dependency needs while voicing the expectation that, gradually, he will assume more and more responsibility for meeting his own needs.

If the nurse assesses that a power struggle exists, she next identifies anxiety levels and needs.[51] Is the client asking for more limits? Is the client testing what controls are present? In what ways can you assist the client to maintain control? It is best to make the covert issue overt. Tell the client that you are not interested in power struggles. State that you would like to see the client remain in control. Compliment the client on whatever degree of control he can maintain, however tenuous that control is.

Psychiatry and psychiatric-mental health nursing rely on verbal, rather than physical abilities. Because nursing is still primarily a female profession and women are not sanctioned to be physically aggressive in our society, many nurses have highly emotional reactions when they need to restrain a client using touching and holding. Anticipatory guidance, or talking through possible feelings, is one way to help nurses deal with this experience of restraining clients.

In the face of aggressive or assaultive behavior, the universal response of all of us is the feeling of fear. Feeling the fear and understanding what it signals can direct a nurse to action. Possible outcomes of this experience of fear are as follows.

1. Countertransference reactions, due to angry feelings, leading to limit-setting without talking-through behavior, as in authoritarian relationships
2. Manifest anxiety reactions, due to helpless feelings, leading to flight from the situation
3. A therapeutic reaction or vigilance for the opportunity to teach and learn about thoughts, feelings, and behaviors[9, 26]

Obviously, this third outcome is the more desirable one.

When afraid, the nurse may "come down hard" on the client in an attacking manner, avoid any confrontation, or approach the feared stimulus in a problem-solving manner. The choices open to us when faced with stressors are the same as those of our clients. Our professional expertise and use of the nursing process help us achieve favorable outcomes even in difficult situations.

Summary

This chapter discusses the wide range and intensity of feelings and minor to severe ramifications of these behaviors. The two-fold orientation of the chapter focuses first on the development and maintenance of these feelings and behaviors, and, secondly, on the application of the nursing process to the care of clients exhibiting paranoid and acting-out disorders. Other foci of this chapter include the following points.

1. Etiological theories from diverse frameworks are advanced to explain the origins of suspicious, hostile, and aggressive behavior and to guide intervention strategies.
2. The dynamics of hostility and suspiciousness, impulsivity and acting-out, and anger and aggression explain the "how" and "why" of these behaviors.
3. The nurse assessing the client with paranoid or acting-out disorders gathers information about altered cognitive or perceptual states, increased psychomotor activity, altered mood or affect, environmental factors causing increased anxiety levels, and history of poor impulse control or drug abuse.
4. The nurse determines the client's ability to remain in control of his behavior.
5. In planning treatment, the nurse sets goals collaboratively with clients based on the needs for trusting relationships, social responsibility, and increased self-esteem.

6. Defusing and deescalating rising feeling states and supporting the client who attempts to control his behavior in socially sanctioned ways are preferable to reactionary handling of aggressive incidents.

7. When control is an issue, manipulation is a possibility.

8. A blending of the nurse's theoretical orientation with client needs leads to interpersonal, behavioral, or cognitive interventions.

9. As a member of the multidisciplinary mental health team, the nurse communicates her observations and interventions to other team members toward the goal of maintaining a consistent, holistic approach to the client.

10. Working with suspicious, hostile, and aggressive clients taps surface and deep emotions in the nurse and other mental health care providers.

11. Evaluation entails a close examination of both client and nurse to determine whether treatment goals were met and to decide what skills and attitudes might achieve more effective outcomes with paranoid and acting-out clients.

Nursing Care Plan

The Client Who Is Hostile and Suspicious

Client Problem	Goal	Intervention
Social/Behavioral Disturbances:		
Psychomotor agitation	To increase self-control	Reduce environmental stimulation. Encourage verbalization of feelings. Suggest diversional activities that channel energy constructively. Approach the client in a calm manner. Offer medication to decrease agitation.
Outbursts of violent behavior	To prevent injury to client, staff, and others	Ensure adequate numbers of staff to contain behavior. Reduce environmental stimulation. Provide chemical or mechanical restraints. Establish one-to-one interaction with staff members involved in the client's violent episode, after behavior is controlled, to review incident for learning.
Manipulation	To facilitate direct communication	Clearly define the nurse–client relationship. Discuss behavioral expectations and consequences. Encourage discussion of feelings by role-modeling. Acknowledge and reward open communication.
Dependency	To promote independent behavior	Initiate frequent interactions, especially during the initial phase of the relationship. Recognize "pseudoindependence" or distancing in relationships as reaction formation to unmet needs.
Drug abuse	Detoxification Abstinence from drug use	Follow a medical detoxification regimen. Encourage satisfying interpersonal relationships. Initiate referral to a rehabilitation program and follow-up with referral.

Client Problem	Goal	Intervention
Cognitive Disturbances: Persecutory or command hallucinations and delusions	To decrease fear and anxiety To clarify reality To promote trust	Use a calm, directive, nonthreatening approach. Follow through consistently on commitments to the client. Make undemanding, frequent, brief contacts with client. Present the nurse's reality in a matter-of-fact tone and manner. Comment on the client's safety but recognize the presence of his fear. Orient the client to person, place, time, and situation. Connect feeling to situation at the onset of the feeling. Encourage reality-oriented conversation and activities.
Disturbances of Mood or Feeling: Increased intensity of feeling	To decrease the intensity of feeling	Approach in a calm, nonthreatening manner. Role-model appropriate verbalization of feeling. Tolerate deviant expressions of affect in place of acting-out behavior. Instruct the client that feelings do not have to lead to bizarre or destructive behaviors. Provide opportunities for alternative activities to release an energizing force of feelings.
Decreased self-esteem	To increase self-esteem	Avoid mutual withdrawal between nurse and client. Encourage and accept expression of thoughts and feelings. Provide opportunities to problem-solve instead of acting impulsively. Discuss behaviors in their perspective. Provide opportunities for the client to experience success. Practice new behaviors in role-rehearsal or role-playing situations. Give merited praise and recognition.
Low frustration tolerance	To increase self-control or the ability to delay gratification	Provide supportive relationship. Gradually increase responsibility at the client's pace. Promote awareness of feeling states that are warning signals of impulsive or explosive behaviors. Discuss alternative behaviors when warning signals occur.

References

1. Bacy-y-Rita G et al: Episodic Control: A Study of 130 Violent Patients. Am J Psychiatr 127:1473–1478, 1971
2. Bandura A: Aggression, A Social Learning Analysis. Englewood Cliffs, Prentice-Hall, 1973
3. Bandura A, Ross D, Ross SA: Imitation of Film-Mediated Aggressive Models. J Abnorm Soc Psychol 66:3–11, 1963
4. Barrett JE, DiMascio A: Comparative Effects on Anxiety of the "Minor Tranquilizers" in "High" and "Low" Anxious Student Volunteers. Dis Nerv Sys 27:483–486, 1966
5. Bowlby J: Attachment and Loss: Attachment, Vol I. New York, Basic Books, 1969
6. Carney FL: Outpatient Treatment for the Aggressive Offender. Am J Psychother 31 (April): 265–274, 1977
7. Carter FM: Psychosocial Nursing, 3rd ed. New York, Macmillan, 1981
8. Chwast J: Psychotherapy of Disadvantaged Acting-Out Adolescents. Am J Psychother 31 (April): 216–226, 1977
9. Clack J: Nursing Intervention into the Aggressive Behavior of Patients. In Burd SF, Marshall MA (eds): Some Clinical Approaches to Psychiatric Nursing, pp 199–205. New York, Macmillan, 1963
10. Clancy J et al: The Hostile-Dependent Personality. Postgrad Med 55:109, 1974
11. Convertino K, Pinto RP, Fiester AR: Use of Inpatient Seclusion at a Community Mental Health Center. Hosp Commun Psychiatr 31 (December): 848–850, 1980
12. DeMeyer-Gapin S, Scott TJ: Effect of Stimulus Novelty on Stimulation Seeking in Antisocial and Neurotic Children. J Abnorm Psychol 86 (January): 96–98, 1977
13. DiFabio S: Nurses' Reactions to Restraining Patients. Am J Nurs 81 (May): 973–975, 1981
14. Durkheim E: The Rules of the Sociological Method. New York, The Free Press, 1938
15. Eron LD: Prescription for Reduction of Aggression. American Psychologist 35 (March): 244–252, 1980
16. Eron LD: Relationship of TV Viewing Habits and Aggressive Behavior in Children. J Abnorm Soc Psychol 67:193–196, 1963
17. Eron LD, Walder LO, Lefkowitz MM: Learning of Aggression in Children. Boston, Little, Brown, 1971
18. Fagan TJ, Lira FT: The Primary and Secondary Sociopathic Personality: Differences in Frequency and Severity of Antisocial Behaviors. J Abnorm Psychol 89:493–496, 1980
19. Fareta G: A Profile of Aggression from Adolescence to Adulthood: An 18-Year Follow-Up of Psychiatrically Disturbed and Violent Adolescents. Am J Orthopsychiatr 51 (July): 439–453, 1980
20. Freud S: Collected Papers of Sigmund Freud. New York, Basic Books, 1959
21. Fromm E: Man for Himself. New York, Holt, Rinehart, 1947
22. Gardos G et al: Differential Actions of Chlordiazepoxide and Oxezepam on Hostility. Arch Gen Psychiatr 18:757–760, 1968
23. Gerta B: Training for Prevention of Assaultive Behavior in a Psychiatric Setting. Hosp Commun Psychiatr 31 (Sept): 628–630, 1980
24. Gluck M: Learning a Therapeutic Verbal Response to Anger. J Psychiatr Nurs Ment Health Serv 19 (March): 9–12, 1981
25. Grace HK, Camilleri D: Mental Health Nursing, A Socio-Psychological Approach, 2nd ed. Dubuque, Iowa, Wm C Brown, 1981
26. Haber J et al: Comprehensive Psychiatric Nursing. New York, McGraw-Hill, 1978
27. Harris TA: I'm OK–You're OK: A Practical Guide to Transactional Analysis. New York, Harper & Row, 1967
28. Hayes SC, Rincover A, Valosin D: Variables Influencing the Acquisition and Maintenance of Aggressive Behavior: Modeling Versus Sensory Reinforcement. J Abnorm Psychol 89:254–262, 1980
29. Hays DA: Anger: A Clinical Problem. In Burd SF, Marshall MA (eds): Some Clinical Approaches to Psychiatric Nursing, pp 110–115. New York, Macmillan, 1963
30. Horney K: The Neurotic Personality of Our Time. New York, WW Norton, 1937
31. Johnson DW: Effects of Warmth of Interaction, Accuracy of Understanding and the Proposal of Compromises on Listener's Behavior. J Counsel Psychol 18 (March): 207–216, 1971
32. Kaplan HI, Sadock BJ: Modern Synopsis of Comprehensive Textbook of Psychiatry/III, 3rd ed. Baltimore, Williams & Wilkins, 1981
33. Kiening Sister M: Hostility. In Carlson C, Blackwell B (eds): Behavioral Concepts and Nursing Intervention, pp 128–104, 2nd ed. Philadelphia, JB Lippincott, 1978
34. Kopp S: An End to Innocence: Facing Life Without Illusions. New York, Macmillan, 1978
35. Lanyon RI, Lanyon BP: Behavior Therapy: A Clinical Introduction. Reading, Mass, Addison-Wesley Publishing Co, 1978
36. Lidz T: A Developmental Approach to Problems of Acting-Out. New York, International Universities Press, 1966
37. Luckey JW, Berman JJ: Effects of New Commitment Laws on the Mental Health System. Am Orthopsychiatr 51 (July): 479–483, 1981
38. McCord W, McCord J, Howard A: Familial Correlates of Aggression in Nondelinquent Male Children. J Abnorm Soc Psychol 62:79–93, 1961
39. Mark VH, Neville R: Brain Surgery in Aggressive Behavior. J Am Med Assoc 226:765–772, 1973
40. Minuchin S: Families of the Slums. New York, Basic Books, 1967
41. Moyer KE: The Psychobiology of Aggression. New York, Harper & Row, 1976
42. Murray R: What to Do with Crying, Clinging, Demanding, Seductive, Abusive and Withdrawn Patients. Nursing Life (Sept/Oct): 32–39, 1981
43. Nashby W, Hayden B, DePaulo BM: Attributional Bias among Aggressive Boys to Interpret Unambiguous Social Stimuli as Displays of Hostility. J Abnorm Psychol 89:459–468, 1980
44. Novaco RW: Anger Control: The Development and

Evaluation of an Experimental Treatment. Lexington, Mass, DC Heath & Co, 1975

45. Pasquali EA et al: Mental Health Nursing: A Bio-Psycho-Cultural Approach. St Louis, CV Mosby, 1981

46. Personal communication and collaboration with Marv A. Glovinsky, Ph.D., Las Vegas, Nevada, Fall, 1981

47. Pihl RO et al: Attribution and Alcohol-Mediated Aggression. J Abnorm Psychol 90:468–475, 1980

48. Quay HC: Psychopathic Personality as Pathological Stimulation-Seeking. Am J Psychiatr 122:180–183, 1965

49. Redfield R: The Folk Society. Am J Sociol 52:298–308, 1946–1947

50. Report of the National Council on Alcoholism, 1976 Long Island Council on Alcoholism Fact Sheet, Garden City, NY

51. Richter JM: Power Struggle in the Clinical Setting. In Kneisl CR, Wilson HS (eds): Current Perspectives in Psychiatric Nursing: Issues and Trends, pp 115–122. St Louis, CV Mosby, 1978

52. Rosen H, DiGiacomo JN: The Role of Physical Restraint in the Treatment of Psychiatric Illness. J Clin Psychiatr 39 (March): 228–232, 1978

53. Roth M: Human Violence as Viewed from the Psychiatric Clinic. Am J Psychiatr 128:397–407, 1972

54. Rubin B: Prediction of Dangerousness in Mentally Ill Criminals. Arch Gen Psychiatr 17:397–407, 1972

55. Sheard MH: Effect of Lithium on Human Aggression. Nature 230:113–114, 1971

56. Smitherman C: Nursing Actions for Health Promotion. Philadelphia, FA Davis, 1981

57. Speck RV, Attneave CL: Family Networks. New York, Pantheon Books, 1973

58. Szurek S: Childhood Origins of Psychopathic Personality Trends. In Szurek SA, Berlin IN (eds): The Antisocial Child: His Family and His Community, pp 2–12. Palo Alto, Science and Behavior Books, 1969

59. Tupin JP et al: The Long-Term Use of Lithium in Aggressive Prisoners. Comp Psychiatry 14:311–317, 1973

60. Walters RH, Willows DC: Imitative Behavior of Disturbed and Nondisturbed Children Following Exposure to Aggressive and Nonaggressive Models. Child Development 39:79–89, 1968

61. Watkins JT: The Rational-Emotive Dynamics of Impulsive Disorders. In Ellis A, Grieger R (eds): Handbook of Rational-Emotive Therapy, pp 135–152. New York, Springer–Verlag, 1977

62. Whaley M, Ramirez L: The Use of Seclusion Rooms and Physical Restraints in the Treatment of Psychiatric Patients. J Psychiatr Nurs Ment Health Serv 18 (January): 13–16, 1980

63. Wilson HS, Kneisl CR: Psychiatric Nursing. Menlo-Park, California, Addison-Wesley Publishing Co, 1979

Chapter 24
Substance Abuse:
The Drug Dependencies

O God that men should put an enemy in their mouths to steal away their brains: that we should with joy, pleasance, revel and applause, transform ourselves into beasts.

Othello

Barbara A. Thurston

Chapter Preview

This chapter deals with the topic of substance abuse and dependency. It discusses the use of substances that affect the central nervous system and the physical and behavioral changes that occur in individuals who abuse and become dependent on them.

These substances are classified as drugs. The generic meaning of the term *drug,* which includes the substance ethyl alcohol (ethanol), is used in this chapter. Because of the socially acceptable status of alcohol, this substance frequently does not elicit as forceful a relationship to drug classification as the image produced by the mention of an illegal drug, such as heroin, or even prescription drugs, such as barbiturates or amphetamines. Nevertheless, the substance alcohol, by its properties and actions, is a drug and needs to be treated as such.

There are factors that all drugs of abuse and dependency have in common, as well as factors that are specific to each drug. This chapter addresses both those commonalities of substance abuse and dependency and the specific factors particular to each drug classification. Wherever possible, however, the emphasis is on the common concepts. This generic concept embraces the idea that the problem of abuse/dependency of a substance and manifestations resulting from the abuse may differ. For example, the manifestations of dependence on heroin differ from dependence on alcohol, but the core problem remains the same; that is, the fact that there is abuse of, or dependence on, a substance.

Individuals who abuse or become dependent on substances are impaired physically, socially, and psychologically at some time in the course of their disorder. The behavior manifested by persons abusing drugs is not tolerated or accepted in most cultures. Prolonged abuse of, or dependency on, drugs and the concomitant adverse behavioral changes that affect the individual's life and well-being usually culminate in a self-destructive course unless the substance use is discontinued or the individual's lifestyle is altered. Ultimately, drug-dependent individuals must learn to adapt to the stresses of life with means other than the abuse of drugs.

This chapter examines systems of classification of substance abuse and dependency and various concepts related to the etiology and dynamics of substance abuse and dependency. A focus of the chapter is the application of the nursing process to individuals who abuse or are dependent on drugs.

Learning Objectives

After completion of the chapter, the reader should be able to accomplish the following.

1. Discuss the application of Selye's theory of stress

and adaptation to the problems of substance abuse and dependency

2. Define substance abuse and dependency and explain current diagnostic categorization
3. Differentiate between various types of substance abuse/dependency disorders
4. Discuss the common etiologic concepts related to substance abuse and dependency
5. Discuss the incidence and significance of substance abuse and dependency
6. Describe the dynamics, physical effects, behavioral changes, medical consequences, social and family problems, and specific group characteristics of abuse/dependency on alcohol, barbiturates and similarly acting sedative/hypnotics, narcotics, cocaine, amphetamine, and similarly acting sympathomimetics, hallucinogens, and cannabis
7. Apply the components of the nursing process to the client who abuses or who is dependent on substances
8. Recognize the nurse's own feelings and attitudes toward substance abuse and dependency disorders

Stress and Adaptation and Substance Abuse

Hans Selye's stress/adaptation syndrome may be applied to problems of substance abuse and dependency, with implications for the treatment and rehabilitation of drug-dependent individuals. (The reader is encouraged to refer to Chapter 1 for a fuller discussion of Selye's theory of stress and adaptation.)

Stress/Adaptation Syndrome

Stress, says Selye, is "the nonspecific response of the body to any demand made upon it."[81] Clearly, the source of the stress and the pleasantness or unpleasantness of the agent or situation of stress do not matter. What does matter is the intensity of the demand for adaptation or readjustment.

Stressors, or stress-producing factors, differ with situations and in the responses they elicit from individuals. Stressors may originate from physical, chemical, physiological, biologic, and emotional sources. They may arise from the internal or external environment of the individual.

The General Adaptation Syndrome (GAS) is composed of three stages.

1. Alarm stage. The body recognizes the internal or external stress that affects its physiological homeostasis, and then prepares to resist by means of "fight or flight."
2. Stage of resistance. The body uses the defense mechanisms of "fight or flight" to repair the damage it suffered and/or adapt to the stressor. If the

body is unable to adapt, it will enter the third stage; if the individual adapts to the stressor, the third stage is prevented.

3. Stage of exhaustion. If this stage of fatigue continues for a period of time, physical or emotional diseases of adaptation (migraine headache, mental disorder) may occur. If this stage is not reversed, the body will be unable to adapt and will become exhausted, and death will ensue.[80, 81]

"Fight or Flight" Mechanisms

Selye emphasizes the importance of making good use of adaptation energy to prevent the diseases of adaptation. The defense mechanisms of "fight or flight" may be applied to interpersonal relationships as well as to physiological problems. That is, a person may manage interpersonal stress by running away from or passively waiting out a situation he cannot change. The choice of the proper defense, however, needs to be tailored to each situation.

To remind himself how to use these adaptation mechanisms wisely, to achieve his goals, particularly when events threaten his equanimity or cause him concern or doubt, Selye has created the following jingle:

> "Fight for your highest
> attainable aim.
> But never put up
> resistance in vain."[81]

The process of reflection and choice of an appropriate response for the situation and circumstances may appear simple, but is really a complex task. Selye believes that each individual has to live his life as his innate freedom of choice directs.[80, 81]

Drug Dependence as a Means of Coping

Applying this theory of stress and proper choice of adaptation methods in interpersonal stress to substance abuse and dependency, it is necessary to consider that drug use, abuse, and dependency serve a purpose for the chemical-dependent individual. There are legitimate reasons for the use of many drugs. Ethyl alcohol is a drug and it is also a legal substance with approved recreational and social use. Many people drink alcoholic beverages without encountering problems. Some drugs are controlled substances, such as narcotics and sedatives/hypnotics, and are used for medical purposes to alleviate physical pain and emotional suffering. These drugs, when taken as prescribed under medical supervision, may be used to diminish the stress of life without serious adverse consequences of abuse and dependency.

For the individual who abuses or is dependent on substances, however, drugs have an added function, more than their specific effects. For these individuals, the drug or drugs have become a way of coping or adapting to any of life's stressors. In other words, drugs are a "way of life" for these individuals.

The individual who abuses substances, for example, may use drugs to relieve feelings of anxiety or unpleasant feelings of any kind, or to experience and to increase pleasant or "high" sensations. Drugs may be used to sustain a world of daydreams or an existence beyond the bounds of reality. Drugs may be used to express feelings of joy, love, anger, or hate, or to repress these emotions. Drugs not only do things *to* people who take them, they also do things *for* people who take them. It is, therefore, important to understand what these substances do for people, in order to effect primary prevention of chemical dependence and to help individuals adapt to, or cope with, the stress of life in a more effective, healthy manner (see insert, Definition of Terms).

Individuals who abuse or who are dependent on substances come from all socioeconomic and cultural groups. The spectrum covers all ages, from youth to old age. The reasons for individuals' misuse of, abuse of, and dependence on drugs generally include an attempt to adapt to the stress of life. Ironically, the process becomes a vicious cycle, because the method of adapting to life's stressors becomes, itself, another stressor.

The use of drugs as a coping mechanism destroys or diminishes an individual's ability to master life's events. "Letting go" of substance abuse, as a method of adaptation, and learning healthy methods of adaptation may result in successful recovery from chemical dependence.

Defining Substance Abuse and Dependency

The Diagnostic and Statistical Manual of Mental Disorders, third edition (DSM-III), classifies the pathological use of substances into two categories.

1. The Substance Use Disorders (see Table 24-1) refer to the maladaptive behavioral changes that may occur in individuals who misuse drugs that affect the central nervous system.
2. The Substance Induced Organic Mental Disorders refer to the physical or direct, acute and chronic effects on the central nervous system by the misuse of the substance.

These categories, although separate for the purpose of classification, are not separate entities. Individuals with a substance use disorder will inevitably experience a substance induced organic mental disorder. For example, an individual who abuses or becomes dependent on alcohol will manifest certain behavioral manifestations or traits, such as inability to cut down or stop drinking, loss of job, or difficulty with family due to excessive alcohol use. The individual will also experience a substance induced organic mental disorder, such as intoxication or withdrawal.[4]

(Text continues on p 348)

Definition of Terms

Physical Dependence (Addiction):	This is a state that is manifested by withdrawal symptoms (abstinence syndrome) when the drug is removed. This state is frequently accompanied by tolerance, the frequent taking of a drug or drugs in increased amounts over a period of time, resulting in a biochemical change in the cells of the nervous system. These cells then need the drug for normal functioning. When the drug is removed or greatly decreased, the level of the drug in the body drops and withdrawal symptoms occur. The specific symptoms that occur depend on the drug or drugs taken.
Psychological Dependence (Habituation):	This is the expression of a severe craving or compulsion to take a drug in order to "feel good." The user has no physical compulsion to take the drug, either because the drug does not produce physical dependence or withdrawal symptoms have been medically treated, such as when a person who has withdrawn from drugs relapses.
Tolerance:	An increased amount of the dose of a drug is necessary in order to obtain the desired effect, or there is a decrease in the desired effect with regular use of the same amount of the drug.
Cross Tolerance:	After tolerance to a drug has developed, tolerance to other drugs in the same or related clases will develop. For example, a person who is tolerant to alcohol will be tolerant to other sedative/hypnotics and minor tranquilizers.
Synergism:	This occurs when two drugs act similarly.
Antagonistic Effect:	This occurs when two drugs have opposing effects.
Additive Effect:	This occurs when two drugs acting similarly are used together and the result is a simple summation, or total, of effect.
Potentiation (Supra-additive effect):	This occurs when the effects of two synergistic, or similarly acting, drugs are greater than the sum of their doses.

(From American Psychiatric Association: Diagnostic and Statistical Manual of Mental Disorders, 3rd ed. Washington, DC, American Psychiatric Association, 1980. Also from Rodman MJ, Smith DW: Pharmacology and Drug Therapy in Nursing, 2nd ed. Philadelphia, JB Lippincott, 1979)

Table 24-1. Substance Use Disorders: DSM-III Criteria

	SUBSTANCES						
	Alcohol	*Barbiturates and Sedative/ Hypnotics*	*Opioids*	*Cocaine*	*Amphetamines and Similarly Acting Sympathomimetics*	*Hallucinogens*	*Cannabis*
Criteria for Abuse							
Pattern of pathological use	Need for daily use for adequate functioning	Inability to reduce or stop use	Inability to reduce or stop use	Inability to reduce or stop use	Inability to reduce or stop use	Intoxication throughout day	Inability to reduce or stop use
	Inability to reduce or stop use	Intoxication throughout day	Intoxication throughout day	Intoxication throughout day	Intoxication throughout day	Intoxication throughout day (possible only with some hallucinogens)	Repeated efforts to control with periods of abstinence or restriction of use to certain times of day
	Repeated efforts to control or reduce by "going on wagon" or restricting to certain times of day	Frequent use, 600 mg or more of secobarbital or 60 mg or more of diazepam	Use of opioids daily for at least 1 month	Episodes of overdose (intoxication so severe hallucinations and delusions occur in a clear sensorium)	Use nearly daily for at least 1 month	Episodes of delusional disorder	Intoxicated throughout day
	Binges	Amnesic periods that occur while intoxicated	Episodes of opioid overdose (intoxication so severe respiration and consciousness impaired)		Episodes of delusional disorder or delirium		Use nearly daily for at least 1 month
	Occasional consumption of a fifth of spirits (or equivalent in beer or wine)						Two or more episodes of delusional disorder
	Blackouts						
	Continuation of drinking despite physical disorder individual knows is increased by drinking						
Impairment in social or occupational functioning	Violence while intoxicated	Fights	Fights	Fights	Fights	Fights	Marked loss of interest in previous activities
	Absence from work	Loss of friends	Loss of friends	Loss of friends	Loss of friends	Loss of friends	Loss of friends
	Loss of job	Absence from work	Absence from work	Absence from work	Absence from work	Absence from work	Absence of work
	Legal difficulties	Loss of job	Loss of job	Legal difficulties	Loss of job	Legal difficulties	Loss of job
	Arrest for intoxicated behavior	Legal difficulties	Legal difficulties		Legal difficulties	Loss of job	Legal difficulties
	Traffic accidents						
	Arguments with family and friends						
Duration	At least 1 month	At least 1 month	At least 1 month	At least 1 month	At least 1 month	At least 1 month	At least 1 month
Criteria for Dependence							
Tolerance	X	X	X	None identified	X	None	X
	or	or	or		or		
Withdrawal	X	X	X	None	X	None	
	Pattern of pathological use or impairment in social or occupational functioning						Pattern of pathological use or impairment in social or occupational functioning

Substance Use Disorders

Substance Abuse

The diagnosis of *substance abuse* depends on the following criteria.

1. A pattern of pathological use, which includes such indicators as a need for daily use for adequate functioning, loss of control over how much of the substance is used, repeated efforts to "cut down" or control the amount of substances used, use of the substance despite physical problems that are worsened by use of the substance, presence of blackouts, drug overdose, or drug intoxication during the day

2. Impairment in social or occupational functioning caused by the pattern of pathological use including indicators such as violence while intoxicated, loss of job, fights, legal difficulties, loss of friends, and family problems due to excessive use of the substance

3. A duration of 1 month of signs of the pattern of abuse

Substance Dependency

Criteria for the diagnosis of *substance dependency*, a more severe form of substance use disorder, require the evidence of physiological dependence, indicated by evidence of tolerance to the drug or withdrawal syndrome. Usually, the three criteria of abuse are also present in dependence but are not necessary for the diagnosis except in alcoholism and cannabis dependence. There are eight classes of substances listed under the criteria for substance dependency. Five of the substances—alcohol, barbiturates and similarly acting sedative/hypnotics, opioids, amphetamines or similarly acting sympathomimetics, and cannabis—are associated with both abuse and dependency. The three remaining substances— cocaine, phencyclidine (PCP), and the hallucinogens—are associated with abuse only, because physiological dependence has not been established.

Substance Induced Organic Mental Disorders

The category of *substance induced organic mental disorders* describes the specific organic brain syndrome (OBS) caused by the substance. The substance may cause more than one syndrome. Table 24-2 depicts the substance induced organic mental disorders by classes of substances. The description of the specific syndromes and the substance use disorders are detailed in the chapter section, Dynamics of Substance Abuse and Dependency. Some symptoms (for example, withdrawal from alcohol and sedative/hypnotics) are similar, whereas symptoms of opioid withdrawal are different. The symptoms of delirium are the same for any organic mental disorder, regardless of etiology, but delirium associated with drugs has a specific cause that needs to be incorporated into the planning of care.

Etiologic Factors

There is no single theoretical concept which explains the etiology of substance abuse and dependency. It is important, rather, to reflect on the complex and varied etiologic factors.

The Drug, the Individual, and the Environment

An initial consideration is that of the drug itself. Each classification of drug, as well as each drug within that class, has particular chemical properties and produces effects particular to its chemical structure. The second consideration is the individual taking the drug. Individuals respond to drugs according to drug dosage, frequency of administration, the route of administration, and genetic, metabolic,

Table 24-2. **Substance Induced Organic Mental Disorders Produced by Abuse/Dependency**

Substance Induced Organic Mental Disorders	COMMON SUBSTANCES							
	Alcohol	Barbiturates and Similar Acting Sedatives/ Hypnotics	Opioids	Cocaine	Amphetamines and Similar Acting Sympathomimetic	P.C.P.	Hallucinogens	Cannabis
Intoxication	X	X	X	X	X	X		X
Withdrawal	X	X	X		X			
Withdrawal Delirium	(DTs)	X						
Delirium					X	X		
Delusional disorder					X	X	X	X
Dementia	X							
Amnestic disorder	X	X						
Hallucinosis	X						X	

physiological, and psychological variables. Certain individuals are more likely to become alcoholic than others (see insert, At Risk for Alcoholism). The third consideration is the environment from which the individual emerges, including the person's family, social factors (*e.g.*, extreme poverty and delinquency), and the culture or subculture.

The overview of several theoretical concepts that have been postulated to explain the nature and cause of substance abuse and dependency includes some concepts specific to the drugs of abuse (*e.g.*, the disease concept of alcoholism) and other concepts with more general applica-

At Risk for Alcoholism

Epidemiologic and social studies of alcohol abuse and dependency demonstrate that certain groups of individuals are at high risk for the development of alcoholism. Although the following criteria from the National Council on Alcoholism point to persons at risk for developing alcoholism, there is no agreement on the extent of the risk for each particular case.[18]

A family history of alcoholism, including parents, siblings, grandparents, uncles, and aunts

A history of teetotalism in the family, particularly where strong moral overtones were present and, most particularly, where the social environment of the patient has changed to associations in which drinking is encouraged or required

A history of alcoholism or teetotalism in the spouse or the family of the spouse

Coming from a broken home or home with much parental discord, particularly where the father is absent or rejecting but not punitive

Being the last child of a large family or in the last half of the sibship in a large family

Although some cultural groups (*e.g.*, the Irish and Scandinavians) have been recorded as having a higher incidence of alcoholism than others (*e.g.*, Jews, Chinese, and Italians), alcoholism can occur in people of any cultural derivation.

Having female relatives of more than one generation who have had a high incidence of recurrent depressions

Heavy smoking (Heavy drinking is often associated with heavy smoking, but the reverse need not be true.)

(From National Council on Alcoholism: Criteria for the Diagnosis of Alcoholism. Am J Psychiatr 129 (August): 47–48, 1972)

tion (*e.g.*, the learning theory). Keep in mind for later consideration that the etiologic concept may be reflected in the treatment and rehabilitation process. For example, those who embrace the disease concept of alcoholism will strongly advise abstinence to treat alcoholism. On the other hand, some of the proponents of learning theory may believe that an individual's behavior may be modified or changed and social or recreational drinking may be resumed.

Social or Environmental Factors

The social or environmental concepts suggest that the social condition or environment from which an individual emerges may contribute to, or predispose an individual to, substance abuse and dependency. For example, there has been a high incidence of abuse of opioid derivatives, such as heroin, in the ghettoes or poverty areas of large cities.[4] The abuse of cocaine and hallucinogens is associated with subculture groups and those seeking "mystical" experiences.[4] There is also a reported high incidence of cocaine abuse in the upper economic bracket and among entertainers and athletes.[4, 36, 77]

Personality Factors

A review of research studies has not substantiated that there is one personality type associated with substance abuse and dependency.[11, 91] Instead, there is a wide variation in personality types involving individuals from all social, cultural, and economic backgrounds.[91] Personality disorders, however, may be intensified by the abuse of, or dependence on, substances, especially noted in the antisocial personality.[4] It is also believed that depressed individuals and those with affective disorders may abuse substances to treat symptoms related to their disorder.[4]

Although current research does not support the concept of an "addictive personality type," there are some factors that are important to those who seek to understand, prevent, and treat substance abuse. Most of the differences between individuals who abuse alcohol and those who abuse other drugs seem to be a reflection of age, sex, race, socioeconomic status, and the use of legal or illegal drugs, rather than intrapsychic dynamics. A common factor in all forms of substance abuse and dependence is a negative self-concept, marked by a sense of failure, inadequacy, guilt, shame, loneliness, and despair.[11]

Self-Destructive Phenomenon

Individuals who abuse and become dependent on substances do so in spite of severe physical, psychological, and social consequences. This lack of concern for one's own well-being has led to the view of drug dependency as a self-destructive phenomenon.[91] It is also difficult to estimate with certainty the incidence of intentional suicide by drug overdose. The risk of suicide is high in individuals who abuse substances, both in the sober and in the intoxicated states.[4, 62, 83, 91]

Pharmacologic and Slang Terms for Common Substances of Abuse

Substance	Generic and Trade Name	Street/Slang Name
Barbiturates	Amobarbital (Amytal) Pentobarbital (Nembutal) Phenobarbital (Luminal) Secobarbital (Seconal)	Barbs, Blockbusters, Bluebirds, Blue Devils, Blues, Christmas Trees, Downers, Green Dragons, Mexican Reds, Nebbies, Nimbles, Pajaro Rojo, Pink Ladies, Pinks, Rainbows, Reds and Blues, Red Birds, Red Devils, Reds, Sleeping Pills, Stumblers, Yellow Jackets, Yellows
Opiates		
Morphine		Cube, First Line, Goma, Morf, Morfina, Morpho, Mud
Heroin	Diacetylmorphine	Big H., Boy, Brown Sugar, Caballo, Chiva, Crap, Estuffa, H., Heroina, Hombre, Horse, Junk, Mexican Mud, Scag, Smack, Stuff, Thing
Central nervous system		
Amphetamines	Amphetamine (Benzadrine) Methamphetamine (Desoxyn, Methedrine) Dextroamphetamine (Dexedrine)	Beans, Bennies, Black Beauties, Black Mollies, Copilots Crank, Crossroads, Crystal, Dexies, Double Cross, Meth, Minibennies, Pep Pills, Speed, Rosas, Roses, Thrusters, Truck Drivers, Uppers, Wake-ups, Whites
Cocaine		Blow, C., Coca, Coke, Flake, Girl, Heaven, Dust, Lady, Mujer, Nose Candy, Paradise, Perico, Polvo Blanco, Rock, Snow, White
Hallucinogens		
LSD	Lysergic acid diethylamine	Acid, Blotter Acid, California Sunshine, Haze, Microdots, Paper Acid, Purple Haze, Sunshine Wedges, Window Panes
Cannabis		
Marihuana		Acapulco Gold, Cannabis, Colombian, Ganga, Grass, Griffa, Hemp, Herb, J, Jay, Joint, Mary Jane, Mota, Mutah, Panama Red, Reefer, Sativa, Smoke, Stick, Tea, Weed, Yerba
Hashish		Goma de Mota, Hash, Soles

Ethnic and Cultural Factors

Substance abuse and dependency is found in all cultures and ethnic groups. There are variations, however, in the incidence and prevalence of the problem, the drug preferred, and the unique aspects relative to treatment, prevention, and rehabilitation. For example, there is a low incidence of alcoholism reported in the Oriental culture and population but a high incidence of opiate dependency in that group.[32, 91] Researchers attribute this low incidence of alcoholism to a possible genetic intolerance to alcohol, manifested by unpleasant physical symptoms when even small amounts of alcohol are ingested.[32] There is also a low incidence of alcohol dependency in the American Jewish population,[91] but a high incidence of alcoholism in the American Indian and Irish populations, and relatively high

incidence in Scandinavian and German populations.[91] The reasons for these phenomena are related to the drinking habits or accepted use of alcohol in the culture.[91]

Since the 1950s, there has been increased research related to alcohol abuse/dependency and culture.[56] The importance of ethnic factors and cultural diversity and their effect on substance abuse dependency are now being emphasized. Knowledge acquired through study and research has special application in drug prevention and treatment programs.

Learning Theory

The learning theory concept, involving a conditional response mechanism, has been applied to substance abuse and dependency. For example, the drug use may initially produce pleasant physical responses, desired social consequences, increased feelings of self-confidence, or relief from tension or anxiety. The conditioned response is always positive in the beginning of the process; however, even after severe negative consequences occur, the repetitive or learned behavior continues, although the initial reasons for the repetitive or learned behavior are no longer in operation.[49, 91]

Biologic Theory

There is a high incidence of alcohol abuse and dependency (alcoholism) in children and family members of alcoholics. Several research studies have suggested a possible inherited predisposition to alcoholism.[17, 31, 32]

Studies using twins with a family history of alcoholism as subjects have yielded interesting results. Monozygotic twins (those who share the same genetic material) were more concordant, that is both twins having the same condition for alcoholism, than dyzogotic twins (those who have the same genetic material as siblings) for alcoholism. The adoptive studies, which involve examination of data of children born of alcoholic parents but separated after birth from their natural parents and raised by nonalcoholic foster parents, indicate that these children are particularly susceptible to becoming alcoholic.[17, 31, 32]

A family history of alcoholism does not necessarily indicate that the cause of alcoholism is genetic in origin. Consider the fact that the majority of all children are raised by their biologic parents and the profound influence of social, cultural, and psychological factors within the family environment on the behavior of children. The question becomes, Does the familial aspect of alcoholism come from a learned pattern of behavior, rather than a genetic predisposition to alcoholism?[31, 32] There may be, in fact, an unfamilial, as well as a familial, type of alcoholism.

At this time, there are no research studies that offer direct evidence that narcotic addiction is genetically transmitted.[35] Nevertheless, researchers are conducting psychobiologic studies in an attempt to identify a common link or aspect of drug addiction. Presently, there is an increase in polydrug users, those who take a variety of substances, including alcohol, with no specific drug of choice.[13]

Disease Concept of Alcoholism

Viewing alcoholism as a disease rather than as a moral problem originated with the work of E. M. Jellinek. A pioneer in the study of alcoholism, Jellinek classified alcoholics into five categories. The disease concept he proposed was based on the statistical analysis of a survey of 2000 male alcoholics. The classes or types of alcoholics that he identified, however, were not meant to reflect theories as to cause or nature of alcoholism.[46, 47] The concept of viewing alcoholism as a disease has had a great impact on the acceptance of alcoholism as an illness or process outside the control of the afflicted individual.

Jellinek's disease concept, labeled by some as the "traditional" model of alcoholism, has been challenged by a more recent concept of alcohol dependence as a behavioral disorder with adverse consequences on the health of individuals. This latter "new" concept has been called the multivariant concept of alcoholism.[67] Most authorities in the field of alcohol abuse continue to view the disease concept of alcoholism as the more valid approach to treatment and eventual recovery.

Incidence and Significance of Substance Abuse and Dependency

The drug of abuse is a main consideration in examining the incidence and significance of substance abuse and dependency. For example, of the many individuals who use the substance alcohol, a legal substance with social approval for recreational use, about 1 in 10 people experience abuse or dependency. On the other hand, among the users of heroin, an illegal substance, there is a higher incidence of users becoming dependent. Also, the time span for abuse or dependency to occur is shorter for narcotic dependency than for alcohol dependency.[4]

The culture or social status from which the drug user comes also has an impact on the incidence of substance abuse. The teenage group culture may experiment with a variety of drugs, including heroin, cocaine, stimulants, alcohol, sedative/hypnotics, PCP, or almost any substance available.[77] During the Vietnam era, servicemen used and abused heroin and cannabis in large quantities with a resulting high incidence of abuse and dependency. Upon returning to the United States, some were able to stop using heroin completely or changed the class of drug of abuse.[4, 72]

The type of drug used in a ghetto may be different than that used by suburban middle-class men or women who, because of class distinctions and social variables, may choose a prescription or legal drug, such as alcohol. Frequently, entertainment or sports celebrities and people of high economic status are associated with abuse of, or dependence on, cocaine.[77]

The age, sex, culture, and social setting from which the individual emerges are factors affecting the incidence and significance of drug abuse. Other considerations in the problem include the availability of the drug, cost of the drug, peer pressure, and the drug-oriented American culture, which extols the use of alcohol and prescription drugs for relief of tension and pain. To counteract this prevalence of substance abuse, health professionals in all fields are uniting to combat abuse and dependency problems in psychological, biologic, and social areas, and through treatment, research, and prevention.[77]

Dynamics of Substance Abuse and Dependency

This section on the dynamics of substance abuse and dependency will describe the chemical substance, or drug, the specific diagnostic criteria, and the particular physical, behavioral, and familial consequences.

Alcohol Abuse and Dependency

Alcohol abuse and dependency is one of the most serious public health problems in our nation. The incidence of alcohol-related accidents resulting in fatalities or in permanent disabilities is awesome. The social impact of the disorder on family members, especially on children, is devastating. Many American adolescents are affected by destructive drinking patterns or suffer alcoholism themselves; many children are born with abnormalities or suffer from fetal alcohol syndrome. (See insert, The Impact of Alcoholism.)

Nature of Alcohol

The chemical substance commonly referred to as alcohol is ethyl alcohol (C_2H_5OH), also known chemically as ethanol and sometimes abbreviated as ETOH.[75] It is a legal chemical substance or drug; that is, the sale and commercial distribution of alcohol-containing beverages differ from the regulation and sale of other classes of drugs.

Ethyl alcohol has pharmacologic properties that produce mind-altering and mood-altering effects on individu-

The Impact of Alcoholism

Alcoholism and alcohol-related problems bear considerable impact and significance in the United States.

Variation and Prevalence of Drinking Problems

Considering all measures of drinking problems and available recent survey data, approximately 10% of adult American drinkers are likely to experience either alcoholism or problem drinking at some point in their lives.

In general, results from these recent surveys indicate that a substantial number of adult American drinkers experience serious drinking problems. Males continue to outnumber females by a fairly wide margin on most indicators of drinking problems.

Level of consumption is related substantially to both alcohol dependence and adverse effects. The higher the level of consumption, the greater the probability that a person will experience dependence symptoms and adverse physical and social consequences. Regular heavy drinking leads to adverse consequences and dependence. Intermittent heavy drinking may also result in adverse consequences.

Biomedical Consequences

Although alcohol-related mortality appears to have remained relatively constant, mortality rates for alcoholics continue to be higher than expected. One recent study reported a mortality rate for alcoholics 2.5 times greater than expected in a group of alcoholics followed over time.

Social Implications

In the United States, traffic accidents are the major causes of violent death. Between 35% and 64% of the drivers in fatal accidents had been drinking prior to the accident. Between 45% and 60% of all fatal crashes involving a young driver are alcohol-related.

Approximately one half of adult fire deaths involve alcohol. Alcoholics are 10 times more likely to die in fires compared with the general population.

Alcoholics are at particularly high risk of committing suicide. Between 15% and 65% of persons who attempt suicide and up to 80% of those who committed suicides had been drinking at the time of the event. The risk of suicide for alcoholics is as much as 30 times greater than the risk of suicide for the general population.

Prevention

The Surgeon General's Report, a World Health Organization Conference, and the Department of Health and Human Services' prevention objectives for the year 1990 indicate increased interest in the prevention of alcohol-related problems.

Intervention

Current prevention programs are aimed at minimizing the occurrences of alcohol-related problems through means other than treatment and rehabilitation. Projects for youth in education and service organizations, projects for public information utilizing mass media and communications, projects replicating earlier successful prevention strategies, and projects involving voluntary organizations and community movements have been undertaken.

Treatment and Rehabilitation

The number of persons receiving treatment for alcoholism and problem drinking has continued to increase. Nevertheless, approximately 85% of the population of aicoholics and problem drinkers are not receiving formal treatment services.

(From selected Highlights of the Fourth Special Report to the U.S. Congress on Alcohol and Health, United States Department of Health and Human Services. Washington, DC, January, 1981)

als. It is a central nervous system depressant similar to barbiturates and ether.[75] Chloral hydrate and paraldehyde are sedative/hypnotic drugs derived from ethyl alcohol.[75] Chloral hydrate is used to induce sleep; paraldehyde was used in the medical management of alcohol withdrawal symptoms prior to the introduction of modern tranquilizers.

Most of the drugs that affect the central nervous system have a use in medicine, but ethyl alcohol is not commonly used as a drug in medical treatment. In addition, other drugs that cause physical and psychologial dependence produce their effect in small quantity dosages. Although alcohol produces its effect in small quantities, it usually requires large quantities over a period of time to cause physical dependence.[18]

There are several types of alcohol-containing beverages. The most common types are beer, wine, and distilled spirits, each containing the same amount of alcohol content. For example, 12 ounces of beer, 4 ounces of dry wine, or 1¼ ounces of whiskey have the same alcohol content.

The alcohol content of distilled spirits is expressed in proof; that is, the concentration of ethyl alcohol in the substance. In the United States, proof is twice the ethanol concentration. One hundred proof if 50% (ethyl) alcohol; 80% proof is 40% (ethyl) alcohol.

Ethyl alcohol is a central nervous system depressant, as are the sedative/hypnotics, antianxiety drugs, and general anesthetics. These drugs cause the following pattern of effects as the dose of the drug is increased—sedation, impairment in mental and motor functioning, a deepening stupor with a decrease in stimulation response (including painful stimulus response), coma, and eventually death from respiratory and circulatory collapse.[73]

Alcohol is often erroneously thought to be a stimulant. The reason for this misconception is that some individuals may become more talkative or hyperactive after drinking alcoholic beverages, display a euphoric mood, have increased self-confidence, or become aggressive. This behavior has been attributed to the disinhibiting effect produced by a low dose of the drug.[73]

Alcohol Concentration in the Body. The physical and behavioral manifestations of the effects of alcohol on the central nervous system is related to the level of alcohol in the blood and the concentration of alcohol in the brain, as well as other contributing factors. The blood level of alcohol is expressed in the number of milligrams of alcohol per milliliter of blood; that is, mg %.[73]

The blood alcohol level is a laboratory blood test to determine the degree of alcohol (ethanol) intoxication. It may be used in medicolegal procedures to rule out intoxication in a person who is comatose. The degree of intoxication of an individual may also be measured by breathalyzers. Presently, research is being conducted by Canadian scientists on detecting alcohol levels in body fluids, such as urine and saliva, by using a litmus paper "dip stick."[64]

The alcohol concentration in the blood depends on the rate of absorption, transportation to the central nervous system, redistribution to the other parts of the body, metabolism, and elimination. Alcohol is absorbed through the mouth, stomach, and small intestine. It is absorbed unchanged into the blood and circulates throughout the body, including the brain; it also crosses the placenta into the fetal circulation. Intoxication occurs when the circulating alcohol interferes with the normal functioning of the nerve cells of the brain.[73]

The rate of absorption into the blood varies with several factors.

1. Substances in the beverage, such as carbonation (CO_2) as in champagne, increase absorption.
2. The rate of ingestion of alcohol can affect the rate of absorption. Drinking alcoholic beverages slowly over a period of time may slow absorption and allow for metabolism of alcohol by the liver. Because the body metabolizes alcohol at a steady rate, when an individual drinks faster than the body can metabolize the alcohol, it accumulates in the blood.
3. The rate of drinking may vary, but alcohol leaves the body at a fixed rate.[73]

Ninety percent of the alcohol absorbed by the body is eliminated by oxidation, which takes place mainly in the liver. The other 10% of the alcohol is eliminated unchanged, through breath, sweat, urine, and other body fluids. The liver of the normal adult metabolizes approximately one drink, 1 oz of distilled spirits, per hour and the excess alcohol that the liver cannot metabolize continues to circulate in the blood. The amount of food in the stomach, especially fatty food, slows absorption, whereas an empty stomach increases absorption. The emotional state of the drinker may also affect absorption of alcohol. For example, stress, fear, anger, and fatigue may increase or decrease absorption. The body size of the drinker affects the concentration of alcohol in the blood. The same amount of alcohol taken by a lightweight person (100 lb) and a heavyweight person (200 lb) will result in greater blood alcohol concentration in the lighter person, because there is more blood volume in the heavyweight person in which the alcohol can be diluted. An individual's body chemistry and cultural influences may also alter the behavioral effects of alcohol.[14]

Tolerance. Prolonged heavy drinking results in physical and behavioral tolerance. *Physical tolerance* or tissue adaptation means that changes occur in the cells of the nervous system, so that more of the drug is required to achieve the desired effect. When physical tolerance develops, the individual may experience withdrawal or abstinence syndrome after cessation or a decrease in consumption of alcohol. Physical tolerance to alcohol never reaches the high dose tolerance of the opiates. Cross tolerance to sedative/hypnotics and other central nervous system depressants also occurs.[73]

Behavioral tolerance to alcohol and other drugs is manifested by the ability to mask the behavioral effects; for example, the acquired ability not to slur words, to walk straight, and to function in ways that would not be possible in a nondependent person. The drinking history of alcoholics frequently reveals the ability to increase tolerance and maintain this increase for a long period of time, perhaps over several years. Frequently, this increase in tolerance is followed by a drop in tolerance, which is irreversible. The individual becomes intoxicated with a smaller amount of alcohol.[13, 14, 75]

Blackout. Persistent heavy drinking frequently results in the chemically induced alcoholic blackout. This is not the same as "passing out," which is defined as a loss of consciousness. In a blackout, the individual appears to function normally while drinking, but he has a loss of memory for what occurs for a period of time. This period of time may be a few hours or several hours. The individual may come out of the blackout period and wonder, "Where did I leave my car last night?" or wake up in a strange city not remembering leaving the home city and wonder, "How did I get here?" "Was I with someone?" These blackouts may be a symptom of alcohol abuse and dependency.[49, 77, 87]

Alcohol Induced Organic Mental Disorders

Intoxication. Intoxication occurs after drinking alcohol and is evidenced in behavior such as fighting, impaired judgment, interference with social or occupational functioning, or other maladaptive behavior. Physiological signs such as slurred speech, incoordination, unsteady gait, nystagmus, and flushed face may accompany intoxication. Psychological signs may be observed, as in mood changes, irritability, talkativeness, or impaired attention.

Alcohol Withdrawal. Alcohol withdrawal, or abstinence syndrome, occurs after reduction in, or cessation of, prolonged heavy drinking. A coarse tremor of hand, tongue, and eyelids may occur, as well as nausea and vomiting, general malaise or weakness, autonomic nervous system hyperactivity (*e.g.*, increased blood pressure and pulse), anxiety, a depressed or irritable mood, and orthostatic hypotension. Sleep disturbances, insomnia, and nightmares may also occur during withdrawal.

Alcohol Withdrawal Delirium. Alcohol withdrawal delirium, referred to as DTs or delirium tremens, is the most serious form of the withdrawal syndrome. It also occurs after cessation of, or reduction in, prolonged heavy drinking and can occur as long as a week after cessation of drinking. The symptoms of delirium include clouding of consciousness (unawareness of environment); inability to shift, focus, and

sustain attention to stimuli in the environment; misinterpretations, illusions, or hallucinations that are usually visual and vivid; incoherent speech; insomnia or daytime drowsiness; increased or decreased psychomotor activity; frequent agitation; and increased blood pressure, sweating, and temperature. Seizures may also occur as a result of alcohol withdrawal (sometimes called "rumfits"). If untreated, this syndrome can cause serious medical complications, such as fluid and electrolyte imbalance, pneumonia, and dehydration.

Alcoholic Hallucinosis. Alcoholic hallucinosis usually occurs within 48 hours after cessation of, or reduction in, drinking. Vivid, and perhaps threatening, auditory hallucinations may develop, but clouding of the consciousness does not occur. The individual's response to the hallucinations is appropriate to its content; that is, he responds with anxiety or fear. Auditory hallucinations are usually experienced as voices, but may be experienced as hissing or buzzing sounds.

Alcoholic Amnestic Disorder. The alcoholic amnestic disorder results from heavy prolonged drinking and is thought to be related to poor nutritional intake. If the disorder is related to thiamine deficiency, it is known as Korsakoff's syndrome. Amnesia consists of impairment in the ability to learn new information (short-term memory) and to recall remote information (long-term memory). Other neurologic signs such as neuropathy, unsteady gait, or myopathy may be present.

Alcoholic Dementia. Alcoholic dementia is associated with prolonged, chronic alcohol dependence. Signs of dementia include loss of intellectual ability that is severe enough to interfere with social or occupational functioning and impairment in memory, abstract thinking, and judgment. The degree of impairment may range from mild to severe and may include permanent brain damage.

Medical Consequences

The heavy consumption of alcohol can adversely affect almost every body system. Various medical conditions may alert the nurse to the early recognition of alcohol abuse problems (see following italicized items).

Gastrointestinal problems occur as a result of the irritating effects of alcohol on the gastrointestinal tract resulting in gastritis or gastric ulcers. Acute or chronic *pancreatitis*, or inflammation of the pancreas, may occur. *Esophagitis* may result from the direct toxic effects of alcohol on the esophageal mucosa, from increased acid production in the stomach, or from frequent vomiting. *Alcohol cardiomyopathy* occurs because of the direct toxic effects of the substance and malnutrition of the individual.[14, 25]

The liver is highly susceptible to the damaging effects of alcohol because it is the primary organ that metabolizes alcohol. Alcohol has been found to be toxic to the liver regardless of the nutritional status of the individual.[6,14] *Alcohol liver disease* has been divided into three major types. In *fatty liver*, deposits of fats (triglycerides) build up in the normal liver cells. This condition is reversible.[6,14] *Alcoholic hepatitis* is a more serious condition involving inflammation and necrosis of the liver cells. This condition is also frequently reversible.[6,14] *Cirrhosis* of the liver is the most serious condition and is irreversible. In cirrhosis, the liver cells are destroyed and replaced by scar tissue. About 90% of deaths from cirrhosis of the liver are associated with chronic alcoholism.[6] There is also a *high risk of cancer*, especially of the mouth, pharynx, larynx, and esophagus, associated with alcoholism.[6,89]

Major and Minor Criteria for the Diagnosis of Alcoholism

The criteria for the diagnosis of alcoholism compiled by the National Council on Alcoholism establish guidelines for the early detection of alcoholism, provide uniform terminology, and assist in preventing overdiagnosis. The criteria also allow for the differentiation between early, middle, and late stages of alcoholism. This staging identifies progression (*i.e.*, worsening over time) of the disease. The criteria for diagnosis of alcoholism are divided into major and minor criteria (see Tables 24-3 and 24-4). The criteria are further grouped into three diagnostic levels.

Diagnostic Level 1. Classical, definite, obligatory; a person meeting this criteria is diagnosed as being alcoholic;

Diagnostic Level 2. Probable, frequent, indicative; a person who meets this criteria is under strong suspicion of alcoholism;

Diagnostic Level 3. Potential, possible, incidental; these manifestations are common but do not by themselves give a strong indication of alcoholism. More significant evidence is needed before a diagnosis is made.

The diagnosis of *alcoholism* may be made if one or more of the major criteria in either track is satisfied, or if several of the minor criteria in both tracks are present.

Abuse of Controlled Substances

Drugs other than alcohol are not as easily attainable and have illegal status. These classes of drugs are regulated by the Controlled Substance Act (Title II, Comprehensive Drug Abuse Prevention and Control Act of 1970, Public Law 91-513). These federal control standards are used to decrease the illegal use and abuse of drugs in the United States.

Illicit drug use in the United States has increased in the past 10 years. The number of active heroin addicts increased to about 500,000 in the mid-1970s from an estimated 50,000 in the mid-1960s. During the same period, the number of people using marihuana increased to 43 million from a former 5 million.[20]

Heroin continues to be an outstanding drug problem greatly feared because of its dependence potential and resulting criminal behavior factors. Cocaine, although expensive and not easily available, is rapidly becoming the desired drug choice of young adults. During 1976, an estimated 2 million Americans used cocaine, an estimated one in 20 Americans over age 12 had used LSD and other hallucinogens, and an estimated 50 million Americans had used marihuana.[95]

Barbiturates and Similar Sedative/Hypnotic Drugs

Effects. The barbiturates and other central nervous system depressants are called antianxiety agents, sedative/hypnotics, and minor tranquilizers. The main difference between a sedative and a hypnotic drug is the degree of sedation, or sleepiness, produced in comparison to the antianxiety-producing effects.[90] The barbiturates are the most common drugs of abuse after alcohol, which is the number one drug of abuse in the United States. The barbiturates and similarly acting drugs are capable of producing intoxication and withdrawal.

Barbiturates are capable of producing physical and psychological dependence and tolerance. The route of administraton may be oral or parenteral (*i.e.*, intravenous or intramuscular). Basically, the organs with greater blood flow absorb the drug first.[90] The majority of commonly used barbiturates are metabolized by the liver. Some barbiturates (*e.g.*, phenobarbital) are not metabolized and are excreted unchanged by the kidneys.[90]

Barbiturates cross the placental barrier and there is potential for the fetus of a drug-dependent mother to experience physical dependence. The physical withdrawal symptoms may occur in the infant up to 7 days after delivery. The following physical symptoms of the drug-dependent infant may appear—high pitched cry, tremors, restlessness, disturbed sleep, increased reflex action, hyperphagia, diarrhea, vomiting, and major motor seizures.[90]

Barbiturates and alcohol produce cross tolerance and, when taken together, will increase absorption and produce additive depression of the central nervous system. Because of this, individuals have taken an overdose of barbiturates while intoxicated with alcohol, perhaps unaware of the additive effects of alcohol and the sedative/hypnotics.

Patterns of Abuse. The barbiturates are frequently used by individuals who abuse or who are dependent on drugs to relieve or counteract the effects of other drugs. For example, barbiturates may be used to relieve symptoms of heroin withdrawal. The individual may be unaware that cross tolerance does not occur between opiates and bar-

(*Text continues on p 359*)

Table 24-3.   **Major Criteria for the Diagnosis of Alcoholism**

CRITERION	DIAGNOSTIC LEVEL
Track 1. Physiological and Clinical	
A. Physiological dependency	
1. Physiological dependence as manifested by evidence of a withdrawal syndrome when the intake of alcohol is interrupted or decreased without substitution of other sedation. It must be remembered that overuse of other sedative drugs can produce a similar withdrawal state, which should be differentiated from withdrawal from alcohol.	
a. Gross tremor (differentiated from other causes of tremor)	1
b. Hallucinosis (differentiated from schizophrenic hallucinations or other psychoses)	1
c. Withdrawal seizures (differentiated from epilepsy and other seizure disorders)	1
d. Delirium tremens, which usually starts between the 1st and 3rd day after withdrawal and minimally includes tremors, disorientation, and hallucinations.	1
2. Evidence of tolerance to the effects of alcohol (there may be a decrease in previously high levels of tolerance late in the course). Although the degree of tolerance to alcohol in no way matches the degree of tolerance to other drugs, the behavioral effects of a given amount of alcohol vary greatly between alcoholic and nonalcoholic subjects.	
a. A blood alcohol level of more than 150 mg without gross evidence of intoxication	1
b. The consumption of ⅕ of a gallon of whiskey or an equivalent amount of wine or beer daily, for more than one day, by a 180-lb individual	1
3. Alcoholic "blackout" periods (differential diagnosis from purely psychological fugue states and psychomotor seizures)	2
B. Clinical: major alcohol-associated illnesses.	
1. Alcoholism can be assumed to exist if major alcohol-associated illnesses develop in a person who drinks regularly. In such individuals, evidence of physiological and psychological dependence should be searched for.	
a. Fatty degeneration in absence of other known cause	2
b. Alcoholic hepatitis	1
c. Laennec's cirrhosis	2
d. Pancreatitis in the absence of choleithiasis	2
e. Chronic gastritis	3
f. Hematologic disorders	
Anemia: hypochromic, normocytic, macrocytic, hemolytic with stomatocytosis, low folic acid	3
Clotting disorders: prothrombin elevation, thrombocytopenia	3
g. Wernicke–Korsokoff syndrome	2
h. Alcoholic cerebella degeneration	1
i. Cerebral degeneration in absence of Alzheimer's disease or arteriosclerosis	2
j. Central pontine myelinolysis ⎤ diagnosis only possible	2
k. Marchiafava-Bignami's disease ⎦ postmortem	2
l. Peripheral neuropathy (see also beriberi)	2
m. Toxic amblyopia	3
n. Alcohol myopathy	2
o. Alcoholic cardiomyopathy	2
p. Beriberi	3
q. Pellagra	3
Track II. Behavioral, Psychological, and Attitudinal	
A. All chronic conditions of psychological dependence occur in dynamic equilibrium with intrapsychic and interpersonal consequences. In alcoholism, similarly, there are varied effects on character and family. Like other chronic relapsing diseases, alcoholism produces vocational, social, and physical impairments. Therefore, the implications of these disruptions must be evaluated and related to the individual and his pattern of alcoholism. The following behavior patterns show psychological dependence on alcohol in alcoholism.	
1. Drinking despite strong medical contraindication known to patient	1
2. Drinking despite strong, identified, social contraindication (job loss for intoxication, marriage disruption because of drinking, arrest for intoxication, driving while intoxicated)	1
3. Patient's subjective complaint of loss of control of alcohol consumption	2

Criteria Committee, National Council on Alcoholism. Am J Psychiatry 129 (August):47–48, 1972

Table 24-4.   **Minor Criteria for the Diagnosis of Alcoholism**

CRITERION	DIAGNOSTIC LEVEL
Track I. Physiological and Clinical	
A. Direct effects (ascertained by examination)	
1. Early	
a. Odor of alcohol on breath at time of medical appointment	2
2. Middle	
a. Alcoholic facies	2
b. Vascular engorgement of face	2
c. Toxic amblyopia	3
d. Increased incidence of infections	3
e. Cardiac arrhythmias	3
f. Peripheral neuropathy (see also Major Criteria, Track 1, B)	2
3. Late (see Major Criteria, Track 1, B)	
B. Indirect effects	
1. Early	
a. Tachycardia	3
b. Flushed face	3
c. Nocturnal diaphoresis	3
2. Middle	
a. Ecchymoses on lower extremities, arms, or chest	3
b. Cigarette or other burns on hands or chest	3
c. Hyperreflexia, or, if drinking heavily, hyporeflexia (permanent hyporeflexia may be a residuum of alcoholic polyneuritis)	3
3. Late	
a. Decreased tolerance	3
C. Laboratory tests	
1. Major—direct	
a. Blood alcohol level at any time of more than 300 mg/100 ml	1
b. Level of more than 100 mg/100 ml in routine examination	1
2. Major—indirect	
a. Serum osmolality (reflects blood alcohol levels) every 22.4 increase over 200 mOsm/liter reflects 50 mg/100 ml alcohol	2
3. Minor—indirect	
a. Results of alcohol ingestion	
b. Hypoglycemia	3
c. Hypochloremic alkalosis	3
d. Low magnesium level	2
e. Lactic acid elevation	3
f. Transient uric acid elevation	3
g. Potassium depletion	3
h. Indications of liver abnormality	
i. SGPT elevation	2
j. SGOT elevation	3
k. BSP elevation	2
l. Bilirubin elevation	2
m. Urinary urobilinogen elevation	2
n. Serum A/G ratio reversal	2
o. Blood and blood clotting	
p. Anemia hypochromic, normocytic, macrocytic, hemolytic with stomatocytosis, low fluid acid	3
q. Clotting disorders: prothrombin elevation, thrombocytopenia	3
r. ECG abnormalities	
s. Cardiac arrhythmias: tachycardia, T waves dimpled, cloven, or spinous, atrial fibrillation, ventricular premature contractions, abnormal P waves	2
t. EEG abnormalities	
u. Decreased or increased REM sleep, depending on phase	3
v. Loss of delta sleep	3
w. Other reported findings	3

(Continues on p 358)

Table 24-4. **Minor Criteria for the Diagnosis of Alcoholism (*Continued*)**

CRITERION	DIAGNOSTIC LEVEL
x. Decreased immune response	3
y. Decreased response to Synacthen test	3
z. Chromosomal damage from alcoholism	3
Track II. Behavioral, Psychological, and Attitudinal	
A. Behavioral	
1. Direct effects	
Early:	
a. Gulping drinks	3
b. Surreptitious drinking	2
c. Morning drinking (assess nature of peer group behavior)	2
Middle:	
a. Repeated conscious attempts at abstinence	2
Late:	
Blatant indiscriminate use of alcohol	1
Skid Row or equivalent social level	2
2. Indirect effects	
Early:	
a. Medical excuses from work for variety of reasons	2
b. Shifting from one alcoholic beverage to another	2
c. Preference for drinking companions, bars, and taverns	2
d. Loss of interest in activities not directly associated with drinking	2
Late:	
a. Chooses employment that facilitates drinking	3
b. Frequent automobile accidents	3
c. History of family members undergoing psychiatric treatment: school and behavioral problems in children	3
d. Frequent changes of residence for poorly defined reasons	3
e. Anxiety-relieving mechanisms, such as telephone calls inappropriate in time, distance, person, or motive (telephonitis)	2
f. Outbursts of rage and suicidal gestures while drinking	2
B. Psychological and attitudinal	
1. Direct effects	
Early:	
a. When talking freely, makes frequent reference to drinking alcohol, people being "bombed," "stoned," or admits drinking more than peer group	2
Middle:	
a. Drinking to relieve anger, insomnia, fatigue, depression, social discomfort	2
Late:	
a. Psychological symptoms consistent with permanent organic brain syndrome (see also Major Criteria, Track 1, B)	2
2. Indirect effects	
Early:	
a. Unexplained changes in family, social, and business relationships; complaints about wife, job, and friends	3
b. Spouse makes complaints about drinking behavior, reported by patient or spouse	2
c. Major family disruptions: separation, divorce, threats of divorce	3
d. Job loss (due to increasing interpersonal difficulties), frequent job changes, financial difficulties	3
Late:	
a. Overt expression of more regressive defense mechanisms: denial, projection, and so on	3
b. Resentment, jealousy, paranoid attitudes	3
c. Symptoms of depression: isolation, crying, suicidal preoccupation	3
d. Feelings that he is "loosing his mind"	2

Criteria Committee, National Council on Alcoholism. Am J Psychiatr 129 (August):47–48, 1972

biturates and may think that, because his tolerance to heroin is high, his tolerance to barbiturates will be high also; therefore, he may unintentionally overdose on barbiturates. Heroin addicts may substitute their habit with barbiturates when heroin is unattainable and, because there is no cross tolerance, may develop physical dependence on both classes of drugs.[90] Barbiturates may also be taken to relieve the anxiety related to flashbacks from LSD abuse or to counteract the symptoms of anxiety, paranoia, and depression due to excessive use of amphetamines.[90]

Individuals may abuse barbiturates and sedative/hypnotics for the many reasons people abuse alcohol, including the relief of anxiety and disinhibiting effects. Some may believe the barbiturates are less detectable than alcohol or find alcohol unpleasant to taste. Many individuals combine or alternate alcohol with the barbiturates or similarly acting sedative/hypnotics.[90] The behavioral differences that may occur in intoxication are usually due to the individual personality of the user or the social setting in which intoxication occurs; for example, violence or aggressive behavior may be more readily exhibited in social settings where alcohol is consumed.[4, 90]

There are two general patterns of abuse/dependency in this class of drugs.

1. Those individuals who obtain the drug through legal means, such as a prescription for medical problems, find the drug useful to relieve anxiety and increase dosage and frequency of consumption. This pattern is often found in individuals from a middle-class background and in females between the ages of 30 and 60 years.
2. Those individuals whose pattern is one of illegal possession of the drug are frequently in their late teens or early 20s and use the drugs to get "high" or get relief from the stimulant effects of the amphetamines.[4]

Criteria for the Diagnosis of Barbiturate Abuse and Dependence.

The criteria for abuse of barbiturates or similarly acting sedative/hypnotics are a pattern of pathological use that causes impairment in social or occupational functioning with a duration of at least 1 month. Dependence is manifested by tolerance or withdrawal.

Barbiturate and Similar Sedative/Hypnotic Organic Mental Disorders

Intoxication. Intoxication occurs after a recent ingestion of barbiturates. Signs and symptoms of barbiturate intoxication are similar to those of alcohol intoxication with the substance initially causing behavioral disinhibition.[4, 90] All of the complications manifested in alcohol intoxication may result from barbiturate intoxication.

Withdrawal. Wtihdrawal occurs hours to several days after decrease in, or cessation of, prolonged heavy use of the barbiturate or similarly acting sedative/hypnotic agent. Signs and symptoms of withdrawal are the same as those of alcohol withdrawal. The signs and symptoms do not necessarily follow a specific sequence of occurrence and the severity of the symptoms depends on individual differences, doses, and duration of use. Abrupt withdrawal from these drugs is not recommended; detoxification should take place in a medical setting.

Withdrawal Delirium. Withdrawal signs and symptoms from the barbiturates are the same as those of alcoholic withdrawal delirium or DTs and usually occur within 1 week after cessation or reduction of the drug. Some individuals experience delirium without seizures, some experience seizures only, and some exhibit both.[90] This condition is a medical emergency requiring hospitalization and medical intervention.

Amnestic Disorder. Amnestic disorder occurs after prolonged heavy use of barbiturates or similarly acting sedative/hypnotics. Predominant signs and symptoms of the disorder are impairment in short-term memory (inability to learn new information) and long-term memory (inability to remember past learned information). Full recovery from this disorder is possible.

Medical Consequences. Severe complications may result from intravenous barbiturate use (see the following italicized items). If the drug is inadvertently injected into subcutaneous tissue, *cellulitis,* in which subcutaneous tissues become swollen, inflamed, and painful, may result. *Vascular complications* occur if the drug is accidently injected into an artery and these may even result in loss of a hand or fingers.[90] The intravenous user may also suffer other medical complications from self-injections, particularly *serum hepatitis, endocarditis, pneumonia, tetanus,* and other *bacterial infections.* Also, *syphilis* or *malaria* may result, as well as *allergic reactions* to substances that may have been added to the drug.[90]

Barbiturates are the drugs frequently used in suicides. There are more than 15,000 deaths secondary to barbiturate poisoning reported yearly.[90] The extent to which these deaths are attributable to accidental or intentional suicide, however, is difficult to ascertain.

Individuals rarely use only one sedative/hypnotic drug; most use a variety of these drugs plus alcohol. It is critical in the detoxification process to assess whether an individual used alcohol, other drugs concurrently with alcohol, or other drugs without alcohol.

The Opiates

Effects. The opiates are narcotics or drugs that produce depressant effects on the central nervous system. Included in this definition is opium and derivatives of opium such as morphine, codeine, and heroin, as well as synthetically produced drugs such as meperidine and methadone.[36]

The pharmacologically active ingredients of opium are the alkaloids, the most common of which are morphine and codeine. The opiates may be taken orally or rectally or they may be smoked; however, they are usually injected intramuscularly or intravenously.

Essentially central nervous system depressants, the opiates produce analgesia, mood changes, and sedation, depress respirations, and inhibit coughing. They are very effective pain relief medications. The physiological actions of heroin are similar to morphine except that studies indicate that heroin is four or five times more potent than morphine.[36]

The body metabolizes heroin and morphine in a similar way. Heroin is converted by the body into morphine, metabolized primarily in the liver, with end products secreted through urine and bile.[78] Tolerance to the opiates develops rapidly and physical dependence occurs after a brief period of use.

Patterns of Abuse. Opiate abusers may be separated into two classes—those who are street abusers and those who abuse the opiate analgesics obtained from medical sources. The latter, in general, are an older, middle-class, well-established group, in comparison with the street abusers who obtain opiates from illegal sources.[7, 91]

The average "street" abuser tends to be male, young, and frequently from a minority group. The individual begins using opiates occasionally, but progresses to daily use and develops dependence and tolerance quickly. Frequently, there is a history of delinquent or antisocial behavior. The illegal status of the drug brings involvement in legal problems. There is a high incidence of death in this group due to suicide, homicide, accidents, and diseases such as infections and tuberculosis. The mortality rate is about 5 to 10 per 1000 for opiate users.[4, 78]

Medical abusers tend to be individuals who are women, from a middle-class environment, or those with pain syndromes who misuse their prescribed drugs and often misuse other drugs as well. Two high-risk groups for this type of abuse are those individuals with pain syndromes and health care workers, especially physicians and nurses.[78] Opioid abuse and dependency is usually preceeded by a period of polydrug use, which continues after opioid use is acquired.[4]

Criteria for the Diagnosis of Opioid Abuse and Dependence. The diagnosis of *opioid abuse* requires a pattern of pathological use of the substance, which causes impairment in occupational or social functioning with a duration of at least 1 month. The diagnosis of dependence requires the presence of either tolerance or withdrawal.

Opioid Organic Mental Disorders

Intoxication. Opiate intoxication is marked by the recent use of opioids, pupillary constriction, drowsiness, slurred speech, impairment in attention or memory, euphoria, dysphoria, apathy, and psychomotor retardation. Problems in social or occupational functioning and impaired judgment may result in maladaptive behavior.

Opioid Withdrawal. Following the prolonged, heavy use of opioids and after cessation or reduction of opioid use, withdrawal symptoms may include tearing, runny nose, dilated pupils, "gooseflesh" (piloerection), sweating, diarrhea, yawning, mild hypertension, tachycardia, fever, and insomnia. Accompanying symptoms may be irritability, depression, restlessness, tremor, weakness, nausea, vomiting, and muscle and joint pains. All of these symptoms may resemble "flu" symptoms.

Duration of the withdrawal period depends on the specific drug. Withdrawal symptoms may elicit a great deal of discomfort but are usually not life-threatening unless the client has a concurrent, serious medical problem, such as cardiac disease.

Medical Consequences. The prolonged use of opiates often results in decreased motivation to quality life experiences and personal and social deterioration that usually involve problems with police and law enforcement agencies as well as family and interpersonal problems.[4, 78]

Serious medical problems may result from drug overdose, from the additives in the street drugs, from poor nutrition and health, and from infections due to unsterile needles and equipment used in self-injection. Some of the common problems encountered are abscesses and infections of skin and muscle, tetanus, malaria, liver disease, hepatitis, gastric ulcers, endocarditis, heart arrhythmias, anemia, infections of bones and joints, pneumonia, tuberculosis, lung abscesses, and kidney failure caused by infections of additives in street drug mixtures. Sexual functioning problems may occur secondary to low testosterone levels during chronic opiate use. In addition, serious emotional problems, such as depression, may result from opioid abuse.[78]

Amphetamine and Cocaine: Central Nervous System Stimulants

Stimulants are drugs that act directly on the central nervous system. The individual taking stimulants becomes more talkative and active, and has an increased sense of wellbeing, self-confidence, and alertness. Stimulants are frequently used to decrease appetite, reduce fatigue, and combat mild depression. A common stimulant is caffeine, an ingredient in coffee, tea, and cola beverages.

Amphetamine is the prototype for this class of drug and other chemically related drugs with similar pharmacologic properties.[4, 36] Cocaine, also a stimulant, is classified as a narcotic and falls under the Controlled Substance Act.[4]

Effects of Amphetamine and Similarly Acting Sympathomimetics. This category includes all substituted phenylethylamine structures such as amphetamine and metamphetamine ("speed"), substances with different chemical structures but amphetamine-like actions, and some substances used as "diet pills." These substances may be taken orally or intravenously.[4] Tolerance develops within hours to days and there is cross-tolerance to most stimulants. It is not known if this tolerance is related to cocaine.[78]

Patterns of Abuse. As with other substances, abusers of amphetamine can be generally classified into medical abusers and street abusers.[36, 78] Medical abusers may obtain these drugs to aid in weight loss or to treat fatigue. Students may use them to help stay awake when studying for exams; truck drivers may use them to stay awake during long distance driving. After the medication is discontinued, fatigue results and need for sleep leads to an increase of dose, eventually leading to chronic use.

Street abusers use amphetamine or similar drugs to get "high" or achieve an altered state of consciousness. The drug may be used alone or with depressant drugs. Another pattern is using the substance in "runs"; that is, taking the drug around the clock for 2 or even 4 days, usually by the intravenous route.[36, 78]

Criteria for the Diagnosis of Amphetamine Abuse and Dependence. Amphetamine abuse is defined by three criteria—a pattern of pathological use, impairment of social and occupational functioning, and the duration of 1 month. The diagnosis of *amphetamine dependence* necessitates the presence of tolerance or withdrawal.

Amphetamine and Similar Sympathomimetic Organic Mental Disorders

Intoxication. Physical symptoms of amphetamine intoxication include increased heart rate, dilated pupils, increased blood pressure, perspiration, chills, nausea, and vomiting. The psychological symptoms of intoxication of this drug are psychomotor agitation, elation, grandiosity, talkativeness, loquacity, and hypervigilance. Individuals who are intoxicated with amphetamine display maladaptive behavior, such as fighting, interference in social and occupational functioning, and impaired judgment.

Delirium. The symptoms of amphetamine delirium usually occur within 1 hour of oral intake or immediately after the intravenous injection and subside within 6 hours. Symptoms of amphetamine delirium include hallucinations (visual, tactile, and olfactory), labile affect, and violent, aggressive behavior.

Delusional Disorder. Prolonged, chronic use of moderate to high doses of amphetamine may result in a delusional disorder. Symptoms of the disorder include persecutory delusions, ideas of reference, aggressiveness, hos-

tility, anxiety, and psychomotor agitation. The delusional individual may experience distortion of body image or tactile hallucinations, such as feeling bugs crawling under the skin, and he may scratch intensely to relieve the sensation. The delusional disorder may last for a week or longer, even for as long as a year.

Withdrawal. Amphetamine withdrawal follows prolonged use with abrupt cessation or reduction in use of the drug. Symptoms of withdrawal include depressed mood, fatigue, disturbed sleep, and increased dreaming. Depressed mood is the main feature of this disorder, and if it is severe, agitation or suicidal ideation may occur. The sleep disturbance is related to an increase in REM sleep and may be present for weeks. The withdrawal syndrome occurs within 3 days of cessation or reduction in the use of the substance and peaks in 2 or 4 days. The symptoms of depression and irritability, however, may continue for months.

Medical Consequences. The medical consequences of abuse of amphetamine and similar drugs are those associated with overdose. Problems may also result from the complications of self-injection, such as tetanus, hepatitis, abscesses, and infections. The signs of cerebral vascular accident may appear as a result of the strong contractions of blood vessels caused by stimulants; the increase in blood pressure may cause intracranial hemorrhage.[78]

Effects of Cocaine. Cocaine is an alkaloid obtained from the plant coca bush, which grows in South America. It is a white, odorless, fluffy powder that looks like snow, giving the substance one of its street names. Cocaine may be taken by sniffing through the nose ("snorting"), where it is absorbed through the mucous membranes. It may be smoked ("free basing"), injected intravenously ("main lining"), or mixed with heroin (called "speedball").[4, 36, 77]

Cocaine use has increased in popularity. A 1977 survey indicated a 43% increase in the number of adults reporting using cocaine.[77] Two of the reasons for the increase in popularity of cocaine are related to the following beliefs of the users.

1. Cocaine is considered a "social drug" in that it facilitates social interaction compared to heroin or lysergic acid diethylamide (LSD), which cause greater orientation to the individual's inner reactions.
2. Many users believe that cocaine is free from side effects; that is, it is a "safe" drug. This belief may very well be a false one.[77]

There is no evidence at this time of physical dependence on cocaine. Tolerance does not appear to develop and a withdrawal syndrome has not been identified.[4, 36, 7] Nevertheless, there are intense psychological effects and the urge to continue use of the drug is strong. Severe hallucinations similar to alcoholic DTs can occur after prolonged heavy use of cocaine. Psychotic depression may also occur when the drug is withdrawn or while it is being used.[36, 77]

Criteria for the Diagnosis of Cocaine Abuse. Cocaine abuse may take up to 8 months to develop. The criteria requires a pattern of pathological use that causes impairment in social or occupational functioning for at least 1 month.

Cocaine Organic Mental Disorders

Intoxication. Cocaine intoxication is marked by recent use of cocaine, maladaptive behavioral effects such as fighting and impaired judgment, and problems in occupational or social functioning. The following physical and psychological symptoms occur within minutes to 1 hour of taking the drug. The psychological symptoms include an increased sense of well-being and confidence, increased awareness of sensory input, psychomotor agitation, elation, talkativeness, pacing, and pressured speech. Physical symptoms are increased heart rate, dilated pupils, increased blood pressure, sweating, chills, nausea, and vomiting.

Cocaine use, especially by intravenous injection, causes a characteristic "rush" or feeling of increased self-confidence and well-being. If severely intoxicated, the individual may experience confusion, incoherent speech, anxiety, paranoid thoughts, headache, and palpitations. Following the physical effects, the user is likely to feel anxious, tremulous, irritable, depressed, and fatigued. This state is known as "crashing" and the user craves more cocaine for relief of these unpleasant symptoms. Recovery from intoxication occurs in 24 hours. There is no apparent withdrawal syndrome.

Medical Consequences. During cocaine intoxication an individual may experience tactile hallucinations which are described as insects crawling up the skin (formication).[4] Severe ulcerations of the skin may result from the user's attempts to dig out these "insects." Overdose of cocaine can produce cardiac arrythmias, convulsions, and respiratory depression.[36] Repeated heavy use by "snorting" the drug can cause tissue ulcerations in the nasal septum.[77, 78]

Hallucinogens

Effects. Hallucinogens are substances that alter mood and perception. They are also called psychomimetics. Ingestion of these drugs results in alterations in time, alterations in space perception, illusions, hallucinations, and delusions. The character and intensity of these reactions depends on the drug dosage and the individual personality of the user. The results are unpredictable—a person may experience a "high" on one occasion and a "bad trip" on another.[36] Lysergic acid diethylamine is the most potent and most common hallucinogenic drug. Lysergic acid comes from ergot, a fungus that spoils rye grain. It was converted to LSD by a Swiss chemist in 1943. The odorless, colorless, and tasteless drug is classified as a hallucinogen drug because it produces hallucinations.[36]

The LSD "trips" start within ½ hour after taking the drug and last for varying lengths of time. It is uncertain how LSD acts on the nervous system, but it is so powerful that only small doses, 100–250 micrograms (one-millionth of a gram), are needed. The drug in liquid form is usually placed on a sugar cube, and has also been put on chewing gum, cookies, and blotting paper.[36]

The misuse of LSD seems to be decreasing, possibly because of the widespread knowledge that side effects such as "flashbacks" and chromosomal damage can result from LSD use. Surveys indicate that about 10% of college students have tried LSD at least once.[36]

Criteria for the Diagnosis of Hallucinogen Abuse. Diagnostic criteria for hallucinogen abuse are pattern of pathological use of hallucinogens with impairment in social and occupational functioning and duration of 1 month. Dependence on hallucinogens has not been established.

Hallucinogen Organic Mental Disorders

Hallucinogen Hallucinosis. After recent ingestion of hallucinogens, a hallucinogen hallucinosis may result and is evidenced by perceptual changes, dilated pupils, increased heart rate, sweating, palpitations, blurring of vision, tremors, and incoordination. Also present are maladaptive behavioral effects such as severe anxiety or depression, "fear of losing one's mind," ideas of reference, paranoid ideation, impaired judgment, and interference with social and occupational functioning. The perceptual changes, the main feature of the hallucinosis, occur in a state of wakefulness and alertness and include subjective intensification of perceptions, depersonalization, illusions, hallucinations, and synesthesias (for example, "seeing noise"). The hallucinations are often visual, colorful, and contain geometric forms and patterns.

The hallucinosis syndrome begins within 1 hour after ingestion of hallucinogens and lasts for several hours. There are individual variations of the experience related to the personality of the user, the setting in which it is used, as well as the user's expectations of the experience. Euphoria is common. The individual is usually aware that the changes in perception are due to the hallucinogen, although, in some instances, the individual fears loss of sanity and believes this will be a permanent state.

Hallucinogen Delusional Disorder. The use of hallucinogens may result in an organic delusional disorder that exists beyond the period of the direct effects of the hallucinogen, lasting longer than 24 hours after cessation of hallucinogen use. The perceptual changes of hallucinogen hallucinosis occur, but the individual believes that these misperceptions and thoughts are based on reality.

Hallucinogen Affective Disorder. An organic affective syndrome due to hallucinogen ingestion may result in a disturbance in mood, more often a depressed mood accompanied by feelings of guilt, fearfulness, and restlessness. The individual may be talkative and unable to sleep. The disorder may last for a brief period or for a prolonged period of time and may be difficult to differentiate from a primary affective disorder.

Medical Consequences. "Flashbacks" may occur following use of hallucinogens. Flashbacks are recurrences of hallucinations when the drug is no longer being used and may occur weeks or months after stoppage of drug use.[4, 36] Individuals who have abused hallucinogens over a prolonged period of time are more likely to experience these recurrences of hallucinations. "Flashback" episodes cause anxiety and the fear of "going crazy." Physical dependence on hallucinogens does not develop. Tolerance develops and disappears quickly. Psychological dependence occurs in some individuals after chronic use. These individuals are known as "acid heads," implying a personality change in the individual as a result of long-term hallucinogen use. The individual becomes more passive, becomes introspective, and may lose the ability to concentrate.[36] There has been research on the possibility of hallucinogen-induced chromosome damage that produces congenital malformations, but this has not been confirmed. Medical problems are related to self-injury during periods of impaired judgment or delusions.

Cannabis

Effects. Cannabis sativa comes from the hemp plant, which is grown in warm climates and from which marihuana and hashish are derived. Tetrahydrocannaberiol, or THC, is the active ingredient in marihuana and hashish. Marihuana is derived from dried plant leaves and is a less potent form of THC than hashish (also spelled hasheesh), which is derived from the resins of the plant flowers.[36]

The most predominant effects of the drug cannabis are euphoria and an alteration in the level of consciousness of the individual without hallucinations. The drug is usually smoked or eaten. The metabolites are excreted in feces and urine.[78] There are federal estimates of 16 to 20 million regular users of marihuana in the United States.[30, 77] During the 1960s, the use of marihuana was popular as a means of anti-establishment protest. Presently, the use of the drug conforms to no specific social group, although many users are teenagers and young adults.[77]

Criteria for the Diagnosis of Cannabis Abuse and Dependence. Cannabis abuse disorder requires a pathological pattern of use that causes impairment in social or occupational functioning for at least a 1-month duration. Dependence on cannabis requires either a pattern of patho-

logical use or impairment in social or occupational functioning plus tolerance.

Cannabis Organic Mental Disorders

Intoxication. Cannabis intoxication is marked by increased heart rate, conjunctival infection (bloodshot eyes), increased appetite (often for sweets or "junk food"), dry mouth, and the psychological symptoms of euphoria, subjective intensification of perceptions, sensation of slowed time, and apathy. Maladaptive behavioral effects of cannabis intoxication include impaired judgment and interference with social or occupational functioning, or other effects such as panic attacks, suspiciousness, paranoid ideation, and excessive anxiety.

Cannabis Delusional Disorder. This delusional syndrome may occur with persecutory delusions during an episode of intoxication or immediately following the use of cannabis. This disturbance does not usually last longer than 6 hours after cessation of the use of the drug.

Medical Consequences. Marihuana inhaled has an irritating effect on the lungs, and may result in acute or chronic bronchitis, and sinusitis in heavy smokers. Increased heart rate and a decrease in the strength of cardiac contractions invariably results from marihuana use, bringing dangerous consequences to individuals with heart conditions. Research has indicated impairment in sperm production and chromosomal damage, but results have not been conclusive. There is also research controversy concerning marihuana causing brain damage. Another danger of marihuana use is the possibility that the use of this substance leads to abuse of more potent drugs, although this fear has not been substantiated.[78]

Application of the Nursing Process to Substance Abuse and Dependency Disorders

The discussion of the use of the nursing process with clients who evidence disorders of substance abuse and dependency focuses on general concepts applicable in all areas of practice. Although the issue of rehabilitation is addressed in relation to psychiatric inpatient settings, it is important to emphasize that nurses encounter problems of substance abuse and dependence in all areas of nursing.

Assessment and Analysis

The Nurse's Attitude and Feelings

The nurse's attitude toward the individual with substance abuse or dependency is a critical component of the interview process. Frequently, individuals with substance abuse problems are very sensitive and perceptive of the attitudes and mannerisms of nurses and other health team members.

The initial approach to interviewing the client needs to be nonjudgmental and objective. It is not unusual for the nurse to want to "rescue" the client; therefore, it is important to become aware of this possible reaction. The nurse's personal value system and personal, unpleasant contact with individuals who abuse substances may arouse judgmental feelings or attitudes toward the client. A therapeutic nurse possesses adequate knowledge about the substance abuse or dependency disorder and approaches the client with compassion and gentle firmness.

The nurse should avoid using words or terms in the interview process which may be interpreted by the client as offensive, such as "drunk," "addict," "alcoholic," and "boozer." Rather, the nurse uses terms with a less negative connotation but which convey the appropriate meaning, such as alcohol use, heroin use, "feeling good," and "feeling high."

The recovery process is another factor that may affect attitudes. Frequently, nurses and other health team members see more initial failures than successes. Relapse and return to drug use after treatment is not uncommon. Nevertheless, recovery does occur in many instances, and those who work in the area of substance abuse and dependence need to develop an attitude of hope. Feelings of hopelessness in the nurse or other health team workers are projected to the client; the reverse is also true.

Approaching the Client

The drug-dependent client who is being interviewed may be embarrassed about his behavior or may display uncooperative behavior. One way for the nurse to encourage cooperation is by demonstrating acceptance and a matter-of-fact manner, one that shows concern for the individual and conveys the message, "I care about your well-being" and "I know you are presently uncomfortable; I want to help you feel better."

The nurse maintains an empathetic approach during the interview and, although the client may be defensive or vague, the nurse does not respond with defensiveness or hostility. Questions should be formulated to elicit specific factual information and should be stated in such a way that they cannot be answered with evasive statements or generalities. The nurse also brings the subject of interview back to the facts being discussed, if the client diverts the conversation.

A format for eliciting information in major areas of assessment is provided in the insert, Assessment Guidelines. These guidelines are not meant to be all-encompassing. The examples of assessment data (in parentheses) are not the only observations that may be noted; there will be others that are not listed in this assessment form.

Because of the denial frequently used by the client who abuses or is dependent on substances, some of the information obtained during the interview may be of questionable validity. A more reliable history or a clearer validation of the information obtained about the substance abuse disorder may be established by interviewing a significant other (spouse, parent, adult, child, employer, roommate) in the client's life. Recognizing that this information may also be somewhat distorted due to the emotional involvement and denial system operating in the spouse or significant other, the information obtained may, nevertheless, offer corroborative data about the client's substance usage and harmful consequences it has incurred. Another important reason for interviewing the significant others is to involve them in the beginning of the treatment and rehabilitation process.

Emergency Conditions

Substance intoxication, overdose, severe alcohol and sedative/hypnotic withdrawal, withdrawal delirium, withdrawal seizures, and prolonged narcotic withdrawal may be life-threatening disorders. The severity of withdrawal or abstinence syndrome depends on many factors, such as the type of drug used, the extent of the addiction, prior drug history, nutritional status, and the status of fluid and electrolyte balance.[78, 91] The client may also have major medical complications the nurse will need to attend to in caring for him.

Intoxication. All of the drugs discussed in this chapter may cause intoxication. If the intoxication is severe, the symptoms may include lethargy and stupor and an overdose of the drug may be a possibility. The intoxicated person may also demonstrate bizarre behavior, panic, fright, confusion, or physical problems such as vomiting or pain.[91] The treatment measures for simple intoxication may consist of careful observation of symptoms, emotional support, and protection from physical injury, until the drug has been metabolized. In most instances, intoxication resolves within a few to several hours.

Overdose. Drug overdose may be a severe medical problem and may necessitate critical care until the emergency situation is resolved.[90] It is more frequent with alcohol, sedative/hypnotics, and narcotic drug use.[90]

Withdrawal Syndrome. Various medications are given for detoxification purposes and relief of withdrawal symptoms. The nurse is knowledgeable about the drug or drugs ingested, dose, route of administration, reactions, and possible side effects and toxic effects of the drugs. Generally, the following drugs are used in treatment of withdrawal syndrome: the barbiturates are used primarily for barbiturate withdrawal and the minor tranquilizers, such as chlordiazepoxide (Librium) or diazepam (Valium), are used for alcohol withdrawal. Codeine, propoxyphene (Darvon), or other opiate-type drugs are given for relief of narcotic with-

(Text continues on p 367)

Assessment Guidelines

Demographic Data:
Name:
Age:
Sex:
Ethnic Group:
Marital Status:
Religious Affiliation:
Significant Other:

What is the reason for coming to the hospital (*e.g.,* symptoms of withdrawal, marital-family crisis, work problems, referred by legal source, wants help to "stop drinking" or using drugs, medical problems)?

What is the motivation for treatment:
General Observations:

Vital Signs:	blood pressure (hypotensive, hypertensive)
Pulse:	rapid, regular, irregular
Temperature:	elevated
Respirations:	rapid, shallow, depressed
Appearance:	
Gait:	unsteady, normal, weaving, shuffling
Eyes:	conjunctival infection, bloodshot, dilated, pinpoint, normal pupils, lacrimation (tearing), vacant stare, poor eye contact, good eye contact
Skin:	perspiration, cool, clammy, dry, bruises, needle tracks, scars, abrasions, gooseflesh, excoriations, reddened palms
Nose:	running (rinorrhea) congested, "red"
Presence of Tremors:	fine or coarse, slight-moderate or severe
Grooming:	neat, unkempt, unshaven, odor, (alcohol, foul)
Behavior:	
Speech:	slurred, incoherent, loud, soft, normal, articulates clearly, monotone, hesitant, pressured, relevant, distractive
Attitude:	quiet, calm, demanding, agitated, irritable, impatient, vague, withdrawn, suspicious, anxious, tearful, happy, silly
Dominant Mood–Affect:	euphoric, depressed, angry, sad, appropriate, inappropriate, normal
Sensorium:	orientation to time, person, place, changes in memory
Perception:	the presence of illusions, hallucinations, delusions, hallucinosis
Potential for Suicide:	Is the individual presently thinking about suicide? Is there a plan or a method to carry out that plan? A history of previous suicide attempts or gestures? Were attempts in intoxicated state or sober state? Is there a family history of suicide? Is there a recent loss or anniversary of a loss? (Assess need for emergency consultation and intervention.)
Potential for Violence:	Does behavior indicate potential for violence? Voice, manner, stance, verbal threats? Assess need for consultation, emergency intervention if necessary. Ask if individual has a history of violence when taking substances or during withdrawal period.
Present Drug History:	The areas that need specific assessment are the type of substance used, the amount taken, and the pattern or use.
Type:	Beer, wine, whiskey, cocaine, heroin, marihuana (cannabis) sedative/hypnotics, hallucinogens. Individual taking one substance only, or a combination? This may mean combination within a class (*i.e.,* alcohol, beer, whiskey and wine, or alcohol and sedative/hypnotics). It may be combinations in different classes (*i.e.,* heroin and alcohol and stimulants or narcotics and sedative/hypnotics). What is the predominant substance of choice? Does the individual use "street" drugs, prescription drugs?)

(Continues on p 366)

Amount:	How much (approximate amount) does the individual drink? How many six packs, quarts, fifths? How much does he use, bags? What route, (oral, intravenous, subcutaneous)? How many pills daily?
What is the pattern of use:	Daily, several times a week? increased on weekends? Only weekends? Binge or episodic drinking? Runs? Intoxicated daily? Has individual ever tried to control or cut down drinking or pattern of substance use? How?

When was last drink?
When was last drug dose: How taken?
What drugs currently taking?
Has individual developed tolerance? (explain)
When did it begin?
Has there been a change in tolerance?
Are withdrawal symptoms present?
Is there a previous history of withdrawal?
Is there a previous history of seizures?
Is there a history of hallucinations? (explain)
Is there a history of hallucinosis?
Was individual ever hospitalized? If yes, what for?
Are there are present medical problems?
Are there any chronic medical problems?
Is there a history of the following: liver disease? hepatitis? diabetes? heart disease? anemia? drug overdose?
Have there been any recent falls, injuries, accidents?
Is the individual taking any prescribed medication?
Has the individual any known allergies?
Past Drug History:
Has the individual ever stopped drinking or using drugs?
How long was the period of abstinence?
Why did the individual abstain, what was the motivation?
At what age did the individual start abusing/using substances?
At what age did the individual first begin having difficulty in life circumstances due to drug intake?
Has the individual ever been in treatment for drug abuse/dependency?
What type of treatment: detoxification, rehabilitation?
How many times in treatment for the above?
Is there a family history of alcohol abuse/dependency?
Is there a family history of other substance abuse/dependency?

Psycho-Social History:

Conjugal:	Married, separated, divorced, never married, widowed? What is spouse's reaction to client's abuse of substances? Does the spouse abuse substances? Is substance use causing marital conflicts?
Parenting:	Are there children? How many, ages, and sex? Have children had school problems, health problems, physical, emotional sleeping problems?
Intrapersonal:	What are the individual's leisure activities, hobbies? Has there been a change in participation in these activities? Has there been a change in friends or a loss of friendships? Do the social activities center around teh substance use/abuse?
Occupation/Employment:	What is individual's occupation? present employment? How long in present employment? Has the individual ever missed work from alcohol use—drug use? Has the individual abused substances while working? Is substance use jeopardizing work or business? How long has individual been employed?

Finances and Living Conditions:	Approximate amount spent on substances, source of income other than employment? Family suffering from less adequate housing or food due to substance abuse or purchases? What are the present living conditions? Is individual living alone, in an apartment, own house, live in a room, is there no address or no permanent living arrangement?
Legal Problems:	Have there been any violations while intoxicated? Are there any present legal offenses pending from substance abuse/dependency? Is present treatment court recommended?

drawal symptoms; if these symptoms are severe, however, drugs such as methadone or morphine may be used. Anticonvulsant drugs, particularly diphenylhydantoin (Dilantin), are given for alcohol and sedative/hypnotic withdrawal seizures. Thiamine is usually given in the alcohol withdrawal treatment phase to prevent Wernicke-Korsokoff syndrome. Multivitamins are frequently administered because of the typically poor nutritional status of the drug-dependent client.[91]

Behavioral Defenses

Defense Mechanisms. Defense mechanisms are processes within the mind (*i.e.*, intrapsychic processes) that are usually unconscious and that relieve the individual from emotional conflict and anxiety.[3]

Denial. Denial is the outstanding defense mechanism used by clients who abuse or who are dependent on substances. It is especially profound in alcohol abuse and dependency.

Denial is an unconscious process used to protect against intolerable feelings, thoughts, wishes, needs, or external reality factors, by blocking knowledge of these factors from conscious awareness.[3] Defense or coping mechanisms are used in normal ways to adapt to threatening situations, such as the normal grief process in terminal illness. The use of defense mechanisms becomes unhealthy when they are used inappropriately and when they interfere with healthy functioning. The individual who abuses drugs often seems unaware of the apparent adverse psychological, social, and physical consequences of the excessive drug use. Frequently, the abuse or dependency disorder develops gradually, especially alcoholism, and the use of denial and other defense mechanisms protects the individual from acknowledging the fact that the disorder is developing. Although denial can be found to some degree in all clients who abuse substances, it is most blatant in alcoholism and allows alcoholics literally to drink themselves to death.

Individuals with alcohol abuse or dependence cannot admit that alcohol is causing serious problems and they continue drinking. One of the reasons attributed to this denial process in alcoholism is the blackouts that occur. Blackouts represent a period of amnesia of part or all of a drinking experience, although the individual appears to others to be functioning and know what he is doing. The guilt feelings the individual experiences as a result of his drinking, the social stigma attached to his behavior or disorder, and the possibility of rejection by others foster the development of denial.[26, 49]

The family and significant others to the individual who abuses alcohol also contribute by denying the drinking as a problem and by assuming caretaking roles rather than allowing the individual to experience the serious consequences of the drinking behavior.[26, 49]

Following are some of the defense mechanisms used by substance abuse/dependency individuals to deny or protect themselves from the acceptance of the disorder.

Projection. Projection is an unconscious mechanism whereby that which is emotionally unacceptable to the self is rejected and attributed to others.[3] The individual does not take responsibility for certain unacceptable behavior and places his behavior outside of himself, blaming persons, places, and things for his behavior.

Rationalizing. Rationalizing is an unconscious mechanism by which the individual justifies, by seemingly believable means, his feelings, behaviors, or motives that would otherwise be intolerable.[3] For example, the individual gives a reason to explain excessive use of a substance other than the fact that he is dependent. The drug usage is not denied; an inaccurate, reasonable explanation is given instead.

Intellectualizing. In order to defend against dealing with unconscious conflicts and their resulting stressful emotions, the process of reasoning is employed.[3] Rather than discussing a personal awareness of his abuse or dependence problem, the individual talks about the problem on an intellectual level; for example, analyzing the problem or giving theories related to the cause.

Minimizing. The individual admits to some drug abuse or dependence but makes it seem to. be a minor problem.

Diversion. The individual uses certain tactics or techniques to change the subject to avoid the topic of abuse and dependency.

Anger. The individual expresses anger or displeasure in response to the subject of drug abuse or dependency. This reaction tends to induce the nurse or health care worker to change the subject, rather than to confront or deal with the anger the discussion produces in the client.

The nurse recognizes that the denial process is a real phenomenon; that is, the individual is not aware of the reality or extent of his substance abuse or dependency disorder. Because the initial experience with the use of the drug was pleasurable and although the pleasant aspects of the experience have diminished and unfavorable consequences have developed, the search for recapturing the pleasure remains. The psychological compulsion to continue the drug use becomes so great that it becomes the priority in a dependent person's life.[49] What begins as a stress–relief or pleasure experience becomes, itself, the stressor. Denial helps the drug-dependent individual maintain some sense of self-worth and remove himself from the harmful consequences of his behavior. In the process, however, he becomes progressively out of touch with the reality of the situation.[49]

Our society may well contribute to this denial process because it is one that promotes the use of substances, especially alcohol, for relief of stress and anxiety, yet rejects the drug-dependent individual as weak-willed and amoral or as a skid-row bum. The drug user's significant others frequently overlook situations of abuse or cover-up the consequences of his behavior. In an effort to protect the individual, they enable the harmful abuse to continue; therefore, the meaning of the descriptive term "enablers" is often used in the field of alcoholism.

Physical and Safety Needs

The physical needs of the client need constant assessment. The potential for infection is increased due to injuries, various medical consequences of the drugs, and factors that may result from substance induced organic mental disorders.

The potential for physical injury is a serious problem. The safety and protection of the patient from harm must be of primary consideration. The substance induced organic mental disorders present altered states of consciousness and impaired reality testing that will require vigilant assessment, thorough analysis, and appropriate nursing intervention.

Sleep disturbances are common, and conditions such as insomnia may result from withdrawal states, from the prolonged pattern of abuse or dependency, or from personal or family stress. Also, nightmares and increased dreaming may occur. Nursing measures to assess and alleviate sleep disturbances are undertaken because the use of sedative/hypnotics is usually discouraged owing to the disorder of abuse.

Feelings of anxiety stemming from underlying conflicts and a variety of reasons related to substance abuse/dependency and cessation of use are present. Assessment and intervention methods need to be individualized.

The presence of depression or feelings of profound sadness due to decreased self-esteem related to substance abuse behavior or its familial, social, and legal consequences requires assessment and individualized treatment. Antidepressant medication may be used in conjunction with other supportive measures. The potential for suicide is a priority consideration and requires appropriate intervention (see Chapters 21 and 34).

Noncompliance with treatment is manifested in many ways that indicate a lack of motivation for treatment and may be due to the denial syndrome and to a lack of understanding of the disorder. The nurse needs to be alert to these manifestations and assist the client to obtain insight into his behavior.

Planning

Developing therapeutic plans facilitates the client's participation in the treatment process and his ultimate recovery. Individualized nursing assessment and intervention help the client obtain the desired behavioral outcomes that will aid in the restoration of his emotional and physical well-being. Ultimately, the recovering individual strives for increased satisfaction in a way of life free from mood-altering and mind-altering substances.

Goal-Setting

Goal-setting for individuals who abuse or who are dependent on substances includes the following.

1. Provision for physical requirements
2. Maintenance of emotional stability
3. Reduction and eventual resolution of the use of pathological defense mechanisms
4. Understanding and acceptance of the substance abuse/dependency disorder
5. Identification with peers
6. Development of hope for recovery
7. Resocialization and increased interpersonal relationship skills
8. Development of increased self-worth and self-esteem
9. Establishment of alternative coping skills
10. Improvement of motivation to continued treatment and prevention of noncompliance
11. Involvement of family and significant others in the treatment and recovery process

Intervention

The Rehabilitation Process

The rehabilitation process usually focuses on the substance abuse or dependence disorder itself. The other problems that the client encounters, such as loss of job, marital conflicts, and legal problems, are often results of the drug abuse. Consequently, the individual does not benefit from the resolution of these problems if the drug dependency continues. Conversely, many problems that stem directly from the drug use, such as physical illness, or family or legal problems, diminish with rehabilitation and continued abstinence. Other significant problems—physical, emotional, and social—are treated concurrently with the substance abuse/dependency disorder.

The rehabilitation process generally involves the following phases: detoxification, the restoration of physical and emotional stability, intervention methods to increase motivation to continue treatment, confrontation of the pathological defenses, intervention methods to increase self-esteem, facilitation of insight into problem areas, planning for discharge, and follow-up care.

An important aspect of the rehabilitation program is for the individual to accept the responsibility for his drug abuse or dependence and to take the necessary actions toward recovery. Underlying the goal of discontinuation of the substance use and maintenance of abstinence is the necessity of a change in the individual's behavior that will lead to a new lifestyle, one of greater personal enrichment.

Breaking Through the Defenses

The breakdown of the pathological defense mechanisms manifested in the denial system is a gradual process. The nurse is alert to recognize and understand the particular defensive maneuver being used by the client. Gradually, the nurse assists the client to come face-to-face with the objective reality that is being denied. A consistent, persistent approach is necessary. This persistent stance of the nurse and other health team members conveys the message that there is never a valid reason for the client to use the substances of abuse and dependency. When the client focuses on other problems in his life to the exclusion of the substance abuse/dependency problem, the nurse and treatment team refocus on the initial abuse or dependency problem. This approach assists the client to understand that other problems may be more effectively defined and resolved as a consequence of attacking the primary problem of substance abuse or dependence.

Understanding and Acceptance of the Disorder

The drug-dependent individual needs to attain an intellectual comprehension of the disorder. One approach is to understand that it is an illness and not a moral problem. Various educational material about the manifestations of substance abuse disorder and clarification of misinformation assist in this process. With an intellectual understanding, the individual is assisted to accept the fact that the disorder is chronic and will not be cured. This requires acceptance of the disorder on an emotional level and recovery on a long-term, but day-by-day, basis. Most rehabilitation programs require abstinence as a prerequisite to recovery.

Identification with Peers

Peer group identification and confrontation of the abuse of or dependence on a substance is a powerful help to recovery. Individuals recognize and internalize the fact that they are not alone in their suffering, and therefore receive emotional support and hope. The group also allows for confrontation by peers who attack pathological defense mechanisms and assist each other in the process of obtaining insight into behavior. The nurse may lead the group, encourage the client to attend the group, or discuss issues that may have surfaced after group attendance and participation.

Development of Hope

Clients enter the rehabilitation program with initial feelings of hopelessness, discouragement, and demoralization. They need to realize that there is the possibility of escape from what may be perceived as a hopeless situation. Identification with others who have the same problems and with those who have recovered or are recovering is significant in initiating a feeling of hope. The positive attitude of the nurse and other mental health team members also instills hope in clients.

Resocialization

The drug user's life becomes drug-centered and, in the process, the individual becomes self-centered. Social skills may be diminished or lacking. It is a priority to assist the client to review and rebuild the capacity for establishing interpersonal relationships that the previous self-centered attitude has eroded.

Development of Self-Worth and Self-Esteem

Generally, the person's self-esteem and self-worth increase with his ability to see the substance abuse problem as an illness. In addition, the individual is helped by taking responsibility for making changes in attitudes and actions and for deriving satisfaction from achievements and relationships.

The nurse also assists the client develop self-discipline. For example, the nurse may help the client organize and adhere to a daily routine which may be difficult for him because of a previously chaotic lifestyle centered around the substance of abuse. The nurse expects and conveys to the client the expectation that he take an active part in the recovery program. She encourages and supports his positive efforts to change. As the client experiences success, self-confidence, and self-esteem, hopefulness develops and he recognizes that there are alternatives to drugs. Motivation for recovery is enhanced as involvement in the program increases. Rehabilitation is a process that continues long after discharge from a treatment facility.

Other Important Therapies

Disulfiram (Antabuse) Treatment. The drug disulfiram (Antabuse) has been used in adjunct with other alcohol dependency treatment methods. The drug interferes with the metabolism of acetaldehyde, a by-product of alcohol metabolism, which produces physical symptoms that, depending on individual variations and conditions, may be severe. The general physical symptoms experienced by the person taking disulfiram, after ingestion of even small amounts of alcohol, include flushing of the skin, pounding headache, feeling faint, weak, and dizzy, nausea and vomiting, tachycardia, chest pain, shortness of breath, hypotension, blurred vision, and confusion.[73]

The taking of the drug disulfiram does not ensure sobriety or cure alcoholism. The chemotherapeutic purpose of the drug is to assist the client to control or not act on the impulse to drink. The client understands that while the drug is being taken, these symptoms can occur after ingestion of alcohol. Therefore, the compulsion to drink during that time is lessened and the client is free to concentrate on other areas in treatment. Because it takes several days for the drug to leave the body completely after the drug use has been discontinued, the client makes the decision to return to drinking on a conscious level rather than attributing it to an impulsive act. Most treatment programs offer disulfiram on a voluntary basis and a written informed consent is usually required. The client must have full understanding of the drug's action and consequences. Candidates for this form of chemotherapy must be carefully screened by the physician and baseline medical tests performed before the drug is administered.

The client must also understand that alcohol in any form (*i.e.*, in foods, cough mixtures, or other medications, as well as shaving lotions or other alcohol-containing substances applied to the skin) must be avoided because the same reaction produced with the intake of ethyl alcohol will occur. A list of these substances is given to the client, along with a medical alert card or bracelet, when he begins taking disulfiram.

Methadone Maintenance. Methadone maintenance is used in opiate dependence in conjunction with other treatment methods, although it is not a "cure." Methadone is a longer-acting narcotic that is substituted for the shorter-acting opiates, such as heroin. Methadone has similar pharmacologic properties to heroin including addiction, sedation, and respiratory depression. It generally acts by blocking the euphoric effects of heroin and other opiates, thereby preventing the impulsive use of heroin.[50, 91] The general purpose of a methadone maintenance program is to assist the client to develop a lifestyle free of "street drugs." This enables him to improve family and social functioning and to decrease or eliminate legal problems, traumatic injuries, and health problems associated with the obtaining and abusing "street drugs."[50, 91] The drug methadone is administered in licensed clinics that have been established to control its distribution and prevent its diversion for illegal use. The clinics maintain a careful screening process for candidates and require that specific criteria for admission be met. Psychological and social rehabilitation of the client takes place concurrently.[50, 91]

Drug Free Communities. Drug free communities are another approach to narcotic dependency treatment and rehabilitation. These therapeutic communities are usually long-term programs lasting up to 1 year. The client is removed from the "street culture" and given a new identity within the group community. In this program, confrontation by group members and ex-addicts assist the client to gain insight into problem areas and find more successful ways of coping with life situations and stresses.[50]

Aversion Conditioning. Aversion conditioning is a behavioral approach related to the conditional response mechanism. For example, the client may be taught not to drink by associating the sight, smell, and taste of alcohol with an unpleasant event. The aversion technique, for example, may be a mild electric shock to the skin.[75, 91]

Other Modalities. Relaxation therapy in various modes is frequently used in programs to teach clients methods to release tension, improve self-image, and relieve insomnia without the use of drugs. Role playing is a technique that includes rehearsed responses to specific situations; for example, where drinking or drug-taking opportunities may be encountered, and hopefully successfully refused, by the client. Social skills and responses to situations such as job interviews may be rehearsed to relieve anticipatory anxiety. Assertiveness training is another useful method to assist the client to meet dependency and interdependency needs and accept personal responsibility and satisfaction in achievements.

Self-Help Groups. The first, and perhaps the most influential, of substance abuse/dependency self-help groups is an organization called Alcoholics Anonymous, or A.A.

This self-help program was founded in 1935 by two men, Dr. Bob, a surgeon by profession, and Bill W., a New York stockbroker. At the time, these men were unable to obtain help from their sufferings of alcoholism from the health professions. They found that, by sharing their life experiences with each other and identifying with each other in their common problem with alcohol, they were able to overcome their compulsion to drink (see inserts, What Is A.A.? and The Twelve Steps of Alcoholics Anonymous).

Al-Anon is a fellowship of spouses, relatives, and friends of alcoholics that started as an outgrowth of A.A. and is now a completely separate organization. Alateen is a component of Al-Anon, and the sponsor of Alateen is usually a member of Al-Anon, although members of Alateen have separate groups and conduct their own meetings. Both groups follow the 12 steps of A.A.

Narcotics Anonymous (N.A.) is a fellowship of recovering addicts. Narcotics Anonymous follows a program adapted from Alcoholics Anonymous; that is, the 12 steps of A.A. are the basis of the program of recovery.[63] Although N.A. follows the same principles of recovery as its model,

the concept has been broadened to include all mood-altering substances.

Evaluation

Evaluation is an ongoing component of the nursing process. The nurse continually assesses the degree to which interventions have been successful in assisting the client resolve problems and meet short-term and long-term goals. The nurse reflects on questions related to the effectiveness of interventions. For example, if the interventions were not successful, why were they ineffective? Were there changes in the client's behavior and was the nurse able to foresee these changes? Evaluation applies to all steps of the nursing process and modifications may be necessary because the changes reflect individual differences and responses to treatment.

Individual treatment plans are initiated together with the client, family, and members of the multidisciplinary team caring for that client. Referrals for continuing care after discharge or a return to the facility for outpatient follow-up care is frequently arranged or advocated. Referrals

What Is A.A.?

Alcoholics Anonymous is a program of recovery from the illness of alcoholism. It is an international fellowship of men and women who meet together to attain and maintain sobriety. It is nonprofessional, self-supporting, nondenominational, multiracial, apolitical, and almost omnipresent. There are no age or educational requirements. Membership is open to any alcoholic who wants to do something about his or her drinking problem.

What Does A.A. Do?

1. The A.A. members share their recovery experience with anyone seeking help with a drinking problem and give person-to-person service or "sponsorship" to the alcoholic coming to A.A. from a treatment or correctional facility or any other referral source.
2. The A.A. program, as set forth in the Twelve Steps to recovery, offers the alcoholic an opportunity to develop a satisfying way of life free from alcohol.
3. This program is discussed at A.A. group meetings:
   a. Open speaker meetings—open to alcoholics and nonalcoholics. (Attendance at an open A.A. meeting is the best way to learn what A.A. does and what it does not do.) At speaker meetings, A.A. members "tell their stories." They describe their experiences with

alcohol, how they came to A.A., and how their lives have changed as a result of the A.A. experience.
   b. Open discussion meetings—one member speaks briefly about his or her experience as an alcoholic and leads a discussion on a selected subject (guilt, resentments, self-pity) or on any subjects or drinking-related problems anyone brings up.
   c. Closed discussion meetings—same format as above
   d. Closed Step meetings—discussion of one of the Twelve Steps
   e. The A.A. members also take meetings into correctional and treatment facilities.
   f. The A.A. members may, in conjunction with court personnel, conduct meetings "about A.A." as a part of A.S.A.P. (Alcohol Safety Action Programs) and D.W.I. (Driving While Intoxicated) programs. These meetings about A.A. are not to be confused with regular A.A. meetings.

What A.A. Does Not Do

A.A. does not

1. furnish initial motivation for alcoholics to recover;
2. solicit members;

3. engage in or sponsor research;
4. join "councils" of social agencies;
5. follow up or try to control its members;
6. make medical or psychological diagnoses or prognoses;
7. provide drying-out or nursing services, hospitalization, drugs, or any medical or psychiatric treatment;
8. offer spiritual or religious services;
9. engage in education about alcohol;
10. provide housing, food, clothing, jobs, money, or any other welfare or social services;
11. provide domestic or vocational counseling;
12. accept any money for its services, or any contributions from non-A.A. sources.

The primary purpose of A.A. is to carry our message of recovery to the alcoholic seeking help. The primary purpose of any alcoholism treatment modality is to help the alcoholic attain and maintain sobriety. Therefore, regardless of the road we follow, we are all heading for the same destination—the rehabilitation of the alcoholic person. Together, we can do what neither of us could accomplish alone.

(From Information on Alcoholics Anonymous, A.A. World Services, New York)

The Twelve Steps of Alcoholics Anonymous

1. We admitted we were powerless over alcohol—that our lives had become unmanageable.
2. Came to believe that a Power greater than ourselves could restore us to sanity.
3. Made a decision to turn our will and our lives over to the care of God as we understood him.
4. Made a searching and fearless moral inventory of ourselves.
5. Admitted to God, to ourselves, and to another human being the exact nature of our wrongs.
6. We're entirely ready to have God remove all these defects of character.
7. Humbly asked Him to remove our shortcomings.
8. Made a list of all persons we had harmed, and became willing to make amends to them all.
9. Made direct amends to such people wherever possible except when to do so would injure them or others.
10. Continue to take a personal inventory and when we were wrong promptly admit it.
11. Sought through prayer and meditation to improve our conscious contact with God as we understood Him, praying only for knowledge of His will for us and the power to carry that out.
12. Having had a spiritual experience as the result of these steps, we tried to carry this message to alcoholics, and to practice these principles in all our affairs.

to halfway houses may be arranged to facilitate readjustment to community and society for clients who require resocialization in a more structured environment. Continued participation in self-help groups is strongly recommended.

Summary

This chapter has discussed the use of substances that affect the central nervous system and the physical and behavioral changes that occur in individuals who abuse or become dependent on these substances. The focus has been on commonalities of substance abuse and dependence and the specific factors particular to each drug classification. Some of the major points of the chapter are as follows.

1. Selye's theoretical framework of the stress/adaptation syndrome may be applied to the problem of substance abuse and dependency.
2. There is no single etiology of drug abuse and dependence; rather, theories examine multiple factors such as personality traits, genetic influences, social, cultural, ethnic, and environmental factors, and a self-destructive phenomenon.
3. Drug dependence may be viewed as a way of coping with life's stressors by individuals who abuse substances.
4. Substance use disorders are divided into the diagnoses of substance abuse and substance dependency.
5. Substance induced organic mental disorders generally include intoxication, withdrawal, and delirium.
6. Each class of substances of abuse is described in terms of its effects, patterns of abuse, diagnostic criteria, organic mental disorders, and medical consequences.
7. A nonjudgmental, objective approach is essential

for establishing rapport with individuals who abuse substances.

8. Rehabilitation and eventual recovery is the focus of treatment planning and intervention with individuals who abuse, or are dependent on, drugs.

9. Problems of substance abuse and dependency are encountered in all areas of nursing practice.

References

1. Ackerman R: Children of Alcoholics. Holmes Beach, FL, Learning Publications, 1978

2. Aldoory S: The Chemical Curtain: Polydrug Abuse Among Women. Alcohol Health and Research World, Vol 2. (Winter): 28–36, 1978

3. American Psychiatric Association: A Psychiatric Glossary. Edited by the Subcommittee of the Joint Commission on Public Affairs. Washington, DC, American Psychiatric Association, 1980

4. American Psychiatric Association: Diagnostic and Statistical Manual of Mental Disorders, 3rd ed. Washington, DC, American Psychiatric Association, 1980

5. Bakdash D: Essentials the Nurse Should Know about Chemical Dependency. J Psychiatr Nurs Mental Health Serv 16 (October): 33–37, 1978

6. Becker CE: Medical Consequences of Alcohol Abuse. Postgraduate Medicine 64 (December): 88–93, 1978

7. Black C: Children of Alcoholics. Alcohol Health and Research World, Vol 3. (Fall): 23–27, 1979

8. Blume S, Dropkin D, Sokolow L: The Jewish Alcoholic: A Descriptive Study. Alcohol Health and Research World, Vol 4. (Summer): 21–26, 1980

9. Brill L, Winick C (eds): The Yearbook of Substance Use and Abuse, Vol II. New York, Human Sciences Press, 1980

10. Broadhurst PL: Drugs and the Inheritance of Behavior. New York, Plenum Press, 1978

11. Carroll JFX: Personality and Psychopathology: A Comparison of Alcohol and Drug-Dependent Persons. In Solomon J, Keeley KA, Wright J (eds): Perspectives in Alcohol and Drug Abuse: Similarities and Differences, pp 59–87. Boston, PSG, Inc, 1982

12. Clopton JR: Alcoholism and the MMPI. J Stud Alcohol 39:1540–1553, 1978

13. Cohen S: Combined Alcohol-Drug Abuse and Human Behavior. In Solomon J, Keeley KA, Wright J (eds): Perspectives in Alcohol and Drug Abuse: Similarities and Differences, pp 89–116. Boston, PSG Inc, 1982

14. Cohen S: The Pharmacology of Alcohol. Postgrad Med 64 (December): 97–102, 1978

15. Cornish RD, Miller MV: Attitudes of Registered Nurses Toward the Alcoholic. J Psychiatr Nurs Ment Health Serv 14 (December): 19–22, 1976

16. Cortina FM: Stroke A Slain Warrior. New York, Columbia University Press, 1970

17. Cotton NS: The Familial Incidence of Alcoholism: A Review. J Stud Alcohol 40:89–115, 1979

18. Criteria Committee, National Council on Alcoholism: Criteria for the Diagnosis of Alcoholism. Am J Psychiatr 129 (August): 127–135, 1972

19. Day S: Fetal Alcohol Syndrome. Alcoholism 1 (September/October): 35–37, 1980

20. DuPont RL: The National Institute on Drug Abuse: Adult Identity Crisis at Five Years of Age. In Brill L, Winick C (eds): The Yearbook of Substance Use and Abuse, Vol II, pp 21–36. New York, Human Sciences Press, 1980

21. Efinger JM: Women and Alcoholism. Topics in Clinical Nursing 5 (January): 10–19, 1983

22. Einstein S: Beyond Drugs. New York, Pergamon Press, 1975

23. Estes NJ, Heinemann EM: Alcoholism: Development, Consequences and Interventions, 2nd ed. St Louis, CV Mosby, 1982

24. Ewing JA, Rouse BA: Drinking—Alcohol in American Society—Issues and Current Research. Chicago, Nelson-Hall, 1978

25. Fenster FL: Alcohol Disorders of the Gastrointestinal System. In Estes NJ, Heinemann EM (eds): Alcoholism: Development Consequences, and Interventions, 2nd ed. St Louis, CV Mosby, 1982

26. Fewell CH, Bissell LeClair: The Alcoholic Denial Syndrome: An Alcohol-Focused Approach. Social Casework 59 (January): 6–13, 1978

27. Fourth Special Report to the U.S. Congress on Alcohol and Health. DeLuca J (ed). Washington, DC, NIAAA (January), 1981

28. Fox V: Recognizing Multiple Simultaneous Drug Withdrawal Syndromes. Paper presented to NCA, AMSA Medical-Scientific Conference, Washington, DC, May, 1976

29. Gareri EA: Assertiveness Training for Alcoholics. J Psychiatr Nurs Ment Health Serv 17 (January): 31–36, 1979

30. Goldman A: Grass Roots. New York, Harper & Row, 1979

31. Goodwin DW: Alcoholism and Heredity. Arch Gen Psychiatr 36 (January): 57–61, 1979

32. Goodwin DW: Is Alcoholism Hereditary? New York, Oxford University Press, 1976

33. Goodwin DW: Two Species of Alcoholic "Blackout." American Journal of Psychiatry 127 (June): 1665–1669, 1971

34. Goodwin DW, Powell B, Stern J: Behavioral Tolerance to Alcohol in Moderate Drinkers. Am J Psychiatr 127 (June): 1651–1653, 1971

35. Gottheil E, Evans BD, Verebey K: Research Relating to Alcohol and Opiate Dependence. In Solomon J, Keeley KA, Wright J (eds): Perspectives in Alcohol and Drug Abuse: Similarities and Differences, pp 179–201. Boston, PSG, Inc, 1982

36. Green HI, Levy MH: Drug Misuse . . . Human Abuse. New York, Marcel Dekker, 1976

37. Greenblatt DJ, Shader RI: Drug Abuse and the Emergency Room Physician. Am J Psychiatr 131 (May): 559–562, 1974

38. Grinspoon L, Hedblom P: The Speed Culture. Cambridge, Harvard University Press, 1975

39. Harrison J: Alcohol and the Impaired Physician. Alcohol Health and Research World 3 (Winter): 2–8, 1978

40. Haughey CW: Alcoholic Cardiomyopathy: Abstinence Makes the Heart Grow Stronger. Nursing 80 10 (September): 54–58, 1980

41. Hoffer R: Heroes and Hangovers: Pro Sports Faces Its Drinking Problem. Alcoholism 4 (November/December): 27–29, 1980

42. Huey LY: Psychiatric Problems of Alcoholics. Postgrad Med 64 (December): 123–128, 1978

43. Hughes R, Brewin R: The Tranquilizing of America. • New York, Harcourt, Brace, Jovanovich, 1979

44. Inglis B: The Forbidden Game. New York, Charles Scribner's Sons, 1975

45. Jaffe J, Peterson R, Hodgson R: Addictions. New York, Harper & Row, 1980

46. Jellinek EM: Disease Concept of Alcoholism. New Haven, United Printing Service, 1960

47. Jellinek EM: Phases of Alcohol Addiction. Quarterly Journal of Studies on Alcohol 13 (December): 673–684, 1952

48. Johansen B: The Tepees are Empty and the Bars are Full. Alcoholism 4 (November/December): 33–38, 1980

49. Johnson V: I'll Quit Tomorrow. New York, Harper & Row, 1973

50. Jones KL, Shainberg LW, Byer CO: Drugs and Alcohol. New York, Harper & Row, 1979

51. Khantzian EJ, McKenna GJ: Diagnosis and Management of Acute Drug Problems. In Brill L, Winick C (eds): The Yearbook of Substance Use and Abuse, Vol II, pp 144–169. New York, Human Sciences Press, 1980

52. Klatsky AL: Alcohol and Hypertension. Hospital Physician 16 (April): 40–43, 1979

53. Koppell F, Stimmler L, Perone F: The Enabler: A Motivational Tool in Treating the Alcoholic. Social Casework 61 (November): 577–583, 1980

54. Loomis T: The Pharmacology of Alcohol. In Estes NJ, Heinemann EM (eds): Alcoholism: Development, Consequences, and Interventions, 2nd ed, pp 93–101. St Louis, CV Mosby, 1982

55. Lipowski ZJ: A New Look at Organic Brain Syndromes. Am J Psychiatr 137 (June): 674–678, 1980

56. Marshall M: Alcohol and Culture: A Review. Alcohol Health and Research World 4 (Summer): 2–7, 1980

57. Martin JC: No Laughing Matter. New York, Harper & Row, 1982

58. Mendelson JH, Mello NK (eds): The Diagnosis and Treatment of Alcoholism. New York, McGraw-Hill, 1979

59. Morehouse E: Working in the Schools with Children of Alcoholic Parents. Health and Social Work 4 (November): 145–161, 1979

60. Morin R: Sexual Dysfunction in the Alcoholic Male. Alcoholism 1 (September/October): 28–31, 1980

61. Morrissey E: Alcohol Related Problems in Adolescents and Women. Postgrad Med 64 (December): 111–119, 1978

62. Murphey GE, Armstrong JW, Jr, Hermele SL, Fischer JK, Clendenin WW: Suicide and Alcoholism. Arch Gen Psychiatr 36 (January): 65–69, 1979

63. Narcotics Anonymous. C.A.R.E.W.A. Publishing Co, 1982

64. New Hampshire Sunday Union Leader: 'Alcohol Dipstick': New Aid to Gauge Levels in the Body. July 24, 1983

65. Nightengale SL: Treatment for Drug Abusers in the United States. Addictive Diseases: an International Journal 3:11–20, 1977

66. Nir Y, Cutler R: The Unmotivated Patient Syndrome: Survey of Therapeutic Interventions. Am J Psychiatr 135 (April): 442–446, 1978

67. Pattison EM, Sobell MB, Sobell LC: Emerging Concepts of Alcohol Dependence. New York, Springer-Verlag, 1977

68. Ramsey ML: Special Features and Treatment Needs of Female Drug Offenders. Journal of Offender Counseling, Services and Rehabilitation (Summer): 357–367, 1980

69. Reddy B, McEltresh OH: Detachment and Recovery from Alcoholism. Alcohol Health and Research World 2 (Spring): 28–33, 1978

70. Richards TM: Working with Children of an Alcoholic Mother. Alcohol Health and Research World 3 (Spring): 22–25, 1979

71. Robertson CC, Sellers EM: Alcohol Intoxication and the Alcohol Withdrawal Syndrome. Postgrad Med 64 (December): 133–138, 1978

72. Robins LN, Helzer JE, Hesselbrock M, Wish E: Vietnam Veterans Three Years After Vietnam: How Our Study Changed Our View of Heroin. In Brill L, Winick C (eds): The Yearbook of Substance Use and Abuse, Vol II, pp 213–230. New York, Human Sciences Press, 1980

73. Rodman MJ, Smith DW: Pharmacology and Drug Therapy in Nursing, 2nd ed. Philadelphia, JB Lippincott, 1979

74. Rosett HL, Ouellette EM, Weiner L, Owens E: Therapy of Heavy Drinking during Pregnancy. Obstet Gynecol 51 (January): 41–46, 1978

75. Royce JE: Alcohol Problems and Alcoholism: A Comprehensive Survey. New York, The Free Press, 1981

76. Santo Y: Differences in Polydrug Abuse Between Men and Women. Alcohol Health and Research World 3 (Winter): 37–39, 1978

77. Schroeder RC: The Politics of Drugs: An American Dilemma, 2nd ed. Washington, DC, Congressional Quarterly Press, 1980

78. Schuckit MA: Drug and Alcohol Abuse: A Clinical Guide to Diagnosis and Treatment. New York, Plenum Medical Book Co, 1979

79. Schuckit MA: The Disease Alcoholism. Postgrad Med 64 (December): 78–84, 1978

80. Selye H: The Stress of Life. New York, McGraw-Hill, 1956

81. Selye H: Stress Without Distress. New York, The New American Library, 1974

82. Silverstein LM et al: Consider the Alternative. Minneapolis, Comp Care Publications, 1977

83. Solomon J, Arnon D: Alcohol and Other Substance Abusers. In Suicide Theory and Clinical Aspects. Massachusetts, PSG Publishing, 1972

84. Solomon J: Perspectives in Alcohol and Drug Abuse:

Similarities and Differences. Boston, PSG Inc, 1982

85. Spotts JV, Shontz FC: Cocaine Users. New York, The Free Press, 1980

86. Strug DL: The Role of Anthropology in the Treatment of Alcoholism and Substance Abuse. Alcohol Health and Research World 4 (Summer): 8–9, 1980

87. Tarter RE, Schneider DU: Blackout Relationship with Memory Capacity and Alcoholism History. Arch Gen Psychiatr 33 (December): 1492–1496, 1976

88. The Drug Abuse Council: Facts about Drug Abuse. New York, The Free Press, 1980

89. Tuyns A: Alcohol and Cancer. Alcohol Health and Research World 2 (Summer): 20–31, 1978

90. Wesson DR, Smith DE: Barbiturates: Their Use, Misuse, and Abuse. New York, Human Services Press, 1977

91. Westermeyer J: A Primer on Chemical Dependency. Baltimore, Williams & Wilkins, 1976

92. Worden M, Rosellini G: Applying Nutritional Concepts in Alcohol and Drug Counseling. Journal of Psychedelic Drugs 11 (July–September); 173–184, 1979

93. Yearwood AC, Hess SK: How Can an Alcoholic Change in 28 Days? Am J Nurs 79 (August): 1436–1438, 1979

94. Zimberg S: Principles of Alcoholism Psychotherapy. In Wallace J, Blume S (eds): Practical Approaches to Alcoholism Psychotherapy, pp 3–18. New York, Plenum Press, 1978

Part VI
Special Topics
In Psychiatric-Mental Health
Nursing

Chapter 25
The Emotionally Disturbed Child

Modern living conditions have made it much more difficult for parents to create a setting in which both their own legitimate needs and the needs of their children can be satisfied with relative ease. That is why love is not enough and must be supplemented by deliberate efforts on the part of the parent. Fortunately most parents love their children and conscientiously strive to be good parents. But more and more of them become weary of the struggle to arrange life sensibly for their children, while modern pressures create more and more insensible experiences which are added to the life of the child.

> Bruno Bettelheim,
> Love Is Not Enough: The
> Treatment of Emotionally Disturbed,
> 1950

Barbara Schoen Johnson

Chapter Preview
Learning Objectives
Emotional Disorders in Children
    Prevalence
    Risk Factors of Disorders
    Dynamics of Childhood Disorders
Application of the Nursing Process to Emotionally Disturbed Children
    Assessment and Analysis
    Planning
    Intervention
    Evaluation
    Advocation for Emotionally Disturbed Children and Their Families
Summary

(The author acknowledges the assistance of Janet Pressler Devaney, Nurse Supervisor, Child Psychiatric Unit, Children's Medical Center, Dallas, Texas, in the writing of this chapter.)

Chapter Preview

There have always been children who are different from the majority of their peers. Frequently, these children exhibit behaviors that result in difficulties for them and those around them. As long ago as 1871, in the schools of New Haven, Connecticut, such children were labeled "contumacious aggressors" and segregated into their own special class.[4] More than a century later, we may continue to question our progress in the area of childhood disorders.

This chapter examines emotionally disturbed children, their needs, problems, and families, and then urges nurses and other mental health caregivers to evaluate their own priorities, abilities, and willingness to meet those needs (see insert, Working with Disturbed Children: Personal Reflections). Through the nursing process—assessment, analysis, planning, intervention, and evaluation—the nurse has an impact on the delivery of mental health care to disturbed children.

Learning Objectives

Upon completion of the chapter, the reader should be able to accomplish the following.

1. Discuss the prevalence and causative or risk factors of emotional disorders in children
2. Describe the behavioral manifestations and dynamics of the emotional disorders of childhood
3. Assess the family functioning and the emotional, social, educational, and cultural problems of the emotionally disturbed child
4. Analyze the assessment data and formulate client or family problems or nursing diagnoses
5. Identify the goals of treatment of disturbed children and their families
6. Describe and compare various intervention modes for disturbed children and their families
7. Discuss the child advocacy role of psychiatric-mental health nurses

Working with Disturbed Children: Personal Reflections

Every field within nursing has its own unique challenges, struggles, and rewards. Working with emotionally disturbed children is no exception. During the years of providing nursing care to these children and their families, I frequently heard this question from my family and friends, "Why do you do that kind of work... how can you do it?"

Why or how does anyone choose their work? It may be because they find the work important in itself and recognize in themselves a talent, understanding, and enthusiasm for the endeavor. Child psychiatric nurses reach an awareness of the families' needs and their own abilities to help family members function more effectively and grow as a family.

The road along which child psychiatric nurses travel in their professional development, however, is frought with difficulties. Novice nurses are often bewildered by the behavior of disturbed children. What does it mean, what could have caused it? they ask.

At times, nurses become angry at the child's parents or guardians whose "parenting" is far from what is considered adequate by professional standards. This anger also extends to the child himself; the child's behavior may be hostile, fearful, demanding, self-defeating, aggressive, withdrawn, regressed, autistic, or destructive. The nurse is often frightened by the child's outbursts or frustrated by the seeming purposelessness of his behavior. Searching for something that will "work"; that is, something that will have an effect on the child's and family's behavior and interaction, may lead the nurse to frustration.

Sometimes, the nurse may feel hopeless and resigned to the fact that the challenge is too great. Feelings of hopelessness, helplessness, and particularly, lack of collegial support contribute to professional burnout. To prevent this occurrence, nurses can form peer support groups within which they can air their feelings and frustrations openly and receive suggestions and rewards from their colleagues.

Nurses must look to their peers in the workplace, their supervisors, their enriching personal lives, and their own strengths and resources for sources of energy, determination, and enthusiasm. The children with emotional disorders and their families cannot provide the rewards to the nurse; they are the ones in need.

Emotional Disorders in Children

Prevalence

The problem of emotional disturbances in children is a monumental one. Because various researchers may employ different criteria against which to measure childhood adjustment and mental health or disorder, precise statistics regarding the prevalence of childhood disorders are difficult to determine. Other factors hampering the determination of the prevalence of childhood psychiatric disorders are difficulties with definition of the disorder, instrumentation, sampling, source of information, ages examined, and location of studies.[41]

Despite these inaccuracies, most frequently quoted estimates of emotional disorders in children assert that 10% of all children in the United States have emotional problems severe enough to disable them as adults.[32] Some would say that the prevalence of these disorders is probably no lower than 11.8%.[41]

Risk Factors of Disorders

Sex and Age

Certain risk factors are associated with the occurrence of emotional disorders of childhood. For example, their occurrence follows trends of sex and age. Boys generally display more disturbances than girls, in a 2:1 ratio, until adolescence, at which time the occurrence of girls' disorders becomes equal to, or greater than, the boys'.[7,41] Studies show that the symptoms of emotional disorders in boys are more disturbing to parents and teachers than girls' behavioral signs; boys are referred for psychiatric treatment more often than girls.[7] For both sexes, there seems to be a slight increase in the rate of emotional disturbance between late childhood (9–12 years) and early adolescence (13–16 years).[41]

Sociocultural Factors

In addition to age and sex factors, there also appears to be a strong link between the prevalence of childhood psychiatric disorder and low socioeconomic class.[7,41] Although this correlation may be thought of as resulting from the case finders' middle-class biases, these biases may actually work in reverse. In other words, a behavior that is seen as a sign of a serious emotional problem in a middle-class child may be disregarded in a child from a low socioeconomic group.[7]

Sociocultural factors in the etiology of psychiatric disorders are probably less important in children than in adults, because most children function within a familial matrix that operates as a remarkably effective buffer to social change. Early childhood seems to be particularly immune to sociocultural influences.[7] Although children may be relatively undisturbed within the family environment when they are young, they increasingly come into contact with the larger society as they grow and develop.

Genetic and Organic Causes

Genetic and organic factors may be manifested in disorders of childhood. Some individuals may, in fact, have a genetic predisposition to handle stress poorly. (The reader is referred to the etiologic factors of depression, schizophrenia, and substance abuse discussed in other chapters of this text.)

Stress

Although it is generally thought that the presence of multiple stressors impacts negatively on the individual, it is possible that stress may exert the opposite effect. Stress may innoculate some children against emotional disorders by causing them and their parents to develop effective coping responses.[17]

Parents and Families

The role of parents and families in the child's growth and development is critical. All people bring their own concerns and anxieties to the task of childrearing. The parents' feelings of fear, guilt, depression, and anxiety, as well as love, make an impression on the child.

An important task of families is maintaining two essential family boundaries—the generational boundary and the division of the two sexes.[20] The generation boundary divides the family into the parents, who nurture, lead, and direct, and the children who are nurtured, follow, and learn. Division of the sexes results in gender awareness, identification, and security.

Disturbances in family functioning are multidimensional; a "problem" of one family member exists not in a vacuum, but as a function of family dynamics. Five areas of family task deficiencies include the following.

1. Individual pathology of a parent, such as a schizophrenic mother or alcoholic father
2. Deviant parental coalitions, such as chronic parental discord
3. Faulty nurturance, such as failure to promote the child's growth toward independence, or child abuse
4. Faulty enculturation, such as parental behavior that is dramatically atypical of the surrounding culture and leads to estrangement of the children
5. Emancipation problems, which are likely to surface in disturbance after the child has reached adulthood, married, and become a parent, thereby continuing the cycle of emotional disorder from one generation to the next.[20]

Several of the family factors associated with conduct disorders of children are parental separation or divorce, marital discord, parental disorder and criminality, and a large number of siblings.[41]

Many countries, including Great Britain, France, Denmark, Holland, Canada, and the United States, are currently experiencing tremendous increases in divorce rates. Two-thirds of the women who divorce in the United States are under the age of 30, and most children are younger than 7 years old at the time of their parents' separation or divorce.[34] What is not known about these and other risk factors of child psychiatric disorders is how they operate independently or interact with each other.

Dynamics of Childhood Disorders

Some emotional disorders are specific to childhood, such as conduct disorders and infantile autism. Others may be variations on adult disturbances. In this chapter, personality disorders will not be discussed, although the reader is encouraged to refer to Chapter 20. Psychophysiological disturbances and the eating disorders of anorexia nervosa and bulimia, which often surface in late childhood or adolescence, are discussed in Chapters 25 and 30.

Adjustment Disorder

The adjustment disorders of childhood are transient disorders of any severity that occur in a child who may or may not have a preexisting emotional disorder. They are acute reactions to an overwhelming, identifiable psychosocial stressor.[3]

A common example of this type of reaction occurs when a child becomes ill, is hospitalized, and is faced with surgery. While in hospital, the child frequently exhibits regressed, fearful, and acting-out behavior. After he is discharged from the hospital and returns home, the child usually continues to show temporary increases in anxiety, hostility, fearfulness, clinging to mother, and disruptions in eating, sleep, and toilet routines. Evidences of such behavior may gradually diminish, after 3 to 6 months posthospitalization.

Attention Deficit Disorder

For the past 20 years, hyperactivity has been perhaps the most frequently diagnosed child psychiatric disorder. Formerly called *hyperkinetic reaction of childhood*, *minimal brain damage*, and *minimal brain dysfunction*, the disorder is now termed *attention deficit disorder*, with hyperactivity or without hyperactivity, according to the Diagnostic and Statistical Manual of Mental Disorders, third edition (DSM-III).[3,51]

Children who are hyperactive are more often called "difficult," "aggressive," and "disruptive" than nonhyperactive children. They also engage more frequently in risk-taking behavior than other children, resulting in mishaps, scratches, scrapes, and broken bones. Hyperactive children are more likely to be academic underachievers, although they don't score significantly lower on intelligence tests, especially individually administered intelligence tests.[51]

Children with attention deficit disorder are referred for treatment for three general types of problems.

1. Problems in learning leading to school failure
2. Difficulty relating to peers
3. Difficulty complying with adult requests and commands[51]

Significant behavior of hyperactive children is their inability to sustain attention, control impulsivity, and control activity level. In fact, the four core symptoms of attention deficit disorder are distractibility, excitability, impulsivity, and excessive activity.[51] Certainly, these behaviors are inappropriate to certain contexts, such as school.

Conduct Disorder

A repetitive and persistent pattern of behavior in which the child violates the basic rights of others or major age-appropriate social dicta is termed a *conduct disorder*.[3] The child with a conduct disorder displays antisocial behavior in the form of physical violence against another person, theft outside the home, fire-setting, assault, or callous or manipulative behavior.

Children with conduct disorders are divided into two main groups.

1. Aggressive, which includes physical violence, theft, and confrontation with the victim, as in muggings and holdups
2. Nonaggressive, in which the child's behavior is passive and nonviolent, such as truancy, running away, and lying

These two groups are further subdivided into socialized and undersocialized. Children with conduct disorders who are socialized show signs of attachment to others, but may be cruel to those to whom they are not attached and feel no guilt about their suffering. Children who are undersocialized fail to establish affectional, empathetic ties with others. Therefore, the child does not feel remorse over his behavior, does not extend himself for another unless there is an immediate reward for him, and readily blames others.

One of the ways that a child may act out his feelings of rejection, isolation, and hostility is through cruelty to animals. Cruelty to animals usually occurs concomitant with certain other symptoms, such as aggressiveness to younger siblings and other small children, firesetting, interest in sex, enuresis, learning problems, hoarding, bulimia, and imperviousness to pain.[58] This behavior is seen most often in young and preadolescent boys (8–10 years). Although cruelty to animals and the associated symptoms may indicate a personality disturbance or mental retardation, they occur most commonly in children from chaotic homes with aggressive, violent parental models.[58]

Firesetting is a dangerous symptom that must be controlled rapidly. Children who set fires also display many other forms of acting-out, including running away, stealing, lying, truancy, and sexual acting-out. One study of 29 children, two girls and 27 boys, aged 5 to 14 years, in which a family crisis-oriented model of therapy was used, demonstrated interruption of the firesetting behavior in all but two children after the initial session.[10] The primary goal of this intervention technique with children who set fires is to bring the firesetting behavior under control by means of reinforcing the child's desire to control this behavior, developing a therapeutic alliance, and using a graphing technique, which helps the child visualize, concretize, and correlate his feelings and behavior.[10]

Anxiety Disorder

Anxiety may be defined as a fear that is not justified by reality or an extreme reaction to a real threat. The younger the child, the more difficult it is for him to separate inner and outer reality.

Children with anxiety disorders experience repressed conflict between intense, but unacceptable, feelings and the defenses against them. The resultant behavior pattern, an anxiety (or neurotic) disorder, is the most successful compromise the child is able to reach. The child may react as if imagined or past events are a real and continuing part of the present.[32]

Two of the most common anxiety disorders in children are phobias and sleep disturbances. A *phobia* is a morbid, irrational, and persistent fear. Childhood phobias are so common that mild, passing fears are considered part of normal development.[32] Frequently, the child may fear school, transportation, such as travel by car or plane, and animals. He may have exaggerated fears of burglars or kidnappers or concerns about dying. Many children fear dogs and become uncomfortable around them. The child with a phobia, however, is preoccupied with the prospects of meeting a dog, in a constant anticipatory anxiety state, and may not want to go to school or even out of the house to insure that he doesn't see a dog. Obviously, a phobia can be quite crippling.

Phobias may result from

1. a real and frightening incident that conditioned the child to the fear;
2. a vicarious frightening experience; or
3. repression of the child's forbidden, secret wish or action leading to guilt and the substitution of another object or person to fear.[32]

School phobia is a symptom that cannot legally be ignored for long. The child may fear some aspect of the school situation, such as the teacher, classroom, trips to and from school, or lunch routine. Often, the child also has some somatic symptom that disappears when he is told that he can stay home from school. School phobia may occur at any age, but is seen more commonly in the lower elementary grades.[32] It may be described as a form of separation anxiety between the child and his parents or as a form of trouble accepting the child's increasing independence.

Sleep disturbances are also tied to separation anxiety, considering that the very young child views sleep as separation. A transitory, common experience of sleep disturbance may be seen, for example, in 2-year olds to 3-year olds who fear losing control over their bodies while asleep which results in wetting the bed. The preschool child's oedipal struggle may become translated into frightening monsters at night. The child may be afraid of sleep itself, for fear that a horrible event, even death, may befall him during his sleep. Nightmares peak during the ages from 4 to 6, and may be the cause of the child's inability to remain asleep. Children awaken from nightmares feeling helpless and afraid and in need of comforting. At the extreme, night terrors leave children feeling panicked and experiencing difficulty reorienting to reality, being comforted, and regaining self-control.[32]

Affective Disorder

Childhood depression often presents as headaches, chest pains, abdominal pain, and other somatic, or bodily, complaints. Depression is often seen in children and adolescents with chronic illnesses, gastrointestinal disorders, and chronic orthopedic problems.[30]

Until recently, it was thought that children rarely, if ever, became depressed. Now, however, we know that children do have depressions. The child's behavior, which may mask his depression, may take the form of acting-out behavior or somatic complaints. The depressed child may express depressive themes in his play, fantasy, dreams, and verbalizations.[30] The various symptoms of depression are specific to the child's age or developmental level. For example, prepubertal children may evidence separation anxiety as a sign of depression; depressed adolescent males may exhibit negativistic and antisocial behavior, sulkiness, social withdrawal, and school difficulties.[12]

Specific risk factors for suicidal behavior in children are

1. the child's depression;
2. the child's concepts about, and preoccupations with, death; and,
3. suicidal tendencies of the child's parents.[43]

The family variables related to suicidal risk in childhood include parental separation, divorce, abuse, communication patterns, and crowding. Children fantasize suicide by stabbing themselves, jumping from heights, hanging themselves, and drowning themselves in a sink.[43]

Self-injury may also be seen in children who are mentally retarded. This behavior may be an attempt to reduce guilt, establish "bodily reality," or direct aggression inward, or it may be a form of autoerotic activity.[62]

Infantile Autism

Autism is a rare pervasive developmental disorder that occurs three to four times more commonly in boys than in girls.[3, 32] It was first described by Leo Kanner in 1943. The distinguishing characteristics of infantile autism are a lack of responsiveness to others and withdrawal from social contact, gross impairment in communication, and bizarre responses to the environment, such as peculiar interest in, or attachment to, animate or inaminate objects and insistence on routines. The onset of these behaviors is evident before 30 months of age.

If the autistic child has speech, it is likely to be echolalic, and he will probably employ his own private language. He may use the third-person pronoun to refer to himself, indicating poor differentiation of self from others, and he may reverse other pronouns.[3,64] The child may also engage in rocking, twirling, or other self-stimulatory behavior.

As infants, autistic children fail to respond to the sight or sounds of others. They give no evidence of a "social smile," or of pleasure in being with the mother or mothering figure. They do not physically reach out; they have no reaction to strangers. Because they are not demanding and don't fuss when separated from parents, these children are sometimes mistakenly called "very good babies." Social games, like peek-a-boo, do not interest autistic children.

The autistic child fails to use speech for the purpose of communication. He may not talk at all, or he may talk in a mechanical, parrotlike manner. He may repeat stereotyped or nonsensical phrases, or he may echo what is said to him. If a certain word results in the child getting what he wants, he may use it over and over—not according to its meaning. The child is unable to generalize word usage. He may, in fact, be so unresponsive that deafness is suspected.[32] His response to sounds is likely to be inconsistent.

The autistic child is usually fascinated with objects, especially ones that spin, twirl, or reflect light and shadow. An important differentiation here is that the normal child values a toy largely because it came from a parent; an autistic child finds joy in the toy's ability to be spun, manipulated, rolled, rocked, or put together.[32]

Autism is a chronic disorder. It seems to be due to biologic factors because its occurrence is associated with maternal rubella, phenylketonuria, encephalitis, and meningitis. About 40% of autistic children have an IQ below 50; about 30% have an IQ of 70 or higher.[3] Even when the child is not retarded, he may be perceived as such because autism hides whatever cognitive ability or potential the child has.[32]

Childhood Onset Pervasive Developmental Disorder

Formerly called *symbiosis psychosis, childhood schizophrenia,* and *atypical children,* childhood onset pervasive developmental disorder develops after 30 months of age and before 12 years. It is a rare disorder, marked by a profound disturbance in interpersonal relations, such as lack of peer relationships, asocial behavior, inappropriate affect, and clinging.

This disorder is also characterized by behaviors such as sudden excessive anxiety, inappropriate or constricted affect, resistance to change, bizarre movements such as posturing or walking on tiptoe, speech abnormalities such as monotony of voice tone, hyposensitivity or hypersensitivity to sensory stimuli, and self-mutilation, such as head banging or biting self.

The child who develops a childhood onset pervasive developmental disorder may appear normal, developmentally, until the age of 2 to 3 years, at which time behavioral pecularities start to become evident. The child's odd postures or mannerisms are especially noticeable when one tries to play or talk with him.[32]

Some severely disturbed children cannot tolerate separation from the mother and become overwhelmed with panic when not with her; this behavior may include agitated, extreme temper tantrums. Normal children experience fears and fantasize but are able to distinguish between real and "pretend" experience. The severely disturbed child loses the distinction, particularly when he is overcome by fear or anxiety.[64]

The severely disturbed child may also show disparity among verbal, motor, social, and adaptive skills appropriate for age. This pervasive developmental disorder occurs more commonly in children with low IQs. It is a chronic and incapacitating disorder.

Psychosis in Children

Childhood psychosis is characterized by the following.

1. Severely disturbed interpersonal relationships, including lack of interest in others, unawareness of others' presence, or inability to separate from others
2. Difficulties communicating with others, including lack of meaningful speech, lack of play, or preoccupation with sensory stimuli or inanimate objects
3. Lack or impairment of contact with reality, such as insufficient distinctions of self from nonself
4. Striving for constancy
5. Uneven development of intellectual, motor, emotional, and social skills[32,54]

The psychotic child lives in a "world of his own," and that private world is unavailable to anyone but himself. He may be preoccupied with sensory stimuli (visual, auditory, or kinesthetic) that have little thought content. For example, a toy car is fun for the psychotic child not because he can pretend he is driving it, but because its wheels spin. "Psychotic children do not make believe," says one author, "they exploit their toys for their physical properties."

Psychosis in children may be thought of as a massive failure of the ego to synthesize and organize the personality.[54] These children are unable to differentiate between inner and outer reality, are often aggressive and unable to tolerate frustration, use language associatively, display stereotypic, compulsive behaviors, and perceive the world as persecuting them.[54]

Application of the Nursing Process to Emotionally Disturbed Children

When children are referred for psychological treatment, the referral may have been initiated by the child's school, parents, health care providers, or the court. A family crisis, acute or chronic physical illness, or other stressors may precipitate the seeking of therapeutic intervention for a troubled child. This section of the chapter examines the application of the steps of the nursing process to the care of emotionally disturbed child clients and their families.

Assessment and Analysis

Family Functioning

In child psychiatric-mental health nursing, the treatment team assesses the disturbed child and his family and then, together, analyzes the information that has been gathered.

Assessment of the family, particularly members of extended family who may help define the family's beliefs and values about child-rearing, is best approached before the assessment of the child. This initial focus on the family, rather than on the individual child, gives a clear message to all involved that no one in the family will be exempt from looking at the "problem" and participating in problem-solving (see the case study, Assessing Eddie H. and His Family).

The nurse assessor or other mental health caregiver asks openended questions such as, "How are things for the family?" This form of questioning allows the family to feel free to respond with whatever information they wish to share. Usually, the parents respond first to opening questions and generally attempt to identify the problem.

Next, the nurse focuses on the child, who is typically the "identified patient" in the family. The question to the child, "How are things going?" often brings a response of "I don't know," "Fine," or "My parents (or teachers) are mad at me."

Case Study

Assessing Eddie H. and His Family

Eddie H., a 7-year-old white male, was brought to the Child and Family Mental Health Clinic by his mother, 30-year-old Hazel W. "Eddie," said his mother, "is rebellious and destructive to school supplies and toys, tells lies to get his younger brother Ralph into trouble, throws temper tantrums, doesn't listen to his teacher, and can't understand the meaning of the word 'no'."

Eddie is the oldest of Hazel's three children, which include 5-year-old Ralph and 4-year-old Lucille. Hazel was married briefly to Eddie's father. Each of the children have different fathers; her current husband, Mr. W., is "out of the picture," she says, and she plans to divorce him as soon as she can afford to do so. Presently living in the home are Hazel, her sons Eddie and Ralph, and sometimes Frank, Hazel's 18-year-old boyfriend. Her daughter Lucille is in foster care.

Additional information was supplied by the family's case worker from the Department of Human Resources. Eddie's behavior is disruptive in school, he spends his time drawing pictures instead of doing his school work, and he seems to block out what is going on in the classroom.

When questioned about an event that precipitated her bringing Eddie to the clinic, Hazel reported that a few days ago he took some powerful pain pills from the medicine cabinet and tried to give them to his younger brother Ralph (who refused them). During the interview Hazel also frequently referred to a car accident 2 years ago, which, she believes, brought on much of the family's troubles. The accident occurred when Hazel was driving a friend's car. She lost control of the vehicle and hit a bridge overpass. The entire family was taken to the emergency department of a local hospital. Eddie had a scalp laceration, Ralph a minor injury, Hazel a broken leg and multiple lacerations, but Lucille suffered internal injuries including a ruptured spleen and "brain damage" resulting from a skull fracture. Hazel was charged with driving while intoxicated (DWI) and Lucille was placed in foster care.

Eddie was a full-term infant, the product of an unplanned pregnancy during which Hazel felt "OK physically," but unhappy, anxious, and apprehensive that the baby might "be abnormal because of Rh." She was upset because the father of the child didn't want the child and often said that the child was not his. Hazel reported that she was in labor for 19 hours but "wouldn't dilate," received Demerol every 2 to 3 hours, and that Eddie was "taken with forceps." He was very sleepy when he was born as a result of the Demerol she received and he experienced difficulty starting to breathe on his own. Hazel said that she "could not afford the gamma globulin shot" after Eddie was born, but that she has had no complications with her later children.

Hazel stated that she believes that Eddie was "spoiled" as a baby and that, as his siblings arrived, he began to have more problems. He sleeps poorly and frequently wakes up screaming with nightmares. He does not talk with his mother and rarely makes eye contact with her.

Eddie's interests include riding his bike, working on art projects, fishing, and being out-of-doors. His relationships with peers are described as poor—he is "beaten up" by his peers from time to time and actively discourages the friendship of his classmates.

According to his mother, Eddie responds to the discipline of standing him in the corner or sending him to his room. Spanking or "getting after him with a switch" sometimes controls him, says Hazel, but for the past few years he "won't cry," which both puzzles and upsets his mother.

Observation in the playroom revealed that Eddie played appropriately, not destructively, with the toys. He seemed anxious and somewhat depressed, but able to interact well. He said that he "never gets mad at anybody," but sometimes worries when his mom gets upset.

When asked to draw a picture of his family doing something (a Kinetic Family Drawing), Eddie quickly responded, "I don't have a daddy, but I'll draw one anyway." He said he drew "kids trick-or-treating at their house and having lots of fun." In fact, the only two members in the drawing were his sister Lucille "dressed up like a princess" and his brother Ralph "as a vampire."

Hazel related that 3 years ago, during a period of extreme stress, she entered a state psychiatric hospital, remained there for 57 days, and then attended outpatient therapy at a neighborhood community mental health clinic. She refused, however, to take the medications prescribed for her, because she thinks that taking medication is a sign of weakness. Presently, she cannot get to the clinic because of lack of transportation.

This family appears to live from crisis to crisis, but the mother, Hazel W., is a resourceful woman who knows how and where to find help when she needs it. She is a very anxious woman who exhibits pressured speech, a great deal of ambivalence, and dependence in her interpersonal relationships. Her current crisis was triggered by a number of factors: losing her job at a convenience store, Eddie's behavior in school and his anger at her for working away from the home, increasing debts, and her noncompliance with her prescribed medications. Eddie is anxious, mildly depressed, not overtly aggressive or destructive, but reacts to the family's stressors with his own behavioral responses of acting-out in school and against his younger brother.

The goals of treatment for Eddie, his mother Hazel, and the other family members include

1. to explore the family's previous coping skills, strengths, and supports during crises;
2. to help the family reach an understanding of this crisis and its effects on the family functioning;
3. to examine the family's alternate coping methods, which could result in a healthier resolution of their current crisis;
4. to provide crisis intervention twice weekly for Hazel and her family for the next few weeks, or until the crisis is resolved;
5. to construct a long-term plan of treatment for Hazel, her son Eddie, and other family members that would teach parenting skills for Hazel and communication and coping skills for all family members.

Sources of Information.   Although parents and teachers are probably better informants for the assessor on the child's observable behavior, such as hyperactivity, academic problems, antisocial behavior, or difficulties with peers, the child is the best source of information about symptoms that reflect subjective experiences.[16] For example, the child should be assessed directly regarding suicidal ideation, disordered moods, feelings of guilt or low self-esteem, and hallucinations.[12]

Throughout the assessment process, the nurse seeks information from the child, parents, siblings, extended family, teachers, and health care professionals. The nurse also notes the congruencies or incongruencies among the perceptions of each of these sources of information.

Communication Patterns.   During the initial assessment interview, the nurse observes the behavior of parents and children and asks, What is their body language communicating? How does the family sit? How do they arrange

themselves in the room? Who speaks for whom? Who is the primary spokesperson for the family? In well-integrated, healthy family systems, each family member is free to speak—there is room for everyone's opinions and ideas. Other ways of determining the openness of the family system are exploring their extrafamilial interactions and influences, their tolerance of differences of opinion among family members, the clarity of the boundaries, and their ability to deal with current issues. (The reader is encouraged to refer to Chapter 17.)

Identifying the Problem.   As the child and his family define the "problem," the nurse assesses its severity, duration, and impact on family functioning, and asks, For whom is the problem most distressing? For example, conduct disorders are likely to be very upsetting to parents, siblings, teachers, and other adults, whereas school phobia may be most disturbing for the child.

The nurse also asks, How functional or dysfunctional

is the problem? A child may be very manipulative with adults and, although the problem is distressing and they don't feel comfortable with him, his growth and development continues satisfactorily. Some mental health problems are dysfunctional for the child and family. When a child has anorexia nervosa, it is not uncommon for everyone in the family to try to placate the anorexic child. If a child exhibits aggressive behavior as is seen in a conduct disorder, the mother may interact with the child as the strict disciplinarian, while the father is trying to create some positive interaction with him; this conflict may certainly lead to marital problems.

Family Relationships. The nurse assesses the family members' genuineness of concern for each other. The family members are asked to describe their relationships and roles, including the child's role in the family. In addition, the family is often requested to perform a certain task, such as planning a family vacation. This experiential task demonstrates the actual relationships, roles, degree of autonomy or enmeshment, and empathy of family members.

Is the child functioning as a family scapegoat? In other words, is he being blamed and held responsible for everything that goes wrong in the family?

Perceptions of the Child. The parents' level of knowledge about the normal processes of child development and behavior influence how realistic their role expectations for him will be. For example, is the 6-year-old male child expected to be "the little man" of the family?

The nurse asks the parents, On what level do you think your child should be functioning now? They are asked to define what is different about this child. They are asked to assess the child's disposition or temperament and his talents and strengths. The latter will be incorporated later into a plan to maximize the strengths.

Sociocultural Influences. Socioeconomic and cultural information from the family give another perspective to the nurse assessor about the family's childrearing and the aftercare planning for the child. This information includes the parents' and other family members' education, occupations, incomes, and the family's cultural beliefs and practices.

Sharing with Parents. During the assessment process, the nurse asks the family whose idea it was to seek help for the child and what intervention measures they have already tried. The nurse acknowledges the seriousness of the problem and compliments the family on their concern and love for the child, which is evident in their seeking treatment for him and the family.

The question, What do you wish your child were like now? yields information about the parents' values, expectations, culture, and attitudes and biases about parenting.

The parents are asked to describe what they hope the treatment team (therapist, caseworker, nurse, and so on) can do for them and their child. Their hopes for their child's future reveal what the parents believe about his career, standards of behavior, and relationships.

The parents need time to ask their own questions. They may fear they "did something wrong," which resulted in the child's becoming hostile, aggressive, or withdrawn. The nurse might briefly explore with them the possibility of a multiplicity of factors in the development of an emotional disorder of childhood.

The Child

History-Taking. Taking a history of factors pertinent to the child's emotional problem includes the following.

1. A history of psychiatric disorders, alcoholism and drug dependence, or organic illnesses in members of the nuclear and extended families
2. A thorough assessment of the growth and development of the child, including prenatal and perinatal factors
3. The time of onset of the problem and any significant events that occurred at or around the time the problem became manifest
4. The child's health and social history

The parents, teachers, and child are asked to describe his strengths and weaknesses and how he is functioning at home, at school, and in the neighborhood. The child's social skills, interests and hobbies, and unusual or troublesome habits are noted.

Physical and Emotional Assessment. A thorough physical examination should be conducted. The child's age, size, nutritional status, speech and hearing, and the presence of "soft" neurological signs are assessed.

A structured mental status examination of the child includes the following.

1. Appearance—dress, gestures, posture, tics
2. Mood or affect—predominant feelings, mood fluctuations, ease or constriction in displaying feelings, appropriateness
3. Manner of relating to the examiner—child's perceptions of the reasons for the interview, rapport with or distance from the examiner, use of play, activity, verbalization, or relationships
4. Modes of thinking and intellectual skills—development of child's thinking, conceptualizations of causality, body image, memory, problem-solving
5. Capacity for play and fantasy—amount and kind of involvement in play, use of play materials, themes of play, spontaneity of play, use of examiner in the play

6. Sensorimotor development—fine and gross motor activities, symmetry of movement, eye–hand coordination, and right–left discrimination[16]

Because children's ability to express themselves verbally is limited, the assessment of children is conducted primarily through the medium of play. A variety of play materials, including dolls, hand puppets, art materials (paint, clay, paper), movement toys (cars, trucks, planes), age-appropriate games, punching bag, toy telephone, rubber-tipped darts, and doll house and furniture are provided as the means through which the child tells his story.[16]

Diagnosis. The word *diagnosis* is derived from the Greek and means "a thorough understanding." A diagnosis should provide the psychiatric-mental health care provider with an understanding of the cause and associated features of the disorder, the age of onset, cause, incidence according to sex, diagnostic criteria, and degree of impairment. It should also lead to treatment implications.

Diagnosis of the disorders of childhood is a particularly difficult problem, because of the following reasons.

1. A child is often inconsistent and unpredictable in his behavior.
2. The child's relationship and degree of comfort with the examiner will definitely affect the results.
3. The child is an immature organism and is constantly developing.
4. The child is affected and being shaped by his parents.

The assessment session sets the tone for the rest of the intervention with child and family. The parents are likely to approach the mental health professionals with some degree of dread; they fear what they will hear about their mistakes in parenting. They have fears that ther child is "crazy" or hopeless. Dealing with and calming these fears, supporting the parents' desire to be "good parents," and teaching them new ways to interact with their child and manage his behavior are some of the nurse's foci in child psychiatric-mental health care.

Planning

Planning with parents and child is a collaborative effort. It begins with the assessment and analysis of the information about the child's developmental level and his and the family's needs and problems; it also involves sharing this information with the family. Planning also takes into account the nature of the emotional disorder and the resources available to the child and family.

Determining Goals

Some of the goals of child and family mental health treatment are as follows.

1. Reducing the symptoms of the child and family
2. Promoting the child's normal development

3. Fostering the child's autonomy and self-reliance
4. Reinforcing the child's behavioral gains
5. Making changes in the child's home or school environment[52]

Priority-Setting

Planning also considers the priorities of psychiatric-mental health care. A 13-year-old, for example, admitted to an inpatient treatment facility following a suicide attempt requires a treatment plan that first attends to the physical safety of the child. Caring for the child with a decreased level of consciousness, assessing blood levels of the drug taken, and instituting antidotal therapy take precedence over psychosocial assessments of the child and family.

Intervention

The form of psychiatric-mental health treatment of children is selected according to the needs and problems of the child and family. In the past, various forms of physiotherapy were employed to treat the emotionally disturbed child. As recently as the 1950s, shock treatments for psychotic children were attained through electricity, pentylenetetrazol (Metrazol), or insulin. Other physiological measures, such as sleep therapy and psychosurgery, have not been an acceptable part of treatment of children.[29]

Prevention

The primary focus of intervention for emotional disorders of childhood is prevention. *Prevention* may be defined as any activity undertaken before individuals are identified as "clients." Estimates suggest that only 10% of the children needing mental health services receive preventive actions.[46] Until recently, it was thought that parenting required no special knowledge or skills; now, adolescents are often able to study parenting in school.

It has been shown that, to be effective, primary prevention programs must take into account the total sociocultural environment in which the child lives.[46] Therefore, brief exposures to interventions will not produce long-term effects in children who continue to live in a disturbed or chaotic environment.

The goals of preventive measures are to

1. reduce the incidence of new cases of the disorder;
2. reduce the incidence of disabilities in the population;
3. raise the immunity of individuals or groups to stress;
4. decrease stress in the environment;
5. improve the quality of life in a targeted population; and,
6. raise the general health of children.[46]

Children and families at risk for emotional disturbance are the targeted populations of preventive efforts. The stress points in the life cycle that may require intervention to prevent disturbance are pregnancy, birth (particularly prematurity), crisis situations such as the maturational crises of adolescence, marriage, retirement, and dying, and the situational crises of serious illness, divorce, and rape.

Individual Therapy

Relationship Therapy. Therapy with emotionally disturbed children may focus on the individual needs and problems of the client. A therapist whose intervention effectiveness depends on the therapist–client relationship must possess a respect for the unique nature of the child.[39]

Approaching the child client may be difficult for nurses and other mental health care professionals due to what Anna Freud called "the fluidity of the child's personality."[22] The child is growing and developing—his needs are not constant.

The role of the therapist may be that of a participant–observer. The therapist hopes to become an important adult in the child's world, someone with whom the child can identify as he moves along in the growth process.[40]

Although Sullivan never treated children, his interpersonal theory has had far-reaching effects on child theory and therapy.[28] His view of maturation processes centers on communication, skills of communication, and the factors that contribute to anxiety, thereby interfering with development.

Brief Psychotherapy. Elective, brief psychotherapy with children is a form of individual psychotherapy based on ego psychology; it is not a fragment of long-term therapy nor an attempt to condense long-term therapy into a short period of time.[61]

This form of therapy is useful in the treatment of relatively healthy children; for example, those suffering from reactive disorders. The therapist or, more significantly, the child delineates a central issue that can be dealt with in the available time period.

The goals of brief therapy focus on the central issue or problem, which is openly discussed with the child and his family, and the termination date is set. The child's relationship with the therapist may become a "model for future relationships—trusting, positive, but limited relationships."[61]

Play Therapy. Nondirective play therapy offers the child an opportunity to experience growth under the most favorable conditions. Because play is the child's natural medium for self-expression, he uses the therapy time to play out his accumulated feelings of fear, tension, confusion, frustration, and aggression.

When the child plays out his feelings, he allows them to surface, faces them, and learns to control, accept, or abandon them. Through this process, the child gradually realizes that he is an individual in his own right and is capable of thinking and making decisions for himself.

Family Therapy

Family therapy is based on the premise that the behavior of an individual within the family cannot be understood or changed without understanding and effecting change within the entire family system.[27] Because behavior does not occur in isolation, intervention is not directed at only one family member.

The family therapist observes the family system in action, noting patterns of interaction among family members, and questions, "What interactional patterns in this family support the child's symptoms?"[27] The therapist then intervenes to change the patterns to ones that support new behavior and personal competence and growth.[27, 42]

The successful treatment of children necessitates the modification of the reinforcement patterns that are part of the child's environment. Therapeutic changes are unlikely to generalize without interventions that extend to the child's home environment. It is important to train parents to become therapeutic agents of change.[44] This training may occur in parent groups that focus on home-related problems and problem-solving.

Behavior Therapy

Behavior therapy is based on the premise that emotional disorders represent learned behavior. Therefore, principles of learning are applied to the modification of these disorders.

Behavioral approaches to therapy with emotionally disturbed children include the use of special techniques such as token economies, "time out" (from positive reinforcement), and rewards for certain behaviors.[2, 14, 50] This mode of treatment also employs less rigorously structured behavioral techniques. Teaching parents and teachers how to use these techniques necessitates that they be observant of child behavior, select the appropriate technique for the behavior, and apply it consistently.[63]

One example of the use of behavior therapy is teaching the autistic child language by training him in verbal imitation, through differential reinforcement, resulting in the establishment of verbal responses in the child. After this has been accomplished, the child is taught the meaning of the verbal response.[35]

Educational Approaches

An emotionally disturbed child's sense of failure is heightened by his staying out of school, because attendance and accomplishment at school make up a significant aspect of the child's developmental strivings for completion. It is estimated that 42% of identified behaviorally disordered children are served in regular classrooms and 44% in special classes. Slightly more than 10% are in separate public schools and the remainder in residential or hospital settings.[21] The dilemma of the school becomes how to control or contain an unstable child and how to teach him what he needs to know.[4]

Goals of special education for the emotionally disturbed child include the following.

1. To decrease the child's deviant behavior
2. To accelerate the child's rate of learning to enable him to "catch up"
3. To reintegrate the child into regular classes as soon as possible[65]

Some of the techniques of working with children with emotional disorders in the classroom are to provide a high degree of structure (which lowers the child's anxiety, gives him the security of defined limits, and serves as a vehicle for expectations for his behavior) and to maximize the development of group cohesiveness and use of peer pressure.[65]

Almost all disturbed children have experienced very little success in school. In the face of repeated failure, it is extremely difficult for the child to think positively about academic learning. The teacher's task is to provide a climate that helps the child become motivated; the teacher accomplishes this task through awareness of the child's individual needs, teaching skills, and use of materials of great interest to the child, and by not defining the child as a failure.[65] It is critical that there exist effective coordination between educational systems and the other systems of health care delivery.[21]

Milieu Therapy

Milieu therapy in a psychiatric inpatient unit or residential treatment facility focuses on the living environment of the child and the relationships between the child and the staff. The living environment of the child and his relationships with other children and the staff are the essential therapeutic features of a milieu.[5] Effective milieu therapy involves an environment organized to provide the child with corrective and restitutive experiences designed to restore his sense of trust in himself and others.[1] These experiences include opportunities for learning, group socialization, reality testing, sublimation, and positive identification with adults. Through the day-to-day living experiences of waking up, attending school, eating meals, participating in play and other activities, watching TV, preparing bedtime snacks, and so forth, the child learns new and more effective ways to relate with others, to deal with his feelings, and to manage his daily activities.

The staff who work in a therapeutic milieu become, in actuality, family surrogates for the child—examples of supportive, respectful, cohesive adults who engage in open, healthy adult-to-adult and adult-to-child communication. The milieu staff, composed of child psychiatric-mental health professionals and paraprofessionals, constantly role-model for the children.

The milieu environment provides safety, security, structure, clear and reasonable limits, behavioral consequences, age-appropriate activities and expectations, pleasant surroundings, and the presence of mature, caring, knowledgeable, ethical staff members who are available to the child 24 hours per day. If seclusion or restraint are an aspect of the milieu, they should be used in a consistent manner and according to well-thought-out rationale.[24] Music, dance, art, and other expressive activities may be incorporated into the milieu.

Psychopharmacology

Psychopharmacology is one facet of a comprehensive therapeutic program. It must be remembered that giving a child medication is not the sole solution to his emotional problems but, combined with family or parental counseling, individual therapy, and special educational plans, medication may provide the child with much greater opportunity to improve his overall functioning. Unfortunately, it is difficult to identify the effects of certain chemotherapeutic agents on the behavior of the child, and for this reason extra precaution in the administration of these agents is required. One survey of clinicians, for example, showed that drugs were being prescribed very conservatively for emotionally disturbed children, and that the drugs that were chosen and administered to children were given in neither large enough doses, nor for as long a duration of time as is considered appropriate for maximal therapeutic effect.[29]

The use of psychopharmacology with children is different from its use with adults. The emotionally disturbed child may be resentful of medication and think that the drugs and their side effects may be a punishment for his bad behavior or a way to force him to comply with adult authority.[33]

The six categories of psychoactive agents, used most commonly and successfully in the treatment of disturbed children are as follows.

1. Hypnotics and Sedatives
   The barbiturates—most widely used since the early 1900s
   Examples—phenobarbital (Luminal), amobarbital (Amytal), pentobarbital (Nembutal), and thiopental (Pentothal)
   Cellular depressants, but can produce paradoxic excitation in children and the aged
   Used to treat anxiety and produce sleep, but not safe for long-term use
2. The Antipsychotic Agents
   The phenothiazines—antihistamines and effective tranquilizers, their use for antipsychotic properties was begun in the early 1950s;

Examples—chlorpromazine (Thorazine), thioridazine (Mellaril), prochlorperazine (Compazine), and trifluoperazine (Stelazine)

To sedate the acutely agitated child; decrease motor activity of hyperactive or hyperaggressive child; decrease impulsiveness, excitability, anxiety, and hyperdistractibility; and create a general calming effect

The most important pharmacotherapeutic agents for psychotic and severely disturbed children, but prolonged use can lead to serious complications; therefore, they must be monitored carefully

3. The Anti-anxiety Agents

Prescribed for anxiety, phobic states, insomnia, irritability, and hyperactivity in children, the diphenylmethane compounds

Examples—diphenhydramine (Benadryl), hydroxyzine (Vistaril)

Useful in treating children with behavior disorders and high anxiety levels

The benzodiazepine compounds

Examples—chlordiazepoxide (Librium), diazepam (Valium)

Sedative action, useful in mild to moderate anxiety states or hyperactivity, but inconclusive data available about their effectiveness, and

Meprobamate (Miltown, Equanil)—used in anxiety states and behavior disorders of children, also inconclusive data available about effectiveness

4. The Psychostimulants—used in the management of hyperactive behavior in conjunction with parental counseling—in adolescents and adults, as an antidepressant; in children, to treat hyperactivity, hyperaggressivity, hyperdistractibility

Example—methylphenidate (Ritalin)

Acts by increasing alertness, concentration, motor activity, decreasing fatigue and sleepiness, suppressing appetite; also used to treat hyperactivity in children

Paradoxical effect on the hyperactive child resulting in calming via unknown mechanism (perhaps by raising the child's low threshhold to stimuli, helping him focus attention and increase concentratin power)

5. The Antidepressants

Examples—imipramine (Tofranil), amitriptyline (Elavil), nortriptylene (Aventyl)

Used to treat depression in children by elevating mood and improving sleep and appetite patterns and to treat enuresis in children

6. The Anticonvulsants

Example—diphenylhydantoin (Dilantin)

Used in childhood behavior disorders with or without associated convulsions, and to treat hyperactive children with organic impairment.[29, 47]

Evaluation

Evaluating psychiatric-mental health care of emotionally disturbed children and their families includes examining the behaviors of children and families following the implementation of therapeutic measures and determining, together with the client and family, whether treatment goals have been reached. "Treatment" in child psychiatry is not synonymous with individual psychotherapy.[14] There are a variety of therapeutic modalities available to children and families, and often, a combination of approaches provides the optimal effect for the client. Periodic reassessment of treatment techniques and their effectiveness is needed, and when indicated, the nurse and other members of the mental health team should be able to shift their approach to maximize the benefits for the child and family.[14]

Advocation for Emotionally Disturbed Children and Their Families

The child is not a "miniature adult, but a developing person" within a family system.[37] His needs are not those of an adult, but those of an individual within an emotional, and often confusing, world.

Children have legal rights, as well as physical and emotional needs. Under British law, children did not have recognized rights separate from their parents. Within the last 10 to 15 years, the courts have significantly expanded the rights of children and have affirmed that children have the same constitutional rights as adults.[11] The rights of the physically and mentally disabled are especially important in relation to children. These include the right to

1. equal educational opportunity provided by the public schools;
2. freedom from involuntary sterilization;
3. equal access to quality medical care;
4. own legal counsel in any proceeding that could lead to the child's institutionalization;
5. care and treatment in the least restrictive setting.[11]

Advocacy for children's rights may be formal, such as when a nurse appears in a court case on a child's behalf. Often, however, the advocacy is informal, in the form of an affirmative role of nurses to promote the respect of children's rights. Strategies that inform parents, professionals, and institutions of children's rights, attempts to overcome budget restrictions, recognition of individuals' rights, and cooperation with other advocates for children and families (case workers, attorneys, and so forth) are examples of informal advocacy for children. Child psychiatric-mental health nurses are in unique positions to advocate for the welfare of children and families; whether a nurse assumes this responsibility is an individual ethical choice.

Summary

This chapter has focused on the prevalence, causative factors, dynamics, behavioral manifestations, and treatment of children with emotional disorders and their families. Some of the emphases of the chapter are as follows.

1. The primary intervention in childhood emotional disorders is that of prevention.

2. Emotional disorders in children comprise a serious mental health problem in the United States with estimates suggesting that about one in ten children are in need of psychiatric-mental health services.

3. Many theories of childhood emotional disturbances postulate an interactive effect of genetic, biologic, physical, intrapsychic, familial, sociocultural, and environmental factors.

4. Assessment of emotional disorders of childhood requires an examination of both family functioning and the individual child.

5. Treatment planning is a collaborative activity involving the child, his family, and the mental health team.

6. Nursing intervention with the emotionally disturbed child requires maturity, thoughtfulness, and an ethical orientation to psychiatric-mental health care.

Nursing Care Plan

The Child with a Psychotic Episode

Client Problem	Goal	Intervention
Poor reality testing, lack of awareness of surroundings and interactions	To promote safety To reinforce reality	Assess the child's judgment. Provide supervision to insure safety; 1:1 supervision may be required.
Confused thought processes, misperceptions	To clarify reality	Use brief, simple comments to explain events, including cause and effect, to child. Explain and restate as necessary the daily schedule to be followed, expectations of his behavior, and what to expect of caregivers. Use specific expectations: "It's time to get up now, come with me to the bathroom..."
Minimal or absent interaction with other children	To encourage peer interaction	Keep the child present in routine activities.
Isolating behavior—lack of eye contact, staring at the wall		Maintain eye contact with the child during conversations. Ask the child to look at the adult or other child while talking.
Disjointed, inappropriate speech	To encourage child's return to contact with reality	Help the child discuss and identify feelings

Client Problem	Goal	Intervention
		Teach appropriate means of expessing feelings.
	To promote appropriate expression of feelings	Give specific instructions for behavior—at the table, in the classroom, and so on—and reward these behaviors.
Ritualistic behavior: rocking, tearing paper, flipping a straw, twirling, placing shoes in a certain order, rubbing the rim of a glass before taking a drink	To decrease ritualistic behavior and anxiety To promote increased reality orientation	Allow certain amount of time to perform these rituals, then move the child into the expected activity. Do not reward rituals by smiling or laughing at the behavior.

Nursing Care Plan

A Child with a Conduct Disorder

Client Problem	Goal	Intervention
Impulsive behavior	To promote greater control of impulses	Teach and role model ways for the child to express needs in an unacceptable manner, such as asking for an object rather than grabbing it.
Poor frustration tolerance resulting in effective coping skills	To encourage delayed gratification of needs and effective/adaptive coping skills	Encourage the child to "take turns" during an activity. Teach the child to "think before acting;" for example, by allowing a pause, which helps him to learn cause and effect. Incorporate a social aspect or interaction into the child's activity. Include the child in group activities with children of similar functioning levels to reduce the child's frustration.
Poor or immature social skills, including poor relationships with peers and adults	To teach acceptable social behavior	Involve the child in a "skill class" covering material such as how to introduce somebody, what to say to others during conversations, and how to compliment someone.
Low self-esteem	To promote increased self-esteem	Build in opportunities to help the child experience success through inpatient milieu management, classroom assignment, and so forth.

(Continues on p 394)

Client Problem	Goal	Intervention
		Assign reasonable tasks that can be accomplished.
		Reward/praise the completion of tasks.
Outbursts of aggressive behavior	To encourage self-control To employ appropriate restraint as needed	Allow the child to role play a situation that "makes him mad" and how he handles his anger; give input about acceptable ways to deal with angry feelings, such as using a punching bag, pounding clay, and so on.
		Encourage the child to express anger verbally, such as "I know that you're angry at Joey . . . What happened that you're angry at Joey? . . . Tell Joey that you're angry at him because . . . "
		Reinforce the child's use of verbal communication to express his feelings, such as "That was super that you used your words to tell Joey that you're angry. You did not throw a chair."
		Establish rules about not hurting self, others, or property.
		Restrain the child physically when necessary.
		Interrupt a physical outburst before an aggressive act occurs; if the child does commit an aggressive act, have him "undo" his behavior as much as possible. For example, if he throws a chair, allow him a period of time to calm down, then have him pick up the chair and place it in its proper position.

References

1. Adler J: General Concepts in Residential Treatment of Disturbed Children. Child Welfare 47 (November): 519–523, 1968

2. Aitchison RA, Green DR: A Token Reinforcement System for Large Wards of Institutionalized Adolescents. Behav Res Ther 12 (September): 181–190, 1974

3. American Psychiatric Association: Diagnostic and Statistical Manual of Mental Disorders, 3rd ed. Washington, DC, American Psychiatric Association, 1980

4. Bardon JI, Bennett VC: Helping Children in School. In Wolman BB (ed): Manual of Child Psychopathology, pp 1058–1087. New York, McGraw-Hill, 1972

5. Barker P, Ward PA: Milieu Therapy in a Child Psychiatry Unit. Nursing Times 68 (December 14): 1579–1581, 1972

6. Bazelon DL: The "Problem Child"—Whose Problem? J Am Acad Child Psychiatry 13 (Spring): 193–201, 1974

7. Besier M: Etiology of Mental Disorders: Sociocultural Aspects. In Wolman BB (ed): Manual of Child Psychopathology, pp 150–188. New York, McGraw-Hill, 1972

8. Bettelheim B: Love Is Not Enough: The Treatment of Emotionally Disturbed Children. New York, The Free Press, 1950

9. Brown AR, Avery C (eds): Modifying Children's Behavior: A Book of Readings. Springfield, IL, Charles C Thomas, 1974

10. Bumpass ER, Fagelman FD, Brix RJ: Intervention with Children Who Set Fires. Am J Psychother 37 (July): 328–345, 1983

11. Burgdorf MP: Legal Rights of Children: Implications for Nurses. Nurs Clin North Am 14 (September): 405–416, 1979

12. Cantwell DP: Childhood Depression: What Do We Know, Where Do We Go? In Guze SB, Earls FJ, Barrett JE (eds): Childhood Psychopathology and Development, pp 67–85. New York, Raven Press, 1983

13. Carr R: The Role of Medication in the Treatment of the Disturbed Child. In Steinhauer PD, Rae-Grant Q (eds): Psychological Problems of the Child in the Family, 2nd ed, pp 635–663. New York, Basic Books, 1983

14. Chess S: Selectivity of Treatment Modalities. In Chess S, Thomas A (eds): Annual Progress in Child Psychiatry and Child Development, pp 448–462. New York, Brunner/Mazel, 1982

15. Crewe HJ: Fears and Anxiety in Childhood. Public Health 87 (July): 165–171, 1973

16. Critchley DL: Mental Status Examinations with Children and Adolescents. Nurs Clin North Am 14 (September): 429–441, 1979

17. Earls FJ: An Epidemiological Approach to the Study of Behavior Problems in Very Young Children. In Guze SB, Earls FJ, Barrett JE (eds): Childhood Psychopathology and Development, pp 1–15. New York, Raven Press, 1983

18. Erikson EH: Childhood and Society, 2nd ed. New York, W. W. Norton, 1963

19. Erlenmeyer-Kimling L, Cornblatt B, Golden RR: Early Indicators of Vulnerability to Schizophrenia in Children at High Genetic Risk. In Guze SB, Earls FJ, Barrett JE (eds): Child Psychopathology and Development, pp 247–264. New York, Raven Press, 1983

20. Fleck S: Some Basic Aspects of Family Pathology. In Wolman BB (ed): Manual of Child Psychopathology, pp 189–204. New York, McGraw-Hill, 1972

21. Forness SR, Sinclair E, Russell AT: Serving Children with Emotional or Behavior Disorders. Am J Orthopsychiatry 54 (January): 22–32, 1984

22. Freud A: Normality and Pathology in Childhood: Assessments of Development. New York, International Universities Press, 1965

23. Galdston R: Mind Over Matter: Observations on 50 Patients Hospitalized with Anorexia Nervosa. J Am Acad Child Psychiatry 13 (Spring): 246–263, 1974

24. Garrison WT: Aggressive Behavior, Seclusion and Physical Restraint in an Inpatient Child Population. J Am Acad Child Psychiatry 23 (July): 448–452, 1984

25. Godsey WC, Cottrell WL, Jr: Using Reality Therapy Techniques with Children and Youth. J Tennessee Medical Association 66 (October): 935–936, 1973

26. Goldman J, Stein CL, Guerry S: Psychological Methods of Child Assessment. New York, Brunner/Mazel, 1983

27. Goren S: A Systems Approach to Emotional Disorders of Children. Nurs Clin North Am 14 (September): 457–465, 1979

28. Green MR: The Interpersonal Approach to Child Therapy. In Wolman BB (ed): Handbook of Child Psychoanalysis: Research, Theory, and Practice, pp 514–566. New York, Van Nostrand Rheinhold, 1972

29. Greenberg LM, Lourie RS: Physiochemical Treatment Methods. In Wolman BB (ed): Manual of Child Psychopathology, pp 1010–1031. New York, McGraw-Hill, 1972

30. Hughes MC: Recurrent Abdominal Pain and Childhood Depression: Clinical Observations of 23 Children and Their Families. Am J Orthopsychiatry 54 (January): 146–155, 1984

31. Kanner L: Child Psychiatry, 3rd ed. Springfield, IL, Charles C Thomas, 1957

32. Kessler JW: Psychopathology of Childhood. Englewood Cliffs, NJ, Prentice-Hall, 1966

33. Koupernik C: Chemotherapy in Child Psychiatry. Br Med J 3 (August 5): 345–346, 1972

34. Leahey M: Findings from Research on Divorce: Implications for Professionals' Skill Development. Am J Orthopsychiatry 54 (April): 298–317, 1984

35. Lovaas OI: The Autistic Child: Language Development through Behavior Modification. New York, Irvington Publishers, 1977

36. Mattsson A: Emotional Problems in Asthmatic Children. Virginia Medical Monthly 100 (November): 1024–1029, 1973

37. McDermott JF, Jr, Char WF: The Undeclared War between Child and Family Therapy. J Am Acad Child Psychiatry 13 (Summer): 422–436, 1974

38. Montanari AJ: A Community-Based Residential Program for Disturbed Children. Hosp Community Psychiatry 20 (April): 103–108, 1969

39. Moustakas CE: Psychotherapy With Children: The Living Relationship. New York, Ballantine Books, 1959

40. Niles GT: Karen Horney's Holistic Approach: A View of Cultural Influences. In Wolman BB (ed): Handbook of Child Psychoanalysis: Research, Theory, and Practice, pp 501–513. New York, Van Nostrand Rheinhold, 1972

41. Offord DR: Classification and Epidemiology in Child Psychiatry: Status and Unresolved Problems. In Stenhauer PD, Rae-Grant Q (eds): Psychological Problems of the Child in the Family, 2nd ed, pp 117–129. New York, Basic Books, 1983

42. Parsons BV, Jr, Alexander JF: Short-Term Family Intervention: A Therapy Outcome Study. J Consult Clin Psychol 41 (October): 195–201, 1973

43. Pfeffer CR, Zuckerman S et al: Suicidal Behavior in Normal School Children: A Comparison with Child Psychiatric Inpatients. J Am Acad Child Psychiatry 23 (July): 416–423, 1984

44. Philipp R: Conducting Parent Training Groups: Approaches and Strategies. In Shamsie J (ed): New Directions in Children's Mental Health, pp 23–30. New York, S P Medical & Scientific Books, 1979

45. Proctor JT: Hysteria in Childhood. Am J Orthopsychiatry 28 (April): 394–406, 1958

46. Rae-Grant N: Prevention. In Stenhauer PD, Rae-Grant Q (eds): Psychological Problems of the Child in the Family, 2nd ed, pp 591–610. New York, Basic Books, 1983

47. Rapoport JL: Stimulant Drug Treatment of Hyperactivity: An Update. In Guze SB, Earls FJ, Barrett JE (eds): Childhood Psychopathology and Development, pp 189–202. New York, Raven Press, 1983

48. Reinherz H, Walker DK et al: Clinical Assessments and Maternal Judgments: Concurrent and Predictive Relationships. Am J Orthopsychiatry 54 (April): 236–249, 1984

49. Ross AO: Behavior Therapy. In Wolman BB (ed): Manual of Child Psychopathology, pp 900–925. New York, McGraw-Hill, 1972

50. Ross AO: Child Behavior Therapy: Principles, Procedures, and Empirical Basis. New York, John Wiley & Sons, 1981

51. Rubinstein RA, Brown RT: An Evaluation of the Validity of the Category of Attention Deficit Disorder. Am J Orthopsychiatry 54 (July): 398–414, 1984

52. Rutter M: Psychological Therapies: Issues and Prospects. In Guze SB, Earls FJ, Barrett JE (eds): Childhood Psychopathology and Development, pp 139–164. New York, Raven Press, 1983

53. Schuster FP: Family-Centered Therapy of the Scapegoat Child. Southwestern Medicine 52 (November): 215–219, 1971

54. Sloate PL, Voyat G: Cognitive and Affective Features in Childhood Psychosis. Am J Psychotherapy 37 (July): 376–386, 1983

55. Sloboda SB: The Children of Alcoholics: A Neglected Problem. Hosp Community Psychiatry 25 (September): 605–606, 1974

56. Stotsky BA, Browne T, Philbirck WA: A Study of Out-come of Special Schooling of Emotionally Disturbed Children. Child Psychiatry and Human Development 4 (Spring): 131–150, 1974

57. Szurek SA, Berlin IN, Boatman MJ: Inpatient Care for the Psychotic Child, The Langley Porter Child Psychiatry Series, Vol 5. Palo Alto, CA, Science and Behavior Books, 1971

58. Tapia F: Children Who Are Cruel to Animals. Child Psychiatry and Human Development 2 (Winter): 70–77, 1971

59. Thomas A, Chess S, Birch HG: Temperament and Behavior Disorders in Children. In Barten HH, Barten SS (eds): Children and Their Parents in Brief Therapy, pp 93–110. New York, Behavioral Publications, 1973

60. Treffert DA: Children and Adolescents: Hospital Treatment Programs, Administering a Residential Program. Hosp Community Psychiatry 19 (August): 237–240, 1968

61. Turecki S: Elective Brief Psychotherapy with Children. Am J Psychother 36 (October): 479–488, 1982

62. Williams C: Self-Injury in Children. Developmental Medicine and Child Neurology 16 (February): 88–90, 1974

63. Winberger HC, Kogan KL: A Direct Approach to Altering Mother–Child Interaction in Disturbed Children. Arch Gen Psychiatr 30 (May): 636–639, 1974

64. Wolman BB: Schizophrenia in Children. In Wolman BB (ed): Manual of Child Psychopathology, pp 446–496. New York, McGraw-Hill, 1972

65. Woodward CA, Johnson Y, Santa-Barbara J, Roberts RS, Pipe M: A Collaborative Special Education Program for Emotionally Disturbed Children: Philosophy, Design and Outcomes. In Shamsie J (ed): New Directions in Children's Mental Health, pp 41–51. New York, S P Medical & Scientific Books, 1979

Chapter 26
The Emotionally Disturbed Adolescent

"Who are you?" said the caterpillar. Alice replied rather shyly, "I-I hardly know, sir, just at present—at least I know who I was when I got up this morning, but I must have changed several times since then."

Lewis Carroll,
Alice in Wonderland

Mary Snyder McElvain

Chapter Preview

This chapter addresses an increasingly important and complex mental health problem in our society. Accepted parameters for normal adolescent development, theories of adolescent disturbance, and the incidence and significance of this problem are presented. The chapter also discusses the dynamics of several important disorders occurring during adolescence.

The steps of the nursing process—assessment, analysis, planning, intervention, and evaluation—are applied to adolescent disorders. There are emphases on assessment of the adolescent based on the nurse's knowledge of developmental variables, on planning with the adolescent and his/her family, including discharge planning, on principles of intervention through a variety of treatment modalities, and on evaluation of the outcomes of nursing interventions. Mental health professionals are encouraged to examine their feelings and attitudes about working with persons in this age group.

Learning Objectives

On completion of the chapter, the reader should be able to accomplish the following.

1. Describe the components of normal adolescent development in the physical, sexual, emotional, and mental spheres
2. Discuss various theories of adolescent development
3. Describe the incidence of various types of adolescent disturbance
4. Discuss the variables of family communication, child-rearing style, personality, social pressures, and sense of alienation as they contribute to the etiology of adolescent disturbance
5. Identify the dynamics of the following adolescent disorders
    Adjustment disorders
    Acting-out behavior
    Substance abuse
    Depression and suicide
    Anxiety disorders
    Eating problems
    Juvenile delinquency
    Psychosis
6. Apply the nursing process to emotionally disturbed adolescent clients
7. Discuss the nurse's own feelings when interacting with an adolescent client and his family

Adolescent Development

In the 20th century, as technology has advanced and economies have reverberated from the impact, our culture has artificially extended the period of adolescence, has made it increasingly difficult for the adolescent youth to contribute to society in a meaningful way; nevertheless, this same society has focused increasing attention on this pivotal age in the life span. At times, adults even look to adolescents for answers to questions or difficult situations that the adult is experiencing for the first time along with the adolescent, such as men in space, home computers, even the Equal Rights Amendment effort.

It now takes some youth until their mid-20s or beyond to assume adult roles. What is happening developmentally during all that time? Adolescent development is a mutually interactive, influential process between individual, family, and society. Adolescents help shape their environment even as their environment helps shape them.

Several myths of adolescent development may be difficult to erase. These myths include the following.

1. Adolescence is a time of universal storm and stress.
2. Rebelliousness is the typical pathway to autonomy.
3. Peer–parent conflict is inevitable during adolescence.
4. Peers replace parents as the major social influence in adolescence.[63]

For most adolescents, development proceeds in an orderly, if not rapid, sequence in which they successfully master growth tasks. "Developmental turmoil" is often, in fact, symptomatic of a disturbance requiring intervention.

Physical Development

Individual differences within each sex are almost as marked as the differences taking place biologically between the sexes. Some adolescents finish maturing physically almost before others begin adolescent biologic development.

Endocrine glands are most involved in adolescent development. The pituitary, ovaries, testes, and cortex of the adrenal gland themselves undergo a growth spurt.[25] The average span of the pubertal process lasts for 5 years.[63]

Sexual Development

Physical development is largely outside the control of the individual except as nutritional, health, and safety (or plastic surgery) practices may alter one's biologic heritage. Sexual, emotional, and mental development takes place within certain genetic and environmental boundaries; however, learning seems to play a large role in the development of sexuality, intellect, and emotional coping.

An important question to ask in relation to adolescent sexual development is, "How does learning sex roles influence overall adjustment, ability to function as adults, and relations with peers and others?"[38] Some research studies have examined the learning of sex roles from parents to answer this question. One study found that father-absent females had a somewhat idealistic and unrealistic picture of the man they wanted to marry, whereas father-present fe-

Age Ranges for Accelerated Growth of Secondary Sex Characteristics and Height

Females		**Males**	
Ovaries	7–9 yr	Volume of testes	$10–13\frac{1}{4}$ yr
Pubic hair	8–14 yr	Penis	$11–14\frac{1}{2}$ yr
Breast buds	8–13 yr	Pubic hair	10–15 yr
Height spurt*	$9\frac{1}{4}–14\frac{1}{2}$ yr	Height spurt*	$10\frac{1}{2}–16$ yr
Median age menarche	12 yr 9 mo	First ejaculation of semen	11–16 yr

* Usually, the peak of height spurt in girls occurs during the year after menarche. The peak of height spurt for boys occurs most frequently after age 14, about the age of first ejaculation of semen.[20]

males were more free to marry someone who differed from their father.[34] Another study found that daughters in families of divorce married early compared to daughters of widows.[35]

Sexuality coexists with the adolescent's search for identity. The process of sexualization begins with dating, which provides an opportunity to practice social roles progressing from hand-holder to kisser to petter to partner in intercourse.[82, 85] The adolescent defines values and standards within these social roles. Personal characteristics, such as being "sexy" or not, become part of the self-concept. Expectations for sexual behavior, sex object, and courtship style evolve out of who one thinks one is and these expectations help determine who one becomes. Sexuality is manifest in relationships with others. Does an individual confide in others of the same or opposite sex or is the individual isolated? Finally, experimentation with sexual conflicts provides an experience for testing autonomous behavior in stressful situations.[85]

Sexual intimacy among adolescents is a concern because of the emotional ramifications and because teenage pregnancies continue to increase while the American birthrate on the whole has declined.[55] Factors that have a significant impact on whether or not an adolescent will be sexually intimate are dating frequency, peer-group-oriented sex education, adolescent sexual experimentation, love relationships with peers, values of peers, a partner who is willing or asking to advance the level of intimacy, and the prospect of marriage.[82] Family attitudes toward sexuality do not appear to be very influential in the adolescent's sexually intimate behavior except as they impact on these other variables.

The media have done much to present, and educate about, human sexuality. The average adolescent watches 2 to 3 hours of television per day, and television seems to reinforce a narrow and rigid view of sex roles.[1] In adult television programming, about 75% of the leading characters are male; in children's programming 89% to 90% of the leading roles are male. Males engage in a wider range and variety of activities than females on television.[83] The subtle message is that the male role is more interesting and appealing.

Emotional Development

Of all of the growth tasks in which the adolescent is engaged, the consolidation of his identity into an independent, fully-functioning adult is probably most challenging and crucial. Self-concept is the cognitive aspect of identity development, self-esteem the affective aspect.[33] When childhood has provided the foundation of positive social interaction and positive self-regard, adolescence is used to refine the self. If childhood, however, has provided little in the way of expectations, too few models, or inconsistent rules, then adolescence is used to define a self previously not started.[33]

The process of achieving emotional independence in adolescence involves multiple intervening factors. Assessment of the parents' readiness to let go, the adolescent's readiness to take hold, and the sense of timing is important. There must be opportunities for trying out new social and intellectual skills and a support system that will remain in place regardless of success or failure in achievement. One observer describes this interplay by explaining, "Adulthood comes about 2 years later than the adolescent claims and 2 years earlier than the parents admit."[33] The adolescent's predominant emotions as he strives for independence from parents are guilt, or "How can I leave them?" and inadequacy, or "Maybe I'm not able."

Child-rearing style provides the context in which emotional development takes place. One way to dichotomize parental discipline is between warmth–control, where parents "guide and show," and warmth–restrict, where parents "order and tell." Studies have shown that warm–restrictive parents tend to have passive, fearful, dependent, and generally well-behaved children. Warm–controlling parents tend to have children who feel responsible, assertive, self-reliant, and independent.[5, 7] Needless to say, there are numerous possible child-rearing styles; however, because responsibility and independence are emotionally healthy traits, it would seem that nurses should practice, advocate, and teach parent–child interactions that foster warm–controlling traits.

The adolescent's self-consciousness is evident if one has ever watched members of this age group at an awards banquet; there is a great deal of blushing, giggling, swaggering, and so forth, all designed to maintain an image. The term for these behaviors is *adolescent egocentrism,* in which the adolescent assumes that others are as consumed with his behavior and appearance as he is. The adolescent continually constructs and reacts to an imaginary audience.[21]

Some adolescents appear to foreclose prematurely on options to develop autonomously before merging with a significant other. Many adolescents marry to escape perceived neglect or domination at home. The deck is often stacked against them. In the first 5 years of marriage, the divorce rate of both males and females who marry younger than 20 is more than twice that of those who marry at later ages, and this rate remains consistently higher than average throughout life.[16]

Counterculture movements attract some adolescents, especially adolescents who are most alienated from themselves and significant others.[14, 69] Mystical and religious cults seem to recruit most successfully among college freshmen and seniors, two years during which major transitions occur. One explanation of this phenomenon is that cults promise definitive answers, give a protecting and structured environment, and provide a "father" who judges right and wrong.[33]

To emerge in adulthood with a positive self-esteem, one must navigate adolescent waters successfully. Emotional development influences and is influenced by extrapersonal circumstances, interpersonal relationships, and intrapsychic stressors.

Mental Development

Jean Piaget's theory of intellectual development describes the final period of formal operational thought, which is consolidated during adolescence. By the time adolescence is reached, the individual's system of mental operations has progressed to a high degree of equilibrium; that is, his ways of thinking, or his cognitive structures, are almost fully formed.[28] These structures may be applied to new problems with resultant new knowledge, but the structures themselves undergo little modification.

Adolescent thought is flexible and effective; an adolescent can imagine many possibilities inherent in a given situation and can deal in abstracts and hypothetical propositions. During adolescence, the individual gains an ability to form concepts, to understand time, and to generalize.[91]

Not all adolescents are capable of formal operational thought and even those adolescents who use formal operations do not do so all of the time. Findings show that only 45% of adolescents reach formal operations by age 15 and 65% by age 30.[49] Factors such as fatigue, boredom, unstimulating environment, or inadequate education may limit an adolescent's ability to use formal operational thought. Cognitive advancement occurs as a function of the following.

1. Appropriate neurological development
2. Proper social environment
3. Experience with objects and events
4. Internal cognitive reorganization[28]

Moral Development

Building on the work of Piaget, Lawrence Kohlberg proposed that moral development proceeds in predictable stages and is part of general cognitive growth and development.[47] He hypothesizes that role-taking is the mechanism by which individuals move through moral stages.[48] Moral issues are universal and timeless and involve issues of justice and fairness.[92]

Kohlberg described a level of conventional morality that involves two stages.

1. The *good boy–good girl orientation* occurs from approximately 10 to 15 years of age, during which time judgments are made on the basis of pleasing others, not pleasing others, or avoiding criticism.
2. The *law and order orientation* occurs at approximately 15 to 18 years of age, during which time judgments are made on the basis of maintaining respect for authority and obeying the law because it is law.[47]

Kohlberg's level of postconventional or principled morality likewise involves two stages.

1. In the *social contract orientation* (ages 18–20 years), judgments are made on the basis of individual rights and standards that have been agreed upon by the whole society.
2. Judgments in the *value of human life orientation* (20 years on) are made on the basis of consequence in accordance with ethical principles such as justice, equality, reciprocity of human rights, and respect for the dignity of human beings.[47]

When working with adolescents, one should gear moral education programs at or above their present levels.[92] The process of struggling to resolve competing ideas helps to teach the adolescent to question and work through conflicts.

Adolescent Disturbance

Theoretical Frameworks

Of all the developmental theorists, Sigmund Freud spends the least amount of time on the adolescent period. According to Freud, at the time of puberty, the Oedipus complex reappears and children must again free themselves from parents as libidinal objects and discover a foreign object of love.[91] During adolescence, a relatively strong id confronts a relatively weak ego. The adolescent reworks parental beliefs, values, and standards. Behavior may reflect disorganization of the superego in preparation for adult restructuring.[31]

Anna Freud states that the following ego defenses are predominant during adolescence.

1. Asceticism—the adolescent becomes idealistic and mistrusts enjoyment
2. Intellectualization—the adolescent achieves mastery through thinking imaginatively
3. Identification—the adolescent may isolate himself from his family and superego in order to find substitutes for abandoned parent objects; that is, he displaces his feelings to idealized adults other than his parents in order to desexualize his parents, and yet learn about adult sexuality.[31]

Erik Erikson looks at adolescent development as a time of review and integration of past stages of development. He has termed the stage of adolescent development *Identity vs Self-Diffusion,* an apt name for the preoccupation with self-image that occurs during this time. In establishing identity, the adolescent looks for ideas and objects to believe in, performs independently, becomes ambitious about some felt capability, and chooses his life work.[91]

Harry Stack Sullivan's interpersonal theory of anxiety focuses on the importance of the early mother–child relationship for the development of the self-system. His theory does not center on the sexual aspects of this early relationship as did Freud's. Sullivan posed three stages of adolescent development.

1. Preadolescence is the stage in which the intimate "chum" relationship occurs. Intimacy here is not necessarily sexual, but is a closeness that permits validation of personal worth. The "chum" relationship is, in essence, a prototype of all future love relationships because it gradually deals with the issue of intimacy.
2. Early adolescence is characterized by heterophilic relationships. The genital drive and an awareness of orgasm appear and responsibility in one's interpersonal relationships becomes an issue.
3. Late adolescence is the stage in which satisfactory genital activity is achieved. This activity is always accomplished within the taboos of a particular culture.[31,91]

The learning theory approach to adolescent development focuses on learning to recognize cues to the drives one feels and using those cues to direct and select behavior. The theme of reworking past experience occurs again in the learning theory approach. There is a contradiction between the teenager's previous learning and new expectations of society so that the teenager uses novel approaches to problem-solve.[54]

Within these developmental theories, one begins to observe a pattern in which separation, sexuality, and responsibility are issues. Conflict in these areas is necessary for a clarification of personal identity. Conflict in these areas is also interpersonal; therefore, it follows that emotionally absent adults in contact with adolescents are as destructive as if they were physically absent. Adolescents need adults with whom they can argue, struggle, and sort out issues. They do not have to be in turmoil and rebel, but must learn to be responsible for their choices.

Theories tell us that, as adolescence progresses positively, the individual matures. Maturity is measured by the capacity to be loving, to wait for emotional satisfaction, to consider the future, and to control hostile and aggressive impulses.[60] Maturity also implies the ability to function autonomously. In families in which adolescent ego autonomy is impaired, parents delineate the adolescent as subject to their control and the adolescent has increased anxiety about his capacity to exist separately from parents. The development of autonomy may even carry a threat of alienation from parents in families of disturbed adolescents.[78]

Adolescents must never be portrayed in terms of a single image. There are vast differences between youths in Malaysia and those in Brooklyn, between those in the Ivy League colleges and those in the ghettos.[70] The nurse must apply generalized theories with caution to a given individual to avoid squeezing "square pegs into round holes."

Incidence and Significance of the Problem

Among adolescents, true psychopathology is relatively rare.[86] The difficulty arises in distinguishing normal strains of the adolescent period from serious disturbance because, if the seriously disturbed teenager does not receive appropriate treatment, the chances are remote that he or she will "grow out of" the problem. This viewpoint seems to be confirmed in a longitudinal study in progress at the University of California at Los Angeles.[63]

One observer has summarized data from several studies with somewhat differing definitions of psychological disorder and concludes that about 20% of adolescents experience disturbances severe enough to interfere with their functioning, 60% experience occasional episodes of anxiety or depression, but not to an extent causing a major disruption in their lives, and the other 20% show no signs of psychological disorder.[88]

There are some statistics that have been gathered to demonstrate the significance of certain problems of adolescence. In one survey of adolescents who were seen in an outpatient clinic, for example, the following diagnostic categories were represented: 4% acute and chronic brain disorder; 10% mentally retarded; 6.5% schizophrenic; 11% to 18% neurotic (males had a smaller pecentage); 23% to 30% personality disorders (females had a smaller percentage); and 36% transient situational disorder.[70] It appears that the majority of adolescents seen in treatment settings fall in the "adjustment reaction" category.

The incidence of acting-out behaviors has been researched among adolescents. In 1976, the Federal Department of Health, Education, and Welfare reported that an estimated one-tenth of 12 to 17-year-olds run away from home at least once.[39] More than half of all serious crimes are committed by youths, age 10 to 17.[83] Drug use statistics vary widely.

Statistics on sexual attitudes and behaviors support general beliefs about adolescent sexuality. Between ages 13 and 15, boys' sexual behavior is more advanced, but by ages 16 to 17, approximately equal numbers males and females engage in petting and premarital intercourse.[24]

Very little of what is experienced as homosexual contact during adolescence or preadolescence will develop into an adult pattern of homosexuality; only 3% to 4% of adolescents who report homosexual experience will become homosexuals as adults.[29]

Even in studies showing that 15% to 25% of adolescents experience "problems" in development, there has been a failure to show what proportion of these individuals are true casualties of adolescence, as opposed to casualties of childhood.[63] In interpreting research about adolescent disturbance, then, one must be careful to note whether statistics are purely descriptive or whether they are inferential, and, if they are the latter, one must note what conclusions are being drawn about the adolescent period.

It is possible to make some summary statements regarding adolescent disturbance. The more behavior problems an adolescent displays, the longer these problems persist beyond an age when they might be expected, and the more they involve cognitive and behavioral difficulties instead of, or in addition to, emotional upsets, then the more likely the young person is to be psychologically disturbed.[88]

Etiologic Theories

A comprehensive, but general, etiologic theory of disturbance in adolescence states that it is caused by the interaction of a certain level of genetic or constitutional disposition (diathesis) and certain kinds of demanding experience (stress).

One theory concerns communication within the family. It states that families with "high expressed emotion" contribute to continued stress in an already disturbed teenager. Specific manifestations of "high expressed emotion" include: parents giving personal criticism of fundamental qualities of the adolescent, rather than aspects of behavior; intruding in the adolescent's life both behaviorally and psychologically; and high degrees of hostility, anger, and resentment.[63]

Another study suggests that children most likely to conform blindly to peer values clearly come from the most extremely authoritarian or permissive families.[63] These theoretical explanations concern childrearing style. It seems that either limits that are too confining or insufficient limit-

setting drives the adolescent out of the family sphere of influence.

A sense of alienation has been linked to psychopathology, delinquency, and low academic achievement. Isolated teenagers are much more likely to lack self-confidence and to overconform to peer values, both of which tend to make them even more likely to be rejected. Isolated teenagers are more prone to mental illness, delinquent behavior, and underachievement.[19, 70] It may be that lack of participation in a social network of peers in early adolescence is a predictor of social deviance or psychopathology in later adolescence or young adulthood.[36]

A disrupted family unit may predispose some adolescents to certain disturbances. The major psychological effects of divorce on adolescents appear to be the following.

1. A sense of rejection and fear of abandonment
2. Intensification of typical adolescent conflicts
3. Fear that own marriage will fail
4. A sense of confusion and disillusionment about life[81]

The factors associated with drug use illustrate the complexity of etiologic theories of adolescent disturbance. Personal, social, and familial factors are associated with how frequently adolescents use drugs and with their likelihood of using drugs at all. The inclination to use drugs is directly related to a high degree of openness to experience, tolerance of deviance, interest in independence, and a low degree of conformity, social inhibition, interest in achievement, and involvement with religion. Socially, the more an adolescent's friends use drugs, the more closely he interacts with these friends, and the more he values these friends' affection and approval, the more likely he is to use drugs. Familial factors include perception of parental drug use, permissiveness or rejection by parents, and a generally negative climate at home.[9, 37, 88] In addition to the above factors in drug use, there is emerging evidence that genetic factors contribute to the disposition to become an addictive drug user. Studies of twins and adoptees identify family patterns that cannot be accounted for by shared experience or parental modeling alone.[88]

Dynamics of Adolescent Disorders

Adjustment Disorders

Adjustment disorders are reactive or situational in nature. They are developmental lags without serious mental disorder. Stress temporarily overwhelms the capacity of the individual to problem-solve. Symptoms of adjustment disorders express a conflict over independence and arise in new life situations that call for increased independence.[44]

Acting-Out Behavior

Acting-out behaviors express conflicts through actions rather than through words. For the adolescent, acting-out behavior is a way of defending against sexual impulses and a direct means of expressing aggressive drives.[63] Acting-out behavior is often impulsive. The adolescent feels overwhelmed by affect and does not think through the consequences of his actions.[31] In this chapter, three behaviors are identified specifically as acting-out—running away, being truant, and problematic sexual activity.

Runaway behavior involves typically immature, timid adolescents who have difficulty directing their anger, or who feel unsafe or unwanted.[31] Seventy percent of runaways interviewed in one study had low achievement and little, if any, involvement with school.[4] The act of running away may either involve much fantasy about the effect the behavior will have on the person or persons left behind or feelings about the family may be too painful to acknowledge in thought.

Truant behavior usually occurs in youngsters who dislike school and are doing poorly academically. Although school phobia, or exaggerated fear of attending school, is probably more common than truancy, it is not necessarily seen as acting-out.

Problematic sexual behavior involves using sex to decrease feelings of loneliness and anxiety.[31] Sexual acting-out among adolescent young women is believed to reflect the breakdown of parental control, a rebellion against authority, and an acute disturbance in the parent–adolescent relationship.[27]

Adolescent pregnancy is an increasingly serious health and sociological problem. One in five births in the United States involves a teenage mother.[67] Teenage pregnancy is often unplanned and unplanned events often conflict with other goals. Pregnancy interferes with the teenager becoming comfortable with her body image. The mental disequilibrium usually associated with any pregnancy can be frightening and alarming to persons whose egos are not fully integrated. Placed within the context of Erikson's psychosocial developmental tasks, the pregnant adolescent is working on generativity before she has accomplished a sense of identity or achieved the task of intimacy.[60]

Prostitution has been explained dynamically by at least two different schools of thought. The psychoanalytic theory focuses on a negative self-image of the female, due to rejection by her father, and states that prostituion is a symbolic way to degrade the self and defend against the need for love. Psychosocial theory suggests that the prostitute rejects society's values rather than rejecting the self. One study reinforces the idea that the sex act is not valued by prostitutes, but instead takes on different meanings. Almost all of the teenage prostitutes interviewed in this study stated that sex was unpleasant for them, something they did only in order to get money.[50]

Substance Abuse

Investigators have found substantial evidence of psychopathology in drug abusers, whereas drug users (*i.e.*, the experimental and social types) are much more like their non-drug-using-peers.[2,90] Whether heavy drug use is a cause or a result of psychosocial difficulties is difficult to determine from available research.[88]

There are several etiologic theories of drug use and any or all of these theories could operate simultaneously.[18] The *peer-influence theory* proposes that youth take drugs to be accepted by contemporaries.[43] The *parental influence theory* claims that drug-taking behavior is learned, especially true of drinking behavior but not strongly proven with marijuana use, and that a poor parent–child relationship seems to be related to the use of illicit drugs other than marijuana.[25]

The *anticipatory socialization theory* asserts that role-taking behavior, in the case of drug use behavior, is perceived as exercising personal direction or independence.[40] The *drug-prone personality theory* is based on a longitudinal study which found that drug users were nonconforming, independent, and adventure-seeking. The non-drug users were conformists, achievement-oriented, and nonimpulsive. What isn't answered is whether these characteristics are cause or effect.[45]

The *deviance theory* maintains that because a deviant subculture is stigmatized and punished, its members adopt values and attitudes to survive in a hostile environment.[8,41] One 5-year longitudinal study, which supports this last theory, found that rebelliousness was the best predictor of drug use.[80]

Depression and Suicide

The normal developmental process presents teenagers with many real losses and threats to their sense of adequacy.[88] Even if development progresses seemingly smoothly, the adolescent may fear not being able to live up to the concept of self he or she has constructed. This fear of failure may lead to a loss of self-esteem resulting in depression. Another "normal" loss in growing up is the loss of the image of parents as perfect; therefore, many adolescents are in a mourning process and feel quite alone.[66]

Depressive disorders emerge primarily in response to the experience of loss in genetically predisposed persons. Individual variation in sensitivity to loss appears to be due to developmental experiences.

A cognitive model of depression proposes that negative thoughts and attitudes are core features of depression. Loss is seen as the loss of some self-attribute necessary for happiness. According to this theory, depression-prone individuals encounter unfavorable life situations disposing them to overreact to being deprived.[62] Depriving early life experiences may include parental absence, dislike of the child, or ignoring the child.[88] The child attributes something lacking in himself, rather than others, when later facing loss.

Another theory relates depression to learned helplessness, or the belief that one's actions have little impact on one's destiny.[76,77] The experience of loss that precipitates depression is a loss of control. When they were children, these individuals felt that they couldn't do anything about unhappy circumstances.

A behavioral model proposes that depression reflects an individual's inability to gain positive reinforcement.[52,53] Developmental experiences have provided insufficient opportunities to learn gratifying ways of responding to people and events.

The symptoms of depression in adolescence are often acting-out behaviors. Acting-out is seen for several reasons—the adolescent's intolerance for intense feelings, his learned behavior, or a lack of verbal skills. Remember that the adolescent is ambivalent about dependency needs versus needs for independence. If a teenager admits that he needs help, he may perceive his request for help as a regression back to childhood.[56] Suicide is acting-out in the extreme.

Eating Disorders

Two startling eating disorders of adolescence are anorexia nervosa, a starvation syndrome, and bulimia, a purge–gorge syndrome. Certainly, nutrition can become problematic for any teenager, as the body requires more nutrients for growth during adolescence or as the teenager responds to dietary fads; however, this chapter examines the two pathological syndromes.

Anorexia nervosa is a self-imposed starvation whose mortality rate is 5%.[17] A fear of not being in control is the central issue in anorexia nervosa. What makes anorexia nervosa especially interesting and also difficult to treat in the clinical setting is that we are still unclear as to how much of the manifestation, both medically and psychiatrically, is a reflection of the effects of hunger and starvation per se.[10] Anorexia nervosa occurs primarily in white adolescent females from middle to upper social classes.[11]

There are predominantly three areas of disturbed psychological functioning in anorexics.

1. Body image
2. Misinterpretation of internal and external stimuli, especially hunger
3. Overwhelming feelings of ineffectiveness

Hilde Bruch, an expert in eating disorders, describes the life of the anorexic as an ordeal of living up to family expectations. The child has, in many cases, been overvalued by parents. The child's view becomes "If you are given much, much is expected of you."[11]

Anorexics' cognitive development remains in Piaget's stage of concrete operations, characterized by egocentricity and magical thinking. The new ways of acting and thinking, which are a normal part of adolescence, are frightening to the anorexic child. She acts out the conviction that by being skinny and in need of protection, she ensures eternal love and care from her parents.[11]

The child who becomes anorexic is usually described as previously being loving, devoted, and well-behaved. The child's compliance probably concealed the fact that she was deprived of living a life of her own. Throughout childhood, her parents failed to acknowledge or confirm the developmental progress she initiated, so that her parents perceive growth and development as their accomplishment, not hers. Other characteristics of the anorexic are excessive involvement in preparing, cooking, and talking about food and being socially isolated during the year preceding the onset of the disorder.[11]

An individual's family may foster excessive concern with bodily needs. Members of the families of anorectics are overinvolved in each other's lives with a resultant loss of individuation.[62] Transactional patterns in these families are characterized by enmeshment, overprotectiveness, rigidity, and lack of conflict resolution.[72]

Bulimia is an episodic, uncontrolled, rapid ingestion of large quantities of food over a short period of time (binge eating). It is commonly associated with anorexia nervosa (25% of anorexics engage in this behavior) and occurs with self-induced vomiting for purposes of weight control. Definite precipitating factors are unknown, but its onset often occurs during the senior year in high school, which is a transitional period. Severe weight loss does not occur in bulimia as it does in anorexia nervosa and amenorrhea seldom occurs.[11,44]

Juvenile Delinquency

Delinquency includes a wide range of illegal acts. An individual's social class has an effect on whether or not a behavior is classified as delinquent. Some youngsters are sociological delinquents, in that they have few psychological problems and are well-integrated members of a delinquent subculture. Other delinquent youngsters, whose deviant behavior results from *psychological* problems, show one of the following three patterns of disturbance.

1. Neurotic delinquency occurs when illegal acts are committed to communicate needs, especially needs for affection and status. Punishment for the acts may relieve guilt feelings.
2. Characterological delinquency involves impulsiveness, low frustration tolerance, inadequate motivation, and a characteristic lack of guilt.
3. Psychotic and organic delinquency results when illegal acts are used as a defense against unrealistic fears of anxiety and annihilation.[79,87]

Gang members are often sociologic delinquents. Youths who join gangs are different from non-gang joiners because they are more likely to have divorced parents or parents with a criminal history, they are more likely to do poorly in school and to have low IQ scores, and they enjoy violence. In fact, physical and verbal aggression are preferred coping mechanisms of gang members.[46] The gang functions as a family substitute for the adolescent whose strong dependency needs are displaced onto the peer group.[13] Sociologic delinquents usually have good family relationships during early life, but lack adequate parental supervision during elementary school and adolescence.[88]

Neurotic delinquency consists of acute, situationally determined lawbreaking, which is precipitated by current psychological distress and stops when distress is relieved. This behavior is especially likely to occur when parents inadvertently foster or reinforce antisocial behavior. Parents may, for instance, model minor disrespect for the law or may be inconsistent in discipline, which tacitly communicates approval of delinquent acts.[88]

Characterological delinquency, like psychopathy, is typically associated with a childhood history of early and severe parental rejection, followed by inadequate discipline and supervision during middle childhood and adolescence. Psychopathy never develops in adulthood in the absence of a developmental history of escalating antisocial behavior.[88]

Psychotic delinquency emerges primarily in schizophrenic youngsters, or in those with minimal brain dysfunction, poor impulse control, or a form of epileptic disorder characterized by psychomotor seizures, all of which may lead to antisocial behavior.[88]

Psychosis

Most forms of schizophrenic disturbance begin during or soon after adolescence. The majority of schizophrenic adolescents initially show a mixed picture in which features of schizophrenia are secondary to, or obscured by, other difficulties, usually depression or antisocial behavior.[88]

Schizophrenic youngsters withdraw from the world of reality, where they are unable to cope, and undergo profound regression to primitive thinking. In the face of overwhelming anxiety, a "retreat into psychosis" provides a degree of relief, comfort, and security.[31] There is a high price for the coping mechanism of psychosis, however protective it may be for the ego.

Application of the Nursing Process to Adolescent Disorders

Assessment and Analysis

Using the theoretical knowledge bases just discussed, the nurse is prepared to assess each individual adolescent according to his developmental progress and special needs, analyze the data, and formulate nursing diagnoses (see insert, Nursing Diagnoses). Assessment of adolescents is challenging because of the wide range of individual variation. It is crucial to assess the whole person and then make comparisons with normal limits of feelings, thoughts, and behaviors in an age group.

Identity Formation

The nurse assesses the adolescent's sense of identity because identity consolidation is the major developmental task of adolescence. Areas of functioning that the nurse explores to assess the adolescent's sense of ego identity include the following.

1. How distinct from others does the individual feel?
2. How is the individual aware of himself/herself? Does this awareness come from all senses? Does the individual describe experiences, memories, perceptions, and emotions?
3. Can the individual make choices from among alternatives?
4. What is the quality of the individual's interactions with others?
5. Does the individual have self-respect?
6. Are the individual's ego functioning and interests stable over time?

When assessing identity formation and maintenance, the nurse will remember that adolescence ends with a sense of ego identity. It is not until around 17 to 22 years that individuals consolidate initial adult identities.[60]

Independent Functioning

Another growth task of adolescence for the nurse to assess is psychological and financial independence or dependence in regard to parents. The 16-year-old may express a desire to "get away from parents," but the 22-year-old may have the means to carry out this theme. Our society does not define or describe the specific steps involved in the process of moving from the status of dependent child to independent adult.[60] Some steps the nurse may look for are as follows.

1. Taking responsibility for completing school work
2. Self-initiation of projects and hobbies
3. Employment that leads to, and eventually results in, self-support
4. Self-assertion in conflict situations

These steps may be attained in varying degrees; some steps may be completed while others have not been attempted. The adolescent in an inpatient unit may have many of these steps curtailed, but the nurse can still assess progress toward independent functioning.

Self-Image

Self-image is the perfect and ideal self that one imagines oneself to be, after identifying with an idealized conception of what the self should be.[93] When the adolescent says, "You don't know the real me," he is likely to be referring to self-image. *Self-concept*, on the other hand, reflects the perceived status of the self; it includes characteristics and personality traits and an evaluation of the worth or desirability of these traits.[22] The adolescent who says, "I care about others, and I'm a good student and I think that's pretty worthwhile," is reflecting self-concept.

Self-awareness is the recognition of one's own exis-

Nursing Diagnoses

Because the emotional problems of adolescents cover such a wide range and lead to such diverse behaviors, the appropriate nursing diagnoses will depend entirely on the data the nurse gathers for each individual. The following examples serve as guidelines to linking certain information with standardized nursing diagnoses.

Possible Nursing Diagnosis	Type of Data Supporting the Nursing Diagnosis
1. Anxiety	1. Perceived threat to self-concept. Conflicts over decisions, choices.
2. Coping, ineffective individual	2. Maladaptive styles.
3. Ineffective family coping	3. Adolescent's problems occur within disturbed family system.
4. Knowledge deficit	4. Regarding health status, economics, relationships. Still in age span when formal learning is occurring.
5. Nutrition, alterations in: less than body requirements	5. If anorexic or bulimic. May be eating junk food rather than balanced diet.
6. Noncompliance	6. May be negative towards authority figures or mistrustful of professional adults.
7. Powerlessness	7. Parents, teachers, health professionals reluctant to relinquish control over decisions affecting adolescent's life. May even be rescued from experiencing consequences of own actions, such as in situations of overprotective guardians. Lack of opportunity for employment or other meaningful contribution to society.
8. Self-care deficit	8. May be unwilling to meet standards of self-care that are required in a given facility. May rebel against following rules for eating, bathing, or grooming in attempt to define identity or be accepted in peer group.
9. Self-concept, disturbance in	9. Struggling to form or consolidate identity. Client may distort strengths and/or weaknesses.
10. Sensory-perceptual alterations	10. If psychotic.
11. Social isolation	11. May have difficulty finding a place in new peer group, especially if hospitalized. May feel like a misfit among peers at school.
12. Thought processes, alterations	12. If psychotic.
13. Violence, potential for	13. May not cope with conflicts verbally, but may instead resort to impulsive acting-out. Obtain history of incidence of lack of control.
14. Potential for injury	14. Suicidal adolescent or substance abuse leading to impaired reality testing.

tence and characteristics and of the evaluations of others toward the self.[23] An adolescent might indicate self-awareness by a statement such as, "When I get scared of other people, I get sort of inconsiderate of them because I want to keep away and not get hurt."

Body image is a mental picture of one's body. As adolescents' bodies change, they must keep restructuring their body images. They must also come to accept a less-than-perfect body unless they are one of the lucky few to have a body that conforms almost exactly to society's current definition of perfect body type. It is hard to convince a distraught teenager that "beauty is in the eye of the beholder." Self-image, self-concept, self-awareness, and body image can be assessed by listening carefully to the adolescent's self-statements as well as by direct questioning about these issues. The disturbed adolescent will always have a disturbance in one or more of these areas.

Strengths

The adolescent is likely to overvalue or undervalue his strengths and talents. He may play down strengths without a firm sense of identity or with a negative self-concept. Conversely, the adolescent may glorify his abilities and worth, thereby showing a characteristic heightened narcissism. This narcissism comes from projecting a model of what he would like to be in an attempt to actualize the ideal image of self.[74] The nurse should assess how realistic the adolescent is in his self-evaluation of strengths, yet remember that increased narcissism is expected.

Impulsivity

Nursing assessment of an adolescent includes the degree of *impulsivity* in behavior because society expects that a person's impulsivity will decrease as he achieves adult status. Also, as this person reaches higher levels of intellectual and moral development, he hopefully retains spontaneity but minimal impulsive behavior. To assess impulsivity the nurse watches an adolescent's reactions to situations for the cognitive component. One might question, "Did the adolescent think of the consequences before acting in a given fashion?" To assess juvenile delinquency, the nurse examines two factors.

1. The social context of the behavior and the life experiences of the perpetrator
2. Whether the behavior constitutes a repeated pattern or is impulsive[91]

Interpersonal Relationships

Adolescence is a time when emancipation conflicts are at a peak. The nurse assesses both the quality and quantity of peer relationships and support groups such as club membership, church affiliations, or job ties, and the nature of family interactional patterns. The diagnosis of adolescent problems is usually child-focused. In most instances, however, the adolescent's difficulties reflect the dysfunctional interaction between the youngster and the parents.[31] This statement does not place blame on parents but recognizes each party as bringing stressors to the interaction.

Sexuality

A final area of assessment is the adolescent's sexuality and sexual behavior. Body image reflects sexual identity. Internalization of body changes takes much longer than the actual physical change. The nurse assesses both physiological variables and the adolescent's cognitive internalization of bodily changes.[60]

Sorting out masculine and feminine identity and the role behavior associated with that sexual identity is a major task. The process of assuming sexual identity and role includes fantasy, role-playing, introjection, projection of self in the role, and finally, role internalization.[73] Role taking occurs in interaction with another person; therefore, many of the areas of functioning already discussed will interface with sexuality and sexual behavior. For example, an isolated adolescent has no one available with whom to try out sexual role behaviors, so fantasy may be this adolescent's primary mechanism.

The nurse also assesses the adolescent's need for knowledge concerning sexual issues. Creating a comfortable climate where discussion may occur about masturbation, homosexuality, sexual intercourse, contraception, pregnancy, or abortion becomes a challenge for the nurse. The cognitive level of the adolescent determines how "in-depth" the discussion may be.

Planning

During the process of assessing and diagnosing the adolescent client, the nurse interacts with him. The nurse begins to establish rapport and trust in the initial contact with the client. The adolescent is particularly sensitive to being listened to, to being understood, and to being accepted. It naturally follows that the adolescent should be included in the planning of professional intervention in his life.

Client Involvement in Decision-Making

In the case of emotional and behavioral difficulties, some person other than the adolescent has probably sought out mental health professionals. It becomes imperative, therefore, that the adolescent be given the opportunity to involve himself in the decision-making. For example, even the adolescent who has been referred for psychiatric treatment by the courts can be given a choice of two or more times when he will be seen by the therapist. The metacommunication to the adolescent when professionals involve him in planning is that maturing includes being active in one's behalf or taking some degree of responsibility for the self.

Goal-Setting

Planning includes learning how to reach goals derived from assessed needs. Two general goals of treatment with adolescents are to identify meanings of behavior and to work through conflicts that act as obstacles to success and happiness.[91]

Planning takes into account the following questions.

1. What alternative services are appropriate to meet the client's assessed needs?
2. What outcome can be expected from each alternative?
3. Which alternative is most cost-effective?
4. Are some alternatives less restrictive than others?
5. Do the alternatives allow the adolescent to continue his education, to be in contact with peers, and to work on the psychosocial growth tasks of adolescence?
6. How long is treatment expected to be necessary?

Family Involvement

The entire family should be incorporated into the treatment of an adolescent's problems.[60] The family system must be considered when planning care because intervention in one part of the system will impact on all other parts of the system. Most state laws require that individuals of certain ages may only be treated with parental consent. If an adolescent insists on strict confidentiality, even from parents, his insistence may be taken as symptomatic of dysfunctional family processes. The therapist points out this fact to the adolescent and tells the adolescent of pertinent legal requirements for treatment. A major decision made in the planning phase will be whether the adolescent will be treated individually, in family therapy, or some combination of both.

Discharge Planning

Discharge planning involves a future orientation that concerns realistic issues of what will happen to the adolescent after treatment. It deals with how the client will manage his own health problems after therapy. In the case of inpatient care, discharge planning includes where the adolescent will live, what difficulties might be anticipated in readjusting to community life, and any available aftercare services.

Intervention

There are several modalities available to the nurse who intervenes with adolescent clients, including specific modalities such as family therapy, group therapy, individual therapy, and behavior modification. Other general principles of intervention, such as effect of the milieu, limit-setting, and communication with adolescents are also used.

Psychotherapy with adolescents focuses on relationship building, to help them experience engaged, trusting, mutual relationships with others, and on reality testing, to correct inaccurate perceptions of the self, environment, and consequences of action. These goals may be achieved in either family, group, or individual psychotherapy.[88]

Family Therapy

With very few exceptions, adequate treatment for disturbed adolescents requires involvement of their parents.[88] Family therapy is a formal involvement of all family members. When the adolescent or parents refuse family therapy, the chances are great that destructive reactions will continue to occur. The family system may resist improvement of the client and sabotage treatment plans in a subtle or not-so-subtle fashion. Parents may feel guilt over their child's problem and become either oversolicitous toward the child or rejecting.[88]

If family therapy is not possible, then at least some effort should be made to informally educate the parents about their adolescent's difficulties and needs. This effort is necessary to help the adolescent be reintegrated emotionally and physically into the family system upon discharge from inpatient care.

In family therapy, the therapist meets jointly with the disturbed adolescent, his or her parents, and as many as possible of the siblings and other relatives who live in the home. Although the adolescent is usually referred to as the "identified patient," the approach focuses more on problems of family interaction than on the young person's abnormal behavior.[88]

Some areas of family functioning addressed during family therapy include the following.

1. Information processing—what kind of information is sought by family members and how is it used?
2. Decision-making—how can the decision-making process be described for a given family?
3. Emotional tenor—what is the emotional atmosphere of the family?
4. Conflict management—how are individual differences handled?
5. Strengths and weaknesses[95]

Intervention strategies that a nurse uses in family therapy sessions include the following.

1. Helping family members articulate feelings and needs in ways that can be heard
2. Refocusing problems as shared difficulties, rather than one person carrying the burden for the entire family unit
3. Facilitating the reminiscence and recall of the parents' own adolescence
4. Refocusing on the marital relationship to defuse parent–child conflict
5. Helping the adolescent to modify and control responses to irritating situations
6. Modeling and facilitating the negotiation process as a way of defining and implementing limits[31]

The family is dealt with as a whole and dysfunction in any of the above areas is related to family processes rather than intrapsychic processes. It is assumed that as the family unit begins to relate in healthier ways, individual behavior will become more satisfying.

Group Therapy

Group therapy is particularly advantageous with adolescents because adolescents function well normally by role-taking in groups. Peer groups allow the adolescent to test behaviors by setting standards and making comparisons. For the adolescent struggling with issues of intimacy, a group setting for relationship building is less anxiety-provoking than a one-to-one relationship. For the psychotic adolescent, group therapy presents reality orientation.[88]

Two therapists of different sexes in group therapy can provide a corrective emotional experience for the adolescent who is reworking oedipal conflicts. Therapists of different sexes may also provide role models for the socially inept or withdrawn teenager. Co-leadership of adolescent groups may be necessary to manage behavioral acting-out and to reinforce limit-setting.

Adolescent group therapy may be called a "special problem group," which is a homogeneous group (all adolescents) whose purpose is to attack directly a problem of concern to all clients in the group. Homogeneous groups seem able to penetrate defenses more quickly. In homogeneous groups, members experience a greater feeling of being understood and accepted, which leads to group cohesion, rather than a sense of discrimination and isolation, which perpetuates defensiveness.[57]

Individual Therapy

Individual therapy may be the preferred mode of treatment if other modalities are not available, if the adolescent needs an intense relationship with a significant other to develop trust, or if the adolescent refuses to communicate in the presence of family members or group members. The particular focus of individual psychotherapy depends upon the assessed needs of the client and the theoretical framework and therapeutic skill of the therapist.

It is a therapeutic challenge to gain adolescents' trust and to motivate them to change. Therapists must demonstrate that symptomatic behavior is self-defeating. The majority of therapeutic approaches to adolescent psychopathology are directed toward psychic reintegration, not toward uncovering and resolving unconscious conflicts. This is a matter of emphasis, however, because often supportive or educative types of treatment also become involved with deeper layers of the personality.[44]

Psychotherapy with adolescents usually combines a dynamic focus on gaining self-understanding and a behavioral focus on symptom removal.[88] The goals of individual therapy with the adolescent include the following.

1. The development of a consistent sense of self
2. The ability to use foresight and to have fun
3. The wish to be with others and the capacity to be alone

4. Thinking that people are neither all to his liking nor are they all unlikeable
5. Confidence in the ability to make choices, with some choices being wrong but not devastating[12]

The therapist provides the adolescent with an adult figure with rational authority and reliability. The choice of topics during therapy sessions is less important than the atmosphere in which the discussion occurs. Because the adolescent dreads to be insignificant, the therapist discusses meaningful, pertinent issues such as trust and competition, sex role satisfaction and responsibility, submissive dependence versus compulsive independence, worthlessness versus omnipotence and denial of abilities, and dedication to suffering.[12]

Behavior Modification

Because many adolescent clients with emotional disturbances are not at the intellectual stage of formal operations (*i.e.,* using logic and making abstractions) and because there is high energy and a propensity for acting-out at this age, it is often useful to plan an emphasis on behavior and observable events in therapy, rather than inferred mental states and constructs.

Techniques of behavior modification that may be used with adolescents include systematic desensitization, positive reinforcement, extinction, role-modeling, and role-playing. Many inpatient residential units for adolescents use a behavioral therapy philosophy. Tokens, or *reinforcers,* are given for certain behaviors and behaviors are tied to privileges the adolescent may earn. Expectations for positive behavior are clearly spelled out as well as consequences for maladaptive behavior. Movement through the treatment program with increasing levels of responsibility and freedom is not arbitrary, but it can be monitored and planned in relation to individual behaviors. Behavior modification programs are matter-of-fact; there is little emphasis on motivation or intent because consequences are based on well-defined behaviors and not on words or feelings. Manipulative behavior between client and staff tends to be decreased when expectations and outcomes are made known to everyone involved.

Therapeutic Milieu

Because residential care for adolescents takes them out of their usual developmental mainstream, the decision to place an adolescent in an institution is not taken lightly. When a decision is made to hospitalize an adolescent, an inpatient unit staff must pay particular attention to the effect of the milieu on a given client. Should adolescents be placed in an all-adolescent unit or in a mixed adult–adolescent unit? Opinions vary but it seems that successful treatment depends less on the mix of the patient population than on whether the unit includes staff who are particularly interested in and knowledgeable about adolescent problems.[88]

The milieu is the total context in which treatment occurs. The physical setting, the atmosphere generated by interpersonal exchanges, and the opportunities available to experience challenge and growth all become important therapeutic tools. Certain principles from milieu therapy and social learning theory explain why the milieu influences behavior.[68] These principles are as follows.

1. The Law of Expectancy. The frequency of a behavior depends on the expectation communicated while or before it occurs. For example, a nurse tells an agitated adolescent that she expects him to maintain control by going to his room to listen to music, rather than hitting a peer with whom he has argued.

2. The Law of Involvement. Acquiring or maintaining new or different behavior requires personal participation in challenges or crises. For example, the nurse guides a practice decision-making session with several adolescents on whether or not they will continue to live with a parent after discharge.

3. The Law of Effect. The frequency of behavior depends on the effects or consequences it produces. For example, visiting privileges are reduced for a patient because of sexual acting-out behavior on the unit.

4. Law of Association by Contiguity. Objects, actions, or environmental changes that occur simultaneously will come to be associated, function in similar ways, or mean the same thing. For example, the peer group praises an adolescent for assertive behavior which both increases the adolescent's self-esteem and gives him a sense of belonging to the group.

When considering the effect of the milieu on adolescents, it is important to stretch out thinking to include nontraditional treatment approaches. One study specifically assessed mental health needs of adolescents and reached the conclusion that more outreach and "off-beat" approaches are needed, such as a milieu in which alcohol abuse, employment problems, and emotional problems are treated simultaneously.[65] If combining services seems too unrealistic, then, at least, we might consider helping the adolescent to integrate the experience of having to deal with several different milieus. Perhaps that's what coping is all about.

Limit-Setting and Follow-Through

Too often, the term *limit-setting* brings to mind verbalizing a hard and fast rule. Instead it should mean a process of determining boundaries in a relationship. Setting limits can be understood as an indication of caring enough to bother with the other. This process becomes very important developmentally with the adolescent who is consolidating ego identity. Questions of "Where do I stand in your opinion?"

and "What controls do I have?" become pivotal guides or limits to behavior in adolescence.

Limit-setting involves reaching consensus about consequences of behavior, verbalizing expectations clearly, and following through consistently with consequences. Limits to behavior must be geared to the abilities of the adolescent to perform those behaviors. For example, expecting an adolescent who is hallucinating to apologize for throwing lunch on the floor will not be as effective as removing her from the lunchroom.

Providing an opportunity to discuss limits and their implementation is another part of follow-through. Strict adherence to rules is not the prime objective in successful treatment on an inpatient unit.[91] The struggle around those rules forms the basis for problem-solving. We often call this struggle "testing." Adolescents may appear to regress and use maladaptive coping measures from past experience when they find themselves in a difficult situation. The process or struggle should be discussed with the adolescent to highlight the usefulness of conflict in forcing some kind of resolution. The nurse presents the possibility of healthier resolution of difficult conflict situations. Reviewing and analyzing how limits are set and why they are broken helps the adolescent understand more about functioning as an adult in the world.

Communication with Adolescents

"But you don't understand!" is such a common statement associated with the adolescent that one may decide adolescents are impossible to understand. Do not, however, allow the adolescent to stop communication from you with his defensive posture. A response to such a statement is, "I would like to understand." Communicating with adolescents entails first listening, then clarifying, restating, and giving nonjudgmental responses.[1]

The nurse working with the adolescent must be able to tolerate ambiguity. The adolescent may not know what to say before he says it, and then it may not "come out right." After all, the adolescent is in the process of consolidation, not closure. It is critical that mental health caregivers show the adolescent that they respect any effort at dialogue.

Both verbal and nonverbal skills are important in communication with the adolescent. For example, attentiveness, smiling, lifting the arm in a "well-done" sign, and hugging are positive warm gestures the nurse may use with adolescents. The nurse must anticipate and understand unconventional language and profanity, and strike a balance between using words familiar to the adolescent and appearing phony or ridiculous by overuse of teenage slang.[91]

The nurse should also expect resistance to her efforts at communication. A young nurse may be viewed as a "sell-out to the establishment" and an older nurse may appear too parental or authoritarian. In either case, trust is difficult to establish. The adolescent's familiar role may be a negative

Therapeutic Dialogue

Interacting with an Adolescent

The following therapeutic dialogue is a portion of the third session between a nurse and Lara, a 14-year-old middle child.

Lara: I couldn't wait to get here today because something awful happened last week. You know how you told me to write things down that were important to me so that I could make the best use of my hour with you?... well, this one I will always remember! I debated a lot about whether I should say anything because it makes my Mom sound terrible, and I don't know whether to be mad or sad, or maybe it's no big thing.

Nurse: You've been really struggling. Let's take a look at it.

Lara: She's a liar.

Nurse: Your Mom?

Lara: Yeh.

Nurse: And that's heavy for you.

Lara: Who wants to think her mother is a big phony? (voice louder)

Nurse: Give me some of the particulars and let's see how you came to that conclusion.

Lara: I went into her drawer to borrow some nylons and found some joints under all her stuff. I mean, my own mother smokes. How can she stand there and tell us not to? Why didn't she tell me? Why couldn't she be honest? She's always wanting me to talk to her, but she never talks to me.

Nurse: Something was hidden from you and you consider that dishonest, even a lie.

Lara: I guess she couldn't come right out and say, "I like grass." I mean, I've never seen her high or anything.

Nurse: So your first reaction was to think she's a liar, but you can understand why a parent might not tell her kid everything she does.

Lara: Yeh, like I don't tell her everything I do. (smiles)

Nurse: You'd like to be close and want to talk to her, but not tell her everything. What else about the joints bothers you?

Lara: She shouldn't be doing it.

Nurse: You've said "should" and "shouldn't" a couple of times today.

Lara: Well, she shouldn't. It's against the law.

Nurse: And why might someone break the law?

Lara: They don't think they'll get caught.

Nurse: What else?

Lara: They think the law is wrong.

Nurse: What else?

Lara: I don't know.

Nurse: I don't know either. We're just speculating. Maybe they're not thinking about the law at the time. Or maybe it's fun to take a risk. People are pretty complicated. Using the words "should" and "shouldn't" can shut our minds to how complex people and relationships are.

Lara: But you're taught since you were a little kid that there are things you should and shouldn't do.

Nurse: And part of growing up is looking at those "shoulds" and "shouldn'ts" and deciding which are valid and important in your life.

Lara: Breaking the law is breaking the law.

Nurse: Yes, laws give us security by providing limits. We also get security from our parents, but now your security is shaken because you don't see Mom as quite so perfect.

Lara: I thought you would tell me to go talk to my mother about the whole thing.

Nurse: You decided what I would say before you came to see me?

Lara: Yeh. These sessions never go like I think they're going to beforehand.

Nurse: You plan to direct them more or to have more control?

Lara: I'd like to!

Nurse: That's something to learn about yourself.

Discussion

When an adolescent brings up conflicts with others, it is so easy to focus on the motives of the other or to defend or attack particular actions in the situation. This nurse never addresses whether it is right or wrong for Mother to smoke marijuana or whether in fact, Mother does! Instead, the nurse keeps the focus on the patient, her struggle as she is disappointed or surprised by others, and the issues of trust and control, which are developmental issues of adolescence. When the nurse asks the client why people might break laws, she is not focusing on others. She is asking the adolescent to reach beyond quick and simple answers in order to expand the adolescent's understanding of others.

As Lara begins this session, she repeats some things the nurse has said previously, indicating that there is some kind of positive relationship developing between nurse and client. Knowing that Lara feels support in the relationship, the nurse can prod Lara later in the interview to consider alternatives and to listen to the nurse's hypothesis regarding insecurity.

At first, Lara catastrophizes with words like "awful" and "terrible." The nurse recognizes the pain involved and invites Lara to continue in a steady, matter-of-fact way ("let's take a look"). When Lara calls her mother a liar and a phony, the nurse ignores the labels. The nurse continues to use language comfortable for the nurse, but not technical jargon or theoretical interpretations. Because the client is operating at a feeling level by calling her mother names, the nurse now gives her an opening to analyze her thinking in order to see how her thinking and feelings are connected. Making the connections won't occur in one session.

When Lara talks about the issues of trust with Mother and the unequal sharing between parent and child, the nurse knows these are parallel issues in nurse–client relationships. The nurse plans to use this example in later sessions to look at Lara's feelings for the nurse. Such interventions should be carefully planned, and will be timed differently by different therapists.

One of the growth tasks of adolescence is moving from the safety of rigid rules to judging circumstances and then choosing actions. Lara, at times, retreats to black-and-white simplifications, and at other times, is capable of tossing ideas back and forth with the nurse. The nurse gently coaxes Lara to expand her thinking, knowing that she will have more options available to her as an adult if she can see more possibilities in situations.

Adolescents often feel impotent in the real world. Lara opens up this issue when she talks of planning the sessions beforehand. Instead of engaging in a power struggle at this point, or becoming defensive, the nurse simply acknowledges Lara's statement and invites Lara to learn about the need she may have to control. The nurse respects Lara and does not pretend to have magic answers.

Questions

1. How might the nurse have begun if the client was less verbal, entered the session tearfully, sullen, or frightened?

2. This nurse focuses on cognitive aspects; for example, how the client decides things, how she uses "should" and "shouldn't" to guide her thinking in a rather narrow way. Where in the interview could the nurse have focused more on feelings? On behaviors?

3. As additional reading, review Alfred Adler's theory on birth order. How might Lara's middle position in her family have influenced her views on fairness and closeness?

4. What are Lara's strengths that the nurse uses in working with her?

image and so tolerating good feelings from staff or accepting kindness involves a huge and difficult change.

Any pretense of unauthentic emotion with an adolescent client is doomed to failure. The nurse should develop qualities of honesty and a sense of humor as well as the ability to say, "I am angry when . . . ," "I am concerned when . . . ," "I am disappointed when . . . ," to describe the nurse's real feelings in a given situation.

Evaluation

Evaluation of the adolescent's progress toward attaining goals as a result of nursing interventions is not a difficult step in the nursing process providing goals were clearly stated in behavioral terms. Adolescent progress often involves movement "one step forward" and "two steps back"; therefore, stating goals in small increments, rather than major changes, aids in evaluating the adolescent's progress.

If gradients of change were specified and planning was done for nursing interventions to help the adolescent attain one gradient at a time, outcomes of nursing interventions for each goal can be evaluated. If all goals have been reached, the adolescent should be discharged from treatment. If there has been success in reaching a portion of treatment goals, the nursing process begins again with another assessment of needs. The nurse and the adolescent may decide to continue to pursue the remainder of the original goals, to set new goals, to change or alter interventions, or to lengthen or shorten the time until the next evaluation. The adolescent's input and cooperation at all stages of the nursing process are important for the adolescent to separate from parental figures and, eventually, to assume responsibility for meeting his own health needs.

The Nurse's Feelings

Whenever impulsiveness, emotional lability, and other issues of self-control are paramount in a treatment setting, nurses need to heighten their vigilance in regard to their own feelings. The nurse may become impatient with the adolescent who is particularly slow to complete growth tasks. Adolescent conflicts within the nurse may be tapped or reawakened. The nurse may unconsciously encourage acting-out by the adolescent because of identification with him and the vicarious satisfaction that defense brings.

Another type of identification is with the parents.

The adolescent client often tries to recreate the home situation using staff in parent roles. In this case, the adolescent may expect adults to reject or abandon him and may attempt to set up a situation in which staff will fulfill his negative expectations.

The nurse may become frightened of the adolescent with tenuous self-control. The nurse who is not secure in his or her own sexual identity may project that insecurity by overreacting to situations or by not providing limits when an adolescent is testing with sexual behavior. It is hard to be on the receiving end of a barrage of hostile remarks, and the nurse may feel like retaliating against the belligerent adolescent.

The examples of many feelings destructive to therapeutic relationships with adolescents may be discouraging. There are, however, just as many instances of positive feelings.

Nurses who are considering working with this age group should carefully examine memories of their own adolescence. It might even be helpful to evaluate to what extent each of the adolescent growth tasks were completed by the nurse. The nurse's own self-awareness, by whatever means attained, is the best way to avoid being caught off guard emotionally or intellectually when interacting with adolescents. Nurses who can be honest with themselves are most likely to be honest with clients.

Positive expectations must also be emphasized in working with adolescents. Adolescents want to be accepted, loved, and understood. If the nurse clarifies which behaviors are likely to lead to satisfying relationships and increased self-esteem, the adolescent can choose whether or not to try out the new behaviors. On the other hand, the adolescent who meets only criticism may have a decided poverty of ideas regarding any other way to behave. The adolescent's message to the nurse caregiver may well be, "Do not lead, I may not follow; Do not push, I may give up; Walk beside and help me discover my way."

Summary

This chapter has introduced some of the parameters of normal adolescent development. Several theories providing frameworks for understanding adolescent disturbance have been presented. Some of the major foci of the chapter have included the following.

1. The adolescent undergoes marked physical change with individual differences within each sex almost as great as the differences between the sexes.
2. Sexual development proceeds by role-taking, which progresses toward sexual intimacy.
3. Emotional development includes defining or refining the self.
4. Mental development consolidates in the intellectual stage of formal operations for many adolescents; moral development is evidenced as the adolescent moves through the levels of conventional morality and postconventional or principled morality.
5. The incidence of adolescent emotional disorders is difficult to identify because of varying diagnostic biases.
6. Etiologic theories of adolescent disturbance examine the variables of family communication, child-rearing style, personality, social pressures, and the sense of isolation.
7. In the assessment phase of the nursing process, the nurse gathers data about the adolescent's sense of identity, independence/dependence, self-image, strengths and talents, impulsivity, support systems, and sexuality.
8. In the analysis phase, the nurse analyzes and categorizes client data and formulates nursing diagnoses.
9. In the planning stage, the nurse includes the adolescent and, hopefully, his family in decisions regarding goals of treatment based on assessed needs.
10. Various intervention strategies for working with disturbed adolescents may include family, group, individual, and milieu therapies, as well as behavior modification, limit-setting, and communication skills.
11. The result of the evaluation phase may be to decide that the adolescent is ready for discharge from treatment or to decide to restart the nursing process with a fresh assessment of needs.
12. Working with adolescents is exciting and demanding and requires a firm awareness of self and a willingness to confront issues such as identification, separation, sexuality, and self-control.

Case Study

Outpatient Treatment for an 18-Year-Old Male Client

When Bob M. came home tearfully from college after only 6 weeks, he reluctantly agreed to see a nurse–therapist. He felt lost, alone, and confused. His mother accompanied him to his first appointment and explained that Bob was very much like her and was a "homebody." Bob did agree to see the nurse–therapist on his own for a series of appointments.

Bob's family history revealed two professional parents and one older sister who had run away from home at age 15 to marry "beneath her social class." Parents had "disowned" the older sister for 1 year and then had begun to speak to her again and to give her gifts and money. Bob idealizes his mother and believes that he is like her. He respects his father but believes that he cannot live up to the standards his father sets; he can never be "good enough" in his father's eyes.

Bob had entered a small college in another state to please his parents. A marginal student, he enjoyed sports but found neither academics nor sports could help him over his panic at being away from home. He didn't feel he belonged in college.

Bob had one or two dates in high school with girls but was shy and uncomfortable around them. He felt quite at ease with males. He felt some pressure to be dating from his parents who tried on a few occasions to arrange dates with daughters of their friends.

When the nurse–therapist first saw Bob individually, Bob had a depressed affect. He described himself as "lazy" with his days spent watching T.V. or "goofing around with friends." He thought he might enroll in a local community college the next semester to overcome his guilt at "disappointing everybody." He was ambivalent about wanting to continue living at home.

The nurse–therapist set the following treatment goals with Bob.

1. To separate from parents by moving to an apartment by himself or with friends
2. To become aware of his own needs as different from the needs of others by deciding on school enrollment
3. To decrease feelings of depression and guilt as reflected in an increased number of positive statements made about himself

4. To take responsibility for his own feelings and behavior through a process of rational decision-making rather than impulsive actions

In the process of 18 months of individual therapy, Bob made progress and had setbacks. He enrolled once again in college, but did not complete the semester due to his inability to discipline himself to attend classes and study. He dated females once or twice, but continued to prefer the company of his group of male friends. He went on a trip to the beach with the group and on a ski trip, both of which he enjoyed. These trips did cause conflict with his parents who reluctantly paid his way. His parents later insisted that he move out of the house and support himself, at which point he found a job at a carwash and moved into an apartment with a friend.

Bob terminated therapy 3 months after his parents stopped paying for his sessions because "my budget is too tight." He felt a sense of accomplishment that he had remained on his own for 6 months and he was thinking of ways he could get into a small business with a chance for advancement. Bob felt positive about his gains in thinking through conflicts rather than running away from his painful emotions. He was starting to verbalize awareness of his similarities and differences from parents and to feel more confident in his own decisions, regardless of whether or not he had parental approval for those decisions.

Questions for Discussion

1. Discuss the interaction of maturational and situational crises in Bob's life.
2. Which etiologic variables of adolescent disturbance help explain Bob's feelings and behavior?
3. How do the issues of separation, sexuality, and responsibility enter into Bob's treatment plan? Are there other important issues?
4. Would you have set the same treatment goals with Bob as the nurse–therapist did? Explain your rationale.
5. Describe specific interventions that might have been used at various stages of Bob's therapy (*e.g.*, communication techniques or behavioral techniques) to accomplish treatment goals.
6. What qualities would the nurse–therapist need to successfully engage Bob in a therapeutic relationship?

References

1. Adams JF: Understanding Adolescence: Current Developments in Adolescent Psychology, 4th ed. Boston, Allyn & Bacon, 1980

2. Admini F, Salasnek S, Burke EL: Adolescent Drug Abuse: Etiological and Treatment Considerations. Adolescence 11:281–299, 1976

3. Baumrind D: What Research is Teaching Us about the Differences Between Authoritative and Authoritarian Child-Rearing Styles. In Hamacheck DE (ed): Human Dynamics in Psychology and Education, 3rd ed. Boston, Allyn & Bacon, 1977

4. Bayh B: Runaway Youth. Washington, DC, US Government Printing Office, 1973

5. Beck AT: Depression: Causes and Treatment. Philadelphia, University of Pennsylvania Press, 1970

6. Beck AT: The Development of Depression: A Cognitive Model. In Friedman RJ, Katz MM (eds): The Psychology of Depression. Washington, DC, Winston, 1974

7. Becker WC: Consequences of Different Kinds of Parental Discipline. In Hoffman ML, Hoffman LW (eds): Review of Child Development Research, Vol 1. New York, Russell Sage Foundation, 1964

8. Braucht G: Psychosocial Typology of Adolescent Alcohol and Drug Users. In the Proceedings of the Third Annual Alcoholism Conference of the National Institute on Alcohol Abuse & Alcoholism. Washington, DC, United States Department of Health, Education and Welfare, 1974

9. Brook JS, Lukoff IF, Whiteman MM: Peer, Family and Personality Domains as Related to Adolescents' Drug Behavior. Psychol Rep 41:1095–1102, 1977

10. Bruch H: Psychological Antecedents of Anorexia Nervosa. In Vigersky RA (ed): Anorexia Nervosa. New York, Raven Press, 1977

11. Bruch H: The Golden Cage: The Enigma of Anorexia Nervosa. Cambridge, Mass, Harvard University Press, 1978

12. Bryt A: Modifications of Psychoanalysis in the Treatment of Adolescents. In Jules H (ed): Adolescence, Dreams and Training, Science and Psychoanalysis, Vol 9, pp 81–88. New York, Grune & Stratton, 1966

13. Burton CA: Juvenile Street Gangs: Predators and Children. In Dacey JS (ed): Adolescents Today. Santa Monica, CA, Goodyear Publishing Co, 1979

14. Carroll JW: Trancedence and Mystery in the Counterculture. Religion in Life 42:361–375, 1973

15. Coche E, Thomas AT: Evaluative Research on a Therapeutic Community for Adolescents. Journal of Youth and Adolescence 4:321–330, 1975

16. Conger JJ: Adolescence and Youth, 2nd ed. New York, Harper & Row, 1977

17. Crisp AH et al: The Long-Term Prognosis in Anorexia Nervosa: Some Factors Predictive of Outcome. In Vigersky RA (ed): Anorexia Nervosa. New York, Raven Press, 1977

18. Cross HJ, Kleinhesselink RR: Psychological Perspectives on Drugs and Youth. In Adams JF (ed): Understanding Adolescence: Current Developments in Adolescent Psychology, 4th ed, pp 363–382. Boston, Allyn & Bacon, 1980

19. Damico SB: The Effects of Clique Membership Upon Academic Achievement. Adolescence 10 (Spring): 93–100, 1975

20. Eichorn DH: Biological Development. In Adams JF (ed): Understanding Adolescence: Current Developments in Adolescent Psychology, 4th ed, pp 56–73. Boston, Allyn & Bacon, 1980

21. Elkind D: Egocentrism in Adolescence. Child Development 38:1025–1034, 1967

22. Encyclopedia of Sociology. Guilford, CN, The Dushkin Publishing Group, 1974

23. Fairchild HP (ed): Dictionary of Sociology. Ames, IA, Iowa State University Press, 1955

24. Finkel ML, Finkel DJ: Sexual and Contraceptive Knowledge, Attitudes, and Behavior of Male Adolescents. Family Planning Perspectives 7:256–260, 1975

25. Forslund MA, Gustafson TJ: Influence of Peers and Parents and Sex Differences in Drinking Behavior by High School Students. Quarterly Journal of Studies in Alcoholism 31:868–875, 1970

26. Freud A: The Ego and the Mechanisms of Defense. New York, International Universities Press (rev ed), 1966

27. Friedman A: Therapy with Families of Sexually Acting-Out Girls. New York, Springer-Verlag, 1971

28. Ginsburg H, Opper S: Piaget's Theory of Intellectual Development, 2nd ed. Englewood Cliffs, NJ: Prentice-Hall, 1979

29. Gordon S, Dickman IR: Sex Education: The Parent's Role. Public Affairs Pamphlet, No. 549. New York, Public Affairs Committee, 1977

30. Green MR: The Problem of Identity Crisis. In Masserman JH (ed): Adolescence, Dreams and Training, Science and Psychoanalysis, Vol 9, pp 74–75. New York, Grune & Stratton, 1966

31. Haber J et al: Comprehensive Psychiatric Nursing, 2nd ed. New York, McGraw-Hill, 1982

32. Halni K et al: Pretreatment Evaluation in Anorexia Nervosa. In Vigersky RA (ed): Anorexia Nervosa. New York, Raven Press, 1977

33. Hamachek DE: Psychology and Development of the Adolescent Self. In Adams JF (ed): Understanding Adolescence: Current Developments in Adolescent Psychology, 4th ed, pp 81–91. Boston, Allyn & Bacon, 1980

34. Hetherington EM: Effects of Father Absence on Personality Development in Adolescent Daughters. Developmental Psychology 7:313–326, 1972

35. Hetherington EM, Parke RD: Child Psychology: A Contemporary Viewpoint, 2nd ed. New York, McGraw-Hill, 1979

36. Hill JP, Monks FJ (eds): Adolescence and Youth in Prospect. Guilford, England, IPC Science & Technology Press Ltd, 1977

37. Huba GJ, Wingard J, Bentler PM: Beginning Adolescent Drug Use and Peer and Adult Interaction Patterns. J Consult Clin Psychol 47:265–276, 1979

38. Huston-Stein A, Welch RL: Sex Role Development and the Adolescent. In Adams JF (ed): Understanding Ado-

lescence: Current Developments in Adolescent Psychology, 4th ed, pp 230–289. Boston, Allyn & Bacon, 1980

39. Intradepartmental Committee on Runaway Youth: Runaway Youth: A Status Report and Summary of Projects. Washington, DC, United States Department of Health, Education and Welfare, 1976

40. Jessor R, Jessor S: Adolescent Development and the Onset of Drinking. Journal of Studies of Alcoholism 36:27–51, 1975

41. Johnson BD: Marijuana Users & Drug Subcultures. New York, John Wiley & Sons, 1973

42. Jones SL: Family Therapy: A Comparison of Approaches. Bowie, MD, Robert J Brady, 1980

43. Kandel DB, Kessler RC, Margulies RZ: Antecedents of Adolescent Initiation into Stages of Drug Use: A Developmental Analysis. Journal of Youth and Adolescence 7:13–40, 1978

44. Kaplan HI, Sadock BJ: Modern Synopsis of Comprehensive Textbook of Psychiatry/III, 3rd ed. Baltimore, Williams & Wilkins, 1981

45. Kay EJ et al: A Longitudinal Study of Personality Correlates of Marijuana Use. J Consult Clin Psychol 46:470–477, 1977

46. Klein MW: Street Gangs & Street Workers. Englewood Cliffs, NJ, Prentice-Hall, 1971

47. Kohlberg L: Development of Moral Character and Moral Ideology. In Hoffman ML, Hoffman LW (eds): Review of Child Development Research. New York, Russell Sage Foundation, 1964

48. Kohlberg L: Moral Stages and Moralization. In Likona T (ed): Moral Development and Behavior. New York, Holt, Rinehart & Winston, 1976

49. Kohlberg L, Gilligan C: The Adolescent as a Philosopher: The Discovery of the Self in a Post-conventional World. Daedalus 100:1051–1086 (Fall), 1971

50. Kurz S: Teenage Prostitutes. Equal Times (Nov. 13):6, 1977

51. Lewinsohn PM: Clinical and Theoretical Aspects of Depression. In Calhoun KS, Adams HE, Mitchell KM (eds): Innovative Treatment Methods in Psychopathology. New York, John Wiley & Sons, 1974

52. Lewinsohn PM: A Behavioral Approach to Depression. In Friedman RJ, Katz MM (eds): The Psychology of Depression. Washington, DC, Winston, 1974

53. Lordi WM: Hospital and Residential Treatment of Adolescents. In Novello JR (ed): The Short Course in Adolescent Psychiatry. New York, Brunner/Mazel, 1979

54. McCandless BR: Adolescents: Behavior and Development. Hinsdale, IL, Dryden Press, 1970

55. McCoy K: Adolescent Sexuality: A National Concern. J Clin Child Psychology 3:18–22, 1974

56. McCoy K: Coping With Teenage Depression: A Parent's Guide. New York, New American Library, 1982

57. Marram GD: The Group Approach in Nursing Practice, 2nd ed. St Louis, CV Mosby, 1978

58. Masterson JF: The Symptomatic Adolescent 5 Years Later: He Didn't Grow Out Of It. Am J Psychiatr 123:1338–1345, 1967

59. Mattheis RF: Holistic Health Concepts. In Haber J et al

(eds): Comprehensive Psychiatric Nursing, 2nd ed, pp 76–136. New York, McGraw-Hill, 1982

60. Mercer RT: Perspectives on Adolescent Health Care. Philadelphia, JB Lippincott, 1979

61. Miller D: Adolescence. New York, Jason Aronson, 1974

62. Minuchin S, Rosman B, Baker L: Psychosomatic Families. Cambridge, Mass, Harvard University Press, 1978

63. Moore DC (ed): Adolescence and Stress. Report of an NIMH Conference. Washington, DC, United States Department of Health and Human Services, P H Service, 1981

64. Norton AH: Evaluation of a Psychiatric Service for Children, Adolescents and Adults. Am J Psychiatr 123:1418–1424, 1967

65. Nuttall EV, Nuttall RL, Polit D, Clark K: Assessing Adolescent Mental Health Needs: The Views of Consumers, Providers, and Others. Adolescence 12 (Summer): 277–285, 1977

66. Pasquali EA et al: Mental Health Nursing: A Bio-Psycho-Cultural Approach. St Louis, CV Mosby, 1981

67. Population Reports, Series J, No 14. Washington, DC, George Washington University Medical Center (March), 1977

68. Rhoades LJ: Treating and Assessing the Chronically Mentally Ill: The Pioneering Research of Gordon L. Paul. NIMH Science Reports, DHHS (ADM)81-1100, 1981

69. Robbins T, Anthony D, Curtis T: Youth Culture Religious Movements: Evaluating the Integrative Hypothesis. Sociol Rev 16:48–64, 1975

70. Rogers D: Issues in Adolescent Psychology, 3rd ed. Englewood Cliffs, NJ, Prentice-Hall, 1977

71. Rosen BM et al: Adolescent Patients Served in Outpatient Clinics. Am J Public Health 55:1563–1577, 1965

72. Rosman BL et al: A Family Approach to Anorexia Nervosa: Study, Treatment, and Outcome. In Vigersky RA (ed): Anorexia Nervosa. New York, Raven Press, 1977

73. Rubin R: Attainment of the Maternal Role. Nurs Res 16:237–245, 1967

74. Rubins JL: The Self-Idealizing and Self-Alienating Process During Late Adolescence. Am J Psychoanal 25:27–37, 1965

75. Sedgwick RA: Family Mental Health, Theory and Practice. St Louis, CV Mosby, 1981

76. Seligman MP: Depression and Learned Helplessness. In Friedman RJ, Katz MM (eds): The Psychology of Depression. Washington, DC, Winston, 1974

77. Seligman MP: Helplessness: On Depression, Development, and Death. San Francisco, WH Freeman, 1975

78. Shapiro RL: Identity and Ego Autonomy in Adolescence. In Masserman JH (ed): Adolescence, Dreams, and Training, Science and Psychoanalysis, Vol 9, pp 18–23. New York, Grune & Stratton, 1966

79. Smiley WC: Classificaton and Delinquency: A Review. Behavioral Disorders 2:184–200, 1977

80. Smith GM, Fogg CP: Teenage Drug Use: A Search for Causes and Consequences. Personality and Social Psychology Bulletin 1:426–429, 1974

81. Sorosky AD: The Psychological Effects of Divorce on Adolescents. Adolescence 12 (Spring): 123–136, 1977

82. Spanier GB: Sexualization and Premarital Sexual Behavior. In Rogers D (ed): Issues in Adolescent Psychology, 3rd ed, pp 240–241. Englewood Cliffs, NJ, Prentice Hall, 1977

83. Stein AH, Freidrich LK: The Impact of Television on Children and Youth. In Hetherington EM et al (eds): Review of Child Development Research, Vol 5. Chicago, University of Chicago Press, 1975

84. Swift P: Inner City Teens. Parade (September 18):5, 1977

85. Wagner CA: Adolescent Sexuality. In Adams JF (ed): Understanding Adolescence: Current Developments in Adolescent Psychology, 4th ed, pp 267–301. Boston, Allyn & Bacon, 1980

86. Weiner IB: Psychological Disturbances in Adolescence. New York, Wiley-Interscience, 1970

87. Weiner IB: Juvenile Delinquency. Pediatr Clin North Am 22:673–684, 1975

88. Weiner IB: Child and Adolescent Psychopathology. New York, John Wiley & Sons, 1982

89. Weiner IB, Del Gaudio AC: Psychopathology in Adolescence: An Epidemiological Study. Arch Gen Psychiatry 33:187–193, 1976

90. Wieder H, Kaplan EH: Drug Use in Adolescents. Psychoanalytic Study of the Child 24:399–431, 1969

91. Wilson HS, Kneisl CR: Psychiatric Nursing. Menlo Park, CA, Addison-Wesley, 1979

92. Windmiller M: Moral Development and Moral Behavior. In Adams JF (ed): Understanding Adolescence: Current Developments in Adolescent Psychology, 4th ed, pp 210–224. Boston, Allyn & Bacon, 1980

93. Wolman BB (ed): Dictionary of Behavioral Science. New York, Von Nostrand, 1973

Chapter 27
Mental Health of the Aging

An Old Lady Has the Last Word

Patriciann Furnari Brady

What do you see nurse, what do you see?
What do you think when you're looking at me?
A crabby old woman, not very wise,
Uncertain of habit, with faraway eyes,
Who dribbles her food and makes no reply
When you say in a loud voice, "I do wish you'd try."
Who seems not to notice the things that you do,
And forever is losing a stocking and shoe
Who resisting or not, must do as you will
Is that what you're thinking; is that what you see?

Then open your eyes, nurse, you're not looking at me.
I'll tell you who I am as I sit here so still,
As I do your bidding, as I eat at your will,
I'm a small child of ten with a father and mother.
Brother and sister who love one another;
A young girl of sixteen with wings on her feet,
Dreaming that soon now a lover she'll meet;
A bride soon of twenty—my heart gives a leap,
Remembering the vows that I promised to keep.
At 25, now I have young of my own who
Need me to build a secure, happy home.
A woman of 30, my young growing fast,
Bound to each other with ties that should last;

At 40, my sons have grown and are gone.
But my man is beside me to see I don't mourn;
At 50, once more babies play around my knees;
Again we know children, my loved one and me.

Dark days are upon me, my husband is dead.
I look to the future, I shudder with dread.
For my young are all rearing children of their own,
And I think of the years and the love I've known

I'm an old woman and nature is cruel.
'Tis her jest to make old age look like a fool.
The body it crumbles; grace and vigor depart.
There is now just a stone where I once had a heart.

But inside this old carcass a young girl still dwells.
And now and again my battered heart swells.
I remember the joys, I remember the pain.
And I'm loving and living life all over again
I think of the years, all too few, gone too fast,
And accept the stark fact that nothing can last.
So open your eyes, nurse. Open and see.
Not a crabby old woman; look closer—

        See Me.

     Author Unknown

Chapter Preview

In 1900, there were slightly more than three million elderly persons in the United States.[3] In 1976, the number of persons aged 65 and older was 22 million or approximately 10.5% of the total population.[24] Statistical projections estimate that by the turn of the century there will be 45 to 48 million elderly living in the United States.[19]

Elderly persons constitute a significant portion of our society. Recognition of the needs of the elderly and an understanding of their physical and psychosocial changes are essential for all practitioners of nursing. The focus of this chapter is to help nurses recognize their own attitudes about the elderly, to identify the physical and psychosocial changes that occur in the aging process, and to apply the nursing process to the care of the elderly.

Learning Objectives

On completion of the chapter, the reader should be able to accomplish the following.

1. Identify those individuals in our society who are identified as the elderly
2. Discuss nurses' attitudes toward the elderly and how these attitudes have an impact on health care
3. Define the process of aging
4. Describe the normal physiological and psychosocial changes occurring during the aging process
5. Identify means for promotion of health and positive adaptation to aging including the following
   Preparing for retirement
   Deciding about residential placement
   Dealing with depression

The Elderly and the Nurse

Identifying the Population

Individuals who have reached the age of 65 are considered elderly in our society. Terms such as *aged, senile old woman,* and *dirty old man* are all part of the systematic stereotyping of, and discrimination against, people because they are old.[4] Nurses must recognize that each individual is unique and that the aging process is also unique for the individual.

Old age is a period of continued developmental growth. The developmental tasks of aging include conservation of strength and resources, when necessary, and adaptation to those changes and losses that occur as part of the aging experience. The ability of the elderly person to adapt and thrive is contingent on his physical health, personality, early life experiences, and the societal supports he receives, such as adequate finances, shelter, medical care, social roles, and recreation.[4]

When one thinks of the elderly, the picture that may come to mind is that of an old person sitting restrained in a wheelchair in a nursing home; however, most elderly individuals live in single family-owned homes. The largest proportion of the elderly live in independent households and the majority of these people live with a spouse or other relatives. According to the 1970 census, fewer than 5% of the elderly live in institutions.[24]

The Nurse's Attitudes

Nursing of the elderly does not command the same level of prestige as nursing in many medical-surgical nursing areas. Unfortunately, geriatric nurses and, particularly, those staff employed in nursing homes often feel and are treated like second-class nurses.[3] They may be thought of as unable to perform in "real" hospital settings; their pay is often below that of nurses who practice in hospitals. Some people believe that it does not take much skill or expertise to take care of old people and that the elderly need custodial care more than anything else.[3] In June, 1966 geriatric nursing was recognized, for the first time, as a vital specialty in nursing by the American Nurses' Association. Standards for Geriatric Nursing Practice were established in 1970 (see insert, The American Nurses' Association's Standards of Geriatric Nursing Practice).

Although the nurse could function as the primary guardian of the aged person's mental health and human dignity, most institutions reward nurses for their medical and technical skills. Psychological and social interventions undertaken by the nurse are deemed worthy and laudable, but more or less voluntary.[20]

Stereotyped attitudes of nurses concerning old people often interfere with treatment by preventing the nurse from seeing the individual as he really is (see insert, Stereotyped Attitudes About the Elderly). If nurses and other health care providers isolate stereotyped attitudes and behaviors directed toward the elderly, they may better understand their reactions to the elderly and become better prepared to care for their aged patients.[5] It has been shown, for example, that the abnormal behavior of patients is often rewarded; hence, a decrease in normal behavior occurs.[38] Recognition of these attitudes is the first step toward improving health care and quality of life for the aging.

The Process of Aging

Each individual, including the elderly individual, develops at his own rate. The age of 65 has been chosen to signify the elderly because of the great number of psychosocial changes heralded by this age. These social changes act as a point of comparison to the younger adult.

As children begin to walk at different ages, the physiological aging process occurs, likewise, at different rates for each individual. The following discussion is presented as a guideline to the aging process.

The American Nurses' Association's Standards of Geriatric Nursing Practice

Standards:

I. The nurse demonstrates an appreciation of the heritage, values and wisdom of older persons.

II. The nurse seeks to resolve her conflicting attitudes regarding aging, death, and dependency so that she can assist older persons and their relatives to maintain life with dignity and comfort until death ensues.

III. The nurse observes and interprets minimal as well as gross signs and symptoms associated with both normal aging and pathologic changes and institutes proper nursing measures.

IV. The nurse differentiates between pathologic social behavior and the usual life-style of each aged individual.

V. The nurse promotes and supports normal physiologic functioning of the older person.

VI. The nurse protects aged persons from injury, infection, and excessive stress and supports them throgh the multiplicity of stressful experiences to which they are subjected.

VII. The nurse employs a variety of methods to promote effective communication and social reactions of aged persons with individuals, family and other groups.

VIII. The nurse, together with the older person, designs, changes, or adapts the physical and psychosocial environment to meet his needs within the limitations imposed by the situation.

IX. The nurse assists the older person to obtain and utilize devices which help them obtain a higher level of function and insures that these devices are kept in good working order by the appropriate person or agencies.

Physiological Changes

The aging process begins at birth. The body does not change obviously, but a variety of cyclic aging changes, on a lesser level, are constantly occurring.[35]

The rapidity of aging depends on a person's heredity, the amount and regularity of exercise, any past illnesses, the presence of one or more chronic illnesses, and the stresses experienced throughout life.[14] Changes attirbuted to aging are as follows.

1. A decrease in rate of cell dimension in specialized cells that regenerate (*e.g.*, epithelial tissue)
2. A deterioration of more specialized nondividing cells, particularly neurons and skeletal muscle cells, leading to a decreased functional capacity
3. Changes in connective tissue leading to increased rigidity and loss of elasticity, producing changes in organ systems
4. A general loss of reserve functional capacity in all organ systems[14]

Respiratory System

There is generally decreased functional reserve capacity of the respiratory system in the elderly.[15] The decreased lung elasticity and changes in the thoracic bones affect the ventilation of the lungs. These are common respiratory system changes that take place with aging; unless illness occurs, elderly people adapt to these changes without difficulty.

Pneumonia and other respiratory illnesses increase in frequency in the elderly due to the inability of the lungs to handle proper ventilation. The reserve capacity of the lungs is increased, however, if the person has continued to exercise regularly.

Cardiovascular System

The heart tends to maintain its size with age; however, in some individuals, it becomes smaller.[24] Reduced cardiac muscle strength and cardiac output frequently occur; however, the anatomic and physiological changes that take place in the aged heart allow it to function adequately, unless the elderly person has coronary artery system disease.[24] Because of the decreased metabolic needs of the aged, the heart functions adequately to meet the needs of the healthy aged individual.

The older American typically shows some degree of atherosclerosis affecting the aorta, coronary arteries, and carotid arteries. Atherosclerotic changes reduce the distensibility and elasticity of the large arteries and limit the

Stereotyped Attitudes About the Elderly

1. Discussing sad and traumatic events of the past makes elderly patients depressed.
2. Rearranging a patient's room provides a more stimulating environment for the elderly.
3. Elderly people prefer to be with people their own age.
4. Elderly patients are not willing to discuss their emotional problems.
5. Elderly people tend to become grouchy and stubborn.
6. As you grow older, you must expect to depend on other people.
7. Most elderly patients are confused at some time during the day.
8. Elderly patients should be encouraged to perform self-care as much as possible.
9. It is bad for the elderly to talk about death and sickness.
10. The elderly tend to be childish and are more secure if treated as a kind adult treats a child.
11. Aged persons do not have sexual feelings or interest in the opposite sex.
12. Old age is a form of sickness requiring medical care and nursing.
13. Elderly patients generally have poor memories.
14. Old people often like to meddle in other people's business.
15. Older people cannot expect to lead completely full or satisfying lives.

ability of the blood vessels to increase the amount of blood available to vital organs.[14] Therefore, any illness that increases the need for blood, such as fever, may produce angina or syncope.

Gastrointestinal System

The bony structures of the mouth begin to shrink with age. Aged people tend to have missing teeth that have been replaced with dentures. As the bony structure of the face changes, the person's dentures may not fit properly and may result in the person having difficulty chewing food properly. Meals become less pleasurable for the individual and he tends to avoid nutritional foods such as meats, vegetables, and fruit. Decreased peristalsis of the gastrointestinal tract causes a feeling of fullness, which, in turn, causes the individual to ingest less food. A slight decrease in the amount of pancreatic enzymes in the aged individual further diminishes the individual's digestion and absorption of nutrients.

Most elderly individuals have daily bowel movements despite reduced peristalsis, reduced muscular activity, and

inadequate exercise.[14] Many elderly persons use a variety of medications to avoid constipation. It is the nurse's responsibility to assist the elderly with diet teaching, thereby assuring maximum nutritional benefits from food and adequate bulk to avoid gastrointestinal problems.

Genitourinary System

During the aging process, the ureters and bladder tend to lose muscle tone. The bladder may lose enough muscle tone to result in incomplete emptying, which increases the risk of urine retention and cystitis. The kidneys concentrate urine inadequately, causing frequent urination and nocturia.

Because of the relaxation of their pelvic muscles, multiparous elderly women frequently experience urinary incontinence. Older men, because of hypertrophy of the prostate and decreased bladder capacity, experience frequency of urination. These conditions frequently affect the lifestyle of the elderly, but appropriate health care intervention helps the elderly adjust to these changes. Although many elderly individuals decrease their fluid intake to alleviate frequency and incontinence, the nurse should explain the hazards of dehydration and should encourage the aged person to take in at least 2000 ml of fluids every 24-hour period, unless contraindicated.[14]

Endocrine System

Estrogen and testosterone are the hormones that generally decrease with age; growth hormones continue to be secreted in the elderly. Some hormones, such as insulin, appear to be secreted at a lower level in the elderly than in younger people.[14]

A decrease of estrogen during menopause causes many of the physiological changes of the female body. Changes in breast tissue result in less glandular tissue, reduced elasticity, and more connective tissue and fat. The uterus becomes smaller and the external genitalia shrink with age and loss of subcutaneous fat.[14]

A decline of testosterone in the aged male occurs, but does not result in an abrupt decline in spermatogenesis.[14] Benign prostatic hypertrophy is a common occurrence in elderly males.

Ears, Nose, and Throat

Visual accommodation is altered in adults around the age of 30 years and progresses throughout all of old age. This visual change is due to the inability of the lens of the eye to adapt to near vision. By the age of 40, most people need corrective lenses for near vision. With age, the pupillary sphincter causes the pupil size to decrease; therefore, bright light becomes necessary for reading. This decreased pupil size also presents an added risk of accidents when the aged person walks in poorly lit areas.[14] Handrails may be necessary to avoid accidents. The lacrimal glands of the older individual produce fewer tears; dry and irritated corneas may result from decreased tearing.[14]

Neurologic System

Neurologic changes of the elderly may be due to physiological or psychological causes. It has been established that, in very aged people, there is a decrease in the size and weight of the brain, with some decrease in the number and functioning of neurons;[14] however, there has been no evidence to support a relation of brain size to neurologic functioning.

Recent studies have shown that those most prone to deficits in mental functioning are individuals with high blood pressure or other deteriorative vascular changes.[3] One study showed that there was minimal evidence of brain impairment in the memory and intelligence performance of men with normal blood pressure, whereas those with high blood pressure manifested marked decline.[39] Of particular relevance is the finding that the individual's intellectual functioning is related more directly to psychological adjustment than to chronological age.[12] Nurses must treat older people as intelligent adults capable of comprehending events unless they have a pathologic condition superimposed on the aging process.[14]

Sleep requirements of the elderly differ from the younger adult in amount and pattern of sleep. The elderly tend to need less sleep and the stages of rapid eye movement (REM) sleep are altered. Assisting the elderly to relax and prepare for sleep and discouraging naps during the day assure more restful sleep patterns for the aged (see case study, Mrs. W.).

Integumentary System

Changes of the skin, hair, and nails are common manifestations of the aging process. Decreased elasticity and dryness are the causes of wrinkled skin. The exposure to sun over a period of years contributes to the aging of the skin. Liver spots (lentigo senilis) and keratosis frequently develop due to sun exposure. The skin becomes dry, inelastic, pallid, and grayish in color due to deficiencies of protein and caloric intake.[37] Frequent baths should be avoided by the elderly because soap causes dryness. Lotion may be used to increase skin moisture. With the thinning of the epidermis, the skin is easily injured and healing is slowed by a decreased blood supply to the dermis.[19]

The toenails and fingernails of the elderly tend to become thick and to split easily. Teaching proper nail care is important to avoid injury to the fingers and toes. For example, the nurse recommends that nails be soaked prior to cutting them.

Graying of the hair begins in the middle years and progresses to the snow white hair of old age. The hair may thin and become fine due to atrophy of the hair roots.

Musculoskeletal System

Joint, muscular, and bone changes are common conditions manifested in the elderly individual. The ability to ambulate and move our extremities is often taken for granted. In the elderly, joint changes and diminished bone and muscle mass give way to increased incidence of fractures and falls, stooped posture and shortened stature, loss of muscle power, misshapen joints, pain, stiffness, and limited mobility.[24]

Fractures in the elderly generally heal as quickly as in the young. Due to decreased activity and nutrition, the elderly may experience increased muscle atrophy and stiffness. Proper health teaching should emphasize the intake of foods high in protein, vitamins, and minerals, which can decrease these health problems. Encouragement of daily exercise, especially walking, may result in decreased muscle atrophy and stiffness.

A common manifestation of bone changes in the elderly is osteoporosis. This condition is found more frequently in older women than men due to the effect that decreased estrogen production has on the bones.

Adaptation to Physiological Change

The nurse working with the elderly focuses on assisting them

1. to understand the normal aging process;
2. to maintain the body through diet, rest and sleep, and exercise;
3. to cope with physiological changes through adaptation.

The nurse's understanding of the normal aging process facilitates the elderly patient's adaptive skills. Planning and implementing nursing care to provide for these needs is the nurse's ultimate goal.

Psychosocial Considerations of Aging

Myths of Aging

There are many myths associated with aging. These are identified as

1. physiological aging;
2. unproductivity;
3. disengagement;
4. inflexibility;
5. senility;
6. serenity.[4]

To facilitate understanding the process of aging, an attempt is made to explore these myths.

Physiological Changes. Physiological changes are part of a continual process begun at birth. The nurse recognizes these changes in the elderly and helps them adapt to changes. Physiological changes require adaptation skills. Most physiological changes of aging bring with them psychological components that cannot be negated, such as threats to self-image, self-esteem, personal identity, and role performance. These aspects of the elderly person's psychological well-being must be addressed by the nurse and the elderly client.

Case Study: Mrs. W.

Mrs. W., a 78-year-old widowed female, was admitted to the medical floor due to complaints of weakness and dizziness. Mrs. W. lives in her own apartment in a senior citizens apartment complex. She had been functioning well at home until approximately 4 days prior to admission. Her daughter, who is married and lives in the same town as Mrs. W., stated that Mrs. W. complained of an inability to sleep at night and of falling asleep during the day. Her daughter feared Mrs. W. was sleeping through meal times. She stated that Mrs. W. formerly was an active person; for example, she knitted many presents for others.

After all medical tests were completed, no physiological cause of the problem was identified. Mrs. W.'s pattern of sleeping during the day continued. Attempts to place Mrs. W. in a wheelchair at the nurses' station during the day did not decrease this behavior. Mrs. W. remained awake from 12:30 am until 5:30 am and continually attempted to get out of bed.

Following a conference of the nursing staff, the following care plan was implemented to intervene in Mrs. W.'s behavior.

Client Problem	Intervention
Inability to sleep at night	Discuss with client her perception of the problem and plans to change her bedtime patterns. Assist Mrs. W. with bedtime routine at 7:00 pm. Offer 8 oz of warm milk at bedtime. Back rub at bedtime. Night light left on in the room. When awake at 12:30 am, permit her to sit at nursing station with knitting for awhile. Then return her to bed. Back rub for relaxation.
Inadequate nutrition due to difficulty waking up in the morning	Wake client at 7:30 am. Assist her with am bath. Determine preference for certain foods. Ambulate in hall following meals. Encourage family to visit, particularly during mealtimes. Provide her with knitting supplies and provide reinforcement for knitting completed. Encourage her to participate in planning daily activity.

The nursing staff implemented this new routine for 4 days. Following day 2, Mrs. W.'s periods of wakefulness during the day increased. Mrs. W. ate all her meals and began to become interested in knitting. She did not exhibit confusion, weakness, or dizziness. Mrs. W. stated she felt like "her old self." Plans were being made for discharge, and Mrs. W. stated she intended to follow this routine at home.

Questions for Discussion

1. What are sleep requirements of an elderly person?
2. Identify the nursing interventions that assist an individual to relax and to sleep.
3. What factors contributed to Mrs. W.'s weakness and dizziness?
4. Discuss why activity was encouraged during periods Mrs. W. was awake.
5. Why was it important for the nurses to ask Mrs. W. her perception of her problem and to encourage her to participate in planning her daily activity?

Unproductivity. Current research supports a broader view of the cognitive process of aging.[3,4,19,24] The variety of life experiences of the elderly contribute to cognitive adjustments to aging. Mental and intellectual functioning of the elderly does not necessarily decline during the aging process and only at death are there apparent changes in intelligence. The changes prior to death, however, may be due to depression rather than physical causes.[20]

The necessity for learning may decrease as one ages. The elderly person's attitude toward learning or his attempts to solve problems on the basis of previous experiences may bring about this change in behavior.[24] The elderly individuals tend to respond slowly to directions and this is often mislabeled as a decrease in intellectual functioning. The manner in which the elderly person perceives outside stimuli is related to his visual and auditory abilities. Due to delayed auditory perception, the aged individual's reaction time may be increased; likewise, as the amount of information associated with decision-making is increased, the time required to reach a decision is increased.[36] It has also been noted that elderly people may be more reflective in making decisions due to consideration of their previous experiences.[4] Nurses should provide the elderly with sufficient time to process information and with the opportunity to be involved in planning their care.

Disengagement and Inflexibility. Personality development of the elderly is often described as inflexible and disengaged. Nevertheless, patterns of personality development of the aged are not dormant. The elderly person attempts to complete the final stage of personality development, which ultimately leads to a preparation for death.

Erikson has identified this final developmental task as Ego Integrity versus Ego Despair.[11] This stage involves a developmental integration of one's life, during which the individual reviews his life experiences and evaluates the successful completion of his life goals. The individual who accepts his life and the achievement of his goals undergoes a new sense of ego integrity. He sees life as having meaning and does not despair for what might have been. He views life as another phase of development that one must accomplish; achieving a positive sense of self becomes his ultimate goal.[32]

Senility and Serenity. The majority of behavioral changes of the elderly are responses to poor adaptation of physiological, psychological, or environmental factors. Mild forms of behavioral changes may be caused by adverse environmental influences, such as social deprivation.[23] For example, sensory-deprived patients are reported to exhibit a loss of mental function, personality disintegration, and psychotic symptoms.[30]

Societal forces place the elderly into dependent roles. Mandatory retirement, financial limitations, highly mobile extended families, government priorities in budget alloca-

tions, incidence of chronic disease, and differential mortality rates for men and women cause dependent role positions, which may precipitate dependence in other areas.[10] In planning and providing care for the healthy elderly, the nurse needs a working knowledge of psychosocial development of the aging individual and, in turn, she must support his independence and positive adaptation.[10]

Promotion of Health and Adaptation to Aging

Health care of the elderly individual requires the acceptance and implementation of a treatment model that is concerned with the psychosocial functioning of the elderly.[1,4] The long-term effects of physical health, longevity of family and social relationships, satisfying and purposeful activities, and successful resolution of psychosocial conflict are difficult to measure, but these factors appear to be instrumental in determining the quality of life for the elderly.[33]

Preventive and Therapeutic Measures

Nursing care of the elderly focuses on those preventive and therapeutic measures that assist the individual to adapt to the changes of growing older. Life review therapy and life-cycle group therapy are two forms of psychotherapy that assist older people in this manner.

Through an extensive autobiography of the individual, life review therapy helps him develop an improved self-image and helps the nurse gain a deeper understanding of him (see Therapeutic Dialogue: Life Review Therapy). The consequences of a life review include expiation of guilt, exorcism of problematic childhood identifications, the resolution of intrapsychic conflicts, the reconciliation of family relationships, the transmission of knowledge and values to those who follow, and the renewal of the idea of citizenship.[4]

Life-cycle group therapy is oriented toward persons experiencing a crisis in their lives. The members of the group are concerned not only with intrinsic emotional problems, but also with preventive and remedial measures as they pass through the life cycle.[4]

Unfortunately, health care deliverers and institutions tend to be organized around the medical model concept of illness. When the behavior of the aged fits neatly into categories that are defined as appropriate illness behavior, then we can discuss, diagnose, and dispose of cases with very little difficulty.[17] Although such illnesses may be present in some elderly patients, opportunities can be provided, even for patients who are slowly deteriorating, to maximize and maintain their essential human dignities through a physical and psychosocial milieu that minimizes the patients' losses.[20]

A variety of treatment techniques, modalities, and

Therapeutic Dialogue

Life Review Therapy

Mr. J., an 84-year-old widower, has been a resident of a nursing home for 2 years. In the last 3 weeks, he frequently mentioned to the nurses that he had a son who died at 9 months of age. The nurses were aware that Mr. J. had two daughters who lived in another town, but were unaware of any children who had died. The nurses feared that Mr. J. was becoming confused; however, he participated in the home's activities and demonstrated no other behavioral changes.

The head nurse, Mrs. Brown, decided to visit Mr. J.'s room, sit with him, and participate in an activity with him to provide an opportunity for him to discuss his son. Mr. J. enjoyed doing puzzles, and she asked him to put one together with her. After 15 minutes of working on the puzzle and discussing activities at the nursing home, the following interaction took place.

Mr. J.: Do you know that I had a son die at 9 months?

Nurse: You had a son who died at 9 months?

Mr. J.: Did you ever hear of the bad flu that went around a long time ago?

Nurse: Did your son die of the flu?

Mr. J.: We were never sure. I couldn't get the doctor there in time. He had a high fever.

Nurse: The doctor didn't arrive in time?

Mr. J.: (tears in his eyes) It was snowing outside, and I had to travel 5 miles to get a doctor. It took me almost 1 hour to get to the doctor and 1 hour to return home. When we got home, I found my wife crying, and I knew he was dead.

Nurse: That must have been a difficult time for you and your wife.

Mr. J.: She cried for 3 days until the funeral. Then she never would talk about Peter. She said it was something we must forget, but I never forgot Peter.

Nurse: You would have liked to talk about Peter?

Mr. J.: He was our only son, and then we had the two girls. I love our girls, but I felt it was my fault he died, and my wife didn't want to talk about it, ever.

Nurse: You felt he died because you couldn't get the doctor there?

Mr. J.: I needed to say I was sorry. It feels good to tell someone that I did the best I could. I'm glad I could tell you.

Mr. J. returned to talking about the puzzle and did not discuss his son in the subsequent weeks. When his daughter came to visit, she confirmed that Mr. J. had a son who died at nine months of age.

Questions for Discussion

Mr. J.'s discussion with the nurse was a type of life review.

1. Discuss the benefits of a life review for the elderly individual.
2. What are the expected results of life review therapy?

---

therapies exist that assist older persons who exhibit cognitive and emotional impairment, including the following.

1. Reality orientation focuses on repetition and learning of basic information, such as the client's name, location, and time of day.
2. Resocialization groups increase the elderly client's contact with others and expands his ability to recognize available choices of living for himself.
3. Remotivation therapy encourages the moderately confused elderly client to take a renewed interest in his surroundings by focusing attention on everyday life not related to his emotional situation.
4. Attitude therapy reinforces the client's desirable behavior and eliminates undesirable behavior.
5. Reinforcement therapy proposes that a person learns to behave in a way that allows him to experience pleasant and rewarding situations.
6. Milieu therapy uses all facets of life of the older individual in the social milieu as opportunities for living-learning experiences.
7. The prevlab program (prevention of loneliness, anxiety, and boredom) is based on the concept that sensory input can be altered in a positive direction for most subacute or chronically ill individuals by introducing high interest items into their immediate environment and by altering or modifying the design and decor of their environment.
8. Self-image therapy is based on the rationale that as a person grows older, he experiences feelings and reactions that impact upon the self.
9. Reality therapy attempts to lead clients away from denying external reality and helps them to recognize that reality not only exists, but that they can fulfill their needs within its bounds.[1]

Adaptation to Change

Besides the physiological and psychological changes of the elderly, there are also lifestyle changes that confront the elderly. These are discussed below.

Retirement

For many individuals, work is a great part of life. Many people view retirement as a crisis. If work is a focal point of one's life, retirement may threaten feelings of identity, integrity, and self-esteem. With retirement may come loss of income, influence, status, creativity, activity, social relationships, and control over the environment.[16]

To plan for retirement, adults need to develop leisure activities that will support their self-esteem. Involvement in groups, such as senior citizen or retirement groups, may provide new areas for experiences in creativity, activity, and social relationships.

Family roles may change during this period. The individual and spouse should plan together and take into consideration their needs and the impact of the changes in their financial situation. Establishing new roles and relationships takes time and requires that others support the client's and family's growth. Our mobile society has altered the extended family; now, the retiree has an opportunity to expend energy on reestablishing and nurturing relationships.

Residential Placement

An individual's need for security and sense of identity may be threatened when it becomes necessary for him to change his lifestyle. Entrance into a residential care facility may threaten the elderly person and subject him to possible psychological stress or anxiety.[2] Significant proportions of the aged are clearly mismatched with respect to their placement in an institutional setting and this results in unmet needs, serious health problems, and sometimes death.[27]

Entrance into a residential home may be regarded as a "crisis rite" for the aged—as an official acknowledgement of their inability to care for themselves, their dependence on others, or their withdrawal into the "sick role." Entrance into an institution also represents the general public's perception of old people, signifying the end of one phase of life (normal society or the outside world) and the beginning of another (institutional care or the "inside").[31] The adaptation of the elderly to such a facility is dependent on pre-admission planning, pre-admission counseling, and matching the individual's needs to the proper facility.

Dealing with Depression

As some elderly individuals attempt to cope with the changes of aging, normal adaptation skills may not suffice. Failure of adaptation skills may lead to depression and depression may lead to suicide.[28]

Suicide in the elderly tends to be a response to situational problems related to the client's aging, rather than an inability to cope.[13] Elderly individuals make fewer suicide attempts, communicate intentions of suicide less frequently, use more lethal methods of suicide, and are more successful than younger suicidal individuals.[28] Single, widowed, separated, and divorced individuals comprise the highest suicidal groups in the elderly population.[25] Crucial factors in determining who among the elderly will attempt suicide appear to be the individual's coping abilities and the strength of his "will to live."[28]

There are eight major causative patterns of suicide in the elderly. Each pattern of suicide is actually a means of reacting to one or more of the changes brought about by the aging process. Suicide among the elderly may be a result of a reaction to the following.

1. Severe illness
2. Mental illness
3. The threat of extreme dependency or institutionalization
4. The death of a spouse
5. Retirement
6. A pathological personal relationship
7. Alcoholism or drug addiction
8. Multiple factors[28]

Precise information is unavailable regarding the number of suicides among the elderly population. Many factors, including family denial and fear of loss of insurance benefits, contribute to this lack of information.[26]

Suicide attempts by the elderly may also be life-threatening behavior, but are not always recognized as such by those caring for them. Life-threatening maneuvers are identified by three characteristics.

1. They can hasten death singly or in combination.
2. They are usually not aggressive behaviors but passive behaviors.
3. They are observed, but unrecognized, by caregivers.[26]

Life-threatening maneuvers by the elderly that are often not recognized as passive suicide attempts include the following.

1. Refusing medication
2. Not following the physician's orders and recommendations
3. Smoking and drinking against medical advice
4. Refusal to eat or ingesting food but retaining little of it
5. Placing the self in a hazardous environment (near drafty doorway, walking on an icy sidewalk)

When the nurse recognizes these behaviors, she begins to develop a relationship with the elderly person to help him adapt to change and learn new adaptation skills. This may be accomplished by encouraging continuity of care, discouraging relocation, fostering interpersonal mutuality, and reinforcing comfort-giving behavior.[26]

Summary

This chapter presents three major areas of information—the elderly and the nurse, the process of aging, and the promotion of health and adaptation to aging. Some of the major concepts of the chapter include the following.

1. Aging is a process of continual physiological change from birth to death and a continual developmental growth process.

2. Through an understanding of the normal aging process, the nurse is better able to assist the elderly to comprehend the inherent physiological and psychological changes and to cope with these changes through adaptation.

3. The nurse is urged to recognize the myths or stereotyped attitudes about aging and to become aware of her own attitudes toward, or beliefs about, the aged.

4. Nursing provides the elderly with the opportunity to continue to grow throughout the process of aging and to meet death as a person at peace with himself.

Psychosocial Assessment Guide

Sondra George Flemming, R.N., M.S.
Coordinator/Instructor, Nursing
El Centro College
Dallas, TX

Name _____

Age _____

Birthdate _____

Present address _____

Date _____

Person supplying information
(if other than client) _____

Relationship _____

Client Profile:
  Birthplace:
  Where have you resided most of your life?
  Occupation:
    Pre-retirement
      Occupation
      How long were you at this job?
      Occupational stresses and hazards
    Post-retirement
      Did you work after retirement?
      Where?
      How many hours per week?
      Occupational hazards
      Employed or self-employed?
      Are you now employed?
    Retirement
      Date of retirement
      Was it voluntary?
      Was it compulsory?
      Was it because of illness?
      Did you have pre-retirement preparation? (Seminars, counseling, etc.)
      Did you have post-retirement counseling?
  Education:
    Grammar   College
    High School   Graduate or professional school
    Later courses, other education, self-education
  Religion:
    Original family affiliation
    Present affiliation
    Are you an active member?

(continued)

Psychosocial Assessment Guide (continued)

Ethnic, racial, or cultural background:
    Are you an immigrant?   Year of immigration:
    Where did you immigrate from?
Marital status:
    Present status
        Single _____ Separated _____ Widowed _____
        Married _____ Divorced _____
    Marriage most current:
        Name of spouse
        Date of marriage
        Closest anniversary attained
        Date of separation, divorce, or widowhood (specify which)
    Marriage, previous:
        Number of previous marriages
        Dates of previous marriages
        Closest anniversary attained
        Dates of separation, divorce or widowhood (specify which)
    Describe your relationship in the present marriage
Economic status:
    Indicate sources of income:
        Employment   Insurance payments
        Social security   Annuities
        Veteran's benefits   Investments
        Railroad retirement   Savings
        Private pension plan   Assistance from family
        Public assistance   Others
        Do you have financial problems?
        Do you have health care coverage?
Home situation:
    Where do you live?
    Who lives with you?
    Any problems with living situation?
    How do you feel about the amount of space you have?
    Do you have:
        many stairs to climb
        toilet facilities
        running water
        bathing facilities
        cooking facilities
        heating and lighting
    Are there any problems with your neighborhood (crime, accessibility)?
    Do you live near areas with loud noises, fumes, and chemicals?
    Are you able to care for yourself in your home environment?
    Care of home:
        Who cares for the home?
        Who watches the house when you are gone?

Transportation and mobility:
    Do you drive a car?   Own one?   Have access to one?
    Do you wear seat belts?   How do you usually get around?
    Is public transportation available? Do you use it?
    Do you have any physical disabilities that affect your mobility?
    Do you feel safe going out during the day?
    Do you feel safe going out during the night?
    Do you have a telephone?
Availability of family or significant others:
    Relatives
    Friends
Hobbies and special interests:
    Hobbies
    Sports and exercise
    Commercial recreation (movies)
    Music
    Language
    Travel
    Vacation habits (frequency, what do you do during vacations)
    Gardening
    Collecting
    Pets
    Use of community centers
    Community involvement (memberships, clubs)
    Energy levels
        Psychological
        Social
        Sexual
How do you spend an average day?
Dietary History:
    How many meals do you eat a day?   Glasses of water per day?
    How many hot meals a day?
    How do you get your meals?
    Are you on a special diet?
    Do you take vitamins?   What kind?
    Who does the shopping for the food?
    Are shopping areas accessible?
    Who does the cooking?
    How do you pay for the food?
Habits (coffee, alcohol, tobacco, soft drinks)
Personal habits (bite nails, tug hair)
Rituals (hot water in morning)
Neurological:
    Alertness
Ability to communicate and understand
Behavior during assessment
Comments:

Physical and Psychological Changes of the Aging: Diagnosis and Intervention

Nursing Diagnosis	Interventions
Respiratory System Breathing patterns, ineffective	1. Protection from respiratory infection 2. Planned exercise program, preferably walking 3. Periods of rest, if exercising and experiencing shortness of breath
Cardiovascular Cardiac output, alteration in, decreased	1. Periodic monitoring of blood pressure 2. Supervision and instruction in diet as directed; for example, a low salt diet 3. Exercise to maintain cardiac output; for example, walking
Gastrointestinal Bowel elimination, alteration in, constipation	1. Instruction to increase foods high in bulk 2. Adequate fluid intake 3. Teach proper use of laxatives
Nutrition, alteration in, less than body requirements	1. Check for properly fitting dentures 2. Encouragement of dental exam 3. Nutrition instruction related to caloric intake 4. Nutritional guidance with food planning 5. Assess elderly client's ability to prepare own food
Genitourinary Urinary elimination, alteration in patterns	1. Fluid intake of approximately 2000 ml/day 2. Decreased fluid intake prior to sleep 3. Bladder training, if necessary 4. Health teaching of proper cleaning technique following voiding to avoid infection 5. Physical examination of male elderly for prostate changes
Eyes, Ears, Nose, Throat: Injury potential, alteration in eyesight	1. Provide glasses and eye examination, as necessary 2. Remove excess furniture, clear cluttered environment 3. Provide properly lighted area for ambulation 4. Handrails to assist with ambulation 5. Night light in bathroom and bedroom at night
Sensory peceptual alteration, auditory	1. Provide access to hearing aid, if necessary 2. Face client when communicating 3. Speak slowly and enunciate clearly 4. Exclude extraneous background noises when communicating with client 5. Use visual aids as necessary

Nursing Diagnosis	Interventions
Neurological System	
Sleep pattern disturbance	1. Discourage naps during day 2. Provide fresh air and exercise during the day 3. Provide relaxing environment prior to sleep
Thought process alteration, slowing of response	1. Provide adequate time to understand communication 2. Allow adequate time for responses 3. Use visual aids for reality orientation 4. Treat as intelligent adults, able to comprehend events
Integumentary	
Skin integrity, impairment, actual and potential	1. Avoid frequent baths with soap 2. Use lotion to increase moisture to skin 3. Teach proper nail care 4. Safety needs to avoid injury to skin

References

1. Barns EK, Sack A, Shore H: Guidelines to Treatment Approaches. The Gerontologist 13:513–527, 1973
2. Beland IL: Clinical Nursing: Pathophysiological–Psychological Approaches. New York, Macmillan, 1970
3. Burnside IM: Nursing and the Aged. New York, McGraw-Hill, 1976
4. Butler RN: Successful Aging and the Role of Life Review. J Am Geriatr Soc 22 (December): 529–535, 1974
5. Campbell ME: Study of the Attitudes of Nursing Personnel Toward Geriatric Patients. Nurs Res 20:147–151, 1971
6. Combs KL: Preventive Care in the Elderly. Am J Nurs 78 (August): 1339–1341, 1978
7. Craven RF: Primary Health Care Practice in a Nursing Home. Am J Nurs 76 (December): 1958–1960, 1976
8. Davis RW: Psychological Aspects of Geriatric Nursing. Am J Nurs 68 (April): 802–804, 1968
9. Dickelmann N: Pre-Retirement Counseling. Am J Nurs 78 (August): 1337–1338, 1978
10. Dresen SE: Autonomy: A Continuing Developmental Task. Am J Nurs 78 (August): 1344–1346, 1978
11. Erikson E: Childhood and Society, 2nd ed. New York, WW Norton, 1964
12. Fischer J: Competence, Effectiveness, Intellectual Functioning and Aging. The Gerontologist 13:62–68, 1973
13. Furukawa C, Somaker D: Community Health Service for the Elderly. Rockville, MD, Aspen Publishing, 1981
14. Graves M: Physiological Changes and Major Diseases in the Older Adult. In Hagstel MO (ed): Nursing Care of the Older Adult: In the Hospital, Nursing Home and Community. New York, John Wiley & Sons, 1981
15. Gray PL: Gerontological Nurse Specialist: Luxury or Necessity. Am J Nurs 82 (January): 82–85, 1982
16. Haber J, Leach A, Schudy S, Sideleau BL: Comprehensive Psychiatric Nursing. New York, McGraw-Hill, 1982
17. Hacker SL: Patients' Effect on Mental Health Professionals. The Gerontologist 12:54–57, 1973
18. Hagstel MO: How Do Elderly View Their World? Am J Nurs 78 (August): 1335–1338, 1978
19. Hagstel MO (ed): Nursing Care of the Older Adult: In the Hospital, Nursing Home and Community. New York, John Wiley & Sons, 1981
20. Herr JJ: Psychology of Aging: An Overview. In Burnside I (ed): Nursing and the Aged. New York, McGraw-Hill, 1976
21. Hirschfeld MJ: The Cognitive Impaired Older Adult. Am J Nurs 76 (December): 1981–1984, 1976
22. Hoff LA: People in Crisis. Menlo Park, CA, Addison-Wesley, 1978
23. Kabrynski B: Innovation in Programs of Care for the Elderly. The Gerontologist 13:50–53, 1973
24. Kart CS, Metress ES, Metress JF: Aging and Health: Biologic and Social Perspectives. Menlo Park, CA, Addison-Wesley, 1978
25. Kastenbaum R, Aisenberg R: The Psychology of Death. New York, Springer-Verlag, 1976
26. Kastenbaum R, Mishara Braue L: Premature Death and Self-Injurious Behavior in Old Age. In Kastenbaum R (ed): Old Age on the New Scene. New York, Springer-Verlag, 1981
27. Leberman M: Institutionalization of the Aged: Effects on Behavior. J Gerontol 24:330–340, 1969
28. Miller M: Suicide After Sixty: The Final Alternative. New York, Springer-Verlag, 1979
29. Murray RB, Zentner JP: Nursing Concepts for Health Promotion. Englewood Cliffs, NJ, Prentice-Hall, 1979
30. Oberleder M: Psychotherapy with the Aging: An Art of the Possible. Psychotherapy 3:139–142, 1966

31. Pasner J: Notes on the Negative Implications of Being Competent in a Home for the Aged. Int J Aging Hum Dev 5:357–362, 1974

32. Pasquali EA, Alesi EG, Arnold HM, Debasio N: Mental Health Nursing: A Bio-Psycho-Cultural Approach. St Louis, CV Mosby, 1981

33. Peterson BH: The Age of Aging. Aust NZ J Psychiatry 7:9–16, 1973

34. Robinson L: Psychiatric Nursing as a Human Experience, 3rd ed. Philadelphia, WB Saunders, 1983

35. Rossman I: Human Aging Changes. In Burnside IM (ed): Nursing and the Aged. New York, McGraw-Hill, 1976

36. Stone V: Give the Older People Time. Am J Nurs 69 (October): 2124–2127, 1969

37. Ubler DM: Common Skin Changes in the Elderly. Am J Nurs 78 (August): 1342–1344, 1978

38. Ullman LP, Krasner LA: A Psychological Approach to Abnormal Behavior. Englewood Cliffs, NJ, Prentice-Hall, 1969

39. Wilkie F, Eisdorfer C: Intelligence and Blood Pressure in the Aged. Science 172:959–962, 1971

Chapter 28
Mental Retardation

Like the surprise and wonder of finding the sky, revolution can't be planned. It happens when you least expect it. Its clerics are not bigger than life but humble and simple souls. Like the person next to you. Revolution is a Rosa Parks, who decides one day not to ride in the back of the bus. Or a navy nurse named Mrs. Nelson, who suddenly refuses to let her children be condemned to a label.

Ron Jones,
The Acorn People,
1976

Peggy J. Drapo

Chapter Preview

This chapter focuses on the definitions, causes, and descriptions of retardation. The many causes and manifestations of mental retardation lead to misunderstanding and often poorly planned care of the retarded.

The chapter defines mental retardation, discusses the varied aspects of daily living and its problems for the person who is retarded, and explains the application of the nursing process to the care of the retarded. It is hoped that a greater awareness of the causes of mental retardation will strengthen the nurse's interest in preventive efforts.

No one chapter in any book can teach all there is to know about mental retardation; it is a nursing specialty in its own right. Another aim of the chapter, therefore, is to stimulate nursing interest in the field so that we may become instrumental in demystifying the problems of mental retardation for the general public.

Learning Objectives

On completion of the chapter, the reader should be able to accomplish the following.

1. Define mental retardation
2. Identify levels of mental retardation as described by Stanford–Binet, Cattell, and Wechsler
3. Discuss the incidence of and significant issues related to mental retardation
4. Identify the leading causes of mental retardation
5. Discuss the effects of the birth of a child with a mental or physical disorder on family relationships
6. Apply the nursing process to the care of a child or adult who is retarded

   Assess the biologic, sociologic, and psychological functioning of the retarded client

   Identify nursing interventions to assist the client to achieve goals

   Formulate plans to reduce the prenatal, perinatal, and postnatal risks of retardation

   Design a care plan for a mentally retarded child or adult

   Design a care plan for an emotionally disturbed retarded client

   Evaluate the effectiveness of nursing intervention with the retarded client
7. Recognize the role of the nurse advocate in the care of clients with mental retardation and related physical disabilities

Defining Mental Retardation

Mental retardation is defined by the American Association of Mental Deficiency (AAMD) as a significantly subaverage general intellectual functioning existing concurrently with deficits in adaptive behavior and manifesting itself during the developmental period.[4] This definition refers to an intelligence quotient, or IQ, two or more standard deviations from the mean average (100) for the population tested. Therefore, two standard deviations below the score would be an IQ of 70 or below. Two standard deviations above the score would be considered IQ ranges for the gifted.

Mental retardation is actually a constellation of symptoms, rather than a disease, although it may result from a disease. Terms used in the descriptions of mental retardation are often confusing. *Subaverage intellectual functioning*, according to the AAMD, means that the client's performance on objective testing is below that expected for his chronological age. *Adaptive behavior* refers to the maturation, learning, and social adjustment of the client. Maturation is the period of development from birth to 18 years. This definition distinguishes mental retardation from other behavior disorders that may occur after the developmental period.[22]

Classification of Mental Retardation

Labeling is a difficult and serious responsibility in the field of mental retardation. Systems of labeling vary, and the danger in attaching labels is that it may affect the care, treatment, and education of retarded persons. Parameters for classification should take into consideration the complex other factors that often surround the diagnosis of mental retardation. These include symptom severity, symptom etiology, syndrome description, adaptive behavior, educability expectations, and behavioral manifestations.[5]

The accepted classification is the use of the labels *mild*, *moderate*, *severe*, and *profound*, rather than old terms of *borderline*, *moron*, *imbecile*, and *idiot*. Depending on the test used, the symptom severity may vary slightly. The scoring accepted by the AAMD places the mildly retarded person in the IQ range of 69 to 55; the moderately or trainable person in the 54 to 40 category; the severely retarded in the IQ range of 39 to 25; and the profoundly retarded at less than 25.[4]

Testing

The standard tests usually employed during childhood are the Stanford–Binet and the Wechsler Intelligence Scale for Children. During the first 3 years, the Cattell, Gesell, and Bayley tests are most often used. The latter three tests are reliable determinates of the child's developmental quotient and are rather accurate predictors of future problems with mental retardation.

According to Stanford–Binet and Cattell, levels of intellectual functioning are as follows.

Mild	68–52
Moderate	51–36
Severe	35–20
Profound	19 and below

The standard deviation for this test is 16.

The Wechsler scale has a standard deviation of 15 and the following levels of intellectual functioning.

Mild   69–55
Moderate   54–40
Severe   39–25
Profound   24 and below

Tests are set up to evaluate certain skills. The Wechsler Intelligence Scale for Children (WISC), for instance, uses subtests that cover verbal skills of general information, general comprehension, arithmetic, similarities, vocabulary, and digit span. Performance is tested by picture completion, picture arrangement, block design, object assembly, coding, and mazes. Performances on tests are compared to average abilities of persons at different chronological ages. The Stanford–Binet uses various tests to measure a wide range of abilities closely associated with various mental ages.[19]

The figures or numbers in IQ ranges do not mean a great deal unless you know that mildly retarded individuals may be able to learn academic skills up to sixth grade level during school years, and are capable of social and vocational adequacy in adulthood if given opportunities and instruction. Moderately retarded persons generally can learn the basics of self-care in childhood, functional academic skills to grade-school level during school years, and, as adults, may be able to accomplish a semi-skilled occupation. The severely retarded need controlled environments in which, by adulthood, they are able to learn the skills of communication, self-protection, health habits, and sheltered workshop vocations. The profoundly retarded usually need complete care and supervision during all of their lives, but may develop some motor and speech development.[26]

Incidence and Significance of the Problem

The incidence of mental retardation in the United States is thought to be approximately 3% of the population or about 6½ million persons;[21] however, these figures are theoretical and other authors suggest that the incidence and prevalence of mental retardation may change with the accumulation of data or with changing definitions. Until it is feasible to collect more data, the most quoted and accepted figure is that of 3% of the population.

The problem confronting professionals who work with the mentally retarded is that mental retardation is not always a separate entity that affects the child. Most often, it is associated with other conditions. Caring for the retarded child means knowing how to care for the accompanying developmental disabilities. The nurse who chooses to work in the field of mental retardation must also be able to care for children with a spectrum of impairments. Nevertheless, all nurses should know the basics of care for individuals with mental retardation because they are living longer and normalization efforts are bringing them out of institutions into the mainstream of society. Increasing numbers of children are being cared for in the home with the help of outreach professionals who help the family learn how to care for their child with handicaps.

For nurses in general, the aspect of prevention of mental retardation is of greatest importance. The goals of the nurse should be, first, to promote preventive efforts and, secondly, to prevent problems related to mental retardation. Nevertheless, before one can prevent disorders from occurring, the nurse must first recognize the causes and manifestations of retardation.

Every outreach team and education team should include a nurse who is knowledgeable about mental retardation and the physical disabilities that are often associated with it. Every newborn nursery nurse, pediatric nurse, and public health nurse should be able to perform an assessment that will discern disabilities, should be skilled and comfortable teaching and listening to families, should recognize risk factors, and should assist families to find resources.

Legislation

Every year, more than 125,000 infants are born who will be diagnosed at some point in their developmental history as mentally retarded. One in 10 persons in America will have a mentally retarded person in their immediate family. Probably because of the growing interest in the rights of members of our society who are mentally or physically handicapped, the federal government has tried to insure through laws what society has neglected to do by itself. Recent legislation such as Public law 94-142, the Education of All Handicapped Children Act of 1977, and the Developmentally Disabled Assistance and Bill of Rights Act of 1975 (P.L. 94-103), are examples of a trend toward more humane treatment of persons with disabilities.

Public Law 94-142 insures that extensive child identification procedures will be carried out to find children who are handicapped and in need of education. The parents are assured of full service and are also assured that those programs will be maintained. Within these programs, children are to be educated in the least restrictive environment and with nondiscriminatory testing and evaluation. The provision of a free, appropriate public education at no cost to the parents or guardians is also assured.

Public Law 94-103 is a bill of similar language that details the rights of the developmentally disabled for services, treatment, and habilitation in institutions and other residential programs.[10]

These bills and others like them were long overdue but are having far-reaching implications for education and services. Currently, many programs serving the retarded are gravely concerned that funding will be reduced or that new legislation will erase the gains made because of the conservative mood of the government. For the legislation that has been passed to succeed, there must be appropriate funding, social incentives, and administrative action. Interest in legislation that affects retarded clients and their families should be a nursing concern.

Ethical and Moral Issues

Mental retardation and physical disability raise significant ethical and moral concerns. Nurses need to evaluate their own feelings in regard to several factors that have customarily been linked with retardation. Some of the nurse's self-directed questions are as follows.

1. How do I feel about the worth of retarded or physically disabled persons? Do I consider them of use to society?
2. Am I willing to support legislation that insures human rights of the disabled? Am I prepared to be an advocate who works to insure that these laws are carried out in more than a token fashion? Am I willing to educate the public, legislators, and the profession to bring the needs of the disabled and legislation in closer proximity?
3. What are my thoughts on institutionalization?
4. Some forms of prevention of mental and physical disability may entail issues such as abortion. What do I believe about the use of abortion as a method of prevention?
5. What are my thoughts and feelings about the use of high technology and high cost efforts to preserve the life of premature infants?
6. Am I willing to support financially, through my taxes, programs that stress prevention?
7. How do I feel about the corrective surgery needs of disabled individuals when these surgeries may prolong their lives?

The recent legislation also raised questions about the educational preparation of nurses. Prior to normalization efforts, the retarded and physically handicapped were placed in specialized institutions for custodial care. If nurses cared to work within this specialized area they had to receive on-the-job training. With the advent of community living, nurses in all health care settings need to be aware of the special needs of handicapped patients. Clinical care opportunities and theoretical information about mental retardation and related disabilities should be included in the basic curricula of nursing education.[14]

Etiology

The causes of mental retardation are multiple. In surveying a list of factors, one is able to envision that nearly all areas of nursing specialization are challenged. Our efforts must be directed at prevention as well as treatment. The etiology of mental retardation arises from two main sources, genetic and acquired factors.

Genetic Factors

Mental retardation is often associated with genetic aberrations. Chromosomal abnormalities, such as errors in the number of chromosomes, result in too many or too few chromosomes. The normal structure of the chromosome may also be changed because of breakage and subsequent loss, or by addition of pieces to a chromosome. Another cause of chromosomal abnormalities may be changes in genes, in which cases no karyotype differences are noticed.

To visualize the chromosomes for study, a cytogenetic lab technician photographs a cell from blood or skin samples during metaphase, enlarges it several thousand times, and then cuts and pastes these enlarged pictures of the chromosomes, matching pairs together. This procedure is called karyotyping. A karyotype is a picture of the chromosomes matched in an order based on length, position of centromere, and banding (see Fig. 28-1). In the banding process, dye is applied to the cells and the dye is absorbed by deoxyribonucleic acid (DNA). Bands of DNA material are visible in the photographs and can be matched to bands on homologous chromosomes. Each pair of chromosomes has a unique banding pattern that is characteristic for humans (see Fig. 28-2). Chromosomal aberrations can be visualized. A broken piece of chromosome without a centromere can reattach and heal, translocate, or become lost. The resulting problems are either an inheritance of too many genes as in translocation, or the loss of the genes. The problem to the fetus depends on the quality and quantity of the genetic material. The karyotype is useful to illustrate these problems; therefore, scientists are able to visualize the abnormal chromosome(s) more readily.

There are normally 46 chromosomes in a human cell. In preparing a karyotype, one begins row 1 with the 3 longest pairs of chromosomes (group A) of which pair number 1 is the longest. Group B contains pairs 4 and 5. The second row (group C) consists of slightly smaller chromosomes which are pairs 6 through 12. The third row contains group D (13–15) and E (16–18). The fourth row is group F (19–20) and G (21–22). The other two chromosomes, known as the sex chromosomes, are the X and Y chromosomes which belong to groups C and G, respectively, located at the bottom of the karyotype. If the karyotype is a female, there are two X chromosomes (XX); for a male, there will be an X and a Y.

Down's syndrome is a condition in which during the process of gametogenesis, nondisjunction occurs (see Fig. 28-3). Normally, the spindle fibers of the cell pull the chromosomes apart from each other and new cells are formed containing half (23) of the complement of chromosomes. Sometimes, this process goes awry. The result is one cell lacking a chromosome and the other cell now containing two. In Down's syndrome, the number 21 chromosome undergoes nondisjunction. The germ cell (ovum) now contains 24 chromosomes instead of the normal 23. If this cell is fertilized by a sperm containing 23 chromosomes, the resulting zygote has 47 chromosomes—22 pairs of autosomes plus one extra number 21 chromosome, and two sex chromosomes. The consequences of this nondisjunction are that it alters not only the physical appearance of the infant

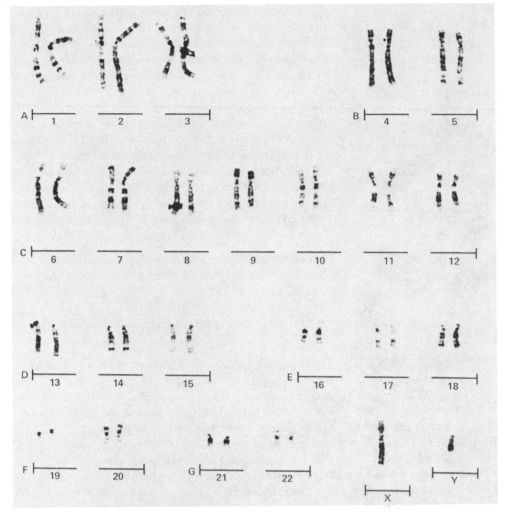

Figure 28-1. *Photo of a normal male karyotype.*

but also causes retardation. Down's syndrome may also oc-cur as a result of nondisjunction in the first cell division of the zygote. These two possibilities account for the high incidence of Down's syndrome and the results are children born with full trisomy 21. A great many of those persons who are institutionalized have Down's syndrome. The reader needs to be aware that some genetic diseases are due to mosaicism; however, this is beyond the scope of this chapter and will not be discussed.

A piece of a chromosome may break off and attach itself to another chromosome. This is called *translocation* (see Fig. 28-4). Down's syndrome is sometimes transmitted by this method also. A piece of a number 21 chromosome breaks off and attaches to another chromosome, such as the number 15. If, during oogenesis, the normal number 21 chromosome and the number 15 chromosome with the translocated number 21 piece are grouped in the same ovum and fertilized, the result is two normal number 21 auto-somes, one from each parent, and two number 15 auto-somes, one of which contains extra number 21 material.

Turner's syndrome (XO) is a situation in which one of the X chromosomes is missing due to nondisjunction, resulting in a female with 45 chromosomes (see Fig. 28-5). If the ovum containing no X chromosome is fertilized by sperm with the Y chromosome, the zygote is not viable; however, if the sperm contains an X chromosome and fer-tilizes an egg containing no X chromosome, the resulting individual has the physical characteristics of a female, but is usually sterile and secondary sex characteristics develop poorly at puberty. Approximately 20% of individuals with Turner's syndrome are mentally retarded.

Another condition called Polysomy of X (three or more X-chromosomes per cell) results in individuals having female sex characteristics. This condition is commonly called "super female." The result is not accentuated fe-maleness, but mental retardation and behavior problems.

Klinefelter's syndrome (multiple X and Y chromo-somes) depicts a masculine appearance because of the pres-ence of a Y chromosome, but the problem results from one or more extra X chromosomes (see Fig. 28-6). At puberty,

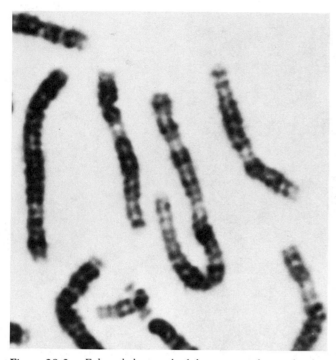

Figure 28-2. *Enlarged photograph of chromosomes showing banding technique.*

female sexual characteristics develop. The male gonads are undeveloped and sterile. Mental retardation and behavioral problems usually, but not always, occur. Males may also be born with an XYY anomaly. This condition may produce a dull mentality, usually in the 80 to 95 IQ range. Internal and external genitalia are often affected and the individual is usually quite tall. Some studies indicate that the aggressiveness attributed to these males with an XYY anomaly is related to their height acquired early in childhood, which resulted in teasing by peers. Other studies attempt to link their behavior with significant psychological differences.

There are over 2000 disorders catalogued by McKusic that are caused by Mendelian inheritance in man.[18] Mendelian inheritance refers to rules governing the transmission of unit factors (genes) that were first described by Gregor Mendel in 1866 as a result of his experiments with garden peas. In essence, his first law states that an individual is formed as a result of the union of a sperm and an egg, each of which receives half of the genetic material found in the somatic cells of the father and mother, respectively. Genes for the traits may either be dominant or recessive.

Chromosomal differences remain the problem but these differences are genic; that is, chemical or submicroscopic in nature. Some of these differences at the cellular level may affect many body systems. Some genetic disorders of metabolism involve the following.

1. Amino acids causing phenylketonuria (PKU)
2. Mucopolysaccharides leading to Hunter's or Hurler's disease
3. Lipids causing Tay-Sachs disease
4. Carbohydrates causing galactosemia
5. Purines causing Lesch-Nyhan syndrome

There are also hereditary, degenerative diseases and endocrine disorders that may cause mental retardation. One endocrine disorder that causes mental retardation is a deficiency of the thyroid hormone leading to cretinism, a failure to develop both physically and mentally.

Some of the above conditions are transmitted in a dominant or recessive fashion. The presence of an abnormal recessive gene, if paired with a normal dominant gene, will not be expressed. If, however, the abnormal recessive gene is paired with an abnormal recessive gene from the other parent, the trait or disorder will occur. A dominant gene will produce its effect whether its homologous allele is dominant or recessive (see Fig. 28-7).

Dominantly inherited genetic disorders are said to be milder than those which are due to recessive or X-linked

Figure 28-3. *Graphic depicting normal cell division and nondisjunction.*

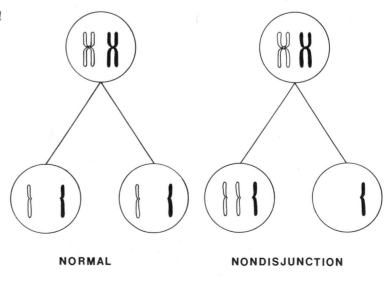

NORMAL   **NONDISJUNCTION**

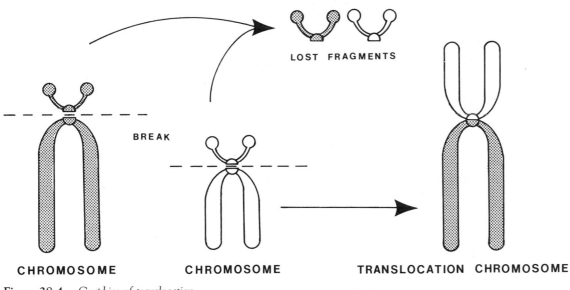

LOST FRAGMENTS

BREAK

CHROMOSOME　　　CHROMOSOME　　　TRANSLOCATION CHROMOSOME

Figure 28-4.　*Graphics of translocation.*

genes, and usually result in structural defects.[15] Mental retardation resulting from a dominantly inherited disorder is usually mild; recessive disorders are more serious (see Fig. 28-8). Phenylketonuria, for instance, is such a disorder. Profound retardation often occurs with inborn errors of metabolism. These errors may appear on the X chromosome also. The Lesch-Nyhan syndrome, for instance, will cause profound retardation. There are about 150 disorders and traits resulting from altered genes on the X chromosome, but the mode of inheritance is slightly different.

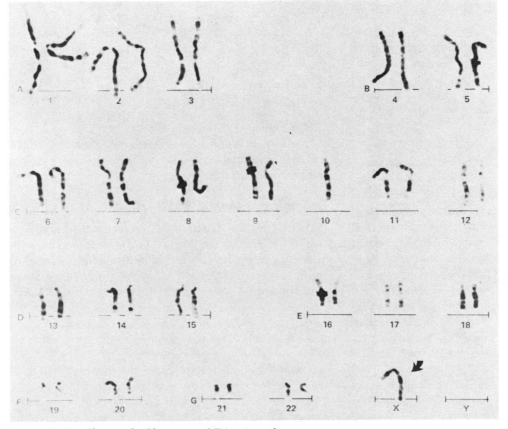

Figure 28-5.　*Photograph of karyotype of Turner's syndrome.*

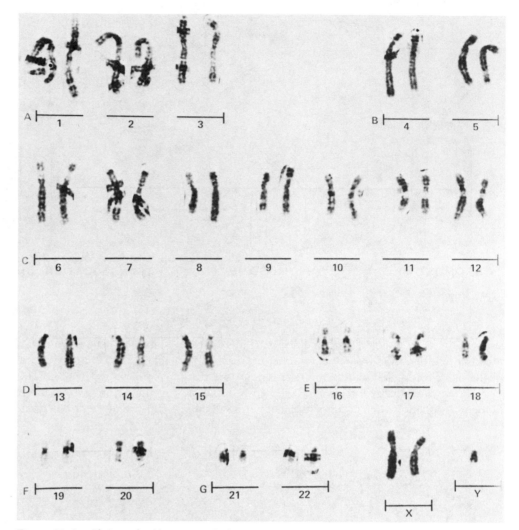

Figure 28-6. *Photograph of karyotype of Klinefelter's syndrome.*

Acquired Factors

Acquired mental retardation involves prenatal, perinatal, and postnatal factors. Prenatal factors are infections, irradiation, toxins, drugs, and unknown causes. Perinatally, one of the most common causes of mental retardation is prematurity. Other factors are anoxia, brain damage, and infection. *Postnatal* conditions include childhood diseases, accidents, infection, anoxia, poisoning, hormonal problems, and influences in the child's environment.

Birth defects such as cerebral palsy, deafness, and blindness may lead to sensory deprivation and may, therefore, result in mental retardation. Early childhood intervention is of great importance in preventing retardation resulting from these problems and will be discussed in more detail later in the chapter.

Psychiatric disorders may retard learning progress because of problematic behavioral activity. Child abuse may cause mental retardation through trauma or deprivation.

It is clear that prevention of mental retardation be-

gins as early as family planning and continues throughout the developmental years. The nursing process is a tool in the preventive efforts.

Dynamics of Mental Retardation

In today's nuclear family, both parents usually pursue a career or job before the birth of a child. Many continue to work outside the home after the birth due to financial or career reasons. Inflaton and high interest rates are tremendous burdens on young people trying to establish a home. The new issues related to women's rights also affect the nuclear family. Sometimes, the mother works outside the home because she wants a career and a life apart from that of housewife and motherhood. Finding adequate child care and resolving conflicts surrounding the changing lifestyle of young couples today create problems. A new child in the family may create unity toward a common goal or may result in such dramatic lifestyle changes that parents are caught up in conflict and strife.[33]

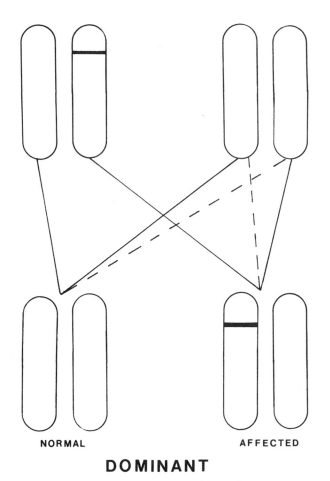

NORMAL   AFFECTED

DOMINANT

Figure 28-7. *Graphic of dominant Mendelian inheritance in man.*

Mothers who choose to breast feed often face difficulties arranging breastfeeding to fit with a job schedule. Guilt and anxiety may be outcomes of trying to manage a home, parenthood, and a career. Old friendships with childless couples are altered, thereby changing social outlets for the young parents. Apartments or other rental properties in which children are welcome are not easily located.

Parents are not, however, without compensation when a child is born. The birth of a beautiful baby is the outcome of prior planning and the wait during the months of pregnancy. Family and friends delight with the new parents during this happy occasion. The fun of planning showers, creating a nursery and layette, and buying baby equipment is shared by all who are close to the couple.

Future life is family-oriented. Friends begin to have families also. New friends are found with common interests. Vacations revolve around activities that can be shared by the family, such as trips to the mountains, the beach, sightseeing, and involving the family in favorite recreation activities. As children are added to the family, the lifestyle continues to evolve.

The birth of a child with a disability is often a cataclysmic event to the family. For a young couple, already in transition, it is particularly traumatic. Every member of the extended family is affected by this event. Support, both psychological and financial, are of prime importance and often difficult to obtain. Misunderstanding about the cause of this disability and the need to place blame by well-meaning family members and friends cause additional stress to the family.

For the friend, family member, or professional who spends limited time within this situation, the viewpoint is not the same as it is for the parents who spend all of their time with the child. A once-busy social life grinds to a halt. The parent, frustrated at trying to find resources and help for the child, is often regarded as an "overanxious parent," a term used by a great many sources, many of them professional.

In order to develop a therapeutic relationship with the family, it is imperative for nurses to understand the normal sequence of stages a parent must work through before intervention can be planned that will be most useful.

Stages of Recognition and Acceptance of a Disability

Some authors believe that parents move through several stages before they are able to recognize and accept the reality of their child's disability. Before parents can begin to receive help they first must develop an awareness that a problem exists. Following this, recognition of the basic problem must occur.[5] For some parents of infants who are severely handicapped, recognition of the disorder is immediate.

The impact of the birth of a handicapped child may cause stress disorders at a time when the parent is also trying to resolve stressful situations of childbirth and maturational status. A mother must resolve several maternal tasks following birth before she feels normal and whole again.[20] These tasks are psychological processes bringing even a normal birth to a full course.

1. Grief work—relinquishing expectations of herself and infant and adapting to reality
2. Infant's performance—measuring the infant's ability to function compared to other infants, before she will lose fearfulness about infant's wholeness
3. Mothering skills—expending energy on developing and performing simple mothering skills
4. Redefining roles—renewing the relationship with the child's father, which is important to her emotional adjustment
5. Resuming other responsibilities—moving from the passive-dependent role to that of taking over responsibilities at home

These normal tasks for the new mother are seriously jeopardized if the child is born with mental retardation or physical disability. The postpartum nurse, through early intervention, may be the first caregiver to assist the family with these maternal tasks.

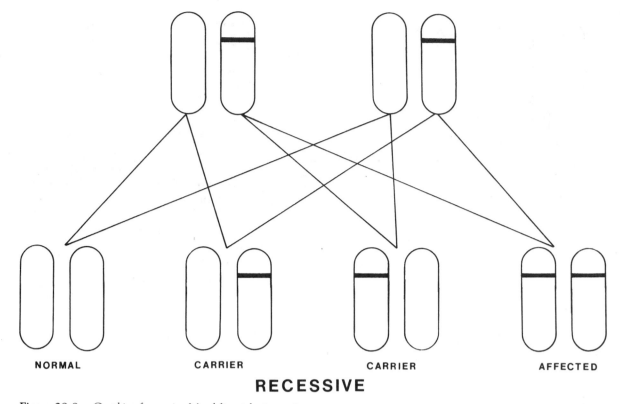

Figure 28-8. *Graphic of recessive Mendelian inheritance in man.*

The next stage is the parent's search for a cause. Whether the cause of the child's condition is genetic in nature, the result of a maternal-environmental condition, or due to infection is important to the family. Blame-placing is an outcome at this point. No one likes to feel that the child's condition may result from a fault on his or her side of the family.

The fourth stage is the searching for a way to heal the child. Until this stage is worked through, the parent may run from one doctor to another or one therapeutic method to another. This often is frustrating to the physician who is the primary caregiver when he discovers that the parent is also putting the child through such things as polyvitamin or megavitamin therapies, patterning, consultation for surgeries, and various adaptive devices, all of which the physician has neither recommended nor planned for this child.

It is only when one reaches the final stage, that of acceptance, that the parent is able to work optimally toward goals of care for this child. Early childhood intervention is of primary importance. A dynamic infant stimulation program can "run defense" for both child and parent. Research has shown that early intervention increases children's learning capacities and social awareness.[11] Likewise, without this therapy the child can, early on, learn helplessness. A handicapped infant is more likely to experience failure and learn to be helpless because those who care for the infant are prone to do everything for the baby. Helping the family overcome this tendency and become more therapeutic is,

more than anything else, the rationale for infant stimulation programs.

By understanding phases and stages that parents experience, the nurse is able to plan effective intervention to expedite the acceptance process. Denial, guilt, and grief, if not worked through successfully, may lead to pathology in the final stages of withdrawal and rejection. These stages, in the extreme, can lead to a lifetime of behaviors that will hinder acceptance of the child.

Application of the Nursing Process to the Mentally Retarded Client

The nursing process is based on assessment, analysis, planning, intervention, evaluation, and revision of the plan. A client does not have to be ill for the nurse to use this process. The nurse easily uses the process to help prevent problems and to maintain wellness. The nursing process is simply a method of applying nursing care in any health care setting. This section of the chapter outlines some ways that nurses use the nursing process to promote optimal wellness of the retarded client.

Assessment and Analysis

During infancy and early childhood, developmental screening is of primary importance in finding children at risk for mental retardation. All of the systems need to be assessed, particularly the neurologic, muscular, and skeletal systems, all of which may offer indications of problem areas.

It is not too early, during the family planning stage, to begin preventive nursing. Nurses who have the opportunity to work with families may begin the assessment of risk factors at this time. A good way to start a risk factor history is through a pedigree chart, which is a diagram in which family health or genetics are arranged in graphic form for easy visualization.

Knowledge of growth and development is necessary in screening infants and children for signs of mental retardation. The insert, Physical Assessment: Checklist for Developmental Defects, is a beginning point for the nurse–assessor. It is meant to serve as a guide to normal growth and development and to the recognition of deviations from the norm. Many children have some of these deviations and are considered normal. Genetic counseling centers urge nurses to refer clients or their families who have two or more minor anomalies for genetic counseling because several small birth anomalies may signify a more major defect elsewhere. Major anomalies, of course, must be referred. Careful follow-up of developmental lags should be accomplished as the child develops. Early intervention is very important to the child and assists the parent in his care. Assessment parameters also include social and peer interaction. Newborns are assessed in the following areas.

Response to light, sound, and pin prick
Orientation to inanimate and animate visual and auditory stimuli
Alertness
Muscle tone and pulling to sit
Cuddling
Defensive movements
Consolability
Excitement
Irritability
Activity
Tremulousness
Color changes of skin
Startle behavior
Self-quieting
Hand-to-mouth movements
Smiling

Assessment of infant's behavior using tools, such as the Brazelton scale, gives clues to the child's developmental outcomes. Abnormalities are easily spotted when this tool is used to assess children at risk for retardation or disability.

Normal Developmental Tasks

Developmental tasks for infants and children are to

1. acquire motor skills;
2. acquire feeding skills;
3. develop effective communication skills;
4. develop beginning control of bowel and bladder function;
5. form simple concepts about the self and environment;
6. develop social and emotional relationships with others whom the child perceives as significant.

Developmental tasks of preschool children are to

1. refine motor skills;
2. further establish communication skills;
3. accomplish toilet training;
4. develop pre-operational thought processes;
5. learn to relate to peers and adults in the outside world;
6. develop value sense;
7. develop sexual identity and modesty;
8. develop ideas of self-worth.

Developmental tasks of school-aged children are to

1. develop and use logical thought;
2. define sex role and self-identity;
3. develop competencies;
4. develop a peer group;
5. expand autonomy;
6. develop internal controls for moral code;
7. develop the ability to handle stress.

Developmental tasks for adolescents are to

1. utilize abstract thought;
2. establish self-identity and sexual role;
3. establish independency and develop interdependent relationships;
4. choose an occupation and prepare for it;
5. develop a personal value system.[23]

When assessing any child or young person, these are the tasks (listed above) that must be observed and evaluated. The person who is retarded has the same needs, and if normalization is to succeed, he must be helped to acquire as many skills as possible.

Eating Ability

The skill required to eat in an acceptable manner is one that must be developed if the child is to achieve autonomy. Many retarded individuals may reach adulthood spilling food, eating with their hands, stealing food from others' plates, and picking up food off of the floor and eating it. An assessment of the individual's eating ability is the forerunner of a program to upgrade the individual's skills. Chances to practice are important and, as the client learns, opportunities to eat in public are effective training methods.

Communication Skills

Language skills are crucial for all individuals. Speech is simply one form of language development. Language skills are still being learned as the retarded person grows to adult-

(*Text continues on p. 446*)

Physical Assessment: Checklist for Developmental Defects

Head

Size—Normal range for male is approximately 34.5 cm at birth → 49 cm at 2 years.

Normal range for female is approximately 34 cm at birth → 48 cm at 2 years.

Microcephaly—limited brain size two standard deviations below norm. May have abnormality of brain tissue.

Hydrocephaly—increase in amount of cerebrospinal fluid. Brain size may be normal or smaller than average. Head size increases due to increased fluid.

The size of head is extremely important because the first 2 years of child's life is vital for brain growth.

Shape—Should be normocephalic. Abnormal findings may be in these areas:

Prominent forehead—as found in Hurler's syndrome.

Premature closing of suture lines—giving rise to oxycephaly, scaphocephaly, plagiocephaly, trigonocephaly.

Late closure of fontanels—most will be closed by 9 to 19 months. Late closure could indicate cretinism, Down's, rickets, osteogenesis imperfecta, hydrocephalus, or syphilis. Mean anterior fontanel diameter 2.1 cm two standard deviations above or below (0.6 and 3.6 cm respectively) are important. Posterior fontanels rarely exceed measurements of 0.5 cm.

Face

Observe for spacing of features, symmetry, and signs of paralysis. The width of a newborn face is approximately 8 cm.

Eyes

Eyes are same level and normally spaced.

Hypertelorism—refers to wide spaced orbits. This is frequently associated with some syndromes of mental retardation. Mean distance between inner canthi for term infant is 2 cm. Three cm is judged as hypertelorism.

Hypotelorism—abnormally close-set eyes. May indicate lack of nasal bridge or trigonocephaly.

Micropthalmia—May indicate encephaloopthalmic dysplasia, toxoplasmosis, or retrolental fibroplasia.

Protruding supraorbital ridge—found in mucopolysaccharidosis and Marfan's disease.

Ptosis of lids—Some neurologic problems may cause this. Sometimes, it is an inherited trait. Family history is important.

Slanting of eyes—Downward slant may be indicative of Treacher–Collins syndrome (antimongolian slant). Upward slant may be Down's syndrome (mongolian slant).

Epicanthal folds—May be present in some normal children. Most will disappear by 10 years of age. May be present as a result of Down's syndrome, glycogen storage disease, renal agenesis, or hypercalcemia.

Eye lashes—very bushy; may indicate some syndrome disorders such as Hurler's syndrome. If absent on inner two thirds, it may indicate Treacher–Collins' disease.

Eye-brows—They grow together in center and may indicate a genetic syndrome such as Cornelia de Lange syndrome.

Color of iris—Permanent color will be established in all children by 1 year. Pinkish coloration may indicate albinism, light or white speckling (Brushfield spots) often found in children with Down's syndrome.

Lens—Absent red reflex may indicate cataracts. These can be due to many problems leading to mental retardation plasmosis. A dislocated lens may be the result of Marfan's syndrome or homocystinuria.

Ears

Normally, the upper part of the pinna should meet an imaginary line that is drawn from the lateral aspect of the eye straight backward. This will indicate if the ear is normally positioned or low set. The rotation of the ear is also important. A vertical line is drawn from the lobe of the ear straight up crossing the horizontal line. The measurement should not be more than a 10 degree angle. Abnormally shaped ears are also found in various disorders and should be reported. Look to see if both ears are at the same level. Are they flat or protruding? Are they bigger or smaller than normal? Check the size and completeness of ear lobes. Check for sinuses or tags of skin on the ear.

Nose

The nose should be observed to be at the middle and upper part of face. In many syndromes, the nose is shaped differently than the normal nose. In some cases, it is broad and flat, small and turned up, or beaklike. Notice if the nose is straight. Are the nares symmetrical? Palpate to examine bone and cartilage. Transilluminate with a flashlight on one nare and look into the other to determine if perforation of the septum exists.

Mouth

Is the mouth symmetrical? Are there clefts in the lip or palate? Drooling starts about 3 months and continues until the child learns to swallow saliva about 9 to 12 months. Examine the palate for a gentle slope. Report a high arched palate. If a notch is felt at the junction of the soft and hard palate, report this as it may cause future speech difficulty. The lower jaw that is excessively small or large may indicate genetic problems that warrant further evaluation. Teeth that are delayed past 1 year of age may be a result of cretinism. Gums that have a black line along the margin may be a sign of metal poisoning. Do not confuse this with the normal dark pigmented coloration on the gums of black children. The tongue that seems large for the mouth may indicate Down's syndrome, cretinism, or Hurler's syndrome. Protrusion of the tongue is a common finding in mental retardation. Note the normal developmental sequence of feeding. The rooting reflex disappears by 3 months. Sucking-swallowing remains for 3 to 5 months. The gag reflex diminishes slightly after child begins to chew or at about 7 months. The bite reflex disappears about 3 to 5 months. Lip closure begins about 6 to 8 months.

Hair

Normally, head hair should begin high over the forehead. Some syndromes have hair growth low on the forehead, such as Hurler's syndrome. Noonan's and Turner's syndrome cause hair to grow far down on the neck. Color is important. White hair may indicate albinism and a white patch may be related to the Waardenburg syndrome. One important factor in prevention is the color changes that occur in diets that are deficient in protein. These children may have red or greyish streaks in their hair. Hair whorls are usually located on the top at the back of the head. Whorls should be noted as to number and location.

Neck

The average length of the trachea is 4 cm. An extra thick or a webbed neck may indicate Noonan's or Turner's syndrome. Extra skin folds at the back of the neck may be indicative of Down's syndrome. Check for reflexes that should have disappeared earlier. Primitive reflexes include a symmetrical tonic neck reflex or an asymmetrical tonic neck reflex, the startle reflex, or the tonic labyrinthine reflex. These will cause future problems particularly in feeding the child.

Chest

Any shape of the chest that is irregular should be reported. When the sternum protrudes from the chest wall (pigeon chest), the child should be evaluated for syndromes such as Marfan's or Marquio's disease. Funnel chest is also found in Marfan's disease. Spinal deformities may be a problem. A horizontal circumference of the thorax at the level of mammary glands with respiration is 34 to 35 cm.

Abdomen and Back

Note whether two arteries and one vein are present in umbilicus. Omphaloceles on the abdomen where the peritoneal contents bulge through a muscular defect are sometimes seen. It is important to know that up to one half of these children have other associated defects. Distribution of hair that is not normal should be reported. A dimpling in the spine can be associated with spina bifida and should be evaluated. The spinal column and hips should be evaluated for defects. Many are related to genetic and developmental problems.

Arms, Legs, Hands, and Feet

The extremities are evaluated for deformities. Children with genetic problems often have defects of the extremities. Specific things to look for are number of fingers and toes, nail growth, any webbing of toes and fingers, and short fingers due to missing phalanges. Enlarged toes and fingers are also significant findings. A large space between the large toe and second toe is important. Any curving inward of small fingers (clinodactyly) should be reported. Fingers that over-ride or cross over each other are sometimes seen in children with trisomy (18) syndrome. The thumb often has the appearance of another finger. Feet are rounded on the bottom and are called "rocker bottom." Dermatoglyphics of hands and toes often vary in children with syndromes. Down's syndrome, in particular, has very different patterns from the normal population. An increased carrying angle of the elbows should alert the nurse to the possibility of gonadal dysgenesis in both sexes.

Genitalia

Examination of the genitalia is important in the developing child. In small children, abnormalities of the genitals may indicate problems with other developmental disabilities. In young boys, abnormal genital enlargement is often the result of neurogenic or idiopathic sexual precocity. In older boys, small genitals can be the result of Klinefelter's syndrome or an endocrine disorder. Secondary sexual characteristics may be missing in young women with Turner's syndrome.

hood and becomes more independent. Information skills about the environment must also be assessed. Many young adults learn to sight read signs related to health and safety in the community. Use of a telephone is important, as are the abilities to tell time and use money. Motivation for, and mastery of, these skills must be assessed.

Some children, because of their other disabilities, do not have effective language skills. They may be able to use a communication board. Assessing the ability for using such a board can be accomplished by working with pictures and having the child point to the object named. If a child cannot use his hands or arms, but has head control, he may point with a pointer taped on a helmet. Pictures should be as similar to the child's environment as possible. For instance, a child who lives in an institution cannot relate to pictures of a bathroom or bedroom such as is found in a home situation, unless he also spends time at home. Using colored pictures or black and white pictures may present problems to children with perceptual motor problems. Assessing the child's perceptual skills is essential before the nurse attempts to use visual aids in health teaching. Children may have trouble learning if there is a problem with eye–hand coordination, figure ground discrimination, position in space, spatial relations, or form constancy. Collaboration with an occupational therapist or a speech therapist is of assistance in this area. The Frostig Developmental Test of Visual Perception is a valuable tool for assessment.

The Child's Environment

Assessment of the child's environment is a valuable piece of data that will assist the nurse to plan effective interventions. All children need stimulation suitable for their physical and emotional needs. Areas that need to be assesssed are as follows.

1. Does the child have opportunities for social stimulation that promote intellectual growth? Is there a caring person in the child's environment with whom he can derive social experiences? Does the child have auditory, visual, and tactile stimulation? What types of stimulation are provided and are they appropriate for the child's particular health needs?

2. Does the child have control of some things in the environment? Does he receive reinforcement for his activities that help build constructive social responses? When he is not able to succeed at a task, is he encouraged to change behavior or activities so that he will succeed?

3. Does the child possess readiness capabilities for interacting with, and benefiting from, the environment? Can he observe, pay attention to, and notice when things are different? Is he persistent in pursuing a problem? Can he imitate and anticipate? Can he see another's point of view? Does the child have the ability to explore, manipulate, or move about? Does the environment seem enriched or is it void of learning experiences?

Planning

The planning stage of the nursing process calls upon all of the communication and interpersonal skills of the nurse. The family of a mentally retarded child may be at any point from shock to acceptance at the time of the nurse's initial contact with them. Meeting the family's needs also favorably affects the retarded child. Initially, the nurse guides the family through the stages of shock, grief, anger, resentment, and finally, acceptance. Planning revolves around the nursing assessment and analysis/diagnosis of the assessment data. Does the family need counseling at this point, the nurse asks, or are they ready to progress to the stage of securing help for the child?

During the child's infancy, the family needs to work with the nurse and other health care professionals to provide stimulation and activities that promote growth and development. Planning may include special training for parents to learn handling and special techniques to enhance the child's physical and mental condition. As the child becomes older, his needs and goals of care change. Services that meet the changing needs of the child must be identified and secured. Long-range plans should be formulated so that the parents have a time frame to help them understand what is required of them as they plan for the child's future.

Issues such as employment needs of the parents, respite care, and institutionalization should be dealt with during the planning stage. The nurse considers the needs of siblings and helps the parents work through their feelings about siblings.

Perhaps plans need to include visits to various agencies with which parents will deal at certain times in the child's development. If the nurse is not familiar with institutional life, a visit should be made to such an institution.

Legislation related to handicapped or mentally retarded persons must also be understood for informed planning with the parents and client. Moral and ethical problems must be addressed by parents, nurses, and other health care providers. A sensitive interview offers insight into how the parents feel about these issues as they pertain to their own child and his condition.

Intervention

Working with the Grieving Family

Nursing intervention is based on a careful and thorough assessment, thoughtful analysis of the client and family data, and collaborative planning. Nurses assist the grieving family to grow in a desired direction. Support of the family is critical.

We know that grief presents symptoms that are both psychological and somatic in nature and can be elicited by an experience of loss. The birth of a child with a handicapping condition triggers the grief response because the expectation or dream the parent had for a normal child is now impossible. Without supportive intervention, a sense of helplessness, hopelessness, and despair may result. Very often, both parents of the child who is handicapped and the normal siblings react in this mourning process by wishing the child were dead. Some families experience additional guilt reactions because of these feelings. Grieving is a process that must take place; it assists families to solve problems and look to the future.

How does the nurse support the family? One of the first responsibilities of nursing is to guide the family through decision-making processes related to issues such as whether the parents should keep the child at home or whether they will allow corrective surgeries for some disability related to the child's diagnosis.

Within the community, there are many sources of assistance for these periods of decision-making. Nurses should be familiar with how to put the family in touch with available resources (see insert, Learning About the Diagnosis of Down's Syndrome: A Dialogue with Two Mothers).

It would be ideal if all families were able to keep their children who are handicapped at home—nurturing, loving, and accepting them and their disabilities. We know that this is not possible in some families. How can nurses present reality to parents?

The nurse helps the parents deal with one issue at a time, one day at a time. Resources for each need can be found. Nurses also help families think through the consequences that each major decision about the child will have for the child and the other members of the family.

Crisis Intervention

During the *crisis period* of the family, often soon after learning of the child's diagnosis, family members are likely to experience confusion, disorganization, helplessness, dependency, anguish, and anger; the client and family are in need of immediate supportive intervention. Information must be presented to the family based on the developmental expectations and capabilities of the child. Services must be secured for the child and support groups must be located to which to refer the parents. A place needs to be made for the child within the family value system.

Crisis intervention is a supportive nursing intervention for the family of a retarded child until the family is able to solve problems by means of their own strengths and abilities. During crisis periods in which families are unable to function in a healthy manner, nursing intervention may mean stepping in and giving direction to the family or simply listening to the family and helping them shape their thinking and behavior.

Meeting Developmental Needs

Problems that the retarded child will face begin in infancy and can best be appreciated by examining the normal needs of all children. If these needs are not met for some reason, the child has troubles. Retarded children are at greater risk of not being able to have their needs provided for.

The retarded child's emotional, sensory, and motor needs are the same as those of "normal" children. Meeting these needs may call upon the creativity of the nurse. The child's emotional adjustment depends on provision of security through affection, acceptance, and approval. It also calls for understanding the intrinsic behavior patterns of the child as he proceeds through growth and development. In an encouraging atmosphere, the child is more likely to attain his fullest potential.[32]

Social development relates to the child's acceptance of the society in which he lives. His role models are his parents, siblings, and friends. The parent's culture and values influence the child. As the child progresses through the maturational process, he needs to develop autonomy and independence. Peer relationships become important and play provides opportunities to help him shape qualities and character. Sexual identification and interest in himself as a sexual person is a lifetime experience, the roots of which begin in infancy.

Progressing through these normal patterns of growth and development are extremely difficult for the mentally retarded or handicapped child. Mentally retarded children need special services that are sometimes difficult to find to help them achieve some degree of autonomy and independence. The retarded child may grow to adulthood being regarded as the "eternal child" and never experiencing independence beyond those of the most basic skills of daily living. For a mentally retarded individual to be considered a peer or a functioning part of society in which he lives has become a possibility only in the past decade.

Teaching the Retarded Child

One of the most pressing needs of parents is to learn techniques to teach their retarded child. Families should be taught positive reinforcement tools, which include using food as a reward, providing feedback to the child about how you see his performance or behavior, social approval such as verbal praise, attention, and affection, and tokens as payment for good behavior that can be redeemed for something desirable to the client.

Other methods to influence the child's behavior are punishment, restriction from a desired event, or ignoring him when he is doing something wrong; that is, not giving feedback to him.

Methods that help the client establish a right way to perform an activity include modeling the desired behavior and allowing the client a time and place to practice. Self-help skills are divided into very basic early, intermediate, and advanced skills.[2] *Basic readiness skills* are such things as looking when called and following a simple command, whereas *basic motor skills* are holding and releasing objects and finger painting. Walking is also a basic motor activity

Learning About the Diagnosis of Down's Syndrome

A Dialogue with Two Mothers

These two women are mothers of children with Down's syndrome. Phyllis B. is a woman in her mid-50s. Her son Kevin, now 20 years old, was born during a second marriage. He has three half-sisters who are school teachers. Mary J. is a young woman in her late twenties. She has a 4-year-old daughter and a 2-year-old son, Larry, who was born with Down's syndrome.

Both women agree that the single most devastating event for them was the way they were informed of their infants' diagnosis. Phyllis relates her story with tears and emotion as readily as if it had been yesterday. The wounds, she informs us, never heal.

She was alone in the postpartum unit on the third day after her son's birth when the obstetrician came in to inform her that her son Kevin was a mongoloid, a term which is no longer used today. She remembers,

"I did not even know what that word meant. He looked perfectly beautiful to me—with his cherub face and chubby little body. Imagine the horror I felt when told my precious child had something wrong with him! I remember the doctor telling me that it was nothing we could do anything about and it would be good if we thought about placing him in an institution and getting on with our lives. He said that such babies often die before they are 10 years old. I remember that I hysterically called my husband to leave work and come to the hospital. I will never forgive the doctor for the callous way he told me about my son's condition. I was a school teacher and I should have known about such things, but if you remember, that was before children like ours were mainstreamed into school and society. I honestly never knew what a child with Down's syndrome was like, and even if I had, how could I relate that knowledge to my precious son?

As a family, we have weathered a great deal, but we have remained together in spite of it all. Kevin is now living independently in a group home in our city, which is a part of the community return program provided by the state school for the mentally retarded in our area. We had him admitted at a younger age, but kept him at home until he was 18 years old. He comes home every weekend possible and he is doing very well there. It seems a most natural thing for us all."

Mary J. is a registered nurse who worked with a local physician prior to the birth of her second child.

Her pain lies in remembering how even her colleague did not seem to be able to talk to her after diagnosing the child. She tells of her anger and resentment that no one could look her in the eye or face her when they spoke. Nurses whom she knew and with whom she had attended classes avoided her room after the baby was born.

When she later took her baby to the physician's office for check-ups, he could not seem to find a single good thing to say about him. Mary says,

"The doctor would almost avoid looking at me or at the baby. I desperately wanted my friend to say one word of kindness about Larry. No one, not even family members, said, 'Isn't he cute.'"

Mary pulls out a large picture of a darling little red-headed boy. It is obvious that he has Down's syndrome, but in spite of it, he is a beautiful baby. She continues,

"I used to dress him up in new little outfits and take him places, just longing to hear someone say a good thing about him. Heck, I knew he had Down's syndrome and I know he has a few problems, but he is not grotesque. He is a doll.

What hurt me the most of all is that most of my friends are doctors and nurses, and their attitudes don't seem to be any different from anyone else's. They should have been the people with therapeutic methods when they confronted me—even in the name of professionalism, if not friendship."

Each woman represents a different era and demonstrates dramatically different stages of grief. Although a great deal has changed in the last 20 years, many things have not; attitudes are still much the same within our profession.

Phyllis relates that services for her child were very rudimentary at the time of his diagnosis, unless one sought full institutional care. Mary, on the other hand, found services in several agencies in the community and that people offered her reading material, but that a great deal of it was outdated and inappropriate. She is presently involved in collecting updated material for young parents and has requested that her colleagues call her when other young couples are facing this diagnosis.

"I can find something warm to say to those parents," she says. "Sure, it is a hurtful experience, but I know some of the good things about these children to tell them about and I know what help they will need."

goal and drinking from a cup is a self-help goal. *Intermediate self-help skills* include threading a belt through loops or washing hands and brushing teeth. Examples of *advanced self-help skills* are tying shoes, bathing, setting a table, and so forth.

Prior to teaching parents to work with their retarded child, the nurse should discuss with the parents their expectations for the child's learning at that particular time. Expectations that are too high risk frustration and failure; expectations that are too low slow the child's progress. The amount of assistance given to a child should also be discussed; parents must be careful not to do everything for a child. Learning to become independent depends largely on the family's allowing the child opportunities to do some planning and carry out tasks by himself. What kind of reward system will the parent choose to increase motivation? Praise, encouragement, and attention are excellent methods.

By dividing needed skills into three categories, parents can form check-off lists of self-help skills, home-care skills, and information skills. An excellent booklet recently published to help parents assist their child become independent, complete with assessment tools, is Toward Independent Living by Bruce Baker, Alan J. Brightman, and Stephen Hirshaw. Publishers are Research Press, 2612 North Mathis Avenue, Champaign, Illinois, 61820. The manual is exceptionally helpful in pointing out ways the parent can set limits for the child's behavior and it gives examples and methods of teaching.

Providing Information

Nurses need to give information. There are many resources available that the nurse can utilize as teaching tools. If there is a university within close enough proximity, the nurse will have a ready source of information. The Association for Retarded Citizens (ARC) is an organization with chapters in every state. Its goals are broad. Experienced parents who belong to the organization strive to help new parents deal with problems. Membership includes interested professionals, community members, family members, friends of the family, and the clients themselves. The ARC educates families about services available for the child with disabilities. Advocacy, and particularly self-advocacy, is a high priority. Prevention of mental retardation is also one of the major goals of the group.

The ARC follows and explains legislation to members. Members are asked to participate fully with legislators when the law affects the needs of the retarded. The ARC endeavors to meet the needs of the retarded in the community and the nation.

Outreach teams are groups of professionals who work out of specialized centers such as state schools, birth defect centers, and school districts. Their membership is made up of any combination of teachers, nurses, occupational therapists, physical therapists, speech therapists, or specially trained aides. These outreach teams travel to the home to

work with family members so that parents can give appropriate intervention to their handicapped child, assisting him to develop as normally as possible or helping him progress by formal assistance. Naturally, the delay of learning during early years places the child greatly behind schedule developmentally.

Handicapped children need many special services. Most communities have speech, hearing, and physical therapy, and occupational therapy services in local or state agencies. Depending on the disability, professional interventions such as dentistry, child psychology, psychiatric services, and social work may be needed. By contacting the School Administration Office in your school area, you can find out the name of service centers if they exist in your state. For instance, the Education Service Center Region XI in Forth Worth, Texas, handles audiovisual materials designed for public awareness and has a computerized listing of all resources available to the handicapped child in the area. These are only a few of the services offered by this center. Schools pay $1.50 per child to participate.

People to People Committee for the Handicapped, Suite 1130, 1522 K Street, N.W., Washington, D.C. 20005, puts out a free Directory of Organizations Interested in the Handicapped. The nearest local agency can be located by contacting any one of the listed organizations serving the particular need of the client. There are many special services available and the nurse with an up-to-date file can be an invaluable resource to the client, the family, and the teacher.

Respite Care

Respite care is one of the services that families will need to utilize in times of family crises, vacations, or even time away from the child for shopping or various appointments at which time both parents need to be away from the home. Respite care is a temporary separation of the child from the family either in the child's home or outside of the home. The time may be for as little as a few hours, or up to 30 or more days in some cases. Home health aides may perform this respite service in the home or the child may be placed in an agency.

Careful, thoughtful investigation must be made prior to placing a child in the hands of another caretaker. Some things to inquire about include the following.

1. Does the aide have special training to work with the child's disability?
2. Are personal references available?
3. What is the total cost?
4. What services can be rendered?
5. Is medical coverage available if necessary?

Agencies providing care for the retarded child should be visited at various times and one should be wary of an agency that does not allow a spontaneous visit. Naturally, an agency should insist that a person from the agency escort the parent around, because it would be dangerous for outsiders to be allowed free access to the facility. Nevertheless, it is reasonable to be able to drop in to the agency for a visit and ask to be escorted to the place where your child would be cared for.

Reinforcing the Family's Strengths

Working with the client and his family requires that the nurse develop a harmonious relationship with them. Through the family assessment, the nurse demonstrates to the family those factors inherent in their situation that can keep the family unit stable. This provides the family with a view of their own strengths. By allowing the family and client an opportunity to express feelings, develop problem-solving skills, and experience the nurse's support, the family begins to trust the caregivers. The nurse's caring attitude helps to validate the self-worth of the client. The family who perceives that the nurse's concern is genuine responds with greater openness.

Evaluation

Evaluation of the plan and the interventions designed for client care should be a responsibility of the total health team, which includes the client and his family. Evaluation is an ongoing activity, aiming toward the next goal the client will reach. Another form of evaluation involves examining terminal behaviors of the client at the end of a formal program. Accurate documentation enhances the evaluation process.

The nurse works with the retarded person and his family in areas related to preventive health practices such as hygiene, accident prevention, disease prevention, nutrition, and grooming. Nurses function in a school situation in which clients are screened for vision, hearing, health problems needing regular attention related to the disability or its complications, and physical assessments. Nurses are also interested in the retarded person's need for vocational education, sex education and birth control measures, securing of resources, monitoring of the client's ongoing health, and skills needed to live in the community, whether at home with parents or in a group home. Nurses and other health care professionals strive to help the client develop and maintain a good self-image.

Vulnerability of the Mentally Retarded Client to Emotional Disorders

Incidence

If we who are "normal" experience stress and health problems leading to emotional disorders, consider the higher degree of risk of the retarded individual. The trauma or congenital defect that led to his particular cerebral dysfunction may also cause hyperactivity. The child who is born with disability is certainly at higher risk for rejection by his significant others. If normal children sometimes are unable

to adjust to the environment in which they live, imagine the problems faced by a person who has no neighborhood peers nor even a sibling with similar problems. Those personality traits that we find hard to accept in normal persons, such as tension and anxiety, prevent retarded individuals from making friendships, further increasing their adjustment difficulties.

Studies of the retarded in institutions before 1960 found a range of 16% to 40% frequency rate of emotional disturbance. Studies conducted during more recent times indicate that among institutionalized children with Down's syndrome, 56% of the total sample display emotional disturbance at the time of their admission to an institution. Among the child population, the rate is 14% to 18%, and up to 40% in the general adult population. These figures would indicate an increased susceptibility to emotional disturbance among the retarded.[19]

Dynamics

It is difficult to define emotional disturbances in mental retardation. Mental retardation may result from many causes and is associated with many physically handicapping conditions. Through the normal growth and developmental phases, children and their needs change continually. Mentally retarded persons are less able to relate to their family and community in general. Root causes of emotional problems in the retarded are hard to separate from those related to mental retardation.

Some of the emotional disturbances that affect the mentally retarded are psychotic disorders, which give rise to several differential diagnosis problems because it is difficult to discern whether the primary diagnosis is a functional psychosis that resembles severe mental retardation or a functional psychosis in the retarded.[19] Behavioral reactions are clusters of symptoms such as hyperactivity. Transitory situational disturbances are reactions to stress in the environment in which clients who do not have emotional disorders are not able to deal with certain troublesome events. When the client is removed from that situation, the symptoms are no longer seen. Psychoneurotic reactions are symbolic behaviors that the client has found useful when dealing with anxiety, and that he continues to use thereafter for any anxiety-causing problems. Personality disorders may occur when the client cannot face frustration and conflicts in a socially acceptable manner. Behavior may vary from passivity to delinquency or antisocial behavior.

Nursing Process and the Emotionally Disturbed Retarded

Assessment and Analysis

Descriptions of psychotic reactions in the mentally retarded generally include bizarre gestures or posture, communication problems, lack of discrimination between inanimate and animate objects, and deviant affective expression. The child may not make eye contact with, or relate to, the examiner. Speech may be monotonous or echolalic, or it may involve a variety of abnormal responses. Motor behavior is repetitive or preoccupied. Children may also engage in unusual motor activity such as hand flapping or tiptoeing. Psychosis is a syndrome of behaviors that cannot be separated from the cause, age of onset, the child's inheritance, and the environment in which the child exists.[19]

Personality disorders produce behaviors that involve an inability to delay gratification, impulsiveness, irresponsibility, and failure to adjust socially by learning from previous interactions with others. These personality disorders are not thought to be related to the causes of mental retardation and are not found in the mentally retarded population in greater proportions than in the normal population.

Planning and Intervention

In the past, it was considered not feasible to treat the retarded with psychotherapy because therapy required good verbal skills. More recent thinking, however, has suggested that treating the client in a humane and accepting manner in therapy is more important than the use of techniques that require the client's use of sophisticated intellectual skills.

Planning should include both the parent and the client, when possible. The treatment of emotionally disturbed retarded clients may require parent counseling, individual or group therapy, and drug therapy. Client–therapist contact may begin on a one-to-one basis and may then enlarge to include a therapy or activity group. Nurse-managed group activities may include planned activities to strengthen self-concept such as a "This Is Your Life" party in which the client is featured. In this activity, each person in the group has a chance during one of the weekly sessions to tell about himself, hobbies, family, and friends. The nurse–group leader helps the client plan his program and the client may invite guests or family members to describe life at home; he may also bring pictures of himself, pets, and friends, examples of his hobbies, and a teacher, school counselor, or work supervisor to talk about him at school or work.

Play therapy is an intervention mode for children who are retarded, and is useful even if the client has limited verbal skills. Music therapy and recreational therapy are activities that can be planned around the client's needs. Through demonstration or modeling, the client may be shown certain behaviors that need to be corrected and then shown the correct behavior. Art therapy is another useful tool incorporating many different media of expression such as clay, finger paints, and designing prints on fabric. As the client's behavior improves, he is gradually moved out of the therapy group and into a transitional group.

Evaluation

Nurses must be accountable for their nursing care through the careful recording of plans, intervention, and client progress. Plans should reflect ways in which goals and objec-

tives are evaluated. Video tapes and progress notes describing outcomes are methods to accomplish this. Meticulous records documenting the behavior of each client and legal consents are time-consuming but worthwhile, particularly when the nurse has a large case load or long-term interaction with clients.

The Nurse's Attitude

The nurse who is an advocate for her clients invests time, energy, and skills promoting those things which she believes will help the client maintain health, prevent injury or illness, and live effectively within his environment (see case study, A Success Story Called Mary). Every client is a unique person with individual needs. The attitude of the nurse sets the tone for client interaction and for movement toward achieving the goals of care.

Because the mentally retarded are moving into the community in ever-increasing numbers and are consumers of health care, nurses must be prepared to care for them. Retarded individuals are more like the general population than they are different from it, but sometimes those differences spell failure in achieving independence.

Professional development is the responsibility of the nurse. Basic curricula to help those nurses meet their career needs are the responsibilities of the educational programs preparing nurses; however, few programs give nursing students the opportunity to become directly involved with the retarded in clinical areas.[14]

Now is the best time in the history of nursing to become involved as an advocate for the client. Moral and ethical issues surrounding the care of the mentally retarded or physically handicapped are churning. Budget reductions are threatening to some programs of prevention and treatment. Prisons are being told to reform and many of those prisoners in state correctional facilities are retarded. One state prison board member in Texas stated that almost a seventh of the prison inmates are retarded.[28] If the needs of the normal prisoner are not met, how much greater are the needs of the retarded inmate being neglected?

The enlightened nurse has a responsibility for the public's awareness of the needs and rights of the mentally retarded and the historic attitudes that have been detrimental to the handicapped. Architectural barriers must be eliminated and the need for recreational facilities must be demonstrated. The client who is mentally retarded and sometimes physically disabled is every nurse's concern. We must share information and treatment ideas with clients, parents, and each other.

Summary

This chapter has focused on a condition affecting about six and a half million persons or about 3% of the population. There are many causes of mental retardation, but categori-

Case Study: A Success Story Called Mary

Her face was a wreath of wrinkles crowned by a blue stocking cap. Black men's galoshes, unbuckled at the top, flopped when she walked, letting both snow and rain inside. An old faded navy coat hung on her thin frame, and the lumps around her ankles indicated she was wearing long underwear under thick brown cotton stockings.

Mary wore that garb the first time I saw her in our nursing clinic, and, according to her case worker, she would wear it with very little variation until summer.

The psychiatric institutions in our community had begun to deinstitutionalize some long-term residents. They placed these individuals in programs throughout the city to help them become independent citizens requiring minimal supervision.

No one could explain to the professionals in our center, where Mary was placed for vocational rehabilitation, why she had been institutionalized in the first place. Mary was a passive, simple person, certainly; however, it was apparent after she attended the center for a short time that she had neither a psychiatric problem nor a serious retardation problem. Nevertheless, she had lived in a psychiatric institution most of her life. Her old admission records were buried somewhere in forgotten or long lost boxes of files. Her case worker could not remember ever having read them.

Mary's dentures were loose and wobbled about in her mouth when she ate or talked. She needed to learn a great deal about community adjustment. The habits and neglect learned over a lifetime were not easy to slough off. Most of the clients who came to the center were younger, but Mary was given a chance to develop a skill and to live in an apartment with two other women. She had no family, as far as anyone knew, and holidays were particularly lonely for her. Her younger roommates were invited home to visit with relatives.

Christmas, though, was not lost on Mary; she was the Santa Claus of the center that first year. She was so happy to be out of the institution and meeting new people that she showered everyone with gifts. She had spent many years attending arts and crafts classes in the institution and had collected boxes full of her handmade crafts—purses, flower vases out of jars, paper flowers, beads of every color, and lots of old shoes covered with macaroni and sprayed with gold paint. She never had a family to whom she could give these presents, so she had saved them. After making her rounds of various offices and department Christmas parties, she returned to her apartment to spend her first Christmas alone.

The rehabilitation center assigned a team to work with Mary's many problems. Mary's transition to community living was not miraculous; it was a slow and tedious process involving several years of classes, counseling, and smoothing out of her many social, emotional, and health problems. New dentures and clothing and improved hygiene and grooming habits have contributed to a more positive self-image. She has learned to prepare nutritious food, manage her own money, shop, and travel about the city. She is more assertive and self-confident and has found a job outside of the vocational center.

Mary still keeps in touch with some of us who worked with her. From time to time she sends us her picture in which we see a woman dressed like everyone else. The old stocking cap and men's galoshes are gone; she looks quite stylish, in fact. Mary has a job in a box factory making labels for orders that are to be shipped. She has her own apartment and is no longer followed by a social worker. She pays taxes like any other wage earner.

Although she still has no family with whom to gather on holidays, she does not sit at home in a lonely apartment sipping tea and eating leftover party cookies. Now she has something useful to do during the holiday season. This year, she tells me, she has a "volunteer job," that of wheeling about older women in a nursing home a few blocks from her apartment. She has been invited to join them for holiday dinners. "Poor ladies," she writes, "they don't have nobody to love them. I have been going to see them since summer, and now they will not be alone. Nobody should be alone at holiday times." Who would know that better than Mary?

cally, two main causes can be listed—genetic and acquired factors. The dynamics of the family into which a retarded child is born are complicated and often crisis-laden. Some of the emphases of the chapter include the following.

1. Genetic factors may be chromosomal abnormalities such as errors in numbers of the chromosomes (nondisjunction) or errors in the structure of the chromosome due to breakage or translocation.

2. According to the laws of Mendelian inheritance, genetic disorders may be passed from generation to generation by traits found on the autosome or the sex chromosome in a dominant or recessive manner.

3. Acquired factors leading to mental retardation may occur prenatally, perinatally, or postnatally; these disorders may arise from trauma, disease, or infec-

tion of the mother during pregnancy or to the child following birth, or from environmental problems such as malnutrition, lead poisoning, or child abuse.

4. Usually, those conditions more readily seen at birth causing multiple physical defects are the most difficult for parents.

5. Most mental retardation is mild in nature and is usually not diagnosed until some time after birth when the child fails to develop academic skills.

6. The feelings ranging from guilt, depression, withdrawal, or rejection to denial or anger are normal following the birth of a retarded child and the nurse must communicate effectively with the parents to help them work through these feelings.

7. When the family has progressed past the crisis stage and is more accepting of intervention for the retarded child, referrals are made to find sources of parent teaching and infant stimulation.

8. Normalization is a widely accepted concept in the area of mental and physical disability that insures that the client will not be segregated from the general population and made more deviant by lack of basic skills and appropriate dress and activities for age.

9. The nurse becomes an advocate for the client and the family by directing them to every resource that meets the needs of the client at each point in his life span and by providing nursing care that accents prevention, support, guidance, and teaching.

10. An advocate is also interested in the rights of the mentally retarded as a citizen, including becoming involved in the legislative process and in ethical issues that affect the client.

11. Knowledge and experience help the nurse to dispel old wives' tales and false beliefs that many people still hold and that continue to separate the retarded from the mainstream of society.

Nursing Process Guidelines for the Preconceptual Period

Assessment and Analysis

Subjective Data:

Nutritional Interview. Lack of protein may be a risk factor. Check the mother's weight and counsel her if she is below 50 kg.

History of Disease or Illness. Has the mother a history of diabetes mellitus, cardiac disease, or chronic renal problems?

Reproductive History. Interview for miscarriages, abortions, previous premature deliveries, a history of any previous delivery of an infant with congenital abnormalities. These are increased risks for the next pregnancy.

Family History (include genetic). The easiest form is a pedigree chart.

Age of Mother. Very young mothers (younger than 16) have higher risk for translocation types of Down's syndrome. Older mothers (over 35) have higher incidence of trisomy 21 (Down's) syndrome.

Education of Parents. Assess social and behavioral areas as well as formal education.

Objective Data:

Results of nutrition testing and metabolic work-ups
Evaluation of pedigree information
Results of testing of Adult Behavior Rating (test that rates adaptive behavior of an adult and examines risk factors prior to conception)

Planning and Intervention

Depending on the results of the assessment, the nurse may plan patient education and referral, which as risk factors warrant, may include the following.

Nutrition education
Referral to appropriate agency for financial assistance
Diet therapy
Genetic counseling
Birth control information and assistance
Family life education

Evaluation

This area is very important in prevention. Follow-up is a major step in the accountability of nursing care. Areas that will enhance evaluation procedures are as follows.

Follow-up visits
Physical assessments (ongoing) for weight gain
Nutritional follow-up
Family interview

Babies are at risk if parents have one or more risk factors that are not corrected.

Nursing Process Guidelines for the Prenatal Period

Assessment and Analysis

Subjective Data:
Complaints of maternal infections, rubella, toxemia
Does the mother use drugs?
Has she been exposed to radiation?
Is there a history of Rh incompatibility?
Diet history
Financial status of parents
Is there a history of psychiatric problems?
Is this child wanted?

Objective Data:
Study lab work for results of the following.

Infections. Maternal infections may cause malformations, low birth weight for baby, or prematurity.
Toxemia. It may result in poorly perfused placenta and poor fetal growth.
Polyhydramnios. It may indicate intestinal obstruction or the possibility that the fetus is unable to swallow.
Oligohydramnios. Possible urinary tract malformation
Amniocentesis. Results may indicate a genetic problem.
Sonogram. Results will provide information on placement of placenta, size of child, and developmental disability.
Maternal psychosis. A suicide threat is a potential danger for the mother. The child is also at risk for harm.

Planning and Intervention

The assessment parameters may indicate nursing care needs. At-risk individuals may need counseling, psychotherapy, and, possibly, termination of pregnancy.

Nursing Process Guidelines for the Perinatal Period

Assessment and Analysis

Subjective Data:
When did labor start? This is important because of trauma damage resulting from long labor.
Last meal eaten. This information is important to anesthesiologist for prevention of aspiration of stomach contents.
Any bleeding or loss of fluids. This information will alert the nurse to dangers of infection or impending miscarriage.
Previous prenatal care. Lack of previous medical care may be a risk factor, because these mothers have not been evaluated for problem areas.

Objective Data:
Monitor for complicatons. Areas to evaluate include hemorrhage, distocia, trauma, placental damage, caesarean section, prematurity, or postmaturity.

Planning and Intervention

Monitor for fetal presentation.
Evaluate maternal-infant condition.
Assist with procedures for birth.
Newborn Apgar score
Newborn care
Notify nursery if problems are expected.
Orders for special lab work if needed

Evaluation

Look at the results of the laboratory work following birth to determine if nursing care was given correctly for each situation. What were the results of cord blood tests? What care is being given to the child as a result of a low Apgar score? Is the recovery of the mother following a normal process? If not, what nursing care is being carried out to assist her?

Nursing Process Guidelines
for the Postnatal Period—Early Childhood Period

Assessment and Analysis

Subjective Data:
The pitch and quality of the child's cry may be indicative, in some cases, of problem areas.
Observe interaction of mother with infant.

Objective Data:
Assessment throughout the child's developmental period must include the following; they should be carefully recorded by maternity, pediatric, or public health nurses for future use.

Apgar scores
Gestational age
Head size
Weight and length
Trauma
Infection
Neurologic assessment results
Physical evaluation for birth defects
Maternal depression
Signs of child neglect or abuse
Prolonged separation from child

Planning and Intervention

Report any abnormalities to physician. Parents and child may be referred to genetic counseling.
Support parents, if defect is found.
Make other referrals, as needed.
Sensory stimulation may be needed for delayed infant.
Behavior modification for client, if needed
Parent education

Evaluation

Ongoing monthly physical and developmental checks are desirable if the child is at risk. These are performed at 6 months, 1 year, 18 months, and 24 months of age. A behavior problem checklist is valuable to maintain and should be followed up in progress notes. Testing of the child's cognitive level should be done early. Language skills and achievement test reports will serve to indicate if the individual program plan is adequate.

References

1. Alexander MM, Brown MS: Pediatric Physical Diagnosis for Nurses. New York, McGraw-Hill, 1974
2. Baker BL, Brightman AJ, Hinshaw SP: Toward Independent Living. Champaign, IL, Research Press, 1980
3. Best GA: Individuals with Physical Disabilities. St Louis, CV Mosby, 1978
4. Capute AJ: Mental Retardation. In Haslam RA, Vallentutti PJ (eds): Medical Problems in the Classroom, pp 217–233. Baltimore, University Park Press, 1979
5. Chinn P, Drew C, Logan D: Mental Retardation: A Life Cycle Approach. St Louis, CV Mosby, 1979
6. Coley IL: Pediatric Assessment of Self Care Activities. St Louis, CV Mosby, 1978
7. Denton AC: Therapeutic Superficiality and Intimacy. In Longo DC, Williams RA (eds): Clinical Practice in Psychosocial Nursing: Assessment and Intervention, pp 23–48. New York, Appleton-Century-Crofts, 1978
8. Erickson ML: Assessment and Management of Developmental Changes in Children. St Louis, CV Mosby, 1976
9. Ferholt JL: Clinical Assessment of Children. Philadelphia, JB Lippincott, 1980
10. Gelman SR: Sociolegal Issues. In Neisworth JT, Smith RM (eds): Retardation Issues, Assessment, and Intervention, pp 85–112. New York, McGraw-Hill, 1978
11. Gitter MJ: Infant Stimulation Programs for the Handicapped: Rationale. In Hernandez-Logan C (ed): Caregiving: A Multidisciplinary Approach, pp 45–49. Palo Alto, CA, RE Research Associates, 1981
12. Hyatt R, Rolnick N: Teaching the Mentally Handicapped Child. New York, Behavioral Publications, 1974
13. Jones R: The Acorn People. New York, Bantam Books, 1977
14. Judkins BL, Harrison A: Nursing Practice, Education, Mental Retardation. New York, Ways of Caring, Inc, 1981
15. Kelly TE: The Role of Genetic Mechanisms in Childhood Handicaps. In Haslam RA, Vallentutti PJ (eds): Medical Problems in the Classroom, pp 193–215. Baltimore, University Park Press, 1979
16. Klaus MH, Kennell JH: Maternal-Infant Bonding. St Louis, CV Mosby, 1976
17. Lewis M: Clinical Aspects of Child Development. Philadelphia, Lea & Febiger, 1971
18. McKusick VA: Mendelian Inheritance in Man: Catalogs of Autosomal Dominant, Autosomal Recessive, and X Linked Phenotypes. Baltimore, Johns Hopkins Press, 1979
19. Menolascino FJ: Challenges in Mental Retardation: Progressive Ideology and Services. New York, Human Sciences Press, 1977
20. Mercer R: The Nurse and Maternal Tasks of Early Postpartum. The American Journal of Maternal Child Nursing 6 (September/October): 341–345, 1981
21. Milunsky A: The Prevention of Genetic Disease and Mental Retardation. Philadelphia, WB Saunders, 1975

22. Neisworth JT, Smith RM: Retardation Issues, Assessment, and Intervention. New York, McGraw-Hill, 1978

23. O'Neil SM, McLaughlin BN, Knapp MB: Behavioral Approaches to Children with Developmental Delay. St Louis, CV Mosby, 1977

24. Philip AS: Neonatology. Flushing, NY, Medical Examination Publishing, 1977

25. Ryan MP: The Family Approach. In Curry J, Peppe K (eds): Mental Retardation Nursing Approaches to Care, pp 27–32. St Louis, CV Mosby, 1978

26. Sattler JM: Assessment of Children's Intelligence. Philadelphia, WB Saunders, 1974

27. Schulman ED: Focus on the Retarded Adult Programs and Services. St Louis, CV Mosby, 1980

28. Separation of Retarded Inmates Urged. Fort Worth Star Telegram, Section 1, p 13A, December 22, 1981

29. Smith JF, Nachazel DP Jr: Ophthalmologic Nursing. Boston, Little, Brown, 1980

30. Thompson JB, Thompson HO: Ethics in Nursing. New York, Macmillan, 1981

31. Urban H, Schassar L, Rogers C, Kirkpatrick N: Meeting the Nutritional Needs of the Multiply Handicapped. Buffalo, United Cerebral Palsy Association of Western New York, p 11–12, 1981

32. Wasserman E, Slobody L: Survey of Clinical Pediatrics, 6th ed. New York, McGraw-Hill, 1974

33. Wernick R: The Family. New York, Time-Life Books, 1974

Chapter 29
Organic Mental Disorder

It is no easy matter to accept that one is growing old, and no one succeeds in doing it without first overcoming his spontaneous refusal. It is difficult, too, to accept the growing old of someone else, of one's nearest and dearest. That of a mother whose kindness, welcome and understanding used to seem inexhaustible, and with whom one begins to hesitate to share one's intimate confidences, because they no longer arouse in her the warm, lively echo they used to. The aging of a father whose judgment and advice always used to seem so sound, but whom one can no longer consult because he must not be worried, or because his faculties are failing. The aging of a friend to whom one no longer talks as one used to, because it would be necessary to shout out loud things that used to be said quite quietly. It is hard to accept the decay of conversation into banality, empty optimism and insignificance.

Paul Tournier,
Learn to Grow Old,
1972

Cheryl Steudtner Detwiler

Chapter Preview

This chapter presents those mental disorders that are attributed to a dysfunctioning or diseased brain. The impact of the various disorders are considered in terms of their incidence and occurrence in the general population. Etiologic factors and clinical manifestations of the organic mental disorders are discussed. Nursing interventions, as derived from the application of the nursing process, are provided with the ultimate goal of achieving optimal care for those individuals affected by these disorders and for their families.

Learning Objectives

On completion of this chapter, the reader should be able to accomplish the following.

1. Define organic mental disorders
2. Discuss the incidence and significance of organic mental disorders
3. Compare the possible etiologies of the organic mental disorders
4. Identify the behaviors associated with various organic mental disorders
5. Apply the steps of the nursing process—assessment, analysis, planning, intervention, evaluation—to clients with organic mental disorders

Defining Organic Mental Disorders

The classification, organic mental disorders, encompasses those abnormal psychological or behavioral signs and symptoms whose origins lie in an identified cerebral disease or dysfunction. This is a fairly recent classification; previously, there has been no real differentiation between the psychotic behavior of a person with an intact, healthy brain and the psychotic behavior of a person with a pathophysiologically impaired brain. It has now become evident that a person with a dysfunctioning, diseased, or injured brain can manifest the same morbid psychological phenomena as the person with a functional psychiatric disorder who is believed to have a physiologically healthy brain.

The critical difference in the two similarly manifested clinical syndromes is that, in an organic mental disorder, the disturbed behavior is secondary to the brain's transient or permanent dysfunctioning or diseased state, not a primary functional problem in and of itself. The key to the diagnosis of these disorders lies in the tangible proof, obtained from the clinical history, physical examination, or laboratory findings, that there exists an organic problem affecting the brain tissue, or that by description, there is an organic brain syndrome present.[1] This organic factor may be a primary disease of the brain, a systemic influence originating in another body system, or an exogenous substance that is either currently affecting the brain tissue or that has left some residual, chronic deficit.

Collecting the data for a definitive diagnosis of an organic mental disorder is difficult, but the implications for treatment make it imperative. When a person with an organic disorder is treated as if he had a functional disorder, the assumption of the therapist is that the brain is an intact, healthy organ when, in fact, it is not.[21] This individual cannot respond nor can he be expected to respond to the therapy in the same manner.

There are situations in which an individual with an organic mental disorder who is demonstrating maladaptive behavior as a result of that malady, may exhibit further psychotic behavior as an emotional reaction to the organic mental disease. In this case, the ensuing disturbed behavior is a result of the individual hosting two disorders, one functional and one organic. This is not an uncommon finding, but a complex problem that necessitates the laborious procedure of collecting and sifting out data to support the diagnosis of an organic mental disorder. This differentiation must be done to initiate valid medical treatment of potentially correctable disorders.[21]

Incidence and Significance of Organic Mental Disorders

The mental health community is becoming increasingly aware of the presence of organic mental disorders, stemming from their increasing occurrence in the mushrooming geriatric population, in the chronic-disease-survivor population, and in the population of acute-care facilities. More than one million persons, or 5% of the American population over the age of 65 years, are affected significantly enough by the dementia of organic mental disease to deter independent living. This translates into statistics that state that 60% of the residents of nursing homes manifest organic mental disease. In addition, another 10% of the American population over 65 years of age is so affected by intellectual impairment that only semi-independent living is possible.[5] Twenty percent of the first admissions to psychiatric hospitals enter with the diagnosis of organic mental disorder, and another 40% of the chronically hospitalized have that diagnosis.

Medical intervention that has prolonged the lives of those requiring critical care and the lives of those with chronic diseases has also created a completely new entity of cerebral damage and dysfunction, which are iatrogenic realities. Systemic metabolic disturbances originating in the cardiovascular, respiratory, or renal systems may affect the homeostasis of the brain. Drug therapies, antineoplastic therapies, and post-trauma resuscitation are therapeutic modalities utilized by the increasingly sophisticated medical community, and these modalities result in a rising psychiatric morbidity.[7] Although there is now an awareness of this psychopathology in the survivors of the intensive-critical/chronic-care treatment regime, at this point, little has been done in terms of investigation to document the magnitude of the problem.[15, 21]

Etiologic Factors

By definition, organic disorders must be shown to be the result of the following.

1. A primary brain disease
2. The brain's response to the influences of systemic disturbances
3. The brain tissue's unique reaction to an exogenous substance
4. The residual effects of, or withdrawal of, an exogenous substance.[1]

Table 29-1 gives examples of the etiologic factors within each category of disorder.

The etiologic factor responsible for the disorder may indicate the potential for the acuteness or chronicity of the organic mental disorder. Previously, the terms *acute brain syndrome* and *chronic brain syndrome* were applied to individuals with organic mental disorders. Because the terms *acute* and *chronic* became erroneously synonymous with the prognostications of reversible and irreversible, these terms are hesitatingly applied to a client with organic mental disorder. There is value, however, in ascertaining the etiologic factor. If, for example, the factor can be eliminated from the individual's system, there is a possibility for a more favorable prognosis. In time, the symptoms may disappear altogether or, at least, there may be a cessation of the progression of symptoms.

It is not to be assumed that any list of plausible etiologic factors actually exhausts the possible reasons for the development of organic mental disorders. There must always be the recognition of the interplay that takes place between the physical and the sociopsychological components of an individual that helps to establish, maintain, or destroy the mental homeostasis of that person. Portnoi, working with the data obtained from Wang, has schematically diagrammed the dynamics of the interactions among the physical, psychological, and sociological spheres (see Fig. 29-1).[13, 20] The discerning practitioner will consider all of these factors when determining the etiologic elements of the client's disorder.

Primary Brain Disease

This category incorporates those indigenous diseases and factors that pathologically affect the brain tissue. Table 29-1 indicates many of the known specific diseases or factors that produce an organic mental disorder.

Organic Brain Syndrome.   Also included in this category are the organic brain syndromes. They are traditionally included in the category of organic disorders, although proof of their existence lies only in the description of their presence rather than in tangible proof of an organic etiol-

ogy. An organic factor is assumed to be the underlying etiology of the disorder and, consequently, tangible proof is not required. (This is an exception to the qualifying definition of organic mental disease.) Should an organic etiology be proven, the organic descriptor is dropped and the etiologic factor is substituted; that is, organic delirium syndrome may become alcoholic delirium syndrome.

The organic brain syndromes are categorized into six groups.

1. Delirium and dementia
2. Amnestic syndrome and organic hallucinosis
3. Organic delusional syndrome and organic affective syndrome
4. Organic personality syndrome
5. Intoxication and withdrawal
6. Atypical or mixed organic brain syndrome

These may also result from other factors; for example, from a systemic metabolic disturbance affecting the whole organism.[1]

Wernicke-Korsakoff Syndrome.   One example of the organic brain syndrome, or amnestic syndrome, is the Wernicke-Korsakoff syndrome. Although it is also seen in hospitalized patients with chronic intravenous therapy, in the United States, this syndrome is more commonly seen in chronic alcoholics whose compulsion for ingestion of alcohol supersedes the need for nutritional intake.[9] This syndrome is usually found in the 40- to 70-year-old alcoholic with a steady and progressive intake of alcohol. In time, this individual develops a Vitamin B_1 (thiamin) deficiency that directly interferes with the production of the brain's main nutrient, glucose.[8]

Dementia.   *Dementia* is a term describing clinical behavior that manifests itself in the insidious development of the following.

1. Memory deficit
2. Intellectual deficit
3. Disorientation
4. Decreased cognitive functioning[4]

Dementias arising in the senium (after 65 years of age) or the presenium (before 65 years of age) constitute a significant portion of the primary brain disease from the organic brain syndrome, dementia, in that there is some tangible proof of their organic etiology.

Alzheimer's Disease.   The most characteristic disease of the senile dementias is Alzheimer's disease. Seen twice as frequently in women than in men, this disease has an unknown etiology although specific physiological findings indicate that there are degenerative changes in the cholinergic neurons and biochemical changes involving the biosynthetic enzyme for acetycholine.[5] Ninety-six percent of the individuals affected with Alzheimer's disease are over the age of 40 and 10% of the American population over the age of 65 are affected with this disease to some degree.[16]

Table 29-1.   **Etiology of Organic Mental Disorders**

Primary brain disease	Cerebral hypoxia/vascular spasms Congenital dysfunction/birth defects Dementias: Alzheimer's, Pick's Huntington's Chorea Infections: menningitis, encephalitis, German measles Intracranial tumors Irritation from blood breakdown products Neurosyphilis Normal pressure hydrocephalus Trauma: hematoma

Systemic disturbances	Infections
	  Systemic
	  Respiratory: pneumonia, atelectasis
	  Cardiac: rheumatic fever, subacute bacterial endocarditis
	Surgery
	  Hypoxia from anesthesia
	  Cardiac (decreased cardiac output), cerebral emboli
	  Transurethral resection
	Organ failure
	  Renal
	  Hepatic > toxin build-up
	  Cardiac: congestive heart failure
	Nutritional deficiencies
	  Vitamins-thiamin: Wernicke-Korsakoff nicotinic acid
	Metabolic imbalance
	  Thyroid
	  Pancreas
	  Parathyroid
	  Adrenal
	  Pituitary
	  Electrolyte imbalance
	  Stress: pain/fear/fever
	  Sleep/sensory deprivation
	  Abnormal reactions to drugs

Exogenous substances	Heavy metals
	  Lead
	  Mercury
	  Manganese
	Tranquilizers
	  Diazepam (Valium)
	  Chlordiazepoxide (Librium)
	Anticholinergics
	  Atropine
	  Scopolamine
	Sedatives/Hypnotics
	Barbiturates
	Antihistamines
	Substance abuse
	  Marijuana
	  Phencycledine (PCP)
	  Cocaine
	  Opium derivatives
	  Amphetamines
	  Alcohol
	Hallucinogenics
	Digoxin
	Antihypertensives
	  Aldomet
	Parkinson drugs
	  Amantadine (Symemtrel)
	  Benztropine mesylate (Cogentin)
	  Trihexphenidyl hydrochloride (Artane)
	  Leva-dopa
	Antidepressants

Withdrawal/residual effects of exogenous substances	Potential exists for any of the drugs listed in the above category

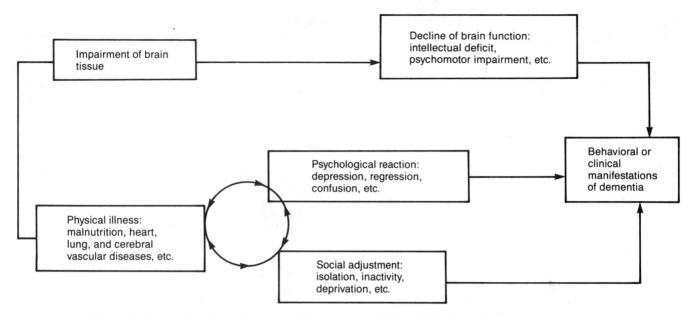

Figure 29-1. *Factors leading to dementia. (From Portnoi V: Diagnostic Dilemma of the Aged. Arch Intern Med (May) 734–737, 1981)*

Amazingly, Alzheimer's disease accounts for 80% of the dementias of old age.[10]

The microscopic findings of senile plaques and neurofibrillary tangels present in the brains of individuals with Alzheimer's disease closely resemble the pathological changes documented in the individual whose brain exhibits "normal aging." This resemblance is so close that differentiation between the disease state of the brain in Alzheimer's disease and the state of the brain in normal aging is not always substantiated in the histological findings at autopsy. Sometimes, the disease can be substantiated only by the documented aberrant behaviors of the individual.

Pick's Disease. Another senile degenerative dementia resembling Alzheimer's disease, although occurring less frequently, is Pick's disease. This disease occurs equally in males and females who are in their early to mid 50s. The actual cause of the disease is unknown, but it is suspected that there are genetic tendencies. The general microscopic findings include atrophies of the frontal and temporal portions of the brain. Why these atrophies occur is not clearly understood but they are believed to be associated with the aberrant behaviors seen in Pick's disease.[16]

Multi-infarct Dementia. Another dementia seen in the senium is multi-infarct dementia. This is a primary disease of the vascular system of the brain. Although atherosclerosis may be an accompanying factor, the main pathology results from multiple infarcts occurring throughout the brain as a result of numerous occlusions within the smaller cerebral arteries. Extensive destruction of brain tissue occurs and, when the infarcts collectively produce a minimum of 50 grams of tissue destruction, the signs and symptoms of this particular dementia appear.[5] Individuals with multi-infarct dementia often have a history of either hypertension or diabetes.[15]

Huntington's Chorea. Huntington's chorea is an example of a dementia occurring in the presenium. It is a familial disease that is passed on through the genes by an autosomal dominant trait. Huntington's chorea manifests itself in individuals between the ages of 45 and 55 years old. The clinical history is the most reliable diagnostic finding, although at autopsy, the brain is seen to have frontal cerebral atrophy. Research laboratory findings suggest that this disease may be the result of biochemical changes within the brain cells.[21]

Systemic Disturbances

Organic mental disorders can be a direct result of the brain's response to a systemic problem present in the individual. It is not always possible to predict the tissue's response to a systemic imbalance, especially because the individual's vulnerability may be heavily influenced by the environmental stress factors that are bombarding him. Although the causes of such systemic disturbances are almost infinite, a partial listing is found in Table 29-1.

Exogenous Substances

The inventory of those substances that may precipitate an organic mental disorder is almost limitless. The problem is compounded when more than one element is present; by itself, an exogenous substance may be innocuous, but when in the presence of, or in combination with, another substance, it may become noxious. Table 29-1 gives a partial listing of these exogenous substances.

Aberrant Behaviors Associated with Organic Mental Disorders

Alzheimer's Disease

Cognitive: Global (or general) intellectual impairment of insidious onset
  Insight into decreasing intellect—depression
Level of consciousness: No clouding until late in disease
Memory: Recent history of memory loss
Appearance: Not affected
Emotional: Depression and anxiety over regressions
Subtle loss of interest in work, family

Pick's Disease

Cognitive: Intellect intact
  Lack of insight into the disease process
Level of Consciousness: Not affected
Appearance: Slovenly
Emotional: Dramatic personality changes
  Socially inappropriate behavior; flip beyond reasonable propriety

Multi-infarct Dementia

Focal signs dependent upon area involved; usually abrupt onset of symptoms resembling a stroke

Huntington's Chorea

Cognitive: Insight into the psychological deteriorative changes
Appearance: Choreiform movements
  Sloppy
Emotional: Moody; apathy to aggressive behavior, inappropriate
  Despair over changes taking place; suicidal
  Decreased interest in job

Wernicke-Korsakoff Syndrome

Cognitive: Cannot learn new information because cannot retain facts
Level of Consciousness: Alert
Memory: Suspended in time; no memory prior to 2 to 3 minutes before this moment
  Extensive memory loss
Appearance: Unsteady gait due to peripheral neuropathies
Communication: Use of confabulation to supply information lost in recent memory gaps

Residual Effects and Withdrawal of Exogenous Substances

The aftermath of exogenous substances can be more devastating than their initial effect. The withdrawal of an exogenous substance may produce unique physiological responses within the neuronal structures of the brain. Accordingly, when the acute response to the substance subsides, the remaining chronic deficits may be more deleterious than the initial ones. The reaction to the absence of an exogenous substance may be seen clinically as one of the organic mental disorders.

Behaviors Associated with Organic Mental Disorders

The behavioral manifestations associated with organic mental disorders are many and varied in nature. There are no essential features predictably present in every patient situation. Frequently, the most significant behavioral problems are due to the individual's emotional reactions when they become aware of the cognitive deficits resulting from an organic mental disorder.[1]

Behavior is the response of the individual as he adjusts to continual changes in his internal and external environment. The physiological soundness of the brain is a necessary ingredient for the successful adaptation of human behavior to these changes. When the organic integrity of the brain is interrupted or interfered with, maladaptive behavior will often follow.[21] This is the essence of what is seen in an individual with an organic mental disorder. Some of the disorders, especially the dementias, have commonalities of behavior but this is not true of most of the acute brain disorders (see insert, Aberrant Behaviors Associated with Organic Mental Disorders).

Generally, the behavioral dysfunctions seen in organic mental disorders can be grouped into either global impairment of intellectual functions or limited impairment of intellectual functions.[10] The behavioral aberrations of organic mental disorders include deficits in the areas of the following.

1. Sensorium
2. Attention
3. Orientation
4. Perceptions
5. Memory capabilities[19]

Sensorium and Attention Deficits

Deficits in the sensorium stem from the individual's inability to use the information collected by his five senses to discern his environment. If this discernment does not take place, the individual experiences confusion that affects his attentiveness to the environment and, ultimately, his level of consciousness. As the level of consciousness decreases, the individual also develops an inability to concentrate on any specific event. His attention span decreases and he becomes highly distractable.

Disorientation

Disorientation occurs when an individual is hampered from successfully receiving and centrally integrating the data obtained from his internal and external environments. When the sensory input falls below the individual's minimum need requirements, and when the brain is affected structurally in such a way that it can no longer perceive and interpret the stimuli adequately, decreased orientation results. The disoriented individual does not know where he is, how he came to be where he is, why he is there, or how he fits into the environmental milieu.

Perceptual Disturbance

Frequently, the individual with an acute organic mental disorder will experience the perceptual abnormalities of illusions and hallucinations. (These behaviors are described in detail in Chapter 22.)

Memory Deficit

Memory disturbances are the most frequently found deficits in organic mental disorders. Recent memory impairment is the most common finding in this disorder; however, remote memory may sometimes be impaired. The inability to register, retain, and retrieve accumulated information is one of the key clinical manifestations of organic mental disorders and may affect the intellectual capability of the individual.[19]

Disorientation and recent memory impairment must be present to confirm the diagnosis of *acute organic mental disorder*. These behaviors, in combination with any of the others described, often appear in a fluctuating manner, waxing and waning in severity from hour to hour or day to day. Empirically, the aberrant behaviors worsen during the hours after sunset, termed the *sundowning effect*.[14] The nurse on night shift will frequently report that the individual mistook hospital personnel for a brother or sister, hallucinated, or became frankly combative.[2]

Degenerative Impairments

Many of the organic mental disorders with a chronic dimension tend to have behavioral manifestations that are predictively associated with their degenerative nature, especially if an irreversible pathology is a known part of the disease progress. None of the organic mental disorders should be isolated and typed initially as acute, chronic, reversible, or irreversible. Any of these disorders may encompass acute, chronic, reversible, and irreversible features or evolve into them. Labeling may negatively influence attempts of the health team to help the client and family. The terminology of chronic and irreversible should be applied only in those disorders, such as Alzheimer's disease, whose known degenerative pathology is an established medical fact.

Many of the degenerative organic mental disorders are difficult to diagnose initially. The impairments that occur are global in nature and the intellectual deterioration is often artfully concealed by the well-preserved social skills of the individual.[10] Nevertheless, some of the symptoms of the diseases listed in the insert, Aberrant Behaviors Associated with Organic Mental Disorders, are worth noting.

Application of the Nursing Process to Clients with Organic Mental Disorders

The nurse may participate in facilitating the recovery of, or improving the quality of life for, a client with an organic mental disorder. The nursing process of assessment, analysis, planning, intervention, and evaluation is discussed as it is applied to the care of individuals with organic mental disorders.

The first step in determining treatment and nursing approaches for this client is a clinical screening for any treatable physical causes of the problem. This involves an extensive history-taking, physical examination, and laboratory work-up. Laboratory and diagnostic evaluation of the client often includes those tests listed in Table 29-2.

When the results of the screening tests prove to be noncontributory, the physician may look to other, more subjective factors. Is the client a victim of sleep and sensory deprivation or overload? Is the client experiencing pain? Is the client postoperative? Is he experiencing an inordinate amount of stress and anxiety from personal losses? Any or all of these elements may be the causative culprit(s) in the disorder. When the contributing factors are determined, they must be aggressively treated or, if possible, eliminated.

Assessment and Analysis

The nursing assessment of a client with an organic mental disorder focuses on the behavior that the client presently exhibits. The client's family is one of the most reliable resources for information about his behavior, because he may not have insight into when the behavior began or insight into its sequential progression. The nurse gathers and compiles behavioral reports because the client's disruptive behavior may at first be overlooked by the family or may be regarded as an idiosyncrasy or as crankiness due to "old age."

The nurse attempts to break down the component parts of the client's behavior and assess how deficient or intact each component is. Intellectual or cognitive deficits may be assessed by the use of the short, portable, mental status questionnaire (SPMSQ) developed by Pfeiffer (see insert). The nurse observes and documents the client's level of consciousness and his sensorium. The amount of stimulation it takes to elicit a response from the client is also to be assessed. This stimulation may range from simply calling

Table 29-2.   **Screening Tests**

TEST	CLINICAL IMPORTANCE
1. WBC with differential	1. Infection
2. Sedimentation rate	2. Infection or vasculitis
3. Urine exam and Toxicology test	
a. Sugar & acetone	a. Diabetes
b. Leucocytes	b. Infection
c. Barbiturates and other toxic substances	c. Toxicity
d. Albumin	d. Renal failure
e. Porphyria screen	e. Renal failure
4. Serum tests	
a. blood urea nitrogen	a. Renal failure
b. Creatinine	b. Renal failure
c. Sugar	c. Diabetes, hypoglycemia
d. T_3, T_4	d. Thyroid disease
e. Electrolytes	e. Evaluation for imbalance including Na^+, K^+, Ca^{++}, Cl^-, $PO_4^=$, parathyroid-induced changes in calcium, phosphorous
f. Mg^+, Br^+	f. If available, bromides are still present in some common drugs and overuse may inadvertantly lead to toxicity.
g. Serum folate level Vitamin B_{12} level	g. Nutritional problems, thiamine deficiency
h. SGOT, SGPT	h. Liver failure
i. VDRL	i. Syphilis
j. Drug levels—specific search for evidence of drugs—ETOH, etc	j. Barbiturate, other drug overdose
5. X-rays, routine	
a. Chest	a. Infection, heart failure
b. Skull	b. Evidence of increased intracranial pressure, fractures, etc.
6. EEG	6. Ictal phenomenon
7. CT scan	7. Brain tumor, subdural hematoma, infection, hemorrhage .
8. Spinal tap	8. Infection, hemorrhage
9. Invasive neuroradiologic procedures	9. Suspicion of tumors, vascular lesions, hydrocephalus

(From Staub R and Black F: Organic Brain Syndromes pp 109–110. Philadelphia, FA Davis, 1981)

the client's name in a normal tone of voice to vigorously shaking him and shouting his name. The attention span of an individual may be appraised by asking him to repeat six or seven digits forward, or by asking him to cross out all the "a's" he finds in a paragraph he is asked to read. Failure to perform tasks such as these indicates that the client is probably having difficulty concentrating.

Information concerning perceptual disorders may be gained by direct observation of the client's behavior and by asking him about any strange or unusual feelings or sensory experiences that he has mentioned. The family may also be able to contribute information about observing such behav-

ior or hearing the client voluntarily express concerns about the "bugs," "roaches," and so forth that he sees.

The assessment includes an evaluation of the client's orientation to his person, environment, time, and date. Simply asking the client for this information by means of the questions, "Who are you?" "Where are you?" and "What are you doing here?" will provide the needed data. The family of the client should also be questioned to ascertain if the client experiences the "sunset effect;" that is, decreased orientation with the onset of the evening hours.

Those who are living with the client or who are in daily contact with him will be able to provide much infor-

Short, Portable Mental Status Questionnaire (SPMSQ)

Instructions:
    Ask question 1 through 10 in this list and record all answers.
    Ask question 4A only if patient does not have a telephone.
    Record total number of errors based on 10 questions.

+   −   1.   What is the date today?_____
                                Month   Day   Year

            2.   What day of the week is it?_____

            3.   What is the name of this place?_____

            4.   What is your telephone number?_____

         4A.   What is your street address?_____
                     (Ask only if patient does not have a telephone)

            5.   How old are you?_____

            6.   When were you born?_____

            7.   Who is the President of the U.S. now?_____

            8.   Who was President just before him?_____

            9.   What was your mother's maiden name?_____

        10.   Subtract 3 from 20 and keep subtracting 3 from each new number you get all the way down

For white subjects with at least some high school education, but no more than high school education, the following criteria have been established:

    0–2 errors   Intact intellectual functioning
    3–4 errors   Mild intellectual impairment
    5–7 errors   Moderate intellectual impairment
    8–10 errors   Severe intellectual impairment

(From Pfeiffer E: A Short Portable Mental Status Questionnaire for the Assessment of Organic Brain Deficit in Elderly Patients, pp 433–441. J Am Geriatr Soc (October 1975))

mation concerning his ability to take care of his personal being and his personal affairs. The social interaction that takes place between the family and the client should be observed and described; it will reveal many of the client's present social assets and deficits.

The nurse spends time with the client to determine the quality of his communication efforts. Many of his social skills may remain long after the intellectual deterioration takes place. Social behavior is usually deeply ingrained by the time adulthood is reached. When talking, people give many nonverbal clues to one another that indicate the proper response. For example, clues such as nodding and smiling indicate a positive atmosphere in which a reciprocal nod or smile is appropriate. It is a kind of mindless, learned response. For this reason, the nurse needs to ask the client questions that solicit more than a "yes" or "no" response.

The client's memory is also evaluated during the nursing assessment. Incidents evoking remote memory are usually easy to elicit from the client. Recent memory, however, may be assessed by the client's response to questions that ask for the recall of the events of the previous day or week.

Assessing these components of the client's behavior and then analyzing the information helps the nurse lay a foundation of understanding of the client problem and a basis for nursing care·planning (see insert, Assessment Guide).

Planning

When the design for care is constructed, a necessary ingredient is the involvement of members of the client's family, which usually includes the spouse and adult children of the client. If the client's prognosis is, realistically, that of continued degeneration, family participation becomes even more crucial as family members assume increasing responsibility for care.

The conflict and the stress brought about by the changes in the family dynamics, as well as the debilitating effects of the organic mental disorder, compel those involved in planning care to also include plans that will encourage family cohesiveness and stability. Necessity demands that discharge planning be initiated early in the treatment process. It must be decided what responsibilities

Assessment Guide

I. Subjective Data
   A. Behavioral changes (often asked of the family)
      1. Is there a change in the behavior? If so,
         a. How does the present behavior differ from former behavior?
         b. When was this change in behavior first recognized?
   B. Emotional changes
      1. are any of the following present?
         a. Depression
         b. Anxiety
         c. Paranoia
         d. Agitation
         e. Grandiosity
         f. Confabulation
      2. Does the client have insight into the fact that "things are not right"?
      3. Is the client complaining of many physical ailments for which there are no bases?
      4. Are certain previous personality traits becoming predominant or exaggerated?
   C. Social changes
      1. Is the client exhibiting embarrassingly loud and jocular behavior?
      2. Is there sexual acting-out beyond the bounds of propriety?
      3. Have the following developed?
         a. Short-temperedness
         b. Irritability
         c. Aggressiveness
      4. Is there an increasing inability to make social judgments?
   D. Intellectual behavior
      1. Has the ability to remember recent events decreased?
      2. Has the ability to problem-solve decreased? (This might be especially apparent in the work or job area.)
      3. Do new environments or even old environments result in the client's disorientation?
      4. Is it difficult for the client to carry out complex motor skills? Do his efforts result in many errors?
      5. Are any of the following language problems present:
         a. Has the language changed?
         b. Does the language ramble and wander from the point of the conversation?
         c. Is the point of the conversation never clearly stated?
         d. Is there difficulty comprehending complex material?
         e. Does the client have trouble remembering names of people and objects?
         f. Does the client have difficulty writing?

II. Objective Observations
   A. Level of consciousness
      1. Is the client confused, sleepy, withdrawn, adynamic, apathetic?
   B. Appearance
      2. Is there decreased personal hygiene?
   C. Attention
      1. Does the client have decreased ability to repeat digits after the interviewer?
      2. Do other stimuli in the environment easily distract the client from the interviewer?
      3. Does the client focus on only one of the stimuli in the environment and is he unable to turn attention from the one stimulus?
   D. Language
      1. Outflow of words decreases.
      2. Patterns of repetitive, tangential, or concrete speech appear.
      3. Writing skills decrease more rapidly than the spoken word.
   E. Memory
      Tests client's ability to remember four unrelated words and recent events. (Confabulation and anger will often be used by the client to move the interviewer away from questions related to memory.)
   F. Constructional ability
      The client is instructed to copy a series of line drawings; he is often unable to do this or his ability to do so will decline dramatically over a period of time.
   G. Cortical function
      1. The client's ability to perform arithmetic is faulty, reveals many errors
      2. Proverb interpretation—usually, the client will give only a concrete interpretation of the proverb.
      3. Similarities—The client will often deny similarities between two objects and give instead a concrete answer. For example, when asked, "What is the similarity between a tiger and a cat,?" the client may reply, "One is small and one is large. There is no similarity."

family members can assume and what "relief" persons, such as neighbors and friends, may be secured to prevent exhaustion of the future primary caregivers.

The general goals of care for the client with organic mental disorder are threefold.

1. To eliminate the organic etiology, if possible
2. To prevent the acceleration of symptomatology
3. To preserve the dignity of the client

These goals are facilitated by the following supportive goals.

1. To maintain peak physical health
2. To promote a structured environment
3. To promote socialization
4. To promote independent functioning
5. To preserve the family unit

Intervention

Maintaining Peak Physical Health

One of the most essential nursing actions in helping the client with an organic mental disorder is to facilitate his optimal level of functioning by maintaining his peak physical health. Realizing that exogenous substances can dramatically initiate aberrant behavior, the nurse must become very sensitive to the client's response to his drug therapy. In addition to knowing the side effects and toxicity reactions of the specific drugs that the client is receiving, the nurse pays particular attention to possible drug interactions.

The nurse also assesses the client daily to recognize any symptoms indicative of an ensuing physical disorder. Cardiovascular and respiratory disorders have a particular impact on those persons already affected by senile dementias.[6] Prompt recognition of symptoms and appropriate intervention by the nurse prevent acceleration of the client's already existent mental deterioration.

The nurse also endeavors to minimize the client's sensory impairments. Poor vision necessitates well-fitting eye glasses that are actually worn by the client and not carelessly set aside. Diminished hearing requires a hearing aid or giving louder, slower, uncomplicated instructions while standing directly in front of the client. The client may participate in activities, but may require a slower pace or simpler instructions prior to the activity to allow the individual sufficient time to compute the significance of the input from his faulty sensory organs. When the nurse recognizes a sensory deficit in the client, she should initiate steps to compensate for it.

Structuring the Environment

Structuring the client's immediate environment is an important nursing intervention. The nurse may increase or decrease the client's level of the sensory input. When the client experiences sensory overload, he may be moved to a quieter area or private room where environmental stimuli are kept at a minimum and where he may rest or sleep. The nurse may place "orientation" clues in the environment; clocks, calendars, and seasonal pictures provide sensory input that is important for the client's orientation to time and place. The number of family members, friends, and hospital personnel entering the environment should be controlled to provide for optimal stimulation. The people and objects within the environment should be as familiar to the client as possible. This may very well imply that the same hospital personnel need to care for the client on a consistent basis.

The perceptual difficulties of hallucinations or illusions may decrease by simply controlling the light in the environment. Light may easily eradicate the "sundown effect." Safety is an important factor that requires that any environmental hazards be eliminated. An agitated individual may become even more panic-stricken if restraints are used as a method to ensure safety. In this situation, the client might benefit from environmental structuring in which someone, either from the hospital or from the family, remain with the client to keep him from injuring himself by such acts as climbing over the bed rails, pulling out tubes, removing dressings, and so forth.

Promoting Socialization

The promotion of the client's socialization may be approached in a variety of ways. The client who is exhibiting signs of fairly severe disorientation may benefit from reality orientation therapy. Through this technique, psychiatric-mental health nurse professionals consistently bombard the client with four or five concrete facts that help to remind him of who he is, where he is, why he is here, and what is expected of him. To assist in accomplishing this goal, "reality orientation boards" are placed throughout the environment. These bulletin boards highlight for the client the date, time, place, and so forth.[11] Although this re-educative program has not been shown to significantly improve the mental status of a client, it does seem to slow the rate of decline.[6]

Another action that promotes the socialization of the individual with an organic mental disorder is that of including him in group work. The group provides a safe, empathetic atmosphere in which the individual may be motivated to utilize all of his faculties to their remaining potential. Food, touch, and music are therapeutic vehicles within the group that add to the re-establishment of self-esteem and resocialization.[6]

Promoting Independent Functioning

The nurse promotes the client's independent functioning by, first, maintaining his peak physical health and, secondly, by helping him accomplish his activities of daily living. It is particularly helpful to facilitate the ease with which clients accomplish their tasks of daily living. Making the materials for daily care available and accessible, keeping the routine of care simple and consistent, and allowing the individual time to complete those tasks that he is able to complete are supportive nursing actions.

Preserving the Family Unit

The nurse does not forget the importance of preserving the family unit. Discussing with the family ways in which relief may be provided by interested neighbors or by home health aides provides a respite for the family from the heavy responsibilities of full-time care of the client with an organic mental disorder. Day care for the client is one possibility that would allow family members to continue with their daily activities and responsibilities. Through day care, the spouse may be able to retain his or her job and income and have the energy to care for the client during evening and weekend hours. Family therapy may help any family who is experiencing undue stress or having difficulty coping with the situation and its demands. Planning family goals and addressing specific family problems add to the preservation of the family unit.[6]

Evaluation

Because the client with an organic mental disorder is constantly in the dynamics of change, nursing actions must be regularly evaluated for their successful outcome and relevance. The client's physical and psychosocial changes may ineffectualize the nurse's efforts that had been previously successful. The nurse also realizes that, when dealing with the degenerative aspects of an organic mental disorder, success may be measured in terms of slowing down the process, rather than stopping or curing the problem.

The Nurse's Attitudes and Feelings

Working with clients who have organic mental disorders may be discouraging for the nurse. In certain situations, neither the institution nor the medical staff desire, or are able, to provide the supportive environment and milieu necessary for the client. For example, the client with an "acute" episode of aberrant behavior may experience attention to his physical needs only, while his psychological needs are merely tolerated. The chronically deficient individual may elicit pity from the staff, not the dynamic intervention that is reserved for the "curables." Any or all of these attitudes may pervade the environment in which the nurse works, making it difficult for her own feelings or philosophy to prevail.

Few patients have such intensive needs in both the physical and psychological realms as do those individuals with organic mental disorders. The nurse hopefully views this as a tremendous challenge for which she draws upon all of the resources available *in* her as well as those available *to* her.

Summary

This chapter has dealt with one of the mushrooming problems of the present time, organic mental disorders. Appearing not only in the aging population but also in the general population as well, these disorders are becoming increasingly prominent in the critical care areas as a result of iatrogenic therapeutic modalities. Some of the major emphases of the chapter are as follows.

1. The possible etiologies of organic mental disorders include primary brain disease, systemic disturbance, influences of exogenous substances, and withdrawal and residual effects of exogenous substances.
2. Aberrant behaviors associated with these disorders may include deficits in the areas of sensorium, attention, orientation, perception, and memory.
3. Symptoms of organic mental disorders may be approached in terms of the nonpredictable findings usually associated with "acute" episodes and the more predictable findings associated with diseases that tend to be long-term in nature.
4. Gathering and analyzing assessment data regarding a client with an organic mental disorder requires participation of family members or friends who have been in close contact with the client.
5. Goal-setting for the client with an organic disorder focuses on elimination of the organic etiology, if possible, prevention of acceleration of his symptoms, and preservation of his dignity.
6. Specific nursing interventions strive to maintain the client's optimal physical health, to structure his environment, to promote socialization and independent functioning, and to preserve the family unit.
7. Hopefully, the nurse approaches the client with an organic mental disorder as a challenge to her professional skills.

Therapeutic Dialogue

Reality Orientation: Presenting Concrete Information

Nurse: (seated beside the client in her room, looking directly at her, with one of the nurse's hands touching the client's arm) Good morning, Mrs. S., I see that you have just finished your bath.

Client: (nodding vigorously and smiling) Yes, Yes. (pats the nurse's hand)

Nurse: Mrs. S., since it is 11:00 in the morning, would you like to walk with me to the day room in this hospital to see the beautiful sunshine?

Client: Yes, oh my yes.

Nurse: Mrs. S., since you are here in St. Luke's hospital, I will walk with you. It is such a pretty day outside. I want you to enjoy the sunshine before noontime when you will eat your lunch.

Client: Yes, dear. Oh my. (Remains sitting until the nurse stands and gently pulls upward on her arm and begins to walk to the door)

Discussion

Often, the client with a senile dementia retains impressive social skills even though she has lost both cognitive capability to understand and orientation to person, time, and place.

In this dialogue, the nurse constantly reminds Mrs. S. who she is, where she is, and where she is going. The nurse also reminds the client of the time through specific facts and references to the sunshine, lunch, and so on, all of which help orient Mrs. S. to time. Note that none of this interaction took place in a manner demeaning to the client. Particularly helpful during this conversation were the "signals" given to Mrs. S., by means of touch and body language, that she should stand and walk, for without these signals, she would have had less comprehension of the conversation.

Nursing Care Plan

The Client with Alzheimer's Disease

Client Problem	Goal	Intervention
Memory: difficulty forming new memories, misplaces articles around the house	To decrease frustration at misplacing articles	Encourage the client to make lists. Keep lists in same, highly visible places. Encourage unobstructive supervision of client by family, such as helping with means to enhance memory.
Sensorium: increasingly upset at night	To minimize sundowning effect	Keep single light on in night room. Decrease activities in late afternoon to lower the client's level of excitability.
Depression: awareness of degenerative, cognitive abilities	To decrease depression	Allow the client to ventilate feelings Point out activities that the client continues to perform adequately Encourage the client's participation in tasks at which he is successful

References

1. American Psychiatric Association: Diagnostic and Statistical Manual of Mental Disorders, 3rd ed. Washingtron, DC, American Psychiatric Association, 1980

2. Guze S: Acute Brain Syndrome. Hospital Medicine 13(4):63–69, 1977

3. Jaspers K: General Psychopathology. Chicago, University of Chicago Press, 1963

4. Katzman R: Dementias. Postgrad Med 64 (August): 119–124, 1978

5. Katzman R: Early Detection of Senile Dementia. Hosp Pract 16 (June): 61–67, 1981

6. Kennie D: Management of Senile Dementia. Am Fam Physician 26(12):105–111, 1980

7. Lipowski ZJ: A New Look at Organic Brain Syndrome. Am J Psychiatry 137 (June): 674–677, 1980

8. Luckman J, Sorenson K: Medical Surgical Nursing: a Psychophysiological Approach. Philadelphia, WB Saunders, 1980

9. McKinney AS: Appropriate Investigations of Stroke and Dementia. Geriatrics 36 (June): 41–48, 1981

10. NIA Task Force: Senility Reconsidered. JAMA 244 (July): 259–263, 1980

11. Nursing Services, Tuscaloosa Veterans Administration Hospital: Guide for Reality Orientation. Tuscaloosa, Alabama, 1974 (mimeographed)

12. Pfeiffer E: A Short Portable Mental Status Questionnaire For the Assessment of Organic Brain Deficit in Elderly Patients. J Am Geriatr Soc 23 (October): 433–441, 1975

13. Portnoi V: Diagnostic Dilemma of the Aged. Arch Intern Med 141 (May): 734–737, 1981

14. Robins P: Management of Irreversible Dementia. Psychosomatics 22 (July): 591–597, 1981

15. Seltzer B, Sherwin I: Organic Brain Syndromes: An Empirical Study and Critical Review. Am J Psychiatry 135 (January): 13–20, 1978

16. Staub R, Black F: Organic Brain Syndromes. Philadelphia, FA Davis, 1981

17. Tomlinson BE, Blessed G, Roth M: Observations on the Brains of Demented Old People. J Neurol Sci 11 (September): 205–242, 1970

18. Verwoerdt A: Clinical Geropsychiatry. Baltimore, MD, Williams & Wilkins, 1976

19. Wang HS: Dementia in Old Age. In Walls CE (ed): Dementia, pp 15–23. Philadelphia, FA Davis, 1977

20. Wells C: Chronic Brain Disease: An Overview. Am J Psychiatry 135 (January): 1–11, 1978

Chapter 30
Psychophysiologic Disorders

We are not ourselves
When nature, being oppress'd, commands the mind
To suffer with the body

Shakespeare,
King Lear, Act II, Scene 4

M. Suzanne Doscher

Chapter Preview

Early beliefs that man was composed of a dichotomous mind and body have given way to a view of man as a system composed of interrelated parts. This chapter focuses on the interrelated parts, or systems—psychological, biologic, and family—that impact on a person's choice to communicate via psychophysiologic responses. The overview of psychophysiologic disorders relates the incidence, possible causes, and examples of types of responses that traditionally have been considered psychophysiologic in nature. The latter sections of the chapter address application of the nursing process—assessment, analysis, planning, intervention, and evaluation—to individuals who communicate psychophysiologically.

Learning Objectives

On completion of the chapter the reader should be able to accomplish the following.

1. Define psychophysiologic behavior
2. Discuss the etiologic influences on psychophysiologic responses
3. Describe the dynamics of the development of psychophysiologic disorders
4. Identify typical behaviors of individuals with common psychophysiologic disturbances of the gastrointestinal, respiratory, cardiovascular, and integumentary systems
5. Describe the physiological responses to depression, grief, loss, and change
6. Apply primary prevention nursing activities to the care of individuals and families at risk for psychophysiologic disorders
7. Apply the steps of the nursing process—assessment, analysis, planning, intervention, and evaluation—to individuals who exhibit psychophysiologic behavior
8. Identify and deal with own feelings and attitudes in the care of individuals with psychophysiologic disorders

Mind–Body Interrelationship

For years, the term *psychosomatic* was used to describe individuals experiencing certain physical disease processes. Diseases such as bronchial asthma, essential hypertension, peptic ulcer, ulcerative colitis, and rheumatoid arthritis were classified under the umbrella of psychosomatic illness. It was assumed that these diseases primarily had a psychological etiology and that other diseases were primarily physical in origin. This view strongly suggested a mind–body dualism in man.

These early beliefs have rapidly given way to the current view of man as a composite of interrelated systems. Disruption or unrest in any one system affects the whole system. This view transcends the boundaries of discrete disease entities and focuses on the interrelationship between psychological and physiological factors present in every person. Strictly speaking then, there are no disease categories considered purely psychosomatic. Emotional factors influence all body processes and organic disease affects changes in the psychological state.[1]

Although clinical experience and scientific reports document the fact that psychological factors play an important role in initiating, exacerbating, or maintaining a number of physical disorders, the individual person may not be consciously aware of the psychological factors affecting organic processes, or vice versa. In two major epidemiologic surveys, 59% to 69% of the subjects did complain of symptoms with both physical and psychological components.[9, 13] It seems that the remaining subjects may have been unaware of the interrelationship of psyche and soma or the meaning of the interrelationship.

Etiology of Psychophysiologic Responses

Given similar life situations, why does one person become physically ill and another person does not? Susceptibility to physical illness depends on many factors. Few, if any, authors would support a single explanation of any disease; multifactorial causation, with a delicate interaction of psychosocial, biologic, and familial factors is, rather, at the root of psychophysiologic responses.

Psychosocial Influences

Psychoanalytic View. The work of Franz Alexander in the 1940s offers the hypothesis that unresolved unconscious conflicts are central to the development of disorders that he classified as psychosomatic. Alexander emphasized that a precipitating event that is of emotional significance to the person triggers an increase in anxiety and activates his underlying conflict. Over time and depending upon the nature of the conflict, specific physiological alterations occur. For example, according to Alexander, a person who pervasively maintains a facade of independence, in an effort to cover up a need to be taken care of, experiences anxiety. The constant arousal of the independence–dependence conflict generates anxiety. The partnership of conflict and anxiety play a key role in the development of peptic ulcer disease.[1]

Psychodynamic View. The psychodynamic approach to the relationship between psychological factors and physical disease asserts that, under stress, persons with certain personality constellations will develop physical disease. This view proposes the individual's personality type is the basis for certain physical illnesses.[4] For example, according to this theory, a person most likely to develop ulcerative colitis is meticulous, compulsive, scrupulously prompt, excessively clean, and passively angry. This idea of the significance of the basic personality has again received popularity in the description of the Type A personality who is prone to coronary heart disease.[5]

Life Experiences. Careful history-taking at the onset of physical illness frequently reveals the accumulation of many life changes in the recent past. Studies indicate that a variety of illnesses coincide with a high life-change profile.[6] Marriage, death of a loved one, retirement, trouble at work, buying a house, and financial changes are but a few of the common and often inevitable events that occur in life (see Table 30-1). The psychological impact of one or more of these events varies among individuals. For some individuals, it seems that an accumulation of these events serves as the foundation for the development of physical illness. The meaning the individual gives to the event(s) and especially the issue of "not being in control" of his life seems to be relevant in the initiation, exacerbation, and perpetuation of the illness.

Family Influences. Mechanisms used to adapt to stress are frequently learned in the family arena. Children are easily and greatly influenced by how their parental role models react and adapt to stressors such as conflict, loss or change, or disappointment. Also, at a time of stress, each child as well as each parent plays a distinct, separate role within the family system.

For some families, the prime mode of adaptation to emotional tension is via physical disorders. Generally, one child is the physical symptom bearer and, in essence, communicates the emotional pain of the entire system. Minuchin believes that the "psychosomatic family" has certain distinct characteristics that are absent from a nonpsychosomatic family.[10] These families are frequently overinvolved (enmeshed) with one another, deny the existence of conflict, have a poor ability to resolve differences, and have a narrow, rigid, and often ineffective repertoire of responses when faced with change.

Biologic Influences

Neuroendocrine Systems. According to biologic theories, physiology rather than psychology plays a key role in the development of somatic disorders. These theories emphasize that the body, particularly the autonomic nervous system and the endocrine system, react in a predictable, organized manner to stress.

Cannon's studies in the 1920s led to the discovery of the adaptive function of adrenalin in assisting the body to strive for "homeostasis" when experiencing stress.[2] Later, in the 1940s, Hans Seyle focused on the role of the pituitary-adrenal mechanism in the body's reaction when defending against stress.[12] Seyle calls this reaction the "general adaptation syndrome." Both Cannon and Seyle believed that if the body experiences a prolonged adaptive struggle to combat stress, the individual is likely to develop a "physical disease of adaptation."

Genetic Factor. It has been hypothesized that all people have one bodily organ or system that is more vulnerable to illness than others.[11] Under stressful circumstances, underlying unconscious conflicts are activated and coping occurs via the development of a physical illness involving the weakest bodily system.

Dynamics and Manifestations of Psychophysiologic Disorders

None of us holds claim to immunity from a short-lived response to anxiety that produces temporary disruption in our physical well-being—preclinical diarrhea, predate hives, preexamination sweaty palms or pounding heart. Although we would like to control these episodes totally, the unconscious and the autonomic nervous systems seem to win out.

Although the response to anxiety, as previously described, is temporary in nature, if it were to remain or recur frequently in relation to events that the individual perceived as stressful, prolonged or chronic physical problems could ensue. All people have unique ways of relieving anxiety; however, if useful, functional "relief valves" are unsuccessful or, perhaps, unknown to the individual, he may unconsciously choose to relieve anxiety by becoming physically ill.

Although anxiety is one feeling state that may be associated with the development and maintenance of physical illness, it certainly is not the only one. Anger that is within or outside the person's awareness and that goes unexpressed can wreak havoc on visceral functioning. Just as mounting prolonged anxiety needs an outlet, the same is true for anger that may be "swallowed down" and allowed to mount. Unfortunately, many people do not receive permission to feel angry and express it in childhood. Therefore, some individuals progress through life operating within the style of "turn the other cheek," "forgive and forget," and denying angry feelings. In some instances, relief is not obtained in a functional way; faulty adaptation occurs when the person's body responds by "becoming ill."

Some individuals feel shame or guilt about expressing or seeking functional ways of meeting their needs for affection, dependency, security, or a sense of belonging. When faced with situations that evoke these dependency longings, these persons experience anxiety and are apt to defend against the anxiety by blocking out, or failing to recognize, the dependency needs. Physical symptoms become the only outlet available to the person and serve to meet his de-

Table 30-1.   **The Social Readjustment Rating Scale**

RANK	EVENT	VALUE	SCORE
1	Death of spouse	100	_____
2	Divorce	73	_____
3	Marital separation from mate	65	_____
4	Detention in jail or other institution	63	_____
5	Death of a close family member	63	_____
6	Major personal injury or illness	53	_____
7	Marriage	50	_____
8	Being fired at work	47	_____
9	Marital reconciliation with mate	45	_____
10	Retirement from work	45	_____
11	Major change in the health or behavior of a family member	44	_____
12	Pregnancy	40	_____
13	Sexual difficulties	39	_____
14	Gaining a new family member (*e.g.*, through birth, adoption, oldster moving in, and so on)	39	_____
15	Major business readjustment (*e.g.*, merger, reorganization, bankruptcy, and so on)	39	_____
16	Major change in financial state (*e.g.*, a lot worse off or a lot better off than usual)	38	_____
17	Death of a close friend	37	_____
18	Changing to a different line of work	36	_____
19	Major change in the number of arguments with spouse (*e.g.*, either a lot more or a lot less than usual regarding childrearing, personal habits, and so on)	35	_____
20	Taking out a mortgage or loan for a major purchase (*e.g.*, for a home, business, and so on)	31	_____
21	Foreclosure on a mortage or loan	30	_____
22	Major change in responsibilities at work (*e.g.*, promotion, demotion, lateral transfer)	29	_____
23	Son or daughter leaving home (*e.g.*, marriage, attending college, and so on)	29	_____
24	In-law troubles	29	_____
25	Outstanding personal achievement	28	_____
26	Wife beginning or ceasing work outside the home	26	_____
27	Beginning or ceasing formal schooling	26	_____
28	Major change in living conditions (*e.g.*, building a new home, remodeling, deterioration of home or neighborhood)	25	_____
29	Revision of personal habits (*e.g.*, dress, manners, association, and so on)	24	_____
30	Troubles with boss	23	_____
31	Major change in working hours or conditions	20	_____
32	Change in residence	20	_____
33	Changing to a new school	20	_____
34	Major change in usual type or amount of recreation	19	_____
35	Major change in church activities (*e.g.*, a lot more or a lot less than usual)	19	_____
36	Major changes in social activities (*e.g.*, clubs, dancing, movies, visiting, and so on)	18	_____
37	Taking out a mortgage or loan for a lesser purchase (*e.g.*, for a car, television, freezer, and so on)	17	_____
38	Major change in sleeping habits (a lot more or a lot less sleep, or change in part of day when asleep)	16	_____

Table 30-1.　　**The Social Readjustment Rating Scale (*continued*)**

RANK	EVENT	VALUE	SCORE
39	Major change in number of family get-togethers (*e.g.*, a lot more or a lot less than usual)	15	_____
40	Major change in eating habits (a lot more or a lot less food intake, or very different meal hours or surroundings)	15	_____
41	Vacation	13	_____
42	Christmas	12	_____
43	Minor violations of the law (*e.g.*, traffic tickets, jaywalking, disturbing the peace, and so on)	11	_____

(From Holmes TH and Rahe RH: The Social Reajustment Rating Scale. J Psychosom Res 11:213–218, 1967)

pendency needs and, possibly, serve to punish him for needs and feelings that he deemed unacceptable.

Types of Psychophysiologic Responses

In the past, there were certain diseases identified as psychophysiologic in nature; however, because humans are not dichotomous minds and bodies, it has been found to be true that psychological factors can play a role in the development or maintenance of any physical disturbance and vice versa.

Accordingly, the Diagnostic and Statistical Manual of Mental Disorders, third edition no longer identifies a group of physical diseases that encompass the diagnostic label "psychophysiologic disorder." Instead, the manual presents the category, "psychological factors affecting physical illness."[8] The health care provider is therefore reminded to eradicate the label and to look at the total person—physical, emotional, and sociocultural aspects of his functioning.

Gastrointestinal Disturbances

Peptic Ulcer. The typical person with peptic ulcer disease has been described as hard-working, strong, unemotional, and independent. These persons are often in executive occupational positions and, despite successes in these positions, are never quite satisfied with their performance or achievement.

Although peptic ulcer disease has no single cause, it is believed that strong dependency longings exist beneath the facade of independence. Gratification in meeting dependency needs may be blocked for external reasons or because of shameful feelings in expressing these needs. It is also thought that a genetic predisposition to gastric hypersecretion may exist in certain individuals.

Ulcerative Colitis. Experiences of intense anxiety or stress, many times associated with loss, frequently precipitate the onset or relapse of ulcerative colitis. Many people with ulcerative colitis tend to guard against becoming emotionally involved with another and are particularly sensitive to rejection, abandonment, or anger from others. When situations develop that evoke angry feelings, the person tends to unconsciously allow the values of staying in control, "being good," and remaining stoic to overshadow the need to express anger directly. Instead, the overactive colon indirectly communicates the feeling. Individuals with ulcerative colitis are frequently quite ambitious, energetic, and highly responsible, yet inwardly, they feel inferior. Outwardly, these people may exhibit characteristics of compulsiveness, conscientiousness, meticulousness, indecisiveness, and a strong sense of duty and honesty.

Anorexia Nervosa. Although the cause of anorexia nervosa is unknown, individual psychological and family issues seem to play major roles in the etiology. Adolescent girls whose parents are either affluent or convey an attitude of success are the most likely group affected by this disease. In early years, these individuals are frequently described as having been "model children," the pride and joy of their parents. In effect, they have not learned to trust their own initiative or to behave in response to their own needs or wants. Rather, the needs of the parents are paramount and the child does not learn that she has needs and wants separate from the parents', nor does she learn how to distinguish between the two sets of needs and wants.

Early issues of separation and individuation are unresolved, and in adolescence, when the struggle for identity and for a sense of independence again surges, the young person experiences intense anxiety and ineptness. One way that she discovers to establish a sense of control, identity, and independence is to starve and lose weight. In essence, the adolescent becomes a powerful master over a weakened slave, the body.

Paralleling the anorexic adolescent's childhood, which is described as trouble-free, is the family constellation described as happy, harmonious, and successful. The apparent marital harmony is, however, but a facade for underlying conflict and dysfunction. This disharmony is circumvented by parents, especially the mother, who is protective and controlling and who seeks self-satisfaction and affection from the "ideal" child. Typically, the families of anorexics are overinvolved in one another's lives and individuation is therefore lost.

Respiratory Disturbance

Asthma. A wide variety of personality types are seen among asthmatics. Some persons with asthma have an intense need to be protected and an exaggerated need to retain dependence and bonding to the mother. If the attachment to the mother figure is threatened in reality or symbolically in later life, insecure feelings and fears associated with abandonment and rejection heighten. Some asthmatic persons are hypersensitive to other persons; others are openly aggressive or hostile.

Cardiovascular Disturbances

Cardiovascular Disease. In addition to the advent of significant medical cardiology knowledge, treatment techniques, and equipment during the past few decades, there has been a new relevance placed on the relationship between personality type and the development of cardiovascular disease (*i.e.*, coronary artery disease, congestive heart failure, and myocardial infarction). Friedman and Rosenman described a "Type A" personality as being associated with high risks of developing cardiovascular disease.[5] "Type A" individuals are described as competitive, driven, hard-working, controlling, and aggressive. Frequently, these individuals occupy managerial or executive positions and, in a sense, their life is their work or "their work drives their life." Self-permission to enjoy life, relax, and have fun is usually at a minimum for these individuals.

Although the concept of the Type A personality certainly has relevance in all levels of cardiovascular disease prevention, it is not the only risk factor associated with the disease. Genetic factors such as predisposition to high cholesterol levels, social factors such as smoking, and factors such as obesity and lack of exercise interrelate with personality variables of individuals at risk. Nevertheless, when the person enters the health care system for treatment, the personality factors usually receive little, if any, attention. In fact, the attention may be in the form of some well-meant but superficial advice to "slow down" or "take life easy." The old concept of the mind–body dualism seems to surface and dominate. Nurses can play a significant role in preventing this hasty approach to psychophysiologic behaviors.

Essential Hypertension. As with other physical disorders, the etiologic basis of essential hypertension is related to more than one variable. The emotional component of repressed hostility, "bottled-up anger," seems to play a significant role in the lives of persons who have essential hypertension.

In encounters with people, especially within meaningful relationships where a typical or functional response may be anger, the individual with essential hypertension allows the guilt component of anger to serve as a barrier to the expression of his real feelings. In a sense, the person consciously or unconsciously chooses to "keep the lid" on his anger. Such pervasive responses of internalizing anger create mounting stress and tension. The avenue for expression of the tension related to repressed anger may be vasoconstriction of the blood vessels, which results in essential hypertension.

This method of viewing anger as an unacceptable emotion may have been learned in early life or through family experiences. Implied messages from significant adults to the young person may have been, "Strong, responsible, mature people don't feel angry, or certainly don't express anger if they feel it." In addition to early learning experiences of individuals who have essential hypertension, the possibility of a genetic predisposition cannot be dismissed when considering etiologic variables. Other variables that seem to relate to the development and maintenance of essential hypertension include socioeconomic status and cultural and ethnic origin.

Skin Disturbances

Unlike other bodily systems, the skin is visible—it is not camouflaged easily. No doubt, all people have experienced or observed the relationship between certain feeling states and skin responses. Physical responses to underlying emotions are readily apparent in the goose flesh of excitement or fear, the blush of the face or neck when one is embarrassed, and the sweating of palms or underarms accompanying anxiety or anger. These responses, under the control of the autonomic nervous system, are common to all persons and assist the body to maintain homeostasis. They generally do not represent the primary mode of communicating feelings.

Some skin disturbances, however, are not transitory in nature; they are severe and longer-lasting. Individuals suffering from these disturbances may engage in frequent itching or scratching or may complain of pain. Disfigurement of the skin in the form of excoriation or loss of pigmentation may ensue. The exact cause of skin disorders of this type is not known. It is proposed that the individual may house an unconscious conflict between wanting and not wanting to express a feeling, and this conflict is not generally in his awareness. During periods of stress, it is not uncommon to observe these individuals with skin disturbances communicating little, if any, verbal or direct emotional unrest. Instead, they frequently suffer exacerbations of skin disorders. This expression often serves as a means of receiving concern and attention from self and others.

Physiological Response In Emotional States

Depression. As it was described in Chapter 21, depression is a state of being that, in a sense, exemplifies the psychophysiologic unity of human beings. Depression may be expressed via the affect, the thought processes, and the physical channels available to the individual. Thoughts and feelings of self-doubt, dejection, or worthlessness impact on the availability and utilization of psychic as well as physical energy. If physical energy is depleted, bodily functions slow and the person is apt to describe himself as weak and "tired all the time."

In addition, it is not uncommon to hear people who are depressed talk about "aching all over" in the joints and muscles. The adage, "I feel like I have the world on my shoulders and I can't get it off," aptly describes both the psychic and bodily experience of many individuals who are depressed.

Another common occurrence in depression is a change in eating habits and gastrointestinal functioning. An individual who is agitatedly depressed and who manifests overt anxiety within the depression is a likely candidate to eat more than usual and to have diarrhea. In contrast, a person whose depression is more retarded in nature is more apt to eat less and have constipation.

Although these physiological alterations are common symptoms in obvious depressive states, an individual's depression may be masked or may appear in the guise of physical illness. Extensive medical testing may reveal no anatomic or physiological rationale for somatic symptoms that may preoccupy the individual. The somatic illness is very real to the person and should signal the astute health care professional to intervene in ways that facilitate the person to get in touch more directly with the underlying depression. Even if there is a structural or functional basis for physical illness, it has been estimated that 70% of persons hospitalized for medical reasons are suffering from depression. This fact has significant implications for the delivery of nursing care, which attests to the belief that man is a biological-psychosocial being.

Grief, Loss, and Change. In varying degrees, loss and change are familiar experiences to all persons at any point in the life cycle. Even the young infant who is weaned from the mother's breast in a sense relinquishes or loses an object that has provided pleasure and nourishment. Similarly, a young child entering school, or a late adolescent entering college, has the opportunity to experience the exciting, frightening, yet potentially satisfying, aspects of growing independence while simultaneously meeting the challenge of facing the accompanying aspects of loss of the familiar and change. As individuals experience loss and change, it is not uncommon for physical problems to surface. The common cold, the "splitting" headaches, and the nagging backache are a few of the possible physical reactions to the stress of loss and change. In some instances, the physical responses may be more severe and more debilitating than these examples.

Although it is true that not all individuals experience a physical response to loss and change, studies have indicated that life changes do positively correlate with health disruptions. After analyzing 5000 case histories of patients' life situations at the onset of illness, Holmes and Rahe developed a social readjustment rating scale (seen earlier in Table 30-1), which focuses on the amount of life-change events present in the subject's life at the onset of illness.[7] The scale delineates a value from 100 to 11 (referred to as Life Change Units, or LCUs) for each life event. The authors found that the higher the value of LCUs, the greater the likelihood that the individual would develop an illness. In fact, almost 80% of those people with over 300 Life Change Units over the past year become sick in the near future.[7]

Indeed, loss and change are inevitable; however, having information about the potential ramifications of the life change events may assist individuals to recognize the risks and plan for ways to cope adaptively rather than becoming physically ill.

Application of the Nursing Process to Psychophysiologic Disorders

Because stress plays a significant role in the initiation, exacerbation, and maintenance of any psychophysiologic response, the nurse has a responsibility to participate in all levels of preventative care. Through primary prevention, the nurse intervenes in ways that assist people to become more aware of potential stressors and to develop or maintain functional methods of adaptation. Secondary prevention focuses on interventions that demonstrate genuine caring and support as the nurse assists the client to improve his physical health, enhance self-knowledge, examine current methods employed to express his needs and feelings, adapt to stress, and consider alternatives for coping other than becoming physically ill. Through tertiary prevention, the nurse supports the client as he tries out new means of expressing his needs and feelings and coping with stress.

Primary Prevention

Promoting health and striving to reduce the incidence and prevalence of disease are at the forefront of nursing care in these last years of the 20th century. Accompanying this charge to nursing is the charge to every person in Western society—to cope with a world of ever-mounting stress and challenge. For nurses the charge is dual—take care of self and assist others to discover ways to adapt that facilitate emotional and physical well-being.

Some individuals choose to adapt to stress or to express emotional needs by becoming physically ill. Bottling up feelings, being frightened or unsure of how to express needs, and receiving reinforcement for such responses may well be at the root of many physical illnesses.

In primary prevention, nurses must direct intervention to the family as a target of care. All people launch on the journey of growth and development in the family unit and learn patterns of behavior that are either functional or dysfunctional. High-risk families for psychophysiologic responses are those in which one or both parents express needs and feelings via psychophysiological illnesses. Regardless of the setting, a thorough nursing assessment and analysis may reveal information suggesting that the client is at risk for using psychophysiologic behavior as a means of coping. Early preventative measures may be influential in choices made as growth and development progress.

Another vulnerable group for the development of psychophysiologic illness are individuals who have experienced multiple life changes. Changes are inevitable in life, yet the nurse engaging in primary prevention can offer information that assists people to cope functionally with change and stress, rather than relinquishing control to the event or stressor.

Planning and Intervening

Goals directed at the primary prevention of psychophysiologic behavior include the following.

1. The development of family relationship patterns that do not foster the use of psychophysiologic behaviors
2. Functional adaptation to life changes

The nurse practices in many settings where she can share her knowledge and skill by role-modeling, teaching, and supporting parents and entire families in fostering functional relationships with one another. The nurse utilizes interventions that facilitate the prevention of psychophysiologic disorders and the promotion of functional family relationships by assisting families to

1. create an atmosphere within the family that is caring, accepting, safe, and supportive;
2. develop and nourish communication patterns that are open and honest and that permit direct expression of feelings and needs;
3. accept, encourage, and respect the expression of differences in ideas and opinions;
4. negotiate and cooperate at times of conflict;
5. employ a flexible approach to problem-solving;
6. achieve a balance between belonging needs and separation needs (autonomy);
7. establish supportive resources beyond the family matrix.

Promoting functional adaptation to life changes may occur in a variety of settings. Opportunities for nursing practice in primary prevention far surpass the traditional hospital setting. Conducting speaking engagements at Parent Teachers Organization meetings, participating in health fairs, teaching prenatal and postnatal classes, and working with persons experiencing transitions in life are some of the settings in which anticipatory guidance may be practiced. Indeed, there are a myriad of life changes and perceptions of the impact of similar events may vary from person to person. The nurse assists individuals to prepare for changes and consider options for coping when stress mounts. Active nursing involvement may assist individuals to cope with the stress in ways other than becoming physically ill.

Secondary Prevention

By the time the nurse meets the individual with a psychophysiologic disturbance who is in need of secondary prevention, the disturbance is already present. Through application of the nursing process—assessment, analysis, planning, implementation, and evaluation—the nurse helps to shorten the duration of the existing disorder, thereby reducing the prevalence of the disorder.[3]

Because most individuals who are in need of treatment for psychophysiologic responses do not seek psychiatric care, the nurse is apt to meet these individuals in secondary care settings, such as outpatient and inpatient nonpsychiatric care settings.

Assessment and Analysis

Viewing the person as a system that is greater than the sum of its parts, or subsystems, assists the nurse in directing assessment at the whole person, rather than centering attention only on the most obvious—the physical body. Indeed, collecting and analyzing data relative to the manifested physical disorder are significant nursing activities. The nurse's knowledge of the possible multiple causes of the illness facilitates the performance of a comprehensive assessment that includes also the psychological, social, and family influences of the individual. Analysis of the assessment data focuses on a thorough examination of the possible interrelationships of all systems assessed. While assessing the individual, the nurse simultaneously uses the self and conveys behaviors that exemplify understanding of therapeutic relationships (The reader is referred to Chapter 4).

The nursing assessment of the individual who exhibits psychophysiologic behavior addresses the major areas of

1. physical examination;
2. history-taking (physical and psychosocial life);
3. emotional themes.

Physical Examination. Performance of a thorough examination is a skill that nurses even 20 years ago did not practice. In most nursing curricula today, the nursing student begins to develop and master physical assessment skills. These skills linked with knowledge of the physical sciences enable the nurse to monitor continuously the individual's physiological status and to plan nursing interventions accordingly.

History-Taking. During the history-taking portion of the assessment process, the nurse aims to assist the client in reporting factual information relative to his current and past health status. In addition, the nurse meets the challenge of blending the more traditional medical model history-taking format, which focuses on areas such as pertinent demographic data, present illness, past health status, and family health, with a psychosociocultural assessment model, which focuses on areas such as the client's perception of himself, his perception of changes in his lifestyle that might be associated with his current health status, his emotional responses to his health, and his relationships with others and his culture. (The reader is referred to textbooks of medical-surgical nursing or physical assessment.)

The client's psychosociocultural assessment includes the following significant assessment areas.

1. What are the client's attitudes toward his physical illness as well as his knowledge about the illness? How does he feel about being ill? What does he think about being ill?
2. What does the client perceive as his strengths and his limitations?
3. How does the client usually adapt to stress or tension?
4. Have significant others in the client's past made use of behaviors similar to his when adapting to stress?
5. What events preceded or precipitated this physical illness?
6. What relationship does the client perceive between his physical illness and his emotions or behavior?
7. What tasks has the illness prevented the client from engaging in?
8. In what ways has the physical disorder changed the client's or his family's lifestyle?
9. What roles have changed in the client's family because of his physical illness?
10. How does the client generally get his emotional needs met?
11. What interpersonal resources are available to the client?

It is useful for the nurse to remember that assessment is not complete after the first nurse–client contact. In fact, based upon the client's physical status and the nurse's perception of his comfort and trust level, the nurse may decide that pursuit of psychosocial assessment is inappropriate during the initial contact. As the client's physical status improves, or as trust and rapport are built between the nurse and client, the nurse actively facilitates the patient's thinking about, and disclosing of, pertinent psychosociocultural history.

Emotional Themes. As an open, trusting nurse–client relationship develops, information becomes evident pertaining to the client's usual ways of behaving within relationships and ways in which the client expresses his needs and feelings. Because all human behavior has meaning, the nursing assessment focuses on analysis of the behavior, which includes speculation and validation of underlying emotional themes.

Through the client's interaction with the nurse, the nurse may perceive that the client has difficulty openly expressing dependency needs. For example, the client may describe himself as very self-sufficient and independent, yet the nurse notices that at least every hour, many times right after she has left his room, the client rings his call light and wants something. Similarly, assessment might indicate that the client has difficulty with openly expressing anger and, instead, seems to "swallow it down," suppress it, and remain physically ill.

Difficulties expressing dependency needs and anger are not the only emotional issues that may interfere with the client's functioning. Other emotions such as pervasive anxiety, guilt, powerlessness, loneliness, and insecurity may seem to be at the core, yet covered by the veneer, of the physical illness. During the assessment and analysis phases, as well as during the practice of the entire nursing process, it is within the nurse's role to approach the client with caring and acceptance while striving to learn about the client and assisting him to know himself in a fuller way.

Planning and Intervening

When planning care, the nurse must prioritize the client's needs and intervene accordingly. In some instances, the client may be acutely physically ill, and his physical condition therefore mandates that the nurse's attention be directed primarily to physical care. Even in these situations, the nurse blends knowledge and skills in the physical aspects of delivering care in a caring, compassionate, and helpful manner. The therapeutic use of self allows the nurse to minister to the physical needs of the client while simultaneously responding to his verbal and nonverbal cues that may indicate underlying emotions such as fear or anxiety. As the client's physical condition improves, the nurse is likely to find that the single most important ingredient of intervention is using the self in a manner that communicates openness, empathy, caring, and acceptance. These behaviors of the nurse are likely to facilitate the client's decision to adapt in ways that are more functional and satisfying.

Because psychophysiologic behavior is communicated by means of various bodily systems, assessment and analysis may reveal that specific goals and interventions need to be directed toward the care of affected bodily organs—cardiovascular, gastrointestinal, or any other. Nevertheless, assessment of the total person may indicate that, in addition to goals related to physical needs, goals also need to address the following.

1. Recognition and ownership of feelings and needs
2. Provision of opportunities to express feelings and needs in an open, direct, functional manner

When intervening to assist the client to meet goals other than those associated with specific physical needs, the nurse recognizes that the client is frequently unaware of the relationship between physical and emotional aspects of his being. Frequently, the mental mechanisms of denial, repression, and suppression are operating; therefore, awareness of feelings and their impact on his behavior and choices are not known consciously by the client. These defenses are frequently strong and serve an important purpose for the client. Therefore, the nurse uses care and caution in approaches to help the client become more insightful (see Therapeutic Dialogue: Approaching the Client Who Has Essential Hypertension).

A good principle of therapeutic practice is never to remove a person's defense unless or until you can offer a replacement that is more functionally sustaining. Sometimes, zealous health care providers think they know the answers to the client's problem and eagerly "lay the cards on the table." This type of zeal can, in fact, be destructive and possibly even reinforce the client's dysfunctional modes of adaptation. Instead, attitudes and behaviors that convey a genuine willingness to help the client discover for himself

Therapeutic Dialogue

Approaching the Client Who Has Essential Hypertension

Nurse: (seated facing client in the outpatient clinic examining room, preparing to take client's blood pressure)

Client: You know, you'd think the kind of life I live would help this blood pressure of mine go down. I couldn't be more sedentary at home. After John goes to work in the morning, it's just me, the house, and the dog. (looking at nurse, soft tone of voice)

Nurse: (placing blood pressure cuff on the table, arms and hands open and resting on lap) Tell me about how you spend a typical day.

Client: Well, my typical day really amounts to fixing meals for my husband and having things ready when he comes home from work. He likes his lunch at 12:00 noon and supper at 6:00 p.m. The two of us don't go out much in the evenings because John likes to be in bed by 10:00 p.m. (questioning tone of voice, maintaining eye contact)

Nurse: So, the structure you operate within revolves mostly around your husband. (pause) What about things you do for yourself?

Client: Well, let me see. (pause, thoughtful expression) I really don't know how to answer that question.

Nurse: Are you saying that your husband is your full-time job? (leaning towards client, maintaining eye contact)

Client: Well, I hadn't thought about it like that, but now that you mention it, it seems like that's so.

Nurse: (nodding) That makes sense to me. Often, when people are busy focusing primarily on others, they tend to overlook themselves.

Client: Yeah, you know, when you take care of people and make sure that all the things that have to happen, happen, there isn't much time and energy left over. (maintaining eye contact)

Nurse: So from your perspective, the only place left to do without your time and energy is you, and what you do for you for yourself.

Discussion

The client's opening comment gives the nurse a clue that Mrs. S. is thinking about the possible relationship between her life situation and her essential hypertension. In an effort to offer support, the nurse directs her attention to Mrs. S. rather than to Mrs. S's. illness; that is, taking her blood pressure. Active listening and genuine interest are demonstrated as the nurse encourages Mrs. S. to describe her thoughts.

Throughout the interaction, the nurse's approach is nonthreatening and accepting as she moves at Mrs. S's. pace. She encourages Mrs. S. to focus on herself—not on her hypertension or her husband—and to reflect on how she goes about "taking care of herself."

The nurse supports Mrs. S. as she considers the new awareness that she apparently chooses to define herself via her husband. The nurse does not push Mrs. S. to explore her possible reaction to this choice; that is, essential hypertension. Although a goal in future interactions may be exploring her reaction, at this time, the nurse appropriately chooses to continue establishing trust and supporting the client in her recent insight.

options to solving his problems are potentially far more constructive and useful.

Because the emotional themes of unmet dependency needs or unexpressed anger frequently underlie the client's psychophysiologic behavior, the following nursing approaches are recommended.

Nursing Interventions for Unmet Dependency Needs

1. Be aware of your own feelings and how you allow these to affect your behavior. Because the client's need is often communicated by means of a facade of independence and demanding or manipulative behavior, the reaction of the nurse may be that of anger and resistance. Develop an awareness and understanding of this dynamic and seek supervision for dealing with your own feelings if necessary.
2. Be accepting of the client's feelings. The client will quickly pick up on nonacceptance, which tends to reinforce his maladaptive position.
3. Begin by meeting the client's dependency needs, then gradually help him meet more of his own needs. Developmentally, the client may well be in a position like a young child who needs consistent caring and mothering. The nurse is in the position to offer the needed nurturing while, at the same time, recognizing the client as a responsible individual.
4. Anticipate the client's dependency needs. Remember that the client's denial of his dependency needs or his feeling that it is not acceptable to ask directly to have his needs met is likely to be strong. Expecting that he will quickly give this up is apt to lead to feelings of anger, distance, and resistance in the nurse and feelings of anger and anxiety in the client. Therefore, recognition and anticipation of needs early in the relationship are useful in meeting the client's needs and building a solid foundation of trust within the relationship. This trust becomes an especially valuable vehicle in facilitating the client to develop greater insight, self-acceptance, and functional independence.
5. As the trusting relationship progresses, support and encourage any cues of functional independence. Assist the client, if need be, but don't usurp his responsibility and ability to think and do for himself. Of great importance is your support, caring, and willingness to follow through with your commitment to him and acceptance of him.
6. Throughout the process, use yourself in modeling and facilitating open communication. Assist the client in thinking about and talking about his thoughts and feelings. As the client becomes aware of his dependent behavior and, hopefully, moves toward growing independence, he is likely to experience feelings of anger, shame, guilt, or anxiety.

Encourage him in identifying and working through these feelings.

Nursing Interventions for Hostility

1. Be aware of your own feelings and how you allow these to affect your behavior. Considering that the client's expression of hostility is usually passive or diverted outwardly to an inappropriate source, the nurse's reaction may be frustration, avoidance, or anger. Allowing these feelings to influence your behavior negatively is likely to prevent the client from exploring his real feelings and the source of his feelings.
2. Be accepting of the client and his feelings. Acceptance is likely to facilitate the client in gradually developing a higher level of insight and eventually adapting in a more functional manner. Consider that the client fears rejection and abandonment if he deals directly with his feelings; therefore, nonacceptance may reinforce his fears. Repressing his anger is the client's prime way of adapting. Repression is usually strong and serves as a significant protective mechanism. Patience and acceptance are important approaches as a relationship builds and develops.
3. Assist the client with recognizing his anger, identifying the source of his anger in current situations, and exploring alternative ways of dealing with his anger. This may be a very slow process because the client learned his maladaptive behavior over a long period of time. Through a trusting nurse–client relationship, the client may decide that open, direct dealing with feelings affords him a welcomed release from the anxiety and tension experienced when he "bottled up his feelings."
4. Consider that the client is apt to direct his anger towards you. This may occur by means of criticism, profanity, or in other derogatory ways. Set limits on the behavior while at the same time showing acceptance of the client and his feelings.

In addition to individual care for the client, the family, likewise, must be a focus of nursing care. Reminding oneself that the client did not exist or develop in a vacuum when he chose psychophysiologic responses as a mode of adaptation is useful in guiding the nurse to broaden her perspective toward the family. There is therapeutic value in the nurse developing a relationship with the family and intervening as needed. The nurse also assists the family to examine ways the whole family system impacts on the client's physical status, as well as how the physical status of the client impacts on the family.

Evaluation

Evaluation is an ongoing process and overlaps with each phase of the nursing process. Because individuals who respond psychophysiologically communicate their needs through various bodily systems, evaluation of the effect of care on the client's physical status is contingent upon the bodily system involved and the degree of progression or regression of the physical malady. Regarding the impact of nursing care on the client's emotional well-being, the nurse–client relationship may be the most valuable measure of the client's status.

The nurse directs her focus to the established goals when engaging in evaluation. For example, a goal for the client might have been to identify thoughts and feelings relative to being physically ill. When evaluating whether or not this goal has been met, the nurse examines interactions with the client and cites progress, regression. or status quo. Evaluation allows the nurse to continue or adjust the plan of care and it is crucial to the delivery of quality nursing care.

Tertiary Prevention

The major focus of tertiary prevention may be to support the individual who is considering whether or not he wants to make changes that could potentially reduce the likelihood of responding to stress by becoming physically ill. It is not uncommon for individuals who respond psychophysiologically to resist change in lifestyle, attitudes, and behavior. Along with change comes loss—loss of a customary, familiar way of adapting; that is, physical illness. In a sense, the physical illness has offered the person a sense of security. The idea of change is frightening, but the nurse is in a position to "be with" the person as she assesses his readiness to consider change and as he chooses whether or not to move through the problem-solving process.

Planning and Intervening

The major goal for tertiary prevention of psychophysiologic behavior is to develop functional adaptation to life stressors, without psychophysiologic behavior.

It is important for the nurse to remember, when planning interventions, that patterns of adaptation are not changed readily. Behavior changes slowly and the nurse must monitor her expectations of self and of the client. Expecting too much of either self or the client only serves as a major obstacle to helping the client consider more functional methods of adaptation. An important goal for the nurse may be to eradicate any expectations that she might hold. This would free the nurse to be herself and to assist the client in being realistic as he examines himself.

Interventions that focus on the change process are the major ones during tertiary prevention of psychophysiologic disorders. The reader is referred to literature on the change process for a thorough presentation of steps in the process. The following interventions are offered for consideration.

1. Assist the individual in examining and clarifying his values and goals.

2. Assist the individual to examine realistically how he currently copes with stress and to consider what, if any, incongruence there might be between his mode of coping and his values and goals.

3. Be honest in sharing your perceptions regarding the negative consequences of his current coping pattern.

4. Assist the person with considering alternative modes of coping. Facilitate identifying pros and cons of all alternatives and help him consider ramifications for self and significant others.

5. Offer support as the person decides to change.

6. Positively reinforce functional change and do not abandon the person when and if he regresses to old modes of adaptation.

Evaluation

When evaluating the care offered during the tertiary phase of prevention with a person who responds psychophysiologically, the nurse directs focus to the modes of adaptation the person chooses in order to cope with stress. It may be useful for the nurse to consider the following questions.

What evidence exists to suggest that the person views stress as a growth-producing experience rather than a destructive one?

What change in lifestyle, attitude, and behavior does the person exhibit?

Has the person given up physical ills as a mode of adapting?

How is he currently adapting?

Is the person open with expressing and dealing with feelings?

Is problem-solving easier for the person?

What changes are evident in the family's style of relating?

Answers to these and similar questions may indicate whether or not the person has decided to adopt a more functional coping pattern and is striving to exercise self-control instead of allowing events and situations to control his life choices.

Summary

This chapter has focused primarily on a view of physical illness as a mode of communicating physiological dysfunction as well as emotional unrest. Suggestions for nursing care during primary, secondary, and tertiary prevention have been offered. Presentation of the following ideas have been included.

1. The human being is a composite of interrelated systems; therefore, the mind and the body cannot be divorced from one another.

2. There is no single cause for psychophysiologic re-

sponses; etiologic theories include psychosocial, biologic, and familial factors.

3. Physical illness may be a means of communicating feeling states and needs such as anxiety, anger, and dependency.

4. The integral relationship between an individual's thinking, feeling, and physical status may be evident in physiological disorders involving the gastrointestinal system, respiratory system, cardiovascular system, and integumentary system, as well as in the individual's response to depression, grief, loss, and change.

5. The nurse has a responsibility to participate in primary, secondary, and tertiary care aimed at preventing psychophysiologic disturbances.

6. During the primary prevention of psychophysiologic behavior, the nurse aims to promote functional family relationships and functional adaptation to life changes.

7. Most individuals in need of secondary prevention for psychophysiologic disorders are nonpsychiatric patients.

8. Assessment, intervention, and evaluation for the psychophysiologically disturbed person focuses on physical and psychosocial life, as well as on the expressions of emotional needs and feelings.

9. The emotional themes of unmet dependency needs or unexpressed anger frequently underlie psychophysiologic behavior.

10. During the tertiary prevention of psychophysiologic behavior, the client's engagement in the process of change is the focus of nursing practice.

Case Study

Planning Care for the Client Who Is Diagnosed with Ulcerative Colitis

Deanna, a well-dressed, pale-appearing secretary in an advertising agency, was admitted to the medical unit with a diagnosis of *Ulcerative Colitis.* During the admission interview with the nurse, Deanna reported that her physical symptoms had started approximately 1 year ago, and that she had experienced a weight loss of 20 pounds and bouts of bloody diarrhea during the past 3 months. With a flat tone of voice she stated, "I have followed the doctor's orders to a tee. Those steroid enemas and Azulfidine just haven't helped enough. I wanted so much to avoid hospitalization, but this mess seems to have gotten the best of me. My doctor says that resting here should help my colon settle down."

While caring for Deanna during her early days of hospitalization, the nurse learned that Deanna had an older and a younger brother who lived approximately 150 miles away, in the same city as her parents. She was the only daughter of a father who managed "a successful business started years ago by his grandfather." Deanna verbalized little about her mother; however, she did state, "I told her about my being hospitalized because I knew she'd expect to know, but I hope she won't come to visit." When the nurse encouraged Deanna to elaborate on this comment regarding her mother, Deanna chose to shift the topic to talking about her work.

She described herself as a very conscientious, reliable, and dependable secretary. The advertising agency for whom she worked had undergone a change in organizational structure during the past year and Deanna's workload had increased considerably. She explained, "I never seem to be able to clear my desk completely anymore. I do the secretarial work for so many more people than when I started working there, 5 years ago. Now that I'm in the hospital with this colon problem, I guess I'll be even further behind when I get back to my job. I'm so tired of all this diarrhea." As Deanna talked about her role at work, the nurse noted that she did not verbalize directly about her feelings relative to the stress she was experiencing, but tended to focus on the fact that her hospitalization would impact negatively on her productivity at work.

Goals of nursing care established early during Deanna's hospitalization include the following.

1. Reducing the inflammation of the colon by assisting Deanna to follow the prescribed medical regime; that is, diet and medication
2. Encouraging and providing opportunities for Deanna to experience adequate comfort and rest
3. Facilitating the development of a nurse–client relationship that would provide emotional support while reducing emotional stress

Deanna's somewhat debilitated physical condition mandated the nurse giving high priority to monitoring Deanna's response to the prescribed diet and sedative, antidiarrheal, steroids, and antibiotic drugs. While encouraging activity within the limit of Deanna's physical capabilities, the nurse geared interventions toward promoting and supporting rest. As with any nurse–client relationship, facilitating trust development and maintaining acceptance of the client were of prime importance as the nurse related to Deanna.

The nurse moved at Deanna's pace as she gradually began to talk about her relationship with her mother and her mother's unreasonableness in her expectations of Deanna. Deanna continued to deny the possible relationship between or among her increased responsibility at work, her reaction to the stress she experienced at work, her conflictual relationship with her mother, and her development of ulcerative colitis.

Questions for Discussion

1. Discuss your values, attitudes, and beliefs that might impact on your care of Deanna.
2. What additional psychosocial assessment data would be useful in planning care for Deanna? Why?
3. Describe Deanna's primary ways of coping with stress (anxiety) at this time. How might the nurse intervene?
4. What possible emotional themes underlie Deanna's psychophysiologic behavior? Formulate a nursing care plan for Deanna, using one of these themes as a basis of problem identification or nursing diagnosis.

Nursing Diagnosis and Long-Term Goals

Clients with Psychophysiologic Disorders

Nursing diagnoses and long-term goals for clients experiencing psychophysiological disorders are offered as examples and are not meant to be conclusive. The nurse is reminded that specific nursing diagnoses are based on assessment of the individual client's behavioral manifestation of a problem and the contributing stressors. Although two clients may, in fact, have the same medical diagnosis (*e.g.*, asthma), the nursing diagnoses for these individuals may vary because of their uniqueness.

After identifying the nursing diagnosis, long-term goals designed to eradicate or modify the actual problem are identified. After identifying long-term goals, the nurse develops short-term goals that involve more specific and measurable outcomes.

Nursing Diagnosis	*Long-Term Goal*
Recurring headaches related to expressing anger in an indirect, passive manner	Facilitate direct, active expression of anger
Painful joints related to anxiety from perceived powerlessness and loss of control in work situation	Promote the adoption of self-control and power over reaction to stress at work
Pruritus and excoriation of the skin related to the loss of significant other	Facilitate the experience of grieving in an adaptive, functional manner
Bronchial constriction and wheezing related to anxiety from marital discord	Facilitate the utilization of problem-solving skills to cope with anxiety
Recurring bouts of diarrhea related to unrealistic self-expectations and expectations of others	Encourage realistic appraisal of strengths and weaknesses of self and others
Pseudo-independent behavior related to denial of dependency needs	Support more functional ways of fulfilling dependency longings
Adoption of sick role related to anxiety from increased role responsibilities as parent	Facilitate the utilization of problem-solving skills to cope with anxiety
Disturbed body image related to anxiety from identity confusion	Encourage realistic appraisal of self

References

1. Alexander F: Psychosomatic Medicine: Its Principles and Applications. New York, WW Norton, 1950
2. Cannon WB: Bodily Changes in Pain, Hunger, Fear and Rage. New York, Appleton, 1920
3. Caplan G: Principles of Preventive Psychiatry. New York, Basic Books, 1964
4. Dunbar F: Emotions and Bodily Changes. New York, Columbia University Press, 1954
5. Friedman M, Roseman RH: Type A Behavior and Your Health. New York, Alfred A. Knopf, 1974
6. Holmes TH: Life Situations, Emotions, and Diseases. Psychosomatics 19 (December): 747–754, 1978
7. Holmes TH, Rahe RH: The Social Readjustment Rating Scale. Journal of Psychosom Res 11:213–218, 1967
8. Leighton AH: My Name is Legion: Foundations for a Theory of Man in Relation to Culture, Vol. I: Sterling County Study of Psychiatric Disorder and Sociocultural Environment. New York, Basic Books, 1959
9. Looney JG, Lipp MR, Spitzer RL: A New Method of Classification for Psychophysiologic Disorders. Am J Psychiatry 135 (March): 304–308, 1978
10. Minuchin S, Roseman B, Baker L: Psychosomatic Families: Anorexia Nervosa in Context. Massachusetts, Harvard University Press, 1978
11. Mirsky IA: The Psychosomatic Approach to the Etiology of Clinical Disorders. Psychosom Med 19:424, 1957
12. Selye H: The Stress of Life. New York, McGraw-Hill, 1956
13. Srole L, Langner TS, Michael ST et al: Mental Health in The Metropolis: The Midtown Manhattan Study. New York, McGraw-Hill, 1962

Part VII
Crisis

Chapter 31
Crisis Theory and Intervention

A small trouble is like a pebble. Hold it too close to your eyes, and it fills the whole world and puts everything out of focus. Hold it at proper viewing distance, and it can be examined and properly classified. Throw it at your feet, and it can be seen in its true setting, just one more tiny bump on the pathway to eternity.

Celia Luce

Sandra L. Patterson

Chapter Preview

In our vocabulary today, crisis and stress are common words that are often used interchangeably; however, stress and crisis are not synonymous. There are many events, in everyone's life, that are stressful—a new career, prematurely gray hair, the loss of a friend, or the acquisition of dentures. As long as the individual is able to cope with the stressful event and is not overwhelmed by it, he does not experience a crisis. On the other hand, any stressful event could precipitate a crisis for the individual depending on his perceptions, his coping skills, and the support available to him. This chapter focuses on crisis theory, and the types and development of crises. Crisis intervention is explored through the application of the nursing process to individuals in crisis.

Learning Objectives

On completion of the chapter, the reader should be able to accomplish the following.

1. Discuss the development of crisis theory
2. Describe the phases of a crisis
3. Differentiate between maturational and situational crises
4. Discuss the goals and methods of crisis intervention
5. Contrast crisis intervention and traditional forms of therapy
6. Apply the nursing process to a client or family in crisis
    Assess the perception of the precipitating event, the coping skills, and the available support system of the client in crisis
    Identify the problems and potential problems of the client in a crisis
    Plan goals and an appropriate time frame for the resolution of a crisis
    Implement nursing actions to resolve a crisis in a healthy, adaptive manner
    Evaluate the effectiveness of the nursing actions
7. Discuss the feelings and needs of the intervener in crises
8. Formulate a comprehensive nursing care plan for the client in crisis

Crisis Theory

Crisis means a turning point, whether in disease or another condition. There are two symbols in the Chinese language to communicate crisis—they are "danger" and "opportunity."

In time of crisis, an individual is not sure what to do. His usual methods of problem-solving are not effective or are unavailable to him. As his anxiety and pain increase, the person becomes more willing to try new ways of problem-solving. In his willingness to try new methods of coping lies the opportunity for growth. Good mental health is thought to be predominantly the result of a life history of successful crisis resolutions.[4] Intervention during crisis has been found to reduce greatly the incidence and severity of mental disorders.

Development of Crisis Theory

Although people have been vulnerable to crises since the beginning of human existence, crisis has been an issue of serious study only in the last 30 years. Caplan defines crisis as a threat to one's homeostasis.[8] During crisis an imbalance exists between the magnitude of the problem and the immediate resources available to deal with it. This imbalance results in confusion and disorganization.[8] The active crisis state lasts a relatively short period of time—approximately 4 to 6 weeks. The individual is unable to tolerate this level of anxiety and imbalance for very long. Quick, appropriate intervention is of paramount importance in helping individuals in crisis return to an optimal state of functioning.

A number of researchers contributed to the development of crisis theory. Lindeman studied the survivors and families of the victims of the disastrous Coconut Grove nightclub fire in Boston in which many people died. Based on those observations and his study of other families who had lost a family member through death, Lindeman described the commonalities of the experience of crisis and bereavement.[22] From this classic study in 1944, some of the basic tenets of crisis theory were developed. Caplan has done the most extensive work on crisis theory and was influenced by the research and writings of Lindeman, Parad, Rapaport, Erikson, and others.[18]

Crisis theory is derived from psychoanalytical theory and the work of ego psychologists. Ego psychology stresses the human ability to learn and grow throughout life.[18] The research, upon which crisis theory is based, involved the study of crisis in bereavement, the reactions of parents to the birth of a normal or premature child, crisis of surgery, crisis experienced by Peace Corps volunteers, responses to the ordinary upsets of early married life, and crisis as a result of war.[8]

Crisis theory emerged in an era of increased social consciousness. John F. Kennedy passionately addressed the Congress and the nation about the need for a national health program with a new approach to mental illness. He maintained that the promotion of mental health was everyone's responsibility—government at every level, private foundations, as well as individual citizens. Congress directed the establishment of a Joint Commission on Mental Illness and Health. As a result of the work of this commission, funds were made available for a nationwide system of community mental health centers whose emphasis was the prevention of emotional disorders. John F. Kennedy has been credited as an instrumental force in the revolution in American psychiatry.[8]

What Happens in a Crisis

According to crisis theory, an individual strives to maintain a constant state of emotional equilibrium. If the person is confronted with an overwhelming threat and is unable to cope, crisis ensues.

This state of disequilibrium, known as crisis, lasts approximately 4 to 6 weeks. Because the crisis state is accompanied by high anxiety, the individual will either adapt and return to his previous state of mental health, develop more constructive coping skills, or decompensate to a lower level of functioning.

The factors that influence the outcome of the crisis are as follows.

1. The individual's previous problem-solving experience
2. How the individual views the problem
3. The amount of help or hindrance from significant others in his life[18]

Maladaptive crisis resolution increases the probability that the individual will unsuccessfully resolve crises in the future.

During the crisis state of disequilibrium, the person is more open to receiving professional help and learning new ways of problem-solving. He is also more likely to make changes in attitude and behavior in a short period of time.

The focus of crisis intervention is on the problem or stressor that precipitated the crisis state rather than on personality traits. Some examples of stressors are marriage, loss of a limb, and death of a child. The person in crisis is viewed as essentially normal, capable of problem-solving, and capable of growth with a little assistance from others.[17, 18, 24, 29]

Phases of a Crisis

To better understand how a crisis develops, we will examine the phases or steps that lead to an active crisis state. The first phase of a crisis is an increase in anxiety in response to a traumatic event.[8] The person tries to use his familiar coping mechanisms to resolve the feeling of increased anxiety. If his coping mechanisms are effective, he will not be in crisis; however, if they are ineffective, he will enter the second phase of crisis, which is marked by an increase in anxiety due to the failure of his usual coping mechanisms.

In the third phase of crisis, the person's anxiety continues to rise and he usually feels forced to reach out and try to find some assistance. If the person is emotionally isolated before he experiences the traumatic event, it is usually impossible for him to avert a crisis.

The fourth phase is the active state of crisis, wherein the person's inner resources and support systems are inade-quate. The precipitating event is not resolved and stress and anxiety mount to an intolerable level.

The individual who is in an active state of crisis demonstrates certain typical behaviors. He has a short attention span, ruminates, and looks inwardly for possible reasons for the traumatic event and how he might have changed or avoided it. This rumination is accompanied by a great deal of anguish, apprehension, and distress. The person's behavior becomes increasingly impulsive and unproductive. His relationships with others usually suffer. The individual becomes less aware of his environment and begins to view others in terms of their ability to help solve his problem. His searching behavior appears confused and disoriented.[5]

Due to the high level of anxiety he is experiencing, the individual may think that he is "losing his mind" or "going crazy."[18] One's perceptive ability is greatly affected by high levels of anxiety, but this is not the same as psychosis. The individual in crisis often needs this explanation and the reassurance that, when he feels less anxious, he will be able to think clearly again.

Types of Crises

Maturational Crisis

There are two types of crisis—*maturational*, precipitated by the normal stress of development, and *situational*, precipitated by a sudden traumatic event. Erik Erikson identified specific periods in normal development when there is a predictable increase in anxiety or stress that could precipitate a maturational crisis.[10] Some common events that may precipitate a crisis during the various developmental stages are birth, mastering control of body functions, starting school, puberty, leaving home, marriage–parenthood; loss of physical youthfulness, and retirement.

A maturational, or developmental, crisis may occur at any of the transitional periods in normal growth and development. Because each stage of development is dependent on the previous stage, the inability to master the tasks of one stage thwarts one's growth and development in subsequent stages of life. Why are these times considered a crisis for some and not for others? One explanation is that some people are unable to make the numerous role changes necessary for the new maturational level.[15] For instance, the birth of the first child constitutes numerous role changes for the parents. Some parents are able to adapt and make the necessary role changes; others, due to a variety of reasons, such as emotional immaturity, marital discord, financial stress, and unmet dependency needs, may not be able to adapt readily to the new roles.

There are three main reasons why an individual may not be able to prevent a maturational crisis. First, the person may not be able to visualize himself in the new role due to inadequate role models. For example, a male child reared without the love and guidance of a father or adult male may have difficulty assuming the role of a loving, guiding, involved parent. Secondly, the individual may lack the interpersonal resources to make the appropriate and necessary changes. For example, the person may lack the flexibility to alter his life goals in order to avoid a mid-life crisis, or he may lack the communication skills needed to maintain a long-term relationship. Thirdly, other people may refuse to recognize the individual's maturational role change. Some parents fail to acknowledge their adolescent's movement toward adulthood and attempt to keep him in a child's role—precipitating a crisis for the adolescent.

In each stage of development, a person needs nurturance from others to work through the tasks of that stage and to obtain the necessary skills for the next level of development.[18] When adequate social support from family and friends is available, the individual is able to channel his increased anxiety and resultant energy into constructive growth and a feeling of accomplishment. Maturational crises are predictable and occur gradually; therefore, it is possible to prepare for these stressful transitional periods and prevent the occurrence of a crisis. Premarital counseling, preparation for parenting, and planning for retirement are examples of anticipatory guidance in crisis prevention.

Situational Crisis

A situational crisis is a response to a traumatic event that is usually sudden and unavoidable. When the stressful event threatens the physical, emotional, or social integrity of the individual, the likely result is a crisis.[1]

A situational crisis usually follows the loss of an established support. The individual's usual way of presenting himself is disrupted, and this disruption consequently threatens the way he views himself. From infancy on, each person develops an image of himself through the feedback he receives from the important people in his environment. Later in his development, the person defines himself according to the various roles he assumes. Throughout life, one's self-image hinges on the continuity of roles and the establishment of new role relationships. The threat or loss of a role viewed as necessary to maintain one's self-image will usually lead to a crisis state. The loss of a job, the loss of a spouse, the birth of a retarded child, or the diagnosis of a chronic or terminal illness will affect the way a person perceives himself.[16]

The most common response to a loss or deprivation is depression. An important point to remember in crisis intervention, however, is that if the person perceives the threat or loss as a challenge, he is more likely to move toward effective problem-solving.[26]

The difficulty in dealing with a situational crisis is compounded when it occurs at the same time the individual is struggling with a developmental crisis.[13] Take note of this as an element in crisis intervention. A client, J. R., related that, without any prior discussion, on his 18th birthday, his father told him it was time for him to be out on his own.

This occurred 2 months before Christmas and J. R. said that he was unsure of where to go or what to do. He felt hurt and abandoned. J. R. packed his suitcase and went to Europe. He spent the most miserable Christmas he could ever remember. Not long after that, his van exploded resulting in a loss of most of his possessions. He also sustained burns on his face and hands. He remembers wandering around in a daze without being able to think clearly. The American Embassy helped him get home. Possibly, J. R. could have coped with the trauma of the fire if he had not been so vulnerable, struggling with his response to being forced to leave home.

Balancing Factors in a Stressful Event

There are certain factors that determine whether a person will enter a crisis state.[1] The balancing factors are as follows.

1. How the person perceives the event
2. What experience he has had in coping
3. His available coping mechanisms
4. The people who can be supportive to him

Aguilera and Messick devised a paradigm to assist the crisis intervener analyze and resolve a crisis situation (see Fig. 31-1).[1] It is important to remember that the paradigm is a guide to help the intervener think clearly about the problem, not a solution to the client's problem. The person in crisis will need assistance working through some of the feelings associated with what has happened to him.

Crisis Intervention

The goal of crisis intervention is to assist the person in distress to resolve his immediate problem and regain his emotional equilibrium. This problem-solving will, hopefully, lead to a higher level of coping ability to deal with future stressful events.

The role of the intervener is one of active participation with the individual in solving his present problem. Because the crisis state is not an illness, the helper does not take over and make decisions for the person unless he is suicidal or homicidal.[16, 18] Crisis intervention is a partnership.[25] The underlying philosophy of crisis intervention is that, with varying degrees of assistance, people can help themselves.[18] To maximize the opportunity for growth, the person in crisis must be actively involved in resolving the problem. Crisis intervention is a thinking, problem-solving approach.[5]

The intervener helps the person in crisis analyze the stressful event, encourages him to express his feelings, and tells him that he has a right to his feelings no matter what they are. He explores methods of dealing with stress with the client and reinforces his strengths and abilities. The

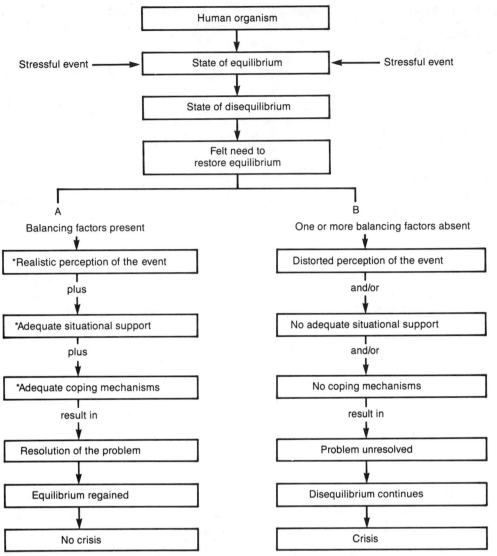

*Balancing factors (From Aguilera DC, Messick JM: Crisis Intervention, 4th ed. St Louis, CV Mosby, 1982)

Figure 31-1. *Paradigm: the effect of balancing factors in a stressful event.*

client is encouraged to seek support from friends, family, and other resource groups in the community. Planning designed to avert possible crises in the future is accomplished through anticipatory guidance.[1]

Crisis Intervention Versus Traditional Therapies

The goal of traditional Freudian therapy is personality change. Its emphasis is on the client's past and exploring his subconscious. The Freudian therapist is usually nondirective and the length of therapy may be years.[1]

Briefer therapy attempts to remove the client's symptoms or prevent the development of more severe neurotic or psychotic problems. Depression and phobias are commonly diagnosed and treated by brief therapy, such as Gestalt therapy, behavior modification, or transactional analysis.[3]

Crisis intervention, on the other hand, assists a person in resolving an immediate problem that he perceives as overwhelming. Sometimes, the crisis stirs up unresolved issues from the client's past. These issues are not dealt with, however, until after the resolution of the crisis.

Crisis intervention emphasizes the healthy aspects of the personality, not pathology. There is no diagnosis of mental illness in crisis work. The individual is evaluated in terms of his ability to cope, his strengths and potentials, and his ability to problem-solve. The major focus of the therapeutic approach is the social structure of the individual, rather than the dynamics of the personality. It is assumed that the person will make appropriate decisions when given the necessary information and support. Crisis intervention requires a much more directive approach than traditional therapies.

Characteristics of the Crisis Intervener

To intervene in crises effectively, a therapist must demonstrate calmness and empathy. Because the person in crisis is often confused, the intervener must be able to identify the facts in a situation and think clearly in order to plan solutions to the problem.

The intervener should also be nonjudgmental and aware of different cultural values. There are different established patterns of response to death, illness, divorce, and pregnancy in various cultural, ethnic, and religious groups.[18] Crisis intervention is effective as long as the intervener does not impose a different lifestyle or value system on the client. A single woman, for example, overwhelmed with an unplanned pregnancy should not be subjected to chastisement or cool indifference in the "helper."

It is essential that the intervener possess courage. The pain involved in a crisis is never pleasant. It is difficult to listen to the tragic things that happen to people; however, that is what the person in crisis needs—someone who will make the commitment to work with him until the problem is resolved, someone who can tolerate the uncomfortableness, the sadness, the anger.

Crisis Intervention and the Nursing Process

Assessment and Analysis

Assessment of the person in crisis is the most important, and often the most difficult, step of crisis intervention. First, the nurse must determine whether the person is really in a crisis state. Tears, anger, and being upset do not automatically mean that the person is overwhelmed and in a crisis state.[18] If, however, the client is experiencing a great deal of anxiety, is having difficulty thinking clearly, and is unable to identify solutions to the problem, then it is helpful to encourage him to talk about the events that immediately preceded his distress.[1] This verbalization frequently calms the client and helps the nurse and client to establish rapport, the beginning of a relationship (see Therapeutic Dialogue: The Client in Crisis). The nurse must focus on the client's immediate problem, not his past history. Usually, when people in crisis reach out for help, the precipitating event occurred within the last 14 days; however, the event may have occurred within the last 24 hours.[1] The situations that can precipitate a crisis are countless—an unwanted pregnancy, the loss of hearing, the diagnosis of a terminal illness, the loss of a girlfriend, or the discovery of a spouse's extramarital affair.

The Client's Feelings

The nurse asks the client to describe the feelings he is experiencing. By accepting the client's feelings without judgment, the nurse assists him to accept his own feelings. The nurse will naturally feel some discomfort in the presence of a person in pain. The human inclination is to stop the person from crying, and to stop talking about what is horrible and upsetting to him. By avoiding the topic of his distress, the client could, at least, appear to be in less pain. Nevertheless, it is beneficial for the person in crisis to express his feelings and experience the pain or frustration firsthand. Therefore, the nurse must learn to tolerate these feelings of discomfort.

Usually, the nurse's increased anxiety stems from fear of saying "the wrong thing" or feeling inadequate to deal with the situation. It is important for the nurse to understand both cognitively and emotionally that, ultimately, the client must make his own decisions. In fact, it is not expedient for the nurse to have all the answers to the client's problem. In order for the individual to grow, much of the work of problem-solving must come from him.

To help the crisis intervener focus on the problem, Aguilera and Messick devised a paradigm of the balancing factors in a stressful event.[1] It is often helpful, as a means of clarifying one's thinking, to write down and then evaluate the individual's perception of the event, his coping mechanisms, and his support systems.

Perception of the Event

The nurse who assesses the client in crisis first determines his perception of the stressful event. How threatened is the person? Is the person realistic or is he distorting the meaning of the event?[1]

Support Systems

After determining the client's perception of the event, the nurse focuses on who will be available to be supportive to the client. The use of questions, such as, "Whom do you trust?" "Who is your best friend?" "Is there a member of your family to whom you are particularly close?" are suggested to identify the client's support systems. It is best to have several supportive people involved with the client. Because a crisis period lasts for a brief time and the nurse will be only temporarily involved, the client needs others on whom he can rely for continued support.

Coping Skills

To assess the individual's coping skills, the nurse asks him what he does when he cannot solve a problem; or, the nurse may ask, "How do you deal with anxiety or depression?"[18] In any event, the nurse must encourage the client to describe his methods of coping as specifically as possible. The nurse then determines whether the client's coping mechanisms are adaptive or maladaptive. Assess the degree to which the individual is affected by the event. Is the person still functioning in his job? Is the person still attending school and fulfilling other roles, such as wife and mother? How are the significant people in the individual's life affected? Are they also upset?[1, 18] The significant others may need crisis counseling as well.

Therapeutic Dialogue

The Client in Crisis

Nurse: (Walks into client's room, notices that Mr. T. is staring out the window with a sad expression on his face.) Mr. T., you look sad to me. Is there something upsetting you?

Client: Oh, you don't have time to listen to me.

Nurse: Mr. T., I have 15 minutes now and I'll have more time later. Let's go for a walk and talk.

Client: (Puts on his robe and continues to look at the floor as he walks down the hall.)

Nurse: I want you to know that I'm available to listen to whatever is troubling you. So, just take a deep breath and get it off your chest.

Client: Well, you know I'm here because my ulcer is acting up, but what is really bothering me is I was fired from my job 2 weeks ago.

Nurse: Well, what are your feelings about that now?

Client: It's strange, it's like my life changed overnight. I've been working for this company for 10 years. I'm just stunned. I feel I'm a failure. Maybe I am a loser. Who is going to want to hire a failure? Until 2 weeks ago, I felt confident, I enjoyed socializing with the people I work with. Now, I feel like they are avoiding me.

Nurse: Do you want to see the people you work with right now?

Client: Well, yes and no. I don't know what to say to them.

Nurse: If you could get support from anyone you wanted to right now, who would it be?

Client: I'm not sure.

Nurse: Who do you trust?

Client: My father, but I'm so ashamed. I don't want to tell him.

Nurse: Let's examine your feelings of being ashamed. Mr. T., have you ever been fired before?

Client: No, never! Work has always been important to me.

Nurse: Tell me about the jobs you have had.

Client: I have worked for 25 years for three different companies. In this last one, I moved up to a mid-management position.

Nurse: Well, it sounds to me like you have had a lot of success in your career. You have worked for 25 years, right? That's a lot of years—25 years and never been fired before now. Mr. T., that doesn't sound like a work record of a failure to me.

Client: Well, my company has been having problems for a while. I just didn't think it would be me that they would let go. I thought Mr. J., my supervisor, appreciated what I have done in my department.

Nurse: How did you receive notice that you were let go?

Client: I received a letter.

Nurse: It never ceases to amaze me how poorly administrators deal with people.

Client: Yes, I always respected Mr. J. I expected more from him than that.

Nurse: Mr. T., after you are feeling better maybe you will want to go in and talk with Mr. J. about what actually happened. But right now, let's talk about your father. The news is full of companies in trouble and people losing their jobs. Don't you think your father will be hurt if you don't tell him?

Client: Yeh, he probably would be.

Nurse: How about giving him a call right now.

Client: Well, I guess I might as well get it over with. I'll call him at his office.

Nurse: I'll be back to talk with you in about an hour.

In this interview, note the distorted perception of the stressful event. Because Mr. T. was fired from his job, he felt that he was a failure. In reality, he had worked for 25 years without this occurrence. The nurse tried to encourage Mr. T. to view the situation in more realistic terms and to mobilize the social support of his father.

Potential Self-Harm

An assessment of the person in crisis is not complete without asking him if he is having thoughts of hurting himself or "doing himself in." Most people will not volunteer this information, but when asked, will readily talk about suicidal thoughts. If the client has ever attempted suicide or has decided how, when, and where he will kill himself, the person needs protection. The suicidal client should not be left alone and needs an experienced therapist (see Chap. 34).

From the assessment data, the nurse should know the nature of the client's feelings, his perception of the precipitating event, whom he has to support and nurture him, how he copes with stress, and what his suicidal or homicidal potential is.

Planning

No matter how critical the time factor, a plan is necessary.[18] Crisis intervention is a structured, objective, problem-solving approach. After collecting the data, the nurse obtains from the client a specific statement of the problem. To insure success of the plan, the client must be actively involved in planning solutions to the problem. An example of planning for a client, without adequate participation of the client and family, follows.

> Mrs. H. was hospitalized with a fractured hip. It was determined that, due to her cardiac condition and the rehabilitation needed for her hip, she could no longer live safely alone in her home. Her son and daughter were both married, had their own families, and were employed full-time.
>
> The daughter stated to the nurse, "I don't think we are going to be able to care for Mother at home." The nurse talked with Mrs. H.'s doctor and together they called the social worker to find a nursing home placement for Mrs. H.
>
> When Mrs. H. learned of the plan, she refused to go to the nursing home. Her family was upset and the nurse was irritated because she felt she had gone out of her way to be helpful.
>
> A difference in cultural values was part of this problem. In the nurse's family, moving into a nursing home when one can no longer live independently was expected and accepted. In the client's family, it was neither. For a crisis to be resolved successfully, the solutions to the problem must be in keeping with the cultural values of the client.

A universal response to crisis is a feeling of helplessness and of being out of control. The basic tenets of crisis intervention state that people can help themselves with varying degrees of assistance from others, and that crisis is an opportunity to grow and develop more constructive coping skills for future use. Therefore, it is essential that the client and significant others are actively involved in the planning stage of problem-solving.

The intervener should convey the attitudinal message that the client will be able to work through his crisis and take charge of his life again. Successful planning is dependent on thorough assessment and diagnosis of the client's level of functioning and his dependency needs. A basic rule of thumb is not to do things for people when they can, but always do for people in crisis what they cannot do for themselves.[18] The more distraught and confused the client is, the more directive the intervener needs to be. Together, the nurse and client define a time frame and goals for resolution of the crisis.

Often, in planning, it is helpful for the intervener to outline the problem and available resources, using the paradigm of the balancing factors in a stressful event. In addition, by using the decision counseling approach, the intervener can clarify with the client the boundaries of the problem.

What are the agreed upon tentative solutions?
Where will the solutions be tried?
What is the time frame?
Who will do what?

Follow-up is critical and should be part of the initial plan.

Goal Setting for the Client in Crisis

The major goal of crisis intervention is to assist the client in reestablishing his equilibrium. To reach that end, the following goals are set.

1. Establishment of a working relationship with the client
2. Identification of the specific problem
3. Reduction of the distortion of the client's perception of the event
4. Improvement of the client's self-esteem
5. Decreasing of the client's anxiety
6. Promotion of the involvement of family and friends
7. Reinforcement of healthy coping mechanisms
8. Validation of the client's ability to solve his problem

It is sometimes difficult, but absolutely essential, for the nurse to accept that the goals of crisis intervention are different from the goals of other therapies. It is not the task of the crisis intervener to deal with all the client's problems or to orchestrate major changes in the client's life.[1,6] The aim of crisis intervention is to assist the individual in solving his immediate problem that was so overwhelming that he was unable to cope. Once he has regained his emotional equilibrium and is able again to cope, the work of crisis intervention has been accomplished.

Intervention

Realizing the Potential for Growth

Crisis intervention has been called "psychological first aid."[20] Nurturance, caring, listening, and willingness to help are powerful and saving forces for people in crisis. Within any crisis situation is the potential for the individual who is faced with an overwhelming stressor to develop a higher level of coping ability than he possessed prior to the precipitating event. Whether this possibility for growth is realized or not attained depends, in part, on the appropriateness of the crisis intervention.

The nurse and client reexamine any feelings that might block adaptive coping. When an individual has extremely negative feelings; for example, about mental illness or physical disabilities, it is particularly difficult for that person to be faced with similar circumstances. The person must deal with those feelings before he can adequately cope with his situation.

Learning to Ask for Help

In a crisis state, it is a natural tendency to feel isolated and withdrawn. Therefore, the client must be helped to communicate directly with significant others in his life. Often, the client has to be taught how to ask for help. The nurse can help demonstrate this skill to the client through role modeling. People who place a high value on their independence may need assistance in recognizing interdependence as a healthy balance.

Using Adaptive Coping

The nurse also teaches and helps the client develop healthier coping skills. During a crisis, an individual is more open and amenable to trying some new means to relieve his anxiety. The nurse encourages the client to use adaptive coping mechanisms, such as the open expression of feelings, progressive relaxation, physical exercise, and drinking warm milk or herb tea to help him relax and sleep, rather than relying on maladaptive coping through excessive alcohol or drug ingestion, social withdrawal, suicide, or homicide.[16,18]

Focusing on the Problem Resolution

As the crisis intervener, the nurse keeps the client focused on the problem and specific goals leading to its resolution. Due to the client's high anxiety level, he may have difficulty focusing on one issue and may need direction to avoid fragmentation of his efforts. After the client has attempted some of the alternative solutions to his problem, he and the nurse evaluate their effectiveness and decide whether additional plans are needed. The nurse reinforces the client's abilities by reviewing the crisis event, how he has been able to cope, and any new methods of problem-solving or coping that he has acquired.

Team Approach

A crisis team approach is sometimes employed in short-term, inpatient psychiatric treatment facilities. A group of four to six clinicians of different educational preparation and experience comprise a crisis team. The team rotates leadership and may consist of a psychiatrist, a psychiatric-mental health nurse, a psychologist, a social worker, a psychiatric aide, a minister, and students in the mental health field. One clinician assumes the role of the primary person responsible for the management of a client; however, continuity of care is built into the system due to the fact that a number of people are involved with the client. The crisis team meets daily to discuss the client's progress. Decisions involving the client are made by the group. The psychiatrist outlines clinical indications for the client and the other team members implement the plan and decide on

time of discharge and method and frequency of follow-up. As in any crisis intervention mode, the goals have to be kept clearly in mind, and, as soon as they are reached, the client is discharged, even if it is his day of admission.[21]

> A young woman, S.L., was admitted to a crisis unit following notification that her husband was reported missing in South Korea. The client had no relatives who could be supportive to her. She had not been able to eat or sleep for the last 3 days. Her only friend brought her to the hospital for admission. S.L. was becoming dehydrated; therefore, the physician ordered IV therapy and a mild sedative to be discontinued the following day. After the initial interview, the team met to discuss the areas in which S.L. needed assistance to facilitate coping with her distress.
>
> In the interview, the crisis team learned that S.L. was ordinarily independent, held a responsible job, and had coped well with living alone in her husband's absence; however, S.L. was expecting her husband home in 2 weeks. It was agreed that S.L. needed more people to be supportive in order for her to deal with this crisis. The nurse made plans to introduce S.L. to other clients who would be particularly supportive, and she encouraged S.L. to contact some of her co-workers. The minister investigated what community support was available. The social worker phoned the Red Cross to see if they could assist in communications with the government. In 3 days, S.L. was eating again and able to sleep better. She had decided to move in with her friend temporarily. S.L. was discharged from the inpatient unit to outpatient status, where she was followed through four weekly appointments.

Crisis Groups

The goal of a crisis group is the same as individual crisis intervention—that the members regain their precrisis functioning ability or develop an even higher level of ability to problem-solve. For some people, a crisis group is more beneficial than one-to-one therapy, paticularly when the person has difficulty with interpersonal relationships. Others who may benefit from a crisis group are people who have difficulty accepting information from psychiatric professionals or from people they see in an authority position.

Advantages of a Crisis Group. Some advantages of a crisis group are that the individual members feel less isolated, and they often make social contact with some of the members in, and outside of, the group. By seeing other people express their feelings, the members realize that other people have similar feelings and problems. Often, the reticent individual can more easily express opinions and feelings after observing other people in a similar situation. Members offer each other suggestions for coping and solving problems; by helping each other within the group, the members' self-esteem is bolstered.

Disadvantages of a Crisis Group. There are some disadvantages, however, of a crisis group. It is difficult to keep each individual's crisis in focus in a group setting. Another problem in crisis groups is the destructive forms of coping or maladaptive problem-solving, which may be suggested by group members. These problems substantiate the need for a trained crisis group leader.[1]

Format and Rules of the Group. Crisis groups are usually scheduled for 1½ to 2 hours, once a week, for 6 weeks. Five to seven members are considered ideal in a crisis group. Some crisis groups are homogeneous, with every member having a similar problem. For example, successful supportive groups have been formed for divorced people, victims of incest, parents in crisis, homosexuals, cancer patients, and many other similar groupings. Some peer groups, organized by lay people rather than by professionally trained people, have also been successful. The best known group among these is probably Alcoholics Anonymous. A heterogeneous group is one in which the members have different problems, but they are all in a crisis. The group may be an open one, in which new members come in and others work through their problems and leave the group. This gives members an opportunity to deal with feelings about intrusion and separation. A closed group does not accept new members after it is formed and continues for a specified time.

Assessment of members and clearly stating the purpose of a group are both crucial aspects of group formation.[18] The members must agree to the rules of the group, such as confidentiality, and they must be able to accept other responsibilities required of group membership. A crisis group can offer an excellent opportunity for people to develop new skills, more successful ways of interacting with others, and ways to increase self-confidence and self-esteem.

Families in Crisis

Seldom does a person live in total isolaton. Usually, a crisis occurs within a family constellation and affects all those who are in close contact with the client. It is not uncommon for parents to be strugglng with mid-life crises at the same time their adolescent is struggling with establishing his separate identity.[12,15] People in crises are either helped or hindered by the people in their social network.[18] Anyone with whom a person routinely interacts, such as friends, family, hairdresser, doctor, teacher, or employer, is part of his social network. The issues of crisis may be viewed within a social framework; until severed social relationships are reestablished, the crisis remains unresolved.[16]

While working with families in crisis, the nurse assesses which member of the family is most obviously upset in the crisis state. Different labels may be used: Who is the scapegoat? Who is the symptom bearer? Who is the identified client?[18] Next, the nurse identifies all members of the individual's social network who were involved before, or are involved now because of, the crisis. Then, the social resources that would be helpful to the client in crisis resolu-

tion are determined. The nurse explains the crisis situation to the person in crisis and how others could assist him.

The intervener is very directive in bringing together the person in crisis and all members of his social system for a conference. During the conference all those involved in the crisis analyze the problem and the effect it has on each family member. Everyone is given an opportunity to verbalize comments or complaints. Available resources and possible solutions are discussed. It is important that, by the end of the conference, the participants have developed a definite plan of action. They must establish exactly who is going to do what and when. The nurse should set a follow-up meeting and help the group decide time, place, participants, and an established purpose of the meeting. The social system approach is very effective in dealing with many-faceted crisis situations, such as family crises.

Frequently, the hospital is the scene of family crises.

A 16-year-old male was admitted to the hospital with the diagnosis of leukemia—he is a juvenile diabetic with a white blood cell count of 300. Previously, he had been active in sports and suddenly he was too tired to do anything but watch television. His father had recently died due to a myocardial infarction. His mother refuses to allow her son to be informed about his illness and planned therapy.

Another admission may look like this.

A 12-year-old girl has attempted suicide by taking an overdose of butalbital (Fiorinal). She has been living with her mother and stepfather; however, she wants to live with her father and stepmother. The mother states that the child's father wants no communication or contact with the child. The mother told the student nurse, "Dont' talk with my daughter about taking the pills. It just upsets her."

Evaluation

In the evaluation process, the nurse and client together evaluate whether the problem has been solved. Has the person regained his equilibrium and his usual level of functioning? It is important for the nurse to know when to "let go" of the client. Before dissolving the partnership, the nurse and client should engage in anticipatory planning so that the client's ability to avoid crisis responses in the future will be maximized.[9,28] The client may need additional information about community services or community resources. After working through the crisis response, some clients are motivated to seek additional therapy to resolve old conflicts and, therefore, referrals may be made.[1,6,18]

The Nurse's Feelings and Attitudes

Nurses often refer people in crisis to other professionals they believe are better qualified to handle the situation.[2] This is unfortunate because nurses are frequently the first health care professionals available to the client. From the standpoint of crisis intervention, the client facing an overwhelming threat needs assistance quickly. Nurses can, and must, provide effective crisis intervention.

The nurse's first experiences in crisis intervention will be neither easy nor comfortable. Often, the novice needs assistance in determining the appropriate expectations for an intervention for both client and nurse.[6] Feelings of apprehension, frustration, anger, and wanting to escape from the situation are not uncommon. Even the most experienced crisis intervener needs a colleague or supervisor who will help him discuss feelings and plan strategies, and will offer support and encouragement.

Anyone who works with people in stressful situations needs to be aware of his own vulnerability to crisis.[7] Symptoms of crisis may go unnoticed in nurses because of their caregiver roles.[14] Nurses who have learned to cope well with the inherent stress of the hospital setting have often created their own support system within the work environment. In one hospice unit, for example, the nurses met together for a few minutes at the beginning and end of each shift to share what was going on with each other. Frequently, they brought in food to share as well. When a nurse was having a difficult time, the others felt comfortable offering her comfort as they would comfort a family member.[30] Support of this nature is advantageous, if not mandatory, in maintaining mental health.[1]

Summary

This chapter has examined how individuals and families respond when faced with an overwhelming stressor and the therapeutic approach to help them avoid or grow from the crisis. The major points of the chapter are as follows.

1. Crisis theory evolved from the study of grief and bereavement by many researchers.
2. An individual who is faced with an overwhelming threat tries his usual coping mechanisms and, if they are unsuccessful in solving the problem, experiences a mounting level of anxiety.
3. A crisis occurs when an individual is unable to solve a problem that he perceives as overwhelming, when his usual coping mechanisms fail to solve the problem, when his perception of the event is distorted, and when he lacks the necessary social support.
4. People experiencing a crisis are more open to learning new coping skills to deal with their problem.
5. There exists the potential for a person in crisis to develop more adaptive coping and, therefore, healthier functioning capabilities after the crisis experience.
6. Maturational crises result from developmental changes and milestones, such as puberty, marriage, old age, and death of a loved one.
7. Situational crises result from sudden, unexpected events, such as divorce, illness, injury, and loss of a job.
8. Crisis intervention is a thinking, directive, problem-solving approach that focuses only on the client's immediate problems.
9. Nurses are often the first health care professionals in contact with the client in crisis; therefore, she is in a unique position to intervene in crises.
10. Any crisis intervener needs a colleague or supervisor with whom he can discuss feelings and plan approaches, and from whom he can receive support and encouragement.

Case Study

J. L. was a 36-year-old woman, a mother of two children (7 and 9 years old), and a full-time student in nursing school. One year before completing her nursing program, J. L. learned that her husband had been having an affair with a 20-year-old woman. He informed J. L. that he was moving out and intended to live with the other woman.

J. L. came to the Community Mental Health Center for counseling because she was not maintaining a passing grade average and feared that she would not be able to remain in school. She was having difficulty coping with both the abrupt changes in her personal life and the pressures of nursing school—and she desperately wanted to finish school.

J. L. felt alienated from everyone. Her parents, particularly her father, thought it must be her fault that her husband left. J. L.'s father remembered the trauma of his parent's divorce and he did not want his grandchildren to grow up like he did. Some of J. L.'s friends were not able to spend much time with her. J. L.'s usual method of coping was to "work hard" and "stay as busy as possible." This coping tactic had not been useful for her lately because of her inability to concentrate, frequent crying spells, and insomnia. J. L. felt she was a failure as a woman and was concerned about her attractiveness to men.

The nurse, as crisis intervener, and J. L. agreed that the immediate problems were the impending divorce and staying in school. Financial options were explored, such as loans, scholarships, and working part-time. J. L. was given permission and encouraged to get the help she needed. The nurse told her, "You have nothing to be ashamed of. You are having a difficult time as anyone would in your situation. Ask your teachers for the help you need." J. L. was encouraged to reach out to some of her classmates for support.

An important point to consider when dealing with people who are getting a divorce is that, often, the person's support system breaks down. Parents grieve the loss of their child's spouse and the family unit. Friends grieve as well; friends will never interact as couples in quite the same way. Friends also experience fears and doubts about their own marriages. The person in crisis needs help in understanding the effects of the divorce on everyone. Through teaching direct commnication and helping the client acknowledge with the parents and friends the natural sadness and loss, grieving is shared. It may be necessary to role play with the client how she might handle a difficult situation. For example, J. L. might role play her encounter with her father. "Dad, I know you are very sad and hurt. This must bring back the feelings you had when your dad and mother got a divorce. I want you to know that I love you. That hasn't changed, and I need you to love me." If communication cannot be worked out with family and friends, the nurse must supply the emotional support to the client.

Other means of support should be explored, such as groups at the college's women's center. J. L. was able to work out better communication with her family and friends, which increased her feelings of being in control and also increased her self-esteem. The children came into counseling for one session to work out communication problems within the family.

The nurse encouraged J. L. to make out a schedule for each day of the week and to include a treat every day—lunch with a friend, coffee in bed, and so forth. J. L. was frequently reminded to think highly of herself and to treat herself with respect. The nurse praised any efforts J. L. made to communicate with others and meet her own needs.

In dealing with J. L.'s feelings about being a failure as a woman because her husband left to live with another woman, J. L. was helped to realize that, for the last several years, she and her husband developed different goals that were in conflict. The reasons for the divorce, she began to understand, had nothing to do with her attractiveness as a woman.

After several weeks, J. L. was a member of a study group and was again making passing grades. She looked better and stated that she felt better. J. L. was able to juggle care of her children, school, work part-time, and socialize occasionally with the help of classmates who were in similar circumstances. J. L. related that the divorce was the most painful experience of her life, but she was stronger than she ever thought possible and felt better able to cope with her present and future life.

Questions for Discussion

1. What does divorce mean in our society today? What are the cultural variations of the meaning of divorce?

2. Discuss the effects of divorce on family members and friends. Why is divorce such a devastating experience for most people?

3. What actions of friends and family might help the client avoid a crisis situation?

4. How could health care workers assist the client and her family?

5. Discuss therapeutic techniques to use when working with a client with a distorted perception of the stressful event.

Nursing Care Plan

The Client Who Is in Crisis

Client Problem	Goal	Intervention
Overwhelming problem	To establish rapport	Establish availability: 1. Time you are available (*e.g.*, 9–5 M–F); emergencies call _____ 2. Emotional availability—caring attitude, willingness to help Provide measures to help the individual to feel important; "I would like for you to feel comfortable. Would you like some coffee or something else to drink? Are you warm enough?" Show acceptance—both verbal and nonverbal. Sit beside the person, not behind a desk.
High anxiety level	To reduce anxiety	Teach healthy coping skills: Suggest walking, drinking herb tea, warm milk, eating comforting foods. Give permission to accept comfort measures as if the person were physically ill. Reassure that strange feelings, such as, "I'm losing my mind," are due to high anxiety.
Confusion	To identify the specific problem	Take a directive approach. "What happened that upset you enough to call? Try to be as specific as you can."
Inability to think clearly	To reinforce use of coping mechanisms that worked in the past To reinforce the problem-solving ability	Example: "Even as stressful as this has been for you, you have managed to continue working." Ask what the person does when things go wrong. Reinforce healthy coping skills. Teach possible coping methods. Diagram the problem according to Aguilera's paradigm. Ask for a commitment from the individual to participate in solving the problem. Then, both parties should agree on specific solutions to attempt (*e.g.*, nurse will call Bread Basket for emergency food; client will call best friend to help with the children for a couple of days).
Distorted perception of the event	To decrease the distortion of perception	Gently point out the facts. Example: One failing grade does not make a failure of a person.
Low self-esteem	To increase self-esteem	Comment on strengths. Individualize approach to client; call by name.
Lack of support from friends and family	To increase involvement of friends and family	Encourage the expression of feelings and direct communication with friends and family.

References

1. Aguilera DC, Messick JM: Crisis Intervention: Theory and Methodology, 4th ed. St Louis, CV Mosby, 1978
2. Ballow M, Rebich C: Crisis Intervention: A Call for Involvement for the Health Professional. J Sch Health 47 (December): 603–606, 1977
3. Bellak L, Small L: Emergency Psychotherapy and Brief Psychotherapy, 2nd ed. New York, Grune & Stratton, 1978
4. Bloom BL: Definitional Aspects of the Crisis Concept. In Porad H (ed): Crisis Intervention: Selected Readings, pp 303–311. New York, Family Service Association of America, 1973
5. Berchopp GW: Crisis Intervention: Theory, Process and Practice. In Lester D, Berchopp G (eds): Crisis Intervention and Counseling by Telephone, pp 89–104. Springfield, IL, Charles C Thomas, 1973
6. Burgess AW, Baldwin BA: Crisis Intervention Theory and Practice: A Clinical Handbook. New York, Prentice-Hall, 1981
7. Caplan G: Mastery of Stress: Psychosocial Aspects. Am J Psychiatry 138 (April): 413–419, 1981
8. Caplan G: Principles of Preventive Psychiatry. New York, Basic Books, 1964
9. Caplan G, Grunebaum H: Perspectives on Primary Prevention. Arch Gen Psychiatry 17 (September): 333–345, 1967
10. Erikson EH: Childhood and Society, 2nd ed. New York, WW Norton, 1963
11. Fitzpatrick JJ, Reed PG: Stress in the Crisis Experience: Nursing Interventions. Occupational Health Nursing (December): 19–21, 1980
12. Gaston SK: Death and Midlife Crisis. J Psychiatr Nurs Ment Health Serv 19(1):31–35, 1981
13. Golan N: Using Situational Crisis to Ease Transitions in the Life Cycle. Am J Orthopsychiatry 50 (July): 542–550, 1980
14. Grant JM: Nurse in Crisis. NZ Nurs J 71(7):18–21, 1978
15. Hall YE, Weaver BR: Nursing in Families in Crisis. Philadelphia, JB Lippincott, 1974
16. Hansell N: The Person in Distress. New York, Human Services Press, 1976
17. Hausman W, Rioch DM: Military Psychiatry. Arch Gen Psychiatry 16 (June): 727–739, 1967
18. Hoff LA: People in Crisis: Understanding and Helping. California, Addison-Wesley, 1978
19. Jacobson GF: Crisis Theory and Treatment Strategy: Some Sociocultural and Psychodynamic Considerations. J Nerv Ment Dis 141 (August): 209–218, 1965
20. Kliman AS: Crisis: Psychological First Air for Recovery and Growth. New York, Holt, Rinehart, 1978
21. Lieb J, Lipsitch I, Slaby A: The Crisis Team: A Handbook for the Mental Health Professional. New York, Harper & Row, 1973
22. Lindeman E: Symptomatology and Management of Acute Grief. Am J Psychiatry 101 (September): 141–148, 1944
23. Mitchell CE: Identifying the Hazard: The Key to Crisis Intervention. Am J Nurs (July): 1194–1196, 1977
24. Narayan SM, Joslin DJ: Crisis Theory and Intervention: A Critique of the Medical Model and Proposal of a Holistic Nursing Model. Advances in Nursing Science 2 (July): 27–39, 1980
25. Phelan LA: Crisis Intervention: Partnership in Problem Solving. J Psychiatr Nurs Ment Health Serv 17(9):22–27, 1979
26. Rapoport L: The State of Crisis: Some Theoretical Considerations. Soc Serv Rev 36 (June): 211–217, 1962
27. Ruditis SE: Developing Trust in Nursing Interpersonal Relationships. J Psychiatr Nurs Ment Health Serv 17(4):20–23, 1979
28. Schulberg HC, Sheldon A: The Probability of Crisis and Strategies for Preventive Intervention. Arch Gen Psychiatry 18 (May): 553–558, 1968
29. Taplin JR: Crisis Theory: Critique and Reformation. Community Ment Health J 1 (March): 13–23, 1971
30. Taylor PB, Gideon MD: But Who Will Minister to You? Nursing 81 11(10):58–61, 1981
31. Wardell SC: Acute Intervention: Nursing Process Throughout the Life Span. Reston, VA, Reston Publishing Company, 1979

Chapter 32
Rape and Sexual Assault

"The world breaks everyone and afterwards many are strong in the broken places."

Ernest Hemingway,
A Farewell to Arms

Sally Francis

Chapter Preview

Rape is a crime of violence that touches everyone at some time, in some way. It is estimated that one of every ten women in the United States is a victim of rape. Consequently, the woman and her family, friends, co-workers, and acquaintances must acknowledge and face their own individual fears of vulnerability, loss of control, perversion, bodily harm, and death. Our hope in a crisis event that affects so many people is that all can "become strong in the broken places" and that psychiatric-mental health nurses will recognize and respond to the needs of the rape victim and her significant others during the mending and healing process.

This chapter will describe rape and sexual assault, its theoretical perspectives, the emotional effects and recovery, and intervention programs. The nursing process will be discussed during the immediate or emergency phase, the intermediate phase, and the recovery phase of the rape crisis. Through application of the nursing process—assessment, analysis, planning, intervention, and evaluation—individuals and families affected by rape or sexual assault can be assisted to grow "strong" in their coping and adaptation.

Learning Objectives

Upon completion of the chapter, the reader should be able to accomplish the following.

1. Identify the typology of rape and sexual assault
2. Define rape trauma syndrome and discuss the behaviors of a victim during the acute, reorganization, and recovery phases of rape trauma syndrome
3. Identify and define unresolved rape trauma and silent rape trauma
4. Discuss primary motivating forces of the assailant in crimes of rape and sexual assault
5. Apply the nursing process to the care of the victim of rape or sexual assault

    Assess the physical and emotional status of clients who have been raped or sexually assaulted

    Identify the actual and potential problems of clients who have been raped or sexually assaulted

    Plan nursing goals and actions designed to prevent or alleviate the rape victim's identified problems

    Formulate a comprehensive nursing care plan for a client who has been raped or sexually assaulted

    Evaluate the effectiveness of the planned intervention

6. Recognize and discuss one's own feelings that may influence the therapeutic use of self with victims of rape and sexual assault

Theoretical Perspectives of Rape and Sexual Assault

Rape and sexual assault can be viewed from historical, legal, psychological, and sociologic perspectives. It is curious that, until recent years, this overwhelming physical assault has received so little attention from research. The mythology of the ancient Greeks contains descriptions of rape which have continued through the centuries. References to rape appear in literature from each century of civilization's development. Nevertheless, it was not until the early 1970s that researchers attempted to describe the victim and rapist in terms that could lead to intervention and that could influence the psychological impact of rape.

Legal Perspective

Definition of Rape and Sexual Assault

Rape is defined as a crime in which forcible penile–vaginal penetration of a female occurs without her consent and against her will. Sexual assault refers to forcible sexual acts performed on a female without her consent and against her will. Specifically, rape is defined as a crime according to the legal statutes of individual state governments. An important concept in identifying rape or sexual assault is the use of force against the will of the female. In this light, the crime of rape or sexual assault is one of force and violence in which sex becomes the means of expressing violence, just as, in a murder, a gun may become the means of expressing violence.

Psychological Perspective

One of the most trraumatizing aspects of the crime of rape or sexual assault involves the victim's feelings about being physically forced to do something against her will. The life-threatening nature of the crime, the helplessness, the loss of control, and the experiencing of self as an object of rage all work together to result in an overwhelming experience of fear and stress for the victim. This experience has been described as the *rape trauma syndrome.*[6] Regaining internal equilibrium and the ability to reorganize one's life into a meaningful and productive whole becomes, therefore, the task of intervention.

Types of Sexual Assault

Burgess and Holstrom have been the leading researchers in the study of rape trauma syndrome.[6] Based on their study of 146 rape victims in the early 1970s, they identified four types of sexual assault: the blitz rape, the confidence rape, accessory-to-sex with inability to consent, and the sex-stress situation.

Blitz rape occurs when the woman has neither previous knowledge of, nor threat of vulnerability from, the rapist. Although blitz rape usually occurs in the woman's home, the attacker may suddenly accost the woman in a parking lot, on the street, or any place where he can strike "out of the blue."

> "I thought I was having a bad dream—that I was screaming. As I regained consciousness, I felt like I was moving up from a dark hole, screaming. It seemed like I slowly realized I wasn't dreaming. I was awake and screaming. A man was holding me down on the sofa where I had fallen asleep earlier in the evening. He had his hands on my face, pushing me down and trying to cover my mouth. He kept telling me to shut up, to stop screaming."

Confidence rape refers to a rape that involves some interaction between the assailant and victim before the rape occurs. Access to the victim is obtained by the rapist by gaining her confidence in some way. For example, the man may ring a doorbell, ask to use the phone for some assistance, and gain entry into the woman's territory, and then rape her.

Accessory-to-sex describes sexual acts with an individual who is unable to consent to sex. The inability to consent results from the female's immature stage of personality or cognitive development, which prevents her from recognizing or understanding the overtures and sexual events. An example of the accessory-to-sex type of sexual assault is a mentally retarded woman who is seduced by the promise of material goods in exchange for sexual activity.

Sex-stress situation refers to events arising after initial consent to sex is given. For example, a woman may agree to a sexual experience with a date who later becomes violent and physically abusive. She then withdraws her earlier consent and he rapes her.

In each of these situations, sexual acts become a means for acting out distorted perceptions held by the male. The female becomes an object who experiences this objectification, powerlessness, and loss of self as a basic, consuming fear. The resultant trauma reaction of the victim, rape trauma syndrome, serves to promote self-preservation; it is a "flight" reaction when fight is not possible. Rape trauma syndrome identifies the psychological work in which the ego must engage to preserve its identity and integration.

Sociological Perspective

Myths About Rape

Although the motivation to rape arises from personality, societal attitudes influence the incidence, prevalence, and treatment of rape and sexual assault. The sociologic perspective includes the myths that society holds about rape. These myths and stereotypical views of rape define how a victim sees herself in relation to society, how society views the victim and the rapist, and the difficulty or ease with which a victim receives support from society. For example, the prevalent myth of rape is that it is motivated by sexual desire and that, in fact, the woman who is raped must have "asked for it." Rapists are seen as exaggerations of the "macho" male. If the victim is a person who society believes would not "ask for it"; for example, a child or an elderly woman, the rapist is viewed as a very sick, disturbed, psychotic individual. A young woman hitchhiking, who is raped but not beaten by a driver who picks her up, is frequently viewed with little sympathy; however, her fears, helplessness, and loss of control can be as traumatizing as the fears experienced by a woman badly beaten in a blitz rape. Not infrequently, women who are raped, as members of the society, share the myths of the society. They experience self-blame and guilt and feel that they should have done something, or not done something, that could have prevented the assault.

> "A part of me was relieved when the police came that I looked so bad, that there was blood, that the door had been broken open, the house was torn up, and there were fingerprints. There couldn't be any doubt that something awful had happened to me."

Who Is to Blame?

Public education programs have made progress in changing society's attitudes about rape and sexual assault. Nevertheless, rape continues to be one of the most frequently underreported crimes. In an attempt to understand public attitudes, several studies have examined how various segments of society attribute blame for the crime of rape.

In one study, four predominate causal attitudes toward rape were identified—blaming the victim, blaming the offender, blaming society, or blaming the situation.[19] Another study included ineffective law enforcement and judicial procedures as potential causes of rape.[10] The multidimensional nature of societal attitudes toward rape has been demonstrated by two studies in which victim blame, offender characteristics, situational characteristics, and societal blame emerged as factors in the development of these attitudes.[9, 18] Other studies have determined that there are sex differences regarding attitudes toward rape.[7, 8] Women tend to place greater blame on society for the occurrence of rape and sexual assault. Feminist writings and popular literature have explored the socialization into sex roles and the role of violence in our society. In a society, they say, that both encourages the treatment of women as sex objects and encourages violence, women cannot avoid attack.[2, 14, 15] What can change is who will be attacked.

Characteristics of Rapists

Who rapes and why? Groth, the leading researcher in the area of rape offenders, concludes that rape is more than an illegal act or an extreme of cultural role behavior.[12] It is a sexual deviation wherein the offender's pathology becomes the etiology of the victim's trauma. Although similar acts may be performed, rapists are not alike. Rapists perform sexual acts in the service of nonsexual needs. It is through these needs, rather than through other behavioral characteristics, that rapists can be classified and described.

The *power rapist* attempts to place a woman in a helpless, controlled situation where she cannot resist or refuse. This situation provides the rapist with a reassuring sense of strength, mastery, security, and control, all of which compensate for his underlying feelings of inadequacy. Usually, the offender has no conscious intention to hurt his victim. His aim, rather, is to have complete control over her. Nevertheless, there may be an increase in aggression over time as the offender becomes repetitive and compulsive in his behavior and more desperate to achieve the feelings of power, control, and adequacy, all of which he lacks.

> "He had a knife but he didn't use it. Thank God he didn't cut me. He used his fists instead and he pulled me around by my hair. All the time he was verbally abusive: called me names and told me if I did what he told me to, he wouldn't kill me. He made me get down on my hands and knees and crawl while he pulled me around by my hair. There was no way out of the room; he was in complete control. When the trial started, there were nine of us who had been raped by this one guy. It was amazing how much alike our stories were. He did the same things, used the same words. The most frightening part was that the police thought there were more; one woman was murdered."

The *anger rapist* uses sexual assault as a means of expressing and discharging feelings of intense anger, frustration, and contempt. The sexual assault is an impulsive act of aggression to retaliate against a world for wrongs that he believes have been committed against him. The assault is not compulsive as is the power rape; instead, it is characterized by more brutality and physical harm due to the expression of rage. The anger rapist derives satisfaction, not from sexual gratification, but from the relief resulting from the discharge of anger and the degradation and humiliation of the victim.

The *sadistic rapist* finds pleasure in the premeditation and ritualistic acts of violence, which usually involve bondage and torture. The rapist's anger and need for control become sexualized through the intense pleasure derived from hurting, degrading, and, frequently, destroying the victim.

The type of rape committed has implications for the treatment of both victim and offender. Anger rape is the most frequently occurring type of rape; however, power rapists make up the larger population of incarcerated offenders. Conviction rates may be higher when there is more physical, bodily harm to introduce as evidence in court proceedings. Just as the physical abuse and harm is distressing to the victim of an anger rapist, the woman who was not outwardly harmed by a power rapist also has fears. These fears can be complicated by the knowledge that there are fewer arrests and convictions of power rapists. The victim of a power rapist may have recurring fears if the offender was not convicted. She cannot, for example, be reassured by the knowledge that "at least, he's locked up." How women cope and adapt to these overwhelming fears is discussed as the rape trauma syndrome.

Rape Trauma Syndrome

Rape Crisis

Rape crisis is the internal and external disequilibrium experienced by the victim of rape or sexual assault. The encounter with a life-threatening situation evokes extreme feelings of fear and vulnerability. Freeing oneself from this fear, redefining one's feelings of vulnerability and helplessness, and regaining control and equilibrium in one's life is the process of adaptation known as *rape trauma syndrome*. The clustering of symptoms in response to the trauma of rape appears to be fairly consistent and occurs during both an acute phase and a period of integration and resolution.[6,17]

Acute Phase: Disorganization

The *disorganization phase* includes the rape victim's immediate reactions that are expressed or controlled, her physical reactions, and her emotional reactions to a life-threatening situation. In the acute phase, the prominent feelings experienced by the woman are fright, anxiety, anger, and disbelief.[7]

These feelings can be seen in an expressive response in which the victim actively displays and discusses feelings. Second-guessing often occurs in this phase, when, for example, the victim asks herself, "Did I do everything I should have to avoid this happening to me?" The second-guessing phenomenon of self-recrimination can be a source of guilt frequently experienced by victims and, in some instances, can lead to a severe depression.

A *controlled reaction* is present when the rape victim appears outwardly calm and composed. Although conventional wisdom might lead us to expect victims of rape or sexual assault to be crying, hysterical, or visibly upset in some other manner, many women do not respond in these ways. A woman who has a controlled reaction to the rape has no less internal suffering and fear, just a different way of handling herself in the acute phase.

> "I went next door to get my neighbor. I remember she said I seemed so calm while we waited for the police. Inside, I was shaking with relief to be with a safe person but I didn't want to talk much until the police came. I

think a shock reaction was setting in. By the time I got to the hospital I was not so much calm as simply exhausted."

Physical reactions during the acute phase vary according to the bodily injury incurred. Often, there are feelings of soreness, which may be generalized as muscle tension eases, or localized to parts of the body that were a focus of the assault. Sleep disturbances, eating pattern disturbances, and symptoms specific to the attack occur frequently.

"In the first days and weeks after the rape, I couldn't fall asleep until it was daylight. My scalp was sore for days and then just sometimes it seemed tender, even after the bruises were gone. I developed little rituals, patterns, for going to bed and for washing my hair. They provided some structure for my anxiety but didn't really take away the fear."

Emotional reactions to rape and sexual assault are primarily the feelings of fear; that is, the fear of bodily harm, death, or mutilation, and other feelings such as anger, humiliation, and self-blame. Frequently, the victim experiences heightened emotional reactions and over-reactions in other situations not related to the rape. Increased irritability, impatience, tearfulness, and anger can cause the victim to feel out of control and out of touch with herself. Incessant thoughts about the event and sudden memory flashes at unlikely and unexpected times add to the victim's feelings of loss of control during this initial phase.

"The first couple of weeks at work I was so busy, I didn't have much time to think about what had happened. Nights at home were the worst part. But there was one person at work that I just couldn't be around. He is a very nice, friendly person but physically, he reminded me of the guy. Just his outgoing, friendly chatter would make me nervous and I'd feel myself withdrawing and feeling threatened and vulnerable. It's an awful way to feel about someone who is just trying to be nice."

The length of the acute phase may vary from a few days to a few weeks. Frequently, the symptoms of the acute phase carry into the long-term adjustment.

Long-term Process: Reorganization

Reorganization refers to the process of adjustment and adaptation during the months following the rape or sexual assault. Of the 81 victims followed-up at 4 years after the rape, Burgess and Holstrom found that 74% of the women felt recovered from the assault.[3] Half of these women felt recovered within months following the attack, and the other half said that it took years before they recovered from the rape. Some of the women (26%) did not yet feel recovered 4 years after the rape. The period of months or years in which reorganization occurs involves regaining equilibrium in physical, psychological, social, and sexual lifestyles. The period of reorganization closely resembles the grief process described by Lindemann.[16]

The intermediate process of regaining equilibrium.has been described as an interim period in which the victim appears to have adjusted and returns to the normal routines of life, school, or work.[17] This interim period is followed by a period of resolution in which feelings toward self and the rapist, feelings about sexuality, and feelings of loss are gradually assimilated.

Issues that are important to the rape victim during the reorganization process include the following.

1. Regaining a feeling of physical well-being and safety
2. Working through fears and phobias
3. Coming to terms with losses, such as loss of self-esteem and loss of trust
4. Assimilating the event into one's sense of self

Unresolved Sexual Trauma

Unresolved sexual trauma occurs when the person experiencing the sexual assault does not deal with the feelings or reactions to the experience. Years after the event, the woman has neither assimilated nor adapted to the sexual assault. Typically, unresolved sexual trauma occurs more often in women who have little or no intervention to support them during the acute phase of rape trauma or who experience subsequent victimization. Women who, at the time of the attack, face chronic life stressors, lack social support, suffer a negative self-esteem, or have undergone prior victimization within 2 years before the attack are also more likely to experience unresolved sexual trauma. Another risk factor in unresolved sexual trauma is the woman's place in the life cycle; young females and those for whom the sexual assault was their first sexual experience may have delayed recovery from rape trauma. The nurse or other mental health professional may suspect unresolved sexual trauma when

1. an individual develops persistent phobic symptoms, such as fear of being alone or going out;
2. an individual experiences retreat from sexual themes, lowered self-esteem, and guilt feelings;
3. a relatively minor event triggers the symptoms of the rape trauma;
4. the anniversary date of the sexual assault brings on symptoms of the rape trauma;
5. an individual totally avoids contact with members of the opposite sex;
6. relationships with family and friends shift in negative ways—toward withdrawal, unusual anger, or silence. The negativity may represent displacement of feelings toward the assailant.

A type of unresolved sexual trauma is seen in a silent reaction to rape, wherein the rape victim has never discussed the sexual assault with anyone.

Recovery from Rape Trauma

A community intervention program can assist the victim of sexual assault recover from rape trauma. This program is a coordinated effort to bring together all the bureaucratic systems—medical, legal, police, and judicial—and the support systems of the victim and family toward the common goal of helping her resolve the crisis and reorganize her life. Public education and community awareness are other essential components of a comprehensive community intervention program.

Aims of community intervention include the following.

1. The police are knowledgeable and concerned about the crime, and effective in apprehending the assailant.
2. Medical care is administered caringly and produces good evidence-collection.
3. The District Attorney's office works closely with the police, medical, and forensic science departments to insure apprehension and conviction of the assailant.
4. The public is educated and assured of the effectiveness of responses from the various systems involved with the victim of rape or sexual assault.

When the aims just listed have been met, victims of sexual assault are more willing to report the assault and have a greater opportunity to work successfully through the events surrounding the attack. It is important that the victim experience careful, caring interactions with each of the systems she encounters after the assault.

Trained counselors available through victim support programs can also assist the individual and her family and friends by providing crisis counseling during the immediate trauma and through the periods of resolution and reorganization. When a crisis center or victim support program is not available, hospital and emergency room nurses can utilize crisis intervention techniques to offer supportive counseling to the woman experiencing rape trauma syndrome.

Application of the Nursing Process to Victims of Rape and Sexual Assault

Assessment and Analysis

Nursing assessment of a victim of rape or sexual assault begins with the nurse's initial encounter with the woman. This may take place in an emergency room, a hospital, physician's office, or a counseling center.[4]

Assessment of the woman's physical status is necessary to determine the extent of external and internal injuries and to begin planning appropriate medical interventions. It is important that the victim's appearance and the condition of her body not be altered, because the physical evidence of the rape or sexual assault is essential in the apprehension and prosecution of the assailant. First aid may be administered to the victim, but further medical attention should be conducted in conjunction with the medical team responsible for the collection of evidence in sexual assault cases.

While assessing the victim's emotional state, the nurse first attends to the primary concerns of the woman and offers information and reassurance in those areas before addressing other issues. Some women will focus on concerns for physical safety. Others will have anxiety about significant others, when, for example, a woman asks, "What will I tell my husband?" Acceptance of these concerns and the provision of supportive care can be calming to the victim and can begin the establishment of a therapeutic alliance. Emotional assessment also includes determination of the victim's perception of the event, her coping behaviors, and her situational and social supports.

Planning

Goal-setting for the victim of rape or sexual assault includes plans to aid the woman during the immediate, interim, and long-range phases of rape trauma syndrome. Immediate concerns are the promotion of the victim's physical well-being and the collection of evidence to be used in legal proceedings. Planning during the first hours after an assault should include the following.

1. Medical attention to the victim
2. Notification of significant people in the victim's life
3. Plans for the victim's leaving the medical facility
4. Plans for the victim's immediate safety
5. Plans for follow-up contact with a crisis counselor during the interim period

The interim period refers to the first few days after an assault. During this time, plans must be made to recontact the victim, refer her to a victim support center, or continue supportive counseling. Long-range plans should include the provision of support at certain times of stress for the woman, such as police investigations, court proceedings, and the anniversary of the attack.

Intervention

Building Rapport and Trust

The primary goal of nursing intervention is the establishment of a therapeutic alliance with the victim of rape or sexual assault. An important means to this goal is through nonjudgmental acceptance of the victim. It is not unusual for the woman to feel "dirty", guilty, or, in other ways, unacceptable. She must feel that the revulsion society expresses about sexual assault in general is not directed at her in particular. The nurse should respond to the woman's verbal and nonverbal expressions of need. Because the victim may misinterpret any questions or comments not directly related to her immediate situation as blaming or rejecting her, the nurse should delay probing questions until the therapeutic alliance is established. The woman's recent experience of objectification intensifies her self-consciousness. She is much more sensitive to the reactions of others, yet less able to interpret others' behavior rationally.

> "My memories of going to the emergency room are blurred. What stands out is how repulsive I felt when I went into the Ob-Gyn waiting room. Who else would be in an Ob-Gyn waiting room in the middle of the night but pregnant women? I had to find a small corridor to be in where no one could see me, where I couldn't upset a woman about to give birth or be confronted with the horrible travesty of sexual intercourse I had just experienced. Later, I could view the irony of the situation—at the time I just felt so exposed and repulsive."

Preparing the Woman for Medical Events

After establishing rapport with the victim of rape or sexual assault, the nurse should begin to prepare her for the events she will encounter in the emergency room and during interactions with hospital, police, and other personnel. Preparation for these events is essential, because most women will not have any prior knowledge or experience to guide them in the immediate crisis. The nurse should give the woman brief, concrete explanations of what is going to happen to her and why. This information provides the victim with a needed sense of control and boundaries. Preparation for the physical examination helps the victim view the exam as essential to her well-being, rather than as further physical intrusion. Her calmness and cooperativeness also assist in the collection of evidence for the apprehension and prosecution of the rapist. In this immediate rape crisis, the nurse determines the emotional needs of the victim.

Does she want a support counselor to stay with her?
Does she want family or friends called?
Does she need assistance from the social services department of the hospital?

Encouraging Ventilation About the Assault

Once the physical needs have been addressed, the victim can use the therapeutic relationship to begin her necessary ventilation about the assault. The woman should be encouraged to talk about the event and about her feelings. Early and full ventilation helps the woman regain a sense of control; by experiencing acceptance in the face of the degrading details of the rape, she is assisted to regain self-worth. When the assault is reported to the police, the victim will be questioned by many individuals, all of whom will be strangers to her. Few of these individuals will have sufficient time to develop a strong therapeutic alliance with her. The initial talking-out of the experience with a nurse

or other mental health professional will prepare the victim for the investigations to follow.

Exploring Physical Safety Concerns

During the immediate contact with the victim of rape or sexual assault, the nurse explores the woman's concerns for her own physical safety. Where will the woman go, after leaving this initial contact? With whom will she leave? How can the nurse intervene to increase the woman's feeling of physical safety at this time?

> "I had to feel safe again. The first things I did were to make physical changes for safety. A locksmith changed and added new locks; a carpenter changed the windows and doors. I was lucky I could afford to do these things, because they helped. I could be alone in my house. But still, the vulnerable feeling stayed with me a long, long time. Even now, 2 years after, I sometimes feel edgy at night and get up to check the locks several times at night. It helps to have a 'safe room'. The police recommend this—have one room, preferably your bedroom with a phone in it. Add deadbolt locks to any door leading into the room. Any suspicious sound or activity, you can lock yourself in the room and call the police."

Anticipatory Guidance for Significant Others

It is likely that the rape victim will express concern for her family and friends. The nurse offers anticipatory guidance to significant others by talking with them and guiding them in their responses to the victim. Helping family and friends explore their feelings, particularly feelings of anger, can free them from the intensity of these feelings and enable them to be more sensitive to, and supportive of, the victim. It is not uncommon for significant others to engage in a "conspiracy of silence," because they believe "the less said, the better." This silent approach only intensifies the victim's feelings of guilt, shame, and her unworthiness of love.

Making Follow-Up Plans

The victim and nurse must agree on an intermediate follow-up plan. The nurse may refer the victim to a counseling center or decide to continue working with the victim through telephone counseling. It is important for the nurse to note several phone numbers at which the woman may be reached. Frequently, the woman does not return home, particularly if the assault occurred in her home, but chooses to stay with family or friends for several days. The victim should not be called at work, unless she agrees to this in advance.

Preparing the Woman for the Interim Phase

The victim of rape or sexual assault should be instructed about the medical follow-up she will need during the interim phase. Although the woman may appear calm and in control at this time, do not assume that she will be able to recall any verbal information given to her. Always give her written instructions for medication and doctors' appointments and reinforce these with verbal instructions. The written information can be reassuring to the woman at the moment and in the future.

> "I know they told me why I had a shot of penicillin. I know I I knew it but when I called my doctor for a follow-up appointment, they scheduled me for blood work. I asked what for. It was as though my mind couldn't deal with the possibility of VD and had rejected that information completely when I was in the emergency room. It made me nervous about what else I had forgotten . . . was I taking the antipregnancy medication the right way, so it would work?"

Promoting Reorganization

It is important that the victim feel she can recontact the nurse in the days following the assault to ask questions, talk, and share feelings. The nurse can assist the woman by giving her specific, written instructions about how to reach her and when are the best times to call.

During the period of reorganization, the nurse intervenes by counseling via telephone or through face-to-face contact or by monitoring the woman's coping and adaptive behaviors. Anticipatory guidance is extremely helpful to the victim during the weeks and months following the attack.

If apprehension of the rapist occurs, the woman should be provided information about the court process. At times, it may be helpful for her to rehearse giving testimony to prepare her for the painful retelling in front of strangers. She may also benefit from exploring how she will feel relating the events in front of strangers. Often, the apprehension of the assailant and the court proceedings occur after the woman has begun reorganizing her life. She may have moved past the acute phase of rape trauma syndrome and may have begun to adapt and live her life once again. The prospect of the trial will renew her feelings of vulnerability and fear. This stress-point in her life can be navigated with the support of a counselor–nurse. The woman needs to be prepared for the potential outcome of the trial, needs to explore her feelings about it, and needs to consider how she will cope with the actuality. Not every case is prosecuted. Not every rapist is convicted.

> "I think I was the craziest during the trial. I kept telling myself it was nothing compared to the real thing but I was even more consumed with thoughts about it all than I had been in the first weeks after the rape. I guess my denial system was not as strong then as it had been right after the rape. It never occurred to me that there might not be a resolution, one way or the other. I had thought about the possibility of the guy getting off, I had thought about how I would feel when I saw him again. But it never occurred to me that there could be a hung jury! No resolution, and the thought of doing it all again was almost more than I thought I could cope with. I was so ready to have it done and over with, finally. Not to have that finality was crushing."

Feelings and Attitudes of the Nurse

Just as society has stereotypical views about rape and sexual assault, so does each individual. The nurse must face her own fears about rape, her anger, and her feelings of helplessness. Understanding and acknowledging these feelings allows the nurse to attend to the victim's feelings. There may be times and circumstances, however, for which the nurse has not prepared. Some events may be so gruesome that the nurse finds them intolerable at the time. A supportive network is as valuable for the nurse as it is for the victim. It is essential that the nurse have someone with whom she can share her feelings about the events she encounters. It is also beneficial for nurses and other health care professionals to take active roles around the theme of sexual assault. Organize a rape prevention seminar for colleagues or friends. Contact police to evaluate your home for physical safety. Taking active steps to insure your own safety can be reassuring and can counteract feelings of helplessness and fears of victimization.[1, 5, 13, 20]

Evaluation

Few women are prepared for rape or sexual assault. The feelings that result from this experience are overwhelming in kind and intensity. Although recovery from rape trauma may follow a generalized pattern of behaviors, each woman brings to the experience a unique array of personal coping skills, personality characteristics, past history with stress, and social networks. The nurse must evaluate each encounter with the victim to monitor the progress of the woman's coping and the effectiveness of the interventions provided. Through this evaluative process, the nurse may determine that another mode of therapy would be more beneficial to the woman. For some women, the assault will precipitate a major breakdown in coping skills, or adequate coping skills will not be available. Individual therapy with a clinical nurse specialist, psychologist, psychiatrist, or social worker may be the referral of choice.

Summary

This chapter has discussed the theoretical perspectives of sexual assault, the findings of recent research about rape and its victims, and the possible therapeutic interventions of nurses and other mental health care providers who work with the victims of sexual assault. Some of the major points included in this chapter are as follows.

1. Theoretical perspectives of rape and sexual assault include historical references, legal definitions, psychological reactions, and sociologic views as means of examining types of assaults and characteristics of assailants.

2. Rape trauma syndrome is the process of adaptation experienced by the victim of rape as she strives to

overcome her feelings of vulnerability, fear, and helplessness, and as she tries to regain her sense of equilibrium.

3. Unresolved sexual trauma and silent reaction to rape delay or inhibit a woman's recovery from the rape crisis.

4. Community intervention programs encompass the medical, legal, police, and judicial institutions with which the victim of rape or sexual assault must interact.

5. Nursing assessment of the victim of rape or sexual assault focuses on the woman's physical and emotional state, concerns for physical safety, anxiety about significant others, perception of the event, coping skills, and the availability of people supportive to her.

6. Planning for the victim who has just been assaulted includes medical attention and the provision of physical safety for her; intermediate and long-range planning consists of continued contact with the victim, supportive counseling, and helping her reorganize her life.

7. The aim of nursing intervention for the victim of rape or sexual assault is to develop a therapeutic alliance that will help her begin to ventilate her feelings and explore what life changes she wishes to make.

8. Preparation for medical events, police investigations, and court proceedings help demystify these procedures for the woman.

9. Anticipatory guidance is necessary for the family and friends of the rape victim to help them explore their own feelings and identify ways to become more supportive of her.

10. Follow-up plans for medical appointments and supportive counseling help the victim reintegrate and reorganize her life.

11. To enhance their therapeutic potential, nurses must recognize and face their own fears and stereotypical views of rape and sexual assault.

Therapeutic Dialogue

Making Contact with the Rape Victim

Ann B., a 20-year-old college student, called the crisis line of a metropolitan hospital. She was referred to the Obstetrics–Gynecology clinic of the hospital and spoke with a staff nurse in the clinic.

Client: I'm calling for some information.

Nurse: Yes, I'm Miss Smith, how may I help you?

Client: I've been staying with a friend for the afternoon. We were going to watch the game on television. He went out to get some things at the grocery. The doorbell rang and a man wanted to use the phone to get his car started. He came in and then, and then, well I don't know what to do. I'm alright, he didn't hurt me but I don't know what to do. He left, I'm O.K., Johnny came back and, and what should I do?

Nurse: I think you are telling me that you've been attacked. I'd like to help, could you tell me your name? Your first name is fine if that's all you want to share now.

Client: Ann.

Nurse: Ann, I am a nurse here in the clinic. When a woman has been attacked she can come here. We can help you and see that you have medical attention. A rape crisis counselor is available to stay with you while you see the doctor and talk with the police.

Client: Oh, do I have to talk to the police? I'm really alright, he didn't hurt me, I don't have any cuts or anything, but I don't know what to do. It was so dumb of me to let him come in. I don't know how I could have been so dumb!

Nurse: Ann, you weren't dumb. You did what many people would do when they wanted to be helpful. Lots of women have done the same thing. You may not have been hurt but you may need medical attention. The best thing you can do now is come in. You don't have to talk to the police if you don't want to. The crisis counselor can talk with you and explain what the police can do and then you can decide. But it would be good to see a doctor. John can come with you and he can be with you. You don't have to come by yourself. We don't have to tell anyone about this, but you do need to see a doctor.

In this initial contact, the nurse is establishing a climate of supportiveness for Ann by providing her with information and being directive in regard to the immediate steps that she must take to meet her health care needs.

Nurse: Ann, I'm going to be here when you come in. I'll look for you and introduce you to the counselor. The doctor will want to examine you. You need to have some medicine so you won't get an infection. Would you like John to bring you?

Client: Yes, I guess so, he can bring me.

Nurse: That will be good. It will be better if you come now. Don't take a bath or shower but just come now as you are. Can I give John directions?

(The nurse then talked with John and gave him directions to the hospital and the clinic.)

Nurse: John, I know this must be upsetting for you.

John: That crazy s.o.b., I'd like to find him and string him up. I don't know how this could have happened. If I'd just stayed home....

Nurse: John, I know you are angry. Right now, though, Ann needs you to be calm. She is blaming herself for what's happened. She may think your anger is at her for doing something she thinks is stupid, letting the man in the house. Ann needs medical attention now and, while you're here, you can talk with the rape crisis counselor to decide what to do next.

Discussion

During an initial contact with a rape victim, it is essential to address the state of disequilibrium that the victim experiences after the attack by providing her with information and specific actions that she can take. These directions offer her structure and a sense of control to counteract her feelings of helplessness and of being overwhelmed. The information should be given in a warm, supportive, personal manner. This form of interaction opens an avenue through which the victim can begin to develop a trusting relationship with the nurse or other health care provider.

In this situation, the nurse assessed John's immediate reactions to the rape and his ability to support Ann during the initial phase of the crisis. After allowing John to express his anger and acknowledging his feelings, the nurse focused on providing directives to him on how he could help Ann at this time. In this way, the nurse assisted John in gaining a sense of control and purposefulness for his feelings.

Note that in this initial contact, the nurse did not probe for information about the attack. The primary goal of the interaction was to begin the process of trust-building and provide information about the specific steps that the woman needed to take. The nurse did not initiate discussion of issues that are common to rape victims, but addressed only those issues brought up by Ann; that is, her feelings of shame and guilt.

After trust has been established and the immediate need for medical attention has been met, Ann and John will be counseled individually to assess their perceptions of the event, their situational supports, and their coping mechanisms. Planning for therapeutic interventions will be based on these assessments. Ann and John will also be counseled together to facilitate their understanding and sharing their feelings. Separately and together, Ann and John will be involved in anticipatory planning for the events and feelings to come.

Nursing Care Plan

The Client Who Is a Victim of Rape or Sexual Assault

Client Problem	*Goal*	*Intervention*
Physical injury and infection	Assessment of physical health care needs	Provide physical care to treat injuries (lacerations, bruises), prevent pregnancy, and treat infection.
		Insure accurate evidence collection to promote apprehension and conviction of the assailant.
		Give clear, concise explanations to the victim about procedures and their rationale.
		Give specific, written directions regarding follow-up medical appointments and medication administration.

Client Problem	Goal	Intervention
Feelings of fear, guilt, self-blame, anger, and vulnerability	Establishment of trust	Approach the client in a consistent and nonthreatening manner. Do not introduce probing questions about the details of the attack until after trust has been established. Communicate nonjudgmental acceptance through nonverbal means (tone of voice, facial expression, touch).
Overwhelming anxiety	Assessment of victim's perception of the rape or sexual attack	Provide opportunities for the victim to talk freely about the event, the feelings aroused, and the meaning of the event to her.
	Development of situational supports	Encourage the victim's family and friends to ventilate their feelings and help them identify ways to demonstrate understanding and acceptance of her.
	Promotion of adequate coping skills	Identify, with the client, ways to restore feeling of physical safety. Develop a plan for ongoing opportunities to talk about the event and subsequent feelings, as they evolve, over time. Provide anticipatory guidance for police investigations, medical questioning, and court proceedings.

References

1. Alexander CS: The Responsible Victim: Nurses' Perceptions of Victims of Rape. J Health Soc Behav 21 (March): 22–33, 1980
2. Brownmiller S: Against Our Will. New York, Simon and Schuster, 1975
3. Burgess AW, Holmstrom LL: Recovery from Rape and Prior Life Stress. Res Nurs Health 1:165–174, 1978
4. Burgess AW, Holmstrom LL: The Rape Victim in the Emergency Ward. Am J Nurs 73 (October): 1740–1745, 1973
5. Burgess AW, Holmstrom LL: Accountability: A Right of the Rape Victim. J Psychiatric Nursing 13 (May): 11–16, 1975
6. Burgess AW, Holmstrom LL: Rape: Crisis and Recovery. Bowie, MD, Robert J Brady, 1979
7. Burt MR: Cultural Myths and Supports for Rape. J Pers Soc Psychol 38 (February): 217–230, 1980
8. Calhoun L, Selby J, Warring L: Social Perception of the Victim's Casual Role in Rape: An Exploratory Examination of Four Factors. Human Relations 29:517–526, 1976
9. Feild HS: Attitudes toward Rape: A Comparative Analysis of Police, Rapists, Crisis Counselors, and Citizens. J Pers Soc Psychol 36:156–179, 1978
10. Feldman-Summers S: Conceptual and Empirical Issues Associated with Rape. In Walker MJ, Bradsky SL (eds): Sexual Assault: The Victim and the Rapist. Lexington, MA, DC Health, 1976
11. Flynn L: Interview: Women and Rape. Medical Aspects of Human Sexuality 8 (May): 183–197, 1974
12. Groth AN, Burgess AW, Holmstrom LL: Rape: Power, Anger, and Sexuality. Am J Psychiatry 134:1239–1243, 1977
13. Holmstrom LL, Burgess AW: The Victim of Rape: Institution Reactions. New York, John Wiley & Sons, 1978
14. Irving J: The World According to Garp. New York, EP Dutton, 1978
15. Irving J: Hotel New Hampshire. New York, EP Dutton, 1981
16. Lindemann E: Symptomatology and Management of Acute Grief. Am J Orthopsychiatry 45:813–824, 1944
17. MacDonald J: Rape: Offenders and Their Victims. Springfield, IL, Charles C Thomas, 1971
18. Resick PA, Jackson TL: Attitudes toward Rape Among Mental Health Professionals. Am J Community Psychology 9:481–490, 1981
19. Walker MJ, Brodsky SL (eds): Sexual Assault: The Victim and the Rapist. Lexington, MA, DC Health, 1976
20. Wilcox BL: Social Support, Life Stress, and Psychological Adjustment: A Test of the Buffering Hypothesis. Am J Community Psychol 9:371–387, 1981

Chapter 33
Violence Within the Family

"Peter, Peter Pumpkin eater
Had a wife and couldn't keep her.
He put her in a pumpkin shell
And there she lived very well."

"There was an old woman who lived in a shoe.
She had so many children she didn't know what to do.
She gave them some broth without any bread.
She whipped them all soundly and put them to bed."

"There was an old woman in Surry,
Who was morn, noon and night in a hurry,
Called her husband a fool,
Drove the children to school,
The worrying old woman of Surry."

The Real Mother Goose, *1916*

Cheryl Lindamood Anderson

Chapter Preview

Abuse of a violent physical or verbal nature can appear in any human relationship. Outbreaks of violence within the family, which has traditionally been viewed as the unit that protects, nurtures, and guides us, are usually quickly denied and concealed. The fact that violence occurs in the parent-to-child relationship has been most readily recognized and researched in the past 2 decades. More recently, study of violence in the child-to-parent or spouse-to-spouse relationship has begun. There is still a great deal that society does not understand about families who are violent.

Violence among family members is a complex issue. It is intertwined with many factors, such as alcohol, poverty, stress, and an ongoing cycle of violence. These factors are not necessarily the causes of violence within the family but may have varying degrees of influence upon the development of family violence.

The overview of violence in the family will be specifically directed at the abused woman and the abused child. It is important to remember, however, that violence may exist among other family relationships as well, either as isolated occurrences or concomitantly with other violent acts. The incidence, traditional and current theoretical applications, and the dynamics of family violence will be discussed in this chapter. A major emphasis of the chapter is the nursing process—assessment, analysis, planning, intervention and evaluation—as it is applied to the abused individual and family.

Learning Objectives

On completion of the chapter, the reader should be able to accomplish the following.

1. Define the six types of child abuse
2. Discuss the difficulty in documenting abuse
3. Identify the predictors of potential child abuse during the prenatal, perinatal, and postnatal periods
4. Identify the predictors of parents who are at high risk to abuse their children
5. Contrast the characteristics of the battering mate and the battered spouse
6. Describe the strengths, limitations, and usefulness of the legal system in dealing with child and spouse abuse
7. Apply the nursing process to the care of the abused individual and the abusing family

    Assess the verbal and nonverbal behaviors of the abused individual and the abusing family member(s)

    List the problems, potential problems, and nursing diagnoses of all family members involved in the abusive situation

Plan nursing goals and actions designed to alleviate the identified problems of the abused or abusing client

Formulate a nursing care plan for the abused or abusing client and his family

Evaluate the effectiveness of the nursing actions

8. Discuss the relevance and application of social theories to the problem of family violence
9. Recognize and discuss one's own feelings, experiences, and behaviors that may affect the nurse's therapeutic effectiveness when working with abused and abusing clients

Child Abuse

Types of Abuse

Child abuse is difficult to define precisely and, as a result, various definitions have emerged. Parents Anonymous recognizes six types of child abuse.

1. Physical abuse—acts of commission, such as burning or beating of a child
2. Physical neglect—acts of omission or inadequate parenting abilities, such as improper feeding or clothing of a child
3. Emotional abuse—attitudes directed towards the child that may be harmful to his emotional development
4. Emotional neglect—the lack of parent–child interaction
5. Sexual abuse—involvement of the child with a parent or adult family member in sex play or actual intercourse
6. Verbal abuse—assaults on the child that are verbally degrading, such as constant ridicule of the child[31]

It is difficult to document any type of abuse through observation, except physical abuse. The fact that there exist scant statistics for all areas of abuse, including physical abuse, illustrates the difficulty faced by health care providers in documenting suspected child abuse. This chapter will describe sexual and emotional abuse, but will concentrate on the topic of physical abuse of children and women.

Physical Abuse

The Model Child Protective Services Act defines an "abused or neglected child" as a child (*i.e.*, a person under the age of 18 years) whose physical or mental health or welfare is harmed or threatened with harm by acts of omission on the part of the responsible caregiver.[19] Physical abuse may be those injuries resulting from excessive corporal punishment. Physical and behavioral indicators of four types of child abuse and neglect are located in Table 33-1.

Table 33-1.   **Physical and Behavioral Indicators of Child Abuse and Neglect**

TYPE OF CHILD ABUSE AND NEGLECT	PHYSICAL INDICATORS	BEHAVIORAL INDICATORS
Physical Abuse	Unexplained bruises and welts: On face, lips, mouth On torso, back, buttocks, thighs In various stages of healing Clustered, forming regular patterns Reflecting shape of article used to inflict (electric cord belt buckle) On several different surface areas Regularly appear after absence, weekend, or vacation	Wary of adult contacts Apprehensive when other children cry Behavioral extremes: Aggressiveness Withdrawal
	Unexplained burns: Cigar, cigarette burns, especially on soles, palms, back, or buttocks Immersion burns (sock-like, glove-like, doughnut-shaped on buttocks or genitalia) Patterned-like electric burner, iron, etc Rope burns on arms, legs, neck, or torso	Frightened of parents Afraid to go home Reports injury by parents
	Unexplained fractures: To skull, nose, facial structure In various stages of healing Multiple or spiral fractures	
	Unexplained lacerations or abrasions: To mouth, lips, gums, eyes To external genitalia	
Physical Neglect	Consistent hunger, poor hygiene, inappropriate dress Consistent lack of supervision, especially in dangerous activities or for long periods of time Unattended physical problems or medical needs Abandonment	Begging, stealing food Extended stays at school (early arrival and late departure) Constant fatigue, listlessness, or falling asleep in class Alcohol or drug abuse Delinquency (e.g., thefts) States there is no caretaker
Sexual Abuse	Difficulty in walking or sitting Torn, stained, or bloody underclothing Pain or itching in genital area Bruises or bleeding in external genitalia, vaginal, or anal areas Venereal disease, especially in preteens Pregnancy	Unwilling to change for gym or participate in physical education class Withdrawal, fantasy, or infantile behavior Bizarre, sophisticated, or unusual sexual behavior or knowledge Poor peer relationships Delinquent or runaway behavior Reports sexual assault by caretaker
Emotional Maltreatment	Speech disorders Lags in physical development Failure-to-thrive	Habit disorders (sucking, biting, rocking, etc.) Conduct disorders (antisocial, destructive, etc) Neurotic traits (sleep disorders, inhibition of play) Psychoneurotic reactions (hysteria, obsession, compulsion, phobias, hypochondria) Behavior extremes: Compliant, passive Aggressive, demanding Overly adaptive behavior: Inappropriately adult Inappropriately infant Developmental lags (mental, emotional) Attempted suicide

(Reproduced from Heindl C, Krall C, Salus M, Broadhurst D: The Nurse's Role in the Prevention And Treatment of Child Abuse and Neglect. Washington, DC, Health, Education & Welfare publication, #(OHDS) 79-30202, 1979)

Sexual Abuse

Sexual abuse of a child includes pornographic photos, rape, molestation, child prostitution, and incest. Sexual abuse is defined as contact or interaction between a child and an adult in which the child is being used as an object of gratification for adult sexual needs or desires.[54] Such an experience may interfere with the child's normal, healthy development by producing a situation with which the child is unable to cope physically, emotionally, or intellectually. Often, a sexually abused child suffers feelings of anxiety, shame, or guilt.

Incidence of Sexual Abuse.   The actual incidence of sexual abuse is unknown because no national statistics exist; however, it has been estimated that its incidence may be higher than the incidence of physical abuse.[54] The National Center on Child Abuse and Neglect estimates a current annual incidence of 60,000 to 100,000 cases per year, generally not including the number of children who are victims of child prostitution or pornography.[9] As many as 80% of sexual abuse victims are abused by people known to them.

Characteristics of Sexually Abusing Adults and Their Victims.   Two general characteristics are common to those who sexually abuse their children—lack of impulse control, sometimes as a result of transient stress or as a characteristic of the abuser, and a confusion of roles, wherein the child is regarded not as a child, but as the object of the adult's needs. These characteristics of the parent-surrogate may be seen in all types of child abuse.[54]

Victims of sexual abuse are frequently characterized as being the oldest daughter of a family, approximately 8 years old when the incestuous relationship begins, and involved in the relationship an average of 5½ years. Later, if the victim enters therapy, she is generally 20 to 25 years old, married, of either blue-collar or white-collar occupational status, having either completed college or lacking a high-school diploma, and presenting to the therapist with marital problems.[54]

Emotional Abuse

Emotional abuse and neglect and verbal abuse may be considered together as emotional maltreatment, due to the similar predictors and consequences of their occurrences. The emotionally maltreated child may or may not be also physically or sexually abused, but physically abused children are always emotionally maltreated. To determine whether a parent–child relationship is emotionally abusive, there must be an action or series of actions or omissions by the parent(s) that can be shown to have caused emotional injury or harm to the child.[26] The causation and extent of injury due to emotional abuse can only be assessed by a qualified professional. It is unfortunate that, often, the true extent of injuries inflicted by emotional abuse cannot be seen until later in life, and, even then, the observable and, perhaps, disordered behaviors of the adult may not be connected to the emotional abuse he received as a child.

An emotionally maltreated and an emotionally disturbed child may display similar behavior, but their parent's actions may help to differentiate the cause of the problem. Parents of an emotionally disturbed child generally recognize that there is a problem and seek help, whereas the parents of an emotionally maltreated child may blame the child for the problem and refuse offers of help. The parents of the emotionally maltreated child may, at times, appear unconcerned about the welfare of their child.[19]

Battered Women

The most common legal definition of *domestic violence* refers to acts of criminal conduct that include the following elements.

1. An intimate relationship between assailant and victim who are, in most cases, or were, married
2. An act of physical violence
3. A private setting[53]

In any marriage, marital conflict is always a possibility. When it occurs, it is due to a difference in individual needs between partners and their capacities to adapt. Wife battering may be regarded as a "failure of adaptation, which means a failure to acquire the necessary social lessons, whether on account of an incapacity to learn, the lack of teaching, or a temporary or permanent destruction of lessons from internal or external influences."[40]

There is increased evidence and recognition that wife battering is often associated with such problems as alcoholism and drug abuse, unemployment and underemployment, and child or parent abuse. It has been estimated that as many as 90% of women batterers were, themselves, victims of abuse as children.[53] Because of the strong association between wife and child abuse, the following sections of this chapter will discuss incidence, theories, dynamics of abuse, and the nursing process in relation to both child and wife abuse victims. The terms *wife abuse* and *spouse abuse* are found most often in this chapter, but abuse occurs between live-in lovers and common-law couples as well; hence, the use of the term *battered women.*

Incidence and Significance of the Problem

Statistics of the number of children and women abused each year within the family network vary widely. The National Center on Child Abuse and Neglect has estimated that approximately 1 million children are maltreated by their parents or caretakers annually—with 100,000 to 200,000 children physically abused, 60,000 to 100,000 children sexually abused, and the remainder of the children victims of neglect. Each year, 2,000 children die in circumstances suggestive of abuse or neglect.[50]

The estimates of the number of women who are abused each year range from 1 million to 28 million.[21, 25] One study reported that nearly 1300 women were killed by their spouses in a period of 1 year.[42] The same study showed that the frequency and level of intensity of the violence vary; 28% of the study subjects reported at least one violent incident in their marriages and 5.3% experienced violence that was considered a beating. The most frequent violent incident reported was pushing or shoving the spouse, followed by slapping the spouse, and, less frequently, beating the spouse.[42]

The actual incidence of child and wife abuse can only be estimated, due to the problems in documenting abuse. Underreporting of abuse in the home may also be due to the fact that those engaged in violent incidents are conditioned to the "normal" part that violence plays in the family system. The ongoing cycle of violence from family generation to generation may make abuse an expected part of life.

The victim's or the abuser's shame or guilt may also contribute to the failure to report the abuse. Such violent acts as being hit with objects, beaten, or attacked with a knife are often too painful to report. Many incidents of wife abuse are not reported because of fear of retaliation or lack of alternatives to make changes in the abusing situation. Many battered women and battering parents describe the abuse as an accident.

Unfortunately, health care providers may also discourage the reporting of abuse by their actions or comments. Although most parents believe that some physical punishment should be given to their children as a means of discipline, society is very judgmental about parents who resort to more severe punishments. A parent may know he is exceedingly harsh with his child's disciplining and seek help, only to face ridicule and debasement from the health care professional.

Every state now has a mandatory law for reporting child abuse with the underlying intention that one who does not report suspected child abuse is committing a misdemeanor (see insert, Legal Issues in Family Violence). In addition, no state requires that the reporter of abuse have actual proof of abuse or neglect before reporting. The law may specify that a person must report "suspected" incidents or include the phrase, "reason to believe," in the report.[7] The report of "suspected" child abuse states that a child may be abused, not that his parents are abusers. Responsibility for the abusive actions should be determined by a qualified professional.

Theories of Violence and Aggression

Impulse and Maladaptation

Various disciplines have participated in developing theories that explain violence in general or a particular aspect of family violence. Freud discussed the "death wish" in some of his later writings. In The Ego and the Id, he postulated the dichotomy of life instincts (eros) and death instincts (thantos).[12] The death instinct, Freud believed, is directed against the organism itself and is therefore a destructive drive that is directed either against the self or others. According to Freud's theory, aggression is not a reaction to stimuli but a constantly flowing impulse rooted in the constitution of the human organism.

Freud's work later provided a framework for Lorenz's study of aggression.[29] Lorenz believed that aggression was an inherited instinct in man and animal that had to be released. He also believed that the unlearned biologic drive of aggression evolved because of its adaptive value to the species. Aggression was therefore not necessarily seen as a destructive force but, in man's case, a distorted maladaptive behavior. Both Freud's and Lorenz's work, however, could be criticized for the ambiguous use of concepts and the lack of differentiation between violence and types of aggression.

Social Learning Theory

Another useful and more recent approach to the study of aggression is the social learning theory. This theory is directed at the question of whether aggression is, or could be, socially learned. Bandura and his associates conducted numerous experiments with children to determine if, once the child saw an aggressive act, he would later incorporate it into his repertoire of behaviors under similar circumstances. In these studies, the children were found to imitate the aggressive behavior they had observed, even when it was unrelated to the solution of the problem.[3]

Psychobiologic Theory

An association between poor mother–infant interaction and potential child abuse is the basis for Restak's psychobiologic theory of the origin of violence.[35] This theory proposes that the infant deprived of motion and physical closeness fails to develop adequate brain pathways that mediate pleasure. Expression of pleasure, therefore, cannot be transmitted through the appropriate parts of the brain because there are fewer possible connections. As the infant is deprived of movement and touch stimuli, fewer impulses are relayed to the immature cerebellum (the coordinator of movement), causing it to develop abnormally. Consequently, fewer connections are made between the pleasure centers of the brain and the cerebellum; and later, the individual may have a more difficult time experiencing pleasure. In this absence of pleasure, the propensity for a dysfunctional state of violence predominates.

Environmental Theory

Through the discipline of sociology, an environmental theory of aggression has emerged.[39] According to this theory, the violent behavior of man or animal is caused by acute social disorganization, which is the result of a lack of mean-

Legal Issues in Family Violence

Child Abuse

Less than 20 years ago, only 11 states had laws requiring the reporting of child abuse. Many times, the professional was hesitant in reporting abuse because of not knowing what or to whom to report. The question of protection rights of the professional who did report also "scared off" physician or nursing personnel who wished to report suspected child abuse.[23]

Today, however, there is a mandatory reporting law for child abuse in all states, subject to a misdemeanor if one fails to report the abuse. Reports can be made to the Child Welfare Service, a county attorney, or a law officer. Problems still exist in reporting cases of abuse because all states have different reporting statutes in regard to the following areas.

1. Types of instances that must be reported
2. Persons who must report
3. Time limits for reporting
4. Manner of reporting (written, oral, or both)
5. Agencies to which reports must be made
6. Degree of immunity conferred on reporters[51]

The major purposes of mandatory reporting laws are to protect the victim of abuse from repeated attacks, to provide social services to families, and to improve the methods of identificaton and investigation of suspected abuse cases. Investigation into the reported child abuse is the second step of involvement in the situation and is a direct consequence of a filed report. An investigation has three purposes.

1. To determine if abuse or neglect is occurring
2. To determine if the child is at risk within the home
3. To determine if that risk is serious enough to warrant intervention guaranteeing the child's safety[51]

Battered Women

Legal protection for the battered woman is less developed. Many times, the legal system encourages the wife to return home rather than file a legal complaint against the batterer.

Different states have various civil remedies for battered women, such as protection orders, restraining orders, or vacate orders that generally include time limits. Other civil remedies can be issued only if the wife is filing for, or has been granted, a divorce. Shelter services are minimal to nonexistent in many states. Special police training to handle domestic abuse is also rare. Few states will issue a warrant for arrest unless the actual violent acts are observed by legal authorities. Spousal abuse is considered a misdemeanor in some states and a felony in one state; most states continue to view spousal abuse as a private matter to be worked out by the couple.[47]

Although some progress has been made concerning the legal issues in family violence, much more is necessary. Children and women are still not safe from abuse within their own family as society appears at times to condone violence against the woman and child. This "private matter" of family violence must be turned into a public matter. Only increased awareness of its presence and consequences will lead to changes in our legal system.

ingful values or the inability of society to impose its values on its members. Children brought up in the inner cities are believed more likely to be socialized into a world of every kind of violence—poverty, malnutrition, lack of jobs, poor education, sickness, and racial discrimination. These children learn aggressive behaviors in order to survive.[39]

Systems Theory

Established theories, considered useful in other areas, are now being applied to the study of family violence. The general systems theory approach, for example, has been applied to family functioning and relationships and, more recently, to family violence.[43] The major assumption underlying this theory is that violence between members of a family is the product of a system rather than a chance aberration or a product of inadequate socialization or disturbed personalities.

Symbolic Interactionism

One interesting approach of another established theory of violence is Athens' application of symbolic interactionism and violent crimes.[2] This theory proposes that people commit violent crimes only after they have formed violent interpretations of the situations that confront them. In addition, some persons are thought to have a violent, and others a nonviolent, self-image. Those who commit violent acts are seen as having violent self-images and a violent "other" to support the violent action. Furthermore, these violent persons cause others of a nonviolent self-image, with nonviolent "others," to commit violent criminal acts.[2]

Additional theoretical applications, such as the conceptual framework of the cycle of violence, the theory of learned helplessness and the battered woman, and the theories of exchange and conflict offer worthwhile contributions to the study of family violence.[8, 41, 46]

Characteristics of Abusing Families

Abusing Parents

Although a potential or actual abuser or victim may not be outwardly obvious, certain common characteristics have been identified. Earlier research in the area of child abuse characterized abusing parents by particular personality deficits and distinguished the battering as controlled or uncontrolled. The four personality types of the psychotic personality, the inadequate personality, the passive-aggressive personality, and the sadistic personality were included in the classification of uncontrolled battering. Controlled battering was classified into two additional categories—the displacement of aggression, and the cold, compulsive disciplinarian.[5]

The psychotic abuser sees the abused child as playing some ideosyncratic role in his fantasies.[5] This type of abuser, one who is psychotic, received much attention in the literature years ago; recent research, however, has discovered that the psychotic abuser is not very common.[10]

The abuser with an inadequate personality is irresponsible, immature, and impulsive. He or she has a very low threshhold for frustration. As parents, these abusers are often separated or relate to one another superficially. Characterizing this family may be a disorderly home, a list of evictions, alcoholism, and the inability to maintain an established line of work. These families are noted for their neglect of children as well as injury to them; the needs of the dependent child conflict strongly with the needs of the immature, impulsive parent.[5]

In families where the abuser is considered passive-aggressive, usually one child is abused. The child is seen as a source of competition or as a representation of the battering parent's failure to meet necessary role expectations. The child may be illegitimate or a step-child of the abuser. The main personality feature of the passive-aggressive abuser is dependency. These abusing parents are generally unresponsive and unemotional regarding the abuse, are defensive about their feelings, are generally depressed, and will never admit to guilt.[5]

Sadistic abusers have long-established patterns of behavior without feelings of guilt, lack of emotional involvement with the act of abuse, no signs of anxiety, and possible masochistic tendencies.[5] Similar to the psychotic abuser, the sadistic abuser is not common.[10]

One example of controlled battering is abuse associated with the displacement of aggression. The abuser who displaces aggression is often the mother who is experiencing marital conflict. This parent finds she cannot express her aggression to its primary object (her spouse) and displaces the aggression onto the defenseless child. After committing the abusive act, the mother generally feels guilty and regrets her actions; however, she may never understand why she acts as she does.[5]

The cold, compulsive disciplinarian is generally characterized by his compulsiveness. This parent asserts his right to punish his own children as he sees fit; he believes this is the privilege of a parent.[5]

Additional indicators of abusing parents may include some of the following behaviors and traits. The abusing parent may

1. seem unconcerned about the child;
2. attempt to conceal the child's injury or protect the identity of the abuser;
3. routinely apply harsh, unreasonable, and age-inappropriate punishment to a child;
4. have been expected to meet high demands from his own parents;
5. be unable to provide emotionally for himself as an adult;
6. expect his children to fill his emotional void;
7. view the child as a small adult capable of meeting his needs.[19]

Abusing Spouses

Some of the characteristics of abusing parents have also been used to describe abusing spouses. The abusing couple, for example, has been described as a sadistic–masochistic relationship. The woman who elected to stay within an abusive situation was considered a masochist, whereas the male batterer was considered the sadist. It may be necessary, though, to reconsider the situation before adopting this view of abusing couples. Many women see no alternatives to leaving an abusive situation due to inadequate finances, lack of job skills, and fear of abuser retaliation.[40]

Men who view spousal abuse as common are characterized as enjoying and participating more in sports and hunting, having had past military service, generally employed with higher incomes but having less job satisfaction, having more education than their wives, having more children than the traditional families, and having a degree of marital happiness.[13] These men also believe that arguing between spouses is common. It is ambiguous whether high or low income or high or low educational level has any influence on the incidence of spouse abuse.[1, 10, 15, 52]

Wife battering commonly begins in the early months of marriage, perhaps with the signs of a pregnancy. The abusive act generally occurs in the home, most commonly in the kitchen or bedroom. Some men do appear to become intoxicated in order to beat their wives later. These men are not believed to be psychotic, but are, instead, unsure of themselves, lacking both necessary self-control and a realistic view of marriage.[10]

Battered wives may be characterized as appearing frightened, distant, or jumpy, often unable to look the helping professional in the eyes, or assuming a stiff, rigid posture.[28] Other characteristics of the abused wife may include emotional and financial dependence, rigid adherence to patriarchal sex roles, low self-esteem, and emotional insecurity.[6] In addition, these women become victims through socially learned behavior as the abuse is continually repeated.[45]

Abused Children

An abusive situation may require only an actor (parent, child, or spouse) and a crisis or severely stressful event. The most frequently reported stress factors from substantiated abuse reports are a broken home, family discord, insufficient income, incapacitating physical handicaps, drug dependency, and mental retardation.[52]

Regardless of the cause, abuse within the home will influence the child either immediately or later. The abused child may be characterized by any of the following behaviors. The abused child

1. appears wary of physical contact with adults;
2. seems frightened of his parents;
3. stares in a vacant or frozen manner;
4. seeks affection from everyone;
5. manipulates adults to get attention;
6. does not cry when approached by an examiner or react in a frightened manner during painful procedures.[19]

As battered children grow older, boys tend to imitate their fathers and girls tend to imitate their mothers. Boys often become aggressive, fight with their siblings or peers, and throw temper-tantrums when they are frustrated. Girls may develop more psychosomatic complaints, and become withdrawn, clinging, passive, and anxious.[48] Some investigators have found correlations between history of abuse as a child and juvenile delinquency, fire-setting, and even murder in later life.[11, 17] Simply witnessing abuse in the home influences the child's later behavior; male children who witness abuse show more abusive behavior as husbands than boys who do not.[36]

Impact on Victim and Family

Impact on the Child

The most obvious and life-threatening consequence of abuse is the physical damage to the victim. The most common physical markings of child abuse are internal and head injuries, spiral fractures, and elbow and knee injuries due to pulling or jerking the child by his extremities.[50] Vaginal tears and bruises are observed on the child who has been sexually abused. Physically abused children may show evidence of neurologic impairment, including spasticity, paraplegia, or blindness. A high incidence of mental and language retardation is also found in children who are abused.[11]

Children who are not directly abused themselves but are caught in the middle of parental marital discord may also demonstrate behavior problems, such as anxiety disorders, truancy, or aggression. The learning of a cycle of violence may also be demonstrated later in parent abuse by adult offspring.

It has been indicated that women raised in an environment of "approved" violence were more prone to marry a violence-prone man.[15] Another study reported that a woman who was frequently struck by her parents as a child would tolerate more strikings from her husband.[6]

Impact on the Woman

The physical impact of abuse on the woman is generally recognized through injuries of the head, neck, or shoulders, with "black eyes" being the most common lesion. Other injuries may result from being pushed against walls or down stairs. During pregnancy, blows may be directed toward the abdominal region, which often represent negative feelings toward an unwanted baby.[10] Sometimes, the battered woman retreats to alcoholism or a mental breakdown. The crime of shoplifting is the most frequent crime perpetrated by the abused wife to escape a bad situation. More severe outcomes, such as suicide of the abused woman, or eventual homicide of the abused spouse, are also possible.[25, 40]

The battered woman's reaction to the abuse may vary greatly; some women seek shelter and temporary or permanent severance of the spousal relationship, others appear to do nothing. Although women initially call the legal authorities, the introduction of the legal system into what is considered by many to be a "private matter" does not necessarily work in favor of the abused woman (see case study, Maria, A Battered Wife). Unless the abuse is witnessed by the police, despite the presence of the woman's bruises or other injuries, no arrest of the abuser may be made. Once the police leave the home, the man may retaliate with another beating because the wife called the police. According to many lawyers, there may not be a feasible legal solution to family violence.[53]

In some cases, a restraining order may be considered for the protection of the wife. Often, however, the restraining order is ignored by the batterer and not encouraged by the judge. Some lawyers advise women to hide. Pressing assault charges may also prove to be ineffective, and, furthermore, may anger the batterer. The imprisonment of the batterer or the levying of a fine may have economic repercussions on the abused woman as well as her husband.

Many women who report the abuse and file a complaint against the batterer drop the complaint shortly thereafter. Fear of retaliation from the batterer and a court system that appears to discourage filing complaint against the batterer leads the woman to change her mind and drop the charges. Many women who leave their home at the time of acute abuse return later, again and again.

Why do women return to a battering situation? Some of the reasons are obvious and some less so—lack of job skills, fear of losing custody of the children on the grounds of abandonment, social isolation, and cultural or religious

Case Study

Maria, A Battered Wife

Maria and James lived together for several years in a common-law relationship. They rented a small but adequate apartment in the poorer section of Los Angeles. Although the first few years together had been good, lately James had begun to drink more heavily and to hit Maria. One night, Maria was hurt badly by his physical abuse and required a 3-day stay in the hospital. Maria realized then that her situation was not going to improve and made plans to file charges against James and move from their apartment.

Pursuing the issue to court was hampered by several legal obstacles, but Maria persisted. In court, the judge asked James to leave Maria alone and James promised that he would comply.

Three months later, Maria had found a new apartment and a job; however, James discovered where Maria lived, barged in on her and hit her, which led to another hospitalization for Maria. Again in court, the judge asked James to leave Maria alone, and, once again, James promised that he would.

Several months later, James returned. Maria tried to fight, but in the struggle, Maria's eye was "put out" with a broom handle. After her hospitali-

zation Maria again returned to court and heard the same exchange between the judge and James. She was terrified and moved to another location, but James found her again and beat her severely. After that hospitalization, Maria told the court she had done everything possible to prevent James from finding her and described her multiple hospitalizations. Still, the judge only asked James to stay away from Maria. When Maria returned to her apartment that night, she took out the small gun she had bought for protection. Unable to use it on another human being, she shot herself. She died before reaching the hospital.

Questions for Discussion

1. What are some of the common characteristics of abusive families illustrated by this violent family?
2. Discuss the legal ramifications and failures involved in this case history. What should have been done?
3. When Maria was in contact with health care professionals, what could have been done to prevent future abuse?
4. Outline a nursing assessment of Maria and James and parallel interventions for them.

---

constraints.[4] The abused woman fears that there is no place to go, that she may be followed and beaten for her actions, that her children may be harmed if they try to protect her from the abuser, and that the future, without her husband, would be worse than the present situation. It is fear, in general, that may be the most understandable, and yet most commonly disregarded, reason for the battered wife's return to the abusing situation.[30] Abused women who return home generally do so on the promise that the husband will reform.[14] Often, the wife loves the batterer and does not wish to file for divorce or leave the husband; in fact, some abused women believe that their marital relationship is better than most.[30] Finally, the view of many is that it is the wife's sole responsibility to keep a marriage intact; therefore, the violent situation continues.[6]

Effects of Violence on Family Members

Some of the most commonly occurring effects of family violence on adult family members include the following.

1. Depression
2. Difficulty obtaining, maintaining, and adjusting to employment
3. Emotional abuse and deprivation

4. Breakup of the family unit
5. Recurrence of violent behavior with a new partner
6. Expansion of violence into the community[4]

The major effects of family violence on children, however, are different from those on adults and include the following.

1. Death by homicide or suicide
2. Emotional injuries, such as lowered self-esteem
3. Depression
4. Runaway episodes
5. Alcohol and drug experimentation
6. Early marriage with continuation of violence[4]

Application of the Nursing Process to Family Violence

Assessment and Analysis of the Battering Family

Assessing and Diagnosing the Battered Child

Whether she is in a prenatal clinic, a postpartum unit, an intensive care nursery, or an emergency room, the nurse is in a unique position to detect potential or actual abuse within families. How the nurse responds to this challenge could save a life. (See insert, Child Abuse: Update on Theories.)

Prenatal Predictors. Assessing potential abuse of a child is guided by the nurse's knowledge of specific behavioral predictors. The following six prenatal predictors are helpful in identifying expectant parents who may later abuse their child.

1. Parental overconcern about the infant's sex
2. Parental overconcern about the infant's performance
3. Denial of the pregnancy

Child Abuse: Update on Theories

Several theories have developed that are specific to the phenomenon of child abuse. The research of over a decade ago emphasized the mental stability or instability of the parent and supported a premise that parents who abuse their children are usually mentally ill. This mental illness model evolved as one of the first potential theoretical frameworks of child abuse. Although this theory is still held by some mental health caregivers, other research has led the way to new discoveries and their potential theoretical frameworks of child abuse.

Research has demonstrated that the factors of stress and environmental violence also influence the occurrence of child abuse. Through the environmental-stress model of child abuse, sociologists began to approach the understanding of child abuse via the high level of violence in the United States and the stress of the family.

The most well-known theory of child abuse may be that promulgated by Helfer and Kempe. In its most simplistic fashion, this theory suggests the possibility of abuse any time a "special child," a "special parent," or stress is present within a family.

Years of continued research of child abuse have illustrated, however, that all three of these theories are limited in scope and characterize perhaps only a small number of abusive families.[4] Not all abused children have mentally incompetent parents; not all stressful families abuse their children; and not all "special children" are abused by their parents. The inability of these theories to describe all abusive families and the knowledge that several factors appear to occur together in the eliciting of abuse have led to the development of the final theory to be discussed, the human ecological model of child maltreatment.

The development of the human ecological theory of child abuse comes from the ideas and work of Garbarino and Belsky, which draws heavily from Bronfenbrenner's model of the ecology of human development.[2,3,5] The basic premise of this theory is that a relationship exists between humans and their environment. This basic idea allows for a much clearer understanding of child abuse that considers the multiple causes of child abuse, such as the individual's personality and environmental stressors. Separate work by Garbarino and Belsky has led to a theoretical framework consisting of four levels of analysis that subsume almost all explanations of child abuse to date. These levels are

1. ontogenic development, which considers the history of abuse in abusing parents, and parental expectations of children;
2. the microsystem, which considers infant/child characteristics and marital stress or conflicts;
3. the exosystem, which considers the world of work and the neighborhood; and
4. the macrosystem, which considers the attitude of society about violence in general.

In summary, the ecological theory of child maltreatment is an extremely useful theory to explain child abuse. This theory considers multiple etiologies including parental characteristics, stress, history of abuse of the abusing parents, characteristics of the neighborhood, infant/child characteristics, and the general attitude of society about violence. Anderson is continuing to apply the ecological model of child maltreatment; Millor's work is focusing on the development of a nursing framework of child abuse.[1,6] Continued insight into the etiologies of child abuse may provide help and hope to some families with the potential for abuse before the cycle of violence begins.

References

1. Anderson C: A Preliminary Profile of Abusive and Non-abusive Mothers. Unpublished Ph.D. dissertation, Texas Woman's University, 1985
2. Belsky J: Child maltreatment: An ecological integration. Am Psychol 35 (April): 320–333, 1980
3. Bronfenbrenner, U: The Ecology of Human Development. Cambridge, Harvard University Press, 1977
4. Campbell J, Humphreys J: Nursing Care of Victims of Family Violence. Reston, Virginia, Reston Publishing Company, 1984
5. Garbarino J: The human ecology of child maltreatment: A conceptual model for research. J Marriage Family 39:721–732, 1977
6. Millor G: Theoretical framework for nursing research in child abuse and child neglect. Nurs Res 30 (March–April): 78–83, 1981

4. Severe maternal depression
5. Lack of support of the expectant mother from the family
6. An earlier wish to terminate the pregnancy that was not carried out[19]

Perinatal Predictors. During the perinatal period, potential child abuse may be signaled by several events surrounding the birth of the child. The mother who has a difficult delivery or lacks an understanding of infant care, or the parents who are unprepared for the infant at home should be more carefully assessed regarding their parenting capabilities.[19]

Other possible indicators of future child abuse can be determined through assessment of parent–child interaction at birth. For example, a new mother who is not adapting readily to her newborn may see her infant as ugly or unattractive, may allow the infant's head to dangle without support, may hold the infant away from her body, may avoid eye contact with her infant or stare fixedly into his eyes, or may fail to coo and "talk" with her infant.[33]

Postnatal Predictors. Sometimes, during the postnatal period, other parental behaviors signal potential child abuse or neglect. When parents are disappointed over the sex of their child or respond either negatively or not at all to their infant, their behavior should be interpreted and monitored as possible child abuse. The nurse who is involved in the care of this family must be alert to the situation and work towards strengthening the parent–infant bond and finding methods of substituting socially acceptable behavior for violent episodes. Other postnatal predictors of potential abuse include situations in which parents resist or are repulsed at changing diapers, parents are unreliable concerning regular medical care, and the father is jealous of the time mother and infant spend together and their mutual affection.[19]

What is known about the parents who abuse their children? It is likely that, as children, the parents suffered abuse or neglect from their own parents. It is also likely that the parents have a poor marital relationship, and that one or both partners have a low self-esteem and are personally or socially isolated to an extreme degree. The abusing parents may also play out a parent–child role reversal in which the child "parents," or takes care of, his parent.[49]

Vulnerable Infants. Certain infants have been identified as susceptible or vulnerable infants to later child abuse, including the following.

1. Low birth-weight infants
2. Infants of unwanted pregnancies
3. Infants of drug-using or alcohol-using parents
4. Infants of a multiple birth
5. Infants with birth defects

6. Children who take on characteristics of a disliked parent or traits the parent dislikes in himself
7. Premature infants in which there is little maternal–infant contact[22, 44]

Infants who meet one or more of these criteria must be considered potential child abuse victims and require continuous assessment and appropriate intervention.

Screening Families for Possible Child Abuse. An Index for Suspicion can be used to screen families for child abuse. Four types of family structures or behavioral patterns known to foster maltreatment of children are classified as the following radar alerts.

Radar alert 1: parents are authoritarian, highly structured, and inflexible in disciplining techniques; attempts at family–staff interaction are either suppressed or rechanneled into superficial conversation
Radar alert 2: drug or alcohol use of parent(s)
Radar alert 3: psychiatric disturbances of documentable psychosis, neurosis, or mental deficiency of parent(s)
Radar alert 4: emotional immaturity of parent(s) and loose or ill-defined family structure[34]

Investigating Child Abuse. Once a report of suspected abuse or neglect is made, an investigation of the family unit commences. The first item in a complete social assessment of the family is the determination of whether or not the abused child is safe in his present surroundings. Assessing the level of danger to the abused child is accomplished by examining the following issues.

1. Are there weapons available to the abuser?
2. Have weapons been used, or may a weapon possibly be used, in the present abusive situation?
3. Is there use of alcohol or a history of abuse of alcohol?
4. Is there talk of murder or suicide?

Following the assessment of the danger to the child, the remainder of the social assessment, including both the strengths and weaknesses of the family, is completed.

Evaluating the Child's Health. During the assessment process, the nurse assists with the medical evaluation of the child, including the proper referrals for physical examination, x-rays, and laboratory studies. Medical personnel are also called upon to cooperate with a representative of the child protective services and to share medical information that will contribute to a thorough social assessment and subsequent interventions.

The nurse is responsible for obtaining specific health data, such as the parental explanation of the child's injury and whether the explanation correlates with the type of injury, and the child's history of previous trauma or health problems. It is important, for example, to further investigate the status of the child who is "accident-prone" or who has frequent health problems.

Physical assessment of the child should focus particularly on the condition of the skin—does the child have bruises, scars, or lacerations? Preventive health practices are determined by questioning whether the child's immunizations are current and whether the child is examined by a physician on a regular basis. Sometimes, abusing parents may list the names of several physicians for the child, because they have sought medical care from a variety of doctors for the various injuries the child has suffered. The child's nutritional status is assessed through his dietary history, and the age-appropriateness and adequacy of the diet.

The Child's Psychosocial Status. Information about the child's social history, family supports, composition of the household, and economic status is gathered by the nurse and other medical and child protective personnel. The nurse asks about the child's typical day's activities, the parent's description of the child, the child's school performance, extracurricular activities, and developmental level of functioning. Specifically, during this phase of the assessment process, the nurse notes whether the parents describe positive or negative aspects of the child's character and whether the parents see the child as doing well in school and at home.

The nurse must pay particular attention to the quality of the parent–child interaction. In addition, the nurse evaluates the degree of parental cooperation with, or resistance to, medical treatment, the degree of parental concern about the situation, and the adequacy of the parents' coping abilities. Do the parents see a need for change in their home situation? Are they aware of their own involvement in the abuse or neglect? Do the parents wish to keep the family intact and work together to solve their problems? Descriptive assessments of the affectional ties within the family and the available supports for the parents are essential pieces of information for health care workers.[19] Are there, for example, any other adults or older children at home who can help assume some family responsibilities?

A child brought into the emergency room as a suspected victim of abuse should be admitted to the hospital. Hospital admission allows time for thorough evaluation and protects the child from the immediate abusive situation. Generally, the parents permit this admission of their child and may feel relieved that the child is removed from the home; however, if the parents do not wish to leave the child at the hospital and health care workers require additional time to complete the evelation of the suspected abuse, the hospital can request a court order to retain the child for a specific length of time.

Diagnosis of Abuse. The nurse and other health care providers should consider several factors when formulating a diagnosis of child abuse. Do the parents present a contradictory history? Is the cause of injury projected onto another person? Did the parents appear to wait an unduly long period of time prior to seeking attention for the child's injury? Is there poor maternal or paternal attachment? Is a history provided that does not adequately explain the injury? Are the parents reluctant to share information with medical personnel? Have the parents "shopped around" from one hospital to another? Are the parents difficult to locate after the child's admission to the hospital?[20]

Certain factors to consider in diagnosing abuse specifically concern the child at risk. Does the child have an unexplained injury? Does the child show evidence of poor care, malnutrition, repeated injuries, fractures, or skin injuries? Does the child appear to take care of the parent?[20]

Legally, there is a mandatory requirement that professionals, and even neighbors of friends, who suspect the occurrence of child abuse must report their suspicions to the appropriate authorities. In the hospital or medical setting, if the responsible health care provider fails to report suspicions of child abuse, it is the nurse's responsibility to do so with the proper direction and authority of the hospital.

Assessing and Diagnosing the Battered Wife

An identification of child abuse may be tied to the abuse of a spouse (man or woman) as well. Some mothers, abused by their mates, abuse their children or a husband abuses both wife and children. An alert nurse may identify abused women in almost any health care facility, such as an outpatient clinic, emergency room, prenatal clinic, or even at home through a visit by a public health nurse. Several guidelines are helpful in making a positive identification of spouse abuse.

Identifying the Battered Woman. The acutely battered woman in the emergency room is likely to come to the hospital without her partner, state that she has no private physician, and present with the complaint of an "altercation" or a "fall." These characteristics, along with a high incidence of skull and facial contusions, assist the nurse in identifying a victim of battering.[1] Sometimes, battered women may enter the emergency room with a battered child, or present with drug overdose or alcohol intoxication, which contributes to the difficulty in formulating an accurate assessment of the underlying problem.[10] A woman who has a history of repeated injuries, particularly around the head, neck, or breasts, or a type of injury that is not adequately explained should alert the nurse's suspicions and encourage her to investigate the woman's situation more closely.[48]

Between the acute battering incidents, the woman may visit her family doctor and complain of insomnia, abdominal pain, headaches, or "nervousness." The woman's anxiety, accompanied by its physical manifestations, is frequently precipitated by her knowledge that the battering is cyclical and that the next episode is approaching. Unfortunately, many clinicians fail to investigate the reasons for these complaints and prescribe sedatives and tranquilizers for the woman.[48]

Nurses and physicians in obstetrical areas are in a unique position to detect battered women, because the injuries of many battered women first occur during pregnancy. Trauma to the abdomen, for example, may be the cause of antepartal hemorrhage or premature labor.[38] Violence during pregnancy may, in effect, be the husband's attempt to terminate the pregnancy and, therefore, eliminate the stress of an additional child in the family.[16]

Diagnosis of Abuse. The history of the battered woman is likely to reveal serious bleeding injuries, broken bones of the vertebrae, pelvis, jaw, or extremities, and burns from scalding water, cigarettes, or hot appliances.[38] As seen in the abused child, the battered woman may show signs of both old and new wounds.[28] If there is sufficient suspicion to warrant the collection of a complete history for signs of possible abuse, it must be approached with sensitivity to the woman's embarrassment, hesitancy, or evasiveness. The nurse or other health care professional should be alert to the usual excuses that her "accident" occurred as a result of walking into a door or having a tooth pulled.[28]

The battered victim may offer clues about her situation, and, therefore, the health care professional should remain alert to their appearance. The abused woman may hint or state directly that she wishes to speak privately with the health care provider. She may appear jumpy, frightened, or unable to make eye contact with medical personnel. If her husband is present, she may flinch with his movements. Any woman with trauma of having been battered, unless there is evidence to the contrary, should be suspected and assessed as an abused woman.[28]

Planning

Planning the treatment of abusing and abused individuals must be approached by health care professionals who are aware of their own feelings concerning battering incidents and who display a nonjudgmental attitude toward the family. Prior knowledge of, and experience with, abusing families will help the nurse create an accepting atmosphere. A judgmental remark uttered irresponsibly will only intensify the family members' shame and guilt. Acceptance and willingness to work openly with the family, on the other hand, will promote the attainment of long-term goals to prevent further abuse.

One of the major goals in working with violent families is the promotion of trust with the abused victim and the abusing parent or spouse. This goal may or may not be reached, depending, in part, on the kinds of experiences the family has already had with health care professionals. Trust is encouraged and accomplished only with time.

Discussion and planning with the violent family should be conducted in a private, quiet place that is a nonthreatening environment for the family. The nurse should encourage the family to verbalize some of their goals. The active participation of the family in the planning process reminds them that the role of the health care provider is not to make the family's decisions or tell them what to do. The family should be asked what changes they want to occur within the family and how they see these changes taking place. Comprehensive planning always incorporates the family's own goals.

Available alternatives for the family are provided by the health care professional. This is an important part of planning treatment with, for example, the battered wife because she may not view her immediate departure from the family as a viable alternative. When a battered woman chooses to remain with her abusing mate, plans must be made to maintain her safety within the home. Sometimes, a woman will delay her decision to leave the battering environment until a later date, when she is financially prepared or has developed greater confidence in her abilities.

Information about another alternative, seeking a shelter, is provided to the battered woman. Within the safety of a shelter, the wife may learn how to become more independent through the development of skills, which will prepare her financially if she decides to leave the family unit. Child care alternatives are also discussed with the woman. Health care personnel may also help the woman locate a new place to stay. Some shelters have emergency funds to help the battered victims with essential, immediate expenses.

Because of the increased demand and their scarceness in the community, most shelters impose a time limit on the woman's stay; therefore, the woman must make some decisions about her future. It is unfortunate that there are relatively few intermediate shelters where a woman can stay as she continues to work out her plans for the future. An intermediate shelter allows the woman to continue to develop her job skills and care for her children within a protected environment.

A heightened awareness of the battering phenomenon by society will lead to greater community involvement and the development of more shelters for the acute and intermediate stages of abuse. This awareness will also promote the activities of support groups, such as Parents Anonymous. Rather than being turned away to rely on their own coping abilities and often to deteriorate into a deeper cycle of violence leading to death, disability, and future generations of violence, abused and abusing individuals will be helped by health care providers to make the necessary changes in their lives.

Intervening with the Violent Family

Dealing with One's Own Anger

Effective intervention can be achieved only after the nurse or other health care provider has established trust and rapport with the abusing family; however, during the nurse's involvement with the family, she is exposed to information about the abuse that is often painful to acknowledge and accept. Admittedly, the nurse may feel a certain amount of anger or disgust when intervening with an abusing family. Working with helpless infants and children who have been beaten, for example, stirs up a wide spectrum of feelings in any person who is concerned with the health and well-being of others. It is, therefore, necessary that the nurse be actively involved in a supportive group with whom she can ventilate and work through her feelings. Prior to any effective intervention with the violent family, the nurse must face the anger within.[44]

Intervening with the Abused Child

Nursing interventions for the abused child begin with the required medical and surgical care; however, it is important that in the midst of his physical care, attention to the child's emotional needs are not forgotten. To initiate a trusting relationship with the abused child, the nurse should explain all tests and procedures to him, in terms he can understand, and in advance of their occurrence. The nurse should talk, sing, and play with the child to establish rapport with him. She is aware that her touch may not be welcome to the child and ascertains first that the child will permit her touch before approaching him.

Planning the Child's Care. After the immediate danger to the child's life has passed, the nurse begins to formulate goals relating to the child's future safety and psychosocial development. These major goals include improvement of the child's self-esteem, development of more positive interpersonal relationships between the child and his family, helping the child to communicate his feelings either verbally or through play, and helping the child channel his aggression constructively.

Therapeutic play opportunities will allow the child to vent his aggression and communicate pent-up feelings.[26] Consistency in limit-setting with the child will help promote a sense of security and predictability.[44] Acceptance of the child, recognizing and commenting on his abilities, and providing activities in which he can excel will help build a more positive self-esteem. If the parents are unable to change their behaviors, the only safe place for the child may be a foster home or a temporary shelter. Consistency and follow-up of care are essential in treating the abused child and his family.

Intervening with the abused child, once the danger period is over, requires comprehensive planning and working toward the accomplishment of a series of long-term goals. Repairing the physical and emotional damage of the child takes time, as does the unlearning of a cycle of violence.

Intervening with the Abusive Parents

Accepting the Parents. Intervening with abusing parents immediately after an abusive incident may severely test the nurse's ability to remain nonjudgmental and accepting of her clients. If the parents have been made to feel they can honestly relate their feelings to a trusting, nonjudgmental professional, they will generally provide some information during the admission interview. The nurse must allow the parents to ventilate their feelings. If the nurse or other professional is not able to allow this ventilation of the abusing parents, another health care professional should be found who is capable of working with the family.

Keeping the Parents Involved with Their Child. When counseling or interviewing the parents, it is best to retreat from the busy emergency room to a quieter, more relaxed setting. The interview should initially be fairly brief. Be honest with the parents and keep them informed of what is happening to their child. Let them know if a report for abuse is filed and what will result from this action.[44] The nurse must, at the same time, communicate her faith in the parent's abilities. Do not begin an interview by pointing out the inadequacies of their parenting skills (after all, they have surely heard this before); just sit, chat, and observe.[32] Full visitation rights of parents to the hospitalized child should be allowed and encouraged, except in extreme cases as determined by the court.[44] Be available to the parents.

Safeguarding the Abused Child. The safety of the child who is returned home after an abusive incident is a major concern of the health care professional. Working on the unmet needs of the parents—their frustrations, stresses, and depressed self-images—can help provide a safer environment for the child. Paying attention to the parent, at some time, without focusing on the child helps to raise the parent's poor self-concept.[44]

Using Community Resources. Health care providers who work with abusive families must know the available resources and services helpful to abusing parents. Referrals to community resources, such as parenting classes, Parents Anonymous, foster grandparents, day care centers, family guidance centers, Planned Parenthood, individual therapy, or group therapy may benefit battering parents (see insert, An Open Letter from a Member of Parents Anonymous). The court may require some parents to undergo psychiatric consultations or therapy before it will allow the abused child to be returned to the home. Such referrals can help the battering parents to communicate their feelings and frustrations more appropriately, develop a more positive self-concept, arrange time for themselves, learn appropriate developmental expectations for their child, and recognize that their problem is not unique.

Approaching the Entire Family. Nursing intervention must be directed at the entire family, not at one particular individual. In fact, the true abuser of the child within the family would not necessarily have to be identified for effective interventions to be implemented with the abusive family.

An Open Letter from a Member of Parents Anonymous

Dear Friends,

I feel to get my point across, I must reach out and touch each of you with some of my innermost feelings. I'll call myself Sally, although Parents Anonymous (PA), the author, and editor have respected the philosophy of PA, which allows me to remain unknown. It has taken me 28 years of searching to find out who I am and like her! I am a Parents Anonymous Parent.

When I heard Parents Anonymous deals with child abuse, I couldn't believe *I* abused my children! I've never left a cut or bruise on my kids; they have no scars—or do they?

In society today, we see child abuse mentioned in the paper when Jane Doe burns her child in hot bath water, or Fred Smith beats his girlfriend's child to death, or Mary Jones, 16 years old and only a child herself, leaves her baby in the care of a stranger, who then disappears with the child. Abuse and neglect can muster feelings like, "Hang 'em from the nearest tree," or "What kind of awful person would do such a thing?" It's true, these things happen every day, everywhere in the world. My questions to you are these: What brings a person to the point of hurting someone they love? Since when is whipping with belts, paddles, hairbrushes, and shoes a "normal" form of discipline? When is leaving children alone 2 to 6 hours a day to avoid babysitting costs, calling them derogatory names, or forcing a child to eat every bit of food an adult puts on his plate "normal" childrearing?

Not only physical and sexual abuse turns our children into abusive adults. Abuse is a cycle and is passed on, in one form or another, from generation to generation. Child abuse "hunters" can only intensify the problem by putting parents in jail, removing children from their home, and so on.

Parents Anonymous is a self-help support group, which simply means the group supports you in your efforts to become better parents. Parents Anonymous is a support system with no guarantee that if you attend six meetings, your abusive traits will go away. What PA does is emotionally support you as you cope with the tasks of being a parent while struggling to live in a tough world.

When I attended my first meeting of Parents Anonymous, I thought that no one could ever understand what I was feeling. I heard some of the problems of members of the chapter and realized that not only did we have a lot in common, I left feeling like things weren't nearly as bad for me as they were for others!

Not everyone can attend group meetings such as MADD, AA, or PA. This should be understood and parents should not be pressured into a group atmosphere. The key word is support and this support can be sought from clergy, therapists, counselors, good friends, or close relatives. It is important to know that somebody cares. Any of us becomes very defensive when confronted with our own family's problems. Being nonjudgmental of the parents and what they've done is an important part of beginning a trusting relationship with the parents. If a child has never "driven you crazy," it will be very hard for you to understand what a parent goes through before and after an abusive episode.

Child abuse has no economic class—as a matter of fact, it can't be pinpointed to any race, creed, or color. There are, however, many common denominators such as stress, employment, and finances, but one significant factor is the generational cycle. If you were abused as a child, chances are you will have a tendency to abuse your children. We were raised hearing tapes . . . "Don't do as I do, do as I say . . . " "A good spanking never hurt you. . . . " As parents, we "replay" those tapes, By seeking help and learning to admit to ourselves that we can never be "perfect" parents, we start to grow as better people and better parents.

I have three children. They are now 10, 6, and 2 years old. My problems are not larger or smaller than when I joined PA (my children were 5 and 2 then). They are just *different* ones now. I've come to grips with the fact that my problems will never go away; they will just keep changing. What I have learned is a new way of coping with them so the stress in my life doesn't affect my children as much. Learning this takes each person their own time and some people never learn it at all. I have learned this with support and guidance from PA chapters.

Parents Anonymous builds self-esteem. If you've heard all your life that you're worthless, you begin to feel that way about yourself. If you don't like yourself, even a little, then nothing much else makes you happy. Parents Anonymous helps you find the "good guy" and the "ugly green monster" in yourself. To recognize and separate these, to learn what triggers your anger, and why your kids "push buttons" are all a part of PA. Through a chapter meeting we can take one, or several, problems to the group each week and get many ideas on what to do the next time it occurs. Options! Support! Hope!

Many parents come with the same frustrations and just knowing "I am not alone" helps. It takes time and patience to work through years of feeling the anger, hurt, despair, and frustration that has led to abuse problems. Parents Anonymous helps work through those times to break the cycle of child abuse in the family.

I started out as a parent in PA with great needs,

and in the chapter in Springfield, Illinois, I discovered the self-worth and strength to get through some really tough times. Now I want to help special families learn to deal with their tough times. With every meeting, training session, seminar, or workshop, I learn more about the ifs and whys of family violence. I have so many caring friends at Parents Anonymous that these groups have become families in themselves. Now, I am a chapter sponsor with great hopes of helping families the way mine was, and still is, by being involved in PA.

My advice to you as nurses who may come in contact with family violence is to remain open. It takes a great deal for a parent to arrive at the point of abuse. Be willing to listen without judgment while remaining honest about your feelings and open to growth. I also warn you to be sufficiently aware of your own feelings, so that you might "pass," if the case or situation warrants it.

I've talked about hope, support, encouragement, openness, honesty, caring, trust, and love. I've told you from my heart how I feel about Parents Anonymous.

I wish each of you success in your nursing education and career and, most of all, in your parenting experiences, which are, however stressful, the most rewarding of all.

Sincerely,

Sally

When intervening with the family, the nurse must maintain the confidentiality of the family, establish realistic goals within a time frame, formulate short-term objectives that are measurable and observable, define specific plans for each involved agency in order to prevent duplication of services, and promote consistency of care through the involvement of as few people as possible.[19]

Intervening with the Abused Spouse

In the immediate phase of intervention, the battered woman's injuries must be treated medically or surgically as required. If her injuries are not severe enough to warrant hospitalization, the health professional must consider letting the woman go home.[38] The importance of thorough assessment and accurate record-keeping in cases of suspected abuse is emphasized.

Interviewing the Abused Woman. If an interview is possible after the battering incident, it is best to interview the woman alone. Never demand a private interview with the woman against the couple's wishes, however, or the battering husband may retaliate later against the wife. In preparing for the interview wiht the abused wife, be ready for what you may hear. Be prepared to listen attentively, or the woman may feel a second sense of rejection.[28] Encourage the woman to share her story. Explore with her what she has done about her situation and what she would like to have done; do not, however, tell her what to do.[28]

The battered woman may express feelings that she expects the abuse as part of being a wife. Wife battering continues to be accepted and expected in many cultures.[21] The battered woman may state or demonstrate that she wishes to stay with her husband. Professionals who express shock or dismay over the wife's reactions only reinforce the battered wife's feelings of shame and guilt.[21] The health care provider must remember that the battered woman's self-respect is at an extremely low level, and she sees no alternatives to her situation.

If the nurse or health care provider believes that the injury is due to battering and not an accident, it is best to ask the victim directly.[21] Before assessing for actual abuse or planning interventions, the health professional may need to examine his or her own feelings about wife abuse.

Identification of the Battered Wife. When a battered woman is identified, the nurse must create a situation in which the woman can be comfortable, supported, and free to discuss her feelings confidentially. The nurse must know and provide the available referrals for the battered wife, such as woman's shelters and legal aid agencies. The nurse may recommend marital counseling for the couple if both see the abusing problem as one needing intervention; however, more often, the woman seeks counseling or group therapy alone and then later drops out. Battered women have a high drop-out rate from psychotherapy because of the following reasons.

1. There was a fear of the partner's retaliation.
2. There was a stigma of being in therapy and a battered wife, as well.
3. The therapy group was seen as another promise for help that would ultimately fail.
4. Some women were seriously locked in the abusive situation and did not wish to further scrutinize their problem.
5. The offer of help was premature through poor timing.[38]

Stages of the Abuse Cycle. The abuse cycle consists of three stages, which may influence the battered woman's use of referrals. The first stage, the *tension build-up stage,* is characterized by increased verbal and minor physical abuse, decreased meaningful communication, and increased levels of anxiety or anxious depression. The battered woman and her partner are more likely to seek help through the complaint of psychosomatic problems and appear, at this time, more amenable to resources.

The second stage, the *acute episode*, begins the acute phase as tension exceeds the couple's ability to cope. Battering may be initiated by either the man or woman, and precipitated by an acute impersonal argument or increased stress from outside the home. During this stage, the battered woman may present in the emergency room in need of first aid. Denial and humiliation may make the diagnosis of abuse difficult, but once it is made, the woman may be amenable to assistance.

The last stage, *reconciliation*, is entered when the couple temporarily resolves the state of increased tension. The reconciliation stage is generally shorter than the previous stage and the battering couple can reenter it again and again. As the couple reconciles more and more frequently, this stage becomes shorter. Resources or referrals are generally not considered or accepted at this time.[1]

The Battered Pregnant Woman. Some battered women are first seen when they are pregnant. The pregnant woman who leaves her husband enters a very complex prenatal period. The progress of the mother and the fetus must be safeguarded through close prenatal supervision.[38] The battered pregnant woman may need to visit the health professional more frequently and may need to be seen without appointments during the more disorganized periods of her life.[38] Intrapartally, caregivers must be made aware of the abusive situation and must focus their care on raising the battered woman's self-esteem and providing understanding and support.

The Postnatal Period. After the battered woman gives birth, pediatric caregivers need to offer additional support. If the abused woman elects to return home with the newborn, the nurse must be committed to including the husband in the plan of care. With the crisis of parenthood, caregivers may need to prepare for future abuse of the wife.[27] Health care providers may have no alternatives except to prepare the wife for possible abuse with plans for her own safety and, perhaps, the child's safety. Before the new mother returns to her home, the nurse encourages the woman to know the location of the nearest shelter, obtain extra keys to the car, keep a few necessities packed and hidden away until needed, and keep handy the name of someone to call for support and assistance. The first arrival of an infant or small child into the home is one of the most common events precipitating the occurrence of wife abuse.[45]

Unplanned Pregnancy. Unplanned or unwanted pregnancies have also been identified as significant precipitating factors in wife abuse. Birth control information and planned parenthood agencies are helpful resources for the battered woman to help her select an appropriate method of child spacing.[38]

Community Education. What can nurses do, on a societal level, to help battered women? Participation in public workshops and forums on wife abuse will help to raise the community's consciousness and prompt the establishment of task forces on battered women. Nurses frequently answer "hot lines" for battered women and organize self-help, support groups. Community education can help the woman by making her aware of nearby shelters, emergency funds, and community mental health centers. The experience, knowledge, and research of nurses can also be utilized by police authorities to help train policemen who answer domestic calls. At present, 20% of deaths of policemen occur while they are trying to break up a family fight.[47]

Unfortunately, social change is a slow process and needs the help of an involved, active community—before the lives of women and children are permanently damaged or destroyed. Nurses are in a position to help.

Evaluation

The effectiveness of the treatment for abusing and abused individuals depends strongly on society and its awareness of the occurrence of battering within the family. The community's involvement with the problem of abuse will influence how readily it provides needed shelters and education about the violent family. Changes within the legal system and special task forces within the police department that deal with the family will determine the effectiveness of treatment for the family who exhibits violence.

The nurse's evaluation of the therapeutic interventions must first address the issue of the client's safety—is the child or woman who has been a victim of abuse presently safe from the likelihood of future abuse? The family's participation in the planning and implementation of treatment will increase the acceptance, and, therefore, the value of the treatment.

There must be an effective network or support group to help rehabilitate the abused and abuser family members. Follow-up with violent families must be continued until the learned pattern of violent behavior is extinguished. The evaluation process should be a continuous one. As more health care professionals become knowledgeable of the situation, progress will be made with the individual, his family, and society.

Summary

This chapter has summarized some of the literature of the past 2 decades in the area of child and woman abuse. Elderly abuse, sibling abuse, and husband abuse were not discussed in the chapter; however, their omission does not imply that they are problems of lesser importance or magnitude.

The information presented about child and woman abuse has included the following major points.

1. The six specific types of abuse recognized by Parents Anonymous are physical abuse, physical neglect, emotional abuse, emotional neglect, sexual abuse, and verbal abuse.

2. Physical abuse is more empirically observable than emotional abuse and, therefore, predominates the available literature on family violence; however, physical abuse may be the least frequently occurring form of abuse within the family.

3. Emotional maltreatment and sexual abuse are probably more common than major physical trauma to children.

4. The incidence, significance and impact of all forms of family violence is tremendous.

5. There exist several decades of multidisciplinary work on the development of theories and the application of these theories to the issue of violence, in general, and family violence, in particular.

6. Although early research on the causes of family abuse emphasized the personality deficits of abusers, more recent studies have focused on the factors of financial stress, drug dependency, and marital discord.

7. The nurse must recognize the characteristics of abusing families and the impact of abuse on the entire family, rather than limit attention to the individual victim.

8. Nursing assessment of the battered child includes the identification of the predictors of abuse and vulnerable infants, the physical and psychosocial information about the child, and specific data about the injury.

9. Assessment of the battered woman often reveals a history of repeated injuries, psychosomatic complaints, and drug and alcohol abuse.

10. It is difficult for the health care professional to document abuse within families.

11. The goals and principles of intervening with the abused child and woman focus on an accepting, objective, and nonjudgmental approach to the family.

12. Health care providers must be familiar with the available community resources and their usefulness to the client and family.

13. Because child abuse and wife abuse often occur together in a family unit, the nurse or other health care professional may need to intervene on behalf of more than one family member.

14. The nurse must become aware of, and face, her own feelings in response to working with the violent family.

15. Nurses need to become involved in the area of social change through consciousness-raising, community education, and the legal process.

Nursing Diagnoses: Family Violence

With an increasing awareness of family violence and its implication to the field of nursing, the potential for violence was introduced in the taxonomy of nursing diagnoses in 1980. Most leading researchers in the field of family violence agree that more direction should be focused on the prevention of violence within families rather than curing the existing dysfunctional family. Several predictors have been identified that may influence a family to become violent. These predictors can readily be observed in many of the clinical areas that employ health care professionals; for example, neonatal intensive care units, postpartum units, and emergency departments.

Specific indicators for potential family violence can be classified as occurring in the prenatal period, intrapartal period, postpartum period, or as characteristics of the infant/child, parent(s), family structure, or community. Additional indicators of the potential for abuse include stress and history of abuse. Each of these predictors may serve as an etiology for various nursing diagnoses regarding the potential for violence.

The following examples of nursing diagnoses may guide the care administered by health care professionals in and out of the hospital setting.

Potential for family violence
(specifically child abuse)
related to

lack of family suport and medical care during pregnancy

increased length of labor and use of general anesthesia during delivery

increased length of separation between mother, father, and infant immediately following delivery

identification of unliked traits in the child that are seen in one or both parents

Potential for family violence
(specifically child or spousal abuse)
related to

increased daily use of alcohol and drugs

an inability to communicate effectively among all family members

lack of social involvements with family and friends

an increase in the perception of stress, or actual stress, currently or continuing for for long periods of time

history of child abuse to one or both parents

The use of nursing diagnoses will enable nurses to better understand, assess, and intervene with the violent family or potentially violent family.

Nursing Care Plan

The Battered Child (Victim of Physical Abuse)

Client Problem	Goal	Intervention
Low self-esteem	To develop improved sense of self-esteem	Communicate acceptance through verbal and nonverbal means. Create situations wherein the child can excel. Reward the child's good work or efforts.
	To interrupt the cycle of guilt that the abuse towards him is deserved	Interview the older child privately and confidentially regarding the abusive situation. Discuss why parents abuse children and what can be done to help the family. Reassure the child that he is not to blame for being abused.
Fearful of others	To establish rapport	Intervene in the abusing situation as a caring, supportive adult. Provide appropriate discipline.

Nursing Care Plan

The Battered Child (Victim of Sexual Abuse)

Client Problem	Goal	Intervention
Reactions to sexual assault may range from fear and panic to complete lack of fear and guilt	To help the child understand what has happened	Assure the child that she is not to blame Interview the child alone if she is verbal.
	To help the child deal with fear and guilt	Encourage the child to recount her experience either verbally or through pictures or drawings, role-playing, or therapeutic play Record particular words of the child and clarify with parents for parents for proper intepretation, if the meaning is questionable.
	To help the parents control emotionalism and work through guilt	Help parents show continued love and support to the child.

Nursing Care Plan

The Battered Wife

Client Problem	Goal	Intervention
Fear and guilt	To establish rapport	Approach her in a nonjudgmental manner. Interview the woman privately and confidentially regarding the abuse.
	To decrease shame and guilt	Be available as a listener and source of support. Provide information about community resources and services, such as nearby woman's shelters and legal aid.
	To provide protection	Assist the client in planning for the development of job skills, care for children, and so on.
	To help woman leave situation (if desired)	Involve the client in assertiveness training workshops and consciousness-raising groups as appropriate. Provide an opportunity for the woman to vent feelings and relate the complete story concerning the abuse. Provide an opportunity for the woman to discuss what she has done about the problem and what she would like to do. Encourage her to set her own priorities.
Low self-esteem	To promote increased self-esteem	Assist the client in identifying her own strengths. Provide positive reinforcement for reaching out, even if she is unsure about future. Help her reach an awareness that she is not alone.

References

1. Appleton W: The Battered Woman Syndrome. Ann Emer Med 9 (February): 84–92, 1980
2. Athens L: Violent Crime: A Symbolic Interactionist Study. Symbolic Interaction 2 (Spring): 56–69, 1978
3. Bandura A: Aggression: A Social Learning Analysis. Englewood Cliffs, New Jersey, Prentice-Hall, 1973
4. Barnett E, Pittman C, Ragan C, Salus M: Family Violence: Intervention Strategies. United States Department of Health and Human Services, Washington, DC, 1980
5. Boisvert M: The Battered Child Syndrome. Social Casework 53 (October): 475–481, 1972
6. Bowerman K: Family Violence: Children Within the Cycle. Austin, TX, Texas Commission on the Status of Women, Office of the Governor, 1978
7. Broadhurst D: The Educator's Role in the Prevention and Treatment of Child Abuse and Neglect. Washington, DC, Health, Education & Welfare publication, #(OHDS) 79-30172, 1979
8. Burr W, Hill R, Nye F, Reiss I (eds): Contemporary Theories About the Family, Vol 2. New York, The Free Press, 1979
9. Child Sexual Abuse: Incest, Assault, and Sexual Exploitation. (Richard Roth, developer) Washington, DC, Health, Education & Welfare publication, #(OHDS) 79-30166, 1978
10. Dunea G: The Joy of Wife Beating. Br Med J 2 (August): 565–566, 1977
11. Freeman M: Violence in the Home. London, Saxon House, 1979
12. Freud S: The Ego and the Id. (Translated by Riviere J, revisions and new edition by Strachey J.) New York, WW Norton, 1962
13. Frieze I: Factors Correlated with Men Who See Spousal Violence as More Common. Handout at Annual Research Conference of the Association for Women in Psychology, Dallas, Texas, 1979
14. Gaylord J: Wife Battering: A Preliminary Survey of 100 Cases. Br Med J 1 (January): 194–197, 1975
15. Gelles R: The Violent Home. Beverly Hills, Sage Publications, 1972
16. Gelles R: Violence and Pregnancy: A Note on the Extent of the Problem and Needed Services. Family Coordinator 24 (January): 81–87, 1975
17. Gorline L, Ray M: Examining and Caring for the Child Who Has Been Sexually Assaulted. The American Journal of Maternal Child Nursing 4 (March/April): 110–114, 1979
18. Gruber A, Heck E, Mintzner E: Children Who Set Fires. Am J Orthopsychiatry 51 (July): 484–487, 1981
19. Heindl C, Krall C, Salus M, Broadhurst D: The Nurse's Role in the Prevention and Treatment of Child Abuse and Neglect. Washington, DC, Health, Education & Welfare publication, #(OHDS) 79-30202, 1979
20. Helfer R, Kempe H: Helping the Battered Child and His Family. Philadelphia, JB Lippincott, 1972
21. Hendrix MJ, LaGodna G, Bohen C: The Battered Wife. Am J Nurs 78 (April): 650–653, 1978
22. Hunter R, Kilstrom N, Kraybill E, Loda F: Antecedents of Child Abuse and Neglect in Premature Infants: A Prospective Study in a Newborn Intensive Care Unit. Pediatrics 61 (April): 629–635, 1978
23. Jacobziner J: Rescuing the Battered Child. Am J Nurs 64 (January): 92–95, 1964
24. Johnson R: Aggression in Man and Animals. Philadelphia, WB Saunders, 1972
25. Langley R, Levy R: Wife Beating: The Silent Crisis. New York, Simon and Schuster, 1977
26. Lauer J, Lourie I, Salus M, Broadhurst D: The Role of the Mental Health Professional in the Prevention and Treatment of Child Abuse and Neglect. Washington, DC, Health, Education & Welfare publication, #(OHDS) 79-30194, 1979
27. Lemasters E: Parenthood as Crises. Marriage and Family Living 19 (November): 352–356, 1957
28. Loraine K: Battered Women: The Ways You Can Help. RN 44 (October): 22–29, 1981
29. Lorenz K: On Aggression. New York, Harcourt, Brace, 1966
30. Martin D: Battered Wives. San Francisco, New Glide Publications, 1976
31. McKeel N: Child Abuse Can Be Prevented. Am J Nurs 78 (September): 1478–1483, 1978
32. Mitchell B: Working with Abusive Parents, A Caseworker's View. Am J Nurs 73 (March): 480–484, 1973
33. Morris M: Maternal Claiming–Identification Processes: Their Meaning for Mother–Infant Mental Health." Parent–Child Relationship: The Role of the Nurse. Paper presented at Continuing Education Workshop, Rutgers University, Newark, New Jersey, 1968
34. Olsen R: Index of Suspicion: Screening for Child Abusers. Am J Nurs 76 (January): 108–110, 1976
35. Restak R: The Brain: The Last Frontier. New York, Doubleday, 1979
36. Rosenbaum A, O'Leary K: Children: The Unintended Victims of Violence. Am J Orthopsychiatry 51 (October): 692–699, 1981
37. Rousaville B, Lifton N, Bieber M: The Natural History of a Psychotherapy Group for Battered Women. Psychiatry 42 (February): 73–78, 1979
38. Sammons L: Battered and Pregnant. The American Journal of Maternal Child Nursing 6 (July/August): 246–251, 1981
39. Scott J (cited) In Endleman S (ed): Violence in the Streets. Chicago, Quadrangle Books, 1968
40. Scott PD: Battered Wives. Br J Psychiatry 125 (November): 433–441, 1974
41. Steimetz S: The Cycle of Violence: Assertive, Aggressive, and Abusive Family Interaction. New York, Praegle Publication, 1977
42. Straus M: Wife Beating: How Common and Why? Victimology: An International Journal 2:443–457, 1977–1978
43. Straus M: A General Systems Theory Approach to a Theory of Violence Between Family Members. Social Science Information 12 (June): 105–125, 1973
44. Tagg P: Nursing Intervention for the Abused Child and His Family. Pediatric Nursing (September/October): 36–39, 1976

45. Walker L: The Battered Woman. New York, Harper Colophon Books, 1979

46. Walker L: Battered Women and Learned Helplessness. Victimology: An International Journal 2:525–534, 1977–1978

47. Battered Women: Issues of Public Policy. A Consultation Sponsored by the United States Commission on Civil Rights, Washington, DC, 1978

48. The Battered Woman. Emer Med 11 (April): 25–29, 1979

49. Maternal Attachment and Mothering Disorders. A Round table discussion sponsored by Johnson and Johnson. Edited by Klaus MH, Kennell JH, 1974

50. Handout on child abuse at the Texas Nurses Association Conference on Family Violence. Dallas, Texas, 1978

51. The Police Perspective in Child Abuse and Neglect. Gaithersburg, MD, International Association of Chiefs of Police, Inc, 1977

52. National Analysis of Official Child Neglect and Abuse Reporting. Washington, DC, DHHS publicaton, #(OHDS) 80-30271, 1980

53. Domestic Violence. A resource paper distributed by the National Indian Child Abuse and Neglect Resource Center. Tulsa, Oklahoma,

54. Sexual Abuse of Children: Selected Readings. Washington, DC, DHHS publication, #(OHDS) 78-30161, 1980

Chapter 34
Suicide

That morning I had tried to hang myself. I had taken the silken cord from my mother's yellow bathrobe as soon as she left for work, and, in the amber shade of the bedroom, fashioned it into a knot that slipped up and down.

Then I saw that my body had all sorts of little tricks, such as making my hands go limp at the crucial second, which would save it, time and again, whereas if I had the whole say, I would be dead in a flash.

Sylvia Plath,
The Bell Jar

Patricia Flatley Brennan

Chapter Preview

Every 11 seconds, an individual attempts to end his life.[21] One of every 10 of these individuals succeeds on the first attempt; another one of those 10 persons will try again and succeed.[19] What is this desperation called suicide? Suicide has been described as

"a response to an invitation, originating from others, that [one] stop living;"[12]

"a behavior that seeks and finds the solution to an existential problem by making an attempt on the life of the subject;"[3]

the failure of all defense mechanisms.

As an isolated act, suicide appears to be an individual's last message to the world. From another viewpoint, suicide is but one of a range of behaviors that directly or indirectly results in the ending of a life.[8] Drug abuse, alcoholism, noncompliance with medical protocols, and excessive risk-taking may all lead to the death of the participant; however, not all persons who engage in such behavior can be called "suicidal." The purpose of this chapter is to help the reader understand the nature of suicidal behavior and to assess and care for persons at risk for suicide.

Through this chapter, the reader is introduced to methods for interpreting the various meanings of suicidal behavior. The etiology of suicidal behavior and the development of suicide in an interpersonal context are examined. The steps of the nursing process—assessment of the client's needs, analysis of the data, planning, identification, implementation of appropriate nursing strategies, and evaluation of the effectiveness of the interventions—are applied to individuals manifesting suicidal behavior.

Learning Objectives

On completion of the chapter, the reader should be able to accomplish the following.

1. Define suicide as a type of self-destructive behavior
2. Discuss factors related to the incidence of suicide and the populations affected
3. Discuss the biologic, sociologic, and psychological theories of the development and dyanmics of suicide
4. Apply the nursing process to the care of clients exhibiting suicidal behavior
    Use communication techniques to assess the meaning of, clues to, and degree of risk of the individual's wish to die
    Formulate short-term and long-term goals for the suicidal client
    Describe the ethical and legal responsibilities of the nurse caring for a suicidal client
    Identify nursing interventions to provide safety, explore stressors, and promote effective coping for the suicidal client
    Evaluate the effectiveness of nursing interventions
5. Recognize and discuss one's own feelings and behaviors that affect the suicidal client, his family, or his survivors.

Incidence of Suicide and Populations Affected

Studies of the records of suicide prevention centers and regional mortality offices paint a picture of the degree and nature of suicidal behavior in the population.[11, 23] Although women make significantly more suicide attempts than men, men are more likely to kill themselves. Women tend to use less lethal methods of suicide than men.

Suicide behavior appears in all age groups (see insert, Adolescent Suicide). Children kill themselves as deliberately and as desperately as the elderly. The likelihood of successful suicide, however, increases with age. Most persons who make attempts to end their lives have experienced a stressful situation prior to the suicide attempt. The most common stressors preceding the suicidal behavior include divorce, rape, death of a significant other, and loss of a significant part of one's life, such as a job.[3, 15, 16, 26]

Social patterns emerge as one examines the demographic information about suicide. The suicide rate among many American Indian tribes is twice that of the national average. Suicide among blacks, especially adolescents and young adults, is increasing. Marriage, once thought to protect an individual from suicide, no longer offers that protection. Increasing economic status has also been associated with an increase in suicide rate.

The demographics of suicide reflect neither the individual's true motivation for taking his own life, nor an accurate picture of the suicidal individual in the community. The statistics of suicide are frequently inaccurate, due to the social stigma of suicide, and this leads to inaccurate reporting of the number of actual suicides.[23] Furthermore, statistical assessments merely describe suicide as a social trend, not as the crisis of an individual and his significant others.

Etiologic Theories

Biologic Factors

The search for explanations of the cause of self-harmful behaviors has yet to identify, definitively, a biologic theory of suicide. Nonetheless, several studies have linked physiological changes in amine levels, brain wave patterns, and adrenal steroids with suicidal behavior in some individu-

Adolescent Suicide

Gregg E. Newschwander, R.N., M.S.N.
Instructor in Adolescent–Young Adult Nursing
Marquette University College of Nursing
Milwaukee, Wisconsin

Suicide is the third leading cause of death among adolescents, exceeded only by accidents and homicide.[3] Reported adolescent suicides, however, may not accurately reflect their true incidence.

When a person commits suicide, the family physician may report it as an accidental death to spare the "reputation" of the family. In addition, many suicides are difficult to distinguish from accidental deaths. Deaths, for example, related to automobile accidents—especially single vehicle crashes—are often attributed to loss of vehicle control or driving while under the influence of alcohol or drugs; therefore, these deaths are listed as "accidental," not suicide.

Adolescent females are more likely to threaten suicide, but males are more likely to carry out the threat. It is estimated that there are as many as 100 unsuccessful suicide attempts by adolescents for each successful one.[1] For example, in 1977, when an estimated 5000 young people took their own lives, nearly a half a million attempted to do so—about 1400 each day.[2]

It is difficult to understand why an adolescent, generally considered full of life and with unlimited future potential, would want to take his or her own life. All adolescents must deal with a multitude of changes and stressors. Why, when faced with a nearly identical set of circumstances, will one adolescent choose suicide while most others will not?

The experience of loss during adolescence may trigger thoughts of suicide. The adolescent's loss may be the termination of a romantic relationship, the loss of a job, loss of a family member, a decline in health, or the life changes that result from increased independence. These events alone, however, cannot be termed the "causes" of adolescent suicide.

Adolescent suicide may be considered, rather, the result of a long-standing inability to form and maintain significant relationships with other people. The adolescent who decides to end his life is, and has been for many years, struggling to achieve a sense of social "cohesion." Typically, this young person has increasing difficulty at home and becomes isolated from his family. Often, he is not succeeding either academically or socially in school. Frequently, the young person has recently failed in a romantic relationship that consumed much of his time and resulted in the loss of a former group of close friends. The adolescent is literally alone. He has become socially "disengaged."

Some adolescents verbally threaten suicide, others do not. In addition, although impulsive suicidal behavior is seen in adolescence, perhaps more frequently than in any other developmental group, most adolescents who are contemplating suicide give some clues reflecting their intentions.

When an adolescent threatens suicide, the threat must be taken seriously. It should not be dismissed as an attention-getting device or challenged in any way—it should be dealt with immediately and openly. The adolescent should be made to understand that he needn't carry out the threat in order to be believed.

Adolescents' clues to suicide reflect changes in three main areas of functioning: personal habits; school behavior; and social relationships. The first area of functioning, personal habits, may be disturbed by changes in the adolescent's appetite, sleep patterns, and personal appearance, and frequent somatic complaints may be heard. The adolescent's school behavior is also affected, as seen by increased truancy, declining academic performance, boredom, apathy, and, possibly, unwarranted aggression or hostility toward teachers and other authority figures. Social relationships, the third area of functioning, are altered by decreased interaction with peers, increased substance abuse, and increased risk-taking and self-destructive behaviors, including carelessness and recklessness. Adolescents contemplating suicide often attempt to "get their lives in order," which might include "passing along" prized possessions.

Although it should be understood that the appearance of one or more of these behaviors does not necessarily indicate a potential for suicide, efforts should be made to explore what the adolescent is experiencing. It is tragic that parents, friends, and relatives are usually shocked when they learn of an adolescent's suicide attempt—not because no warning signals were given, but because the clues were not recognized and dealt with.

Intervention with the suicidal adolescent centers on communication. The adolescent needs someone to listen to, *and hear*, what he has to say. The simple fact that there is someone who really cares about him may be enough to discourage a suicide attempt. It is through the development of a supportive, caring relationship that the adolescent will be helped to find other ways to cope with the problems he faces.

As a relationship with the young person is being established, his family must also be included in counseling. The family is a major source of support for the adolescent—one which, he may believe, has been lost. The suicide threat or attempt has a great impact on family members. As a unit, the family may experience anger and dismay at the deliberate attempt, guilt at having failed the adolescent, and, possibly, resentment for having been "socially embarrassed."

It is a sad commentary that suicide is a leading cause of death in what is generally considered a "healthy population." Nurses, physicians, teachers, and parents must become more aware of the warning signs of adolescent suicide and must begin to act on them—with understanding and foresight.

1. Gallagher JR, Heald FP, Garell DC: Medical Care of the Adolescent, 3rd ed. New York, Appleton-Century-Crofts, 1976
2. McKenry PC, Tishler CL, Christman K: Adolescent Suicide and the Classroom Teacher. Journal of School Health 50 (March): 130–32, 1980
3. United States Bureau of the Census, Characteristics of American Children and Youth: 1976. Current Population Reports, Series P-23, Number 66. Washington, DC, U.S. Government Printing Office, 1978

als.[10] One of the confounding factors in the search for a biologic basis for suicide is that suicide is frequently, although not always, linked with depression. Although the biochemical basis of depression, including genetic and biochemical precursors, is well-established, not all persons who attempt to kill themselves are depressed.

Evidence of an elevation in the urinary excretion of adrenal steroids has been found in depressed suicidal patients.[22] Other studies have discovered lowered cerebral concentration of indolamine metabolites on autopsy of established suicides. Contrary to popular belief, the influence of the moon's lunar cycles on the body does not lead to suicide.

Sociologic Viewpoint

Durkheim, the father of modern suicidology, based his observations of suicidal behavior on the social statistics available in Europe in the late 19th century.[5] He studied suicide as a social phenomenon and drew explanations for suicidal behavior from social trends, such as reactions to social order, or the lack of social order.

Durkheim postulated that all suicidal behavior falls in one of three categories—anomic, egoistic, and altruistic. Both anomic and egoistic forms of suicide represent an individual's isolation from society. *Anomic* suicide stems from the normlessness of society, which leaves the individual without a sense of social order. A lack of meaning or purpose in life leads to *egoistic* suicide. *Altruistic* suicide occurs when the individual gives up his life for some greater good. The overdose of a solitary poet, in response to his despair at the modern world, is an example of anomic suicide. Egoistic suicide is exemplified in the behavior of those who lost fortunes and jobs during the depression. Soldiers on a "suicide mission" approach death as an altruistic suicide.

Psychological Influences

Psychoanalytic View

Early psychological theories of suicide proposed that suicide was the result of the individual's drive or desire for death.

Freud defined two drives basic to all people—*Thantos*, the drive toward death, and *Eros*, the drive toward life. Suicidal behavior resulted when the "death drive" of the individual took precedence over the "life drive." This shift in the driving forces of an individual, Freud believed, occurred in response to the real or imagined loss of a loved one. The image of the loved one, with all its concomitant feelings, was internalized. The individual who felt abandoned by the lost love experienced anger, and this anger, lacking an outlet, was turned toward the self. The ultimate act of self-destruction resulted as the depressive response to a loss.

"Partial Suicide"

Menninger viewed suicide as more than the depressive response to a loss.[14] He hypothesized a tripartite source of suicide in everyone—the wish to kill, the wish to be killed, and the wish to die. The core of the suicide act, he postulated was anger and despair. Menninger viewed suicide not merely as a single act, but also as a group of behaviors he termed "partial suicide," such as polysurgeries, substance abuse, and self-mutilation. When the individual lacked one of the three components of suicide, a "partial suicide" occurred.

Interpersonal View

Later psychological theorists, although not rejecting Freud's and Menninger's ideas entirely, have viewed suicide as the result of an interpersonal, as well as an intrapsychic, crisis. Suicide has been described as a time-limited crisis that occurs in an individual who is severely distraught.[20] The individual experiences ambivalence about living and chooses suicide as the most effective response to others.

Dynamics of Suicide

A person contemplating suicide generally perceives himself as isolated, hopeless, and helpless. The isolation may be evident in actual physical distance from others or as a psychological barrier between the individual and other people. The suicidal person is unable to initiate or respond to social interactions. Through the act of suicide, the individual communicates his final message to others.

As a result of discussions with suicidal clients and examination of suicide notes, theorists have gleaned an understanding of the emotional component of suicide. The emotional state of the suicidal person is characterized by depression, anger, and feelings of hopelessness and helplessness. The suicidal person experiences a desire to kill himself or to be dead simultaneously with a wish to be saved or rescued. Talking about suicide or making a suicidal gesture carries in it a message to others. The meaning of the message is unique.

Escapist suicides occur as a desire to remove oneself from an intolerable situation. In *aggressive suicide,* the individual uses the self-induced death as a means of causing suffering or revenge to another. An *oblative suicide* stems from the desire to transform the self to a more pleasurable reality. In *ludic suicide,* death is the unintended result of taking excessive chances with one's life.

The etiology of suicide and the meaning of suicidal behavior serve to heighten the nurse's awareness of the dynamics of suicide. Suicidal behavior occurs in individuals with many psychiatric diagnoses, such as depression, schizophrenia, anxiety disorders, and adjustment reactions. The nurse uses the understanding of the dynamics of suicidal behavior as a basis for providing care to the suicidal client and his family.

Application of the Nursing Process to Suicide

Assessment of the Suicidal Client and Analysis of the Data

Accurate assessment is the key to the care of the suicidal client. Through observation and careful listening, the nurse examines the client's behavior and verbalizations for clues of suicidal intent. In the assessment process, the nurse explores the client's request for help, the presence and nature of a suicide plan, the client's mental state, the availability of support systems, and the client's lifestyle. Nursing knowledge and judgment guides the nurse to evaluate suicide risk amidst a complex set of behaviors and thoughts.

Clues to Suicide

Most people who try to kill themselves give a clue of their intention to others.[21] Some people leave suicide notes; others give cryptic verbal messages to friends or family. Clues to suicide are found in the behavior of the individual and may be classified as direct or indirect and verbal or nonverbal. Table 34–1 offers some examples of these clues to suicide.

A person may display one clue or any combination of clues to communicate suicide intention. Individuals who give direct clues to suicide have not been found to be more likely to make suicidal attempts than those who give indirect clues or no clues at all.

Behavioral Changes. Clues to suicide are frequently subtle and difficult to interpret. Change in expected patterns of behavior is, perhaps, the most important indicator of suicide risk. The turmoil of a person considering the option of suicide is evident in his behavior; he is likely to exhibit anxiety, insomnia, poor concentration, anorexia, and somaticism. Expressions of anger and despair are also common behavioral indicators of the person's distress.

A sudden calmness in the distraught client may indicate that he has made a decision to die. Depressed people frequently think about suicide but lack the energy to act on their thoughts until the vegetative symptoms of fatigue, anorexia, and psychomotor retardation lift. The apparent improvement in the depressed client's behavior lulls those around him to assume that the risk of suicide has passed, when, in fact, the client has decided to kill himself.

Persons who are close to the suicidal individual are in the best position to monitor changes in his behavior. The nurse on the inpatient unit or a member of the client's family may be the first one to notice changes in behavior that may indicate a risk of suicide. The nurse should also be aware that certain factors, such as being older than 50 years of age, overwhelming stressors in one's life, and alcohol abuse increase the risk of suicide.

Risk Periods. Certain times of the year have been identified as "peak periods" for suicide. Suicides increase in the spring. Some believe that suicides increase around holiday periods.[17] For some individuals, the decision to die is

Table 34-1. **Clues to Suicide**

	VERBAL	NONVERBAL
Direct	"I can't stand it—I'm going to kill myself." "I could die without pain by taking all my pills."	Actions such as taking pills, cutting wrists, making a noose Writing suicide notes
Indirect	"My family would be better off without me." "Pray for me." "I won't be here when you get back."	Risk-taking lifestyles Giving away personal posssessions Purchasing a cemetary plot Sudden onset of sense of peacefulness

linked to disappointment or a sense of isolation during the holiday seasons, which are considered to be a time for family togetherness. For others, the holiday rituals decrease their loneliness and despair and lead to a diminishing of the will to die.

In inpatient psychiatric settings, certain times are risk periods for increased incidence of suicide, especially between 10:30 am and 6:30 pm, around "change of shift" time, and between Friday morning and Monday evening.[25] These times are usually periods of decreased observation by, and interaction with, staff members.

Goals of Assessment

Clues and acts of self-harmful behavior do not always indicate that the individual wishes to die. These behaviors must be viewed as the individual's attempt to communicate a dramatic message.[9] In order to understand and respond to the message being communicated, the nurse observes and identifies the client's behavior and explores the meaning of the behavior with the client. The goals of assessment are as follows.

1. To establish the probability that the individual will make an act of self-harm
2. To determine the meaning of the self-destructive behavior
3. To initiate a therapeutic relationship with the client

Interviewing

Assessment of the suicidal client is an interpersonal process; that is, the nurse makes direct, verbal contact with the client. During the initial interaction, the nurse uses the skills of the dyadic, or one-to-one relationship to establish an atmosphere of warmth, concern, and interest. Calling the client by name demonstrates an attitude of respect and caring. Verbally acknowledging the client's perception of the situation and his own fears and desperation helps to convey the nurse's willingness to understand his situation. Touch may be used judiciously to establish a bond of reassurance and support. To carry out a complete assessment, the nurse asks clear, direct questions and responds to both the feeling and the content expressed by the client. It is best to avoid euphemisms such as "ending it all" and "doing yourself in" in the interview. The essence of an effective and accurate assessment of the suicidal client lies in clear, specific communication.

Values and Attitudes of the Nurse

Because suicide assessment is a dyadic process, the nurse's own values, moral beliefs, and attitudes toward self-destructive behavior have great influence on her response to the client. Before working with clients at risk for suicide, the nurse examines her own feelings about suicide and people who choose to terminate their own lives. The following questions address some of the issues that the nurse must consider.

Is suicide ever justifiable?
Are people who attempt suicide with nonlethal methods merely trying to get attention?
Are all suicides preventable?

Answering these questions and discussing the responses with peers will help the nurse identify her own feelings and reactions to the suicidal person. This self-awareness will help the nurse respond to the client with greater objectivity and empathy.

Although suicide is no longer a criminal act, most societies and cultural groups consider suicide an immoral act. Religious groups generally believe that suicide is a sin and promulgate rules against suicidal behavior. At times of social crisis, such as war, proscriptions against suicide may give way to the value of giving one's life for a greater good. The social sanctions against suicide help to dissuade potential victims from carrying out suicidal acts. At the same time, these social sanctions contribute to the stigma attached to suicidal persons and their families.

Gathering Information from Family

Assessment of suicidal risk also includes discussions with the family members or friends of the client. This is particularly important if the client is comatose following the ingestion of pills or self-induced trauma. Data gathered from significant others aid the nurse in identifying the precipitants to the client's suicidal act and his patterns of behavior. Health care workers who have aided the client (emergency room nurses, ambulance drivers) may also provide valuable information. Questions directed to the family or friends must be phrased in a manner that protects the client's rights to confidentiality. Contact with the family or significant others permits the nurse to offer support to those experiencing the crisis with the suicidal individual while gathering data about the crisis.

Clients who are hospitalized in general medical–surgical units, as well as in psychiatric units, may discuss suicidal thoughts or wishes before making an attempt on their lives. The assessment process of a suicidal client who is in an inpatient psychiatric unit does not differ markedly from that of a suicidal client in any other setting. Questions addressing past or present suicidal ideation provide additional data about the client's prior coping strategies as well as previously undetected suicide risks.

Psychological Autopsy

In a *psychological autopsy*, staff review the events preceding a successful suicide.[20] This process has taught mental health workers that clues to suicide are usually present, but that frequently they do not realize the significance of the clues. It is important that nurses review the client's behavior, even when the behavior appears to lack significance. The patterns of behavior and the changes in these patterns hold the clues to thoughts not yet verbalized by the client who is contemplating suicide.

Means of Seeking Help

Assessment of the client at risk for suicide begins with an examination of how the person initially sought help. Did the person call a suicide hotline? Did he call his physician? Did he call a friend who brought him into the hospital? The greater the individual's volition in seeking help, the greater the chance that early intervention will prevent a death by suicide.

The Client's Intent. Determining the meaning of the self-destructive thoughts or acts for the individual is an ongoing process. Initially, the nurse uses questions and active listening to identify the nature of the immediate crisis and the effect the person desires from the act of self-harm. The nurse listens for clues to the client's intent in his words—does he seek relief from stress? . . . escape from an intolerable situation? . . . revenge against a loved one? . . . death? By examining the individual's desired goal, the nurse gains a framework within which she can assess and intervene to provide safety and to meet the need expressed by the client.

Because clients at high risk of killing themselves display severe anxiety and poor concentration, the exploration of the meaning of suicide is limited initially to overt, conscious motives. In-depth exploration of the factors leading to the suicide attempt is delayed until after the crisis has passed and the person is no longer at risk of acting on his suicidal impulses.

All people think about suicide; however, to certain individuals, suicidal ideation is not an intellectual tour through the options of life and death, but an actual plan of ending one's life. In the assessment process, the nurse distinguishes between clients who use self-destructive behavior to end their lives and those who use self-destructive behavior to reach some other goal. Through a systematic suicide assessment, the nurse examines the content of the client's suicide ideation for the how, where, when, and what of self-destruction.

Suicide Plan

The nurse assessing a suicidal individual asks him directly if he has a plan for ending his life. Suicidal plans include a description of the method (shooting, hanging, overdose, self-immolation), location (at home, in the client's room), agent (gun, type of pills), and time (on discharge, when the client's wife is at work) of the proposed suicide. The more specific the plan verbalized by the client, the greater is the risk of suicide.

In addition, certain plans are more lethal than others. Suicide by shooting or hanging carries a greater potential of success than suicide by cutting one's wrist. For example,

compare the plan of the young man who stated he would hang himself with a bed sheet in his room as soon as the staff member left, with that of a middle-aged woman who threatened to "take a few pills and end it all." Suicide plans are evaluated based on the specificity of the plan and the lethality of the method.

Mental State

After determining whether or not an individual has a plan for ending his life, the nurse evaluates the client's mental state, which includes anxiety level, mood, and thought organization. Clients with a moderate-to-severe level of anxiety are at the greatest risk of deliberately acting on the suicide thoughts. In a panic state of anxiety, the person may make impulsive, haphazard attempts at suicide; low levels of anxiety rarely cause the person to act dramatically to alter his life situation. Immediately prior to a suicide gesture, the anxiety level of the client may drop. Generally, the mood of the suicidal person is depressed and hopeless. Suicide risk is increased when disorganized thinking and impaired judgment leave the individual vulnerable to an accidental suicide.[2]

Support Systems

The nurse explores with the client the interpersonal support systems that are available to him. Although the presence of family members or friends usually lowers the risk of suicide, problems in the relationships with significant others may have precipitated the suicidal gesture.[1] The nurse must realistically assess the supports available to the client, because his sense of isolation or estrangement may make him incapable of using the available support systems.

Lifestyle

After examining the individual's mental state, the nurse then examines the client's lifestyle. What type of coping mechanisms does the client use—defense-oriented or task-oriented? Has there been a change in the client's interest in food, sex, sleep, or interpersonal relationships? A marked decrease in the appetites of life usually precedes suicidal behavior; an increase in these appetites can also herald a sign of a warning. Another factor to consider is the stability of the client's lifestyle. Is the suicide ideation the result of a sudden, catastrophic crisis, or has the person been slowly dying for years? A history of a stable lifestyle, including job and social functioning, reduces the risk of suicide.

Recording and Reporting

Suicide risk is often described as high, moderate, or low degree of risk. All persons involved in the care of the suicidal client must be alerted to his status and suicide risk. The nurse communicates this information by reporting the degree of suicide risk and the plan developed to protect the client from his suicidal impulses. The formulation of nursing diagnoses is an essential component of the nursing process (see insert, Examples of Nursing Diagnoses: The Suicidal Client).

Careful, accurate documentation of the six factors of suicide clues, means by which the client sought help, suicidal plan, mental state, support systems, and lifestyle provides for continuity of care and meets the nurse's legal responsibilities. Documentation includes notations in the client's chart and the written nursing care plan.

Planning

Planning involves bringing together the nurse's skill and judgment with the client's participation to formulate an appropriate approach to treatment. The nurse assesses the degree of suicide risk, validates this assessment with the client and other team members, and discusses with the client the type of nursing care most appropriate to meet his needs.

The nurse designs, with the client, the measures needed to protect him while supporting the maximum degree of autonomy that he is capable of. Nurses sometimes limit their response to the suicidal client to the provision of safety measures because of the overwhelming fear that the client may actually die while under the nurse's care.

At the same time, repeated contacts with chronically suicidal clients lead to feelings of frustration and anger in the nurse. The sense of futility that nurses experience while caring for the person with repeated nonlethal suicide attempts may lead them to underestimate the client's need for safety.

Short-Term Goals

Nursing care plans for the client with suicidal thoughts or behaviors are directed toward providing safety and interpersonal support to the client. Short-term goals include

1. Client will not act on the suicidal plan.
2. Client will talk with the nurse about suicidal thoughts.
3. Client will keep a "no suicide contract" with the nurse.

Examples of Nursing Diagnoses: The Suicidal Client

Nursing Diagnosis

Moderate risk of suicide related to rejection from husband

High risk of suicide related to pattern of response to auditory hallucination

Dysfunctional coping, characterized by multiple suicide attempts, related to impulsivity.

Long-Term Goals

Long-term goals focus on helping the client to resolve the issues that precipitated the suicide crisis and to develop less destructive coping mechanisms. Examples of long-term goals include the following.

1. Client will be free of suicide ideation.
2. Client will use task-oriented reactions to stress.
3. Client will take steps to resolve relationships and lifestyles that increase the suicide risk.

Treatment Settings

When planning care, the nurse considers both the immediate environment of the client in treatment and the usual living situation of the client. In the inpatient setting, the nurse uses the resources of nursing and non-nursing team members collaboratively to formulate and implement the treatment plan. The plan must be developed within the policy and procedural guidelines of the institution. Community care of the suicidal client demands that the nurse and client together discuss supports to which the client has access, such as family members or crisis hotlines. Planning within the community setting requires that the nurse recognize the limits of her ability to protect the client and be knowledgeable in the appropriate referral to community resources.

Ethical and Legal Responsibilities

When planning care for a suicidal individual, the nurse has both legal and ethical responsibilities to the client and to the caregiving agency. The situation in which the client is encountered influences the legal responsibilities of nurses in community settings. In a personal or private relationship, the nurse's responsibilities to the suicidal individual are primarily ethical, whereas in a caregiving agency, such as a clinical facility, the nurse also has a legal responsibility to fulfill.

Nurses are legally bound to follow agency policies and procedures regarding suicide precautions, and a nurse may be found negligent for omitting or not following necessary precautionary procedures. The importance of documentation in verifying the observation of suicide precautions cannot be overemphasized.

The law and administrative orders in most states define the legal basis of nursing care. Based on the interpretation of these laws, the nurse is responsible for making professional nursing assessments and analysis and for implementing the appropriate nursing actions in the care of the suicidal client.

Intervention

Nursing Intervention for the Suicidal Client

The nurse encounters the suicidal client in the hospital, in emergency rooms, on psychiatric units, and through telephone calls to crisis intervention hotlines. Although the settings in which nursing care is provided vary, nursing actions center on three areas of concern.

1. Providing safety for the client
2. Exploring, with the client, the lifestyles or stressors that precipitated the suicide crisis
3. Assisting the client in developing new ways of coping

Intervening in the Community

Suicide Prevention Services. The pioneering work of the Los Angeles Suicide Prevention Center illustrated the effectiveness of crisis intervention services in helping potentially suicidal people postpone the decision to kill themselves.[19] Since the late 1950s, volunteer groups and professional clinics have established crisis services to deal with the suicidal person. These services provide anonymous telephone hotlines and limited face-to-face counseling to persons at risk of suicide. Workers in a crisis intervention service use communication skills and crisis theory to help the individuals postpone the decision to kill themselves and to obtain needed therapy.

Community members other than those providing formal crisis intervention services encounter and work with suicidal individuals. Clergy, public health nurses, and occupational health nurses all provide support and counseling to the suicidal individual. In England, The Samaritans have offered support and counsel to the suicidal person since the early 1900s.[20] This group of lay volunteers was founded by a clergyman who discovered that suicidal persons benefit from the availability of a compassionate listener.

Mobilizing Coping Skills. The nurse works with the suicidal client in the community to mobilize his existing coping strategies. To achieve this goal, the nurse explores with the client his perception of the situation at the time of the contact, encourages the client to report feelings and needs, and asks him to define what actions he views as necessary. In a calm, direct manner the nurse emphasizes the client's desire to continue living as evidenced by his request for help. While acknowledging the client's desire for both death and life, the nurse makes clear her willingness to help the client respond to his desire to live.

The Need for Hospitalization. A client at high risk for suicide in the community should be encouraged to enter a psychiatric inpatient unit of a hospital or treatment facility. The nurse may enlist the assistance of family members or friends to convince the client of the need for hospitalization. If the client refuses hospitalization, the nurse continues to talk with the client to identify a person with whom he can remain until the crisis has passed. The nurse must never indicate to the client that she, or anyone else, can magically protect him from his impulses.

Understanding the Meaning of the Crisis. To respond effectively to the client, the nurse must understand the meaning of the suicide crisis to the client and to those around him. By exploring precipitating stressors and by responding to the client's words and feelings, the nurse helps the client identify the meaning of the suicide crisis. The nature of the crisis is that it is time-limited, and the client is most likely to be receptive to assistance during the crisis period.[1]

The nurse asks the client what type of assistance he needs. Questions such as "What can I do for you?" and "What would be helpful to you?" indicate the nurse's interest and decrease the client's sense of despair and hopelessness. The use of the problem-solving process helps the client to establish a plan of assistance, such as arranging for further treatment. The client should be encouraged to contact the crisis service whenever needed. The initial contact with the suicidal client is not terminated until he can state a specific plan of action for preventing self-destructive behavior in the future.

Intervening in the Hospital or Treatment Center

Providing Environmental Support. The suicidal client in the hospital may have already made one suicide attempt but remains at risk to make another, or he may have entered the hospital as a means to resist acting on his suicidal impulse. In addition to the interpersonal support used in the community setting, the nurse uses the safe environment of the hospital to provide environmental support to the client.

Clients at high risk for suicide are placed on a closed unit or in some type of protected environment. Closed units provide for safety by restricting access to potentially hazardous objects such as scissors, glass bottles, light bulbs, and knives. Care is taken to preserve the client's sense of dignity; personal or clothing objects such as belts and shoe laces are removed from him only when absolutely necessary. The nurse administering to the highly suicidal client must insure that all medications are consumed. It is necessary to remember that the client may sequester medications for use in a suicide attempt.

The highly impulsive client may require closer observation even while in a protected environment. Nursing personnel may need to remain in close proximity of the client or even keep him in direct view. Nurses should not hesitate to employ environmental supports, such as a quiet room, to provide safety for the client. Explain the purpose of the support to the client in brief, direct sentences. Inform the client that you are concerned for his safety and will help him control his impulses to harm himself.

Verbalizing Concern and Offering Help. While providing environmental support to the client, the nurse uses interpersonal techniques to decrease his sense of isolation.

Verbal contact with the client every 1 to 2 hours reinforces the nurse's interest and concern. Realistic reassurances can be offered to him, such as informing him that the suicidal crisis will pass, and that the staff will work with him to help him resist the suicidal urge.

Conversation with the client should address the healthy, functional parts of the client. This focus may include activities of daily living, such as his self-care, eating, and dressing. It is wise to avoid extensive discussion and exploration of the reasons for the suicidal behavior until the client's risk of suicide has decreased.

The severe isolation of the high-risk suicide client can be combatted by regular, frequent contact with consistent personnel. Nurses and other psychiatric staff must approach the client; he will not actively seek out the staff. The number of staff working with the client should be limited to the lowest necessary number. The nurse should inform the client when she will be available to him, how often she will make contact, and how to notify the nurse if he desires contact.

Promoting Decision-Making and Autonomy. Suicidal clients are frequently preoccupied with their suicidal thoughts. Simple decisions required to carry out activities of daily living can be overwhelming and perplexing. The nurse helps the client make decisions, such as what to wear or when to bathe, thereby helping him to maintain a level of self-esteem and autonomy. Aiding the client in decision-making decreases his isolation by providing contact with a helping professional; it also maintains a sense of dignity through self-direction.

Suicidal Behaviors and Thought Disorders. Clients with thought disorders have trouble organizing their thoughts and are at risk of making impulsive, psychotic, self-destructive gestures. Schizophrenic clients may use self-harmful behaviors as a means of testing reality or in response to auditory hallucinations.[2] The nurse must first explore and identify the content of the client's disordered thoughts. By presenting reality and making the environment safe, the nurse decreases the likelihood that the client will respond to the disordered thoughts that prompt self-harm.

The "No Suicide" Contract. The nurse establishes a "no suicide contract" with the client at moderate to low risk of suicide.[24] In this contract, the client repeats to the nurse a statement that he will not accidentally or on purpose kill himself. The "no suicide" contract specifies the length of time the contract is valid and is renewed before it expires.

If a client is unable to make the "no suicide" contract, his ambivalence is evident in this attempt to alter the wording of the contract. For example, the client might say, "I will *try* not to kill myself" or "I *might* be able to keep the agreement." Insistence on the exact words of the contract promotes honesty and reinforces to the client that it is his responsibility, not the nurse's, to control the suicide impulse. If a client is unable to make a "no suicide" contract, environmental supports, such as a closed psychiatric treatment unit, may be offered. Praise should be offered for the client's ability to make and maintain the contract.

Suicide as a Message. The suicide crisis should be viewed as a dramatic, but ineffective, means of communication. The client is trying to tell others an important message. An immediate need of the client's is to identify the stressors contributing to the suicide risk. Talking with the client about the stressors provides him with reassurance that the anger, despair, and frustration are being heard. The nurse helps the client break the problem into small pieces of solvable units, see the options available to him, and make his choices. Take care to focus on the healthy, functional parts of the client—focus not only on the suicide risk of the client, but on his realistic strengths and abilities.

Clients who make or threaten suicide gestures have poorly developed coping patterns. Nursing interventions are directed toward strengthening existing coping skills or toward developing new coping strategies. This process begins by helping the client understand and accept the implications of his suicide attempt. Verbally discussing possible substitutions of coping mechanisms for the suicide helps the client identify other ways of dealing with the stresses in his life. The nurse identifies and reinforces those effective methods of coping that the client already possesses and of which he may be unaware due to his distorted image of himself.

Postvention

Despite the availability of effective psychiatric and nursing care, some persons can and do kill themselves. The suicide act is an interpersonal act and touches all those significant to the client. Nursing intervention does not end with a completed suicide act; the nurse continues to work with the survivors in resolving their reactions to the suicide.

The term *survivor–victim* is used to describe the dual role of the survivors of suicide.[20] Those left behind in a suicide act experience anger, frustration, guilt, and ambivalence in addition to the grief associated with a death.[6] Family members describe a sense of shame and embarassment following a suicide, accompanied by an estrangement from well-meaning relatives who do not know how to respond to the loss through suicide.

Resynthesis of Survivor–Victims. Using Resnick's model of resynthesis, the nurse guides the survivor–victims through the stages of resuscitation, rehabilitation, and renewal.[18] In the *resuscitation* stage, the first 24 hours following notification of the suicide, the nurse offers assistance with the shock of the death. Emphasis is placed on the funeral and burial as well as helping the survivor–victims to acknowledge the death of the person who committed suicide. During *rehabilitation*, the nurse uses group or individual intervention to allow the survivor–victims to mourn the death as well as to express their unique reactions to the suicide. The *renewal* phase, characterized by acceptance, is a time used for helping the survivor–victims reintegrate the suicide experience into their lives.

Conducting the Psychological Autopsy. When a client suicides, the nursing and other psychiatric-mental health staff also experience feelings of anger and guilt.[13] Frequently, a suicide elicits a sense of failure among nursing personnel. In a *psychological autopsy,* staff gather to review the client's behaviors and actual death act. The psychological autopsy does not attach blame; rather, it is a process to examine what clues, if any, were missed and to learn from the evaluation of a particular situation. Following the suicide of a client by overdose, the staff of one inpatient unit met on three occasions to discuss the death and their reactions to it. Staff members verbalized feelings of frustration at their lack of power to keep the client from killing himself as well as anger at the client for "doing it to them." Examination of clues revealed that the client, a chronically depressed young man, had not established a therapeutic alliance with any of the staff on the unit. No changes in eating or sleeping patterns were observed during his hospitalization. Based on the final evaluation of this client and his behavior in the treatment facility, the staff modified the existing assessment protocol on their unit to include a verbatim report of an interaction with every potentially suicidal client during every shift.

Evaluation

Evaluation of the care of the suicidal individual includes examining the assessment, planning, and intervention phases of the nursing process.

The first goal in the care of the suicidal client is identification; that is, did the nurse correctly identify all clients at risk for suicide? Expertise in suicide assessment comes not only from following a systematic process, but also from actually performing suicide assessments and receiving verification from colleagues. Evaluation of the assessment process should reveal that the nurse accurately assessed the suicide risk of all persons in her care.

Evaluation of the planning and implementation of care provided for persons at risk of suicide is an ongoing process. The information gathered in the daily evaluation of nursing care plans forms the basis of the assessment of the client's suicide risk.

Evaluation is an inherent factor in the assessment process. The nurse examines the goal statements for appropriateness. Through evaluation based on the goals of therapy, the nurse determines whether intervention strategies should continue to promote safety, begin exploration of the precipitants to the suicide, or focus on the development of new coping strategies. Evaluation helps the psychiatric-mental health staff to identify which actions were effective in the care of the client.

Nurses participate in the evaluation of care individually when reviewing their own treatment plans and the attainment of goals. Care of the suicidal client may also be evaluated during team conferences and peer review sessions, or through "change of shift" reports and psychological autopsies.

Summary

All forms of self-destructive behaviors are potentially life-threatening. This chapter has focused on the assessment, planning, intervention, and evaluation of the person at risk for suicide. Some of the major points of this chapter include the following.

1. Suicide occurs as a response to life situations in an intrapersonal or interpersonal context.
2. Although some evidence suggests a biochemical basis for suicidal behavior, the most commonly held etiologic theories define suicide as the result of an interpersonal or intrapsychic crisis.
3. The suicidal person experiences feelings of ambivalence, anger, isolation, and desperation.
4. The suicide act has many meanings and serves to communicate a dramatic message to others.
5. The nurse uses the nursing process to determine the degree of suicide risk of an individual and to discover the message expressed through the suicidal behavior.
6. In assessment, the nurse examines six factors: the presence of clues to suicide, the means by which the person sought help, the suicidal plan, the person's mental state, his support systems, and his lifestyle.
7. Nursing care is planned in conjunction with the suicidal individual and other resource personnel, including psychiatric staff and the client's significant others.
8. Nursing interventions, based on the degree of suicidal risk of the client, focus on providing safety and establishing a therapeutic alliance.
9. One goal of nursing care is to help the client express his unique message.
10. The nurse uses dyadic skills to help the client learn less destructive means to cope with stressors.
11. Nursing intervention continues after a completed suicide through postvention activities with the "survivor–victims" of the suicide.
12. Evaluation of nursing care is based on two questions: Were the clues identified early enough to permit intervention? Was the intervention appropriate and effective?
13. Nurses and other psychiatric-mental health care providers need opportunities to express their feelings of anger and frustration at the behaviors of suicidal clients, and work through these feelings to achieve objectivity and empathy.

Therapeutic Dialogue

Assessing Suicidal Risk

Nurse: (during admission interview) Mike, I'd like to know more about why you came to the hospital.

Client: Well, after I lost my job, I just stayed around the house. The kids, you know (looking at the floor), after they go to school, I'm pretty much alone. And my wife, well, it's awful, but she's gotta work. We really need the money.

Nurse: Uh, huh. (trying to reestablish eye contact with client) You're alone most of the day, and your wife and children are busy with work and school. Sounds like you've felt lonely and a bit worthless.

Client: You don't know what it's like! (meeting nurse's eye contact) There's just no other choice. They're all caught up in their own things. They don't need me, I'm just a burden. (mournful facial expression)

Nurse: Mike, you're telling me that you feel like a "burden" and that you have no other choice. What is the choice?

Client: Well, I thought it would be better for them, and anyway, what's left for me? I'm not a man any more.

Nurse: You seem quite desperate. I wonder if you've thought of killing yourself?

Client: Uh, no, uh, well, there's the insurance but she wouldn't hear of it. She's the one that called the doctor. I just don't know. (twisting wedding ring on his finger)

Nurse: (slowly and softly) Sometimes, when a person's life seems worthless and hopeless, he sees suicide as a reasonable choice.

Client: Yeah—I know. (hesitates) I had those pills from my wife's operation and the kids were at school. I would've been alone, and I could've slept.

Nurse: Let me make sure I understand you—you've been thinking about killing yourself and had a plan. Is that right?

Client: Well, yeah, but she came home for her purse and saw the pills out and started yelling. I wasn't really sure—I still don't know. Then she made me come here.

Nurse: How are you feeling now that you're here?

Client: I guess it's okay. She really is right.

Nurse: Do you still have thoughts of killing yourself?

Client: I don't know. Sometimes. I don't know.

Nurse: I'm sure the past few weeks have been rough for you. For now, I want to work with you to keep you from killing yourself, and to help you figure out what you want to do to make things different.

Discussion

The client in this interview displays a moderate risk of suicide. He experiences suicidal thoughts, has a specific plan of moderate lethality but low accessibility to the means or method. The client demonstrates a depressed affect with feelings of hopelessness and worthlessness. His risk of suicide is also judged as a moderate risk based upon the significant factors of job loss, role change, and loss of status. The client expresses ambivalence about dying and appears to have a supportive family structure. The fact that the client agreed to be hospitalized for psychiatric treatment suggests that he has some degree of motivation.

The nurse uses therapeutic communication techniques to establish rapport with the client and to gather assessment data. She responds to both the feelings and the content expressed by the client. The nurse directly inquires about the client's suicidal thoughts and involves him in establishing a treatment plan that will promote autonomy and provide support.

Nursing Care Plan

The Suicidal Client: Moderate Risk

Client Problem	Goal	Intervention
Moderate risk of suicide	Client will not act on suicide impulse.	Suicide assessment each shift and as needed. Document level of risk and appropriate plan on client's chart.

Client Problem	*Goal*	*Intervention*
		Establish a no-suicide contract with the client. Renew the contract each shift and as needed.
		Establish a support plan with client (*e.g.*, have client check in with, and speak to nurse, every half-hour).
		The primary nurse is to explore client's feelings and motives regarding suicide once a day.
		If suicide risk increases, implement a high-risk plan and inform involved psychiatric-mental health staff.
	Client will maintain activities of daily living and social interaction.	Assist client with decision-making by pointing out options and supporting his decision.
		Make a written activity schedule with client for a 2-to-4-hour period.
		Focus the client's discussion on events and activities of the day. Explore the client's satisfactions and disappointments.
		Encourage the client to attend unit activities and meals (accomplished through verbal discussion and encouragement or by accompanying the client to the activity).

References

1. Aguilera D, Messick J: Crisis Intervention, 4th ed. St Louis, CV Mosby, 1982
2. Anderson N: Suicide in Schizophrenia. Perspectives in Psychiatr Care 11:106–112, 1973
3. Baechler J: Suicides. New York, Basic Books, 1979
4. Burgess AW, Baldwin B: Crisis Intervention Theory and Practice. Englewood Cliffs, NJ, Prentice Hall, 1981
5. Durkheim E: Suicide (trans). Glencoe, IL, The Free Press, 1951
6. Hatton C, Valente SM: Bereavement Group for Parents who Suffered a Suicidal Loss of a Child. Suicide Life Threat Behav 11 (Fall): 114–150, 1981
7. Farberow N: Suicide. Morristown, NJ, General Learning Corporation, 1974
8. Farberow N (ed): The Many Faces of Suicide. New York, McGraw-Hill, 1980
9. Farberow N, Schneidman E (eds): The Cry for Help. New York, McGraw-Hill, 1961
10. Hankoff L: Physiochemical Correlates. In Hankoff L, Einsidler B (eds): Suicide Theory and Clinical Aspects. Littleton, MA, PSG Publishing, 1979
11. Holinger PC: Violent Deaths as a Leading Cause of Mortality: An Epidemiologic Study of Suicide, Homicide, and Accidents." Am J Psychiatry 137 (April): 472–476, 1980
12. Jourard S: Suicide: An Invitation to Die. Am J Nurs 70:269, 1970
13. Marshall K: When a Patient Commits Suicide. Suicide Life Threat Behav 10 (Spring): 23–40, 1980
14. Menninger K: Man Against Himself. New York, Harcourt, Brace and World, 1938
15. Miller M: The Geography of Suicide. Psychol Rep 47, Part 1 (December): 699–702, 1980
16. Miller M: Suicide After Sixty: The Final Alternative. New York, Springer-Verlag, 1979
17. Phillips D, Lio J: The Frequency of Suicides Around Major Public Holidays: Some Surprising Findings. Suicide Life Threat Behav 10 (Spring): 41–50, 1980
18. Resnick HP: A Clinical Approach to the Survivors in a Death by Suicide. In Cain A (ed): Survivors of Suicide. Springfield, IL, Charles C Thomas, 1972
19. Resnick HP, Rubin H: Emergency Psychiatric Care (NIMH). Bowie, MD, The Charles Press Publishers, 1975
20. Schneidman E: An Overview: Personality, Motivation, and Behavior. In Hankoff L, Einsidler B (eds): Suicide Theory and Clinical Aspects. Littleton, MA, PSG Publishing, 1979
21. Schneidman E, Farberow N (eds): Clues to Suicide. New York, McGraw-Hill, 1957
22. Snyder S: Biological Aspects of Mental Disorders. New York, Oxford University Press, 1980
23. The Reliability of Suicide Statistics: A Bomb Burst. Suicide Life Threat Behav 10 (Summer): 267–269, 1980
24. Twiname BG: No Suicide Contract for Nurses. J Psychiatr Nurs Ment Health Serv 19 (July): 11–12, 1981
25. Vollen K, Watson C: Suicide in Relation to Time of Day and Day of Week. Am J Nurs 75 (March): 263, 1975
26. Wilson M: Suicidal Behavior: Toward an Explanation of the Differences in Female and Male Rates. Suicide Life Threat Behav 11 (Fall): 131–139, 1981

Part VIII
Mental Health Intervention with the Medical Patient

Chapter Preview

Trauma, surgery, or an acute illness requiring a hospital stay is a stressful event. Both the individual patient and the involved family face the stresses of the illness heaped upon preexisting personal and interpersonal life stressors. The individual's usual problem-solving abilities, energy and resources, and available supports influence his ability to cope with the stress of a major physiological onslaught. The injured or seriously ill person often experiences the psychological themes of denial, threatened body image, and emotional lability. Nurses generate interventions that assist the individual and his family by preserving and nurturing adaptive responses.

Learning Objectives

On completion of the chpater, the reader should be able to accomplish the following.

1. Describe the personal, environmental, and injury-related stressors confronting the person experiencing trauma, surgery, or critical illness
2. Describe a problem-solving method of coping with the stressor of illness or injury
3. Apply the nursing process to the care of persons experiencing trauma or critical illness
    Describe the behaviors of patients at the various phases of their injury—impact, resistance, and resolution
    Formulate nursing diagnoses for the injured or acutely ill patient
    Identify goals and interventions that assist the individual and family cope with specific trauma reactions
    Evaluate the effectiveness of nursing interventions
4. Discuss the major concerns of family members of severely injured or critically ill patients during hospitalization
5. Describe the effect that working with trauma and seriously ill patients and their families has on the nurse
6. Identify coping measures that assist the nurse who cares for victims of trauma and critical illness

Impact of Trauma and Surgery

Severely traumatized patients and those undergoing major surgeries account for millions of hospital days per year in the United States. The cost of trauma—financially, physically, and emotionally—to the injured and their families is staggering. Aside from the physical effects of the trauma or surgery, the individual suffers emotional or psychological consequences, which comprise a stress response.

Stress is a part of everyday life. People respond to stress in a total or holistic manner as they try to reestablish or maintain a steady state, or equilibrium. This stress/stress response cycle is characterized by the following.

1. The stressful event or stressors
2. The interpretation or perception of the meaning of the event
3. Conditioning factors or characteristics of the individual, such as his past experiences and goals
4. The individual's available coping mechanisms[40]

Stressors Confronting the Seriously Ill Patient

The seriously ill patient experiences stress due to a combination of preexisting life stressors, stressors inherent to hospitalization, and injury- or illness-related stressors. Stress may have a negative connotation, such as death of a loved one, or a positive connotation, such as an increase in salary. Both of these examples suggest a change of some sort, and any change interrupts the individual's equilibrium, thereby creating stress. Not all changes result in maladaptation, however; stress may induce a person to grow and develop more effective responses to his environment.

Stressful Life Events

Certain life events that occur normally throughout the course of a lifetime may add to the stress of the seriously ill patient. Death of a spouse, divorce, or financial problems are highly stressful events due to the amount of change that occurs at those times.[20] These stressful life events drain the resources of the individual. When they are closely spaced events, they increase the likelihood of illness. It is not unusual, for example, for the surgical patient to give a history of recent major life stress. Inadvertently, the nurse may focus on the present event, the patient's illness or injury, and ignore or dismiss the importance of the previous stressful events in his life. Nevertheless, those previous events may have precipitated the current illness, and definitely have an impact on the healing capabilities of the individual.

Stressors Due to Hospitalization

Hospital-related stressors compound the injured or ill patient's preexisting life stresses. These stressors include unfamiliarity of the surroundings, loss of independence, separation from loved ones, and financial problems. It has been found that people reporting high levels of life stress also report high levels of hospital-related stress.[43] In addition, these people who experience higher-than-normal levels of stress require a longer period of convalescence before returning to their previous or usual activities.[45] Often, the patient may be unaware of the amount of stress with which

Chapter 35
Trauma, Surgery, and Critical Care

"Surgical Ward"

They are and suffer; that is all they do;
A bandage hides the places where each is living,
His knowledge of the world restricted to
The treatment that the instruments are giving.

And lie apart like epochs from each other
—Truth in their sense is how much they can bear;
It is not talk like ours, but groans they smother—
And are as remote as plants; we stand elsewhere.

For who when healthy can become a foot?
Even a scratch we can't recall when cured,
But are boist'rous in a moment and believe

In the common world of the uninjured, and cannot
Imagine isolation. Only happiness is shared,
And anger, and the idea of love.

WH Auden,
WH Auden: Collected Poems

Cynthia Ann Pastorino

he is coping. In this situation, nurses may help the patient develop insight into his life and recognize and manage his stress.

Illness-Related Stressors

If stressful life events and hospitalization have not overwhelmed the patient, consider the stressors confronting the critically ill patient; that is, the *illness-related stressors*. These stressors include physical, chemical, biologic, and physiological assaults.[41] Physical stressors include changes in environmental temperature and disturbances in the patient's natural body rhythms of rest and activity. The constant activity of the critical care areas of the hospital, such as the noise and lights throughout the day and night, cause the patient to lose those indicators of night and day. While environmental effects confuse the patient, drugs may add to his disorientation by disturbing normal body functions. Pain and other physiological factors contribute to the problem.

ICU Syndrome. Illness-related stressors also contribute to a phenomenon, most often seen in the intensive care unit (ICU), called "ICU psychosis," "ICU syndrome," or "ICU-itis." The onset of this syndrome is heralded by a change in orientation (person, place, or time), usually preceded by major physiological assault (trauma or surgery) and accompanied by sleep deprivation.[17] Patients at risk for the development of this syndrome tend to be over 50 years of age, have a personal history of inflexible modes of coping under stress, and have been in the intensive care unit for more than 3 days.[30] The onset of this syndrome usually occurs 3 to 7 days post surgery or trauma.

With improved surgical techniques, diligent postoperative monitoring, and increased sensitivity of staff to psychological needs of patients, the incidence of this syndrome has decreased dramatically over the years. If the ICU syndrome is left untreated, or unrecognized, however, the change in cognition develops into full-blown psychosis with the patient experiencing visual hallucinations, paranoid ideation, and strange bodily sensations.[7] Nursing interventions to prevent the development of this syndrome will be discussed later in this chapter.

Stressors related to life events, hospitalization, and illness or injury elicit both a physiological and psychological stress response. Ineffective coping perpetuates the stress syndrome and results in maladaption, at the least, and illness or death, at the extreme. How these stressors are perceived governs the effectiveness of the patient's response.

Perception and Problem-Solving

Understanding how stressors are perceived and how problems are defined and solved is crucial in assisting patients through surgery, trauma, or any other crisis event. Adults who have been responsible and functioning in society have learned how to meet their need and have learned how to make sense out of their environment. These same adults, however, when hospitalized, are lost in a strange place. The patient's predicament may be likened to driving in a foreign city in search of a specific place. The ill or injured patient is ignorant of the hospital's rules and customs and is dependent upon caregivers who are unfamiliar to him, yet he attempts to understand and react appropriately to the strange environment.

Perception of an event is a highly individualized phenomenon based on the person's values, instincts, personality, past experience, problem-solving ability, and many other factors.[14] These factors contribute to the individual's ability to define the problem, generate possible solutions, and choose the solution that is most likely to be effective.[21]

When a patient's resources (*i.e.*, his attention span or verbal abilities) are compromised, satisfactory resolution of the stressful situation or problem is hampered. For example, when a patient is treated with analgesics, his problem-solving ability is likely to be affected.

Several obstacles may hinder the individual's effective resolution of a problem, including the following.

1. The problem may tax the individual beyond his capacity to respond.
2. The problem may be insoluble.
3. The solutions to the problems are contradicotry.[21]

When stress is overwhelming, the patient cannot mobilize sufficient energy to overcome it. An example of this effect of overwhelming stress is the compromised ability of a person to cope with several successive family deaths. An insoluble problem, for instance, may be extensive multisystem organ failure. Contradictory solutions to problems pose an ever-present quandary in patient care; for example, how to provide comfort to a patient with extensive orthopedic injuries who also has head trauma. Nevertheless, solutions must be found, because the stress will perpetuate itself if the problem remains unresolved.

Conditioning Factors

The intensity and duration of the stress response depends not only on perception and problem-solving, but also on other characteristics of the individual. These characteristics, or conditioning factors, include genetic predispositions, nutritional status, types and variety of coping mechanisms, available situational supports, cultural inheritance, health history, and developmental level.[1]

An individual with a deficit in these factors is at risk for more adverse effects of trauma, surgery, or critical illness. For example, a diabetic patient undergoing major surgery is more likely to experience complications and a prolonged recovery period than a nondiabetic patient. Likewise, an injured person who uses only acting-out behavior as a coping method and who hasn't any friends has limited resources at a time when he needs maximum resources.

The Critically Ill Person and the Nursing Process

Assessment and Analysis

Nursing care of patients who have suffered trauma or serious illness or who have major surgery rely on a data base of information concerning previous life experiences, responses to stressful life events, and other factors. The particular response of the patient to trauma or surgery depends on several factors.

1. The extent and type of injury
2. The meaning that the injury has for the individual
3. Other situational factors[27]

The overall goal of nursing care of these patients is to return them to the highest possible level of functioning, with healing of both physical and psychological wounds. This healing requires a gradual shift from life-or-death considerations to self-actualization considerations. At the time of injury, the person's energy expenditure is at the level of compensation, or constantly trying to "catch up" with physiological and psychological needs. As these needs become satisfied, the injured person can direct his energies toward coping with the environment and, finally, toward growth.[33] Nursing care focuses on conserving the patient's energy to enable growth to occur. Patient response to injury or critical illness is studied through the phases of impact, resistance, and resolution.[40]

Impact

At the time of serious illness or injury, the individual is placed in an unfamiliar environment and is expected to adapt, although his bodily energies are focused at the life–death level. Some of the behavioral manifestations of the phase of impact include denial, threatened body image, loss of control, and altered cognitive abilities.

Denial. Denial is perhaps the most frequent initial response to injury or serious illness. Patients may deny the extent of their injuries, the consequences of the injuries, or that they are injured at all. It is not uncommon for a person with a fractured leg to attempt to walk on it, despite the severe pain. Patients who are spinal-cord injured may rationalize the paralysis as temporary and may imagine movement. Even in the face of obvious clues (monitors and so on) and frank conversation to the contrary, patients may verbalize being "okay."

Denial is used to minimize the degree of threat of the injury and to "buy time" needed for the patient to call on his resources.[26] Denial allows the patient to focus energies on physiological healing while preserving other energies for later needs. Denial may be maladaptive when it is so encompassing that it threatens the patient's health, or when it requires great amounts of energy to maintain the denial.

Often, denial and awareness coexist and usually progress to some kind of reality-testing.[45] Although a patient may use denial when talking to others, this does not necessarily imply that he is deceiving himself.

Threatened Body Image. Threatened body image is another frequent response to trauma, serious surgery, and illness. The whole, functioning body that the patient once knew and loved is now changed. The patient may feel betrayed by his body. In the critical care unit, as well as in general units of the hospital, the person is connected to intravenous infusions, catheters, monitors, traction, and respirators, all of which provide basic functions that were once taken for granted.[4]

Body image, which develops from early childhood, is largely associated with freedom of movement and autonomy.[24] Our culture greatly esteems the ability to function independently. An important criterion of independence is movement, yet movement is greatly restricted in the critically ill.[32] In injured patients, not only is the mental picture of oneself altered, but the means of assessing the amount of damage done is also denied.

Behavioral manifestations of threatened body image vary and change over time. The patient often verbalizes a feeling of change in body function or structure, he may have a pet name for the body part involved, he may refuse to look at the affected part, or he may be depressed, anxious, or guilty.[15, 18]

Loss of Control. While the patient is seriously ill and basically dependent, he experiences loss of control and helplessness. The more serious his illness and the further removed he is from his family, the greater his feelings of helplessness are.[37] If the patient attempts to solve problems originating in the hospitalization or illness, and the desired outcomes are not attained, the patient's feelings of helplessness will increase and he may give up trying.[36] For example, a patient may cooperate with painful breathing exercises to prevent pulmonary complications of bedrest, but develops pneumonia anyway; he then sees no relationship between his actions and the outcome, which magnifies his feelings of being out of control and powerless.

Behavioral manifestations of loss of control may include verbalization of powerlessness, such as, "I don't see why I should try, it won't work anyway," worthlessness, such as, "I don't know why you bother with me," and passivity. The patient may be unable to recognize any area of his life over which he may exert some measure of control.

Altered Cognitive Abilities. During the impact phase, the patient may experience a change in cognitive abilities and sensory overload. *Sensory overload* is a phenomenon whereby the individual, having lost the ability to distinguish, weigh, and interpret environmental cues, attempts to attend to all stimuli. Ordinarily, people are aware of few stimuli at any one time, and all others are ignored. The ill person, however, feels the hardness of the strange bed, the roughness of the sheets, the pinching of the tape, the burning of the intravenous solution, the pain of the incision, the lightness of the room, the noise of the monitor, the conversations of the staff, and so on. The ICU syndrome is detected by a change in cognitive ability in persons stressed by major assault, sleep deprivation, and limited coping strategies.

It is not uncommon for critically ill persons to have fantasies of being dead (not dying) and being held prisoner.[37] These feelings are very confusing and frightening for the patient. It is not difficult, though, to understand why a patient might experience these feelings, because he is restrained, looking through the bars of the bed's siderails, and may be unable to speak because of a new tracheostomy.

Resistance

The next phase, resistance or stabilization, is characterized by increasing attempts by the individual to come to terms with the injury, illness, or surgery. The individual's energy stores are depleted and he is unable to focus his energy in any direction. The emotional responses of this phase include anger and hostility, guilt, vulnerability, and grief.

Anger and Hostility. The patient's anger and hostility may be directed at himself, family members, staff, or those who have been spared injury.[25] Whereas once the patient was passive, he now becomes hostile and difficult to please. If the injury is permanent, the patient may be reluctant to express any anger for fear of alienating future care providers.[46] Often, the patient succeeds in turning away loved ones who may be bewildered by these outbursts.[19]

Guilt. The patient's emotional outbursts may trigger feelings of guilt at having been angry, at having been injured, or at any wrongdoings.[25] The patient may feel guilt or shame for his behavior early in the hospital stay. Nurses may hear the patient talk about what he "should have" or "wished he would have" done, as he expresses responsibility for the injury, illness, or surgery. The conclusions reached by the patient may be far-fetched; for example, when the automobile-accident victim states he "should have taken the bus" when he never before rode the bus.

Vulnerability. The feeling of vulnerability implies that the individual is not coping well; it is characterized by a distressing mood and by feelings of being flawed, breakable, or exposed to harm. The patient may express lack of confidence in significant others and caregivers.[45] He scrutinizes each staff member for clues as to whether or not he or she can be trusted. Although clinically he may be improving, the patient sees little future for himself. He may feel abandoned, in part because of the less frequent visits by health care workers and families during the patient's im-

provement. These feelings of vulnerability seem to increase and decrease depending on the patient's energy.

Grief. During the resistance phase, the patient has time to think about the injury and begins to talley his losses. The patient grieves for all that has been changed or lost, and the losses are many. These losses, which may be potential, actual or irreversible, include the following.

1. Changes in body parts or functioning; that is, self-care activities, agility, consciousness, mental acuity, and others
2. Changes in rest or comfort
3. Changes in self-concept; that is, self-esteem, body image, personal identity, and role performance
4. Changes in significant other; that is, availability of support group and emotional and financial security
5. Changes in availability of inanimate objects, such as personal belongings
6. Control over the environment
7. Existential changes, such as choice, hope, freedom, and individuality
8. Changes in life dreams and goals
9. Changes in certainty or predictability.[16]

The realization of the extent of the losses may come as a surprise to the patient, especially if he has used denial previously. If the injury, illness, or surgery has resulted in a permanent handicap or disfigurement, the patient has a constant reminder of the loss and, therefore, the potential for constant grieving.[46] The feeling of grief may flood the patient at unpredictable times, and this unpredictability further increases his feelings of distress. The increased awareness of the impact of the trauma or surgery signals the beginning of the third stage of the response syndrome: resolution.

Resolution

During the resolution phase of the response to critical illness or trauma, the patient comes to terms with the assault. Coping is defined as the satisfactory resolution of distress. Through these stages of stress, patients try a variety of coping measures until equilibrium is attained. This equilibrium may not be achieved for months after the injury or serious illness, or may not be achieved at all. Exhaustion results from failure to cope with the injury or illness, and is characterized by depleted energy stress, continued distress, and impaired psychophysiological functioning.[40] Exhaustion is precipitated by errors in problem-solving, altered perception, and deficits in biologic functioning.

Coping generates energy for growth. The goal of the resolution phase is the establishment of quality of life to the patient's ability and satisfaction. By this time in the course of the injury or illness, the patient has defined more clearly the problems, has generated some options for himself, and is attempting to reconstruct his life. The patient has plans for reentry into a social life and his energies are now directed toward growth. Major themes of the patient during the resolution phase include framing memories of the accident or illness, divided time, and existential and spiritual concerns.

Framing Memories of the Accident or Illness. In an attempt to pull together the events surrounding the injury or illness, the patient will begin to frame memories of the accident or illness. He may also express embarrassment about some of his past behavior, or fear of the trauma happening again. The patient attempts to place the accident or surgery in perspective, and in his past. This is accomplished through telling and retelling his story. Some people may even keep a scrapbook of souvenirs from their hospital stay.

Divided Time. With the trauma or surgery safely in the past, the injury is used as a marker with which to divide time.[36] The patient places events "before the accident" (or illness or surgery) or "after the accident," as though the event were a convenient way to remember other unrelated events. A daughter's wedding is now remembered as occurring "before my accident," or Uncle Joe died "after my accident."

Existential and Spiritual Concerns. Along with framing memories and using the assault to divide the past, individuals may also experience increased attention to existential and spiritual concerns.[42] Some patients view the accident or surgery as a lesson. The patient may realize unfulfilled hopes and dreams and set new goals. These goals often revolve around promises to give to charity or attend church services more often. The trauma may have provided an opportunity for the patient to grow.

Effect on the Critically Ill Patient's Family

The individual patient is not alone in experiencing the stress of trauma or major illness; the family, as a unit, also encounters stressors. These family stressors include interpersonal problems, debt, unemployment, problems with child care, and illness of other family members.[5] The family also experiences hospital-related stressors, such as loss of social contact with the injured member, role changes, changes in eating and sleeping habits, and relocation to a strange environment.[3] These stressors often affect the health of family members and may cause exacerbations of their preexisting health problems.[23]

Assessing Family Members. The nurse assesses the family's strengths and weaknesses by examining the following.

1. Adaptation, or use of resources in a crisis
2. Partnership, or shared decision-making

3. Growth, or the self-fulfillment achieved by family members through mutual support
4. Affection
5. Resolve, or the commitment to each other[39]

How the family perceives this illness and its effect on family life will determine the amount of threat that is experienced. If the family perceives the patient's illness or injury as affecting all family roles, life dreams, and relationships, then the family is at risk for emotional problems. The basic needs of the family are to hope, to know, and to be close.

Family Responses. Typical responses of the family with a critically ill member are high anxiety levels, denial, anger and rage, and, finally, resolution.[8]

Manifestations of high anxiety levels are observed in the family members' tense facial expressions and posture.[8] "Is he alive?" is their main concern. The family members often huddle together, supporting each other and attempting to make sense out of what has happened. The nurse functions as the main source of information about the hospital and about their injured or ill family member. The nurse is the family's lifeline to the injured member; the family attempts to interpret every piece of information they receive.

Denial serves the same purpose for the family as it does for the individual—it maintains hope. At times, one family member is designated the "strong one" and denial helps that member maintain the posture of strength.[11] Family members using denial say, "He looks okay," when the patient has multiple monitors, IVs, and massive dressings. They see the patient as they want to see him—alive and basically well.

The family's anger and rage may be focused at the patient, the hospital, society, or other family members. Not infrequently, a family member will react to some trivial irritant, such as the tone of someone's voice, with an explosion of anger. In reality, the family unit has been severely disrupted by the patient's injury or critical illness. Families need reassurance that their anger is understandable and needs to be expressed.

Hopefully, the family adaptively resolves the crisis. They make plans to resocialize the injured or ill family member into the fold. The members once again laugh with each other and begin to act as a family unit. (See Therapeutic Dialogue: Recognizing and Responding to the Anxiety of Family Members.)

Planning

Goal-Setting

Planning nursing care for patients experiencing trauma or critical illness poses serious problems for the care provider. Much attention is focused on the patients' technical and physical needs; obviously, the priority is the patient's life.

Nursing Diagnosis of the Critically Ill

Diagnosis	Supporting Data
Sleep Pattern Disturbance	Critically ill and surgical patients are frequently awakened throughout the day for assessment of physiological parameters and necessary activities. Patients may verbalize feeling tired, or may be restless, confused, apathetic, and unable to perform customary activities, such as bathing, turning, or feeding self.
Impaired Verbal Communication	Patients may be unable to communicate because of facial or neck trauma, tracheostomy, fatigue, disorientation, or fear. Speech may require more energy than is available for the patient, resulting in halting speech or shortened phrases. This results in frustration for staff and patient and reliance on nonverbal communication, which, by its nature, may be incomplete or misinterpreted.
Impaired Thought Process	Patients demonstrate a decrease in attention span, memory deficits, and a change in problem-solving ability related to excessive sensory stimulation when acutely ill.
Disturbance in Body Image	The patient's body image is challenged by illness or trauma, resulting in feeling unfamiliar with self and capabilities. The patient can become preoccupied with the involved body parts, feel negative about the body, and fear rejection of others because of perceived changes in his body.
Impaired Home Maintenance Management	The patient/family express difficulty in being able to care for patient because they are unfamiliar with care regimens, lack the resources (personal, financial) to provide assistance, or the regimens are too complex, difficult, or disruptive to family's lifesytle.
Dysfunctional Grieving	The grieving process is normal after injury/trauma, especially when that injury has lasting effects. The inability to resolve the feeling of grief may result in a lack of physical progress and exhaustion of the patient and family. Patients may verbalize distress, guilt, anger, and, in general, may experience disruption of the usual patterns of living, eating, sleeping, and work.

Nevertheless, just as protocols for physical care must be planned, so must nurses recognize and plan care to meet the patient's psychosocial needs. General goals to promote the mental health of patients and families include the following.

1. Maintaining previously adequate coping styles and encouraging flexibility of coping
2. Preventing untoward side effects, such as distrust, despair, and ICU syndrome
3. Maintaining the patients' support system.

Therapeutic Dialogue

Recognizing and Responding to the Anxiety of Family Members

Nineteen-year-old M. C. was involved in a major automobile accident. He underwent extensive surgery for abdominal and multiple orthopedic injuries. His condition is stable at this time.

Father: How's he doing?

Nurse: He spoke to me awhile ago and said he was okay, but was having pain in his leg.

Mother: Did you give him a shot? He doesn't like needles.

Nurse: He had a shot about 1 hour ago, so . . .

Mother: Well, the other nurse said he can have it anytime!

Nurse: No, not really . . .

Father: Well, I wish you'd all get your stories straight!!

Nurse: We seem to be getting off on the wrong foot here. I know you must be scared and worried half to death about M. I would be, too, about my child. And the intensive care unit is pretty confusing—especially with all the different doctors and nurses and machines.

Father: Everyone says something different.

Nurse: Sometimes that's true; sometimes we don't hear everything because we're so worried.

Mother: Well, that's true . . .

Nurse: I think there's a way we can get together. We have what we call a care plan where we write down the most important aspects of M's care. I think you can help us by letting us know about M. so we can help him better. Some things we may not be able to do while he's here in intensive care, but when he goes back to the orthopedic unit, the nurses there will know just how to care for him.

Discussion

Being in the intensive care unit is an anxiety-producing experience for both the family and the patient. Although the patient's parents verbalized their need for information, their anxiety and fear hindered their understanding.

There are times when the communication process goes badly, as when the nurse and parents began to discuss the patient's injections for pain. The nurse recognized the parent's emotional need, redirected the conversation (although it would have been easy to become angry or defensive), and proceeded with a more constructive interchange. The family also hinted at other avenues that need to be explored; for instance, what other incidents led the family to hear conflicting stories, and the need for reassurance that their son's pain management is of great concern to the nursing staff.

Incorporating Psychosocial Concerns into Care

Although these goals just listed may seem obvious within the context of this chapter, the "real-world" situation is often problematic. When the focus of care is crisis-oriented and the priority is the preservtion of life, psychological issues assume less importance. It is, therefore, imperative that nurses and other caregivers incorporate psychological support into the patient's care beginning with his entrance into the hospital.

Social workers, chaplains, and clinical nurse specialists often serve as liaisons between hospital staff and the patient and family and help facilitate the development of trust and understanding. These health care professionals usually have flexibility in the geographic area in which they work and may be able to link the intensive care unit with the general hospital units for the patient and family. The concept of continuity of care is vital in the care of seriously ill patients. When staffing problems prohibit continuing care by the same nurse, a written plan of care becomes increasingly essential. If nurses use standardized care plans or guides, interventions directed at emotional/psychosocial issues should be listed along with other items.

Nurses should be rewarded for attending to patients and families' emotional needs. Often, the outcome of the psychological intervention is not realized until long after the patient has left the intensive care unit. Skill in addressing and alleviating the patient's and family's emotional problems should be incorporated into the nursing career ladder along with technical skills. Critical care nurses also need to be allowed and encouraged to visit former patients as they recover on the general hospital units. This visiting allows the nurse to evaluate the effectiveness of her psychosocial interventions and reinforces their importance. Visiting with the critical care nurse also provides the patient with the opportunity to fill in blank areas of his memory and put the experience into perspective.

Intervention

Nursing interventions for critically ill patients and families involve three main areas for consideration—structuring the environment, sharing information, and providing emotional support.

Structuring the Environment

Monitoring Environmental Stimuli. Structuring or controlling the environment involves monitoring the amount and intensity of environmental stimuli reaching the patient. Stimuli easily amenable to restructuring include lowering the noise level of the unit, providing a light and dark cycle to promote sleep, condensing nursing activities so that the patient is minimally interrupted, and providing privacy for the patient. Calendars and clocks will help patients stay aware of the passage of time.

Providing Safety and Comfort. From the family's perspective, waiting rooms need to be geographically close to the patient and should have nearby bathrooms and comfortable chairs.[28] Although these may seem like minor points, to the family who waits for hours and days, they become very important.

The patient and family need to feel safe in their new environment. The family may bring objects from home, such as pillows, pajamas, or pictures of loved ones, which will increase their feelings of being safe. These objects also make a statement about the patient as a person and reaffirm his personhood to himself and others.

Sharing Information

Because the way in which individuals and families cope with stress is based on the processing of information or stimuli, it is essential that caregivers share information with them. This sharing of information helps the individual define the problem, generate options, and think of consequences to those options. The sharing process also provides patients with feedback on their progress toward the achievement of their goals.

Preparing the Patient and Family. Information sharing begins at admission with a discussion of the hospital admitting procedure. Where to wait while the patient is undergoing surgery and how various members of the health care team function are examples of information needed by family members to help them cope with hospitalization.[6, 38]

Information shared with family members during the initial hours of treatment usually involves the patient's general condition, such as vital signs and comfort level, and an interpretation of that information. If the patient is scheduled for surgery, he and his family should be provided information about the surgery, and what to expect pre- and postoperatively. Although patients vary in their abilities to recall the information given preoperatively, they have a need to know.[31]

Sensory Preparation for Medical Events. The use of sensory information, coupled with relaxation measures, is a potent nursing intervention for helping patients cope with treatments and hospitalization.[22] Sharing information about how the treatment will look, taste, feel, sound, or smell prepares the patient for those sensations so that they are not alarming. For example, when a patient is going to ambulate after surgery, knowing that the incisional area usually feels tight to most postoperative patients helps him to interpret the sensation as "normal."

Facilitating the Patient's Move Out of Intensive Care. When the patient is to be moved from the intensive care unit to another unit of the hospital, he may both welcome and dread the move. Although the move usually signifies an improvement in the patient's condition, it also means a loss of the now-familiar critical care area and relationships with the critical care nursing staff. To ease the transfer, patients need to know, upon admission, that their stay in the intensive care unit is temporary, that the general medical or surgical unit is different from the intensive care unit, and that the plan of care formulated with the patient in intensive care will be continued, with modifications, on the other hospital unit.[35]

Probably the most effective nursing intervention is a combination of information giving and caring.[29] Although sharing of information assists the patient and family in problem-solving, caring and providing emotional support are also essential for patient healing.

Providing Emotional Support

The nurse's provision of emotional support helps the patient resolve the multiple responses to his injury or illness. The caring attitude softens any "bad news" or difficulties that the patient encounters. Patient goals include the following.

1. Maintenance of hope
2. Establishment of feelings of control
3. Grieving for losses
4. Reentry into the social world

Maintaining Hope. The ability of a patient to maintain a feeling of hope is related to his level of trust; both help the individual face adverse times. It has been said that both trust and hope are strong enough to withstand truth.[45] These thoughts are useful to consider when the nurse is caring for a person or family who deny the seriousness or consequences of the illness.

Because the patient's denial is protective at this time, the nurse supports his response. On the other hand, the nurse realizes that inaccurate information undermines the patient's trust and shatters hope. If the nurse has established, through listening and sharing, a warm and caring relationship with the patient and family, this warmth will cushion the realities of their situation.

The patient's and family's need to be physically close to each other signifies hope in a tangible way.[11] Very often, patients remark, "I guess they're still there—they haven't given up on me yet." Tailoring visiting hours and supporting families when they spend the night with the injured patients are only two ways to foster hope. If there is no hope for survival, there can still be hope for peaceful death.

Maintaining Control. The nurse helps the patient establish and maintain feelings of control by continually involving patient and family in decision-making and by informing them of areas in which they can be in control. Simple nursing measures, such as placing the call light and telephone within reach and in the patient's control, will alleviate some feelings of powerlessness. A call light that slips off the bed is terrifying to a patient. Minimal use of restraints, while assuring patient safety, will also ensure feelings of control. If the patient is able to maintain a record of his breathing and leg exercises, intake and output, or turning, he will have a feeling of accomplishment and may be diverted from the stress of the injury through this activity.[9]

Mourning the Losses. The patient's grief for losses incurred through his illness or injury may become evident as anger or hostility, as well as sad feelings. The explosive anger of the resistance phase is, in part, related to the patient's losses. Continuing anger of the patient may drive away family and hospital staff. The patient needs to know that his anger is understandable, but that the energy consumed by his anger might better be channeled into rehabilitation or constructive activities.

Vulnerability is, in a sense, precipitated by the patient's ineffective coping and diffusion of energy. The feeling of being open to hurt is distressing because the patient and family increase their surveillance and lose sight of the objectives of care. Nurses need to protect the individual from unwise energy expenditure, and reinstill the feeling of hope by acknowledging and praising any small increment of progress or lack of regression.

If the patient's losses entail a significant change in lifestyle—according to the patient's, not the staff's, perception—he will need to learn new ways of managing his resources of energy and supports. Perhaps, if the patient is a college professor, teaching a class of 100 students might be beyond his capabilities, but he might be able to manage a class of 25 students.

Probably the most important intervention to help patients deal with loss is to encourage them to ventilate their feelings and grief. Patients whose illness or injury leaves them very much unlike their former selves face a constant reminder of their loss; their families are also constantly reminded of the loss. The patient and family's mourning is not a once-and-forever thing.[46] Although patients may adapt to illness or handicap, most probably continue to wish for lost functions and abilities.

Reentering the Social World. When the patient has progressed to leaving the hospital or rehabilitation center,

he needs to rehearse for social situations. Most patients carefully decide whom they will see or visit while convalescing, and when they will allow visitors. For patients who have a lasting handicap or change in appearance, this rehearsal for reentry into society is vital.

If a disfiguring surgery, such as a mastectomy, is planned, the nurse and patient have the luxury of time to explore the significance of the body part to the patient and the meaning of the surgery, and to plan for the postoperative course. Unfortunately, this period of time to deal with the upcoming event is not possible when an individual undergoes trauma. The victim of trauma may not be aware of the extent of his injuries and the consequences of the trauma for some time after the accident. As he becomes aware of the extent and ramifications of his injury, he may retreat from social contacts. Patients and families benefit from visits from recovered patients and members of self-help groups, such as Reach to Recovery for mastectomized women. Within these groups, patients can help and be helped by sharing common problems and concerns. These groups provide patients with hope, guidance, and an opportunity for catharsis.[36]

Evaluation

The ultimate effect of nursing interventions may be difficult to determine because much of the patient's healing continues after he is discharged from the health care setting. The establishment of a lifestyle satisfactory to the patient may or may not be possible. Realistic expectations for the patient probably exist somewhere between being locked into his anatomy, or limited by it, and the feeling that anything is possible.[46]

If good coping means good solutions for old problems, adequate solutions for new problems, and resourceful solutions for unexpected problems, then effective nursing measures elicit these adaptive responses.[45] Nursing intervention has been effective when the patient trusts, hopes, feels in control, and is ready to take on the world (or his portion of it). Early recognition of, assessment of, and intervention with, patients and families who lack resources, are overwhelmed with stressors, or react in a rigid manner are necessary. These patients and families may need more intensive counseling continuing beyond hospitalization.

Effects on the Nurse

Working with people who are anxious, depressed, physically ill, or stressed by normal life events can be both exhilarating and draining to the nurse. When profession-related stressors are coupled with job-related stressors, such as rotating shifts, the result is devastating because of the energy drain on nurses. No area of nursing is immune from this energy drain, nor does this drain affect nurses in critical care areas more than on general medical or surgical units.[12]

Nurses need to provide the same supportive actions

for themselves and each other that they provide for patients. The physiological indicators of professional stress syndrome include changes in eating habits, insomnia, lethargy, muscle tension, rashes, and gastrointestinal symptoms. Psychologically, the nurse feels disoriented, fragmented, frustrated, and indecisive. The nurse may exhibit angry, suspicious, or all-knowing behavior and may begin taking excessive risks.[12]

To prevent professional stress syndrome, nurses are encouraged to

1. become aware of the stresses in their lives;
2. establish peer group support;
3. if possible, change work activities or settings;
4. pursue recreational interests;
5. set realistic goals;
6. attend conferences and seminars away from the hospital interruptions;
7. take and give credit for a job well done.[11]

"Burnout" perpetuates more "burnout;" inadequate staffing perpetuates itself via a high level of nurse turnover. When they have less negative feelings with which to deal, nurses will have more energy for patient care and personal growth.

Summary

This chapter examines the stresses of, and responses to, major trauma, surgery, and critical illness. Some of the emphases of the chapter are as follows.

1. The assessment of the patient's response to trauma, surgery, or critical illness depends on his usual coping methods, problem-solving ability, and conditioning factors, such as available supports, previous health status, developmental level, and cultural background.
2. The response to trauma or serious illness varies from individual to individual, but generally follows a course of shock or impact, through resistance, and hopefully, to resolution.
3. Some of the emotional responses of patients to injury or critical illness include denial, body image disturbances, feelings of loss of control, vulnerability, angry outbursts, and grief.
4. Family members of the critically ill patient also experience overwhelming anxiety, denial, anger, and rage.
5. Psychosocial interventions should be incorporated in the plan of care for the critically ill patient and his family, beginning with the patient's entrance into the hospital.
6. The focus of nursing intervention is the promotion of hope, control, trust, appropriate grieving, and reentry into the social world through sharing information, structuring the environment, and supporting the individual and family.
7. To provide optimal care to the injured or seriously ill, the nurse also needs to care for herself and accept peer support and recognition.

Case Study

Recovering from the Loss of a Limb

D. R. is a 70-year-old man who underwent an above-the-knee amputation secondary to arterial occlusion. Immediately after recovering from the anesthetic in the intensive care unit, he became confused and combative. Within 24 hours of surgery, he was alert and oriented to person, time, and place. He was returned to the general surgical unit where his vital signs and general medical status stabilized. Because of the extent of other concurrent medical conditions, however, D. R. was expected to have a prolonged hospital stay.

The loss of his leg rekindled feelings of other losses D. R. had experienced in his life—especially the loss of his beloved wife 5 years previously. He repeatedly recounted stories of their life together and of their three children. His feelings of grief affected how he felt about life in the hospital. He grieved over his loss of control over the environment, the

meal selections, his daily schedule, visiting hours, and lack of contact with friends. During this time, the loss of his leg with resultant loss of mobility, though temporary, seemed to him an insurmountable obstacle. He wished he had died.

D. R.'s personal turmoil influenced his perceptions of the caregivers. He was distrustful of them, felt that they didn't know what they were doing, and that they withheld information from him. He maintained close ties with one nurse, but even when this nurse talked with him, he continually increased the volume on the television. He later referred to these days as "those dark times."

His adjustment to his new body took many weeks. At first, he did not look at his stump or touch the dressings. Gradually, he began to supervise the dressing changes, but was not interested in more active participation for some time.

The turning point in his adaptation, or coming

to terms with his surgery, began about 10 days post-operatively. Within one day, he felt relatively pain-free, was given a peanut butter sandwich (his favorite food) for lunch, received out-of-town visitors, and began to work with a new physical therapist. In therapy, he saw others "in worse shape than I'm in," and those who were "just as bad as me, but getting somewhere." The therapy sessions provided a means for him to measure his progress and encouraged his maximum effort. He thrived on the challenge.

Then D. R. began to redefine what had happened to him. Perhaps, he said, he "could still golf after all." He began dressing his stump and became very assertive about his care. The time arrived for his discharge to a rehabilitation hospital.

The rehabilitation hospital was definitely not home but, because it encouraged self-care, D. R. could be responsible for himself. Although he complained about the "rules," he realized the benefits. He spoke of the "dark times" at the acute care hospital and began to place that experience in perspective. He recognized his capabilities and accepted help for what he was unable to do. He finally consented to allow his grandchildren to see him, because, he asserted, "I'm still the same old grandpa—even with only one leg."

D. R. was discharged from the rehabilitation hospital 8 weeks after his amputation. At that time, he had a prosthesis and was able to take care of himself very well. If he were granted one wish, he would still wish to have two legs, but he had gained a respect for "what I can do if I set my mind to it." His son, with whom he had never had a deep relationship, became his most fervent supporter. He began to establish new relationships with a few people in his neighborhood.

Discussion

Mr. D. R.'s recovery from an amputation of his leg reflects the course of hospitalization and resolution of grief of many trauma patients. The loss of his limb was compounded by the loss of his wife 5 years before the surgery. He suffered the effects of hospitalization and experienced loss of control over daily events. The nurses strove to reestablish his sense of control over the situation and provided information, emotional support, and even, peanut butter sandwiches. The combined efforts of the nurses, other members of the medical team, D. R., and his family helped reduce his feelings of isolation and challenged and encouraged him to continue.

Nursing Care Plan

Responses to Trauma

Client Problem	Goal	Intervention
Sensory overload	The patient will experience reduced sensory input.	Decrease sensory stimulation—turn down lights, provide privacy, decrease number of people who come in contact with the patient.
		Interpret meaning of sensory input to patient—explain how procedures will look, feel, taste, smell, sound; explain meaning of alarms.
Feelings of vulnerability	Patient will demonstrate a more hopeful attitude.	Establish a relationship with patient through a calm, caring demeanor.
		Encourage verbalization of feelings.
		Reinstill feelings of hope, by acknowledgement of small increments of progress, or lack of regression.
		Protect the patient's energy stores by providing rest, adequate nutrition, and pacing activities according to his capabilities.
		Focus on small, easily tackled problems.

Client Problem	Goal	Intervention
Feelings of loss of control, helplessness	Client will reestablish feelings of control.	Identify aspects of care in patient's direct control—for instance, arrange room according to patient's desire, place call light and phone within reach, serve patient's food preferences *Together* plan the day, incorporating the patient's wishes Ask the family to bring into hospital patient's personal items from home
Grieving for losses incurred	Client and family will resolve their grieving.	Establish trust and hope through an honest, caring relationship. Acknowledge the losses incurred. Help the patient and family verbalize the meaning of losses. Help generate options—what have the patient and family gained from this experience?
Fear of being seen in public due to disfiguring surgery	Client will experience a reopening of his social world.	Plan a gradual widening of his social circle—initially, only family and very close friends permitted to visit, then other acquaintances. Walk with the patient in the hall or to the hospital lobby. Arrange for a visit by a self-help group of recovered patients for sharing and support.

References

1. Antonovsky A: Health, Stress, and Coping. San Francisco, Jossey-Bass Publishers, 1979

2. Auden WH: Selected Poetry of W. H. Auden. New York, The Modern Library, 1958

3. Breu C, Dracup K: Helping the Spouses of Critically Ill Patients. Am J Nurs 78 (January): 50–53, 1978

4. Caldwell E: The Psychologic Impact of Trauma. Nurs Clin North Am 13 (June): 247–254, 1978

5. Craven R, Sharp B: The Effects of Illness on Family Functions. Nursing Forum 11 (Spring): 186–193, 1972

6. Dzeurbejko M, Larkin J: Including the Family In Preoperative Teaching. Am J Nurs 78 (November): 1892–1894, 1978

7. Eisendrath S: ICU Syndrome Revisited. Critical Care Update! 9 (May): 31–35, 1982

8. Epperson M: Families In Sudden Crisis. Soc Work Health Care 2 (Spring): 265–273, 1977

9. Gal R, Lazarus R: The Role of Activity In Anticipating and Confronting Stressful Situations. J Human Stress 1(4):4–19, 1975

10. Gardner E, Hall R: The Professional Stress Syndrome. Psychosomatics 22 (August): 672–680, 1981

11. Geary M: Supporting Family Coping. Supervisor Nurse 10 (March): 52–59, 1979

12. Gentry WD, Parkes K: Psychologic Stress In Intensive Care Unit and Non-Intensive Care Unit Nursing. Heart Lung 11 (January–February): 43–47, 1982

13. Giacquinta B: Helping Families Face The Crisis of Cancer. Am J Nurs 77 (October): 1585–1588, 1977

14. Goosen G, Bush H: Adaptation: A Feedback Process. Advances In Nursing Science 1 (July): 51–66, 1979

15. Gordon M: Manual of Nursing Diagnosis. New York, McGraw-Hill, 1982

16. Gunta K: The Assessment of Losses Related to the Immobility of Orthopedic Patients. Master's Paper, Marquette University, Milwaukee, Wisconsin, 1981

17. Helton MC, Gordon SH, Lunnery SL: The Correlation Between Sleep Deprivation and the Intensive Care Unit Syndrome. Heart Lung 9 (May–June): 464–468, 1980

18. Henkler F: Body-Image Conflict Following Trauma and Surgery. Psychosomatics 20 (December): 812–820, 1979

19. Hohmann G: Psychological Aspects of Treatment and Rehabilitation of the Spinal Cord Injured Person. Clin Orthop 112 (October): 81–87, 1975

20. Holmels TH, Rohe RH: The Social Readjustment Rating Scale. J Psychosom Res 11:213–218, 1967

21. Howard A, Scott R: A Proposed Framework for the Analysis of Stress in The Human Organism. Behav Sci 10:141–160, 1965

22. Johnson J, Fuller SS, Endress MP, Rice V: Alluring Pa-

tients' Responses to Surgery: An Extension and Replication. Res Nurs Health 1 (May–June): 111–121, 1978

23. Klein R, Dean A, Bogdonoff M: The Impact of Illness Upon The Spouse. J Chronic Dis 20 (April): 241–248, 1967

24. Kolb L: Modern Clinical Psychiatry. Philadelphia, WB Saunders, 1977

25. Krupnick J, Horowitz M: Stress Response Syndromes. Arch Gen Psychiatry 38 (April): 428–435, 1981

26. Lazarus R: Positive Denial: The Case For Not Facing Reality. Psychology Today 13 (November), pp 44–60, 1979

27. Mattsson E: Psychological Aspects of Severe Physical Injury And Its Treatment. J Trauma 15 (March): 217–234, 1975

28. Molter N: Needs of Relatives of Critically Ill Patients. Heart Lung 8 (March–April): 332–338, 1979

29. Mumford E, Schlesinger H, Glass G: The Effects of Psychological Intervention on Recovery From Surgery And Heart Attacks. Am J Public Health 72 (February): 141–151, 1982

30. Nadelson S: The Psychiatrist In The Surgical Intensive Care Unit. Arch Surg 111 (February): 113–117, 1976

31. Reading A: Psychological Preparation for Surgery. J Psychosom Res 25:57–62, 1981

32. Rubin R: Body Image and Self-Esteem. Nursing Outlook 15 (June): 20–23, 1968

33. Ryden MB: Energy: A Crucial Consideration In The Nursing Process. Nursing Forum 16:71–82, 1977

34. Seligman M: Helplessness. San Francisco, WH Freeman, 1975

35. Scalzi C: Nursing Management of Behavioral Responses Following an Acute Myocardial Infarction. Heart Lung 2 (January–February): 62–69, 1973

36. Scarlon-Schilpp A, Levesque J: Helping The Patient Cope with the Sequelae of Trauma. J Trauma 21 (February): 135–139, 1981

37. Schnaper N: The Psychological Implications of Severe Trauma. J Trauma 15 (February): 94–98, 1975

38. Selva MC: Effects of Orientation Information on Spouses' Anxieties And Attitudes Toward Hospitalization And Surgery. Res Nurs Health 2:127–136, 1979

39. Smilkstein G: The Family Apgar. J Fam Pract 6 (June): 1231–1239, 1978

40. Smith M, Selye H: Reducing The Negative Effects of Stress. Am J Nurs 79 (November): 1954–1957, 1979

41. Stephenson C: Stress In The Critically Ill Patient." Am J Nurs 77 (November): 1806–1811, 1977

42. Tomlinson W: Psychiatric Complications Following Severe Trauma. J Occup Med 16 (July): 451–454, 1974

43. Vollicer B: Hospital Stress And Patient Reports of Pain and Physical Status. J Human Stress 4 (June): 28–37, 1978

44. Vollicer B, Burns M: Pre-existing Correlates of Hospital Stress. Nurs Res 26 (November–December): 408–415, 1977

45. Weisman A: Coping With Cancer. New York, McGraw-Hill, 1979

46. Zola cK: Denial of Emotional Needs to People with Handicaps. Arch Phys Med Rehabil 63 (February): 63–67, 1982

Chapter 36
The Child at Risk:
Illness, Disability, and Hospitalization

Whenever I approach a child his presence inspires two feelings in me. Affection for what he is now, and respect for what he may one day become.

Louis Pasteur

There is virtue in the search for some form of precise intervention, but there remains the discomforting awareness that the future environmental demands that all children must face, whatever their degree of vulnerability to psychopathology, are so great that a broader program of intervention seems necessary. Skill and competence develop, as Bruner has observed, by small daily acretions of experience from infancy throughout childhood. Such skills lead to new mastery, and this, in turn, encourages the development of other skills that generate a deep competence that may be the necessary inoculant that stays the ravaging effects of disorder.

Norman Garmezy,
in Anthony EJ, Koupernik C (eds):
The Child in His Family:
Children at Psychiatric Risk,
1974

Sally Francis

Chapter Preview

This chapter focuses on a child's illness, disability, and hospitalization, events in a child's life which place him and his family at risk for psychosocial disturbance and disruption to ongoing development. Because a child is an integral part of a family, the adaptation required in response to the stresses of illness will be influenced by, and required of, the family as well as the child. The interaction between nurse, parent, and child is foremost in the delivery of nursing care to the child. The nursing process—assessment, analysis, planning, intervention, and evaluation—supports the child's and family's positive adaptation to these crisis events.

Communication and self-understanding are essential to the nurse's personal coping with the illness of a child and to the nurse's professional role of assisting the child and family at risk. Additionally, the nurse's role as an advocate for the child and family within the health care environment is discussed.

Learning Objectives

On completion of the chapter, the reader will be able to accomplish the following.

1. Discuss the overlay of illness, disability, and hospitalization on the developmental needs of children
2. Describe the influences of hospitalization, parent–child attachment, and communication on the child's and family's positive adaptation
3. Apply the nursing process to the care of ill, disabled, or hospitalized children

   Assess the child's developmental level, environmental influences on the child (including the child's family), and idiosyncratic attributes of the child

   Discuss the concepts of trust, understanding, and mastery, on which the nurse bases nursing plans and interventions

   Formulate nursing diagnoses for children at risk due to illness, disability, or hospitalization

   Evaluate the psychosocial care of physically ill, disabled, or hospitalized children and their families
4. Describe the nurse's role of advocacy for children in health care and their families
5. Discuss the nurse's use of personal coping measures and collegial support in the provision of psychosocial care to children at risk due to illness, disability, or hospitalization.

Development and the Overlay of Illness, Disability, and Hospitalization

All individuals arrive at adulthood having developed from the dependency of an infant who must rely on the external world for survival. Successful passage through the phases of development leads to a sense of self as both separate from the external environment and capable of using the external world to provide for one's own survival. The individual becomes self-reliant, as well as interdependent with others in the environment. This is accomplished through the years of childhood as the individual acquires skills and resolves developmental crises.[16]

The crises of illness, disability, and hospitalization are frequently added to the normal, although monumental, developmental vicissitudes. These events may place the individual at risk not only for physical survival, but also for successfully managing the developmental tasks that lead to satisfying, productive adulthood.

The events of illness, disability, and hospitalization place the child at risk, but they also provide opportunities for the child and family to acquire skills for coping with, mastering, and adapting to stress.[12, 31] The stresses on the child are also stresses experienced by the family.[33, 41, 69, 74]

A developing child is an integral part of a family unit; the stresses of illness, disability, and hospitalization are disruptions for the family as well as for the child; for example, the family's daily routines are altered by trips to the health care setting. The parents' relationship is altered by sleeping arrangements and family responsibilities divided between home and hospital. Siblings experience disruptions as they become secondary to the ill child and are cared for by neighbors or relatives.[32, 35, 38] Hospital bills, medication costs, and time off work result in unusual financial strains on the family. As one child takes on the patient role, other family members shift in their roles and functions within the family.[37] These disruptions in the family's daily living, routines, and roles require adaptation by all members of the family.

Adaptation becomes more complex when the illness represents a chronic condition or disability. The family unit must make ongoing adjustments with each phase of the child's illness.[63] Consider the family in which a child is diagnosed with leukemia. At the time of diagnosis of the disease, there is an acute phase of stress and disequilibrium. The family begins adjusting with the onset of remission of the child's illness. As the remission extends over time, the family adapts; however, disruption occurs again when the child relapses, necessitating adjustment that may be followed by another period of the disease's remission. Stress, disequilibrium, adjustment, and adaptation may take place several times as the disease process and treatments continue.[71, 81]

When the chronic illness or disability extends over months and years, the child and family must make new adjustments and adaptations with each developmental phase through which the child passes.[27, 47, 73] For example, the child with congenital abnormalities must cope with disruptions in daily living resulting from staged surgical corrections, while the evolving processes of body image, sexual identification, self-esteem, and mastery take on different emphases with each stage of psychosexual development. This overlay of illness on developmental behaviors is also seen when the usual storm and stress of adolescence is compounded in the child with diabetes who uses noncompliance with treatment as a vehicle for expressing typical adolescent rebellion.[68]

The parents' feelings of grief and guilt for what the child is, or could have been, further complicate the family's adaptation. The family may mourn the loss of the fantasized child. The family's feelings about the disability and perceptions of the stresses influence its adjustment to the stressors.[63] The support available to the family and the understanding and acceptance of their feelings also influence adaptation.

Adaptation is the end state of adjusting to the changes brought about by the illness, disability, and hospitalization. How the child and family perceive the stress influences their manner of coping. The nurse affects the perceptions, understandings, and responses to stress of the child and family and, subsequently, their adaptation. By providing support and assistance in the mastery of stress, the nurse mediates the adaptive responses of the family. To facilitate this help for the family, the nurse must understand the effects of hospitalization, parent–child attachment, and communication as factors influencing the child at risk.

Hospitalization

Whether as a mental health consultant or as a pediatric clinician, the nurse often becomes involved with a child and family on admission into the hospital. Admissions generally take one of three forms.

1. Emergency admissions for which there is little time for advance preparation
2. Planned admissions for elective events, such as diagnostic work-ups and surgery
3. Episodic admissions; that is, one of multiple hospitalizations for a chronic condition.

Entry into the health care system is a time of stress for the child and family. The amount of stress experienced by the child and family and the opportunities for mediation of the stress vary with the type of admission. The nurse has a greater opportunity to initiate planned interventions with a child's planned or episodic admissions than with emergency admissions.

Admission to the hospital carries the potential for psychological upset, which will have a disruptive effect on the child's development (see insert, The Psychosocial Needs of Children in Hospitals). This disruption, in fact, occurs in

The Psychosocial Needs of Children in Hospitals

A Historical Perspective

Reports of hospital conditions during the first part of the 20th century described stringent aseptic conditions, enforced to counteract the threat of untreatable cross-infections. In these hospitals, children were isolated from one another, contact with staff was restricted, and parents were permitted very limited visiting.

The studies of maternal–child separations in the 1940s by Rene Spitz and Anna Freud brought the term *maternal deprivation* into focus. James Robertson, a colleague of Anna Freud's, applied the study of mother–child separations to hospitalized children. His findings, published in 1958, documented adverse effects of hospitalization on children and brought about reforms in pediatric care in English hospitals.

In the United States, interest in the emotional care of hospitalized children developed throughout the 1950s. Impetus came from the first major United States study to document the psychological effects of hospitalization on children. Conducted by Dane Prugh in Boston, the study found that adverse psychological disturbance resulting from a child's hospitalization could be mediated by unlimited parental visiting, provision of play and preparation programs for children, and support of staff and parents.

Research and clinical concern continued in the 1960s and led to the formation of a multidisciplinary organization focused on the psychosocial needs of children in health care—the Association for the Care of Children in Hospitals. (In 1980, the name of this organization was changed to the Association for the Care of Children's Health to reflect changing patterns of health care, such as the expanded role of outpatient care in chronic illness.)

The thrust of research from the mid-1960s through the 1970s focused on the use of preparation to decrease children's anxiety in health care. Clinical settings also developed or expanded therapeutic play programs as means of providing emotional support to children. The development of the clinical nurse specialist role and primary nursing in pediatrics further strengthened the provision of care based on the developmental needs of children. Research studies by Douglas, reported in 1975, and a supporting study by Quinton and Rutter, documented the prolonged trauma experienced by some children, and identified children at psychiatric risk, as a result of hospitalization.

Unfortunately, the research findings of the past 3 decades have not found uniform expression in the organization and delivery of health care to hospitalized children in the 1980s. Concern for the psychosocial needs of children and families expressed in the provision of play and preparation programs, rooming-in, primary nursing, and clinical nurse specialists have yet to become elements common to all pediatric settings.

about 25% of all pediatric hospitalizations. Children with multiple admissions during the first 4 years of life are the most vulnerable to the effects of psychological upset; however, another 25% of children admitted to the hospital appear to benefit psychologically from hospitalization. The remaining 50% of children admitted into hospitals are neither unusually negatively affected, nor benefited psychologically, by hospitalization.[13, 57, 58, 82]

The statistics just mentioned affirm an imperative of pediatric health care—to examine a child's experiences in hospitalization. The goal of this examination is to minimize the potential negative psychological effects and to maximize the opportunities for psychological benefit from hospitalization. Benefits can occur when the child and family view hospitalization as a stressful event that can result in positive adaptation, an event which can lead to growth in self-confidence, self-esteem, and mastery. As hospitalization supports the physical well-being of the child, it can support, and can, in fact, enhance the child's emotional well-being.

Hospitalization at the time of initial diagnosis of a chronic illness or disability begins the process of adjustment for the family. Whether diagnosis is made at the time of the child's birth or later, the family experiences initial feelings of shock and disbelief. Disruption occurs and adjustment begins. The Rochester Child Health Group conducted extensive studies of families with a child with a chronic condition and families of well children and proposed that early identification of families at risk for successful adaptation is an essential intervention to assist the child with a chronic condition.[64] One scale, devised to detect families at risk rates components of psychosocial family functioning and identifies the following highest risk factors for the family with a chronically ill child.

1. Parental age under 20 years
2. Family income under $5000
3. Parents married less than 2 years
4. Marriage described as weak
5. Child with a chronic condition is their first child
6. Parents having less than high school educations
7. Family having no involvement with the community
8. Maternal grandmother offering no support
9. Husband and wife having had no experience with chronic illness and have negative feelings about chronic conditions[36]

The identification of families at risk turns attention to the child who is hospitalized.

Parent–Child Attachment

Research evidence clearly indicates the necessity for the presence of the child's primary emotional support figure during the child's hospitalization.[9, 61, 72] The anxiety aroused in the child by unfamiliar surroundings, people, and painful events is secondary to the anxiety aroused by separation from the child's primary object relation. Although this is evident for young children, it is also applicable to older children for whom regression is a normal response to the physical and emotional demands of illness and hospitalization.[15] Providing emotional support to the child must first include efforts to continue the support provided by the child's primary attachment. Except in unusual instances, this primary attachment is to the parents, particularly the mother.

On admission of the child into health care, the nurse plays an important role in the continuance of the parent–child attachment. The nurse explains to the parents the need for *rooming-in;* that is, allowing the parents unlimited stay in the child's room. The nurse refers the parents to the social work department to acquire financial assistance, or to other services, such as child care, that will make the parent's rooming-in possible.

After assuring continuation of the parent–child attachment, the nurse next directs her efforts toward decreasing the parents' anxiety. Young children mirror the anxiety of their parents. Interventions to reduce the parents' distress result in the reduction of a child's anxiety.[70]

The nursing process is based on the child's needs and the parents' ability to meet the health care and emotional needs of their child. This is not always as easy as it appears. The nurse continually examines her personal feelings toward the parents. For example, it may be easier to provide comfort and support to a 2-year-old child who has ingested cleaning fluid than to be supportive of the negligent parents; however, the parents' perceptions of health care, formulated during this initial hospitalization, will influence the family's positive adaptation to future multiple admissions, surgical procedures, and clinic visits. The acceptance and support offered to the parents by the nurse help them clarify their own feelings of guilt. This may lead to greater receptiveness to the nurse's instructions for home care and to role modeling and education promoting more effective parenting, limit-setting, and discipline for their child.

The nurse who does not acknowledge her own feelings of blame toward the parents may unconsciously exclude them from participation in the child's physical and emotional care. As the parents become increasingly uncomfortable in the climate provided by the nurse, they may withdraw from the nurse's efforts at instruction and, perhaps, withdraw from their child. By ignoring or discounting feelings evoked by the parents, the nurse unwittingly sabotages her own efforts to implement the nursing process and to promote the child's adaptation.

Communication

The nurse conveys attitudes and feelings that influence the behavior of the recipients of care. Communication is a key element in caring for children at risk from illness, disability, and hospitalization.[1, 39] Verbal communications convey warmth, acceptance, empathy, and caring; however, the communication of these attitudes through nonverbal means is more important.

The nurse has many functions and duties to perform in pediatrics. These activities include the administration of drugs, therapies, treatments, and other tasks relating to machines and equipment. How the nurse performs these functions communicates a level of caring that influences the child's and family's coping. For instance, the necessary physical restraint of a child during a lumbar puncture can convey caring and support of the child's efforts, however limited, for self-control, or can indicate punitive retaliation against the child's actions, which are judged as willfully immature and hostile. The difference is observed in the nurse's physical handling of the child, tone of voice, and facial expressions. Through these communications, the nurse can convey a supportive, humanistic concern for the child as a person or can convey a mechanical, task-oriented outlook, in which the child is perceived as an object to be controlled. The former attitude is health-inducing, because it promotes the child's coping with stress; the latter attitude, in its dehumanization of the child, adds to the child's psychological stress and places the child at further risk.

Successful communication with a child and family is built on an understanding of their problems, needs, and strengths obtained from the nursing assessment, and on the recognition and acceptance of personal feelings and attitudes.

Application of the Nursing Process to the Child at Risk Due to Illness, Disability, and Hospitalization

Each child and family are different from all others. Each course of hospitalization of a child differs from others. There are many physical diagnoses and concomitant treatments. The degree of physical disability and psychological distress resulting from illness varies from child to child.

The complexity of facts and possibilities and the feelings they arouse may overwhelm us; however, by keeping the goal—minimizing psychosocial distress in pediatric nursing—in focus, the nurse maintains and acts on the commitment to children at risk from illness, disability, and hospitalization. The nurse assists the child's and family's positive adaptation by performing tasks within the perspective of providing emotional support. The nursing process provides a framework within which information is organized and nursing intervention is planned.

Assessment of the Child and Analysis of Data

The nurse has an opportunity to assist the child and family in defining the stressors as opportunities for growth, rather than as events that are overwhelming, beyond personal control, and leading to disorganization and disturbance. How the nurse best supports the child's positive adaptation is addressed through the nursing process, beginning with the first step, assessment.

The goal of assessment is to gather and organize information in such a way that it assists the nurse in caring for the child at risk in health care. The assessment incorporates information about both the child and the family and about the resources available in the health care setting (see insert, Assessment Outline).

Developmental Level

The assessment of the child begins with an understanding of the child's developmental level. What psychosocial issues is the child dealing with? How does the child process events and information? What fears, general and specific to health care, are typical of children at a particular age?[3] (See insert, Common Fears and Anxieties of Children in Health Care.) Chronological age, combined with an understanding of theories of psychosexual, ego, and cognitive development, provide guidelines for nursing assessment.[16, 21, 22, 28, 52]

Environmental Influences

Environmental influences affecting the child's response to the stresses of illness, disability, and hospitalization are assessed by gathering information about the child's specific illness or disability, the child's previous life experiences, and the child's family.

Nature of the Illness or Disability. Research has not substantiated a causal relationship between a specific illness or disability and a psychological disorder in a child. Nevertheless, knowledge about specific diagnoses does provide the nurse with information about the typical kind of hospitalization that is required, treatments that are prescribed, and medical events that the child will encounter. Furthermore, the nurse's knowledge of the illness or disability gives

Assessment Outline

I. Assessment of the child
   A. Developmental level
   B. Environmental influences
      1. Specific illness or disability
      2. Child's previous life experiences
      3. Child's family
   C. Idiosyncratic (personal) attributes
II. Assessment of the health care setting
   A. Resources in the physical environment
   B. Departmental and program resources
   C. Resources in the affective environment

Common Fears and Anxieties of Children in Health Care

Developmental Phase	Fears, Anxieties
Infancy	Separation anxiety
Toddlers	Separation anxiety
	Fear of the unknown
	Fear of strangers
Preschool Ages	Separation anxiety
	Anxiety about body intrusions, intense need for body intactness
	Anxieties aroused by egocentric thought, fantasies, magical thinking
	Fear of punishment aroused by guilt, as child feels he is the cause of the illness or disability
	Fear of body mutilation
Schoolage	Fear of body injury
	Fear of pain
	Fear of loss of respect, love, and emerging self-esteem
	Anxiety related to guilt continues
	Fear of anesthesia
Adolescence	Fear of loss of identity and control
	Anxiety about body image and changes in physical appearance
	Fear of loss of status in peer group
	Anxiety related to long-term implications of illness or disability

her indications about the pain and physical discomfort, about the type and number of intrusive procedures that the child will experience, and about the changes in the child's appearance—outward physical signs of the disease or disability and required treatments—to which the child and family must adjust.[55, 66, 78]

The nature of the child's illness or disability gives the nurse information about the acuteness or chronicity involved, information about the probable number of hospital admissions required, and some indication of prognosis for life expectancy. This and other information related to a specific illness or disability has implications for the nurse in planning and carrying out interventions to support the child's adaptation.

Previous Life Experiences. The child's response to the stress of illness and hospitalization at a given point in time is influenced by prior experiences, particularly those perceived as stressful. For some young children, hospitalization may be the first stressful experience encountered by the child and family. The repertoire of responses and skills available to the child will therefore be limited because there has been little prior need for, or practice with, responding to stress.

Other children may have had many opportunities to develop coping skills in response to stress. The child whose family moved a great distance 2 months prior to the child's hospitalization, or whose mother began full-time work after giving birth to the family's second child, will certainly have had practice with coping. Despite their suggested callousing effects, these recent changes in the child's life may intensify the child's vulnerability and feeling of insecurity.

Previous stressful life experiences may influence the child's perception of the immediate stress. What, for example, is the possible meaning of hospitalization to a 10-year-old girl whose maternal aunt died in a hospital, 3 months prior, with cancer? Knowing about the child's previous life experiences, perceived as stressful by the child and family, assists the nurse in understanding the child's responses to the immediate stress and impacts the nurse's plans and interventions.

The Child's Family. The greatest environmental influence in the life of a child is the child's family. The family constellation, the ability to organize daily activities, the socioeconomic level, the cultural–ethnic makeup, and the previous life experiences of the family have implications for the delivery of nursing care to the child. Several of these factors relate to the child's vulnerability to psychological disturbance resulting from hospitalization. For example, children from chaotic, disorganized families experiencing chronic family stresses—referred to as families with high psychosocial disadvantage—have the greatest risk for psychiatric disturbance resulting from hospitalization.[13, 58]

Assessment of the family's cultural–ethnic orientation has obvious implications for the delivery of nursing care.[7, 34] What language does the family speak? What language can they read? Can they understand the language that the nurse speaks? Perhaps less obvious are the cultural implications for behavioral responses to health care. For example, in families with strong hispanic orientations, it is more difficult for a mother to remain with her child in the hospital and to make decisions if she is not accompanied by her husband.[40]

The religious orientation of families and strong ties with a particular religion influence a family's perceptions and coping with stresses of illness. For example, the refusal of blood transfusions by members of Jehovah's Witnesses may complicate medical care and increase the anxiety of staff, which, in turn, compounds the stress of the family.

The previous life experiences of the family will alert the nurse to changes to which the family may still be adjusting and which may have depleted their resources for dealing with the stress of the child's illness. Of particular concern is information about loss and grief. Is the family mourning the illness or death of a significant person at the time of the child's hospitalization? How emotionally available are the parents and family members to the child as the child experiences the stresses of illness, disability, and hospitalization?

> The mother of an 18-month-old child was observed sleeping throughout the remainder of the day of the child's admission to the hospital and the following day. The mother seldom roused when the child cried or fretted. In talking with the mother, the nurse explored possible reasons for the extended sleep.
>
> Suspecting a depressive reaction, the nurse questioned the mother about recent events in the family's life. Although there had not been other illness in the family, the mother's aunt, a close emotional support to her, had died immediately in a car accident 2 days previously. This information not only assisted the nurse's assessment and plans for care of the child, it also facilitated the nurse's interaction with, and personal reactions to, the family. The information enabled the nurse to extend empathy and acceptance to the mother, rather than to judge her a "bad" mother because she was unresponsive to her child.

Idiosyncratic (Personal) Attributes of the Child

Assessment of the developmental level of the child and the environmental influences on the child must be augmented with an understanding of the child as an individual. What is the temperament and personality of the child?[79] Does the child typically move toward new experiences or is he shy?

What is the child's pain tolerance?[66] What coping mechanisms does he use to defend against stress?[88] What words does the child use to refer to body parts and functions? Does the child have a transitional object that provides comfort such as a blanket or doll? What are the child's preferences—dietary, play activities, nap and bedtime routines? By what name does the child prefer to be called? What was the child like prior to the illness; that is, his premorbid personality? Answers to these questions will be unique to each child. Gathering and analyzing information about the child specific to his personality and temperament increases the nurse's understanding of the child and the child's responses to the stressors in illness, disability, and hospitalization. It also allows the nurse to implement nursing actions in ways that minimize the strangeness of the health care setting and convey to the child and family the nurse's deep commitment to the child as a person, not an object, in health care.

The nurse analyzes the assessment data to determine the health problems of child and family and to formulate nursing diagnoses. Analysis also helps the nurse understand and clarify personal feelings toward a child and family. Understanding that a child's physical expression of anger is a typical response of 2-year-olds, that a child's refusal to find comfort in the nurse's arms is usual when he is initially reacting to separation anxiety, and that this particular child is described as "a difficult baby" by the mother helps the nurse remain supportive of the child. Through understanding based on assessment of the child, the nurse remains supportive, rather than withdrawing due to personalizing the child's rejection of her nursing efforts.

Assessment of the Health Care Setting

The Physical Environment

A final aspect of assessment that influences the implementation of the nursing process is the health care setting's ability to meet the psychosocial needs of the child and family. What resources are provided by the physical environment?[46] What departmental or program resources are available? Finally, what is the affective environment of the health care setting? The assessment of the child and family, combined with an assessment of the health care setting's ability to provide for the needs of the child, impact the plans and interventions of the nurse.

No setting is ideal. All hospitals and health care settings have assets and limitations that affect the delivery of care to patients. One setting may be particularly supportive of the needs of young children, but meet few of the typical needs of adolescents. For example, the pediatric unit may have a large playroom but no space that affords privacy or peer interaction for the teenagers. If there are limited provisions for rooming-in, what will the nurse have to do to make the parent comfortably available to the child? If there is not a playroom on the pediatric unit, what can the nurse improvise as space for children to be actively engaged in constructive play?

Department and Program Resources

Departments within the health care setting offer resources the nurse utilizes in planning care. For example, the dietary department assists in meal planning to meet individual preferences; this will both enhance the child's nutritional intake and provide more familiar, comfortable mealtimes. The social work department provides financial referrals for families and support and counseling for parents. The child life–child development department (sometimes known as play therapy or children's activities departments) provides developmental assessments, supervised play and activities based on assessments, and support for children's understanding and mastery of the health care experience. The volunteer department is available as "parent surrogates" for children whose parents must return to work. Foster grandparent programs are used in this capacity in many children's hospitals in the United States.

The Affective Environment

A final consideration is the affective environment of the health care setting. Does the formal philosophy of the health care setting and nursing department emphasize the psychosocial needs of children and families? Does the informal group attitude welcome parents or feel they are a nuisance? How much support will the nurse receive from the other staff and departments as she tries to meet the psychosocial needs of families?[5] The answers to these questions help the nurse plan for the time and energy she must expend as she integrates psychosocial care into the physical care of children.

Planning

Development of Trust, Understanding, and Mastery

Treatment plans are drawn from the information provided in the assessment of the child and family and the health care setting. The process of planning includes setting of goals, utilization of resources, and discharge planning.

Three concepts are common to the processes involved in planning for the child at risk—trust, understanding, and mastery. If the nurse uses these concepts in planning and organizing interventions, the psychosocial needs of the child and family will be integrated into nursing care.

The nurse must ask, How can I assist in the child's and family's development of trust? How can I assist in their understanding? How can I assist in their development of mastery of the stresses they encounter in health care? What goals can I establish around these concepts? How can I plan to utilize the resources available to assist in their trust, understanding, and mastery? What discharge plans are necessary to continue their mastery? These concepts of trust, understanding, and mastery are essential to nursing planning and interventions that support psychosocial needs.

Goal-Setting

Without goals, the nurse has limited knowledge and direction with regards to where the nursing process is going. Although treatment plans for physical care of pediatric diagnoses may be standardized in some settings, plans for psychosocial care cannot be standardized. The interplay between the diagnosis, the child, the family, and the health care setting necessitates individualization of treatment plans. The nurse plans the performance of required physical care in an emotionally supportive manner.

Although treatment plans should not be standardized, they should share some common goals. The primary goal should be to minimize the potential for psychosocial disturbance in the child as the state of physical health is being restored or supported. A second goal should be to maximize the opportunities for psychosocial benefit as the state of the child's physical well-being is restored or supported. A further goal common to treatment plans in pediatrics should be the provision of assistance to the child's development of trust, understanding, and mastery of the stressful experiences in health care.

Goals specific to an individual child, which may lead to positive adaptation, should also be made in the planning process. These goals should include the utilization of resources available in the health care setting.

> A 5-year-old child is admitted for intravenous antibiotic therapy to treat cystic fibrosis. The admission is one of many admissions the child has experienced; the hospital and treatment are familiar to the child; however, the child has great difficulty with intrusive procedures. As the nurse plans for the child's care, a specific goal for this child will be "to develop positive coping with intrusive procedures." Resources available in this particular setting that the nurse plans to utilize are primary nursing assignments and the child life–child development program.

Primary nursing facilitates the child's development of trust. The formation of a therapeutic alliance with the primary nurse assists the child in perceiving intrusive procedures as necessary steps to feeling better, rather than as retaliation or punishment. The child life–child development program provides unhurried opportunities for the child to play out feelings and anxieties aroused by medical procedures. This play, often referred to as *medical play*, facilitates the child's mastery of aggressive, angry feelings. The presence of the child life specialist during medical play provides support and boundaries for the child's expression of feelings.

Discharge Planning

Discharge planning begins with the assessment of the child and continues throughout hospitalization. For example, instructing parents in home care is most successful when a therapeutic alliance has been formed with the family, a process which begins on admission. The child's specific illness or disability may dictate particular referrals needed.

Informing the child and family about the referral, the particular agency, or the treatment provides preparation for discharge. Discharge planning also includes preparing the family for changes in the child's behavior, those that are specific to the diagnosis or expected as common reactions to hospitalization.[19] Discharge plans should also include follow-up contact to assess the child's adjustment and any concerns of the parents.

Finally, discharge planning should include the concept of closure; that is, the ending of an experience marked by a sense of resolution, which can include feelings expressed by the individuals toward one another. This is particularly important for a child who has experienced a lengthy hospitalization. Closure of the hospital experience gives the child permission to move on in the process of adaptation—to move back into the family and home and other relationships while retaining the esteem of the people left behind in the health care setting.

> A simple closure device is saying to the child, "John, you have done it! You have been here with people you didn't know and you had things done to you that hurt. But you did it! And you made new friends in the playroom, you painted your mom some pictures, and you took your medicine which helped you feel better. And now you get to go home. You did it! And you helped me and the doctor help your kidney. Thank you!!"

This small speech, accompanied by a congratulatory handshake, conveys a strong message of mastery to a 7-year-old, yet takes very little time from the nurse's busy routines.

Intervention

Nursing interventions to support a child at risk due to illness, disability, and hospitalization are directed to

1. external or environmental factors, which influence the child and family's experience of the stressors;
2. influencing the child and family's perceptions of the stressful experience (see insert, Family-to-Family Support).

The concepts of trust, understanding, and mastery are applied to both internal and external factors. For example, providing rooming-in for the parent of a 4-year-old, an environmental intervention, enhances the child's ability to trust. Providing the child with preparation for surgery enhances the child's understanding and mastery by influencing the way in which the child thinks and feels about the surgical procedure.[75]

Setting Priorities

Nurses establish priorities based on the assessment, goals, and plans for individual patients. Establishing priorities gives the nurse a guide and mandate for allocating the resources of time and energy. The nurse's priorities should reflect the degree of vulnerability of a child for psychosocial disturbance in illness, disability, and hospitalization. Children most vulnerable to psychiatric disturbances are those

Family-to-Family Support

A diagnosis such as *diabetes* may be perceived as devastating by one family. The child is viewed as a normal child no longer. The parents respond with overprotectiveness, hovering, and restricting the child's activity. When introduced to another family who has a similar-aged child with the same diagnosis, the newly-diagnosed family has a model of coping on which to base their understanding of what can be reasonably expected for their child. They can see that their child, in fact, can continue usual activities just as the other child has done.

This parent-to-parent support can be utilized in many situations of different diagnoses. Careful assessment of the families should be made to assure their positive potential. Some settings utilize parent support groups and provide training to parent models to increase their effectiveness with families of children newly diagnosed with illness or disability.

in the first 4 years of life who have had multiple hospital admissions and who are from psychosocially disadvantaged families. These children should have the greatest allocation of the nurse's time and energy that can be devoted to psychosocial care. Needless to say, these priorities must coincide with the priorities for required physical care.

Other priorities are those children, of any age, who are assessed as vulnerable to stress in illness, disability, and hospitalization. Vulnerability is seen in the following.

Children who have recently experienced severe stress, such as a death in the family, parents' divorce, or parental illness

Children who have experienced a recent series of stressful events

Children who are in mild to moderate psychological distress prior to the hospital admission

Children who cannot understand communication as it is usually performed in the health care setting, who communicate in another language, or who have severe hearing or visual deficits

Children who have limited life experiences and limited repertoires of behaviors with which to respond to stress

Children who have experienced recent illness or hospitalization that may or may not be related to the present condition

Children who have defects from birth such as blindness or deafness[2, 65]

Finally, the nurse considers as priorities those interventions that, for all patients, will be growth-producing.[56, 77, 83] The child's psychosocial growth is enhanced as the child experiences positive adjustment to the stresses of illness, disability, and hospitalization.

Not all nursing interventions can be planned in advance; some take place in an acute, crisis manner. As the nurse gains experience working with children at risk, greater flexibility in intervening in acute, emergency situations will result. Nevertheless, the nurse must first have a firm commitment to, and understanding of, the possible and desirable interventions.

A 6-year-old with esophageal varices began hemorrhaging. The child was alert as the 'stat' call was made; the room filled with staff and a cardiac monitor was rushed in. The child looked at the monitor, which had not yet been activated, and cried out in extreme fear "I'm dying! I'm dead! The line is straight, the line is straight!!"

Those participating in this acute emergency will certainly be sensitive to the need for simple explanations in future emergencies when the child is alert and aware of the activities.

In a global sense, and in each specific instance, the nurse must ask, How can I promote this child's development of trust, understanding, and mastery? These three concepts will be used to organize nursing interventions.

Interventions to Support and Develop Trust

Interventions to support and develop trust involve external factors, such as changes in the physical environment, in conjunction with interpersonal behaviors, such as communication. The nature and flavor of the interventions vary according to the assessment data. Development of trust with a 15-month-old focuses on the presence of the parenting figure; development of trust with a 15-year-old depends on verbal communications and their congruence with nonverbal messages.

Interventions in the physical environment include the following.

Maintenance of tie with primary emotional support figures (rooming-in)

Continuity of care in nursing assignments, particularly primary nursing

Maintenance of tie with family (sibling visiting)

Maintenance of tie with peer group, for older children and adolescents

Structuring delivery of care so that intrusive procedures are not done in the patient's bed or in the patient's room

Structuring delivery of care so that as many routines and rituals associated with activities of daily living as possible (meals, naps, bathing, bedtime, and so forth) can be continued during hospitalization.

Nursing interventions to support trust, which are based on interpersonal behaviors, include the following.

Spending nonstructured, non-task-oriented time with child patient and parents

Postponing intrusive procedures, whenever possible, until the child and parents recognize the nurse as a trusted individual

Communicating openness and "trustworthiness" through nonverbal signals and congruence of verbal and nonverbal messages

Using communication skills of active listening, inviting requests, attending, showing warmth, self-disclosure, and feedback

Interventions to Support and Develop Understanding

Developing and supporting the child's and family's understanding directly affects their levels of stress as the nurse mediates their perceptions of the stressors. Observation of young children in health care shows that their fantasies of what will happen are often more frightening than the real events. Through preparation the child learns about the reality—what the child will see, hear, feel, and be expected to do. Sensory preparation has been found to be successful in decreasing children's anxiety during health care procedures.[30] Sensory preparation is preparation that imparts information about what will be felt, seen, and heard.

The nurse reduces the child's anxiety by relating to his concrete feelings rather than explaining the medical routines. For example, an explanation of what happens during the surgery is not appropriate, because the child will not feel during this time. Explaining that a mist that feels cool and soft will be blowing in his face when he awakens after surgery is important, however. Experiencing the feeling of the mist during presurgery preparation enhances sensory preparation for the child.

Understanding, developed through preparation and patient education, has been extensively reported in research and clinical literature.[51, 82, 85, 87] Interventions to promote understanding include the following.

Preadmission preparation[18, 68]

Stress-point preparation, which is preparation immediately before each potentially stressful experience such as injections, venipunctures, or going to a new location in the hospital[85]

Preparation for diagnostic procedures[14]

Preparation for surgical procedures[75]

Patient education to teach child and parents about inpatient and home care; for example, teaching a child newly diagnosed with diabetes to give insulin[48]

The nurse integrates the concept of developing understanding through preparation into all nursing tasks. This means that at each point of potential stress, the nurse will give the child some advance knowledge of what to expect, particularly what the child will feel. How the nurse presents the information depends on the child's cognitive development, what the child can expect sensorially, and a brief explanation of why.

The question of "why" is important to interventions to develop understanding, for the child as well as for parents and other family members. Children's concepts of illness and causality follow developmental trends aligned with cognitive development as described by Piaget.[6, 11, 49] Additionally, a child's definition of illness is somewhat dependent on his mother's understanding of the illness and her previous health care experiences.[42] This means that young children functioning at the concrete operational level need brief, specific, unambiguous, object-related explanations of why things are being done to them.

Older children who can grasp cause and effect relationships will benefit from simple analogies.[54] Adolescents who have begun abstract thinking may require more detailed information with explanations of the implications of the treatment. Giving suitable explanations for health care events lets the child understand that there is a plan for his care, that he is not being subjected to disturbing events at the whim of more powerful individuals, and that there are boundaries and limits that are known and shared. The impact of regression in health care must also be considered in the child's understanding. It is not unusual for individuals to regress to a lower level of cognition during stress.[8]

A further aspect of interventions to support understanding relates to the structuring of events.[86] As much as possible, the nurse should structure routines of care to follow a course that can be made known to the child. It is desirable, wherever possible, to follow routines the child experiences at home. For school-aged children, simple charts of the daily activities and calendars to mark the days and special events will help them understand the process and reinforce the ending of the hospitalization.

By developing a child's understanding of what is to happen, when it is to happen, and why, the nurse intervenes in the child's perception of the stress. Fantasies become anchored in reality. Overwhelming fear of the unknown becomes a manageable known. Parents' perceptions take on more realistic concerns, thereby decreasing the anxiety they project to the child.

A wide array of media has been developed for pediatric preparation and patient–parent education. These media include movies, filmstrips, coloring books, and children's books. Although there is still much to be researched in the use of media for preparation of children for health care events, those materials that most closely approximate the reality and provide behavioral modeling for the child most effectively decrease children's anxiety.[43]

Interventions to Support and Develop Mastery

A final group of interventions uses the development of trust and understanding to activate the child's coping with stressors. *Mastery* is the term that describes the positive coping with stress, which encourages adaptation.

Illness, disability, and hospitalization present as life crises, events that disrupt reality as experienced by the child and family. These life events involve changes to which the child must react. Coping is the process, or series of steps and sequences, through which the child comes to terms with the changes in reality. Coping devices are the choices in ways of using resources, new structures, and integrations developed by the child to respond to the changes in the environment. Defense mechanisms are also part of the overall coping effort.[63]

Changes and stressors in the environment demand coping of the child. Adaptation is the result of coping, a return to equilibrium. Mastery is positive adaptation; it is the successful use of coping devices to come to terms with the environment. Mastery is the child's ability to respond to, and use, the environment constructively.[26, 44, 45]

One of the early studies of coping with psychosocial stress in illness involved patients, of all ages, in a medical center for polio care.[84] Effective coping was found to be patterns of behavior, thoughts, feelings, and actions, that facilitate one or more of the following functions.

1. Keeping distress within manageable limits
2. Generating encouragement and hope
3. Maintaining or restoring a sense of personal worth
4. Maintaining or restoring relations with significant others
5. Enhancing prospects for physical recovery
6. Enhancing prospects for favorable situations—interpersonal, social, economic—after maximum physical recovery has been attained

In one study of chronic illness in children, four adaptive patterns were identified in children, from the onset of their illnesses, who did not develop debilitating psychological symptoms during the course of their diseases. These adaptive patterns were

1. intellectualization;
2. identification with medical staff;
3. denial in the service of hope;
4. idiosyncratic rituals.[25]

Interventions to support these adaptive patterns from the onset of the illness or disability lead to mastery. *Intellectualization* involves the sense of organization it contributes to the ego's assimilation of anxiety (see insert, Supporting Children's Use of Intellectualization). *Identification with medical staff*, when combined with intellectualization, fosters a strong desire to care for one's own body.

> Identification is seen when a child develops a trusting bond with a particular nurse. The child likes the nurse and knows from pleasurable interchanges between them that the nurse likes him. Because this nurse believes a particular treatment will be helpful to him and his body, the child, too, adopts this belief and wants to do what will help him.

Supporting Children's Use of Intellectualization

A common misconception of young children is that they have somehow caused their illness.[15, 49] Telling the child many times, in different ways, that she did not cause the illness develops appropriate intellectualization, which reduces guilt and anxiety.

A 3-year-old playing with a doll picked it up, gave it a big swat on the bottom and said, "You've been bad! You have to go to the hospital!" An observing health care provider said to the child and her mother, "Lots of children think they have been bad and that's why they come to the hospital. But you know, you haven't been bad; those other kids haven't been bad. You came to the hospital so your hurt in your stomach would be helped to go away. Your mother knows you weren't bad. She brought you to the hospital so we can help you feel better and help the hurt go away." The mother then picked up the child and gave her a big hug, echoing these statements and adding, "Mommy and Daddy love you." Later, the child was playing with the doll and imitated the words and actions of the mother. This child was using intellectualization; that is, thinking about her experience in ways appropriate to her developmental level, as a coping mechanism.

Intellectualization in an older child was graphically illustrated when an 11-year-old requested that pictures be taken of him while he underwent a lumbar puncture. Previously, he had great difficulty with the procedure, was uncooperative, and could not maintain positioning. He could not mentally visualize what was being done to him. The pictures provided him with a device for seeing what was being done, thinking about what was happening, and understanding why positioning and his cooperation were important. The pictures were additionally important as concrete means to think about the experience after it was over and develop mastery. For several days after the procedure, the boy would say to adults entering his room, "Say, do you want to see what I did?" He would then display his pictures with pride at his accomplishment.

Denial in the service of hope alleviates the painful external reality of sickness and allows courage and hope to assist the endurance of unreasonable suffering.

Idiosyncratic rituals are patterns of behavior developed by children to cope, or get through, particular aspects of illness or treatments. The rituals serve to bind staff and patient together in a shared, nonpathological routine. Unless the ritual self-destructively interferes with the patient's care, the staff should not disrupt the rituals because they offer a playful, yet formalized, sequence that provides boundaries for the child's anxiety. The ritual enhances the child's feeling of belongingness and of personal distinctiveness.

A 6-year-old having difficulty with intravenous injections begins chanting, "I think I can, I think I can, I think I can," when he sits down in the treatment room and continues this chant throughout the procedure. This chant is taken from the children's book, *The Little Engine That Could.* At the conclusion of procedures, the child and nurse exclaim together, "I knew I could!" This ritual is repeated whenever the child has intravenous infusions started. It brings shared mastery to the child and nurse, as well as recognition and praise for the child's attempts to hold his arm immobile and cooperate as a team member in his physical care.

Another example of rituals is one hospital's use of finger puppets. Laboratory technicians follow finger sticks for blood tests with the presentation of a finger puppet to be worn over the child's bandaid. If the technician forgets, children often remind the technician and ask for the puppet. The finger puppet is a pleasurable, ritualized ending to this procedure.

In considering these adaptive patterns of behavior that allow the child to manage and master the changes in the environment, one sees that the patterns relate both to the internal and external perceptions. Interventions may support mastery through mediating the child's internal environment or external, physical environment. Play is a most useful means for supporting mastery. Provision for a child's play becomes an essential intervention in the nursing process.

Play. What is play? It is not the equivalent of adult recreation.

"The playing adult," says Erikson, "steps sideward into another reality; the playing child advances forward to new stages of mastery. I propose the theory that the child's play is the infantile form of the human ability to deal with experience by creating model situations and to master reality by experiment and planning."[16]

Play, he further states, is "an indispensable harbor," one that is used for "overhauling of shattered emotions after periods of rough going in the social seas." Play is a device for mastery of anxiety-producing aspects of hospitalization and illness or disability. Piaget views play as a means of assimilation. New experiences, such as the stressful events of illness, are assimilated and accommodated into the child's structure.[53] One study looked specifically at the use of play in hospitals by children 3 to 8 years of age. The youngest children first established a trusting relationship

Reinforcing the Child's Self-Esteem

"Amy, I know it hurts you to have your injections. When you held your leg still, counted to three, squeezed your mom's hand, and said, 'Ouchie!' you helped me! Thank you!!"

It is not uncommon to observe children's anger expressed in play. Children will say to a doll, "I'm the nurse and I'm going to give you a shot. Don't you cry or I'll give you another one!" The nurse who observes such expressed anger may feel dismay to realize her careful support of the child has, seemingly, gone unrecognized by the child.

However, what is really happening is ventilation of natural anger and retaliation in an acceptable way. It is important to know that children do have anger, should be allowed to express it, and that it need not represent a personal rejection of the nurse's efforts. If one finds it difficult to accept the display of children's anger, the nurse might need to question her personal support system and look for ways to feel good about herself that are not dependent on a child's total acceptance.

In one setting where psychosocial care is a priority, the nurses try to have some pleasant physical interaction with young children after an invasive procedure. The nurse will say, "Judy, I know the needle I gave you hurt. I wish I didn't have to hurt you but that is the only way to give this medicine. Now that the hurt is over, can I give you a hug? I want to help you feel good, too." Most children eagerly and positively respond to this request. Parents also seem to appreciate this extra display of caring for their child. Occasionally, a child will refuse. If the nurse takes this refusal as a personal rejection, further distress is placed on the child. When the nurse accepts the child's refusal and says "That's o.k., Judy, some other time maybe we can do something nice together—when you want to," the nurse conveys a deep acceptance of the child as an individual, as well as a belief in the child's basic worth, and hope for a better time to come for them.

---

with the adult in the play setting and then moved to manipulation of toy objects. Older children used toys rather than the adult to orient, establish familiarity, and then achieve pleasure in the mastery of function. Once familiarity was established, they moved into supportive peer play.[80]

The play environment and the child's use of play can be used in assessment and to support trust and understanding.[76] Play interventions support mastery by affording the child the opportunity to be actively involved in structuring, controlling, and recreating the stresses of the hospital and illness events. This is most dramatically seen in the use of *medical play*, dramatic play using props of real medical equipment in which the child plays about being a patient and a caregiver. When this play is nondirective (*i.e.*, not designed toward a specific learning objective), the process of mastery is facilitated.

Expression of Feelings. Other interventions that support mastery encourage and allow the child's expression of feelings through art, storytelling, the use of children's books, and peer-group discussions.[17, 20, 29, 62, 67] Efforts to facilitate communication between parents and child in order to overcome the "conspiracy of silence" lead to shared mastery of feelings.

Positive Feedback to Child and Family. The nurse further supports mastery through interventions that mediate the child's self-esteem. The Roy Adaptation Nursing Model discusses this as interventions in the self-concept mode.[60] One's self-concept is determined through interactions with others. The nurse intervenes through positive feedback to

the child and family about their successes, however small (see insert, Reinforcing the Child's Self-Esteem).

School Activities. Providing school activities for the child while hospitalized or homebound builds the child's self-esteem as he successfully learns new academic skills and information. Provision of school activities is an intervention in the physical environment that enhances the internal perceptions of the child.

Helping Families at Risk. An additional intervention that enhances mastery has been identified from research on the effects of chronic illness and disability.[64] Three interventions found beneficial in decreasing risk to the child's adjustment to chronic conditions and development include the following.

1. Early identification of families at risk; for example, families with low functioning are two times as likely to have a child whose adjustment to illness is poor, as compared to other families of children with chronic conditions

2. Determining and making known to the family and health care staff the individual in charge; that is, the primary orchestrator of the child's care

3. Provision of an "outreach person" to meet the needs of the family on an intensive, sustained, caring, and creative basis.

This outreach individual influences the child's and family's perceptions of themselves and gives support and feedback on their successes in coping with specific stressors. Through her role in a specialty clinic, the nurse may function as this person or the nurse may advocate and demonstrate the need for such a person in the child's health care.

Evaluation

The final component of the nursing process, evaluation, is actually an ongoing process that begins with the child's entry into the health care system. Evaluation serves as a "feedback loop" for the nursing process. At any point in the process, or system, evaluation is used to determine the success or correctness of other parts of the system.

Evaluation in the nursing process is based on observation and analysis. Observing a child's behavior and analyzing it and thinking about its meaning and probable causes confirms or modifies the analysis of assessment data and subsequent plans. Evaluating the child's response to interventions may lead to developing other interventions, planning the continuation of present interventions, or developing a new plan of care.

Self-Reflection

Evaluation also offers the nurse an opportunity for self-reflection. How am I doing? How do I feel? How am I coping? What stresses am I experiencing in working with this child and family? The use of self as a therapeutic tool in working with the child at risk is a primary organizing factor in the nursing process. The self as an open, accepting, and warm person actualizes the development of trust. Understanding, developed through preparation, depends on clear, appropriate communication between the nurse and child and family. Ego strength in the nurse is necessary to allow, and accept, the child's negative feelings.

At times, the nurse's defense mechanisms may aid in coping. At other times, their use may interfere with her personal coping and with assisting the child and family in positive coping. An example of this interference is the nurse's use of denial of pain when, in truth, bearing the child's pain is difficult for her. When a nurse says to a child, "There, that was just a little stick. It didn't really hurt so bad. Don't cry," she is really saying that she hates to hurt children, please don't cry, because then she will have to face the fact that she did hurt the child. The nurse is really saying, "Please help me continue my denial of this unpleasant part of my job." The nurse must continually evaluate the effectiveness of her defense or coping mechanisms and processes.

Working with ill or disabled children in a hospital or health care setting can be emotionally painful and draining. There are times of helplessness—the child's physical pain continues, the disability cannot be reversed, the progress of the disease cannot be arrested, perhaps death is an approaching reality. Anger is a natural expression of helplessness. How and where the nurse directs anger is important to consider. Evaluating one's professional and personal effectiveness is enhanced by awareness of other defensive or coping mechanisms such as denial, repression, projection, intellectualization, and overidentification.

Need for Personal and Professional Supports

Working with children can stir up the "child" in each of us. Unresolved issues in our developmental past may be brought into preconscious awareness and may evoke unpleasant feelings. Acknowledging and accepting these feelings, understanding one's self, and developing personal support systems and professional support systems within the work setting aid in the process of caring for children at risk.[5]

The Nurse's Role As an Advocate

Knowledge of the psychosocial needs of children in health care has progressed, whereas the application of such knowledge has lagged behind. What are the explanations for this lag? The primary reason is that health care systems are bureaucracies and change is always slow. Decisions about the allocation of funds and resources are frequently made by individuals far removed from the literature and research findings. The medical model, built on concrete observations and manipulation of observable data, is frequently resistant to the "soft" sciences. Changing routines of care to meet psychosocial needs of children acknowledges that the provision of health care can be detrimental to children's development; those caring for children are reluctant to admit that while helping, they do inflict pain. Regardless of these and other explanations, the need to provide for the psychosocial requirements of children and families exists. As an advocate, the nurse educates about, facilitates, and models more effective care of individual children and all children in health care.

Advocacy takes place when the nurse shares information with other health care providers that helps them understand the child and family. This may be done through verbal communication, as when giving a change-of-shift report or in written communications in the nursing progress notes and Kardex. Advocacy may also take the form of volunteering to present nursing inservice education programs organized around psychosocial issues. Frequently, advocacy for individual children takes the form of sharing information that makes caring for the child easier for other staff and, consequently, for the child. For example, the nurse may share "tricks of the trade" with a lab technician who must collect blood samples from the child or with a physician who is starting an IV.

Advocacy also takes place when the nurse shares information with the parents. It is not uncommon to see parents placing unrealistic demands for behavior on their child. "You're a big boy now, don't cry!" the parents might say to their child. By explaining pain and the usefulness of expressing pain for the child's emotional and physical well-being, the nurse promotes quality care of the child.

At times, advocacy is best accomplished when one can help others identify, intellectually and emotionally, with the child and family. One child used a ritual of stalling and gaining control before he could participate in intrusive procedures. He seemed to need more time than other children typically requested. This need for time was interpreted by one staff member as simply stalling that served no useful purpose, other than taking up her time. Another nurse observed, "Did you ever dive off the high-dive board when you were little? I can remember climbing the ladder, getting to the top, walking out to the end of the board, and I just couldn't make myself jump. I wanted to. I would back up a little, take forward steps, and then stand again. I just couldn't do it at first. I'd take another try and finally I would be able to. I think this is what Jeff does. He's just getting himself ready for the big plunge." The first nurse, with a strong remembrance, exclaimed, "I used to do that when I was doing backward dives off the high dive. Was I ever scared!" With an analogy she could appreciate, this nurse was able to understand the child's need for "just a little more time" to get ready for frightening events.

Advocacy also occurs during staff meetings when a group of health care providers discusses ideas and reaches decisions about routines of care for child patients and their families. Speaking up on ways to provide health care that meet both the institution's needs and the psychosocial needs of children and families demonstrates for others the importance and possibility of combining and meeting both needs. How to accomplish this comes from many sources— reading journals, talking with people from other health care settings, attending educational conferences—all of which impart information about how best to care for children and families in pediatric settings.

Accepting the role of advocate comes with realizing that advocacy can minimize the potential for psychosocial disturbance and can maximize the opportunities for benefit to children by facilitating physical care. By reducing the emotional stress component of the patient's illness, the child is left with more of his metabolic resources in reserve to deal with the onslaught of disease.[10]

Summary

This chapter has discussed the child in health care from the perspective of stress/adaptation theory. Illness, disability, and hospitalization are life crises for a child and family; the impact of these events can affect the developmental progress of a child. Some of the major points of the chapter include the following.

1. Long-lasting psychological disturbance has been found in 25% of pediatric hospital admissions.
2. Children with multiple admissions to the hospital

in the first 4 years of life are the most vulnerable to psychological disturbance.

3. The influences of hospitalization, parent–child attachment, and communication are factors that the nurse recognizes and analyzes when applying the nursing process.
4. Assessment of the child at risk for psychosocial disturbance in health care includes gathering information about the child's developmental level, the environmental influences on the child, such as the nature of the specific illness or disability, the child's previous life experiences, and the child's family, and personal attributes of the child.
5. Planning and interventions for the child who is ill, disabled, or hospitalized are evaluated for effectiveness in supporting the child's and family's development of trust, understanding, and mastery of the stresses involved in health care.
6. Preparation for experiences encountered in health care and the use of play are common, yet critical, psychosocial interventions.
7. Mastery allows the child to be active on his own behalf, to turn from a passive victim to a participating role.
8. Interventions to support mastery are those that allow the child active exploration of feelings, as in nondirective play and expressive arts, and that enhance the child's and family's self-concept and self-esteem.
9. Evaluation of the effectiveness of nursing intervention is based on observation and analysis of the child's and family's behavior and self-reflection.
10. The nurse's acceptance of the advocacy role, coupled with the responsibility to minimize potential psychological disturbances and to maximize growth potentials, affords the challenges and rewards of the nursing of children.

References

1. Anthony EJ, Koupernik C (eds): The Child in His Family: The Impact of Disease and Death. New York, John Wiley & Sons, 1973
2. Anthony EJ, Koupernik C (eds): The Child in His Family: Children at Psychiatric Risk. New York, John Wiley & Sons, 1974
3. Astin EW: Self-Reported Fears of Hospitalized and Non-Hospitalized Children Aged Ten to Twelve. Matern Child Nurs J 6 (Spring): 17–24, 1977
4. Azarnoff P, Woody PA: Preparation of Children for Hospitalization in Acute Care Hospitals in the United States. Pediatrics 68 (September): 361–368, 1981
5. Beardslee WR, DeMaso DR: Staff Groups in a Pediatric Hospital: Content and Coping. Am J Orthopsychiatry 52 (October): 712–718, 1982

6. Bibace R, Walsh ME: Development of Children's Concepts of Illness. Pediatrics 66 (December): 912–917, 1980

7. Blitzer EC et al: Another Myth: Reduced Hospital Visiting By Inner-City Mothers. Pediatrics 71 (April): 504–509, 1983

8. Blos P: Children Think About Illness: Their Concepts and Beliefs. In Gellert E (ed): Psychosocial Aspects of Pediatric Care, pp 1–18. New York, Grune & Stratton, 1978

9. Bowlby J: Separation: Anxiety and Anger. New York, Basic Books, 1973

10. Bovard EW: The Effects of Social Stimuli on the Response to Stress. Psychol Rev 66 (September): 267–277, 1959

11. Campbell JD: Illness is a Point of View: The Development of Children's Concepts of Illness. Child Dev 46 (March): 92–100, 1975

12. Caplan G (ed): Prevention of Mental Disorders in Children. New York, Basic Books, 1961

13. Douglas JB: Early Hospital Admissions and Later Disturbances of Behavior and Learning. Dev Med Child Neurol 17 (August): 456–480, 1975

14. Droske S, Francis S: Pediatric Diagnostic Procedures. New York, John Wiley & Sons, 1981

15. Eissler RS, Freud A, Kris M, Solnit AJ (eds): Physical Illness and Handicap in Childhood. New Haven, Yale University Press, 1977

16. Erikson E: Childhood and Society. New York, WW Norton, 1950

17. Fassler J: Helping Children Cope: Managing Stress Through Books and Stories. New York, The Free Press, 1978

18. Ferguson BF: Preparing Young Children for Hospitalization. Pediatrics 64 (November): 656–664, 1979

19. Fletcher B: Psychological Upset in Posthospitalized Children: A Review of the Literature, Matern Child Nurs J 10 (Fall): 185–195, 1981

20. Frank JL: A Weekly Group Meeting for Children on a Pediatric Ward: Therapeutic and Practical Functions. Int J Psychiatry Med 8(3):267–283, 1978

21. Freud A: Normality and Pathology in Childhood: Assessments of Development. New York, International Universities Press, 1965

22. Freud A: The Ego and Mechanisms of Defense. New York, International Universities Press, 1966

23. Freud A: The Role of Bodily Illness in the Mental Life of Children. In Eissler RS, Freud A, Kris M, Solnit A (eds): Physical Illness and Handicap in Childhood, pp 1–12. New Haven, Yale University Press, 1977

24. Garmezy N: The Study of Competence in Children at Risk for Severe Psychopathology. In Anthony EJ, Koupernik C (eds): The Child in His Family: Children at Psychiatric Risk, p 94. New York, John Wiley & Sons, 1974

25. Geist RA: Onset of Chronic Illness in Children and Adolescents: Psychotherapeutic and Consultative Intervention. Am J Orthopsychiatry 49 (January): 4–23, 1979

26. Gohsman BN: The Hospitalized Child and the Need for Mastery. Issues in Comprehensive Pediatric Nursing 5 (March–April): 67–76, 1981

27. Goslin ER: Hospitalization as a Life Crisis for the Preschool Child: A Critical Review. Journal Comm Health 3 (Summer): 321–346, 1978

28. Greenspan S: The Clinical Interview of the Child. New York, McGraw-Hill, 1981

29. Hughes MC: Chronically Ill Children in Groups: Recurrent Issues and Adaptations. Am J Orthopsychiatry 52 (October): 704–711, 1982

30. Johnson JE, Kirchhoff KT, Endress M: Easing Children's Fright During Health Care Procedures. Am J Matern Child Nurs 1 (July/August): 206–210, 1976

31. Kliman G: Psychological Emergencies of Childhood. New York, Grune & Stratton, 1968

32. Knafl KA, Dixon DM: The Role of Siblings During Pediatric Hospitalization. Issues in Comprehensive Pediatric Nursing 6 (January–February): 13–22, 1983

33. Knox JE, Haynes VE: Hospitalization of a Chronically Ill Child: A Stressful Time for Parents. Issues in Comprehensive Pediatric Nursing 6 (July–August): 217–226, 1983

34. Korbin JE, Johnston M: Steps Toward Resolving Cultural Conflict in a Pediatric Hospital. Clinical Pediatr 21 (May): 259–263, 1982

35. Lavigne JV, Ryan M: Psychologic Adjustment of Siblings of Children with Chronic Illness. Pediatrics 63 (April): 616–627, 1979

36. Lawson BA: Chronic Illness in the School-aged Child: Effects on the Total Family. Am J Matern Child Nurs 2 (January–February): 49–56, 1977

37. Litman TJ: The Family as a Basic Unit in Health and Medical Care: A Social-Behavioral Overview. Soc Sci Med 8 (September): 495–519, 1974

38. McKeever P: Siblings of Chronically Ill Children: A Literature Review with Implications for Research and Practice. Am J Orthopsychiatry 53 (April): 209–218, 1983

39. Marten GW, Mauer AM: Interaction of Health-Care Professionals with Critically Ill Children and Their Parents. Clin Pediatr 21 (September): 540–544, 1982

40. Martinez RA (ed): Hispanic Culture and Health Care. St Louis, CV Mosby, 1978

41. Mattsson A: Long Term Physical Illness in Childhood: A Challenge to Psychosocial Adaptation. Pediatrics 50 (November): 801–811, 1972

42. Mechanic D: The Influence of Mothers on Children's Health Attitudes and Behavior. Pediatrics 33 (March): 444–453, 1964

43. Melamed B, Siegel L: Reduction of Anxiety in Children Facing Hospitalization and Surgery by Use of Filmed Modelling. J Consult Clin Psychol 43 (August): 511–521, 1975

44. Murphy L, Moriarty AE: Vulnerability, Coping and Growth. New Haven, Yale University Press, 1976

45. Murphy L et al: The Widening World of Childhood. New York, Basic Books, 1962

46. Olds A: Psychosocial Considerations in Humanizing the Physical Environment of Pediatric Outpatient and Hospital Settings. In Gellert E (ed): Psychosocial Aspects of Pediatric Care, pp 111–132. New York, Grune & Stratton, 1978

47. Orr DP, Weller SC, Satterwhite B, Pless IB: Psycho-

social Implications of Chronic Illness in Adolescence. J Pediatr 104 (January): 152–157, 1984

48. Paulson JA: Patient Education. Pediatr Clin North Am 28 (August): 627–635, 1981

49. Perrin EC, Gerrity S: There's A Demon in Your Belly: Children's Understanding of Illness. Pediatrics 67 (June) 841–849, 1981

50. Perrin EC, Perrin JM: Clinicians' Assessments of Children's Understanding of Illness. Am J Dis Child 137 (September): 874–878, 1983

51. Petrillo M, Sanger S: Emotional Care of Hospitalized Children. Philadelphia, JB Lippincott, 1972

52. Piaget J: The Language and Thought of the Child. New York, Meridian Books, 1953

53. Piaget J: Play, Dreams and Imitation in Childhood. New York, WW Norton, 1962

54. Pidgeon V: Characteristics of Children's Thinking and Implications for Health Teaching. Matern Child Nurs J 6 (Spring): 1–8, 1977

55. Pless IB, Roghmann KJ: Chronic Illness and its Consequences: Observations Based on Three Epidemiologic Surveys. J Pediatr 79 (September): 351–359, 1971

56. Poster EC: Stress Immunization: Techniques to Help Children Cope with Hospitalization. Matern Child Nurs J 12 (Summer): 119–134, 1983

57. Prugh D et al: A Study of the Emotional Reactions of Children and Families to Hospitaliation and Illness. Am J Orthopsychiatry 23 (February): 70–106, 1953

58. Quinton D, Rutter M: Early Hospital Admissions and Later Disturbances of Behavior: An Attempted Replication of Douglas' Findings. Dev Med Child Neurol 18 (August): 447–459, 1976

59. Rie HE, Boverman H, Grossman BJ, Ozoa N: Immediate and Long-Term Effects of Interventions Early in Prolonged Hospitalization. Pediatrics 41 (April): 755–764, 1968

60. Riehl J, Roy Sr C: Conceptual Models for Nursing Practice. New York, Appleton-Century-Crofts, 1974

61. Robertson J: Young Children in Hospitals. New York, Basic Books, 1958

62. Robertson M, Barford F: Story Making in Psychotherapy with a Chronically Ill Child. In Schaefer CE (ed): Therapeutic Use of Child's Play. New York, Jason Aronson, 1976

63. Robinson K et al: Concepts of Stress for Nursing. Issues in Mental Health Nursing 4 (July–September): 167–176, 1982

64. Roghmann K, Pless IB (eds): Child Health and the Community. New York, John Wiley & Sons, 1975

65. Rutter M: Prevention of Children's Psychosocial Disorders: Myth and Substance. Pediatrics 70 (December): 883–894, 1982

66. Savedra M et al: Description of the Pain Experience: A Study of School-Aged Children. Issues in Comprehensive Pediatric Nursing 5 (September–December): 373–380, 1981

67. Schaefer CE (ed): Therapeutic Use of Child's Play. New York, Jason Aronson, 1976

68. Schowalter J: Psychological Reactions to Physical Illness in Adolescence. J Am Acad Child Psychiatry 16 (Summer): 500–516, 1977

69. Schulman J: Coping with Major Disease: Child, Family, Pediatrician. J Pediatr 102 (June): 988–991, 1983

70. Skipper JK, Leonard RC: Children, Stress and Hospitalization: A Field Experiment. J Health Soc Behav 9 (December): 275–287, 1968

71. Spinetta JJ: Behavioral and Psychological Research in Childhood Cancer: An Overview. Cancer 50 (November supplement): 1939–1943, 1982

72. Spitz R: Hospitalism: An Inquiry into the Genesis of Psychiatric Conditions in Early Childhood. The Psychoanalytic Study of the Child 1:53–74, 1945

73. Steele S (ed): Nursing Care of the Child with Long-Term Illness. New York, Appleton-Century-Crofts, 1977

74. Steinhauer PD, Mushin DN, Rae-Grant Q: Psychological Aspects of Chronic Illness. Pediatr Clin North Am 21 (November): 825–840, 1974

75. Tarnow J, Gutstein S: Children's Preparatory Behavior for Elective Surgery. J Am Acad Child Psychiatry 22 (July): 365–369, 1983

76. Terr L: Forbidden Games: Post-Traumatic Child's Play. J Am Acad Child Psychiatry 20 (Autumn): 741–760, 1981

77. Tesler M, Savedra M: Coping with Hospitalization: A Study of School-Aged Children. Pediatric Nursing 7 (March–April): 35–38, 1981

78. Tesler M et al: Coping Strategies of Children in Pain. Issues in Comprehensive Pediatric Nursing 5 (September–December): 351–359, 1981

79. Thomas A, Chess S: Temperament and Development. New York, Brunner/Mazel, 1977

80. Tisza V, Hurwitz I, Angoff K: The Use of a Play Program for Hospitalized Children. J Am Acad Child Psychiatry 9 (July): 515–531, 1970

81. Travis G: Chronic Illness in Children: Its Impact on Child and Family. Stanford, Stanford University Press, 1976

82. Vernon D et al: The Psychological Responses of Children to Hospitalization and Illness. Springfield, IL, Charles C Thomas, 1965

83. Vipperman JF, Rager P: Childhood Coping: How Nurses Can Help. Pediatric Nursing (March/April) 6:11–18, 1980

84. Visotsky H, Hamburg D, Goss M: Coping Behaviors Under Extreme Stress. Arch Gen Psychiatry 5 (November): 423–448, 1961

85. Visintainer M, Wolfer J: Psychological Preparation for Surgical Pediatric Patients: The Effect on Children's and Parents' Stress Responses and Adjustment. Pediatrics 56 (August): 187–202, 1975

86. Volz DD: Time Structuring for Hospitalized School-Aged Children." Issues in Comprehensive Pediatric Nursing 5 (July–August): 205–210, 1981

87. Wear E, Covey J, Brush M: Facilitating Children's Adaptations to Intrusive Procedures. In Fochtman D, Foley G (eds): Nursing Care of the Child with Cancer. Boston, Little, Brown, 1982

88. Yates A: Stress Management in Childhood. Clin Pediatr 22 (February): 131–135, 1983

89. Ziemer MM: Coping Behavior: A Response to Stress. Topics in Clinical Nursing 4 (July–September): 4–12, 1982

Chapter 37
Issues in Women's Health Care

Your health is bound to be affected if, day after day, you say the opposite of what you feel, if you grovel before what you dislike and rejoice at what brings you nothing but misfortune . . . [Our soul] can't be forever violated with impunity.

Boris Pasternak,
Doctor Zhivago

Rhea P. Williams

Chapter Preview

Women are the largest group of consumers of health care. They comprise about 60% of all patient visits to a doctor.[26] Women present a variety of common, yet unique, health issues. For many years, these concerns have been closeted as "female problems." Over the past 2 decades, however, the interest in women's health care has grown steadily and encouraged open discussion of women's health care needs.

To provide competent and sensitive care to women, the nurse must be aware of these health care issues and their meanings to women. This chapter focuses on the psychological significance of women's health care issues, problems, and needs. It examines the politics of women's health care and discusses the notions of self-concept, loss, anxiety, powerlessness, and stress as they relate to women in health care. The issues of childbearing and parenting, menopause, and the surgical interventions of hysterectomy and mastectomy are studied and the nursing process is applied to each of these issues in women's health care.

Learning Objectives

On completion of this chapter, the reader should be able to accomplish the following.

1. Identify needs and conflicts of the female client seeking health care
2. Compare and contrast the traditional and emerging roles of women
3. Discuss the politics of women's health care
4. Describe adaptation of the health care system to the needs of women
5. Discuss the application of mental health principles to the concepts of loss, anxiety, self-concept, stress, and powerlessness
6. Apply the nursing process—assessment, planning, intervention, and evaluation—to the health care of women facing childbearing and parenting, surgical interventions (mastectomy and hysterectomy), and menopause.

Developing Roles of Women

The 1980s are both an exciting and a difficult time to be a woman. As their horizons broaden, women claim greater freedom to make choices and define their own courses of action. Despite society's changes, however, this is also a difficult era for women working for their equal place, because they are becoming increasingly susceptible to the pressures and stresses of contemporary society.

In response to changes in society, today's woman is undergoing significant life changes. She faces questions such as

"What are my expectations of myself?"
"Am I prepared and capable?"

"Need I change?"
"What are the consequences?"

Change invariably brings conflict. Conflict produces stress; unresolved conflict produces distress, which can lead to disruption or pathology. To ease this stress and distress, the nurse must understand the many conflicts and needs of the woman seeking health care.

Traditional Role of Women

Traditionally, from infancy, a little girl was programmed or socialized into the feminine role. The proclamation at delivery, "It's a girl," started the socialization process. Infant girls are held, cuddled, and kissed more often than male babies.[6] These behaviors directed toward baby girls may foster the emotional and dependent responses seen in the traditional female.

Girls have also been socialized into the female role in other ways. Girls were dressed in pink, a color shown to contribute to calmer and more passive behavior. Wearing a dress was part of learning to act feminine, because this article of clothing was certainly meant to discourage roughhousing, ball playing, and other forms of active child play. Little girls were given dolls, toy brooms, dishes, and similar toys to help them enter the domestic experience. In her early play, she was frequently reminded to be ladylike and not to be a tomboy. She was praised for being "Mommy's helper." She was taught to have low aspirations; too much education or success, she was warned, might scare away the boys.

Female role models depicted in books and the mass media were often emotional and dependent thinkers. The important names learned in history class were, overwhelmingly, those of men. A woman, the little girl was taught, was best suited as someone's wife and mother. Girls took classes in home economics and typing, and were encouraged to fear math and anything mechanical. The woman's ultimate status would be dependent on her husband's, not her own, skills. Her unmarried sisters were viewed as "poor dears" or misfits.

The traditionally socialized girl was a conforming person, bound by cultural values and social expectations. In accordance with the expectation that they would devote their lives to others, women were trained to be sensitive to, and respond to, other people.[19] Women were defined by the image of their domestic responsibilities; that is, they were perceived as actual or potential wives and mothers to the exclusion of other roles. The image of the ideal wife and mother as a warm, nurturant, supportive person defined what all women were supposed to be.[3]

Emerging Role of Women

Although the socialization process held clear-cut expectations, there were always women who didn't fit this clear-cut role. Coupled with the messages that they should be feminine, women were exposed to other messages. During school and through the media, girls learn the value society places on achievement, success, competition, leadership, and productivity. Parents are proud of their daughters' achievements in school, but often deliver the double message, "Do well, but don't do too well."[19]

Throughout the last 2 decades, women have questioned their place in society. They have asked, "Why should I not do as well?" Women have struggled with their dissatisfaction and with, what Betty Friedan, in 1963, called, "the problem that has no name."[11] The women's movement brought about many alterations in the traditional woman's role.

Every woman is affected by the uncertainty of the woman's role today. Some women cling to traditional values and defend the roles of wife, mother, and homemaker as fulfilling, rewarding, and important ones. They would argue for a return to the past.

The modern woman, liberated from the confines of tradition, perceives the role of women as changing. She believes in her ability to achieve whatever she desires and become whatever she wants to become.

There are also those women caught in the middle. They have internalized the traditional role of women, but still feel a nagging dissatisfaction. They frequently question, "Is that all there is?" The internalization of traditional values is too binding to bring about an immediate role change; therefore, this group of women experiences a "role addition." The woman who is in, or approaching, the middle years during the 1980s is, particularly, at risk for conflict. Although she has been socialized as a traditional female, she is bombarded by her own feelings, the media, and literature about the modern female. Her ambivalence and conflict about women's roles may be passed along to her daughter in the form of mixed messages, such as, "Girls can be anything . . . but act ladylike."

The emerging role of women has many consequences for the mental health of women. Nurses must help women deal with conflict, change, and stress.

The Politics of Women's Health Care

Women make up the largest number of health care consumers in a system dominated by male physicians, a system that over the years, has kept women in a passive role. Women are often, therefore, the recipients of care delivered from a male viewpoint at the most private and vulnerable times of their lives.

Women's acceptance of male dominance in medical care is not surprising in light of their traditional socialization. The physician represents everything one admires—intelligence, independence, omniscience, decisiveness, dominance, and power. He commands respect. He often calls the woman by her first name and may refer to her as a "good girl," but he is always called Dr. ____. Many women feel that their symptoms are treated less seriously than those of men, because most medical problems of women are approached as though they are psychosomatic in origin.[10]

The medical profession's literature is replete with examples of a sexist view of women. Eighteenth and nineteenth century medicine regarded women as feeble creatures who needed to invest their limited energies in their primary task of reproduction. Overdevelopment of the brain, it was felt, might atrophy the uterus.[18]

In a textbook of obstetrics and gynecology published as recently as 1971, women are seen as self-sacrificing, dependent beings whose mental health and life fulfillment are derived from the achievements of their loved ones, primarily their husbands and children. The book also explains that a woman's visit to a physician often places her in a "parent–child" situation. The woman is depicted as placing her trust and faith in the knowledgeable physician much in the same way she trusted her parents when she was a child.[34]

Even the modern day, popular authority on child care, Dr. Benjamin Spock expresses the view that women are innately passive. He believes that women derive more pleasure from life when they are noncompetitive.[28] One can only speculate how these attitudes influence the advice given to so many women.

There are also those who believe that visiting a doctor is a feminine way of coping with stress and ailments of any nature. If the doctor in attendance has been successfully socialized into the medical profession, the woman patient is likely to meet a physician who views her as a dependent, emotional person to be looked after.

Medicine's traditional beliefs and teaching have contributed to the inferior status of women. Because physicians are highly esteemed by society, their beliefs about women help to perpetuate those views.[18]

The subordination of women is also reflected in the sexual structure of the organization of medicine; in a field where women comprise the majority of health care workers, the power control of the medical hierarchy is solidly in the hands of the male physician.[10] In light of such confining medical and social stigma, nurses have a responsibility to plan and implement strategies to assist women to become more independent and powerful in matters of their own health care.

Adaptation of the Health Care System

The Women's Health Movement

The traditional system of providing health care to women is now being questioned. Prompted by the women's movement, the women's health movement has played a major role in the adaptations of the health care system. The women's health movement originally focused on the issues of birth control, abortion, and maternity care, but has expanded to include all aspects of preventive health, including nutrition and exercise, respiratory health problems, occupational health, and aging. The literature of the women's health movement combines shared experiences, health information, and political comment.[12]

There are three prominent views of the women's movement about the status of women within the health care system.[10] The *liberal feminists* want greater numbers of women to be admitted to medical schools. Women physicians, they insist, should be more capable of treating the health problems presented by women patients, if only because the female body and mind is more familiar to them.

The *radical feminists* criticize the power of physicians and hospital administrators. Women, they say, should understand their bodies and know what they can reasonably expect from physicians. From this philosophy sprung the health movements' self-help groups.

Marxist feminism holds the most extreme views of the women's health movement. This group believes that the structure of the American health system is oppressive to women as workers and as patients, but that the structure cannot be understood without an analysis of the total system. Furthermore, they believe that the only way to liberate the potential for improved care and preventive measures is to retire the capitalist order and replace it with a democratic socialist one.

Nursing's Adaptation to Women's Health Needs

In addition to society, nursing is also involved in a period of transition as it attempts to adapt its practice to the needs of women. Leonide Martin's message is important for all nurses working with women.

> The nurse is in a particularly favorable position to bring about many of the changes women desire in their health care. As an occupational group consisting mainly of women, nurses have a built-in propensity to understand and respond empathetically to women's concerns. Men in nursing also have an advantage in responding sensitively to women's health needs through their close association with many women and the socialization process of the profession. Professional norms and values internalized through nursing education emphasize the patient as an individual and promote practice which considers the person's unique needs, relation to the family and community, psychological and social factors as well as physical, and concentrate much of nursing care on the meaning and impact of illness rather than the illness itself. Nursing also emphasizes education about health and maintenance of well being as a major function of the profession.[19]

Applying Mental Health Principles to Women's Health Needs

By reviewing women's past and present roles and expectations, persistent themes of change, role addition, and conflict surface. these stressors (change, conflict, and so forth)

produce physiological and psychological stress. For example, when one's self-concept is threatened, the individual becomes distressed; to restore and maintain a state of eustress, or optimal stress level, the individual's self-concept must adapt.

Self-Concept

The *self-concept* is the composite of an individual's beliefs and feelings about himself at a given time. This self-concept is formed from perceptions of others' reactions to the individual, and directs his behavior. Specifically, there are two components of self-concept—the physical self and the personal self.[7]

The physical self or body image is the person's appraisal of his physical being; that is, his image of himself physically. The physical self includes one's physical attributes, appearance, physical performance, sexuality, and level of wellness.

The personal self involves the person's expectation of himself—his dreams, his standards, his evaluation of himself, and his need to maintain a consistent or stable self-image that says, "I can and should be; therefore, I am and will be tomorrow." When an individual's self-concept is high, his self-esteem, or his perception of his worth, is also high.

How a woman sees herself and feels about herself is an important issue for nurses to assess because it influences her health care needs. The traditionally socialized woman has learned to continually seek the approval of others; for this woman, what others think of her is critical in the development of her self-concept.

Development of Self-Concept

The development of the self-concept may be discussed in parallel with the developmental stages described by Erikson.[9] At each stage of development, the individual passes through a growth period wherein new coping mechanisms are learned and used to promote adaptation to his environment. During each of these periods, the individual takes on a new view of himself, thereby adapting his self-concept.

These life periods have been called "crisis points" in a person's life. Resolution of each crisis encountered builds on the resolution of the previous crises and, in turn, contributes to how the person will meet the next crisis.

For the female, particularly, these crisis points may have been resolved with ambivalence. The 3-year-old to 5-year-old, faced with the task of initiative versus guilt, strives to determine what kind of person she will be. She questions, "What can I be?" This time of subtle, but distinct, differences between male and female is reflected in the toys given to children and the play that is encouraged or discouraged. When a girl senses more excitement in boys' play and prefers to play like a boy, she may develop a subconscious feeling of guilt. Her initiative may falter when she is reprimanded, and her self-concept suffers.

The next stage of development, industry versus inferiority, is a critical one for girls. Schools send messages about what girls can achieve; for example, it is not unusual to hear that "girls can't do math." If a feeling of inferiority or inadequacy develops at this stage, the girl's self-concept is impaired, and her future adult functioning may be affected.

During the period of intimacy versus isolation, all individuals strive to develop an important, intimate relationship. Often, however, this relationship allows a woman to experience her self-worth only through another, a situation leading to isolation.

When a woman has achieved only through the accomplishments of others, she may face another crisis during the stage of generativity versus stagnation. The need to be needed can lead to emptiness and depression when the children are gone.

At the final stage of development, ego integrity versus despair, the woman must examine whether who she was as a younger woman and is presently is a good enough person. When this task is accomplished successfully, the woman's self-concept is secure and filled with affirmative reflection; if she develops despair, she views her life with much regret.

Loss

The experience of a loss to the physical or personal self often leads women to seek assistance from health care agencies. *Loss* is defined as a state of being deprived of, or being without, something one has had.[22] For example, a woman who has experienced unsuccessful resolutions of various developmental crises is deprived of a secure sense of self. On the other hand, she may lose positive attitudes about the self, such as pride, esteem, attractiveness, independence, or control, as well as more obvious losses, such as loss of body parts and loved ones.

An individual who suffers a loss goes through a well-defined grief response. A frequent consequence of this response is depression. A greater number of women experience depression than men, and this depression is often related to the loss of a love object.[26]

Anxiety

Anxiety is a response to a threat to the personal self—particularly the self that yearns to maintain a consistent and stable self-image. Tradition has always been a core of the culture, and, therefore when the feminine tradition is threatened, both women and men may become uncertain of their places and roles. An individual's perception of threat, however, varies according to many factors, which include sociocultural background, education, financial resources, support system, self-esteem, and previous experience with change. The stressors that cause the anxiety response and the response itself are highly individualized.

A woman's attempt to adapt to threatening stressors may be either successful or unsuccessful. She may face up to

the stressor ("fight") or withdraw from the situation by physically or mentally removing herself ("flight"). Often, the woman who deals directly with the threat may appear to be a healthy, self-actualizing person, or she may present with various psychophysiological diseases, such as insomnia, hyperactivity, ulcer disease, or hypertension. The woman who withdraws from stressors, on the other hand, is often depressed and dependent.

Stress

Contemporary society bombards women with numerous stressors. These stressors may interfere with fulfillment of individual needs. Women's responses to these stressors makes stress an inevitable force in their lives. Because prolonged stress is unbearable to the person's equilibrium, the individual must adapt to these forces and maintain eustress and a feeling of well-being.

The differences in response to stress, on the basis of sex, are shown in Table 37-1. As you examine this chart you could speculate that, in response to stress, hormonal changes in women seem to play a part in their increased incidence of anxiety and depression.

Powerlessness

Roy describes *powerlessness* as "the perception on the part of the individual of a lack of personal or internal control over events within a given situation."[25] Each woman perceives herself as what she would like to be and what she expects herself to be. This includes some sense of power or control over her being. When the individual does not fulfill her expectancy and self ideal, an important part of the self-concept, she is likely to feel powerless.[25]

Table 37-1.   **Sex Differences: Male and Female Responses to Stress**

	WOMEN	MEN
Stress	↓ Epinephrine ↑ Behavioral inhibition	↑ Epinephrine ↓ Behavioral inhibition
Normal conditions	↑ Circulating estrogens ↑ Circulating high-density lipoprotein	↑ Circulating androgens ↓ Circulating high-density lipoprotein
Exercise	↓ Physical working capacity ↓ Lung capacity ↓ Blood volume	↑ Physical working capacity ↑ Hemoglobin capacity ↑ Energy expenditure (aerobic)

(With permission from Martinson I, Anderson S: Male and Female Response to Stress. In Kjervik D, Martinson I (eds): Women in Stress: A Nursing Perspective, p 91. New York, Appleton-Century-Crofts, 1979)

Childbearing and Parenting

Childbearing is a significant event in the life of a woman; parenting is a significant role addition. Both childbearing and parenting lead to important consequences regarding a woman's self-concept. Positive adaptation to these events enhances a woman's level of wellness.

Childbearing and parenting were once seen as natural and expected norms of adult female functioning. In 1970, nine out of ten married women between the ages of 40 to 44 had at least one child; this infers that practically every fertile couple claimed parenthood.[3] Today, however, these presumed expectations of women are being questioned. The emerging roles of women and dependable methods of birth control allow women to explore choices and make conscious decisions about whether, and when, to bear children and parent. Even in our so-called modern society, however, these decisions are seldom reached easily. Both internal and external pressures affect a woman's decision to mother. Indeed, pregnancy is a biologic process invested with great social meaning and surrounded by values, customs, and law in all human societies.[29]

The present period in society is a time of transition, when values are changing—a time when old and new norms coexist. It is so much a part of feminine identity to bear children that, for both traditional and nontraditional women, the decisions of whether to mother and when to mother are frequently met with significant conflict.[3]

Crisis Events

Both childbearing and parenting are crisis events. Pregnancy is a major turning point or crisis in the life of a woman, especially the primigravida, calling for far-reaching psychological adaptations.[2]

The crisis of parenthood occurs when old patterns of coping are inadequate to deal with these sharp or decisive life changes. Some of the problems resulting from these changes include the following.

1. Adjusting to being "tied down" or restricted to the home
2. Getting accustomed to being awake at all hours
3. Inability to keep up with the housekeeping and decline in housekeeping standards
4. Tiredness and exhaustion
5. Feelings of neglecting the spouse[8, 17]

The elements of fantasy and romance, which are so prominent in our culture, contribute to the crises of pregnancy and parenting.

In one study of the perceptions of motherhood, it was found that prospective mothers do imagine what it will be like to have a baby and be a mother. Some of these views are unrealistic with elements of imagination, idealization, and romance. Many prospective mothers imagine the storybook baby who smiles and coos much of the time. Prospective mothers seldom think about a crying baby and the daily work involved in caring for a newborn. New parents are seldom prepared for the impact of parenting on their individual lives and their lives as a couple.[33]

Whether the periods of childbearing and parenting develop into crises or not, most women must make adjustments and adaptations. The nurse, through the nursing process, helps the woman adapt to the roles of childbearing and parenting in a changing society.

The Nursing Process

Assessment and Analysis

To determine the woman's perceptions and present level of adaptation to pregnancy and parenting, the nurse completes an assessment of both biologic and psychosocial components. Using an accepted theoretical reference for biologic assessment, the nurse determines the client's biologic state of adaptation and subsequent energy for psychosocial adaptations.

One aspect of the psychosocial component of assessment is the consideration of cultural influences. Examples of some cultural differences are identified in the insert, Cultural Beliefs and Practices: Childbearing and Parenting.

The following assessment tool for pregnancy and parenting is based on the Roy adaptation model of nursing.

Psychosocial Assessment

I. Assessment of self-concept
   A. How do you feel about being pregnant?
   B. How do you feel about the changes in your body since you became pregnant (example: abdomen, breast, weight gain, skin, and so on)?
   C. What do you think people think of you now that you are pregnant?
      1. Husband
      2. Family
      3. Friends
      4. Coworkers
   D. Many women find that they act or feel different when they are pregnant.
      1. Have you noticed any difference in your moods or temperament?
      2. How do you react to this?
   E. Contraception
      1. Was this a planned pregnancy?
      2. Did you use a contraceptive before you became pregnant?
      3. Have you thought of using a contraceptive after the baby is born?
      4. Do you need any information about birth control?
   F. How do you feel about becoming a mother?
   G. Do you think the new baby will change your present functioning as a person?

II. Assessment of role mastery
  A. Educational background
  B. Job
    1. Are you working outside the home?
    2. Do you plan to return to work outside the home after the baby is born?
    3. If yes, how do you think this will affect your job and your mothering?
  C. If this is a first pregnancy,
    1. What do you like most about being a wife?
    2. Do you think this will change when the baby comes?
    3. What are you looking forward to most about being a mother?
    4. What are you looking forward to least about being a mother?
    5. Have you ever taken care of a baby before?
    6. Do you feel confident about baby care?
    7. Have you attended any baby care classes?
    8. Do you think newborn babies sleep very much?
    9. How do you think you might feel about having to get up in the middle of the night with the baby?
    10. Have you thought about the baby crying? What do you think you will do when the baby cries?
  D. If second (or third, fourth, and so on) baby,
    1. Did you find that your role as a wife changed after your first child?
    2. What do you enjoy most about being a mother?
    3. What do you enjoy least about being a mother?
    4. Do you think the new baby will change your present functioning as a mother?
III. Assessment of interdependency or interrelationships
  A. 1. Have family and friends given you special attention since you have been pregnant?
     2. How do you feel about it?
  B. Has your relationship with your husband changed since pregnancy (or motherhood)?
  C. Has your relationship with friends and coworkers changed since pregnancy (or motherhood)?
  D. Do you plan to have any help when you return home with the baby?
  E. What will you expect whoever helps you to do?
  F. In what ways do you expect your husband to help?
  G. Are there any particular cultural practices or customs around childbearing or childrearing in your family that you will follow?
  H. In what way can we help?

Identifying Adaptation Problems. The assessment data are analyzed to determine actual and potential problems. These problems must be validated with the woman. In many instances, what may be considered a problem for many women (or for the nurse) may not be a problem for

another woman. Some common adaptation problems that might be anticipated by the nurse include the following.

1. Increased self-esteem due to body image changes
2. Anxiety (related to)
   a. Ambivalence about combining parenting and career responsibilities
   b. Guilt about plans to return to work outside the home after birth of baby
3. Lack of knowledge about
   a. Biologic changes during pregnancy and puerperium
   b. Infant care
4. Unrealistic perceptions of motherhood
5. Bonding problems (*e.g.*, inadequate bonding)

Planning

After validation of problems, the nurse and woman client formulate realistic objectives for the adaptation process. The woman's participation in goal formulation allows her to accept the goals as part of herself. The nurse remembers that goals are the client's behavioral outcomes. By providing the woman with optimal control over these outcomes, the nurse helps to enhance the woman's self-concept and self-esteem. In some instances, however, the nurse may have to provide more input into the goal-setting for those women experiencing high levels of anxiety or crisis.

Goal Statements. A general objective for the care of a client experiencing pregnancy or parenthood follows.

> The woman will make a positive adaptive response (state specific behavioral outcome) to pregnancy or parenting, while achieving and maintaining a secure self-concept (state measurable behavior(s) to detect secure self-concept).

An example of a specific objective for the nursing care of this client might be the following.

> The woman will state realistic perceptions of infant behaviors and show confidence (through her statements and actions) in dealing with the infant's behavior by the end of the fourth trimester.

After validating the actual or potential problems and determining the objectives, the nurse is ready to intervene.

Intervention

Personalizing Care. The nurse examines both the apparent cause of the client problem and the corresponding influencing factors, or variables, that make the problem unique and personal to the client. Pregnancy and parenting, for example, may be viewed as two of life's most personal experiences. As the nurse and client examine and deal with each influencing factor, either to change or to support them, the nurse intervenes to provide truly personalized nursing care. For example, sensitivity to the woman's sociocultural and spiritual practices helps to individualize care and make it more acceptable to her.

Supporting the Significant Other. The nurse also supports the woman client's significant other during intervention. This requires initially determining the father's perceptions of the pregnancy and parenting. In addition, his feelings about the traditional and emerging roles of women and his own role as father will be important information for the nurse to use in planning care.

Promoting Optimal Control. The nurse intervenes in a way that promotes the woman's feelings of being in control. One nursing approach used to attain this goal is an attitude of collaboration of care; that is, doing things with, not to, the client. The use of therapeutic communication will enable her to explore her feelings and to identify her problems and their best solutions.

Choosing the Setting and Timing. The setting in which the nurse intervenes may influence whether the woman client experiences adaptation or maladaptation. Some interventions are presented most effectively in a group setting, whereas others are most effective if presented on a one-to-one level.

The timing of interventions is also a critical factor in planning nursing care. The identified psychological tasks of pregnancy indicate that a woman faces certain tasks during each of the three trimesters of pregnancy.[29] These tasks suggest that the woman's interest in, and need for, information will vary according to each trimester of pregnancy.

Offering Information. The provision of learning opportunities for the woman client usually revolves around the biologic facts of pregnancy and the puerperium, and preparation for childbirth and child care activities. This information should include some of the known realities of parenting, such as a realistic picture of the wide range of normal infant behavior, and the mother's role. The nurse should also offer information about resources that can assist the woman during the pregnancy and parenting experience; for example, child care resources and various support groups for the family. An increase in knowledge increases the client's security and self-confidence, and therefore strengthen's her self-concept. Praise reinforces the client's increased knowledge and self-esteem.

Communicating Therapeutically. Therapeutic communication allows the woman to explore her feelings about pregnancy and parenting. By encouraging open communication with significant others, the nurse helps her examine the effects of pregnancy and parenting on relationships.

Although, today, greater numbers of men are participating in child care activities, the nurse cannot assume that all fathers will wish to do so; each family's plans for parenting should be discussed and clarified. The woman is also encouraged to explore her own career plans, and to find solutions for herself.

Evaluation

The evaluation process leads the nurse to review the objectives or goals of intervention and reassess the client's behaviors. How closely, the nurse asks, do the outcome behaviors resemble those stated in the objectives? How well has the woman client adapted to childbearing and parenting in today's society? Does her adaptation represent, for her, a high level of wellness?

This organized problem-solving process, the nursing process, and identified intervention strategies offer the nurse guidelines for assisting women to cope with the tasks and challenges of childbearing and parenting (see Nursing Care Plan: Adaptation to Parenting).

Surgical Alterations: Hysterectomy and Mastectomy

Each year, thousands of women in the United States enter hospitals to undergo surgical procedures that strike at the internal and external symbols of feminine identity. In 1978, 644,000 women in America underwent hysterectomies.[30] It is estimated that 11,000 new cases of breast cancer were diagnosed in 1981 and that most of these were treated by various forms of mastectomy.[1]

Hysterectomy and mastectomy mean far more to these women than simply the physical recovery after a surgical procedure. These operations can have far-reaching, and sometimes devastating, effects on a woman's self-concept. Although health care practitioners may anticipate many common responses such as grief, anxiety, fear, depression, anger, and powerlessness, the ultimate effect of the surgery is unique for each woman. Her experience of the grief process depends on the reason for the surgery and the woman's perception of femininity, her lifestyle, support system, sociocultural orientation, stress responses, and personality factors.

These surgeries, hysterectomy and mastectomy, need not produce pathological responses. A knowledgeable, understanding nurse can help the woman client deal with these stressors and grow as a result of the experience.

Common Responses to Surgical Alterations

From the time of their childhood on, women have been informed about their "special, private part within," the uterus. They anticipate the growth of their breasts and await the external sign, menstruation, which signifies that the

(*Text continues on p 593*)

Cultural Beliefs and Practices: Childbearing and Parenting

Most of these cultural beliefs and customs are reflective of the traditional culture and are not universally practiced by all members of the cultural group. Variables such as degree of acculturation, educational and income levels, and amount of contact with older generations influence the extent to which these customs are practiced.

Cultural Group	Pregnancy	Childbirth	Parenting
Mexican-American[15]	1. Pregnancy desired soon after marriage 2. Expectant mother influenced strongly by mother or mother-in-law 3. Cool air in motion considered dangerous during pregnancy 4. Unsatisfied food cravings thought to mark the baby 5. Some pica observed in the eating of ashes or dirt (not a common practice) 6. Milk avoided because it causes large babies and, thus, difficult deliveries 7. Many predictions about the sex of the baby 8. Unacceptable and frightening to have pelvic examination by male doctor 9. Use of herbs to treat common complaints of pregnancy 10. Drinking chamomile tea thought to assure effective labor and uncomplicated separation of the placenta, starting during the 8th month of pregnancy	*Labor* 1. Use of "partera" or midwife preferred because they do not rush the delivery. 2. After the delivery of the baby, the mother's legs brought together to prevent air from entering the uterus. *Postpartum* 1. Diet restricted after delivery, for first 2 days only boiled milk and toasted tortillas permitted, then followed by pieces of chicken or chicken soup for next 2 to 3 days; no fruits or vegetables, which are considered too "acid" or "cold;" pork and chili thought to harm breast milk, therefore avoided for 40 days 2. Bed rest for 3 days after delivery 3. Mother's head and feet protected from cold air—bathing permitted after 14 days 4. Mother often cared for by her own mother 5. Forty-day restriction on sexual intercourse	*Newborn* 1. Breast feeding begun after the 3rd day; colostrum may be considered "filthy" 2. Olive oil or castor oil given to stimulate the passage of meconium 3. Male infant not circumcised 4. Female infant's ears pierced 5. Belly band used to prevent umbilical hernia 6. Religious medal worn by mother during pregnancy; placed around infant's neck 7. Infant protected from the "evil eye" 8. Various remedies used to treat Mal ojo and fallen fontanel

Oriental[5]	1. Pregnancy considered time when mother "has happiness in her body"
	2. Pregnancy seen as natural process
	3. Strong preference for female physician
	4. Belief in theory of hot and cold
	5. May omit soy sauce in diet to prevent dark-skinned baby
	6. Prefer soup made with ginseng root as general strength tonic
	7. Milk is usually excluded
		Labor
		1. Mother attended during labor by other women
		2. Father does not actively participate during labor
		
		Postpartum
		1. Must protect self from Yin (cold forces) for 30 days
		   Ambulation limited
		   Shower prohibited
		   Chinese mother avoids fruits and vegetables
		2. Diet
		  a. Some patients are vegetarians.
			1. Concept of the family is important and valued
			2. Father is head of the household; wife plays a subordinate role.
			3. The birth of a boy is a particularly joyful event.

Cultural Group	Pregnancy	Childbirth	Parenting
	from diet because it causes stomach distress	b. Korean mother is served seaweed soup with rice. c. Chinese diet high in hot foods (*e.g.*, chicken soup made with pig knuckles)	
Afro-American[4]	1. Acceptance of pregnancy depends on economic status 　Middle income family usually shows acceptance of pregnancy 　Pregnancy of lower income family may be accepted or rejected depending on circumstances 2. Pregnancy thought to be state of "wellness," which is often the reason for delay in seeking prenatal care, especially by lower income blacks who seek medical care only when "sick" 3. Old wives tales include having your picture taken during pregnancy will cause stillbirth; 　birthmarks are the result of emotional frights or the unsatisfied craving of a certain food during pregnancy; 　reaching up will cause the cord to strangle the baby 4. Craving of certain foods 　Nutritionally acceptable foods include chicken, greens 　Unacceptable foods or pica include clay, starch, dirt	*Labor* 1. Use of "Granny midwife" 2. Stoic behavior exhibited to avoid calling attention to selves 3. Mother may arrive at hospital in far-advanced labor 4. Often, cries to the Lord; for example, "Lord have mercy." 5. Emotional support often provided by other women, especially own mother *Postpartum* 1. Vaginal bleeding seen as sign of sickness; tub baths and shampooing of hair prohibited 2. Sassafras tea thought to have healing power 3. Liver thought to cause heavier vaginal bleeding because of its high "blood" content 4. Pregnancy may be viewed by black men as a sign of their virility 5. Self-treatment for various discomforts of pregnancy 　Constipation treated with epsom salts, castor oil 　Nausea, vomiting and headache treated with herb teas 　Heartburn treated with vinegar, baking soda	*Newborn* 1. Feeding very important: 　"Good" baby thought to eat well 　"Good" mother thought to have baby who eats well 　Early introduction of solid foods 　May breast or bottle feed; breastfeeding may be considered embarrassing 2. Parents fearful of spoiling baby 3. Commonly call baby by nicknames 4. May use excessive clothing to keep baby warm 5. Belly band used to prevent umbilical hernia 6. Abundant use of oil on baby's scalp and skin 7. Strong feeling of family, community, and religion

　　The discussion of cultural practices is not intended to stereotype clients. It is important, rather, that the nurse become familiar with the woman client as an individual and validate which cultural beliefs are meaningful to her.

　　Equipped with this knowledge, the nurse supports and nurtures those beliefs that promote physical or emotional adaptation; however, if certain beliefs are identified that might be harmful, the nurse should carefully explore those beliefs with the client, and use them in the reeducation and modification process.

Nursing Care Plan

Adaptation to Parenting

Assessment (Nursing Diagnosis)

Inadequate Maternal–Infant Bonding

Behaviors
1. Holds infant tensely, at arm's distance
2. Refers to infant as "it"
3. States, "He's so little"
4. Asks, "Why does he cry so much?" and "Nurse will you change his diaper?" (makes a face when nurse changes diaper)
5. Watches television most of time while infant in room, including during feeding
6. Asks that infant be returned to nursery right after feeding

Influencing Factors
1. 19-year-old mother
2. No previous experience with infants
3. Hoped for a female infant
4. Maternal physiological discomfort

Planning (Objectives/Goals)

Short term
   The mother will begin to show signs of maternal infant bonding by the end of the shift, as evidenced by calling the infant by name and holding the infant closely.
Long-term
   The mother will continue to show signs of increased bonding with infant before discharge, by participating in infant care and using affectionate terms when referring to infant.

Intervention

Intervene to provide physiological comfort and meet mother's dependency needs.
Initiate conversation with mother.
Use therapeutic communication techniques to assess mothers feelings about the infant; for example, "Beth, tell me how you are feeling now that your baby boy is here," or, "Sometimes mothers feel disappointed when the baby is not the sex they had hoped for."
Accept mother's feelings without judgment.
Call the infant by name.
Provide brief, frequent opportunities for the mother to be with the infant, suggest times when favorite shows are not on television.
Make positive statements about the infant.
Demonstrate to mother how to hold infant, explain that baby can see her best when baby is held close.
Explain crying behavior of infants and suggest specific techniques for comforting infant.
Praise mother for any positive maternal–infant interactions; for example, "you look so good together; he looks so comfortable in your arms."
Assess the mother's readiness for learning infant care and begin teaching specific infant care activities.
Provide the mother with opportunities for return demonstration of baby care.
Praise her efforts to care for baby.
Gradually increase length of time mother spends with the baby.
Encourage the mother to ask questions about infant behavior, needs, and care, and her own needs.

uterus within functions. Loss of either of these organs, uterus or breast, causes the woman to experience loss and grief.

Grief and Loss

The grief process results from the losses to both the physical self and the personal self. Besides the loss of the body part, the uterus or breast, the woman also faces the perceived or actual loss of good health, especially if cancer is diagnosed. When a woman's breast is removed, she may fear that others will discover she has had a mastectomy and she may have concerns about her physical attractiveness. Undergoing a hysterectomy may cause the woman to worry that she will experience acceleration of the aging process, weight gain, or decreased sexual interest. Her personal self may question whether her dreams for longevity will be realized. She may examine her life plans and ask, "Can I now really expect this for myself?"

Anxiety and Fear

Anxiety and fear follow both the woman's realization of the need for the surgery and her realization, afterwards, that the surgery has taken place. The impact of an altered state of wellness may cause the woman to turn inward. She must use a great deal of mental energy to deal with the unknown—energy that is drawn from every aspect of her life.

Anger and Powerlessness

Anger is another part of the grief response. If the woman believes that she has somehow done, or not done, something to cause her illness, she may direct her anger at herself, often leading to depression. Often, she directs her anger at medical personnel if she believes she has not been told the truth about her condition. For example, she may wonder whether the hysterectomy was absolutely necessary. If the woman is unclear about a one-step biopsy and mastectomy procedure, she may awaken from surgery feeling deceived by the surgeon. Anger and powerlessness, or frustration at the lack of control of her body, must be acknowledged and dealt with.[31]

Depression

Depression is also a stage of the grief reaction and may be a pronounced response to surgical alterations. The meaning of these surgeries to the woman and the perceived loss of femininity are often causes of her depression following mastectomy and hysterectomy.

Factors in the Response to Surgical Alterations

Reason for the Surgery

The indications for hysterectomy are surrounded by controversy. Some women and physicians share the opinion that, if a woman has completed her family or desires no more children, a hysterectomy relieves her of a useless, bleeding organ that may become cancerous. On the other hand, some believe that American surgeons are performing too many hysterectomies.[24]

When a woman is ambivalent about the need for an operation, she loses a certain degree of trust in the physician and experiences increased anxiety. If a woman begins to question the necessity of the operation after she has undergone the surgery, she may express anger toward herself and others. Women seem to be more accepting of a total hysterectomy (removal of the uterus) than a total hysterectomy and bilateral salpingo-oopherectomy (removal of the uterus, ovaries, and fallopian tubes).

Before undergoing a hysterectomy, a woman may have lived with the symptoms and the thought of surgery for a period of time. Anticipatory grieving and the mobilization of resources often occur during the presurgical period. If nurses, physicians, and significant others use this time to prepare the woman physically and psychologically, she is more likely to experience successful postoperative adaptation.

A mastectomy is generally performed when a life-threatening disease, breast cancer, is detected. With more treatment options now available to women with breast cancer, the necessity of a mastectomy may be debated. Once the woman and her physician decide on the need for this surgery, however, she is forced to face the reality of having a life-threatening illness. Usually, little time elapses between suspicion of breast cancer and determination of need for the operation. The crisis nature of this situation provides a woman with little time to deal with her acute feelings of grief, anxiety, powerlessness, and depression, or to mobilize her strengths. Immediate intervention by family, friends, nurses, and other health care professionals is crucial to help the woman cope effectively with the disease and the treatment that will follow.

Perception of Femininity

Our culture emphasizes women's breasts as a sign of femininity. As a girl grows into womanhood, the development of her breasts give her and "the world" external evidence of her femaleness. The functioning of the internal female organs comprises another value in the process of becoming a woman. Menstruation is the first visible sign of the functioning uterus and corroborates its existence.[24] The breast and the uterus, then, are likely to symbolize a woman's femininity and to form an essential component of her body image. Her reaction to losing either breast or uterus will depend, to a great extent, on the value she places on these organs as symbols of being a worthwhile woman. For example, it has been found that women who have considerable emotional investment in their breasts are more likely to suffer severe depression after mastectomy.[27]

Studies have also demonstrated that some women view the uterus as a badge of femininity and, after hysterectomy, perceive themselves as less attractive and fear rejection by their spouses or other men. In addition to reproduction, they attribute to the uterus the functions of excretion, regulation of body processes, expression of sexuality, and maintenance of health, vitality, youth, and attractiveness.[14] The woman who values her body as a measure of self-worth and social acceptance may have more difficulty incorporating the loss of a breast or uterus into an acceptable altered body image than the woman who places greater value on intellectual qualities.[14]

Lifestyle

Lifestyle variations influence the woman's acceptance of surgical alterations. For example, the woman whose body image and role in life are dependent on her external appearance, such as a model or dancer, may be more severely threatened by potential or actual breast loss than a woman whose career is not based on physical attributes.[31] Likewise, for the woman who has not completed her family, the prospect of a hysterectomy comes as a severe blow. The threat of cancer and its potentially debilitating physical effects alter a woman's lifestyle and role performance. It is usually difficult for an independent woman to alter roles and accept help from others.

Support System

An individual's self-concept is partially dependent on the response of others; what others think of us is important in affirming our self-esteem. As she alters her perception of herself in the face of these surgeries, the woman also tries to determine what others now think of her.

The reaction of others following her surgery is a critical determinant of her emotional adaptation to the event. For example, it has been found that, following hysterectomy, a woman is more apt to be depressed if her significant male is distant or detached, shows little concern for her feelings, or believes that she is less attractive than before her surgery.[24] Similarly, when a woman undergoes a mastectomy, her feelings about the loss of her breast are deeply affected by the reaction of her significant male. Most women interpret a negative response from a significant male as physical rejection and interpret avoidance as pity.

In addition to coping with the loss of the specific organ, the significant others must cope with their feelings about the presence of cancer, if that diagnosis has been made. Family members and friends suffer many of the same anxieties, fears, and grief responses as the woman client; their feelings and reactions affect her adaptation.

Sociocultural Orientation

We live in a cancer-fearing society. The American Cancer Society reports that most people associate cancer with death and pain.[31] Women with breast cancer who wish to enter or re-enter the job market may face discrimination through company policies. Although such discrimination policies are illegal, the American Cancer Society of California has reported discrimination against cancer patients in all aspects of employment.

Because the American culture places such a high value on breasts, many women believe that the size and shape of their breasts define their acceptability as women.[31] Recent social trends, however, may help ameliorate society's traditional emphasis on the breast as woman's most valuable attribute.

Various cultural groups hold particular views about the uterus and its functions in maintaining health, youth, and attractiveness. Following a hysterectomy, therefore, a woman of one of these cultural groups might perceive herself as unattractive, unhealthy, and aging.

Response to Stress

An individual's reactions to the crises of life are unique responses influenced by her own personality, philosophy of life, and characteristic coping behavior. Emotionally charged surgical procedures, such as hysterectomy and mastectomy, challenge one's ability to cope and maintain ego integrity. The nurse is able to support and facilitate psychosocial adaptation to these surgical alterations through the systematic approach of the nursing process.

The Nursing Process

Assessment and Analysis

The woman undergoing surgical alterations experiences both physical and emotional trauma and fatigue, which impede healing of the body and mind. Care provided to both body and mind begins with the physical and psychosocial nursing assessment. As the woman client begins to feel better physically, she also begins to improve psychologically. Freedom from pain, infection, and complications greatly ease emotional distress. It is often through the preoperative and postoperative physical care that the nurse begins to build a trusting relationship with the client. The development of a trusting relationship is essential before psychosocial assessment and intervention can be accomplished.

The psychosocial assessment example that follows is based on the Roy adaptation framework. Suggested questions and observations regarding the assessment of self-concept, role, and interrelationships are included. The nurse varies or alters the questions according to the client's response and the nurse's comfort level. Some of these issues are best approached preoperatively, others postoperatively; some in a formal manner, others informally. Exploring these areas helps the nurse obtain information needed to plan nursing interventions, which, eventually, promote the client's positive adaptation (see insert, Excerpts from an Interview with a Postoperative Mastectomy Client).

The nurse should inform the client that obtaining this information will help to anticipate some of her needs and insure optimal care. When possible and appropriate, the nurse also involves the client's sexual partner in the assessment process to identify concerns and feelings about the proposed surgery and the degree of support available to the woman.

Psychosocial Assessment

I. Assessment of self-concept (and body image)
   A. How would you describe yourself?
      1. Your appearance?
      2. Your outlook on life?
   B. How would you describe your general state of health?
   C. What is your understanding of why this operation is necessary?
   D. Can you recall your reaction when you first learned that this operation was necessary?
   E. Can you describe what will happen during the operation?
   F. Do you anticipate any changes?
      1. In your body's functioning?
      2. In your body's appearance because of the operation?
   G. How do you feel about these anticipated changes?
   H. How would you describe a feminine woman?
   I. How would you describe your usual response to a stressful situation?
   J. Do religious practices have meaning for you?
   K. How has your present illness affected your religious beliefs and practices?
   L. What questions do you have about the surgery or anything related to the surgery (preoperatively)?
   M. How are you feeling about your surgery now (postoperatively)?
   Observations:
   A. Words used to describe herself
   B. Ease or uneasiness as she speaks
   C. Age
   D. Personal appearance
   E. Nonverbal behaviors and affect
   F. Willingness to look at operative site
   G. Use of religious articles
II. Assessment of role mastery
   A. What is your educational background?
   B. Do you work outside the home?
   C. Will you describe the type of activities necessary for your job?
   D. With whom do you live?
   E. Will you describe your responsibilities at home?
   F. What kinds of activities do you engage in for fun?
III. Assessment of interrelationships
   A. Describe how you view your relationship to
      1. Men
      2. Women
   B. Has your present illness affected your relationship with anyone in your life?
      1. Husband or significant other?
      2. Family?
      3. Friends?
      4. Coworkers?
   C. How did your family and friends react when they first learned about your surgery?
   D. Do you anticipate any changes in your relationships after the surgery?
      1. With husband?
      2. With family?
      3. With friends?
      4. With coworkers?
   E. Do you anticipate needing help with usual routines when you return home?
   F. Whom do you expect to help you?
   G. How do you feel about needing this help?
   Observations:
   A. Visitors? How often? Who?
   B. Family involvement
   C. Response to others in the hosptial environment (*e.g.,* doctors, nurses, roommate)
   D. Willingness to accept help or do for self

Identifying Adaptation Problems.   After analysis of the assessment data, the nurse identifies and validates problems and potential problem areas with the woman client.

Some psychosocial adaptation problems experienced by women undergoing hysterectomy and mastectomy include the following.

1. Decreased self-esteem due to perceived or actual body image changes
2. Lack of knowledge about anatomic and physiological changes after surgery
3. Anxiety about future health
4. Depression
5. Decreased self-confidence in ability to perform role functions after surgery
6. Fear of rejection by others
7. Denial of implications of surgery
8. Dysfunctional dependence or independence

Planning

The plan for her health care must be acceptable to the woman client. Participation in the decision-making process fosters the development of her self-esteem. A broad or general goal for the client undergoing hysterectomy or mastectomy follows.

> The client will perceive herself as a worthwhile individual who understands what is happening to her, and possess a realistic outlook and the ability to problem-solve in the future.

The nurse also formulates specific, measurable objectives for each actual or potential problem of the client.

> The client will make positive statements about her appearance before discharge from the hospital.
> The client will correctly describe the function of the uterus and the effects of its removal on her body.

Intervention

Before intervening with women clients undergoing hysterectomy or mastectomy, the nurse must look at her own feelings about the loss of female organs, cancer, and these surgical alterations. Confronting and dealing with her own responses will prepare the nurse to promote the client's

Excerpts from an Interview with a Postoperative Mastectomy Client

I. Assessment of self-concept:
  A. How would you describe yourself?
    1. Your appearance?
      "Not very good. Awful, I look awful."
    2. Your outlook on life?
      "Cheerful, with a coverup."
  B. What is your understanding of why this operation was necessary?
    "To keep me alive, and keep the cancer from spreading."
  C. Can you recall your reaction when you first learned that this operation was necessary?
    "I thought, 'This couldn't be real.' I was angry and hysterical."
  D. Do you anticipate any changes?
    1. In your body's functioning?
      "Yes. I wonder if I will be able to do everything I did before."
    2. Your body's appearance?
      "Oh yes. How will I look in my clothes? Will everyone notice the difference?"
  E. How do you feel about these anticipated changes?
    "Bewildered and confused."
  F. How would you describe your usual reaction to a stressful situation?
    "I always try to keep my cool."
  G. Do religious practices have meanings for you?
    "Yes. It's what will carry me through this experience. It's made me stronger."
  H. How are you feeling about your surgery now?
    "I am grateful to be alive. Sometimes I wonder, 'Did they get it all, and are they lying to me?'"
II. Assessment of role
  A. Educational background?
    "B.S."
  B. Do you work outside the home?
    "No."
  C. With whom do you live?
    "My husband and two children; they are teenagers."
  D. Will you describe your activities at home?
    "General housework, care of the family, and gardening."
  E. What kind of activities do you do for fun?
    "Swimming, sailing."
III. Assessment of interrelationships
  A. Has your present illness affected your relationship with your husband, family, friends, or coworkers?
    "No. But I now appreciate them more."
  B. Do you anticipate any changes in your relationships with your husband?
    "Yes, some. I wonder how he will look at me. I don't feel sexy."
  C. Do you anticipate needing help with your usual routines when you return home?
    "No, I will be able to manage fine myself."

Discussion

It is important to remember that the assessment data do not need to be gathered at one time. Some client responses require immediate intervention; others lead to further questioning and analysis. The client may need to express her feelings about one issue before moving on to the next.

This assessment interview shows some typical, yet unique, responses from a client who has undergone mastectomy. The nurse analyzes the data and notes the client's reference to her "coverup" and her concerns about survival, body image, and role performance. Beginning interventions include encouraging further expression of feelings and giving concrete and direct information. This might also be an appropriate time to involve her with a Reach to Recovery volunteer.

The nurse also notes the client's concern about her relationship with her husband and deems that an area of high priority for intervention.

The client's responses indicate that she is independent and feels she will need no help with usual activities upon her return home. It is expected that the recovery period will extend beyond the hospital stay. The nurse is responsible for exploring the client's perceptions of the recovery period and offering concrete suggestions about activities to the client and her family.

adaptation to these losses. The nurse must face the question, "Am I strong enough to hear what the client has to say?" Although the general guidelines that were discussed in the section Childbearing and Parenting, are also appropriate here, some specific interventions for the woman with surgical alterations follow.

Communicating Therapeutically. The use of therapeutic communication allows the woman freedom to express her feelings about these surgical procedures. This expression of her feelings will be encouraged by the non-judgmental statements and open-ended questions of a warm, caring health care provider. The nurse also encourages the woman to discuss her feelings and concerns with her loved ones. If the woman is unable to express her feelings verbally, she may be encouraged to express them through the medium of writing. Informing the woman of your availability when she is ready to talk will help her realize that you are genuinely interested in her well-being.

The nurse empathizes with the woman client and accepts her feelings as real and worthy of attention (see Theapeutic Dialogue: Exploring the Feelings of a Woman

Therapeutic Dialogue

Exploring the Feelings of a Woman After Mastectomy

Two days ago, Mrs. C. B. underwent a mastectomy of the right breast. The nurse who has been caring for her since her admission to the hospital now enters the client's room and finds her crying.

Nurse: (with hands on Mrs. B.'s shoulder, waits quietly for a few minutes)

Client: (still crying, but more softly, looks at the nurse)

Nurse: (softly, conveying care, and maintaining eye contact) Mrs. B., you seem upset. Is there anything you would like to talk about?

Client: My whole life has changed.

Nurse: Your whole life has changed?

Client: Well, yes, just look at me . . . (pauses and looks down at her chest) I don't even feel like a woman anymore.

Nurse: You feel that, without your breast, you are not a woman?

Client: I . . . I don't know, it's hard to say. (a period of silence) I feel so confused.

Nurse: Will you tell me a little more about what being a woman means to you?

Discussion

The client postmastectomy frequently has a need to cry. Crying will help her release pent-up emotions and should be accepted by others. Standing near her, making physical contact, and using periods of silence help the woman feel accepted and cared for. By acknowledging and encouraging the expression of her feelings, the nurse explores with the client what being a woman means to her.

After Mastectomy). For example, the nurse conveys, through words and attitude, "I can understand how you could feel that way. . . ."

Providing Physical Care. Providing for the woman's physical well-being and comfort is the basis for competent nursing care. Freedom from incisional pain, abdominal distention, and fatigue will allow the client to rest, mobilize her resources, and, eventually, deal with the physical and emotional implications of her surgery. The nurse also assists the client to maintain her personal appearance, which, in turn, enhances her self-esteem.

Fostering Independence. In the early stages of her recovery, the woman is permitted, and even encouraged, to satisfy her dependency needs. This period of dependent behavior allows her time to mobilize her strengths. The nurse then begins to foster the client's independence as soon as, and to whatever degree, she is able to do for herself. Praising her independent behavior reinforces its occurrence.

There are times, however, when the woman's regression and dependency should be supported. Certain predictable, stressful times require the presence of a caring health professional. During the woman's first look at her mastectomy scar, for example, she needs privacy and the nurse's presence, acceptance, and, perhaps, touch.

Discharge Teaching. Several areas of concern should be addressed with the woman client undergoing surgical alterations prior to her discharge from the hospital. This should include information about the drugs she will be taking, the available community resources, and the perceived effects of surgery on sexual activity.[48] After mastectomy, the woman will need information about the fitting of a prosthesis.

Two examples of valuable community resources are as follows.

1. The American Cancer Society's Reach for Recovery. Through this program, women who have undergone mastectomy help other breast cancer patients during their initial recovery period; the woman client's physician must make the referral.
2. Encore (Encouragement, Normalcy, Counseling, Opportunity Reaching out Energies revived). This program of the YWCA focuses on exercises performed on land and in water that aid women in rebuilding their physical and emotional strengths after mastectomy.

A summary of other programs available in various cities may be found in The Breast Cancer Digest.[31]

Evaluation

If objectives are realistic and interventions are appropriate for each identified client problem, the nurse will assess positive signs of emotional adaptations to hysterectomy and mastectomy. Often, the adaptive process is just beginning at the time of the woman's discharge from the hospital; the continued support of family, friends, and community resources is necessary. During the evaluation process, the nurse may identify adaptation problem areas of the client in which the nurse is unable to intervene. Such problems should be referred to another health care professional with the necessary expertise.

Menopause

The menopause is that period in a woman's life that marks the permanent cessation of menstrual activity. It can be diagnosed retrospectively, after one year has elapsed.[23] Menopause is not a disease, however, but a normal physiological process.

The terms *menopause, female climacteric,* and *change of life* have been used interchangeably not only to describe the biologic occurrence, but also to symbolize the fact that one is middle-aged and quickly approaching old age.[13] Because of the myths surrounding menopause, many women anticipate this time in their lives with dread and respond to it as if in physical and emotional pain (see insert, Myths and Misconceptions About Menopause). The continuous message in American society, that these are years of declining usefulness and value, proves stressful to women. It is important, then, for nurses and other health care providers to understand the impact of this physiological process and its associated stressors for the woman client and to promote psychological adaptation and well-being.

Significant Life Changes

"Change of life" is an accurate description of the middle years because of the many major changes taking place in the life of the middle-aged adult.[13] The significant life changes that expose a woman to stress at this time include the following.

1. Children reaching maturity and leaving home
2. Possible alteration in marital (or other significant) relationship
3. Returning to the work force (and possible unpreparedness for, or reassessment of, one's place in the work force)
4. Significant physical changes

The menopause occurs at a time in a woman's life—at the average age of 49 years in the United States—when the traditional role assigned to her by society, that of mothering, is essentially complete. A woman's crisis during menopause, therefore, is often one of lost identity. With no clearly defined and socially accepted role for the later years, the middle-aged woman sees menopause as a symbol of profound loss.[19] She may increasingly question her self-worth as she seeks to redefine herself, an inevitable characteristic of the developmental task of the middle years. During this stage of generativity versus stagnation, a woman's need to be needed when the children are gone can lead to emptiness and depression.

As their children mature and leave home, the woman and her husband must adapt to being a couple again. Their communication may have centered on the children for so long that they now find it difficult to express needs as individuals. The perimenopausal woman may even discover she has no supportive person to help her. Often, couples face the prospect of divorce during these years because they have, sometimes unknowingly, drifted apart.

The perimenopausal woman often faces the dilemma of how to use her excess time. In the past, women frequently turned to volunteerism. Faced with the reality of today's economy, however, many women are forced to enter the work force; for some of these women, it may be the first time in their lives to hold a job outside the home. In the 1980s, unfortunately, many of these women are ill-prepared to enter the work force. They often hold low-paying and boring jobs, another contributor to low self-esteem. As a result of societal changes, future generations of menopausal women may be less affected by this potential stressor.

Physical Changes

Changes in body functioning occur during the middle years. The most obvious change, cessation of menstruation, results as the ovaries finally stop functioning. Other physical effects may include vasomotor instability, atrophic vaginitis, osteoporosis, coronary atherosclerosis, and skin and muscle changes. If a woman has been dependent on a youthful body for affirmation of her femininity, she may find it difficult to accept the changes associated with menopause.

Perception of the Menopause

When the woman perceives the menopause as a loss, such as the loss of the mothering role or the loss of purpose, youth, femininity, and self-esteem, she will experience a grief response.

Some of the more frequently observed responses to the menopause include emotional lability, anxiety, feelings of tension and nervousness, insomnia with resultant fatigue, vague bodily aches, and depression. An individual woman's reaction to the menopause, however, is highly variable. Some women respond to the climacteric with no notable behavioral changes, whereas others respond to it with all the typically described behaviors. A woman's response seems to depend greatly on her feelings about herself and

Myths and Misconceptions About Menopause

1. Menopause brings on depression and mental illness.
2. Menopause is a deficiency disease.
3. The hot flashes associated with menopause occur at any time and they are unbearable.
4. A menopausal woman will become old, fat, and wrinkled overnight.
5. The menopausal woman loses interest in sex, and becomes sexless.
6. Menopausal women drive their husbands to other, younger women.
7. The menopausal woman is always tired.
8. Menopause is the end of womanhood, because womanhood is equated with fertility.
9. Menopause is *the* change of life.

her womanhood. If youth, motherhood, and femininity have been the major sources of her self-esteem, she may have a more severe, and, perhaps, destructive, reaction to the menopause than a woman with a number of interests and fulfilling activities outside her home.[13]

On the other hand, many women do not view the end of fertility as a tragedy. Moving into the middle years can be a special time for a woman.[19] Such women are questioning sexual stereotypes and confining social roles.

The Nursing Process

The nurse's role in helping the perimenopausal woman meet her needs is to approach her as a unique individual reacting to physical and environmental stressors. The nurse or other health care provider strives to minimize the impact of these stressors and maximize the client's adaptation and growth.

Assessment and Analysis

A thorough assessment of biopsychosocial factors is important to determine to what extent the client's present distress results from the impact of the menopausal experience. Biologic assessment includes a complete menstrual history and consideration of the presenting physical symptoms. To obtain the psychosocial assessment, it is again suggested that you use the Roy adaptation framework to help you organize data about the woman's self-concept, role, and interrelationships, which are affected during the perimenopausal years. The following serves as a guide to this important information.

I. Assessment of self-concept
   A. How would you describe yourself?
      1. Your appearance?
      2. Your outlook on life?
   B. Have you noted any changes in your body during the past years? (if not, do you anticipate any changes?)
   C. How do you feel about these changes?
   D. How would you describe your general state of health?
   E. Describe what comes to mind when you hear or think of the term "menopause."
   F. During this time of their lives, women sometimes report feeling "different." Have you noticed any differences?
      1. In your mood or temperament?
      2. In your energy level?
   G. How do you feel about these differences?
   H. How have you reacted in the past to changes occurring in your life?
   I. How would you like to describe yourself?
      1. In the next few years?
      2. Ten years from now?
II. Assessment of role mastery
   A. Educational background
   B. Marital status and number of children

C. Do you presently have children living at home?
   D. Did you work outside the home while your children were growing up?
   E. Can you describe how you felt when your last child left home?
   F. Are you presently working outside the home?
   G. What do you like most about your job?
   H. What do you like least about your job?
   I. What other interests do you have outside the home and your job?
   J. How important are these interests to you?
III. Assessment of interdependency or interrelationships
   A. Marital status and years of marriage
   B. Who is the most important person to you?
   C. For whom are you responsible?
   D. (If married) Have you noted any changes in your marital relationship?
      1. During the last year?
      2. Since your children left home?
   E. How would you describe your present relationship with your children?
   F. How do you feel about this relationship (or these relationships)?
   G. To whom would you turn if you needed help?

Depending on the woman and her concerns, other assessment data may be necessary to complete the picture within this framework.

Identifying Adaptation Problems.   Analysis and validation of the assessment data often reveal the following psychosocial problems and potential problems for the menopausal client.

1. Decreased self-esteem
2. Anxiety, due to perception of losses
3. Depression, due to perception of losses
4. Anxiety, due to lack of knowledge about expected physical changes
5. Anxiety about future roles

Planning

Together, the nurse and the woman client formulate a realistic plan to promote adaptation during the menopause and, thereby, enhance her self-esteem. The woman's desired view of herself in the future guides long-range planning. Specific behavioral objectives are determined conjointly to address each identified problem. An example of a specific objective is that the menopausal client will state that she views herself and her physical appearance in a positive manner.

Intervention

Women in the menopausal years during this transitional time in American society are often dependent on others for their feelings of worth. The nurse incorporates these significant others into the plan of care.

Communicating Therapeutically. The nurse realizes that it is important that the client expresses how she feels about this time of her life and how the perceived changes are affecting her. The woman needs to examine the multiple influences in her life and discover which factors are creating stress. For effective and therapeutic communication, the nurse must encourage open expression of the woman's feelings within a nonjudgmental atmosphere.

Health Teaching. The nurse draws from her knowledge of the physiological bases of menopause to clarify the myths and misconceptions that surround it. The individual who understands what is going on within her body is better able to cope with it. The nurse explains health maintenance through proper nutrition, rest, and exercise, and various treatment modalities, such as the use of estrogen therapy.

Anticipatory Guidance. The client is guided in using problem-solving techniques to identify her strengths and resources. The nurse supports, praises, and thereby reinforces the woman's positive attempts to determine solutions to her own problems. Encouraging the menopausal client to share her experiences with other women may help to demystify the event.

Evaluation

The nurse evaluates the responses of the woman client by reviewing the behavioral outcomes. Is there evidence that her self-esteem has increased? Does the woman now express more positive feelings about herself and her abilities? Is she able to view the menopause as another natural occurrence in her life during which her own inner strength and support system will guide her to new horizons?

Summary

This chapter emphasizes the importance of the psychosocial significance of certain adaptations and interruptions in women's health. Some of the foci of the chapter have included the following.

1. Today's female seeking health care faces conflicts related to the traditional and emerging roles of women in our society.
2. Women's traditional place within the health care system has been a subordinate one, but that is presently being questioned.
3. Many of women's health problems are related to how the individual perceives her physical and personal selves.
4. The nurse frequently deals with the recurring themes of loss, anxiety, stress, and powerlessness in the health care of women.
5. Application of the nursing process to the specific

issues of childbearing and parenting, the surgical alterations of hysterectomy and mastectomy, and the menopause includes consideration of the psychosocial significance of these events.

6. Psychosocial assessment of the woman client in the health care setting is based on the Roy adaptation framework, addressing the client's self-concept, role, and interrelationships.
7. General interventions to promote adaptation to these common health alterations include therapeutic communication, mutual goal-setting, health care teaching, and anticipatory guidance.
8. By designing nursing care to meet the needs of the whole person, nurses can have a significant impact on the woman client experiencing childbearing and parenting, surgical alterations, or menopause, as well as an impact on her significant others.

References

1. American Cancer Society: Facts and Figures. New York, American Cancer Society, 1981
2. Bibring B et al: A Study of the Psychological Process in Pregnancy and the Earliest Mother–Child Relationships. Psychoanalytic Study of the Child 14:25–26, 1959
3. Bradwick JM: In Transition. New York, Holt, Reinhart, 1979
4. Carrington BW: The AfroAmerican. In Clark AL (ed): Culture, Childbearing, Health Professionals, pp 35–51. Philadelphia, F. A. Davis, 1978
5. Chung HJ: Understanding the Oriental Maternity Patient. Nurs Clin North Am 12 (March): 67–75, 1977
6. deChateau P: The Influence of Early Contact on Maternal and Infant Behavior in Primiparae." Birth and the Family Journal 3 (Winter): 149–155, 1976–1977
7. Driever MJ: Theory of Self-Concept. In Roy SC (ed): Introduction to Nursing: An Adaptation Model, pp 169–179. New Jersey, Prentice-Hall, 1976
8. Dyer ED: Parenthood as Crisis: A Restudy. In Parad H (ed): Crisis Intervention, Selected Readings, pp 312–323. New York, Family Service Association of America, 1965
9. Erikson E: Childhood and Society, 2nd ed. New York, WW Norton, 1963
10. Fee E: Women and Health Care: A Comparison of Theories. In Dreifus C (ed): Seizing Our Bodies, pp 279–297. New York, Vintage Books, 1977
11. Friedan B: The Feminine Mystique. New York, WW Norton, 1963
12. Fruchler RG et al: The Women's Health Movement, Where Are We Now? In Dreifus C (ed): Seizing Our Bodies, pp 271–278. New York, Vintage Books, 1977
13. Galloway K: The Change of Life. Am J Nurs 75 (June): 1006–1011, 1975
14. Hogan R: Human Sexuality: A Nursing Perspective. New York, Appleton-Century-Crofts, 1980
15. Kay MA: The Mexican American. In Clark AL (ed):

Culture, Childbearing, Health Professionals, pp 88–108. Philadelphia, FA Davis, 1978

16. Lake A: Our Own Years, What Women Over 35 Should Know About Themselves. New York, Random House, 1979

17. LeMasters EE: Parenthood as Crisis. In Parad H (ed): Crisis Intervention, Selected Readings, pp 312–323. New York, Family Service Association of America, 1965

18. Levinson R: Sexism in Medicine. Am J Nurs 76 (March): 426–431, 1976

19. Martin LL: Health Care of Women. Philadelphia, JB Lippincott, 1978

20. Martinson IM, Anderson S: Male and Female Response to Stress. In Kjervik DK, Martinson I (eds): Women in Stress: A Nursing Perspective, pp 89–95. New York, Appleton-Century-Crofts, 1979

21. Maslow AH: Motivation and Personality. New York, Harper & Row, 1954

22. Peretz D: Development, Object-Relationships, and Loss. In Schoenberg B et al (eds): Loss and Grief: Psychological Management in Medical Practice, pp 3–19. New York, Columbia University Press, 1970

23. Perlmutter JF: A Gynecological Approach to Menopause. In Notman MT, Nadelson C (eds): The Woman Patient: Medical and Psychological Interfaces, pp 323–335, Vol 1. New York, Plenum Press, 1978

24. Roeske NA: Hysterectomy and Other Gynecological Surgeries: A Psychological View. In Notman MT, Nadelson C (eds): The Woman Patient: Medical and Psychological Interfaces, Vol 1, pp 217–231. New York, Plenum Press, 1978

25. Roy Sr C: Problems in Self Ideal and Expectancy: Powerlessness. In Calliota R: Introduction to Nursing: An Adaptation Model, pp 224–231. New Jersey, Prentice-Hall, 1976

26. Scaff M: The More Sorrowful Sex. Psychology Today 12 (April): 44–52, 89–90, 1979

27. Schoenberg B, Carr AC: Loss of External Organs: Limb Amputation, Mastectomy, and Disfiguration. In Schoenberg B et al (eds): Loss and Grief: Psychological Management in Medical Practice, pp 119–131. New York, Columbia University Press, 1970

28. Spock B: Decent and Indecent. New York, Fawcett World, 1971

29. Tanner LM: Developmental Tasks of Pregnancy. In Bergersen BS et al (eds): Current Concepts in Clinical Nursing, Vol 2, pp 292–297. St. Louis, CV Mosby, 1969

30. US Department of Health and Human Services: Facts at Your Fingertips. Washington, DC, DHSS, 1978

31. US Department of Health and Human Services: The Breast Cancer Digest. Bethesda, MD, National Cancer Institute, May, 1980

32. Weideger P: Menstruation and Menopause: The Physiology and Psychology, The Myth and the Reality. New York, Alfred A Knopf, 1976

33. Williams R: The Perceptions of Motherhood as Viewed by Primigravidas. M. N. Thesis, University of California at Los Angeles, 1972

34. Willson JR, Beecham CT, Carrington ER: Obstetrics and Gynecology, 4th ed. St Louis, CV Mosby, 1971

Chapter 38
Death and Dying

You hurry on—
but for one brief moment
saw the anguished night of darkness,
heard the echoes of fear and terror,
felt both human strength and weakness.

You hurry on—
but for one brief moment
knew that you made all the difference.
And—for one brief moment prayed.

P. Mahon

Patricia N. Mahon

Chapter Preview

Death is an inevitable event that every living organism faces as the finality of life and living. Death, said Jung, is probably the only irreversible and unequivocal process we experience that is directed toward a goal, a state of complete rest.

This chapter discusses the theoretical, philosophical, religious, and "American" viewpoints of death and dying. The stages of dying are described in relation to the dying client, his significant others, and the professionals involved in his care. The chapter also examines mourning and societal rites. Nursing care of the dying client and his family—both physical and psychological care—is explored.

Learning Objectives

On completion of the chapter, the reader should be able to accomplish the following.

1. Discuss theoretical, philosophical, religious, and "American" perspectives of death and dying
2. Discuss the meaning of death to the client, his family and friends, and the health care professionals caring for him
3. Compare the behavior of clients, significant others, and health care providers during various levels of awareness of dying
4. Provide examples of clients' and family members' behavior during each stage of dying
5. Discuss the implications of certain special circumstances of death, such as sudden death and death of a child
6. Describe physical and psychological nursing care of the dying individual and his family

Perspectives of Death and Dying

Theoretical Viewpoints

The meaning of death has troubled man from the beginning of time; its meaning and relationship to life have been the philosopher's enigmas. From the time of the ancient Greeks, death's mysterious relationship with life has been examined. The major religions of the world deal intimately with death and view it as a commencement or transformation to another type of existence. At one end of the continuum, death may be perceived as the ultimate threat of nonexistence; at the other end, as a blessed relief for those in painful agony.

Psychologists and sociologists have theorized about death and have made it a topic of study. Freud believed that the ego of man was incapable of understanding the possibility of his own future nonexistence. He proposed that people experience, simultaneously, anxiety over death and a death instinct.[9] In strong disagreement with Freud, Carl Jung presented the idea that the most important and positive aspect of individuation, or unique development of self, is recognition and acceptance of one's mortality and fulfillment of the tasks to prepare for death.[17] The integration of death into the process of living may be viewed existentially as an essential aspect of development and a way to diminish the individual's vulnerability to a neurotic denial process.[28]

Systematic investigations into the generally tabooed topic of death began after the appearance of Feifel's book, The Meaning of Death, in 1959.[7] In the 5 years following the book's publication, its impact was reflected in the scientific community in the appearance of a greater amount of social, psychological, and medical literature on death, dying, and grief than had appeared in the previous century. In 1973, the Center for Death Education and Research at the University of Minnesota published a bibliography of more than 2600 references on the topic of death and related issues.[12]

One author examined the individual denial reactions to death and categorized them according to degrees:

1st degree—denial of the clinical facts
2nd degree—denial of the implications of the clinical facts
3rd degree—denial of extinction or nonexistence[38]

An individual may reach a level of "middle knowledge" or vascillation between complete denial and acceptance. On the other hand, an individual may experience both acceptance and denial of death at the same time, which may serve as an adaptational process in the preparation for death.[8]

The American View of Death

The thought of death elicits anxiety and denial in modern man. Death has become an enemy that evokes our greatest fears. American society, with its emphasis on the "to be" and the young, has little room for the concept of "no future." Death, therefore, has the power to stir our fear and hostility and to set into motion a process of denial. Many view death as the final loss of identity, complete extinction, or the annihilation of the individual's significance.

The coping mechanisms of our culture have attempted to disguise death or pretend that its finality does not exist. An example of this pretense is the elaborate burial rite in which the body is prepared "to look natural" for the funeral at the cost of many thousands of dollars. In addition, the language or phrases we use to communicate that an individual has died reflects yet another ritual of denial. The phrases, such as "he passed on" or "she's gone," utilized by lay and professional persons alike, are common attempts to avoid discussing death directly. The American funeral has been sarcastically described as "grief therapy" for those who try to "buy off" the grief process in dollars and cents.[27]

The American way of death primarily incorporates the Judeo-Christian orientation of our society. There are basically two reactions to death in our contemporary world—avoidance and preoccupation with death as a destructive force. Death delivers with it separation, from the body as well as from loved ones, and reawakens the childhood threat of abandonment.[26] Most individuals readily admit that they will die, but view their own death and the deaths of their loved ones as events that are far removed and in the distant future. The prevalent attitude in our society, says Kubler-Ross, is "It shall happen to thee and thee but not to me."[21]

In direct counteraction to these views of death is the "happy death movement," which attempts to promote a change in the American society's taboo on death.[25] The three main components of this movement are immortality, positivity, and expressivity. Immortality is associated with a belief in an afterlife, positivity is the breaking away from secularism and materialism of society, and expressivity is the open expression of feelings about dying. There will, however, always be individuals who, at any cost, emotional or monetary, will wish to prolong life. There will be others who will not, or cannot, express feelings about living or dying. Still others may see themselves as failures if they are unable to "grow" in this final chance for achievement and end their lives as they have viewed themselves during life.

Death is inevitable, no matter what ritual, thoughts, or actions we attempt to use to magically control or alter the reality. Both professionals and lay persons continue to experience the ambivalences of death and continue to move closer to a new understanding and realistic acceptance of what is inevitable as a stage of potential growth. We must use the strengths of the new philosophy of caring for the dying, while maintaining objectivity about its limits.[2]

Meaning of Death

Meaning of Death to the Client

Relocation of Care

Medical progress in the past few decades has proven to be a double-edged sword to the dying individual. This progress has not only altered the care and treatment of the dying, but has relocated the place of death and the interaction of the dying with loved ones. Rarely does an individual die in the privacy of home and family; rather, he is subjected to the institutional "public square" of the impersonal hospital. This transfer to the institution of what was once an intimate, personal, and private process reinforces our denial of death and breeds isolation and loneliness for the dying individual.

Fear of Abandonment

Loneliness is the experience that results from the dying person's exposure to the abandonment of others and the isolation in the institutional setting.[19] The lengthier the process of dying, the greater the feelings of abandonment and isolation that are experienced by the dying individual (see Therapeutic Dialogue: Living with a Terminal Illness). The dying patient manifests three basic levels of fear—fear of pain, fear of loneliness, and fear of meaninglessness.[41]

The interaction between the dying patient and his family or staff has been described as "premortem dying."[40] The individual's isolation is potentiated by the nonverbal gestures of dimming the lights and drawing the blinds, and the verbal gestures of whispering and giving stereotyped answers to the patients' questions. Despite increasing public and professional attention to the subject of death and dying, dying still remains a lonely and isolated event in which the patient often feels "dehumanized, impersonalized, and mechanized."[20]

The "Sick Role"

The process of dying also places the individual in a dependent position with many role expectations. Society has carved out a unique position for the ill individual. The expectations associated with the illness role include the rights to be dependent, to accept help from those whom the patient previously has not known, and to have the anticipation that he will be cared for. To possess these rights, patients must conform to the bureaucratic structure and expected behaviors of the health care system. Those who do not conform to the role expectations and bureaucratic structures cause much annoyance to health care providers and may be viewed as demanding or "difficult patients," or may be subtly avoided.

By accepting the sick role, the individual patient loses control over his environment, loses the right to make decisions about basic functions such as eating and sleeping, and loses his familiar and secure social roles, such as father, mother, boss, worker, breadwinner. These losses, which are inherent in the sick role, and the change in role expectations place the individual in a vulnerable, dependent, childlike position, and may prompt him to view himself at the mercy of the professional staff. (The insert, The Living Will, illustrates one recently adopted alternative to a terminal patient's complete loss of control.)

The Stigma of Nonexistence

The dying person not only confronts new experiences and new roles, he is also saddled with a stigma; he represents what all of us fear—our own nonexistence.[15] Instead of dealing with our death fears, we tend to view the dying individual as "different," thereby protecting ourselves, in some magical way, form the horror of death. This process of stigmatization further isolates the dying individual and compounds the loneliness of the dying process.

Therapeutic Dialogue

Living with a Terminal Illness

Dave is a 16-year-old diagnosed with terminal bone cancer. In the last year, he has undergone two surgeries and chemotherapy. This interview took place at a recreational center where Dave spends time with his friends. Dave was expecting the interviewer and was aware of the topic of the interview.

Nurse: Hi Dave, I'm Dr. M.

Client: Yeah, hi . . . I've been expecting you. Let's go sit under the tree by the courts.

Nurse: You look like you're having fun.

Client: Yep, it's about time . . . I was letting myself die too long . . . until I finally got a little smarts and I said to myself, this death thing . . . you've been just going down, down . . . you've got to LIVE! You know you can make the decision to die, like my doctor said, just give up, lay there and finally die.

Nurse: Did that happen to you?

Client: Oh yeah, for a long time all I did was stay in bed in my room . . . didn't do a thing.

Nurse: Just stayed alone . . . and did you experience anger?

Client: Yep, when I was laying there I used to think over and over again, why me, why me . . . why did I get picked out for cancer? It seemed like I just finally said to myself, "Dave, you're just gonna have to die or live—not live just like I was—you're gonna have to really LIVE!! I just can't do everything I used to do before. So I went back to my regular school and did most of what I used to. Most my friends knew I was going to die—and it was hard—nobody would say anything at first and they didn't invite me to do all the things we all used to. But it got better—I guess they just forgot about me dying.

Nurse: That was difficult.

Client: Yep, for a while it made me more scared, but now it's O.K. . . .

Nurse: You might have to have more surgery. . . .

Client: That's what they wanted . . . but after my last surgery when I finally woke up . . . I said to myself, "No way am I ever going to go back for any more. My mom said that I had the choice, and I don't want to go through all that pain any more for nothing. I know that they can't cure it . . . and that's O.K. It hurts my mom, but she understands.

Discussion

One of the greatest stressors experienced by the dying is the isolation from family and friends. Sometimes, this occurs when significant others avoid conversations dealing with the client's feelings about his illness and impending death. Nurses and other health care professionals can fill this need for openness and truthfulness by accepting the client's expressions. The nurse listens to, acknowledges, and refrains from making judgments about these expressions.

The individual who is living with a terminal illness faces multiple, real losses. Interpersonal or social support should not have to be one of these losses when health care providers intervene therapeutically.

The Living Will

In caring for the dying, it is critically important to respect the individual's decisions and wishes. The Living Will is one attempt to communicate to family, friends, and physician that one wishes to be allowed to die when that event becomes inevitable.

Although it has little legal power except in California, the Living Will is a legal document and, therefore, must be signed in the presence of two witnesses; notarization is not necessary. It is suggested that the individual who wishes to utilize the Living Will provide copies to his physician and significant others and discuss with them his decision about terminal care. The individual must also carry a copy of the Living Will on his person to guarantee that his wishes will be known to health care providers. A copy of the Living Will follows.

TO MY FAMILY, MY PHYSICIAN, MY LAWYER, MY CLERGYMAN

TO ANY MEDICAL FACILITY IN WHOSE CARE I HAPPEN TO BE

TO ANY INDIVIDUAL WHO MAY BECOME RESPONSIBLE FOR MY

HEALTH, WELFARE OR AFFAIRS

Death is as much a reality as birth, growth, maturity and old age—it is the one certainty of life. If the time comes when I, _____ can no longer take part in decisions for my own future, let this statement stand as an expression of my wishes, while I am still of sound mind.

If the situation should arise in which there is no reasonable expectation of my recovery from physical or mental disability, I request that I be allowed to die and not be kept alive by artificial means or "heroic measures." I do not fear death itself as much as the indignities of deterioration, dependence, and hopeless pain. I, therefore, ask that medication be mercifully administered to me to alleviate suffering even though this may hasten the moment of death.

This request is made after careful consideration. I hope you who care for me will feel morally bound to follow its mandate. I recognize that this appears to place a heavy responsibility upon you, but it is with the intention of relieving you of such responsibility and of placing it upon myself in accordance with my strong convictions, that this statement is made.

Signed _____

Date _____

Witness _____

Witness _____

Copies of this request have been given to _____

_____

_____

_____

_____

It is almost an impossibility to be truly prepared for death, because we cannot imagine ourselves as nonexistent. Although fear of death is a part of the human experience, we find that, many times, the older individual seems to be less fearful than the young person and, consequently, is more often concerned about the deaths of his loved ones, friends, and pets. In a lengthy terminal illness, an individual may even welcome death as a release from pain. A client's religious belief or philosophical orientation may alter his acceptance of death and may individualize his dying process.

The acceptance of death as an inevitable and individual process may begin early in life for one person, whereas, for another, this realization may not be reached until he experiences the physical signs and deterioration of aging. A small group of individuals may attempt to deny death to the very ends of their lives.

Meaning of Death to Family Members and Loved Ones

The Experience of Loss

The loss of a loved one is experienced not only through death, but also through lengthy illness, divorce, and separation. The experience of each loss requires adjustment to the specific life circumstance. All losses in life, including the loss of a loved one through death, involve a part of the "self"; therefore, the experience is unique for each individual. Survivors experience difficulty in reintegrating as a family unit and as individuals. The dying process and the loss ensued are often more difficult experiences for the survivors than for the dying person. Every family in which a loss by sudden, unexpected, or expected death has occurred is defined as a family at risk or in crisis.[4]

Anticipatory Grief

During the hospitalization of a terminally ill family member, the other family members begin to experience intense feelings of loss. This phenomenon is termed *anticipatory grief* and occurs when the family and loved ones know for sure that the individual will die.

Anticipatory grief is a phenomenon within our contemporary world that has been identified by professionals concerned with the mental health of the public. Identifying and nurturing anticipatory grief are vital aspects of pre- and post-death counseling and the reconstruction and reintegration of the survivor's emotional and social life. This phenomenon aids in the grief transition and acceptance of the death of the loved one, and therefore frees the survivor's energy to function in the decision-making of everyday living. Although anticipatory grief work may function as a positive experience in the adjustment of the survivor, it presents itself as a double-edged sword to the dying individual. The dying individual must not only deal with his own loss, but must also attempt to cope with the loss of emotional support of the loved one.

Another backlash of anticipatory grief is felt when the loved one's actual death and funeral are confronted. Historically, funeral rites have functioned as ceremonies to provide emotional support to the survivors and to strengthen familial, friendship, and community bonds. When anticipatory grief has helped the survivors separate from the dying client, their expected mourning behaviors are minimized and they may be criticized for coldness or lack of love of the dead individual. Traditional funeral rites will not disappear because of anticipatory grief work, but, for a large number of individuals, they will change significantly.

Coping with the Loss

From the earliest investigations, it has been observed that under "normal" circumstances, "normal" individuals will experience "normal" grief reactions and return to a "normal" state of functioning. It has, however, been observed that if the pattern is disrupted in any way, such as when there is a lack of evidence that death has occurred (*e.g.*, war deaths) or when the primary denial reaction is not overcome, then a maladaptive reaction to the loss may occur, such as a major pathological depression or even psychosis in certain instances.

Family members and friends begin to cope with the loss of an individual through death before the actual death occurs and continue to deal with their loss after the death. *Coping behavior* may be defined as all of the mechanisms utilized by individuals to deal with significant threats to their psychological stability and to enable them to function in daily living.[37] Coping behaviors are responses to environmental factors that assist the individual regain control or master the situation and successfully adapt to the stressor.

The Process of Mourning

During the initial stage of mourning impact, the mourning individuals have difficulty determining their own needs and lack the initiative or energy to search out the needed helping service. The second phase, or middle stage of mourning, may extend beyond one year after the death, during which the family and friends acutely feel the losses. During this second phase, the mourner experiences loneliness and a need to speak about the deceased. The third phase, accommodation, overlaps the first two phases, from 3 months to 2 years after the loss. Those who have experienced anticipatory grief appear to have less severe grief reactions and enter the accommodation stage earlier.

The dying individuals and their families may move through the stages of dying identified by Kubler-Ross—denial, anger, bargaining, depression, and acceptance—although not necessarily at the same time or at the same pace. Successful mourning brings comfort when the family or friends attain a sense of peace or acceptance with the death. To grieve is to allow expression of the sorrow and other feelings but not to grasp on to the feelings as an excuse to avoid the gift of life that the mourners still possess.

In the process of grieving, the deep feelings of ambivalence; that is, love, anger, and guilt toward the lost loved one, are the emotions seen in a major depression. Although these emotions of the grieving person are, in varying degrees, identical to those of major depressions, they differ in origin and process. The grief process is healthy, necessary, and growth-producing; major depressions are personality structure-oriented and growth-blocking processes.

The length of the grieving reaction and the final adjustment made to a new social environment depends on the success of what is called the "grief work"; that is, freedom from the bondage to the deceased, reorientation to the environment in which the deceased is no longer present, and establishment of new relationships.[24] Some individuals resist accepting the discomfort and distress of mourning. They may choose to avoid the intense pain connected with the grief experience and the expression of the feelings associated with grieving. The avoidance or disruption of normal grieving may be the prelude to a morbid grief reaction. This morbid reaction may be reflected in both physiological and behavioral responses, ranging from psychosomatic conditions such as asthma, ulcerative colitis, and rheumatoid arthritis, to antisocial behavior and even psychosis.[24]

There are certain factors that must be considered when dealing with a bereaved individual because they can aid in understanding and predicting reactions and facilitating the helping relationship. These critical factors include the following.

1. The degree of significance the deceased played in the life of the survivor
2. How others react behaviorally to the death
3. The ages of the deceased and the survivor
4. The emotional and physical state of the survivor
5. Previous loss experiences
6. The presence of close friendships
7. Role changes necessitated by the death
8. The degree of the survivor's dependence upon the deceased

In addition, professionals must recognize the typical behaviors seen in a healthy response to the death of a significant other. Grief may be manifested in tears, overwhelming feelings of loss, desires to withdraw, imagined guilts over omissions, and a multitude of physical symptoms such as anorexia, headache, and dizziness. Health care professionals must accept grief-related behaviors because these behaviors help individuals reorganize and resume productive, functional living. These behavioral expressions loosen the ties to the deceased, which, in turn, frees the survivor to form new ties. It is particularly helpful for survivors to understand that the emotions they are experiencing are

common phenomena and that the deep hurting does come to an end.

The grieving process does not necessarily take place only after the physical death of the loved one. During a long illness, family members and significant others may actively move through the stages of mourning and may "let the other go"; in this way, they accept the person's death before his death actually takes place. Therefore, when the death finally occurs, the survivors may express, through verbal and nonverbal behavior, a sense of relief and peaceful acceptance.

Although none of us are able to control the inevitability of death, we can control the process by which the separation from life and loved ones takes place; we can create either a life-accepting or life-rejecting stage of development.

Meaning of Death to the Health Care Professional

Outside their own natural life experiences, many health professionals are as unprepared to deal with death and dying as is the lay person. Health education focuses on health, living, and the extension of life and neglects to teach coping skills in the care of the dying and their families. Because the underlying and subconscious goal in the ministering to the sick is health, a dying individual is difficult for health care providers to handle. Symbolically, the health care professional may experience death as a frontal attack on the professional goal of health promotion and life.

In addition to the professional threat, working with the dying stirs a more personal reminder of our own death, nonexistence, and abandonment. Nurses and other health care providers may avoid the dying by busying themselves with other patients, make short and only necessary contacts with the dying individual, move the dying person out of their constant vision and hearing, or overtly avoid the dying person and his family on the hospital unit.

One study found that a number of factors affected the physician's behavior toward the dying patient, including the patient's age, the patient's response to therapy, the rank or social worth of the patient, the ability of the patient or family to pay for services, the patient's attractiveness, the appeal of the disease, and the physician's own personality; that is, his optimism, conservativism, or radicalism.[23]

Nurses seem better able to face death than their coworkers. As one nurse succinctly stated,

> We readily care for those whom we can help cure, and it feels good... knowing a patient is going to die doesn't mean we can't receive just as much reward....[36]

In an investigation involving 15,400 nurses, it was found that a significant number felt that a dying person most needed to be allowed to die in peace, which included the right to refuse treatment. Sixty percent of the nurses believed that the patient should be told as soon as possible that he is dying.[29] One nurse therapist utilized role-playing to help the nursing staff in the coronary care unit deal with death. Staff members played the roles of the dying patient, the family, and the staff to reenact and work through difficulties they experienced in patient care situations. The therapist identified two major reactions: 1) the majority of the nursing staff were willing to deal directly with the patient and his problems with dying; and, 2) others attempted to ignore the problem of death and become involved with technical tasks, and proceeded to tell the patient that he was doing well.

It is necessary for the health care professional to accept and recognize his own mortality and examine his personal meaning of death to be effective in caring for the dying. Even when these steps have been accomplished, death is still difficult to view and the feelings accompanying it are painful.

Theories of Dying

Research and theory development regarding death and dying has increased dramatically in the past 20 years. Glaser and Strauss conducted a long-term sociologic study of dying and, from this intensive investigation, they published their work describing aspects of the process of dying.[13, 14]

Levels of Awareness of Dying

The dying client and his family, friends, and professional staff may experience awareness that the client is dying but each may be at different levels at any given time. The levels of awareness are as follows.

1. Closed awareness, or "keeping the secret." The client in this situation is not aware that he is dying but the family and professional staff are.
2. Suspicion awareness. The client has a suspicion that death may occur but cannot obtain sufficient information to verify it.
3. Mutual pretense awareness, or "let's pretend time." All individuals involved in the situation are aware of the active dying process, but a ritual of pretense is carried out by all.
4. Open awareness. All involved in the situation are aware of the active dying process and demonstrate their awareness in actions, communications, and the taking care of unfinished business.[13]

Expected Death Patterns

In a later publication, Glasser and Strauss discussed death expectations and professional care patterns.[14] A terminal patient, for example, cared for on a particular service (emergency room, cardiac intensive care unit, oncology unit, and so forth) is expected to die over an expected time period and in a predictable way.

Professional staff may assess when a patient will die and may, therefore, plan their work in light of their expectations. The death patterns have been divided into five categories:

1. Too sudden death
2. Vacillating pattern
3. Certain to die on time
4. Short-term reprieve
5. Lingering.

When the health professional's assessment closely parallels the actual death pattern of the patient, the professional staff's work with all patients, the dying individual and other patients, is made easier and care is delivered more smoothly.[14]

Process of Dying

The time involved in the process of dying has also been subdivided into last weeks, last days, and last hours. During the last weeks, nurses need to rearrange care activities for the patient, while he ties up the loose ends and begins to take leave of life. The phenomenon of social isolation of the dying patient is more evident during these last weeks. During the last days, the family and professional staff are faced with the decision of whether to prolong the life of the individual and make decisions concerning where the final stage of his dying will occur—home, hospital, or nursing home.

During the last hours, three levels of behavior—the death watch, the death scene, and the final death—occur. The death watch is carefully handled by the caregivers to prevent an unpleasant death. Physiological control through promotion of sleep, elimination of pain, and relief from restlessness is the focus of care. It is of utmost concern to the health care providers and family and friends that the patient not die alone. The death scene is usually brief and terminates at the actual physiological death with the ritual pronouncement of death. Family members are usually most intimately involved in this final stage of dying.

Stages of Dying

What of the patient? Once diagnosed as dying—what comes about next? In 1969, Kubler-Ross presented a framework for understanding the process of dying. Her extensive case study investigations with the terminally ill, their families, and professional staff for the past twenty years and her many books and workshops on death and dying have profoundly affected how society thinks about death.

Kubler-Ross identified five possible stages of dying experienced by the patient and his loved ones.

Stage 1—denial
Stage 2—anger

Stage 3—bargaining
Stage 4—depression
Stage 5—acceptance

Denial

In the first stage of dying, the initial shock and its concomitant denial are reactions to the overwhelming threat of nonexistence. Denial is a necessary and protective mechanism that may be present for a few minutes or may be utilized for periods of months.

Anger

The initial stage is followed by felt and expressed anger. The dying person's anger is directed at self, God, and others who have a future and do not face the loss of existence.

Bargaining

The anticipation of the losses through death brings about a time of bargaining. Through this bargaining, the individual attempts to postpone or reverse the dreaded moment of death. The individual may pray for more time to complete important goals in his life, to see a new grandchild born, or take the special trips he had always planned. During this time, promises are made to alter lifestyles, go to church more often, and give to charity; the individual usually promises something in exchange for life.

Depression

When the full impact of his diagnosis is felt and the loss can no longer be delayed, the individual moves into the stage of depression. This depression is a therapeutic state and a necessary way of aiding the individual to detach from life and living and thereby accept his death.

The depression of the process of death and dying is viewed differently from the pathological depressions seen in the process of life. Pathological depressions must be treated and their cause or causes must be dealt with; in the process of dying, depression is a necessary stage of growth rather than a regression.

Acceptance

To accept death is to pass beyond the emotional turmoil inherent in its process. The word, acceptance, is an ambiguous word. The individual who "gives up" refusing medication, treatment, or food can, in a sense, be said to have accepted death. Or has he just "refused" life? Though the physical fact of the cessation of life is the same, the emotional freedom and sense of peace that accompany acceptance may not exist with the person who "gives up."

Kubler-Ross' theory of the stages of dying is currently being questioned, because of her lack of a controlled research design. The stages she described, says one critic, have not been clearly demonstrated and no strong evidence presented to support that individuals do, in fact, move through stages in dying.[18] Nevertheless, the greatest value

of Kubler-Ross' work may be an increased sensitivity to the needs of the dying person and attention to the possibility that adaptive stages may be at work in the terminal process.

Disengagement

The theory of disengagement has evolved with the growth of the field of gerontology. This theory proposes that the elderly or dying person acts voluntarily in giving up his or her roles in life, slowly loses interest in the active world, and pulls away or withdraws from significant others. The individual would not be defined as happy and may, in fact, experience emotional deprivation, but is at peace. This state is comparable to the stage of acceptance described by Kubler-Ross.

According to the disengagement theory, society and the individual mutually engage in the process of withdrawal from each other as a normal aspect of aging and the ending of life. This theory further states that an individual will deal with aging and dying similar to the way he dealt with other problems and losses in his life.[3]

Other studies have shed doubt on the idea of mutual withdrawal of the disengagement theory. One investigator, for example, found that aging individuals generally move toward activity and social contacts, and questioned whether the disengagement process is a result of environmental conditions, rather than a natural process of tying up loose ends and preparing to withdraw from life.[5]

From the work with the terminally ill, we can learn something about living—if death is a final separation, what of other separations in life, such as divorce, graduations, loss of a job, a move? If there is a parallel in the processes, then each of us in daily living are preparing ourselves for the final "letting go."

Death and Special Circumstances

Sudden Death

Much work has been done with the survivors of victims of sudden or unexpected deaths. Sudden deaths are related to a greater amount of emotional turmoil and shock in the survivors than with those whose significant other was ill. The survivors of victims of sudden death have no time to engage in anticipatory grief and often have no alerting warning time. The most disturbing and unbalancing feature of a sudden death is the element of unexpectedness.

Many times, interpersonal circumstances existing prior to the death, such as periods of emotional stress, anger, or hurt, may result in severe guilt feelings in the survivors. The immediate reactions of the survivors are usually severe and include disbelief, guilt, fear, remorse, and despair.[16, 35] There is a high incidence of suicide in the surviving mate after the sudden death of the spouse.[31]

The sudden death of a significant other is viewed as a disaster, similar to that of the news of a catastrophic event. This reaction is a "disaster syndrome," which includes the initial shock followed by motor retardation, flattened affect, somnolence, amnesia, guilt feelings, exhaustion, numerous bodily complaints, and feelings of worthlessness.[10, 42]

The "psychological autopsies" on the parents of adolescents who committed suicide demonstrated three basic phases in the survivors' grief process. These phases include the following.

1. Resuscitation from the initial shock, which lasts up to 24 hours
2. Rehabilitation, which extends from 1 to 6 months after the death
3. Renewal, which is a healthy tapering off of the mourning, lasting 6 months or more[33]

To help families cope with sudden death, nurses may direct survivor care toward the goals of intervening in the distortion of the reality of the event, identifying consistent support systems for the family, and enhancing the coping mechanisms of the family members.[32]

Death of a Child

The death of one's child is probably the most threatening loss that a person can experience. The parent visualizes his child as he visualizes his future and the extension of the self. With the child's death, the bubble of the future is burst and nothing remains. The parents are desolate.

One of the most difficult tasks of any health professional is attempting to help the parents of a dying child. Each parent reacts in a unique manner to the imminent death of his or her child. The impending death of an only child produces more severe reactions ranging from psychosis to total denial. Self-recrimination and self-degradation may surface in response to perceived "selfishness" in having only one child. This dynamic has the potential of impacting the stability of the marriage.

Guilt is likely to be a prominent manifestation of the parents when their child dies and they feel responsible for what led up to the death. A common feeling is that one has nothing left to live for.

In viewing family grief, attention must also be paid to the grieving siblings. It is much too easy to overlook the emotional needs of the young. The parents' natural reaction is to remember only what is good about their dying or dead child, which may lead to a difficult family situation when the dying child is raised to "sainthood" in the eyes and feelings of the parents. The surviving siblings must then attempt to match that idealized image or may begin to exhibit antisocial, or another form of disordered, behavior in a desperate call to win their parents' love again.

Nursing Care of the Dying Patient and His Family

The goals of nursing care of the dying individual are synonymous with those designed for all individuals who cannot meet their own needs. The dying person must be treated as a unique individual, not as a diagnosis or entity, within the institution's confines. The nursing care should foster the optimum quality of life for the individual at that point in time; he and his family need to be dealt with in a secure and protected atmosphere.

Physical Care

The priority of nursing care for the dying patient is meeting his physical needs. This priority must be met before the nurse can continue to intervene meaningfully on an interpersonal level to provide emotional care of the dying patient and his family. Prevention or alleviation of physical problems reassures the dying individual and his loved ones that they need not be anxious about the adequacy of his care. Physical care of the dying includes attention to the following.

1. Hair. Cared-for hair has a great influence on the self-image and self-esteem of the individual.
2. Mucous membranes. Nose, mouth, and eyes need to be kept moist and clean. The use of oils and mouthwashes is desirable.
3. Skin. Skin should be clean, lotion should be applied to provide moisture, and pressure areas should be protected from skin breakdown and decubitus formation.
4. Elimination. The nurse should keep the incontinent patient clean, dry, and odor-free, and should assess him for the presence of an impaction. The nurse's attitude when dealing with the incontinent patient may communicate rejection or protective care.
5. Positioning. Frequent positioning is needed to protect the patient from skin breakdown, and to insure that the airway is not partially or totally obstructed.
6. Nutrition and hydration. Small, frequent feedings of the patient's favorite foods are likely to be accepted. Ice chips or favorite soft drinks need to be constantly available to him.[2]

(Extensive discussions of the physical care of the dying may be found in medical-surgical nursing texts.)

Psychological Care

Psychological care of the dying individual is not a specific, delineated set of activities or interventions, but an ongoing, individualized interpersonal process based on the personality of the individual and his specific situation and circumstances (see insert, Emotional Care of the Dying Patient). The goals and needs of the patient and the philosophy of the health care professional generate the specific interventions of care. Five psychological factors that need to be incorporated into the care of the dying are as follows.

1. Information
2. Autonomy
3. Safe conduct
4. Meaningfulness
5. Appropriate death.[2]

Providing Information

Patients and family members wish to be kept informed about what is happening to them. Information that is solicited, but withheld, is a professional's method of controlling the situation, the dying individual, and his family. Without appropriate information, the patient cannot take an active part in decisions made regarding his personal self.

The nurse's role in working with dying individuals and their loved ones is one of liaison between the patient, his family, the physician, and the hospital. The nurse also assumes the vital role of clarifier, explainer, and interpreter of symptoms, communications, hospital rules, and expectations.

Maintaining Autonomy

The ill or dying individual finds himself in a situation of extreme dependency. A balance between autonomy and dependency must be maintained as long as the patient is able to remain involved. Areas of involvement, including various aspects of self-care and decision-making, allow the individual a degree of personal power and control. An individual may be totally dependent for his physical care yet maintain autonomy through his decision-making. This is an important aspect in a health approach, rather than an illness approach, to the dying individual (see previous insert, The Living Will).

Offering personal control means allowing the individual a voice in the decisions in his care. Control over the environment; that is, where to place objects, who is acceptable as visitors, when and what will be eaten, and when treatments and medications will be administered, are examples of behaviors that can lead to the assumption of control. The nurse provides the patient with the basic rights of all individuals, including that of informed consent and the alternative of saying "no" to those things that intimately affect him.

As with any behavior, extremes of the autonomy–dependency continuum may exist. Individuals who are basically dependent may react by exhibiting dictating, controlling behaviors toward health care professionals and family. A more intense look at the individual may reveal a frightened and lonely individual whose greatest fear is that of abandonment. This dynamic of behavior has probably

Emotional Care of the Dying Patient

Assessment and Analysis

Is the patient aware of his terminal diagnosis?
At which stage of death and dying is the individual?
Does the individual have helpful support systems (*i.e.*, family, significant other)?
Does the individual express "unfinished business" that needs to be completed?
Is a referral needed to deal with financial, emotional, or legal problems?
What are the individual's positive coping skills?

Planning

Be available, on a daily basis, to the individual.
Sit down and LISTEN. Use open statements, such as "You look sad—is there something you'd like to talk about?" "Is there something I can do for you today?" Or, the nurse may have to follow an intuitive hunch, pull up a chair next to the patient's bed, facing him, and ask, "Do you mind if I sit awhile?"
If financial, emotional, or legal problems exist, identify the area of concern and the individual's wish for assistance.
Be available to the family and significant others for information, understanding communication, and support.
Allow for as much physical and emotional independence as the individual needs and is capable of.

Intervention

Spend time daily with individual, creating an accepting atmosphere.
LISTEN rather than talk; allow for the expression of feelings.
Allow and support the individual's own decision-making; that is, planning time of care, visitors, and so forth.
Use touch when patient indicates through verbal or nonverbal behavior (crying, relating sad stories) that it is needed.
Meet with family and significant others to answer questions, listen to feelings, provide information, and give support.
Allow as much time as the dying individual needs with family and significant others.
Make appropriate referrals, based on individual's wishes, to social worker, lawyer, minister or priest, and so forth.
Aid the individual in completing "unfinished business."

existed throughout the individual's life with family members and significant others and will probably not change during this aspect of life.

If the client's behavior represents a major change in the way he has reacted or acted in the past, the nurse demonstrates quiet acceptance, gentle limit-setting, and trust through reliable and predictable administration of nursing care. Listening, role modeling, and open communication with the loved ones is necessary to maintain a balance of integrity and support a continued interaction with the dying individual. The nurse facilitates family interactions and provides a place for the expression of feelings.

Assuring Safe Conduct

Safe conduct is the cautious and prudent behavior that guards another individual through peril or the unknown.[40] A promise not to abandon the dying individual comprises the corner stone of assurance of safe conduct. Social isolation is a component of the potent feeling of abandonment that may be experienced if safe conduct is not aided.

In the provision of safe conduct, the nurse meets the physiological needs that the patient cannot meet himself and supports a relationship in which the patient can express and explore feelings. The experience of safe conduct requires the reinforcement and nurturance of the patient's existing positive coping skills.

Supporting Meaningfulness

Frequently, the dying patient's world is filled with loneliness, isolation, and feelings of rejection. This triad is the source of feelings of meaninglessness in an existence that holds no purposeful actions or goal attainment activity for an individual.

Alleviation of pain, the lessening of discomfort, and positive give-and-take relationships are supportive of the dying individual during the remainder of his life. During the phases of the dying process, the presence of at least one significant other—at times, that person may be the nurse—is necessary for open sharing and expression of feelings. Dying persons, when given the opportunity and appropriate milieu, tend to be frank and direct in expressing their feelings and thoughts.

Communication with the dying individual should be composed of active listening and a minimum of idle chatter. Many times, all that is needed is a mutual silence in which the nurse is comfortable. During the active listening, the nurse carries on the ongoing assessment of the client's feelings and coping abilities. The dying individual may express concern about specific problems or unfinished business that he must complete before reaching any sense of peace or acceptance. Together with the nurse or other health care provider he can then make appropriate plans.

The exploration of feelings may be appropriate at any time in the dying process. When dealing with human beings, it is too global to assume that certain feelings are occurring because the individual is dying. Examining expressed feelings opens the way for sharing deeper or more submerged ones, thereby releasing energies that may be used in more successful coping.

When curing is not possible, the nurse can be involved in a healing-caring process. Through a healing-caring process, the dying individual is given the opportunity to maintain connectedness to the world.[6] One aspect of the healing-caring process is the nurse's role in aiding the dying individual to maintain relationships with family and significant others; such relationships may require learning new methods of interacting, even at this stage in life.

Through assessment and analysis of client and family data, the nurse makes decisions about the needs of the dying individual. These needs may vary from active communication and exploration of feelings to the acceptance of the need for withdrawal, reflection, and separation from life.

The search for meaning, which many dying individuals undertake, is an introspective process examining not only the meaning of death, but also the meaning of life. The patient may reaffirm philosophical or religious orientations of his earlier life or make major alterations in his religious or philosophical beliefs during this time. The values of his accomplishments, achievements, and relationships are examined. Relationships with family members and significant others may take on increased importance and immediacy. When all the pieces begin to fit together and some order has been put to life and death, dying can become a meaningful growth experience.

The act of leave-taking or saying goodbye may be possible when the dying patient feels a sense of order to his life and death. The nurse's role in this stage is one of support to the dying individual, family members, and significant others.

Promoting an Appropriate Death

An "appropriate death" for the client involves the following criteria.

1. Reduction of conflict
2. Reinforcement of significant relationships
3. Behavior compatible with the individual's ego ideal
4. Realization of basic instincts and wishes[40]

The appropriate death for an individual is one that reflects, and is integrated into, his lifestyle and its past meaning. The event is not alien to the client's past behavior or some magical change in behavior. It is reflective of the dignity of the individual and his personality.

Summary

This chapter has examined the philosophical, theoretical, religious, and "American" viewpoints of death. Some of the major points of the chapter are as follows.

1. Contemporary reactions to death involve avoidance and preoccupation with death as a destructive force.
2. Advances in medical practice have altered the nature and location of treatment of the dying.
3. The dying client faces the fears of abandonment, initiation into the "sick role," and stigmatization, all of which further isolate him.
4. Family and friends of the dying experience feelings of loss and anticipatory grief to prepare for the death of their loved one.
5. As a result of the grieving process, the survivors free themselves from the bonds of the deceased, reorient themselves to their environment from which the deceased is absent, and establish new relationships.

6. Working with the dying elicits both a personal and a professional threat in health care providers.
7. Kubler-Ross identified five stages of dying experienced by the patient and his family—denial, anger, bargaining, depression, and acceptance.
8. Sudden, unexpected death allows no time for the survivors to engage in anticipatory grief.
9. Competent physical nursing care of the dying patient reassures the family and significant others and adds to their emotional well-being.
10. Psychological nursing care of the dying is based on the patient's and family's goals and needs and incorporates the provision of information, autonomy, safe conduct, meaningfulness, and appropriate death.

Personal Reflections on Death

Felicitas Alfaro, R.N., M.Ed.
Instructor of Nursing
El Centro College
Dallas, Texas

When I stop to analyze or reflect on the major events of my life, I necessarily have to think about the significant losses that I have experienced and the tremendous impact they had on me and my development.

Six to seven hours after I was born, my mother died. When I was 2 weeks old, my oldest sister and my father brought me home to a family of two sisters and nine brothers ranging in age from 2 to 25 years. They all played a role in raising me, as did my aunts and even a friendly neighbor or two.

I grew up hearing, "That's the baby of the family—poor thing—you know her mother died when she was born." Often, I was introduced as "this is my baby sister—the one that was born when my mother died." There was no malice here, just fact; however, for many years I felt guilty. I used to think that if I'd never been born, then my mother would have never died and my brothers and sisters would have had a mother. It was not until I was in college that I was truly able to verbalize this and work it through, to realize that I had no control over my being born or over my mother's life or death.

When I was 8 years old, my oldest brother died of cancer at the age of 33. He had struggled for 7 years. The last few months of his life were the most uncomfortable. A couple of my older brothers and my oldest sister helped his wife with his care. He died at home—surrounded by those who loved him most. I remember it being a Valentine's Day because his daughters and I were comparing our Valentine's Day cards.

As an adult looking back, I am struck by the vivid memories of my brother's colostomy, his pneumonectomy scar, the whispers and the crying at home when the doctor pronounced him dead—and the Valentine's Day cards.

By the time I graduated from high school, one of my paternal aunts, who had taught me to sew and to embroider, was found to have metastatic bronchiopulmonary carcinoma. Because she had no children, she and my uncle moved in with my other aunt. My sister, cousins, and I took turns helping with her care until she died—again, very peacefully at home.

My father died a couple of months later of a massive heart attack. It was New Years Day afternoon and we were getting ready to go to mass. I remember him walking by my room and on out to the back door where he collapsed after looking out one last time. I ran to him, sat him up and held him in my arms. He died there, but I didn't know it because I had never seen anyone actually die.

A neighbor helped me bring him into the house to his bed. I called my brother, who is a mortician, to come quickly. He arrived within minutes. He knew my daddy was dead, but he also knew that I still thought he was alive.

Daddy was pronounced "D.O.A." I could not cry just as I was not able to look at him in his coffin. After the shock wore off, all I felt was anger. I was very angry at God—I could not and did not want to understand. Then I was very depressed.

The depression was what drove me to see the

doctor I had had as a child. He was hispanic and he knew my family well. He was very sensitive and gentle with me and helped me to realize that I had to get out of the "poor me's" and get on with living.

I became a volunteer in the clinics at the county hospital and it was that experience that led me to become a nurse—the one thing I had sworn I would never be.

Since then, I have lost all my aunts and uncles and several very close and dear friends, as well as a sister-in-law who died suddenly and tragically.

I have to think of all that uncalled-for guilt of a child who did not understand. I reflect on the years when anger would surface and then subside. I'm glad that it is finally resolved. I'm thankful for all the love and support from my family and friends, the love and support that I believe is a reflection of God's love and support.

It is the enduring love, the steadfast love, the patient love, the quiet love of those around us that keeps us going.

The interesting thing is that, even after many years, I still cry and I still miss them. The feelings never go away—the changes in understanding and the tears are different—but the feelings never go away. I'm sure some of you can understand what I am saying.

References

1. Becker E: The Denial of Death. New York, The Free Press, 1973
2. Burns N: Nursing and Cancer. Philadelphia, W. B. Saunders, 1982
3. Butler RN, Lewis MI: Aging and Mental Health. St Louis, CV Mosby, 1982
4. Caroff P, Dobrof R: The Helping Process and Bereaved Families. In Schaenberg B et al (eds): Bereavement: Its Psychosocial Aspects. New York, Columbia University Press, 1975
5. Carp FM: A Future for the Aged: Victoria Plaza and Its Residents. Austin, TX, University of Texas Press, 1966
6. Castles MR, Murray RB: Dying in an Institution: Nurse/Patient Perspectives. New York, Appleton-Century-Crofts, 1979
7. Feifel H: The Meaning of Death. New York, McGraw-Hill, 1959
8. Feifel H (ed): New Meanings of Death. New York, McGraw-Hill, 1977
9. Freud S: Thoughts for the Times on War and Death, Part II: Our Attitudes toward Death, pp 289–300. Standard Edition 14 (1915). London, Hogarth, 1957
10. Friedman P, Lum L: Some Psychiatric Notes on the 'Andria Doria' Disaster. Am J Psychiatry 114: 426–432, 1958
11. Fulcomer DM: The Adjustment Behavior of Some Recently Bereaved Spouses. Unpublished Doctoral Dissertation, Chicago, Northwestern University, 1942
12. Fulton R (ed): A Bibliography on Death, Grief, and Bereavement. Minneapolis, Center for Death Education and Research, 1973
13. Glaser BG, Strauss AL: Awareness of Dying. Chicago, Aldine Publishing, 1965
14. Glaser BG, Strauss AL: Time for Dying. Chicago, Aldine Publishing, 1968
15. Goffman E: Stigma. New Jersey, Prentice-Hall, 1963
16. Goldstein S, Heidmann EM: Sudden Death and Coronary Heart Disease. Cardiovascular Nursing 12: 11–15, 1976
17. Jung CG: Modern Man in Search of a Soul. New York, Harcourt, Brace, 1933
18. Kastenbaum R: Death, Society, and Human Experience. St Louis, CV Mosby, 1977
19. Kneisel CR: Dying Patients and Their Families: How Staff Can Give Support. Hospital Topics 45: 37–39, 1957
20. Kubler-Ross E: On Death and Dying. New York, Macmillan, 1971
21. Kubler-Ross E: On Death and Dying. JAMA 221: 174–179, 1972
22. Kubler-Ross E: Death—the Final Stage of Growth. New Jersey, Prentice-Hall, 1975
23. Lasagna L: Physicians' Behavior Toward the Dying Patient. In Brins O et al (eds): The Dying Patient. New York, Missel Sazeton, 1970
24. Lindemann E: Symptomatology and Management of Acute Grief. Am J Psychiatry 1011 (September): 141–148, 1944
25. Lofland LH: Toward a Sociology of Death and Dying. Beverly Hills, Sage, 1976
26. May WF: The Sacred Power of Death in Contemporary Experiences. In Macks A (ed): Death in American Experience. New York, Schacken, 1973
27. Mitford J: The American Way of Death. Greenwich, CT, Fawcett, 1963
28. Pattison EM: Help in the Dying Process. In Wilcox S, Sutton M (eds): Understanding Death and Dying: An Interdisciplinary Approach, 2nd ed. Sherman Oaks, CA, Alfree, 1981
29. Popoff D: What Are Your Feelings About Death and Dying? Nursing 75 5: 15–25, 39–50, 55–62, 1975
30. Ramsey P: The Indignity of 'Death with Dignity.' In Steinfels P, Veatch RM (eds): Death Inside-Out: The Hastings Center Report, Institute of Society, Ethics and Life Sciences. New York, Harper & Row, 1975
31. Rinear EE: The Nurse's Challenge When Death Is Unexpected. R.N. 38 (December): 50–55, 1975

32. Ryan MA: Helping the Family Cope with a Cardiac Arrest. Nursing 74 4 (August): 80–81, 1974

33. Schneidman ES: The Death of Man. New York, Quadrangle, 1973

34. Silverman P et al (eds): Helping Each Other in Widowhood. Health Sciences 7, 1974

35. Surawicz FG: Psychological Aspects of Sudden Cardiac Death. Heart Lung 2 (November–December): 836–840, 1973

36. Ufema JK: Dare to Care for the Dying. Am J Nursing 76: 88–90, 1976

37. Visotky HM, Hamburg DA, Gross ME, Lebovitz BA: Coping Behaviors under Extreme Stress: Observations of Patients with Severe Poliomyelitis. Arch Gen Psychiatry 5: 423–448, 1961

38. Weisman A: On Dying and Denying. New York, Behavioral Publication, 1972

39. Weisman AD: The Psychiatrist and the Inexorable. In Feifel H (ed): New Meanings of Death. New York, McGraw-Hill, 1977

40. Weisman AD, Hackett TD: Predictions to Death: Death and Dying as a Psychiatric Problem. Psychosom Med 23: 232–256, 1961

41. Williams JC: Understanding the Feelings of the Dying. Nursing 76 6: 52–56, 1976

42. Wolfenstein M: Disaster: A Psychological Study. Glencoe, Del, The Free Press, 1957

Part IX
Professional Issues
in Psychiatric-Mental
Health Nursing

Chapter 39
Legal Implications of Psychiatric-Mental Health Nursing

Like the five blind men, each grasping a different part of the fabled elephant and each describing a different beast, so the perceivers of the therapeutic state have seen in it diverse realities. Some have viewed it as a humanistic boon. Others have portrayed it as the first rational endeavor for the scientific control of deviant behavior. Still others have compared it to the infamous Star Chamber proceeding—the royal Tudor court that dispensed arbitrary punishments without proper regard for the safeguards that the law usually provided for the liberty of the subject.

Nicholas Kittrie,
In Informed Consent:
A Guide for Health Care Remedies, *1981*

Virginia Trotter Betts
S. Robin Shanks

Chapter Preview

Probably no other specialty area of nursing demands as great a need for knowledge of the law and its impact upon nursing practice than psychiatric-mental health nursing does. Consumers of health care are becoming increasingly knowledgeable about legal issues, rights, and remedies, and have improved access to legal counsel through legal clinics, the American Civil Liberties Union, and other protective rights-conscious groups (see insert, Past and Present Legal Trends in Mental Health for a historical perspective). Therefore, psychiatric nurses and other health care professionals must be aware that their practice must meet not only their own professinal standards, but that those professional standards must also bear close adherence to legal standards as developed through case or statutory law.

Psychiatric nurses are responsible both for the services that they perform and for those that they do not perform. They are responsible for accurate assessments, careful plans, competent implementation, and purposeful evaluation. If psychiatric nurses are not aware of the national expectations for clinical practice, the impact on clinical practice of new laws arising from cases decided in the court system, and proposed and past legislation affecting mental health care, it seems unlikely that they can provide the quality of care to consumers that would safeguard clients' rights, protect the client's safety, or further the influence or power of the nurse on the interdisciplinary mental health team.

This chapter has many purposes, the first of which is to define a standard of quality psychiatric care as set by professional nurses and to demonstrate how this standard has been impacted by current case law. Another important purpose of the chapter is to clarify, for the practicing mental health nurse and for the nursing student, some of the differences in important legal concepts that may seem somewhat similar to the novice. Some of these concepts include the differences between the following.

1. The competency to stand trial versus the competency to handle affairs
2. The tort actions of malpractice and assault and battery
3. Voluntary and involuntary civil clients and their rights
4. Criminal or civil status of clients in inpatient institutions

It is imperative that nurses learn to value, respect, and seek out knowledge about laws, legislation, and the legal processes that regulate, impede, and facilitate the practice of professional nursing. The major goal of this chapter is to prepare nurses to include legal principles in their psychiatric-mental health nursing practice, both to benefit and protect the nurse and to enhance the quality of care that the client receives.

Learning Objectives

On completion of this chapter, the reader should be able to accomplish the following.

1. Identify and discuss some legal issues basic to accountable nursing practice, including the following
   Nursing practice and malpractice
   Informed consent
   Confidentiality
   Record keeping
2. Identify the basic rights of the mentally ill
3. Differentiate between voluntary and involuntary civil commitment
4. Differentiate between criminal and civil commitment
5. Discuss the differences between the competency to stand trial and general legal competency
6. Differentiate between the rights of voluntary and involuntary clients
7. Identify nursing implications for the right to refuse treatment and other important client rights
8. Plan actions for ensuring accountability for psychiatric-mental health nursing practice through the following
   Use of the ANA Standards of Practice
   Integration of quality assurance into practice
   Seeking of appropriate legal consultation

Legal Issues Basic to Accountable Psychiatric-Mental Health Nursing Practice

Nursing Practice and Malpractice

Nursing Practice Acts

Nursing as a profession is given effect in each state by the promulgation of the Nurse Practice Act by each state legislature. Each state Nurse Practice Act defines nursing, describes the scope of nursing, and identifies limits on the practice of nursing within that state. Although the Nurse Practice Act in each state may differ, the definition of nursing in the Tennessee Nurse Practice Act is clearly a definition not too dissimilar to many of the acts in the nation. The act immediately highlights some recognized independent nursing practices as well as some dependent areas of nursing practice (see insert, TCA 63-7-103: "Professional Nursing" Defined).

It is important to review the specific activities that are mandated in the Nurse Practice Act. Clearly, only "the administration of medications and treatment as is prescribed by a licensed physician or dentist" is a service that could be considered dependent for the nurse; that is, it is

Past and Present Legal Trends in Mental Health

For the last few hundred years, society has dealt with its mentally disturbed members in a variety of ways. The principal method, until recently was to segregate them from the general population.

This isolation from society was reflected in K. Jones' *Lunacy, Law & Conscience.*
"16th century, deranged were expelled, shipped off, executed;
17th century, insane were locked up in jails and houses of correction;
18th century, madmen were confined in madhouses;
19th century, lunatics were sent to asylums;
20th century, mentally ill are committed to hospitals"[9]

Present day laws regarding the treatment of the mentally ill evolved from the Common Law of England. During the 11th century, the King of England was responsible for the care of the insane if there were no kinsmen. By the beginning of the 14th century, the church and the lord of the manor were responsible for the mentally ill. Then, in the early 14th century, Edward II proclaimed the king's responsibility toward the mentally ill and the national law of guardianships extended to this class of people, and they were again made the duty of the crown. The term *parens patriae* was used by W. Blackstone to refer to the power and the responsibility of the state to care for the disabled members of society. In Blackstone's words, "The king has the general superintendance of all charities."[12]

At first, the mentally disabled who came to the New World were dealt with informally by the colonists. Families locked up their mentally ill relatives in back rooms or outhouses. Others who had nowhere to go wandered from place to place or they were confined in jails with criminals, drunkards, and other social outcasts. The *parens partriae* power of the king then was officially assumed by the states.[12]

In 1752, Philadelphia Hospital was opened. Not only was it this country's first general hospital, but it also provided treatment to the mentally ill in addition to the sick and poor. During this same time period, Pinel's and Luke's work in France and London, referred to as moral treatment of the mentally ill, traveled across the Atlantic. Pinel's "moral treatment" implied a mental condition that was curable in an appropriate psychological and social environment.[21]

Subsequently, other hospitals opened, but by the middle of the 19th century, it was obvious that the corporate hospitals were unable to meet the needs of the mentally disabled.[21] This, in turn, caused social crusaders such as Dorothea Dix to assist with funding, building, and enlarging public mental hospitals. Despite their humanistic purposes, the construction of these hospitals actually allowed for an era of custodial treatment by the unwarranted commitment of thousands of homeless people in overcrowded hospitals with little regard for any legal protective processes.

To combat these increasingly unacceptable conditions, the patients' rights movement developed; both movements supported the concept of deinstitutionalization of the mentally ill. During the last decade, the deinstitutionalization concept and its implementation has been at the forefront of mental health care delivery. Community mental health centers have opened their doors to provide necessary psychiatric treatment to persons who do not require inpatient hospitalization. As a result of this community approach, inpatient psychiatric numbers have decreased over 50% since the early 1950s. Within the past 10 years, the criteria for judicial commitment have been narrowed considerably. A person can no longer be judicially committed merely because of the presence of mental illness or the need for psychiatric treatment.

Deinstitutionalization has mandated the development of over 2000 public mental health centers to provide care for the mentally ill for whom inpatient care is not necessary, leaving hospital facilities to care for those who are not functioning safely in society due to mental illness. The integration of the mentally ill into the general population has engendered a great deal of political and social controversy and conflict. This conflict is not likely to be resolved until the stigma attached to mental illness is replaced by an increased understanding of mental health and illness by society or until the health delivery system develops community support services such as housing, employment, and accessible aftercare that facilitates social integration of the formerly hospitalized mental health client population.

Many legal rights and remedies for the mentally ill are in rapid states of evolution. One of the most frequently litigated issues is the right to refuse psychotropic medication. New statutes resulting from judicial decisions will have a major impact on the care and treatment of the mentally ill in our society in the future.

TCA 63-7-103: "Professional Nursing" Defined

The practice of professional nursing means the performance for compensation of any act requiring substantial specialized judgment and skill based on knowledge and application of principles of nursing derived from biologic, physical, and social sciences including:

a. responsible supervision of a patient requiring skill and observation of symptoms and reactions and accurate recording of the facts;

b. the maintenance of health or prevention of illness of others;

c. supervision and teaching of others;

d. administration of medications and treatments as prescribed by a licensed physician or dentist;

e. application of such nursing procedures as they involve understanding of cause and effect. The foregoing shall not be deemed to include acts of medical diagnosis or the development of a medical plan of care and therapeutics for a patient.

(From Tennessee Code Annotated, §63-7-101 et seg)

dependent on the acts (orders) of someone else.[24] All the rest of the mandated activities are acts that the nurse can, should, and must do on her own initiative because patients need and should reasonably expect these nursing actions. Nurses are responsible and accountable for these nursing acts and are responsible for performing them in a manner that is safe for the patient.

Nursing Malpractice

It is important to define nursing malpractice. *Malpractice* is a particular kind of tort action that is brought by a consumer plaintiff against a defendant professional from whom the consumer plaintiff feels that he has received injury during the course of the professional–consumer relationship. Malpractice is professional negligence.

In order for a plaintiff consumer to receive money damages by successfully suing a professional nurse for malpractice, the consumer plaintiff must prove the five elements of nursing negligence.

1. The nurse professional had a duty to use due care toward the plaintiff.

2. The nurse professional's performance fell below the standard of care and was therefore a breach of that duty.

3. As a result of the failure to meet the standard of

care, the plaintiff consumer was injured and the nurse's action was the proximate cause of the injury.

4. The act that the nurse engaged in could foreseeably have caused an injury.

5. The plaintiff consumer must prove his injuries.

In a malpractice action against the nurse, the proof of the standard of care becomes an essential and important ingredient. Expert witness testimony is usually presented by both sides to give the jury the perspectives of experts on professional practices and standards. The appropriate expert witness for psychiatric nursing practice is another psychiatric nurse who would have knowledge about what the standard of care in the particular case should have been.

Such expert testimony is presented in the case and is submitted with all other testimony and evidence to the jury for a decision. The jury is asked by the Court to apply the reasonable man test to the facts in the case at hand. The *reasonable man test,* as applied to the nurse defendant, is what the reasonably prudent nurse would have done under similar circumstances if that nurse came from the same or similar community (see insert, Practice or Malpractice?). Therefore, in order to decrease liability for malpractice, a psychiatric nurse must keep her professional practice within the bounds that her nurse peers would consider reasonable and appropriate. The law of negligence seeks a peer standard for reasonableness of action—not a quality performance standard of excellence.

In the history of malpractice litigation, nurses have been protected from direct suits by clients due to nurses being seen as either dependent on the physician for orders or as employees of an institution. Attorneys, using the "deep pocket theory" of recovery, tended to sue as direct defendants either the well-insured physician or the employer-hospital rather than the nurse. Now, with the advent of consumerism, the recognition of professional nursing as an independent discipline, and the awareness that most nurses are self-insured against malpractice liability, there is an increasing trend to sue the individual nurse as a co-defendant along with the physician and the hospital.[13]

This trend has many implications for nursing practice and for the profession. As nurses are being held increasingly responsible and monetarily liable for nursing practice and malpractice, nursing must and will take control of nursing practice issues such as staffing, educational qualifications and competencies, and role definition on the health care team.

When nurses are found liable for less-than-adequate nursing care, employers are usually found liable to the plaintiff under the legal theory of respondeat superior. *Respondeat superior* states that the acts of employees are attributable to the employer for the purpose of being responsible for damages to injured third parties.[17] Eventually, because of joint liability and increased monetary risk, hospitals will insist

Practice or Malpractice?

A 23-year-old, married, graduate student, Mr. C. T., became severely depressed over a 3-week period of time. He was increasingly despondent, unable to study, and discussed suicide with his family and friends on frequent occasions during the 3-week period. He finally became so immobilized that he requested voluntary admission to the psychiatric unit of the local general hospital.

The unit was a 32-bed, open-ward therapeutic community treatment center and the nursing model was primary nursing. Mr. C. T.'s primary nurse, Ms. D., met him on admission and completed a nursing history in a hurried manner. She did not include the client's wife in the history-taking process, nor did she directly inquire about suicidal thoughts, gestures, or plans despite his obvious depression.

Ms. D.'s nursing history and her participation in the interdisciplinary team conference to develop the treatment plan for the client included information about his health status, drug allergies, the stressors of graduate school, and his deteriorated eating and sleeping habits. Information from and about the client's family was omitted, as well as the client's and his wife's perceptions of the severity of the problem and their goals for hospitalization.

After 10 days on the unit, Mr. C. T. evidenced an improved mood and energy level. He approached the nurse, Ms. D., with a request for a weekend pass. Ms. D. championed his request in the team meeting noting 1) his increased energy, 2) his compliance and "good" behavior, and 3) his voluntary admission status.

The team, relying on Ms. D's judgment agreed that she could facilitate his pass. Without further assessment or activity, Ms. D. provided him with the weekend pass. The client left the unit at 2:00 p.m., went to his home, and took an overdose of medication, part of which was provided for him for his pass

and part of which he had acquired on his own prior to admission. He died before he was discovered by his wife when she returned home from work; she had not been informed that a pass was to be granted to her husband.

The wife sued the primary nurse, the hospital, and the attending physician for negligence and wrongful death.

If you were called as an expert witness to evaluate Ms. D.'s standard of care and her possible liability, both personally and jointly, what would you consider?

1. Inadequate history-taking and initial assessment, especially lack of family participation in the process
2. Limited scope of assessment
3. Poor understanding of dynamics of depression indicated in client assessment
4. Lack of understanding of the meaning of "voluntary" status
5. No planning with the family for goals for treatment or continuity of care
6. Limited evidence of use of the ANA Standards of Practice

It is doubtful that this primary nurse and her treatment team colleagues met the "reasonable man" test in the case of Mr. C. T. As his caretakers they had a duty to do so. They breached their duty and his harm was foreseeable. Their inappropriate actions toward him were legally significant factors in his death and death is a monetarily compensable injury.

Therefore, it is likely that, by proving each element of negligence, the client's wife will be able to recover money damages from the defendants. Malpractice does occur in psychiatric settings due to acts of both commission and omission.

on, rather than resist, nursing's efforts to direct and control its practice in order to provide a higher quality of client care. Quality client care provided by nursing greatly decreases malpractice litigation and successful recovery against both professional and corporate defendants.

Informed Consent—A Basic Right

All consumer clients have a right to informed consent prior to health care interventions. The performance of health care treatments or procedures without the informed consent of the client can result in a tort action against the physician and the health care agency for assault and battery. *Battery* is the unpermitted touching of another.[17] Consent is an

absolute defense to battery and informed consent is required in health care situations. *Informed consent* can be defined as that knowing consent that is given in an interaction or series of interactions between the treating physician and the client that allows the client to fully consider information about the treatment that is being proposed (*e.g.*, the way it will be administered, its prognoses, its side effects, its risks, the possible consequences of refusing the treatment, and a discussion of other treatment alternatives).[20]

In the case of Cantebury v. Spence, the Court said that the client could truly be informed only if the physician shared with him all those things that "the patient would find significant" in making a decision on whether to permit or to participate in a particular treatment regimen.[5] Elements of informed consent include the following.

1. Adequate and accurate knowledge and information
2. An individual with legal capacity to consent
3. Voluntarily given consent[10]

Special Consent Considerations in Psychiatric Settings

A major problem with consent arises with psychiatric clients because the validity of their competence to agree to a procedure is usually questioned. Many mental health clients certainly are capable of giving informed consent. They are aware of their surroundings, they understand what is being said, they are making their decisions based on what they think is best for them, and they are doing it without coercion.

Nevertheless, it is clear that some clients are not able to give informed consent. Clients already determined by the court to be incompetent for the purposes of handling their civil and business affairs are certainly in question as to their ability to make treatment decisions. Some clients who have not been so adjudicated are also so clearly impaired by their psychiatric illness that a true understanding of what is being said is not possible, and they are therefore unable to give valid consent. Because of this unreliability, major nursing considerations in the psychiatric-mental health practice area surrounding the issue of informed consent are the constant monitoring and observing of clients for the following.

1. Competence when they are asked to give informed consent
2. Continuing understanding of the information that they have been given
3. Power and opportunities to revoke consent at any time during a particular course of treatment[20]

Substituted Consent. When it is determined that a client is unable to give informed consent, providers of health services should obtain substituted consent for the necessary treatment or procedure. *Substituted consent* is that authorization given by another person on behalf of one who is in need of a procedure of treatment. Substituted consent can come from a court-appointed guardian or, in some instances, from the client's next of kin.

If the client has not previously been adjudicated incompetent to handle his own affairs and if there is no next of kin available to give substituted consent, the health care agency may initiate a court proceeding to appoint a guardian so that the procedure or treatment can be carried out.[20]

It is important for nurses, along with other health care providers, to know the statutory requirements for obtaining substituted consent. It is also necessary for the nurse functioning in the role of client advocate to know whether a client has been adjudicated incompetent and whether consent from a next of kin or a guardian is a legally acceptable substitution for the consent of the client. Assuring legally adequate informed consent prior to treatment should be an important part of the psychiatric nursing care plan.

The Nurse's Role

In the area of informed consent, the nurse acts as the client advocate, the physician's colleague, and the hospital's excellent employee by her continuing evaluation of an individual's ability to give informed consent, as well as his voluntariness to participate and continue in a particular treatment modality. It is not the nurse's responsibility to obtain informed consent because that is an activity between the client and the primary physician. It is the nurse's prerogative to pursue actively the observations as outlined above to protect the client's rights as he is engaged in treatment. Clearly defining the nurse's role in obtaining a client signature on a consent form needs to be addressed in every agency. A joint signing between the physician and client at the time of the decision is a preferred method of documenting consent and many agency policies and consent forms reflect this perference.

Confidentiality

In nursing practice, it is well acknowledged that the data generated through both interpersonal relationships and indirect sources with and about clients are confidential. It is a professional and an ethical duty to use the knowledge that is gained about clients for the enhancement of their care rather than for other purposes, such as gossip, personal gain, or mere curiosity. The confidentiality of verbal, as well as written, material must be maintained and this is especially true in the care of the mentally ill.

Despite the modernization of society, there continues to be a tremendous stigma attached to anyone who is labeled with a diagnosis of mental illness. Any kind of breach of confidentiality of data about clients, their diagnoses, their symptoms, their behaviors, and the outcomes of treatment can certainly affect the course of the rest of their lives in terms of employment, promotions, marriage, attainment of insurance benefits, and so forth. Psychiatric nurses cannot be too careful with their records, their reports, and their plans.

Responsible Record Keeping

According to the Bill of Rights of the American Hospital Association, each patient has a right to a written record that enhances his care.[2] The client record should state all those concerns that must be addressed in the care of the client including those history items that impact on the current status of the client. The record should not be so in depth as to be voyeuristic, but it should not be so limited as to narrowly construe the client's condition.

Records are legal documents that can be used in court; therefore, all nursing notes and progress records should reflect descriptive, nonjudgmental, and objective statements. Examples of significant data include here-and-now observations of the client through the use of the nurse's senses, accurate reporting of what is said and what is done for the client, and a description of the client outcomes of the care provided.[11]

Verbal communication and data sharing are important, especially on treatment teams and units that use interdisciplinary approaches to client care. The verbal sharing should be straightforward, forthright, descriptive, and unopinionated, and should be shared only with those individuals who are involved in the care and treatment of the client. It is wise in a psychiatric institution to have an established methodology of reminding staff about their professional and legal responsibilities for confidentiality, such as an annual signing of a form that promises the maintenance of client confidentiality.

Privileged Communication

Privileged communication is provided by statute in each state. The statute delineates which categories of professionals are given the legal privilege not to be required to reveal conversations and communications with a citizen. Although statutes differ state by state, the statutes customarily provide privilege to physicians, attorneys, clergymen, and, in some states, psychologists, nurses, and other health care providers. Psychiatric nurses should be aware of statutory privileged communication and, if the nursing privilege is limited or nonexistent, they should understand what typical boundaries to set in therapeutic interviews. In the absence of statutory privileges for nurses, communications between the nurse and the client may be required to be repeated in court through the subpoena process. Therefore, sharing sensitive or incriminating data should not be encouraged.

There have been some cases involving the issue of the appropriate circumstance to warrant breach of the confidential relationship with a client. A leading case in this area is Tarasoff v. Regents of University of California.[22] In these types of cases, courts have said that the mandate on therapists to hold clients' verbalizations in confidence is cut off when those confidences include threats on the lives of third persons.

Courts have held that, although the duty of confidentiality between client and therapist is one that should be recognized, a higher duty to protect the public safety intervenes and subsumes the duty of confidentiality. There are no nursing cases *per se* on this point, but it is important to know that threats to third persons cannot be ignored or unattended, especially when there is some reasonable opportunity for the client to follow through on these threats.

Providing Legally Acceptable Nursing Care: Rights Issues

Basic Rights of Psychiatric Clients

An important issue in psychiatric-mental health nursing care is the recognition of the basic rights of clients. This is particularly true because the treatment of the mentally ill tends to be more coercive, less voluntary, and less open to public awareness and scrutiny than is the treatment and hospitalization of other types of clients.

When a psychiatric client enters a hospital, he loses his freedom to come and go, to schedule his day, to choose his activities, and to control his activities of daily living. If he is also adjudicated incompetent, he loses his freedom to manage his financial and legal affairs and make many important decisions.[7]

Because of the loss of these important freedoms, the courts and the advocates of psychiatric clients closely guard and value those rights that the psychiatric client retains. Some of these rights include the right to communicate with an attorney, the right to send and receive mail without censorship, the right to visitors, the right to the basic necessities of life, and the right to safety from harm while hospitalized.

Certainly, treatment issues arise that indicate a need for a limitation on visitors or for client inclusion in a behavior modification type of treatment program that requires the earning of tokens to secure certain privileges or articles; however, clients have a right to challenge such restrictions and the treatment facility may have to prove the value or necessity of such rights abridgements.[7]

Use of restraints and seclusion as treatment approaches are considered suspect because such approaches reflect a flavor of possible punishment; therefore, the when's, where's, why's, and how long's of restraints and seclusion need to be addressed by policy in every psychiatric facility. Many states have developed statutes to define the use of restraints and seclusion within psychiatric units.

Clients have limited rights to be paid for work within institutions. Forced or even voluntary labor by clients without payment violates the principles of law in our society. The amount of payment considered adequate for client labor is still not clearly defined in each state.[7]

Clients have the right not to be subjected to experimental treatments nor to be subjects in research projects without their informed consent. Because of the complexity of informed consent issues with psychiatric clients as discussed previously, institutions having programs involving research or experimental treatment approaches must have institutional review boards to evaluate such projects and programs and to approve or disapprove them based upon strict client-protection criteria. Humane research approaches that entail no undue risks to clients but that have strong expectations of client benefit and that allow clients to withdraw from the project at any time are usually viewed favorably by these human subjects committees if clients give voluntary consent to participate.[7]

Nursing Implications for Provision of Rights

Nursing has long espoused a philosophy that one of its important roles in the health care system is to act as an advocate for the client. The advocacy role is nowhere more important than in the psychiatric care system as an assessor of, and spokesman for, the protection of client rights.

Discussing rights within treatment teams, including these rights in the nursing care plan, and ensuring that methodologies for rights protection are included in facility and unit policies and procedures are nursing activities that fulfill the client advocate role. One important resource that nursing should request is ongoing legal advice and consultation in the area of client rights.

Client Status and Specific Legal Issues

When psychiatric clients are hospitalized, their status as to the type of admission they represent is vitally important. It is important because various admission statutes reflect differing client rights as well as staff treatment responsibilities. Civil commitment admissions are denoted as

1. voluntary admissions,
2. emergency admissions, and
3. involuntary commitments (indefinite duration).

Each state has specific statutory regulations pertaining to each admission status and these statutes control state procedures for admissions, discharges, and commitments for treatment.

Voluntary Admissions

When clients present themselves at psychiatric facilities and request hospitalization, they are considered *voluntary admission* clients. Likewise, clients who are evaluated as being of danger to themselves or to others or being so seriously mentally ill that they cannot adequately meet their own needs in the community but who are willing to submit to treatment and are competent to do so have *voluntary admission* status.

Voluntary clients have certain rights that differ from the rights of other hospitalized clients. Specifically, voluntary clients are considered competent unless otherwise adjudicated and, therefore, have the absolute right to refuse treatment including psychotropic medications unless they are dangerous to themselves or others as in a violent destructive episode within the treatment unit.[18]

Voluntary clients do not have an absolute right to discharge at any time but may be required to request discharge. This time delay provides the health care team an opportunity to initiate a procedure to change the client's admission status to involuntary if the client meets the necessary statutory requirements. Many clearly mentally ill people can be voluntarily treated but cannot be required by the state to be treated in any setting if the client refuses. Therefore, there are numerous mentally ill people whose behaviors cause family, community, and social problems but who do not and cannot receive psychiatric care if they are unwilling to be voluntary clients.

Involuntary Admissions

An individual is considered to have *emergency involuntary admission* status when that individual acts in such a manner as to indicate that he is both mentally ill and, due to his illness, likely to harm himself or others, and is taken into custody and detained in a psychiatric facility.[23] The exact procedure for the initial evaluation is defined by state statute, as is the possible length of detainment and attendant treatment available.

All emergency admission individuals are admitted to facilities for the purposes of diagnosis, evaluation, and emergency treatment. At the end of the statutorily limited admission period, the client must be discharged, must be changed to voluntary status, or must attend a "probable cause" civil hearing, which will be held to determine his need for continuing treatment on an involuntary basis.

During the time of the emergency admission, the client's right to come and go is restricted, but he must have the right to consult with an attorney in order to prepare for his probable cause hearing. He may be forced to take psychotropic medications, especially if he continues to be dangerous to himself or to others, but more invasive procedures, such as electroconvulsive therapy (ECT) or psychosurgery, are not permitted. No treatment should impair the client's ability to consult with an attorney at the time of his probable cause hearing.[23]

An individual who refuses psychiatric hospitalization or treatment but poses a danger to himself or others, who is mentally ill, and for whom less drastic treatment means are unsuitable may be adjudicated to *indefinite involuntary admission* status in a psychiatric hospital for an indefinite period for the purpose of treatment.[23] The exact legal procedure may differ in each state but the standards for commitment are similar (see Two Case Studies: Committable–Not Committable).

Certainly, to deprive an individual of liberty to the extent of involuntary commitment is a serious matter and the legal protections are strict. A major case, Addington v. Texas, decided in 1979, requires that, in a civil hearing prior to involuntary commitment, the standard of proof of "mentally ill and dangerous to self or others" must be beyond that of a "preponderance of the evidence" (the prior civil commitment standard) and must be, instead, "clear and convincing evidence" (a much higher standard).[1] This Supreme Court standard of the protection of the right to liberty must be reflected in the statutes of each state concerning commitment procedures.

Two Case Studies: Committable–Not Committable

A Case of Mental Distress—Not Committable

Mrs. A., a 65-year-old widow, had lived alone for 25 years. Her neighbors frequently expressed concern among themselves and to the local authorities about Mrs. A.'s unusual lifestyle and eccentric behavior. Their complaints were generally based on tales told to them by neighborhood children. The observations of the neighborhood children included reports that Mrs. A. slept during the day then stayed up all night, ate strange foods like raw meat and 10 pounds of sugar every 2 weeks, and talked to herself aloud. The only public place in which Mrs. A. was ever seen was in the church on Sunday mornings.

Finally, a neighbor called the police who picked up Mrs. A. while she was in her yard placing tree branches in strange patterns on her lawn. She was then admitted as an emergency admission to the local state mental hospital. The various psychiatric team members' assessments and psychological diagnostic testing results were presented at the probable cause hearing, along with testimony of other experts plus testimony from the neighbors. The descriptive nursing observations of Mrs. A.'s behavior for the 5 days prior to the civil commitment hearing were a most important part of the expert evidence and testimony.

The mental health assessment indicated that Mrs. A.'s rather odd behavior was the result of her suffering from primary degenerative dementia. The court found that, even though Mrs. A. exhibited rather bizarre behaviors at times, her mental condition, as indicated by the testimony, did not generate a tendency for her to harm either herself or others. Likewise, the testimony did not indicate that her condition would prevent her from using community resources in a manner adequate for continued self-care.

Therefore, the court determined that Mrs. A. was not judicially committable to an inpatient psychiatric unit. Nevertheless, the court did find the need for followup care by a visiting nurse from the local mental health center to monitor Mrs. A.'s nutrition, self-care, and any further progression of her mental illness that might eventually require hospitalization.

A Case for Involuntary Civil Commitment

Jim, a 20-year-old single white man, lived at home with his parents while attending college classes at the community college. For the past 2 months, Jim's behavior had become increasingly bizarre to the point that, presently, he did not sleep, did not eat, and did not attend class. He left his parents' house at all times of the day and night, which caused a great deal of disturbance. When his father attempted to reason with him, he became increasingly agitated and stormed out of the house.

The parents were not aware of any drug usage; however, they are aware of the fact that Jim had been drinking large amounts of beer. Jim lost a lot of weight and failed to care for his personal hygiene.

Although Jim had become very agitated, he had never made any threats toward anyone nor had he exhibited any assaultive behavior. He became increasingly preoccupied with the Bible; and, when his parents questioned his strange behavior, he responded that he was an apostle and that he was only doing what God told him to do. About 1 month ago, Jim's parents persuaded him to visit the local mental health center, but, when the therapist suggested inpatient treatment at a psychiatric hospital, Jim stormed out of his office.

One night, with Jim standing on the patio "preaching the gospel," and disturbing the whole neighborhood, his parents, feeling completely helpless and frightened, called the local police department. The police transported Jim to the state psychiatric facility where he stayed for 5 days on an emergency admission status, after which time he attended his probable cause hearing.

During the hearing, Jim was still hyperactive to the point that he could not sit still. Based on the testimony of both the physician and the nurse regarding Jim's mental condition and behavior, the court found that Jim met the standards for civil judicial commitment on two grounds. First, his hyperactivity secondary to his mental illness was resulting in loss of appetite, loss of weight, and insomnia to the extent that his physical health was compromised. Secondly, his increasing agitation and preoccupation with religion, also secondary to his mental illness, was potentially an antecedent to a situation in which he could lose control and harm others. Therefore, Jim was returned to the psychiatric hospital for continued treatment on a nonvoluntary, civilly committed basis with no judicial pronouncements about his competency status.

It is for that classification of clients who are indefinitely involuntarily committed that many of the issues of psychiatric client rights have been pursued. Therefore, these other "evolving" rights will be discussed in a later section.

Legal Issues of Special Client Populations

Forensic Psychiatric Clients

Mental health professionals become involved with clients who are charged with criminal acts in two major instances: first, for the evaluation of a defendant's competency to stand trial and concommitant pretrial treatment if needed, and secondly, for the evaluation of a defendant's mental condition at the time of an alleged crime and concommitant treatment if the defendant pleads and is acquitted on an insanity defense. This specialized area of mental health care is called *forensic psychiatry.*

Competency to stand trial refers to the mental condition of an individual defendant at the time of the trial. Mental health professionals determine whether the defendant is competent by assessing the following.

1. The defendant's ability to assist his attorney with his defense
2. The defendant's understanding of the nature and consequences of the charge against him
3. The defendant's understanding of courtroom procedures

In many states, community mental health centers have forensic teams who visit the jails and provide these evaluations for the court, and most states have a forensic inpatient unit that provides these evaluations as well.

If the defendant is evaluated as being incompetent to stand trial, treatment begins with the defendant being judicially criminally committed to a psychiatric hospital with a forensic unit. Treatment of incompetent defendants includes, but is not limited to, medication, individual and group psychotherapy, and groups designed to educate the defendant about courtroom proceedings as well as his current legal predicament. An important point to remember is that a defendant can be exhibiting signs and symptoms of mental illness but can still be competent to stand trial.

A decision handed down by the United States Supreme Court in Jackson v. Indiana in 1972 has resulted in state statutes designed to protect the rights of persons with criminal charges who continue to be incompetent to stand trial by virtue of their mental illness.[8] These defendants can no longer be detained for an indefinite period of time without the benefit of the same type of civil commitment hearing to which all civilly committed clients have a right. In other words, these pretrial defendants should be returned to court as soon as they are competent to stand trial, and this should be the primary goal of pretrial treatment.

If the defendant chooses to plead an insanity defense,

mental health professionals are involved in the evaluation of the defendant's mental condition at the time of an alleged crime. Four different standards or tests are used for an insanity plea to be a valid defense.

The earliest standard that achieved wide acceptance in the United States was the M'Naughten Rule, which was established in England in 1843. This is the "right–wrong test," which states, in essence, that, if at the time of his criminal act the defendant suffered from a disease of the mind that so affected his reason that he was unaware of the nature and quality of his act or that his act was wrong, then he is to be found not guilty by reason of insanity.

The second test, the irresistible impulse rule, broadened M'Naughten. This test retained the language of M'Naughten but also provided that a person acting in response to an irresistible impulse also lacked criminal responsibility even though he knew the wrongfulness of his act.

The third test, the Durham Rule, provided that a person lacked criminal responsibility if his acts were the product of a mental disease or defect. This rule was not widely used.

The fourth test, which was adopted by the American Law Institute, is most widely used today. It provides that a person is not responsible for a criminal act if he was suffering from a mental illness at the time of the act, if he was unable to appreciate the wrongfulness of his act, and if he was unable to conform his conduct to the requirements of the law.

After the forensic team uses these statutory standards in their evaluation of the defendant, they are then called to court to testify based on their evaluation of the defendant's mental status at the time of the crime. The jury uses the team's expert testimony when deciding about the client's guilt or innocence and when deciding about the appropriateness of the insanity plea.

If a defendant is found not guilty by reason of insanity, the legal implication is that, because of a mental condition, the defendant could not form the deliberate intent necessary to constitute mens rea. *Mens rea* is the mental element necessary for a defendant to be convicted of a crime; it involves a notion of deliberate criminal intent and foresight of the consequences.

When an individual is found not guilty by reason of insanity, he is involuntarily admitted to a forensic unit for an evaluation period, usually ranging from 60 to 90 days. During this time, mental health professionals evaluate the client's need for hospitalization and any other appropriate disposition. On completion of the evaluation, the court is notified of the recommendations, at which time a hearing may be scheduled to determine the court's order for release or for continuation of mandatory commitment for treatment. As soon as the client is considered not committable, he will be released into the community, possibly with some mandatory requirements for aftercare treatment.

There is a great deal of controversy involving the verdict of not guilty by reason of insanity, much of which has surrounded the John Hinckley acquittal in the assassination attempt of President Reagan. As a result of this controversy, some states have passed "a guilty but mentally ill" plea. This plea has not yet passed constitutionality scrutiny; therefore, although it is popular in principle, it may not be the final answer to a difficult balancing problem between the rights of victims and the rights of mentally ill offenders.

Ideally, the mental health team responsible for providing forensic evaluations and services is composed of a psychiatrist, a clinical psychologist, a social worker, a psychiatric-mental health nurse clinical specialist, and other nursing personnel who are active in the client's evaluation and treatment.

Nurse clinical specialists can be very valuable members of the mental health team. They are specially trained to do mental status examinations as well as function as individual and group therapists. In some states, they are qualified to be trained in competency evaluations and to testify in court as expert forensic witnesses.

Registered nurses are, likewise, valuable in the evaluation and treatment of these clients. Their nursing assessments, nursing observations, nursing interventions, knowledge of medication, and accurate documentation contribute to the formulation and implementation of a treatment plan to ensure that these clients with very special needs are given the highest quality of care possible.

Juvenile Psychiatric Clients

A special population of psychiatric clients are minors or juveniles. Until the recent past, parents or guardians have had almost an absolute privilege to admit their minor children under 18 years of age for mental health treatment. This absolute right has been eroded somewhat by state recognition of some rights of more mature children (12–18 years) to protest such treatment.[7]

In 1979, the United States Supreme Court, in Parham v. JR et al, gave a more definite standard for juvenile admissions to which state statutes and hospital policy should conform.[16] The Supreme Court held that juveniles can be authorized for admission by their parents, but that accompanying the admission, some "neutral fact finder" should determine whether statutory requirements for admission are satisfied. Further, an adversarial hearing for admission is not required nor does due process require that the fact finder be legally trained or a hearing officer.[16]

By ruling in this way, the Court balanced competing interests of the rights of parents and guardians to control the lives of their children with the right of children to due process prior to a limitation upon their liberty.

Psychiatric-mental health nurses need to be mindful of these procedural protections for the benefit of their juvenile clients. Limiting hospitalization to statutory require-

ments is an important advocacy activity for juvenile psychiatric clients.

Major Evolving Legal Rights

Right to Treatment

The idea that psychiatric clients have a legally actionable right to psychiatric treatment began to develop in the late 1960s and culminated in the early 1970s in the Circuit Court case of Wyatt v. Stickney.[25] The case provided innovative statements about the rights of civilly committed mentally ill patients in state hospitals. The Court stated that such patients do have certain treatment rights, which include the following.

1. Treatment must give some realistic opportunity to improve or be cured.
2. Custodial care is insufficient to meet treatment requirements.
3. A lack of funding does not excuse a state from treatment responsibilities.
4. Commitment without treatment violates the due process rights of patients.

Perhaps the most important pronouncement in Wyatt concerns the three determinates for the adequacy of treatment, which are 1) a humane environment, 2) a qualified staff in adequate numbers, and 3) individualized treatment plans.[25] This case gave the nation guidance about treatment rights; however, because it was not reviewed by the Supreme Court, it is not totally generalizable.

O'Connor v. Donaldson was a case decided by the Supreme Court and is commonly thought to be the leading case for the right to treatment.[15] However, O'Connor instead states that no state can confine a nondangerous mentally ill individual in a state hospital who is capable of surviving safely in the community by himself or with the help of willing responsible family or friends.[15] There is still no clear national standard on the right to treatment of the involuntarily civilly committed or on the right of the state to commit involuntarily the mentally ill for the purpose of treatment. Newer cases will decide these issues.

Treatment in the Least Restrictive Environment

Over time, through dicta and decisions, Courts have given guidance to the mental health system on many matters, including standards about the settings in which treatment should occur. As early as 1969, in Covington v. Harris, the Courts held that an individual who is to be treated involuntarily should receive such treatment in a setting that is least restrictive to his liberty but that will still meet his treatment needs.[6]

Least restrictive environments can be community resources instead of hospitalization, open wards instead of locked wards, or outpatient care instead of inpatient care.[7] The importance of this client right to nursing is that nurses need to constantly assess the client's condition and status so that more or less restrictive treatment alternatives can be applied based upon the client's evolving needs.

Right to Refuse Treatment

As discussed previously, the doctrine of informed consent implies that clients have a right to choose or refuse medical and health treatment. Certainly, health care providers, through interpersonal relationships and client education, may try to convince clients about the need for certain treatments but only in rare or life-threatening instances do Courts intervene in the negative treatment decisions of clients.

Voluntary Clients. Following this principle of judicial noninterference, voluntary clients who have not been adjudicated incompetent have an absolute right to refuse treatment and to choose between treatment alternatives. They cannot be forced to take medications, be research subjects, or be involved in invasive treatments, such as ECT or psychosurgery. Only in rare cases of severe behavioral acting out that threatens self or others can voluntary clients be forced to take psychotropic medications.

Involuntary Clients. The rights of involuntarily committed clients to refuse treatment are less clearly defined than are the rights of voluntary clients. Rennie v. Klein and Rogers v. Okin are the leading cases to give guidance on this unsettled issue.[18, 19] The Courts have been prone to state that involuntary clients cannot refuse tried and true treatments that promote recovery, such as psychotropic medication; however, there must be protections applied for more risky procedures with more extreme side effects or consequences, such as ECT, insulin shock, or psychosurgery. In Mills v. Rogers (on appeal of Rogers v. Okin), the Supreme Court seemed to favor a standard that there would be no absolute right of involuntary patients to refuse treatment but that treatment decisions would be left to the judgment of professionals who would consider patient rights in their treatment decisions.[14]

Clearly, it is important for the psychiatric nurse to know that there is much continuing controversy and litigation about the rights of involuntary clients to refuse treatment; therefore, being current on the most recent case law about this issue is a must. Unit and facility policies need to remain current and should clearly reflect that, as the treatment becomes more invasive, as it has increased risk, or as it demonstrates questionable results, the more likely it is that the client's right to refuse must be honored.

Right to Aftercare

Care in the community following psychiatric hospitalization is greatly needed to prevent readmissions and to ensure the rehabilitation of former inpatients. There is no absolute legal right at this time to aftercare programs unless such a right is provided by state statutes. It is not inconceivable that case laws may evolve to mandate aftercare services as a right of the mental health client.

In conjunction with other members of the interdisciplinary team, it is a nursing responsibility to plan for aftercare treatment. As knowledgeable and responsible citizens, nurses voice their concern at all levels of the political system to see that psychiatric clients have access to adequate aftercare services such as outpatient counseling, medication follow-up, vocational placement, and sheltered living environments.

Strategies for Assuring Quality and Accountability in Nursing Practice

American Nurses' Association's Standards of Practice

The nursing profession—through its professional organization, the American Nurses' Association (ANA)—has developed clinical standards of practice for both generic and specialty areas of practice. The generic standards apply to all professional nursing practice and serve as guidelines or norms for practice. A review of the generic standards indicates that nurses must use the nursing process in therapeutic relationships with clients. In other words, nurses will assess, diagnose, document, report, plan, implement, and evaluate client care with the client, the family, and the client's significant others.[4] The focus of nursing practice is on the client's attainment or restoration of physical and mental health. Practitioners of nursing are uniquely able to view the client holistically and to engage in a process *with* the client that has, as its aim, care and growth. The use of ANA Standards of Practice as a baseline for performance evaluation will assure such practice.

Quality Assurance Programming

Another major strategy for the assuring of quality and accountability in nursing is the involvement of nursing in quality assurance programs. In the 1970s, the American Nurses' Association developed a national program emphasizing that nurses would implement the standards of nursing practice through development of, and participation in, systematic quality assurance endeavors.[3]

The American Nurses' Association developed a conceptual model for quality assurance that is represented in Figure 39-1.[3] The use of the model as the conceptual basis for quality assurance facilitates nurses' and other health care practitioners' understanding of quality assurance and demonstrates that quality care be assured to consumers and is not merely an exercise used for accreditation or reimbursement verification.

There are numerous nursing activities that fit into the ANA quality assurance model—client care audit, peer re-

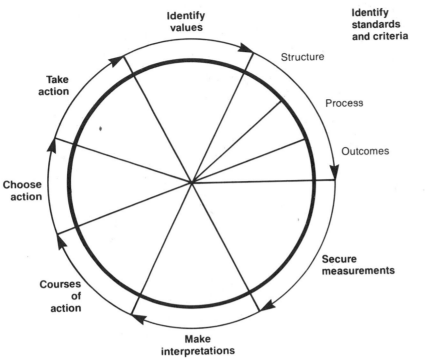

Figure 39-1. *Quality assurance model.*

view, client classification and acuity rating, the nursing clinical ladder, medical care evaluation, and nursing care planning, to name a few. Psychiatric audit is a procedure through which client care in psychiatric settings can be measured for its effectiveness in providing care to population categories in psychiatric settings. The ANA Model for Quality Assurance can be useed in a psychiatric audit as a way of conceptualizing the audit activity as a dynamic process. The process includes values classification, criteria development, client care measurements, identification of care successes and failures, development of alternative care approaches, and the introduction of change into the psychiatric setting.[3] The dynamic audit process is never complete until a complete reaudit is accomplished to evaluate the effectiveness of change.

Audit criteria should be written to include the measurement of the health team's awareness of the legal rights and remedies available to clients. Criteria that address meeting the client's legal needs are very important, especially in the psychiatric setting. It is most important that nurses voluntarily and enthusiastically join in quality assurance programs for the purpose of systematically evaluating client care in an effort to improve care for all consumers.

Seeking Legal Consultation

A further strategy that needs to be employed by health professionals on the psychiatric unit is knowing how and when to obtain appropriate legal consultation on an ongoing basis. First, it would be important as a baseline to have an attorney who is aware of the issues in mental health

law make an assessment of the institution's policies and procedures and to provide that review for the staff in a problem-solving, rather than policing, manner.

Secondly, some arrangements should be made to have such an attorney offer continuing education programs on a regular basis in order to review with the staff updates on court decisions and recent legislation that would impact on care in the psychiatric unit. Also, having legal consultation readily available on a case (client) consultation basis when the staff is endeavoring to ensure legal accountability is extremely valuable. Most institutions should provide this kind of legal consultation, if requested, not only for the benefit of their clients but also to protect the institution from potential liability.

Summary

The legal impact on the practice of psychiatric-mental health nursing is both immense and subtle. The psychiatric nurse who evaluates her practice in an attempt to improve the nursing profession and the health of her clients does so not from legal demands but from professional standards. Nevertheless, nursing practice must meet certain legal standards and must adjust its course as new legal standards evolve. It is the capable and challenged nurse who includes legal knowledge in client care and it is to her that many clients will turn for information, advocacy, and protective justice.

Some of the major points of this chapter include the following.

1. Nurses have both independent and dependent areas of nursing practice and are liable for maintenance of a responsible standard of care to clients in both of these areas of practice.
2. A failure to meet the standard of care that results in an injury to a client–consumer makes the nurse liable for nursing negligence or malpractice.
3. Nurses have a duty to participate in the issues of informed consent, which are basic rights of clients; failure to obtain informed consent from a client prior to a procedure can result in a civil action against the physician and the health care agency on the theory of assault and battery.
4. Clients also have a right to rely on the appropriateness and confidentiality of their medical records and data.
5. Confidentiality is an ethical, professional, and legal responsibility and is, in many instances, mandated by statute.
6. Privileged communication is determined by statute for certain professional groups and their clients.
7. Some cases indicate that confidentiality must be breached when the public safety is in jeopardy, as when clients threaten to harm third persons.
8. To provide legally acceptable nursing care in psychiatric-mental health settings, nurses must be informed about a variety of issues, including recognized client rights, and they must take responsibility with other health team members to see that client rights are protected.
9. Client rights may differ due to
   the civil or criminal nature of commitment proceedings;
   the voluntariness of a civil commitment;
   the purpose of the criminal commitment;
   the age of the client.
10. It is most important that psychiatric-mental health care givers identify client status and client rights and secure adequate consultation as client rights evolve.
11. Three strategies for enhancing the quality of psychiatric-mental health nursing care and, thereby, assuring quality care and accountability by nursing to consumers are as follows.
    Nurses must practice by using the ANA Standards of Practice as their normative base.
    Nurses must develop, and participate in, quality assurance programming, including psychiatric audits.
    Nurses must request and secure ongoing continuing education and consultation with an attorney who is knowledgeable in mental health law.

Legal Nursing Care Plan

Goal	Plan	Outcome Evaluation
To prevent nursing negligence	Provide at minimum "reasonable man" standard of care in assessment, planning, implementation, and evaluation of nursing practice. Know elements of negligence and problem solve to prevent occurrences. Give safe care both in independent and dependent areas of nursing practice.	Malpractice suits are at a minimum and client feedback reflects satisfaction with nursing care. Staff inservice periodically reviews legal malpractice problems and strategies. Care shows nursing initiation of assessment, planning, implementation, and evaluation of health care and judicious implementation of the physician's treatment and drug orders.
To ensure client rights to informed consent	Know the elements of informed consent. Observe the client for behaviors that would indicate consent was valid—knowledge, competence, capacity. Record and report any discrepancies in consent or behavior, re-	Staff inservice periodically reviews issues of informed consent for psychiatric clients. Nurse acts as client advocate in informed consent and has interdependent role of assessment of consent, competence, and consent revocation with physician.

Goal	Plan	Outcome Evaluation
	vocation of consent, and so on to the client's physician.	Client record reflects specific nursing assessment of current behaviors and appropriate nursing action is taken if consent is questioned or invalidated.
To protect the client's right to confidentiality of health data	Records/charts are protected and data are not shared without client authorization. The record is the legal document and should be chronological, comprehensive, and complete to facilitate care. No verbal communication about the client should be shared except between treatment team members. Nurses rarely have statutory privileged communication with clients but both confidentiality/privilege must be breached if the client threatens harm to third persons.	The unit has policy/procedure for staff confidentiality and that procedure is reviewed by all staff yearly. The client record reflects nursing process and descriptive charting. Policy/procedures reflect nurse's duty to protect third persons in cases of prior threats.
To protect client rights	Knowledge of client rights should be made known to all staff. Ensure that ward policy/procedure do not violate client rights. Periodically review rights, issues of violations, and mechanisms that provide rights accountability. Specifically review/reevaluate changes in voluntary/nonvoluntary status and civil/criminal commitment proceedings and treatment consequences.	Inservice programs on client rights are held periodically. Legal consultant periodically reviews unit policy/procedure manual to guard against rights violations and to advise staff as to protective mechanisms for full rights provisions. Staff inservice periodically covers statutory/case law on admission status, procedures, and treatment. Quality assurance materials reflect items that measure the status of client's rights.
To protect evolving client rights	The nurse must know and policies must reflect the following. Voluntary clients are seeking treatment and nondangerous involuntary clients cannot be confined without receiving treatment. Treatments needs to be, or occur, in methods and settings that are least restrictive to the client's liberty. Voluntary clients who are nondangerous may refuse all treatments including medications, ECT, and psychosurgery. Nonvoluntary clients who are nondangerous have limited rights	The legal consultant reviews and advises on new legislation and case law implications for mental health care. Psychiatric treatment reflects differing modalities and choices for the consumer. Medicine and nursing are concerned about the client's right to refuse treatment and this is reflected in policies, client records, and orders. Policies and procedures clearly reflect differing rights in voluntary and nonvoluntary clients and between medication and more invasive procedures.

Goal	Plan	Outcome Evaluation
	to refuse medication and have greater rights to refuse more invasive procedures such as ECT and psychosurgery. Competence to consent and procedures for substituted consent are always at issue with involuntarily committed clients.	Consent procedures are clearly defined, known, and utilized by all involved staff.
To provide legally sound and professionally accountable nursing care	Secure legal consultation for new decision-update, review of policy/procedures, and case consultation when needed.	A yearly staff legal inservice for case update is held. A legal consultant is retained and is available to staff on an "on call" basis. The ANA Quality Assurance Model is used by the unit in a quality assurance program. There is an ongoing audit on each diagnostic category of frequent client population. Each client care plan and audit tool includes one or more elements of legal knowledge and specific need in the area of psychiatric-mental health care.

References

1. Addington v. Texas. 99 Supreme Court 1813, 441 United States 418, 1979
2. American Hospital Association: A Patient's Bill of Rights. Chicago, The American Hospital Association, 1974
3. American Nurses' Association: Quality Assurance Workbook. Kansas City, American Nurses' Association, 1976
4. American Nurses' Association: Standards of Practice. Kansas City, American Nurses' Association, 1973
5. Canterbury v. Spence. 464 Federal, Second 772, 1972
6. Covington v. Harris. 419 Federal, Second 617, 1969
7. Ennis B, Emery R: The Rights of Mental Patients. New York, Avon Books, 1978
8. Jackson v. Indiana. 406 United States 715, 1972
9. Jones K: Lunacy, Law, and Conscience. London, Routledge and Kegan Paul, 1955
10. Karmowitz v. Michigan Department of Mental Hygiene. 2 Prison Law Reporter 433
11. Kerr AH: Nurses Notes, That's Where the Goodies Are. Nursing '75, February, pp 34–41, 1975
12. Kittrie N: The Right to be Different. Baltimore, Johns Hopkins University Press, 1974
13. Menzes WC: The Neglected Nurse: Rx for the Medical Malpractice Victim. Tulsa, Tulsa Law Review 12(104):104–128, 1976
14. Mills v. Rogers. 102 Supreme Court, 2442, 1982
15. O'Connor v. Donaldson. 422 United States 563, 1975
16. Parham, Commissioner, Department of Human Resources of Georgia et al v. I.R. et al. 442 United States 584, 1979
17. Prosser W: Law of Torts. St Paul, MN, West Publishing, 1971
18. Rennie v. Klein. 653 Federal Second 836, 1981
19. Rogers v. Okin. 634 Federal Second 650, 1980, 478 Federal Supplement 1342 (D. Mass), 1979
20. Rosoff AJ: Informed Consent: A Guide for Health Care Remedies. Rockville, MD, Aspen Systems Corporation, 1981
21. Sharill NL: Patients' Rights vs. Patients' Needs: The Right of the Mentally Ill to Refuse Treatment in Colorado. Denver Law Review 58:567–608, 1981
22. Tarasoff v. Regents of University of California. 592 P. 2nd 553, 1974
23. Tennessee Code Annotated, §33-6-103
24. Tennessee Code Annotated, §63-7-101 et seq
25. Wyatt v. Stickney. 325 Federal Supplement 781, 1971

Chapter 40
Research in Psychiatric-Mental Health Nursing

The nurse contributes to nursing and the mental health field through innovations in theory and practice and participation in research.

American Nurses' Association
Standards of Psychiatric and Mental Health Nursing Practice
(Standard XI: Research), 1982

Mary Anne Sweeney
James McColgan, Jr.

Chapter Preview

This chapter presents an overview of the research process in nursing. Special emphasis has been placed on two key areas that integrate research skills with a well-rounded nursing practice base. The first area highlights the utilization of published research reports. Nurses need to utilize the professional literature—to learn the outcomes of studies that have already been completed. In addition, they need to develop an ability to critique research reports, and to incorporate important elements of the research process into routine nursing practice. The second area of emphasis focuses on involvement in varied steps of the research process, because learning is enhanced by participation. Practical suggestions have been included with the beginning researcher in mind.

Learning Objectives

After completion of the chapter, the reader should be able to accomplish the following.

1. Define nursing research and recognize broad distinctions among the main types of research
2. Discuss the varied ways that the research process can be incorporated into the role of the nurse
3. Locate published nursing research reports and other sources of research-related information
4. Read, evaluate, and utilize information from research studies
5. Develop a strategy for active participation in nursing research-related activities

Understanding Nursing Research

Definition and Purpose of Research

One way of gathering and processing information related to nursing is through the use of the research process. Although you may not have realized it, you have been doing "research" for quite some time. Unfortunately, the mention of the word "research" may trigger an immediate, but unfavorable, response in many professionals.

If, however, we put the research process into its proper perspective, we can deal with it more effectively. Research is one way to gather and process information, and it is used routinely by all types of professional groups. Research is the use of a series of formalized steps to gather objective information; the research process is a series of steps that can be followed by nurses, psychologists, biologists, or any professionals interested in obtaining data or information. *Nursing research* is the "application to the study of all nursing problems with the goal of expanding the theoretical basis of nursing through the discovery of new knowledge."[6]

The Research Process

The steps of the research process provide structure and consistency in the approach to information gathering. The flexibility available at each step of the research process enables a study to be specifically tailored to each new situation. Because the major objective of conducting a research study is to add new knowledge to what is already known about nursing, some of the reasons for the formality and safeguards of the process become clear. It is critical to insure that the information gained in the study is as accurate as possible. The information should also be useful because it is unbiased by the investigator's particular point of view. Many safeguards have been devised to help researchers collect "good" or "clean" information and to help them sort out its true meaning.

Scientific Method Applied to Nursing

The scientific method has been found to be the most effective way of determining relationships between variables, thereby enabling the scientist to understand, predict, and, to a degree, control.[3] The use of a scientific process of obtaining objective information can be applied by its practitioners to any professional discipline.

The nursing role is presently expanding to include the use of scientific research methods at many different levels of expertise. Nursing students, faculty members, and clinical nursing practitioners in all types of different nursing settings are becoming increasingly involved with nursing research in the course of their normal work routine (see insert, Examples of Research Studies Conducted by Nurses in Psychiatric Nursing and Mental Health Topics).

Examples of Research Studies Conducted by Nurses in Psychiatric Nursing and Mental Health Topics

A Study of Psychiatric Patients' Knowledge About Their Prescribed Medications

A Study of Alcoholic Patients' Perceptions of the Role of the Nurse

The Nurse's Therapeutic Use of Touch as Related to Withdrawn Patients

Factors Affecting Staff Nurses' Use of Limit Setting with Disruptive Patients

A Study of the Confidence Level of Nurses in Caring for Patients with Depression

Client Expectation and Perception of the Nurses' Role in Relationship to Client Satisfaction

Observable Signs of Anxiety or Distress During Psychiatric Interviews Conducted by Nurses

Nurses' Attitudes Toward the Suicidal Patient

Nursing Interventions with Long-Term Patients in Regard to their Physical Appearance: An Evaluative Study

Nurses, in general, are fortunate that their work entails a variety of interesting experiences and situations. The selection of research topics can be as varied as the types of professional work nurses perform. It usually takes only a brief period of time of perusing through research journals to discover a study that is both interesting and useful to the reader.

For instance, two faculty members at Wayne State University in Detroit, Michigan were interested in looking at factors that influenced the success of registered nurse students when they returned to school for a baccalaureate degree. They examined a specific set of charcteristics and found, among other things, that the type of the student's initial nursing program discriminated significantly between students who completed the baccalaureate degree and those who did not.[5]

The best introduction to the realm of research is to read about it. You are encouraged to find examples in the literature of studies that cover issues or questions that are important to you. The selected references listed in the insert, Selected References for Locating Research-Related Nursing Information, will help you locate the material you need. Your objective should be to locate, read, and assess the results of a research project, and then use the new knowledge in your nursing activities.

There are a number of ways to implement the research process according to the objectives of the individual conducting the study. Table 40-1 summarizes the main points in six of the most frequently encountered types of research. The most prevalent type of research in the nursing literature is the survey, and it can take many forms, such as descriptive and explanatory studies. The report should clearly state, usually in the introductory section of the report, the type of research being reported. After reading your first few research reports, compare your particular study with the criteria presented in Table 40-1.

Selected References for Locating Research-Related Nursing Information

Books

Abdellah F, Levine E: Better Patient Care Through Nursing Research, 2nd ed. New York, Macmillan, 1978

Diers D: Research in Nursing Practice. Philadelphia, JB Lippincott, 1979

Downs F, Newman M: A Sourcebook of Nursing Research, 3rd ed. Philadelphia, FA Davis, 1984

Hardyck C, Petrinovich L: Understanding Research in the Social Sciences. Philadelphia, WB Saunders, 1975

Kerlinger F: Foundations of Behavioral Research. New York, Holt, Rinehart, 1973

Mayo C, LaFrance M: Evaluating Research in Social Psychology. Monterey, CA, Brooks/Cole, 1977

Meltzoff J, Kornreich M: Research in Psychotherapy. Chicago, Aldine Publishing, 1970

Polit D, Hungler B: Nursing Research, 2nd ed. Philadelphia, JB Lippincott, 1983

Sweeney MA, Olivieri P: Introduction to Nursing Research. Philadelphia, JB Lippincott, 1981

Verhonick P, Seaman C: Research Methods for Undergraduate Students in Nursing. New York, Appleton-Century-Crofts, 1978

Journals

Nursing Research
10 Columbus Circle, NY, NY 10019

Advances in Nursing Science
Aspen Systems Corporation, PO Box 335, Dover, NJ 07801

Research in Nursing and Health
John Wiley & Sons, Publisher, 605 Third Ave., NY, NY 10016

Western Journal of Nursing Research
Phillips-Allen, Publishers, 1330 S. State College Blvd., Anaheim, CA 92806

Journal of Psychosocial Nursing and Mental Health Services
Charles B. Slack Inc., 6900 Grove Road, Thorofare, NJ 08086

Journal of Nursing Education
Charles B. Slack Inc., 6900 Grove Road, Thorofare, NJ 08086

International Journal of Nursing Studies
Pergamon Press, Maxwell House, Fairview Park, Elmsford, NY 10523

Indexes

Nursing and Allied Health Literature Index and its annual cumulation, Cumulative Index to Nursing and Allied Health Index 1956 + (Glendale, CA, Adventist Medical Center Library)

Nursing Studies Index 1900–1959 by Virginia Henderson, 4 volumes (JB Lippincott, 1972)

Index Medicus and its annual cumulation, Cumulated Index Medicus, 1960 + (National Library of Medicine)

Abstracts

Abstracts of Reports by Studies in Nursing in each issue of Nursing Research 1960–1978

Nursing Research Abstracts (England), 1979 +

Psychological Abstracts, 1927 +

Excerpta Medica, 1947 +

Table 40-1.   **Characteristics of Various Research Approaches**

	PHILOSOPHICAL	HISTORICAL	CASE STUDY	METHODOLOGICAL	STUDY	EXPERIMENTAL
Time Frame	Present–past	Past	Present–past	Present	Present	Present–future
Researcher's objectives	Trace development and/or present status of abstract ideas.	Discover exciting facts and combine to draw conclusions.	In-depth analysis of subject; usually includes historical aspects	Develop instruments to measure variables; test statistical procedures for appropriateness.	Discover new facts about subjects; make conclusions and interpretations	Prediction of events; discover cause-and-effect relationships under controlled condition
Data collection source	Documents	Personal and public documents and records; artifacts; interviews in limited circumstances	Combination of data from subjects, documents and artifacts	Subjects utilized for pretesting, reliability, and validation of instruments	Subjects	Subjects
Type of research report	Narrative only	Narrative, sometimes includes objects or artifacts	Narrative with occasional numerical data; can include objects or artifacts	Numerical with accompanying narrative statements	Narrative that usually includes numerical data	Narrative with great emphasis on numerical results

Utilizing Published Research

The Research Report

The first step in utilizing research results in nursing practice requires the development of a strategy to read and understand published reports. Once you are comfortable in reviewing the purpose and content of research reports, you can begin to evaluate the report's results and place the findings appropriately within nursing theory and practice.

The four areas of published research reports that require your attention are the introduction, methodology, results, and discussion. Each area contains essential information for comprehension of the research project and its possible applications to nursing practice.

Introduction

The introduction of the research report describes the problem that was investigated and related background information. The problem statement is usually placed within the first paragraph of the report. Usually, a declarative statement describes the overall purpose of the study. For example, the author might state that "the purpose of this study is to investigate the relationship between blood pressure and varied levels of psychological stress."

An interrogative statement of the research problem may be used that questions the nature of the relationship between the variables or factors being studied. An example

of this is the statement, "What is the relationship between blood pressure and different levels of psychological stress?" It is particularly important, at this point, to determine a simple definition of what the study is about. The variables being investigated are defined in general terms within the introduction, but are refined in the methodology section of the study.

The introduction of the study should lead the reader to understand not only what is currently investigated, but why it is an important topic for scrutiny. The background of the problem is presented by a review of related literature. The scope of the literature review should be fairly exhaustive and should demonstrate a comprehensive grasp of the topic. This literature review should include key studies that have been conducted about the problem, the findings of previous investigations, and the identification of questions concerning the problem that have yet to be answered. Although the review of the literature is not intended to provide an expert level of knowledge concerning the problem area, it should engender an appreciation for where the problem under investigation "fits" into the realm of nursing theory and practice.

Methodology

The methodology portion of the research report describes the mechanics by which the investigation was conducted. It includes an explanation of the population and sample, instrument, data collection methods, and data analysis procedures. The detailed information in this portion of the study is needed to provide a clear understanding of the procedures so they can be evaluated or replicated by other researchers.

Population and Sample.

The population is the entire group of subjects possessing the qualities desired by the researcher. The sample is the group of people who were actually selected from the population to participate in the research project. The research report should describe, in as much detail as possible, both the population and the criteria used to select the sample from this group. This description should include how many individuals were selected, how they were chosen, and the procedures used to obtain consent from the individuals for participation in the study.

Research Instrument.

The description of the research instrument includes discussion of its format, reliability, and validity. The instruments might be a questionnaire, an interview schedule, or machinery (*e.g.*, a sphygmomanometer). In the first two types of instruments, the number, type, and some examples of the items should be included in the research report. Because of the variety of instruments available to researchers, knowledge of the instrument format is important for understanding this aspect of data collection.

Reliability of an instrument refers to its consistency. Its ability to collect the same kind of data in repeated administrations, and in a variety of situations, is important. One of the more common ways of determining reliability is termed *test–retest reliability*. To establish this type of reliability, the researcher administers the instrument, and then, after a period of time (from 2 weeks to several months), administers the same instrument to the same sample group again. If the instrument has a high degree of test–retest reliability, it will yield similar results on both occasions. The reader of the research report needs to know if the instrument is one that produces consistent results before believing its findings.

Validity is the ability of the instrument to truly measure the variables under investigation. There are various types of validity–face, content, construct, and criterion-related. Face validity is established if the instrument merely appears or looks related to what is being studied. Content validity refers to the degree to which items contained in the instrument collect representative information related to the content of the variable being measured.

Construct validity is more difficult to establish. Constructs are concepts that are not directly observable, such as human reasoning or intelligence. To establish construct validity, the researchers compare their results with an alternate means of measuring the variable. For example, the instrument is administered to a group that is also observed by judges for the concept. The amount of agreement between the data collected by the instrument and the observations of the judges is the level of construct validity.

Criterion-related validity is used to predict future performance. This validity is established by *post facto* identification of characteristics related to successful performance of a task. These characteristics are formulated into an instrument that should then identify individuals who will successfully perform the tasks desired. The varied types of validity are important in assessing the value of the instrument used to obtain useful information from subjects.

Data Collection.

After describing the instrument, the research report should describe the data collection methodology. This description concerns how the study group was selected and how the information was actually collected. In this portion of the report, the reader should find sufficient details to replicate the research project.

The description of the data collection method may be general or complex, depending on the instrument format employed. The methodology of using mechanical instruments or paper and pencil measures with established reliabilities and validities may be described in general terms if the instrument's specific administration procedures have been followed by the researcher. More complex descriptions of the methodology are required when researchers adapt an instrument or its administration procedure to meet their particular needs. In the former case, the reader may be referred to the original instrument; in the latter, the researcher should report the methodology in sufficient detail to enable the reader to replicate it.

Data Analysis.

The final area within the discussion of the methodology is the data analysis plan. The data analysis plan describes processing of the raw data and the procedures, usually statistical, that will be employed to tabulate the data. Processing may range from hand scoring of items on a test to the coding of data for computer analysis.

The statistical procedures used by researchers are classified as descriptive or inferential. *Descriptive statistics* are used to summarize the characteristics of the data collected. The most commonly used descriptive statistics are frequencies and mean (or average) scores.

Inferential statistics are used to test hypotheses and compare the results from this group with larger populations. Unlike most descriptive statistics, inferential statistics require the application of mathematical formulas. For this reason, a computer is often employed for this type of data analysis. There are many types of inferential statistical tests designed to analyze specific types of data. Each reports a numbered value for its specific statistic that is compared to a table of values for that test. If the value of the statistics falls at or above the table's designated value for the level of significance desired (usually 0.05), the existence of a relationship between the variables is supported. The research report should name the statistical test that was used and specify the acceptable level of significance.

Results

The implementation of the data analysis plan is reported in the results of the report. The discussion should focus first on the overall characteristics of the data by using descriptive statistics. The discussion itself should highlight important characteristics rather than reporting each item singly. Most of the data may be presented in tabular form; there are usually several tables in this section, but the key points will be discussed in the text as well.

The analysis and interpretation of the data should follow a logical sequence. Often, research reports will analyze and interpret data following the sequence established by the order of the hypothesis or research questions. The key point is to present a clear picture of the study results. The analysis of the data should report both the obtained statistical values and the level of significance. The author should state whether a hypothesis was supported or, in the case of research questions, a relationship was implied.

Keep in mind that research in which hypotheses or relationships are not supported also has value. The lack of significant findings in a research project has important implications, too. From this discussion of results, you should learn not only what the researchers found out from the subjects, but also how they interpret these results. The interpretation section will discuss the meaning of the findings.

Discussion

The final area of a research report that contains important information for the reader is the discussion. In the discussion, the researchers describe the conclusions they have drawn from the entire sutdy and suggest implications of this information in regard to nursing practice. The conclusions must be specific and must be clearly based upon results. The conclusions proposed by the researchers describe what has been learned from the research project. In discussing the implications of the findings, the researcher suggests uses for the information. Implications also include predictions of the impact the results may have on the theory or practice of nursing. The report usually concludes with suggestions concerning the future direction of research in this area.

The discussion portion of a research report is considered by many readers to be the substance of a research project, but it must be considered within its overall context. The conclusions and implications of a research project must be viewed in relation to specific information about such factors as the size of the study group, the soundness of the instrument, and the data analysis plan. Weakness in any of these areas reduces the value and applicability of the research conclusions and implications. The form in the insert, Research Reading Guidelines may be useful in helping you extract and summarize information from research studies.

Research Reading Guidelines

1. Reference Identification (in format for listing in Bibliography):
2. Introductory Material:
   A. Research Problem (in your own words):
   B. Purpose of the study:
   C. Summary of the relevant points of the literature cited:
3. Methodology:
   A. Overall plan or design of the study (in your own words):
   B. Description of the following:
      1. Subjects:
      2. Variables (or factors) being studied:
      3. Instrument:
      4. Procedures (what was done to the subjects):
4. Results:
   A. Summary of the main results:
   B. Any additional interesting features:
5. Evaluation:
   A. Your comprehension level of article
      _____ fairly easy to understand
      _____ some difficulty
      _____ very complicated
   B. Overall value of the study to the field
      _____ very worthwhile
      _____ average
      _____ questionable contribution

Protection of Subjects' Rights

The ethics surrounding the conduct of research projects must be considered. The nurse conducting a research project has the dual role of researcher and nurse. As a researcher, the nurse must implement the project's methodology and collect the desired data. As a nurse, the researcher continues to have the nursing responsibility of promoting the health needs of the person. The issues with which the nurse researcher should be concerned are the individual's right not to participate, informed consent, and confidentiality.

Right to Refuse to Participate

An individual has the right to refuse to participate in any research project for any reason. This is a right possessed solely by the individual. No other individual or institution may deny or override this right. Furthermore, an individual may not be coerced into agreeing to participate in a research project. Nurses should be aware of the client's involvement in a research project, and the circumstances surrounding this involvement, even when they are not directly involved in the research themselves.

Right to Informed Consent

Informed consent is the term used to explain that the individual has the right to be fully informed about what participation in the research project involves, how it might affect him, the time commitment required, and any possible risks that may be involved. To obtain informed consent, the nurse researcher must explain these aspects of the study to the individual in nontechnical language. Although the researchers must be careful not to affect or bias the information that will be forthcoming from the client, they should answer all questions as fully and honestly as possible. Obtaining informed consent from potential research subjects can be time-consuming for the researcher, but it will pay dividends by increasing the level of each subject's level of participation.

Right to Confidentiality

Confidentiality and anonymity are often considered synonymous by researchers; however, they are not. Confidentiality involves the right of the individual to privacy concerning the data that he provides to the researcher. Anonymity involves the individual's right of privacy as a participant in the research group. Researchers may provide confidentiality to a research participant's data by various methods such as replacing the name on each instrument with a code number. The most common manner in which well-meaning researchers violate a subject's anonymity is by specifically identifying the source of the study group in their research report. For example, a researcher who identifies the study group as "the senior class of nursing students at Plain State College" has not provided anonymity to the research subjects. Although the research report must contain specific information concerning the criteria for selection of the study groups and its characteristics, the specific source of the study group need not be revealed.

The nurse researcher must be cognizant of the rights of subjects involved in research projects. As a professional, the nurse must coordinate both the requirements of these rights and the research process itself. Above all, as a nurse, the researcher must be supportive and protective of subjects' rights.

Participating in Nursing Research

Developing Necessary Skills

There are three broad steps to follow in order to develop the skills that are necessary to participate in nursing research. The amount of participation increases as one progresses through the three steps, and they should be approached in the order in which they appear.

Step 1. Read all the studies you can.
The steps you have just learned to apply in utilizing published research studies will help you develop greater understanding of the process and increase your depth of knowledge. The confidence you display in identifying varied steps of the research process will increase markedly as you read and critique more examples in the professional literature. Use the journals listed in the insert, Selected References for Locating Research-Related Nursing Information as a starting point for locating nursing-related research articles.

Step 2. Practice individual steps of the research process.
You do not have to undertake a complete study to gain experience in research-related activities. Start with one step of the research process that involves a skill you could develop to do your job better. Perhaps the skill involves summarizing and analyzing data. Look over the data analysis section of the research studies you have been critiquing. Then take some of your patient-related data and try to summarize it just as the authors did in one of the published reports. In other words, construct a table that presents the key points, and then make several summary statements about the information in your table.

Perhaps you need to present a summary of the current literature regarding a procedure at a team conference. Study the introductory sections of published research studies to see how varied articles are summarized, condensed, and combined. Note how the authors give credit to the original sources, and how they present reports with conflicting results.

Step 3. Replicate a published study.
The best way to acquire an understanding of the research process is to become actively involved in it. A good way to begin is to use a previously conducted

study as an example. Use it as a step-by-step pattern just as a tailor would when making a garment. Follow and update as needed. For instance, check the literature to see if any related articles have been published since the date of this study. Use the same instrument, if possible, or a close facsimile. Your tables will already be laid out, but the data will be new. You'll learn a lot about the practical steps of conducting a project while having your own set of "back up" instructions.

Nurses who are just starting out in research often think that they must "reinvent the wheel." Replication of previously conducted studies is a necessary step in the process of building sound theoretical knowledge. Replications of studies are also appearing more frequently in the nursing literature. The following suggestions will help you become actively involved in your own project.

Tips on Conducting Small Research Projects

The following ten steps will help you get started on your way to becoming a professional who utilizes research in a meaningful way in any area of nursing practice.

1. Define a topic that you want to find out more about. Your interest level will help "spur you on" to explore the topic further. Note two things—the types of articles you tend to read when you look through professional journals, and the aspects of nursing that you "puzzle over" or think about a lot. The first step is to summarize your idea or interest in a few words, such as "communicating with confused patients" or "exploring nurses reactions to dying patients." The idea doesn't need to be crystal clear, just a start in a direction that is interesting to you.

2. Find several studies that have been published on this general topic or ones that are closely related to it. Remember in your search that you may find a related study that has been done by researchers in another discipline, such as psychologists or social workers. Use these studies as a basis for your "research folder." Summarize the main points of the study or make a copy that you can put in your folder for later reference. Find several articles that relate to the topic that may not be formal "research" studies and add them to your folder too. The more you know about a particular topic, the better. Note which articles your authors mention most often in their bibliographies and gather those works as well.

3. Pick out one aspect of one of the studies in your folder and draw up a plan to reconstruct this in a limited fashion. Use a study or parts of several studies as a pattern to follow. For instance, suppose one study on communicating with confused patients contrasts two different types of nursing intervention. Use the two approaches as a part of your nursing care and observe the results. Keep some notes in your folder about your findings. Talk with other nurses to find out their views and experiences on the subject. With your previous reading and thinking about the topic, you will quickly be able to spot and explore new ideas. Add all this to your growing folder.

4. Talk to colleagues about your interest and the material you've gathered. See if you can find someone who would like to work with you on this type of study. It is often more stimulating to work with one other "researcher" or even a small group. That way, you can share the work and have "built in" audiences for discussing varied aspects of the project. If you want to pursue it by yourself, try to locate someone with some research experience with whom you can consult and discuss ideas.

5. Write out a simple study plan. Define what you intend to study and outline the steps you plan to take to complete your project. Keep it simple and straightforward. You can do another project later if you have more than one aspect of the topic you wish to investigate.

6. Polish your proposal outline with advice from some "expert" source—a basic textbook or someone who has previously conducted a research project. Don't be afraid to investigate your resources because many health care institutions are providing help for employees who want to carry out small-scale studies. Try to project the time it will take you to complete the tasks on this polished version of the outline. Then multiply every number by 2 in order to give yourself leeway. Check your project "calendar" periodically to help keep track if you're on schedule. You'll need a tentative budget too, but you can keep the costs of important work to a minimum as other researchers have demonstrated.[2]

7. Identify the steps you need to follow in gaining permission to conduct your study. Usually, you will need to submit a written request to a review committee. Use your outline as a basis for the proposal to this group.

8. Watch for advertisements of workshops, continuing education classes, or university courses in research-related topics. You may even find some needed consultation or a research partner there.

9. Keep a record of all your study activities in case you want to write about the study at a later time.

10. Offer to give a small inservice program on your topic. You can communicate your procedures and findings—and hopefully stimulate more interest and discussion about the project.

Summary

This chapter has explained the research process as an effective way to gather and process information and has examined some of the components of nursing research. Other major points of the chapter include the following.

1. The research process can be applied by any professionals interested in obtaining data or information.
2. The safeguards of the steps of the research process provide structure and consistency to information-gathering.
3. Research reports contain four areas.

   The introduction describing the problem investigated and related background information

   The methodology describing the population and sample, research instrument(s), and procedures for data collection and data analysis

   The results of the report describing the analysis, and interpretation of the data

   The discussion describing the conclusions drawn from the study and the implications of the findings in relation to nursing practice
4. The individual subject possesses the right to refuse to participate in the research, the right to informed consent, and the right to confidentiality.
5. The expanding role of nurses today includes participation in nursing research and the application of research results to nursing practice.

References

1. Downs FS: A Source Book of Nursing Research, 3rd ed. Philadelphia, FA Davis, 1984
2. Holstrom L, Burgess A: Low-Cost Research: A Project on a Shoestring. Nurs Res 31 (March/April): 123–125, 1982
3. Munhall P: Nursing Philosophy and Nursing Research: In Apposition or Opposition? Nursing Res 31 (May/June): 176–181, 1982
4. Polit DF, Hungler BP: Nursing Research: Principles and Methods, 2nd ed. Philadelphia, JB Lippincott, 1983
5. Raderman R, Allen D: Registered Nurse Students in a Baccalaureate Program: Factors Associated with Completion. Nurs Res 23 (January/February) 71–73, 1974
6. Sweeney MA, Olivieri P: An Introduction to Nursing Research: Research, Measurement, and Computers in Nursing. Philadelphia, JB Lippincott, 1981
7. Treece EW, Treece JW: Elements of Research in Nursing, 3rd ed. St Louis, CV Mosby, 1982
8. Waltz CF, Bausell RB: Nursing Research: Design, Statistics, and Computer Analysis. Philadelphia, FA Davis, 1981

Chapter 41
Trends in Psychiatric-Mental Health Care

The only way to maintain any semblance of equilibrium during the super-industrial revolution will be to meet invention with invention—to design new personal and social change-regulators. Thus we need neither blind acceptance nor blind resistance, but an array of creative strategies for shaping, deflecting, accelerating or decelerating change selectively. The individual needs new principles for pacing and planning his life along with a dramatically new kind of education. He may also need specific new technological aids to increase his adaptivity. The society, meanwhile, needs new institutions and organizational forms, new buffers and balance wheels.

Alvin Toffler,
Future Shock, 1970

Patricia Flatley Brennan

Chapter Preview

Although institutional care of the mentally ill has existed since the middle ages, psychiatric nursing as a legitimate clinical focus is only 100 years old.[7] Throughout the 500 years of psychiatry, practitioners of the mental healing arts faced many challenges, which the psychiatric and mental health nursing specialty changed and grew in response to. Current obstacles faced by psychiatric-mental health nurses stem from changes in social awareness and population demographics, economics and legislation, technology, and the health care system itself. These obstacles demand responses from practitioners in the form of newer, more sophisticated, less costly, and more effective modes of treatment. The responses to these challenges by psychiatric-mental health nurses take the form of changes in providers, changes in practice settings, changes in the nature of care, and changes in the foci of care.

Some challenges in the past, caused by new forms of treatment such as electroconvulsive therapy or Sodium Amytal interviews, required nursing skills to promote safe and effective patient response to treatment. Other challenges, such as the need for psychiatric nursing support throughout the general hospital, were met through the inception of a new breed of practitioners, the clinical liaison nurse. Still other challenges were met by the community itself. The community, having grown tired of the lack of responsiveness from professional providers, encouraged the development of support groups. These self-help groups place new demands on psychiatric and mental health nurses, not for direct service, but for consultation, education and referral.

Learning Objectives

On completion of the chapter, the reader should be able to accomplish the following.

1. Explain the influence that changes in the following have on psychiatric and mental health nursing
   Population demographics and social awareness
   Economics and legislation
   Technology
   The health care systems
2. Assess the response of psychiatric-mental health nursing to the challenge posed by change
3. Describe the foundation documents supporting the new order of psychiatric and mental health nursing
4. Define the roles of psychiatric-mental health nursing
5. Identify foci for psychiatric-mental health nursing research
6. Trace the trends in inpatient and community psychiatric nursing practice
7. Prepare responses to current and future challenges within target groups

The Challenges

Since 1950, significant events and attitude shifts have occurred that impact on the nature and function of psychiatric and mental health nursing. Despite a close alliance, the field of psychiatric nursing and the field of mental health nursing are not identical. The specialty of mental health nursing resulted from the merger of community-based psychiatric nursing and psychiatric emphases in community health nursing.[11] For the purpose of this section of the chapter, however, the two fields will be discussed together, and events that affected only one field will be identified as such.

Social Awareness and Population Demographics

Changes in society's attitudes toward certain groups often accompany, or are followed by, changes in the demographic parameters of those groups. The 1960s were a time of great social change and of tremendous growth in the awareness of the social rights of many groups. The rights and needs of various groups were highlighted through civil action, enactment of laws protecting the rights of certain groups, and an increased awareness of the complexity of society. The affected groups include the elderly, women, families, and minority groups. The phenomena of change within these groups cannot be viewed in isolation of the whole of society; rather, we must examine change from the standpoint of both intragroup and intergroup influences.

The Elderly

The over-65 age group comprises an ever-growing proportion of society. Numbering greater than 25 million in 1982, the elderly will account for over 50 million by the year 2030.[10] One person out of nine in America is over 65. This group presents new challenges to all economic and social support systems.

Scientific research and social activism challenge many commonly held assumptions about the elderly. Myths of inevitable senility, lack of sexuality, and lowered productivity among all aged persons are being dispelled. Limited economic resources, a need for specialized, not more, health services, and changes in social support systems certainly bring a new configuration to the lifestyle of the aging person. Living arrangements vary, but less than 5% of all persons over 65 reside in nursing homes.[19] The number of elderly persons living independently is also increasing.[19] The economic status of the elderly spans a wide range, with the median income well below $10,000.[19] Although the remaining life span of a person at age 65 has increased steadily, women continue to outnumber men in the over-65 age group.

The mental health concerns of the aging population pose several unique challenges. Previously healthy adults may develop the need for mental health care arising from loss, the physiological changes associated with aging, or the developmental demands of aging. Chronically mentally ill persons, hospitalized during the 1950s, now reside among the geriatric population. Therefore, two related but separate specialty fields have emerged in the care of the elderly—psychogeriatrics and geropsychiatry. *Psychogeriatrics* refers to special psychiatric care for clients in the over-65 age group; *geropsychiatry* is the care of the aging psychiatric client.[16] This distinction is not artificial, because each group of elderly persons requires special understanding and demands the application of a different body of knowledge. In addition, nonclinical services, such as Eldercare and the Meals-on-Wheels programs, have emerged and indirectly meet the mental health needs of the elderly population.

The Gray Panthers movement of the 1960s addressed social prejudice and discrimination affecting the elderly. Of the several "isms" that social activists brought to the attention of the public, the Gray Panthers advocated liberation from the ill effects of agism. *Agism* is a social stereotype that prevents the elderly from achieving the fullness of living. Maggie Kuhn, an aging person herself, led the fight for full recognition of the abilities, talents, and liveliness of the older person. This process led to the enactment of laws protecting the older person from discrimination in the work place, in residences, and in health care.

The Family

Through the past 25 years, we have learned that there are many definitions of the word "family." Society at large has become more accepting of alternative family styles, although the traditional nuclear family is still desired and, even, revered. Alternative family styles have become increasingly common and these families make their claim on the service and skills of mental health professionals. The 1980 census found an increasing number of single heads-of-households and families headed by a single parent. In many cases, that parent was a single woman—single by divorce, separation, widowhood, or choice. Unmarried couples living together and other group-living situations forced redefinition of what actually composes the family.

Awareness of the importance of the family in psychological development was enriched by the growth and acceptance of the family therapy movement. Family concepts were also incorporated into the treatment approaches to the individual and the group. Changes in family composition forced treatment providers to consider the special needs of the aging parent caring for a disabled child or the anguish experienced at the end of a long-term, live-in relationship.

The growth in family theory led to a reconsideration of the origins and etiology of psychopathology. Intrapsychic dynamics were not abandoned; rather, the care of the mentally ill was expanded to encompass exploration and experience of the individual's family relationships. Family assessments became an essential component of each contact with a health care provider. The changing family not only demanded a new type of treatment, but also forced a revision of the traditional modes of treatment.

The Feminist Movement

Women comprise the majority of psychiatric clients as well as the majority of society.[9] The activism of the 1960s brought an awareness of the roles and rights of women. Many books and journals appeared that promulgated the new order of women. Women as persons, first, then as members of social groups and families, and finally, as workers, were viewed with a new understanding.

The special issue of women and psychotherapy deserves consideration. The women's movement has demanded new definitions of the concepts of mental health and mental illness.[8] Feminist psychology challenges traditional concepts of human development and the very nature of psychotherapy. Viewed from a feminist perspective, many of the "problems" experienced in living result from an oppressive, male-dominated society that rewards males and sanctions females.

The women's movement's cry for androgeny and equality led to the introduction of nonsexist language, a reduction in the sexual biases found in advertising, education, and entertainment, and a greater acceptance of the values of both "maleness" and "femaleness." Although the feminist movement has been accused of contributing to the demise of traditional values and the nuclear family, it has also been credited with helping the society as a whole achieve a higher level of mental health. The failure of the ratification of the Equal Rights Amendment, however, threatens the permanence of the gains initiated by 20th-century feminists.

Minority Groups

America, supposedly the great melting pot, took a look at itself over the last few decades and discovered that very little melting had actually occurred. Many racial, sexual, and cultural groups make up this complex social group. Blacks, Native Americans, Orientals, and Hispanics, for example, represent major cultural subgroups. The recent influx of refugees from third world countries expands the diversity of cultural minorities in need of health care services. Each group has its own characteristic focus and special features. More importantly, however, different cultures define mental illness in their own terms.

The activism of the 1960s and the "me-ism" of the 1970s engendered an awareness of the danger and damage of social prejudices, as well as the pride and power of membership in a minority. The melting envisioned by our forefathers gave way to a peculiar sense of nationalism, in which minority groups demanded civil rights and social acceptance without giving up the uniqueness of the subculture. Prejudice and exploitation continue to exist. The effect of minority awareness can be measured by legislation prohibiting discrimination and by the economic gains of some members of minority groups. Social prejudice and inequity cannot be legislated away.

Biases and stereotypes influence the practitioner's assessment and treatment of culturally different clients. Attempts have been made to devise bias-free psychological tests in order to evaluate clients' psychological status more accurately. Some argue that effective mental health treatment can only be designed and delivered by providers with cultural backgrounds similar to the client. Others believe that clinical education and supervision can ameliorate the effects of culturally biased assumptions in the treatment dyad.

Economics and Legislation

Mental health services grew and flourished during the 1960s. Federal commitment to the needs of the mentally ill translated into large amounts of federal funding for the development and maintenance of services for mental health and mental illness. Monies were allocated for primary, secondary, and tertiary prevention efforts, as well as for education of mental health personnel and for research into the cause and treatment of mental illness. Direct expenditures for mental illness, including drug and alcohol treatment, reached $20 billion per year in the 1970s.[21] This figure does not reflect money lost through sick time, use of other social services, or the economic costs of family disruption.

Sources of Funding

Beginning in the late 1970s, private insurers and federally related insurance agencies such as Civilian Health and Medical Program of the Uniformed Services (CHAMPUS), entered the funding arena. Reimbursement for mental health services is a mandated benefit in many states, a requirement for any private insurance carrier in that state.

The turbulent economic environment of the 1980s now threatens the economic viability of the mental health care system as it presently stands. Direct federal support of mental health services, education, and research is rapidly diminishing. Mental health care services are particularly vulnerable to changes in funding because the hoped-for private sector support may be hampered by the lingering social stigma of mental illness.

The changing economic environment directly impacts on the mental health system from another perspective—the client's. Economic stressors such as high unemployment, bankruptcy, and job insecurity strain the mental health of the worker. Viewed from a systems framework, the stressors experienced by an individual in one role spill over into the other elements of the individual's role set. Unemployment threatens insurance benefits, leaving the worker less able to purchase necessary services. Just as the federal government is hoping that the private sector will assume more of the responsibility for the funding of mental health services, the private sector is least able to afford it.

Block Grants

A discussion of the economics of mental health care is not complete without an understanding of the block grant process. Traditionally, funding for community mental health center services initiated at the federal level, with direct funding of local community mental health centers and some supplemental funding coming from the states. The Reagan administration's fiscal plan, presented in 1981 and implemented in fiscal year 1983, is based on the premise of shifting the responsibility for funding from the federal level to the state level. This change in attitude means that the state governments are now charged with the responsibility of administrating mental health services. Money from the federal government will be awarded to the states, under a system of block grants, in a lump sum to be dispensed in the manner decided upon by the state.[20]

A *block grant* is a federal allocation given to a state's government for a special purpose, such as mental health services. Each state will receive one block grant to fund all mental health and drug and alcohol abuse treatment services. The amount of money received by the state is a proportion of the monies received for similar services during prior fiscal periods. Each state then determines for itself exactly how it will use the money. The actual dollar amount of the block grant is expected to be less than the earlier allocations. It is not the administration's intention to replace or reduce state expenditures under the block grant program; rather, block grants will supplement state funds for mental health services.[18]

Other factors resulting from changes in the economy impinge on the mental health system. The number of jobs available for vocational rehabilitation has decreased, preventing optimal habilitation of many mentally ill persons. The "social drift" hypothesis questioned whether the mentally ill congregated in the lower socioeconomic classes by chance or if persons in the lower social classes were more vulnerable to mental illness.[7] Resolution of this debate will not solve the mental health problems of the poor, who are both statistically more in need of mental health care services and least able to pay for such services. The economically disadvantaged are currently the focus of a glut of poorly designed services, many of which overlap the others, and none of which truly accomplishes what was originally envisioned by the service designer.

Mental health services today are more costly to provide than they were 25 years ago. The much needed economic parity for nurses has, in part, contributed to the rise in the costs of mental health services. The salaries of other mental health professionals have risen along with nursing salaries, prompting the phenomenon of "substitutibility" among the mental health professional groups.[16] With salaries rising and the measurable differences between professional groups declining, is it any wonder that mental health center administrators seek the most cost-effective staff member regardless of clinical discipline?

Legal Protection of Clients' Rights

The past 20 years have seen a growth in the clients' rights legislation. These laws led to the most significant restructuring of the legal environment of mental health care since the M'Naughten ruling.[22] Clients' rights legislation attempts to protect the client from undue restriction of personal safety or freedom. One of the negative effects of the client's rights legislation has been to preclude the involuntary treatment of persons who are in need of psychiatric care but who are not displaying behavior dangerous to self or others.

Technology

Technology developments of the past 25 years have created a world heretofore only imagined. Computers are commonplace, supplementing and, at times, substituting for human processes of decision-making, verbal communication, and discrimination. Advances in electronics now make possible the instant replay of a football game or a family therapy session. Television enables in-home education, entertainment, and public awareness of events as they happen. No part of daily living remains unaffected by technology.

These advances produce a mixed blessing of better, cheaper, faster living along with information overload, hazardous by-products of energy materials, and complex stressors. The television, which brings the excitement of a sports competition into the home, also brings the terror of a bombing raid. Computer technology provides rapid access to massive amounts of data about individuals but also threatens the individual's right to privacy. The speed with which information is processed precludes the more gradual integration of knowledge into one's repertoire of skills and strategies. Modern persons are asked to develop stress responses to stressors newly created in the name of technological advancement.

Technology and Mental Health Care

Computer technology has impacted the very nature of psychiatric care in addition to influencing the method of delivering, charging for, and evaluating care. Computer programs simulate the interaction between the therapist and the client.[23] Recordings of client progress, pharmacotherapy protocols, and psychological evaluation can be recorded and stored in a computer data base. Computers assist mental health practitioners to reach clinical decisions regarding diagnosis and treatment.

Computer systems that conduct psychological tests and immediately score the results offer great assistance to community-based practitioners. Standard psychological tests, such as the Minnesota Multiphasic Personality Inventory or the Beck Depression Inventory, are stored in the memory bank along with the appropriate normative information. To undergo testing, the individual client sits at a computer terminal. The screen displays one question at a time to which the client is asked to respond. At the conclusion of the test the individual responses are recorded and analyzed. The therapist-practitioner has immediate access to very sophisticated information to aid in diagnosis and evaluation.

The electronic media play a large role in the development of feelings and attitudes among the general public. The public perception of the complex of psychiatric players, including the nurse, the client, and the mental health system, is molded in part by the images conveyed through movies and television.[15] Television can also serve the public's need for mental health education. Special interest programs alert viewers to the signs of stress or to effective parenting strategies. In rural areas, mental health professionals can receive their continuing education via television. Television technology has invaded the therapy session with the use of videotaped sessions. Closed-circuit systems permit the taping and immediate review of clinical therapy sessions. Videotape techniques have become standard, not only in the training of neophyte therapists, but also as a means to enhance a group's or family's progress in self-awareness.

Developments in basic science research permit sophisticated laboratory screening for such disorders as depression or schizophrenia. In the dexamethasone suppression test, for example, cortisol levels are evaluated 16 hours after the administration of oral dexamethasone. Elevated serum cortisol indicates that the expected response to dexamethasone did not occur, a phenomenon consistent with depression.[13] Laboratory screening for mental illness aids in the accurate diagnosis and prompt treatment of individuals with those disorders.

The Health Care System

Although it is difficult to isolate the health care system from its many component parts and interacting related systems, it is necessary to try to do so in order to understand trends and issues in psychiatric-mental health nursing.

General Medical Care

Advances in life support systems and in surgical techniques have saved the lives of persons who, less than 5 years ago, would have died. This process of aiding in the survival from catastrophic illness and injuries has made options for life support and choices of health services more complex than ever. The economic factors of life support systems, coupled with the moral and legal ambiguity surrounding life support, add additional stress to the family members and significant others of the patient. Life support issues also cause stress among health care providers, as evidenced by the recent upsurge in the literature on the topic of burnout in the human service professions.

During the past 20 years, the medical environment has witnessed a growth in the understanding of the mind–

body interaction. Psychophysiologists have taught that the presence of physical or emotional stress results in stress responses from both his body and his mind. There is, at present, a new (or renewed) awareness of the psychological needs of the hospitalized patient and a search for the physiological roots of mental distress. Traditional therapies, which relied only on the mind or the body as the site of intervention, have been challenged. Although the response to this challenge has not been a complete cessation of purely somatic therapies, many more therapies are currently being scrutinized.

Mental Health Care

Rising frustration with traditional health care providers led some groups of individuals to form self-help groups. Individuals sharing common problems or life situations banded together for the purpose of exchanging support, coping hints, and encouragement. At times, the outrage at the common enemy, traditional healers, provided an external impetus for cohesiveness among these groups. Self-help groups of the 1980s are not antiprofessional care providers; rather, they call on professional providers in a collaborative, consultative manner. Some self-help groups have received recognition from professional health care providers and are now viewed as reasonable adjuncts or alternatives to traditional professional care.

Community Mental Health. The community mental health care system is the fastest growing subgroup of the health care system. Three major factors influenced the inception and establishment of the community mental helath system. First, the discovery of chlorpromazine and the antipsychotic medications during the 1950s enabled previously dependent clients to live outside of the hospital. Secondly, the massive, 70% reduction in state hospital beds since 1955 placed a demand on communities to provide shelter and services for chronically disturbed clients.[21] Thirdly, the commitment of the federal government to the care of the mentally ill during the Kennedy and Johnson administrations provided funding for the development and staffing of community mental health centers. The legacy of the community mental health movement of the past 25 years is an awareness of the tremendous mental health needs of communities and the lack of an organized, effective method for meeting the needs.

The community mental health center movement also brought about an awareness of the factors within the community that influence the development and treatment of mental illness. The original design of 1500 mental health centers scattered throughout the country was never realized; nonetheless, the consciousness-raising caused by this movement will have impact for years. The private-profit and not-for-profit sectors responded to the need for community-based treatment facilities with the development of isolated treatment centers located within the community. The net-

work of treatment and research centers envisioned by community mental health planners never materialized, however; in part, because of the lack of clear-cut evaluation standards and processes.[17]

Community-based psychiatric treatment has not replaced inpatient care of the mentally ill. Client care episodes in inpatient psychiatric facilities have actually increased by 40% over the past 10 years.[21] Note that this increase reflects client care episodes, not the number of clients treated or their duration of stay. The major increase in the number of psychiatric beds has occurred in the private facilities. Due to the gross inaccuracies in statistical reporting, and the continuing, although decreasing, social stigma of mental illness, it is impossible to tell how many clients are receiving treatment for psychiatric disorders in general inpatient hospital settings.

Gaps in Understanding. This section discussing the challenges to psychiatric-mental health nursing care would not be complete without an examination of the trends that did *not* occur. No new forms of somatic therapy have been evaluated and proven effective for such pervasive disorders as anxiety and depression; instead, a resurgence of older, somatic therapies is occurring. Science has given us greater understanding of what happens neurochemically in the presence of illness, yet we still do not know why one person develops schizophrenia and another develops an ulcer. Research tells us that dyadic relationships make people better, yet we know little how the dyad works. It is left to the future practitioners of psychiatric-mental health nursing not only to react to the demands of society, but to proact to ensure the mental health of society.

The Responses

Psychiatric and mental health nurses are called upon to meet many challenges arising from population changes, an unstable economy, patients' rights legislation, developments in technology, and changes in the way health care is delivered. The process of meeting challenges can occur proactively; that is, in a preplanned, well-designed manner based on an assessment of the needs of society and of available resources, or reactively; that is, in reaction to the challenges presented from health care consumers, colleagues, and employers. A proactive response to change demands vigilance and creativity; a reactive response to a challenge requires rapid mobilization of resources and adaptability. Psychiatric-mental health nursing's responses to challenges can be seen by examining four areas of change—changes in care providers, changes in roles in practice settings, changes in the activity of psychiatric-mental health nurses, and changes in the focus of care. Before examining the responses to challenges, let us examine the supporting guides for change.

Guides for Change

Within established professions, the direction for change and the needs for meeting the challenges of the future arise from within the profession. As the nursing profession grows and becomes more fully established as a profession, nurses assume greater responsibility for self-direction. The development of nursing as a self-directed profession can be traced through the American Nurses' Association's publication of four documents:

1. The Statement on Psychiatric and Mental Health Nursing Practice (1967, revised 1976)
2. The Standards of Practice of Psychiatric and Mental Health Nursing Practice (1973, revised 1982)
3. The Code for Nurses with Interpretive Statements (1976)
4. Nursing: A Social Policy Statement (1980)[2, 4, 5, 6]

These documents present to the public a definition of nursing practice in psychiatric-mental health care, a clarification of the various roles of nursing personnel, and the established standards of nursing practice. Through the use of these documents, nurses promulgate their functions, and colleagues and consumers learn what can be achieved through nursing care.

We, as psychiatric-mental health nurses, comprise one special group among the 1.5 million nurses in the United States. We share the professional colleagueship with all nurses, thereby maintaining a responsibility for intra-professional collaboration and service. We hold claim to a specialized body of knowledge within nursing practice and yet acknowledge that psychiatric-mental health nursing concepts permeate the whole of nursing practice. Psychiatric-mental health nurses also share a professional peership with other disciplines within the mental health complex, including social workers, psychologists, physicians, and adjunctive therapists. Although our practice is derived from many of the applied human sciences, our mandate for practice rests within the nursing profession. Therefore, we develop and draw from the documents of professional nursing to guide our practice and our response to the challenges.

Definition of Psychiatric-Mental Health Nursing

The Statement on Psychiatric and Mental Health Nursing Practice defines psychiatric nursing as

> a specialized area of nursing practice employing theories of human behavior as its science and purposeful use of self as its art.[6]

Nursing practice in psychiatric-mental health care shares many functions with other disciplines, yet holds several unique features, notably a biopsychosocial approach to client and community, and the systematic use of the nursing process. The Statement serves to interpret psychiatric nursing practice to interested others within the mental health field. In addition to an explanation of nursing, critical variables such as subspecialization and the scope of practice are defined. Nursing roles in psychiatric and mental health care include direct care functions, such as psychotherapy, provision of the therapeutic milieu, and community action, and such indirect care functions as education, administration, and research.

Standards of Psychiatric-Mental Health Nursing

The Standards of Psychiatric and Mental Health Nursing Practice define the minimally acceptable practices of psychiatric and mental health nurses. Subsequent to the development of the Statement on Psychiatric and Mental Health Nursing, the practice division established criteria describing psychiatric and mental health nursing practice. These criteria serve as guides denoting the nature of activities that nurses are prepared to implement competently. Standards serve both to direct professional activities and to evaluate the quality of professional care. Self-direction and professional accountability contribute to a profession's ability to meet the challenges of the present and of the future. Many agencies have incorporated the Standards of Practice into the job descriptions or evaluation criteria for practicing nurses. Nurses in private practice use the standards as guides defining the nature and scope of their practice. The standards have also been entered in legal testimony as evidence of the expected professional practice of a nurse.

Code of Ethics for Nursing

The Code of Ethics for Nursing defines ethical conduct for practicing nurses in all clinical areas, not only for psychiatric-mental health nurses. The changes and challenges impacting on target populations and, therefore, on the nature of psychiatric and mental health nursing practice pose dilemmas for every practicing nurse. Issues of patient confidentiality, protection of society, and patients' right to treatment confront the nurse in daily practice. The Code neither supplants individual decision-making, nor provides universally applicable answers to the nurse's ethical dilemma. Rather, the Code serves as a decision-making guide concerning ethical practice.

The Social Policy Statement

A landmark document entitled Nursing: A Social Policy Statement emerged in 1980, slightly more than 100 years after the first training school for nurses was organized. This document delineates the nature and scope of nursing practice and serves all nurses as "an affirmation of nursing's social responsibility."[4] Although it does not replace any of the documents noted earlier, the Social Policy Statement renews and organizes the commitment of nursing to the public society it serves. Based on the premise that a social contract forms the legal right to practice, the statement defines nursing practice issues, specialization, articulation with other disciplines, and the role of theory within the social environment of nursing.

Nursing: A Social Policy Statement has particular significance for psychiatric and mental health nurses. Several leaders within psychiatric nursing contributed to the development of this document. The very nature of psychiatric and mental health nursing practice is social, involving a dyadic encounter between nurse and client.[11] The proliferation of mental health professionals within the past 25 years demands a delineation of the borders, boundaries, and dimensions of psychiatric-mental health nursing. Nursing: A Social Policy Statement provides a professional mandate for the establishment of these delineations by validating the right of self-determination among the various nursing specialty groups. It also legitimizes many of the activities already carried out by psychiatric and mental health nurses. Graduate education, certification at the generalist and the specialist levels, and clinical research have been guided by the leadership of psychiatric and mental health nurses.

Other Guides

Other guides for nursing practice are found in legislation, in agency policy, and within the nurse–client relationship. Nurse practice acts define the legal nature of nursing practice, and have undergone major revisions over the past 25 years. The revisions of the laws speak more directly to expanded nursing practice in all areas, and not specifically to psychiatric–mental health nursing practice. Under the nurse practice acts of most states, however, psychiatric-mental health nurses find legal support for independent nursing functions and independent nursing practice. Agency policy, under the aegis of state and federal laws, establishes the parameters of practice within a given institution. Within the client care dyad, the nurse finds the specific directions for individualizing practice. The psychiatric-mental health nurse then draws from the professional group, the employing agency, and the client situation to formulate practice. The nurse's internalization of theory, understanding of behavioral dynamics, and own self-awareness complete the composite of guides required for professional practice and the ability to meet the challenges posed by society.

The Care Providers

Twenty-Five Years Ago

Psychiatric nurses today make up a very different configuration as compared with those of 25 years ago. As a group, we are older than other nurses, better educated—that is, with a greater proportion of master's-prepared nurses among our ranks—and more varied in our practice settings. The psychiatric nurse of 1957 grappled with the issues of moving the chronic mentally ill person out to the community and how to manage a client with mania without the use of the medication, lithium carbonate. Peplau's work on anxiety and psychiatric nursing and Maxwell Jones' therapeutic milieu were both about 5 years old. Electroconvulsive therapy was the treatment of choice for depression and sedation was a treatment for any type of emotional disorder. Medical-surgical concepts applied in the psychiatric setting served most nurses well, and the only nurse who worked in the community was the local public health nurse. Independent practice of nurses was almost unheard of, and the impact of economics on nursing practice was negligible.

Psychiatric-Mental Health Nursing in the 80s

The 1980s are witnessing many changes in the education and practice of psychiatric and mental health nurses. The growth of the profession provided the necessary intraprofessional support needed to meet the challenges of changing populations, unstable economics, technological advancements, the demands of a changing health care environment, and nurses' own health problems (see insert, Autobiography of a Recovering Alcoholic Nurse). The psychiatric-mental health nursing response can be seen in the changes in the education, practice roles, and practice settings of psychiatric nurses.

Basic Education. The integrated curriculum stands as education's response to the challenge of abandoning the mind–body dichotomy of medical care. Although many definitions of the integrated curriculum exist, the concept essentially refers to the unification of nursing concepts that transcend isolated clinical areas. In an integrated curriculum, for example, students do not take a separate course in the nursing care of patients with selected medical problems. Interpersonal nursing concepts form the core of nursing practice—the nurse–client relationship. Accordingly, concepts traditionally reserved for the psychiatric nursing course, such as anxiety, stress management, and depression, are addressed throughout the nursing curriculum. The integrated curriculum has recently come under attack by nursing practice and educational leaders.[12, 14] Although the integrated curriculum enhanced the psychosocial skills of all nurses, the cost may have caused a decline in the number of nurses capable of, and interested in, entering psychiatric nursing care.

Advanced Education. The federal government has fostered the development of psychiatric-mental health nursing at the bachelor's and master's levels of nursing education. The federal government's support of community mental health centers, following the deinstitutionalization process, demanded practitioners who were skilled in the care of the mentally ill in the community. Grants available through the Nurse Training Acts of the 1960s and 1970s and through the National Institute of Mental Health (NIMH) funded master's level nursing education. As late as 1980, NIMH traineeships provided tuition and stipend sub-

Autobiography of a Recovering Alcoholic Nurse

Doris Leffler, RN, CAC
Senior Nurse
Coordinator, Alcoholism Recovery Program
Friends Hospital
Philadelphia, Pennsylvania
February 23, 1984

I was born in New York City and raised as an only child, although I have a brother who is 15 years older. My environment, though stimulating, was generally hectic and offtimes chaotic. I was shy, self-conscious and insecure. My father was a quiet, outwardly easy-going man and rarely demonstrative in his feelings, while my mother, on the other hand, was outgoing, assertive, and often capricious.

I attended private school and was an average student. Upon graduation, I was accepted, on a probationary basis due to my grades, in a 3-year diploma nursing program at a New York City hospital. Because this was what I had wanted most in my life, I worked exceptionally hard and within the 6-month probationary period, I received my cap.

Going to class and working on the hospital ward was a very hectic, demanding, and anxiety-provoking schedule. When it became difficult to sleep, Seconals (secobarbitol) became my friend. During my third year of nursing school, I became acquainted with amphetamines while doing my psychiatric affiliation at a state hospital. I found another friend in alcohol. Alcohol gave me a warm, comfortable feeling, filled the void of emptiness, conquered all my fears and insecurities, and allowed me to function.

My life, however, seemed perfect to colleagues and friends. With a husband and three healthy children, no one at home or elsewhere knew I was frightened, lonely, and empty, drinking every evening, taking tranquilizers throughout the day and sleeping pills at night.

In 1972, I was employed as a psychiatric nurse in a 500-bed general hospital located in a mid-sized northeastern suburb. It was there that I met Helen H., another psychiatric nurse. I was very much in awe of Helen when we first met; she was vibrant, articulate, and one of the best nurses I had known. More than anyone else, she taught me the techniques of nursing. Though 20 years my senior, Helen became my good friend.

Helen and I were working buddies and drinking buddies, joking about who drank more and which one of us had a problem with alcohol. And yet I had a fear of Helen; when she drank she became hostile and nasty. Even with our joking, I knew Helen drank too much and I knew she was sick, perhaps alcoholic. If this were true of her, I speculated, was it also true of me? In January 1975, Helen committed suicide, alone in her car with a drink in her hand.

The hospital opened an alcoholism recovery unit shortly afterward and the coordinator of the program, also named Helen, Helen P., a registered nurse and recovering alcoholic, became not only my friend but was instrumental in educating me about the disease of alcoholism.

Helen P., or HP as I later learned to call her, frequently visited the psychiatric unit seeking patients, because this was the unit that most commonly admitted alcoholics and drug users. HP spent much of her time talking with me, querying about my patients and myself. She knew how to ask questions and how to share of herself, never accusing or belittling, but rather comparing one's feelings with compassion and dignity. I knew she understood me, and over the months, I began to trust her more and more and face some of my fears. If HP was afflicted with the disease of alcoholism, then I, too, must be an alcoholic.

Denial is the foremost symptom of the disease of alcoholism and nurses have massive denial. They are taught how to be caretakers, how to heal others but not themselves. More aware of the disease and its symptoms, I made a conscious decision to look at myself.

As a recovering alcoholic for the past 9 years, I have experienced considerable behavioral changes. I have learned to deal with life on life's terms, I have learned that feelings do not have to consume me, that it's allright to be imperfect, and, in fact, to be human is to be imperfect. I have learned to share my feelings—to follow the principles of life we use in dealing with our patients.

Attending support groups, I realized that recovering nurses did not share with others about their professional problems. In June 1982, a small group of recovering nurses in Philadelphia formed a nurses' support group. It was a safe place to verbalize feelings of inadequacies and fears and concerns of working with addictive drugs while continuing to practice safely. Within a year's time, the group grew from five to 30 active members. Some relapsed, but the group, without being judgmental, continued supporting them into treatment.

It was obvious to me that these nurses were able to maintain abstinence from alcohol and drugs for a while, but still had difficulty at work. I believed that if their supervisors were educated about the disease of addiction, nurses had a better chance of recovering and of maintaining their jobs. The nurses were encouraged to share their addiction problems with their supervisors and peers. Hospital administrators became interested and willing to learn more about the disease.

A protocol was instituted in a few major hospitals. A nurse found to be diverting drugs or manifesting signs of drug use, such as personality changes, social changes, mental status changes, and a general job shrinkage, is confronted by two people, and one, if possible, is a recovering person. The nurse is asked to surrender his or her license to the hospital. If the nurse if willing to do this, a consultation is set up with a recovering nurse capable of recommending treatment. Usually, to the frightened, impaired nurse, willing to do almost anything, treatment is a welcome encounter. A medical leave is granted and the nurse's job is held open. If possible, prior to discharge from a rehabilitation center, the nurse meets with the hospital and nurse representa-

tives. In that meeting, a moral contract, outlining the commitments of both the nurse and hospital, is agreed upon.

Although 15% of nurses practicing today have a substance abuse problem, we are seeing recovering nurses dealing with their illnesses, and returning to their profession strengthened and capable of performing their duties. These nurses usually deliver excellent care and educate patients openly about pain and pain medication.

For nursing to be truly a caring profession, nurses must learn to care for their own in the struggle with the devastating disease of addiction. Increased awareness of addiction in the health professions and renewed education about substance abuse in general are positive trends. We are finally beginning to recognize this illness as being treatable, and if we treat ourselves, we can more effectively treat others.

sidy for Master of Science in Nursing candidates, in significantly greater amounts than what was available to other nursing specialties. Current federal cutbacks, however, portend the end of such funding. Funding for graduate study is in short supply, but programs addressing special needs of the elderly or the chronically mentally ill are most likely to be successful in obtaining funds.

Graduate education flourished under the period of federal funding from 1964 to 1980. In response to the need for clinical practitioners, consultants, researchers, and educators, special programs developed. Programs addressed such roles as clinical nurse administrator (University of Pennsylvania), psychiatric liaison nurse (Yale University), clinical nurse practitioner (Rutgers University), and clinical nurse specialist (University of Wisconsin). Although the need for such programs remains strong, recent reductions in the federal funding available for student subsidy and program development threaten both the viability of existing programs and the inception of any new programs.

Advanced preparation for the psychiatric-mental health nurse begins with the master's degree. Post-master's training options include special institutes, continuing education, and doctoral study. Special institutes focus on the development of a particular set of skills and therapeutic technique, such as family therapy. Continuing education emphasizes incidental knowledge or skill acquisition. Through doctoral study, nurses prepare for future roles as expert practitioners, clinical researchers, administrators, or nurse scientists.

Changes in Roles in the Practice Setting. The most obvious evidence of psychiatric-mental health nursing's response to social challenges can be seen in the practice

setting. Although psychiatric nurses comprise less than 5% of the entire active nursing workforce, their practice efforts permeate every type of health care setting possible.[2] Within each of these settings, nurses fulfill many roles, including staff nurse, clinical nurse specialist, liaison, consultant, administrator, and psychotherapist.

Staff Nurse. Inpatient psychiatric nursing presently receives renewed interest. During the heyday of the community mental health movement, some suggested that the need for inpatient care was on the decline, a fact that most psychiatric staff nurses would quickly dispute. The nature of inpatient psychiatric care has changed over the past 25 years, with a greater focus on the nurses' role in the development of the milieu, the application of the nursing process to aid clients in maintaining activities of daily living, and in the provision of leadership for formal and informal client therapeutic groups. The number of colleagues of the staff nurse has increased, especially the number of nonphysician, mental health professionals.[21]

Psychiatric inpatient facilities have been affected by the shortage of nursing resources. The nurse–patient ratio is generally lower in psychiatric settings than in other settings. The increase in nurses attracted to other clinical specialities reduces the number of nurses available to fill psychiatric-mental health nursing positions.[2] A minimum of 1 year of general nursing practice is often requested before a nurse enters the psychiatric-mental health field. This requirement, coupled with the biases about mental illness, tends to lower the number of nurses available to care for the mentally disturbed. In addition, salaries in psychiatric facilities tend to be lower than those in general hospital settings.[2] The impact of community mental health concepts on the nature of staff nurse functioning can be seen in the increased emphasis on discharge planning, follow-up skills, and goals that can be accomplished during short-term treatment. Psychiatric nursing readily adopted the primary mode of delivering nursing care.

Clinical Nurse Specialist. The advent of the clinical nurse specialist in psychiatric-mental health nursing redefined many nursing roles in both the community and inpatient settings. The activities of the clinical nurse specialist vary from educational to therapeutic to consultative in nature, and are many times defined by the agency and the nurse's personality and role interests. Clinical nurse specialists may hold a line or a staff position, although the managerial position of a clinical nurse specialist is currently more economically viable. The clinical nurse specialist concept possesses theoretical soundness, but the role has yet to be tested using a cost-effectiveness process.

Psychiatric Liaison Nurse. The liaison nurse serves patients in a general hospital setting with select psychosocial needs. Skills of consultation, nursing process, and brief psychotherapy are essential to a full actualization of the role of the psychiatric liaison nurse.[20] The client of the liaison nurse may be a patient, a family member, or a staff member. Initially, the liaison nurse faced many battles to secure her place on the hospital staff; presently, most large hospitals have a psychiatric liaison nurse or, at least, a person fulfilling part of the duties of the liaison nurse. The unit-based psychiatric-mental health clinical nurse specialist may assume liaison responsibilities outside the psychiatric unit. The term *liaison* specifically refers to the mental health treatment, consultation, and educational functions in a nonpsychiatric environment.

Nurse as Psychotherapist. The growth of master's and doctorally prepared psychiatric-mental health nurses has produced many nurse-psychotherapists. Some nurse-psychotherapists practice independently; others practice in groups practices or in community mental health centers. Increases in the number of nurse-psychotherapists forced recognition of two problems never before faced by psychiatric-mental health nurses—reimbursement for services and certification for practice. During the 1970s some private and one government agency began reimbursing nurses directly for mental health services provided independently of a physician. This achievement meant that consumers now had a viable alternative to physician-directed mental health care. Desire for reimbursement required that nurses could certify their competancy for independent practice. Not only did insurance companies demand such verification, but health care consumers also began inquiring about the credentials of the providers.

Establishing and verifying the credentials of professionals is a process managed internally by the profession. The American Nurses' Association certifies two levels of psychiatric-mental health nurses—the generalist, prepared at the bachelor's level, and the specialist, prepared at the master's level. This credential signifies to the profession, to colleagues in other professions, and to consumers that the holder demonstrated the standards and competency to practice at the identified level.

Nurses in independent practice use a variety of psychotherapeutic models—psychoanalytic, Christian healing, systems, and the like (see insert, "The Integration of Spirituality with Psychotherapy"). No theory of psychiatric-mental health nursing exists now; this lack of current theory stands as a challenge to the independent nurse practitioners of the future.[12]

Nurse Leader. Within facilities devoted to psychiatric care, nurses hold management positions. Rarely, however, are psychiatric-mental health nurses found in nursing leadership positions in general hospitals. Although mental health nurses in clinics may hold positions of leadership in nursing departments, very few nurses serve as clinic administrators.

The leadership roles of the psychiatric-mental health nurse are not limited to either inpatient or community settings. Psychiatric-mental health nurses hold such leadership positions as academic deans, directors of state nurses' associations, and in one case, director of a center for nursing research. Psychiatric-mental health nurses also possess and encourage a professional alliance that crosses disciplinary boundaries, and they frequently hold influential positions within interdisciplinary groups.

Activities

Issues Influencing Activities

The practice of psychiatric-mental health nursing draws heavily from developments in related fields. Growth in family theory helped broaden the understanding of family dynamics in the care of the mentally disturbed. Selected trends now indicate a need for psychiatric-mental health nurses to integrate more fully the care of the chronically mentally ill person. Economic instability and fiscal restrictions decrease the likelihood of job training and remotivation activity for clients. Fewer persons will be eligible for insurance coverage, while, at the same time, the economy threatens to increase the incidence and prevalence of stress-related illnesses. The rise in community-based treatment and the shortened hospital stay point to the need for a greater focus on daily living skills. Traditional psychotherapy has yet to either prove its effectiveness or reduce its cost in the care of the mentally ill. The future focus of psychiatric-mental health nursing care must be directed to finding more cost-effective ways of delivering services that will enable persons with emotional disorders to maintain daily independent lives that are satisfying and fulfilling.

Legal Issues. Client's rights legislation of the 1970s brought into focus a crying need—that of the client's right to choose and freedom to select care providers, treatment options, and other medical services. Throughout the country, new statutes were enacted guaranteeing basic rights to

The Integration of Spirituality with Psychotherapy

Margaret T. Crepeau, R.N., Ph.D
Marquette University College of Nursing
Milwaukee, Wisconsin

Among the new trends in psychiatric nursing, from primal scream to computers, it is a gift to be able to include the integration of a faith in God, or spirituality, and psychotherapy. The results are so rich, so rewarding, that it is a joy to share them, and to distinguish the elements in Christian psychotherapy from processes and strategies in traditional therapies.

On the surface, Christian psychotherapy doesn't appear very different from any other form of competent verbal therapy. But at its heart is the belief that the God who forgives, heals, and frees His broken people is an active participant in every therapy session. The differences are perhaps in content or interpretation of issues, and usually in taking the last few minutes of a session to annoint and pray with the client. These unique foci in content are as follows.

1. Emphasis on forgiveness of self and others as a key to healing
2. Getting in touch with, and letting go of, painful memories by seeing these episodes with the compassionate eyes of Christ
3. A gentle, but responsible, acknowledgement of one's own sins and how these affect a hurting life
4. Being open to the reality of grace through healing prayer

The emphasis on forgiveness in integrating spirituality with psychotherapy is a crucial one. In traditional psychotherapy, the endpoint of treatment has often been simply to get in touch with one's anger, resentment, and bitterness toward those who have been hurtful and express those feelings in an "appropriate way." Until one has really gone back and forgiven the people who have been responsible for hurts, however, it seems the anger, resentment, and bitterness do not go away.

Beginning with MacNutt's classic book, *Healing*, therapists who are working with clients toward deep inner healing recognize the power and intense freedom that accompany forgiveness.[2] Forgiveness, above all, needs to begin with self. Many can find it in their hearts to forgive others, but they somehow cling to the idea that they, themselves, are not forgivable. These destructive patterns of self-hatred, which are written out of the scripts of perfectionism, legalism, moralism, unhealthy guilt, and projecting to God a punishing image, are gently and brilliantly dealt with in Brennan Manning's A Stranger to Self-Hatred.[3] All healing is centered on forgiveness of self and others.

The Linns' Healing of Memories portrays the process through which clients allow the Lord to reveal those conscious and hidden memories through which He desires to heal the broken-hearted.[1] The idea is made real that out of painful experiences have also come gifts and strengths that otherwise would not have been developed. The techniques of imaging and visualizing are used, but with the added picture of Christ in each scene. The examples can be dramatic, as in the case of a young woman who had had many unhappy affairs and was locked in a vicious cycle of self-hatred and depression. A long-repressed memory surfaced of her coming into the house at the age of 16, after a date and some very innocent kissing, and her father thundering at her from the second floor stairway, "You're a whore!" The blatant falseness of this was superseded by a lethal blow to her spirit in which she believed she was unclean and unable to love. As she went back in time and understood the dynamics that had contributed to her father saying such a thing, and forgave him and herself, she quickly made progress toward valuing herself and rediscovering a joy and purity in herself that truly changed her life. The healing of memories is often a radical turning point in the lives of people who have too long believed that nothing or no one could help them.

The acknowledgement of one's own sins and the consequences of sin in life is seemingly difficult in an age and a society that denies, for the most part, the existence of sin. (This is suggested eloquently in Menninger's Whatever Became of Sin?[4]) What is often forgotten or distorted is that Freud himself believed men are basically responsible for the choices they make and, therefore, for the way in which they attempt to alleviate their inner loneliness and pain. In practice, it is astounding that, once clients are freed from unhealthy guilt, there is a real willingness and relief to accept responsibility for patterns of pride, rebellion, arrogance, unforgiveness, impurity, and other subtle, and not so subtle, sins that have kept them for years in prisons of blaming others, clinging to hurt and sickness, and, in general, choosing to be a "poor me" victim.

A recent example of this blaming pattern is of a young woman who came to therapy with complaints of scrupulosity because of past involvement with the occult. She held a self-righteous contempt for her husband because of his violence toward her and their son in the early years of the marriage. As the husband joined her in the sessions, it became clear that her only method of communicating with her husband was through constant criticism, castrating judgments, and derogatory statements. Once she could stop seeing her husband only as the "bad" one, and begin to see an element of her own verbal violence in interactions, they were together able to ask each other's forgiveness and explore tenderness and support of one another that they hadn't dreamed was possible.

The healing prayer that accompanies each session is as varied as the myriad stories that accompany each person into therapy. Usually, it is a gentle lifting of all the elements of that session into the heart of God for transformation into light, freedom, and forgiveness. Barbara Shlemon's Healing The Hidden Self is a beautiful example of a type of prayer through all the developmental stages from conception to adulthood.[6] Leanne Payne's The Broken Image describes a very deep type of prayer used with persons with problems with sexual identity.[5] As the Spirit moves each therapist, so develops the prayer. It is acknowledged that some people prefer to be in therapy for many months without the dimension of prayer because they do not feel ready for it.

In whatever way the integration of spirituality and psychotherapy develops, it remains true today, as in ancient times, that the body, mind, and spirit are one, and the Lord God of all creation is healing His people in new and extraordinary ways. Nurses, along with other health professionals who are committed to bringing their gifts of faith to their healing ministries, have long been conscious of the unique broad knowledge base that nursing has as its foundation. Nurses in many areas are also aware that only lip service has been given, in many instances, to the concept of "total patient care." What has been missing is the hunger of the spirit to be fed and healed. Christian psychotherapy is one such avenue for psychiatric-mental health nurses to feed the hungry, give sight to the blind, and heal the broken.

References

1. Linn M, Linn D: Healing of Memories. New York, Paulist Press, 1974
2. MacNutt F: Healing. Notre Dame, IN, Ave Maria Press, 1974
3. Manning B: A Stranger to Self-Hatred. Denville, NJ, Dimension Books, 1982
4. Menninger K: Whatever Became of Sin? New York, Hawthorne Books, 1975
5. Payne L: The Broken Image. Westchester, IL, Cornerstone Books, 1981
6. Shlemon B: Healing the Hidden Self. Notre Dame, IN, Ave Marie Press, 1982

the mentally ill. No longer could treatment and restrictive confinement be induced at the request of the family.

The client's rights legislation has had two major consequences. Clients by law are entitled to comprehensive assessment and treatment in a timely fashion. Emergency court-ordered treatment for the mentally ill came under strict guidelines. The burden of proof of a person's mental incapacity rested with those initiating a treatment request.

Client's rights legislation, however, extends far beyond emergency court-ordered treatment. Informed consent agreements now detail the outcomes of treatment, anticipated therapies, and specific criteria for the use of chemical, physical, or environmental restraints. Treatment plans, progress, and evaluation must be discussed with the client.

Advocates and Gatekeepers

The nurse serves as the client's advocate when she actively pursues treatment and services that are in the best interest of the client. This advocacy occurs in several ways. Teaching a client about treatment options enables him to make informed decisions about the treatment situation. In multidisciplinary conferences, nurses coordinate the skills of the mental health team or report to the team about the client's status. Perhaps the most essential act of advocacy occurs when the nurse helps the client enter and navigate the mental health treatment maze.

Community mental health introduced the concept of the "gatekeeper." Gatekeepers are persons who, by their positions or abilities, facilitate or control the movement of other persons in or out of the mental health system. All nurses, by the nature of their preparation in mental health concepts, can function as gatekeepers. The permeable boundaries of the mental health system are known to health professionals. Nurses can aid others in defining and entering these boundaries.

Despite the much needed benefits brought on by the client's rights legislation, these laws can work to the disadvantage of the individual in need of care. Sometimes, the person who is most in need of treatment cannot be helped because he refuses treatment voluntarily and is not committable under the existing legislation. The paranoid person, or the elderly recluse, may not demonstrate behavior that is potentially harmful to self or others, and would therefore not qualify for court-ordered treatment. It becomes the nurse's role when such a person is encountered, to help the person recognize the need for treatment. In the absence of treatment, the nurse may provide assistance and guidance to family members in helping them understand and cope with the disturbed family member.

Clinical Activities

The set of activities of the psychiatric-mental health nurse within the dyadic relationship has emerged as viable and essential over the past 25 years. The nurse uses the skills of the dyadic relationship to aid individuals, groups, and families in achieving effective living. The nurse participates in the care of the client receiving somatic therapies. Education, research, and leadership activities complete the set of activities of the psychiatric-mental health nurse. These activities are defined in the Standards of Psychiatric and Mental Health Nursing.

Both the nature of the activities and the proportion of time spent in each activity is now changing. Milieu development in an inpatient setting remains a critical function. Medication administration is changing to include a greater emphasis on client participation and client education. The dyadic relationship remains the core arena for psychiatric-mental health nursing practice.

The cry has gone out for research that would validate the effectiveness and value of the dyadic relationship. Although nurses have studied the therapeutic dyad from a process framework; that is, focusing on personal growth, self-awareness, and so forth, they have not examined the range of therapeutic effectiveness of dyads. Nurses seem to place a higher value on therapy than on counseling in relation to activities of daily living. Therapy is valuable, certainly, but nurses may be missing the major contribution of psychiatric-mental health nursing—encountering a person in a corrective emotional experience.

Cost-Effective Care

Economic constraints, both in the practice setting and in education, have forced psychiatric-mental health nurses to develop a sense of cost-effectiveness about their care. Nurses are now questioning how much it costs to provide emotional support, to reduce anxiety, to teach problem-solving, and to formulate a nursing care plan. This awareness of the cost of client care is healthy; gone are the days of expansiveness in treatment inspired by the federal allocations of the 1960s and 1970s. Cost containment and cost-effectiveness of services are essential to the future availability of services. To preserve the gains brought about by the community mental health movement, we require an accountable, more cost-wise group of practitioners.

Focus of Care

The net effect of changes in social awareness and population demographics has been a redefinition of the target populations served by the mental health systems. Target populations are the selected groups that will be the recipients of mental health services. Traditional target populations include youth (through primary prevention activities), the elderly, and those having identified mental disorders. The identification of additional target populations led not only to the design of new services for the specific group, but also to an increased vigilance in case finding and to alternative forms of treatment.

Target Group: Women

Social awareness of women's issues brought to light the myriad of subgroups of women who need special services. Victims of sexual assault, battered women, and women in transition comprise some of the newly-defined target groups. Mental health services are provided in community-based shelters in consultation with police, and through special groups in the workplace. Inpatient therapies for depressed women, for example, now include action-oriented foci, such as assertiveness training and preparation for return to the workplace.

Target Group: The Elderly

The growing number of well and ill elderly persons demands a specialized response. Geropsychiatric service units in the hospital and in the community offer care for the complex needs of the aged mentally ill. Psychogeriatric services address the psychiatric needs of the elderly in the areas of loss, organic dysfunctions, and other health problems and concerns. Care of the older person requires collaboration of nurses with many other health care professionals.

Target Group: Criminals

Of the four major resolutions approved during the International Congress of Nurses (ICN) in 1981, two dealt specifically with mental health nursing issues.[1] In response to the worldwide increase of substance abuse, crime, suicide, and other stress-related disorders, ICN publicly acknowledged a commitment to the instruction and practice of preventive mental health care. The second resolution defined the nurse's role in the care of criminals. The decline in the availability and access to the mental health system will spill over into a greater demand for services from the criminal justice system—not because the mentally disturbed are potential criminals, but because individuals who need mental health care and cannot get it become desperate. Referrals from the criminal justice system will be more difficult to meet, thereby further taxing the health care providers already serving this population.

Target Group: The Mentally Retarded

Federal cutbacks and court rulings adjudicating the least restrictive treatment setting for the disabled will create a demand for community-based nursing services for disabled persons. Nursing is ill-prepared for this demand at present. Most psychiatric and mental health nursing curricula do not address the issue of mental retardation. The courts and funding regulations stipulate the necessity of providing nursing care in community-based treatment settings, but nursing will need to move quickly to meet this demand in the care of the mentally retarded.

Target Group: Youth

Although the birth rate is declining, the number of persons under age 24 is higher than ever. Mental health activities directed toward youth have usually focused on the primary and secondary levels of prevention. Economics currently threaten both the viability of most primary prevention activities and secondary activities that involve screening for emotional disorders. Subgroups among adolescents that require specialized services include suicidal adolescents, psychotic adolescents, and adolescents with behavioral disorders. Funding will be most available for prevention activities within existing structures, such as through the schools.

Target Group: The Chronically Mentally Disturbed

The proportion of chronically mentally ill, as defined by the number of readmissions for hospitalization or the duration of treatment, is increasing at an accelerated rate.[17]

The chronically mentally disturbed pose special challenges for the psychiatric-mental health nurse because of the complexity of their needs and the difficulty of providing services. In the face of economic cutbacks, many formerly held conceptions of the right to treatment and the potentially curable disorders must be modified. The chronically mentally ill populations of most large cities are the poorest, the most in need of service. Services need to be directed to both the disturbed person and his social support group. Because many of the chronically mentally ill lack supportive networks, attention must be paid to developing supports through nontraditional methods.

Summary

This chapter has explored some of the significant challenges to the mental health care of society. These challenges demand the delivery of a greater amount and a greater variety of mental health services under a shrinking funding source. The major foci of the chapter include the following points:

1. Nursing's response to the challenges to mental health care has been to provide a variety of practitioners who are capable of serving clients in an inpatient or community setting.
2. Another significant nursing response to this challenge is to integrate psychiatric-mental health nursing concepts into the generic preparation of all nurses.
3. Psychiatric-mental health nurses assume leadership and practice roles in all types of health care delivery systems.
4. Presently, the most significant threat to the psychiatric-mental health nursing practice is one shared by all mental health practitioners—economic destruction.
5. Despite economic disasters and the high cost of service, mental health professionals must not lose their awareness of the pain and suffering caused by mental disorders, and they must use the available political, social, and professional avenues to alleviate that suffering.[17]
6. The demand for skill in mental health consultation will increase.
7. The need for psychiatric nurses who specialize in the care of the chronically mentally disturbed and mentally disturbed youths will continue to outdistance the number of nurses prepared in these areas.
8. Psychiatric-mental health nurses will develop new funding sources to maintain and promote the graduate educational programs necessary to carry out nursing research.

References

1. American Journal of Nursing: ICN 81. Am J Nurs 81 (September): 1664–71, 1981
2. American Nurses' Association: Code for Nurses with Interpretive Statements. Kansas City, The American Nurses' Association, 1976
3. American Nurses' Association: Facts About Nursing 80–81. New York, American Journal of Nursing Company, 1981
4. American Nurses' Association Commission on Nursing Practice: Nursing: A Social Policy Statement. Kansas City, The American Nurses' Association, 1980
5. American Nurses' Association Division of Psychiatric and Mental Health Nursing: Standards of Psychiatric and Mental Health Nursing Practice. Kansas City, The American Nurses' Association, 1982
6. American Nurses' Association Division of Psychiatric and Mental Health Nursing: Statement on Psychiatric and Mental Health Nursing Practice. Kansas City, The American Nurses' Association, 1976
7. Bloom B: Community Mental Health. Monterey, CA, Brooks/Cole Publishing, 1977
8. Brodsky A, Hare-Mustin R: Women and Psychotherapy: An Assessment of Research and Practice. New York, Guilford Press, 1980
9. Carmen E, Russo N, Miller J: Inequity and Women's Mental Health: An Overview. Am J Psychiatry 138 (October): 1319–30, 1981
10. Cohen G: The Older Person, The Older Patient, and the Mental Health System. Hosp Community Psychiatry 33 (February): 101–103, 1982
11. Curtin L: Privacy-Belonging to Oneself. Perspect Psychiatr Care 19 (March–April): 112–115, 1981
12. Fagin Claire. "Psychiatric Nursing at the Crossroads: Quo Vadis?" Perspect Psychiatr Care 19 (March–April): 99–106, 1981
13. Harris E: The Dexamethasone Suppression Test. Am J Nurs 82 (May): 784–785, 1982
14. Hipps O: The Integrated Curriculum: The Emperor is Naked. Am J Nurs 81 (May): 976–980, 1981
15. Kalish P, Kalish B: Image of Psychiatric Nurses in Mo-

tion Pictures. Perspect Psychiatr Care 19 (March–April): 116–129, 1981

16. Lewis R: A Review and Preview of the State of the Art. Paper presented at Perspectives in Psychiatric Care '82, Washington, DC, 1982

17. Mechanic D: Mental Health and Social Policy, 2nd ed. Englewood Cliffs, NJ, Prentice Hall, 1980

18. Mental Health Reports 5: 21 (October 21), 1981

19. Redick R, Taube C: Demography and Mental Health Care of the Aged. In Birrin J, Sloan RB (eds): Handbook of Mental Health and Aging. Englewood Cliffs, NJ, Prentice Hall, 1980

20. Robinson L: Liaison Nursing. Philadelphia, F. A. Davis, 1974

21. Sharfstein S: Medicaid Cutbacks and Block Grants: Crisis or Opportunity for Community Mental Health? Am J Psychiatry 139 (April): 466–470, 1982

22. Slovenko R: Law and Psychiatry. In Kaplan H, Freedman A, Sadock B (eds): Comprehensive Textbook of Psychiatry III. Baltimore, Williams & Wilkins, 1980

23. Spitzer R, Endicott J: Computer Applications in Psychiatry. In Arieti S (ed): American Handbook of Psychiatry. New York, Basic Books, 1974

Chapter 42
Career Profiles in Psychiatric-Mental Health Nursing

Barbara Schoen Johnson

Deborah Antai-Otong, R.N., M.S., Certified Clinical Specialist in Adult Psychiatric Mental Health Nursing

Position: Psychiatric Triage Nurse
Agency: Veterans Administration Medical Center
Location: Dallas, Texas

I am currently a Psychiatric Clinical Specialist working as a psychiatric triage nurse. This position is invaluable to the medical center and serves numerous purposes for the institution.

As a nurse, regardless of the educational level, one knows that assessment skills are essential in the decision-making process, nursing diagnoses, planning, and disposition of the patient in any health care facility. As I walk to and from the waiting area, I begin assessing the patient immediately. These observations include the patient's affect, dress, gait, general appearance, and the presence or absence of a significant other. The essential tools for my role also include accurate and prompt assessment of the patient's problems, knowledge of services available to the patient, and genuine caring for the needs of the individual.

Sometimes brief crisis intervention is needed by the patient and significant others; this includes the prevention of harmful acts that may arise from the stressful situation. Communication with the psychiatric units, staff psychiatrists, and other mental health facilities in the community is another important aspect of my job as the psychiatric triage nurse. Some of my correspondence involves transferring patients from one unit to another or admissions of patients from other medical facilities. This role also involves acting as liaison between a consulting psychiatrist from the medical unit and the various psychiatric units.

As you have probably gathered, I enjoy utilizing my expertise as a clinical specialist in the role of the psychiatric triage nurse. Some of the most rewarding aspects of my job include administrative support, autonomy, and space for professional growth. From the administrative perspective, I receive respect for, acknowledgment of, and confidence in my skills as a clinical specialist to make autonomous decisions regarding patient evaluation, care, and disposition.

Another responsibility of this position includes having input into various administrative meetings. These meetings keep me abreast of hospital policies that facilitate the delivery of quality patient care. The least rewarding aspect of my job is the lack of control of patient visits.

It is almost impossible to predict how my day will turn out because of the nature of the triage setting. Some days I need roller skates to manage the large number of patients, and other days I manage fine with a regular pair of shoes. The unpredictable nature of my job is an inherent factor in working as a triage nurse, but it is not unbearable and sometimes adds to the excitement and spontaneity of the job.

Why did I decide to become a psychiatric nurse? Actually, I decided to become a psychiatric nurse by accident. My goal in nursing at one time was to become a critical care nurse. This area of nursing was exciting and fulfilling because decisions had to be made under pressure and the results of my actions were immediate. I enjoyed also the mechanical aspects of working with ventilators and reading monitors. I wanted to specialize in cardiovascular nursing!

My goals started changing after I had a clinical rotation in a psychiatric outpatient unit of a large metropolitan hospital. I was fascinated by the manner in which the psychiatric team worked together in groups with patients and staff. I was amazed at the manner in which patients shared their feelings and thoughts about their everyday problems. I decided during this wonderful rotation that these people were special because of their ability to assist patients who were experiencing difficulty in their lives to feel and function better.

I was also impressed by the role of the Master's level psychiatric nurse who worked on this unit. At first, I thought, "What an easy job!" She sat in the groups with other staff members and sometimes she led groups. I thought, "I have been working in the wrong area of nursing." After about 4 to 6 weeks on the unit, I realized that there was more work than I saw on the surface. I started thinking about my personal problems and realized that my problems were not any different from those of some of the patients on the unit, except that the patients were unable to cope with their problems outside a psychiatric facility and I was. I also realized the importance of mental health and how essential it is to all aspects of human life, including critical care nursing. I decided that this area of nursing would be my "niche" and that eventually I would attend graduate school and focus my energies on psychiatric-mental health nursing.

What is the future of psychiatric-mental health nursing? Its future depends on several factors. First, existing groups of psychiatric nurses need to be willing to promote a professional image by developing and promoting research in the mental health field and by sharing their findings with other health disciplines through workshops, staff development, and community involvement. Second, the profession of psychiatric nursing has to provide avenues for sharing ideas, providing support, and facilitating changes through special interest psychiatric mental health groups. History has demonstrated that change is more readily achieved in numbers than through individual efforts. Finally, psychiatric-mental health nurses must accept themselves as competent, intelligent, powerful, and resourceful individuals who can work with other professionals in facilitating change in psychiatric nursing and health care delivery.

Finally, I would tell the nurse who is entering a career in the area of psychiatric-mental health nursing today that education is the key in developing the necessary tools for functioning fully as a psychiatric nurse. The field of psychiatric nursing is quite complex and intriguing and requires an individual who knows herself and has a solid foundation in understanding human behavior. This knowledge is gained through basic and continuing education and reflection on one's individual strengths and weaknesses. If the profession wants to be identified as credible, education and self-examination are essential for growth and viability.

Rhenna L. Armstrong, *R.N.*

Position: Psychiatric Staff Nurse
Agency: Fort Logan Mental Health Center
Location: Denver, Colorado

Giving to others was a quality instilled in me as a very young child by my parents. Being poor, more often than not the only thing I had to bestow on another individual was my ability to care for the person. A significant amount of my free time as a young person was spent visiting the sick and elderly—talking with them and listening to their plight. When I was 14 years old, I used to go to the Puerto Rican state mental hospital and vist the female ward. I didn't know anyone there but I felt compelled to go back Sunday after Sunday and listen to those suffering people who appeared to be forgotten by everyone. I never saw another visitor or even the attendants interacting with the patients. The ward was constructed like a jail, complete with bars. Each cell had one very small window but no bathroom facility, only a large drain in the middle of the floor. There was no furniture of any kind; not even a bed was provided.

I remember one woman sitting, completely nude, on the floor laughing and singing about her past sexual encounters. I felt an overwhelming sadness for her. Not only was she in a deplorable physical setting, but also her own behavior was adding to her degradation. I can distinctly remember how glad I felt that she was too "crazy" to realize how embarrassing and degrading her situation was.

Sixteen years later, my life had changed dramatically. I was married, had four children, and found my time occupied with all of those things demanded of a wife and mother. One day, I happened to read a newspaper ad placed by the Fort Logan Mental Health Center. It offered to train, with pay, eligible persons as psychiatric technicians. I was thrilled about being part of such an organization. Fort Logan was the ideal therapeutic community, a model for the nation, and recognized worldwide for its work in mental health. I loved my work. The clients were treated with respect. Their physical and emotional welfare was our utmost concern. There were no locked doors, restraints, or shock treat-

ments. Each unit and all surroundings were beautifully decorated and maintained.

The multidisciplinary team approach was at its best. All recognized and acceptable modes of therapies were practiced and results could be measured. During my training and the ensuing 5 years, I was able to define and polish my natural abilities and acquire quality skills. I grew as a therapeutic staff member and as a person.

My responsibilities as a wife and mother, however, required that I leave my role as a psychiatric technician. Two years ago, I returned to Fort Logan as a registered nurse. Fort Logan is now a state mental hospital. Most of the units are locked units and most of the clients are overtly mentally ill.

The unit in which I work is a 24 bed, in-patient evaluation, and short-term treatment care facility. Our clients arrive in a crisis state, emotionally out of control and displaying inappropriate behavior that is frequently aggressive to themselves and to others. This behavior reflects the client's loss of mental and emotional controls, his inability to do effective problem-solving, and his inappropriate coping mechanisms. The task of the mental health team (*i.e.*, psychiatric nurse, mental health worker, medical doctor, psychiatrist, psychologist, social worker, and occupational and recreational therapist) is to assume the responsibility of control that the client has lost, and thus set limits on inappropriate behavior.

This is a critical period for both the client and the staff. For the client, the loss of control elicits strong fears that may be manifested as anger, other types of acting-out behaviors, or withdrawal. The ultimate goal of our team is to help the client regain some measure of control over his own actions. The achievement of this goal depends on the application of the holistic approach. While the use of psychotropic medications may be an integral part of a client's therapy program, the treatment of the client with kindness, dignity, and respect for his rights as a human being allows him to recognize the fact that there are people who care about him. This display and subsequent recognition of caring cannot be minimized for it quiets or erases many fears and allows the client to assume some of the responsibility for control of his life. I feel that the client's functioning in activities of daily living and hygiene levels is a good measure of his own estimation of self-worth. It is very important for the psychiatric nurses, as well as other team members, to serve as role-models for the client. We must encourage, educate, and at times assist the client with these activities of daily living.

Because of the client's stay is short (10 days–3 months), we as a team need to be aggressive and efficient in out therapeutic efforts. Many of the clients have physical problems that challenge the nurse to stay abreast of the current nursing procedures and maintain nursing skills at a maximum level.

In addition to my medical nursing skills, I have realized for many years that my ability to care about these individuals is my most valuable asset as a psychiatric nurse. I find it extremely rewarding when a confused or agitated client clears and tells me "thanks for putting up with me when I was such a mess." This reaffirms my belief that a client, regardless of how severe or critical his condition is on admission, will remember his behavior during this period of crisis. He also remembers what staff members said to him and how he was treated. This inter-

action between staff and client serves as the basis for developing the trusting relationship needed to assist him in regaining control of his life.

Precisely because we are a short-term unit, the frustration level at times can be high. Seldom do we observe a client progress to the level of his set goals or learn of his progress at the referral centers or in the community.

The future of psychiatric-mental health nursing will require a highly professional nurse with sharp medical and psychiatric skills, a thorough knowledge of legal implications pertinent to psychiatric nursing, and dedication to patient advocacy. The rewards offered by a career in psychiatric nursing center around personal growth and an immense gratification that you have had a part in helping another human being in one of the most difficult and socially least understood illnesses.

When I serve as preceptor for nursing nursing students or new nurses entering psychiatric nursing, my main goal is to relieve their fear of the clients. I believe that the main difference between the nurse and the client is the client's inability to problem-solve. It is imperative to show genuine acceptance of the client and to treat him as you wish to be treated. It may not be on the first day or the first week but, with consistency, fairness, and kind firmness, a trusting relationship will develop and a behavioral change or modification in the client will occur. We are a valued tool in the client's recovery.

Mary Ellen Yarrish, R.N.

Position: Staff Nurse
Agency: Brookhaven Psychiatric Pavilion, Brookhaven Recovery Services
Location: Farmers Branch, Texas

At no time during my student days or my early nursing days did I ever think my career would turn toward psychiatric nursing, and especially not toward treatment of alcohol and drug abuse. What I saw as a student nurse in a large state hospital were the devastating effects of abuse—the "organic brains" or "wet brains," as alcoholics call them. It seemed to me that this had been a choice the patients had made and they should have known better. I saw DTs in my own small community hospital as a frightening, unpreventable consequence of alcohol withdrawal. DTs seemed unmanageable for both the patient and the nurse. Treatment seemed little more than incarceration and restraint, when necessary, until such time as the alcoholic could be discharged to his or her family to begin another round of drinking, with eventual termination in trauma, insanity from neurological damage, or death from physical complications.

With that introduction, how did I become involved with substance abuse? It was purely circumstance. My neighbor, also a nurse, began working in an alcohol treatment hospital. Her description of working conditions and a 4 p.m. to midnight opening fit my life-style and needs. I had done private duty and PRN nursing but I liked the idea of consistency of hours, assignment, diagnosis, and treatment in this new position. What began as a part-time job became a love affair with this field of nursing. Fourteen years later I'm still doing this work. Gradually over the years my history-taking skills, my assessment skills, and decision-making skills became fine-tuned. Probably the most significant skill gained through experience in this field is that of assessing the patient's potential for severe withdrawal. Many patients arrive at a treatment facility with combinations of chemicals in their systems; alcohol, cocaine, tranquilizers, and marijuana seem to be the most common. Usually nursing personnel are the first to see the patient and evaluate the initial course of action, which may include everything from transfer for emergency care to routine admission.

This speciality has become one in which I am able to combine all my nursing knowledge. Alcoholism and drug abuse are diseases of body, mind, and spirit; therefore, my nursing care involves meeting the holistic needs of our patients.

Currently I am a charge nurse on the 3 to 11 shift on our 27-bed substance abuse recovery unit. My role involves many of the traditional tasks, such as taking orders, preparing patients for tests, coordinating staff activities, and collaborating with staff on patient care. I especially enjoy admitting new patients to our unit. Alcoholics and substance abusers are usually in family, legal, health, job, or psychological crisis on the day of arrival to our unit. On our team of nurses and mental health technicians, we meet this new patient with acceptance, competence, and professionalism. I see myself as someone who must display and convey these qualities to the newly admitted patient. I try to allow adequate time, sometimes an hour or more to listen, assess, and reassure our new patient. Sometimes before I do any of this, I respond by administering medication. It is my belief that these initial few hours set the stage for the beginning of confidence and trust, prerequisites toward reaching out and allowing us to help.

It was been my privilege to work closely with a team of professionals—psychiatrists, counselors, mental health technicians, psychologists, social workers, and personnel from other therapies who contribute to our busy, dynamic program. Our group-oriented program involves training sessions, education, group therapy, and participation in community-based Alcoholics Anonymous and Narcotics Anonymous Programs. Part of my job is in teaching a session to the patients on the physical effects of alcohol and drugs. I take pride in being able to translate complicated medical jargon and physiological processes into understandable, meaningful information. As a result of this session patients are able to approach lab results with greater ease and understanding. It would be difficult to describe the changes I see in patients as withdrawal symptoms subside, toxicity lessens, and denial decreases. These signs of recovery begin to appear in the return of emotional balance; families reconnect, anger dissipates, and humor and joy replace depression, fear, and defensiveness.

Although this job has many rewards and advantages, I should not lead you to belive that every day is a fulfilling, rewarding experience. Some days are so frustrating that I don't want to go back for another day—on those days, many patients are needy, dependent, angry, complaining, and generally difficult. On that same day we may get news of the relapse (return to drugs or drinking) of one of our discharged patients. Some days the team has been split by manipulative patients. Some days we even manage to split ourselves and become divided, discouraged, and ineffective. Our most important asset as a team is unity and cooperation among ourselves.

Sometimes personal concerns spill over into work. I remember one day getting off the phone at the nursing station in tears. Patients who were leaving for an AA meeting were signing out in front of me. They could see that I was wiping away my tears. I couldn't talk, and they didn't talk. Suddenly across the desk came a folded note that said, "We don't know what's wrong, but we're sorry your're hurt and we love you." These people are truly special. They have been hurt and have hurt others, but they grow and change as they learn to reach out for help and to help others. I'm glad to be part of that growth.

We may be qualified to administer medications, but the larger meaning for me is the ability to minister to people searching for change, knowledge, and healing. To those of you who are reluctant to try this area of psychiatric nursing, I suggest that you talk with those of us who enjoy and appreciate the privilege of working with other professionals in medical and psychiatric programs. Equally rewarding is working with community-based self-help groups such as Alcoholics Anonymous, Alanon, and Narcotics Anonymous, whose programs continue to save lives through nonmedical intervention and support.

Nancy M. Horvath, R.N.

Position: Coordinator, Health Medicine Unit
Agency: La Palma Intercommunity Hospital
Location: La Palma, California

The Health Medicine Unit deals with psychosomatic illnesses, disorders of adaptation, or disorders characterized by chronicity, disability, and history of inadequate response to purely medical interventions. We serve patients recovering from chronic disorders such as pain, those with eating disorders, and those in need of medication reduction or stress reduction. The primary emphasis is to gain control of the medical condition, increase the individual's level of functioning in all areas of his life (familial, social, vocational, emotional, physical), and develop new health habits that will impact on both the medical condition and the individual's daily life. Therefore the program is designed to increase the patient's level of adaptation. We work with clients to decrease untoward responses to environmental stressors by developing problem-solving strategies. Our secondary goal is to assist the client in changing his attitude toward himself.

My role as the coordinator for this program is to assist in the evaluation of prospective patients, to oversee and facilitate the functioning of the interdisciplinary team, and to participate in program development and budgeting.

My decision to enter psychiatric-mental health nursing stemmed from my own frustatrions early in my training. In caring for patients there was always a void. There never seemed to be enough time—I could get treatments done but then couldn't spend the time to allay fears of surgery. There was too much emphasis on the non-functional body part. The one area in which I experienced at least partial satisfaction was Pediatrics. Meeting my needs to nurture seemed to be my most logical choice until I was exposed to the wonders of psychiatric nursing. Frustration again set in but this time because I needed to choose between a specialty area that filled the "missing piece" and an age group that met my need to nurture. All of the pieces and needs came to-

gether for me when I spent part of a day on a field trip to a children's psychiatric facility. The next 14 years of my nursing career were spent exclusively involved in adolescent psychiatric units. My career then started taking a few turns toward administrative positions.

The most rewarding aspect of my present position is being an integral part of a growth process that includes both clients and staff. I get the greatest feeling—a natural high—when a client who had come in totally disorganized and been nonfunctional for several years learns new skills, develops the ability to generalize, and then leaves the program and returns to work. It is a high for me to work with new staff, assist them in developing interpersonal skills, and watch them effectively treat the whole person.

What's my major frustration at this point in my career? Trying to find ways for clients to receive appropriate treatment and still meet reimbursement needs for the organization.

Just as my career has taken a turn, I think psychiatric-mental health nursing will need to take a turn. In all areas of health care we are faced with more complex cases, shorter lengths of stay, and tighter budgets. In psychiatric nursing this translates to a higher medical component, a need for more day (or rather evening) treatment programs, and generally doing more with less. Psychiatric units will remain, but the emphasis will need to shift to med-psych units and behavioral medicine units. This may also mean a shift in out-patient treatment to more involvement with self-help groups that are supervised by clinicians.

My advice to a nurse now entering psychiatric nursing would be to first have a solid base in medicine, then develop skills in the area of stress reduction, and, if interest lies in administration, develop skills in marketing and program development.

Suzanne Lego, *R.N., PH.D., C.S.*

Position: Nurse Psychotherapist
Agency: Private Practice
Location: New York, New York, and Demarest, New Jersey

When I started my private practice in psychotherapy in 1965 there were not too many of us around. I had just completed the Rutgers University Graduate Program in Advanced Psychiatric Nursing. Dr. Hildegard Peplau, often called the "Mother of Psychiatric Nursing," had designed the program to prepare nurses to practice psychotherapy. As a staff nurse in Pittsburgh I had read about the program and decided it was the place for me. I'd often wondered what went on in the private offices of psychiatric residents with the patients that I knew on the unit, and believed *that* was where the action was. So I came East to Rutgers, totally unprepared for the rigorous program I entered. As graduate students we saw individual patients for 1 year, 2 years if we wanted, and taped every session (two sessions per week). This went on over holidays, every week, rain or shine. We spent 2 days a week in supervision—all day long hearing our own and our classmates' tapes. The faculty who supervised us were all clinicians themselves, and they experienced pressure to become expert clinicians, to write clinical papers, and to publish. Furthermore, our patients were all chronic "state hospital" patients. My analyst at the time described this as comparable to "putting medical students in the OR the first week of school and teaching them brain surgery." Dr. Peplau believed that if we thoroughly understood basic, primitive psychopathology, everything else later would be easy, and I still believe this to be true.

As students we were very strongly encouraged to be in therapy and required to be in a group for the 2 years of graduate study. We were also required to attend national conferences and told that when the speaker finished reading a paper we were to be on our feet making comments or asking questions.

In 1965 when I graduated, I stayed on to teach for a year in the program. I continued seeing my patients and group, and in this year two of my patients were discharged from the "state hospital." They were to become my first two private patients. I saw them in my apart-

ment, and gradually over the next 10 years I began to see others. In the meantime I taught, was a nursing supervisor, a clinical specialist, and then a therapist in a child guidance clinic. I completed my Ph.D. in nursing and entered a postdoctoral psychoanalytic program.

By 1974 (9 years after graduation from my Masters program) I was seeing too many private patients to continue using my apartment. I clearly needed an office. I rented an office suite in Greenwich Village just across Washington Square Park from my apartment. It seemed a very grown-up thing to have my own office with a waiting room. I rented the second office in the suite to colleagues. Two years later, around the time of graduation from the analytic program, I took an even bigger step, giving up my teaching job and supporting myself entirely in my private practice. I was not the only nurse to support herself in private practice in the 1970s. My friend and colleague, Sheila Rouslin, did the same thing and has written a very interesting chapter on the subject in a book she co-authored with William Herron, *Issues in Psychotherapy* (Bowie, MD, Brady, 1982). In this chapter she described the unconcious feelings of dependency and aggression that can be activated by stepping out of a "parental" employment situation into independent practice.

Today many psychiatric nurses have private patients, and a smaller number have fulltime practices like mine. There are several advantages to private practice. The first obvious one is financial remuneration. Agencies do not pay nurses as much per session as they can earn privately. (The average fee per session is $40 to $50.)

A second advantage is flexibility. Nurses in private practice can choose the type of theoretical framework, the patients they want to work with, the hours they want to fill, when they wish to take vacations, and how long they wish to see patients (assuming the patient is agreeable). In an agency this is often decided for the therapist.

Some nurses in private practice are discouraged by the disadvantages. First, the nurse is totally responsible for the patient. There is no "team" to help with decisions, although supervision should be and is used. Second, the patient who lives at home may not be in the best environment, so the private practitioner does not have a "therapeutic milieu" in which to practice, as might exist in a hospital. Third, some private practitioners find it lonely working all day in an office without the company of colleagues. Finally, there is the threat of decreased income if there is a decrease in case load.

The reader may wonder where the patients come from and how they are referred. My patients are sent to me by other current patients, past patients, colleagues, former students, and people who attend the lecture and seminars I frequently present to professional groups. In the event they need medication, they are seen by a psychiatrist who is a friend and colleague.

I now live in New Jersey and have two offices—one in Greenwich Village and one in my home. I divide my time between these two offices, spending 2 days in each office per week. I reserve the fifth day, Friday, for travel and speaking engagements.

In my 25 years in psychiatric nursing I believe I've sampled nearly every role and every setting common to the practice of our specialty. I've worked in places I've loved, and in some that I haven't liked so much. Private practice for me is by far the most satisfying. I like being in charge of my own practice and in a sense "the master of my fate." My patients are interesting, stimulating, and often challenging. I've never doubted for a minute that the trip East in 1963 was the most important one I ever made!

Elinor L. Bethke, R.N., M.S.

Position: Psychiatric Nurse Clinical Specialist
Agency: Private Practice
Location: Monte Vista, Colorado

I am a small town person. I grew up in a small eastern Oregon town and now live and work as a psychiatric nurse in rural southern Colorado. I am used to living in a town with one main street, one school system, a lot of small but active churches, a local 30-bed hospital, and one movie theater. When I go to the grocery store, I see my neighbors and my clients. My daughter's teacher is a neighbor, and the yearly rodeo is our town's big event. I am content with small town living; when I travel to the city, I love the atmosphere and the choices, but it does not pull at my heart.

I have lived in Monte Vista for 12 years, but I am still an outsider in some ways. My family history is elsewhere, while many of my friends and clients have one or two generations of family here. This area is known as the San Luis Valley. It is a large mountain valley, elevation 7800 feet, population 34,000. There are ten small towns here dependent on farming, ranching, and recreation.

While a baccalaureate student at the University of Oregon School of Nursing, I started each new clinical rotation wondering if the new area would be special for me and my skills. I liked many specialities, but none was pivotal until psychiatric nursing in my junior year. My clinical placement was at the State Hospital in Salem, Oregon. An important influence was my nursing instructor, Eleanor Hein—a great teacher and motivator for personal and professional growth. I was challenged and comfortable with the work and felt purposeful.

My nursing career plans from then on focused on psychiatry. I decided to obtain a master's degree in Psychiatric Nursing, and my choice of a graduate program was influenced by my husband's being with the U.S. Forest Service. I remember researching graduate schools, putting the schools and cities on a map, and looking for national forests within a 100-mile radius.

I chose the University of Colorado School of Nursing in Denver. While waiting to get into the graduate program, I worked for 1 year as a staff nurse in in-patient psychiatric facilities. Graduate school gave me a wide range of clinical experiences, including a flying psych clinic into the rural area of central Colorado. My focus in rural mental health was supported by my professors, Madeline Leininger and Dort Gregg.

In 1969, I began work as a psychiatric nurse clinical specialist in a comprehensive community mental health center in the Denver area. Job opportunities were plentiful, with federal monies supporting community mental health care. At this time in Colorado, master's level nurses were starting to work in community outpatient clinics. We nurses were more independent than the psychiatrists and psychologists expected. A psychiatric nurse began to be seen as a mixture of a public health nurse, social worker, and psychotherapist.

In 1973, I moved to Monte Vista, Colorado, with my husband and daughter. Soon after settling here, I was actively sought by the newly established local comprehensive mental health center. The job opportunity was ideal; I could determine my own hours and also my work focus. I had a young daughter and was able to balance home and work. Community mental health helped weave me into the local area. I worked with many social agencies, learned a great deal about the people, and furthered my clinical skills.

After working 11 years in community mental health, I felt it was time to be more independent. I decided to start a private practice. It helped that I had had many good professional relationships and was a known psychotherapist in the area. I now have my own office at home, and I also work with a group of physicians in a nearby town. My clients are mostly adults; many are women. I do individual and couple therapy, and my cases usually last 3 months to a year. My special interests are women's issues, depression, psychological issues of chronic illness, and relationship counseling. I have been in private practice for 4 years.

Using psychotherapy for personal growth and at times of transition is not considered an option by many people. Here in a rural area, psychotherapy is often considered a serious intervention used only for severe mental illness. Family life is traditional, and the family system is strong and extended. Families feel responsible to maintain and care for a member who has a serious mental illness. Problems can be severe and long term before help is sought. An example is a 19-year-old anorectic woman whom I saw recently. Her height is 5′7″ and her weight is 75 pounds. She has been at this weight for 3 months and had been at 90 pounds or less for 2 previous years without seeking treatment. Her family has been caring for her on their own.

Because I do psychotherapy in a rural area I must be particularly careful to protect my clients' privacy. Living and working in a small community, I understand and practice confidentiality in my own personal life. It can be lonely. People in small communities love to exchange news about each other. My friends tease me about how I do not gossip. I cannot. My carefulness is irritating to me. I am, by nature, a private person, but I would be less so if I were in a different field.

People here have intertwined histories. I often deal with interconnections that make therapy more difficult. Sometimes I feel everyone knows everyone else. Friendships, work relationships, and family relationships cross between people and can result in situations in which I cannot be the therapist.

I work independently and have to learn to deal with isolation. I travel 200 miles over a mountain pass for supervision. In the winter this travel is quite difficult. I am fortunate to have professionals outside the valley who trust my judgment and support my work. My telephone is invaluable for ongoing connection with other professionals.

Working in psychotherapy has been important to me personally. My work has helped me know many special people. I think these qualities or attributes make an effective therapist: personal awareness and continued self-growth; interest in other people and the ability to listen and remember people's stories about themselves; assessment skills; and a nonjudgmental attitude, with the ability to be surprised and delighted by people's spirit. Over the years I have spent hours and hours listening to people. I continue to want to listen, understand, affirm, and connect with others. I do not have all the answers, but I do believe behavior makes sense and that change is possible and positive.

To a nursing student or nurse practitioner considering continuing in psychiatric nursing, I want to encourage you. I consider nurses to be strong in assessment skills, with a wide range of clinical experiences. Nurses start early as students to provide direct nursing care. I have found many other professionals in the mental health field to have limited clinical work in their educational preparation. Nurses usually have had experience with mild to severe mental and behavioral dysfunction. There is a seriousness about the treatment contract between nurses and their clients or patients. I like the level of responsibility that exists.

For student nurses looking at this field, my cautions are the following: the days of federally supported and state-supported mental health care are over or greatly changed; the field of mental health is saturated with many types of providers; and credentials will be more and more necessary for third party collections, for licensure, and for being recognized as legitimate therapists by the community.

James J. Casey, R.N.

Position: Head Nurse, Adolescent Psychiatric Department
Agency: Valley Hospital Medical Center
Location: Van Nuys, California

My current job title is that of Head Nurse of the Adolescent Psychiatric Department, Valley Hospital Medical Center, Van Nuys, California. I have been employed in my current position for about 2 years. Before this, I worked in Child and Adult psychiatric hospital milieus at the University of Texas Medical Branch, Galveston, Texas, an adult transitional living center, a geriatric nursing facility, and an in-patient adolescent milieu at the UCLA Medical Center, Los Angeles, California.

I chose the field of psychiatry for a number of reasons. I was instantly attracted to psychiatric services during my clinical rotation in school because of the human contact and interaction with the staff and patients. I am not very mechanically inclined, and thus had little desire to work in such settings as the ICU, OR, Surgery, or any department that had machines, instruments, or monitors. I also enjoy working with an interdisciplinary team—one that consists of nurses, physicians, therapists, social workers, recreational and occupational therapists, art and dance therapists, and other adjunctive staff members. The team operates by meeting weekly, in which each patient's case is presented and discussed by the entire treatment team and a uniform therapeutic direction is instituted. Thus, the left hand knows what the right hand is doing, and patients find it difficult to manipulate a specific individual or an entire treatment staff.

I also perceive an interesting phenomenon in psychiatric departments regarding nurse–physician relations. I, and overwhelmingly my co-workers, feel somewhat as peers, not subordinates, or "do-fers," as nurses on medical floors so often complain about. Perhaps this is due to the value of communication with the patients, and, or course, the nursing staff maintains around the clock observation of the ward. Yes, the physicians read our nurses' notes and solicit information about their patient when entering the nurses' station. The general consensus of nurses in psychiatry is that they feel as though they are a valued commodity. This does wonders for

one's sense of autonomy, integrity, and self-esteem. And this, in turn, creates a more harmonious, pleasant working atmosphere.

Life in psychiatry is not always a bed of roses. Yes, we too are inundated by reams of paperwork, triplicate forms, and momentum-halting bureaucratic policies and procedures. As frustrating as this is, psychiatric nurses realize that necessary evils do exist.

Another unfortunate occurrence is the premature discharge of a patient. Because of a restrictive insurance policy, a patient may be discharged before his hospital treatment is complete. This causes emotional trauma for both patient and family. It is a frustrating feeling to have worked with a youngster, attempting to deal with adolescent crises, and abruptly be told that the patient must leave the hospital because there is no funding left.

The treatment team must also deal with the non-supportive family—the family that seldom or never comes to visit their son or daughter, the family that signs their youngster out of the hospital just when progress is seemingly being made. Imagine how frightened and angry the teenager must feel. Imagine the despair of returning home and knowing that nothing in the family system has changed.

Moving to the other side of the spectrum, there are quite a number of positives involved in psychiatric nursing. One is the privilege of working with a group of dynamic, motivated staff, people who are vital and optimistic regarding the progress and prognosis of the patient. There is also a certain sense of accomplishment watching a teenager mature. It fulfills our desire to help when a patient who was "out of control" a year or so ago returns to visit cleanly groomed, and back in school or steadily employed. There is a gratifying feeling in knowing that we were able to help the youngster become a productive member of society.

I have settled upon adolescent psychiatry as my subspecialty because of its intrinsic challenge. The teenagers are always trying to outthink, outguess, and outwit the nurses and therapists, seldom leaving a dull moment on the ward. Another reason that I prefer adolescent psychiatry is that I feel the prognoses for the adolescent are generally more optimistic than for other age groups of patients. I feel that this, in turn, creates a more enthusiastic, motivated nursing team to relate with the patient.

Currently, there are many psychiatric hospitals with varied treatment regimes/philosophies, including behavior modification programs, analytical milieus, token economies, level systems, immediate reward/consequence units, and a variety of others too numerous to mention. Allow me to describe to you our theories and philosophy of treatment in our program at Valley Hospital. Our program is oriented to facilitate an increase in personal responsibility in the adolescent, as well as to help delineate clarity in personal and parental identity and roles. This is done through individual psychotherapy and family therapy, as well as therapy in the milieu itself. To understand more fully our view of adolescent difficulties, as well as the adolescent process, our Unit Philosophy is offered for your review.

We belive that adolescents with character disorders have developed coping styles that protect their narcissism (their self-interest) but promote isolation from object relations (social interest). Such isolation increases separation anxiety and prevents reality testing that otherwise would promote identity consolidation. The above sense of isolation further facilitates the use of primitive, preverbal communication that is manifested as acting out behavior (substance abuse, promiscuity, delinquency, running away, *etc.*) Thus, techniques that promote object relating (social contact) must be devised to overcome this self-imposed isolation.

From the above, our task is stated as follows:

1. At the most primitive level (psychoses and beginning work with character disordered individuals), the task is containment of troublesome impulses. These means of containment range from physical restraint, medication, and time-out rooms, to time-outs, groundings, and loss of privileges. All of these refer to various aspects of physical impulse containment; these are all at the narcissistic level of treatment.
2. The above accomplished, we then move to the more difficult but essential work of facilitating object relatedness (social contact). This is done by

progression in intensity from the most primitive human contact during physical restraint, to encouraging verbal communication by talking to the individual while in time-out, to having them put their feelings into words through writing in a daily journal, to, finally, achieving daily, time-limited talks with unit staff. To further facilitate object relatedness (social contact, and thus decrease separation anxiety), the staff will help the patient focus on object relatedness with remarks stated in an uncritical manner, keeping in mind the narcissistic sensitivity to humiliation.

Thus, our task is twofold:

1. To contain impulsiveness.
2. To promote object relatedness (people relatedness).

To achieve both tasks results in an increase in a personal sense of centeredness or integration of self-identity, with a decrease in the quality of isolation, thus enabling the adolescent to utilize social support more appropriately and decrease the use of acting out as well as to increase the use of verbal communication to sustain object relations and contain troublesome impulses. This offers the youngster and his or her family an alleviation of pathologic symptoms and a reasonable hope for a productive life outside a hospital setting.

The future of psychiatric nursing, is, of course, uncertain at best, but let me expound on a few factors. Unlike general medicine, which has already undergone drastic changes under the DRG system, adolescent psychiatry remains virtually untouched by financial restrictions. Thus far, the situation remains optimistic. Insurance companies realize that the hospital team cannot undo in 2 or 4 weeks the severe pathology that the family system has ingrained for 15 or so years. Therefore, as hospital stays grow shorter, adolescent in-patient psychiatric length of stays continue to be relatively lengthy. One must hope that the insurance companies recognize the wisdom of their decisions and keep the status quo.

I would like to tell the nursing students that psychiatric nursing is a wide open field with innovative theories, revolutionary therapeutic and diagnostic techniques, and a multitude of challenges. It is not a restrictive science—it is one that invites a creativity of thought and deed. If you enjoy working with people, possess good common sense, are a creative thinker, and relish a good challenge, choose Psychiatric Nusing.

Marilee K. Jones R.N., C.S., M.S.N.

Position: *Program Director, Day Treatment Center*
Agency: *Cincinnati Veterans Administration Medical Center*
Location: *Cincinnati, Ohio*

My appointment as Program Director of a Day Treatment Center was the attainment of a 10-year goal for me. I had turned to psychiatric nursing after exhausting my fascination with surgical nursing. Psychiatric nursing seemed mysteriously exciting. I went to work on a psychiatric in-patient unit, obtained a Master's degree in Psychiatric Mental Health Nursing, and became a head nurse on an acute in-patient unit. The bonding process was complete. As I became experienced in psychotherapeutic techniques and comfortable in dealing with acutely psychotic patients, I learned to appreciate the clients and their families as people. I also learned to be pragmatic. From this pragmatism grew my awareness of a need for a place to send chronic patients that would provide support and direction without expecting cures. It seemed that the after care facilities offered only time limited, highly focused programs that weren't appropriate for our recidivistic population.

Then I accepted a newly created position as a Clinical Nurse Specialist at the Mental Health Clinic. At the urging of the Mental Health Clinic Director, I initiated two re-socialization groups and a Vietnam Era group. The director and I both hoped to prove the need for a Day Treatment Center. Space was a problem, and for the next 4 years my volunteer assistant Carol and I carried our coffee pot to wherever we could negotiate space. We offered goal-oriented group therapy and were able to demonstrate improved compliance and decreased hospitalization among our patient members. We also witnessed some unexpected behavioral changes.

The first year that Carol and I took a group downtown to tour the Christmas displays, passers-by looked askance at us. "Who do you think, they think, we are?" queried one of the group. "They probably aren't even giving us any thought," I responded with my fingers crossed. We seemed a motley cluster: all ages, all sizes, all colors, and in varied attire. The gentleman asking was impeccably dressed but had bleached his hair in spots

and wore it in a Mohawk. I felt most persons could guess who we were. The following year, on the same excursion with some of the same patients, we were given an identity by a waitress scurrying to seat us. "Come right over here. You're a jury, aren't you. Who's your judge?" We had arrived and at a level no one had anticipated.

Now the Day Treatment Center is funded. We have a staff of two social workers, an Associate Degree nurse who is also an activity therapist, a secretary, and a half-time geropsychiatrist, besides Carol and me. We have the entire third floor of the clinic. This gives us a kitchen and dining area, a group room, arts and crafts room, classroom library, and offices. All of the rooms are multipurpose. Our membership is composed of half-psychiatric and half-geriatric veteran clients. To maximize benefits to as many as possible, our programs last half a day and members attend the programs one to four times a week. We teach classes in Coping Skills, Health, and Personal Management. We have re-socialization groups, medication groups, and special interest groups, and the members publish a monthly newspaper. Each member is assigned a staff person as a case manager. Socialization excursions occur about every 3 weeks. The purpose of the excursions is to expose members to new experiences, to offer an opportunity to practice newly acquired social skills, and to increase members' familiarity with the city.

Group therapy is the main therapeutic modality. Patients openly share concerns, losses, joys, and triumphs. The leader acts as a catalyst and a rudder to stabilize and direct the group. The rules are simple. Members are to be clean, sober, and should refrain from acting or talking "crazy." Acceptance of one another permits confrontation when appropriate, which includes confronting the leader. Once, when I reminded a member who was speaking in numbers that he was not to speak that way in group, another member spoke up. "Marilee, this is only his third time. I didn't stop talking crazy for 3 months. Give the man a chance." It is difficult to describe the special warmth and companionship that evolves in groups. We've celebrated birthdays, weddings, graduations, and births. We've shared surgery, cancer, divorce, and death. Gains are minor and ever so slow for many. With others, such as the Vietnam veterans, changes come in leaps. Many of the geriatric patients make noticeable changes by the second encounter. My job is neither simplistic nor glamorous. It combines the action verbs—push, pull, shove, stroke, hug, clap, laugh, and cry.

As the director I case manage 20 clients and lead four groups. This permits me to utilize my clinical skills and maintain an awareness of the milieu. Although my number of clients is greatly reduced, it keeps me apprised of the tasks involved and assists me in evaluating staff and client performance. I have administrative duties that include budgeting, staffing, supervising, record keeping, and reporting. I am responsible for maintaining a therapeutic milieu and ensuring that each client receives a goal-directed, individualized treatment program that is documented as well as implemented. There is a great deal of paper work, system work, and committee work. I get a great deal of satisfaction from seeing patients progress, the staff develop, and the program grow. I even enjoy the statistics.

While psychiatric nursing isn't mysterious, it has moments of excitement. It is a real privilege to be able to share so closely in the lives of others. This has included courtship, marriage, and parenthood with some. Once, a baby took his first steps in my office! A few clients have completed college, and some discovered the world of work or retirement. There have also been those who returned to drug abuse, committed suicide, or didn't change at all. I get calls and cards from patients I haven't seen in years. I also get cursed, threatened, and reported. Like anything you invest yourself in, it brings moments of extreme pleasure and moments of frustration or pain.

Skilled psychiatric nurses have an excellent opportunity to step into administrative positions and to demonstrate cost-effective health care delivery. It isn't a good career choice for those who seek power or prestige, or for those who need distance and space. It is a good choice for those who can be open and humble and for those who have energy, creativity, a sense of humor, and a belief in the future.

Karen J. Rodeheffer, B.A. (Social Work); Diploma in Nursing; Certified in Psychiatric and Mental Health Nursing

Position: *Supervisory Nurse for Psychiatric Team*
Agency: *The Menninger Foundation*
Location: *Topeka, Kansas*

I don't think I'm someone you'd describe as a typical psychiatric nurse; but maybe each of us views ourself this way. At any rate, I wasn't someone who knew in high school that nursing was a clearly defined career choice. In fact, I didn't even consider nursing at that time. I thought I wanted to be a music teacher, but after 1 year of college I knew that wasn't a good fit. At that time I changed to social work; I got my B.A. and completed one semester of graduate school. I still wasn't satisfied that this was the direction I wanted to go, so I decided to quit school and get some practical experience.

As a family planning specialist in a city–county health department, I found I enjoyed contact with clients and families, and I was able to utilize my social work training. However, it seemed to me that the nurses in the clinic did more for the client. With their nursing care—a holistic approach dealing with *both* physical and emotional concerns—they met a lot of the patient's personal needs in a manner that I couldn't. (I also liked their pay better!) As a result, I became dissatisfied with what seemed to be limitations in my role. It was at that point that I decided to go back to school to become a nurse—not just any nurse, but a psychiatric nurse. This was not an easy decision; I was moving from one career track where I was beginning to feel comfortable and skilled, to something unknown. However, I came to see my nursing training as augmenting, not replacing, my previous skills.

During my nursing education, I found in fact that my social work background put me at ease in relating to patients and their families, something that was unfamiliar to many of my younger classmates. (At that point, our 8-year age difference seemed like a generation.) My skill in dealing with the emotional health of patients at times made my instructors uneasy; they weren't sure that I would focus enough on the physical problems of the patient. I'm sure that they would be relieved and surprised when I now stress to other nurses that they need to be

aware of the physical problems of patients in addition to their psychological difficulties. The holistic approach to patient care has become an integral part of my nursing philosophy and practice!

There was little doubt in my mind as to what area I would enter following graduation. I also knew where I wanted to work: I wanted to go into psychiatric nursing at the Menninger Foundation. The reputation of nursing at this hospital was good. More importantly, I had heard that it was a place where I would receive thorough supervision and would be expected to continue to learn. In spite of my former training and experience, I was still a novice when I first began as an R.N. on the 3 to 11:30 shift on a 24-bed, long-term, adult psychiatric care unit (something the unit's more experienced mental health technicians wouldn't let me forget!). Looking back now 8 years later, I've come a long way from that slightly rigid, anxious to please, superorganized beginner. Through support of co-workers, supervisors, the treatment team, and my own growth process, I've made a lot of changes in style, comfort, and conceptualization. Most of all, I've become much more skilled in working with a wider range of patient behaviors, knowing appropriate interventions, and yet being tolerant in letting the patient move at his or her own pace. I think, and have been told by others, that this is a major strength in my practice.

Just to be sure that I would continue toward my career goals, I set up a yearly contract, and annually I would go in and evaluate my progress with the Director of Nursing and set new goals for the next year. It wasn't that this also didn't go on in my own supervision, but somehow I needed it to be formalized as part of my own motivation—doing it in my own way.

During what I would now call some of my more formative years, there were opportunities outside the hospital to broaden my skills. Through personal experiences I became interested in women's issues, and volunteered as a rape counselor. I served on an advisory committee

676

for the county jail, making me more aware of a whole new set of emotional crises for people. Watching my little sister in the Big Brother/Big Sister program grow from the age of 9 to 18 and graduate from high school broadened my understanding of long-term relationships and the role of consistency, not to mention the genuine caring that is involved. My participation in the state nursing association (KSNA) during this time also played an important role in developing my identity as a nurse.

As my nursing skills developed, I was encouraged to look beyond the scope of my responsibilities as a staff nurse on the unit. I became the chairperson of a professional nurse committee within the hospital, which made me more comfortable in being a leader with my peers. My main accomplishment with this committee was incorporating the ANA Psychiatric Nursing Standards into our own standards of practice. This project is one that not only made me quite proud of my job here, but also solidified my pride in my profession in general. One hospital-wide activity that I enjoyed, but wouldn't want to repeat, was being the move coordinator for my unit when our hospital moved several miles to a new campus. Teaching a patient how to pack and touring groups of patients through unfinished construction with hard hats was something they never taught in nursing school!

Although I really liked my work with patients on the evening shift, I was faced with a common dilemma of many nurses: needing to take a position on days in order to advance my career as a nurse, and to incorporate some priorities of my personal life as well. This position as the nurse leader for the nursing care of a 12 patient team is one that I've now held for 3½ years. While different from the evening position, I find that it does allow me an opportunity to stay clinically involved with patients in giving direct care. Additionally, I now have more opportunity to supervise and teach other nursing staff and nursing students. My role on the interdisciplinary team allows me to be an advocate for nursing as well as for the patients.

One of the aspects I enjoy about psychiatric nursing is the diversity it provides, even in day-to-day activities. One of my favorite activities is working with patient groups. It was exciting to start and co-lead a diet and exercise group for patients and a talk group about women's issues for female patients, and to be the staff liaison for the patient government, and to teach yoga classes for patients. I like to think that the role modeling I try to do with patients, for example, around creative use of their leisure time, is another aspect of my holistic approach to patient care. In fact, I firmly believe that the nurse, because of his or her direct contact with patients, provides an important role model for them, whether intentional or not.

If I had to pick the group of patients that I like to work with the most, and where I do my best work, it would be schizophrenic patients. The nurse's role in the hospital strongly emphasizes patient teaching, and with the schizophrenic patient, teaching goes on through day-to-day involvement. The patients have taught me a lot too—the importance of limit-setting; being nurturing but not infantilizing; and being caring but with boundaries. I suppose that the element of caring, so much a part of our philosophical belief at Menninger's, is one thing that makes me so comfortable with my role as a nurse in this setting.

The expertise that I have developed in this area has led me to be a part of the foundation's Survival Skills workshops that are conducted for families who have chronically mentally ill (mainly schizophrenic) members. The workshop's use of a psycho-educational model, which emphasizes families' learning to cope with their members' illnesses parallels my work on the unit with patients. Therefore, my part of the workshop is to present coping strategies to the familes—how to deal with the day-to-day behaviors the patients present, and how to interact in a manner that works out best for both the patient and the family.

As much as I like direct patient care, I also enjoy teaching and supervising other nursing staff and nursing students. The time set aside for supervision with discussion of clinical issues as well as relationships within the staff group is a time to get one's battery recharged, not just for the supervisee but for me too! In a work setting that is at times very draining, supervision decreases the chance of burnout and discouragement, and helps to minimize the acting out of countertransference feelings one might have toward a particular patient. What I try to give to those I supervise are some of the things that were and are important in my own supervision—support and encouragement to grow as an individual and a practitioner; direction and limit-setting when it's needed; and challenging the person to learn, and the end goal of giving better patient care.

My experience in working on an interdisciplinary team has been a positive one. I feel that I've had professional respect and a collegial working relationship with the various team members, which include a psychiatrist team leader, a psychologist, social worker, activity therapist, and, of course, other nursing staff. As much as I like my work, there have been—and are—moments of frustrations, discouragement, and disappointment. For instance, along with the power, respect, and responsibility I have earned on the team, it is frustrating to see a less experienced resident join the team and become the assistant team leader because of his or her discipline.

One of the most frustrating parts of my work with patients is that long-term treatment is a slow, often tedious process in which patient gains are hard to see on a day-to-day basis. Likewise, it's frustrating for me as a nurse who has trained to help people get better to encounter a patient who isn't interested in changing.

Like many professional women, I have had to deal with how to combine a career with family priorities. Very soon I shall be taking an extended leave of absence from my full-time work to stay home with our baby, and it will be difficult to leave behind patients and staff in whom I have invested a great deal. However, because of the flexibility of my nursing skills, I won't have to make a complete choice; in the interim, until I return to work full time, I will be working with some schizophrenic patients in the community making weekly visits, monitoring medication, and helping with their activities of daily living.

In summary, psychiatric nursing for me has been a profession that has given me the opportunity to develop my career potential as I choose. For example, while I have not chosen to continue my formal education—at least at this point—I did take the ANA certification for psychiatric and mental health nursing as a way to upgrade my professional development. Having lattitude to define my role and make my own choices places risks and responsibility for future direction and outcome on me for my career development, For me, the direction I've taken fits my own interest and skills. Back to the original question—why would I want to become a nurse?—if someone asked me now, I'd be able to tell them.

Patricia D. Barry, R.N., M.S.N.

Position: *Psychiatric Liaison Nursing Clinical Specialist*
Location: *West Hartford, Connecticut*

"Psych liaison nursing is the greatest job there is in nursing." These words were spoken by a woman who was a Chief Nurse in the Veterans Administration Hospital system. I agree! My background in psychiatric liaison nursing has given me the ability to choose from an almost unlimited number of work opportunities related to its conceptual bases in personality development, biopsycho-social phenomena, stress and its management, and groups and systems theory.

When I attended a diploma nursing program in northern Vermont more than 20 years ago, I was a more than occasional source of consternation to my nursing instructors because I became "overinvolved" with my patients and insisted on describing the emotional state of my nursing care study patients—even though I had not yet completed my psychiatric affiliation. Indeed, in every medical–surgical position I filled following graduation, the most rewarding aspect of my work was the psychosocial support of patients and families in distress because of physical illness.

I trekked back to school in the mid-1970s to complete my bachelor's degree, and then went on to study psychiatric liaison nursing at Yale University. The course work in general psychiatry was an excellent and necessary foundation, but it wasn't fun for me. However, the courses and clinical work in liaison psychiatry dealing with emotional outcomes of illness, theories of stress, coping, bereavement, family and general system theory, staff responses to stress, and so on, were a joy for me. I had been looking for this information for years. I became determined that as soon as I finished graduate school I would pull together these concepts and research findings from the fields of nursing, medicine, psychology, and social work and write a book for nurses on psychosocial assessment and intervention theory.

After graduation I took a part-time position in a baccalaureate nursing program and developed a course that became the outline for the book-I-hoped-would-be.

In addition, I was able to conduct a weekly clinical case conference in the medical–surgical setting to discuss the students' emotionally complex patients. As another part of the position, I was a clinical instructor in a residential drug and alcohol treatment center, an excellent site to use liaison psychiatry theory.

During that year I began to consult in various health care settings about staff nurse stresses associated with patient care. I had believed for 20 years that nurses would be able to give better care to their patients if some of their own patient-related and system-related stresses were addressed. I was very happy to begin helping both nurse managers and staff members to help themselves.

Because of NLN standards, the nursing school where I was working changed to an integrated curriculum. This change required the full-time participation of psychiatric faculty. I enjoyed the teaching, but I missed working directly with my own patients. Because I had been wanting to develop a psychiatric liaison clinical specialist position in one of the local hospitals, I decided to leave the university.

By then, my book had been accepted for publication. In order to allow time to write, I worked 3 days a week in the hospital and 3 days a week writing at home. On my writing days I continued to consult to a variety of institutions. These consultations or seminars pertained to the stresses associated with major change, interpersonal aspects of nursing management, and conflict resolution. Many hospitals were decentralizing their nursing department, resulting in major role changes and different expectations of nursing managers. My services were sought for management development and team-building during the change process.

The psychiatric liaison clinical position was the most enjoyable job I have ever held. There were 28 nursing units in the hospital where I worked; each unit called on me to assist in a multitude of roles.

A typical day in my position could include the following schedule:

7–8	Returning telephone calls left on answering machine. Checking on consultation requests. Scheduling appointments.
8–9	Meeting with head nurse regarding negative response by nursing staff to new medication delivery system.
9–11	Sessions with hospitalized patients seen on prior consultations. (I usually followed five patients at a time.)
11–12	Ongoing staff support group or one-time staff meeting requested for problem resolution.
12:30–1:30	New patient consultation. This required follow up with primary nurse, attending physician, or house officer and usually two or three other caregivers in order to ensure a successful systems intervention.
1:30–2:30	Support group with new nursing graduates.
2:30–3	Meeting with staff development instructor from the cardiac intensive care unit to discuss program development on "Emotional Aspects of Myocardial Infarction."
3–4	Crisis intervention consultation and referral of nursing staff member who was recently widowed.

The position called for a high level of stamina, creativity in designing workable interventions for a wide variety of problems, and a capacity for self-support. Being able to prioritize situations that are described by others as "crises" is important in avoiding excessive fatigue. It is essential that a psychiatric liaison clinical specialist have consultation available to him or her in order to discuss the complex systems issues that occur in health care settings and organizations.

Three and a half years after developing and thoroughly enjoying the position, I was asked to edit a nursing textbook. I had increasingly been asked to consult to other instituions. In addition, I wanted to begin a counseling practice. With feelings of both happiness and sadness, I decided to leave the hospital.

I was very concerned about whether I could remain solvent. I knew that developing either a counseling or consulting practice takes time—at least a year for each. I began an active networking process. I called people who were well-respected and prominent in either nursing management or the clinical counseling field. I sought their advice and contacted the people they thought I should speak with. Two and a half years later both practices are very gratifying and successful.

I see approximately 12 patients a week during two clinical days, and usually average four or five consultations or seminars a month. These programs are wonderfully varied. Recent consultations or seminars have included the following:

1. Psychosocial Nursing Assessment and Intervention seminars in 15 major cities.
2. Counseling Techniques for Nursing Managers presentation to regional meeting of nursing administrators.
3. Giving and Taking Criticism and related seminars for a major U.S. computer corporation.
4. Consultation to a general hospital that is developing the position of liaison nurse in order to work with all hospital departments to reduce manager and employee stress levels.
5. Stress management program for all department managers in large suburban community.
6. Ongoing professional support group for professionals working with Alzheimer's patients and families.

The advantages of my current work are many. Interestingly, they can also be viewed as disadvantages, depending on the perspective. First of all, I am in charge of my own schedule. Other than my clinical days that are consistent each week, I can schedule seminars at my own convenience. Accordingly, I can also overschedule myself. It feels very good, as we all know, to be needed, but sometimes the wisdom of knowing when to say no is elusive.

The range of topics that I am asked to address keeps me actively involved in a number of interesting subjects. The scope of topics, however, does not allow me to be a specialist in any of them. Rather, I am a generalist, retaining my skills and developing new ones, but not deepening my knowledge base as much as I would prefer.

Another important consideration for me is the availability of friends who do similar work to my own. I have several therapist, as well as consultant, friends. Although I don't see them as much as I would like, they are a phone call away. Knowing that they experience similar challenges and frustrations in their own lives has been an ongoing source of quiet and necessary support for me. In addition, I belong to a group counseling practice. We meet once a week for case discussion in a supportive and caring environment filled with camaraderie.

I could not ask for a more fulfilling work life. It challenges all of my abilities and pushes me to continue my own development. I am deeply grateful to be allied with nursing. Because of its woman-oriented value system, I have been able to retain my femininity and womanly traditions. It has been a marvelous choice of profession.

Joyce Helen Godels, B.S.N., M.S. *in Psychiatric Nursing*

Position: *Assistant Professor*
Agency: *College of Nursing, Medical University of South Carolina*
Location: *Charleston, SC*

I am a teacher. I facilitate (I hope) the process of learning in undergraduate nursing students in a baccalaureate nursing program in the southeastern United States. In collaboration with several fellow faculty members I develop, implement, and evaluate nursing courses in my area of expertise, which is psychiatric-mental health nursing. I am responsible, again in collaboration, for deciding *what* a student needs to know and how best to facilitate the learning of those concepts and skills. I enjoy direct student contact in classroom, clinical, and one-to-one supervision settings. My interactions with students are influenced by my theoretical framework, which is based on Bowen's Family Systems Model. I believe that students learn more from the process that occurs between teacher and student than from any information or content the teacher is able to impart. In addition to meeting my direct teaching responsibilities, I participate in faculty committees that assist in making sure we are giving students what we say we are giving them—and doing that reasonably well. Some of the faculty committees facilitate getting the administrative work of the university done.

The series of events that influenced my decision to enter psychiatric-mental health nursing began on day one of my first psychiatric nursing course. I couldn't believe what I heard. There were names for the experiences I had had in my life, and—even more amazingly—these experiences were common to everybody. I became hooked on intrapersonal and interpersonal dynamics. Later, as I began implementing the strategies I was learning I found that they worked—not always and not perfectly—but they worked. I became aware of the potential for personal growth in the nurse–patient interaction. The varying and even conflicting psychiatric theories only served to pique my interest, and before I knew it I had been a psychiatric-mental health nurse for 20 years. Even though 16 of those years have been spent teaching

psychiatric-mental health nursing, I have carried a small private caseload of clients much of that time.

Two aspects of my work stand out as the most rewarding. On the one hand, learning about myself, which has been facilitated by all the conferences, classes, confrontations, collaborations, conversations, and long hours spent thinking alone, is the single most rewarding aspect of my professional career. On the other hand, the opportunity for relationships with individuals—whether clients or co-workers—willing to share their experiences about the human condition is the highlight. Although using psychiatric jargon to talk about human behavior is an occupational hazard of nurses working in mental health, opportunities to talk to real people about real experiences are an occupational benefit.

The area of my discontent relates to quality control—or the lack of it—that exists in the psychiatric field generally. Because of the difficulties inherent in applying the rules of research to the therapeutic relationship, some of the interventions that occur under the guise of being therapeutic are based less on a consistent theoretical framework for practice than on the shifting emotional states of the therapists. Of all the times that these interactions occur, I feel the worst about those in which I have participated.

By observing trends in health care one can predict that wellness and prevention are likely to be the foci in psychiatry, as in other health care professions. I believe that nursing education programs have always been built upon the concepts of "caring" and facilitating wellness rather than "curing." For this reason, nurses are particularly suited, by educational background, to participate in providing health care the objective of which is to move toward higher level wellness and prevent illness. Psychiatric-mental health nurses are no exception. The increasing number of success stories regarding psychiatric nurses in private practice may also indicate a future trend.

In summary, as a teacher I find the students' attempts to understand concepts new to them to be very stimulating. The student's fresh perceptions about infor- mation that has become familiar to me results in new awarenesses, and the opportunity to observe and to be part of the student's process of learning about self is, for me, an exhilarating experience.

Glossary

Acting in a kind of resistance that circumvents therapy through blocking, forgetting, changing the subject; trying to elicit the therapist's approval or disapproval while trying to recall or express feelings.

Acting out the client substitutes some kind of action for feeling or thinking; common forms of acting out include running away, use of alcohol or drugs, sexual promiscuity, and aggressive behavior.

Adolescence the stage of development during which the physiological changes of puberty, the emergence of the self-concept, and the integration of the biopsychosocial aspects of the individual occur.

Affect mood or feeling tone.

Aggression any behavior that expresses anger or its related emotions.

Akathisia a syndrome characterized by motor restlessness.

Anal period late infancy or toddlerhood, the period from ages 2 to 3 or 4 years, during which the child is involved in the development of social, emotional, and physiological control.

Anger a physical and emotional state in which a person experiences a sense of power to compensate for an underlying feeling of anxiety.

Anorexia nervosa self-imposed starvation.

Antianxiety agents psychotropic drugs used in the treatment of overt anxiety.

Anticipatory grief the experience of intense feelings of loss that occur when the family and friends know for certain that their loved one will die.

Antidepressant agents psychotroic drugs used in the treatment of depression.

Antipsychotic (or neuroleptic) agents psychotropic medication used primarily to treat psychoses, that is, severe emotional disorders.

Anxiety the initial response to psychic threat, evidenced as feelings of discomfort, uncertainty, apprehension, dread, restlessness, and uncertainty.

Assertiveness the employment of expressive, goal-directed, spontaneous, and self-enhancing behavior.

Assessment the gathering, classifying, and categorizing of client information which forms the basis of nursing planning.

Autocratic leadership the exercise of significant authority and control over group members, including the lack or rare use of input from the group and minimal group interaction and participation.

Avoidance the management of anxiety-laden experiences through evasive behaviors.

Battery the unpermitted touching of another.

Behavior a wide range of overt and covert responses that include emotions and verbalizations.

Behavioral contract an agreement between client and psychiatric-mental health caregiver for a specific behavior.

Behavioral rehearsal role playing, that is, the client rehearses new responses to problem situations after learning new adaptive responses portrayed through modeling.

Behavioral therapy a form of treatment that deals with changing the individual's maladaptive behavior by a planned, objective approach, such as respondent conditioning.

Bisexuality an equal, or almost equal, preference for either sex as a sexual partner.

Blocking the client suddenly "blanks out" and is unable to finish a thought or idea, that is, he represses painful knowledge and feelings.

Body image a mental picture of one's body.

Bulimia episodic, uncontrolled, rapid ingestion of large quantities of food over a short period of time, or binge eating.

Catharsis the emotional re-experiencing of painful, frightening, or angry feelings that are associated with the client's symptom or behavior.

Coitus sexual intercourse, or penetration of the vagina by the penis.

Collaboration working with others, as an equal, toward a common goal.

Communication a personal, interactive system, a series of ever-changing, ongoing transactions in the environment.

Compliance adherence to prescribed treatment regimes.

Consciousness the perceptions, thoughts, and feelings existing in a person's immediate awareness.

Coping mechanisms (also called ego defense mechanisms, mental mechanisms, and defense mechanisms) mechanisms that function to protect the ego from overwhelming anxiety and that usually operate on an unconscious level.

Counter transference an experience in which the therapist transfers his feelings for significant others onto the client.

Crisis a turning point, a state of disequilibrium usually lasting 4 to 6 weeks.

Crisis intervention a thinking, direct, problem-solving form of therapy that focuses only on the client's immediate problems.

Cryptic language abbreviated language, such as speaking aloud only every fifth or tenth word of one's thoughts.

Cunnilingus oral-genital stimulation performed on a woman.

Delusion a fixed, false belief that cannot be corrected by reasoning.

Dementia clinical behavior manifested in the insidious development of memory and intellectual deficits, disorientation, and decreased cognitive functioning.

Democratic leadership the encouragement of group interaction and participation in group problem-solving and decision-making; the group is marked by common goals, solicitation of opinions, ideas, and input and provision of feedback.

Denial an unconscious coping mechanism wherein a person denies the existence of some external reality.

Depression pathologically intense unhappiness.

Development the orderly evolution of events moving from simple to more complex.

Differentiation a tendency of living, open systems to increase in complexity over time.

Discrimination a specific response occurring in a given situation.

Disengagement a theory that proposes that the elderly or dying person acts voluntarily in giving up his roles in life, slowly loses interest in the active world, and withdraws from significant others.

Displacement an unconscious coping mechanism through which a person transfers an emotion from its original object to a substitute object.

Disqualifying an individual fails to attend to another's message by silence, ignoring it, or changing the subject.

Distress damaging or unpleasant stress.

Double-bind communication the sending of an incongruent message that includes a directive to do something and a nonverbal message to do the opposite, while the receiver of the message is not permitted to comment on it.

DSM III the American Psychiatric Association's *Diagnostic and Statistical Manual, Third Edition.*

Dyspareunia pain with sexual intercourse.

Dystonia involuntary, jerking, uncoordinated body movements.

Early latency the ages from 6 to 9 years, or early school-age years, during which the child focuses on learning, the acquisition of knowledge, the development of the social role outside the protection of home and family.

ECT electroconvulsive therapy, a form of treatment for depression.

Ego the structure of the human personality that has the greatest contact with reality.

Enculturation the process by which an individual learns the expected behavior of the culture.

Entropy the tendency of a system to be closed to the environment.

Erogenous zones the areas of the body that are particularly sensitive to erotic stimulation, such as the neck, breasts, inner thighs, and genital areas.

Ethnic groups a group of people with a common origin and holding basically similar values, beliefs, and means of communication.

Evaluation the process of determining the value of something in the attainment of preset goals.

Exhibitionism an erotic desire to expose one's genital or erogenous areas to others.

Existential crisis a crisis in which the individual is faced with life, in the form of aloneness, the absurdity of existence, and the responsibilities inherent in his attained freedom, and is confronted with a reorganization of the meaning of life.

Extinction the withholding of reinforcers, thus reducing the probability of the occurrence of the response.

Fading gradual reduction of the process of facilitating or accentuating the reinforcer.

Family a primary group whose members are related by blood, marriage, adoption, or mutual consent, who interact through certain familial roles, and create and maintain a common subculture.

Family structure the organization of the family.

Family therapy a form of treatment based on the premise that the member of the family with the presenting symptoms signals the presence of pain in the whole family.

Fantasy a coping mechanism through which a person engages in nonrational mental activity and thus escapes daily pressures and responsibilities.

Fellatio oral-genital stimulation performed on a man.

Flight of ideas a stream of thought characterized by a rapid association of ideas and play upon words.

Folie à deux a delusional system shared by two persons, most commonly sisters.

Foreplay the petting and fondling activities engaged in during the excitement phase of the sexual response cycle.

Formal group a group with structure, authority, and limited interaction, such as a business meeting.

Free association a primary method of treatment in psychoanalysis, the free expression of thoughts and feelings as they come to mind.

Gender identity how one chooses to view oneself as a male or female in interaction with others.

Gender role how a person's gender identity is expressed socially, in behavior with others of the same and opposite sex.

General Adaptation Syndrome (GAS) the body's manifestations of stress that evolve in three stages: alarm reaction, stage of resistance, and stage of exhaustion.

Generalization the phenomenon by which adaptive behavior specific to one situation may occur in similar situations.

Geropsychiatry the care of the aging psychiatric client.

Group three or more persons with related goals.

Group norm the development, over time, of a pattern of interaction within a group to which certain behavioral expectations are attached.

Group therapy a form of treatment in which individuals explore their problems and styles of communication in a safe, confidential atmosphere where they can receive feedback from other group members and undergo change.

Hallucination a false sensory perception, that is, without external stimuli, or a sensory perception that does not exist in reality, such as seeing "visions" or hearing "voices."

Homosexuality a male's preference of a male as a sexual partner.

Hostility a feeling of antagonism accompanied by a wish to hurt or humiliate others.

Id the most primitive structure of the human personality that houses the instincts.

Identification a coping mechanism through which a person unconsciously adopts the personality characteristics, attitudes, values, and behavior of another person.

Illusion a misinterpretation of a real sensory experience.

Imagery a therapeutic approach in which the client pictures significant memories and present events that, combined with relaxation and role playing, increase awareness of events and behavior.

Imitation the conscious process of identifying with another person.

Impotence the inability to achieve or maintain erection sufficiently to perform coitus.

Informal group a group of members who are not dependent on each other, such as a hobby group.

Informed consent the knowing consent given in a interaction or series of interactions between the treating physician and the client that allows the client to consider fully information about the treatment that is being proposed.

Insight conscious awareness of the painful, angry, or socially unacceptable thoughts or feelings that the client repressed.

Intellectualization an unconscious coping mechanism through which a person uses his intellectual abilities such as thinking, reasoning, and analyzing to blunt or avoid emotional issues.

Interpretation a person's insight or understanding of his feelings and behavior.

Interview a purposeful, goal-directed interaction between two people.

Laissez-faire leadership a style of leadership in which group members are free to operate as they choose.

Latency the ages from 9 to 12 years, or late school-age years, during which occurs the harmonization of various aspects of the self-concept, especially through clubs, sports teams, and scouts.

Latent content that content which is not discussed, which occurs on a feeling level, and which is seldom verbalized.

Lesbianism a female's preference of a female as a sexual partner.

Libido an energy source associated with the physiological or instinctual drives such as hunger, thirst, and sex.

Listening focusing on all of the behaviors expressed by a client.

Lithium carbonate a psychotropic drug used in the treatment of bipolar disorder (formerly termed manic-depressive illness).

Malpractice a tort action brought by a consumer plaintiff against a defendant professional from whom the consumer plaintiff feels that he has received injury during the course of the professional–consumer relationship.

Mania a mood disturbance characterized by elation, hyperactivity, agitation, and accelerated thinking and speaking.

Manifest content the spoken words during an interaction.

Masochism a paraphilia in which the person's preferred sexual object is the experience of pain.

Masturbation self-stimulation of erogenous areas to the point of orgasm.

Maturational (or developmental) crisis a crisis precipitated by the normal stress of development, such as pregnancy, birth, or adolescence.

Melancholia depression, at one time thought to result from an excess of "black bile" in the body.

Mental health a state of emotional well-being in which a person functions adaptively and comfortably within his society and is satisfied with himself and his achievements.

Mental health team the groups of mental health caregivers, including nurses, occupational and recreational therapists, social workers, psychiatric nurse clinical specialists, dance and art therapists, psychologists, psychiatrists, pastoral counselors, and paraprofessionals, who work together to design and implement a therapeutic milieu for clients.

Mental retardation a significantly subaverage general intellectual functioning existing concurrently with deficits in adaptive behavior and manifesting itself during the developmental period.

Milieu environment or setting; in psychiatric-mental health nursing, the therapeutic milieu is the people and all other social and physical factors within the 24-hour environment with which the client interacts.

Milieu therapy a group therapy approach that uses the total living experience of a client to accomplish therapeutic objectives.

Modeling imitation as a method of behavior change.

Negative reinforcer a harmful reinforcer that the client evades or avoids, thus strengthening or facilitating adaptive behavior.

Negentropy a tendency toward openness to the environment, both inside and outside the family.

Neologism a new, private word with idiosyncratic meaning.

Noncompliance the failure of the client and his family to adhere to prescribed treatment regimes, such as the failure to take prescribed psychotropic medication after discharge from the treatment facility.

Nursing diagnosis a statement of a client's response pattern to a health disruption.

Objective data data or information that can be measured, observed, or validated.

Oedipal period the preschool years, from age 3 or 4 to 6 years, during which stage the child's developmental needs include dealing with sexual and aggressive impulses and coming to terms with parental and societal demands.

Oral period the first 2 years of life, or infancy, during which the personality structure of the individual is centered around the issue of impulsivity.

Paraphilia the investment of an adult's sexual interest in objects, events, or particular types of people.

Personality an individual's consistent and stable pattern of behavior.

Personality disorder a maladaptive personality style.

Physical dependence (addiction) a state manifested by withdrawal symptoms when the drug is removed.

Planning the structuring of needs and problems in an orderly manner to achieve an end or a goal.

Pleasure principle the employment of pleasure-seeking behaviors that reduce tension when the physiological or instinctual drives are released.

Positive reinforcer a reward, that which strengthens a behavior.

Preconscious that material which is not immediately accessible to a person's awareness.

Primary group a group of members with face-to-face contact and boundaries, norms, and explicit and implicit interdependent roles, such as a family.

Primary prevention therapeutic approaches such as infant stimulation and parenting education programs that aim to prevent mental illness or disorder before it occurs.

Primary process thought processes deriving from the id and characterized by an illogical, confused form and preverbal, or preoperational, content.

Problem-solving using anxiety in the service of learning adaptive behavior.

Projection an unconscious coping mechanism through which a person displaces his feelings, usually feelings perceived as negative, onto another person.

Prompting the creation of a condition that facilitates or accentuates the reinforcer.

Psychoanalysis a form of long-term therapy that uses strategies such as dream interpretation, hypnosis, and free association.

Psychodrama a form of group therapy in which clients explore problems through dramatic methods.

Psychogeriatrics the special psychiatric care for clients in the over-65 age group.

Psychological dependence (habituation) the expression of a severe craving or compulsion to take a drug in order to "feel good."

Psychopathology the difference or gap between the existing emotional developmental level of an individual and the expected emotional development level that corresponds to his chronological age.

Psychopharmacology the use of psychotropic, or psychoactive, drugs to treat various emotional disorders.

Psychosis an extreme response to stress that may be characterized by impaired reality testing, delusions, hallucinations, and affective, psychomotor, and physical disturbances.

Psychosomatization the visceral or physiological expression of anxiety.

Psychotherapy the use of a group of techniques to modify feelings, attitudes, and behavior in people by means of understanding self and being understood by another, to achieve relatedness, and to relieve emotional pain.

Punishment that which suppresses the maladaptive pattern of behavior.

Rape a crime in which forcible penile–vaginal penetration of a female occurs without her consent and against her will.

Rape trauma syndrome the process of adaptation in which the rape victim frees herself of overwhelming fear, redefines her feelings of vulnerability and helplessness, and regains control and equilibrium.

Rationalization an unconscious coping mechanism through which a person substitutes socially acceptable reasons for the real or actual reasons motivating his behavior.

Reaction formation an unconscious coping mechanism through which a person acts in a way opposite of how he feels.

Reality principle the ability to delay pleasure in favor of more socially acceptable behavior.

Reconstructive therapy deep psychotherapy or psychoanalysis that delves into all aspects of the client's life and may take 2 to 5 years or more of time.

Re-educative therapy psychotherapy that involves new ways of perceiving and behaving and exploring alternatives in a planned, systematic way, often requiring more than short-term therapy.

Regression an unconscious coping mechanism through which a person avoids anxiety by returning to an earlier, and more satisfying or comfortable time in his life.

Reinforcer anything that increases the probability of a response.

Relationship a state of being related or affinity between two individuals.

Repression a coping mechanism through which a person forces certain feelings or thoughts into his unconscious.

Resistance the client resists recalling information or recalling feelings.

Sadism a paraphilia in which the person's preferred sexual object is the act of inflicting pain on someone else.

Scapegoating the process in which a family tends to view one of its members as "different" and the cause of its trouble.

Schizophrenia a severe disturbance of thought or association, characterized by impaired reality testing, hallucinations, delusions, and limited socialization.

Secondary group a group of members who do not have relationship bonds or emotional ties, an impersonal group such as a political party.

Secondary prevention therapeutic approaches such as crisis intervention, counseling, and inpatient hospitalization that reduce prevalence of emotional disorders through early case-finding and prompt intervention.

Self-concept a composite of a person's beliefs and feelings about himself at a given time.

Sex roles culturally determined patterns associated with male and female social behavior.

Sexual identity the basic recognition of one's sex.

Sexuality the expression and experience of the self as a sexual being.

Shaping a behavioral reinforcement technique used to condition close approximations of some desired adaptive behavior.

Situational crisis a crisis precipitated by a sudden traumatic event, such as divorce, job loss, or birth of a child with a congenital defect.

Stress the nonspecific response of the body to any demand made upon it, according to Hans Selye.

Stressors stress-producing factors, including physical stressors such as heat, cold, and illness and psychological stressors such as failure, success, and loss.

Subculture a group of people who may be distinguishable by ethnic background, religion, social status, or other similar characteristics, and simultaneously share certain features with larger segments of society.

Subjective data data that reflect the client's feelings, perceptions, and "self talk" about his problems.

Superego the structure of the human personality that contains the values, legal and moral regulations, and social expectations that thwart the free expression of pleasure-seeking behaviors.

Supportive therapy psychotherapy that allows the client to express feelings, explore alternatives, and make decisions in a safe, caring relationship.

Suppression a coping mechanism through which a person consciously excludes certain thoughts or feelings from his mind.

Suspiciousness hypersensitivity, alertness, and hypervigilance.

Tardive dyskinesia a late symptom associated with the long-term use of high-dose phenothiazine drugs; symptoms include buccolingual movements such as "fly catcher" movements, pursing of lips, jaw movements, and involvement of limbs and trunk.

Termination the dissolution of a relationship.

Tertiary prevention therapeutic approaches such as halfway houses and residential placements that aim to reduce long-term disability from emotional disorder through a program of rehabilitation, after care, and resocialization.

Theory conceptual system that describes and explains selected phenomena.

Therapeutic relationship a relationship in which the nurse and client participate with the goal of assisting the client to meet his needs and facilitate his growth.

Time out a period of time during which the client is removed from any form of reinforcement.

Token reinforcement a therapeutic approach that delays the use of direct reinforcers through the administration of tokens, which can then be redeemed for actual reinforcers.

Tolerance a state wherein an increased amount of a drug is necessary to obtain the desired effect or there is a decrease in the desired effect with regular use of the same amount of a drug.

Transcendental self a self that exists beyond one's individual self-image, or a self in relation to the larger universe.

Transference a tool or technique of psychotherapy whereby the client transfers feelings and attitudes held toward significant others onto the therapist.

Transsexuality the belief that one is psychologically of the sex opposite his or her anatomical gender.

Transvestitism a sexual desire to dress in the clothing, or adopt the mannerisms, of the opposite sex.

Treatment alliance the ability to work together and to be invested emotionally in the task of therapy.

Triangle a form of cross-generational clinging, such as a coalition formed by a mother and son against the father.

Unconditioned response the response elicited by an unconditioned stimulus, for example, salivation is an unconditioned response in a hungry dog elicited by an unconditioned stimulus, food.

Unconditioned stimulus that which elicits an unconditioned response, for example, food is an unconditioned stimulus that elicits an unconditioned response, salivation, in a hungry dog.

Unconscious that material which is inaccessible to a person's awareness.

Unresolved sexual trauma a state in which a person experiencing a sexual assault does not deal with the feelings or reactions to the experience.

Vaginismus a spastic contraction or tightening of the vagina before or during penetration for coitus.

Voyeurism a desire to watch others in sexually vulnerable or erotic positions.

Withdrawal the behavioral or psychological retreat from anxiety-provoking experiences.

Working through a part of the final phase of therapy in which the client's insights are discussed and reworked over time.

Index

Page numbers followed by a t indicate a table; page numbers followed by an f indicate a figure.